THE POEMS OF

WILLIAM BLAKE

EDITED BY

W. H. STEVENSON

TEXT BY

DAVID V. ERDMAN

Longman
—
Norton

LONGMAN GROUP LIMITED
London

*Associated companies, branches and representatives
throughout the world*

W. W. NORTON & COMPANY INC.
New York

Longman Edition

*First published 1971
First paperback edition 1972
Third impression 1975*

ISBN 0 582 48445 6 Cased
ISBN 0 582 48459 6 Paper

Norton Edition

First published 1972

ISBN 393 04381 9

Library of Congress Catalog Card Number 73-178130

*Printed in Hong Kong by
Wing Tai Cheung Printing Co Ltd*

CONTENTS

Illustrations

William Blake in 1825   *Frontispiece*
   (Reproduced by kind permission of the Nonesuch Press
   Limited, from the frontispiece of *Life of Blake* by Mona
   Wilson, published in 1927)

MAPS

Acknowledgements

We are indebted to the following for permission to reproduce copyright material:

Brown University Press for an extract from 'The Welsh Triades' from *A Blake Dictionary* by S. Foster Damon; Eyre & Spottiswoode Ltd. for an extract from *Hidden Riches* by D. Hirst.

Note by the General Editor

This series has been planned to apply to the major English poets the requirements, critical and scholarly, that a serious reading of their poems entails today. Whereas the editorial emphasis has often been on what may be called textual refinements, sometimes carried to grotesque extremes, the Annotated English Poets series concerns itself primarily with the *meaning* of the various texts in their separate contexts. With the aids provided in the table of dates, the headnotes and the footnotes, the modern reader should have all, or almost all, that he requires both for aesthetic appreciation and for proper emotional response to the whole poetic corpus of each poet represented.

Our ideal of comprehension, for the reader, combined with comprehensiveness, for the poet, has three logical consequences:

1. Since an essential clue to an author's intentions at any point is provided, on the one hand, by what he has already written and, on the other hand, by what he will write later, an editor will print his poems as far as possible in the order in which they were composed.

2. A poet writing in a living language, such as English, requires elucidation of a different kind from that suitable to the poet of a dead language, such as Sanskrit, Latin or Old English: with minor exceptions vocabulary and syntax can be taken for granted, but sources, allusions, implications and stylistic devices need to be spelt out.

3. Since the reader in any English-speaking country will tend to pronounce an English poet of the past (at any rate to Chaucer) as if he was a contemporary, whatever impedes the reader's sympathetic identification with the poet that is implicit in that fact—whether of spelling, punctuation or the use of initial capitals—must be regarded as undesirable. A modern pronunciation demands a modern presentation, except occasionally for rhymes (e.g. *bind-wind*) or obsolete archaisms (*eremite, hermit*).

Some exceptions have had to be admitted to the principles summarized above, but they have been few and unimportant.

F. W. BATESON

PREFACE

This edition comprises all Blake's verse, including the scattered verses and epigrams. The successive editions of G. L. Keynes, and lately that of David V. Erdman, have brought increasing certainty to Blake's text, but in spite of the vast and continuing work of critical scholars, no editor, since A. P. Sloss and J. P. R. Wallis, forty years ago, produced their edition of the *Prophetic Works*, has attempted to annotate all Blake's poems line by line and detail by detail. Sloss and Wallis themselves did not attempt the whole of the poetry; Harold Bloom's *Commentary*, in the Erdman–Bloom edition of 1965, is explicatory discussion rather than detailed annotation. Perhaps scholars have been remiss in leaving this task undone for so many years; perhaps they have been wise. Blake's thought and expression are notoriously complex; it is easy to make them appear more complex still. I have tried in this edition not to interpret or expound any 'system' in his works, but to give whatever information is necessary for the exposition of each poem or passage, so that the reader may be able to interpret more easily for himself. Blake's beliefs and doctrines have only been explained where it would be difficult for the reader to recognize them; and then only when they are clearly demonstrable. The more general 'influences' have not been my concern; instead, I have considered it my task to provide essential details of fact and background. I have only quoted or summarized the studies of other scholars where comprehension depends on it; although, needless to say, my debt to their works in forming my own understanding is incalculable. It would have been impossible in one volume to specify every one of Blake's verbal allusions (especially to Milton and the Bible), even if one could be sure of having identified them all; I have had to confine myself to the more necessary or revealing references—not so many, it is hoped, that they will confuse the reader.

At the end of the book will be found an index to certain footnotes of major importance, which are identified in the body of the notes by reference words in small capitals. The Sloss and Wallis edition contained an extensive *Index of Symbols*, in which the editors summarized the meanings, as they saw them, of the mythological names which are scattered through the poems, and of Blake's special terms. The danger of this kind of index lies in its dissociation of the name or word from its context, so that it appears to be pre-existent, an idea fixed in Blake's mind quite apart from the poem into which he then inserts it. The shifts of meaning,

and the central meanings themselves, are often unintelligible outside a
given context. On the other hand, it would be impossible to annotate
such words as *spectre*, *druid* or *state* for each poem, each context and each
shade of meaning. I have therefore given an extended note on each of
the important words listed in the Index, setting it either in the place of
first appearance or, if more appropriate, in the most illuminating context.

The text and textual notes are the result of an invaluable collaboration
with Professor Erdman. Since the purpose of this edition is not primarily
textual investigation, it is necessary that the text accepted should be the
most reliable one available. Professor Erdman supplied a copy of the text
of his own edition of *The Poetry and Prose of William Blake* before its
publication, followed this up with a series of minor corrections, and gave
carte blanche for the use of his own textual footnotes. The inestimable
value of this displays itself. All the strictly textual notes included here are
given on Professor Erdman's authority, and many in his own words. They
are limited to matters of literary interest, and do not cover all the points
of textual complexity. For these the reader is referred to Erdman's own
complete edition where many matters, here passed over in silence, are
fully discussed.

The text here printed differs from Professor Erdman's complete edition
in three ways. In accordance with the general policy of the series as out-
lined by the General Editor on p. ix, the spelling and punctuation have
been modernized. This has proved a task of considerable nicety. Blake's
own punctuation in the Illuminated Books is at best rhetorical and at
worst quite irrational; and in the MSS, most of all in *The Four Zoas*, it is
often non-existent. The problem of punctuating has much exercised Mr.
Bateson, Professor Erdman and myself, and we have concluded that it is
often insoluble. We can only hope to have reached a not intolerable com-
promise, even though it has meant losing the individual flavour of
Blake's page. In particular, we have written out in full such forms as
turnd, *hovring*, as *turned*, *hovering*, etc. There has been some debate as to
the significance of Blake's usage in such cases, but the evidence is inde-
cisive, and (except in a few places, such as in rhymes) the reader's ear,
rather than Blake's spelling, will determine the number of syllables.
Blake's abbreviations seem intended to save manual labour more often
than to indicate the omission of a sound.

The second deviation from the Erdman text is in the arrangement of
the First, Second and Seventh Nights of *The Four Zoas*. The rearrange-
ment of the sheets of the First and Second Night, discussed in more de-
tail in the headnote to the First Night, is my own considered decision. It
is necessary for an editor to present a settled text; it may well be that
Blake had not made up his mind about this matter, but the present ar-

rangement seems to me to incorporate his apparent intentions with least distortion.

Night VIIb has long been a source of disagreement among scholars. I have included it in the main text, although it is often said to be an earlier version of the Seventh Night, rejected in favour of VIIa. I do not doubt that it is earlier, but do not accept that it was rejected. Clearly the present numeration, with two 'Seventh Nights', is unsatisfactory, but the poem was left in a very incomplete state. This is only one of several questions which must lie open to an individual assessment of the rather confusing facts. It is a fact that Blake did not destroy or erase these pages of his text, and *The Four Zoas* seems to me to present sufficient problems without our complicating them by hypotheses on the changes that Blake might have been about to make. Professor Erdman, who in his own edition puts VIIb in an appendix, has agreed that these arrangements of Nights I, II and VIIb are plausible.

Thirdly, I have adopted in my text of *Milton* the order of plates of the two earliest copies, omitting the five plates added in later copies (these are given in an appendix to the poem), and putting plates 25–27 in their earlier order. One minor advantage of this choice is that it enables an editor to print, legitimately, the famous Preface, which Blake left out of the two later copies. I have chosen the earlier version because it is easier to follow; those who wish to read the later one may do so by making the necessary adjustments, as shown in the text and notes.

I must record my great debt to M. J. Tolley, whose encyclopædic knowledge of Blake's biblical allusions, which he very kindly placed at my disposal, has been invaluable. Without it I would have been unable to elucidate a number of problems, and even then I have been unable to use all the thousands of references which Mr Tolley has collected. In the search for Blake's meaning, the clarification of an apparently unintelligible phrase is often made unexpectedly simple when one sees that Blake was merely drawing on the comprehensive biblical knowledge which was commonplace in his age, but which so easily confuses the more ignorant scholar of today.

My debt to other Blake scholars is immeasurable, as every page witnesses. I am only sorry that the nature of this edition precludes a complete apparatus of critical reference, which would show the extent of my debt. Many people have been troubled with requests for information on the many subjects which Blake studies involve, and I wish to thank all these for their help, advice and criticism: S. Barrington-Ward, A. E. Barker of the S.P.C.K., D. Bullock, D. Burnett, Professor J. Ferguson, J. A. Gardiner, J. Gillespie, Mrs D. Lewis, Professor M. M. Mahood, Professor D. E. S. Maxwell, P. Moore, Professor S. Piggott, J. E. Pretty, Mrs

M. P. Wright; and J. Packman, who as Deputy Librarian of the Ibadan University Library during the relevant period was very helpful in obtaining for me the many singular books I ordered. I must also thank Mrs C. O. Atanda and O. A. Sanni for the care with which they unravelled a very involved manuscript.

Finally, I must thank F. W. Bateson, who gave me in the first place the remarkable opportunity of tackling this edition, and who has helped it along ever since. In particular I am grateful for his shrewd comments on my draft, and for his patience with an editor who was not always percipient enough to accept them.

W. H. STEVENSON

Chronological Table
of the Life and Work of William Blake

1741	Heinrich Füsslich (later anglicized as Henry Fuseli) and James Barry born (later artist-friends of B.).
1745	William Hayley born.
1752	(*October 15*) James Blake and Catherine Harmitage married.
1753	(*July 10*) James Blake born.
1755	John Flaxman and Thomas Stothard born.
1757	(*November 28*) William Blake born, at 28 Broad Street, near Golden Square, London (now Broadwick St, W.1).
1760	(*March 20*) John Blake born.
1762	(*June 19*) Richard Blake born (died in infancy).
1764	(*January 7*) Catherine Elizabeth, the only sister, born.
1767	(*August 4*) Robert Blake, William's favourite brother, born.
1767 or '68	B. begins to attend Henry Parr's drawing school in the Strand (he attended no other school).
1768–69	Begins to write some of the lyrics later printed in *Poetical Sketches*.
1772	(*August 4*) Apprenticed to James Basire, engraver.
1773	Engraves plate called 'Joseph of Arimathea' after a drawing from Michaelangelo (first state; B.'s earliest engraving known).
1774	After difficulties with other apprentices, sent to make drawings in Westminster Abbey.
1775	Outbreak of War of Independence in America.
1777	According to the 'ADVERTISEMENT' in *Poetical Sketches*, the last of these poems were written in this year.
1778	John Varley, B.'s friend from 1819, born.
1779	(*October 8*) End of apprenticeship; admitted to the Royal Academy as student, under G. M. Moser. Made engraving of *Edward and Elenor*, and water-colour of *The Penance of Jane Shore*. Begins to receive engraving work from booksellers, including Joseph Johnson. Meets Flaxman.
1780	Original drawing for the *Glad Day* engraving. Exhibited at the Royal Academy for the first time – a water-colour of *The Death of Earl Goodwin*. (*June 6*) Caught up in the Gordon Riots of June 2–8, and witness of the burning of Newgate Prison.

1782   (*August 18*) Marries Catherine Sophia Boucher (b. 1762), whom he met in 1781. They go to live at 23 Green Street, Leicester Fields (now Leicester Square).

About this time, a member of the circle of artists regularly entertained by Mrs. Harriet Mathew.

1783   *Poetical Sketches* printed at the expense of John Flaxman and Rev. A. S. Mathew, but not published; the copies given to B. for private distribution.

1784   Goes into partnership with James Parker in a print-shop at 27 Broad Street. Exhibits at the Royal Academy.

(ca. *July 2*) B.'s father dies.

(*Autumn*) Writing 'An Island in the Moon'.

1785   Late in the year, leaves the partnership and goes to live at 28 Poland Street. Exhibits again at the R.A.

1787   (*February 11*) Burial of B.'s brother Robert, died of consumption.

1788   'W. Blake's original stereotype' – probably the sets of small tracts *All Religions are One* and *There is no Natural Religion*.

1788–89   Writes *Tiriel*: annotates Fuseli's translation of Lavater's *Aphorisms* and Swedenborg's *Wisdom of Angels*. Associated with the Swedenborgian Society.

1789   (*June*) Beginning of the French Revolution.

Thel and *Songs of Innocence* engraved.

1790   Hostile annotation of Swedenborg's *Divine Providence*.

later 1790–91   *French Revolution*, printed for Joseph Johnson but not published.

1791   (*April 18*) Rejection of Bill in Commons to abolish slave trade (this campaign is reflected in *Visions*).

Illustrates Mary Wollstonecraft's *Original Stories from Real Life*. Begins engravings for Stedman (see 1796).

By the second quarter of the year, has moved to 13 Hercules Buildings, Lambeth.

First Part of Paine's *Rights of Man* (Pt. II, 1792).

1791–92   *America*, first form, written and partly engraved.

Begins to write lyrics in Notebook, on pp. 115–109 (reversed): and *Visions*. Probably also new endings to *Tiriel* and *Thel*.

1792   (*April 23*) Commons pass motion calling for end of slave trade.

(ca. *September 7*) Death of B.'s mother.

(*September 20*) Invasion of France halted at Valmy; reflected in *A Song of Liberty*, written to conclude *Marriage* (now

	(*November 22*) Two letters to Butts, indicating dissatisfaction with Hayley's interference with his private work at Felpham.
1803	(*January 30*) Letter to B.'s brother James, complaining of Hayley's envy, referring to Catherine's illness, and stating intention of leaving Felpham.

(*April 25*) Letter to Butts mentioning 'the Spiritual Acts of my three years Slumber on the banks of the Ocean' and 'my long Poem descriptive of those Acts . . . an immense number of verses on One Grand Theme'.

(*May 10*) War with France renewed.

(*August 12*) Warrant issued for B.'s arrest on a charge of assault and seditious words, 'taken out against me by [Scholfield, whose] enmity arises from my having turned him out of my garden'. About this time, writing some of the 'Pickering MS' poems.

(*September*) Returns to London, and goes to live in rooms at 17 South Molton Street.

1804   (*January 11–12*) Trial and acquittal at Chichester Quarter Sessions.

Titlepages of *Milton* and *Jerusalem*, intended to have 12 and 28 chapters respectively. Probable completion of *Milton* (engraved *c.* 1809), with composition of 'Bard's Song' which opens the poem.

Visit to Truchsessian Gallery, where 'I was again enlightened with the light I enjoyed in my youth, and which has for exactly twenty years been closed from me'.

1805   'Pickering MS' copied?

(*October 18*) Flaxman writes to Hayley that 'Mr Cromek has employed Blake to make a set of forty drawings from Blair's poem of *The Grave*, twenty of which he proposes to have engraved by the designer . . .'

Samuel Palmer and Frederick Tatham, B.'s disciples in old age, born.

1806   Cromek steals the idea of B.'s *Canterbury Pilgrims* and gives it to Stothard.

B. H. Malkin's *A Father's Memoirs of his Child*, including in the dedicatory epistle biographical details of B., and giving as example of his verse 'How sweet I roamed' and 'I love the jocund dance' from *Poetical Sketches*; 'The Divine Image', 'Holy Thursday', 'Laughing Song' from *Innocence*; 'The Tiger' from *Experience*.

(*June*) Letter to *Bell's Weekly Messenger* defending Fuseli's art. Death of James Barry.

1807 (*May*) Stothard's *Canterbury Pilgrims* exhibited.
Cromek writes an insulting letter to B., having previously given the engraving work on *The Grave* to Schiavonetti.

1808 (*January 18*) Writes to Ozias Humphrey that he has completed painting of *The Last Judgment*, and describing it.
Publication of Cromek's edition of *The Grave*, with portrait of B. by Phillips, and dedicatory poem to the Queen by B.
(*August 7*) B.'s *Grave* designs attacked by Robert Hunt in *The Examiner*.
Notebook epigrams continue; further annotation to Reynold's *Discourses*.

1809 (*May 15*) MS date on advertisement of B.'s exhibition, which includes his *Canterbury Pilgrims* painting, and the *Spiritual Forms* of *Pitt* and *Nelson*.
(*May–September*) Exhibition at 28 Broad Street; *Descriptive Catalogue* also printed for this exhibition, which fails to attract the attention and fame hoped for. Visited by Crabb Robinson and Southey.
(*September 17*) Attack on the exhibition in *The Examiner*, describing B. as an 'unfortunate lunatic' and his paintings as 'the wild effusions of a distempered brain'.
(*December*) Death of Johnson, the bookseller.

1809–10 Engraving of *Milton* (first stage, without the extra plates).
More Notebook epigrams; B. begins an engraving of the *Canterbury Pilgrims*: plans a further exhibition for 1810, and drafts the so-called 'Public Address' in the Notebook, and also the commentary 'The Vision of the Last Judgment, For the Year 1810: Additions to Blake's Catalogue of Pictures &c'.

1810 (*March*) Death of Ozias Humphrey.
(*June 7*) Death of Schiavonetti from consumption.

1810–12 ?Work on text of *Jerusalem* (engraved 1819–20); last changes to *Vala*, renamed *The Four Zoas*.

1811 (*July 24*) Crabb Robinson records that Southey had visited B. and had seen *Jerusalem*.
(*December 26*) Reduced plate of part of *Canterbury Pilgrims* engraved.

1812 *The Prologue ... of the Canterbury Pilgrims* published, to draw attention to B.'s full engraving.
(*March 12*) Death of Cromek from consumption.

	Exhibits three pictures at Associated Artists in Water Colour.
1814	Begins to engrave Flaxman's designs for Longmans' edition of *Hesiod*.
1815	End of Napoleonic war; period of general economic depression follows. B. very poor: engraves designs for Wedgwood's chinaware catalogues, 1815–17.
	Visits Royal Academy to draw the Laocoön.
1816	Designs for *L'Allegro* and *Il Penseroso*.
1817	*Hesiod* published.
1818	(*June 9*) Letter with price-list of illuminated books, not incl. *Marriage* or *Jerusalem*; *Innocence* and *Experience* quoted separately; *Milton* in its enlarged form of 50 plates.
	Everlasting Gospel (approx. date).
1818	Begins series of *Job* water-colours for Butts.
1819	Meets Varley; draws 'Visionary Heads'.
1820	First copy of *Jerusalem* printed.
	Designs and engraves woodcuts for Thornton's *Virgil* (the only woodcuts B. ever did).
	September issue of *London Magazine* contains a facetious allusion to *Jerusalem* by Thomas Wainewright.
1821	Sells collection of prints.
	Paints new series of *Job* water-colours for Linnell.
	Removes to lodgings at 3 Fountain Court, Strand.
1822	Receives donation of £25 from the Royal Academy.
	The Ghost of Abel, B.'s last illuminated book.
1823	(*March 25*) Agreement with Linnell to engrave *Job* designs, at L.'s risk; B. assured of £100, plus up to £10 from the profits (if any).
1824	*Pilgrim's Progress* designs.
	Death of James Blake.
	Letter of uncertain date refers to B.'s illness.
	(*October 9*) Samuel Palmer introduced to B.
1825	(*March*) *Job* completed. Begins Dante drawings, making 100 between 1825 and 1827, and engraving seven.
	(*April 16*) Death of Fuseli.
	(*December 10*) Crabb Robinson's first visit to B.
1826	(*February 1*) Writes to Linnell referring to renewed illness: so also 31 March and 19 May.
	(*March*) Publication of *Job*.
	(*July 2, 5, 16, 29*) Writes to Linnell on attacks and recessions of illness.

(*December 7*) Death of Flaxman.

1827   Begins Dante engravings.

(*April 12*) Writes to Cumberland: 'I have been very near the gates of death, and have returned very weak and an old man, feeble and tottering, but not in spirit and life . . .' Gives price-list of illuminated books: *Jerusalem, Thel, Visions, Songs* (combined), *America, Europe, Urizen*. Promises to engrave C.'s visiting-card (eventually his last engraving).

Satiric annotations to Thornton's *New Translation of the Lord's Prayer.*

(*July 3*) Writes to Linnell: 'I must not go on in a youthful style . . . I have been yellow, accompanied by all the old symptoms'.

(*August*) Colours copy of his *Ancient of Days* engraving for Tatham.

(*August 12*) Dies, at 6 p.m., 'the exact moment almost unperceived' (Gilchrist).

1831   (*October 18*) Death of Catherine Blake.

(For full details and documentation of B.'s life, see G. E. Bentley: *Blake Records*, Oxford 1969.)

Abbreviations

NB	Blake's Notebook (also known as the 'Rossetti MS')
Marriage	*The Marriage of Heaven and Hell*
Visions	*Visions of the Daughters of Albion*
Erdman 1965, 1966	The Poetry and Prose of William Blake, ed. D. V. Erdman and H. Bloom, New York 1965; 2nd (corrected) impression, 1966.
Keynes 1957	The Poetry and Prose of William Blake, ed. G. L. Keynes, London 1957 (revised edn, Oxford 1966)
L, R (in notes on designs	left, right
pl.	plate (i.e. a page of an illuminated book)
st.	stanza
1st rdg. del.	first (deleted) reading

Plate numbers thus: Pl. 45 (31) refer to an alternative arrangement explained in the headnote to the particular poem.

Line references to poems by Blake are given in italic numerals, e.g. *Thel 15.*

B.'s ampersands are retained in *The Four Zoas, Milton* and *Jerusalem,* as in these poems they materially reduce the number of 'turned' lines.

THE POEMS

1 Poetical Sketches

This collection is the fruit of B.'s association with the artist's circle of the Rev. A. S. Mathew and his wife. (B.'s biographer, Alexander Gilchrist, gave the name inaccurately as 'Henry Mathew', following J. T. Smith.) Although some at least of the poems had been written before this association (they are given here in the order of the 1783 edition), it was doubtless the enthusiasm of Mathew and his friends that caused some fifty copies of the poems to be printed–though they seem only to have circulated privately. If the 'Advertisement' is accurate, the outside dates of composition are 1768–77; there is therefore a gap of six years before the printing in 1783. Perhaps Mathew (who probably wrote the 'Advertisement') stretched a point; the more sophisticated poems may have been written under the influence of the 'salon', but there is no evidence for this. B. was certainly writing the poems which appear in *An Island in the Moon* around 1784.

Poetical Sketches contains a number of B.'s most obviously attractive–and derivative–work. Yet there is little direct borrowing, and it would be truer to say that, even at this early stage, he has formed for himself a style as individual as Collins's and Akenside's–though he has learnt from such writers of his father's generation as well. The notes on *To Spring* and 'My silks and fine array' illustrate the typical difficulty of relating apparently secondhand phrases to any precise original, and show that B. rather made a chosen style of his own than plagiarized other poets. The classic study is Margaret Lowery's *Windows of the Morning* (Yale, 1940).

MISCELLANEOUS POEMS

1 TO SPRING

O thou with dewy locks, who lookest down
Through the clear windows of the morning, turn
Thine angel eyes upon our western isle,
Which in full choir hails thy approach, O Spring!

¶ 1 i *1. dewy locks*] The association of *morning* and *dew* is a commonplace of Elizabethan poetry, and the Petrarchan tradition as a whole; and the image of the god or goddess (often Aurora herself) rising from bed and looking out on to the world is almost as widespread. B. has adopted this dawn convention to a Spring dawn in particular; it is significant that he goes on much farther than the conventions in realizing the figure of his 'angel'–her *locks, eyes, feet, garments*, etc. The blank verse, with its near-regularity, its shortness of clause, contrasted with the looseness of its line endings, follows Akenside rather than Milton.

3

5 The hills tell each other, and the listening
   Valleys hear; all our longing eyes are turned
   Up to thy bright pavilions. Issue forth,
   And let thy holy feet visit our clime.

   Come o'er the eastern hills, and let our winds
10 Kiss thy perfumed garments; let us taste
   Thy morn and evening breath; scatter thy pearls
   Upon our love-sick land that mourns for thee.

   O deck her forth with thy fair fingers. Pour
   Thy soft kisses on her bosom, and put
15 Thy golden crown upon her languished head,
   Whose modest tresses were bound up for thee.

                    II TO SUMMER

   O thou, who passest through our valleys in
   Thy strength, curb thy fierce steeds, allay the heat
   That flames from their large nostrils! Thou, O Summer,
   Oft pitched'st here thy golden tent, and oft
5 Beneath our oaks has slept, while we beheld
   With joy thy ruddy limbs and flourishing hair.

   Beneath our thickest shades we oft have heard
   Thy voice, when noon upon his fervid car
   Rode o'er the deep of heaven; beside our springs
10 Sit down, and in our mossy valleys, on
   Some bank beside a river clear, throw thy
   Silk draperies off, and rush into the stream:
   Our valleys love the Summer in his pride.

   Our bards are famed who strike the silver wire;
15 Our youth are bolder than the southern swains;

i 5–6. This is, evidently, 'biblical', with its naive personification and its antithetical clauses: but it is B.'s own, not derived directly from any passage in the Bible.

i 7. *pavilions*] Used in the Bible rarely, and only of dark places; but Milton has 'pavilions numberless . . . celestial tabernacles' (*Paradise Lost* v 653–4).

i 9. *Come . . . hills*] In the convention of, e.g. *Hamlet* I i 166: 'the morn . . . Walks o'er the dew of yon high eastward hill', itself not an original image.

i 13.] *her* I.e. 'our land's'.

i 15. *languished head*] Occurs twice in Milton: *Comus* 744 and *Samson Agonistes* 118–19, where Samson '. . . lies at random, carelessly diffused, / With languished head unpropped'.

ii 6. Cp. Notebook (1791–92, p. 162, no. xxxvi): 'the ruddy limbs and flaming hair'.

Our maidens fairer in the sprightly dance.
We lack not songs, nor instruments of joy,
Nor echoes sweet, nor waters clear as heaven,
Nor laurel wreaths against the sultry heat.

III TO AUTUMN

O Autumn, laden with fruit and stained
With the blood of the grape, pass not, but sit
Beneath my shady roof! There thou may'st rest,
And tune thy jolly voice to my fresh pipe,
5 And all the daughters of the year shall dance.
Sing now the lusty song of fruits and flowers:

'The narrow bud opens her beauties to
The sun, and love runs in her thrilling veins;
Blossoms hang round the brows of morning, and
10 Flourish down the bright cheek of modest eve,
Till clustering Summer breaks forth into singing,
And feathered clouds strew flowers round her head.

The spirits of the air live on the smells
Of fruit; and joy, with pinions light, roves round
15 The gardens, or sits singing in the trees.'
Thus sang the jolly Autumn as he sat;
Then rose, girded himself, and o'er the bleak
Hills fled from our sight—but left his golden load.

IV TO WINTER

O Winter, bar thine adamantine doors!
The north is thine; there hast thou built thy dark
Deep-founded habitation. Shake not thy roofs,
Nor bend thy pillars with thine iron car.

5 He hears me not, but o'er the yawning deep
Rides heavy; his storms are unchained. Sheathed
In ribbed steel, I dare not lift mine eyes;
For he hath reared his sceptre o'er the world.

Lo! now the direful monster, whose skin clings
10 To his strong bones, strides o'er the groaning rocks;
He withers all in silence, and his hand
Unclothes the earth and freezes up frail life.

He takes his seat upon the cliffs; the mariner
Cries in vain. Poor little wretch! that deal'st

15 With storms—till heaven smiles, and the monster
      Is driven yelling to his caves beneath Mount Hecla.

V TO THE EVENING STAR

      Thou fair-haired angel of the evening,
      Now, while the sun rests on the mountains, light
      Thy bright torch of love! Thy radiant crown
      Put on, and smile upon our evening bed!
5   Smile on our loves; and, while thou drawest the
      Blue curtains of the sky, scatter thy silver dew
      On every flower that shuts its sweet eyes
      In timely sleep. Let thy west wind sleep on
      The lake; speak silence with thy glimmering eyes,
10 And wash the dusk with silver. Soon, full soon,
      Dost thou withdraw; then the wolf rages wide,
      And the lion glares through the dun forest.
      The fleeces of our flocks are covered with
      Thy sacred dew: protect them with thine influence.

VI TO MORNING

      O holy virgin, clad in purest white,
      Unlock heaven's golden gates and issue forth!
      Awake the dawn that sleeps in heaven; let light
      Rise from the chambers of the east and bring
5   The honeyed dew that cometh on waking day.
      O radiant morning, salute the sun,
      Roused like a huntsman to the chase; and, with
      Thy buskined feet, appear upon our hills.

VII FAIR ELENOR

      The bell struck one and shook the silent tower;
      The graves give up their dead: fair Elenor

iv *16. Hecla*] In Iceland (there is also a Hecla on S. Uist in the Outer
Hebrides).
v *2. while*] Revised by B. in one copy; printed *whilst.*
vi *1–4.* Cp. Spenser's *Epithalamion* 148–51: 'Lo where she comes along with
portly pace, / Like Phoebe from her chamber of the East, / Arising forth
to run her mighty race, / Clad all in white, that seems a virgin best.'
vii. This poem, and *Gwin* (p. 14) embody the full Gothic strain deriving
from the ballads and Walpole's *The Castle of Otranto*, at this time fashion-
able and becoming more and more popular. This poem has all the classical
Gothic elements (later to be used, e.g. by Coleridge in *Christabel*, and Keats
in *Isabella*)—midnight, a fair maiden, a castle, vaults, a horrific bloody head,
ghostly voices, and a macabre ending.

Walked by the castle gate, and looked in.
A hollow groan ran through the dreary vaults.

5 She shrieked aloud, and sunk upon the steps
On the cold stone her pale cheek. Sickly smells
Of death issue as from a sepulchre,
And all is silent but the sighing vaults.

Chill death withdraws his hand, and she revives;
10 Amazed, she finds herself upon her feet,
And, like a ghost, through narrow passages
Walking, feeling the cold walls with her hands.

Fancy returns, and now she thinks of bones,
And grinning skulls, and corruptible death,
15 Wrapped in his shroud; and now fancies she hears
Deep sighs and sees pale sickly ghosts gliding.

At length, no fancy, but reality
Distracts her. A rushing sound, and the feet
Of one that fled, approaches—Ellen stood,
20 Like a dumb statue, froze to stone with fear.

The wretch approaches, crying, 'The deed is done;
Take this, and send it by whom thou wilt send;
It is my life—send it to Elenor—
He's dead, and howling after me for blood!
25 'Take this,' he cried; and thrust into her arms

A wet napkin, wrapped about; then rushed
Past, howling: she received into her arms
Pale death and followed on the wings of fear.

They passed swift through the outer gate; the wretch,
30 Howling, leaped o'er the wall into the moat,
Stifling in mud. Fair Ellen passed the bridge,
And heard a gloomy voice cry, 'Is it done?'

As the deer wounded, Ellen flew over
The pathless plain; as the arrows that fly
35 By night, destruction flies and strikes in darkness.
She fled from fear, till at her house arrived.

Her maids await her; on her bed she falls,
That bed of joy, where erst her lord hath pressed:

vii *20. froze*] Acceptable grammar in 1780.
vii *34–6.* Cp. *Psalm* xci 5–6: 'Thou shalt not be afraid for the terror by
night; nor for the arrow that flieth by day; Nor for the pestilence that
walketh in darkness; nor for the destruction that wasteth at noonday.'

'Ah, woman's fear!' she cried; 'Ah, cursed duke!
40   Ah, my dear lord! ah, wretched Elenor!

'My lord was like a flower upon the brows
Of lusty May! Ah, life as frail as flower!
O ghastly death, withdraw thy cruel hand,
Seek'st thou that flower to deck thy horrid temples?

45   'My lord was like a star in the highest heaven,
Drawn down to earth by spells and wickedness;
My lord was like the opening eyes of day,
When western winds creep softly o'er the flowers.

'But he is darkened; like the summer's noon,
50   Clouded; fallen like the stately tree cut down;
The breath of heaven dwelt among his leaves.
O Elenor, weak woman, filled with woe!'

Thus having spoke, she raised up her head,
And saw the bloody napkin by her side,
55   Which in her arms she brought; and now, tenfold
More terrified, saw it unfold itself.

Her eyes were fixed; the bloody cloth unfolds,
Disclosing to her sight the murdered head
Of her dear lord, all ghastly pale, clotted
60   With gory blood; it groaned, and thus it spake:

'O Elenor, behold thy husband's head,
Who, sleeping on the stones of yonder tower,
Was reft of life by the accursed duke!
A hired villain turned my sleep to death.

65   'O Elenor, beware the cursed duke,
O give not him thy hand, now I am dead;
He seeks thy love—who, coward, in the night
Hired a villain to bereave my life.'

She sat with dead cold limbs, stiffened to stone;
70   She took the gory head up in her arms;
She kissed the pale lips; she had no tears to shed;
She hugged it to her breast, and groaned her last.

VIII SONG

How sweet I roamed from field to field
    And tasted all the summer's pride,
Till I the prince of love beheld,
    Who in the sunny beams did glide.

vii 61. *behold*] Printed 'I am', and corrected by B. in some copies.

5 He showed me lilies for my hair,
    And blushing roses for my brow;
He led me through his gardens fair,
    Where all his golden pleasures grow.

With sweet May dews my wings were wet,
10   And Phoebus fired my vocal rage.
He caught me in his silken net,
    And shut me in his golden cage.

He loves to sit and hear me sing,
    Then laughing sports and plays with me—
15 Then stretches out my golden wing,
    And mocks my loss of liberty.

IX SONG

My silks and fine array,
    My smiles and languished air,
By love are driven away;
    And mournful lean Despair
5 Brings me yew to deck my grave:
Such end true lovers have.

His face is fair as heaven,
    When springing buds unfold;
O why to him was't given,
10   Whose heart is wintry cold?
His breast is love's all-worshipped tomb,
Where all love's pilgrims come.

Bring me an axe and spade,
    Bring me a winding sheet;
15 When I my grave have made,
    Let winds and tempests beat.
Then down I'll lie, as cold as clay;
True love doth pass away.

viii. Dr B. H. Malkin, who wrote on B. and his work, quoting some poems, in his *A Father's Memoirs of his Child* (in the dedication), said that this poem was written before B. was fourteen. Other poems in *Poetical Sketches* seem more immature than this; but there is no direct evidence to disprove Malkin's assertion.

ix. At first appearance a poem compiled at second-hand by collecting Elizabethan phrases and images. In fact, though there are commonplaces in the lover's threat that he will die of love (but here the lover is female), and the references to yew (but in Elizabethan verse, with its Mediterranean sources, the cypress is more usual than the English churchyard yew), to

X SONG

Love and harmony combine,
And around our souls entwine,
While thy branches mix with mine,
And our roots together join.

5   Joys upon our branches sit,
Chirping loud and singing sweet;
Like gentle streams beneath our feet,
Innocence and virtue meet.

Thou the golden fruit dost bear,
10   I am clad in flowers fair;
Thy sweet boughs perfume the air,
And the turtle buildeth there.

There she sits and feeds her young,
Sweet I hear her mournful song;
15   And thy lovely leaves among,
There is Love: I hear his tongue.

There his charming nest doth lay,
There he sleeps the night away;
There he sports along the day,
20   And doth among our branches play.

XI SONG

I love the jocund dance,
The softly-breathing song,
Where innocent eyes do glance,
And where lisps the maiden's tongue.

5   I love the laughing vale,
I love the echoing hill,

grave and shroud, and also the view of the lover as pilgrim, and though
the poem has a general resemblance to such others as Shakespeare's 'Come
away, death', the only close allusion it contains is the likeness of *13–14* to
Vaux's 'I loth that I did love' (in Tottel's Miscellany, though Blake will
have read it in Percy's *Reliques*): 'A pikeax and a spade, / And else a shrowd-
ing shete.' There is perhaps also an echo of the dirge for *Cymbeline*, without
its conceit: 'all lovers must / Consign to thee, and come to dust'.
x. This and the following poem have the style, though not the substance,
of Isaac Watts's verse for children (for an example, see *Innocence*, 'Cradle
Song', p. *56n* below).
x *16. his*] Printed 'her' and altered by B. in one copy.

Where mirth does never fail,
   And the jolly swain laughs his fill.

I love the pleasant cot,
10   I love the innocent bower.
Where white and brown is our lot,
   Or fruit in the midday hour.

I love the oaken seat
   Beneath the oaken tree,
15   Where all the old villagers meet,
   And laugh our sports to see.

I love our neighbours all,
   But, Kitty, I better love thee;
And love them I ever shall;
20   But thou art all to me.

XII SONG

Memory, hither come,
   And tune your merry notes;
And, while upon the wind
   Your music floats,
5   I'll pore upon the stream,
Where sighing lovers dream,
And fish for fancies as they pass
Within the watery glass.

I'll drink of the clear stream,
10   And hear the linnet's song;
And there I'll lie and dream
   The day along:
And, when night comes, I'll go
To places fit for woe;
15   Walking along the darkened valley
With silent melancholy.

XIII MAD SONG

The wild winds weep,
   And the night is a-cold;
Come hither, Sleep,
   And my griefs enfold.
5 But lo! the morning peeps
   Over the eastern steeps,
And the rustling birds of dawn
The earth do scorn.

Lo! to the vault
10   Of paved heaven,
With sorrow fraught
My notes are driven;
They strike the ear of night,
Make weep the eyes of day;
15   They make mad the roaring winds,
And with tempests play.

Like a fiend in a cloud
With howling woe,
After night I do crowd,
20   And with night will go;
I turn my back to the east,
From whence comforts have increased;
For light doth seize my brain
With frantic pain.

XIV SONG

Fresh from the dewy hill, the merry year
Smiles on my head and mounts his flaming car;
Round my young brows the laurel wreathes a shade,
And rising glories beam around my head.

5   My feet are winged, while o'er the dewy lawn,
I meet my maiden, risen like the morn.
Oh, bless those holy feet, like angels' feet;
Oh, bless those limbs, beaming with heavenly light!

Like as an angel glittering in the sky,
10   In times of innocence and holy joy—

xiii. There are six 'Mad Songs' in Percy's *Reliques*, though none quite like
B.'s (note esp. the characteristic sentiment of the last two lines). Cp. from
Percy's songs (Series II, Book II, nos. 17–22): 'Fears and cares oppress my
soul; / Hark how the angry Furies howl! / Pluto laughs, and Proserpine is
glad / To see poor naked Tom of Bedlam mad' ('Old Tom of Bedlam',
st. 2). 'Ah! 'tis in vain! 'tis all, 'tis all in vain! / Death and despair must end
the fatal pain: / Cold, cold despair, disguis'd like snow and rain, / Falls on
my breast; bleak winds in tempests blow; / My veins all shiver, and my
fingers glow: / My pulse beats a dead march for lost repose, / And to a
solid lump of ice my poor fond heart is froze' ('The Lady Distracted with
Love', attrib. Tom D'Urfey, st. 4). The difference between B.'s source and
his invention is plain.
xiii. 4. enfold] Printed *unfold*, but altered by B. to *infold* in one copy. The
spelling above is modernized from this.

The joyful shepherd stops his grateful song
To hear the music of an angel's tongue.

So when she speaks, the voice of heaven I hear;
So when we walk, nothing impure comes near;
15 Each field seems Eden, and each calm retreat;
Each village seems the haunt of holy feet.

But that sweet village where my black-eyed maid
Closes her eyes in sleep beneath night's shade,
Whene'er I enter, more than mortal fire
20 Burns in my soul and does my song inspire.

XV SONG

When early morn walks forth in sober grey,
Then to my black-eyed maid I haste away;
When evening sits beneath her dusky bower,
And gently sighs away the silent hour,
5 The village bell alarms—away I go,
And the vale darkens at my pensive woe.

To that sweet village, where my black-eyed maid
Doth drop a tear beneath the silent shade,
I turn my eyes; and, pensive as I go,
10 Curse my black stars and bless my pleasing woe.

Oft when the summer sleeps among the trees,
Whispering faint murmurs to the scanty breeze,
I walk the village round; if at her side,
A youth doth walk in stolen joy and pride,
15 I curse my stars in bitter grief and woe
That made my love so high, and me so low.

O should she e'er prove false, his limbs I'd tear,
And throw all pity on the burning air;
I'd curse bright fortune for my mixed lot,
20 And then I'd die in peace and be forgot.

XVI TO THE MUSES

Whether on Ida's shady brow,
    Or in the chambers of the east,
The chambers of the sun, that now
    From ancient melody have ceased;

xiv, xv. Two conventional songs in the idiom of eighteenth-century
sensibility. The 'black eyes' belong to the convention, but Blake's wife
Catherine is said to have had black eyes. (Note the 'Kitty' of xi.)

5   Whether in heaven ye wander fair,
    Or the green corners of the earth,
Or the blue regions of the air,
    Where the melodious winds have birth;

Whether on crystal rocks ye rove,
10   Beneath the bosom of the sea
Wandering in many a coral grove,
    Fair Nine, forsaking poetry!

How have you left the ancient love
    That bards of old enjoyed in you!
The languid strings do scarcely move,
15   The sound is forced, the notes are few.

XVII GWIN, KING OF NORWAY

Come, kings, and listen to my song,
    When Gwin, the son of Nore,
Over the nations of the north
    His cruel sceptre bore.

5   The nobles of the land did feed
    Upon the hungry poor;
They tear the poor man's lamb and drive
    The needy from their door.

'The land is desolate; our wives
10   And children cry for bread;
Arise, and pull the tyrant down;
    Let Gwin be humbled.'

Gordred the giant roused himself
    From sleeping in his cave;
15   He shook the hills, and in the clouds
    The troubled banners wave.

Beneath them rolled, like tempests black,
    The numerous sons of blood,
Like lions' whelps, roaring abroad,
20   Seeking their nightly food.

xvii. Cp. 'Fair Elenor' (pp. 6–8). Gordred here may derive from Chatterton's *Godred Crovan*; the style is very Chattertonian. The ballad form is Percy's rather than Chatterton's (who borrowed it from Percy), but B. would know it also from its general circulation. Yet B.'s use of the ballad is noticeably literary; he misses the spare vigour of the Scottish ballad, which suggests that his immediate mentor was Chatterton.

Down Bleron's hills they dreadful rush,
　Their cry ascends the clouds—
The trampling horse, and clanging arms
　Like rushing mighty floods.

25　Their wives and children, weeping loud,
　　Follow in wild array,
　Howling like ghosts, furious as wolves,
　　In the bleak wintry day.

　'Pull down the tyrant to the dust,
30　　Let Gwin be humbled,'
　They cry, 'And let ten thousand lives
　　Pay for the tyrant's head.'

　From tower to tower the watchmen cry,
　　'O Gwin, the son of Nore,
35　Arouse thyself! the nations black,
　　Like clouds, come rolling o'er.'

　Gwin reared his shield, his palace shakes,
　　His chiefs come rushing round;
　Each, like an awful thunder cloud,
40　　With voice of solemn sound.

　Like reared stones around a grave
　　They stand around the King;
　Then suddenly each seized his spear,
　　And clashing steel does ring.

45　The husbandman does leave his plough,
　　To wade through fields of gore;
　The merchant binds his brows in steel
　　And leaves the trading shore;

　The shepherd leaves his mellow pipe
50　　And sounds the trumpet shrill;
　The workman throws his hammer down
　　To heave the bloody bill.

　Like the tall ghost of Barraton,
　　Who sports in stormy sky,
55　Gwin leads his host as black as night,
　　When pestilence does fly,

　With horses and with chariots;
　　And all his spearmen bold,
　March to the sound of mournful song,
60　　Like clouds around him rolled.

Gwin lifts his hand; the nations halt;
  'Prepare for war,' he cries—
Gordred appears; his frowning brow
  Troubles our northern skies.

65   The armies stand, like balances
  Held in the Almighty's hand:
'Gwin, thou hast filled thy measure up,
  Thou'rt swept from out the land.'

And now the raging armies rushed,
70   Like warring mighty seas;
The heavens are shook with roaring war,
  The dust ascends the skies!

Earth smokes with blood and groans and shakes,
  To drink her children's gore,
75   A sea of blood; nor can the eye
  See to the trembling shore.

And on the verge of this wild sea
  Famine and death doth cry;
The cries of women and of babes
80   Over the field doth fly.

The king is seen raging afar
  With all his men of might;
Like blazing comets, scattering death
  Through the red feverous night.

85   Beneath his arm like sheep they die,
  And groan upon the plain;
The battle faints, and bloody men
  Fight upon hills of slain.

Now death is sick, and riven men
90   Labour and toil for life;
Steed rolls on steed, and shield on shield,
  Sunk in this sea of strife.

The god of war is drunk with blood,
  The earth doth faint and fail;

xvii *65. like balances*] Cp. *Paradise Lost* iv 1011–14: '. . . read thy lot in
yon celestial sign, / Where thou art weighed, and shown how light, how
weak / If thou resist. The Fiend looked up, and knew / His mounted scale
aloft: nor more; but fled . . .'
xvii *78. famine and death doth cry*] The use of a singular verb after a com-
bined subject like this was not unknown: it was at this time attracting the
attention of the more pedantic grammarians.
xvii *88. hills of slain*] A phrase used several times by Chatterton.

95 The stench of blood makes sick the heavens;
  Ghosts glut the throat of hell.

 O what have kings to answer for
  Before that awful throne,
 When thousand deaths for vengeance cry,
100 And ghosts accusing groan?

 Like blazing comets in the sky
  That shake the stars of light,
 Which drop like fruit unto the earth,
  Through the fierce burning night;

105 Like these did Gwin and Gordred meet,
  And the first blow decides;
 Down from the brow unto the breast
  Gordred his head divides.

 Gwin fell; the sons of Norway fled,
110 All that remained alive;
 The rest did fill the vale of death;
  For them the eagles strive.

 The river Dorman rolled their blood
  Into the northern sea,
115 Who mourned his sons, and overwhelmed
  The pleasant south country.

XVIII AN IMITATION OF SPENSER

 Golden Apollo, that through heaven wide
  Scatter'st the rays of light and truth's beams,
 In lucent words my darkling verses dight,
  And wash my earthy mind in thy clear streams,
5 That wisdom may descend in fairy dreams,
 All while the jocund hours in thy train
  Scatter their fancies at thy poet's feet;
  And when thou yields to night thy wide domain,
 Let rays of truth enlight his sleeping brain.

10 For brutish Pan in vain might thee assay
  With tinkling sounds to dash thy nervous verse,

xvii 97–8. An interjection characteristic of B.
xviii. This is an 'imitation' in the normal eighteenth-century sense: not a parody, but an attempt to reproduce the manner of the original in a contemporary form. B. aims at the elaborateness of imagery and allusion (for once using classical mythology) as well as the diction and the archaism; but does not seek to add verses to *The Faerie Queene* or even to maintain Spenser's rhyme-scheme.
xviii 8. *when thou yields*] This should strictly be 'yieldest', but it saves the rhythm. B., unlike Spenser, was not colloquially familiar with 'thou' forms.

2*

Sound without sense; yet in his rude affray
    (For ignorance is Folly's leesing nurse,
    And love of Folly needs none other curse)
15 Midas the praise hath gained of lengthened ears,
    For which himself might deem him ne'er the worse
    To sit in council with his modern peers,
And judge of tinkling rhimes and elegances terse.

And thou, Mercurius, that with winged brow
20   Dost mount aloft into the yielding sky,
And through heaven's halls thy airy flight dost throw,
Entering with holy feet to where on high
Jove weighs the counsel of futurity;
    Then, laden with eternal fate, dost go
25 Down, like a falling star, from autumn sky,
And o'er the surface of the silent deep dost fly.

    If thou arrivest at the sandy shore,
Where nought but envious hissing adders dwell,
    Thy golden rod, thrown on the dusty floor,
30 Can charm to harmony with potent spell.
Such is sweet eloquence, that does dispel
    Envy and hate that thirst for human gore,
And cause in sweet society to dwell
Vile savage minds that lurk in lonely cell.

35   O Mercury, assist my labouring sense,
That round the circle of the world would fly!
    As the winged eagle scorns the towery fence
Of Alpine hills round his high aery,
And searches through the corners of the sky,
40   Sports in the clouds to hear the thunder's sound,
And see the winged lightnings as they fly,
    Then, bosomed in an amber cloud, around
Plumes his wide wings and seeks Sol's palace high.

    And thou, O warrior maid invincible,
45 Armed with the terrors of almighty Jove!

xviii 13. *leesing*] In Spenser, 'lesing' or 'leasing' (lie, falsehood) is always a substantive, but B. not unexpectedly sees it as an adjective formed from a verb.
xviii 14. *other*] Printed 'others' and corrected by B. in some copies.
xviii 15. *eares*] Printed 'cares' and altered by B. in one copy.
xviii 25. *down, like a falling star*] Cp. *Paradise Lost* i 744–5, where Mulciber 'with the setting sun / Dropped from the zenith, like a falling star.'
xviii 41. *see* is grammatically parallel with *hear* in line 40.

Pallas, Minerva, maiden terrible,
Lov'st thou to walk the peaceful solemn grove,
In solemn gloom of branches interwove?
Or bear'st thy ægis o'er the burning field,
50   Where, like the sea, the waves of battle move?
Or have thy soft piteous eyes beheld
The weary wanderer through the desert rove?
Or does the afflicted man thy heavenly bosom move?

XIX BLIND-MAN'S BUFF

When silver snow decks Susan's clothes,
And jewel hangs at the shepherd's nose,
The blushing bank is all my care,
With hearth so red and walls so fair.
5   'Heap the sea-coal; come heap it higher;
The oaken log lay on the fire.'
The well-washed stools, a circling row,
With lad and lass, how fair the show!
The merry can of nut-brown ale,
10   The laughing jest, the love-sick tale,
Till tired of chat, the game begins;
The lasses prick the lads with pins;
Roger from Dolly twitched the stool,
She falling, kissed the ground, poor fool!
15   She blushed so red, with sidelong glance
At hob-nail Dick, who grieved the chance.
But now for blind-man's buff they call;
Of each encumbrance clear the hall—
Jenny her silken kerchief folds,
20   And blear-eyed Will the black lot holds.
Now laughing stops, with 'Silence! hush!',
And Peggy Pout gives Sam a push.
The blind-man's arms, extended wide,
Sam slips between—'O woe betide
25   Thee, clumsy Will!'—but tittering Kate
Is penned up in the corner straight!
And now Will's eyes beheld the play,
He thought his face was t'other way.
Now, Kitty, now; what chance hast thou,
30   Roger so near thee trips, I vow!
She catches him—then Roger ties
His own head up—but not his eyes;
For through the slender cloth he sees,
And runs at Sam, who slips with ease
35   His clumsy hold, and, dodging round,

Sukey is tumbled on the ground!
See what it is to play unfair!
Where cheating is, there's mischief there.
But Roger still pursues the chase—
40 'He sees! he sees!' cries softly Grace;
O Roger, thou, unskilled in art,
Must, surer bound, go through thy part!
Now Kitty, pert, repeats the rhymes,
And Roger turns him round three times;
45 Then pauses ere he starts—but Dick
Was mischief bent upon a trick:
Down on his hands and knees he lay,
Directly in the blind-man's way—
Then cries out, 'Hem!'—Hodge heard and ran
50 With hood-winked chance—sure of his man;
But down he came. Alas, how frail
Our best of hopes, how soon they fail!
With crimson drops he stains the ground,
Confusion startles all around.
55 Poor piteous Dick supports his head,
And fain would cure the hurt he made;
But Kitty hasted with a key,
And down his back they straight convey
The cold relief—the blood is stayed,
60 And Hodge again holds up his head.
Such are the fortunes of the game,
And those who play should stop the same
By wholesome laws, such as: all those
Who on the blinded man impose
65 Stand in his stead, as long a-gone
When men were first a nation grown;
Lawless they lived—till wantonness
And liberty began to increase,
And one man lay in another's way;
70 Then laws were made to keep fair play.

xx KING EDWARD THE THIRD

PERSONS

King Edward	Lord Audley
The Black Prince	Lord Percy
Queen Philippa	Bishop
Duke of Clarence	William, Dagworth's
Sir John Chandos	man
Sir Thomas Dagworth	Peter Blunt, a common
Sir Walter Manny	soldier

SCENE 1, *The Coast of France. King Edward and Nobles before the Army.*

King. O thou, to whose fury the nations are
But as dust, maintain thy servant's right.
Without thine aid, the twisted mail and spear,
And forged helm, and shield of seven times beaten brass,
5 Are idle trophies of the vanquisher.
When confusion rages, when the field is in a flame,
When the cries of blood tear horror from heaven,
And yelling death runs up and down the ranks,
Let liberty, the chartered right of Englishmen,
10 Won by our fathers in many a glorious field,
Enerve my soldiers; let liberty
Blaze in each countenance, and fire the battle.
The enemy fight in chains, invisible chains, but heavy;
Their minds are fettered; then how can they be free,
15 While, like the mounting flame,
We spring to battle o'er the floods of death?
And these fair youths, the flower of England,
Venturing their lives in my most righteous cause,
O sheathe their hearts with triple steel, that they
20 May emulate their fathers' virtues.
And thou, my son, be strong; thou fightest for a crown
That death can never ravish from thy brow,
A crown of glory: but from thy very dust
Shall beam a radiance to fire the breasts
25 Of youth unborn. Our names are written equal
In fame's wide trophied hall; 'tis ours to gild
The letters and to make them shine with gold
That never tarnishes: whether third Edward,
Or the Prince of Wales, or Montacute, or Mortimer,

xx. The debts of this dramatic fragment to Shakespeare are evident; but by this time Shakespeare was accepted as a 'classic', and to imitate him when writing a historical play was blameless and almost inevitable. At the same time, much of the verse is standard late eighteenth-century; the same influences are visible here as in most of the *Poetical Sketches*–a predominance of the conventions of B.'s day, coloured by a reading of Percy and Chatterton, and of the Elizabethans. B. included two incidents from Edward III's reign in a series of historical engravings mentioned in a draft prospectus of 1793.

xx. *Scene 1*] B. does not number the scenes.

xx. *1.9. liberty*] British Freedom was one of the staple elements of eighteenth-century patriotism.

xx *1.28–30.* This sentiment illustrates B.'s egalitarianism rather than the feelings of a medieval king, or of most authors contemporary with B.

30 · Or even the least by birth, shall gain the brightest fame,
    Is in his hand to whom all men are equal.
    The world of men are like the numerous stars,
    That beam and twinkle in the depth of night,
    Each clad in glory according to his sphere.
35 But we that wander from our native seats
    And beam forth lustre on a darkling world
    Grow larger as we advance, and some perhaps
    The most obscure at home, that scarce were seen
    To twinkle in their sphere, may so advance,
40 That the astonished world, with up-turned eyes,
    Regardless of the moon, and those that once were bright,
    Stand only for to gaze upon their splendour!

            [*He here knights the Prince and other young Nobles.*

    Now let us take a just revenge for those
    Brave lords, who fell beneath the bloody axe
45 At Paris. Thanks, noble Harcourt, for 'twas
    By your advice we landed here in Brittany—
    A country not yet sown with destruction,
    And where the fiery whirlwind of swift war
    Has not yet swept its desolating wing.
50 Into three parties we divide by day,
    And separate march, but join again at night:
    Each knows his rank, and heaven marshal all. [*Exeunt.*

        SCENE 2, *English Court. Lionel, Duke of Clarence,*
            Queen Philippa, Lords, Bishop, etc.

    Clarence. My Lords, I have, by the advice of her
    Whom I am doubly bound to obey, my parent
    And my sovereign, called you together.
    My task is great, my burden heavier than
5   My unfledged years;
    Yet, with your kind assistance, Lords, I hope
    England shall dwell in peace; that while my father
    Toils in his wars, and turns his eyes on this

xx 1.*43*. STAGE DIRECTION] This event happened soon after Edward's land-
ing in Normandy.
xx 1.*46*. *Brittany*] In fact, in the Creçy campaign, Edward landed at Saint-
Vaast-de-la-Hogue on the Cotentin peninsula. He had landed in Brittany
in 1343.
xx 1.*50*. *Into three parties*] As reported by Froissart (the ultimate source of
most eighteenth-century histories of this war).

His native shore, and sees commerce fly round
10 With his white wings, and sees his golden London
And her silver Thames, thronged with shining spires
And corded ships, her merchants buzzing round
Like summer bees, and all the golden cities
In his land overflowing with honey,
15 Glory may not be dimmed with clouds of care.
Say, lords, should not our thoughts be first to
        commerce?
My Lord Bishop, you would recommend us agriculture?
Bishop. Sweet prince, the arts of peace are great,
And no less glorious than those of war,
20 Perhaps more glorious in the philosophic mind.
When I sit at my home, a private man,
My thoughts are on my gardens and my fields,
How to employ the hand that lacketh bread.
If industry is in my diocese,
25 Religion will flourish; each man's heart
Is cultivated, and will bring forth fruit.
This is my private duty and my pleasure.
But, as I sit in council with my prince,
My thoughts take in the general good of the whole,
30 And England is the land favoured by commerce;
For commerce, though the child of agriculture,
Fosters his parent, who else must sweat and toil,
And gain but scanty fare. Then, my dear lord,
Be England's trade our care; and we, as tradesmen,
35 Looking to the gain of this our native land.
Clar. O my good lord, true wisdom drops like honey
From your tongue, as from a worshipped oak!
Forgive, my lords, my talkative youth that speaks
Not merely what my narrow observation has
40 Picked up, but what I have concluded from your lessons.
Now, by the Queen's advice, I ask your leave

xx 2.9. *commerce*] This emphasis on the importance of commerce is an
eighteenth-century commonplace: cp. James Thomson's *Liberty* v 569–73:
'The times I see, whose glory to supply / For toiling ages, commerce
round the world / Has winged unnumbered sails and from each land /
Materials heaped that, well employed, with Rome / Might vie our gran-
deur, and with Greece our art!'
xx 2.37. *a worshipped oak*] It was a commonplace of eighteenth-century
historical knowledge drawn from Caesar's *Gallic Wars*, that the Druids
had worshipped in oak groves. Clarence's simile is out of character, but
the anachronism shows how 'the past'–of all ages–was one notion in
Blake's mind.

To dine to-morrow with the Mayor of London:
If I obtain your leave, I have another boon
To ask, which is the favour of your company;
45 I fear Lord Percy will not give me leave.
Percy. Dear sir, a prince should always keep his state,
And grant his favours with a sparing hand,
Or they are never rightly valued.
These are my thoughts, yet it were best to go;
50 But keep a proper dignity, for now
You represent the sacred person of
Your father. 'Tis with princes as 'tis with the sun,
If not sometimes o'er-clouded, we grow weary
Of his officious glory.
55 *Clar.* Then you will give me leave to shine sometimes,
My lord?
Lord. Thou hast a gallant spirit, which I fear
Will be imposed on by the closer sort! [*Aside.*
Clar. Well, I'll endeavour to take
60 Lord Percy's advice; I have been used so much
To dignity that I'm sick on't.
Queen Phil. Fie, fie, Lord Clarence; you proceed not to
business,
But speak of your own pleasures.
I hope their lordships will excuse your giddiness.
65 *Clar.* My lords, the French have fitted out many
Small ships of war, that, like to ravening wolves,
Infest our English seas, devouring all
Our burdened vessels, spoiling our naval flocks.
The merchants do complain and beg our aid.
70 *Percy.* The merchants are rich enough;
Can they not help themselves?
Bish. They can, and may; but how to gain their will
Requires our countenance and help.
Percy. When that they find they must, my lord, they
will;
75 Let them but suffer awhile, and you shall see
They will bestir themselves.
Bish. Lord Percy cannot mean that we should suffer
This disgrace; if so, we are not sovereigns
Of the sea; our right, that heaven gave
80 To England, when at the birth of nature
She was seated in the deep, the ocean ceased
His mighty roar, and fawning played around
Her snowy feet, and owned his awful queen.

xx 2.*78–9. sovereigns | Of the sea*] An eighteenth-century sentiment.

Lord Percy, if the heart is sick, the head
85 Must be aggrieved; if but one member suffer,
The heart doth fail. You say, my Lord, the merchants
Can, if they will, defend themselves against
These rovers: this is a noble scheme,
Worthy the brave Lord Percy, and as worthy
90 His generous aid to put it into practice.
Percy. Lord Bishop, what was rash in me is wise
In you; I dare not own the plan. 'Tis not
Mine. Yet will I, if you please,
Quickly to the Lord Mayor, and work him onward
95 To this most glorious voyage, on which cast
I'll set my whole estate,
But we will bring these Gallic rovers under.
Queen Phil. Thanks, brave Lord Percy; you have the
        thanks
Of England's Queen, and will, ere long, of England.
                                        [*Exeunt.*

SCENE 3, *At Crécy. Sir Thomas Dagworth and*
            Lord Audley, meeting.

Aud. Good morrow, brave Sir Thomas; the bright morn
Smiles on our army, and the gallant sun
Springs from the hills like a young hero
Into the battle, shaking his golden locks
5 Exultingly. This is a promising day.
Dagw. Why, my Lord Audley, I don't know.
Give me your hand, and now I'll tell you what
I think you do not know—Edward's afraid of Philip.
Aud. Ha, ha, Sir Thomas! you but joke;
10 Did you e'er see him fear? At Blanchetaque,
When almost singly he drove six thousand
French from the ford, did he fear then?
Dagw. Yes, fear—that made him fight so.
Aud. By the same reason I might say, 'tis fear
15 That makes you fight.
Dagw. Mayhap you may; look upon Edward's face—
No one can say he fears. But when he turns
His back, then I will say it to his face,
He is afraid; he makes us all afraid.

xx 3.*10. e'er*] Printed 'ere'.
Blanchetaque] A ford near Abbeville where Edward's army forced a crossing
of the Somme on the way to Flanders, and thus avoided being trapped
against the sea by the larger French army. Froissart records 1,000 horsemen
and 6,000 footmen, but does not give this personal glory to Edward.

20   I cannot bear the enemy at my back.
     Now here we are at Crécy; where, to-morrow,
     To-morrow we shall know. I say, Lord Audley,
     That Edward runs away from Philip.
     Aud. Perhaps you think the Prince too is afraid?
25   *Dagw.* No; God forbid! I'm sure he is not—
     He is a young lion. Oh, I have seen him fight,
     And give command, and lightning has flashed
     From his eyes across the field. I have seen him
     Shake hands with death, and strike a bargain for
30   The enemy; he has danced in the field
     Of battle, like the youth at morrice play.
     I'm sure he's not afraid, nor Warwick, nor none,
     None of us but me; and I am very much afraid.
     Aud. Are you afraid too, Sir Thomas?
35   I believe that as much as I believe
     The King's afraid; but what are you afraid of?
     Dagw. Of having my back laid open; we turn
     Our backs to the fire, till we shall burn our skirts.
     Aud. And this, Sir Thomas, you call fear? Your fear
40   Is of a different kind then from the King's;
     He fears to turn his face, and you to turn your back.
     I do not think, Sir Thomas, you know what fear is.

              Enter Sir John Chandos.

     Chand. Good morrow, Generals; I give you joy.
     Welcome to the fields of Crécy. Here we stop,
45   And wait for Philip.
     Dagw. I hope so.
     Aud. There Sir Thomas; do you call that fear?
     Dagw. I don't know; perhaps he takes it by fits.
     Why, noble Chandos, look you here—
50   One rotten sheep spoils the whole flock;
     And if the bell-wether is tainted, I wish
     The Prince may not catch the distemper too.
     Chand. Distemper, Sir Thomas! what distemper?
     I have not heard.
55   *Dagw.* Why, Chandos, you are a wise man,

xx 3.23. *Edward runs away*] Edward was intending to join his allies in
Flanders. Until he could do so he was avoiding the superior French army,
but he reached an advantageous position at Crécy and unexpectedly
turned to face them.
xx 3.51. *bell-wether*] The leader of the flock, given a bell so that other sheep
can follow him.

I know you understand me; a distemper
The King caught here in France of running away.
Aud. Sir Thomas you say you have caught it too.
Dag. And so will the whole army; 'tis very catching,
60 For when the coward runs, the brave man totters.
Perhaps the air of the country is the cause.
I feel it coming upon me, so I strive against it;
You yet are whole, but after a few more
Retreats, we all shall know how to retreat
65 Better than fight. To be plain, I think retreating
Too often takes away a soldier's courage.
Chand. Here comes the King himself; tell him your
    thoughts
Plainly, Sir Thomas.
Dagw. I've told him before, but his disorder
70 Makes him deaf.

     Enter King Edward and Black Prince.

King. Good morrow, Generals. When English courage
    fails,
Down goes our right to France;
But we are conquerors everywhere; nothing
Can stand our soldiers; each man is worthy
75 Of a triumph. Such an army of heroes
Ne'er shouted to the heavens, nor shook the field.
Edward, my son, thou art
Most happy, having such command; the man
Were base who were not fired to deeds
80 Above heroic, having such examples.
Prince. Sire! with respect and deference I look
Upon such noble souls, and wish myself
Worthy the high command that Heaven and you
Have given me. When I have seen the field glow,
85 And in each countenance the soul of war
Curbed by the manliest reason, I have been winged
With certain victory; and 'tis my boast,
And shall be still my glory. I was inspired
By these brave troops.
90 *Dagw.* Your Grace had better make
Them all generals.
King. Sir Thomas Dagworth, you must have your joke,
And shall, while you can fight as you did at
The ford.
95 *Dagw.* I have a small petition to your Majesty.
King. What can Sir Thomas Dagworth ask, that Edward
Can refuse?

Dagw. I hope your Majesty cannot refuse so great
    A trifle; I've gilt your cause with my best blood,
100   And would again, were I not forbid
    By him whom I am bound to obey: my hands
    Are tied up, my courage shrunk and withered,
    My sinews slackened, and my voice scarce heard;
    Therefore I beg I may return to England.
105   *King.* I know not what you could have asked,
      Sir Thomas,
    That I would not have sooner parted with
    Than such a soldier as you have been, and such a friend.
    Nay, I will know the most remote particulars
    Of this strange petition; that, if I can,
110   I still may keep you here.
    Dagw. Here on the fields of Crécy we are settled,
    Till Philip springs the timorous covey again.
    The wolf is hunted down by causeless fear;
    The lion flees, and fear usurps his heart—
115   Startled, astonished at the clamorous cock;
    The eagle, that doth gaze upon the sun,
    Fears the small fire that plays about the fen;
    If, at this moment of their idle fear,
    The dog doth seize the wolf, the forester the lion,
120   The negro in the crevice of the rock
    Doth seize the soaring eagle; undone by flight,
    They tame submit—such the effect flight has
    On noble souls. Now hear its opposite:
    The timorous stag starts from the thicket wild,
125   The fearful crane springs from the splashy fen,
    The shining snake glides o'er the bending grass,
    The stag turns head and bays the crying hounds;
    The crane o'ertaken fighteth with the hawk;
    The snake doth turn and bite the padding foot;
130   And, if your Majesty's afraid of Philip,
    You are more like a lion than a crane.
    Therefore I beg I may return to England.
    King. Sir Thomas, now I understand your mirth,
    Which often plays with wisdom for its pastime,
135   And brings good counsel from the breast of laughter.
    I hope you'll stay, and see us fight this battle,
    And reap rich harvest in the fields of Crécy,
    Then go to England, tell them how we fight,
    And set all hearts on fire to be with us.
140   Philip is plumed and thinks we flee from him;
    Else he would never dare to attack us. Now,
    Now the quarry's set, and death doth sport

In the bright sunshine of this fatal day.
Dagw. Now my heart dances, and I am as light
145 As the young bridegroom going to be married.
Now must I to my soldiers, get them ready,
Furbish our armours bright, new-plume our helms,
And we will sing, like the young housewives busied
In the dairy. My feet are winged, but not
150 For flight, an please your grace.
King. If all my soldiers are as pleased as you,
'Twill be a gallant thing to fight or die;
Then I can never be afraid of Philip.
Dagw. A raw-boned fellow t'other day passed by me;
155 I told him to put off his hungry looks—
He answered me, 'I hunger for another battle.'
I saw a little Welshman with a fiery face;
I told him he looked like a candle half
Burned out; he answered, he was 'pig enough
160 To light another pattle.' Last night, beneath
The moon I walked abroad; when all had pitched
Their tents and all were still,
I heard a blooming youth singing a song
He had composed, and at each pause he wiped
165 His dropping eyes. The ditty was, 'If he
Returned victorious, he should wed a maiden
Fairer than snow, and rich as midsummer.'
Another wept, and wished health to his father.
I chid them both, but gave them noble hopes.
170 These are the minds that glory in the battle,
And leap and dance to hear the trumpet sound.
King. Sir Thomas Dagworth, be thou near our person;
Thy heart is richer than the vales of France.
I will not part with such a man as thee.
175 If Philip came armed in the ribs of death,
And shook his mortal dart against my head,
Thou'dst laugh his fury into nerveless shame.
Go now, for thou art suited to the work,
Throughout the camp; inflame the timorous,
180 Blow up the sluggish into ardour, and
Confirm the strong with strength, the weak inspire,
And wing their brows with hope and expectation:
Then to our tent return and meet to council.

[*Exit Dagworth.*

Chand. That man's a hero in his closet, and more
185 A hero to the servants of his house
Than to the gaping world; he carries windows

In that enlarged breast of his that all
May see what's done within.
Prince. He is a genuine Englishman, my Chandos,
190 And hath the spirit of liberty within him.
Forgive my prejudice, Sir John; I think
My Englishmen the bravest people on
The face of the earth.
Chand. Courage, my Lord, proceeds from self-
dependence;
195 Teach man to think he's a free agent,
Give but a slave his liberty, he'll shake
Off sloth, and build himself a hut, and hedge
A spot of ground. This he'll defend; 'tis his
By right of nature. Thus set in action,
200 He will still move onward to plan conveniences,
Till glory fires his breast to enlarge his castle,
While the poor slave drudges all day, in hope
To rest at night.
King. O liberty, how glorious art thou!
205 I see thee hovering o'er my army, with
Thy wide-stretched plumes; I see thee
Lead them on to battle;
I see thee blow thy golden trumpet, while
Thy sons shout the strong shout of victory!
210 O noble Chandos, think thyself a gardener,
My son a vine, which I commit unto
Thy care; prune all extravagant shoots, and guide
The ambitious tendrils in the paths of wisdom;
Water him with thy advice, and heaven
215 Rain freshening dew upon his branches. And,
O Edward, my dear son, learn to think lowly of
Thyself, as we may all each prefer other—
'Tis the best policy, and 'tis our duty.

[*Exit King Edward.*

Prince. And may our duty, Chandos, be our pleasure.
220 Now we are alone, Sir John, I will unburden
And breathe my hopes into the burning air,
Where thousand deaths are posting up and down,
Commissioned to this fatal field of Crécy.
Methinks I see them arm my gallant soldiers,
225 And gird the sword upon each thigh, and fit
Each shining helm, and string each stubborn bow,
And dance to the neighing of our steeds.

x 3.*218. Exit*] Printed 'Exeunt'.

Methinks the shout begins, the battle burns;
Methinks I see them perch on English crests,
230 And roar the wild flame of fierce war upon
The thronged enemy. In truth, I am too full.
It is my sin to love the noise of war.
Chandos, thou seest my weakness. Strong nature
Will bend or break us; my blood, like a springtide,
235 Does rise so high to overflow all bounds
Of moderation; while reason, in his
Frail bark, can see no shore or bound for vast
Ambition. Come, take the helm, my Chandos,
That my full-blown sails overset me not
240 In the wild tempest; condemn my venturous youth,
That plays with danger, as the innocent child,
Unthinking, plays upon the viper's den.
I am a coward in my reason, Chandos.
Chand. You are a man, my prince, and a brave man,
245 If I can judge of actions; but your heat
Is the effect of youth and want of use;
Use makes the armed field and noisy war
Pass over as a summer cloud, unregarded,
Or but expected as a thing of course.
250 Age is contemplative; each rolling year
Brings forth fruit to the mind's treasure-house,
While vacant youth doth crave and seek about
Within itself, and findeth discontent;
Then, tired of thought, impatient takes the wing,
255 Seizes the fruits of time, attacks experience,
Roams round vast nature's forest—where no bounds
Are set, the swiftest may have room, the strongest
Find prey; till tired at length, sated and tired
With the changing sameness, old variety,
260 We sit us down and view our former joys
With distaste and dislike.
Prince. Then if we must tug for experience,
Let us not fear to beat round nature's wilds
And rouse the strongest prey; then if we fall,
265 We fall with glory. I know the wolf
Is dangerous to fight, not good for food,
Nor is the hide a comely vestment; so
We have our battle for our pains. I know
That youth has need of age to point fit prey,

---

xx 3.*236. his*] Printed 'her', corrected by B. in some copies (cp. 291–93).
xx 3.*243. I am a coward in my reason*] 'My spirit leads me to do daring acts
which my reason counsels me to avoid.'

270 And oft the stander-by shall steal the fruit
Of the other's labour. This is philosophy;
These are the tricks of the world; but the pure soul
Shall mount on native wings, disdaining
Little sport, and cut a path into the heaven of glory,
275 Leaving a track of light for men to wonder at.
I'm glad my father does not hear me talk;
You can find friendly excuses for me, Chandos.
But do you not think, Sir John, that if it please
The Almighty to stretch out my span of life,
280 I shall with pleasure view a glorious action,
Which my youth mastered?
    Chand. Considerate age, my Lord, views motives,
And not acts; when neither warbling voice,
Nor trilling pipe is heard, nor pleasure sits
285 With trembling age, the voice of conscience then,
Sweeter than music in a summer's eve,
Shall warble round the snowy head and keep
Sweet symphony to feathered angels, sitting
As guardians round your chair. Then shall the pulse
290 Beat slow, and taste, and touch, and sight, and sound,
            and smell,
That sing and dance round reason's fine-wrought
            throne,
Shall flee away and leave him all forlorn—
Yet not forlorn if conscience is his friend. [*Exeunt.*

SCENE 4 *in Sir Thomas Dagworth's Tent. Dagworth and
            William his Man.*

Dagw. Bring hither my armour, William;
Ambition is the growth of every clime.
Will. Does it grow in England, sir?
Dagw. Aye, it grows most in lands most cultivated.
5 *Will.* Then it grows most in France; the vines here
Are finer than any we have in England.
Dagw. Aye, but the oaks are not.
Will. What is the tree you mentioned? I don't think
I ever saw it.
10 *Dagw.* Ambition.
Will. Is it a little creeping root that grows in ditches?
Dagw. Thou dost not understand me, William.
It is a root that grows in every breast;
Ambition is the desire or passion that one man
15 Has to get before another in any pursuit after glory;
But I don't think you have any of it.

Will. Yes, I have; I have a great ambition to know every thing, sir.

Dagw. But when our first ideas are wrong, what follows
20 must all be wrong of course; 'tis best to know a little, and to know that little aright.

Will. Then, sir, I should be glad to know if it was not ambition that brought over our King to France to fight for his right?

25 *Dagw.* Though the knowledge of that will not profit thee much, yet I will tell you that it was ambition.

Will. Then if ambition is a sin, we are all guilty in coming with him and in fighting for him.

Dagw. Now, William, thou dost thrust the question
30 home; but I must tell you that guilt, being an act of the mind, none are guilty but those whose minds are prompted by that same ambition.

Will. Now I always thought that a man might be guilty of doing wrong without knowing it was wrong.

35 *Dagw.* Thou art a natural philosopher and knowest truth by instinct, while reason runs aground, as we have run our argument. Only remember, William, all have it in their power to know the motives of their own actions, and 'tis a sin to act without some reason.

40 *Will.* And whoever acts without reason may do a great deal of harm without knowing it.

Dagw. Thou art an endless moralist.

Will. Now there's a story come into my head that I will tell your honour, if you'll give me leave.

45 *Dagw.* No, William, save it till another time; this is no time for story-telling. But here comes one who is as entertaining as a good story.

Enter Peter Blunt.

Peter. Yonder's a musician going to play before the King; it's a new song about the French and English, and the
50 Prince has made the minstrel a squire, and given him I don't know what, and I can't tell whether he don't mention us all one by one; and he is to write another about all us that are to die, that we may be remembered in Old England, for all our blood and bones are in France. And
55 a great deal more that we shall all hear by and by; and I

xx 4.49. *a new song*] The song of Scene 6?
xx 4.52. *another . . .*] Perhaps *A War Song to Englishmen*, printed separately, no. xxiii.

came to tell your honour, because you love to hear war-
songs.
Dagw. And who is this minstrel, Peter, dost know?
Peter. Oh, ay, I forgot to tell that; he has got the same
60 name as Sir John Chandos, that the prince is always
with—the wise man, that knows us all as well as your
honour, only ain't so good natured.
Dagw. I thank you, Peter, for your information, but not
for your compliment, which is not true. There's as much
65 difference between him and me as between glittering
sand and fruitful mould or shining glass and a wrought
diamond, set in rich gold, and fitted to the finger of an
emperor. Such is that worthy Chandos.
Peter. I know your honour does not think anything of
70 yourself, but everybody else does.
Dagw. Go, Peter, get you gone; flattery is delicious, even
from the lips of a babbler. [*Exit Peter.*
Will. I never flatter your honour.
Dagw. I don't know that.
75 *Will.* Why, you know, sir, when we were in England, at
the tournament at Windsor, and the Earl of Warwick
was tumbled over, you asked me if he did not look well
when he fell? And I said, No, he looked very foolish; and
you was very angry with me for not flattering you.
80 *Dagw.* You mean that I was angry with you for not
flattering the Earl of Warwick. [*Exeunt.*

SCENE 5, *Sir Thomas Dagworth's Tent. Sir Thomas*
Dagworth. To him—
Enter Sir Walter Manny.

Sir Walter. Sir Thomas Dagworth, I have been weeping
Over the men that are to die today.
Dagw. Why, brave Sir Walter, you or I may fall.
Sir Walter. I know this breathing flesh must lie and rot,
5 Covered with silence and forgetfulness.
Death wons in cities' smoke and in still night,
When men sleep in their beds, walketh about.
How many in walled cities lie and groan,
Turning themselves upon their beds,
10 Talking with death, answering his hard demands!
How many walk in darkness, terrors are round
The curtains of their beds, destruction is
Ready at the door! How many sleep

xx 5.6 *wons*] dwells–a Spenserism.

In earth, covered with stones and deathy dust,
15 Resting in quietness, whose spirits walk
Upon the clouds of Heaven, to die no more!
Yet death is terrible, though borne on angel's wings.
How terrible then is the field of death
Where he doth rend the vault of Heaven
20 And shake the gates of Hell!
O Dagworth, France is sick, the very sky,
Though sunshine light it, seems to me as pale
As the pale fainting man on his death-bed,
Whose face is shown by light of sickly taper.
25 It makes me sad and sick at very heart;
Thousands must fall today.
Dagw. Thousands of souls must leave this prison house,
To be exalted to those heavenly fields,
Where songs of triumph, palms of victory,
30 Where peace, and joy, and love, and calm content,
Sit singing in the azure clouds and strew
Flowers of Heaven's growth over the banquet-table.
Bind ardent hope upon your feet like shoes,
Put on the robe of preparation,
35 The table is prepared in shining Heaven,
The flowers of immortality are blown.
Let those that fight, fight in good stedfastness,
And those that fall shall rise in victory.
Sir Walter. I've often seen the burning field of war,
40 And often heard the dismal clang of arms,
But never, till this fatal day of Crécy,
Has my soul fainted with these views of death.
I seem to be in one great charnel-house,
And seem to scent the rotten carcases.
45 I seem to hear the dismal yells of death,
While the black gore drops from his horrid jaws.
Yet I not fear the monster in his pride—
But oh, the souls that are to die to-day!
Dagw. Stop, brave Sir Walter; let me drop a tear,
50 Then let the clarion of war begin.
I'll fight and weep, 'tis in my country's cause;
I'll weep and shout for glorious liberty.
Grim war shall laugh and shout, decked in tears,
And blood shall flow like streams across the meadows
55 That murmur down their pebbly channels and
Spend their sweet lives to do their country service.
Then shall England's verdure shoot, her fields shall
   smile,
Her ships shall sing across the foaming sea,

Her mariners shall use the flute and viol,
60   And rattling guns, and black and dreary war,
Shall be no more.
Sir Walter. Well, let the trumpet sound, and the drum
      beat;
Let war stain the blue heavens with bloody banners;
I'll draw my sword, nor ever sheathe it up,
65   Till England blow the trump of victory,
Or I lay stretched upon the field of death. [*Exeunt.*

SCENE 6, *in the Camp. Several of the Warriors
met at the King's Tent with a Minstrel, who sings
the following Song:*

O sons of Trojan Brutus, clothed in war,
Whose voices are the thunder of the field,
Rolling dark clouds o'er France, muffling the sun
In sickly darkness like a dim eclipse,
5   Threatening as the red brow of storms, as fire
Burning up nations in your wrath and fury.

Your ancestors come from the fires of Troy,
(Like lions roused by lightning from their dens,
Whose eyes do glare against the stormy fires)
10   Heated with war, filled with the blood of Greeks
With helmets hewn, and shields covered with gore,
In navies black, broken with wind and tide.

They landed in firm array upon the rocks
Of Albion; they kissed the rocky shore.
15   'Be thou our mother, and our nurse,' they said;
'Our children's mother, and thou shalt be our grave;
The sepulchre of ancient Troy, from whence
Shall rise cities, and thrones, and arms, and awful
      powers.'

Our fathers swarm from the ships. Giant voices
20   Are heard from the hills, the enormous sons
Of Ocean run from rocks and caves—wild men,
Naked and roaring like lions, hurling rocks,
And wielding knotty clubs, like oaks entangled,
Thick as a forest, ready for the axe.

25   Our fathers move in firm array to battle,
The savage monsters rush like roaring fire;
Like as a forest roars with crackling flames,

xx 6.1. *sons of Trojan Brutus*] Referring to the legend that Trojans, escaping
from Troy when it fell, came to Britain and founded a nation under Brutus.

When the red lightning, borne by furious storms,
Lights on some woody shore; the parched heavens
_30_   Rain fire into the molten raging sea.
The smoking trees are strewn upon the shore,
Spoiled of their verdure. Oh, how oft have they
Defied the storm that howled o'er their heads!
Our fathers, sweating, lean on their spears and view
_35_   The mighty dead—giant bodies, streaming blood,
Dread visages, frowning in silent death.

Then Brutus spoke, inspired; our fathers sit
Attentive on the melancholy shore.
Hear ye the voice of Brutus: 'The flowing waves
_40_   Of time come rolling o'er my breast,' he said;
'And my heart labours with futurity.
Our sons shall rule the empire of the sea.

'Their mighty wings shall stretch from east to west,
Their nest is in the sea; but they shall roam
_45_   Like eagles for the prey; nor shall the young
Crave or be heard; for plenty shall bring forth,
Cities shall sing, and vales in rich array
Shall laugh, whose fruitful laps bend down with fulness.

'Our sons shall rise from thrones in joy,
_50_   Each one buckling on his armour. Morning
Shall be prevented by their swords' gleaming,
And evening hear their song of victory.
Their towers shall be built upon the rocks,
Their daughters shall sing, surrounded with shining
            spears.
_55_   'Liberty shall stand upon the cliffs of Albion,
Casting her blue eyes over the green ocean;
Or, towering, stand upon the roaring waves,
Stretching her mighty spear o'er distant lands,
While, with her eagle wings, she covereth
_60_   Fair Albion's shore and all her families.'

XXI PROLOGUE,

intended for a dramatic piece of
KING EDWARD THE FOURTH.

Oh, for a voice like thunder, and a tongue
To drown the throat of war! When the senses

xxi. _Title._ No trace of such a play survives, and the word 'intended' in the
title implies that it was never written.
xxi _1. O for a voice_] Cp. Shakespeare's well-known prologue to _King
Henry V_, line 1. B.'s prologue is clearly not a practical stage piece.

Are shaken, and the soul is driven to madness,
Who can stand? When the souls of the oppressed
5   Fight in the troubled air that rages, who can stand?
When the whirlwind of fury comes from the
Throne of God, when the frowns of his countenance
Drive the nations together, who can stand?
When sin claps his broad wings over the battle,
10   And sails rejoicing in the flood of death;
When souls are torn to everlasting fire,
And fiends of hell rejoice upon the slain,
Oh, who can stand? Oh, who hath caused this?
Oh, who can answer at the throne of God?
15   The kings and nobles of the land have done it!
Hear it not, Heaven, thy ministers have done it!

XXII PROLOGUE to KING JOHN.

Justice hath heaved a sword to plunge in Albion's breast;
for Albion's sins are crimson dyed, and the red scourge
follows her desolate sons. Then patriot rose; full oft did
patriot rise, when tyranny hath stained fair Albion's
5   breast with her own children's gore. Round his majestic
feet deep thunders roll; each heart does tremble, and
each knee grows slack. The stars of heaven tremble: the
roaring voice of war, the trumpet, calls to battle!

xxi 4. *Who can stand?*] Cp. *Malachi* iii 2: 'Who may abide the day of his
coming? And who shall stand when he appeareth?'
xxii. Although written as prose, *Prologue to King John* should be recognized
as belonging to an intermediate kind, the *prose-poem*, a form which was
popular in B.'s age. Several examples of attempts in this medium by B.
exist: in *Poetical Sketches* itself, two other pieces called 'The Couch of
Death' and 'Contemplation'; and two pieces in MS, beginning 'Then she
bore pale desire . . .' and 'Woe, cried the muse . . .' These four pieces have
been omitted; this *Prologue*, more dramatically rhetorical, is import-
ant, not as literature, but as an illustration of a stage in the development of
B.'s style, which soon rejected prose-poetry, but retained, in his long-lined
verse, many of its features. Solomon Gessner's *The Death of Abel*, translated
into English by Mary Collyer in 1761, was the leading work in the vogue,
which continued well into the nineteenth century, but produced little of
any literary value. The essence of the prose-poem is that it has the diction
and sentiments of poetry–the poetry of sensibility–and tries to capture the
effects of the poetic use of metre in the freer rhythms of prose. B.'s pieces
are by no means bad examples of the style, but they illustrate its major
inherent defect—an almost complete lack of any technical discipline, with a
resultant excess of rhetoric and sentimentality.

Brother in brother's blood must bathe, rivers of death!
10 O land, most hapless! O beauteous island, how forsaken!
Weep from thy silver fountains; weep from thy gentle
rivers! The angel of the island weeps! Thy widowed
virgins weep beneath thy shades! Thy aged fathers gird
themselves for war! The suckling infant lives to die in
15 battle; the weeping mother feeds him for the slaughter!
The husbandman doth leave his bending harvest! Blood
cries afar! The land doth sow itself! The glittering youth
of courts must gleam in arms! The aged senators their
ancient swords assume! The trembling sinews of old age
20 must work the work of death against their progeny; for
tyranny hath stretched his purple arm, and 'Blood', he
cries; 'the chariots and the horses, the noise of shout, and
dreadful thunder of the battle heard afar!'—Beware, O
proud! thou shalt be humbled; thy cruel brow, thine iron
25 heart is smitten, though lingering fate is slow. O yet may
Albion smile again, and stretch her peaceful arms, and
raise her golden head, exultingly! Her citizens shall
throng about her gates, her mariners shall sing upon the
sea, and myriads shall to her temples crowd! Her sons
30 shall joy as in the morning! Her daughters sing as to the
rising year!

XXIII A WAR SONG TO ENGLISHMEN

Prepare, prepare the iron helm of war;
Bring forth the lots, cast in the spacious orb;
The angel of fate turns them with mighty hands,
And casts them out upon the darkened earth.
5   Prepare, prepare.

Prepare your hearts for death's cold hand; prepare
Your souls for flight, your bodies for the earth!
Prepare your arms for glorious victory!
Prepare your eyes to meet a holy God!
10   Prepare, prepare.

Whose fatal scroll is that? Methinks 'tis mine!
Why sinks my heart, why faltereth my tongue?
Had I three lives, I'd die in such a cause,

xxii *12–13. Thy widowed virgins*] Brides widowed on the day of their wed-
ding, a theme found in a number of ballads in Percy's *Reliques*.
xxiii. In appearance and sentiment the most juvenile of the *Poetical
Sketches*; hence, perhaps, its obscure place in the collection. See *Edward III*
iv *52n.*

And rise, with ghosts, over the well-fought field.
15   Prepare, prepare.

The arrows of Almighty God are drawn.
Angels of death stand in the lowering heavens.
Thousands of souls must seek the realms of light,
And walk together on the clouds of Heaven.
20   Prepare, prepare.

Soldiers, prepare! Our cause is Heaven's cause;
Soldiers, prepare! Be worthy of our cause;
Prepare to meet our fathers in the sky;
Prepare, O troops, that are to fall today.
25   Prepare, prepare.

Alfred shall smile and make his harp rejoice;
The Norman William and the learned Clerk,
And Lion-Heart, and black-browed Edward, with
His loyal queen shall rise and welcome us!
30   Prepare, prepare.

2 Poems written in a copy of *Poetical Sketches*

Three poems written in a copy of *Poetical Sketches* which was inscribed
'from Mrs Flaxman May 15 1784'; discovered and transcribed by G. L.
Keynes in 1910. It is at present in Wellington, N.Z. The second song is a
variant of 'Laughing Song' in *Innocence* (p. 57).

I SONG 1ST BY A SHEPHERD

Welcome, stranger, to this place,
Where joy doth sit on every bough,
Paleness flies from every face;
We reap not what we do not sow.

5   Innocence doth like a rose
Bloom on every maiden's cheek;
Honour twines around her brows,
The jewel health adorns her neck.

II SONG 2ND BY A YOUNG SHEPHERD

When the trees do laugh with our merry wit,
And the green hill laughs with the noise of it,
When the meadows laugh with lively green,
And the grasshopper laughs in the merry scene;

 5 When the greenwood laughs with the voice of joy,
    And the dimpling stream runs laughing by,
    When Edessa, and Lyca, and Emilie,
    With their sweet round mouths sing *Ha, ha, he*!

    When the painted birds laugh in the shade
10 Where our table with cherries and nuts is spread,
    Come live and be merry and join with me,
    To sing the sweet chorus of *Ha, ha, he*!

III SONG BY AN OLD SHEPHERD

    When silver snow decks Sylvio's clothes,
    And jewel hangs at shepherd's nose,
    We can abide life's pelting storm
    That makes our limbs quake, if our hearts be warm.

 5 Whilst virtue is our walking-staff,
    And truth a lantern to our path,
    We can abide life's pelting storm
    That makes our limbs quake, if our hearts be warm.

    Blow, boisterous wind; stern winter, frown—
10 Innocence is a winter's gown;
    So clad, we'll abide life's pelting storm
    That makes our limbs quake, if our hearts be warm.

3 Songs from *An Island in the Moon*

The amusing skit known as *An Island in the Moon*, from its opening phrase and its setting in a supposed lunar world indistinguishable from Europe, England and London, exists in a holograph MS of *c.* 1784, as shown chiefly by an allusion to a fantastic fashion in ladies' hats in the autumn of that year. As a whole, *An Island in the Moon* parodies the activities and idiosyncrasies of B.'s circle of friends; the following selection contains all the songs that are sung in the course of their gatherings, with the immediate prose context. The characters are identified where possible in the notes.

I CHAPTER 3

    In the moon as Phœbus stood over his oriental garden-
    ing, 'Oh, ay, come, I'll sing you a song' said the Cynic.
    'The trumpeter shit in his hat' said the Epicurean.

¶ 3.i 2. *the Cynic*] Quid the Cynic is B. himself.
i 3. *the Epicurean*] Suction the Epicurean and Sipsop the Pythagorean are the others of a trio of philosophers: they have not been certainly identified, but Suction may well be Robert Blake.

3+B.

'And clapped it on his head' said the Pythagorean.
5 'I'll begin again', said the Cynic:
     Little Phœbus came strutting in
     With his fat belly and his round chin.
     What is it you would please to have?
     Ho! Ho!
10   I won't let it go at only so and so—

Mrs Gimblet looked as if they meant her. Tilly Lally
laughed like a cherry clapper. Aradobo asked, 'Who was
Phœbus, sir?' Obtuse Angle answered, quickly, 'He was
the god of physic, painting, perspective, geometry, geo-
15 graphy, astronomy, cookery, chemistry, mechanics,
tactics, pathology, phraseology, theology, mythology,
astrology, osteology, somatology—in short, every art and
science adorned him as beads round his neck.' Here
Aradobo looked astonished and asked if he understood
20 engraving. Obtuse Angle answered, 'Indeed he did.'
'Well,' said the other, 'he was as great as Chatterton.'
Tilly Lally turned round to Obtuse Angle and asked who
it was that was as great as Chatterton. 'Hey, how should
I know?' answered Obtuse Angle. 'Who was it, Ara-
25 dobo?' 'Why, sir,' said he, 'the gentleman that the song
was about.' 'Ah,' said Tilly Lally, 'I did not hear it;
what was it, Obtuse Angle?' 'Pooh', said he, 'Nonsense.'
'Mhm', said Tilly Lally. 'It was Phœbus,' said the
Epicurean. 'Ah, that was the gentleman,' said Aradobo.
30 'Pray, sir', said Tilly Lally, 'who was Phœbus?' Obtuse
Angle answered, 'The heathens in the old ages used to
have gods that they worshipped and they used to sacrifice
to them. You have read about that in the Bible.' 'Ah,'
said Aradobo, 'I thought I had read of Phœbus in the
35 Bible.' 'Aradobo, you should always think before you
speak,' said Obtuse Angle. 'Ha, ha, ha, he means
Pharaoh!' said Tilly Lally. 'I am ashamed of you
making use of the names in the Bible,' said Mrs Sigta-
gatist. 'I'll tell you what, Mrs Sinagain, I don't think
40 there's any harm in it,' said Tilly Lally. 'No,' said
Inflammable Gas, 'I have got a camera obscura at
home—what was it you was talking about?' 'Law,' said
Tilly Lally, 'what has that to do with Pharaoh?'
'Pho, nonsense—hang Pharaoh and all his host,' said
45 the Pythagorean, 'sing away, Quid.'
    Then the Cynic sung:

i 41. *Inflammable Gas*] Joseph Priestley, Unitarian minister and radical,
who discovered oxygen.

Honour and genius is all I ask,
And I ask the gods no more.
No more! No more! ⎱ *The three philosophers*
50   No more! No more! ⎰ *bear chorus.*

Here Aradobo sucked his underlip.

II FROM CHAPTER 6

'Ah,' said Sipsop, 'I only wish Jack Tearguts had had the
cutting of Plutarch. He understands anatomy better
than any of the ancients; he'll plunge his knife up to the
hilt in a single drive and thrust his fist in, and all in the
5   space of a quarter of an hour. He does not mind their
crying—though they cry ever so, he'll swear at them and
keep them down with his fist and tell them that he'll
scrape their bones if they don't lay still and be quiet.
What the devil should the people in the hospital, that
10   have it done for nothing, make such a piece of work for?'
'Hang that,' said Suction, 'let us have a song.'
Then the Cynic sang:

When old Corruption first begun,
Adorned in yellow vest,
15   He committed on Flesh a whoredom—
O what a wicked beast!

2
From them a callow babe did spring,
And old Corruption smiled
To think his race should never end,
20   For now he had a child.

3
He called him Surgery, and fed
The babe with his own milk;
For Flesh and he could ne'er agree—
She would not let him suck.

4
25   And this he always kept in mind,
And formed a crooked knife,
And ran about with bloody hands
To seek his mother's life.

i 47. A parody of a song in James Harris's *Daphnis and Chloe* (1762).
ii 1. *Jack Tearguts*] 1st rdg del. Jack Hunter. A famous surgeon, 1728–93,
the founder of modern surgery.

5
And as he ran to seek his mother
30 He met with a dead woman;
He fell in love and married her—
A deed which is not common.

6
She soon grew pregnant, and brought forth
Scurvy and Spotted Fever:
35 The father grinned and skipped about
And said, 'I'm made for ever.

7
'For now I have procured these imps,
I'll try experiments.'
With that he tied poor Scurvy down
40 And stopped up all its vents,

8
And when the child began to swell
He shouted out aloud:
'I've found the dropsy out, and soon
Shall do the world more good.'

9
45 He took up Fever by the neck
And cut out all its spots,
And through the holes which he had made
He first discovered guts.

'Ah,' said Sipsop, 'you think we are rascals, and we
50 think you are rascals. I do as I choose—what is it to any-
body, what I do? I am always unhappy too, when I think
of surgery. I don't know: I do it because I like it. My
father does what he likes and so do I. I think somehow
I'll leave it off. There was a woman having her cancer
55 cut and she shrieked so that I was quite sick.'

III From chapter 8

Steelyard the Lawgiver, sitting at his table taking ex-
tracts from Hervey's *Meditations among the Tombs* and
Young's *Night Thoughts*. 'He is not able to hurt me', said
he, 'more than making me constable or taking away
5 the parish business. Hah! "My crop of corn is but a
field of tares."

iii 1. *Steelyard*] John Flaxman, B.'s friend for many years; sculptor and
Swedenborgian.
iii 5. *My crop . . . tares*] from *Reliquiæ Wottonianæ* (1685): Chidiock Tych-
bourn's lines written on the eve of his execution (1586).

Says Jerome, 'happiness is not for us poor crawling reptiles of the earth.' Talk of happiness and happiness; it's no such thing—every person has a something:

10 Hear then the pride and knowledge of a sailor—
  His spritsail, foresail, mainsail, and his mizzen.
  A poor frail man, God wot, I know none frailer—
  I know no greater sinner than John Taylor.

'If I had only myself to care for, I'd soon make Double
15 Elephant look foolish—and Filigree work. I hope shall live to see "The wreck of matter and the crush of worlds," as Young says'.

. . . Then said Miss Gittipin, 'Mr Scopprell, do you know the song of Phœbe and Jellicoe?' 'No, miss,' said
20 Scopprell. Then she repeated these verses while Steelyard walked about the room:

  Phœbe dressed like beauty's queen,
  Jellicoe in faint peagreen,
  Sitting all beneath a grot
25 Where the little lambkins trot;

  Maidens dancing, loves a-sporting,
  All the country folks a-courting,
  Susan, Johnny, Bet, and Joe,
  Lightly tripping on a row.

30 Happy people! who can be
  In happiness compared with ye?
  The pilgrim with his crook and hat
  Sees your happiness complete.

 'A charming song indeed, miss!' said Scopprell. Here
35 they received a summons for a merrymaking at the Philosophers' house.

IV CHAPTER 9

'I say, this evening we'll all get drunk.' 'I say, dash, an anthem, an anthem!' said Suction:

   Lo! the bat with leathern wing,
   Winking and blinking,
5   Winking and blinking,
   Winking and blinking,
   Like Doctor Johnson.

iii *16*. Really Addison's *Cato* v.i.28.
iv *3*. From William Collins's *Ode to Evening* *9-10*.

   Quid––'Oho!' said Doctor Johnson
    To Scipio Africanus,
10   'If you don't own me a philosopher,
    I'll kick your Roman anus'.

   Suction–'Aha!' to Doctor Johnson
    Said Scipio Africanus,
    'Lift up my Roman petticoat
15   And kiss my Roman anus'.

   And the cellar goes down with a step.
         (*Grand Chorus*)

   'Ho, ho, ho, ho, ho, ho, ho, hooooo, my pooooooor
siiides! I I should die if I was to live here!' said Scopprell,
'Ho, ho, ho, ho, ho–'

20 *1*st *Vo* Want matches?
  2^d *Vo* Yes, Yes, Yes!
  *1*st *Vo* Want matches?
  2^d *Vo* No–––––––––
  *1*st *Vo* Want matches?
25 *2*^d *Vo* Yes, Yes, Yes!
  *1*st *Vo* Want matches?
  2^d *Vo* No–––––––––

  Here was great confusion and disorder. Aradobo said
that the boys in the street sing something very pretty and
30 funny about matches. Then Mrs Nannicantipot sung:

    I cry my matches as far as Guildhall.
    God bless the Duke and his Aldermen all.

  Then sung Scopprell:

    I ask the Gods no more,
35   no more, no more.

  Then said Suction, 'Come, Mr Lawgiver, your song,'
and the Lawgiver sung:

    As I walked forth one May morning,
    To see the fields so pleasant and so gay,
40   Oh, there did I spy a young maiden sweet
    Among the violets that smell so sweet,
     Smell so sweet,
     Smell so sweet,
    Among the violets that smell so sweet.

45 'Hang your violets, here's your rum and water!' 'Oh,
ay,' said Tilly Lally: 'Joe Bradley and I was going along

one day in the sugar house. Joe Bradley saw—for he had
but one eye—saw a treacle jar. So he goes of his blind side
and dips his hand up to the shoulder in treacle. "Here,
50 lick, lick, lick!" said he. Ha, ha, ha, ha, ha! For he had
but one eye! Ha, ha, ha, ho!' Then sung Scopprell:

>   And I ask the gods no more,
>   no more, no more,
>   no more, no more.

55   'Miss Gittipin,' said he, 'you sing like a harpsichord.
Let your bounty descend to our fair ears, and favour us
with a fine song'
        Then she sung:

>   This frog he would a wooing ride—
60   Kitty alone, Kitty alone.
>   This frog he would a wooing ride—
>   Kitty alone and I.
>   Sing cock I carry, Kitty alone,
>   Kitty alone, Kitty alone,
65   Cock I carry, Kitty alone,
>   Kitty alone and I.

    'Charming, truly elegant' said Scopprell,

>   And I ask the gods no more.

        'Hang your serious songs,' said Sipsop, and he sung
70 as follows

>   Fa ra so bo ro
>   Fa ra bo ra
>   Sa ba ra ra ba rare roro
>   Sa ra ra ra bo ro ro ro
75   Radara
>   Sarapodo no flo ro.

        'Hang Italian songs, let's have English,' said Quid.
'English genius for ever! Here I go':

>   Hail matrimony, made of love,
80   To thy wide gates how great a drove
>   On purpose to be yoked do come!
>   Widows and maids and youths also,
>   That lightly trip on beauty's toe
>   Or sit on beauty's bum.

85   Hail, fingerfooted lovely creatures,

iv 59. *This frog*] A well-known traditional folk-song or nursery rhyme.

The females of our human natures,
Formed to suckle all mankind—
'Tis you that come in time of need;
Without you we should never breed,
90   Or any comfort find.

For if a damsel's blind or lame,
Or nature's hand has crooked her frame,
Or if she's deaf or is wall-eyed;
Yet if her heart is well inclined,
95   Some tender lover she shall find
That panteth for a bride.

The universal poultice this,
To cure whatever is amiss
In damsel or in widow gay;
100   It makes them smile, it makes them skip;
Like birds just cured of the pip
They chirp and hop away.

Then come, ye maidens, come, ye swains,
Come and be eased of all your pains
105   In matrimony's golden cage.

'I–go and be hanged', said Scopprell, 'How can you
have the face to make game of matrimony?'

Then Quid called upon Obtuse Angle for a song, and
he, wiping his face and looking on the corner of the
110 ceiling, sang:

To be or not to be
Of great capacity,
Like Sir Isaac Newton
Or Locke or Doctor South,
115   Or Sherlock upon Death—
I'd rather be Sutton.

For he did build a house
For aged men and youth
With walls of brick and stone.
120   He furnished it within
With whatever he could win,
And all his own.

He drew out of the stocks
His money in a box,
125   And sent his servant
To Green the bricklayer,
And to the carpenter;
He was so fervent.

iv *116.* Founder of the Charterhouse (1611).

The chimneys were three score,
130   The windows many more;
And for convenience
He sinks and gutters made,
And all the way he paved
To hinder pestilence.

135   Was not this a good man,
Whose life was but a span,
Whose name was Sutton,
As Locke or Doctor South
Or Sherlock upon Death
140   Or Sir Isaac Newton?

The Lawgiver was very attentive and begged to have
it sung over again and again till the company were
tired and insisted on the Lawgiver singing a song him-
self—which he readily complied with:

145   This city and this country has brought forth many
    mayors,
To sit in state and give forth laws out of their old
    oak chairs,
With face as brown as any nut with drinking of
    strong ale;
Good English hospitality, oh, then it did not fail!

With scarlet gowns and broad gold lace would make
    a yeoman sweat,
150   With stockings rolled above their knees, and shoes as
    black as jet;
With eating beef and drinking beer, oh, they were
    stout and hale;
Good English hospitality, oh, then it did not fail!

Thus sitting at the table wide, the Mayor and
    Aldermen
Were fit to give law to the City; each ate as much as
    ten.
155   The hungry poor entered the hall to eat good beef
    and ale;
Good English hospitality, oh, then it did not fail!

Here they gave a shout and the company broke up.

V CHAPTER II

Another merry meeting at the house of Steelyard the
Lawgiver.
After supper Steelyard and Obtuse Angle had pumped

3*

Inflammable Gass quite dry. They played at forfeits and
5 tried every method to get good humour. Said Miss Gitti-
pin, 'Pray, Mr Obtuse Angle, sing us a song'; then he
sung:

Upon a Holy Thursday, their innocent faces clean,
The children walking two and two in grey and blue
and green;
10 Grey-headed beadles walked before with wands as
white as snow,
Till into the high dome of Paul's they like Thames
waters flow.

Oh, what a multitude they seemed, these flowers of
London town!
Seated in companies they sit, with radiance all their
own.
The hum of multitudes were there, but multitudes of
lambs,
15 Thousands of little girls and boys raising their inno-
cent hands.

Then like a mighty wind they raise to heaven the voice
of song,
Or like harmonious thunderings the seats of heaven
among.
Beneath them sit the reverend men, the guardians of
the poor:
Then cherish pity, lest you drive an angel from your
door.

20 After this they all sat silent for a quarter of an hour. And
Mrs Nannicantipot said, 'It puts me in mind of my
mother's song:'

When the tongues of children are heard on the green,
And laughing is heard on the hill,
25 My heart is at rest within my breast,
And everything else is still.

'Then come home, my children, the sun is gone down
And the dews of night arise;
Come come, leave off play, and let us away
30 Till the morning appears in the skies.'

'No, no, let us play, for it is yet day,
And we cannot go to sleep;

v 8. *Upon a Holy Thursday*] Cp. *Songs of Innocence* (pp. 57–66 below) for
this and the next two poems.

Besides, in the sky the little birds fly,
And the meadows are covered with sheep.'

35 'Well, well, go and play till the light fades away,
And then go home to bed.'
The little ones leaped and shouted and laughed,
And all the hills echoèd.

Then sung Quid:

40 'Oh, father, father, where are you going?
Oh, do not walk so fast!
Oh, speak, father, speak to your little boy,
Or else I shall be lost.'

The night it was dark, and no father was there,
45 And the child was wet with dew;
The mire was deep, and the child did weep,
And away the vapour flew.

Here nobody could sing any longer, till Tilly Lally
plucked up a spirit and he sung:

50 Oh, I say, you Joe,
Throw us the ball.
I've a good mind to go
And leave you all.
I never saw saw such a bowler—
55 To bowl the ball in a tansy
And to clean it with my handkercher
Without saying a word!

That Bill's a foolish fellow,
He has given me a black eye;
60 He does not know how to handle a bat
Any more than a dog or cat.
He has knocked down the wicket
And broke the stumps,
And runs without shoes to save his pumps.

65 Here a laugh began, and Miss Gittipin sung:

Leave, oh, leave me to my sorrows;
Here I'll sit and fade away,
Till I'm nothing but a spirit,
And I lose this form of clay.

70 Then if chance along this forest
Any walk in pathless ways,
Through the gloom he'll see my shadow,
Hear my voice upon the breeze.

75   The Lawgiver all the while sat delighted to see them in
such a serious humour. 'Mͬ Scopprell,' said he, 'you
must be acquainted with a great many songs.' 'O, dear
sir! Ho, ho, ho, I am no singer – I must beg of one of these
tender-hearted ladies to sing for me.' They all declined
and he was forced to sing himself:

80   There's Doctor Clash
And Signor Falalasole;
Oh, they sweep in the cash
Into their purse-hole.
Fa me la sol. La me fa sol.

85   Great A, little A,
Bouncing B,
Play away, play away,
You're out of the key.
Fa me la sol. La me fa sol.

90   Musicians should have
A pair of very good ears,
And long fingers and thumbs,
And not like clumsy bears.
Fa me la sol. La me fa sol.

95   Gentlemen, gentlemen,
Rap, rap, rap!
Fiddle, fiddle, fiddle!
Clap, clap, clap!
Fa me la sol. La me fa sol.

100   'Hm,' said the Lawgiver, 'funny enough. Let's have
Handel's "Water Piece". Then Sipsop sung:

A crowned king,
On a white horse sitting,
With his trumpets sounding,
105   And banners flying,
Through the clouds of smoke he makes his way;
And the shout of his thousands fills his heart with
rejoicing and victory,
And the shout of his thousands fills his heart with
110   rejoicing and victory,
Victory, victory! – 'twas William, the prince of Orange!

4 Songs of Innocence

In 1784-85 B. was partner in a print shop, where an illustrated book of verse of high artistic value would have been a useful addition to his stock. During this period these *Songs* began to be written, though they were not published in time to be useful in the shop, i.e. not until 1789-90. *Songs of Innocence* was original in its method of printing and exceptional in poetic value; but in form it is a kind of chap-book of poems in the tradition of Isaac Watts's *Divine Songs for Children* (1715), familiar to the children of two centuries-though B.'s book is distinguished by its lavish embellishment with engraved ornaments and illustrations. B. consistently rates freedom and joy in a child's life above discipline; but a distinction must be made between the overtones which the sophisticated reader can detect and the simpler effects the poems would have on the parents and children for whom they were intended. That B. himself saw the difference is plain, since he went on to produce *Songs of Experience*, in which such 'overtones' are made explicit. The bitterness of *Experience* should not make us doubt the sincerity of the *Songs of Innocence*, which he continued to issue separately even after the combined *Songs of Innocence and of Experience* had appeared *c.* 1794.

Date: on the titlepage, *1789*: probably engraved 1789-90. Three poems, 'Nurse's Song', 'The Little Boy lost' and 'Holy Thursday' appear in the MS *An Island in the Moon* (pp. 50-51 above), *c.* 1784. An early text of 'Laughing Song' (see p. 40 above) is dated May 1784. The poems' terminal dates are thus 1784-90. The form of the designs suggests a certain order, with two provisos: (*a*) that though the earliest designs were probably simpler than the style B. later developed, he doubtless reverted to the simple style when it suited him-i.e. the complex designs are probably later, but the simple designs may have been engraved at any date up to 1790; (*b*) we have no way of knowing how long the period was over which the engraving was done-years, months, or weeks. The simplest designs-'Echoing Green', 'Laughing Song', 'Spring', 'Little Boy Lost' and 'Found', 'The Little Black Boy', 'The Shepherd'-have a block illustration which resembles the illustration in a printed book. Another simple type is used in 'Holy Thursday', 'Nurse's Song', 'The Chimney Sweeper', 'A Dream', 'A Cradle Song' and 'The Schoolboy': this has a good deal of interlinear ornament, often with a simple illustration at head and foot. Three poems- 'The Divine Image', 'Infant Joy', 'The Blossom'-have a much more complex design, in which it and the text are presented as a whole upon the plate; and it is very probable that these were engraved distinctly later than the others so far mentioned. 'Night' and 'The Lamb' are intermediate; the design does not affect the layout of the text, but the page is a harmonious whole.

The dates of engraving were not necessarily those of composition. If 'Blake's original stereotype was 1788' (see p. 864 below), he must have

had some of the poems assembled before the technique was worked out,
and the order of engraving would only by chance follow that of composi-
tion. External evidence is slight. 'The Chimney Sweeper' may belong to
the period of agitation on behalf of child-sweeps, for the tone of the poem
is less naive than it seems; in any case B. had no need of an agitation
to show him the sweeps. 'The Little Girl Lost' and 'Found', and 'The
Voice of the Ancient Bard' both have a 'prophetic' tone which marks
them as the latest; 'The Little Girl' poems seem to belong to the period of
Thel (1788–89). In view of this uncertainty of dating, except for a few of
the earliest and latest poems, the order below is one of B.'s own–that of
one of the early copies. It has the advantage of presenting the simpler and
probably earlier poems first: the only liberties with this order have been
to move 'The Little Girl' poems and 'The Ancient Bard' to the end; in
this copy they followed 'A Dream' and 'The Little Black Boy' respec-
tively. B. never settled the order of these poems, though this is probably a
sign of experiment rather than of carelessness. But in eight early copies
(*c.* 1789–94), the following pairs are found seven times, which suggests that
B. found the association pointed:

A Dream	The Lamb
'Little Girl' poems	The Blossom
The Divine Image	Nurse's Song
The Chimney Sweeper	Holy Thursday
Spring	The Shepherd
The Schoolboy	Infant Joy
Laughing Song	
The Little Black Boy	
The Voice of the Ancient Bard	

A facsimile, in colour, is available (ed. G. L. Keynes, 1967).

[*Frontispiece*]

1 INTRODUCTION

Piping down the valleys wild,
Piping songs of pleasant glee,
On a cloud I saw a child
And he laughing said to me:

5   'Pipe a song about a lamb.'
So I piped with merry cheer;
'Piper, pipe that song again.'
So I piped; he wept to hear.

¶ 4. *Frontispiece.* The piper with his flock; the child of the 'Introduction'
hovers in the air over him.
i. Twining stems in both margins make ovals in which happy scenes of
'Innocence' are shown.

'Drop thy pipe, thy happy pipe;
10   Sing thy songs of happy cheer.'
So I sung the same again,
While he wept with joy to hear.

'Piper, sit thee down and write
In a book that all may read.'
15   So he vanished from my sight:
And I plucked a hollow reed,

And I made a rural pen,
And I stained the water clear,
And I wrote my happy songs
20   Every child may joy to hear.

II THE SHEPHERD

How sweet is the shepherd's sweet lot—
From the morn to the evening he strays!
He shall follow his sheep all the day,
And his tongue shall be filled with praise.

5   For he hears the lambs' innocent call,
And he hears the ewes' tender reply;
He is watchful while they are in peace,
For they know when their shepherd is nigh.

III INFANT JOY

'I have no name—
I am but two days old.'
What shall I call thee?
'I happy am,
5   Joy is my name.'
Sweet joy befall thee!

Pretty joy!
Sweet joy but two days old—

ii. This poem drifts from the pastoral to the religious, in keeping with its twin traditions—simple but polite pastoral poetry, in the same vein of sentimental mimicry that produced the Dresden shepherdess; and the *Divine Hymns for Children* of Isaac Watts, which put lessons for children into a genuine ballad form (for example, see 'Cradle Song' below). The design shows a youthful shepherd with his flock.

iii. The design shows an open flower, in which an angel admires a child on its mother's lap.

iii 5. *Joy . . . name*] Joy was not a common name for girls in B.'s time; he is using the abstract noun. The child may be boy or girl.

Sweet joy I call thee.
10   Thou dost smile,
I sing the while—
Sweet joy befall thee!

IV A CRADLE SONG

Sweet dreams, form a shade
O'er my lovely infant's head,
Sweet dreams of pleasant streams,
By happy silent moony beams.

5   Sweet sleep, with soft down
Weave thy brows an infant crown;
Sweet sleep, angel mild,
Hover o'er my happy child.

Sweet smiles in the night
10   Hover over my delight.
Sweet smiles, mother's smiles,
All the livelong night beguiles.

Sweet moans, dovelike sighs,
Chase not slumber from thy eyes.

iv. The text is on two plates; most of the second is taken up with a picture
of a mother watching her child in his cradle. Note the close parallel with
Watts's 'Cradle Hymn' (discussed in V. de S. Pinto: *The Divine Vision*
(1957), pp. 71–6):

Hush! my dear, lie still and slumber;
Holy angels guard thy bed!
Heavenly blessings without number
Gently falling on thy head.

Sleep, my babe; thy food and raiment
House and home thy friends provide,
All without thy care or payment,
All thy wants are well supplied.

How much better thou'rt attended
Than the Son of God could be,
When from heaven he descended
And became a child like thee.

Soft and easy is thy cradle;
Coarse and hard thy Saviour lay;
When his birthplace was a stable,
And his softest bed was hay . . .

iv 4. By] Either 'lit by' or 'together with'.

15   Sweet moans, sweeter smiles,
        All the dovelike moans beguiles.

        Sleep, sleep, happy child:
        All creation slept and smiled.
        Sleep, sleep, happy sleep,
20   While o'er thee thy mother weep.

        Sweet babe, in thy face
        Holy image I can trace;
        Sweet babe once like thee
        Thy maker lay and wept for me,

25   Wept for me, for thee, for all,
        When he was an infant small.
        Thou his image ever see,
        Heavenly face that smiles on thee—

        Smiles on thee, on me, on all,
30   Who became an infant small.
        Infant smiles are his own smiles,
        Heaven and earth to peace beguiles.

V LAUGHING SONG

    When the green woods laugh with the voice of joy,
    And the dimpling stream runs laughing by;
    When the air does laugh with our merry wit,
    And the green hill laughs with the noise of it;

5   When the meadows laugh with lively green
    And the grasshopper laughs in the merry scene;
    When Mary and Susan and Emily,
    With their sweet round mouths, sing *Ha, ha, he*!

    When the painted birds laugh in the shade
10 Where our table with cherries and nuts is spread,

iv *15–16*. i.e. 'Sweet moans! but your mother's sweeter smiles will beguile the moans away'.
Beguiles should strictly be 'beguile', but the rhyme forces a plural form. B. was not pedantic on these matters.
iv *17–24*. First, the mother's care ('weeping') for her sleeping child is like the creator's care for his unknowing creation. Then the child is like the infant Jesus: the creator's care caused him to become like a child, to look after the woman who then became his mother, as well as all creation.
v. For an earlier form, see p. 40 above. The design above the text shows a gay party around a table.
v *7. Mary . . . Emily*] Cp. the names in the earlier version–'Edessa, Lyca and Emilie'. For once, B.'s alteration brings the poem nearer to the everyday world.

Come live and be merry and join with me,
To sing the sweet chorus of *Ha, ha, he*!

VI THE LITTLE BLACK BOY

My mother bore me in the southern wild,
And I am black, but oh, my soul is white;
White as an angel is the English child,
But I am black as if bereaved of light.

5   My mother taught me underneath a tree,
And sitting down before the heat of day
She took me on her lap and kissed me,
And pointing to the east began to say:

'Look on the rising sun: there God does live
10 And gives his light, and gives his heat away;
And flowers and trees and beasts and men receive
Comfort in morning joy in the noon day.

'And we are put on earth a little space,
That we may learn to bear the beams of love,
15 And these black bodies and this sun-burnt face
Is but a cloud, and like a shady grove.

'For when our souls have learned the heat to bear
The cloud will vanish, we shall hear his voice,
Saying: "Come out from the grove, my love and care,
20 And round my golden tent like lambs rejoice."'

Thus did my mother say, and kissed me;
And thus I say to little English boy:
When I from black and he from white cloud free
And round the tent of God like lambs we joy,

25 I'll shade him from the heat till he can bear
To lean in joy upon our Father's knee;
And then I'll stand and stroke his silver hair,
And be like him and he will then love me.

vi. A poem in the spirit of contemporary radical anti-slavery writing. It apparently hints at the commonplace of 'the benighted heathen'; but note that the black boy leads the white boy to God, not vice versa. The design above the poem illustrates st. 2; the design after the poem illustrates the last stanza.

In the copy which is otherwise followed here for the order of *Songs of Innocence*, 'The Voice of the Ancient Bard' is the next poem: it has been put at the end on account of its undoubted lateness. But it normally went with this poem (see headn.).

VII THE ECHOING GREEN

The sun does arise,
And make happy the skies;
The merry bells ring
To welcome the spring;
5   The skylark and thrush,
The birds of the bush,
Sing louder around,
To the bells' cheerful sound,
While our sports shall be seen
10   On the Echoing Green.

Old John with white hair
Does laugh away care,
Sitting under the oak,
Among the old folk.
15   They laugh at our play,
And soon they all say,
'Such, such were the joys,
When we all, girls and boys,
In our youth-time were seen
20   On the Echoing Green.'

Till the little ones weary
No more can be merry;
The sun does descend,
And our sports have an end.
25   Round the laps of their mothers,
Many sisters and brothers,
Like birds in their nest,
Are ready for rest—
And sport no more seen,
30   On the darkening Green.

VIII NURSE'S SONG

When the voices of children are heard on the green,
And laughing is heard on the hill,

vii. Above the text, a family (four adults and a large group of children of
all ages) sit or play round a leafy tree. The margins contain figures of
children and branches with leaves and fruit; beneath the text the father and
mother lead the children home.

vii *11–13. Old John*] The conventional 'old shepherd'; B.'s later notion of
old age under an oak tree as evil has not yet grown.

viii. Cp. 'Nurse's Song', *Experience*, p. 214 below; and an early version in
Island in the Moon, p. 50 above. Beneath the text, the nurse sits and watches
the children dance in a ring.

My heart is at rest within my breast,
And everything else is still.

5   'Then come home, my children, the sun is gone down
And the dews of night arise;
Come, come, leave off play, and let us away
Till the morning appears in the skies.'

'No, no, let us play, for it is yet day,
10   And we cannot go to sleep;
Besides, in the sky the little birds fly,
And the hills are all covered with sheep.'

'Well, well, go and play till the light fades away,
And then go home to bed.'
15   The little ones leaped and shouted and laughed,
And all the hills echoed.

IX HOLY THURSDAY

'Twas on a Holy Thursday, their innocent faces clean,
The children walking two and two in red and blue and
green;
Grey-headed beadles walked before with wands as white
as snow,
Till into the high dome of Paul's they like Thames
waters flow.

5   Oh, what a multitude they seemed, these flowers of
London town!
Seated in companies they sit, with radiance all their own.

ix. Annual services for all the Charity Schools in London–i.e. schools (for
poor and destitute children) whose income was the voluntary subscriptions
of the rich–had been held since 1704: but only in St Paul's since 1782.
'Holy Thursday' strictly speaking is Ascension Day; these services were
held on the first Thursday in May *except* when that was Ascension Day.
Thus the occasion was 'Holy Thursday' by its own worth, not by the
tradition of ecclesiastical nomenclature. The emotional effect of the singing
of perhaps 6,000 children, evidently felt by B., is testified to by a number
of observers. This poem is found in *An Island in the Moon*, c. 1784, see
p. 50; cp. also 'Holy Thursday' in *Experience*, p. 219. The designs above
and below the text show the children in procession.
ix 2. *red*] 1st version (p. 50) has 'grey'. There were charity schools wear-
ing red, grey, blue and green; one wore orange. B. would make the altera-
tion for poetical reasons therefore, not for accuracy.

The hum of multitudes was there, but multitudes of
  lambs,
Thousands of little boys and girls raising their innocent
  hands.

Now like a mighty wind they raise to heaven the voice of
  song,
10 Or like harmonious thunderings the seats of Heaven
  among.
Beneath them sit the aged men, wise guardians of the
  poor:
Then cherish pity, lest you drive an angel from your
  door.

X ON ANOTHER'S SORROW

Can I see another's woe,
And not be in sorrow too?
Can I see another's grief,
And not seek for kind relief?

5 Can I see a falling tear,
And not feel my sorrow's share?
Can a father see his child
Weep, nor be with sorrow filled?

Can a mother sit and hear,
10 An infant groan, an infant fear?
No, no, never can it be,
Never, never can it be!

And can he, who smiles on all,
Hear the wren with sorrows small,
15 Hear the small bird's grief and care,
Hear the woes that infants bear,

And not sit beside the nest
Pouring pity in their breast,
And not sit the cradle near
20 Weeping tear on infant's tear,

And not sit both night and day,
Wiping all our tears away?
Oh, no, never can it be,
Never, never can it be!

x 11. beneath] There is no permanent gallery in St Paul's, but on these
occasions wooden stands were built to accommodate the thousands of
children present.
x. See note on iv 'A Cradle Song'.

25 He doth give his joy to all,
He becomes an infant small.
He becomes a man of woe,
He doth feel the sorrow too.

 Think not thou canst sigh a sigh,
30 And thy maker is not by;
Think not thou canst weep a tear,
And thy maker is not near.

 Oh, he gives to us his joy
That our grief he may destroy;
35 Till our grief is fled and gone,
He doth sit by us and moan.

XI SPRING

 Sound the flute!
Now it's mute;
Birds delight
Day and night;
5 Nightingale
In the dale,
Lark in the sky,
Merrily
Merrily merrily, to welcome in the year.

10 Little boy
Full of joy;
Little girl
Sweet and small;
Cock does crow,
15 So do you;
Merry voice,
Infant noise,
Merrily, merrily, to welcome in the year.

 Little lamb
20 Here I am;
Come and lick
My white neck.
Let me pull
Your soft wool,

xi. Above the text, a mother under a leafy tree holds up her baby to see the feeding sheep around them. Beneath the text, the child sits and plays with a lamb.

25   Let me kiss
         Your soft face;
         Merrily, merrily, we welcome in the year.

XII THE SCHOOLBOY

     I love to rise in a summer morn,
     When the birds sing on every tree;
     The distant huntsman winds his horn,
     And the skylark sings with me.
5   Oh, what sweet company!

     But to go to school in a summer morn—
     Oh, it drives all joy away!
     Under a cruel eye outworn
     The little ones spend the day,
10   In sighing and dismay.

     Ah, then at times I drooping sit,
     And spend many an anxious hour;
     Nor in my book can I take delight,
     Nor sit in learning's bower,
15   Worn through with the dreary shower.

     How can the bird, that is born for joy,
     Sit in a cage and sing?
     How can a child, when fears annoy,
     But droop his tender wing,
20   And forget his youthful spring?

     Oh, father and mother, if buds are nipped,
     And blossoms blown away,
     And if the tender plants are stripped
     Of their joy in the springing day
25   By sorrow and care's dismay,

     How shall the summer arise in joy,
     Or the summer fruits appear?
     Or how shall we gather what griefs destroy,
     Or bless the mellowing year,
30   When the blasts of winter appear?

xii. This poem seems to belong to *Experience* because of its unhappy mood; yet even after B. had issued the double volume, he kept 'The Schoolboy' in *Innocence* in thirteen copies. Perhaps the reason is that the poem expresses the child's feelings, and not the disillusioned adult's recollections of them.

xii. *Design*: a group of boys play marbles or taws at the foot; behind them a shrub twists its way up the R margin.

XIII A DREAM

Once a dream did weave a shade,
O'er my angel-guarded bed,
That an emmet lost its way
Where on grass methought I lay.

5　Troubled, wildered and forlorn,
Dark, benighted, travel-worn,
Over many a tangled spray
All heart-broke I heard her say:

'Oh, my children, do they cry?
10　Do they hear their father sigh?
Now they look abroad to see,
Now return and weep for me.'

Pitying, I dropped a tear;
But I saw a glow-worm near,
15　Who replied, 'What wailing wight
Calls the watchman of the night?

'I am set to light the ground,
While the beetle goes his round.
Follow now the beetle's hum;
20　Little wanderer, hie thee home.'

XIV THE BLOSSOM

Merry, merry sparrow,
Under leaves so green,
A happy blossom
Sees you, swift as arrow,
5　Seek your cradle narrow
Near my bosom.

xiii. This poem has been likened to Watts's song 'The Ant, or Emmet',
beginning: 'These emmets, how little they seem in our eyes! / We tread
them to dust, and a troop of them dies...' (cp. Pinto, *Divine Vision*, p.
77); yet it seems nearer the well-known nursery rhyme 'Ladybird, lady-
bird, fly away home' in its mood and sentiment, though the versification
is like Watts's.

xiii *8. heart-broke*] Standard eighteenth-century English (as commonly in
Jane Austen).

xiii *13. Pitying*] But the glow-worm was more practical, and showed a
light.

xiv. The extreme simplicity of this poem has puzzled interpreters, who
have had to delve deep for its symbolism. It is more than doubtful that B.
would embody such symbolism so deeply in a book planned for children;

Pretty, pretty robin,
Under leaves so green,
A happy blossom
10   Hears you sobbing, sobbing,
Pretty, pretty robin,
Near my bosom.

XV THE LAMB

Little lamb, who made thee?
Dost thou know who made thee,
Gave thee life and bid thee feed
By the stream and o'er the mead—
5   Gave thee clothing of delight,
Softest clothing, woolly bright,
Gave thee such a tender voice,
Making all the vales rejoice?
Little lamb, who made thee,
10   Dost thou know who made thee?

Little lamb, I'll tell thee,
Little lamb, I'll tell thee!
He is called by thy name,
For he calls himself a Lamb;
15   He is meek and he is mild,
He became a little child:
I a child, and thou a lamb,
We are called by his name.
Little lamb, God bless thee,
20   Little lamb, God bless thee!

in any case, he usually indicates quite clearly when he has an important notion to propound. B. speaks of the flower which looks on (i.e. it is a sentient being) at the human and the birds who laugh and weep together; all creation is united. This is one of B.'s favourite themes, both in this simple form in his early works, and more metaphysically in his last epics. The design shows a flame rising like a plant from the ground up the right margin and above the title; on its 'branches' sits a woman with a child; cherubs sport around: Cp. 'The Sick Rose' in *Experience*, p. 216.

xv. The text is set in the midst of a scene with a byre and a spreading, leafy tree in the background, while a naked child feeds one of a flock of sheep in the foreground; saplings reach up on either side of the text and entangle their branches beneath the title. Cp. 'The Tiger', *Experience*, p. 214.

xv 13. *called by thy name*] ('callèd' in two syllables): the phrase is from *Isaiah* xliii 7, *Jeremiah* xiv 9, xv 16, where the Israelites are 'called . . .' But B. gives the phrase a Christian meaning, and passes over the sense 'named as God's people'.

XVI THE LITTLE BOY LOST

'Father, father, where are you going?
Oh, do not walk so fast!
Speak, father, speak to your little boy,
Or else I shall be lost.'

5   The night was dark, no father was there,
The child was wet with dew;
The mire was deep, and the child did weep,
And away the vapour flew.

XVII THE LITTLE BOY FOUND

The little boy lost in the lonely fen,
Led by the wandering light,
Began to cry, but God ever nigh
Appeared like his father in white.

5   He kissed the child and by the hand led,
And to his mother brought,
Who in sorrow pale through the lonely dale
Her little boy weeping sought.

XVIII NIGHT

The sun descending in the west,
The evening star does shine;
The birds are silent in their nest,
And I must seek for mine.
5   The moon like a flower
In heaven's high bower,
With silent delight,
Sits and smiles on the night.

xvi. The child is led astray by a will-o'-the-wisp, which he thinks is his father. The poem, with very minor variations, appears in *An Island in the Moon*. The design above the poem shows the boy, in a short gown, following the light past a bare tree. Cp. 'A Little Boy Lost' in *Experience*, p. 217.

xvii. *The Little Boy Found*] This poem is not in *An Island in the Moon* Kathleen Raine has found a source in Salzmann's *Elements of Morality*, although the translation Blake knew was not published by 1789. Above the poem, the boy walks through the grim wood with his rescuer; an aura is seen round both heads.

xvii 2. *the wandering light* of the previous poem.

xvii 4. *like his father*] Note the illustration; B. approved the Swedenborgian idea that God is essentially the *human* being, in unbroken perfection.

Farewell, green fields and happy groves,
10 Where flocks have took delight;
Where lambs have nibbled, silent moves
The feet of angels bright.
Unseen they pour blessing,
And joy without ceasing,
15 On each bud and blossom,
And each sleeping bosom.

They look in every thoughtless nest,
Where birds are covered warm;
They visit caves of every beast
20 To keep them all from harm;
If they see any weeping,
That should have been sleeping,
They pour sleep on their head
And sit down by their bed.

25 When wolves and tigers howl for prey
They pitying stand and weep—
Seeking to drive their thirst away,
And keep them from the sheep.
But if they rush dreadful,
30 The angels most heedful
Receive each mild spirit
New worlds to inherit.

And there the lion's ruddy eyes
Shall flow with tears of gold,
35 And pitying the tender cries,
And walking round the fold,
Saying: 'Wrath by his meekness,
And by his health sickness,
Is driven away
40 From our immortal day.

'And now beside thee, bleating lamb,
I can lie down and sleep;
Or think on him who bore thy name,

xviii 10. took] Like 'heart-broke', xiii 8, an acceptable form.
xviii 11. moves] Unlike the above, a flaw: unusual but not unknown in B.
The rhyme causes it.
xviii 17. thoughtless] i.e. unreflecting–without the cares of thinking man.
Cp. 'The Fly' 3, Experience xix.
xviii 27. thirst] The angels not only seek to repel the beasts of prey; they
also try to remove the cause of their ferocity–a thirst for blood.
xviii 37. his] Christ's: see line 43.

Graze after thee and weep.
45 For washed in life's river
My bright mane for ever
Shall shine like the gold,
As I guard o'er the fold.'

XIX THE CHIMNEY SWEEPER

When my mother died I was very young,
And my father sold me while yet my tongue
Could scarcely cry *'weep 'weep, 'weep 'weep*!
So your chimneys I sweep, and in soot I sleep.

5   There's little Tom Dacre, who cried when his head,
That curled like a lamb's back, was shaved; so I said,
'Hush Tom, never mind it, for when your head's bare,
You know that the soot cannot spoil your white hair.'

And so he was quiet, and that very night,
10 As Tom was asleeping he had such a sight—
That thousands of sweepers, Dick, Joe, Ned, and Jack,
Were all of them locked up in coffins of black;

xviii 45. *life's river*] The vision of the River of Life was seen by Ezekiel (xlvii 1–13), and used in *Revelation* xxii 1–2: 'And he shewed me a pure river of water of life, clear as crystal, proceeding out of the throne of God and of the Lamb.' The image derives its power from the necessity of the river in a desert land, both for washing and for life. It involves such traditions as Naaman's washing away his leprosy; the baptisms of John the Baptist; the healing of the blind man in the pool of Siloam; and the apocalyptic 'blood of the Lamb' which washes away evil as a river washes clothes clean.

The design on the second pl. (sts 4–6) shows figures walking, with auras about their heads, in a leafy park.

xix. Cp. the 'contrary' poem in *Experience* (p. 218). In 1788, Jonas Hanway brough to Parliament the plight of these children. They were often 'apprenticed' (i.e. sold) at the age of about seven; they were brutally and unscrupulously used by their masters, not clothed, fed or washed; when sweeping, in constant danger of suffocation or burning, besides the skin cancer caused by the soot which was literally never washed from their bodies; they were encouraged to steal, and were often turned out in the streets by their masters to 'cry the streets' on the chance of employment, or for mere begging; their dirt and their reputation for stealing made them social outcasts. Lines *1–8, 11–12* were literally true. The design at the foot illustrates lines *15–16*. James Montgomery's miscellany *The Chimney-Sweeper's Friend, and Climbing-Boy's Album* (1824) included the poem 'Communicated by Mr. Charles Lamb, from a very rare and curious little work . . . Blake's *Songs of Innocence*'.

And by came an angel, who had a bright key,
And he opened the coffins and set them all free;
15   Then down a green plain leaping, laughing they run,
And wash in a river and shine in the sun.

Then naked and white, all their bags left behind,
They rise upon clouds and sport in the wind.
And the angel told Tom, if he'd be a good boy,
20   He'd have God for his father and never want joy.

And so Tom awoke, and we rose in the dark,
And got with our bags and our brushes to work.
Though the morning was cold, Tom was happy and
warm;
24   So if all do their duty, they need not fear harm.

XX THE DIVINE IMAGE

To mercy, pity, peace and love
All pray in their distress;
And to these virtues of delight
Return their thankfulness.

5   For mercy, pity, peace and love
Is God our father dear;
And mercy, pity, peace and love
Is man, his child and care.

For mercy has a human heart;
10   Pity, a human face;
And love, the human form divine;
And peace, the human dress.

Then every man of every clime
That prays in his distress,
15   Prays to the human form divine—
Love, mercy, pity, peace.

xx. This poem was said by an unnamed friend of B.'s to have been written
in the Hatton Garden (Swedenborgian) Church; but the church was not
built in 1789. The poem is very Swedenborgian, nevertheless. The design
is a curling flame (cp. 'The Blossom') which rises bottom R, under the
text and up the L margin, branching beneath st. 3, the main branch crossing
the plate up the R margin and over the text; at top and bottom idyllic
figures are seen. Cp. 'A Divine Image', p. 143; and 'The Human Abstract',
Experience, p. 216.
xx 1. i.e. in praying to God, one prays to the sum of these virtues personi-
fied in man. In Swedenborgian thought, God is the Divine Man, and vir-
tues are the virtues of man. Cp. 13–15. God's nature is found in humankind
in a debased form.

And all must love the human form
In heathen, Turk or Jew.
Where mercy, love and pity dwell
20   There God is dwelling too.

XXI THE LITTLE GIRL LOST

In futurity
I, prophetic, see
That the earth from sleep
(Grave the sentence deep)

5   Shall arise and seek
For her maker meek,
And the desert wild
Become a garden mild.

In the southern clime,
10   Where the summer's prime
Never fades away,
Lovely Lyca lay.

xxi, xxii. In the copy of *Innocence* which is here normally followed, this
pair of poems comes after 'A Dream' (p. 64) ; and this association is very
common (see headn.). But the poems seem late in composition; they (and
the 'Ancient Bard') introduce for the first time the notion of *prophecy* (2).

The poems contrast the innocence of the child who is not afraid of
nature and its life with the fears of her parents. At its simplest, this is a very
naive idea; but the design in the R margin of the first of the three pls
shows a youth and girl (her hair in a bun–i.e. artificially dressed) embracing
beneath a sapling with delicately arched branches. This implies that the
'nature' which Lyca does not fear includes her own instincts as well as
those of the beasts around. Yet she rests lightly in them, and the savage
beast her parents fear becomes, in the 'Found' poem, a sort of fairy prince.
Cp. 'A Little Girl Lost', *Experience*, p. 221: these poems were also later
transferred there. For an elaborate Neo-Platonic exegesis, see Raine:
Blake and Tradition (1969), Ch. 5.

Other designs: on the 2nd pl. between the two poems, Lyca lying down
in the forest. Beside *1–14* of 'Found', a tiger: the rest of the poem is on the
3rd pl. At the foot, children play with a lion and lioness; twisted massive
tree-trunks rise up the R margin, delicate stems up the L.

xxi *4. Grave*] Engrave.

xxi *7–8. desert . . . garden mild*] Cp. *Marriage* (Argument) *6–8*; both derive
from *Isaiah* xxxv 1 (quoted in *Marriage* note, p. 103 below).

xxi *12. Lyca*] The name occurs in 'Song 2nd by a Young Shepherd' (p.
41) but is altered there on its appearance as 'Laughing Song' (p. 57).

Seven summers old
Lovely Lyca told.
15 She had wandered long,
Hearing wild birds' song.

'Sweet sleep, come to me
Underneath this tree;
Do father, mother weep,
20 "Where can Lyca sleep?"'

'Lost in desert wild
Is your little child.
How can Lyca sleep,
If her mother weep?

25 'If her heart does ache,
Then let Lyca wake;
If my mother sleep,
Lyca shall not weep.

'Frowning, frowning night,
30 O'er this desert bright
Let thy moon arise,
While I close my eyes.'

Sleeping Lyca lay—
While the beasts of prey
35 Come from caverns deep,
Viewed the maid asleep.

The kingly lion stood
And the virgin viewed;
Then he gambolled round
40 O'er the hallowed ground.

Leopards, tigers play
Round her as she lay,
While the lion old,
Bowed his mane of gold,

45 And her bosom lick;
And upon her neck,

xxi *17. Sweet sleep . . .*] Similar to 'A Cradle Song' (p. 56), *1, 5*.
xxi *19-24.* Lyca is unafraid; instead, she sympathizes with the fears of her
mother. In her innocence she understands better that there is nothing to
fear.
xxi *30. bright*] Refers to *moon*–'let the moon rise bright over the desert'.
xxi *40. hallowed*] By her innocence.
xxi *45. lick*] Should strictly be 'licks'; perhaps B. was still thinking in the
plural of the *Leopards, tigers* of *41*. See 'A Cradle Song' *15–16n*.

From his eyes of flame
Ruby tears there came;

While the lioness
50   Loosed her slender dress,
And naked they conveyed
To caves the sleeping maid.

XXII THE LITTLE GIRL FOUND

All the night in woe
Lyca's parents go
Over valleys deep,
While the deserts weep.

5   Tired and woe-begone,
Hoarse with making moan,
Arm in arm seven days
They traced the desert ways.

Seven nights they sleep
10   Among shadows deep,
And dream they see their child
Starved in desert wild.

Pale through pathless ways
The fancied image strays—
15   Famished, weeping, weak,
With hollow piteous shriek.

Rising from unrest
The trembling woman pressed,
With feet of weary woe;
20   She could no further go.

In his arms he bore
Her armed with sorrow sore—
Till before their way
A couching lion lay.

25   Turning back was vain;
Soon his heavy mane
Bore them to the ground;
Then he stalked around,

xxi 50–1. *Loosed her slender dress, and naked* . . .] She loses her contact with
artificiality and returns to the natural life to which her innocence entitles
her.
xxii. See note on previous poem.

Smelling to his prey.
30 But their fears allay,
When he licks their hands,
And silent by them stands.

They look upon his eyes
Filled with deep surprise,
35 And wondering behold,
A spirit armed in gold;

On his head a crown,
On his shoulders down
Flowed his golden hair—
40 Gone was all their care.

'Follow me,' he said,
'Weep not for the maid;
In my palace deep,
Lyca lies asleep.'

45 Then they followed
Where the vision led,
And saw their sleeping child
Among tigers wild.

To this day they dwell
50 In a lonely dell,
Nor fear the wolvish howl,
Nor the lions' growl.

XXIII THE VOICE OF THE ANCIENT BARD

Youth of delight, come hither,
And see the opening morn,
Image of truth new born.
Doubt is fled, and clouds of reason,
5 Dark disputes and artful teasing.

xxii *30. allay*] Intransitive.
xxii *36. A spirit*] An early example of B.'s vision of a non-human creature
in a human form; cp. the lily, cloud, worm and clay in *Thel*, pls 1–5,
which may belong to the same period as this poem (by its theme and treat-
ment). But note also its fairy-tale origins, remarked in the comment on
the 'Lost' poem.
xxiii. This poem was transferred to *Experience*, yet occasionally appears in
Innocence in copies issued as late as 1815. Certainly the last engraved of the
Songs of Innocence, and engraved in a different script, it is the first to be
devoted entirely to the spirit of prophecy. The design below the text
shows an aged bard speaking or singing to the music of his large triangular
celtic harp, while young people stand round listening.

4+B.

Folly is an endless maze,
Tangled roots perplex her ways—
How many have fallen there.
They stumble all night over bones of the dead,
10   And feel they know not what but care—
And wish to lead others when they should be led.

5 Tiriel

Date: *c.* 1798; from the same period as *Thel*. B. uses, in both poems, names
from the same obscure source (see *1n*). The MS is fastened in a cover
marked 'Tiriel/MS by Mr. Blake': this suggests that it went into another
reader's hands, but it was never published or engraved. The last lines
(*334ff*) were written probably two or three years later (as was the last plate
of *Thel*), and may represent an attempt to improve an unsatisfactory
ending, or to bring the poem into line with B.'s style and expression of
the period 1790–3. But even so, the poem seems to have satisfied neither B.
nor any other publisher sufficiently to be engraved or printed.

Theme. The poem as a whole concerns the tragic discovery of Tiriel,
King of 'the west', that his world, and the society that he has built up
around himself, are worthless. He has enslaved his brother Zazel; another
brother, Ijim, is a grim, fierce, solitary figure living alone in the wilds.
At the beginning of the poem, Tiriel is seen spurned by his children
after the death of his wife Myratana; he fails to find solace with the
senile Har and Heva, his parents; Ijim does not recognize him and
scornfully carries him back to his palace. There he again curses his
children, and forces one of his daughters, Hela, to take him back
to Har. On the way they pass Zazel and his sons, who take the chance of
insulting him; and when he comes at last to Har, Tiriel curses him too, and
dies.

The poem is thus much less obviously didactic or moralistic than most of
B.'s long poems. The theme is not clearly related to any political, philo-
sophical, religious or moral doctrine. There are a number of echoes of
King Lear and, resemblances to the Oedipus plays (Raine, *Blake and
Tradition* i.36 ff.), and it seems that B. was attempting to write a 'pure'
but 'Gothic' tragic poem about aged tyranny.

There is facsimile of the MS, ed. G. E. Bentley (1967).

¶ *5.1. Tiriel*] The name appears, with Zazel and Bne Seraphim (cp. *Thel
1n*) in *De Occulta Philosophia* II xxii, by Cornelius Agrippa, a sixteenth-
century German alchemist. There was an English translation as early as 1651.
Tiriel is there associated with the planet Mercury and the elements sulphur
and mercury: Zazel with Saturn and the element earth: Bne Seraphim
with Venus. Zazel appears also in the occult Hebraic–Christian tradition
as a demon of earth, who eats dust and to whose power corpses are left.
In alchemical tradition, mercury represents the *prima materia*, the crude,
unformed base of nature.

I

And aged Tiriel stood before the gates of his beautiful
    palace
With Myratana, once the Queen of all the western
    plains;
But now his eyes were darkened, and his wife fading
    in death.
They stood before their once delightful palace, and
    thus the voice
5 Of aged Tiriel arose–that his sons might hear in their
    gates:

'Accursed race of Tiriel, behold your father.
Come forth and look on her that bore you; come,
    you accursed sons!
In my weak arms I here have borne your dying
    mother.
Come forth, sons of the curse, come forth, see the
    death of Myratana!'

10 His sons ran from their gates and saw their aged
    parents stand,
And thus the eldest son of Tiriel raised his mighty
    voice:

'Old man, unworthy to be called the father of
    Tiriel's race—
For every one of those thy wrinkles, each of those
    grey hairs,
Are cruel as death, and as obdurate as the devouring
    pit—
15 Why should thy sons care for thy curses, thou
    accursed man?
Were we not slaves till we rebelled? Who cares for
    Tiriel's curse?

2. *Myratana* has been traced (1969) by Mary S. Hall to Jacob Bryant's *New System*, in which *Myrina* is a Queen of the Amazons in Mauretania (the *West* of Africa). Some of Blake's own illustrations to *Tiriel* may be held to support the Amazonian association.
western plains] B. consistently thought of the west as beautiful, the east as ominous–the associations being largely political. America, land of freedom, and the fabled land of Atlantis, lay in the west; the oppressive kingdoms of the modern and ancient worlds lay in the east.
3. *darkened*] B. spells it 'darkned', and perhaps intends the pronunciation 'dark-néd'

His blessing was a cruel curse; his curse may be a blessing.'

He ceased: the aged man raised up his right hand to the heavens,
His left supported Myratana shrinking in pangs of death;

20 The orbs of his large eyes he opened, and thus his voice went forth:

'Serpents, not sons, wreathing around the bones of Tiriel!
Ye worms of death feasting upon your aged parents' flesh,
Listen and hear your mother's groans! No more accursed sons
She bears; she groans not at the birth of Heuxos or Yuva.

25 These are the groans of death, ye serpents, these are the groans of death—
Nourished with milk, ye serpents, nourished with mother's tears and cares.
Look at my eyes, blind as the orbless skull among the stones,
Look at my bald head! Hark, listen, ye serpents, listen!
What, Myratana? What, my wife? O soul, O spirit, O fire!

30 What, Myratana, art thou dead? Look here, ye serpents, look!
The serpents sprung from her own bowels have drained her dry as this.
Curse on your ruthless heads, for I will bury her even here.'

So saying he began to dig a grave with his aged hands;
But Heuxos called a son of Zazel to dig their mother a grave:

35 'Old cruelty, desist, and let us dig a grave for thee.
Thou hast refused our charity, thou hast refused our food,

---

21. *serpents, not sons*] *King Lear* IV ii 40, 'Tigers, not daughters'; and the word 'serpents' is recurrent in the play. See also *202*.
22. *parents*'] B. has no apostrophe: the word may be singular or plural.
34. *a son of Zazel*] As later contexts show, a slave tribe. See *1n*.

Thou has refused our clothes, our beds, our houses
    for thy dwelling,
Choosing to wander like a son of Zazel in the rocks.
Why dost thou curse? Is not the curse now come
    upon your head?
40 Was it not you enslaved the sons of Zazel, and they
    have cursed
And now you feel it. Dig a grave and let us bury our
    mother.'

'There take the body, cursed sons, and may the
    heavens rain wrath
As thick as northern fogs around your gates, to choke
    you up,
That you may lie as now your mother lies, like dogs
    cast out,
45 The stink of your dead carcases annoying man and
    beast,
Till your white bones are bleached with age for a
    memorial.
No, your remembrance shall perish, for when your
    carcases
Lie stinking on the earth, the buriers shall arise from
    the east
And not a bone of all the sons of Tiriel remain.
50 Bury your mother; but you cannot bury the curse of
    Tiriel.'

He ceased and darkling o'er the mountains sought his
    pathless way.

II

He wandered day and night; to him both day and
    night were dark;
The sun he felt, but the bright moon was now a use-
    less globe.
O'er mountains and through vales of woe, the blind
    and aged man
55 Wandered, till he that leadeth all led him to the vales
    of Har.

52–3. *to him . . . a useless globe*] A reminiscence of the imagery, rather than
the words, of *Samson Agonistes* 80–9, esp.: 'The sun to me is dark, / And
silent as the moon . . .'
55. *the vales of Har*] Cp. *Thel* 125 (and an allusion in *Song of Los* (Africa)
36, 45). In each case the notion of 'second childhood' is apt, though not
essential.

And Har and Heva like two children sat beneath the oak.
Mnetha (now aged) waited on them, and brought
    them food and clothing;
But they were as the shadow of Har, and as the
    years forgotten;
Playing with flowers, and running after birds they
    spent the day,
60 And in the night like infants slept delighted with
    infant dreams.
Soon as the blind wanderer entered the pleasant
    gardens of Har
They ran weeping like frighted infants for refuge in
    Mnetha's arms.
The blind man felt his way and cried, 'Peace to these
    open doors!
Let no one fear, for poor blind Tiriel hurts none but
    himself.
65 Tell me, O friends, where am I now, and in what
    pleasant place?'

'This is the valley of Har,' said Mnetha, 'and this
    the tent of Har.
Who art thou, poor blind man, that takest the name
    of Tiriel on thee?
Tiriel is King of all the west; who art thou?–I am
    Mnetha,
And this is Har and Heva, trembling like infants by
    my side.'

70 'I know Tiriel is King of the west, and there he lives
    in joy.
No matter who I am, O Mnetha; if thou hast any
    food
Give it to me, for I cannot stay; my journey is far
    from hence.'

Then Har said: 'O my mother Mnetha, venture not
    so near him,
For he is the king of rotten wood and of the bones of
    death.
75 He wanders without eyes, and passes through thick
    walls and doors.
Thou shalt not smite my mother Mnetha, O thou
    eyeless man!'

61. The next line del: 'The aged father & mother saw him as they sat at
play'.
76. Note Har's horrible childishness, though he is an aged man.

'A wanderer, I beg for food. You see I cannot weep;
I cast away my staff, the kind companion of my
    travel,
And I kneel down that you may see I am a harmless
    man.'

80 He kneeled down; and Mnetha said: 'Come, Har
    and Heva, rise;
He is an innocent old man and hungry with his
    travel.'

Then Har arose and laid his hand upon old Tiriel's
    head:

'God bless thy poor bald pate. God bless thy hollow
    winking eyes.
God bless thy shrivelled beard. God bless thy many-
    wrinkled forehead.
85 Thou hast no teeth, old man; and thus I kiss thy
    sleek bald head.
Heva, come kiss his bald head, for he will not hurt
    us, Heva.'

Then Heva came and took old Tiriel in her mother's
    arms:

'Bless thy poor eyes, old man, and bless the old father
    of Tiriel;
Thou art my Tiriel's old father; I know thee through
    thy wrinkles,
90 Because thou smellest like the fig tree; thou smellest
    like ripe figs.
How didst thou lose thy eyes, old Tiriel? Bless thy
    wrinkled face.'

Mnetha said: 'Come in, aged wanderer; tell us of thy
    name.
Why shouldest thou conceal thyself from those of
    thine own flesh?'

'I am not of this region,' said Tiriel dissemblingly;

77. Before this line a del. line: 'O venerable O most piteous O most
woeful day': and between 77 and 78, another del. line: 'But I can kneel
down at your door. I am a harmless man'.
91. After this, a two-line del. paragraph:
    The aged Tiriel could not speak, his heart was full of grief
    He strove against his rising passions. But still he could not speak.
94. The next line del.: 'Fearing to tell them who he was. Because of the
weakness of Har'.

95 'I am an aged wanderer, once father of a race
Far in the north, but they were wicked and were all
destroyed,
And I their father sent an outcast. I have told you all;
Ask me no more, I pray, for grief hath sealed my
precious sight.'

'O Lord,' said Mnetha, 'how I tremble! Are there
then more people,
100 More human creatures on this earth, beside the sons of
Har?'

'No more,' said Tiriel, 'but I remain on all this globe,
And I remain an outcast. Hast thou anything to
drink?'

Then Mnetha gave him milk and fruits, and they sat
down together.

III

They sat and ate, and Har and Heva smiled on Tiriel:

105 'Thou art a very old, old man, but I am older than
thou.
How came thine hair to leave thy forehead? How
came thy face so brown?
My hair is very long; my beard doth cover all my
breast.
God bless thy piteous face–to count the wrinkles in
thy face
Would puzzle Mnetha. Bless thy face, for thou art
Tiriel.'

110 'Tiriel I never saw but once. I sat with him and ate.
He was as cheerful as a prince and gave me
entertainment;
But long I stayed not at his palace, for I am forced to
wander.'

99. The peace of the vale of Har is false; it arises from ignorance, and separation, from the world, not from mature achievement. Cp. *139*.
104. *ate*] B. spells it 'eat', in the old fashion.
109. A two-line del paragraph follows:
  Tiriel could scarce dissemble more & his tongue could scarce
  refrain
  But still he feard that Har & Heva would die of joy & grief.
110. Tiriel speaks.

'What! wilt thou leave us too?' said Heva. 'Thou
    shalt not leave us too.
For we have many sports to show thee, and many
    songs to sing,
115 And after dinner we will walk into the cage of Har,
And thou shalt help us to catch birds, and gather
    them ripe cherries.
Then let thy name be Tiriel, and never leave us
    more.'

'If thou dost go,' said Har, 'I wish thine eyes may
    see thy folly.
My sons have left me; did thine leave thee?—
    Oh, 'twas very cruel!'

120 'No, venerable man,' said Tiriel, 'Ask me not such
    things:
For thou dost make my heart to bleed. My sons were
    not like thine
But worse. Oh, neve rask me more or I must flee away.'

'Thou shalt not go,' said Heva, 'till thou hast seen
    our singing birds,
And heard Har sing in the great cage, and slept upon
    our fleeces.
125 Go not, for thou art so like Tiriel that I love thine
    head,
Though it is wrinkled, like the earth parched with the
    summer heat.'

Then Tiriel rose up from the seat and said: 'God
    bless these tents.
My journey is o'er rocks and mountains, not in
    pleasant vales.
I must not sleep nor rest, because of madness and
    dismay.'

115. Har's sports are not innocent, though he is childish. The bird would
rather find its cherries by its own efforts, in freedom.
119. The implication is that Tiriel is their child, though *88–91* are not
clear: cp. *276–80, 332–3.*
127. Followed by a del. line: 'God bless my benefactors for I cannot tarry
    longer.'

129. A three-line del. paragraph follows (cp. *137–9*):

    Then Mnetha led him to the door & gave to him his staff
    And Har & Heva stood & watchd him till he enterd the wood,
    And then they went & wept to Mnetha but they soon forgot
      their tears.

4*

130 And Mnetha said: 'Thou must not go to wander
            dark, alone,
       But dwell with us and let us be to thee instead of
            eyes,
       And I will bring thee food, old man, till death shall
            call thee hence.'

       Then Tiriel frowned and answered: 'Did I not
            command you, saying
       Madness and deep dismay possess the heart of the
            blind man,
135 The wanderer who seeks the woods leaning upon his
            staff?'

       Then Mnetha trembling at his frowns led him to the
            tent door
       And gave to him his staff and blessed him; he went
            on his way.

       But Har and Heva stood and watched him till he
            entered the wood,
       And then they went and wept to Mnetha; but they
            soon forgot their tears.

IV

140 Over the weary hills the blind man took his lonely way.
       To him the day and night alike was dark and
            desolate,
       But far he had not gone when Ijim, from his woods
            come down,
       Met him at entrance of the forest in a dark and
            lonely way:

       'Who art thou, eyeless wretch, that thus obstructs the
            lion's path?
145 Ijim shall rend thy feeble joints, thou tempter of dark
            Ijim!
       Thou hast the form of Tiriel, but I know thee well
            enough.
       Stand from my path, foul fiend. Is this the last of
            thy deceits,
       To be a hypocrite, and stand in shape of a blind
            beggar?'

145. Ijim] B. took the name from *Isaiah* xiii 21, where A.V. reads 'satyrs',
creatures of the wilderness (who will dance among the ruins of Babylon:
the context is irrelevant). B.'s Ijim is an old-fashioned Puritan–honest but
grim, always a ready adversary of Sin (*145–8*).

The blind man heard his brother's voice and kneeled
down on his knee:

150 'O brother Ijim, if it is thy voice that speaks to me,
Smite not thy brother Tiriel, though weary of his life.
My sons have smitten me already, and if thou smitest
me
The curse that rolls over their heads will rest itself on
thine.
'Tis now seven years since in my palace I beheld thy
face.'

155 'Come, thou dark fiend, I dare thy cunning. Know
that Ijim scorns
To smite thee in the form of helpless age and eyeless
policy.
Rise up, for I discern thee, and I dare thy eloquent
tongue!
Come, I will lead thee on thy way and use thee as a
scoff.'

'O brother Ijim, thou beholdest wretched Tiriel;
160 Kiss me, my brother and then leave me to wander
desolate.'

'No, artful fiend – but I will lead thee. Dost thou
want to go?
Reply not, lest I bind thee with the green flags of the
brook.
Ay, now thou art discovered I will use thee like a
slave.'

When Tiriel heard the words of Ijim he sought not to
reply.
165 He knew 'twas vain, for Ijim's words were as the
voice of Fate.

And they went on together, over hills, through
woody dales,
Blind to the pleasures of the sight and deaf to
warbling birds.
All day they walked and all the night beneath the
pleasant moon,
Westwardly journeying, till Tiriel grew weary with his
travel:

154. Written in the margin, with the del. half-line: 'Seven years of sorrow
then the curse of Zazel . . .'
162. flags] Water irises.

170 'O Ijim, I am faint and weary, for my knees forbid
       To bear me further. Urge me not, lest I should die
           with travel.
       A little rest I crave, a little water from a brook,
       Or I shall soon discover that I am a mortal man,
       And you will lose your once-loved Tiriel. Alas, how
           faint I am!'

175 'Impudent fiend,' said Ijim, 'Hold thy glib and
           eloquent tongue.
       Tiriel is a king, and thou the tempter of dark Ijim.
       Drink of this running brook, and I will bear thee on
           my shoulders.'

       He drank and Ijim raised him up and bore him on
           his shoulders.
       All day he bore him, and when evening drew her
           solemn curtain
180 Entered the gates of Tiriel's palace, and stood and
           called aloud:

       'Heuxos, come forth! I here have brought the fiend
           that troubles Ijim.
       Look: knowst thou aught of this grey beard, or of
           these blinded eyes?'

       Heuxos and Lotho ran forth at the sound of Ijim's
           voice,
       And saw their aged father borne upon his mighty
           shoulders.
185 Their eloquent tongues were dumb and sweat stood
           on their trembling limbs;
       They knew 'twas vain to strive with Ijim; they bowed
           and silent stood.

       'What, Heuxos, call thy father, for I mean to sport
           tonight.
       This is the hypocrite that sometimes roars a dreadful
           lion;
       Then I have rent his limbs and left him rotting in the
           forest
190 For birds to eat. But I have scarce departed from the
           place
       But like a tiger he would come and so I rent him too.

189–192. These changes resemble the varied forms taken by Orc in the
Preludium to *America, 13–16.* Cp. the changes of Proteus (Ovid, *Meta-
morphoses* viii).

Then like a river he would seek to drown me in his
    waves,
But soon I buffeted the torrent; anon like to a cloud
Fraught with the swords of lightning, but I braved
    the vengeance too.

195 Then he would creep like a bright serpent, till around
    my neck
While I was sleeping he would twine; I squeezed
    his poisonous soul.
Then, like a toad or like a newt, would whisper in
    my ears;
Or like a rock stood in my way, or like a poisonous
    shrub.
At last I caught him in the form of Tiriel, blind and
    old,
200 And so I'll keep him. Fetch your father, fetch forth
    Myratana!'

They stood confounded, and thus Tiriel raised his
    silver voice:

'Serpents, not sons! Why do you stand? Fetch hither
    Tiriel,
Fetch hither Myratana, and delight yourselves with
    scoffs.
For poor blind Tiriel is returned, and this much
    injured head
205 Is ready for your bitter taunts. Come forth, sons of
    the curse!'

Meantime the other sons of Tiriel ran around their
    father;
Confounded at the terrible strength of Ijim they
    knew 'twas vain.
Both spear and shield were useless and the coat of
    iron mail;
When Ijim stretched his mighty arm, the arrow from
    his limbs
210 Rebounded, and the piercing sword broke on his
    naked flesh.

194–7. These appearances are similar to Satan's, in *Paradise Lost* iv 800 and
ix 494ff, where he appears to Eve whispering like a toad in her ear as she
sleeps, and then as a serpent.
202. why . . . Tiriel] *1st rdg del.* 'you see and know your father'. See *21* n.
210. Followed by 10 del. lines: (*continued on p. 86*)

'Then is it true, Heuxos, that thou hast turned thy
    aged parent
To be the sport of wintry winds?' said Ijim. 'Is
    this true?
It is a lie, and I am like the tree torn by the wind.
Thou eyeless fiend—and you dissemblers! Is
    this Tiriel's house?
215 It is as false as Matha, and as dark as vacant Orcus.
Escape, ye fiends, for Ijim will not lift his hand
    against ye!'

So saying, Ijim gloomy turned his back, and silent
    sought
The secret forests, and all night wandered in desolate
    ways.

V

And aged Tiriel stood and said: 'Where does the
    thunder sleep?
220 Where doth he hide his terrible head, and his swift and
    fiery daughters?
Where do they shroud their fiery wings and the
    terrors of their hair?
Earth, thus I stamp thy bosom! Rouse the earth-
    quake from his den,
To raise his dark and burning visage through the
    cleaving ground
To thrust these towers with his shoulders. Let his
    fiery dogs

Then Ijim said. 'Lotho Clithyma. Makuth fetch your father
Why do you stand confounded thus Heuxos why art thou Silent

O noble Ijim thou hast brought our father to our eyes
That we may tremble & repent before thy mighty knees
O we are but the slaves of Fortune & that most cruel man
Desires our deaths. O Ijim, [*tis one whose aged tongue*
Decieve the noble &] if the eloquent voice of Tiriel
Hath workd our ruin we submit nor strive against stern fate

He spoke, & kneeld upon his knee. Then Ijim on the pavement
Set aged Tiriel. In deep thought whether these things were so.

The words in italics were deleted before the whole passage was cancelled.
215. *Matha, Orcus*] The first is borrowed from Ossian, out of context.
Orcus was the Roman god of the underworld, and the name was applied
to the region of the underworld itself.
as Matha] The MS has an ' &' for *as*.

225 Rise from the centre belching flames and roarings,
      dark smoke.
Where art thou, pestilence that bathest in fogs and
      standing lakes?
Rise up thy sluggish limbs, and let the loathsomest of
      poisons
Drop from thy garments as thou walkest. Wrapped in
      yellow clouds
Here take thy seat in this wide court; let it be strown
      with dead,
230 And sit and smile upon these cursed sons of Tiriel.
Thunder and fire and pestilence, hear you not
      Tiriel's curse?'

He ceased: the heavy clouds confused rolled round the
      lofty towers,
Discharging their enormous voices at the father's
      curse.
The earth trembled, fires belched from the yawning
      clefts,
235 And when the shaking ceased a fog possessed the
      accursed clime.

The cry was great in Tiriel's palace; his five
      daughters ran
And caught him by the garments, weeping with cries
      of bitter woe.

'Ay, now you feel the curse you cry; but may all
      ears be deaf
As Tiriel's, and all eyes as blind as Tiriel's to your
      woes.
240 May never stars shine on your roofs, may never sun
      nor moon
Visit you, but eternal fogs hover around your walls.
Hela, my youngest daughter; you shall lead me from
      this place,

231. *Tiriel's curse*] Another echo of *King Lear*, though the solemn curse is
well known in legend. The imagery of flame, smoke and fog recalls in
particular the curse of *King Lear* II iv: 'You nimble lightnings, dart your
blinding flames / Into her scornful eyes, infect her beauty, / You fen-
suck'd fogs, drawn by the powerful sun, / To fall and blast her pride.'
But in Tiriel the curse has a visible effect, as befits the legendary narrative
(235).
242. *Hela*] The name seems to have begun as *Hili*—certainly not *Hela*: so
until 258. From 268 *Hela* is decided on. The name is that of the goddess of
death through age in Norse mythology; Gray mentions her in *The
Descent of Odin*.

And let the curse fall on the rest and wrap them up
    together!'

He ceased; and Hela led her father from the noisome
    place.
245 In haste they fled, while all the sons and daughters of
    Tiriel,
Chained in thick darkness, uttered cries of mourning
    all the night.
And in the morning, lo, an hundred men in ghastly
    death!
The four daughters stretched on the marble pave-
    ment, silent—all
Fallen by the pestilence. The rest moped round in
    guilty fears;
250 And all the children in their beds were cut off in one
    night.
Thirty of Tiriel's sons remained, to wither in the
    palace—
Desolate, loathed, dumb, astonished, waiting for
    black death.

VI

And Hela led her father through the silent of the
    night,
Astonished, silent, till the morning beams began to
    spring:

255 'Now, Hela, I can go with pleasure and dwell with
    Har and Heva,
Now that the curse shall clean devour all those guilty
    sons.
This is the right and ready way; I know it by the
    sound
That our feet make. Remember, Hela, I have saved
    thee from death;
Then be obedient to thy father, for the curse is taken
    off thee.
260 I dwelt with Myratana five years in the desolate rock,
And all that time we waited for the fire to fall from
    heaven,
Or for the torrents of the sea to overwhelm you all.
But now my wife is dead and all the time of grace is
    past.

You see the parents' curse. Now lead me where I
    have commanded.'

265   'O leagued with evil spirits, thou accursed man of
    sin!
True, I was born thy slave. Who asked thee to save
    me from death?
'Twas for thy self, thou cruel man, because thou
    wantest eyes!'

'True, Hela: this is the desert of all those cruel ones.
Is Tiriel cruel? Look, his daughter—and his
    youngest daughter—
270   Laughs at affection, glories in rebellion, scoffs at love.
I have not eat these two days. Lead me to Har and
    Heva's tent,
Or I will wrap thee up in such a terrible father's curse
That thou shalt feel worms in thy marrow creeping
    through thy bones;
Yet thou shalt lead me. Lead me, I command, to
    Har and Heva.'   '.

275   'O cruel! O destroyer! O consumer! O avenger!
To Har and Heva I will lead thee then. Would that
    they would curse;
Then would they curse as thou hast cursed. But they
    are not like thee.
Oh, they are holy and forgiving, filled with loving
    mercy,
Forgetting the offences of their most rebellious
    children;
280   Or else thou wouldest not have lived to curse thy
    helpless children.'

'Look on my eyes, Hela, and see—for thou hast
    eyes to see.
The tears swell from my stony fountains; wherefore
    do I weep?
Wherefore from my blind orbs art thou not seized
    with poisonous stings?
Laugh, serpent, youngest venomous reptile of the
    flesh of Tiriel,
285   Laugh! For thy father Tiriel shall give thee cause to
    laugh,
Unless thou lead me to the tent of Har, child of the
    curse.'

266. slave] 1st rdg del. child.

'Silence thy evil tongue, thou murderer of thy
    helpless children!
I lead thee to the tent of Har–not that I mind thy
    curse,
But that I feel they will curse thee, and hang upon
    thy bones
290 Fell shaking agonies, and in each wrinkle of that face
Plant worms of death, to feast upon the tongue of
    terrible curses.'

'Hela, my daughter, listen; thou art the daughter of
    Tiriel.
Thy father calls. Thy father lifts his hand unto the
    heavens,
For thou hast laughed at my tears, and curst thy
    aged father.
295 Let snakes rise from thy bedded locks and laugh
    among thy curls!'

He ceased: her dark hair upright stood, while snakes
    enfolded round
Her madding brows. Her shrieks appalled the soul of
    Tiriel:

'What have I done? Hela, my daughter, fearest
    thou now the curse,
Or wherefore dost thou cry? Ah, wretch to curse
    thy aged father!
300 Lead me to Har and Heva, and the curse of Tiriel
Shall fail. If thou refuse, howl in the desolate moun-
    tains!'

VII

She howling led him over mountains and through
    frighted vales
Till to the caves of Zazel they approached at eventide.

Forth from their caves old Zazel and his sons ran,
    when they saw
305 Their tyrant prince blind, and his daughter howling
    and leading him.

They laughed and mocked; some threw dirt and
    stones as they passed by,
But when Tiriel turned around and raised his awful
    voice

Some fled away, but Zazel stood still and thus began:
'Bald tyrant, wrinkled cunning, listen to Zazel's
    chains!
310 'Twas thou that chained thy brother Zazel. Where
    are now thine eyes?
Shout, beautiful daughter of Tiriel; thou singest a
    sweet song!
Where are you going? Come and eat some roots and
    drink some water.
Thy crown is bald, old man; the sun will dry thy
    brains away,
And thou wilt be as foolish as thy foolish brother
    Zazel.'
315 The blind man heard, and smote his breast and
    trembling passed on.
They threw dirt after them, till to the covert of a
    wood
The howling maiden led her father, where wild beasts
    resort,
Hoping to end her woes; but from her cries the tigers
    fled.
All night they wandered through the wood, and when
    the sun arose
320 They entered on the mountains of Har; at noon the
    happy tents
Were frighted by the dismal cries of Hela on the
    mountains.
But Har and Heva slept, fearless as babes on loving
    breasts.
Mnetha awoke; she ran and stood at the tent door,
    and saw
The aged wanderer led towards the tents. She took
    her bow
325 And chose her arrows, then advanced to meet the
    terrible pair.

VIII

And Mnetha hasted and met them at the gate of the
    lower garden:
'Stand still, or from my bow receive a sharp and
    winged death!'

308. *1st rdg.* 'They fled away & hid themselves but some stood still &
thus scoffing begun'.
309. *cunning*] *1st rdg del.* cunning wretch.

Then Tiriel stood, saying: 'What soft voice threatens
  such bitter things?
Lead me to Har and Heva; I am Tiriel, King of the
  west.'

330 And Mnetha led them to the tent of Har, and Har
  and Heva
Ran to the door. When Tiriel felt the ankles of aged
  Har
He said: 'O weak mistaken father of a lawless race,
Thy laws, O Har, and Tiriel's wisdom end together in
  a curse.
Why is one law given to the lion and the patient ox,
335 And why men bound beneath the heavens in a reptile
  form—
A worm of sixty winters creeping on the dusky
  ground?
The child springs from the womb, the father ready
  stands to form

329. The rest of the MS is written hurriedly, with another pen, perhaps
some years later. See headnote.
334. Tiriel's speech from this line on has quite a different character from
the rest of the poem. It is one of the sets of rhetorical questions much liked
by B. around the period 1790–93—similar passages occur in *The French
Revolution 181–9, Visions* from *44 passim, America 118–29,* and also in
Thel 118–27. These speeches are usually given to a voice of righteous
indignation, and it is thus unusual to find Tiriel the speaker here.
   Line *334* is similar to the line 'One Law for the Lion & Ox is Oppres-
sion', written under the design on *Marriage* pl.24.
335–6. These lines replace the following twelve cancelled lines:

Dost thou not see that men cannot be formed all alike [...]
Some nostrild wide breathing out blood. Some close shut up
In silent deceit. Poisons inhaling from the morning rose
With daggers hid beneath their lips & poison in their tongue
Or eyed with little sparks of Hell or with infernal brands
Flinging flames of discontent and plagues of dark despair
Or those whose mouths are graves whose teeth the gates of
  eternal death.
Can wisdom be put in a silver rod or love in a golden bowl
Is the son of a king warmed without wool or does he cry with a
  voice
Of thunder does he look upon the sun & laugh or stretch
His little hands into the depths of the sea to bring forth
The deadly cunning of the flatterer & spread it to the morning

In the last line, *flatterer* originally read 'scaly tribe'.

The infant head, while the mother idle plays with her
    dog on her couch.
The young bosom is cold for lack of mother's
    nourishment, and milk
340 Is cut off from the weeping mouth. With difficulty
    and pain
The little lids are lifted and the little nostrils opened.
The father forms a whip to rouse the sluggish senses to
    act,
And scourges off all youthful fancies from the new-
    born man.
Then walks the weak infant in sorrow, compelled to
    number footsteps
345 'Upon the sand', etc.
And when the drone has reached his crawling length
Black berries appear that poison all around him.
    Such was Tiriel,
Compelled to pray repugnant, and to humble the
    immortal spirit
Till I am subtle as a serpent in a paradise,
350 Consuming all, both flowers and fruits, insects and
    warbling birds,
And now my paradise is fallen, and a drear sandy
    plain
Returns my thirsty hissings in a curse on thee, O Har,
Mistaken father of a lawless race. My voice is past.'

He ceased, outstretched at Har and Heva's feet in ·
    awful death.

6 Thel

Date: c. 1789–90 for pls 1–5. The titlepage gives the date 1789; B. probably
aspired to something longer after writing *Songs of Innocence.* Such dates
generally mean no more than that the titlepage was engraved in that year.
Thel's Motto and pl.6 are very different in tone and style from pls 1–5 as
well as being etched in a slightly different script; this points to a date
c. 1791 for these two plates, perhaps pl. 6 replacing an earlier one. B. may
have left *Thel* (and the *Tiriel* MS) unfinished when he was swept into the
writing of *Marriage, The French Revolution,* and *America,* and it is possible
that when he came back to complete it other and more personal
theories had set him afire, so that he left *America* incomplete, finished

345. etc.] This must refer to a passage now lost.
347. After this, the del. line: 'Hypocrisy the idiot's wisdom & the wise
mans folly'.

Thel, and then went on to write a new and (at that time) more satisfactory story about an innocent girl in *Visions*. This would put the completion of *Thel* about 1791–92.

Fifteen copies of *Thel* exist, most of them dating from the time of first publication, though two, more richly finished, are from about 1815. There is a colour facsimile in the Blake Trust series (1965).

Sections i–iii preach two simple messages. First, B.'s lifelong belief that, to those with eyes to see, even the slightest object can bring a vision of eternal life. Thel sees four creatures, anthropomorphically, as human. Second, the particular message of *Thel* in its early form. Thel is a timid girl, afraid because of the transience of life. One by one, a lily, a cloud, a worm and even a piece of clay try to persuade her that life given in the service of others knows no fear; that even death then becomes a fulfilment and a realization of new life. But Thel is still too fearful to accept this. Finally, 'the matron clay' offers to show her the secrets of the grave—and at this point the early text breaks off.

The remainder (i.e. iv. pl.6) is strongly tinged with Neo-Platonic influences (see *104n, 112n*). Thel is no longer a girl wandering in some mythical valley, fearful of her present life; she is a spirit destined to go down to mortal life, and she is afraid of it. The two themes have been made to fit, but do not do so perfectly.

Thel's Motto

> Does the eagle know what is in the pit
> Or wilt thou go ask the mole?
> Can wisdom be put in a silver rod,
> Or love in a golden bowl?

Pl. 1   I

> The daughters of Mne Seraphim led round their
>   sunny flocks,
> All but the youngest. She in paleness sought the
>   secret air,

¶ 6. Pl.I. *Motto*] For date see headnote. For this cryptic verse cp. *Visions* 144ff, esp. *150–1*: 'Does not the eagle scorn the earth and despise the treasures beneath? / But the mole knoweth what is there . . .' In some copies the *Motto* is placed at the end.

Lines *3–4* are the same as a del. line after *Tiriel 334 (q.v., n)*. Thus *1–2* mean that each individual creature has its own place and its own vision: *3–4* mean that wisdom and love are infinite, and unlimitable, qualities.

1. Mne Seraphim] Various emendations have been suggested for this curious name. The text has always stood thus; it is not an emendation, but apparently a variation on the name referred to by the mystical alchemist Cornelius Agrippa (1486–1535), 'Bne Seraphim'. B. only uses the name this once, and it therefore does not develop any special significance. Cp. *Tiriel 1n*: B. derived 'Tiriel' from the same source.

To fade away like morning beauty from her mortal
    day.
Down by the river of Adona her soft voice is heard,
5 And thus her gentle lamentation falls like morning
    dew:
'O life of this our spring, why fades the lotus of the
    water?
Why fade these children of the spring, born but to
    smile and fall?
Ah, Thel is like a watery bow, and like a parting
    cloud,
Like a reflection in a glass, like shadows in the water,
10 Like dreams of infants, like a smile upon an infant's
    face,
Like the dove's voice, like transient day, like music
    in the air;
Ah, gentle may I lay me down, and gentle rest my
    head,
And gentle sleep the sleep of death, and gentle hear
    the voice
Of him that walketh in the garden in the evening
    time.'

15 The lily of the valley breathing in the humble grass
Answered the lovely maid, and said: 'I am a watery
    weed,
And I am very small, and love to dwell in lowly vales;
So weak, the gilded butterfly scarce perches on my
    head;
Yet I am visited from heaven, and he that smiles on
    all
20 Walks in the valley and each morn over me spreads
    his hand,
Saying, "Rejoice, thou humble grass, thou new-born
    lily flower,
Thou gentle maid of silent valleys and of modest
    brooks;
For thou shalt be clothed in light and fed with
    morning manna,
Till summer's heat melts thee beside the fountains
    and the springs

---

14. *him that walketh*] From *Genesis* iii 8: 'And they heard the voice of the
Lord God walking in the garden in the cool of the day'. Cp. also 'Intro-
duction' to *Experience* (p. 209): 'The Holy Word / That walked among
the ancient trees.' In *Thel* 'the voice' is not a tyrant's.

25 To flourish in eternal vales." Then why should Thel
        complain,
Pl. 2 Why should the mistress of the vales of Har utter a sigh?'
    She ceased and smiled in tears, then sat down in her
        silver shrine.
    Thel answered: 'O thou little virgin of the peaceful
        valley,
    Giving to those that cannot crave, the voiceless,
        the o'ertired.
30 Thy breath doth nourish the innocent lamb; he
        smells thy milky garments,
    He crops thy flowers, while thou sittest smiling in his
        face,
    Wiping his mild and meekin mouth from all
        contagious taints.
    Thy wine doth purify the golden honey; thy perfume,
    Which thou dost scatter on every little blade of grass
        that springs,
35 Revives the milked cow and tames the fire-breathing
        steed.
    But Thel is like a faint cloud kindled at the rising sun:
    I vanish from my pearly throne, and who shall find
        my place?'
    'Queen of the vales', the lily answered, 'ask the
        tender cloud,
    And it shall tell thee why it glitters in the morning sky,
40 And why it scatters its bright beauty through the
        humid air.
    Descend, O little cloud, and hover before the eyes of
        Thel.'

    The cloud descended, and the lily bowed her modest
        head,
    And went to mind her numerous charge among the
        verdant grass.
                        [*Design*]

26. *Vales of Har*] Cp. *Tiriel* 55ff, 320ff: a place of pastoral simplicity; in
Tiriel also a place of false simplicity and senile innocence.
32. *meekin*] Either (*a*) a variety of 'meek', from the rare word 'meeken'
(which is, however, normally a verb–'to make meek'): or (*b*) less
probably the word 'meäking', recorded by the *English Dialect Dictionary*,
as used in Shropshire and Gloucestershire only, and meaning 'low-spirited,
poorly'–hence, here, 'humble'. It may have come to B. through Chatter-
ton, but I have not found it.
43. *went to mind* . . .] The lily is a person with a duty–not merely an object.
The *design* here shows Thel speaking to the lily.

Pl. 3   II

'O little cloud', the virgin said, 'I charge thee,
    tell to me
45 Why thou complainest not, when in one hour thou
    fade away.
Then we shall seek thee but not find; ah, Thel is like
    to thee,
I pass away; yet I complain, and no one hears my
    voice.'

The cloud then showed his golden head, and his
    bright form emerged,
Hovering and glittering on the air before the face of
    Thel:

50 'O virgin, knowest thou not? Our steeds drink of the
    golden springs
Where Luvah doth renew his horses. Lookest thou
    on my youth,
And fearest thou because I vanish and am seen no
    more,
Nothing remains? O maid, I tell thee, when I pass
    away
It is to tenfold life, to love, to peace, and raptures holy.
55 Unseen descending weigh my light wings upon balmy
    flowers,
And court the fair-eyed dew to take me to her
    shining tent.
The weeping virgin trembling kneels before the risen
    sun,
Till we arise linked in a golden band and never part,
But walk united, bearing food to all our tender
    flowers.'

60 'Dost thou, O little cloud? I fear that I am not like
    thee;
For I walk through the vales of Har, and smell the
    sweetest flowers,
But I feed not the little flowers; I hear the warbling
    birds,
But I feed not the warbling birds. They fly and seek
    their food.

51. *Luvah*] He reappears much later, in *The Four Zoas*, but no special sig-
nificance need be given to him here except, as is obvious, that he is the
Apollo-like figure who drives the chariot of the sun across the sky.

But Thel delights in these no more, because I fade
    away;
65 And all shall say, "without a use this shining woman
    lived—
Or did she only live to be at death the food of
    worms?"'

The cloud reclined upon his airy throne and
    answered thus:

'Then if thou art the food of worms, O virgin of the
    skies,
How great thy use, how great thy blessing! Every-
    thing that lives
70 Lives not alone, nor for itself. Fear not and I will call
The weak worm from its lowly bed, and thou shalt
    hear its voice.
Come forth, worm of the silent valley, to thy pensive
    queen.'

The helpless worm arose, and sat upon the lily's leaf,
And the bright cloud sailed on to find his partner in
    the vale.

III

Pl. 4   [Design]

75 Then Thel astonished viewed the worm upon its dewy
    bed:

'Art thou a worm, image of weakness? Art thou but a
    worm?
I see thee like an infant wrapped in the lily's leaf.
Ah, weep not; little voice, thou canst not speak, but
    thou canst weep.
Is this a worm? I see thee lay helpless and naked
    weeping,
80 And none to answer, none to cherish thee with
    mother's smiles.'

The clod of clay heard the worm's voice and raised
    her pitying head;
She bowed over the weeping infant and her life
    exhaled

Pl. 4. *Design* illustrates *73–4*.
77. *an infant wrapped in the lily's leaf*] B. used this subject for engraving,
but disapprovingly, in his emblem-book *The Gates of Paradise*.

In milky fondness; then on Thel she fixed her
    humble eyes:

'O beauty of the vales of Har, we live not for
    ourselves;
85 Thou seest me, the meanest thing, and so I am
    indeed;
My bosom of itself is cold and of itself is dark,
Pl. 5 But he that loves the lowly pours his oil upon my
    head,
And kisses me, and binds his nuptial bands around
    my breast,
And says; "Thou mother of my children, I have
    loved thee,
90 And I have given thee a crown that none can take
    away".
But how this is, sweet maid, I know not, and I cannot
    know,
I ponder, and I cannot ponder; yet I live and love.'

The daughter of beauty wiped her pitying tears with
    her white veil
And said: 'Alas! I knew not this, and therefore did I
    weep.
95 That God would love a worm I knew, and punish the
    evil foot
That wilful bruised its helpless form. But that he
    cherished it
With milk and oil I never knew, and therefore did I
    weep,
And I complained in the mild air, because I fade
    away
And lay me down in thy cold bed and leave my
    shining lot.'

100 'Queen of the vales', the matron clay answered, 'I
    heard thy sighs.
And all thy moans flew o'er my roof but I have
    called them down.
Wilt thou, O Queen, enter my house—'tis given
    thee to enter
And to return. Fear nothing; enter with thy virgin
    feet.'

[*Design*]

Pl. 5. *Design* shows Thel watching the matron and worm.

Pl. 6   IV

The eternal gates' terrific porter lifted the northern
        bar.
105 Thel entered in and saw the secrets of the land
        unknown.
She saw the couches of the dead, and where the
        fibrous roots
Of every heart on earth infixes deep its restless
        twists—
A land of sorrows and of tears where never smile was
        seen.

She wandered in the land of clouds, through valleys
        dark, listening
110 Dolours and lamentations; waiting oft beside a dewy
        grave
She stood in silence, listening to the voices of the
        ground,
Till to her own grave plot she came, and there she
        sat down,
And heard this voice of sorrow breathed from the
        hollow pit:

'Why cannot the ear be closed to its own destruction,

Pl. 6. For the late date of this pl. see headnote.
104. the northern bar] This phrase derives ultimately from a passage in the
Odyssey, xiii *109–12*, describing the 'cave of the Naiads'. This cave has two
gates; the northern, for mortals, the southern for gods. See *Milton* pl.27.*13*,
p. 534 below, for full quotation. The passage was given an allegorical
interpretation by the Neo-Platonists, who read it as an allusion to the
descent of souls to earth (by the northern gate), and the occasional visits by
gods and spirits (by the southern gate). Such a reading was available to B.,
through the writings of Thomas Taylor (*Dissertation on the Eleusinian and
Bacchic Mysteries*, *c.* 1790). By the addition (probably replacing an early
sect. iv) of this plate, B. has turned the legend of Thel into a story of the
fear of a soul which dare not enter the mortal world. See also *112n*. The
imagery of *104–8* is quite unlike anything in the early B.; note esp. the
words evocative of evil, common in his verse after about 1794 (*Urizen*)
but rare before: *secrets of the land unknown: couches of the dead: fibrous roots:
infixes deep its restless twists.*
112. grave plot] Taking their cue from Plato himself, the Neo-Platonists
emphasized the notion that this mortal world is a sort of death; that real
life is only known in Heaven; and that this world is no more than a cave
of the dead, a grave.
114–23. About 1791–93 B. became very fond of sets of rhetorical questions.
Cp. *Tiriel 334*ff; and in *Visions 63–70, 83–110, 116–53, 205–10.* ·Here

115   Or the glistening eye to the poison of a smile?
Why are the eyelids stored with arrows ready drawn,
Where a thousand fighting men in ambush lie?
Or an eye of gifts and graces, showering fruits and
        coined gold?
Why a tongue impressed with honey from every wind?
120   Why an ear a whirlpool fierce to draw creations in?
Why a nostril wide inhaling terror, trembling and
        affright?
Why a tender curb upon the youthful burning boy?
Why a little curtain of flesh on the bed of our desire?'

The virgin started from her seat, and with a shriek
125   Fled back unhindered till she came into the vales of
        Har.

The End

[Design]

7 The Marriage of Heaven and Hell

Date. By hand on pl. 3 of one copy, *1790*. *Song of Liberty* 1792–93, from the
historical allusions. Pls 4, 7–10, 14–20, have a later style of lettering than the
rest (as has the *Song* pls 25–27), and may have been composed about the
same time as the *Song*, or more probably merely later than the rest. One
copy has an engraving as frontispiece dated 5 June 1793, but this is only
an extreme *terminus ante quem*. There is a Blake Trust facsimile (1960).
Theme. This book marks the end of B.'s adherence to Swedenborg's doc-
trines, though by no means of Swedenborg's influence on B. After the
opening poem, B. parodies Swedenborg's manner and themes, arguing
again and again that Swedenborg was handling the right material in the
wrong way. Emanuel Swedenborg (1688–1772) was a Swedish engineer
who claimed divine revelations. His writings are not altogether to be ig-
nored and were the source of much inspiration to B., who derived from
them his ideas of the Divine Humanity, of the spiritual world as true
reality, with this world a limited image of it; of the power of ordinary
mortals to enter the spiritual world if they choose to purify themselves. But
Swedenborg's visions are prosaic; his angels and devils are conventional,
as are his morals and most of his theological principles. He was too stolid

they form a cry of the lost creation, 'Why must mankind be imaginative?'.
They would rather remain sunk in the cave, unable to sense any reality
beyond material nature.
122–3. These lines were del. in two copies; thirteen remain with the lines
retained. They do not fit the general sense (see *n.* above) and seem to
mean 'Why must desire be restrained?'–a contrary idea.
Design at the end: three children ride on a serpent.

for the Blake of 1790, during his period of enthusiasm for the new age of political freedom. To Swedenborg 'Divine Humanity' meant that Christ was God without reservation; to B. it meant that divinity resided in every human soul. In this book he relegates Swedenborg to the position of 'the Angel sitting at the tomb: his writings are the linen clothes folded up' (pl.3). The 'clothes' have served their purpose, and can be put away; in the new age, which B. heralds, only naked and pure beauty and truth will remain. B.'s chief opinions here argued are (a) that the energies of natural desire, not behaviour according to a predetermined code, will lead to the proper way of life; and (b) that each individual's imagination is 'the truth' for him—sacred, and not to be denied by others. He retained both ideas for the rest of his life, but they underwent serious modification; he did not long believe, as he did in 1790, in the necessity for complete moral individualism.

After the *Argument* B. gives a series of parodies of Swedenborg, who often wrote in just this way, a philosophical discourse being followed by a *Memorable Relation*, a narrative of what he saw and said on one of the many occasions when he was carried up to heaven. These are parodied here in B.'s *Memorable Fancies*. Two examples will suffice to show the kind of thing B. had in mind, both bearing some similarity to B.'s *Fancy* on pls 17–20. They are drawn from *The True Christian Religion*, paras 161 and 388.

I once heard, in the spiritual World, a Noise like the Grinding of a Mill . . . Then I observed something like an arched Roof above the Ground, the Entrance to which was through a Cave, and entered in; and lo! there was a large Room, and an aged Person sitting therein, surrounded with Books, and holding before him the Word or Holy Scripture, wherein he was searching what might be serviceable to his Doctrine; about him lay several sheets of Paper, whereon he wrote such Passages as favoured his Purpose; in the next Apartment were a number of Scribes, who collected the scattered Sheets, and copied out the Contents on one entire Paper. [*The Doctrine was of the implacable wrath of God against sin; Swedenborg replies that* 'Grace on God's Part, as it is infinite, so also is it eternal'.] As I uttered these words, the Old Man was inflamed to such a Height of Passion, that he sprung forwards from his Chair, and called his Scribes to turn me out of his House; and as I walked out of my own Accord, he threw after me the first Book that he could lay his Hands on, and the Book proved to be the Word.

[*A Dragon*] led me through a gloomy Wood to the Top of a Hill, whence I might behold the Amusements of the Dragons; and I saw an Amphitheatre . . . they who sat on the lowest Seats appeared to me, at a Distance, like Satyrs and Priapusses, some with a covering to conceal their Privy Parts, and some naked without a Covering; on the Benches over those sat Whoremongers and Harlots . . . and I saw, as it were, Heifers, Rams, Sheep, Kids and Lambs, driven into the Area of the Circus, and when they were in, a Gate was opened, and there rushed in, as it were, young Lions, Panthers, Tigers, and Wolves, who attacked the Flock with great Fury, and tore them in Pieces, and killed them; but the Satyrs, when the bloody Slaughter was over, scattered Sand over the Place ...

A SONG OF LIBERTY (p. 102) though related in spirit, is very different in theme. It looks as if B. composed it in order to finish the book with a rousing chorus, though it also exists alone (but *Marriage* does not exist without the *Song*). Whereas the substance of most of the book is religious, *A Song of Liberty* is political. It resembles a summary of *America* (which it may well be), in that it describes the failure of 'the starry king's' attempt to destroy 'the son of fire', as Albion's Angel and Urizen fail to destroy Orc in *America*. B. is not now concerned with Swedenborg directly; he has almost forgotten him. But the principles of the body of the book– freedom, youthful energy and imagination–are still very active, though at this point their outlet is political. But B.'s mind was never compart-mented, and political freedom involves social and moral freedom as well. Erdman has related the *Song* to events in Sept. 1792, when the anti-revolutionary armies of the central European powers, under the Duke of Brunswick's command, were halted and turned back in their attempted invasion of France. B. characteristically sees this as symbolic of a wider victory of the powers of truth, heralding the advent of a New Age. The biblical 'verses' of poetic prose are part of the tradition established by Solomon Gessner (see p. 38 above).

Pl. 2   I THE ARGUMENT

 Rintrah roars and shakes his fires in the burdened air;
 Hungry clouds swag on the deep.

 Once meek, and in a perilous path,
 The just man kept his course along
5 The vale of death.
 Roses are planted where thorns grow,

¶ 7. Pl.1 is the titlepage.
Pl.2. *Argument* (that false religion has invaded the paths of truth). *Design:* In the R margin, a leafy tree; a gowned youth reaches down to a gowned girl to give her its fruit.
i *1. Rintrah*] A shadowy figure here, apparently a sort of wrathful thunder-'god': he reappears in *Europe 36, 49, 54* as 'furious king'; and, much later, in *Milton* pls 7–13, as ploughman, and still furious. It would be a mistake, however, to read these future developments into this allusion.
i *2. swag*] 'Sway, hang unsteadily'–an obsolete word.
i *3–5.* This seems to be an allusion to Christian's journey through the Valley of the Shadow of Death, in *Pilgrim's Progress*, when he had to walk on a knife-edge path; deviation from it would have meant his destruction.
i *6.* Cp. the well-known passage in *Isaiah* xxxv 1: 'The desert shall rejoice, and blossom as the rose'. But the similarity is only verbal; the sentiment is quite different.

And on the barren heath
Sing the honey bees.

Then the perilous path was planted;
10   And a river and a spring
On every cliff and tomb;
And on the bleached bones
Red clay brought forth.

Till the villain left the paths of ease
15   To walk in perilous paths and drive
The just man into barren climes.

Now the sneaking serpent walks
In mild humility,
And the just man rages in the wilds
20   Where lions roam.

Rintrah roars and shakes his fires in the burdened air;
Hungry clouds swag on the deep.

———————

II

Pl. 3   [*Design*]

As a new Heaven is begun, and it is now thirty-three years
since its advent, the eternal Hell revives. And lo!

i *9. planted*] Planted with flowers (*6–8*).
i *13*. i.e. clay–the flesh of the earth, fertile soil–appeared on the rocks, the
'dry bones' of the earth. Cp. *Ezekiel* xxxvii, the vision of the valley full of
dry bones, which were clothed with flesh by the word and spirit of God.
But 'clay' may also mean, by a literal translation from Hebrew, 'Adam'.
i *15. perilous paths*] So-called; they are now perilous no longer, and villains
choose to enjoy the pleasures they find there, using the force of their un-
scrupulousness to drive out the just men who were there when the place
was really perilous. The *sneaking serpent* of *17* claims humility by following
the pilgrimage–but he is a hypocrite, because it is a pilgrimage of hardship
no longer.
Pl.3. *Design*: A female figure, stretching in enjoyment of vital flames.
ii *1. a new Heaven*] B. wrote '1790' in the margin of one copy. Swedenborg
claimed that a new dispensation had been granted by God, and revealed to
him in 1757–the year of B.'s birth. But B. says that the thirty-third year
(1790)–the age of Christ at the end of his ministry, when his resurrection
ushered in the new dispensation of Christ–is producing, not another
heaven on the old model, but a resurgence of 'hellish' energy, as B. goes
on to display it. This kind of irony is characteristic of the whole book. The
following references to Swedenborg show that B. now thinks of him, not
as the bearer of the new gospel, but merely as an assistant at its coming.

Swedenborg is the angel sitting at the tomb; his writings
are the linen clothes folded up. Now is the dominion of
5 Edom, and the return of Adam into Paradise; see Isaiah
xxxiv & xxxv chap:

Without contraries is no progression. Attraction and
repulsion, reason and energy, love and hate, are neces-
sary to human existence.

10 From these contraries spring what the religious call
good and *evil*. Good is the passive that obeys reason:
Evil is the active springing from energy.

Good is Heaven; Evil is Hell.

[*Design*]

Pl. 4   THE VOICE OF THE DEVIL

All bibles or sacred codes have been the causes of the
15 following errors:

1. That man has two real existing principles, viz, a body
and a soul.

2. That energy, called evil, is alone from the body, and
that reason, called good, is alone from the soul.

20 3. That God will torment man in eternity for following
his energies.

But the following contraries to these are true:

1 Man has no body distinct from his soul, for that called

ii 5. *Edom*] The disinherited descendants of Esau, often reviled in the Old
Testament, come into their rights. In *Genesis* xxvii 40, when Jacob has
cheated Esau of his birthright, Isaac still grants Esau one blessing, that,
though he must ·serve Jacob, 'it shall come to pass when thou shalt have
dominion, that thou shalt break his yoke from off thy neck'. The passage
in *Isaiah* is apocalyptic, describing the destruction of the enemies of Israel
including Edom (i.e. 'dominion *over* Edom') and the restoration of the
land of the chosen people. The lines quoted in the note to *Argument 6*
come from this well-known passage.

ii 7. *contraries*] In this paragraph B. argues that opposite principles are
necessary; it is wrong to choose one (e.g. Reason, Love) as good and de-
clare the opposite evil. But he also takes the more perverse attitude that the
commonly supposed good is evil, and the commonly supposed evil, which
he associates with all things impulsive and energetic, is good. Both lines
of thought appear throughout the book.

ii. *Design*: L, a woman in childbirth; two figures R; a woman supine, and
a man kissing her as he runs past.

Pl.4. *The Devil*] B.'s new Messiah (see ii 7*n*.).

5 + B.

25 body is a portion of soul discerned by the five senses, the chief inlets of soul in this age.

2 Energy is the only life and is from the body, and reason is the bound or outward circumference of energy.

3 Energy is eternal delight.

[*Design*]

Pl. 5   [*Design*]

30 Those who restrain desire do so because theirs is weak enough to be restrained; and the restrainer or reason usurps its place and governs the unwilling.

And being restrained it by degrees becomes passive, till it is only the shadow of desire.

35 The history of this is written in *Paradise Lost*, and the governor (or reason) is called Messiah.

And the original archangel, or possessor of the command of the heavenly host, is called the Devil or Satan, and his children are called Sin and Death.

ii *25. inlets of soul*] This is basically the Swedenborgian idea that all things on earth are 'correspondences' of their equivalents in heaven; alternatively, that the things we see on earth are embodiments of divine or eternal truths. B. removes the theological implications which Swedenborg took for granted and leaves this idea (which is also a common Platonic and Neo-Platonic notion).

ii *26. Energy is the only life*] This is B.'s own development. Swedenborg's morality was very conventional.

ii. *Design*: An angel coming over the sea snatches a child from a chained angel surrounded by flames. A rising sun beyond the sea. (This became the colour-print 'The good and evil angels'; in it the fettered evil angel was made blind.)

Pl.5. *Design*: Above the text, a falling man, horse and military equipment drop into the flames of hell (cp. *Song of Liberty 15*).

ii *32. usurps*] The notion of the false god who usurps the place of truth is important to B. throughout his life, recurring in *Urizen, The Four Zoas, Milton, Jerusalem* and scattered references up to the last year of his life, when he parodied Thornton's new version of the Lord's Prayer thus: 'Thy Kingdom on Earth is not, nor thy Will done, but Satan's, who is God of this World, the Accuser'. In 1790, B.'s beliefs were tending against Christianity, but the image is the same.

ii *39. Sin and Death*] a reference to the famous passage in *Paradise Lost* ii *643ff.*

40 But in the *Book of Job* Milton's Messiah is called Satan.
For this history has been adopted by both parties.

It indeed appeared to reason as if desire was cast out;
Pl. 6 but the Devil's account is that the Messiah fell, and
formed a heaven of what he stole from the abyss.

45 This is shown in the Gospel, where he prays to the
Father to send the comforter (or desire) that reason
may have ideas to build on, the Jehovah of the Bible
being no other than he who dwells in flaming fire. Know
that after Christ's death he became Jehovah.

50 But in Milton the Father is destiny, the Son a ratio of
the five senses, and the Holy Ghost vacuum!

Note. The reason Milton wrote in fetters when he wrote
of angels and God, and at liberty when of devils and Hell,
is because he was a true poet, and of the Devil's party
55 without knowing it.

A MEMORABLE FANCY

As I was walking among the fires of Hell, delighted with
the enjoyments of genius (which to angels look like tor-
ment and insanity), I collected some of their proverbs,
thinking that, as the sayings used in a nation mark its
60 character, so the proverbs of Hell show the nature of
infernal wisdom better than any description of buildings
or garments.

ii *40. the Book of Job*] The Messiah of *Paradise Lost* is identified with Reason,
which in turn is associated with the 'Right' and 'Good', and therefore
with the Satan of *Job*, the Tempter whose function is to distinguish 'wrong'
from 'right'. This is not the true, energetic Satan of B.'s imagination. See
p. 116 below, pl.17 iv *125 n.*
Pl.6. (begins at *Messi/ah*).

ii *48. he who dwells . . .*] i.e. Jehovah is Satan, living in the eternal fires of
energy and desire; his power gives life, and even Jesus (here his enemy,
not his incarnation) must ask him for benefits.

ii *50. ratio*] .e. a 'rationale', a logical abstraction derived hypothetically
from what the senses observe. The Son is shown by Milton as if he were a
product, rather than the lord, of the material universe 'closed by your
senses five' (ii. *70*).

ii *51. vacuum*] Because he is ignored by Milton.

ii *52. in fetters*] B. was the first to propose that Milton has erected a
'human' Satan who attracts the reader's sympathies far more than the
apparently despotic God or the colourless Christ.

ii. *A Memorable Fancy*] A parody of Swedenborg's *Memorable Relations*.
B. is more concerned with fancy and imagination than with merely re-
lating accurately what he saw. See headnote.

When I came home, on the abyss of the five senses,
where a flat-sided steep frowns over the present world, I
65   saw a mighty devil folded in black clouds, hovering on
Pl. 7   the sides of the rock. With corroding fires he wrote the
following sentence now perceived by the minds of men,
and read by them on earth:

How do you know but every bird that cuts the airy way
70   Is an immense world of delight, closed by your senses
five?

III PROVERBS OF HELL

In seed time learn, in harvest teach, in winter enjoy.
Drive your cart and your plough over the bones of the
dead.
The road of excess leads to the palace of wisdom.
Prudence is a rich ugly old maid courted by incapacity.
5   He who desires but acts not breeds pestilence.
The cut worm forgives the plough.
Dip him in the river who loves water.
A fool sees not the same tree that a wise man sees.
He whose face gives no light shall never become a star.
10   Eternity is in love with the productions of Time.
The busy bee has no time for sorrow.
The hours of folly are measured by the clock, but of
wisdom no clock can measure.
All wholesome food is caught without a net or a trap.

Pl.7 (cor/roding). B.'s later style of lettering (?1792/3–1805) begins here (see
headnote). It may be more than coincidence that he chooses to discuss his
printing technique on this plate.
ii 66. corroding fires] B. is probably thinking of his own trade of engraving
with corrosive acid on a metal plate.
iii. Proverbs] Collections of aphorisms were popular eighteenth-century
reading; B.'s own annotations on Fuseli's translation of J. K. Lavater's
Aphorisms are extant.
iii 2. The image is of the farmer ploughing land under which lie the burial
grounds of past ages.
iii 6. Used also, but deleted, in the draft of 'The Fly' (Songs of Experience,
p. 220 below); as the second stanza:

> The cut worm
> Forgives the plough
> And dies in peace,
> And so do thou.

iii 8. An important principle in B.'s thought.

Bring out number, weight and measure in a year of
   dearth.
15 No bird soars too high, if he soars with his own wings.
A dead body revenges not injuries.
The most sublime act is to set another before you.
If the fool would persist in his folly he would become wise.
Folly is the cloak of Knavery.
20 Shame is Pride's cloak.
Pl. 8 Prisons are built with stones of Law, brothels with bricks
   of Religion.
The pride of the peacock is the glory of God.
The lust of the goat is the bounty of God.
The wrath of the lion is the wisdom of God.
25 The nakedness of woman is the work of God.
Excess of sorrow laughs. Excess of joy weeps.
The roaring of lions, the howling of wolves, the raging of
   the stormy sea, and the destructive sword are por-
   tions of eternity too great for the eye of man.
The fox condemns the trap, not himself.
Joys impregnate. Sorrows bring forth.
30 Let man wear the fell of the lion, woman the fleece of the
   sheep.
The bird a nest, the spider a web, man friendship.
The selfish smiling fool and the sullen frowning fool
   shall be both thought wise, that they may be a
   rod.
What is now proved was once only imagined.
The rat, the mouse, the fox, the rabbit, watch the roots.
   The lion, the tiger, the horse, the elephant, watch
   the fruits.
35 The cistern contains: the fountain overflows.
One thought fills immensity.
Always be ready to speak your mind, and a base man
   will avoid you.
Everything possible to be believed is an image of truth.
The eagle never lost so much time as when he submitted
   to learn of the crow.

iii 16. Not 'dead men tell no tales', but 'if a man is alive, you must expect
him to react to what you do to him'.
iii 18. *Proverbs* xvi 22: 'the instruction of fools is folly'; xxvi 11: 'a fool
returneth to his folly'. But B.'s idea is different; cp. B's Proverb 52.
Pl.8. iii 33. i.e. imagination is prior, and superior, to reason, which follows
on behind.
iii 39. i.e. every creature has its own nature, and it is folly to try to make it
something else. This is the argument of pl.3: it follows from it that what is

Pl. 9   The fox provides for himself, but God provides for the
        lion.
  41   Think in the morning. Act in the noon. Eat in the even-
        ing. Sleep in the night.
        He who has suffered you to impose on him, knows you.
        As the plough follows words, so God rewards prayers.
        The tigers of wrath are wiser than the horses of instruc-
        tion.
  45   Expect poison from the standing water.
        You never know what is enough unless you know what
        is more than enough.
        Listen to the fool's reproach: it is a kingly title.
        The eyes of fire, the nostrils of air, the mouth of water,
        the beard of earth.
        The weak in courage is strong in cunning.
  50   The apple tree never asks the beech how he shall grow,
        nor the lion the horse, how he shall take his prey.
        The thankful receiver bears a plentiful harvest.
        If others had not been foolish, we should be so.
        The soul of sweet delight can never be defiled.
        When thou seest an eagle, thou seest a portion of genius:
        lift up thy head!
  55   As the caterpillar chooses the fairest leaves to lay her
        eggs on, so the priest lays his curse on the fairest joys.
        To create a little flower is the labour of ages.
        Damn braces. Bless relaxes.
        The best wine is the oldest. The best water the newest.
        Prayers plough not. Praises reap not.
  60   Joys laugh not. Sorrows weep not.
Pl. 10 The head Sublime, the heart Pathos, the genitals Beauty,
        the hands and feet Proportion.
        As the air to a bird or the sea to a fish, so is contempt to
        the contemptible.
        The crow wished everything was black; the owl, that
        everything was white.
        Exuberance is beauty.
  65   If the lion was advised by the fox, he would be cunning.

good for one creature or person may not be good for another. Cp. Proverb
50.
Pl.9. iii 43. i.e. plans are discussed first, then the work is done.
iii 48. *the beard of earth*] Associating old age and the grave.
iii 50. Cp. Proverb 39.
iii 53. So in *Visions 9–10* and *America 72*.
Pl.10. iii 65. i.e. the lion would be cunning, but not kingly (cp. Pro-
verb 40).

Improvement makes straight roads, but the crooked
roads without improvement are roads of Genius.
Sooner murder an infant in its cradle than nurse unacted
desires.
Where man is not, nature is barren.
Truth can never be told so as to be understood and not
be believed.

70   Enough, or too much!

[Design]

IV

Pl. 11   *[Design]*

The ancient poets animated all sensible objects with gods
or geniuses, calling them by the names, and adorning
them with the properties, of woods, rivers, mountains,
lakes, cities, nations, and whatever their enlarged and
5 numerous senses could perceive.
And particularly they studied the genius of each city
and country, placing it under its mental deity.
Till a system was formed, which some took advantage
of and enslaved the vulgar by attempting to realise or
10 abstract the mental deities from their objects. Thus
began priesthood – choosing forms of worship from poetic
tales.
And at length they pronounced that the gods had
ordered such things.
15   Thus men forgot that all deities reside in the human
breast.

[Design]

iii *70. Enough! . . . much*] Perhaps an ironic remark on the 'Proverbs.'
iii. *Design*: A devil with a scroll teaches two young women, who write.
Pl.11. iv. *Design*: The sea (in some copies enclosed in a cave); a tritonlike
male figure; and on an island, a woman with a child.
iv *11. Choosing forms . . .*] i.e. converting poetry into rigid rituals.
Pl.13. iv *15. all deities . . . breast*] i.e. are creations of the human imagina-
tion, which is infinite. Swedenborg held that supreme divinity resided in
Christ; that is, he was unitarian in rejecting the doctrine of a divided
Trinity, but different from the Unitarians in seeing Jesus Christ, not merely
as the ideal man, but as entirely God. This leads to an emphasis on the
nearness of true humanity and godhead, which B. here develops into the

Pl. 12   A MEMORABLE FANCY

The prophets Isaiah and Ezekiel dined with me, and
I asked them how they dared so roundly to assert that
God spake to them; and whether they did not think at
20   the time that they would be misunderstood, and so be
the cause of imposition.

Isaiah answered, 'I saw no God, nor heard any, in a
finite organical perception; but my senses discovered the
infinite in everything, and as I was then persuaded, and
25   remain confirmed, that the voice of honest indignation is
the voice of God, I cared not for consequences but wrote.'

Then I asked: 'Does a firm persuasion that a thing is
so, make it so?'

He replied, 'All poets believe that it does, and in ages
30   of imagination the firm persuasion removed mountains;
but many are not capable of a firm persuasion of any-
thing.'

Then Ezekiel said, 'The philosophy of the east taught
the first principles of human perception; some nations
35   held one principle for the origin and some another. We
of Israel taught that the Poetic Genius (as you now call
it) was the first principle, and all the others merely de-
rivative—which was the cause of our despising the priests
and philosophers of other countries, and prophesying

statement that godhead springs from the state of Humanity which is fully
and imaginatively realized. Further, gods that men worship are their own
imaginative ideals. This was a lifelong view of B.'s: he did not mean it to
devalue worship, but to emphasize that the true vision of perfection—which
is Human perfection—is impossible in this world. Then to elevate such
worship into an absolute demand is to elevate a partial truth (thus making
it false).

iv. *Design*: An aged figure: a rolling sea carries a youth.

Pl.12. iv *17*. *The prophets*...] B. parodies Swedenborg's *Relations* of
familiarity with heavenly spirits. This is not to say that B. entirely dis-
believed in this possibility; the succeeding conversation is not parody, but
expresses what B. believed to be true. B. did not persuade himself that this
dinner-party had occurred; this is an imaginative creation in which he
envisages the conversation that would have taken place at such a party—
with a little humour at Swedenborg's expense. Note the sentence beginning
'All poets believe . . .'.

iv *36*. *The Poetic Genius*] i.e. B. says that the God of *Genesis* i is not the
Miltonic despot, but the supreme imaginative genius; all works of the
imagination, such as poetry—and including such poetic inventions as the
gods of human religions—derive from this first Genius.

Pl. 13 that all gods would at last be proved to originate in ours
41 and to be the tributaries of the Poetic Genius. It was
this that our great poet King David desired so fervently
and invoked so pathetically, saying by this he conquers
enemies and governs kingdoms. And we so loved our
45 God, that we cursed in his name all the deities of sur-
rounding nations, and asserted that they had rebelled;
from these opinions the vulgar came to think that all
nations would at last be subject to the Jews.

'This,' said he, 'like all firm persuasions, is come to
50 pass, for all nations believe the Jews' code and worship
the Jews' God, and what greater subjection can be?'

I heard this with some wonder, and must confess my
own conviction. After dinner I asked Isaiah to favour the
world with his lost works; he said none of equal value was
55 lost. Ezekiel said the same of his.

I also asked Isaiah what made him go naked and bare-
foot for three years. He answered, 'The same that made
our friend Diogenes the Grecian.'

I then asked Ezekiel why he ate dung, and lay so long
60 on his right and left side. He answered, 'The desire of
raising other men into a perception of the infinite. This
the North American tribes practise, and is he honest

Pl.13. (gods/would).

iv 42. King David] The reference is not to a particular passage, though B.
may have had II Samuel xxii (i.e. Psalm xviii), or Psalm lx in mind; both
are specifically related to the strength of the Lord in certain victories of
David's.

iv 56. naked and barefoot] Isaiah xx: at the time of an Assyrian invasion
which penetrated well into the Israelite territory from the N, capturing
Ashdod (now Isdud, on the coast west of Jerusalem), Isaiah 'walked naked
and barefoot three years for a sign and wonder upon Egypt and upon
Ethiopia; so shall the king of Assyria lead away the Egyptians prisoners and
the Ethiopians captives'. Diogenes's assumption of extreme poverty is said
by B. to have had the same inspiration, though Isaiah claimed his to have
been a response to the Word of God.

iv 59. ate dung] Ezekiel iv: Ezekiel was taken into exile from Jerusalem with
King Jehoiachin; five years later Jerusalem, under King Zedekiah, rebelled
again. At this time, in Babylon, in obedience to the Word, Ezekiel made a
model of the coming siege of Jerusalem, and then lay on his left side for
390 days, to signify the number of years Israel would be held captive, and
then forty days on his right, to signify the length of Judah's captivity. Then
he ate barley cakes, carefully measured, and baked them on dung, to sig-
nify the rationing and hardship that would come during the siege of
Jerusalem.

5*

who resists his genius or conscience only for the sake of
present ease or gratification?'

Pl. 14   [*Design*]

65   The ancient tradition that the world will be consumed
in fire at the end of six thousand years is true, as I have
heard from Hell.
      For the cherub with his flaming sword is hereby com-
manded to leave his guard at the Tree of Life; and when
70   he does, the whole creation will be consumed, and appear
infinite and holy, whereas it now appears finite and cor-
rupt.
      This will come to pass by an improvement of sensual
enjoyment.
75   But first the notion that man has a body distinct from
his soul is to be expunged. This I shall do by printing in
the infernal method by corrosives, which in Hell are
salutary and medicinal, melting apparent surfaces away,
and displaying the infinite which was hid.
80   If the doors of perception were cleansed everything
would appear to man as it is—infinite.
      For man has closed himself up, till he sees all things
through narrow chinks of his cavern.

Pl. 15   A MEMORABLE FANCY
      I was in a printing-house in Hell and saw the method
85   in which knowledge is transmitted from generation to
generation.

iv *62. North American*] It is not clear what B. had in mind. North American
religions are animist, relating the spiritual world to visible objects, and do
not consider 'the infinite' in the abstract. Perhaps he refers to the ordeals
of initiation into 'manhood'.
Pl.14. *Design*: A sleeper (or a corpse): a figure, arms outspread, hovers
over, and flames rise behind.
iv *66. six thousand years*] Taking the Creation as 4004 B.C., this would be
1996, or beyond B.'s own day–but near enough, perhaps, for B. to con-
sider it 'our own times'. The *Revelation* term is 'A thousand years', sig-
nifying a long time, and making the total, not six, but five thousand. But
six thousand years is, as B. says, a traditional figure.
iv *68. the cherub*] Genesis iii 24: God 'placed at the east of the garden of
Eden Cherubims, and a flaming sword which turned every way, to keep
the way of the tree of life'. (The plate reads 'at tree'. . .)
iv *77. the infernal method*] See note on pl.7, ii 65, *corroding fires*.
Pl.15. iv *84. printing house*] The trend of this passage is to emphasize the
infinite beauty of the process.

In the first chamber was a dragon-man, clearing away the rubbish from a cave's mouth; within, a number of dragons were hollowing the cave.

90   In the second chamber was a viper folding round the rock and the cave, and others adorning it with gold, silver and precious stones.

In the third chamber was an eagle with wings and feathers of air; he caused the inside of the cave to be in-

95   finite. Around were numbers of eagle-like men, who built palaces in the immense cliffs.

In the fourth chamber were lions of flaming fire, raging around and melting the metals into living fluids.

In the fifth chamber were unnamed forms, which cast

100   the metals into the expanse.

There they were received by men who occupied the sixth chamber, and took the forms of books and were arranged in libraries.

[Design]

Pl. 16   *[Design]*

The giants who formed this world into its sensual

105   existence, and now seem to live in it in chains, are in truth the causes of its life and the sources of all activity; but the chains are the cunning of weak and tame minds, which have power to resist energy – according to the proverb, 'the weak in courage is strong in cunning.'

110   Thus one portion of being is the *prolific*, the other, the *devouring*. To the devourer it seems as if the producer was in his chains, but it is not so; he only takes portions of existence and fancies that the whole.

But the prolific would cease to be prolific unless the

115   devourer as a sea received the excess of his delights.

Some will say, 'Is not God alone the prolific?' I answer, 'God only acts and is in existing beings or men.'

iv *101. men . . . books . . . libraries*] Note how prosaic and dull men are, after the dazzling animals.

iv. *Design*: An eagle grasps a serpent (perhaps struggling) in the sky.

Pl. 16. *Design*: Ugolino, who with two sons and two grandsons was sealed in a prison all (*Inferno* xxxi). The design seems to allude to *the giants* of iv. *104–5*; see also *The Gates of Paradise* pl. 12 (p. 844 below). This section is quite different from the earlier engraved pl. 11, and embodies an idea which was no doubt conceived at a different time. There is, however, still the same attitude, that of free energy being preferable to a tame acceptance of reason and custom.

Pl. 17
120
These two classes of men are always upon earth, and they should be enemies; whoever tries to reconcile them seeks to destroy existence.

Religion is an endeavour to reconcile the two.

Note. Jesus Christ did not wish to unite but to separate them, as in the parable of sheep and goats. And he says, 'I came not to send peace, but a sword.'

125
Messiah or Satan or Tempter was formerly thought to be one of the antediluvians who are our energies.

A MEMORABLE FANCY

130
An angel came to me and said, 'O pitiable foolish young man! O horrible! O dreadful state! Consider the hot burning dungeon thou art preparing for thyself to all eternity, to which thou art going in such a career.'

I said: 'Perhaps you will be willing to show me my eternal lot, and we will contemplate together upon it, and see whether your lot or mine is most desirable.'

135
So he took me through a stable and through a church and down into the church vault, at the end of which was a mill. Through the mill we went, and came to a cave; down the winding cavern we groped our tedious way, till a void boundless as a nether sky appeared beneath us, and we held by the roots of trees and hung

---

iv *119. enemies*] i.e. it is wrong to claim that one or the other is 'the good', and so to force the opposite to conform. Both are essential. The argument also involves B.'s belief in preserving the essential individuality of different natures–'One law for the lion and ox is oppression' (iv. *293*).
Pl.17 (*tries/to*).

iv *122. Jesus Christ*] the allusions are to *Matthew* xxv 32–3 and x 34.

iv *125. Messiah or Satan or Tempter*] (See 'The Book of Job', ii *40n* above). B. says the Messiah was formerly, but mistakenly, thought to be one of those whose energy infused the world with life. But he was not; he was the Tempter of *Job* whose wish was to judge right and wrong, not to allow people to enjoy their lives fully.

iv. *Memorable Fancy*] See headnote and the quotation from Swedenborg there for a parallel to this 'Fancy'.

iv *134. he took me . . .*] A place for animals leads to a church, which leads to a place for hard labour and slavery (B. usually has Milton's phrase 'grinding at the mill with slaves' in mind when using this word), which leads to a 'tedious cavern'. B. imagines a flat earth, with an abyss like a 'nether sky' underneath it, and the roots of trees serving instead of their trunks and branches as a sort of downwards vegetation. This is the opposite of Swedenborg's common experience of being carried up to heaven.

140 over this immensity. But I said, 'If you please we will
commit ourselves to this void, and see whether provi-
dence is here also; if you will not; I will.' But he
answered, 'Do not presume, O young man; but as we
here remain, behold thy lot which will soon appear
145 when the darkness passes away.'

Pl. 18   So I remained with him sitting in the twisted root of an
oak. He was suspended in a fungus which hung with the
head downward into the deep.

By degrees we beheld the infinite abyss, fiery as the
150 smoke of a burning city; beneath us at an immense
distance was the sun, black but shining. Round it were
fiery tracks on which revolved vast spiders, crawling after
their prey, which flew or rather swum in the infinite
deep, in the most terrific shapes of animals sprung from
155 corruption; and the air was full of them, and seemed
composed of them. These are devils, and are called
Powers of the Air. I now asked my companion which
was my eternal lot; he said, 'Between the black and
white spiders.'

But now, from between the black and white spiders a
160 cloud and fire burst and rolled through the deep,
blackening all beneath, so that the nether deep grew
black as a sea, and rolled with a terrible noise. Beneath
us was nothing now to be seen but a black tempest, till
looking east between the clouds and the waves, we saw a
165 cataract of blood mixed with fire and not many stones'-
throw from us appeared and sunk again the scaly fold of
a monstrous serpent. At last to the east, distant about
three degrees, appeared a fiery crest above the waves;
slowly it reared like a ridge of golden rocks, till we dis-
170 covered two globes of crimson fire, from which the sea
fled away in clouds of smoke; and now we saw it was the
head of Leviathan. His forehead was divided into streaks
of green and purple like those on a tiger's forehead; soon
we saw his mouth and red gills hang just above the rag-
175 ing foam, tingeing the black deep with beams of blood,
advancing toward us with all the fury of a spiritual

Pl. 19 existence.

My friend the angel climbed up from his station into
the mill. I remained alone, and then his appearance was

Pl.18 (*twisted*/*root*).
iv *149*. The place indicated by the angel as a place of horror becomes a
place of inspiration (perhaps through its assignment to B.).
Pl. 19. (*toward* / *us*).

180   no more, but I found myself sitting on a pleasant bank
beside a river by moonlight, hearing a harper who sung
to the harp; and his theme was, 'The man who never
alters his opinion is like standing water, and breeds
reptiles of the mind.'

185   But I arose, and sought for the mill, and there I found
my angel, who, surprised, asked me how I escaped?

I answered, 'All that we saw was owing to your meta-
physics; for when you ran away, I found myself on a
bank by moonlight hearing a harper. But now we have

190   seen my eternal lot, shall I show you yours?' He laughed
at my proposal; but I by force suddenly caught him in
my arms, and flew westerly through the night, till we
were elevated above the earth's shadow. Then I flung
myself with him directly into the body of the sun. Here I

195   clothed myself in white, and taking in my hand Sweden-
borg's volumes sunk from the glorious clime, and passed
all the planets till we came to Saturn. Here I stayed to rest
and then leaped into the void between Saturn and the
fixed stars.

200   'Here,' said I, 'is your lot, in this space, if space it may
be called.' Soon we saw the stable and the church, and I
took him to the altar and opened the Bible, and lo! it was
a deep pit, into which I descended, driving the angel be-
fore me. Soon we saw seven houses of brick, one we

Pl. 20   entered; in it were a number of monkeys, baboons, and all
206   of that species, chained by the middle, grinning and
snatching at one another, but withheld by the shortness
of their chains. However I saw that they sometimes grew
numerous, and then the weak were caught by the strong

210   and with a grinning aspect, first coupled with them and
then devoured, by plucking off first one limb and then
another till the body was left a helpless trunk. This after
grinning and kissing it with seeming fondness they de-
voured too; and here and there I saw one savourily

iv *180. I found myself sitting*...] This pleasant state was what he had
created for himself; the horrors of the deep were created by the diseased
imagination of the angel, which bred 'reptiles of the mind'.

iv *192. flew westerly*] B. always thought of the West as the land of hope
(except in *Tiriel*): this is an early example of it. Note that they are now
flying, not crawling.

iv *198. the void*...] Uranus was discovered in 1781, but B. evidently did
not know of this, or chose to ignore it. Traditionally, in the Ptolemaic
cosmology, Saturn was the outermost of the planetary spheres, and beyond
it only the sphere of the 'fixed stars' and, outermost, the firmament.

Pl.20 (*were a/number*)

215 picking the flesh off of his own tail; as the stench terribly
annoyed us both we went into the mill, and I in my
hand brought the skeleton of a body, which in the mill
was Aristotle's *Analytics*.

So the angel said: 'Thy fantasy has imposed upon me
220 and thou oughtest to be ashamed.'

I answered: 'We impose on one another, and it is but
lost time to converse with you whose works are only
Analytics.'

[Design]

OPPOSITION IS TRUE FRIENDSHIP.

Pl. 21   *[Design]*

I have always found that angels have the vanity to
225 speak of themselves as the only wise; this they do with a
confident insolence sprouting from systematic reasoning.

Thus Swedenborg boasts that what he writes is new,
though it is only the contents or index of already-
published books.

230 A man carried a monkey about for a show, and be-
cause he was a little wiser than the monkey, grew vain,
and conceived himself as much wiser than seven men. It
is so with Swedenborg; he shows the folly of churches
and exposes hypocrites, till he imagines that all are
Pl. 22 religious, and himself the single one on earth that ever
236 broke a net.

Now hear a plain fact: Swedenborg has not written
one new truth. Now hear another: he has written all the
old falsehoods.

240 And now hear the reason. He conversed with angels,

iv *217. skeleton*] i.e. philosophical works are no more than grotesque
notions, with whatever life they had in them extinct.

iv *218. Aristotle's Analytics*] B. may only have known the name, which
carries enough meaning to damn the books in his eyes.

iv. *Design*: The serpent of pl.18 coiling over the sea.

iv. *Opposition is true Friendship*] Del. by colouring in six of the nine
copies.

Pl.21. *Design*: The resurrection figure of *America* pl.6, in some copies here
against a background of pyramids: a youth rising from a mound on which
bones are scattered, and looking upwards.

Pl.22 (*single/one*)

iv *240. conversed with angels*] As in the second passage quoted in the head-
note, Swedenborg treated the devils in his visions with disdain.

who are all religious, and conversed not with devils who all hate religion, for he was incapable through his conceited notions.

245 Thus Swedenborg's writings are a recapitulation of all superficial opinions and an analysis of the more sublime, but no further.

Have now another plain fact: any man of mechanical talents may from the writings of Paracelsus or Jacob Behmen produce ten thousand volumes of equal value

250 with Swedenborg's—and from those of Dante or Shakespeare an infinite number.

But when he has done this, let him not say that he knows better than his master, for he only holds a candle in sunshine.

A MEMORABLE FANCY

255 Once I saw a devil in a flame of fire, who arose before an angel that sat on a cloud; and the devil uttered these words:

'The worship of God is honouring his gifts in other men,
Pl. 23 each according to his genius, and loving the greatest men
260 best. Those who envy or calumniate great men hate God, for there is no other God'.

The angel, hearing this, became almost blue, but mastering himself he grew yellow, and at last white pink and smiling, and then replied,

265 'Thou idolater, is not God One, and is he not visible in Jesus Christ? And has not Jesus Christ given his sanction to the law of ten commandments; and are not all other men fools, sinners, and nothings?'

The devil answered, 'Bray a fool in a mortar with

iv 248. *Paracelsus or Jacob Behmen*] (i.e. Boehme); the former (1493–1541) was a noted, and quarrelsome, physician and mystic philosopher, the second (1575–1624) a shoemaker; untutored but a great mystic. There is evidence in *Urizen* (1794) that B. knew Boehme and though the offhand tone of this remark suggests that at this time he had no close acquaintance with his writings, the letter-poem of 12 Sept. 1800 (p. 469 below) implies that B. read both authors in youth.

iv 255. *devil . . . angel*] The devil expresses B.'s point of view, the angel that which B. takes to be the orthodox.

Pl.23 (the/greatest)

iv 269. *Bray a fool*] Proverbs xxvii 22: 'Though thou shouldest bray a fool in a mortar among wheat with a pestle, yet will not his foolishness depart from him'—the devil is quoting scripture for his own purposes. *Bray* (now dialect only) = 'beat'.

270 wheat, yet shall not his folly be beaten out of him. If
Jesus Christ is the greatest man, you ought to love him in
the greatest degree. Now hear how he has given his sanc-
tion to the law of ten commandments: did he not mock
at the Sabbath, and so mock the Sabbath's God? Murder
275 those who were murdered because of him? Turn away the
law from the woman taken in adultery? Steal the labour
of others to support him? Bear false witness when he
omitted making a defence before Pilate? Covet when he
prayed for his disciples, and when he bid them shake off
280 the dust of their feet against such as refused to lodge
them? I tell you no virtue can exist without breaking
these ten commandments. Jesus was all virtue, and acted
Pl. 24 from impulse, not from rules.'
When he had so spoken I beheld the angel who
285 stretched out his arms embracing the flame of fire, and
he was consumed and arose as Elijah.
Note. This angel, who is now become a devil, is my par-
ticular friend. We often read the Bible together in its
infernal or diabolical sense, which the world shall have if
290 they behave well.
I have also the Bible of Hell—which the world shall
have whether they will or no.

[*Design*]

One Law for the Lion and Ox is Oppression.

iv 273. *did he not mock*] This set of apparent contradictions, showing Christ
in opposition to the religious laws of his day, was worked out in full, many
years later, in *The Everlasting Gospel* (1818 approx.). But although the
contradiction was still the same, B.'s religious ideas were by then much
developed and matured. The events referred to may be found in: *Mark*
ii 27 ('the sabbath was made for man . . .'); *John* viii 2–11 (the woman taken
in adultery); *Matthew* xxvii 13–14 ('and he answered him to never a
word'); *Matthew* x 14 ('and whosoever shall not receive you . . . when ye
depart . . . shake off the dust of your feet').
Pl.24 (*im/pulse*).
iv 286. *as Elijah*] i.e. like Elijah, who (2 *Kings* ii 11) went up by a whirlwind
into Heaven. Since he was first separated from Elisha by a chariot and
horses of fire, he is commonly said to have ascended in the fiery chariot–as,
indeed, the text may intend, though it does not say so.
iv 291. *the Bible of Hell*] It may be that B.'s two *Prophecies*, i.e. *America* and
Europe, and his '*Genesis*' (*The Book of Urizen*), together with the other
similar poems of the next few years–but not, probably, *Visions*–were
intended as parts or all of the *Bible of Hell*. The deliberate imitation of
Biblical themes and, to a less extent, of Biblical manner, makes this probable;
but these poems were never so labelled.   [*Note on Design see over*

Pl. 25   v A SONG OF LIBERTY

1. The Eternal Female groaned; it was heard over all the earth.

2. Albion's coast is sick, silent; the American meadows faint.

3. Shadows of prophecy shiver along by the lakes and the rivers, and mutter across the ocean. France, rend down thy dungeon!

4. Golden Spain, burst the barriers of old Rome!

5. Cast thy keys, O Rome, into the deep—down falling, even to eternity down falling,

6. And weep.

7. In her trembling hands she took the new-born terror, howling.

8. On those infinite mountains of light, now barred out by the Atlantic sea, the new-born fire stood before the starry king.

9. Flagged with grey-browed snows and thunderous visages, the jealous wings waved over the deep.

10. The speary hand burned aloft, unbuckled was the

iv. *Design*: Nebuchadnezzar (*Daniel* iv 25, 33), insane and half-beast, crawling on all fours. The following line probably alludes to this design

iv *287. One Law . . . Oppression*] Cp. *Tiriel 334*: and *Visions 108* (where Bromion accepts what B. here rejects).

Pl.25. *A Song of Liberty*

v 1. *The Eternal Female*] A figure who was later much developed; in this context she is a kind of earth-mother, producing destined events.

v 3. *thy dungeon*] The Bastille, destroyed in 1789. B. makes much of its terror in his unpublished *The French Revolution*.

v 5. *keys*] The keys of Rome are the traditional symbol of Papal power.

v 6. *And weep*] B.'s shortest verse echoes the Bible's: 'Jesus wept' (*John* xi 35). Original reading: 'And weep and bow thy reverend locks'.

v 7. *the new-born terror*] The fiery youth, another figure later fully developed, into Orc who appears in most poems from *America* (1793) to *Vala* (begun ca. 1797). He is the spirit and champion of revolution.

v 8. *mountains of light . . . sea*] Atlantis, the fabled land of beauty and civilization, which was overcome by a deluge. B. came to use the Atlantis story as a myth of devouring chaos.

the starry king] The king of the stars, of the vacant law-governed universe. Although B. may think of a star as bright, his use of the word *starry* almost always implies the universe of Newton—silent, fixed, and dead.

v 9. *flagged*] Weighed down, wearied.

v 10. *speary*] A 'poetic' word, formed after such Miltonic adjectives as 'massy'. The antique power of oppression tries to do away with the power of youth and freedom.

shield, forth went the hand of jealousy among the flam-
Pl. 26 ing hair, and hurled the new-born wonder through the
starry night.

11. The fire, the fire, is falling!

12. Look up, look up! O citizen of London, enlarge thy
countenance; O Jew, leave counting gold! Return to thy
oil and wine, O African, black African! (Go, winged
thought, widen his forehead!)

13. The fiery limbs, the flaming hair shot like the sink-
ing sun into the western sea.

14. Waked from his eternal sleep, the hoary element
roaring fled away.

15. Down rushed, beating his wings in vain, the jealous
king; his grey browed counsellors, thunderous warriors,
curled veterans, among helms, and shields, and chariots,
horses, elephants, banners, castles, slings and rocks,

16. Falling, rushing, ruining! Buried in the ruins, on
Urthona's dens.

17. All night beneath the ruins; then, their sullen flames
faded, emerge round the gloomy king.

18. With thunder and fire, leading his starry hosts
Pl. 27 through the waste wilderness, he promulgates his ten
commands, glancing his beamy eyelids over the deep in
dark dismay,

19. Where the son of fire in his eastern cloud, while the
morning plumes her golden breast,

20. Spurning the clouds written with curses, stamps the
stony law to dust, loosing the eternal horses from the dens
of night, crying:

Pl.26 (*and/hurled*)

v 13. The fire falls in the ocean, but instead of being quenched, boils the
sea ('the hoary element', always hated by B., see verse 8*n*).

v 15. The sudden collapse of power recurs in *America*, cancelled plate *b*
(which may well be earlier than this), and in *Europe 66–70*, but the story is
not exactly the same.

v 16. *Urthona*] A shadowy figure as yet; in *America* (Preludium) he is
father of the Shadowy Female; and is generally associated with grim
strength, even in his further development in *The Four Zoas* where, how-
ever, B. alters his character. Here he seems to be little more than an old
earth spirit, probably an associate of the evil King.

v 18. *leading . . . wilderness*] *America 62*. The leading away of his followers
by the king also recurs in *Europe 71*ff, and (in a different myth) in *Urizen
515*.

Pl.27 (*wilderness/he promulgates*)

v 20. *stony law*] The ten commandments were inscribed on 'tablets' of
stone, written with the 'finger of God' (*Exodus* xxxi 18).

Empire is no more! And now the lion & wolf
shall cease.

Let the priests of the raven of dawn no longer, in deadly
black, with hoarse note curse the sons of joy. Nor his
accepted brethren whom, tyrant, he calls free, lay the
bound or build the roof. Nor pale religious lechery call
that virginity that wishes but acts not.
For everything that lives is holy.

8 The French Revolution
A Poem in Seven Books

This is B.'s only book apart from *Poetical Sketches* to appear in printed
form, but like the *Sketches*, it was never published; the unique extant
copy – of the First Book only – is a page-proof, not a copy of a published
edition. If the poem was ever completed, the remaining six books indicated
on the titlepage (dated 1791) are lost; but there is no evidence that they
were ever written, in spite of the *Advertisement*.

The poem deals with the very earliest stages of the Revolution, before
the fall of the Bastille, when all turned on the challenge of the Third
Estate (which on 17 June 1789 constituted itself National Assembly) to the
king and nobility. B. did not possess an accurate knowledge of the day-to-
day course of events, and, as the notes show, he might be in confusion
about them. However, his main purpose was to give an imaginative
history of the attempt by the aristocracy to browbeat the commons, of the
commons' defiance, and of the sense of catastrophe pervading the whole
period, even before violence had broken out. Therefore, his misunder-
standing of the positions and characters of Orleans and Lafayette is not
only to be expected; it is irrelevant to his purposes.

The essential events were that on 17 June 1789, after refusing to act for
some weeks, the Third Estate constituted itself a National Assembly and
on the 20th, in the famous tennis-court resolution, the Assembly became

v. *Chorus*] This resembles a poetic-prose version of the chorus of a choral
ode, such as that which ends Dryden's *Song for St Cecilia's Day*, and many
others.
v. *Chorus*] *bound . . . roof*] Marks of enclosure and limitation.
v. *Chorus*] *religious lechery . . .*] Cp. *America 68–9*. B. uses the word 'lechery'
because he means that the so-called virginity which is prudery is not pure
at all, but depraved.
v. *Chorus*] *everything . . . holy*] Cp. *Visions 215, America 71*.

openly defiant. On the 19th and 21st the king had a private session with his council, and on the 23rd an open 'royal session' with the States-General, in which he spurned their independence of his will–and, after his departure, was again defied. On the 27th the king at last ordered the three Estates to hold combined meetings–since many of the less reactionary nobles and clergy had already gone to join the commons in the Assembly. On 8 July, and again on the 13th, 14th (Bastille day) and 15th the Assembly protested at the quantity of troops being brought to the neighbourhood of Paris. On the 15th, after they had not been used to save the Bastille, their withdrawal was ordered.

The titlepage date, 1791, was that of intended publication. At the rate events move in the one book we have, the whole poem of seven books would scarcely have covered more than a year, and perhaps less, so that the poem was probably drafted somewhere in mid-1790. The stress laid here on events which later proved less important suggests a nearness to them. On the other hand, B.'s error in supposing that the troops were moved before the Bastille fell suggests that memories were already beginning to blur. Erdman in *Blake: Prophet against Empire* (1954) has proposed Joel Barlow's *Vision of Columbus*, an imaginative, quasi-Dantesque vision of the history of America, as a source for B.'s imaginative-historical narrative in *America*, but it may also have influenced *The French Revolution*.

Advertisement.

The remaining Books of this Poem are finished, and will be published in their order.

BOOK THE FIRST

The dead brood over Europe, the cloud and vision
    descends over cheerful France.
O cloud well appointed! Sick, sick, the Prince on his
    couch, wreathed in dim
And appalling mist, his strong hand outstretched, from
    his shoulder down the bone,
Runs aching cold into the sceptre too heavy for mortal
    grasp. No more
5 To be swayed by visible hand, nor in cruelty bruise the
    mild flourishing mountains.

Sick the mountains, and all their vineyards weep, in the
    eyes of the kingly mourner;
Pale is the morning cloud in his visage. 'Rise, Necker:
    the ancient dawn calls us

¶ 8.2. *the Prince*] Louis XVI.
7. *Rise, Necker!*] The king speaks. Necker was Director-General of Finance; his economy and reforms had made him unpopular with the aristocracy–he

To awake from slumbers of five thousand years! I awake,
    but my soul is in dreams;
From my window I see the old mountains of France, like
    aged men, fading away.'

10   Troubled, leaning on Necker, descends the King, to his
    chamber of council; shady mountains
In fear utter voices of thunder; the woods of France
    embosom the sound;
Clouds of wisdom prophetic reply, and roll over the
    palace roof heavy.
Forty men, each conversing with woes in the infinite
    shadows of his soul,
Like our ancient fathers in regions of twilight, walk,
    gathering round the King;
15   Again the loud voice of France cries to the morning, the
    morning prophecies to its clouds.

For the Commons convene in the Hall of the Nation.
    France shakes! And the heavens of France
Perplexed vibrate round each careful countenance!
    Darkness of old times around them
Utters loud despair, shadowing Paris; her grey towers
    groan, and the Bastille trembles.
In its terrible towers the Governor stood, in dark fogs
    listening the horror;
20   A thousand his soldiers, old veterans of France, breath-
    ing red clouds of power and dominion.
Sudden seized with howlings, despair, and black night,
    he stalked like a lion from tower

was also Swiss and a Protestant—and it was at his instance that the States-
General was called. He was later (11 July) dismissed by Louis for his
relatively democratic sympathies. But he was no politician, and did not
wish to see the power of the Third Estate increase for its own sake, but only
in so far as it would be useful assistance towards his own reforms.

13. forty men] No particular group seems to be implied. ....

16. The Commons . . . Nation] B. translates 'Tiers Etat', reasonably, by the
English equivalent 'Commons'. They had been meeting during May and
June in the large chamber at Versailles intended for general meetings of all
the Estates together, as no separate hall had been provided for them. Its
name was not 'Hall of the Nation' but *Salle des Menus Plaisirs du Roi.*
B. does not refer to any particular session, but imagines a Commons
meeting occurring at the same time as a royal council.

19. in dark fogs] These are figurative; the weather was not foggy.

20. a thousand] A gross overestimate; the garrison was about 130.

To tower, his howlings were heard in the Louvre; from
court to court restless he dragged
His strong limbs; from court to court cursed the fierce
torment unquelled,
Howling and giving the dark command; in his soul
stood the purple plague,
25 Tugging his iron manacles, and piercing through the
seven towers dark and sickly,
Panting over the prisoners like a wolf gorged; and the
den named *Horror* held a man
Chained hand and foot, round his neck an iron band,
bound to the impregnable wall.
In his soul was the serpent coiled round his heart, hid
from the light, as in a cleft rock;
And the man was confined for a writing prophetic: in
the tower named *Darkness*, was a man
30 Pinioned down to the stone floor, his strong bones
scarce covered with sinews; the iron rings
Were forged smaller as the flesh decayed, a mask of
iron on his face hid the lineaments
Of ancient Kings, and the frown of the eternal lion was
hid from the oppressed earth.
In the tower named *Bloody*, a skeleton yellow remained
in its chains on its couch
Of stone, once a man who refused to sign papers of
abhorrence; the eternal worm
35 Crept in the skeleton. In the den named *Religion*, a
loathsome sick woman, bound down
To a bed of straw; the seven diseases of earth, like
birds of prey, stood on the couch,
And fed on the body. She refused to be whore to the
Minister, and with a knife smote him.
In the tower named *Order*, an old man, whose white
beard covered the stone floor like weeds
On the margin of the sea, shrivelled up by heat of day
and cold of night; his den was short
40 And narrow as a grave dug for a child, with spiders'
webs wove, and with slime

25. *seven towers*] B.'s list of towers, their names and their prisoners, is
imaginative: there were, however, seven prisoners in the Bastille at the
time of its fall.
31. *a mask of iron*] B. has brought the old seventeenth-century story of the
Man in the Iron Mask, supposedly disguised because of his royal blood,
down to his own day.
35. *the den named Religion*] B.'s names for the towers now become ironic.

Of ancient horrors covered, for snakes and scorpions
    are his companions; harmless they breathe
His sorrowful breath: he, by conscience urged, in the
    city of Paris raised a pulpit,
And taught wonders to darkened souls. In the den
    named *Destiny* a strong man sat,
His feet and hands cut off, and his eyes blinded; round
    his middle a chain and a band
45 Fastened into the wall; fancy gave him to see an image
    of despair in his den,
Eternally rushing round, like a man on his hands and
    knees, day and night without rest:
He was friend to the favourite. In the seventh tower,
    named the *Tower of God*, was a man
Mad, with chains loose, which he dragged up and
    down; fed with hopes year by year, he pined
For liberty; vain hopes: his reason decayed, and the
    world of attraction in his bosom
50 Centred, and the rushing of chaos overwhelmed his
    dark soul. He was confined
For a letter of advice to a King, and his ravings in
    winds are heard over Versailles.

But the dens shook and trembled, the prisoners look up
    and assay to shout; they listen,
Then laugh in the dismal den, then are silent, and a
    light walks round the dark towers.

For the Commons convene in the Hall of the Nations;
    like spirits of fire in the beautiful
55 Porches of the sun, to plant beauty in the desert
    craving abyss, they gleam
On the anxious city; all children new-born first behold
    them; tears are fled,
And they nestle in earth-breathing bosoms. So the city
    of Paris, their wives and children,
Look up to the morning Senate, and visions of sorrow
    leave pensive streets.

But heavy-browed jealousies lower o'er the Louvre,
    and terrors of ancient Kings

48. *Mad*] One of the prisoners, when released, had to be taken to an asylum.
B. may not have known this, however; his descriptions are otherwise
quite imaginary.
59. *Louvre*] As this and the preceding lines show, B. seems to think that
the king's council was held in Paris. In fact, most of its meetings were at
Versailles.

60 Descend from the gloom and wander through the
        palace, and weep round the King and his nobles.
    While loud thunders roll, troubling the dead, kings are
        sick throughout all the earth.
    The voice ceased: the Nation sat. And the triple forged
        fetters of times were unloosed.
    The voice ceased: the Nation sat: but ancient darkness
        and trembling wander through the palace.

    As in day of havoc and routed battle, among thick shades
        of discontent,
65 On the soul-skirting mountains of sorrow cold waving:
        the nobles fold round the King,
    Each stern visage locked up as with strong bands of iron,
        each strong limb bound down as with marble,
    In flames of red wrath burning, bound in astonishment
        a quarter of an hour.

    Then the King glowed: his nobles fold round, like the
        sun of old time quenched in clouds;
    In their darkness the King stood, his heart flamed, and
        uttered a withering heat, and these words burst
        forth:

70 'The nerves of five thousand years' ancestry tremble,
        shaking the heavens of France;
    Throbs of anguish beat on brazen war foreheads, they
        descend and look into their graves.
    I see through darkness, through clouds rolling round
        me, the spirits of ancient kings
    Shivering over their bleached bones; round them their
        counsellors look up from the dust,
    Crying: "Hide from the living! Our bonds and our
        prisoners shout in the open field,
75 Hide in the nether earth! Hide in the bones! Sit
        obscured in the hollow skull.

62. *the voice*] i.e. the prophetic voice of France (*15*).
65. B. seems to be thinking of the royal council on 21 June, after the Third
Estate had, on 20 June, in the famous Tennis Court session, declared itself
a National Assembly. But it is equally likely that B. did not attempt any
historical correctness.
70. *Five thousand years' ancestry*] An exaggeration of course; the Bourbons
could trace their monarchy back to the first Capetian king, Robert, briefly
king of France in 922-25, and his more successful grandson Hugh (reigned
987-96).

Our flesh is corrupted, and we wear away. We are
    not numbered among the living. Let us hide
In stones, among roots of trees. The prisoners have
    burst their dens,
Let us hide; let us hide in the dust; and plague and
    wrath and tempest shall cease." '

He ceased, silent pondering, his brows folded heavy,
    his forehead was in affliction,
80   Like the central fire: from the window he saw his vast
    armies spread over the hills,
Breathing red fires from man to man, and from horse
    to horse; then his bosom
Expanded like starry heaven, he sat down: his nobles
    took their ancient seats.

Then the ancientest peer, Duke of Burgundy, rose
    from the monarch's right hand; red as wines
From his mountains, an odour of war, like a ripe
    vineyard, rose from his garments,
85   And the chamber became as a clouded sky; o'er the
    council he stretched his red limbs,
Clothed in flames of crimson, as a ripe vineyard
    stretches over sheaves of corn,
The fierce Duke hung over the council; around him
    crowd, weeping in his burning robe,
A bright cloud of infant souls; his words fall like
    purple autumn on the sheaves.

'Shall this marble-built heaven become a clay cottage,
    this earth an oak stool, and these mowers
90   From the Atlantic mountains, mow down all this great
    starry harvest of six thousand years?

76. 'numbered ... living'] Biblical language, but not a quotation.   '*Let
us hide ...*'] Cp. *Revelation* vi 15–16: 'The kings of the earth, and the
great men ... hid themselves in the dens and in the rocks of the mountains;
And said ... Fall on us, and hide us ...'.
80. his vast armies] As the tension grew during the sitting of the States-
General, more and more regiments were brought in and encamped around
Paris, and their presence became a major source of complaint by the Third
Estate and their supporters, who felt the troops were meant to intimidate
them.
83. Burgundy] B.'s word *ancientest* refers no doubt to the historic title;
however, although the name was great, the duchy was absorbed by the
Crown in the 15th century; the last Duke died in 1714. B. makes much
use of the association of the name and region with wines.
90. six thousand years] Cp. *Marriage* iv 66 *n*.

And shall Necker, the hind of Geneva, stretch out his
    crooked sickle o'er fertile France,
Till our purple and crimson is faded to russet, and the
    kingdoms of earth bound in sheaves,
And the ancient forests of chivalry hewn, and the joys
    of the combat burnt for fuel;
Till the power and dominion is rent from the pole,
    sword and sceptre from sun and moon,
95   The law and gospel from fire and air, and eternal
    reason and science
From the deep and the solid, and man lay his faded
    head down on the rock
Of eternity, where the eternal lion and eagle remain
    to devour?
This to prevent, urged by cries in day, and prophetic
    dreams hovering in night,
To enrich the lean earth that craves, furrowed with
    ploughs; whose seed is departing from her;
100 Thy Nobles have gathered thy starry hosts round this
    rebellious city,
To rouse up the ancient forests of Europe, with clarions
    of loud breathing war;
To hear the horse neigh to the drum and trumpet, and
    the trumpet and war shout reply;
Stretch the hand that beckons the eagles of heaven;
    they cry over Paris, and wait
Till Fayette point his finger to Versailles; the eagles of
    heaven must have their prey.'
105 The King leaned on his mountains, then lifted his
    head and looked on his armies, that shone

93–4. The Duke is trying to defend the indefensible.
100–1. *starry hosts . . . ancient forests*] Both images are constantly used by B.
to denote profound evils in religious and political systems.
104. *Fayette*] The Marquis de Lafayette, already in 1789 a popular figure on
account of his exploits against the old enemy, England, in the American
War of Independence. But he was not in command of the French army.
B. imagines Burgundy looking to him to repress revolt: in particular,
'pointing his finger at Versailles' to use the army to scatter the Assembly.
Its use against the Assembly was widely expected after the fall of the
Bastille on 14 July (on 8 July the Assembly had requested its withdrawal);
but the next day Louis agreed to move the army, and on 17 July it was
withdrawn.
105. In the original, the sequence of lines is: *1–104, 116–20, 105–15, 121ff.*
W. F. Halloran has made a convincing case for the rearrangement which,
as can be seen without further elaboration, makes better sense.

Through heaven, tinging morning with beams of
    blood, then turning to Burgundy troubled:

'Burgundy, thou wast born a lion! My soul is
    o'ergrown with distress
For the nobles of France, and dark mists roll round
    me and blot the writing of God
Written in my bosom. Necker rise, leave the kingdom,
    thy life is surrounded with snares;
110 We have called an Assembly, but not to destroy; we
    have given gifts, not to the weak;
I hear rushing of muskets, and brightening of swords,
    and visages reddening with war,
Frowning and looking up from brooding villages and
    every darkening city;
Ancient wonders frown over the kingdom, and cries
    of women and babes are heard,
And tempests of doubt roll around me, and fierce
    sorrows, because of the nobles of France;
115 Depart, answer not, for the tempest must fall, as in
    years that are passed away.'

He ceased, and burned silent, red clouds roll round
    Necker, a weeping is heard o'er the palace;
Like a dark cloud Necker paused, and like thunder on
    the just man's burial day he paused;
Silent sit the winds, silent the meadows, while the
    husbandman and woman of weakness
And bright children look after him into the grave, and
    water his clay with love,
120 Then turn towards pensive fields; so Necker paused,
    and his visage was covered with clouds.

Dropping a tear the old man his place left, and when
    he was gone out
He set his face toward Geneva to flee, and the women
    and children of the city
Kneeled round him and kissed his garments and wept;
    he stood a short space in the street,
Then fled; and the whole city knew he was fled to
    Geneva, and the Senate heard it.

109. *Necker . . . kingdom*] Necker was dismissed on July 11th, his position
having been undermined by the reactionary party, and left for Switzerland
(see *122*).
121. *the old man*] Necker was fifty-seven in 1789.
122. *Geneva*] Necker actually went to Basle.
124. *the Senate*] The National Assembly.

125 But the nobles burned wrathful at Necker's departure, and wreathed their clouds and waters
    In dismal volumes; as risen from beneath the Archbishop of Paris arose,
    In the rushing of scales and hissing of flames and rolling of sulphurous smoke.

    'Hearken, Monarch of France, to the terrors of heaven, and let thy soul drink of my counsel;
    Sleeping at midnight in my golden tower, the repose of the labours of men
130 Waved its solemn cloud over my head. I awoke; a cold hand passed over my limbs, and behold
    An aged form, white as snow, hovering in mist, weeping in the uncertain light,
    Dim the form almost faded, tears fell down the shady cheeks; at his feet many, clothed
    In white robes, strewn in air censers and harps, silent they lay prostrated;
    Beneath, in the awful void, myriads descending and weeping through dismal winds,
135 Endless the shady train shivering descended, from the gloom where the aged form wept.
    At length, trembling, the vision sighing, in a low voice, like the voice of the grasshopper whispered:
    "My groaning is heard in the abbeys, and God, so long worshipped, departs as a lamp
    Without oil; for a curse is heard hoarse through the land, from a godless race
    Descending to beasts; they look downward and labour and forget my holy law;

125. *wrathful*] Either at losing him; or at all liberals, their wrath increased by this success. Such a generalization, on whichever side, cannot easily be made of *all* the nobles.

126. *the Archbishop of Paris*] He played no important part in these events, but did persuade a large group of clergy from joining the Commons in mid-June.

127. The casting of an archbishop in the rôle of a devil is in keeping with B.'s anti-ecclesiastical views.

130. This dream recalls the dream of Eliphaz in *Job* iv 13–16: 'When deep sleep falleth on men, fear came upon me, and trembling, which made all my bones to shake. Then a spirit passed before my face; the hair of my flesh stood up: it stood still, but I could not discern the form thereof . . .'.

139. Note that the vision complains, not of the degradation and poverty of God's people, but of their neglect of ritual and the risk of the rulers losing their prestige.

140   The sound of prayer fails from lips of flesh, and the
            holy hymn from thickened tongues:
        For the bars of Chaos are burst; her millions prepare
            their fiery way
        Through the orbed abode of the holy dead, to root up
            and pull down and remove,
        And Nobles and Clergy shall fail from before me, and
            my cloud and vision be no more;
        The mitre become black, the crown vanish, and the
            sceptre and ivory staff
145   Of the ruler wither among bones of death; they shall
            consume from the thistly field,
        And the sound of the bell, and voice of the sabbath,
            and singing of the holy choir,
        Is turned into songs of the harlot in day, and cries of
            the virgin in night.
        They shall drop at the plough and faint at the harrow,
            unredeemed, unconfessed, unpardoned;
        The priest rot in his surplice by the lawless lover, the
            holy beside the accursed,
150   The King, frowning in purple, beside the grey
            ploughman, and their worms embrace together. ''
        The voice ceased, a groan shook my chamber; I slept,
            for the cloud of repose returned,
        But morning dawned heavy upon me. I rose to bring
            my Prince heaven-uttered counsel.
        Hear my counsel, O King, and send forth thy generals,
            the command of Heaven is upon thee;
        Then do thou command, O King, to shut up this
            Assembly in their final home;
155   Let thy soldiers possess this city of rebels, that threaten
            to bathe their feet
        In the blood of nobility, trampling the heart and the
            head; let the Bastille devour
        These rebellious seditious; seal them up, O Anointed,
            in everlasting chains. '

        He sat down, a damp cold pervaded the nobles, and
            monsters of worlds unknown
        Swam round them, watching to be delivered; when
            Aumont, whose chaos-born soul

159. Aumont] The Duke of Aumont, later a commander of the National
Guard in Paris, and in charge of the troops leading Louis from Versailles
to Paris on 5 October–which B. probably saw as a pro-revolutionary act,
contradicting Aumont's earlier membership of the Second Estate of
nobility.

160 Eternally wandering, a comet and swift-falling fire,
           pale entered the chamber;
       Before the red Council he stood, like a man that returns
           from hollow graves.

       'Awe-surrounded, alone through the army a fear and
           a withering blight blown by the north,
       The Abbé de Sieyès from the Nation's Assembly. O
           princes and generals of France,
       Unquestioned, unhindered—awe-struck are the soldiers;
           a dark shadowy man in the form
165 Of King Henry the Fourth walks before him in fires, the
           captains like men bound in chains
       Stood still as he passed, he is come to the Louvre, O
           King, with a message to thee;
       The strong soldiers tremble, the horses their manes
           bow, and the guards of thy palace are fled.'

       Up rose awful in his majestic beams Bourbon's strong
           Duke; his proud sword from his thigh
       Drawn, he threw on the earth! the Duke of Bretagne
           and the Earl of Bourgogne
170 Rose inflamed, to and fro in the chamber, like
           thunder-clouds ready to burst.

       'What, damp all our fires, O spectre of Henry,' said
           Bourbon; 'and rend the flames
       From the head of our King! Rise, Monarch of France;
           command me, and I will lead
       This army of superstition at large, that the ardour of
           noble souls quenchless
       May yet burn in France, nor our shoulders be ploughed
           with the furrows of poverty.'

163. The Abbé de Sieyès] A liberal political scientist, who was a priest only
by necessity. He took the side of the Third Estate from the beginning, and
sat in it as a Parisian deputy, and not, as an abbot, in the First Estate. On
12 June he was the spokesman to the other two houses, carrying a proposal
(which was rejected) that the three Estates should meet together. This may
be the incident in B.'s mind; Sieyès was not an emissary to the royal
council.

165. King Henry the Fourth] 'The people's king', the famous late-sixteenth-
century king who had a reputation, not for liberalism, but for care for his
country, and common sense; it may be for this reason that B. sees his
spirit as directing the revolution.

168. Bourbon's strong Duke] A great name, but it is not clear who B. meant.

169. the Duke of Bretagne and the Earl of Bourgogne] Fictitious Dukes of
Britanny and Burgundy.

175 Then Orléans generous as mountains arose, and
      unfolded his robe, and put forth
His benevolent hand, looking on the Archbishop, who
      changed as pale as lead;
Would have risen but could not, his voice issued harsh
      grating; instead of words harsh hissings
Shook the chamber; he ceased abashed. Then Orléans
      spoke, all was silent,
He breathed on them, and said, 'O princes of fire,
      whose flames are for growth not consuming,
180 Fear not dreams, fear not visions, nor be you dismayed
      with sorrows which flee at the morning;
Can the fires of nobility ever be quenched, or the
      stars by a stormy night?
Is the body diseased when the members are healthful?
      Can the man be bound in sorrow
Whose every function is filled with its fiery desire? Can
      the soul whose brain and heart
Cast their rivers in equal tides through the great
      Paradise, languish because the feet
185 Hands, head, bosom, and parts of love, follow their
      high-breathing joy?
And can nobles be bound when the people are free, or
      God weep when his children are happy?
Have you never seen Fayette's forehead, or Mirabeau's
      eyes, or the shoulders of Target,

175. Orléans] A distant cousin of the king, and head of the house of Or-
léans, the junior branch of the royal family. He gained the reputation of
being a democrat, renounced his title early in favour of the name *Philippe
Egalité*, but could not escape execution in the Terror of 1793. His democ-
racy was largely adopted for self-advantage and self-advertisement.
177. Cp. a similar effect in *Paradise Lost* x. 517–9.
183–5. B. stresses the belief that the soul acts through the body, and is not
separated from it. Cp. *Marriage*, pl.4 ii *23* (p. 105 above): 'Man has no body
distinct from his soul; for that called body is a portion of soul discerned
by the five senses, the chief inlets of soul in this age'.
184. their rivers] i.e. of brain and heart; an image of the systems of nerves
and blood-vessels.
187. Each person in the next lines represents a part of the 'body' of France–
eyes, shoulders, feet, etc.
Mirabeau] The famous revolutionary leader, eldest son of a marquis, but
soon, with Sieyès and Bailly, one of the champions of the National
Assembly. On 23 June he led the Assembly's defiance of the king's orders.
Target] A lawyer and member of the Assembly, occasionally its President,
but not an important figure.

Or Bailly the strong foot of France, or Clermont the
    terrible voice, and your robes
Still retain their own crimson? Mine never yet faded,
    for fire delights in its form.
190   But go, merciless man, enter into the infinite labyrinth of
    another's brain
Ere thou measure the circle that he shall run. Go, thou
    cold recluse, into the fires
Of another's high flaming rich bosom, and return
    unconsumed, and write laws.
If thou canst not do this, doubt thy theories, learn to
    consider all men as thy equals,
Thy brethren, and not as thy foot or thy hand, unless
    thou first fearest to hurt them.'

195   The Monarch stood up, the strong Duke his sword to its
    golden scabbard returned,
The nobles sat round like clouds on the mountains,
    when the storm is passing away:

'Let the nation's ambassador come among nobles,
    like incense of the valley.'

Aumont went out and stood in the hollow porch, his
    ivory wand in his hand;
A cold orb of disdain revolved round him, and covered
    his soul with snows eternal.
200   Great Henry's soul shuddered, a whirlwind and fire
    tore furious from his angry bosom;
He indignant departed on horses of heaven. Then the
    Abbé de Sieyès raised his feet
On the steps of the Loùvre, like a voice of God following
    a storm, the Abbé followed
The pale fires of Aumont into the chamber, as a father
    that bows to his son;
Whose rich fields inheriting spread their old glory, so the
    voice of the people bowed
205   Before the ancient seat of the kingdom and mountains
    to be renewed.

'Hear, O heavens of France, the voice of the people,
    arising from valley and hill,

188. Bailly] A middle-aged scholar, President of the National Assembly.
Clermont] Count of Clermont-Tonnerre, a representative of Paris for the
Second Estate, who left that house to join the Third Estate in forming the
National Assembly, taking others with him.
196. B. has little sense of protocol; the nobles would not dare to sit when
the king stood.

6+B.

O'erclouded with power. Hear the voice of valleys, the
    voice of meek cities,
Mourning oppressed on village and field, till the village
    and field is a waste.
For the husbandman weeps at blights of the fife, and
    blasting of trumpets consume
210   The souls of mild France; the pale mother nourishes her
    child to the deadly slaughter.
When the heavens were sealed with a stone, and the
    terrible sun closed in an orb, and the moon
Rent from the nations, and each star appointed for
    watchers of night,
The millions of spirits immortal were bound in the ruins
    of sulphur heaven
To wander enslaved; black, depressed in dark ignorance,
    kept in awe with the whip,
215   To worship terrors, bred from the blood of revenge and
    breath of desire,
In bestial forms, or more terrible men, till the dawn
    of our peaceful morning,
Till dawn, till morning, till the breaking of clouds,
    and swelling of winds, and the universal voice,
Till man raise his darkened limbs out of the cares of
    night, his eyes and his heart
Expand. Where is space? Where, O sun, is thy dwelling?
    where thy tent, O faint slumberous Moon?
220   Then the valleys of France shall cry to the soldier,
    "Throw down thy sword and musket,
And run and embrace the meek peasant." Her nobles
    shall hear and shall weep, and put off
The red robe of terror, the crown of oppression, the
    shoes of contempt, and unbuckle
The girdle of war from the desolate earth; then the
    priest in his thunderous cloud
Shall weep, bending to earth embracing the valleys, and
    putting his hand to the plough,
225   Shall say, "No more I curse thee; but now I will bless
    thee: no more in deadly black
Devour thy labour, nor lift up a cloud in thy heavens,
    O laborious plough,

209. *blights of the fife*] Cp. *Visions 125*. B.'s complaint: the French peasantry
did not especially complain of losses through military demands; their
chief anxieties arose from taxation.
214. B.'s concern over slavery is also shown in similar terms in *Visions 21–3*.
216. *bestial*] B., as usual, spells it 'beastial'.

That the wild raging millions, that wander in forests,
and howl in law-blasted wastes,
Strength maddened with slavery, honesty bound in
the dens of superstition,
May sing in the village, and shout in the harvest, and
woo in pleasant gardens
230 Their once savage loves, now beaming with knowledge,
with gentle awe adorned;
And the saw, and the hammer, the chisel, the pencil,
the pen, and the instruments
Of heavenly song sound in the wilds once forbidden,
to teach the laborious ploughman
And shepherd delivered from clouds of war, from
pestilence, from night-fear, from murder,
From falling, from stifling, from hunger, from cold,
from slander, discontent and sloth,
235 That walk in beasts and birds of night, driven back by
the sandy desert
Like pestilent fogs round cities of men: and the happy
earth sing in its course,
The mild peaceable nations be opened to heaven, and
men walk with their fathers in bliss."
Then hear the first voice of the morning: "Depart,
O clouds of night, and no more
Return; be withdrawn, cloudy war, troops of warriors
depart, nor around our peaceable city
240 Breathe fires, but ten miles from Paris, let all be peace,
nor a soldier be seen!" '

He ended; the wind of contention arose and the clouds
cast their shadows, the princes
Like the mountains of France, whose aged trees utter
an awful voice, and their branches
Are shattered, till gradual a murmur is heard
descending into the valley,
Like a voice in the vineyards of Burgundy, when
grapes are shaken on grass;
245 Like the low voice of the labouring man, instead of the
shout of joy;
And the palace appeared like a cloud driven abroad;
blood ran down the ancient pillars,
Through the cloud a deep thunder, the Duke of
Burgundy, delivers the King's command:

227. B.'s subject is now not merely France, but the savages of the world.
240. This demand was made by Mirabeau, not Sieyès, on 8 July (see
259-67).

'Seest thou yonder dark castle, that moated around,
keeps this city of Paris in awe.
Go command yonder tower, saying, "Bastille depart,
and take thy shadowy course.
250   Overstep the dark river, thou terrible tower, and get
thee up into the country ten miles.
And thou black southern prison, move along the dusky
road to Versailles; there
Frown on the gardens," and if it obey and depart,
then the King will disband
This war-breathing army; but if it refuse, let the
Nation's Assembly thence learn
That this army of terrors, that prison of horrors, are the
bands of the murmuring kingdom.'

255   Like the morning star arising above the black waves,
when a shipwrecked soul sighs for morning,
Through the ranks, silent, walked the Ambassador
back to the Nation's Assembly, and told
The unwelcome message. Silent they heard; then a
thunder rolled round loud and louder;
Like pillars of ancient halls, and ruins of times remote
they sat.
Like a voice from the dim pillars Mirabeau rose; the
thunders subsided away;
260   A rushing of wings around him was heard as he
brightened, and cried out aloud,
'Where is the General of the Nation?' The walls
re-echoed: 'Where is the General of the Nation?'–
Sudden as the bullet wrapped in his fire, when brazen
cannons rage in the field,
Fayette sprung from his seat saying, 'Ready!'; then bow-
ing like clouds, man toward man, the Assembly
Like a council of ardours seated in clouds, bending over
the cities of men,
265   And over the armies of strife, where their children are
marshalled together to battle;
They murmuring divide, while the wind sleeps beneath,
and the numbers are counted in silence,

---

249. This passage is of course heavy with dramatic irony, since the Bastille
was sacked three weeks after this supposed council.
251. *thou black southern prison*] Perhaps *La Force*, a little way to the south of
the Bastille; but more probably *L'Abbaye*, in St Germain des Prés, south
of the river (but west of the Bastille). L'Abbaye was stormed by a mob on
29 June, who released eleven soldiers imprisoned there.

While they vote the removal of war, and the pestilence
    weighs his red wings in the sky.

So Fayette stood silent among the Assembly, and the
    votes were given and the numbers numbered;
And the vote was that Fayette should order the army to
    remove ten miles from Paris.

270 The aged sun rises appalled from dark mountains, and
        gleams a dusky beam
    On Fayette, but on the whole army a shadow; for a
        cloud on the eastern hills
    Hovered, and stretched across the city and across the
        army, and across the Louvre.
    Like a flame of fire he stood before dark ranks, and
        before expecting captains
    On pestilent vapours around him flow frequent
        spectres of religious men weeping
275 In winds driven out of the abbeys, their naked souls
        shiver in keen open air,
    Driven out by the fiery cloud of Voltaire, and
        thunderous rocks of Rousseau,
    They dash like foam against the ridges of the army,
        uttering a faint feeble cry.
    Gleams of fire streak the heavens, and of sulphur the
        earth, from Fayette as he lifted his hand;
    But silent he stood, till all the officers rush round him
        like waves
280 Round the shore of France, in day of the British flag,
        when heavy cannons
    Affright the coasts, and the peasant looks over the sea
        and wipes a tear.
    Over his head the soul of Voltaire shone fiery, and
        over the army Rousseau his white cloud
    Unfolded, on souls of war-living terrors silent listening
        toward Fayette,

267–9. The motion could be no more than a request to the king, who was
in fact asked by the Assembly to remove the troops stationed between
Versailles and Paris. He did not, although the troops were ineffective and
unused when the Bastille fell a few days later. They were not under the
command of Lafayette, on 15 July (the day the troops were removed)
became Commandant General de la Milice Parisienne (the National Guard)
which was superseding the army in the task of restoring order.
276. i.e. superstition is driven out by the force of reason as displayed in
Voltaire and Rousseau. B. later attacked them as advocates of Deism
(Jerusalem pl.52).

His voice loud inspired by liberty, and by spirits of the
   dead, thus thundered:

285 'The Nation's Assembly command that the Army
   remove ten miles from Paris;
   Nor a soldier be seen in road or in field, till the
   Nation command return.'

Rushing along iron ranks glittering the officers each
   to his station
Depart, and the stern captain strokes his proud steed,
   and in front of his solid ranks
Waits the sound of trumpet; captains of foot stand
   each by his cloudy drum;
290 Then the drum beats, and the steely ranks move, and
   trumpets rejoice in the sky.
Dark cavalry like clouds fraught with thunder ascend
   on the hills, and bright infantry, rank
Behind rank, to the soul-shaking drum and shrill fife
   along the roads glitter like fire.

The noise of trampling, the wind of trumpets, smote
   the palace walls with a blast.
Pale and cold sat the King in midst of his peers, and his
   noble heart sunk, and his pulses
295 Suspended their motion, a darkness crept over his
   eyelids, and chill cold sweat
Sat round his brows faded in faint death, his peers pale
   like mountains of the dead,
Covered with dews of night, groaning, shaking forests
   and floods. The cold newt
And snake, and damp toad, on the kingly foot crawl,
   or croak on the awful knee,
Shedding their slime, in folds of the robe the crowned
   adder builds and hisses
300 From stony brows; shaken the forests of France, sick
   the kings of the nations,
And the bottoms of the world were opened, and the
   graves of arch-angels unsealed;
The enormous dead lift up their pale fires and look
   over the rocky cliffs.

301. the bottoms of the world were opened] A curious image, but used again,
in *Marriage iv.127*ff, and a number of times in the long epics, to indicate a
catastrophe falling on the powers of evil. It seems to be derived from a
picture of a flat world, with heaven above, and a complementary abyss
beneath.

302. enormous] Dreadful, monstrous.

A faint heat from their fires revived the cold Louvre; the
   frozen blood reflowed.
   Awful up rose the King, him the peers followed, they
      saw the courts of the palace
305   Forsaken, and Paris without a soldier, silent, for the
      noise was gone up
   And followed the army, and the Senate in peace sat
      beneath morning's beam.
               End of the First Book.

9 A Divine Image

Date. 1790-91. This poem is an early 'Song of Experience', which was
replaced by 'The Human Abstract' (p. 216 below) in *Experience* (both
poems are 'contrary' to 'The Divine Image' of Innocence, p. 69). The
design shows a blacksmith hammering at a wall round the sun-a subject
redrawn in *Jerusalem* pl.73.
   Facsimiles: Keynes, *W.B.'s Engravings*, pl.118: *Innocence and Experience*,
1967.

       Cruelty has a human heart,
       And jealousy a human face—
       Terror, the human form divine,
       And secrecy, the human dress.

5   The human dress is forged iron,
       The human form, a fiery forge.
       The human face, a furnace sealed,
       The human heart, its hungry gorge.

10 Poems from the Notebook, *c*. 1791-2

For many years B. used a notebook, which had apparently belonged to his
brother Robert (who died in 1787), both as a sketch-book and as a hand-
book for drafts of lyric poems. (This notebook used to be called 'the
Rossetti MS', because D. G. Rossetti once owned it.) At first, in the early
1790s, starting from the back, B. used it for fair copies, ready for transcrib-
ing, and the first poems in the series which follows are of this sort, with
few corrections in the MS. But, as the textual notes show, the later poems
are much corrected and sometimes preserve the whole process of compo-
sition. The first poems seem to reflect the same social indignation as
Visions (*c*. 1791-92), rather than the revolutionary excitement of *The
French Revolution* (*c*. 1790-91). The fragments on 'Fayette' and the French
Queen are the only poems certainly datable: they belong to the time

between the news of Lafayette's imprisonment, 25 October 1792, and the King's execution in January 1793. The series may have been begun at any time after 1789, but on these grounds seems to run from 1791 to late 1792. Most of the *Songs of Experience* derive from the Notebook; but there are also many poems in it which B. did not engrave. The poems are printed in the order in which they appear in the Notebook, since this is the most probable date order we have, and in the form which, as far as can be ascertained, was B.'s latest intention at the time. For these poems B. turned the Notebook upside down; he used the other end for sketches for the emblem book *The Gates of Paradise*, which was engraved in 1793. In later years he came to fill in all the gaps, gradually, and in no particular order. (This early sequence of poems is marked by its orderliness on the page.)

The themes which were exercising B. at this period were social–freedom from jealousy, freedom of love and affection, and freedom from want. These themes are aired in the poems which were appearing at the same time as these lyrics–*Visions* and *America*. From time to time it has been conjectured that some of the lyrics arise from personal experiences. It may be so; but the 'I' of a lyric is often no more than a literary convention, and external evidence is required to prove such interpretations. In B.'s case there is no such evidence, and it is necessary, as with Shakespeare's *Sonnets*, to resort to the circular process of reconstructing the supposed events from the poems themselves.

There is a facsimile, ed. G. L. Keynes (s1935); a more detailed one, ed. David V. Erdman, is expected in 1971.

I

A flower was offered to me,
Such a flower as May never bore;
But I said, 'I've a pretty rose-tree,'
And I passed the sweet flower o'er.

5 Then I went to my pretty rose-tree,
To tend her by day and by night;
But my rose turned away with jealousy,
And her thorns were my only delight.

II

Never pain to tell thy love,
Love that never told can be;

¶ 10. i. This appears as 'My Pretty Rose Tree' in *Experience* (p. 211).
i 6. *To ... night*] In the silent of the night *1st rdg.*
i 7. *turned ... jealousy*] *1st rdg* was turned from me; *2nd rdg* was filled with Jealousy.
ii *1–4*. Del. in MS; but essential to the poem. In 'Earth's Answer' (pp. 153 and 210) lines del. were restored in engraving.
ii *1. pain*] *1st rdg del.* seek.

For the gentle wind does move
Silently, invisibly.

5   I told my love, I told my love,
I told her all my heart;
Trembling, cold, in ghastly fears—
Ah, she doth depart!

Soon as she was gone from me,
10   A traveller came by
Silently, invisibly—
Oh, was no deny!

III

'Love seeketh not itself to please,
Nor for itself hath any care,
But for another gives its ease
And builds a Heaven in Hell's despair.'

5   So sung a little clod of clay,
Trodden with the cattle's feet;
But a pebble of the brook
Warbled out these metres meet:

'Love seeketh only self to please,
10   To bind another to its delight,
Joys in another's loss of ease,
And builds a Hell in Heaven's despite.'

IV

I laid me down upon a bank
Where love lay sleeping;
I heard among the rushes dank
Weeping, weeping.

5   Then I went to the heath and the wild,
To the thistles and thorns of the waste,
And they told me how they were beguiled,
Driven out and compelled to be chaste.

ii *12. Oh . . . deny*] *1st rdg del.* He took her with a sigh (*a reading preferred by many editors, although the cancellation is clear*).
iii. This is 'The Clod and the Pebble' in *Experience* (p. 211). Cp. the clod of clay in *Thel* iii (p. 98).
iv. Cp. *Marriage* ('Argument'), p. 103 above, where the just are driven out into the wild, and their own place taken by the hypocrite.

6*

V

I went to the garden of love,
And I saw what I never had seen:
A chapel was built in the midst,
Where I used to play on the green.

5 And the gates of this chapel were shut,
And *Thou shalt not* writ over the door;
So I turned to the garden of love
That so many sweet flowers bore,

And I saw it was filled with graves,
10 And tomb-stones where flowers should be—
And priests in black gounds were walking their rounds,
And binding with briars my joys and desires.

VI

I saw a chapel all of gold
That none did dare to enter in;
And many weeping stood without,
Weeping, mourning, worshipping.

5 I saw a serpent rise between
The white pillars of the door;
And he forced and forced and forced—
Down the golden hinges tore;

And along the pavement sweet,
10 Set with pearls and rubies bright,
All his slimy length he drew,
Till upon the altar white

Vomiting his poison out,
On the bread and on the wine.
15 So I turned into a sty
And laid me down among the swine.

v. This is a draft of 'The Garden of Love' in *Experience*, p. 212.
v *11. gounds*] A Cockney pronunciation, giving an internal rhyme; B.
dropped it in the engraved version.
vi. The imagery of the previous poem makes it clear that the 'chapel of
gold' is the temple of innocent love, defiled by the repression described in
the previous poem. Love is perverted into something monstrous, and the
sight revolts the poet.
vi *8. Down . . . tore*] 1st rdg del. Till he broke the pearly door.

VII

I asked a thief to steal me a peach;
He turned up his eyes.
I asked a lithe lady to lie her down,
'Holy and meek!' she cries.

5   As soon as I went
An angel came;
He winked at the thief
And smiled at the dame—

And without one word said
10   Had a peach from the tree,
And still as a maid
Enjoyed the lady.

VIII

I heard an angel singing,
When the day was springing,
'Mercy, pity, peace,
Is the world's release.'

5   Thus he sung all day
Over the new-mown hay,
Till the sun went down
And haycocks looked brown.

I heard a devil curse
10   Over the heath and the furze,
'Mercy could be no more
If there was nobody poor.

'And pity no more could be
If all were as happy as we.'

vii. A fair copy exists, dated *Lambeth 1796*, which has the text given above
and is identical to the NB final reading.
vii *1. to steal*] *1st rdg* if he'd steal.
vii *9. said*] *1st rdg del.* spoke.
vii *11. And still as a maid*] This may mean 'she pretended to know nothing
about it, and to be still a maid afterwards.' *1st rdg* And 'twixt earnest and
game; *2nd rdg* 'game' become 'joke' (to rhyme with spoke, *9*).
vii *12. 1st rdg* He enjoyed the dame.
viii. Cp. 'The Divine Image' in *Innocence* (p. 69) and an earlier attempt at
a contrary poem to it, 'A Divine Image' (p. 143). B.'s third attempt, 'The
Human Abstract' (p. 157 below) was finally engraved in *Experience* (p. 216).
The angel in this poem is one of the deluded creatures referred to in
Marriage.

15   At his curse the sun went down,
        And the heavens gave a frown.

        Down poured the heavy rain
        Over the new-reaped grain;
        And misery's increase
20   Is mercy, pity, peace.

IX A CRADLE SONG

        Sleep, sleep, beauty bright,
        Dreaming o'er the joys of night;
        Sleep, sleep; in thy sleep
        Little sorrows sit and weep.

5   Sweet babe, in thy face
        Soft desires I can trace,
        Secret joys and secret smiles,
        Little pretty infant wiles.

        As thy softest limbs I feel,
10   Smiles as of the morning steal
        O'er thy cheek and o'er thy breast,
        Where thy little heart does rest.

        Oh, the cunning wiles that creep
        In thy little heart asleep!
15   When thy little heart does wake,
        Then the dreadful lightnings break

viii *15. At his curse*] *1st rdg del.* Thus he sang &. . . .
viii *19–20.* These lines were much corrected. *1st rdg:*

        And Mercy & Pity & Peace descended
        The farmers were ruined & harvest was ended.

2nd rdg:

                And Mercy Pity & Peace
                Joyed at their increase
                With Poverty's increase
                Are

This extension was rejected; three further corrections produced the present
reading.
ix. A 'contrary' to 'A Cradle Song' in *Innocence* (p. 56); in *Experience,*
'Infant Sorrow' was used instead (pp. 150 and 213 below).
ix *1–4.* The first st. much altered, the second couplet written first.
ix *4. 1st rdg* 'Thou wilt every secret keep', amended twice, then *del.*
ix *5–8.* This st. written fourth, later numbered second. An earlier del. at-
tempt at 2nd st. began 'Yet a little while the moon / Silent. . . .'
ix *8. 1st rdg del.* Such as burning youth beguiles.

From thy cheek and from thy eye,
O'er the youthful harvests nigh.
Infant wiles and infant smiles
20   Heaven and earth of peace beguiles.

X CHRISTIAN FORBEARANCE

I was angry with my friend;
I told my wrath, my wrath did end.
I was angry with my foe;
I told it not, my wrath did grow.

5   And I watered it in fears,
Night and morning with my tears;
And I sunned it with smiles,
And with soft deceitful wiles.

And it grew both day and night
10   Till it bore an apple bright—
And my foe beheld it shine,
And he knew that it was mine,

And into my garden stole,
When the night had veiled the pole.
15   In the morning glad I see
My foe outstretched beneath the tree.

XI

I feared the fury of my wind
Would blight all blossoms fair and true.
And my sun it shined and shined,
And my wind it never blew;

5   But a blossom fair or true
Was not found on any tree;
For all blossoms grew and grew
Fruitless, false, though fair to see.

XII

Why should I care for the men of Thames,
Or the cheating waves of chartered streams,

ix *17. 1st rdg del.* O the cunning wiles that creep.
ix *19. Infant*] *1st rdg* Female (both times).
x. This appears in *Experience* (p. 212) as 'A Poison Tree'.
xi. A poem in praise of life-giving energy as against sterile prudence.
xi *1. fury*] *1st rdg del.* roughness.
xii. An emigrant's song.

Or shrink at the little blasts of fear
That the hireling blows into my ear?

5   Though born on the cheating banks of Thames,
Though his waters bathed my infant limbs,
The Ohio shall wash his stains from me;
I was born a slave, but I go to be free.

XIII INFANT SORROW

My mother groaned, my father wept—
Into the dangerous world I leapt,
Helpless, naked, piping loud,
Like a fiend hid in a cloud.

xii 7. *1st rdg del.* 'I spurned his waters away from me.' Nancy Bogen has
pointed out that the Ohio was not a popular emigrant region, but its
opportunities were highly praised in *A Topographical Description of the
Western Territory* (1792), by G. Imlay (later Mary Wollstonecraft's lover).
xiii. *Experience* gives the same title to a poem made up of the first two sts
only (p. 213). The text above is that reached after much alteration from the
fair copy, which was as follows (sts 1–2 were unaltered and are not repro-
duced):

                And I grew day after day
10   Till upon the ground I stray
                And I grew night after night
                Seeking only for delight

                [But upon the nettly ground
                No delight was to be found] *del.*
15   And I saw before me shine
                Clusters of the wandering vine
                And beyond a myrtle tree
                Stretched its blossoms out to me

                But a priest with holy look
20   In his hand a holy book
                Pronounced curses on his head
                Who the fruit or blossoms shed

                I beheld the Priest by night
                He embraced my myrtle bright
25   I beheld the priest by day
                Where beneath my vine he lay

                Like a serpent in the night
                He embraced my myrtle bright
                Like a serpent in the day
30   Underneath my vine he lay

5   Struggling in my father's hands,
      Striving against my swaddling bands,
      Bound and weary, I thought best
      To sulk upon my mother's breast.

      When I saw that rage was vain
10 And to sulk would nothing gain,
      Turning many a trick and wile
      I began to soothe and smile.

      And I soothed day after day
      Till upon the ground I stray;
15 And I smiled night after night,
      Seeking only for delight.

      And I saw before me shine
      Clusters of the wandering vine,
      And many a lovely flower and tree
20 Stretched their blossoms out to me.

      My father then with holy look,
      In his hands a holy book,
      Pronounced curses on my head
      And bound me in a myrtle shade.

25 Like to holy men by day
      Underneath the vines he lay;
      Like a serpent in the night
      He embraced my blossoms bright.

      So I smote him and his gore
30 Stained the roots my myrtle bore;
      But the time of youth is fled
      And grey hairs are on my head.

> So I smote him and his gore
> Stained the roots my myrtle bore
> But the time of youth is fled
> And grey hairs are on my head

B.'s first alteration was to make *priest* and *serpent* plural; then he changed *priests* to *father*, and began to make the ensuing pronouns singular again, but before he had finished this the poem was abandoned. At some point he also added the present third st. Thus, as the text stands, *he* and *his* in 23–9 read *they* and *their*, and *a serpent* (27) reads *serpents*: had B. finished his adjustments, all would have been singular. The continuing process involves 'In a myrtle shade' (p. 153) and 'To my Myrtle' (p. 159). All three are together an early attempt at a cyclic poem (cf. 'A Mental Traveller', p. 578 below); see *Erdman* (4th printing) pp. 720–1.

XIV

Silent, silent night,
Quench the holy light
Of thy torches bright;

For, possessed of day,
5   Thousand spirits stray
That sweet joys betray.

Why should joys be sweet,
Used with deceit,
Nor with sorrows meet?

10   But an honest joy
Does itself destroy
For a harlot coy.

XV

O lapwing, thou flyest around the heath,
Nor seest the net that is spread beneath.
Why dost thou not fly among the cornfields?
They cannot spread nets where a harvest yields.

XVI [EXPERIMENT]

Thou hast a lap full of seed
And this is a fine country;
Why dost thou not cast thy seed
And live in it merrily?

5   Shall I cast it on the sand
And turn it into fruitful land?
For on no other ground
Can I sow my seed,
Without tearing up
10   Some stinking weed.

xiv. Perhaps intended as a 'contrary' to 'Night' in *Innocence* (p. 66).
xv. On p. 101 (rev.) of the NB, B. made a memo:

on 1 Plate ⎰ O Lapwing &c
            ⎱ An answer to the Parson
              Experiment
              Riches
              If you trap &c

No known engraved plate contains these poems; no poem is entitled
'Experiment', but *Erdman 1965* suggests 'Thou hast a lap full of seed', the
next poem.
xvi. See note above.
xvi 5. *Shall I*] *1st rdg del.* Oft I've

XVII EARTH'S ANSWER

Earth raised up her head
From the darkness dread and drear.
Her light fled
(Stony dread!)
5 And her locks covered with grey despair.

'Prisoned on watery shore,
Starry jealousy does keep my den;
Cold and hoar,
Weeping o'er,
10 I hear the Father of the ancient men.

'Does spring hide its joy
When buds and blossoms grow?
Does the sower
Sow by night,
15 Or the ploughman in darkness plough?

'Break this heavy chain
That does freeze my bones around.
Selfish, vain,
Eternal bane,
20 That free love with bondage bound.'

XVIII IN A MYRTLE SHADE

Why should I be bound to thee,
O my lovely myrtle tree?
Love, free love, cannot be bound
To any tree that grows on ground.

xvii. An 'answer' to the 'Introduction' of *Experience* (q.v. pp. 209–10).
xvii *3. light fled*] *1st rdg del.* eyes fled; *2nd rdg del.* orbs dead.
xvii *10. 1st rdg.* I hear the Father of the ancient men; *2nd rdg.* . . . the ancient father of men; in *Experience* the original rdg is adopted.
xvii *11.* Before this, a st. del. (but eventually engraved in *Experience*, q.v.).
xvii *13–14. sower / Sow by night*] *1st rdg.* sower sow / His seed by night.
xvii *17. freeze*] *1st rdg del.* close.
xvii *19–20. 1st rdg.*:   Thou my bane
                      Hast my love with bondage bound.
xviii. Adapted from the middle verses of the cyclic poem, no. xiii. Written in the MS in the order of sts 2–1–3–4. St.2 (then the opening) originally began:

        To a lovely myrtle bound
        Blossoms showring all around

but these lines were del.

5　　O how sick and weary I
　　Underneath my myrtle lie,
　　Like to dung upon the ground,
　　Underneath my myrtle bound.

　　Oft my myrtle sighed in vain
10　　To behold my heavy chain;
　　Oft my father saw us sigh,
　　And laughed at our simplicity.

　　So I smote him, and his gore
　　Stained the roots my myrtle bore,
15　　But the time of youth is fled
　　And grey hairs are on my head.

XIX LONDON

　　I wander through each dirty street
　　Near where the dirty Thames does flow,
　　And mark in every face I meet
　　Marks of weakness, marks of woe.

5　　In every cry of every man,
　　In every infant's cry of fear,
　　In every voice, in every ban,
　　The mind-forged manacles I hear—

　　How the chimney-sweeper's cry
10　　Every blackening church appals,
　　And the hapless soldier's sigh
　　Runs in blood down palace walls;

　　But most through midnight streets I hear
　　How the youthful harlot's curse
15　　Blasts the new-born infant's tear,
　　And smites with plagues the marriage hearse.

xviii *11. my father saw*] *1st rdg del.* the priest beheld (see note on xiii).
xix *1, 2. dirty*] In *Experience* (p. 213) reads 'chartered'.
xix *3. mark*] *1st rdg del.* see.
xix *6. infant's . . . fear*] *1st rdg del.* voice of every child.
xix *8. mind-forged manacles*] *1st rdg del.* german-forged links (i.e. Hanoverian).
xix *9. How*] *1st rdg del.* But most (altered to transfer the climax to st.4).
xix *10. 1st rdg del.* Blackens o'er the churches' walls.
xix *13-16.* The poem originally ended at *12* (see *9n*); the remaining st. was squeezed in the space left by the next poem. This st. underwent much revision, but the main theme was the same throughout.

XX TO NOBODADDY

Why art thou silent and invisible,
Father of jealousy?
Why dost thou hide thyself in clouds
From every searching eye?

5   Why darkness and obscurity
In all thy words and laws,
That none dare eat the fruit but from
The wily serpent's jaws?
Or is it because secrecy
10 Gains females' loud applause?

XXI

The modest rose puts forth a thorn,
The humble sheep a threatening horn;
While the lily white shall in love delight,
Nor a thorn, nor a threat, stain her beauty bright.

XXII

When the voices of children are heard on the green,
And whisperings are in the dale,
The days of youth rise fresh in my mind—
My face turns green and pale.

xx. Between this and the previous poem are written sts 2 and 3 of xxvii, and the added verses of xix.

xx. *Nobodaddy*] Doubtless 'Nobody's Daddy'–a name used again in lii and the 'Klopstock' poem (p. 467). He largely resembles Urizen, who is also 'Father of Jealousy' (*Visions 114, 187*), whom B. was developing at this time. The title was squeezed in later.

xx 2. *Father*] *1st rdg del.* Man.

xx 9–10. An afterthought, crowded in as one line. Their sentiment suggests a date (for the addition) of 1794–the period of *Europe*–or later; but this may be begging the question.

xxi. Draft for 'The Lily' of *Experience* (p. 214).

xxi 1. Various alterations; the most important are that the adjective to *rose* is successively *envious* and *lustful* before *modest*.

xxi 2. *humble*] *1st rdg del.* coward.

xxi 3. After this line, 2 del. lines:

> And the lion increase freedom & peace
> The priest loves war & the soldier peace.

The first of these seems to be the original end of the poem, with internal rhymes in *3* and *4*. The changes alter the sense of the poem considerably.

xxii. This is 'Nurse's Song' of *Experience* (p. 214).

xxii 3. *days*] *1st rdg del.* desires.

5　'Then come home, my children, the sun is gone down
　And the dews of night arise;
　Your spring and your day are wasted in play,
　And your winter and night in disguise.'

XXIII

Are not the joys of morning sweeter
Than the joys of night,
And are the vigorous joys of youth
Ashamed of the light?

5　Let age and sickness silent rob
　The vineyards in the night,
　But those who burn with vigorous youth
　Pluck fruits before the light.

XXIV THE TIGER

Tiger, tiger, burning bright
In the forests of the night,
What immortal hand and eye
Dare frame thy fearful symmetry?

5　Burnt in distant deeps or skies
　The cruel fire of thine eyes?
　Could heart descend or wings aspire—
　What the hand dare seize the fire?

And what shoulder, and what art
10　Could twist the sinews of thy heart?
　And when thy heart began to beat,
　What dread hand—and what dread feet?

When the stars threw down their spears
And watered Heaven with their tears,
15　Did he smile his work to see?
　Did he who made the lamb make thee?

Tiger, tiger, burning bright
In the forests of the night,
What immortal hand and eye
20　Dare frame thy fearful symmetry?

xxiv. This text is the NB fair copy, which stands opposite a much revised draft. For final text, see *Experience* (p. 214); for details of the revisions, see p. 170. (St. 2 is an addition to the fair copy.)

XXV THE HUMAN IMAGE

Pity would be no more
If we did not make somebody poor;
And mercy no more could be,
If all were as happy as we.

5   And mutual fear brings peace,
Till the selfish loves increase.
Then cruelty knits a snare
And spreads his baits with care.

He sits down with holy fears
10   And waters the ground with tears;
Then humility takes its root
Underneath his foot.

Soon spreads the dismal shade
Of mystery over his head;
15   And the caterpillar and fly
Feed on the mystery.

And it bears the fruit of deceit,
Ruddy and sweet to eat,
And the raven his nest has made
20   In its thickest shade.

The gods of the earth and sea
Sought through nature to find this tree.
But their search was all in vain—
There grows one in the human brain.

25   They said this mystery never shall cease:
The priest promotes war and the soldier peace.

xxv. Draft for 'The Human Abstract' of *Experience* (p. 216): cp. also viii above and 'A Divine Image' (p. 143). All are 'contrary' to 'The Divine Image' in *Innocence* (p. 69). Above this draft are the following del. lines which seem to be continued in this poem (the title was inserted later):

How came pride in Man
From Mary it began
How contempt & scorn

What a world is Man
His Earth . . .

xxv 1. *Pity*] 1st rdg del. Mercy.
xxv 2. 1st rdg del. If there was nobody poor.
xxv 8. *baits*] 1st rdg del. nets.
xxv 24. *There grows one*] 1st rdg del. Till they sought.
xxv 25-6. Derived from xxi; the st. was unfinished.

There souls of men are bought and sold,
And milk-fed infancy for gold,
And youth to slaughter-houses led,
30   And beauty for a bit of bread.

XXVI

Love to faults is always blind,
Always is to joy inclined,
Lawless, winged and unconfined,
And breaks all chains from every mind.

5   Deceit to secrecy confined,
Lawful, cautious and refined,
To every thing but interest blind—
And forges fetters for the mind.

XXVII THE WILD FLOWER'S SONG

As I wandered the forest,
The green leaves among,
I heard a wild flower
Singing a song:

5   'I slept in the earth,
In the silent night,
I murmured my fears
And I felt delight.

'In the morning I went
10   As rosy as morn
To seek for new joy,
But I met with scorn.

xxv *27–30* seem to belong to this poem, though now separated from it by part of xxvi.

xxvi. It is not certain that these two sts were intended to make one poem, although they read as if they were; they were written on opposite pages. The title was added after composition and then del.: 'How to know Love from Deceit'.

xxvi *6. 1st rdg del.* Modest prudish and confind.

xxvi *8. 1st rdg del.* And chains and fetters every mind.

xxvii. The first st. is written here; sts 2–3 are on p. 109 of the NB, between xix and xx.

xxvii *3. flower] 1st rdg del.* thistle.

xxvii *5. slept] 1st rdg del.* was fond.   *earth] 1st rdg del.* dark.

XXVIII THE SICK ROSE

O rose, thou art sick;
The invisible worm
That flies in the night,
In the howling storm,

5   Hath found out thy bed
Of crimson joy,
And her dark secret love
Does thy life destroy.

XXIX SOFT SNOW

I walked abroad in a snowy day;
I asked the soft snow with me to play.
She played and she melted in all her prime—
And the winter called it a dreadful crime.

XXX TO MY MYRTLE

To a lovely myrtle bound,
Blossoms showering all around,
Oh, how sick and weary I
Underneath my myrtle lie!

5   Why should I be bound to thee,
O my lovely myrtle tree?

xxviii. Draft of the *Experience* poem (p. 217).

xxviii 7. *And his dark*] *1st rdg del.* O dark; *2nd rdg.* And his dark; *3rd rdg.* And her dark.

xxviii 8. *Does thy*] *1st rdg del.* Doth.

xxix 4. *1st rdg del.* Ah that sweet love should be thought a crime.

xxx. Developed along with xviii. Altogether, B. wrote the following:

      O how sick & weary I
      Underneath my myrtle lie
5 Why should I be bound to thee
6 O my lovely myrtle tree
      Love free love cannot be bound
      To any tree that grows on ground
1 To a lovely myrtle bound
2 Blossoms showring all around
      Like to dung upon the ground
      Underneath my myrtle bound
3 O how sick and weary I
4 Underneath my myrtle lie.

Of these, the first two were erased before the ink was dry; the unused couplets were del., and the lines numbered to make the poem given above. Cp. the condensation of lii.

XXXI

'Nought loves another as itself,
Nor venerates another so,
Nor is it possible to thought
A greater than itself to know.

5 'And, father, how can I love you
Or any of my brothers more?
I love you like the little bird
That picks up crumbs around the door.'

The priest sat by and heard the child;
10 In trembling zeal he seized his hair;
He led him by the little coat,
And all admired his priestly care.

And standing on the altar high:
'Lo, what a fiend is here!' said he,
15 'One who sets reason up for judge
Of our most holy mystery.'

The weeping child could not be heard;
The weeping parents wept in vain—
They stripped him to his little shirt
20 And bound him in an iron chain,

And burned him in a holy place,
Where many had been burned before.
The weeping parents wept in vain—
Are such things done on Albion's shore?

XXXII MERLIN'S PROPHECY

The harvest shall flourish in wintry weather,
When two virginities meet together.

xxxi. Draft of 'A Little Boy Lost' in *Experience* (p. 217).
xxxi *10*. Followed by two del. lines:

> The mother followed weeping loud
> 'O that I such a fiend should bear.'

xxxi *19-20. 1st rdg del.*:

> They bound his little ivory limbs
> In a cruel iron chain

xxxi *21. place*] *1st rdg del.* fire.   *holy place*] The biblical name for the sanctuary in the Temple.
xxxi *24. Are such things*] *1st rdg.* Such things are.
xxxii. 'Merlin's Prophecy', in Geoffrey of Monmouth's *History of the King's of Britain*, is a series of such cryptic sayings. The Fool, in *King Lear*

The king and the priest must be tied in a tether
Before two virgins can meet together.

XXXIII DAY

The sun arises in the east,
Clothed in robes of blood and gold;
Swords and spears and wrath increased,
All around his bosom rolled—
Crowned with warlike fires and raging desires.

XXXIV THE FAIRY

'Come hither, my sparrows,
My little arrows—
If a tear or a smile
Will a man beguile;
5   If an amorous delay
Clouds a sunshiny day;
If the step of a foot
Smites the heart to its root—
'Tis the marriage ring
10   Makes each fairy a king.'

So a fairy sung.
From the leaves I sprung;
He leaped from the spray
To flee away,
15   But in my hat caught,
He soon shall be taught;
Let him laugh, let him cry,
He's my butterfly—
For I've pulled out the sting
20   Of the marriage ring.

III ii, rounds off his jingle with 'This prophecy Merlin shall make . . .'–
using the tradition B. was to adapt to his own ends. B. equates 'virginity'
and 'purity', but not in the conventional manner, saying that law and
custom destroy the purity of natural love (cp. 'A Little Girl Lost' in
Experience (p. 221)).
xxxiii *1. sun*] *1st rdg del.* day.
xxxiii *4. bosom*] *1st rdg del.* ankles.
xxxiv. *The Fairy*] An earlier *del.* title was 'The Marriage Ring'.
xxxiv *18–20.* There were two previous readings:

1st rdg.   He's my butterfly
                   And a marriage ring
                   Is a foolish thing.

XXXV

The sword sung on the barren heath,
The sickle in the fruitful field;
The sword he sung a song of death
But could not make the sickle yield.

XXXVI

Abstinence sows sand all over
The ruddy limbs and flaming hair;
But desire gratified
Plants fruits of life and beauty there.

XXXVII

In a wife I would desire
What in whores is always found—
The lineaments of gratified desire.

XXXVIII

If you trap the moment before it's ripe,
The tears of repentance you'll certainly wipe;
But if once you let the ripe moment go,
You can never wipe off the tears of woe.

XXXIX ETERNITY

He who binds to himself a joy
Does the winged life destroy;
But he who kisses the joy as it flies
Lives in eternity's sunrise.

2nd rdg.

He's my butterfly
And I've pulled out the sting
And a marriage ring
Is a child's plaything.

The fairy speaks the first stanza. Fairies in B. are usually mischievous, even spiteful; this one thrives on the 'feminine wiles' (3–5) of love and marriage. But B. catches the fairy. He is master of love; feminine arts have no terrors for him, and he can enjoy love in his own way.

xxxviii. See xv note.

xxxviii 1. *trap*] *1st rdg del.* catch.

xxxix. See xv note. This verse is followed in the MS by the note: 'The Kid' / 'Thou little kid didst play, &c': but no poem beginning like this has been found.

XL THE LITTLE VAGABOND

Dear mother, dear mother, the church is cold,
But the alehouse is healthy and pleasant and warm;
Besides I can tell where I am used well;
The poor parsons with wind like a blown bladder swell.

5   But if at the church they would give us some ale,
And a pleasant fire our souls to regale,
We'd sing and we'd pray all the livelong day,
Nor ever once wish from the church to stray.

Then the parson might preach and drink and sing,
10 And we'd be as happy as birds in the spring;
And modest dame Lurch, who is always at church,
Would not have bandy children nor fasting nor birch.

Then God, like a father, rejoicing to see
His children as pleasant and happy as he,
15 Would have no more quarrel with the Devil or the
       barrel,
But kiss him and give him both drink and apparel.

XLI THE CHIMNEY-SWEEPER

A little black thing among the snow,
Crying *'weep, 'weep,* in notes of woe!
'Where are thy father and mother, say?'
'They are both gone up to the church to pray.

5   'Because I was happy upon the heath
And smiled among the winter's snow,
They clothed me in the clothes of death
And taught me to sing the notes of woe.

'And because I am happy, and dance and sing
10 They think they have done me no injury—
And are gone to praise God and his priest and king,
Who make up a heaven of our misery.'

xl. Draft of 'The Little Vagabond' in *Experience* (p. 218). The title first
read 'A Pretty Vagabond'.
xl *4. 1st rdg del.* Such usage in heaven makes all go to hell.
xl *16. 1st rdg del.* But shake hands and kiss him and there'd be no more hell.
xli. Draft of 'The Chimney Sweeper' in *Experience* (p. 218), contrary of
'The Chimney Sweeper' in *Innocence* (p. 68). The draft is on two pages
of the NB.
xli *6. winter's snow] 1st rdg del.* winter wind.
xli *12. 1st rdg del.* Who wrap themselves up in our misery.

XLII LACEDEMONIAN INSTRUCTION

Come hither, my boy, tell me what thou seest there?
'A fool tangled in a religious snare'.

XLIII RICHES

The countless gold of a merry heart,
The rubies and pearls of a loving eye,
The indolent never can bring to the mart
Nor the secret hoard up in his treasury.

XLIV AN ANSWER TO THE PARSON

Why of the sheep do you not learn peace?
'Because I don't want you to shear my fleece'.

XLV HOLY THURSDAY

Is this a holy thing to see
In a rich and fruitful land—
Babes reduced to misery,
Fed with cold and usurous hand?

5 Is that trembling cry a song?
Can it be a song of joy,
And so great a number poor?
'Tis a land of poverty!

And their sun does never shine,
10 And their fields are bleak and bare,
And their ways are filled with thorns.
'Tis eternal winter there!

For where-e'er the sun does shine,
And where-e'er the rain does fall,
15 Babe can never hunger there,
Nor poverty the mind appal.

xlii. This reads like one of Plutarch's *Moralia*, versified; but an original has not been traced.
xliii. See note on xv.
xliii 4. *secret*] *1st rdg del.* cunning.
xliv. See note on xv. The verse alludes to tithes, the dues collected by the parson of the established church from his parishioners. B., in common with many other radicals, especially those of nonconformist origin, regarded tithes as 'fleecing' the poor.
xlv. A draft of 'Holy Thursday' in *Experience* (p. 219), and contrary to 'Holy Thursday' of *Innocence* (pp. 50 and 60).

XLVI THE ANGEL

I dreamt a dream—what can it mean?
And that I was a maiden queen,
Guarded by an angel mild.
Witless woe was ne'er beguiled!

5   And I wept both night and day,
And he wiped my tears away;
And I wept both day and night
And hid from him my heart's delight.

So he took his wings and fled.
10   Then the morn blushed rosy red;
I dried my tears and armed my fears
With ten thousand shields and spears.

Soon my angel came again;
I was armed, he came in vain.
15   For the time of youth was fled,
And grey hairs were on my head.

XLVII

Little fly,
Thy summer play
My thoughtless hand
Hath brushed away.

5   Am not I
A fly like thee?

xlvi. Draft of 'The Angel' in *Experience* (p. 219), and 'contrary' to 'A Dream' in *Innocence* (p. 64). Lines *15–16* are taken from xviii.

xlvii. Draft of 'The Fly', in *Experience* xix (p. 220).

xlvii *1–4*. A simpler version, in a short-line rhythm, of the original 1st st., now del.:

> Woe alas! my guilty hand
> Brushed across thy summer joy
> All thy gilded painted pride
> Shattered fled . . .

xlvii *3. thoughtless*] *1st rdg del.* guilty.

xlvii *5*. Before this st., a st. del.:

> The cut worm
> Forgives the plough
> And dies in peace
> And so do thou.

The first two lines of this st. are a 'Proverb of Hell' (p. 109).

Or art not thou
A man like me?

10   For I dance
And drink and sing;
Till some blind hand
Shall brush my wing.

If thought is life
And strength and breath,
15   And the want
Of thought is death,

Then am I
A happy fly,
If I live,
20   Or if I die.

XLVIII MOTTO TO THE SONGS OF INNOCENCE AND OF EXPERIENCE

The good are attracted by men's perceptions,
    And think not for themselves—
Till experience teaches them to catch
    And to cage the fairies and elves.

5   And then the knave begins to snarl,
    And the hypocrite to howl—
And all his good friends show their private ends,
    And the eagle is known from the owl.

XLIX

Her whole life is an epigram, smack-smooth and neatly
    penned,
Plaited quite neat to catch applause, with a sliding noose
    at the end.

xlvii *13–16.* This st. was written last, and numbered to go in here. Line *13* originally read *Thought is life*: the change is significant.
xlvii *15. And*] *1st rdg del.* But.
xlviii. Not in fact used in *Songs of Innocence and of Experience.*
xlviii *1. Good*] Here a term of approval—not the satiric 'good' of *Marriage,* who live by moral law, but those who live true and good lives, by instinct—until Experience bruises them and teaches them to hit back. Then villains show their villany.
xlviii *4. fairies*] Mischievous creatures: cp. **xxxiv.**

L

An old maid early, ere I knew
Ought but the love that on me grew;
And now I'm covered o'er and o'er
And wish that I had been a whore.

5   Oh, I cannot, cannot find
The undaunted courage of a virgin mind,
For early I in love was crossed
Before my flower of love was lost.

LI SEVERAL QUESTIONS ANSWERED

He who binds to himself a joy
Doth the winged life destroy;
But he who kisses the joy as it flies
Lives in eternity's sunrise.

5   The look of love alarms
Because 'tis filled with fire;
But the look of soft deceit
Shall win the lover's hire.

Soft deceit and idleness—
10   These are beauty's sweetest dress.

What is it men in women do require?—
The lineaments of gratified desire.
What is it women do in men require?—
The lineaments of gratified desire.

An ancient proverb

15   Remove away that blackening church,
Remove away that marriage hearse,
Remove away that ——— of blood—
You'll quite remove the ancient curse.

l. The two sts were written in reverse order, but numbered *2–1.*
li. These sts were drafted on previous pages, and assembled on p. 99, in the
order 4, 2, 3, 1, 5. The first, drafted on p. 105, is there entitled 'Eternity'.
li *10. These . . . dress*] The 1st rdg, altered on p. 103, was:

> Which are beauty's sweetest dress?
> Soft deceit and idleness.

li *17. that* ——— *of blood*] In the draft on p. 107: *1st rdg.* that place of blood;
2nd rdg. that man of blood. On p. 99 only a long dash. Cp. xix *12.*

LII

'Let the brothels of Paris be opened,
With many an alluring dance,
To awake the physicians through the city,'
Said the beautiful Queen of France.

5 Then old Nobodaddy aloft
Farted and belched and coughed,
And said, 'I love hanging and drawing and quartering
Every bit as well as war and slaughtering'.

Then he swore a great and solemn oath:
10 'To kill the people I am loth;
But if they rebel they must go to hell:
They shall have a priest and a passing bell'.

The King awoke on his couch of gold,
As soon as he heard these tidings told:
15 'Arise and come, both fife and drum,
And the [*famine*] shall eat both crust and crumb'.

The Queen of France just touched this globe,
And the pestilence darted from her robe;
But our good queen quite grows to the ground,
20 And a great many suckers grow all around.

LIII

Who will exchange his own fireside
For the stone of another's door?
Who will exchange his wheaten loaf
For the links of a dungeon floor?

lii, liii. These two poems were made out of a long series of sts, heavily
corrected, on similar themes. For details of the process of composition, see
Erdman 1965, pp. 779–80. Deleted lines and sts are given below.

lii *3. physicians*] 1st rdg del. pestilence.

lii *8.* After this line another quatrain, written as three lines and del. im-
mediately:

> Damn praying and singing
> Unless they will bring in
> The blood of ten thousand by fighting or swinging.

lii *16. famine*] Del. but not replaced.

lii *18.* Followed by a del. couplet:

> But the bloodthirsty people across the water
> Will not submit to the gibbet and halter.

lii *20. And . . . around*] This line replaces: 'There is just such a tree at Java
found'.

5   Fayette beheld the King and Queen
      In curses and iron bound;
      But mute Fayette wept tear for tear,
      And guarded them around.

      Oh, who would smile on the wintry seas,
10   And pity the stormy roar?
      Or who will exchange his newborn child
      For the dog at the wintry door?

liii. Stanzas composed and del., not re-used (see note opposite).

    (*a*) Fayette, Fayette, thou'rt bought and sold
        For well I see thy tears
        Of pity are exchanged for those
        Of selfish slavish fears.

    (*b*) Fayette beside King Louis stood
        He saw him sign his hand
        And soon he saw the famine rage
        About the fruitful land

        Fayette beheld the Queen to smile
        And wink her lovely eye
        And soon he saw the pestilence
        From street to street to fly.

    (*c*) Fayette beside his banner stood
        His captains false around
        Thou'rt bought and sold . . .

    (*d*) Who will exchange his own heart's blood
        For the drops of a harlot's eye . . .

    (*e*) Will the mother exchange her newborn babe
        For the dog at the wintry door?
        Yet thou dost exchange thy pitying tears
        For the links of a dungeon floor.

    (*f*) Fayette, Fayette, thou'rt bought and sold
        And sold is thy happy morrow
        Thou gavest the tears of pity away
        In exchange for the tears of sorrow.

liii 2. *stone*] *1st rdg.* steps.

liii 4. *dungeon floor*] Lafayette, being unable to maintain order and constitutionalism in the face of revolutionary violence in Paris in August and September 1793, fled abroad, but was arrested by the Austrians and imprisoned (until 1797). To French patriots he was a fallen idol, his flight an admission of treachery. It was, rather, 'a tame conclusion; but the only possible one for a man who so steadfastly refused to move with the times' (J. M. Thomson). It was good nature, rather than treachery, which got him into trouble. See also p. 131.

liii 6. *curses*] *1st rdg.* tears.

7+B.

APPENDIX

Revisions of *The Tiger* (see pp. 156 and 214)

There are two states of the draft in the NB; the first on the lower righthand side of p. 109 (reversed); the second opposite it on the righthand side of p. 108 (reversed). St. 5 of the first draft is on the lefthand side of p. 108 rev., between the two drafts; st. 2 of the second draft is above it. The final state of the second draft is printed on p. 156. The following shows the earliest state of the first draft, with alterations to it in footnotes:

1 Tyger Tyger burning bright
In the forests of the night
What immortal hand or eye
Could frame thy fearful symmetry

5 2 In what distant deeps or skies
Burnt the fire of thine eyes
On what wings dare he aspire
What the hand dare sieze the fire

3 And what shoulder & what art
10 Could twist the sinews of thy heart
And when thy heart began to beat
What dread hand & what dread feet

(At this point several false starts were made on the next st., thus:)

Could fetch it from the furnace deep
And in thy horrid ribs dare steep

(*thy* altered to *the*)

In the well of sanguine woe

In what clay & in what mould
Were thy eyes of fury rolld

(All these del.)

13 4 What the hammer what the chain
In what furnace was thy brain
15 What the anvil what the *arm arm grasp clasp* dread grasp
Could its deadly terrors *clasp grasp* clasp

4. Could] *Del.*: Dare *written in the margin, and also del.*
5. In what] *Del., but deletion line erased: 2nd rdg del.* Burnt in.
6. Burnt the] *Del.*: The Cruel *substituted in margin.*
13. What . . . what] *Del.*: Where . . . where *substituted.*
15. The italicized words were written one after another as shown, and del. in turn; 'dread grasp' was finally written above the line.
16. Could] Del. 'Dare' written in margin, not also del. as in line 4.   *clasp*]
italicized words del.

  6 Tyger Tyger burning bright
   In thee forests of the night
   What immortal hand & eye
20 Dare form thy fearful symmetry

 5

   3 And *is*
    did he laugh
    dare he *smile* laugh his work to see
22   What the *shoulder* ankle what the knee
   4 *Did* Dare he who made the lamb make thee
   1 When the stars threw down their spears
25 2 And waterd heaven with their tears

18. thee] *Sic*; doubtless a slip of quick copying.
20. form] del. frame *substituted*.
21–25. This st. written separately (see note at head); numbered with the rest of the sts to show its place; the couplets numbered to indicate a different order.
21. The alterations were made along and above the line. Italicized words were del.
22. This line entirely del., before the composition of the next line.

The second draft was then written out as a fair copy (see no xxiv, p. 156), except for the displacement of the second st. as described above:

    Tyger Tyger burning bright
    In the forests of the night
    What Immortal hand & eye
    Dare frame thy fearful symmetry
  5 Burnt in distant deeps or skies
    The cruel fire of thine eyes
    Could heart descend or wings aspire
    What the hand dare sieze the fire

    And what shoulder & what art
  10 Could twist the sinews of thy heart
    And when thy heart began to beat
    What dread hand & what dread feet

    When the stars threw down their spears
    And waterd heaven with their tears

This is the version engraved in *Experience* (p. 214), with the addition of punctuation, and the following changes:
3. & became *or.*
4. Dare became *Could.*
5. Burnt in distant became *In what distant* (as 1st draft).
6. The cruel became *Burnt the* (as 1st draft).

15   Did he smile his work to see
    Did he who made the lamb make thee

    Tyger Tyger burning bright
    In the forests of the night
    What immortal hand & eye
20   Dare frame thy fearful symmetry

12. & what] So in all drafts and the engraved poem; but in one late copy
of *Experience* altered to *formd thy* in ink; and in the version printed in 1806
by B. H. Malkin in *A Father's Memoirs of his Child* (see p. 215), it is given as
forged thy, very likely on B.'s authority. After this st., the st. beginning
What the hammer . . . from the first draft was included in the engraved
poem, incorporating the alterations of *Could* to *Dare*.

11 Visions of the Daughters of Albion

Date: *c*. 1791–92. The slavery issue (*21*) was alive in 1791, and the plates
are recognizably earlier than *America*. 'Lambeth' (where B. moved 1790–
91), does not appear on the titlepage, as it does in all poems from *America*
to *The Book of Los*.

Theme. In Macpherson's collections of heroic prose poems which he called
translations from the ancient Gaelic of the bard Ossian (1760–63) there is
the story of *Oi-thona*, 'the virgin of the waves'. She married the great
hero Gaul, who was called away. As the *Argument* says: 'Oi-thona was left
alone at Dunlathmon, the seat of the family. Dunrommath, Lord of Uthal,
supposed to be one of the Orkneys, taking advantage of the absence of her
friends, came, and carried off, by force, Oi-thona, who had formerly
rejected his love, into Tromathon, a desert island, where he concealed her
in a cave.' So far the parallel with Oothoon is clear, but Macpherson's
story continues quite differently. Gaul, coming to Tromathon to take his
revenge, 'found Oi-thona disconsolate, and resolved not to survive the
loss of her honour'; in the ensuing battle she disguised herself as a warrior
and was killed. B. was interested in the situation, not in the outcome in
battle. True love would have no place for jealousy, and no outcome in
war. He asks, by implication, 'Why should Oi-thona trouble about her so-
called honour?', and he has imagined her taking a more daring attitude–
and the trouble such an attitude would lead to. B. knew her, and may
have picked up from Mary Wollstonecraft her enthusiasm for the eman-
cipation of women.

But freedom, to B., was indivisible; it is not merely the rights of women
he is concerned with. The oppression of Oothoon, 'soft soul of America'
(*3*)–the land of freedom (and slavery)–is bound up with the campaign of
the early 1790s against both the slave trade, which culminated in a motion
in the Commons (which proved ineffective at the time) on 23 April 1792,
calling for the abolition of the trade, and the nearer cruelties in the ex-
ploitation of child labour (*20–4, 31*). All these ideas have coalesced in B.'s
mind to produce a characterstic synthesis of distinct themes.

Visions falls into three clear parts, where (echoing Spenser): 'The daughters of Albion hear her woes, and echo back her sighs' (*43, 113* and *218*). Only the first part is narrative; the second is made up of three speeches, one from each of the characters, and the third is one long effusion from Oothoon, the protagonist.

The narrative section begins, like *Thel*, with a maiden who wanders uncertainly; but unlike Thel, Oothoon dares: she accepts the love of the flower which wants to be picked by her so that she may enjoy it. As she puts it between her breasts, its love enters her heart and she flies fearlessly to Theotormon, her lover. Like the flower, she has dared to give herself in love. But her joy is turned to disaster. Bromion, a storm-and-sea figure, rapes her and gloats to Theotormon. Worse still, Theotormon now rejects her as defiled, taking her to be as foul as Bromion, and ties them up, back to back, away from love and life. Oothoon has flown 'over Theotormon's reign' because he is her accepted lover, as his jealousy implies. For her part, although Bromion's attack causes her 'woe' (*17*) at first, most of her speech in the rest of the poem is given to justifying the innocence of free and promiscuous love. Theotormon's jealousy and oppression form a greater evil than Bromion's violence. Thus the first section, and the narrative, ends.

The middle section is a disputation, each character speaking in turn. Oothoon tries to inspire Theotormon with the vision of delight she saw in the flower; he, full of doubt and fear, does not accept her vision; and the blunt and brutish Bromion says, in effect, 'Who cares?' The third section is all Oothoon's (and B.'s)–a long outburst against hypocrisy in marriage and restraint in love. Finally (*216*) we are recalled to the pathetic, unmoving trio in the cave by the seashore.

The eye sees more than the heart knows.

THE ARGUMENT

I loved Theotormon,
And I was not ashamed;
I trembled in my virgin fears,
And I hid in Leutha's vale.

I plucked Leutha's flower,
And I rose up from the vale;
But the terrible thunders tore
My virgin mantle in twain.
[*Design*]

¶ 11. *Titlepage.* The legend 'The eye . . . knows' is inscribed at the foot, under the figure of Oothoon running over the waves of a stormy sea (see *14–15*).

Argument. Design: Illustrates lines *11–12* of the poem. Oothoon, kneeling, her hands on her breasts, kisses the spirit that leaps from the flower. Reproduced in A. Blunt: *Art of W.B.*, pl.20b.

Pl. 1   VISIONS

    Enslaved, the daughters of Albion weep–a trembling
        lamentation
    Upon their mountains, in their valleys sighs toward
        America.
    For the soft soul of America, Oothoon, wandered in
        woe
    Along the vales of Leutha, seeking flowers to comfort
        her;
5   And thus she spoke to the bright marigold of Leutha's
        vale:

        'Art thou a flower? Art thou a nymph? I see
            thee now a flower,
        Now a nymph! I dare not pluck thee from thy
            dewy bed.'

        The golden nymph replied: 'Pluck thou my
            flower, Oothoon the mild.
        Another flower shall spring, because the soul of
            sweet delight
10   Can never pass away.' She ceased and closed her
            golden shrine.

    Then Oothoon plucked the flower, saying, 'I pluck
        thee from thy bed,
    Sweet flower, and put thee here to glow between my
        breasts,
    And thus I turn my face to where my whole soul
        seeks:'

1. *The daughters of Albion*] Englishwomen, imaginatively seen.
3. *soft soul of America, Oothoon*] Slavery exists in different forms in Britain and in America (where the light of freedom had risen).
4. *Leutha*] This name appears in *Europe* 170, *Song of Los* 28, *Book of Los* 2, *Jerusalem* pl. 83.*82*, and *Milton* pl. 11.*28*ff. (qv. for note on Leutha in the later poems). Fragment *d* of *America* (p. 208) seems to imply that the vale of Leutha is an unreal land, a land of dreams. In that case, Oothoon is 'living in a dream-world', but the vision she has there sends her 'exulting' into reality. Yet note that B. treats 'Leutha's vale' and 'Theotormon's reign' as if they belonged to the same world.
9–10. *The soul . . . pass away*] *Marriage of Heaven and Hell* pl.9, 'Proverb' 53, and *America* 72 have 'can never be defiled'.
11. The plucking of a flower, usually a rose, is traditionally symbolic of the attainment of sexual love (see *Argument*, design).
13. *Thus I turn my face*] As the marigold turns its face to the sun; cp. 'The Sunflower' in *Songs of Experience.*

Over the waves she went in winged exulting swift
    delight,
15 And over Theotormon's reign took her impetuous
    course.

Bromion rent her with his thunders; on his stormy bed
Lay the faint maid, and soon her woes appalled his
    thunders hoarse.

Bromion spoke: 'Behold this harlot here on Bromion's
    bed,
And let the jealous dolphins sport around the lovely
    maid!
20 Thy soft American plains are mine, and mine thy
    north and south.
Stamped with my signet are the swarthy children of
    the sun;
They are obedient, they resist not, they obey the
    scourge;
Their daughters worship terrors and obey the violent.

[Design]

Pl. 2 Now thou mayest marry Bromion's harlot and protect
    the child
25 Of Bromion's rage that Oothoon shall put forth in nine
    moons time.'

Then storms rent Theotormon's limbs; he rolled his
    waves around
And folded his black jealous waters round the
    adulterate pair.
Bound back to back in Bromion's caves, terror and
    meekness dwell.

At entrance Theotormon sits, wearing the threshold
    hard

15. *Theotormon's reign*] The sea (see *19, 26–7, 216–7*).
16. *Bromion*] A wind-and-storm figure who has, like the classical winds
his caves.
19. *jealous dolphins*] Sea-creatures belonging to the jealous Theotormon.
21 *Stamped . . . signet*] An allusion to the branding of slaves.
Pl.1. *Design*: The three figures of the poem; Oothoon and Bromion ex-
hausted (after the rape?), Theotormon dejected.
26. *Storms . . . limbs*] Bromion's winds drive Theotormon's sea into a storm.
28. *back to back*] Imprisoned together, but unable to see or embrace. The
design at the end of the poem illustrates *28–30*.

30   With secret tears; beneath him sound like waves on a
           desert shore
       The voice of slaves beneath the sun, and children
           bought with money,
       That shiver in religious caves beneath the burning fires
       Of lust that belch incessant from the summits of the
           earth.

       Oothoon weeps not, she cannot weep, her tears are
           locked up,
35   But she can howl incessant, writhing her soft snowy
           limbs
       And calling Theotormon's eagles to prey upon her
           flesh:

       'I call with holy voice kings of the sounding air,
       Rend away this defiled bosom that I may reflect
       The image of Theotormon on my pure transparent
           breast.'

                        [Design]

40   The eagles at her call descend and rend their bleeding
           prey.
       Theotormon severely smiles; her soul reflects the
           smile,
       As the clear spring muddied with feet of beasts grows
           pure & smiles.

       The daughters of Albion hear her woes, and echo back her sighs.

30. secret tears] In B.'s mind oppression, possessiveness, jealousy, secretive-
ness, hypocrisy and deceit were all bound up together. He often treats
tears as hypocritical (cp. 'Infant Sorrow' and 'The Human Abstract' in
Experience, and Urizen 333). Note also Oi-thona's words, 'I sit in my tears
in the cave! Nor do I sit alone, O Gaul! the dark chief of Cuthal is there'
(Macpherson's Ossian: Oi-thona).
30-3. Theotormon is like those 'religious' people whose repressed lust
issues in oppression, figured here as volcanic, e.g. in the worse cruelties of
slavery.
38. Rend ... bosom] Her physical 'defilement' by Bromion is nothing
against her untouched inner love for Theotormon. B. asserts that adultery
and innocence need not be contradictory. The illustration (pl. 3) recalls
the Promethean source of the image–an eagle hovers over Oothoon to
tear her with its beak.
Design. A slave tries to lift himself from the ground; a tree leans away from
him, his pickaxe lying beside it.

'Why does my Theotormon sit weeping upon the
    threshold,
45 And Oothoon hovers by his side, persuading him in
    vain?
I cry, "Arise, O Theotormon, for the village dog
Barks at the breaking day, the nightingale has done
    lamenting,
The lark does rustle in the ripe corn, and the eagle
    returns
From nightly prey and lifts his golden beak to the
    pure east,
50 Shaking the dust from his immortal pinions to awake
The sun that sleeps too long. Arise, my Theotormon,
    I am pure!
Because the night is gone that closed me in its
    deadly black."
They told me that the night and day were all that I
    could see;
They told me that I had five senses to enclose me up,
55 And they enclosed my infinite brain into a narrow
    circle
And sunk my heart into the abyss, a red round globe
    hot-burning,
Till all from life I was obliterated and erased.
Instead of morn arises a bright shadow, like an eye
In the eastern cloud, instead of night a sickly charnel-
    house,
60 That Theotormon hears me not. To him the night
    and morn
Are both alike—a night of sighs, a morning of fresh
    tears,
Pl. 3 And none but Bromion can hear my lamentations.

'With what sense is it that the chicken shuns the
    ravenous hawk?

43. i.e., Oothoon's legendary sorrows are echoed in the hearts of English-women.

51. I am pure] The heart of Oothoon's declaration. But Theotormon has not similarly learnt to dare to be free.

54-7. five sense to enclose me up...] Cp. *Urizen 210-269*; *Song of Los* (*Africa*) *35*. In *Urizen* B. develops the image fully as part of the narrative of the Fall, and the creation of the restricted world of mortal life.

58. a bright shadow] The earthbound eye of man sees only the physical appearance of the sun, and does not experience the full spiritual joy of dawn.

7*

With what sense does the tame pigeon measure out
   the expanse?
65 With what sense does the bee form cells? Have not
   the mouse and frog
Eyes and ears and sense of touch? Yet are their
   habitations
And their pursuits as different as their forms and as
   their joys.
Ask the wild ass why he refuses burdens and the meek
   camel
Why he loves man. Is it because of eye, ear, mouth or
   skin,
70 Or breathing nostrils? No: for these the wolf and
   tiger have.
Ask the blind worm the secrets of the grave, and
   why her spires
Love to curl round the bones of death; and ask the
   ravenous snake
Where she gets poison, and the winged eagle why
   he loves the sun.
And then tell me the thoughts of man that have
   been hid of old.

75 'Silent I hover all the night, and all day could be
   silent,
If Theotormon once would turn his loved eyes upon
   me;
How can I be defiled when I reflect thy image pure?
Sweetest the fruit that the worm feeds on, and the
   soul preyed on by woe,
The new-washed lamb tinged with the village smoke,
   and the bright swan

63ff. At this period B. was fond of passages of rhetorical questions; note
especially the endings of Thel and Tiriel. Here Oothoon dwells on the
importance of insight, as given in different ways to individual creatures,
and as against general laws of science, which make all things seem alike.
Thus she emphasizes the right of every individual to go his own way and
fulfil his own potentialities and impulses.
77. i.e., 'How can adultery with Bromion defile me? Love is in the inner
being, not in the body only'. The reverse of this is expressed in 132ff, where
'proper' sexual union in marriage is abhorred when it is loveless.
78–81. Sweetest the fruit . . .] The perfect being is that which most attracts,
and most clearly shows, the envious attacks of destructive forces. Cp. 'The
Sick Rose' in Experience.

80 By the red earth of our immortal river. I bathe my
  wings,
And I am white and pure to hover round
  Theotormon's breast.'
Then Theotormon broke his silence, and he answered:
'Tell me what is the night or day to one o'erflowed
  with woe?
Tell me what is a thought, and of what substance
  it is made?
85 Tell me what is a joy and in what gardens do joys
  grow.
And in what rivers swim the sorrows, and upon what
  mountains

[Design]

Pl. 4   *[Design]*

Wave shadows of discontent, and in what houses
  dwell the wretched
Drunken with woe, forgotten and shut up from cold
  despair?
'Tell me where dwell the thoughts forgotten till
  thou call them forth,
90 Tell me where dwell the joys of old, and where the
  ancient loves.
And when will they renew again and the night of
  oblivion past—
That I might traverse times and spaces far remote
  and bring
Comforts into a present sorrow and a night of pain.
Where goest thou, O thought? To what remote land
  is thy flight?
95 If thou returnest to the present moment of affliction
Wilt thou bring comforts on thy wings, and dews and
  honey and balm,
Or poison from the desert wilds, from the eyes of the
  envier?'

Design: Oothoon stretched backwards on a cloud; an eagle hovers over her,
striking at her heart with its beak.
Pl.4. *Design*: Theotormon, dejected, on the seashore; Oothoon, swept up
by a wave but shackled at her ankle, hangs over him, supplicating.
80. red earth] See *Marriage* 'Argument' *13*, and *Milton* 19:*10*.
82–97. Theotormon's response is to ask for facts, for the 'substance' of
things which by their nature are intangible.

Then Bromion said, and shook the cavern with his
   lamentation:

'Thou knowest that the ancient trees seen by thine
   eyes have fruit,
100 But knowest thou that trees and fruits flourish upon
   the earth
To gratify senses unknown, trees, beasts and birds
   unknown—
Unknown, not unperceived, spread in the infinite
   microscope,
In places yet unvisited by the voyager, and in worlds
Over another kind of seas, and in atmospheres
   unknown?
105 Ah, are there other wars beside the wars of sword
   and fire?
And are there other sorrows besides the sorrows of
   poverty?
And are there other joys beside the joys of riches and
   ease?
And is there not one law for both the lion and the ox?
And is there not eternal fire–and eternal chains–
110 To bind the phantoms of existence from eternal life?'

Then Oothoon waited silent all the day, and all the
   night,
Pl. 5 But when the morn arose, her lamentation renewed.

The daughters of Albion hear her woes, and echo back her sighs.

'O Urizen, creator of men, mistaken demon of heaven
115 Thy joys are tears, thy labour vain, to form men to
   thine image.
How can one joy absorb another? Are not different
   joys
Holy, eternal, infinite? And each joy is a love.

98–110. Bromion is more certain than Theotormon, at least in knowing
that, if anything does lie beyond the spiritual world, he can't lay his hands
on it. He will not meddle there, but will stay with what he knows.
114. Urizen] The earliest reference to Urizen, with the possible exception
of *America* cancelled pl.*b*.5 (p. 206).
118–9. The great mouth . . . the narrow eyelids] Both treat giving with scorn.
119–20. Cp. *The Four Zoas* II *599–600:*

   I have chosen the serpent for a councellor & the dog
   For a schoolmaster to my children.

'Does not the great mouth laugh at a gift, and the
        narrow eyelids mock
At the labour that is above payment? And wilt
        thou take the ape
120 For thy counsellor, or the dog for a schoolmaster
        to thy children?
Does he who contemns poverty, and he who turns
        with abhorrence
From usury, feel the same passion—or are they
        moved alike?
How can the giver of gifts experience the delights of
        the merchant,
How the industrious citizen the pains of the
        husbandman?
125 How different far the fat-fed hireling with hollow
        drum,
Who buys whole cornfields into wastes and sings
        upon the heath!
How different their eye and ear! How different the
        world to them!
With what sense does the parson claim the labour
        of the farmer?
What are his nets and gins and traps, and how does
        he surround him

121. *He who contemns poverty*] I.e. he who despises the poor man for his
poverty—not the reformer or genuine philanthropist who values the man
and hates the poverty. The emotions of the two sorts of men are of entirely
different kinds.

125–6. *Who buys . . . wastes*] Gamekeepers, who preserve game birds and
vermin such as foxes, to be hunted by rich men, and so keep what could be
good farmland as wild country; or the recruiting sergeant, who denudes
the land of labour and causes tracts of it to lie untilled. Cp. 'The sword
sung on the barren heath' (p. 162). Or the 'drumming on the heath' may
refer to military displays or tattoos.

128. *The parson* took tithes, the legally-enforced church tax. B. is ironical.

128–33. An excellent example of one of B.'s trains of thought. Beginning
with country evils, he includes the unjustifiable custom of tithing. This
leads him to attack the parson further, for taking in the people with vague
abstract pious hopes. The religion and law of oppression are based on
such deception. This brings Oothoon back to her subject, for one of the
results of this oppression is the rigid code of marriage which causes so much
misery. The thought of William Godwin and Mary Wollstonecraft (see
headnote) is clearly visible in this sequence, which also shows how B. can
be carried away by intensity of feeling and vividness of imagery.

130 With cold floods of abstraction and with forests of
     solitude,
     To build him castles and high spires, where kings
     and priests may dwell,
     Till she who burns with youth and knows no fixed
     lot, is bound
     In spells of law to one she loathes. And must she
     drag the chain
     Of life in weary lust? Must chilling murderous
     thoughts obscure
135 The clear heaven of her eternal spring, to bear the
     wintry rage
     Of a harsh terror, driven to madness, bound to hold a
     rod
     Over her shrinking shoulders all the day, and all the
     night
     To turn the wheel of false desire, and longings
     that wake her womb
     To the abhorred birth of cherubs in the human form,
140 That live a pestilence and die a meteor and are no
     more—
     Till the child dwell with one he hates, and do the
     deed he loathes,
     And the impure scourge force his seed into its
     unripe birth
     Ere yet his eyelids can behold the arrows of the day?

                    [Design]

     'Does the whale worship at thy footsteps as the hungry
     dog,
145 Or does he scent the mountain prey, because his nos-
     trils wide
     Draw in the ocean? Does his eye discern the flying
     cloud
     As the raven's eye, or does he measure the expanse
     like the vulture?
     Does the still spider view the cliffs where eagles hide
     their young?
     Or does the fly rejoice, because the harvest is brought
     in?
150 Does not the eagle scorn the earth and despise the
     treasures beneath?
     But the mole knoweth what is there, and the worm
     shall tell it thee.

Design: A woman, covered by a sheet, buries her head in her pillow.

Does not the worm erect a pillar in the mouldering
    churchyard

Pl. 6 And a place of eternity in the jaws of the hungry
    grave?

Over his porch these words are written: "Take thy
    bliss, O man!

155 And sweet shall be thy taste and sweet thy infant joys
    renew."

'Infancy, fearless, lustful, happy, nestling for delight
In laps of pleasure! Innocence, honest, open, seeking
The vigorous joys of morning light, open to virgin
    bliss!

Who taught thee modesty, subtle modesty, child of
    night and sleep?

160 When thou awakest, wilt thou dissemble all thy secret
    joys—

Or wert thou not awake when all this mystery was
    disclosed?

Then com'st thou forth a modest virgin, knowing to
    dissemble

With nets found under thy night pillow to catch
    virgin joy,

And brand it with the name of whore, and sell it in
    the night,

165 In silence, even without a whisper, and in seeming
    sleep.

Religious dreams and holy vespers light thy smoky
    fires—

Once were thy fires lighted by the eyes of honest
    morn.

And does my Theotormon seek this hypocrite modesty,

152–3. the worm] The worm builds where everything decays, and it creates
out of decay, rather than destorying.

156–8. nestling for delight . . .] B. will not distinguish between the sensual
delights of the infant at the breast and those of the adult. Both arise from
the innocence of nature.

158. virgin bliss] Cp. *162, 163, 170, 173*, and also *A Song of Liberty* (Chorus)
and *America 68–70*. Virginity is *innocence*, not abstinence. It is found in the
free, childlike enjoyment of one's nature; and where this enjoyment is, it
is irrelevant whether or not the person is 'virgin' (in the physical and thus
earthly sense). The real 'whore', who degrades humanity, is the 'respect-
able' person who teaches the innocent to fear and despise this innocence of
'virgin bliss', the true and natural destiny of all creatures.

159. modesty, child . . .] i.e. modesty is the child of night, etc.

    This knowing, artful, secret, fearful, cautious, trembling hypocrite?

170 Then is Oothoon a whore indeed, and all the virgin joys
    Of life are harlots, and Theotormon is a sick man's dream,
    And Oothoon is the crafty slave of selfish holiness.

    'But Oothoon is not so, a virgin filled with virgin fancies,
    Open to joy and to delight wherever beauty appears.

175 If in the morning sun I find it, there my eyes are fixed

[Design]

[Pl. 7]   *[Design]*

    In happy copulation; if in evening mild, wearied with work,
    Sit on a bank and draw the pleasures of this freeborn joy.

    'The moment of desire! The moment of desire! The virgin
    That pines for man shall awaken her womb to enormous joys

180 In the secret shadows of her chamber. The youth, shut up from
    The lustful joy, shall forget to generate and create an amorous image
    In the shadows of his curtains and in the folds of his silent pillow.
    Are not these the places of religion, the rewards of continence,
    The self-enjoyings of self-denial? Why dost thou seek religion?

185 Is it because acts are not lovely that thou seekest solitude,

---

170. *A whore indeed!*] i.e. if she adopts the attitude of *160*ff as virtuous, and accepts Theotormon on these grounds—the grounds he asks for.
Design: A man (Theotormon), half-sitting, waves a scourge; a woman (Oothoon) springs away from him, not in fear but in misery.
Pl.7. *Design*: Four huddled figures, gowned; two with their heads hidden, one looking sadly upwards, one almost hidden beside them.
185. But of course 'acts *are* lovely', and Theotormon should *not* turn away.

Where the horrible darkness is impressed with
     reflections of desire?

'Father of Jealousy, be thou accursed from the earth!
Why hast thou taught my Theotormon this accursed
     thing,
Till beauty fades from off my shoulders, darkened
     and cast out,
190 A solitary shadow wailing on the margin of non-
     entity?

'I cry, Love! Love! Love! Happy, happy love,
     free as the mountain wind!
Can that be love that drinks another as a sponge
     drinks water,
That clouds with jealousy his nights, with weepings
     all the day,
To spin a web of age around him, grey and hoary,
     dark,
195 Till his eyes sicken at the fruit that hangs before his
     sight?
Such is self-love that envies all, a creeping skeleton
With lamplike eyes watching around the frozen
     marriage bed.

'But silken nets and traps of adamant will Oothoon
     spread
And catch for thee girls of mild silver or of furious
     gold;
200 I'll lie beside thee on a bank and view their wanton
     play
In lovely copulation, bliss on bliss with Theotormon,
Red as the rosy morning, lustful as the first-born
     beam,
Oothoon shall view his dear delight, nor e'er with
     jealous cloud
Come in the heaven of generous love, nor selfish
     blightings bring.

187. Father of Jealousy] Urizen.
189–90. This is an image B. returns to again and again. Cp. *Ahania 174–6*,
and Enion in *The Four Zoas* I *131*, II *593*, etc. Oi-thona also, like
Lucrece, mourned her fate and went to her death.
195. The jealous man cannot enjoy the woman he possesses; she be-
comes in his eyes the creature he does not want her to be.

205   'Does the sun walk in glorious raiment on the secret
          floor

Pl. 8   Where the cold miser spreads his gold? Or does the
          bright cloud drop

          On his stone treshold? Does his eye behold the beam
          that brings

          Expansion to the eye of pity? Or will he bind himself

          Beside the ox to thy hard furrow? Does not that mild
          beam blot

210   The bat, the owl, the glowing tiger, and the king of
          night?

          The sea-fowl takes the wintry blast for a covering to
          her limbs,

          And the wild snake the pestilence to adorn him with
          gems and gold –

          And trees and birds and beasts and men behold their
          eternal joy.

          Arise, you little glancing wings, and sing your infant
          joy!

215   Arise and drink your bliss! For everything that lives
          is holy.

          Thus every morning wails Oothoon. But Theotormon
          sits

          Upon the margined ocean, conversing with shadows
          dire.

          The daughters of Albion hear her woes, and echo back her sighs.

          The End

          [Design]

          [Full-page Design]

205–8. The jealous man – and the miser is another example – cannot ex-
perience magnanimity. Cp. *118*ff.
209. *thy*] Urizen's – he makes the task heavier than it should be.
210. *bat, owl, tiger*] All are night creatures, and the 'mild beam' of mag-
nanimity, of the life-giving sun, blots them out.   *King of night* is obscure.
Design: Three figures sit on the seashore; one with head down, the others
(one with an arm round another's shoulder) look up at a herald-like figure
in a flaming cloud. Perhaps the daughters of Albion.
Full-page design: Oothoon and Bromion in a cave mouth at the seashore,
bound and shackled back to back. Theotormon sits beside them, his head
buried wretchedly in his arm. In some copies this is a frontispiece.

12 America

A Prophecy

Date. 1791–93: on the titlepage, *Lambeth 1793.* Three 'cancelled plates' exist which represent an earlier state in the composition of this poem. The titlepage of the completed poem is dated from Lambeth where B. had moved by March 1791, and the mood of most of the poem is that of 1791–92 –the joyful certainty that a Golden Age was returning through the force of political revolution in America and France. This is not the mood of the last lines of the 'Preludium' (usually omitted: see Prel. *37*n). It appears that *A Song of Liberty* was composed later than the text of pls 8 and 16. The version of the cancelled plates (see pp. 205–8) alludes more definitely to the rulers of Albion – Parliament and King – than the final version; by Jan. 1793 (when England declared war on France) it was becoming more dangerous to be a radical. It is possible that the plates were not quite completed until 1794 (B.'s titlepage dates often anticipate), but he included *America* in his *Prospectus* of 10 Oct. 1793.

Theme. B wrote two *Prophecies–America* and *Europe.* The term has, in common usage, been extended loosely to all his longer poems, but these two are different in kind from the imaginative history of *The French Revolution*, and, more especially, such poems as *Urizen*, which is to the 'Books of Moses' in the Bible what *America* and *Europe* are to the 'Books of the Prophets'. The *Prophecies* are spiritual interpretations of contemporary events. This is an entirely acceptable understanding of prophecy, though unusual among B.'s contemporaries. His own idea of it is summarized in the words he gives to Isaiah (*Marriage*, pl.12): 'my senses discovered the infinite in everything'.

In *America*, B. has moved away from the narrative form of *The French Revolution*, in which he followed actual events closely, though enwrapping them in imaginative detail. In *America* there is a clear narrative, covering the struggle between the government of George III in London and the colonies; but few of either the events or the participants are historical, or even human. The *Prophecy* itself begins with the defiance of Washington, but continues as a struggle, first (in epic manner) in wordy defiance and then in battle, between the spirit of freedom, Orc, supported by the guardian Angels of the thirteen colonies, and their enemy Albion's Angel– the tutelary spirit of Albion (i.e. Britain). Albion's Angel threatens Washington (*1–18*); but Orc arises out of the Atlantic to take their part (*19–51*). After they have challenged one another (*52–75*) Albion's Angel calls in vain on his thirteen minions in the colonies, but they too defy him (*76–129*). Then war begins in the heavens, casting its shadows on the earth beneath and affecting, as it does so, the colonial governors (*142*), the British army (*147*), Washington and his friends (*158*) and the New England citizens (*170–3*). The weapons used are pestilence (by Albion's Angel) and fire (by Orc). When Orc begins to drive the plagues back over Albion itself, a higher figure intervenes–Urizen, the aged tyrant-god of snow and storm. He freezes the entire action (*204–17*); but the poem ends with a promise (*218*) that Orc's fires will in the end melt Urizen's frost.

The 'Preludium', though using the figure of Orc, was probably the last part to be written. B.'s hopes are now less immediately political; he is turning, as in the later Lambeth books, to more universal images. Orc's rape of the delighted 'female' is not directly a reflection of the American War of Independence. In *America* and *Europe*, more than in any other of B.'s books, the text and designs are integral, the text being written across the face of the design which fills the page. For this reason the position of the designs cannot be indicated by lines. A facsimile is available in the Blake Trust series (1963).

Frontispiece

Pl. 1   PRELUDIUM

The shadowy daughter of Urthona stood before red
        Orc,
When fourteen suns had faintly journeyed o'er his
        dark abode.
His food she brought in iron baskets, his drink in cups
        of iron.

¶ 12. *Frontispiece.* A breached wall, before which a winged figure sits manacled, his head bowed. A woman with two children watches him unhappily. Reproduced in Keynes: *W.B.'s Engravings*, pl.83.
Pl.1. *Design*: Top L, Orc, chained, under a tree; two horrified figures, male and female, look at him. Roots go down L of text to a dejected figure bottom L.
1. *daughter of Urthona*] Cp. *Song of Liberty 1* and *Europe* (*Prel.*) *1*. She is here a shadowy figure, the virgin daughter of the grim Urthona who imprisons Orc (the sympathetic gaoler's daughter is well known in folktale). In the *Song* and *Europe* she becomes a mother-spirit; in all these poems she is passive rather than active, but usually the vehicle of world-shaking, glorious events. Cp. *17n.*   *Orc*] The first use of the name, although the nameless youth of *A Song of Liberty* is recognisably the same. He is a vigorous youth; his home is fire and he here resembles Prometheus, punished endlessly for the freedom of his spirit, yet undefeated. He is often seen as a serpent; this aspect appears in *15*, and (*Prophecy*) *54–5*.
2. *fourteen suns*] May refer to Orc's age–arrival at puberty and independent life; several years later this is the sense given in the rewriting of this legend (*Four Zoas* v *79*). Fourteen years elapsed between the publication of Rousseau' *Social Contract* (1762) and the Declaration of Independence (1776).

Crowned with a helmet and dark hair the nameless
    female stood—
5 A quiver with its burning stores, a bow like that of
    night,
When pestilence is shot from heaven (no other arms
    she need),
Invulnerable though naked, save where clouds roll
    round her loins
Their awful folds in the dark air. Silent she stood as
    night;
For never from her iron tongue could voice or sound
    arise,
10 But dumb till that dread day when Orc assayed his
    fierce embrace.

'Dark virgin', said the hairy youth, 'thy father stern
    abhorred
Rivets my tenfold chains while still on high my spirit
    soars.
Sometimes an eagle screaming in the sky, sometimes
    a lion
Stalking upon the mountains, and sometimes a whale
    I lash
15 The raging fathomless abyss; anon a serpent folding
Around the pillars of Urthona, and round thy dark
    dark limbs,
On the Canadian wilds I fold. Feeble my spirit folds.
For chained beneath I rend these caverns; when thou
    bringest food

8. silent . . . night] Cp. *Paradise Lost* ii 670, where Death is seen: 'black it
stood as night'.
11. thy father stern, abhorred] Urthona, a shadowy but grim figure; cp. *Song
of Liberty 16, Europe 10* (neither specific). He is always an earth-spirit, and
in the early books is ominous, being allied to the evil sky-god Urizen. In
Four Zoas B. turns him into an entirely different figure, though he is
still a stern earth-spirit.
13–15. eagle, lion, whale, serpent] Creatures both free and potentially danger-
ous; of air, earth, water and (in B.) fire respectively.
17. Canadian wilds] Cp. *32–4*; the maiden is associated with America, soon
to be awakened to freedom and joy, besides being a figure of universal
significance.
Design: Beneath the text Orc climbs out of rock. The sun rises behind his
head; a vine shoots up the L margin. The following four lines are in-
scribed across the rock; they were excluded from all copies except the
earliest and the two latest, presumably representing a moment or period

I howl my joy, and my red eyes seek to behold thy
    face—
20 In vain! these clouds roll to and fro, and hide thee from
    my sight.'

Pl. 2 Silent as despairing love, and strong as jealousy,
The hairy shoulders rend the links, free are the wrists
    of fire;
Round the terrific loins he seized the panting
    struggling womb.
It joyed. She put aside her clouds and smiled her
    first-born smile,
25 As when a black cloud shows its lightnings to the
    silent deep.

Soon as she saw the terrible boy, then burst the virgin
    cry:

'I know thee, I have found thee, and I will not let thee
    go.
Thou art the image of God who dwells in darkness of
    Africa,
And thou art fallen to give me life in regions of dark
    death.
30 On my American plains I feel the struggling afflictions
Endured by roots that writhe their arms in to the
    nether deep;
I see a serpent in Canada, who courts me to his love;
In Mexico an eagle, and a lion in Peru;
I see a whale in the South-Sea, drinking my soul away.
35 Oh, what limb-rending pains I feel! Thy fire and my
    frost
Mingle in howling pains, in furrows by thy lightnings
    rent;
This is eternal death, and this the torment long
    foretold.'

of disillusionment – probably the public outcry and official witch-hunt
against radical groups, in 1792–94 – which B. did not wish to recall:
38 The stern bard ceas'd, asham'd of his own song: enrag'd he
    swung
His harp aloft sounding, then dashed its shining frame against
A ruin'd pillar in glittring fragments: silent he turned away,
41 And wander'd down the vales of Kent in sick & drear
    lamentings.
Both forms of the page are reproduced in Keynes: *W.B.'s Engravings*, pls
84, 85.

Pl. 3   A PROPHECY

The Guardian Prince of Albion burns in his nightly
    tent;
Sullen fires across the Atlantic glow to America's
    shore,
Piercing the souls of warlike men, who rise in silent
    night.
Washington, Franklin, Paine and Warren, Gates,
    Hancock and Greene

5 Meet on the coast glowing with blood from Albion's
    fiery Prince.

Washington spoke: 'Friends of America, look over
    the Atlantic sea;
A bended bow is lifted in heaven, and a heavy iron
    chain
Descends link by link from Albion's cliffs across the
    sea to bind
Brothers and sons of America, till our faces pale and
    yellow,

10 Heads depressed, voices weak, eyes downcast, hands
    work-bruised,

Prophecy: Pl.3. *Design*: Ornamented with running figures: the *A* curls
into stalks of wheat. Between 5 and 6 a figure with a flaming torch;
flames around the lower text.

1. *Guardian Prince of Albion*] Albion's Angel, or tutelary spirit, the evil
angel, instrument of warlike oppression (he is in a tent). Cp. *Song of Los*
(*Africa*) 52, where B. brings the narrative of world history up to this point.

4. *Washington*, etc.] Benjamin *Franklin* (1706–90) was the famous American
'man of parts', who tried to reconcile homeland and colonial differences,
but when that became impossible, played a valuable part for the colonies
in administration and diplomacy. Thomas *Paine* (1737–1809), born in
England, famous pamphleteer and political writer; he produced the
antimonarchic works *Common Sense* in 1776 and *The Rights of Man* in 1792.
Joseph *Warren* (1741–75) was a leader killed at Bunker Hill. Horatio *Gates*
(1728–1806), born in England, commanded the army which defeated
Burgoyne at Saratoga, but was himself defeated in 1780 by Cornwallis.
John *Hancock* (1737–93) was a merchant of Boston, a member of the first
Congress. Nathaniel *Greene* (1742–86) was one of the best generals of the
war.

5. *glowing with blood*] Reflecting and feeling the threatening blood-red
light from Albion.

8–11. These lines reflect B.'s concern for slavery, as well as for political
oppression. The *sultry sands* also suggest the slavery of the Israelites under
Pharaoh.

Feet bleeding on the sultry sands, and the furrows
    of the whip
Descend to generations that in future times forget. '

The strong voice ceased; for a terrible blast swept
    over the heaving sea.
The eastern cloud rent; on his cliffs stood Albion's
    wrathful Prince,
15 A dragon form clashing his scales! At midnight he
    arose,
And flamed red meteors round the land of Albion
    beneath.
His voice, his locks, his awful shoulders, and his
    glowing eyes
Pl. 4   Appear to the Americans upon the cloudy night.

Solemn heave the Atlantic waves between the gloomy
    nations,
20 Swelling, belching from its deeps red clouds and raging
    fires.

Albion is sick; America faints. Enraged the zenith
    grew.
As human blood shooting its veins all round the orbed
    heaven
Red rose the clouds from the Atlantic in vast wheels of
    blood,
And in the red clouds rose a wonder o'er the Atlantic
    sea—
25 Intense, naked, a human fire, fierce glowing as the
    wedge
Of iron heated in the furnace. His terrible limbs were
    fire,
With myriads of cloudy terrors, banners dark and towers
Surrounded; heat but not light went through the
    murky atmosphere.

13. Albion's Angel, hearing their defiance, stands up to threaten the
Americans.
14. wrathful] The early, cancelled plate (see headnote) reads 'fiery'. But
Orc is 'fiery', and so the attribute is inappropriate.
Pl.4. Design: Text *19–28* on a bank of clouds. Above *19* a dragon follows
an aged figure who dives, sceptre in hand, through lightning towards the
waves at the foot. Beneath, a man, woman and child cower under a fallen
tree R. A wide space between *28* and *29*.
18–19. The design, which divides the text, makes the scene-change clear.
Attention shifts to mid-Atlantic, where Orc rises from the waves.

The King of England looking westward trembles at
the vision.

Pl. 5 Albion's Angel stood beside the Stone of Night, and
saw

31 The terror like a comet, or more like the planet red
That once enclosed the terrible wandering comets in
its sphere.
Then, Mars, thou wast our centre, and the planets
three flew round
Thy crimson disc; so ere the sun was rent from thy
red sphere.

35 The spectre glowed, his horrid length staining the
temple long
With beams of blood, and thus a voice came forth and
shook the temple:

Pl. 6 'The morning comes, the night decays, the watchmen
leave their stations;
The grave is burst, the spices shed, the linen wrapped
up;

29. *The King of England*] This is the only reference to George III himself
in the final text of *America* (but see pl.*b*, p. 206); like Washington and his
colleagues, he is out of his depth in this conflict.

Pl.5. *Design*: Text encircled above, L and beneath a 'judgment' sequence:
one figure carries scales, one casts a prisoner down, one (R) carries a great
sword. Bottom L, the condemned figure falls; centre, a serpent spirals
round him.

30. *the Stone of Night*] Cp. *Europe 102*; B. envisages a kind of pulpit, a
place of false authority.

34. *so ere the sun . . .*] i.e. 'so it was ere . . .' A fragment of myth not
developed elsewhere by B. This ends the extended simile of *31–4*.

35. *staining the temple long*] The temple has not been mentioned so far,
except by implication in the 'Stone of Night' *30*. B. has in mind such so-
called Druid temples of vast stones as Stonehenge and Avebury (q.v.
Europe 72n), whose influence for oppression and obscurity overspreads
Albion. *Spectre* is the favourite 'Gothic' word for an apparition, and is a
term yet undeveloped by B. See also the 'Chapel of Gold' poem, p. 146.

36. *a voice*] Orc's.

Pl.6. *Design*: Above the text, the 'resurrection' figure (as in *Marriage*,
pl.21), seated on a mound amid bones; he has awoken and looks upwards.
Beneath the text, lowly animal life–a frog, and a lizard catching a fly near
a wild plant.

37–8. Note the resurrection allusions (including the design) to Christ
leaving the tomb, the scattering of the spices which covered his body, the
discovery by the disciples of the linen clothes carefully wrapped up and
laid aside, and the departure of the guard to report.

The bones of death, the covering clay, the sinews
    shrunk and dried
40 Reviving shake, inspiring move, breathing,
    awakening,
Spring like redeemed captives when their bonds and
    bars are burst.
Let the slave grinding at the mill run out into the
    field;
Let him look up into the heavens and laugh in the
    bright air;
Let the enchained soul shut up in darkness and in
    sighing,
45 Whose face has never seen a smile in thirty weary
    years,
Rise and look out—his chains are loose, his dungeon
    doors are open.
And let his wife and children return from the
    oppressor's scourge—
They look behind at every step and believe it is a
    dream,
Singing, "The sun has left his blackness, and has
    found a fresher morning,
50 And the fair moon rejoices in the clear and cloudless
    night;
For empire is no more, and now the lion and wolf
    shall cease."'

Pl. 7   In thunders ends the voice. Then Albion's Angel
      wrathful burnt

39–40. The bones of death . . .] Cp. *Ezekiel* xxxvii 1–10, esp. vv. 7–8: 'There was a noise, and behold a shaking, and the bones came together, bone to his bone. And when I beheld, lo, the sinews and the flesh came up upon them, and the skin covered them above: but there was no breath in them.' B.'s bodies breathe and awake.
42. the slave grinding at the mill] Cp. *Judges* xvi 21, where Samson is bound and made to 'grind at the prison house': *Matthew* xxiv 41: 'two women shall be grinding at the mill; the one shall be taken and the other left': and *Samson Agonistes* 41: 'Eyeless in Gaza at the mill with slaves'.
mill] Here, as generally in B., a biblical word, implying slavery such as Samson's, grinding corn, rather than the mills of the Industrial Revolution, which B. scarcely knew.
51. Verse 20 of *A Song of Liberty.*
Pl.7. Design: A delicate tree L hangs over the text, its branches ending in catkins or similar flowers. Birds of paradise sit in the branches. Below, a ram and two children, asleep by a stream; the light of sunrise behind.

> Beside the Stone of Night; and, like the eternal lion's
>   howl
> In famine and war, replied: 'Art thou not Orc, who
>   serpent-formed
> 55 Stands at the gate of Enitharmon to devour her
>   children?
> Blasphemous demon, Antichrist, hater of dignities,
> Lover of wild rebellion and transgressor of God's law,
> Why dost thou come to Angels' eyes in this terrific
>   form?'
>
> Pl. 8 The terror answered: 'I am Orc, wreathed round the
>   accursed tree.
> 60 The times are ended, shadows pass, the morning 'gins
>   to break.
> The fiery joy, that Urizen perverted to ten commands

54. Orc, serpent-formed] A usual characteristic of Orc. But the image is two-sided, for the serpent may represent the admirable virility of the anti-tyrannical Satan, and the beauty of the serpent itself: or be itself a poisonous or constrictive creature.

55. Stands at the gate . . . children] Cp. *Revelation* xii 1–4, 'And there appeared a great wonder in heaven: a woman clothed with the sun, and the moon under her feet, and upon her head a crown of twelve stars: And she being with child cried, travailing in birth. . . . And behold a great red dragon . . . stood before the woman . . . for to devour her child as soon as it was born.' B. reverses the moral status of the woman and the dragon, who is Satan. Note the anatomical sense of *gate*.

57. transgressor of God's law] To Orc, and B., a virtue.

Pl.8. *Design*: Above the text: Urizen in his clouds, the sea beneath. Reproduced in Keynes: *W.B.'s Engravings*, pl.86.

59. wreathed round the accursed tree] The tree of the forbidden fruit in the Garden of Eden: in *Paradise Lost* Satan, disguised as the serpent, tells Eve that he had tasted the fruit and, to get at it (ix 589) 'About the mossy trunk I wound me soon'. In a Norse myth which B. certainly knew later in life and may have known in 1793, the mighty ash Yggdrasil supports the world, and a dragon gnaws one of its roots; but it is not 'accursed'.

60. times] A word commonly used in biblical apocalyptic literature when the writer is not willing to foretell exact dates. B. takes over the usage, though he often uses the word as if it meant a specific period.

61–3. Echoed in *A Song of Liberty 18, 20, Chorus* (which may have been composed later than this). The image of Moses leading the chosen people under the Law through the wilderness was very powerful to B. In *Urizen 513–16* Fuzon, this time hostile to Urizen, leads Urizen's children out of Egypt; in *Jerusalem* Exodus imagery is much used.

What night he led the starry hosts through the wide
    wilderness—
That stony law I stamp to dust, and scatter religion
    abroad
To the four winds as a torn book, and none shall
    gather the leaves;
65 But they shall rot on desert sands and consume in
    bottomless deeps
To make the deserts blossom and the deeps shrink to
    their fountains,
And to renew the fiery joy and burst the stony roof;
That pale religious lechery, seeking virginity,
May find it in a harlot, and in coarse-clad honesty
70 The undefiled, though ravished in her cradle night
    and morn.
For every thing that lives is holy, life delights in life,
Because the soul of sweet delight can never be defiled.
Fires enwrap the earthly globe, yet man is not
    consumed;
Amidst the lustful fires he walks; his feet become like
    brass,
75 His knees and thighs like silver and his breast and head
    like gold.'

Pl. 9 'Sound, sound, my loud war-trumpets and alarm my
    Thirteen Angels!
Loud howls the eternal wolf; the eternal lion lashes
    his tail.

66. *the deserts . . . the deeps*] The first echoes the well-known *Isaiah* xxxv 1:
'the desert shall rejoice, and blossom as the rose'. The second perhaps
alludes to *Revelation* xxi 1: 'and there was no more sea', but also to B.'s
normal dislike of the sea, which to him was a fearsome, devouring element.
68–71. These lines repeat ideas also found in *Visions 163–4, 215*, and *Song
of Liberty (Chorus)*.
72. Cp. *Visions 9–10* and *Marriage* Proverb 53 (p. 110).
74–5. From two incidents in *Daniel*: (a) Daniel's escape in Nebuchadnezzar's
furnace (iii 25–7); in the Bible this is God's deliverance from the destruc-
tive flames, but here Orc is at home in the fierceness of the 'lustful' ele-
ment: (b) *Daniel* ii 32–3; Daniel recalls the king's dream to him, reminding
him that he dreamt of an image, whose 'head was of fine gold, his breast
and arms of silver, his belly and his thighs of brass, his legs of iron, his feet
part of iron and part of clay'. There is no clay in Orc's substance.
Pl.9. *Design*: Little room for design: beneath, ears of wheat sweep over the
body of a child: reproduced in Keynes: *W.B.'s Engravings*, pl.87.
76ff. Albion's Angel does not address Orc again, but calls on his delegates
in America to rouse themselves on his behalf.

America is darkened, and my punishing demons
    terrified
Crouch howling before their caverns deep like skins
    dried in the wind.
80   They cannot smite the wheat, nor quench the fatness
    of the earth;
They cannot smite with sorrows, nor subdue the
    plough and spade;
They cannot wall the city, nor moat round the castle
    of princes;
They cannot bring the stubbed oak to overgrow the
    hills.
For terrible men stand on the shores, and in their robes
    I see
85   Children take shelter from the lightnings; there
    stands Washington
And Paine and Warren, with their foreheads reared
    toward the east.
But clouds obscure my aged sight. A vision from afar!
Sound, sound, my loud war-trumpets and alarm my
    Thirteen Angels.
Ah, vision from afar! Ah, rebel form that rent the
    ancient
90   Heavens, eternal viper self-renewed, rolling in clouds!
I see thee in thick clouds and darkness on America's
    shore,
Writhing in pangs of abhorred birth. Red flames the.
    crest rebellious
And eyes of death. The harlot womb oft opened in
    vain
Heaves in enormous circles; now the times are returned
    upon thee,
95   Devourer of thy parent, now thy unutterable torment
    renews.
Sound, sound, my loud war-trumpet and alarm my
    Thirteen Angels!

80–3. They cannot smite...] The Angel's work is destruction, and his
minions cannot carry it out.

82–3. wall ... moat ... stubbed oak] All these represent either war or
domination, or both. The *oak* was sacred to the Druids, who worshipped
in oak groves; to B. the Druids were the aboriginal oppressive priests
(cp. *Europe 72n*). From the oak warships were made.

90. viper self-renewed] The snake renews itself when it sloughs its skin. B.
again (as in *31–4*) hints at a myth which he does not develop.

Ah, terrible birth! A young one bursting! Where is
    the weeping mouth?
And where the mother's milk? Instead those
    ever-hissing jaws
And parched lips drop with fresh gore. Now roll
    thou in the clouds!
100   Thy mother lays her length outstretched upon the
    shore beneath.
Sound, sound, my loud war-trumpets and alarm my
    Thirteen Angels!
Loud howls the eternal wolf; the eternal lion lashes
    his tail.'
Pl. 10 Thus wept the angel voice, and as he wept the terrible
    blasts
Of trumpets blew a loud alarm across the Atlantic
    deep.
105   No trumpets answer, no reply of clarions or of fifes.
Silent the Colonies remain and refuse the loud alarm.
On those vast shady hills between America and
    Albion's shore,
Now barred out by the Atlantic sea, called Atlantean
    hills,
Because from their bright summits you may pass to
    the golden world,
110   An ancient palace, archetype of mighty emperies,
Rears its immortal pinnacles, built in the forest of God
By Ariston, the king of beauty, for his stolen bride.

97–8. the weeping mouth . . . the mother's milk] Orc (*19–28*) was born from a
womb of clouds and flame, not a 'human' mother. *Thy mother* (*100*) is
usually Enitharmon (see *55n, Europe* 'Prel.'). Orc is seen, now as a youth,
now as a serpent.

Pl.10. *Design*: Orc amidst his flames, which rise round text and between
lines *106–7*. In Keynes, *W.B.'s Engravings* pl.88.

108. Atlantean hills] Atlantis was said to have been drowned by the Atlantic;
to B. the fabled land is always a beautiful land, and the sea, particularly the
Atlantic, an evil, destructive element (cp. *66n*). There was a Neo-Platonic
idea that Atlantis was one of the highest points on earth; B. echoes this in
109.

110. emperies] A 'poetic word' evoking the richness of ancient empires and
not, for once, their inhumanity.

112. Ariston] A shadowy figure. Ariston, King of Sparta, obtained by deceit
as his third wife th̄ beautiful wife of a friend, according to Herodotus
(*History* ii: 61ff), where B. could find the story. He does not develop it or
the figure of Ariston, (but see the rejected *Vala* fragment, p. 466). Plato, in
the *Critias*, says that Poseidon, lord of Atlantis, stole a mortal bride.

Here on their magic seats the Thirteen Angels sat
    perturbed,
For clouds from the Atlantic hover o'er the solemn
    roof.

Pl. 11 Fiery the Angels rose, and as they rose deep thunder
    rolled
116 Around their shores, indignant burning with the fires
    of Orc;
And Boston's Angel cried aloud as they flew through
    the dark night.

He cried: 'Why trembles honesty, and like a
    murderer
Why seeks he refuge from the frowns of his immortal
    station?
120 Must the generous tremble and leave his joy to the idle,
    to the pestilence,
That mock him? Who commanded this? What God?
    What angel?
To keep the generous from experience, till the
    ungenerous
Are unrestrained performers of the energies of nature;
Till pity is become a trade, and generosity a science
125 That men get rich by, and the sandy desert is given to
    the strong.
What God is he, writes laws of peace and clothes him
    in the tempest?
What pitying Angel lusts for tears, and fans himself
    with sighs?
What crawling villain preaches abstinence and wraps
    himself
In fat of lambs? No more I follow, no more obedience
    pay!'

113. the Thirteen Angels] The guardian spirits of the thirteen colonies, counterparts of Albion's Angel. From now on they, rather than Washington and his companions, are the symbols of the colonies in revolt.

Pl.11. Design: The plate is designed as a starry night scene, with the text in two blocks upon it; three lines at the top and the rest in the middle, leaving a wide margin L. Clouds and stars surround the text; a male figure (Boston's Angel?) rides on a flying swan between *118* and *119*: at the foot, three children ride on a snake. In Keynes, *W.B.'s Engravings* pl.89.

117. Boston's Angel] Boston was a town eminent in the opposition to the London government.

128. B. denounces the increasing moral propaganda of the Anglican establishment.

Pl. 12 So cried he, rending off his robe and throwing down
            his sceptre
131   In sight of Albion's Guardian; and all the Thirteen
            Angels
         Rent off their robes to the hungry wind and threw
            their golden sceptres
         Down on the land of America. Indignant they
            descended
         Headlong from out their heavenly heights, descending
            swift as fires
135   Over the land. Naked and flaming are their lineaments
            seen
         In the deep gloom. By Washington and Paine and
            Warren they stood,
         And the flame folded roaring fierce within the pitchy
            night
         Before the demon red, who burnt towards America,
         In black smoke, thunders and loud winds, rejoicing
            in its terror,
140   Breaking in smoky wreaths from the wild deep, and
            gathering thick
         In flames as of a furnace on the land from north to
            south.

Pl. 13 What time the thirteen Governors that England sent
            convene
         In Bernard's house, the flames covered the land.
            They rouse, they cry,
         Shaking their mental chains they rush in fury to the
            sea
145   To quench their anguish; at the feet of Washington
            down fallen,

Pl.12 *Design*: Around the text, Death's stone door: an old man on crutches
enters it, and an ancient tree grows above it and overhangs the text.
138. the demon red] Orc; the flames (as commonly in B.) revitalize the land.
B. often uses *towards* to signify a gesture of recognition–e.g. *Visions 2.*
Pl.13 *Design*: The sea: above, the shore, and an eagle descending on a
female body. Roots and weed L reach down to the seashore, where fish
come to a male body.
143. Bernard's house] Sir Francis Bernard (1712–79) was Governor of
Massachusetts Bay from 1760 to 1771. This meeting seems to be B.'s
invention.
144. Shaking their mental chains] They shake their chains (chains of the
mind, and seen in the mind–but all the more real for that) but, in spite of
their anguish, do not throw them off.

They grovel on the sand and writhing lie, while all
The British soldiers through the thirteen states sent
   up a howl
Of anguish, threw their swords and muskets to the
   earth and ran
From their encampments and dark castles, seeking
   where to hide
150 From the grim flames and from the visions of Orc;
   in sight
Of Albion's Angel, who enraged his secret clouds
   opened
From north to south, and burnt outstretched on wings
   of wrath, covering
The eastern sky, spreading his awful wings across the
   heavens;
Beneath him rolled his numerous hosts—all Albion's
   Angels camped
155 Darkened the Atlantic mountains, and their trumpets
   shook the valleys,
Armed with diseases of the earth to cast upon the
   abyss,
Their numbers forty millions, mustering in the
   eastern sky.

Pl. 14 In the flames stood and viewed the armies drawn out
   in the sky
Washington, Franklin, Paine and Warren, Allen,
   Gates and Lee,
160 And heard the voice of Albion's Angel give the
   thunderous command.

147. *the British soliders*] An imaginative vision. B. does not mean that the
Loyalist troops panicked at the outset of the war. He invents the incident
to illustrate Orc's power and the inevitable defeat of the army.

Pl.14. *Design*: Between *166* and *167* an ancient tree, roots down margin
and branches up it: a branch overhangs a figure who sits with a serpent and
teaches a youth. Beneath the text, a fire-breathing serpent. In Keynes,
W.B.'s Engravings pl.90.

160–73. B. alludes to *Paradise Lost* vi 834–9: 'Full soon / Among them he
arrived, in his right hand / Grasping ten thousand thunders, which he
sent / Before him, such as in their souls infixed / Plagues. They, astonished,
all resistance lost, / All courage; down their idle weapons dropped . . .'
Thus Albion's Angel, emissary of a tyrant king, takes the place of Milton's
Messiah, emissary of Jehovah. Both are armed with plagues, which over-
whelm their defiant opponents: but while in Milton Satan's forces are
routed, in B. Orc retaliates effectively.

8 + B.

His plagues, obedient to his voice, flew forth out of
    their clouds,
Falling upon America, as a storm to cut them off,
As a blight cuts the tender corn when it begins to
    appear.
Dark is the heaven above, and cold and hard the earth
    beneath;
165 And as a plague-wind filled with insects cuts off
    man and beast,
And as a sea o'erwhelms a land in the day of an
    earthquake,

Fury, rage, madness, in a wind swept through
    America,
And the red flames of Orc that folded roaring fierce
    around
The angry shores, and the fierce rushing of the
    inhabitants together.
170 The citizens of New York close their books and lock
    their chests;
The mariners of Boston drop their anchors and
    unlade;
The scribe of Pennsylvania casts his pen upon the
    earth;
The builder of Virginia throws his hammer down in
    fear.

Then had America been lost, o'erwhelmed by the
    Atlantic,
175 And earth had lost another portion of the infinite.
But all rush together in the night, in wrath and
    raging fire;
The red fires raged, the plagues recoiled, then rolled
    they back with fury
Pl. 15 On Albion's angels; then the pestilence began in
    streaks of red
Across the limbs of Albion's Guardian, the spotted
    plague smote Bristol's
180 And the leprosy London's Spirit, sickening all their
    bands.

175. another portion] Besides Atlantis (*108n*).
Pl.15. Design: Below and in margin, figures representing vitality and life:
figures encircled with flames; a bunch of grapes; a flower reaching up-
wards from the ground.
179. Bristol] At this time one of Britain's major cities, selected because of
its importance in American trade.

The millions sent up a howl of anguish and threw off
　　their hammered mail,
And cast their swords and spears to earth, and stood a
　　naked multitude.
Albion's Guardian writhed in torment on the eastern
　　sky.
Pale, quivering toward the brain his glimmering eyes,
　　teeth chattering,
185 Howling and shuddering, his legs quivering, convulsed
　　each muscle and sinew,
Sickening lay London's Guardian and the ancient
　　mitred York,
Their heads on snowy hills, their ensigns sickening in
　　the sky.
The plagues creep on the burning winds, driven by
　　flames of Orc,
And by the fierce Americans rushing together in the
　　night,
190 Driven o'er the guardians of Ireland and Scotland
　　and Wales.
They, spotted with plagues forsook the frontiers, and
　　their banners seared
With fires of hell deform their ancient heavens with
　　shame and woe.
Hid in his caves the Bard of Albion felt the enormous
　　plagues,
And a cowl of flesh grew o'er his head and scales on his
　　back and ribs;
195 And rough with black scales all his angels fright their
　　ancient heavens.
The doors of marriage are open, and the priests in
　　rustling scales

181. The millions] In contrast to the thirteen governors (*144*) the masses
throw off the armour given them to serve Albion's Angel in. B. expresses
his hope that 'the millions' will respond to the new vision.
193. the Bard of Albion] An obscure reference, probably not intended to
reflect any particular event. The poet laureate 1757–85 was William White-
head; after him, Thomas Warton until 1790, and then until 1813 Henry
James Pye, an indifferent poet who got the post by Pitt's influence. This
passage may be wishful thinking; or B.'s opinion of laureate verse.
196–203. The doors of marriage are open] The revolution brings social as well
as political freedom; B. could never separate different manifestations of the
same principle. Marriage is here seen as a restriction on human freedom
by priestly oppressors.

Rush into reptile coverts, hiding from the fires of Orc
That play around the golden roofs in wreaths of fierce
        desire,
Leaving the females naked and glowing with the lusts
        of youth.

200   For the female spirits of the dead, pining in bonds of
        religion,
Run from their fetters reddening, and in long drawn
        arches sitting
They feel the nerves of youth renew, and desires of
        ancient times
Over their pale limbs as a vine when the tender grape
        appears.

Pl. 16 Over the hills, the vales, the cities, rage the red
        flames fierce;
205   The heavens melted from north to south; and Urizen,
        who sat
Above all heavens in thunders wrapped, emerged his
        leprous head
From out his holy shrine, his tears in deluge piteous
Falling into the deep sublime. Flagged with grey-
        browed snows
And thunderous visages, his jealous wings waved over
        the deep;
210   Weeping in dismal howling woe he dark descended,
        howling
Around the smitten bands, clothed in tears and
        trembling, shuddering cold.
His stored snows he poured forth, and his icy
        magazines
He opened on the deep, and on the Atlantic sea,
        white, shivering.
Leprous his limbs, all over white, and hoary was his
        visage,

201. *in long-drawn arches sitting*] An image of church-bound women.
203. *a vine . . . appears*] Cp. *Song of Songs* ii 13: 'The vines with the tender grape give forth a good smell'.
Pl.16. *Design*: Above, a gowned, suppliant female figure, with tiny human figures on it. Twisted trees behind. Beneath, the word FINIS woven into a twisted mass of thorns, flowers, and a serpent.
205. *Urizen*] His first appearance in action in B.'s poetry (cp. the allusion in *Visions 114*). His servant, Albion's Angel, has failed, and he must act for himself.
208–9. Cp. *A Song of Liberty 9*.

215 Weeping in dismal howlings before the stern
    Americans,
Hiding the demon red with clouds and cold mists from
    the earth—
Till angels and weak men twelve years should govern
    o'er the strong,
And then their end should come, when France
    received the demon's light.

Stiff shudderings shook the heavenly thrones. France,
    Spain and Italy
220 In terror viewed the bands of Albion and the ancient
    guardians
Fainting upon the elements, smitten with their own
    plagues.
They slow advance to shut the five gates of their
    law-built heaven,
Filled with blasting fancies and with mildews of
    despair,
With fierce disease and lust unable to stem the fires
    of Orc;
225 But the five gates were consumed, and their bolts and
    hinges melted,
And the fierce flames burnt round the heavens and
    round the abodes of men.

Finis

217. *twelve years*] A difficult period to calculate. The years from the American victory at Yorktown (1781) to the end of the rule of 'weak men' with Louis XVI's execution in Jan. 1793 are probably meant.
222. *the five gates*] The gates of the five senses, which limit man's appreciation of infinity. This revolution is an Armageddon–a new vision and a new life will follow.
223. *blasting and mildew*] In *Deuteronomy* xxviii, among the curses which will befall the nation of Israel if they are disobedient; verses 21–2: 'The Lord shall make the pestilence cleave unto thee. . . . The Lord shall smite thee with a consumption, and with a fever, and with an inflammation, and with an extreme burning, and with the sword, and with blasting, and with mildew; and they shall pursue thee until thou perish.'

Cancelled Plates

Of the three plates, *a* is almost identical with pl.3 of the *Prophecy*, but (i) the names in *4* are arranged differently; (ii) *14* has *fiery* instead of *wrathful*; (iii) *16* has *fierce* instead of *red*. There are also one or two minor differences in punctuation. But *a* runs on to *b*, which is quite different from pl.4; for a suggested reason, see headnote, p. 187. There is a further fragment, *d*, found in two copies of a collection of designs; it has been printed from the bottom half of a plate of the same width and style of lettering as *America*, but the text has been covered by pigment. The last line might be the end of a poem, the awakening from a dream or vision.

The alterations in *c* have generally changed words with approved connotations to others connoting gloom and evil. They are written on the page in pencil and are all incorporated here in a modernized text.

b

　　Reveal the dragon through the human, coursing swift as fire
　　To the close hall of counsel, where his angel form renews.

　　In a sweet vale sheltered with cedars, that eternal stretch
　　Their unmoved branches, stood the hall built when the
　　　　moon shot forth—
5　　In that dread night when Urizen called the stars round his
　　　　feet,
　　Then burst the centre from its orb and found a place beneath,
　　And earth, conglobed, in narrow room rolled round its
　　　　sulphur sun.

　　To this deep valley situated by the flowing Thames,
　　Where George the Third holds council, and his Lords and
　　　　Commons meet,
10　　Shut out from mortal sight the Angel came. The vale was
　　　　dark
　　With clouds of smoke from the Atlantic, that in volumes
　　　　rolled
　　Between the mountains; dismal visions mope around the
　　　　house.

　　On chairs of iron, canopied with mystic ornaments
　　Of life by magic power condensed, infernal forms art-bound,
15　　The council sat; all rose before the aged apparition.
　　His snowy beard that streams like lambent flames down his
　　　　wide breast
　　Wetting with tears, and his white garments cast a wintry
　　　　light.

　　Then as armed clouds arise terrific round the northern
　　　　drum,
　　The world is silent at the flapping of the folding banners.
20　　So still terrors rent the house: as when the solemn globe
　　Launched to the unknown shore, while Sotha held the
　　　　northern helm,
　　Till to that void it came and fell; so the dark house was rent,
　　The valley moved beneath; its shining pillars split in twain,
　　And its roofs crack across down-falling on the angelic seats.

c

Then *Albion's Angel rose* resolved to the cave of armoury:
His shield, that bound twelve demons and their cities in its orb
He took down from its trembling pillar; from its cavern deep
His helm was brought by London's Guardian, and his thirsty
    spear
5 By the wise spirit of London's river. Silent stood the King
    breathing damp mists,
And on his aged limbs they clasped the armour of terrible
    gold.
Infinite London's awful spires cast a dreadful cold
Even on rational things beneath, and from the palace walls
Around Saint James's chill and heavy, even to the city gate.

10 On the vast stone whose name is Truth he stood, his cloudy
    shield
Smote with his sceptre: the scale-bound orb loud howled;
    the ancient pillar
Trembling sunk, an earthquake rolled along the mossy pile.

In glittering armour, swift as winds, intelligent as clouds,
Four winged heralds mount the furious blasts and blow their
    trumps;
15 Gold, silver, brass and iron clangours clamouring rend the
    shores.
Like white clouds rising from the deeps, his fifty-two armies
From the four cliffs of Albion rise, mustering around the
    Prince;
Angels of cities and of parishes and villages and families,
In armour as the nerves of wisdom, each his station holds.
20 In opposition dire a warlike cloud the myriads stood
In the red air before the Demon—*seen even by mortal men,*
Who call it fancy, or shut the gates of sense and in their chambers
Sleep like the dead. But like a constellation risen and blazing
Over the rugged ocean, so the angels of Albion hung,
25 A frowning shadow, like an aged king in arms of gold,
Who wept over a den, in which his only son outstretched
By rebels' hands was slain; his white beard waved in the
    wild wind.

On mountains and cliffs of snow the awful apparition
    hovered;
And like the voices of religious dead, heard in the mountains,
30 When holy zeal scents the sweet valleys of ripe virgin bliss,
Such was the hollow voice that o'er America lamented.

Pl.*c 1. Then . . . rose*] Del.; but the replacing words are now cut away.
c 2–3. Marked 6 and 7, but the four lines to be inserted above them are now
cut away. So also words to be added after *5.*
c 5. damp mists] *1st rdg del.* with flames: *2nd rdg del.* hoar frosts.
c 6. aged] *1st rdg del.* shining.

c 7. cold] *1st rdg del.* gleam.
c 9. chill and heavy] *1st rdg del.* glow the fires: *2nd rdg del.* till by the freeze.
c 11. ancient] *1st rdg del.* eternal.
c 13. clouds] *1st rdg del.* flames.
c 15. clangours] *1st rdg del.* ardours.
c 17. mustering] *1st rdg del.* glowing.
c 19. holds] *1st rdg del.* fires.
c 21–3. The italicized matter was del. and not replaced.
c 25. a frowning . . . King] *1st rdg.* Over the frowning shadow, like a King.
c 31. America] *1st rdg del.* the red Demon.

Fragment d

As when a dream of Thiralatha flies the midnight hour,
In vain the dreamer grasps the joyful images; they fly
Seen in obscured traces in the Vale of Leutha. So
The British Colonies beneath the woeful princes fade.
And so the princes fade from earth, scarce seen by souls of
    men:
But, though obscured, this is the form of the angelic land.

13 Songs of Experience

The *Songs of Innocence* developed from a pastoral convention of children's
verse which B. at first sight seems to have accepted, not only in its form, but
also largely in its ideas, although with a sophistication of Swedenborgian-
ism that Coleridge recognized (letter to C. A. Tulk, 12 Feb. 1818). Even as
early as *Songs of Innocence*, however, his ideas and beliefs were quite radical–
there are already signs of this in such poems as 'The Schoolboy' and 'The
Voice of the Ancient Bard' in *Innocence*. The *Songs of Experience* arise from
a desire to set the adult experience of real life against the innocent pre-
suppositions of children who have not experienced it–and against the less
innocent indoctrination they receive from their parents. The collection is
therefore largely in parallel with the *Songs of Innocence*, each of these poems
having a poem in *Innocence* to which it is more or less closely related.
Whereas B. issued *Innocence* alone, and continued to do so for many
years, he only issued *Experience* in the combined volume *Songs of Innocence
and of Experience*. It is dated 1794 on its combined titlepage; in a prospectus
of 10 Oct. 1793 the two collections are given as separate volumes of
twenty-five designs each, priced at five shillings. But perhaps B. anticipated
himself in this prospectus, and decided, when he actually came to the
binding, to attach *Experience* firmly to *Innocence*. Thus the two 'Nurse's
Songs' are verbally very similar, whereas the poems on the 'Little Boy
Lost' are only connected by the title–and by the ironic contrast of their
subject-matter, the notion of God.

The *Songs of Experience* are unusual in B. in that we possess a corrected MS or fair copies of almost all the poems in his Notebook (included pp. 143ff even where identical), where they are mixed with many more poems and fragments of the same date which were not used in this collection. Many of these do not parallel *Innocence* at all, and B. included some of these independent poems in *Experience*. Of the poems which make up *Experience*, only the 'Introduction', 'Ah, Sunflower', 'A Little Girl Lost' and 'To Tirzah' (a very much later poem) are not found in the NB. The order printed here is that of the MS, except that 'Earth's Answer', which follows 'Infant Sorrow' in the MS, is in its inevitable place following the Introduction, to which it is a sequel (though the Introduction was probably written later – would which explain some of its obscurities).

The themes of *Experience* are those of the period in which B. wrote *Marriage*, *Visions* and *America*: tyranny, by brutality or deceit, the lack of freedom and openness in love, and enslavement, especially of children.

A complete facsimile was published in 1967, ed G. L. Keynes.

SONGS of *INNOCENCE* and of *EXPERIENCE*
Showing the Two Contrary States of the Human Soul

[*Frontispiece*]

I INTRODUCTION

Hear the voice of the bard,
Who present, past, and future sees—
Whose ears have heard
The Holy Word
5   That walked among the ancient trees,

Calling the lapsed soul
And weeping in the evening dew—

Frontispiece. The shepherd of the frontispiece to *Innocence* has caught the winged child and set him firmly on his head, holding the child's arms so that he cannot fly away.

i *1*. This bard (i.e. Blake) has heard B.'s oppressive tyrant-father-god, who produces a 'Holy Word' to bully mankind.

i *5. walked*] As Adam and Eve 'heard the voice of the Lord God walking in the garden in the cool of the day' (*Genesis* iii 8).

i *6. lapsed soul*] *lapsèd* in two syllables; the soul that has 'fallen into sin', that has fallen away from the joy of Heaven. The Creator thinks the Fall is due to 'sin'; it is actually due to his own insistence on the restricted visions and values of a law-governed creation.

8*

That might control
The starry pole

10 And fallen, fallen light renew.

O Earth, O Earth, return!
Arise from out the dewy grass!
Night is worn,
And the morn

15 Rises from the slumberous mass.

Turn away no more.
Why wilt thou turn away?
The starry floor,
The watery shore

20 Is given thee till the break of day.

II EARTH'S ANSWER

Earth raised up her head
From the darkness dread and drear.
Her light fled
(Stony dread!)

5 And her locks covered with grey despair.

'Prisoned on watery shore,
Starry jealousy does keep my den;
Cold and hoar,
Weeping o'er,

10 I hear the Father of the ancient men.

'Selfish Father of men!
Cruel jealous selfish fear!
Can delight
Chained in night

15 The virgins of youth and morning bear?

'Does spring hide its joy
When buds and blossoms grow?

i 8. *that might control*] i.e. 'the Holy Word, that walked . . .' and 'that
might control. . . .'
i *18–20.* The joys offered are illusory. Blessing is not to be found 'on the
starry floor' and 'the watery shore'–the lands of night. The images are
similar to those of *Europe*, where Los and Enitharmon rejoice and feast in a
night which is only apparently endless.
ii. Cp. *Visions 114–17*; and draft (p. 153).
ii *13–15.* i.e. 'can innocent, free, youthful beings know delight when they
are chained in night?' The subject of the sentence is *virgins*.

Does the sower
Sow by night,
20 Or the ploughman in darkness plough?

'Break this heavy chain
That does freeze my bones around.
Selfish, vain,
Eternal bane—
25 That free love with bondage bound.'

III MY PRETTY ROSE-TREE

A flower was offered to me,
Such a flower as May never bore;
But I said, 'I've a pretty rose-tree,'
And I passed the sweet flower o'er.

5 Then I went to my pretty rose-tree,
To tend her by day and by night;
But my rose turned away with jealousy,
And her thorns were my only delight.

IV THE CLOD AND THE PEBBLE

'Love seeketh not itself to please,
Nor for itself hath any care,
But for another gives its ease
And builds a Heaven in Hell's despair.'

5 So sang a little clod of clay,
Trodden with the cattle's feet;
But a pebble of the brook
Warbled out these metres meet:

'Love seeketh only self to please,
10 To bind another to its delight,
Joys in another's loss of ease,
And builds a Hell in Heaven's despite.'

iii. It has been suggested that the poem is autobiographical, and concerns the behaviour of Catherine, B.'s wife, when he refused another woman's advances; but there is no direct evidence for this beyond the poem itself. The suggestion is plausible, but it is always possible that this an an impersonal lyrist's 'I'. The allegory, however, explains itself.

iii. *Design*: Beneath the text two figures, a woman sleeping under a tree, the man opposite her bowed in dejection. This poem is engraved on the same plate as 'Ah, Sunflower' (p. 221) and 'The Lily' (p. 214).

iv. *Design*: Above the text, cattle and sheep drinking at a brook; beneath it, a duck, and two frogs on the edge of the water.

See draft, p. 145.

V THE GARDEN OF LOVE

I went to the garden of love,
And saw what I never had seen:
A chapel was built in the midst,
Where I used to play on the green.

5   And the gates of this chapel were shut,
And *Thou shalt not* writ over the door;
So I turned to the garden of love,
That so many sweet flowers bore,

And I saw it was filled with graves,
10   And tomb-stones where flowers should be—
And priests in black gowns were walking their rounds,
And binding with briars my joys and desires.

VI A POISON TREE

I was angry with my friend;
I told my wrath, my wrath did end.
I was angry with my foe;
I told it not, my wrath did grow.

5   And I watered it in fears,
Night and morning with my tears;
And I sunned it with smiles,
And with soft deceitful wiles.

And it grew both day and night
10   Till it bore an apple bright—

v. See draft, p. 146, and the 'Chapel of Gold' poem which follows it in
the NB. The chapel is built by the priests, who wish to contain the true
joys of life, and to keep the key in their own power. Above the text, a
priest in monk's robes, with shaven head, kneels with his prayer-book, and
young people kneel behind him.

v 6. Cp. *Europe 134*. The reference is to *Deuteronomy* vi 8–9: 'And these
words, which I command thee this day, shall be in thine heart. . . . And
thou shalt write them upon the posts of thy house, and on thy gates'.

v 11. *gowns*] Pronounced *gownds* in 18th-century Cockney (see p. 146).

v 12. *binding*] As gardeners bind plants to sticks to make them upright.

vi. *Design*: Beneath the text, an outstretched, supine figure under a bare,
rugged tree. Apart from its stark force, this poem is interesting in the light
it throws on B.'s feelings of horror about trees, especially–as the designs
suggest–leafless trees. He probably felt a sentient power and latent life in
what is to most people an almost inanimate object. In the NB draft (p. 149),
the poem is entitled 'Christian Forbearance'.

vi 9. *And it grew*] Cp. *Ahania 102, 109*: *Four Zoas* viia *31*ff: *Jerusalem*
pl.*28.14*.

And my foe beheld it shine.
And he knew that it was mine,

And into my garden stole,
When the night had veiled the pole.
15   In the morning glad I see
My foe outstretched beneath the tree.

VII INFANT SORROW

My mother groaned, my father wept—
Into the dangerous world I leapt,
Helpless, naked, piping loud,
Like a fiend hid in a cloud.

5   Struggling in my father's hands,
Striving against my swaddling bands,
Bound and weary, I thought best
To sulk upon my mother's breast.

VIII LONDON

I wander through each chartered street
Near where the chartered Thames does flow,
And mark in every face I meet
Marks of weakness, marks of woe.

5   In every cry of every man,
In every infant's cry of fear,

vii. The contrary poem to 'Infant Joy', in *Innocence* (p. 55); see draft on p. 150.

vii. *Design*: Beneath the text, a mother leans forward to take hold of her child who is reaching upwards and away from her out of his cradle.

vii 7. The child prefers his mother's soft rule to his father's sternness—and so the woman's power is greater.

viii. See draft on p. 154.

viii. *Designs*: Above the poem, a child leads an old blind man, who leans on sticks, along a drab street. Beside sts 2 and 3, a child warms himself by a wood fire.

viii 1. *chartered*] Like all ancient cities, London is proud of its charters, through which it holds certain liberties and privileges—and which once represented its source of freedom. But these charters have not granted liberty or privilege to most of the city's people. There may also be a hint of the meaning of *charter* as a form of *hire* (recorded by the OED only from 1806, but likely to have been in use earlier).

In every voice, in every ban,
The mind-forged manacles I hear—
How the chimney-sweeper's cry
10   Every blackening church appalls,
And the hapless soldier's sigh
Runs in blood down palace walls;
But most through midnight streets I hear
How the youthful harlot's curse
15   Blasts the new-born infant's tear
And blights with plagues the marriage hearse.

IX THE LILY

The modest rose puts forth a thorn,
The humble sheep a threatening horn,
While the lily white shall in love delight,
Nor a thorn nor a threat stain her beauty bright.

X NURSE'S SONG

When the voices of children are heard on the green,
And whisperings are in the dale,
The days of my youth rise fresh in my mind,
My face turns green and pale.
5   Then come home, my children, the sun is gone down
And the dews of night arise;
Your spring and your day are wasted in play,
And your winter and night in disguise.

XI THE TIGER

Tiger, tiger, burning bright
In the forests of the night,
What immortal hand or eye
Could frame thy fearful symmetry?

viii 7. *ban*] A public prohibition; here chiefly an angry swear-word (*OED*, *ban* III 6).
viii 8. *mind-forged*] The phrase 'german-forged', suggesting the strength of skilled workmanship (see draft, p. 154), is replaced by this, emphasizing that the fetters are not inevitable, but created in the twisted minds both of the oppressor and of the sufferer who accepts the chains. Perhaps originally an allusion to the German tyranny of the Hanoverian dynasty, or the German mercenaries they employed.
ix. The rose is a traditional symbol of love, the lily of purity. B. says that true purity does not repulse or torment lovers. See no. iii *n* (*design*).
x. See draft, p. 155, and the contrary in *Innocence*, p. 59.
x. *Design*: A doorway framed in grape-clustered vines: a woman combs a youth's hair; behind, a girl sits reading

5   In what distant deeps or skies
     Burnt the fire of thine eyes?
     On what wings dare he aspire?
     What the hand dare seize the fire?

     And what shoulder and what art
10   Could twist the sinews of thy heart?
     And when thy heart began to beat,
     What dread hand? And what dread feet?

     What the hammer? What the chain?
     In what furnace was thy brain?
15   What the anvil? What dread grasp
     Dare its deadly terrors clasp?

     When the stars threw down their spears
     And watered Heaven with their tears,
     Did he smile his work to see?
20   Did he who made the Lamb make thee?

     Tiger, tiger, burning bright
     In the forests of the night,
     What immortal hand or eye
     Dare frame thy fearful symmetry?

xi. See draft, p. 156, and details of composition in the appendix (p. 170).
This is the contrary poem to 'The Lamb' in *Innocence* (p. 65).
xi 5. *deeps or skies*] The spaces of primal, unformed creation–in *Genesis* i 2
'darkness was upon the face of the deep' over which the Spirit moved;
and soon the deep was divided into heaven above and deep beneath.
xi *12*. In the first stage of composition, the sentence continued: 'Could
fetch it from the furnace deep' (p. 170), but this was cancelled, and the line
remains in the air. In one copy B. altered this line to 'What dread hand
formed thy dread feet?' In a printed version it appears, very likely with
B.'s approval, as '. . . forged thy . . .'. But, though the anomaly may have
bothered B., he did not change the plate. See p. 172*n*.
xi *17–20*. A famous stanza which has produced many interpretations. The
stars have been said to throw down their spears in fear, or rebellion, or
allegiance. *Four Zoas* v *224*, 'the stars threw down their spears and fled
naked away' shows that when B. recalled the phrase some years later it
implied to him an act of horror and rejection by the starry spirits. Much
ink has been spilt in answering the question in *20*–surely a futile activity,
since the question is clearly rhetorical. B. is not asking for an answer, but
in question form presenting the paradox, that lamb and tiger visibly
exist in the same creation.
xi *20. Lamb*] B. often capitalized words; but as NB has 'lamb' here, the
change seems to be a deliberate allusion to 'the Lamb of God'.

XII THE HUMAN ABSTRACT

Pity would be no more,
If we did not make somebody poor;
And mercy no more could be,
If all were as happy as we;

5 And mutual fear brings peace,
Till the selfish loves increase.
Then cruelty knits a snare
And spreads his baits with care.

He sits down with holy fears
10 And waters the ground with tears;
Then humility takes its root
Underneath his foot.

Soon spreads the dismal shade
Of mystery over his head;
15 And the caterpillar and fly
Feed on the mystery;

And it bears the fruit of deceit,
Ruddy and sweet to eat,
And the raven his nest has made
20 In its thickest shade.

The gods of the earth and sea
Sought through nature to find this tree.
But their search was all in vain—
There grows one in the human brain.

XIII THE SICK ROSE

O rose, thou art sick:
The invisible worm
That flies in the night,
In the howling storm,

xii. Cp. draft, p. 157: in NB entitled 'The Human Image'. Contrary of
'The Divine Image' in *Innocence* (p. 69): *Human* here means *mortal*, a
creature of the material world; an *abstraction* is an unreality, the opposite
of the definiteness of an image, which can take a divine form. Cp. also 'A
Divine Image' (p. 143).

xii 7-20. Cp. *Ahania 102*ff, and 'A Poison Tree' (p. 212). This is the first
appearance in B.'s published works of the Tree of Mystery which grows
monstrously and inescapably, and overwhelms its unwitting creator. Here
the image runs away with B.'s imagination and distracts his pursuit of the
poem, as set out in st. 1.

xii. *Design*: At the foot of the text, an aged man struggles with a net that
has caught him under a tree.

5   Has found out thy bed
       Of crimson joy;
       And his dark secret love
       Does thy life destroy.

XIV A LITTLE BOY LOST

       'Nought loves another as itself
       Nor venerates another so,
       Nor is it possible to thought
       A greater than itself to know.

5   'And, father, how can I love you
       Or any of my brothers more?
       I love you like the little bird
       That picks up crumbs around the door.'

       The priest sat by and heard the child;
10   In trembling zeal he seized his hair;
       He led him by his little coat,
       And all admired the priestly care.

       And standing on the altar high,
       'Lo what a fiend is here!' said he.
15   'One who sets reason up for judge
       Of our most holy mystery.'

       The weeping child could not be heard;
       The weeping parents wept in vain—
       They stripped him to his little shirt
20   And bound him in an iron chain,

       And burned him in a holy place,
       Where many had been burned before.

xiii. Contrary of 'The Blossom', in *Innocence* (p. 64). The design shows a rose, fully blown yet closed, drooping over, round and beneath the text; a caterpillar eats one of its leaves, and a spirit tries to escape from its closed blossom. The stem is very thorny. Reproduced in A. Blunt, *Art of W.B.* Cp. 'The Garden of Love' (p. 212), and draft, p. 159.

xiv. Contrary of the pair 'The Little Boy Lost' and 'Found' in *Innocence*, p. 66. Cp. also 'On Another's Sorrow', p. 61: and Watts's lines 'On Obedience to Parents': 'Have ye not heard what dreadful plagues / Are threatened by the Lord, / To him that breaks his father's law / Or mocks his mother's word? / What heavy guilt upon him lies, / How cursed is his name! / The ravens shall pick out his eyes, / And eagles eat the same.'

xiv 15. *reason*] B. is often said to be the enemy of reason; it would be better to say, 'of rationalism'. Here 'reason' means roughly common sense.

The weeping parents wept in vain—
Are such things done on Albion's shore?

XV THE LITTLE VAGABOND

Dear mother, dear mother, the church is cold;
But the ale-house is healthy and pleasant and warm.
Besides I can tell where I am used well;
Such usage in Heaven will never do well.

5   But if at the church they would give us some ale,
And a pleasant fire, our souls to regale,
We'd sing and we'd pray, all the livelong day,
Nor ever once wish from the church to stray.

Then the parson might preach and drink and sing,
10 And we'd be as happy as birds in the spring;
And modest dame Lurch, who is always at church,
Would not have bandy children nor fasting nor birch.

And God, like a father rejoicing to see
His children as pleasant and happy as he,
15 Would have no more quarrel with the Devil or the
      barrel,
But kiss him and give him both drink and apparel.

XVI THE CHIMNEY-SWEEPER

A little black thing among the snow
Crying *'weep, 'weep*, in notes of woe!
Where are thy father and mother, say?
'They are both gone up to the church to pray.

xiv *24*. No, not literally; imaginatively, yes, in all the cruelties and enslave-
ment perpetrated on children's minds and bodies in the discipline and
labour which destroy their real life.
xiv. *Design*: At the foot, a group of kneeling figures, bowed, before flames
which may come from a sacrificial fire.
xv. *Design*: Above the poem, among trees, an aged man with radiant head
embraces a young man: underneath, a group of people, probably a family,
sit round a fire in a field. The upper scene may illustrate the Prodigal
(vagabond) Son.
xvi. *Design*: Illustrates *1*.
xvi. Contrary of 'The Chimney Sweeper' in *Innocence* (p. 68): see draft on
p. 163.
xvi *2*. *'weep, 'weep*] i.e. *sweep!*, the cry of the children sent out on the
chance of getting work (see p. 68); also a pathetic pun.

5   'Because I was happy upon the heath
    And smiled among the winter's snow,
    They clothed me in the clothes of death
    And taught me to sing the notes of woe.

    'And because I am happy and dance and sing,
10 They think they have done me no injury—
    And are gone to praise God and his priest and king,
    Who make up a Heaven of our misery.'

                XVII HOLY THURSDAY

        Is this a holy thing to see
        In a rich and fruitful land—
        Babes reduced to misery,
        Fed with cold and usurous hand?

5   Is that trembling cry a song?
        Can it be a song of joy—
        And so many children poor?
        It is a land of poverty!

        And their sun does never shine,
10   And their fields are bleak and bare,
        And their ways are filled with thorns;
        It is eternal winter there!

        For where'er the sun does shine,
        And where'er the rain does fall,
15   Babe can never hunger there,
        Nor poverty the mind appal.

                XVIII THE ANGEL

        I dreamt a dream—what can it mean?
        And that I was a maiden queen,
        Guarded by an angel mild—
        Witless woe was ne'er beguiled!

xvi 5. *Because*] The poem originally began here. It implies that adults are
not merely careless–they do not like to see natural, youthful joy.
xvi 9. 'Because I am occasionally seen enjoying myself.....' There was a
traditional May Day dance of sweeps and milkmaids in London.
xvii. Cp. the contrary poem in *Innocence* (p. 60), and the draft on p. 164.
xvii *Designs*: Above, a clothed woman, under a tree, against a lakeland
background, looks down at the body of a child. On the right of the text,
children clinging to their mother, all weeping; in the bottom left corner,
the body of another child.
xvii 4. i.e. fed impersonally, in an orphans' institution.
xviii. Cp. the contrary, 'A Dream', in *Innocence* (p. 64), and the draft on

5   And I wept both night and day,
           And he wiped my tears away,
           And I wept both day and night
           And hid from him my heart's delight.

           So he took his wings and fled.
10   Then the morn blushed rosy red;
           I dried my tears and armed my fears
           With ten thousand shields and spears.

           Soon my angel came again;
           I was armed, he came in vain.
15   For the time of youth was fled,
           And grey hairs were on my head.

XIX THE FLY

           Little fly,
           Thy summer's play
           My thoughtless hand
           Has brushed away.

5   Am not I
           A fly like thee?
           Or art not thou
           A man like me?

p. 165. A poem on the theme of perverse virginity. The 'maiden queen' accepts the angel's affections (st. 2) but does not reciprocate them or even let him see that she likes them. Therefore he goes (st. 3); she prepares to receive him—not openly, but in a duel of love: but (st. 4) it is too late—she is too old (at least in part because she has put herself beyond love).

xviii. *Design*: Above the text, a reclining woman, gowned, pushes away a cupid who stands behind her, reaching towards her: a serpent coils above her.

xviii 4. An obscure line. She is full of woe (st. 2); she was not 'beguiled', taken in, by his love—she did not surrender.

xviii 5. Weeping is commonly hypocritical in B.

xviii 12. *ten thousand* tricks of coquetry—fending off and challenging.

xviii 16. Cp. 'An old maid early' in the NB, p. 167.

xix. Cp. draft, p. 165. This poem is written in the short lines, common in nursery rhymes, of such *Innocence* poems as 'The Blossom' and 'Spring'. It is followed in the NB by the 'Motto to the Songs of Innocence and of Experience' (p. 166), which also deals with the theme of perception.

xix. *Design*: Under the text, a mother (or nursemaid) teaches a child to walk, holding both its hands; an older child in the background plays with shuttlecock and racket.

xix 3. *thoughtless*] i.e. 'unreflecting' as well as careless.

10
For I dance
And drink and sing,
Till some blind hand
Shall brush my wing.

15
If thought is life
And strength and breath,
And the want
Of thought is death;

20
Then am I
A happy fly,
If I live,
Or if I die.

XX AH, SUNFLOWER

Ah, sunflower, weary of time,
Who countest the steps of the sun,
Seeking after that sweet golden clime
Where the traveller's journey is done;

5
Where the youth pined away with desire
And the pale virgin shrouded in snow
Arise from their graves and aspire
Where my sunflower wishes to go.

XXI A LITTLE GIRL LOST

Children of the future age,
Reading this indignant page,
Know that in a former time
Love, sweet love, was thought a crime.

xix. *13–20.* The fourth st., as the NB shows, was written later than the rest, and inserted here. The 'If ... Then' sequence gives an appearance of a logical conclusion to the poem that is misleading, since the third st. was originally intended to read straight on to the last. Now the last two sts may be approximately paraphrased: 'If the essence of human nature and life is reflection and consideration, I will have none of it: I am content to live the simple, instinctive life of the fly'.

xx. Clytie (Ovid: *Met.* iv) was in love with Hyperion who, however, loved Leucothoe and visited her in disguise. Clytie, in her jealousy, betrayed Leucothoe, whose angry father had her killed. Clytie's jealousy was repaid by Hyperion's scorn, and, still a virgin, she pined away and dwindled into a sunflower, whose face is said always to be turned to the sun in its journey across the sky. See no. iii *n* (*design*).

xx *6. shrouded in snow*] Her desires frozen.

xxi. One of the four poems not in the NB (see headnote). The contrary poem to 'The Little Girl Lost' (which, however, with its companion

5 In the age of gold,
   Free from winter's cold,
   Youth and maiden bright
   To the holy light,
   Naked in the sunny beams delight.

10 Once a youthful pair,
   Filled with softest care,
   Met in garden bright,
   Where the holy light
   Had just removed the curtains of the night.

15 There in rising day
   On the grass they play;
   Parents were afar,
   Strangers came not near,
   And the maiden soon forgot her fear.

20 Tired with kisses sweet,
   They agree to meet
   When the silent sleep
   Waves o'er heaven's deep,
   And the weary tired wanderers weep.

25 To her father white
   Came the maiden bright,
   But his loving look,
   Like the Holy Book,
   All her tender limbs with terror shook.

30 'Ona, pale and weak,
   To thy father speak.
   Oh, the trembling fear,
   Oh, the dismal care,
   That shakes the blossoms of my hoary hair.'

XXII TO TIRZAH

'Found' poem, was later transferred to *Experience*). The earlier poem, unlike this, was not openly and simply concerned with love, except by implication and in its illustration. Coleridge (*Letters*, ed. E. H. Coleridge, ii 685ff) among other comments on *Innocence* and *Experience*, wished the poem had been omitted, 'from the too probable want of [Innocence] in many readers'. Its theme is a simplified version of the theme of *Visions*.

xxi *5–16*. Note the stress on the open day–not the secret night–as their time for making love.

xxi *28*. His love is 'moral'–he looks loving because the book tells him to 'love and forgive'–not in true sympathy with her joy.

xxii *To Tirzah*. This poem is found in later copies of *Experience*, but is printed here in its proper chronological place, near *Milton* and *Jerusalem* (see p. 590).

14 Europe

a Prophecy

Date. The titlepage reads *Lambeth 1794.* This seems probably correct, though B.'s titlepage dates are often earlier than those of actual completion. The closeness of *Europe* to the final *America*, its use (65ff) of an incident from an earlier stage of *America*, and a probable allusion to an event of 1792 (*121*) do not suggest lateness. The middle 'dream' section (*60–150*) may well be the earliest part, since it is an imaginative historical reconstruction, as *America* is. The 'Preludium' lacks the optimism of the 'Preludium' of *America*, and may be a little later; it is closer to the mood of the four omitted lines at the end of the 'Preludium' of *America*. The rest of *Europe* is original imaginative myth; the trend from *The French Revolution* to *Urizen* shows a clear movement from 'historical' to 'pure'.

The central figures of *Europe* are Orc, Albion's Angel, the 'nameless shadowy female', Enitharmon and Los. Though there are also allusions to Urizen and others, the first two are the main contestants in *America*, and in the middle section of *Europe* they carry on their fight. Albion's Angel subsumes all the oppressive and tyrannical elements in British rule and society; Orc is the spirit of freedom, the 'fiery youth', often likened to the rebel serpent, Satan. The 'shadowy female' appears only in the 'Preludiums' to the two *Prophecies*; here she is seen to have given birth to numerous sons of Orc, whom Enitharmon has snatched away and corrupted (though in the last lines of the 'Preludium' 'the female' speaks more hopefully). She is derived from the 'prima materia' of the alchemists – matter in chaos, the world-mother of stars and all nature; dark, moist, cloudy, female, prolific. The nature of Los is not fully displayed; he is primarily Enitharmon's consort.

But *Europe* is Enitharmon's poem. She is its corrupt, luxury-loving queen, B.'s first representation of the figure he was to develop throughout his poetry – the dazzling female, rich in beauty and spirit, who seeks to dominate and bind man by the 'soft delusions' of her seductive power. In *America* Urizen is the tyrant who rules by force and death; Enitharmon's power is more subtle and more to be feared. In her we may also see the perversion of religious teaching into a demand for subservience – as in the work of Wilberforce, Hannah More, and their Society for the Prevention of Vice.

Europe has a poem within a poem. The outer part, *1–54* and *151–209* of the *Prophecy*, describes Enitharmon's night of pleasure in the heavens, and its violent ending. The inner, *60–150*, describes her dream (*55–9* being a link).

(*a*) Enitharmon's night of pleasure begins about the time of the birth of Christ, which B. associates (*1–4*) with the emergence of Orc. Enitharmon ignores this, and calls her children around her to enjoy themselves. In the middle she falls asleep, and dreams. On awakening she ignores the ominous dream and continues to call her children: but the dream has lasted 1800 years; the time of Orc's breaking free (promised in *America*, both 'Preludium' and *Prophecy*) has come. The night ends, and as dawn breaks, Orc spreads his free and rebel spirit over Europe; Los rises to support Orc but his creative labours (reflecting the war which followed the French nation's assertion of freedom, and the artist's contribution to the cause).

(*b*) Enitharmon's dream, had she taken note of it, would have warned her. It is a piece of narrative belonging to the same story as that of the *Prophecy* of *America*, and involving the same figures, Albion's Angel and Orc. In an earlier version of *America* (cancelled pl.*b*), Orc's appearance results in the collapse of the council chamber on the head of Albion's Angel (as in *A Song of Liberty*)—a clear reference to the wretched state of the British government about 1780 after the defeat in America. In the final version of *America* this collapse is omitted, probably being held over for this part of *Europe*. Instead, B. describes the recoiling plagues which were driven back on to Albion, and the dream of Europe takes up the story at this point (*62*). Albion's Angel has failed in America; he now tries to re-establish himself in Albion. He leads his followers (*72*) to the 'serpent temple'—an imaginative vision of the abuse by the British ruling class of their religious power and authority. There he looks round (*102–3*) and sees the strength of the laws of his master Urizen everywhere apparent–and this also satisfies Enitharmon in her sleep (*131*). But it is too late; Orc's flames are burning the rotten structure down (*138–9*), and in despair Albion's Angel tries to bring on the destruction of his lawless enemies by blowing the Last Trumpet. Instead he and his angels are cast down, and in their fall 'as leaves of autumn' Enitharmon wakes, and continues her 'night of joy' already described.

There is a facsimile of *Europe* in the Blake Trust series (1969). The note on designs at the end of the headnote to *America* (p. 188) applies also to *Europe*.

Pls, i, ii   *[Frontispiece and Titlepage]*

Pl. iii   'Five windows light the caverned man: through one
         he breathes the air;

¶ 14. *Frontispiece.* The famous 'Ancient of Days' design: an aged figure kneels in a sphere, reaching down with dividers in his left hand (to circumscribe the world). The *titlepage* is dominated by a coiling serpent.
Prefatory Poem. 1. five windows] The outlets of the five senses: nose, ears, tongue, eyes, and the whole body with its sensitivity to touch.

Through one, hears music of the spheres; through one
    the eternal vine
Flourishes, that he may receive the grapes; through
    one, can look
And see small portions of the eternal world that ever
    groweth;
5   Through one, himself pass out what time he please—
    but he will not;
For stolen joys are sweet, and bread eaten in secret
    pleasant.'
So sang a fairy mocking as he sat on a streaked tulip,
Thinking none saw him; when he ceased I started
    from the trees
And caught him in my hat as boys knock down a
    butterfly.
10   'How know you this,' said I, 'small sir? Where did
    you learn this song?'
Seeing himself in my possession, thus he answered me:
'My master, I am yours; command me, for I must
    obey.'
'Then tell me what is the material world, and is it
    dead?'
He laughing answered: 'I will write a book on leaves
    of flowers,
15   If you will feed me on love-thoughts, and give me
    now and then
A cup of sparkling poetic fancies. So when I am tipsy,
I'll sing to you to this soft lute and show you all alive
The world, when every particle of dust breathes forth
    its joy.'
I took him home in my warm bosom. As we went
    along
20   Wild flowers I gathered, and he showed me each
    eternal flower;

2. *the eternal vine*] Beyond the window – i.e. outside the material world –
and the tongue (in tasting, and perhaps in speaking also) can reach out and
taste its immortal fruit.

6. *For stolen joys . . . pleasant*] Cp. *Proverbs* ix 17: 'Stolen waters are
sweet, and bread eaten in secret is pleasant.' Man refuses eternal pleasures
for stolen, secret, earthly substitutes. The fairy does not approve. Cp. also
Visions, esp. *178–86*.

19–22. each eternal flower] Cp. *Visions 6–20*: in both passages the flower
can be seen as a mere plant, or as a living spirit. But Oothoon's flower is
glad to be picked, while these 'whimper'; yet their scent is like a cloud of
spirits.

He laughed aloud to see them whimper because they
    were plucked.
(They hovered round me like a cloud of incense.)
    When I came
Into my parlour and sat down, and took my pen to
    write,
My fairy sat upon the table, and dictated EUROPE.

Pl. 1   [*Design*]

PRELUDIUM

The nameless shadowy female rose from out of the
    breast of Orc,
Her snaky hair brandishing in the winds of
    Enitharmon;
And thus her voice arose:

'O mother Enitharmon, wilt thou bring forth other
    sons
5 To cause my name to vanish, that my place may not
    be found?
For I am faint with travail,
Like the dark cloud disburdened in the day of dismal
    thunder.

'My roots are brandished in the heavens, my fruits
    in earth beneath

Pl.1. 'Preludium'. *Design*: Above the text, a traveller walks round a path
among rocks, unsuspecting, while a villain lies in wait, knife in hand.
Other figures of dread surround the text.

p *1. From out . . . Orc*] i.e. from Orc's embrace: since the 'Preludium' of
America she has become worn out by child-bearing. But the new age then
foretold has not been born, since Enitharmon takes the children into her
corrupting care. See headnote para. 1.

p *4. other sons* besides Orc, to beget children on her, equally hopelessly (see
1n, and *24–6*).

p *6. travail*] B. has *travel*, but the meaning is clearly 'child-bearing'. The
OED records the spelling 'travel' in this sense for the eighteenth century;
the two words shared the two spellings for centuries, both diverging from
the general sense 'work'.

p *8. brandished in the heavens . . . beneath*] The image is similar but not identi-
cal to that of *Marriage* pl.17–trees whose branches flourish in the sky
above the earth, put out roots in the same way, but inverted, to flourish
downwards in the abyss or in the earth. The idea of an inverted existence
beneath the earth in the spreading roots of the Tree of Mystery in the abyss
is fully developed (several years later) in *Four Zoas* viia. Cp. also the idea
of inversion in the *Prophecy*, *97–101* below.

Surge, foam, and labour into life, first born and first
    consumed,
10 Consumed and consuming!
Then why shouldst thou, accursed mother, bring me
    into life?

'I wrap my turban of thick clouds around my
    labouring head,
And fold the sheety waters as a mantle round my
    limbs.
Yet the red sun and moon
15 And all the overflowing stars rain down prolific pains.

Pl. 2 'Unwilling I look up to heaven, unwilling count the
    stars.
Sitting in fathomless abyss of my immortal shrine,
I seize their burning power
And bring forth howling terrors, all-devouring fiery
    kings—

20 'Devouring and devoured, roaming on dark and
    desolate mountains
In forests of eternal death, shrieking in hollow trees.
Ah, mother Enitharmon,
Stamp not with solid form this vigorous progeny of
    fires!

'I bring forth from my teeming bosom myriads of
    flames,
25 And thou dost stamp them with a signet; then they
    roam abroad
And leave me void as death.
Ah, I am drowned in shady woe, and visionary joy.

p 9. *first born and first consumed*] See 1n. In *America* (Prel.) there was a vision
of hope in the union of the Female and Orc. But the children who should
have realized that hope are stolen by Enitharmon as soon as they are born.
p 12–13. i.e. 'I hide myself away in clouds and deep waters'.
p 14–19. 'The heavenly bodies make me bring forth children against my
will.'   *Prolific*] In the sense of 'causing abundant production', not the
casual sense of 'many'.
p 23–5. *Stamp not . . . thou dost stamp . . .*] Cp. *Visions 21*, which refers to
the practice of branding slaves. B. may be taking this further, and thinking
also of the practice of marking sheep and cattle before turning them loose
on common land–they are not the less enslaved for being free to 'roam
abroad'.

'And who shall bind the infinite with an eternal
    band,
To compass it with swaddling bands? And who shall
    cherish it
30 With milk and honey?
I see it smile and I roll inward and my voice is past.'

        She ceased, and rolled her shady clouds
        Into the secret place.

[Design]

Pl. 3   A PROPHECY
      The deep of winter came,
      What time the secret child
Descended through the orient gates of the eternal day.
War ceased, and all the troops like shadows fled to
    their abodes.

p *28. who shall bind the infinite?*] B. wrote these five words beside a rough
sketch in the NB (p. 96) of the 'Ancient of Days' design which is the
frontispiece of *Europe*. The Female at last is reassured; Enitharmon cannot
hope to destroy utterly the infinity of life in Orc's children, nor bind and
swaddle every one of them so that all are at her mercy.
p. *Design*: Beneath and to the R of the text, an aerial scene in which one
figure chokes two others, while a fourth escapes over a cloud.
Pl.3 *Prophecy*] For the meaning of the word 'Prophecy', see *America*, head-
note, p. 187. The title is ornamented with various flying figures, esp. a
winged woman, gowned, flying in a dejected attitude. An aged man
huddles in a sphere.
1–4. The opening deliberately recalls Christmas: in 'the deep of winter';
the child born from heaven secretly upon earth; the traditional association
of the season with peace. Cp. esp. Milton's *Nativity Ode*, 29–31, 61–3: 'It
was the winter wild, / While the Heaven-born Child / All meanly wrapt
in the rude manger lies . . . // But peaceful was the night / Wherein the
Prince of Light / His reign of peace upon the earth began. . . .' Milton
also spends several sts (xix–xxv) describing the discomfiture of the heathen
gods, which B. summarizes in *4*. But B. is not concerned with the Nativity
of Christ, but with the onset of a night of leisure and corrupted joys for
Enitharmon and her companions. The '1800 years' of *56*, however, bring
us down from the time of Christ to the events of the middle section of the
poem, *c.* 1794. B. looks to Orc rather than Christ for salvation, but likens
them in their appearance on earth, and depicts Enitharmon as living in a
fool's paradise for 1800 years between 'the secret child's' birth and the
catastrophe of the end of the poem.

5 Then Enitharmon saw her sons and daughters rise
      around.
    Like pearly clouds they meet together in the crystal
      house,
    And Los, possessor of the moon, joyed in the peaceful
      night,
    Thus speaking, while his numerous sons shook their
      bright fiery wings:

    'Again the night is come
10 That strong Urthona takes his rest,
    And Urizen unloosed from chains
    Glows like a meteor in the distant north.
    Stretch forth your hands and strike the elemental
      strings!
    Awake the thunders of the deep,
Pl. 4 The shrill winds wake—
16 Till all the sons of Urizen look out and envy Los!
    Seize all the spirits of life and bind
    Their warbling joys to our loud strings.
    Bind all the nourishing sweets of earth
20 To give us bliss, that we may drink the sparkling wine
      of Los;
    And let us laugh at war,
    Despising toil and care,
    Because the days and nights of joy in lucky hours
      renew.'

    'Arise, O Orc, from thy deep den,
25 First-born of Enitharmon, rise!
    And we will crown thy head with garlands of the
      ruddy vine;
    For now thou art bound;
    And I may see thee in the hour of bliss, my eldest
      born.'

9–28. Los speaks; the sons of Urizen may speak *17–23,* and Enitharmon *24–8.* It is clear that Enitharmon speaks those lines; B. makes definite divisions in the plate at *9/10, 23/24;* pl.3 ends at *14.* B. has no inverted commas. The scene shows Los and Enitharmon at peace; while Los enjoys peace, though aware of Urizen, Enitharmon revels in dominion (*27, 35*). She begins to speak, unaware of the envy of Urizen's sons (*17–23*), as later she is unaware that her dream (*55–150*) is a vision of reality. Like Marie Antoinette, she does not wish to know the realities outside her world.

24. Orc] Orc is bound and in Enitharmon's power. For the nature and relationships of Los and Enitharmon to Orc, see headnote.

The horrent demon rose, surrounded with red stars of
   fire,
30 Whirling about in furious circles round the immortal
   fiend.
Then Enitharmon down descended into his red light,
And thus her voice rose to her children – the distant
   heavens reply:

Pl. 5   *[Full-page design]*

Pl. 6 'Now comes the night of Enitharmon's joy!
Who shall I call? Who shall I send?
35 That woman, lovely woman, may have dominion?
Arise, O Rintrah, thee I call, and Palamabron, thee.
Go, tell the human race that woman's love is sin,
That an eternal life awaits the worms of sixty winters
In an allegorical abode where existence hath never
   come.
40 Forbid all joy, and from her childhood shall the little
   female
Spread nets in every secret path.

'My weary eyelids draw towards the evening; my
   bliss is yet but new.

29. the horrent demon] Orc.
Pl.4. Design: Beneath smaller dancing figures, a female figure spreads
or lifts a cloth over a prone youth who lies with head buried but radiant.
Pl.5. Full-page illustration. Design: This represents death by famine: two
female figures in front of a stone fireplace on which a large cauldron boils;
the body of a child before them on the hearth. (The positions of this and
pl.7 vary in different copies.)
Pl.6. Design: Most of the plate (above the text) is a scaly, crowned male
figure with a sword, attended by two female angels.
34. Who shall . . . send?] From *Isaiah* vi 8 (the vision of God in the temple,
who asks:) 'Whom shall I send, and who will go for us?' B. brings the
phrase in line with the grammar of normal speech.
36. Rintrah . . . Palamabron] Sons of Los and Enitharmon (see p. 243). In
Marriage (*Argument*) *1* 'Rintrah roars', thus assuming his usual aspect of
wrath (cp. *44*). Their character in *Europe* is still not developed; nor is it
until *Milton*, perhaps ten years later, and by that time Los, Enitharmon and
Orc have changed out of recognition. The two should therefore be under-
stood as the following lines depict them rather than by reference elsewhere.
39. allegorical] To B. the word usually implies false propaganda.

Pl. 7   [*Full-page design*]

Pl. 8   'Arise, O Rintrah, eldest born, second to none but Orc.
         O lion Rintrah, raise thy fury from thy forests black;
   45   Bring Palamabron, horned priest, skipping upon the
               mountains;
         And silent Elynittria, the silver-bowed queen.
         Rintrah, where hast thou hid thy bride?
         Weeps she in desert shades?
         Alas, my Rintrah, bring the lovely jealous Ocalythron.

   50   'Arise, my son, bring all thy brethren, O thou king of
               fire.
         Prince of the sun, I see thee with thy innumerable
               race
         Thick as the summer stars,
         But each ramping his golden mane shakes,
         And thine eyes rejoice because of strength, O Rintrah,
               furious king!'

Pl. 9
   55   Enitharmon slept
         Eighteen hundred years. Man was a dream—
         The night of nature and their harps unstrung.
         She slept in middle of her nightly song,
         Eighteen hundred years, a female dream.

Pl.7. *Full-page illustration*: Plague. A bellman, black and silent, stalks past a
door inscribed 'LORD HAVE MERCY ON US'. In front, a man bends anxiously
over a seated woman; another woman throws up her hands and falls.
Cp. pl.5*n*.

45. skipping . . . mountains] Out of context, from *Song of Songs* ii 8: 'The
voice of my beloved! behold, he cometh, leaping upon the mountains,
skipping upon the hills'.

54. rejoice because of strength] Not a biblical quotation, though it sounds like
one. B., soaked in the A.V. as he was, has caught its idiom exactly, even to
its occasional awkwardness of phrase.

Pl.8. *Design*: Beneath the text, an aged male figure, (a Druid?), holds
out his hands in horror at something off L, while a young, gowned
woman, kneeling, clasps his knees.

Pl.9. *Design*: Above the text, but springing from beneath and R, stalks of
blighted barley, with two racing figures, male and female, scattering the
blight among the ears. (Cp. *Exodus* ix 31: 'The flax and the barley was
smitten; for the barley was in the ear. . . .')

59. eighteen hundred years] Cp. *1–4n*. Enitharmon falls asleep and dreams;
her dream (*60–150*) is the story of B.'s world of the 1790s. Her reality is in

60　Shadows of men in fleeting bands upon the winds
　　Divide the heavens of Europe,
　　Till Albion's Angel, smitten with his own plagues,
　　　fled with his bands.
　　The cloud bears hard on Albion's shore
　　Filled with immortal demons of futurity.
65　In council gather the smitten Angels of Albion.
　　The cloud bears hard upon the council house, down
　　　rushing
　　On the heads of Albion's Angels.

　　One hour they lay buried beneath the ruins of that
　　　hall;
　　But as the stars rise from the salt lake they arise in
　　　pain,
70　In troubled mists o'erclouded by the terrors of
　　　struggling times.

Pl. 10　In thoughts perturbed, they rose from the bright
　　　ruins, silent following
　　The fiery king, who sought his ancient temple
　　　serpent-formed

the heavens, and our world is a dream to her. B. passes over the inter-
vening 1800 years since the birth of Christ (and Orc) as 'fleeting bands upon
the winds'.

62. *Albion's Angel*] This brings us to the situation in *America 177*; but the
outcome is different, perhaps deriving from the earlier narrative of *America*
(q.v. headnote and cancelled pl.*b*). There, Urizen intervenes to save Albion's
Angel; here, and in the cancelled plates of *America*, the effect of the disaster
to British arms (defeat in the American colonies) is the collapse of Parlia-
ment – conceived by B. as the actual fall of the roof of the chamber on the
legislators' heads (probably the House of Lords).

69. *the salt lake*] The Dead Sea.

Pl.10. *Design*: A serpent, with flaming head and tongue, spirals up the L
margin.

72. *the fiery king*] Albion's Angel or guardian spirit. He goes to seek in-
spiration from the ancient religion of Albion.

temple serpent-formed] The following lines illustrate B.'s notions of the
DRUIDS. The *serpent temple*, supposedly built by Druids, was at Avebury,
Wilts. The archaeologist William Stukeley (1687–1765), writing on this
ring of great stones which surrounds the village of Avebury, distorted the
evidence to show that it and neighbouring stones take the form of a serpent,
spreading over the area. (B. drew this 'serpent temple' at the end of
Jerusalem, and the image affected him powerfully, as he imagined its power
spreading, not merely over a few hills, but over the entire island.) Stukeley

That stretches out its shady length along the island
    white.
Round him rolled his clouds of war; silent the Angel
    went,
75 Along the infinite shores of Thames to golden
    Verulam.
There stand the venerable porches that high-towering
    rear
Their oak-surrounded pillars, formed of massy stones,
    uncut

and others used such 'evidence' to show that this supposed British serpent-worship was related, and even senior, to ancient religions of the east where the serpent symbol was also found.

It was assumed by all (Roman and Danish 'claims' having been dismissed) that Avebury and Stonehenge were 'Druid temples', since there was no knowledge of any religions or societies in 'Ancient Britain' but that of the Druids. (a) According to Caesar, and other classical authorities, the Druids worshipped in oak groves, and the oak and mistletoe were sacred to them. (b) According to the assumptions of scholars of the seventeenth and eighteenth centuries, they also built the many stone circles to be found in Britain, in particular the vast stone temples of Avebury and Stonehenge. These scholars saw Stonehenge in particular as a place of sacrifice, identifying a certain stone as the altar. Caesar had said that on occasion the Druids slaughtered human victims; as it is unlikely that the Druids, apparently forest-priests, used the stone temples (which were built perhaps 1500 years before their time), Caesar is not likely to associate the Druids with these temples. He describes instead sacrifices of criminals and captives, on occasions of tribal danger, by burning in a huge wickerwork image; this monstrosity is referred to by B. in *Jerusalem* 47.7, etc. (c) The Druids, by B.'s time, had entered popular literary lore as the 'wise men' of 'Ancient Britain', and as such were often confused with the bards—and sometimes with hermits. All would be represented as aged, gowned, learned even to the extent of prophecy, and venerable. B. uses this, though to him the religion of the Druids, with its legends of human sacrifice, and its priesthood (which, according to classical sources, was secret and restricted), was abhorrent, while the bards represented poetry and imagination. (The standard authority on 'druid-lore' and scholarship from medieval to modern times, with a chapter devoted to B.'s notions, is A. L. Owen, *The Famous Druids*, 1962.)

73. *island white*] 'Albion' is derived from Latin *albus* 'white'.
75. *Verulam*] An important town in Roman times, traditionally an ancient religious site, near modern St Alban's. Sir Francis Bacon, whose philosophy B. especially detested, became Lord Verulam. The site is N. of London; B. has thus transferred the 'serpent temple' nearer home.
77. *oak-surrounded*] Showing Druid influence (see *72n*).

With tool, stones precious–such eternal in the
    heavens,
Of colours twelve, few known on earth, give light in
    the opaque,
80 Placed in the order of the stars. When the five senses
    whelmed
In deluge o'er the earth-born man, then turned the
    fluxile eyes
Into two stationary orbs, concentrating all things;
The ever-varying spiral ascents to the heavens of
    heavens
Were bended downward, and the nostrils' golden
    gates shut,
85 Turned outward, barred and petrified against the
    infinite.
Thought changed the infinite to a serpent, that which
    pitieth
To a devouring flame, and man fled from its face and
    hid
In forests of night. Then all the eternal forests were
    divided
Into earths, rolling in circles of space, that like an
    ocean rushed
90 And overwhelmed all except this finite wall of flesh.
Then was the serpent temple formed, image of infinite
Shut up in finite revolutions, and man became an
    angel,
Heaven a mighty circle turning, God a tyrant
    crowned.

—Now arrived the ancient Guardian at the southern
    porch
95 That, planted thick with trees of blackest leaf, and in
    a vale
Obscure, enclosed the Stone of Night. Oblique it
    stood, o'erhung

78. eternal in the heavens] Quoted, out of context, from *2 Corinthians* v 1.
79. colours twelve] In *Revelation* xxi 10–21, the new Jerusalem is adorned
with twelve different kinds of jewel.
80–5. A brief note of the restrictive 'creation' of eyes, ears and nose, de-
scribed in full in *Urizen 218–38*.
86. Thought] To B. 'thought' usually means 'anxious thought' or 'calcu-
lation'. Here it changes the true infinite into an endless, constricting coil:
cp. 91–2.
96. the Stone of Night] The pulpit-stone, where the voice of authority speaks.

With purple flowers and berries red, image of that
    sweet south,
Once open to the heavens and elevated on the human
    neck,
Now overgrown with hair and covered with a stony
    roof.
100 Downward 'tis sunk, beneath the attractive north that
    round the feet,
A raging whirlpool, draws the dizzy enquirer to his
    grave.

Pl. 11   Albion's Angel rose upon the Stone of Night.
    He saw Urizen on the Atlantic;
    And his brazen book
105   That kings and priests had copied on earth
    Expanded from north to south.

Pl. 12 And the clouds and fires pale rolled round in the
    night of Enitharmon
Round Albion's cliffs and London's walls (still
    Enitharmon slept);
Rolling volumes of grey mist involve churches,
    palaces, towers,

97. *purple flowers and berries red*] B. clearly intends deadly nightshade,
though he describes the commoner woody nightshade, which has red
berries. Deadly nightshade berries are a purple so dark as to be nearly black.
97–101. *sweet south . . . attractive north*] There are many interpretations, e.g.
by Neo-Platonists and Swedenborg, of the relative significances of north
and south. B.'s sense here is plain, and his own. The true order is reversed;
the human mind, that once was open to the eternal sun in infinity, is now
enclosed in a bony skull, drawn northwards by magnetic attraction, so that,
in a topsy-turvy world, the grim north is 'up' and 'the sweet south' is
'down'. We think we are upright, but (like the Female in *Preludium 8*) we
are upside-down in the abyss.
Pl.11. *Design*: The text is at the foot of the pl., most of which is taken up by
the design. A figure (not unlike George III) in ecclesiastical robes, wearing a
triple-crowned mitre in allusion to the Pope, and with batlike wings extended,
sits reading from a book, above two angelic female figures, with eagle wings,
who throw their sceptres down before him, keeping their eyes downcast.
Pl.12. *Design*: A spider's web hangs from the right margin; it would cover
the lower half of the pl., but the text obscures it, so that only its upper half
is seen between *126–7*. Flies and other insects are on it, also two spiders;
one is descending on a thread to a figure bottom right, beside dock leaves
which dwarf him; he is cocooned in the spider's threads.
109. *churches, palaces, towers*] Places where rulers live. The *grey mist* is a
mental fog.

110 For Urizen unclasped his book, feeding his soul with
          pity.
       The youth of England hid in gloom curse the pained
          heavens, compelled
       Into the deadly night to see the form of Albion's
          Angel.
       Their parents brought them forth and aged ignorance
          preaches canting
       On a vast rock, perceived by those senses that are
          closed from thought—
115 Bleak, dark, abrupt it stands and overshadows London
          city.
       They saw his bony feet on the rock, the flesh con-
          sumed in flames;
       They saw the serpent temple lifted above, shadowing
          the island white;
       They heard the voice of Albion's Angel howling in
          flames of Orc,
       Seeking the trump of the last doom.

120 Above the rest the howl was heard from
          Westminster, louder and louder.
       The Guardian of the secret codes forsook his ancient
          mansion,
       Driven out by the flames of Orc; his furred robes and
          false locks
       Adhered and grew one with his flesh, and nerves and
          veins shot through them.
       With dismal torment sick, hanging upon the wind, he
          fled
125 Grovelling along Great George Street through the
          Park gate. All the soldiers
       Fled from his sight; he dragged his torments to the
          wilderness.

110. Urizen . . . book] Cp. design on pl.11, and *Urizen 86–8*: the book con-
tains his Law.
114. i.e. 'perceived by the imaginative use of the senses which have shut
out mere earthly vision' (as in dreams)'.
121. The Guardian of the secret codes] Cp. *America 193–5*, where a similar
plague attacks the Bard of Albion. On 15 June 1792, Lord Thurlow was
dismissed as Lord Chancellor, and B. may well refer to him: see D. V.
Erdman, *W.B.*, *Prophet against Empire* p. 199. The dismissal was an act
of the king, on the advice of the Tory prime minister, Pitt, and this does
not suggest direct action by Orc—but the flames are everywhere.
125. i.e. going away from Parliament.

Thus was the howl through Europe.
For Orc rejoiced to hear the howling shadows;
But Palamabron shot his lightnings trenching down
    his wide back,
130 And Rintrah hung with all his legions in the nether
    deep.

Enitharmon laughed in her sleep to see (Oh, woman's
    triumph!)
Every house a den, every man bound; the shadows
    are filled
With spectres, and the windows wove over with
    curses of iron.
Over the doors *Thou shalt not*, and over the
    chimneys *Fear* is written.
135 With bands of iron round their necks fastened into
    the walls
The citizens, in leaden gyves the inhabitants of
    suburbs
Walk heavy; soft and bent are the bones of villagers.

Between the clouds of Urizen the flames of Orc roll
    heavy
Around the limbs of Albion's Guardian, his flesh
    consuming.
140 Howlings and hissings, shrieks and groans, and voices
    of despair
Arise around him in the cloudy
Heavens of Albion. Furious
Pl. 13 The red-limbed Angel seized, in horror and torment,
    The trump of the last doom; but he could not blow
    the iron tube!

131. Enitharmon laughed] She fails to see what is happening to Albion's
Angel (*138–42*).
134. Over the doors . . . written] Cp. the reminders of the Law in *Deuter-*
onomy vi 8–9, xi 18–20: '[Ye shall] lay up these my words in your heart and
in your soul, and bind them for a sign upon your hand, that they may be
as frontlets between your eyes. And ye shall teach them your children,
speaking of them when thou sittest in thine house, and when thou walkest
by the way, when thou liest down, and when thou risest up. And thou
shalt write them upon the door posts of thine house, and upon thy gates....'
Cp. also 'The Garden of Love' (*Experience*) 6 (p. 212).
Pl.13. *Design*: Below the text, a man chained in a massive stone dungeon
lifts his fettered hands in horror as his gaoler goes out up the steps–perhaps
for ever.

145   Thrice he assayed presumptuous to awake the dead to
          Judgement.
        A mighty spirit leaped from the land of Albion
        Named Newton; he seized the trump and blowed the
          enormous blast.

        Yellow as leaves of autumn, the myriads of angelic
          hosts
        Fell through the wintry skies seeking their graves,
150   Rattling their hollow bones in howling and
          lamentation.

        ───────

        Then Enitharmon woke, nor knew that she had
          slept,
        And eighteen hundred years were fled
        As if they had not been.
        She called her sons and daughters
155   To the sports of night
        Within her crystal house,
        And thus her song proceeds:

        'Arise, Ethinthus, though the earth-worm call—
        Let him call in vain,
160   Till the night of holy shadows
        And human solitude is past.

Pl. 14 'Ethinthus, queen of waters, how thou shinest in the
          sky!

147. Newton] Chosen as the Angel's aide-de-camp because he was one of
the great rationalists hated by B., though his many admirers often saw
Newton as heralding a new and enlightened age. The effect of the Trumpet
is not, as expected, to destroy Orc, but to overthrow the angels (*148–50*).
149. Fell . . . graves] Whereas at the Day of Judgment, the spirits of the
dead are said to rise from their graves, here the evil angels fall and seek
their graves. The dissolving image is an apt dream-ending. Cp. Milton's
Nativity ode 232–4: 'The flocking shadows pale / Troop to th'infernal
jail, / Each fettered ghost slips to his several grave'.
158. Ethinthus] Only a name, though also used in *Four Zoas* viii 352, and
Jerusalem pl.12.25. B. only uses the name when he needs many of them.
Pl.14. *Design*: Caterpillars, various insects, and serpents creep on and
around plants with entwining tendrils, in the line-end spaces on the right,
between *175–6*, and at the foot.
162. Ethinthus . . . how thou shinest in the sky!] Cp. Macpherson's Ossian,
Cath-Loda ii: 'U-thorno, that rises in waters! on whose side are the meteors
of the night!'.

My daughter, how do I rejoice! For thy children
  flock around
Like the gay fishes on the wave, when the cold moon
  drinks the dew.
165 Ethinthus, thou art sweet as comforts to my fainting
  soul,
For now thy waters warble round the feet of
  Enitharmon.

'Manathu-Vorcyon, I behold thee flaming in my
  halls.
Light of thy mother's soul, I see thy lovely eagles
  round;
Thy golden wings are my delight and thy flames of
  soft delusion.

170 'Where is my luring bird of Eden, Leutha, silent love?
Leutha, the many-coloured bow delights upon thy
  wings—
Soft soul of flowers, Leutha!
Sweet smiling pestilence, I see thy blushing light;
Thy daughters many-changing
175 Revolve like sweet perfumes ascending, O Leutha,
  silken queen.

'Where is the youthful Antamon, prince of the
  pearly dew?
O Antamon, why wilt thou leave thy mother
  Enitharmon?
Alone I see thee, crystal form,
Floating upon the bosomed air
180 With lineaments of gratified desire.
My Antamon, the seven churches of Leutha seek thy
  love.

167. *Manathu-Vorcyon*] See *158n*; this name also occurs in *Four Zoas* viii 352.
169. *soft delusion*] Enitharmon's favourite feminine weapon with which she achieves her 'woman's triumph' (*131*) of binding and controlling mankind.
170. *Leutha*] Cp. *Visions 4n*. Here she is clearly characterized as beautiful and treacherous.
176. *Antamon*] Another shadowy figure; see also *Song of Los (Africa) 28* (q.v. i.*28n*) *Four Zoas* VIII *346*, *Milton 28, 13–18* and *Jerusalem 83.28*. His character in *Milton* is quite different from that in *Europe*.
180. *With lineaments . . . desire*] A phrase B. liked; cp. NB (1793) nos. xxxvii and li, pp. 162, 167 above.
181. *the seven churches*] Seven churches are addressed in *Revelation* i–iii: B. probably intended no fully developed idea in this expression.

'I hear the soft Oothoon in Enitharmon's tents.
Why wilt thou give up woman's secrecy, my
    melancholy child?
Between two moments bliss is ripe.
185   O Theotormon, robbed of joy, I see thy salt tears flow
Down the steps of my crystal house.

'Sotha and Thiralatha, secret dwellers of dreamful
    caves,
Arise and please the horrent fiend with your melo-
    dious songs.
Still all your thunders golden-hoofed and bind your
    horses black.
190   Orc, smile upon my children.
Smile, son of my afflictions;
Arise, O Orc, and give our mountains joy of thy red
    light.'

She ceased, for all were forth at sport beneath the
    solemn moon,
Waking the stars of Urizen with their immortal
    songs—
195   That nature felt through all her pores the enormous
    revelry,
Till morning oped the eastern gate;
Then every one fled to his station, and Enitharmon
    wept.

But terrible Orc, when he beheld the morning in the
    east,
Pl. 15 Shot from the heights of Enitharmon,
200   And in the vineyards of red France appeared the light
    of his fury.

182–6. An allusion to *Visions*.
187. Sotha and Thiralatha] Mentioned in the cancelled plates to *America*,
b.21 and *d.1*: but still shadowy sons of Los. See also p. 244.
Sotha] May be derived from *Sothis*, a name for Sirius, the dog star.
190. Orc, smile . : .] Enitharmon asks the bound Orc to smile, although she
herself is the cause of his 'afflictions'.
193. for all . . . sport] Mended on the pl. from 'and all went forth to sport'.
196. gate] *1st rdg.* . . . . gate, and the angel trumpet blew. (Refers back to
147, and ties Enitharmon's dream and her waking life.) In an intermediate
stage, this line is altered by this deletion, but *193* is unchanged.
199. heights of Enitharmon] *1st rdg.* heights of Enitharmon, before the Trum-
pet blew.
200. red France] Orc's appearance in Europe was foretold in *America 218*.

The sun glowed fiery red!
The furious terrors flew around
On golden chariots raging, with red wheels dropping
    with blood;
The lions lash their wrathful tails;
205 The tigers couch upon the prey and suck the ruddy
    tide;
And Enitharmon groans and cries in anguish and
    dismay.

Then Los arose; his head he reared in snaky thunders
    clad,
And with a cry that shook all nature to the utmost
    pole
Called all his sons to the strife of blood.

Finis—[Design]

15 The Song of Los

AFRICA : ASIA

Date. The titlepage has *Lambeth 1795*. The two parts of the poem are
separate and may have been composed at different times. The engraved
script resembles that of *America* and *Europe* rather than the more restrained
script of *Urizen* where, however, B. may have been limited by space.
Asia picks up the narrative of the dream in *Europe* (which may be *Europe's*
earliest part) and ends with the enthusiasm of 1793 rather than the specula-
tions of *Urizen* (dated 1794 on titlepage). *Asia* is written in the short-line
metre of *Urizen* and may be B.'s first experiment with that metre. *Africa*
metrically resembles *Europe* with its varied length of line; but these re-
semblances in metre may not help with dating the poem. The matter of
Africa is uncertain enough to suggest that when it was written the myth of
Urizen was not settled; Los, though named 'Eternal Prophet' at the begin-
ning (the last part written?), is an indeterminate character; his 'sons'–
Sotha, Diralada, etc.–disappear when the myth of *Urizen* is complete. In
this edition *The Song of Los* is placed before *Urizen* on the conjecture that
both parts were written before *Urizen*, which may well have captured B.'s
imagination before he had begun to engrave *The Song of Los*, which had
then to wait. Hence *Urizen* is dated 1794 by B., and the *Song* 1795.
    The two *Prophecies* and *The Song of Los* form a group which sketches a
spiritual history of the world in the order *Africa–America–Europe–Asia*.
Africa begins with Adam and ends with the first line of *America* (A.D. 1775),
and describes how Urizen spread his Law over the earth, gradually cor-
rupting mankind. *Asia* ends the story. It has been concerned (as a whole)

Design. A young man carrying and leading two children upstairs through
flames.

9*

with the rising of Orc, whose fiery power spreads from west to east,
consuming the evil works and systems of Urizen one by one. In *America*
he has defied Albion's Angel and defeated him; in *Europe* he does so again
in Britain itself, and moves over to France; in *Asia* the kings of the East
undergo his attack.

Pls. 1–2   *[Frontispiece and Titlepage]*

Pl. 3   I AFRICA

I will sing you a song of Los, the eternal prophet;
He sung it to four harps at the tables of Eternity
          In heart-formed Africa.
Urizen faded; Ariston shuddered.
5   *And thus the song began:*

Adam stood in the garden of Eden
And Noah on the mountains of Ararat;
They saw Urizen give his laws to the nations
By the hands of the children of Los.

10   Adam shuddered; Noah faded. Black grew the sunny
          African,
      When Rintrah gave abstract philosophy to Brahma in
          the east.

¶ 15. Pl.1. *Frontispiece.* A priest bows at an altar before a diseased sun.
Pl.3. i. *Africa.*
i *1. Los, the eternal prophet*] He is scarcely mentioned again, and the poem
is only hung on his name. Los becomes a 'prophet' in *Urizen*, after first
appearing as Enitharmon's consort in *Europe.*
i *2. tables*] i.e. Los is a minstrel or bard, singing to a company at dinner.
four harps] The four continents of B.'s *prophecies*–*America, Europe* and the
two contained in this *Song.*
i *4. Ariston*] A very shadowy figure; *America 112* ascribes beauty to him
(see *n* and *Four Zoas* appendix, p. 466).
i *6–9.* The Law has ruled man since the Creation; in *Urizen* adherence to
Law among the immortals causes mortal creation. The *sons of Los* are the
mythical names mentioned in the succeeding lines–Rintrah, Palamabron,
etc.–who are named as 'law-givers'; they have corrupted his prophecy
into Urizenic Law. They misapply Los's poetic gift.
i *10. shuddered . . . faded*] The resemblance to *4* is probably a coincidence of
verbal memory.
i *11. abstract philosophy to Brahma*] B. may seem unfair to Brahma; when he
appears (in the Vedic myth) as a god, he has no philosophical significance.
He was a somewhat Urizenic figure in that he was held to be the eldest of
living things, from half of whose divided body the world eventually came.

> (*Night spoke to the cloud:*
> '*Lo, these human-formed spirits in smiling hypocrisy war*
> *Against one another; so let them war on, slaves to the eternal*
> *elements*'.)

15 Noah shrunk beneath the waters;
Abram fled in fires from Chaldea;
Moses beheld upon Mount Sinai forms of dark delusion.

To Trismegistus Palamabron gave an abstract law,
To Pythagoras, Socrates, and Plato.

20 Times rolled on o'er all the sons of Har; time after time
Orc on Mount Atlas howled, chained down with the
    Chain of Jealousy.
Then Oothoon hovered over Judah and Jerusalem,
And Jesus heard her voice (a man of sorrows); he
    received
A gospel from wretched Theotormon.

25 The human race began to wither, for the healthy built
Secluded places, fearing the joys of love,
And the diseased only propagated.

In later thought, Brahma is indeed abstract, the all-pervading deity; but far from being rationally philosophical, the concept is now mystical. But B. is taking his cue from Sir William Jones (1746–94) who, in *Asiatick Researches* (1794) attributed 'a technical system of logick' to Brahma (see Raine, *B. and Traidition* i 351, 425).

i *18. Trismegistus*] The mythical source of alchemical wisdom; mentioned by Plato, and supposed to be either a form of the Egyptian god Thoth or else a divine man; 'thrice great' as priest, philosopher and king. See *Jerusalem* pl.91.35n, for his 'Table' that was as unduly revered as a holy book.

i *19. Pythagoras, Socrates and Plato*] B. links the mystical, the down-to-earth enquirer, and his more legalistic disciple together and implies that all thinkers of the classical world were Aristotelian in outlook and method. Of the three, only Plato can be accused of wishing to find such 'an abstract Law'.

i *20. sons of Har*] Apparently, 'mortal men'. This seems to be an attempt to draw B.'s *Tiriel* myth into the larger myth of the Lambeth books; but apart from the reference in *36*, little is made of it.

i *21. Orc on Mount Atlas*] As in the design on pl.1 of *America*, and the text of the *Preludium* there, Orc is a Promethean figure, chained on the mountains (though Prometheus was chained on the Caucasus). For the Chain of Jealousy, see *Urizen 378–95*.

i *22–4. Oothoon . . . Theotormon*] A reference to *Visions*. Jesus, like Theotormon, is resigned to sorrow and will not accept Oothoon's gospel of release from law.

So Antamon called up Leutha from her valleys of
      delight,
   And to Mahomet a loose Bible gave.
30 But in the north to Odin Sotha gave a code of war,
   Because of Diralada, thinking to reclaim his joy.

Pl. 4 These were the churches, hospitals, castles, palaces,
   Like nets and gins and traps to catch the joys of Eternity,
   And all the rest a desert;
35 Till like a dream Eternity was obliterated and erased.

Since that dread day when Har and Heva fled,
   Because their brethren and sisters lived in war and lust;
   And as they fled they shrunk
   Into two narrow doleful forms,
40 Creeping in reptile flesh upon
   The bosom of the ground,
   And all the vast of nature shrunk
   Before their shrunken eyes.

Thus the terrible race of Los and Enitharmon gave
45 Laws and religions to the sons of Har, binding them
      more

i 28. *Antamon and Leutha*] Also linked, and also shadowy, in *Europe 176–7*:
for Leutha, see *Visions 4*.
i 29. *a loose Bible*] The Koran; the name has been supposed to mean 'a
collection of loose sheets'.
i 30. *Odin . . . Sotha*] *Odin*, the Germanic high god, lord of the dead,
whose servants assembled in Valhalla. He was not strictly a god of war,
but was commonly supposed to be so. B. could read Norse mythology in
P. H. Mallet's *Northern Antiquities* (1770). *Sotha* 'held the northern helm'
in *America* pl.*b.21* (p. 206).
i 31. *Diralada*] Perhaps another form of *Thiralatha*, also linked with Sotha
in *Europe 187* (cp. also *America* pl.*d*).
i 32. *These*] i.e. 'these laws' built the churches, etc.
Hospitals] Places of 'charity', for the poor or the destitute or aged; their
inmates were often despised and often exploited, most notably at Bedlam
Hospital for the insane.
i 36–43. *Har and Heva*] See *20n*. In *Tiriel* no explanation is given of the
senility of Har and Heva; here B. invents one. Their flight resembles the
flight of Lot from Sodom (*Genesis* xix); but B. changes the story to a
flight not from wickedness, but from energetic life which Har and Heva
can only see as 'war and lust'. Refusing life they degenerate to mortal
form.   *Design*: The passage is illustrated at the foot of the page, by two
escaping figures clinging together, running from something off the pl. to
the left.

And more to earth; closing and restraining,
Till a philosophy of five senses was complete.
Urizen wept and gave it into the hands of Newton and
    Locke.

Clouds roll heavy upon the Alps round Rousseau and
    Voltaire,
50 And on the mountains of Lebanon round the deceased
    Gods
Of Asia, and on the deserts of Africa round the fallen
    angels.
The Guardian Prince of Albion burns in his nightly
    tent.

[*Design*]

Pl. 5   [*Full-page illustration*]

Pl. 6   II ASIA
The kings of Asia heard
The howl rise up from Europe,
And each ran out from his web,
From his ancient woven den;
5   For the darkness of Asia was startled
At the thick-flaming, thought-creating fires of Orc.
And the kings of Asia stood
And cried in bitterness of soul:

i *48. Newton and Locke*] To B. Newton was the leading rationalist cos-
mographer, Locke the rationalist philosopher, and both therefore anathema.
Urizen's weeping, as so often in B., is hypocritical, as he is the father of
the evil he pretends to lament.

i *49. Rousseau and Voltaire*] Both lived for a long time in or near Geneva,
of which Rousseau was a native. Here they seem to be associated with Law
and Reason, as they are in B.'s later writings; in *French Revolution 276* they
are pro-revolutionary spirits.

i *52.* The line repeats *America 1.* B. has brought his narrative from the
Creation down to the first *Prophecy*; the story is continued in the two
Prophecies and *Asia.*

Pl.*5. Full-page illustration.* A reclining king and queen on flowers (known
as 'King and Queen of the Fairies').

Pl.6. ii. *Asia.*

ii *1. The kings of Asia*] I.e. of the tyrannical monarchies traditional in Asia.

ii *2. The howl*] The howl of Albion's Angel, attacked by the flames of Orc
(*Europe 118*). Orc's influence is spreading over Asia, having begun in the
west in America.

ii *3–4. web . . . den*] In B., symbols of obscurantism and oppression.

'Shall not the king call for famine from the heath,
10   Nor the priest for pestilence from the fen?
To restrain, to dismay, to thin
The inhabitants of mountain and plain—
In the day of full-feeding prosperity
And the night of delicious songs.

15   'Shall not the counsellor throw his curb
Of poverty on the laborious
To fix the price of labour,
To invent allegoric riches?

'And the privy admonishers of men
20   Call for fires in the city,
For heaps of smoking ruins,
In the night of prosperity and wantonness?

'To turn man from his path,
To restrain the child from the womb,
Pl. 7   To cut off the bread from the city,
26   That the remnant may learn to obey;

'That the pride of the heart may fail;
That the lust of the eyes may be quenched;
That the delicate ear in its infancy
30   May be dulled, and the nostrils closed up—
To teach mortal worms the path
That leads from the gates of the grave.'

Urizen heard them cry,
And his shuddering waving wings

ii *13–14. prosperity . . . delicious songs*] Decadent luxury, to those who enjoy it.

ii *18. allegoric riches*] Riches declared to exist by the rulers, but not seen by those who labour.

ii *19. And the privy admonishers . . .*] The *Shall not?* of *9* and *15* is assumed here.

ii *20. fires in the city*] B. had seen the Gordon riots of 1780, when the mob ran loose in London, and will have remembered the burning of Joseph Priestley's house in Birmingham, supposedly at the instigation of 'privy admonishers', in July 1791.

ii *20–2. fires . . . wantonness*] So (in another context) in *Milton* pl.5.*40–1* (a late addition to Milton, over ten years later than *Song of Los*).

ii *29–32. That the delicate ear . . . May be dulled*] 'So that man, living a life of brutal hardship, may be prevented from seeing visions of immortality.'

ii *33–40. Urizen heard*] As he heard Albion's Angel's cry in *America 205*, and in *Europe 103*ff. Always on the retreat, he now tries to entrench himself in the East.

35 Went enormous above the red flames,
    Drawing clouds of despair through the heavens
    Of Europe as he went;
    And his books of brass, iron and gold
    Melted over the land as he flew,
40 Heavy-waving, howling, weeping.

    And he stood over Judæa,
    And stayed in his ancient place,
    And stretched his clouds over Jerusalem.

    For Adam, a mouldering skeleton,
45 Lay bleached on the Garden of Eden;
    And Noah as white as snow
    On the mountains of Ararat.

    Then the thunders of Urizen bellowed aloud
    From his woven darkness above.

50 Orc, raging in European darkness,
    Arose like a pillar of fire above the Alps,
    Like a serpent of fiery flame.
            The sullen earth
            Shrunk.

55 Forth from the dead dust rattling, bones to bones
    Join; shaking, convulsed, the shivering clay breathes,
    And all flesh naked stands: fathers and friends;
    Mothers and infants; kings and warriors:

ii 41–9. *he stood over Judæa*] B. ties the end of the sequence *Africa–America–Europe–Asia* to its beginning (cp. *44–7* and *Africa 6–10*). The religion of Mosaic Law was always a stronghold of Urizenic power, and he returns to it, when his political power is overthrown.

ii 49. *woven darkness*] The darkness of Urizen's web of religion (cp. *Urizen 457*ff). The image is of an inescapable, self-guided net.

ii 51–2. *pillar of fire . . . serpent*] From *Exodus* xiii 21–2, 'And the Lord went before them . . . by night in a pillar of fire': and *Numbers* xxi 6–8, 'And the Lord sent fiery serpents among the people': and Moses, to save their lives, was directed by the Lord to make 'a fiery serpent, and set it upon a pole: and it shall come to pass, that every one that is bitten, when he looketh upon it, shall live'. Thus Orc, in his typical characteristics of fire and serpent-form, recalls the deliverance of God; but Orc is not a law-giver, and he leads to freedom, not law.

ii 55. *bones to bones*] An allusion to the resurrection of the dry bones in the vision of *Ezekiel* xxxvii: cp. *America 39–40n*, and contrast the fall of the angels in *Europe 148–50*.

The grave shrieks with delight and shakes
60 Her hollow womb, and clasps the solid stem;
Her bosom swells with wild desire,
And milk and blood and glandous wine
In rivers rush and shout and dance
On mountain, dale and plain.

The Song of Los is Ended.

Urizen Wept.

Pl. 8   *[Design]*

16 The First Book of Urizen

Date. 1794, the titlepage date, is probably the actual date of engraving. Six
of the seven known copies were certainly printed before 1800; the altera-
tions in the last of these (the so-called 'copy A') are shown in the notes, as
this was the most carefully revised. In one other copy the heading 'Chap:
II' is deleted and 'III' becomes 'II', yet the two headings 'Chap: IV' re-
main. The text printed here is an early version without deletions. Ten
plates are entirely pictorial, in various sequences; they are noted in the
order which has become conventional. This is not altogether satisfactory
as it was based on the British Museum copy, which lacks two plates, so that
these had to be included arbitrarily. Yet since B. himself never fixed any
order, no editor should pretend to be final in the matter.
Theme. Urizen is an attack on legalism in thought and religion, in the form
of a myth designed as the *Genesis* of B.'s 'Bible of Hell' (see *Marriage* iv, *291*,
p. 121), and describing the Creation and Fall. The poem is set out in chap-
ters and verses, the title echoes *Genesis* ('The First Book of Moses'), and
there are many allusions to the biblical narrative of creation. B.'s notion of
the earthly soul as spirit in a material prison was a Neo-Platonic common-
place, but he draws particularly on material originating with the German
mystic Jacob Boehme (1575–1624), whose writings were more widely
known in B.'s time than they are now. B. uses the following ideas from
Boehme: (*a*) creation caused by introspection in an eternal being; (*b*) crea-
tion as part of the Fall; (*c*) a fall in two stages, the second stage being the

ii 59. *The grave shrieks with delight*] The grave becomes a womb, and takes
delight in giving up the dead in a new birth, having rediscovered the joys
of fertility ('clasps the solid stem').
ii 62. *glandous*] A word unknown to the *OED*. B. in various places equates
rivers with the veins and nerves of the body. Perhaps the 'glandous wine'
is lymph (*Urizen* 291) or seed (*Milton* 19.55–60).
ii *Urizen wept*] See *Song of Liberty* 6, 'And weep'; B. imitates the shortest
verse in the Bible, *John* xi 35: 'Jesus wept'.
Pl.8. *Design*: Los leans on his hammer and looks down, satisfied, at the sun.

division of Adam into male and female (*314n*). Other connections are shown in the footnotes. But B. reshaped these concepts: (*a*) he envisaged an Eternity peopled by a 'republic' of immortals with infinite faculties; (*b*) the creation *is* Urizen himself, expelled from Eternity on account of his law-giving (a blend of the tyranny of Jehovah and the fate of Lucifer); (*c*) B. has *two* always distinct major figures, Urizen and Los; (*d*) above all there is a constant social and moral emphasis, which is absent from his religious and mystical sources. *Genesis* presents creation as God's benevolent and generous act, the evils of later life arising from self-willed disobedience to God's just commands. In *Urizen* the evil lies, not in disobedience, but in the despotic command itself; hence creation cannot be the act of a benevolent being. B. traces the source of this despotism back to Urizen's primeval selfishness and self-withdrawal (*6–7, 50–7, 75–84*). This is the beginning of the myth, which is expanded to show that from this self-centred separation of souls spring all other evils, such as Los's jealousy. Boehme has much to say of the inward-looking of the mind, but nothing of tyranny and social or personal unhappiness.

Urizen, an immortal, first separates himself from the other Eternals, and then seeks to dominate them by his laws. He flees from their anger, and Los, an unfallen immortal, is set to watch him. Urizen's state is chaotic, and Los has to save what he can. Urizen's enclosure becomes our universe, his own form hardens into the fixed form of man. In Ch. v Los wearily forgets the infinite life; he too becomes self-centred and a series of divisive changes follows. His single form fragments into male (Los) and female (Enitharmon); the child Orc is born and jealousy begins. So the Fall is complete, and the remaining events occur in the separated world of Urizen. In Ch. vii he awakes and, exploring his world, sees the appearance of the four elements (his 'sons'), various creatures, and then human beings–all constricted under his Net of Religion. Most men cower in their cities, but some, following the fire-element (to them a god) Fuzon, escape a little way in an Exodus which closes the poem.

There is a facsimile in the Blake Trust Series (1958).

Pl. 1   [*Titlepage*]

Pl. 2 PRELUDIUM TO THE [FIRST] BOOK OF URIZEN

> *Of the primeval priest's assumed power,*
> *When Eternals spurned back his religion,*
> *And gave him a place in the north,*
> *Obscure, shadowy, void, solitary.*

¶ 16. *Titlepage*] Urizen as Jehovah, reading a book in front of the Tables of Law. Pls. 1, 2: 'First' in the title deleted in 'copy A' and one other. Pl.2. *Design*. A woman, gowned to ankles and wrists, her hair in a bun (marks of propriety and orderliness) leads a naked infant as they float through the air.

Eternals, I hear your call gladly.
Dictate swift-winged words, and fear not
To unfold your dark visions of torment.

Pl. 3   CHAPTER I

    1. Lo, a shadow of horror is risen
In Eternity. Unknown, unprolific,
Self-closed, all-repelling. What demon
Hath formed this abominable void,
   5 This soul-shuddering vacuum? Some said,
'It is Urizen'. But unknown, abstracted,
Brooding secret, the dark power hid.

    2. Times on times he divided and measured
Space by space in his ninefold darkness,
 10 Unseen, unknown. Changes appeared
In his desolate mountains, rifted furious
By the black winds of perturbation.

    3. For he strove in battles dire,
In unseen conflictions with shapes,
 15 Bred from his forsaken wilderness,
Of beast, bird, fish, serpent and element,
Combustion, blast, vapour and cloud.

    4. Dark revolving in silent activity,
Unseen in tormenting passions,
 20 An activity unknown and horrible,
A self-contemplating shadow,
In enormous labours occupied.

    5. But Eternals beheld his vast forests.
Age on ages he lay, closed, unknown,

Pl.3. *Design*. Above the text, an Immortal exulting in the flames of life.
Chapter i. Urizen's self-separation.
1–7. unknown, unprolific, self-closed, all-repelling, abstracted, brooding, secret,
dark; vacuum, void, indicate the kind of evil in Urizen, especially in contrast
with infinite life (*36–9*). Boehme saw the 'Eternal Will' bringing an
'Eternal Nature'–a creation before Creation–into being through intro-
spection. But whereas in Boehme the Eternal Will is the sole existent
Being, expanding in love, Urizen's act is separation, a crime against love.
8. divided and measured] The act of a restrictive mind, a contradiction of
infinity.
9. ninefold] A Neo-Platonic use (see *Four Zoas* i *150n*) adopted by B., indi-
cating incompleteness (ten being a 'complete' number).
23. forests] Places of oppressive darkness, gloom, and inhuman 'vegetative'
life.

25 Brooding, shut in the deep; all avoid
    The petrific abominable chaos.

    6. His cold horrors silent, dark Urizen
    Prepared; his ten thousands of thunders
    Ranged in gloomed array stretch out across
30 The dread world, and the rolling of wheels
    As of swelling seas sound in his clouds,
    In his hills of stored snows, in his mountains
    Of hail and ice; voices of terror
    Are heard, like thunders of autumn,
35 When the cloud blazes over the harvests.

CHAPTER II

    1. Earth was not, nor globes of attraction.
    The will of the Immortal expanded
    Or contracted his all-flexible senses.
    Death was not, but eternal life sprung.

40 2. The sound of a trumpet! The heavens
    Awoke and vast clouds of blood rolled
    Round the dim rocks of Urizen, so named,
    That solitary one in immensity.

    3. Shrill the trumpet, and myriads of Eternity
Pl. 4 Muster around the bleak deserts,
46 Now filled with clouds, darkness and waters
    That rolled perplexed, labouring, and uttered
    Words articulate, bursting in thunders
    That rolled on the tops of his mountains:

50 4. 'From the depths of dark solitude; from
    The eternal abode in my holiness,

---

28. prepared] Cp. Satan's preparations in *Paradise Lost* vi 507–23, of primordial cannon which (522–3): 'Secret they finished, and in order set / With silent circumspection, unespied'—and contemporary mobilisations. *Chapter ii. The Law-giving.*
36. globes of attraction] The phrase combines two related notions: (*a*) B.'s dislike of enclosure and restriction, and (*b*) Newton's system, which asserted that such order, control and gravity governed the universe.
40. trumpet] Cp. *Exodus* xix 16: on Sinai, on the day when the law was given to Moses, 'there were thunders and lightnings, and a thick cloud upon the mount, and the voice of the trumpet exceeding loud'; and the Israelites, like the 'myriads of Eternity' (*44*) were gathered round.
44. Deleted in 'copy A'.
Pl.4. Only found in three of the seven copies. *Design.* A nude man crouches under a heavy, dark rainfall.

Hidden, set apart in my stern counsels
Reserved for the days of futurity,
I have sought for a joy without pain,
55   For a solid without fluctuation.
Why will you die, O Eternals?
Why live in unquenchable burnings?

5. 'First, I fought with the fire, consumed
Inwards, into a deep world within—
60   A void immense, wild, dark and deep,
Where nothing was, nature's wide womb.
And self-balanced stretched o'er the void
I alone, even I, the winds merciless
Bound. But condensing, in torrents
65   They fall and fall; strong I repelled
The vast waves and arose on the waters,
A wide world of solid obstruction.

6. 'Here alone I, in books formed of metals,
Have written the secrets of wisdom,
70   The secrets of dark contemplation
By fightings and conflicts dire
With terrible monsters sin-bred,
Which the bosoms of all inhabit—
Seven deadly sins of the soul.

75   7. 'Lo, I unfold my darkness and on
This rock place with strong hand the book
Of eternal brass, written in my solitude.

8. 'Laws of peace, of love, of unity,
Of pity, compassion, forgiveness.
80   Let each choose one habitation,
His ancient infinite mansion,
One command, one joy, one desire,
One curse, one weight, one measure,
One King, one God, one Law.'

52. *set apart*] In *Exodus* xix 9 God says to Moses, 'I come unto thee in a
thick cloud'; and the people are kept away from God on threat of death,
except for Moses, who is set apart to speak to God. Urizen takes the part
both of God the Law-giver and Moses the Law-speaker.
57. *unquenchable burnings*] As in *Marriage* ii 55–57, the fiery excitement of
a life of continual impulse and desire gratified and renewed looks like Hell
to Urizen and those like him.
58. *I fought with the fire*] Instead of living with and in it–the fire of life.
65–6. Illustrated in pl.12.
68. *books formed of metals*] The materials are rigid and unyielding. Urizen's
books also appear in *Europe 102*, *Ahania 111–22*, and *Four Zoas* vi and vii a.

CHAPTER III

85   1. The voice ended; they saw his pale visage
     Emerge from the darkness, his hand
     On the Rock of Eternity unclasping
     The book of brass. Rage seized the strong,

     2. Rage, fury, intense indignation—
90   In cataracts of fire, blood and gall,
     In whirlwinds of sulphurous smoke
     And enormous forms of energy;
     All the seven deadly sins of the soul
Pl. 5 In living creations appeared
95   In the flames of eternal fury.

     3. Sundering, darkening, thundering,
     Rent away with a terrible crash,
     Eternity rolled wide apart,
     Wide asunder rolling
100 Mountainous, all around
     Departing, departing, departing—
     Leaving ruinous fragments of life,
     Hanging, frowning cliffs, and all between
     An ocean of voidness unfathomable.

105 4. The roaring fires ran o'er the heavens
     In whirlwinds and cataracts of blood,
     And o'er the dark deserts of Urizen;
     Fires pour through the void on all sides
     On Urizen's self-begotten armies.

82–4. *one command* . . .] Cp. *Marriage* pl.24: 'One law for the lion and ox
is oppression'.
Chapter iii. Urizen casts himself out of Eternity.
85–8 are illustrated at the top of pl.5.
93. *seven deadly sins*] See *74*; these powers, which Urizen fears, are indeed
terrible, 'enormous', and now when roused cause great ruin. It does not
follow that, in their place in the infinite joy of life, they are necessarily
'sins' at all. Urizen has created Sin.
93–5. Deleted in 'copy A'.
Pl.5. *Design.* See *85n.*
96. *sundering*] This is the great catastrophe; in Infinite life there is no divi-
sion, only variety in unity. Hereafter, complete unity is impossible. All the
Eternals can do is to limit the disaster.
109. *On Urizen's self-begotten armies*] This line erased in 'copy A'; in all
copies *he* in *113–16* and *122* has been *they* ('the armies'). These changes
limit the evil to one figure, Urizen alone: but most of pl.6 is covered by a
design of *three* figures, encircled by snakes and falling into flames: with the

110   5. But no light from the fires: all was darkness
        In the flames of eternal fury.

        6. In fierce anguish and quenchless flames,
        To the deserts and rocks he ran raging
        To hide, but he could not; combining
115   He dug mountains and hills in vast strength;
        He piled them in incessant labour,
        In howlings and pangs and fierce madness—
        Long periods in burning fires labouring,
        Till hoary, and age-broke, and aged,
120   In despair and the shadows of death.

        7. And a roof, vast, petrific, around
        On all sides he framed, like a womb;
        Where thousands of rivers in veins
        Of blood pour down the mountains to cool
125   The eternal fires beating without
        From Eternals; and like a black globe
        Viewed by sons of Eternity, standing
        On the shore of the infinite ocean,
        Like a human heart struggling and beating,
130   The vast world of Urizen appeared.

        8. And Los round the dark globe of Urizen
        Kept watch for Eternals, to confine
        The obscure separation alone;
        For Eternity stood wide apart,
Pl. 6   As the stars are apart from the earth.

136   9. Los wept, howling around the dark demon,
        And cursing his lot; for in anguish

word 'combining' (*114*) the plural was too deeply rooted for B. to
eradicate it thus even by eliminating two figures from the design.
113–14. Raging / To hide] Cp. *Revelation* vi 15–16: 'And the kings of the
earth, and the great men . . . hid themselves in the dens and in the rocks of
the mountains; and said . . . Fall on us and hide us. . . .'
114. combining] Urizen has 'begotten' armies–i.e. many spirits have been
formed out of his single personality. Now, to produce the 'vast strength'
required, they recombine in him.
119. age-broke, and aged] Age does not exist in eternity.
122. like a womb] An image of constriction; the child must escape from the
womb in order to live.
128. the infinite ocean] The separating 'ocean of voidness' (*104*).
131. Los is the guardian set by the immortals. In *Urizen* B. sees him as a
blacksmith (*180*ff) and as 'eternal prophet', in that his task is to guard, as
well as he can, the spiritual welfare of a fallen creature, Urizen.
Pl.6. Design. See 109n.

Urizen was rent from his side,
And a fathomless void for his feet
140 And intense fires for his dwelling.

10. But Urizen laid in a stony sleep
Unorganized, rent from Eternity.

11. The Eternals said: 'What is this? Death?
Urizen is a clod of clay.'

Pl. 7   12. Los howled in a dismal stupor,
146 Groaning, gnashing, groaning,
Till the wrenching apart was healed.

13. But the wrenching of Urizen healed not.
Cold, featureless, flesh or clay,
150 Rifted with direful changes,
He lay in a dreamless night,

14. Till Los roused his fires, affrighted
At the formless unmeasurable death.

Pl. 8   CHAPTER IV[a]

1. Los, smitten with astonishment,
155 Frightened at the hurtling bones

2. And at the surging, sulphureous
Perturbed Immortal, mad-raging

3. In whirlwinds and pitch and nitre
Round the furious limbs of Los.

160 4. And Los formed nets and gins
And threw the nets round about.

138. rent from his side] B. conceived of the eternal existence as permitting
the mingling of the 'spiritual bodies' of the Eternals, and Urizen was
literally a part of Los's life.
142 summarizes Urizen's state. B., as an artist, stresses the need for meaning-
ful, 'organized' form: the 'unorganized' being has no ability to act,
create or associate. Los, the creative watchman, limits the disaster by
creating an organic form for Urizen–a fallen, restricted form, but better
than non-existence.
Pl.7. *145. Los howled*] The design that fills most of this plate shows Los,
against a background of flames, wrapping his arms round his head in agony.
147–8. Los expects a temporary separation, until Urizen recovers his
sanity: but Urizen cannot cure himself without Los's creative aid.
Chapter iv [a–b]. The creation of Urizen's organic form. (B. heads and
numbers two Chs iv: the [a] and [b] are not his. See headnote.)
Pl.8. *Design.* A crouched skeleton (beneath the text).
155. frightened] i.e. 'took fright'.

5. He watched in shuddering fear
The dark changes and bound every change
With rivets of iron and brass.

165 6. And these were the changes of Urizen.

Pl. 9   *[Full page illustration]*

Pl. 10   CHAPTER IV [b]
1. Ages on ages rolled over him.
In stony sleep ages rolled over him,
Like a dark waste stretching, changeable,
By earthquakes riven, belching sullen fires.
170 On ages rolled ages in ghastly
Sick torment, around him in whirlwinds
Of darkness. The eternal prophet howled,
Beating still on his rivets of iron,
Pouring solder of iron, dividing
175 The horrible night into watches.

2. And Urizen (so his eternal name)
His prolific delight obscured more and more
In dark secrecy, hiding in surging
Sulphureous fluid his fantasies.
180 The eternal prophet heaved the dark bellows,
And turned restless the tongs, and the hammer
Incessant beat, forging chains new and new,
Numbering with links hours, days and years.

3. The eternal mind, bounded, began to roll
185 Eddies of wrath ceaseless round and round,
And the sulphureous foam surging thick

163. *bound every change*] Urizen changes, Proteus-like, before Los. This meaningless transformation would never end, but Los takes every new form as it appears and gives it permanence. This is B.'s rewriting of the creation of the animal world in *Genesis* i 20–5.
Pl.9. *Full-page illustration.* Urizen, eyes shut, tries to climb through crushing rocks.
Pl.10. *Design.* A figure struggles among crushing rocks.
174. *solder*] Here and elsewhere B. spells it *sodor*.
175. *watches*] As, in *Genesis* i, time was divided into days.
177. *prolific*] 'creative': cp. 2.
180. *the eternal prophet*] Cp. *131n.*
184–262. These lines, metrically adapted, recur in *Four Zoas* iv *208–45, 279–82* (pp. 346–7, 350 below).
184. *the eternal mind*] The mind of Urizen.

Settled, a lake, bright and shining clear,
White as the snow on the mountains cold.

4. Forgetfulness, dumbness, necessity,
190 In chains of the mind locked up,
Like fetters of ice shrinking together,
Disorganized, rent from Eternity.
Los beat on his fetters of iron,
And heated his furnaces and poured
195 Iron solder and solder of brass.

5. Restless turned the Immortal, enchained,
Heaving dolorous, anguished, unbearable,
Till a roof, shaggy wild, enclosed
In an orb his fountain of thought.

200 6. In a horrible dreamful slumber,
Like the linked infernal chain,
A vast spine writhed in torment
Upon the winds, shooting pained
Ribs, like a bending cavern,
205 And bones of solidness froze
Over all his nerves of joy.
And a first age passed over,
And a state of dismal woe.

Pl. 11 7. From the caverns of his jointed spine,
210 Down sunk with fright a red
Round globe hot-burning, deep,
Deep down into the abyss—
Panting, conglobing, trembling,
Shooting out ten thousand branches
215 Around his solid bones.
And a second age passed over,
And a state of dismal woe.

8. In harrowing fear rolling round,
His nervous brain shot branches

189–92. Urizen has forgotten Eternity; he is divided from his kind and can no longer speak to them; he is bound by the chains of inevitable cause-and-effect.

198. a roof, shaggy, wild] The head with its hair: cp. *Europe 99.*

207. And a first age . . . woe] Cp. 'And the evening and the morning were the first day' (*Genesis* i 5).

Pl.11. Beneath the text, Los sinks back, weary, beside the form of Urizen who (shown as a bowed skeleton on pl.8) here is 'skin-and-bone' but begins to have fleshy form.

209–17. a red | Round globe] The heart, then the blood vessels.

220 Round the branches of his heart
     On high into two little orbs;
     And fixed in two little caves
     Hiding carefully from the wind,
     His eyes beheld the deep.
225 And a third age passed over,
     And a state of dismal woe.

     9. The pangs of hope began,
     In heavy pain, striving, struggling.
     Two ears in close volutions
230 From beneath his orbs of vision
     Shot spiring out and petrified
     As they grew. And a fourth age passed,
     And a state of dismal woe.

     10. In ghastly torment sick,
235 Hanging upon the wind

Pl. 12   *[Full-page illustration]*

Pl. 13 Two nostrils bent down to the deep.
        And a fifth age passed over,
        And a state of dismal woe.

        11. In ghastly torment sick,
240   Within his ribs bloated round
        A craving hungry cavern.
        Thence arose his channelled throat,
        And like a red flame a tongue
        Of thirst and of hunger appeared.
245   And a sixth age passed over,
        And a state of dismal woe.

        12. Enraged and stifled with torment,
        He threw his right arm to the north,
        His left arm to the south,
250   Shooting out in anguish deep;
        And his feet stamped the nether abyss
        In trembling and howling and dismay.
        And a seventh age passed over,
        And a state of dismal woe.

229. *close volutions*] The spirals of the inner ear.
Pl.12. *Full-page illustration.* Illustrates 65–6; Urizen floats in the deep.
Pl.13. *Design.* In the middle of the page, a figure thrusts apart the clouds
of a starry night sky.

CHAPTER V

255 1. In terrors Los shrunk from his task.
His great hammer fell from his hand;
His fires beheld and sickening
Hid their strong limbs in smoke.
For with noises ruinous loud,
260 With hurtlings and clashings and groans
The Immortal endured his chains,
Though bound in a deadly sleep.

2. All the myriads of Eternity,
All the wisdom and joy of life,
265 Roll like a sea around him,
Except what his little orbs
Of sight by degrees unfold.

3. And now his eternal life
Like a dream was obliterated.

270 4. Shuddering, the eternal prophet smote
With a stroke, from his north to south region.
The bellows and hammer are silent now;
A nerveless silence his prophetic voice
Seized; a cold solitude and dark void
275 The eternal prophet and Urizen closed.

5. Ages on ages rolled over them.
Cut off from life and light, frozen
Into horrible forms of deformity,
Los suffered his fires to decay.
280 Then he looked back with an anxious desire,
But the space undivided by existence
Struck horror into his soul.

Chapter v. Los's fall and division.
255. In *Genesis* 'God saw that it was good': here Los sees his work with horror.
257. His fires beheld . . .] The fires are personified.
261. The Immortal] i.e. Urizen, as elsewhere.
268–9. his eternal life . . . obliterated] One of B.'s favourite phrases, also in *Visions 57, Song of Los (Africa) 35.*
270–82. The fall of Los: he is first confounded by the sight of what he has had to do, and remains motionless for 'ages on ages'. He 'looks back' with regret. This period, unfilled by creative activity, becomes an impassable void between Los and the eternal world. The 'eternal prophet' (*178, 275*) must henceforth prophesy of eternity from outside. The passage may also suggest the mental fate of an inspired man who fails to respond to his inspiration. Cp. also *314n.*

6. Los wept, obscured with mourning;
His bosom earthquaked with sighs;
285   He saw Urizen, deadly black,
In his chains bound, and pity began,

7. In anguish dividing and dividing—
For pity divides the soul;
In pangs, eternity on eternity,
290   Life in cataracts poured down his cliffs.
The void shrunk the lymph into nerves,
Wandering wide on the bosom of night,
And left a round globe of blood
Trembling upon the void.

Pl. 14   [*Full-page illustration*]

Pl. 15 Thus the eternal prophet was divided
296   Before the death-image of Urizen.
For in changeable clouds and darkness,
In a winterly night beneath,
The abyss of Los stretched immense,
300   And now seen, now obscured to the eyes
Of Eternals, the visions remote
Of the dark separation appeared.
As glasses discover worlds
In the endless abyss of space,
305   So the expanding eyes of Immortals
Beheld the dark visions of Los,
And the globe of life-blood trembling.

283. Los wept] The tears are false; see below.
286. pity began] Cp. 'The Human Abstract' (p. 216): 'Pity would be no more / If we did not make somebody poor'. Pity is a distraction; the soul is divided between it and the action a 'pitiable' state demands. This is seen as Los's division into active male and tearful female–the latter deluding the former.
288. Repeated in *Milton* pl.8.*19*, with the addition 'and man unmans'.
Pl.14. *Full-page illustration.* A male figure (Los) dives downwards, pushing through clouds.
Pl.15. *Design.* See *300n.*
299. The abyss of Los] The space between Urizen and the land of the Eternals (*132–3*).
300–7. Though the Eternals' vision is infinite, they must stretch their faculties to the extreme to see Urizen, drifting further and further away. The design on this page shows them looking out of the clouds at a watery globe: one reaches down and trails his fingers in it; another is causing waves with his beard.

Pls. 16, 17   [*Two full-page illustrations*]

Pl. 18 8. The globe of life-blood trembled,
            Branching out into roots—
310   Fibrous, writhing upon the winds,
            Fibres of blood, milk and tears,
            In pangs, eternity on eternity.
            At length in tears and cries embodied,
            A female form trembling and pale
315   Waves before his deathy face.

            9. All Eternity shuddered at sight
            Of the first female now separate,
            Pale as a cloud of snow,
            Waving before the face of Los.

320   10. Wonder, awe, fear, astonishment,
            Petrify the eternal myriads
            At the first female form now separate;
Pl. 19   They called her *Pity*, and fled:

            11. 'Spread a tent, with strong curtains around them.
325   Let cords and stakes bind in the void
            That Eternals may no more behold them.'

            12. They began to weave curtains of darkness,
            They erected large pillars round the void,
            With golden hooks fastened in the pillars.
330   With infinite labour the Eternals
            A woof wove, and called it *Science*.

Pl.16. *Full-page illustration.* Los falling, crouched, through flames.
Pl.17. *Full-page illustration.* Enitharmon rising from her globe of blood.
Pl.18. *Design.* Los with his hammer, among flames.
314. A female form] Illustrated by pl.17. The last part of the Fall; Los is now locked in the restricted world, and divided. In Boehme, Adam fell in the same two stages. Before division Adam, like Los, was a being without sex, male and female in one whole. But instead of producing new creations out of the two principles within him, Adam desired to externalize what should have been his inner nature–he fell in love with himself. In his sleep, the female was separated from him. Now he, like Los, was in 'Generation', a world where the divided pair could only reproduce an endless succession of repeated self-images (*337n*).
Pl.19. *Design.* See *333n*.
331. Science] i.e. learning and knowledge; that derived through our restricted senses is a barrier, rather than a window, to true understanding.

CHAPTER VI

1. But Los saw the female and pitied.
He embraced her, she wept, she refused.
In perverse and cruel delight
335 She fled from his arms, yet he followed.

2. Eternity shuddered when they saw
Man begetting his likeness
On his own divided image.

3. A time passed over; the Eternals
340 Began to erect the tent,
When Enitharmon, sick,
Felt a worm within her womb.

4. Yet helpless it lay, like a worm
In the trembling womb,
345 To be moulded into existence.

5. All day the worm lay on her bosom;
All night within her womb
The worm lay, till it grew to a serpent
With dolorous hissings and poisons
350 Round Enitharmon's loins folding.

6. Coiled within Enitharmon's womb
The serpent grew, casting its scales;
With sharp pangs the hissings began
To change to a grating cry.
355 Many sorrows and dismal throes,
Many forms of fish, bird and beast,
Brought forth an infant form
Where was a worm before.

7. The Eternals their tent finished,
360 Alarmed with these gloomy visions,
When Enitharmon groaning
Produced a man-child to the light.

Chapter vi. The world of generation begins, with the birth of Orc.
333–5. Enitharmon's perverse flirtation, illustrated on this plate by a bowed
Los before a self-averting Enitharmon, is common in B. at this period: cp.
NB lyrics, pp. 47ff above: contrast Oothoon, *Visions 173–7, 191–204.*
337. begetting his likeness] After the fall there is no *new* creation; only repe-
tition. In eternity, love is a complete blending of loving persons: but this
is the self-love of Los for himself in Enitharmon–not love, but in-turned
desire.

8. A shriek ran through Eternity,
And a paralytic stroke,
365 At the birth of the human shadow.

9. Delving earth in his resistless way,
Howling, the child with fierce flames
Issued from Enitharmon.

10. The Eternals closed the tent.
370 They beat down the stakes; the cords
Pl. 20 Stretched for a work of Eternity;
No more Los beheld Eternity.

11. In his hands he seized the infant,
He bathed him in springs of sorrow,
375 He gave him to Enitharmon.

CHAPTER VII

1. They named the child Orc; he grew,
Fed with milk of Enitharmon.

2. Los awoke her. O sorrow and pain!
A tightening girdle grew
380 Around his bosom. In sobbings
He burst the girdle in twain;
But still another girdle
Oppressed his bosom. In sobbings
Again he burst it. Again
385 Another girdle succeeds.
The girdle was formed by day;
By night was burst in twain.

3. These falling down on the rock
Into an iron chain
390 In each other link by link locked.

365. the human shadow] Formed entirely in the fallen world, and unable to
partake of infinity. It is a 'shadow' of true, infinite humanity, but shows
that the fallen world is self-perpetuating.
366. delving earth] Forcing his way through Enitharmon's body.
resistless] 'irresistible'.
Pl.20. *Design.* A babe (Orc?) falling amid flames (cp. *Book of Los 86–8*).
371. a work of Eternity] A piece of eternal work–not necessarily to last for
eternity, but potentially so.
Chapter vii. The chain of jealousy: 'Life' awakes on earth.
379. A tightening girdle] Jealousy inevitably follows the division of the soul
into more than two entities. Ignoring it strengthens it into an unbreakable
chain, which is used to bind its innocent object–Orc.

4. They took Orc to the top of a mountain—
Oh, how Enitharmon wept!
They chained his young limbs to the rock
With the Chain of Jealousy
395   Beneath Urizen's deathful shadow.

5. The dead heard the voice of the child,
And began to awake from sleep.
All things heard the voice of the child,
And began to awake to life.

400   6. And Urizen, craving with hunger,
Stung with the odours of nature,
Explored his dens around.

7. He formed a line and a plummet
To divide the abyss beneath;
405   He formed a dividing rule;

8. He formed scales to weigh;
He formed massy weights;
He formed a brazen quadrant;
He formed golden compasses
410   And began to explore the abyss,
And he planted a garden of fruits.

9. But Los encircled Enitharmon
With fires of prophecy
From the sight of Urizen and Orc.

415   10. And she bore an enormous race.

---

393. They chained his young limbs] Orc is always represented as bound. In *America* (Prel.) this fact is merely a preliminary to his bursting free—primarily a political allegory, with no mention of jealousy. B. has here used the image for a new purpose. The Chain is developed in *Four Zoas* v–viib, but (except *Milton* pl.20.61 and casual refs.) is then dropped.

396. The dead] Ironically, those prepared for 'birth' in the fallen world. Such life as they have is derived from the vitality of Orc. The concept of fossils as ancient life, which might be inferred from this, had not been established in 1794.

402. explored his dens] A parody of scientific enquiry; Urizen explores with a dim lamp, illustrated at the foot of pl.23. This exploration is much developed in *Four Zoas* vi.

413. fires of prophecy] Is it strange to see B. connecting prophecy with jealousy?

CHAPTER VIII

1. Urizen explored his dens—
Mountain, moor and wilderness,
With a globe of fire lighting his journey,
A fearful journey, annoyed
420 By cruel enormities, forms

Pls. 21, 22   [*Two full-page illustrations*]

Pl. 23   Of life on his forsaken mountains.

2. And his world teemed vast enormities
Frightening, faithless, fawning
Portions of life, similitudes
425 Of a foot, or a hand, or a head,
Or a heart, or an eye, they swam—mischievous
Dread terrors, delighting in blood.

3. Most Urizen sickened to see
His eternal creations appear,
430 Sons and daughters of sorrow on mountains,
Weeping, wailing. First Thiriel appeared,
Astonished at his own existence,
Like a man from a cloud born. And Utha,
From the waters emerging, laments.
435 Grodna rent the deep earth howling—
Amazed, his heavens immense cracks
Like the ground parched with heat. Then Fuzon
Flamed out, first begotten, last born.
All his eternal sons in like manner;
440 His daughters from green herbs and cattle,
From monsters, and worms of the pit.

Chapter viii. The elements of Urizen's world.
Pl.21. *Full-page illustration* of *379–90.*
Pl.22. *Full-page illustration* of *189–90.*
Pl.23. *Design.* See *402n.*
424. Portions of life; similitudes] The common Platonic notion of this world as
a poor imitation of an ideal heaven; especially when seen unimaginatively,
with Urizen's eyes.
429–30. His eternal creations . . . sorrow] What in eternity had been true
creation was here no more than a wretched self-copy. The four figures that
follow are not men, but the four elements: Grodna from Earth; Thiriel–
Air; Fuzon–Fire; Utha–Water: their birth is illustrated on pl.24.

4. He in darkness closed viewed all his race,
And his soul sickened. He cursed
Both sons and daughters; for he saw
445 That no flesh nor spirit could keep
His iron laws one moment.

5. For he saw that life lived upon death.

Pl. 24   *[Full-page illustration]*

Pl. 25 The ox in the slaughter-house moans,
The dog at the wintry door,
450 And he wept, and he called it pity,
And his tears flowed down on the winds.

6. Cold he wandered on high, over their cities,
In weeping and pain and woe.
And wherever he wandered in sorrows
455 Upon the aged heavens,
A cold shadow followed behind him,
Like a spider's web, moist, cold, and dim,
Drawing out from his sorrowing soul,
The dungeon-like heaven dividing
460 Wherever the footsteps of Urizen
Walked over the cities in sorrow;

7. Till a web dark and cold throughout all
The tormented element stretched
From the sorrows of Urizen's soul.
465 (And the web is a female in embryo.)
None could break the web—no wings of fire,

8. So twisted the cords, and so knotted
The meshes, twisted like to the human brain.

444–6. he saw . . . one moment] Urizen's tragedy, since he had proclaimed
his laws as the ideal of life. His laws are inevitably followed by his curse.
Cp. Paul's criticism of the law (*Galatians* iii 10–11): 'For as many as are of
the works of the law are under the curse: for it is written, Cursed is every
one that continueth not in all things . . . in the book of the law . . . But
that no man is justified by the law in the sight of God, it is evident: . . .'
Pl.24. Full-page illustration of *429–38*.
Pl.25. Design. A mass of writhing figures, human and serpentine, in the sea.
449. The dog at the wintry door] Illustrated on pl.26.
465. a female in embryo] An odd phrase; the probable meaning is that the
web is like a pregnant female, enclosing a life in its 'womb'. This line was
deleted in 'copy A'.

9. And all called it *The Net of Religion*.

CHAPTER IX

470   1. Then the inhabitants of those cities
Felt their nerves change into marrow,
And hardening bones began
In swift diseases and torments,
In throbbings and shootings and grindings
475   Through all the coasts—till weakened
The senses inward rushed, shrinking
Beneath the dark net of infection;

2. Till the shrunken eyes, clouded over,
Discerned not the woven hypocrisy;
480   But the streaky slime in their heavens
Brought together by narrowing perceptions
Appeared transparent air; for their eyes
Grew small like the eyes of a man,
And in reptile forms shrinking together
485   Of seven feet stature they remained.

3. Six days they shrunk up from existence,
And on the seventh day they rested;
And they blessed the seventh day, in sick hope—
And forgot their eternal life.

490   4. And their thirty cities divided
In form of a human heart.
No more could they rise at will
In the infinite void, but bound down
To earth by their narrowing perceptions

469. Net of Religion] B. objects, not to the inspiration of religion, but to ecclesiastical control of men's beliefs and lives. The Net is developed in *Four Zoas* vi *241*ff.
Chapter ix. Mankind appears.
470. those cities] The cities of Egypt (*452, 490*). See also *505n.*
479. the woven hypocrisy] The Web of Religion, which is more than a mere temporary human scheme, an error in the universe's foundations.
484. reptile forms] Crawling upon the face of the earth.
485. seven feet stature] Perhaps a reference to the primeval giants of *Genesis* vi 4, 'There were giants in the earth in those days'.
486. six days they shrunk up] A parody of the six days of expanding creation in *Genesis*.
490–1. The cities become Africa (*Song of Los* iii *3*—'heart-formed Africa').
492. no more could they rise] In eternity, Urizen's creations (see *36–9* and *429n*) would have had infinite faculties. Now they, with him, are bound in the fallen world.

Pls. 26, 27   [*Two full-page illustrations*]

Pl. 28 They lived a period of years,
496   Then left a noisome body
         To the jaws of devouring darkness.

         5. And their children wept, and built
         Tombs in the desolate places,
500   And formed laws of prudence, and called them
         The eternal laws of God.

         6. And the thirty cities remained,
         Surrounded by salt floods, now called
         Africa (its name was then Egypt).

505   7. The remaining sons of Urizen
         Beheld their brethren shrink together
         Beneath the net of Urizen.
         Persuasion was in vain;
         For the ears of the inhabitants
510   Were withered, and deafened, and cold,
         And their eyes could not discern
         Their brethren of other cities.

         8. So Fuzon called all together
         The remaining children of Urizen,
515   And they left the pendulous earth:
         They called it Egypt, and left it.

         9. And the salt ocean rolled englobed.

         The End of the first book of Urizen

Pl.26. *Full-page illustration* of *449*.
Pl.27. *Full-page illustration.* Urizen rushing away.
Pl.28. *Design.* Illustrates *454–8*.
500. laws of prudence] Laws formed for caution's sake, to escape the risks of imaginative living in a fallen world. It is safer to be legal.
505. The remaining sons, in contrast with the inhabitants of the cities. These 'sons' retained some desire for life and preferred the desert to 'the fleshpots of Egypt'. Fuzon is B.'s Moses as leader: as Urizen in ch. i was Moses as law-bearer.
513. Fuzon is the fire-element or god (*438*): the Israelites in the Exodus worshipped a fire-Jehovah in the pillar of fire and smoke (*Exodus* xiii 21–2): and Boehme also emphasised the virtues of this forceful element even under the Fall.
517. A Blakean summary of chaos.

17 The Book of Ahania

Date. The engraved titlepage has 'Lambeth 1795'. In 1796 B. was engaged in designing and engraving Young's *Night Thoughts*, and so *Ahania* is not likely to be later; unless the simpler presentation than usual–like *The Book of Los*, it is engraved in the conventional manner, not by B.'s technique of 'Illuminated Printing'–indicates a hurried completion in 1796 in order to make way for *Night Thoughts*. Only one copy is known; its few designs are colour-printed. Like *Urizen* and *The Book of Los*, *Ahania* is presented in 'biblical' form, with chapters and verses (though in metre).

Theme. *Ahania* has a broken-backed narrative, but is valuable for the beautiful lament of Ahania with which it ends, besides such material as the growth of the Tree of Mystery. As narrative, it demonstrates the petering-out of the *Urizen* myth (later reshaped in *Vala, or The Four Zoas*). The poem is a sequel to *Urizen* and describes Fuzon's revolt, which divides Urizen's soul; and Urizen's retaliation, which destroys Fuzon. The narrative falls into two pieces, Ch. iv introducing yet another theme. (*a*) The poem begins with Fuzon (a figure similar to the Orc of *America*) as protagonist; but when Fuzon becomes 'a pale living corse on the Tree' (*131*) there is little more to tell. (*b*) B. branches out, in Ch. iv, in another direction entirely, reintroducing Los for the first time in the poem, and showing him again at his formative work, as in *Urizen*: but this too leads to a dead end. (*c*) Urizen, in Fuzon's revolt, was struck by a fiery beam which divided his soul into male and female; his female portion, Ahania, is driven apart from him, 'a faint shadow wandering / In chaos' (*38–9*), and is forgotten while B. deals with the other matter. But in Ch. v she reappears, and this chapter is devoted to her lament for the joys of their lost life together. Ultimately she is the chief imaginative creation of the poem, and it is named after her, not Fuzon.

Pl. 1   [*Titlepage*]

Pl. 2   CHAPTER I

      1: Fuzon, on a chariot iron-winged,
      On spiked flames rose; his hot visage
      Flamed furious; sparkles his hair and beard
      Shot down his wide bosom and shoulders.

¶ 17. Pl.1. *Titlepage.* The design shows a flying female figure.

1. *Fuzon*] Cp. *Urizen* 437, 513: the rebellious son of Urizen who, Moses-like, leads the other free sons away from their father's influence. Note the likeness of Fuzon to the Orc of *America* and *Europe* (but not of *Urizen*, where Orc is only a child). Fuzon has been equated by Erdman with Robespierre, who hunted down the enemies of the French Revolution with a violence which recoiled on himself.

3–4. *sparkles his hair . . . shoulders*] The syntax is confusing: a comma after *his hair* might help; the precise intent is uncertain, though the general sense is clear.

5   On clouds of smoke rages his chariot,
    And his right hand burns red in its cloud,
    Moulding into a vast globe his wrath,
    As the thunder-stone is moulded,
    Son of Urizen's silent burnings.

10 2: 'Shall we worship this demon of smoke,'
    Said Fuzon, 'this abstract non-entity,
    This cloudy god seated on waters,
    Now seen, now obscured—king of sorrow?'

    3: So he spoke in a fiery flame,
15 On Urizen frowning indignant,
    The globe of wrath shaking on high.
    Roaring with fury he threw
    The howling globe; burning it flew,
    Lengthening into a hungry beam. Swiftly

20 4: Opposed to the exulting flamed beam
    The broad disc of Urizen upheaved
    Across the void many a mile.

    5: It was forged in mills where the winter
    Beats incessant; ten winters the disc
25 Unremitting endured the cold hammer.

    6: But the strong arm that sent it remembered
    The sounding beam; laughing it tore through
    That beaten mass, keeping its direction,
    The cold loins of Urizen dividing.

30 7: Dire shrieked his invisible lust.
    Deep groaned Urizen, stretching his awful hand

8–9. Fuzon, a child of Urizen, creates weapons of violence after the manner of his father.

19. *Lengthening into a hungry beam*] The missile was created as a *globe*, a form which, as *Urizen* amply shows, B. hated as representing the self-contained and inward-turning mind. B. now wants the missile to be arrow-like, sharp and piercing; so in flight the globe turns into a fiery beam, perhaps with phallic implications (*30*).

23–9. Once more cold, winter and death are defeated by light, heat and youth.

30–7. Fuzon's blow induces lust in Urizen. Ahania, therefore, who before was a part of his personality united to him in love, is externalized as an *object* of his lust: and further, his lust and her separation make him jealous

Ahania (so name his parted soul)
He seized on his mountains of jealousy.
He groaned, anguished, and called her Sin,
35   Kissing her and weeping over her,
Then hid her in darkness, in silence,
Jealous though she was invisible.

8: She fell down, a faint shadow wandering
In chaos and circling dark Urizen—
40   As the moon anguished circles the earth—
Hopeless, abhorred, a death-shadow,
Unseen, unbodied, unknown,
The mother of pestilence.

9: But the fiery beam of Fuzon
45   Was a pillar of fire to Egypt,
Five hundred years wandering on earth:
Till Los seized it and beat in a mass
With the body of the sun.

Pl. 3   CHAPTER II
1: But the forehead of Urizen gathering,
50   And his eyes pale with anguish, his lips
Blue and changing, in tears and bitter
Contrition he prepared his bow,

of her. Thus lust, sex, sin and jealousy in Urizen appear simultaneously. The image—of separation of the feminine principle of the soul through the soul's undue introspection—is found in Boehme, where it is one of the processes of creation.

32. Ahania] In B.'s later terminology, she is Urizen's 'emanation', the feminine part of his immortal united personality, divided and separated from him. No longer enriched by her presence, he is impoverished by her separateness.

38ff. Ahania now begins an existence apart from Urizen, longing for him but unable to find him, as she laments in ch. v.

45. a pillar of fire] As Israel wandered for forty years, so here Egypt had wandered for 500 before the creation of the sun, led by a pillar of fire which became the sun. The biblical reference is *Exodus* xiii 22: cp. *Song of Los* (*Asia*) *51n*, *Urizen 513n.*

47–8. Los seized it] This disposes of the pillar of fire, and also connects to the narrative of *The Book of Los 145ff.* Line *48* means 'beat *it into* a mass....'

52. contrition] Urizen's remorse is inevitably hypocritical—a virtue easily assumed in a morally meaningless form.

2: Formed of ribs, that in his dark solitude
When obscured in his forests fell monsters
55   Arose. For his dire contemplations
Rushed down like floods from his mountains
In torrents of mud settling thick
With eggs of unnatural production
Forthwith hatching—some howled on his hills,
60   Some in vales, some aloft flew in air.

3: Of these an enormous dread serpent,
Scaled and poisonous horned,
Approached Urizen even to his knees,
As he sat on his dark rooted oak.

65   4: With his horns he pushed furious.
Great the conflict and great the jealousy
In cold poisons, but Urizen smote him.

5: First he poisoned the rocks with his blood,
Then polished his ribs, and his sinews
70   Dried, laid them apart till winter;
Then a bow black prepared. On this bow,
A poisoned rock placed in silence,
He uttered these words to the bow:

6: 'O bow of the clouds of secrecy,
75   O nerve of that lust-formed monster,
Send this rock swift, invisible, through
The black clouds, on the bosom of Fuzon.'

7: So saying, in torment of his wounds,
He bent the enormous ribs slowly,
80   A circle of darkness; then fixed
The sinew in its rest, then the rock,
(Poisonous source) placed with art, lifting difficult
Its weighty bulk. Silent the rock lay.

8: While Fuzon, his tigers unloosing,
85   Thought Urizen slain by his wrath.
'I am God,' said he, 'eldest of things!'

53–5. The syntax is irregular; B. only has a comma after 'monsters'. It
is tempting to make sense by regarding 'fell' as a verb, and 54 as a paren-
thesis, but the resultant construction is unfamiliar in B. Perhaps some-
thing is missing.
64. oak] Sacred to the Druids, and thus the tree of Urizenic false religion.
78–83. Compare the youthful fire of Fuzon's attack with the misery, pain
and labour of Urizen's retaliation.
84–6. his tigers unloosing] Tigers are commonly associated in B. with wrath (as
in 37). Fuzon's assumption of godhead (86) is a sure sign of his corruption.

9: Sudden sings the rock, swift and invisible
On Fuzon flew, entered his bosom.
His beautiful visage, his tresses
90 That gave light to the mornings of Heaven
Were smitten with darkness, deformed
And outstretched on the edge of the forest.

10: But the rock fell upon the earth,
Mount Sinai, in Arabia.

CHAPTER III

95 1: The globe shook; and Urizen, seated
On black clouds, his sore wound anointed.
The ointment flowed down the void
Mixed with blood; here the snake gets her poison.

2: With difficulty and great pain Urizen
100 Lifted on high the dead corse;
On his shoulders he bore it to where
A tree hung over the immensity.

90. That gave light . . . heaven] A reminiscence of the image, rather than the words, of *Isaiah* xiv 12: 'How art thou fallen from heaven, O Lucifer, son of the morning!'
94. Mount Sinai] Where the abhorred Law was given. See *Galatians* iv 24–6: 'Which things are an allegory: for these are the two covenants; the one from the mount Sinai, which gendereth to bondage, which is Agar. For this Agar is mount Sinai in Arabia, and answereth to Jerusalem which now is, and is in bondage with her children. But Jerusalem which is above is free, which is the mother of us all.' Thus Paul also uses the phrase in a symbol of the bondage of Mosaic law, in contrast with the freedom of heaven.
95. the globe shook] A rhetorical device, indicating that more fearful events are still to come. The *globe* is the world, not Fuzon's globe of 7ff.
102. A tree] This is the first appearance in the narrative poems of the Tree of Mystery: cp. 'A Human Abstract' and 'A Poison Tree' in *Experience*. Its characteristics are its obscurity, its poisonous nature, and its self-generation in a labyrinth of roots (note the Miltonic source quoted at *Four Zoas* viia *31*, where the idea is further developed). The Tree also appears in *Jerusalem* pl.28.*13–19*, much altered in detail but recognizably the same image, which expresses B.'s horror of the mindless grasp of compulsive religious error that creeps around men's minds. In this context it also resembles the cross of Christ (*129*); and Fuzon in *128–29* resembles Prometheus.

11*

3: For when Urizen shrunk away
From Eternals, he sat on a rock
105   Barren, a rock which himself
From redounding fancies had petrified.
Many tears fell on the rock,
Many sparks of vegetation;
Soon shot the pained root
110   Of mystery under his heel.
It grew a thick tree; he wrote
In silence his book of iron,
Till the horrid plant bending its boughs
Grew to roots when it felt the earth
115   And again sprung to many a tree.

4: Amazed started Urizen, when
He beheld himself compassed round
And high roofed over with trees.
He arose; but the stems stood so thick
120   He with difficulty and great pain
Brought his books, all but the book
Pl. 4   Of iron, from the dismal shade.

5: The tree still grows over the void,
Enrooting itself all around,
125   An endless labyrinth of woe:

6: The corse of his first begotten
On the accursed TREE OF MYSTERY—
On the topmost stem of this tree
Urizen nailed Fuzon's corse.

CHAPTER IV

130   1: Forth flew the arrows of pestilence
Round the pale living corse on the tree;

112. *His book of iron*] Cp. *Europe 104, Urizen 77–88, Four Zoas* viia *109*ff.
In these the book is always brass; it has been suggested that the book of
brass contains moral law, and the book of iron the laws of oppression: but
B. did not distinguish between forms of tyranny, whether moral, political
or religious, and the distinction is not explicit and very improbable.
116–22 recur in *Four Zoas* viia *36–9* (adapted to the septenary metre). There
is a curious and unexpected likeness between Urizen and Robinson Crusoe,
who grew a grove round his dwelling to keep away possible enemies, and
then found it a great labour to carry stores in and out.
130. arrows of pestilence] Fuzon also becomes a source of pestilence, which
began with the separation of Ahania from Urizen (*43*). The origin of the
arrows is not very clearly explained; see *143–7*.
131. living] The first indication that Fuzon is not dead; at *100* B. says he is.

2: For in Urizen's slumbers of abstraction
In the infinite ages of Eternity,
When his nerves of joy melted and flowed,
135 A white lake on the dark blue air,
In perturbed pain and dismal torment
Now stretching out, now swift conglobing.

3: Effluvia vapoured above
In noxious clouds. These hovered thick
140 Over the disorganized Immortal,
Till petrific pain scurfed o'er the lakes
As the bones of man, solid and dark.

4: The clouds of disease hovered wide
Around the Immortal in torment,
145 Perching around the hurtling bones,
Disease on disease, shape on shape,
Winged, screaming in blood and torment.

5: The eternal prophet beat on his anvils,
Enraged in the desolate darkness;
150 He forged nets of iron around
And Los threw them around the bones.

6: The shapes, screaming, fluttered vain;
Some combined into muscles and glands,
Some organs for craving and lust;
155 Most remained on the tormented void,
Urizen's army of horrors.

7: Round the pale living corse on the tree
Forty years flew the arrows of pestilence.

8: Wailing and terror and woe
160 Ran through all his dismal world;
Forty years all his sons and daughters
Felt their skulls harden; then Asia
Arose in the pendulous deep.

---

135. As earlier in *Urizen 187*.
140. *the disorganized Immortal*] Urizen–a phrase reminiscent of *Urizen*.
141. *scurfed*] Formed into a scum on the surface.
161–2. *forty years . . . skulls harden*] Cp. *158*, 'forty years'. Perhaps a verbal reminiscence of *Psalm* xcv 8, 10: 'Harden not your heart, as in . . . the wilderness', and 'Forty years long was I grieved. . . .' But the Psalm is God's admonition to the Israelites, referring to the forty years which they spent wandering as a punishment for their lack of faith.
Asia] Africa arose in *Urizen 490–504*.

9: They reptilize upon the Earth.
165   10: Fuzon groaned on the tree.

CHAPTER V

1: The lamenting voice of Ahania,
Weeping upon the void
And round the tree of Fuzon.
Distant in solitary night
170   Her voice was heard, but no form
Had she: but her tears from clouds
Eternal fell round the tree,

2: And the voice cried: 'Ah, Urizen, love,
Flower of morning, I weep on the verge
175   Of non-entity. How wide the abyss
Between Ahania and thee!

3: 'I lie on the verge of the deep.
I see thy dark clouds ascend,
I see thy black forests and floods,
180   A horrible waste to my eyes.

4: 'Weeping I walk over rocks,
Over dens and through valleys of death.
Why didst thou despise Ahania,
To cast me from thy bright presence
185   Into the world of loneness?

5: 'I cannot touch his hand,
Nor weep on his knees, nor hear
His voice and bow, nor see his eyes

164. *reptilize*] i.e. become crawling, earth-tied creatures who cannot spread wings in infinity. Lines *164–5*, written as two distinct and numbered verses, are a rhetorical device to enhance the awe and fearfulness of the situation. Chapter v. All movement in the action has ceased, and the chapter is given up to Ahania's lament.

170–71. *no form / Had she*] A creature cannot exist without form, which it needs to make it a living, active organism. When it loses form, it becomes chaotic and is in danger of annihilation. B. hated fixity, but believed in form; i.e. the living form of living creatures. Ahania is a part of Urizen's soul; cast out from him, she can have no true existence.

174–5. *I weep on the verge / Of non-entity*] Cp. *Visions 189–90*: 'Till beauty fades from off my shoulders, darkened and cast out, / A solitary shadow wailing on the margin of non-entity'. A characteristically Blakean re-use of an image.

188. *his voice and bow*] In B. bows are often said to 'sound' or 'sing'.

And joy, nor hear his footsteps and
190　My heart leap at the lovely sound.
　　　I cannot kiss the place
　　　Whereon his bright feet have trod,
Pl. 5　But I wander on the rocks
　　　With hard necessity.

195　6: 'Where is my golden palace,
　　　Where my ivory bed,
　　　Where the joy of my morning hour?
　　　Where the sons of Eternity, singing

　　　7: 'To awake bright Urizen, my King?
200　To arise to the mountain sport,
　　　To the bliss of eternal valleys;

　　　8: 'To awake my King in the morn
　　　To embrace Ahania's joy
　　　On the breadth of his open bosom—
205　From my soft cloud of dew to fall
　　　In showers of life on his harvests?

　　　9: 'When he gave my happy soul
　　　To the sons of eternal joy;
　　　When he took the daughters of life
210　Into my chambers of love;

　　　10: 'When I found babes of bliss on my beds,
　　　And bosoms of milk in my chambers
　　　Filled with eternal seed.
　　　Oh, eternal births sung round Ahania
215　In interchange sweet of their joys!

　　　11: 'Swelled with ripeness and fat with fatness,
　　　Bursting on winds my odours,
　　　My ripe figs and rich pomegranates
　　　In infant joy at thy feet,
220　O Urizen, sported and sang.

194–231. These lines are an echo of Oothoon's lament in *Visions*, esp. *173–7*, *198–204.*
211–5. These lines are difficult to visualize; they give a general impression of a profusion of delight, particularly in love and birth.
217–19. my odours, / *My ripe figs,* . . . / *In infant joy*] An example of B.'s belief in the essential unity of creation.

12: 'Then thou with thy lap full of seed,
With thy hand full of generous fire,
Walked forth from the clouds of morning
On the virgins of springing joy,
225   On the human soul to cast
The seed of eternal science.

13: 'The sweat poured down thy temples;
To Ahania returned in evening
The moisture awoke to birth
230   My mother's joys, sleeping in bliss.

14: 'But now, alone over rocks, mountains,
Cast out from thy lovely bosom.
Cruel jealousy! selfish fear!
Self-destroying, how can delight
235   Renew in these chains of darkness,
Where bones of beasts are strown
On the bleak and snowy mountains,
Where bones from the birth are buried
Before they see the light ?'

Finis

[*Design*]

18 The Book of Los

Date. Engraved titlepage 'Lambeth 1795' (see *Ahania* headnote). It is not
possible to say which of the two poems is earlier. The closeness of the
opening of *Ahania* to the end of *Urizen*, in contrast with the inconsistencies
between *The Book of Los* and *Urizen* suggest the order (commonly ac-
cepted) followed in this edition. The poem, also preserved in a unique
copy, was printed like *Ahania* by conventional etching.
Theme. After 26 lines which are presented as integral to the poem but
which function as a 'Preludium' (though not so named), the narrative

221. *lap full of seed*] Urizen's dual character–as a builder when fallen, but
a farmer in eternity–is fully developed in *Four Zoas*. This line is the first
indication of his 'eternal' nature; in *Urizen* it is not hinted at.
226. *science*] Knowledge, understanding, of any profound kind.
233–5. Cp. 'Earth's Answer' in *Experience* (p. 210), where a Urizenic
figure is also addressed: 'Selfish Father of men, / Cruel jealous selfish
fear: / Can delight / Chained in night / The virgins of youth and morninf
bear?'
Pl.5. *Design.* A heap of beheaded corpses (fruit of the guillotine?).

begins. Los is found watching Urizen's shadow; but soon his indignation—
an error prophets are prone to—gets the better of him. He is angry, chained
as he is, at the freedom of the flames of eternal life around him. Like a man
in the midst of a heath fire, he stamps out the flames under his feet until he
has made a clear, unburning space for himself. But he has driven eternity
away, and, as in a nightmare, the fires (dark fires without light) freeze into
solid rock, which imprisons him until his impatience bursts it. Then, lost
in error, he falls in an indefinite void until in his flailing efforts he begins
to acquire a shape. Head, lungs and nerves spread out formlessly like a
polypus in the void, which then turns into an ocean. He has come through
fire, earth, air and water. His struggles again change the elements; the
fluid around him divides into solid and gas, and light appears.

We are then recalled to Los's first task, for now he sees Urizen—or
rather his spine, the only shaped part of him. Los begins his blacksmith's
labours, and creates a brilliant globe which is yet an illusion. To it he binds
Urizen's spine as if it were a heart, and an illusory pseudo-human form
begins to develop round the spine and the sun-heart. At this point the
poem ends: a strange poem, unsatisfactory in its lack of completeness,
compelling in a dreamlike logic.

Pls. 1–2 *[Frontispiece and Titlepage]*

Pl. 3 CHAPTER I

   1 : *Eno, aged mother,*
   Who the chariot of Leutha guides,
   Since the day of thunders in old time
   2 : *Sitting beneath the eternal oak,*
5 *Trembled and shook the steadfast earth,*
   And thus her speech broke forth:

   3 : *O times remote,*
   When love and joy were adoration,
   And none impure were deemed—

¶ 18. Pl.1. Eno crouched against a stone, with a background of rocks.
Pl.2. *Design*: Los huddled in a cave.
Pl.3. The first twenty-six lines are engraved in a smaller script than the rest.
1. *Eno, aged mother*] Only a name; also mentioned in a draft of the first line
of *The Four Zoas*, though later excluded; and in *Four Zoas* i *139–48* as 'a
daughter of Beulah' who took care of lost souls.
2. *the chariot of Leutha*] See *Visions 4n*. Leutha does not here appear to be
the devious and insidious female of *Europe 170–5*, though she is scarcely
characterized by this allusion.
4. *Sitting beneath the eternal oak*] Usually a sign of evil influence; though
not, it seems, here. The *eternal* oak may be conceived as distinct from the
pernicious trees of the Druids; Eno speaks as a prophetic female bard.

10   *Not eyeless covet,*
    Nor thin-lipped envy,
    Nor bristled wrath,
    Nor curled wantonness.

    4: *'But covet was poured full;*
15 *Envy fed with fat of lambs;*
    Wrath with lions' gore;
    Wantonness lulled to sleep
    With the virgin's lute,
    Or sated with her love.

20 5: *'Till covet broke his locks and bars,*
    And slept with open doors;
    Envy sung at the rich man's feast;
    Wrath was followed up and down
    By a little ewe lamb,
25 *And wantonness on his own true love*
    Begot a giant race'.

    6: Raging furious, the flames of desire
    Ran through heaven and earth, living flames,
    Intelligent, organized, armed
30 With destruction and plagues. In the midst
    The eternal prophet, bound in a chain,
    Compelled to watch Urizen's shadow,

    7: Raged with curses and sparkles of fury.
    Round the flames roll, as Los hurls his chains,
35 Mounting up from his fury, condensed,
    Rolling round and round, mounting on high
    Into vacuum, into non-entity,
    Where nothing was. Dashed wide apart
    His feet stamp the eternal fierce-raging
40 Rivers of wide flame; they roll round
    And round on all sides making their way
    Into darkness and shadowy obscurity.

9–26. Lines *9–13* in particular are paradoxical. The idea is that the appetites now known as Covet, Envy, etc., in the Golden Age had their desires satisfied. By implication, it was only when these desires were in themselves 'deemed impure' that they were repressed and broke out in excess: until then (as in *20–6*) they were joyfully fulfilled.

27. *the flames of desire*] The scene is that of *Urizen 110*: Urizen has been cast out of heaven, and Los is set to watch him. But there Los is not said to be chained, though his task is in exile.

34–44. Los stamps on the flames, driving the rivers of flame apart so that he stands alone in the midst of fire.

8: Wide apart stood the fires. Los remained
In the void between fire and fire.
45 In trembling and horror they beheld him;
They stood wide apart, driven by his hands
And his feet, which the nether abyss
Stamped in fury and hot indignation.

9: But no light from the fires. All was
Pl. 4 Darkness round Los. Heat was not; for bound up
51 Into fiery spheres from his fury
The gigantic flames trembled and hid.

10: Coldness, darkness, obstruction, a solid
Without fluctuation, hard as adamant,
55 Black as marble of Egypt, impenetrable,
Bound in the fierce raging Immortal.
And the separated fires froze in,
A vast solid without fluctuation,
Bound in his expanding clear senses.

CHAPTER II

60 1: The Immortal stood frozen amidst
The vast rock of Eternity—times
And times, a night of vast durance:
Impatient, stifled, stiffened, hardened;

2: Till impatience no longer could bear
65 The hard bondage: rent, rent, the vast solid
With a crash from immense to immense

3: Cracked across into numberless fragments.
The prophetic wrath, struggling for vent,
Hurls apart, stamping furious to dust
70 And crumbling with bursting sobs, heaves
The black marble on high into fragments

4: Hurled apart on all sides, as a falling
Rock. The innumerable fragments away
Fell asunder, and horrible vacuum
75 Beneath him and on all sides round.

47. i.e. 'his feet stamped the nether abyss'.
49. *no light from the fires*] So in similar passages, *America 28* and *Urizen 110*.
50. *Darkness*] Los has driven away the fierceness of the flames; but he can-
not partake of their vitality, now he is separate from them. Hence the effect
seen in 53ff. Los's impatience is now first seen; in *Urizen* his enthusiasm
wanes (255): but prophetic impatience is a feature of Los, especially in
Milton and *Jerusalem*.

5: Falling, falling! Los fell and fell,
Sunk precipitant, heavy, down, down,
Times on times, night on night, day on day
(Truth has bounds, error none), falling, falling,
80 Years on years, and ages on ages.
Still he fell through the void, still a void
Found for falling day and night without end.
For though day or night was not, their spaces
Were measured by his incessant whirls
85 In the horrid vacuity bottomless.

6: The Immortal, revolving, indignant,
First in wrath threw his limbs, like the babe
New-born into our world. Wrath subsided,
And contemplative thoughts first arose;
90 Then aloft his head reared in the abyss,
And his downward-borne fall changed oblique,

7: Many ages of groans, till there grew
Branchy forms, organizing the human
Into finite inflexible organs,

95 8: Till in process from falling he bore
Sidelong on the purple air, wafting
The weak breeze in efforts o'erwearied.

9: Incessant the falling mind laboured,
Organizing itself, till the vacuum

79. *Error*] Los's 'prophetic wrath' (*68*, see *50n*) does not keep him from
error, since he has repulsed the 'living, intelligent flames of desire' (*27–30*).
The importance to B. of human vitality and human form is repeatedly
made clear; here the image shows that, not only is error boundless in a
loose sense, it is of the essence of error that it is abstract, shapeless, without
the boundaries which would give it some meaning, if only a negative one.
81. *Still he fell*] Cp. the fall of Mulciber, *Paradise Lost* i 740–4: 'and how he
fell / From Heaven they fabled ... / from morn / To noon he fell, from
noon to dewy eve, / A summer's day ...' and of Satan, ii 932–4: 'All un-
awares, / Fluttering his pennons vain, plumb-down he drops / Ten thou-
sand fathom deep, and to this hour / Down had been falling. ...'
88–9. *wrath subsided ... arose*] Los's error has been leading him (like
Satan; see *81n*) into endless chaos; now he begins to take a form which
organizes his fallen being into a body, which has its uses in that he can
achieve some control of error.
93–4. *organizing the human / Into finite inflexible organs*] This summarizes
the Fall; the Human form is infinitely variable–though not chaotic.
99–100. *Organizing itself*] Note the *self*-centredness of this; Los has lost con-
tact with all others.   *the vacuum became element*] Los does not fall into
the sea; his mind forms the sea around him.

100   Became element, pliant to rise,
       Or to fall, or to swim, or to fly;
       With ease searching the dire vacuity.

CHAPTER III

1 : The lungs heave incessant, dull and heavy;
    For as yet were all other parts formless,
105 Shivering, clinging around like a cloud,
    Dim and glutinous as the white polypus
    Driven by waves and englobed on the tide.

2 : And the unformed part craved repose.
    Sleep began; the lungs heave on the wave,
110 Weary, overweighed, sinking beneath
    In a stifling black fluid: he woke,

3 : He arose on the waters, but soon
    Heavy falling, his organs like roots
    Shooting out from the seed, shot beneath,
115 And a vast world of waters around him
    In furious torrents began.

4 : Then he sunk, and around his spent lungs
    Began intricate pipes that drew in
    The spawn of the waters. Outbranching,
Pl. 5 An immense fibrous form, stretching out,
121 Through the bottoms of immensity raging.

5 : He rose on the floods; then he smote
    The wild deep with his terrible wrath,
    Separating the heavy and thin.

106. polypus] A loathsome, formless, poisonous creature, an image of Error
which B. found satisfying: cp. *Four Zoas* viib *286*, *Jerusalem* pl.66.*48*. A
jellyfish is an organism of the polypus type, in a free-floating stage. A very
few, such as the 'Portuguese man-o'-war' are 'colonial'. The association
of the jellyfish with *lungs* is derived from the pulsation of the 'float' of this
and other kinds of jellyfish; for the association with the ramifications of
'intricate pipes' (*118*) see *Four Zoas* iv *265n* and *Jerusalem* pl.66.*48n*.
122. He rose on the floods] Cp. *Genesis* i 2: 'And the earth was without form,
and void; and darkness was upon the face of the deep. And the Spirit of
God moved upon the face of the waters.' B. begins a parallel account of
the Creation. The division of air and solid, and the appearance of light from
the firmament (*129*) reveal, not a world, but Urizen, whom Los was to
guard: and the Creation parallel ends. Note that Los, not the law-giver
Urizen, is here the Creator (cp. *Urizen* viii–ix).

125   6: Down the heavy sunk, cleaving around
        To the fragments of solid; up rose
        The thin, flowing round the fierce fires
        That glowed furious in the expanse.

CHAPTER IV

        1: Then light first began; from the fires
130   Beams, conducted by fluid so pure,
        Flowed around the immense. Los beheld
        Forthwith, writhing upon the dark void,
        The backbone of Urizen appear,
        Hurtling upon the wind
135   Like a serpent, like an iron chain
        Whirling about in the deep.

        2: Upfolding his fibres together
        To a form of impregnable strength,
        Los, astonished and terrified, built
140   Furnaces; he formed an anvil,
        A hammer of adamant. Then began
        The binding of Urizen day and night.

        3: Circling round the dark demon, with howlings,
        Dismay and sharp blightings, the prophet
145   Of Eternity beat on his iron links.

        4: And first from those infinite fires
        The light that flowed down on the winds
        He seized—beating incessant, condensing
        The subtle particles in an orb.

150   5: Roaring, indignant, the bright sparks
        Endured the vast hammer; but unwearied
        Los beat on the anvil, till glorious
        An immense orb of fire he framed.

129-31. Cp. *Paradise Lost* vii 263-5: '. . . and God made / The firmament,
expanse of liquid, pure, / Transparent, elemental air. . . .'
133. the backbone of Urizen] Cp. *Urizen* 196ff; the two poems are not con-
sistent. In *Urizen* Los has already been working at his anvil for some time,
and has created the spine which he here discovers.
145. his] Urizen's.
148-64. orb] This passage is somewhat confused through the ambiguity of
orb. Los is a blacksmith, hammering a globe into shape; heating it first in his
fire, hammering it, quenching it in his water-trough, and turning it over
as he holds it in his tongs to look at it. Confusingly, both the fire and the
globe which is being made is called an *orb*: in *156* at least the *orbs* are the
fire, not the creation. Note the word *condensing* here (*148*); the word always
implies corruption through the constriction of free forms.

6: Oft he quenched it beneath in the deeps,
155 Then surveyed the all-bright mass. Again
Seizing fires from the terrific orbs
He heated the round globe, then beat,
While, roaring, his furnaces endured
The chained orb in their infinite wombs.

160 7: Nine ages completed their circles,
When Los heated the glowing mass, casting
It down into the deeps; the deeps fled
Away in redounding smoke. The sun
Stood self-balanced. And Los smiled with joy.
165 He the vast spine of Urizen seized
And bound down to the glowing illusion.

8: But no light, for the deep fled away
On all sides, and left an unformed
Dark vacuity. Here Urizen lay
170 In fierce torments on his glowing bed,

9: Till his brain in a rock, and his heart
In a fleshy slough formed four rivers,
Obscuring the immense orb of fire
Flowing down into night—till a form
175 Was completed, a human illusion,
In darkness and deep clouds involved.

The End of the
Book of Los

19 Verses written with illustrations to Gray's *Poems*

These poems were inscribed in B.'s volume of water-colour illustrations to Gray's *Poems* which, it has long been conjectured, was given to Mrs Flaxman in 1800. The second seems to refer to Flaxman's assistance in B.'s

163–4. *the sun | Stood self-balanced*] As in *Genesis* i, light appears first, and the sun several stages later. The *self*-balancing (cp. *99n*) is from *Paradise Lost* vii 242: 'And Earth, self-balanced, on her centre hung'. Here the sun, instead of giving light to the earth, is made into Urizen's heart.
166. *And bound down to*] Bound is paired with *seized*, and does not strictly require the grammatical object *it*.
171–6. The globe (as in *Urizen 209–15*) is Urizen's heart; but Urizen becomes our world, with the four rivers of Paradise (*Genesis* ii 10) at its centre–all in an illusory imitation of Humanity (which is not finite, fixed dark nor asleep). The 'rivers', besides, are blood vessels.

arrangements to move to Felpham; cp. B.'s letters of 12 and 14 Sept. 1800. But Irene Tayler has recently (1968) found evidence that B. did the Gray illustrations in 1797.

Around the springs of Gray my wild root weaves:
Traveller, repose, and dream among my leaves.

*

TO MRS. ANN FLAXMAN

A little flower grew in a lonely vale;
Its form was lovely but its colours pale,
One standing in the porches of the sun,
When his meridian glories were begun,
5 Leaped from the steps of fire, and on the grass
Alighted where this little flower was.
With hands divine he moved the gentle sod
And took the flower up in its native clod;
Then planting it upon a mountain's brow—
10 "Tis your own fault if you don't flourish now.'

20 Verses written *c.* 1798–1802

among the marginalia to Reynolds's *Discourses*

A copy of Reynolds's *Discourses* (1798), heavily annotated by B., is in the British Museum. B.'s earliest comments are in pencil; these he later expanded and amended in ink. It is thus possible to distinguish two main stages of annotation. The verses below are from the early stage, written probably when B. read the book when he first got it and in any case before 1802 when he refers to the *Discourses* in a letter to Butts (22 Nov. 1802), in a manner which shows he has read them. The *Discourses* were delivered separately to the students of the Royal Academy by Sir Joshua Reynolds as President from 1769 to 1790. The first complete collection was edited by Malone in 1797; B.'s is the 2nd edn of 1798. For later poems from the marginalia, see p. 593 below.

I ADVICE OF THE POPES WHO SUCCEEDED THE AGE OF RAPHAEL

Degrade first the arts if you'd mankind degrade,
Hire idiots to paint with cold light and hot shade;
Give high price for the worst, leave the best in disgrace,
And with labours of ignorance fill every place.

¶ 20. i. Written on the titlepage, under the remark: 'This man was hired to depress art'. The title was added probably *c.* 1808–10.

II

When France got free, Europe 'twixt fools and knaves
Were savage first to France, and after, slaves.

III

When Sir Joshua Reynolds died
All nature was degraded;
The King dropped a tear into the Queen's eye
And all his pictures faded.

21 Vala, *or* The Four Zoas

Date. Either title is commonly used: the titlepage date 1797 probably
indicates the year of beginning. B. worked on the poem for many years,
and some of the latest additions were borrowed from *Jerusalem*, perhaps
c. 1810 or even later. The poem in its first form probably dates from
1797–1800, with most of the changes complete by 1803, and only isolated
passages added later.

Text. The text exists only in one MS and a few fragments; it has many
deletions and additions, major and minor, which complicate the textual
problem. The major editions are: a facsimile, ed. G. E. Bentley (Oxford
1963); *Vala*, ed. H. M. Margoliouth (Oxford 1956)–an attempt to dis-
entangle the poem in its original form from the later accretions; and
Erdman 1966. In the present edition, lines are numbered by Nights; the
page numbers of the MS are given thus [20], to make reference to and
from certain other editions easier.

In 1796 B. was engaged to illustrate a grand edition of Edward Young's
popular *The Complaint, or Night Thoughts* (1742–45). The poem *Vala* is
written largely on proof sheets of his engravings for this edition; like
Night Thoughts, it is in nine 'Nights'. The MS is illustrated with sketches;
where these refer directly to the poem, a brief description is given in the
notes. Each Night ends in a full-page drawing (see viia *361n* and *852n*):
but the reader should study the facsimile.

Theme. The poem is about the *Eternal* or *Universal Man*: he is its universe
as well as its subject. That is, B. envisages all the universe as making up
one giant Man. His 'elements'–his reason, his passion, etc.–are fragments
of his personality, and also assume human form, of a lesser kind. In turn,
they have their 'children'–a 'child' of any figure (great or small) is one
who follows the pattern of behaviour set by that figure. Thus Urizen and

ii. A comment on the reference by Malone (Reynolds's editor) to 'the
FEROCIOUS and ENSLAVED republic of France!', quoting Pope on those who
'thought that all but SAVAGES were slaves'. Cp. also Pope's Epistle *To
Augustus*, 263–4:'We conquer'd France, but felt our captive's charms; / Her
Arts victorious triumph'd o'er our Arms'.

his 'sons' become 'sons of Los' in viia *488–9* when Los draws them into his influence. The entire universe that we see–seas, continents, trees, fields, birds, animals, men and women; even the stars and planets–are parts of this Universal Man. In eternity, the senses are not fixed or limited, and can be microscopic or telescopic at will; thus one might see trees and rivers, microscopically; or universally, the whole Man of whom the trees and rivers are veins and hair. But the Man falls sick, his elements fight and are divided against one another, and separate into different entities–as we are now divided.

B. uses this concept, for which he could have found a source in Swedenborg, though he was aware of its ultimate derivation in Jewish mysticism (see *Jerusalem 27*) as the basis of an allegory. He sees the Man as divided into four beings, each representing a major faculty of the whole: Urizen embodies conscious Thought; Luvah embodies Passion and Desire; Urthona, Imagination and Wrath; Tharmas, Compassion. These are the 'Four Zoas' of the title; the name is convenient, though it is not used in the poem (see ix *281n*). Each has his emanation (see i *17n*), the feminine part of his being–which is not a separate being, but an essential counterpart of the masculine within each personality–respectively Ahania, Vala, Enitharmon and Enion. (Note also that, after the fall, Urthona appears as Los, and Luvah as Orc.) The basis of the allegory is stated in ix *363–9* (p. 443; the four are there referred to as 'gods'): when one of the faculties of a man, or of Man, is elevated or elevates itself at the expense of the others, the man will collapse. The universality of the Man enables this to be an allegory either of psychological distress or of social and political enmity, and B. uses it as both.

In B.'s story of the Zoas, while the Man is asleep, Urizen and Luvah struggle for dominion over him; Urizen wins, and the other three Zoas are shattered. The Man, now sick, hands his authority to the only active Zoa left–Urizen–and falls into a coma. (That is; reason and passion should be balanced, but they fought for control of man, and reason won; thus the personality is overturned.) Urizen uses his authority to control all life, for he is afraid of uncertainty, and most of all, in his solitary power, of Luvah. But Luvah, split into two fallen forms, the male Orc and the female Vala, reappears through an earthly birth to Los and Enitharmon; and the result is that Urizen's controlled world falls into the power of the supposedly repressed Vala–into the capricious domination of a cruel, designing, sensual, selfish female. Male violence, in Orc (i.e. fallen Luvah), Urizen has easily overcome. Only when he is on the brink of ultimate disaster does the Man come to himself (in ix), when he directs Urizen to his proper place and regenerates all his elements.

A second myth tells how the Man's sickness began even before this, when Vala seduced him. Luvah (Vala's male counterpart) has become jealous, and the rest of the story of division follows. In this case, the allegory reads thus: when Man allows his soft, pleasure-loving desires–good in their place–to get the better of him, his passions and lusts will go wild, resulting in a reaction of conscious mental self-control, which in turn will over-balance him. Hence the title *Vala*: although much of the poem deals with Urizen, she is the source of the evil, the poem reaches its climax in her power, and her regeneration is accordingly the most fully treated in ix. The two narratives are not contradictory, but are never fully blended together.

The allegory goes no further than this, and the story as such takes charge. Elements of allegory appear from time to time, but Urizen and the others become persons on their own, with recognizable characteristics—and that is how the poem is to be read—as a legend, a narrative in its own right, with only an undercurrent of allegory.

Accordingly, B. felt free to alter the legend or myth to include new elements which may destroy the allegorical pattern, but which add new truths as he comes to see them. The process has two stages: in the first, material is added which is absorbed into the poem; in the second, there are clearly distinct additions. The basic narrative sequence described above was probably written by 1800, the pervasive additions by 1804, and the others in the following ten years or so.

The new material introduces a wider Eternity than that of the Universal Man—who thus, paradoxically, is now no longer strictly 'universal', and who, in the last state of the text, is particularized as Albion, to assimilate him to the myth of *Jerusalem*. In this Eternity there is the *Council of God*, the assembly of many Universal Men—B. intends them to be a republic of heaven (i *164-9*) as in *Urizen*, but he moves towards a pattern of an assembly led by Jesus, the Divine Mercy—a clearly Christian scheme, if somewhat unusual. The assembly watches the action from afar; the 'Divine Hand' directs some of the events, especially the most critical; and 'watchers in Beulah' (the land on the borders of heaven and earth) are set. In particular, B. introduces his own version of the Atonement; Jesus takes the place of Luvah, the figure most oppressed by Urizen, so that all Urizen's assaults fall on Jesus—and his divinity is indestructible.

These additions are in part incorporated into the MS text, and in part added to it. The still later additions are clearly superimposed; in particular, the use of Welsh place-names with Hebrew personal names in the First Night, and the development of Rahab in viii. These, and their local effects on the narrative, are described in their place.

At an early stage, B. appears to have worked into the narrative of Los and his counterpart Enitharmon some reflections derived from his married life. *Enitharmon* may be derived from *Catherine*; the two figures often behave like husband and wife; and their quarrelling and reconciliation, with the image of the closed gates of Enitharmon's heart, may have some autobiographical origin. But we have no external evidence for any of this.

The four Zoas, apart from their allegorical significance, fall into a balanced order of which B. makes much use, setting out patterns of con-trast, which are sometimes essential in order to recognize the Zoas and understand their relationships. They convey little symbolic meaning, but are useful for recognition and identification. A table of the chief distinctions follows: any figure who assumes a characteristic not rightly his is disturbing the order of nature.

	URTHONA/LOS	LUVAH/ORC	URIZEN	THARMAS
emanation	Enitharmon	Vala	Ahania	Enion
nature	imaginative, wrathful	passionate, desiring	rational, controlling	compassionate
occupation and status	blacksmith, 'eternal prophet'	wine-grower, prince of love	farmer, prince of light	shepherd, mariner
element	earth	fire	air	water
place in the body	heart/ear	loins/nose	brain/eyes	bowels/tongue
compass-point	north	east	south	west

The First Night

The First Night is the most confused part of the poem, the most altered, and the least finished. Its text contains, in part, some of the earliest and some of the latest writing in *The Four Zoas*. However, even as it stands, some kind of narrative order and purpose may be perceived. Textual alterations were never completed, and our present text is merely the latest stage B. reached, not his 'final' intentions. It is printed here in the *Erdman* text, with editorial rearrangements as stated below. Its narrative falls into four sections, which in a chronological order would be *A–D–B–C*; but B. begins *in medias res*.

(*A: 1–12*) A 'correct' epic opening, in which B. declares his theme and intentions.

(*B: 17–122*) The theme of Night i is the fall of Urthona into disunity. He is one of 'the Four Mighty Ones', the four elemental spirits who make up the character of the Eternal Man. B.'s purpose is to set him in his place in the story: but first he must be brought into the fallen world, the scene of the story. This is managed through Tharmas and Enion (Tharmas is another of the Four, Enion his emanation or female counterpart). In this section we see Tharmas and Enion quarrel, until they break apart into an unhealable disunity (in Eternity their substance is united). The source of the quarrel is that Tharmas has taken pity on another female, variously named as Jerusalem or Enitharmon (see *19n*), of whom Enion is jealous. She traps Tharmas in a sort of cocoon, but his 'spectre'–not his real self–rises before her, and after their savage mating she conceives, and Los and Enitharmon are born. But these are the fragmented parts of Urthona, and his appearance beside Tharmas and Enion in the fallen world is thus contrived.

(*C: 123–63*) The quarrelsome twins, Los and Enitharmon, are set in the fallen world, after they have used and rejected their mother Enion, who until the end of viii wanders, a lost and faded being, 'on the verge of non-entity', sought in vain by Tharmas. Two passages (*84–98, 139–48*) describe the heavenly concern for all this spiritual disintegration.

(*D: 164–269*) We are now taken to the 'Council of God', where the origins of these troubles are narrated by messengers. It had all begun in an abortive conspiracy between Urizen and Luvah, the two of the 'Four' not involved in (*B*) above, to seize control of Man. The conspiracy had soon broken up in a quarrel, of which the first effect was that Urthona was horrified, the second that his being disintegrated, and the fragments–who became Los and Enitharmon–took refuge respectively with Enion and Tharmas, who then began the quarrel with which the poem opens.

Urizen, whose hostility to Luvah is one of the consistent features of *Four Zoas*, then causes Luvah's ruin. Luvah's anger falls, not on Urizen, but on himself and the Man, whose being is thus entirely shattered and ready to be dominated, in ii, by the one remaining Zoa, the cold, tyrannical, calculating Urizen.

The purpose of the 'Council of God' passage is threefold. (*a*) In B.'s original poem there had been no scheme of four Zoas–the title is a late pencil alteration, and the phrase is not used in the poem. Before this there was nothing to prevent Enion from being the mother of Los and Enitharmon. But now Tharmas and Los are 'brothers'; both are members of the 'Four'. How then can one (Los) be the child of another (Tharmas)? The new version has arranged that the fleeing fragments of Urthona are 'incorporated' into Enion, ready to be born as her children. B. has also effected the identification of Urthona and Los; in earlier poems they were different persons. (*b*) B. has provided a standard narrative of the Man's first fall; there are many versions later in the poem, but this one is told by credible witnesses. (*c*) B. has introduced the theme he had come to see as essential–that the Divine Mercy is in control, whatever disasters the Man might bring on himself.

All the 'Council of God' passage is added in extra pages, and it is difficult to know where the Second Night begins. There is a large heading on p. 23, but here B. has deleted the word *First* and left the erasure blank. After i *163* there is a marginal insertion *Night the Second*, together with a new introductory line (our ii *1*), which are not deleted. Unfortunately the First Night is marked to end *later* (on pp. 18 and 21, the latter superseding the former; lines i *255–69* are a still later addition in pencil). Thus the present arrangement of the text is editorial. Since pp. 19–22 are an isolable passage; since their material is more suitable for a late position in the First Night (which it holds if, as in many editions, ii begins on p. 23); and since the addition of our line ii *1* implies some intervention between i *163* and ii *1*, it seems reasonable to place our lines *164–269*, written on pp. 18–22, after i *163*. The MS is at present in an arrangement made since B.'s time; but for those who wish to follow it, the order of the MS is i *1–163*, ii *1–210*, i *164–269*, ii *211*ff. (This merely exchanges the two sheets, pp. 19/20 and 21/22, in their accepted correct order, and leaves the beginning of ii in doubt.)

[1]   THE FOUR ZOAS
              The Torments of Love & Jealousy in
                  The Death and Judgement
                  of Albion the Ancient Man

                    by William Blake 1797

[2]   Rest before Labour

[3]   *Οτι ουκ εστιν ημιν η παλη προς αιμα και σαρκα, αλλα
             προς τας αρχας, προς τας εξουσιας, προς τους
             κοσμοκρατορας του σκοτους του αιωνος τουτου, προς
             τα πνευματικα της πονηριας εν τοις επουρανιοις.*
                                      Εφες: vi κεφ. 12 ver.

                    NIGHT THE FIRST
The song of the aged mother which shook the heavens with wrath,
Hearing the march of long resounding strong heroic verse,
Marshalled in order for the day of intellectual battle.

Four mighty ones are in every man: John xvii 21–3
      a perfect unity

¶ 21.i. Night i poses the severest textual problems in the whole of B.'s
verse. The first ten pages of text (pp. 3–12) have been written on, largely
erased, and a later text–itself with many alterations–then superimposed.
Only the most significant alterations are noted here. B. cancelled a number
of lengthy passages, which are given in an appendix on pp. 461–7 below.
p. 1. Title: 1st rdg del. Vala or The Death and Judgement of the Ancient
Man [etc.]. The new title is in pencil.
p. 2. The only words in this page, which has a sketch of a reclining male
figure.
p. 3. Superscription] The Greek text of *Ephesians* vi 12: 'For we wrestle not
against flesh and blood, but against principalities, against powers, against
rulers of the darkness of this world, against spiritual wickedness in high
places'. That is, the evil in the world will be traced in this poem to the
corruption of Man's spiritual powers. B. writes the Greek without accents
or breathings.
i 1–3. Syntax and heavy inking mark these lines as a subtitle of the lengthy
eighteenth-century kind. They are the result of much emendation and
abbreviation, as the appendix shows (p. 461).
i 4–6. See headnote, p. 287 above, and *Jerusalem* pl.98.28ff. These lines
are most important for an understanding of the persons of the poem and
their interrelations.
    John xvii 21–3 reads: 'That they all may be one; as thou, Father, art in
me, and I in thee, that they also may be one in us: that the world may
believe that thou has sent me. And the glory which thou gavest me I have
given them; that they may be one, even as we are one: I in them, and thou
in me, that they may be made perfect in one; and that the world may

5   Cannot exist, but from the universal
            brotherhood of Eden,   John i 14
     The universal man, to whom be   καὶ· ἐσκήνωσεν· ἐν ἡμῖν
            glory ever more. Amen.
     What are the natures of those living creatures the Heavenly
            Father only
     Knoweth; no individual knoweth nor can know in all Eternity.

     Los was the fourth immortal starry one, & in the earth
10   Of a bright universe empery attended day & night,
     Days & nights of revolving joy. Urthona was his name
[4] In Eden; in the auricular nerves of human life
     Which is the earth of Eden, he his emanations propagated,
     Fairies of Albion, afterwards gods of the heathen. Daughter of
            Beulah, sing
15   His fall into division & his resurrection to unity.

know that thou hast sent me, and hast loved them, as thou hast loved me.'
To B. the opening words, and the whole sense, of this passage have a
visionary meaning far wider—and more literal—than 'that they may all
agree with one another'.

i 5. *John* i 14 reads: 'And the Word was made flesh, and dwelt among us,
(and we beheld his glory, the glory as of the only begotten of the Father,)
full of grace and truth'.

i 6. The Greek is quoted from the above passage—'and dwelt among us'.

i 8. *No individual knoweth nor*] replacing *Individual Man knoweth not*. Note
the cancellation of the word *Man*: 'individuals' are not necessarily mem-
bers of the earthly human race.

i 9–13. *Urthona, Los*] The poem opens with a glimpse of Los, or Urthona,
in his unfallen state of joy. In Eden (the eternal paradise) his domain is the
earth, the basis of life itself (fire, air and water belong to the other Zoas).
He is the prophet and poet, and propagates his poetry, his 'emanations'
(which have the living human form), in the living *auricular nerves* of the
ear of the 'eternal man', as a gardener propagates plants and flowers, which
then grow.

i 14. *afterwards*] Because the fairies of old legend are imaginative truth;
but the imagination was lost, and the legends corrupted into systems of
gods and goddesses. Cp. *Marriage* iv. *15n*, p. 111.

Albion] B.'s later name for the Eternal Man.

i 15. *His fall*] Los's fall, in the first place; the beginning of the story, as told
later in this Night, of how Urthona divided into two beings, Los and Eni-
tharmon, born into a corrupted world through Tharmas and Enion. But
the fall was also Albion's, and in the Ninth Night Albion (with all his
constituent elements, the Zoas) is resurrected and reunited. Between this
line and the next, the following two lines are inserted, but seem to be del.
by light strokes: 'His fall into the generation of decay & death, & his /
Regeneration by the resurrection from the dead.'

Begin with Tharmas, parent power, darkening in the west:
'Lost! Lost! Lost are my emanations. Enion, O Enion!
We are become a victim to the living, we hide in secret.
I have hidden Jerusalem in silent contrition. O, pity me.

i *16. Tharmas*] See p. 290 above. Tharmas's characteristics of compassion and pity fit him to be 'parent' of Los in the fallen world.

i *17. Enion*] Tharmas's counterpart, wife or emanation—terms all used in the course of the poem; but the third was B.'s final choice.

i *17.* EMANATION] At first B.'s term for the feminine counterparts of the Zoas; they are almost always female. There is no sex in Eternity, but the emanation is an idealization of the specifically feminine virtues, the 'wifely' parts of the personality, as B. sees them. She is gentle, tender and caring; but she is weak and, as here, her anxiety may lead her to jealousy and bitterness. Thus she requires protection and guidance. Secondly, 'emanation' was a term used by the Neo-Platonists for a spiritual exhalation of the personality; B.'s emanations, though more strongly individualized, are also essentially parts of the total personality, and may be sent out from it for a while for some purpose, but always belong to it. Only when the emanation is *lost*, unable to return, is there tragedy; this is an important situation in all the long epics. Thirdly in, *Jerusalem* (esp. pl.54.*1–3*) there is a trend towards using the word, in a less personal way, of creations of the mind or the imagination; when these are lost, the personality is unable to reach out to others, and becomes enclosed in itself. In *Jerusalem* this concept coexists with the earlier, more personal use of the word, which is normal in *Four Zoas* and *Milton*.

The term 'emanation' may have been suggested to B. by the same Epicurean source as that referred to under *spectre* (*Jerusalem* pl.6.*1n*). But the emanation is not merely a feminine equivalent of the male spectre. The emanation is a real part of the eternal being; the spectre is only a shade. But when a mythical figure loses his emanation, and the spectre also breaks from him, he may dwindle almost to nothing, with the two fragments, male and female, seeming to usurp his entire personality. (E.g. Tharmas in Night i, and Los and Enitharmon in Night viia. In both cases, monstrous children are the consequence.)

i *19. Jerusalem*] A confusing alteration, here, *21* and *62*. Lines *19–20, 1st rdg*, were:

I have hidden thee Enion in Jealous Despair. O Pity Me
I will build thee a Labyrinth where we may remain for ever alone.

Cp. also *21n, 23n, 62n*. The idea is simply that Enion is jealous of another female figure–Enitharmon or Jerusalem: but Tharmas has only provided refuge out of pity. Lines *217–20* show that this is true: pity and compassion are Tharmas's essential nature, but Enion's jealousy is not assuaged and disaster follows. In *23*, and the story of *217*ff, the other female is Enitharmon: it is difficult to see why B. brought in Jerusalem, the emanation of the Man (Albion) himself.

20   I will build thee a labyrinth also; O, pity me. O Enion,
      Why hast thou taken sweet Jerusalem from my inmost soul?
      Let her lay secret in the soft recess of darkness & silence.
      It is not love I bear to Enitharmon, it is pity.
      She hath taken refuge in my bosom, & I cannot cast her out.

25   'The men have received their death wounds & their emanations
          are fled
      To me for refuge, & I cannot turn them out for pity's sake,'
      Enion said. 'Thy fear has made me tremble, thy terrors have
          surrounded me,
      All love is lost; terror succeeds & hatred instead of love,
      And stern demands of right & duty instead of liberty.

30   'Once thou wast to me the loveliest son of heaven—but now
      Why are thou terrible? And yet I love thee in thy terror till
      I am almost extinct, & soon shall be a shadow in oblivion
      Unless some way can be found that I may look upon thee & live.
      Hide me some shadowy semblance, secret whispering in my ear
35   In secret of soft wings, in mazes of delusive beauty.
      I have looked into the secret soul of him I loved
      And in the dark recesses found sin, & cannot return.'

      Trembling & pale sat Tharmas, weeping in his clouds:

      'Why wilt thou examine every little fibre of my soul,
40   Spreading them out before the sun like stalks of flax to dry?
      The infant joy is beautiful, but its anatomy
      Horrible, ghast, & deadly. Nought shalt thou find in it
      But death, despair, & everlasting brooding melancholy.

      'Thou wilt go mad with horror if thou dost examine thus
45   Every moment of my secret hours. Yea, I know

i 20. *labyrinth*] A sign of evil, not primarily because of its classical associ-
ations, but through B.'s characteristic hatred of anything secret, hidden and
tortuous.
i 21. *sweet Jerusalem*] 1st rdg. Enitharmon.
i 22. *lay*] Commonly used in B.'s time where we would expect 'lie'.
i 23. *Enitharmon*] B. has not altered this to *Jerusalem*, as in 19; perhaps an
oversight, perhaps not.
i 26. *pity*] Tharmas's particular characteristic.
i 27–30. So in *Jerusalem* pl.22.1, and 10–12, where the passage is adapted
to another context.
Thy fear] i.e. 'my fear for thee': she fears she may lose him.
i 34. *Hide me some shadowy semblance*] Perhaps 'in' or 'as' is missing after
'me'.
i 39–43. So in *Jerusalem* pl. 22.20–4. See 27n.

That I have sinned & that my emanations are become harlots.
I am already distracted at their deeds, & if I look
Upon them more, despair will bring self-murder on my soul.
O Enion! thou art thyself a root growing in hell,
50   Though thus heavenly beautiful, to draw me to destruction.

'Sometimes I think thou art a flower expanding,
Sometimes I think thou art fruit breaking from its bud
In dreadful dolour & pain, & I am like an atom,
A nothing left in darkness! Yet I am an identity.
55   I wish & feel & weep & groan. Ah, terrible! terrible!'

[5]   (In Eden females sleep the winter in soft silken veils,
Woven by their own hands to hide them in the darksome grave.
But males immortal live, renewed by female deaths. In soft
Delight they die, & they revive in spring with music & songs.)
60   Enion said, 'Farewell, I die, I hide from thy searching eyes.'

So saying, from her bosom weaving soft in sinewy threads
A tabernacle for Jerusalem, she sat among the rocks,
Singing her lamentation. Tharmas groaned among his clouds
Weeping, then bending from his clouds he stooped his innocent
      head,
65   And stretching out his holy hand in the vast deep sublime,
Turned round the circle of destiny with tears & bitter sighs,
And said, 'Return, O wanderer, when the day of clouds is o'er.'
So saying, he sunk down into the sea, a pale white corse.
In torment he sunk down & flowed among her filmy woof,
70   His spectre issuing from his feet in flames of fire
In gnawing pain, drawn out by her loved fingers. Every nerve
She counted, every vein & lacteal, threading them among
Her woof of terror. Terrified & drinking tears of woe,
Shuddering she wove—nine days & nights sleepless; her food was
      tears.

i 53. *an atom*] The concept of the atom (in 1800 still a philosophical rather
than a scientific concept) was, in B.'s view, the product of a misguided
mind, analysing instead of imagining.
i 62. *for Jerusalem*] 1st rdg del. of delight: 2nd rdg del. for Enitharmon.
i 63–8. The illustration at the foot of the page shows Tharmas, brooding,
on the surface of the sea.
i 65. *holy*] B.'s irony.
i 66. The *circle of destiny* is mentioned only in this passage. It is the fallen
material world, where the main action will take place. The failure of
Tharmas and Enion has trapped them in an everturning cycle of life and
death. A similar cycle is described in *The Mental Traveller* (p. 578).
i 70. *spectre*] A corrupt, unreal form; see iv 63n.
i 72. *lacteal*] Vessels similar to veins, which carry lymph.

75 Wondering she saw her woof begin to animate, & not
    As garments woven subservient to her hands but having a will
    Of its own, perverse & wayward. Enion loved & wept.

    Nine days she laboured at her work, & nine dark sleepless nights;
    But on the tenth trembling morn, the circle of destiny complete,
80 Round rolled the sea englobing, in a watery globe self-balanced,
    A frowning continent appeared, where Enion in the deserts
    Terrified in her own creation, viewing her woven shadow
    Sat in a dread intoxication of repentance & contrition.

    —There is from great Eternity a mild & pleasant rest
85 Named *Beulah*, a soft moony universe, feminine, lovely,
    Pure, mild & gentle, given in mercy to those who sleep
    Eternally, created by the Lamb of God around
    On all sides, within & without the Universal Man.
    The daughters of Beulah follow sleepers in all their dreams
90 Creating spaces lest they fall into eternal death.
    The circle of destiny complete, they gave to it a space
    And named the space *Ulro*, & brooded over it in care & love.

    They said: 'The spectre is in every man insane & most

76. *garments*] See *56–9*.
i *80. self-balanced*] *Paradise Lost* vii 242: 'Earth, self-balanced, on her centre
hung'. Cp. also *Book of Los 163–4*.
i *82. terrified*] Not, like God in *Genesis* i, pleased.
her woven shadow] Tharmas in his 'cocoon'.
i *83. dread*] Replaces 'sweet'.   *repentance and contrition*] 1st *rdg* false
woven bliss, *del. for* self woven sorrow, *itself del*. The apparent contradic-
tion is solved when one realizes that one can relish sorrow, and indulge in
repentance. After this line the following was inserted, then deleted:

    He spurned Enion with his foot, he sprang aloft in clouds,
    Alighting in his drunken joy in a far distant grove.

i *84*. B. looks up from his narrative of the world of Tharmas to show that
even in the worst disasters the divine care is operating. Such passages are
late additions; the sense of hope they bring was not in the poem in its
first state.
i *84–90. Beulah*] See *Milton* pl.30.1*n*.
i *90. spaces*] Cp. *Milton* pls *8.42–4, 10.6–7*. Such spaces limit and contain
the soul, but do so in order to prevent its complete disintegration–a
temporary but inevitable expedient which must be accompanied by more
positive redemptive measures.
i *92. Ulro*] The sense is unusual; normally Ulro is the place of chaos and
non-entity, beyond the hope that is implied here.
i *93. The spectre . . . deformed*] So in viia 300 and *Jerusalem* pl.33.4.

Deformed. Through the three heavens descending in fury & fire
95 We meet it with our songs & loving blandishments, & give
To it a form of vegetation. But this spectre of Tharmas
Is eternal death! What shall we do? O God, pity & help!'
So spoke they, & closed the gate of the tongue in trembling fear.

[6] She drew the spectre forth from Tharmas in her shining loom
100 Of vegetation. Weeping in wayward infancy & sullen youth,
Listening to her soft lamentations soon his tongue began
To lisp out words, & soon in masculine strength augmenting he
Reared up a form of gold, & stood upon the glittering rock,
A shadowy human form winged, & in his depths
105 The dazzlings as of gems shone clear, rapturous in fury,
Glorying in his own eyes. Exalted in terrific pride,
[7 & Opening his rifted rocks, mingling together they join in burning
143]   anguish,
Mingling his horrible darkness with her tender limbs. Then high
she soared
Shrieking above the ocean. A bright wonder that nature
shuddered at—

i *94. the three heavens* of female beauty; cp. *257–8*, and especially *Milton*
extra pl.*5.10* and note. Here, B. means that the 'insane spectre' may begin
to be tamed through female beauty–if it is used, not deceitfully or as a
trap, but as a source of true joy. This means remaining for a while in
earthly bounds ('a form of vegetation', *96*), but the condition may be the
beginning of rebirth.
i *98. the gate of the tongue*] B. explains the image in *Jerusalem* pl.*38.24*:
'the affectionate touch of the tongue is closed in by deadly teeth'. Cp.
Europe, prefatory poem and *Milton* pl.*2.10*n.
i *98–9.* Ten deleted lines follow; see appendix, p. *461*.
i *104. a shadowy human form*] deceptively beautiful, but only a shadow.
i *106.* Forty-seven deleted lines follow on pp. *6–7*: see appendix. The un-
deleted portion of p. *7* is duplicated on a small leaf, (now bound into the MS
as p. *143*), and was there revised further. We take these revisions as B.'s
latest and incorporate them into the text. The earlier text is given in the
appendix.
i *106–15.* This passage describes the beginning of sexuality: a fierce,
antagonistic meeting of separate beings, not the total union of body and
spirit known in Eternity. This was still more clearly shown in the un-
shortened version (see appendix, p. *462*). Note that in the final version, the
spectre, with his *rifted rocks, metals* and *rocky features,* seems to be a per-
sonification of the earth (though Tharmas is said to own the sea, and
Urthona the earth).
i *110.* The illustration on p. *7* shows a woman-serpent, looking upwards in
terror or agony.

110   Half woman & half beast. All his darkly waving colours mix
        With her fair crystal clearness; in her lips & cheeks his metals rose,
        In blushes like the morning, & his rocky features softening;
        A wonder lovely in the heavens or wandering on the earth,
        With female voice warbling upon the hollow vales,
115   Beauty all blushing with desire, a self-enjoying wonder.

        For Enion brooded, groaning loud; the rough seas vegetate.
        Golden rocks rise from the vortex vast
        And thus her voice: 'Glory, delight & sweet enjoyment!–born
        To mild Eternity, shut in a threefold shape delightful,
120   To wander in sweet solitude enraptured at every wind.'

[8]   Till with fierce pain she brought forth on the rocks her sorrow
            & woe:
        Behold, two little infants wept upon the desolate wind.

        The first state weeping they began, & helpless as a wave
        Beaten along its sightless way, growing enormous in its motion to
125   Its utmost goal, till strength from Enion like richest summer
            shining
        Raised the bright boy & girl, with glories from their heads
            out-beaming,
        Drawing forth drooping mother's pity, drooping mother's sorrow.

        They sulk upon her breast; her hair became like snow on mountains
        Weaker & weaker, weeping woeful, wearier and wearier,
130   Faded, & her bright eyes decayed, melted with pity & love.

[9a]   And then they wandered far away. She sought for them in vain;
        In weeping blindness stumbling she followed them, o'er rocks
            and mountains
        Rehumanizing from the spectre in pangs of maternal love.
        Ingrate they wandered, scorning her, drawing her spectrous life,
135   Repelling her away & away by a dread repulsive power,
        Into non-entity revolving round in dark despair,
        And drawing in the spectrous life in pride and haughty joy.
        Thus Enion gave them all her spectrous life.

i *117. vortex*] The *x* is missing where the page is torn; this and the previous
line are an insertion written as one line, and some words may be missing
after *vast.*

i *119. threefold*] Less than the eternal fourfold.

i *122. two little infants*] Los and Enitharmon.

i *127.* Thirteen deleted lines follow: see appendix, p. 464.

i *133. Rehumanizing*] *Un-* and *re-humanize* are terms occasionally used in
Four Zoas (e.g. viii 107), but rarely elsewhere. Although odd terms, they
define themselves, when one remembers that to B. the true human form
was divine perfection.

i *134–6.* Illustrated at foot of the page.

Then Eno, a daughter of Beulah, took a moment of time
140   And drew it out to seven thousand years with much care and
           affliction
       And many tears, & in every year made windows into Eden.
       She also took an atom of space & opened its centre
       Into infinitude, & ornamented it with wondrous art.
       Astonished sat her sisters of Beulah to see her soft affections
145   To Enion & her children, & they pondered these things
           wondering;
       And they alternate kept watch over the youthful terrors.
       They saw not yet the Hand Divine, for it was not yet revealed,
       But they went on in silent hope & feminine repose.

       But Los & Enitharmon delighted in the moony spaces of Eno.
150   Nine times they lived among the forests, feeding on sweet fruits,
       And nine bright spaces wandered, weaving mazes of delight,
       Snaring the wild goats for their milk, they ate the flesh of lambs,
       A male & female, naked & ruddy as the pride of summer.
       Alternate love & hate his breast, hers scorn & jealousy
155   In embryon passions. They kissed not nor embraced for shame
           and fear.
       His head beamed light & in his vigorous voice was prophecy,
       He could control the times & seasons, & the days & years;
       She could control the spaces, regions, desert, flood & forest,
       But had no power to weave a veil of covering for her sins.
160   She drave the females all away from Los,
       And Los drave all the males from her away.
       They wandered long, till they sat down upon the margined sea,
       Conversing with the visions of Beulah in dark slumberous bliss.

                    *   *   *

i *139–43. Jerusalem* pl.48.*30–41* seems to be based on these lines. Cp. also
Milton pl.8.*43*; and pl.28.*44*ff, where B. describes the elasticity of time and
space.
i *150. Nine*] Proclus, a Neo-Platonic commentator on Homer, sees the ten
years' wanderings of Odysseus as symbolizing the soul's nine ages of wan-
dering and one of homecoming. The last year makes up the perfect num-
ber; one less is imperfection. There is evidence that B. had read this com-
ment, or knew about it; he uses nine and multiples of nine in this way on
a number of occasions (e.g. the twenty-seven churches of *Milton* pl.37.*35*ff).
times] i.e. ages. B. uses the word as if it had a specific meaning such as
'century' has.
i *152. eat . . . lambs*] Cp. ii *196–8.*
i *155. for shame and fear*] Here and in the following lines the 'Adam-and-
Eve' nature of the pair is suggested, linking with the deleted creation pas-
sage after *127* (see appendix).
i *160–1.* So with Urizen and Ahania in ii *419–20.*

[21]   Then those in great Eternity met in the Council of God
165   As one Man. For contracting their exalted senses
         They behold multitude, or expanding they behold as one,
         As one Man, all the universal family, & that one Man
         They call Jesus, the Christ. And they in him & he in them
         Live in perfect harmony, in Eden the land of life,
170   Consulting as One Man above the mountain of Snowdon sublime.

         For messengers from Beulah come, in tears & darkening clouds,
         Saying: 'Shiloh is in ruins, our brother is sick. Albion, he
         Whom thou lovest, is sick; he wanders from his house of Eternity.
         The daughters of Beulah terrified have closed the gate of the
                   tongue,
175   Luvah & Urizen contend in war around the holy tent.'

         So spoke the ambassadors from Beulah & with solemn mourning
         They were introduced to the Divine Presence & they kneeled
                   down

i *164*, p. 21. Two extra leaves, pp. 21–2 and 19–20, contain *164–269*; the
leaves have been incorrectly arranged in the MS. The leaves and hand-
writing are distinctive, but B. gave no specific instructions where they
were to be inserted. See headnote to First Night.

i *170*. *Snowdon*] (Replacing 'Gilead'): a mountain in the land of the pro-
phetic bards, who knew the patriarchal tradition, and transmitted in their
art the true religion. Gilead was probably rejected because B. later thought
that he wanted a place more directly connected with Albion.

i *172*. SHILOH] In *Joshua* xviii 1, the place where, after the conquest of
Canaan, the Israelites gathered, set up 'the tabernacles of the congregation'
and divided up the unallotted parts of Canaan. (Note *holy tent* several times
in *175–246*.) Shiloh was for a long time one of the great holy cities of
Israel. After the division of the nation into two kingdoms, Shiloh was in
the Northern, Jerusalem in the Southern. B. uses Shiloh either to contrast
two sister-nations (e.g. Britain and France, *Jerusalem* pl.55.29) who may
be opposed but who should be friends, or to mark the lost or faithless
but still beautiful city, where God should be worshipped, but is not–as
here, where the city is spiritually 'in ruins'. Cp. also *Jerusalem* pl.63.6n.
As the reference to Snowdon in *170* shows, B. had come to associate
Wales, the land of the bardic tradition and early Christianity, with Israel.
Cp. *To the Jews*, in *Jerusalem* pl.27. He had come into contact with British
Israelite ideas from the Welsh nationalist Owen Pugh, but though Pugh
may have given him some ideas, B. was no British Israelite; he used these
ideas imaginatively to draw attention to eternal equivalences. The Holy
Land is not far away in distance and time, but is spiritually present in
Britain.

174. *Albion* is the 'Eternal Man'. i Cp. *98*.

In Conway's Vale, thus recounting the wars of death eternal:

'The Eternal Man wept in the holy tent. Our brother in Eternity,
180   Even Albion, whom thou lovest, wept in pain; his family
Slept round on hills & valleys in the regions of his love.
But Urizen awoke, & Luvah woke, & thus conferred:

'"Thou, Luvah," said the prince of light, "behold our sons and
           daughters
Reposed on beds. Let them sleep on. Do thou alone depart
185   Into thy wished kingdom where in majesty & power
We may erect a throne. Deep in the north I place my lot,
Thou in the south. Listen attentive. In silent of this night
I will enfold the eternal tent in clouds opaque, while thou,
Seizing the chariots of the morning, go outfleeting, ride
190   Afar into the zenith, high bending thy furious course
Southward, with half the tents of men enclosed in clouds
Of Tharmas & Urthona. I remaining in porches of the brain
Will lay my sceptre on Jerusalem the emanation,
On all her sons & on thy sons, O Luvah, & on mine,
195   Till dawn was wont to wake them. Then my trumpet sounding
           loud,
Ravished away in night my strong command shall be obeyed.
For I have placed my sentinels in stations: each tenth man
Is bought & sold, & in dim night my word shall be their law."'

[22]   'Luvah replied: "Dictate to thy equals: am not I
200   The prince of all the hosts of men, nor equal know in Heaven?
If I arise into the zenith, leaving thee to watch
The emanation & her sons, the Satan & the Anak,
Sihon and Og, wilt thou not, rebel to my laws, remain
In darkness building thy strong throne, & in my ancient night,
205   Daring my power, wilt arm my sons against me in the Atlantic,
My deep, my night—which thou assuming hast assumed my
           crown?
I will remain as well as thou, & here with hands of blood

i *178. Conway's Vale*] In North Wales, not far from Snowdon. The phrase
is an alteration from *Beth Peor* (see *170n, 172n*). Beth Peor was the place
where Moses died; B. thought of the bards and Moses in the same terms
here, as great leaders with prophetic powers. See also Gray's *The Bard*.
i *182*. The usurpation story in its standard form. Other versions, usually
with a personal slant, occur at intervals–e.g. ii *14, 213*, iii *41*, viia *233*.
When Man sleeps, the elements within him, which he should direct, take
advantage of him, but fall into disunity among themselves.
i *202–3. Satan and the Anak, / Sihon and Og*] See *Jerusalem* pl. *48.63n*. They
are, here, 'angels' as yet unfallen.

Smite this dark sleeper in his tent; then try my strength with
    thee."'

'While thus he spoke his fires reddened o'er the holy tent;
210 Urizen cast deep darkness round him, silent brooding death,
Eternal death to Luvah. Raging Luvah poured
The lances of Urizen from chariots; round the holy tent
Discord began, & yells & cries shook the wide firmament.

Beside his anvil stood Urthona dark, a mass of iron
215 Glowed furious on the anvil prepared for spades & coulters. All
His sons fled from his side to join the conflict. Pale he heard
The eternal voice. He stood; the sweat chilled on his mighty
    limbs.
He dropped his hammer. Dividing from his aching bosom fled
A portion of his life, shrieking upon the wind—she fled
220 And Tharmas took her in, pitying. Then Enion in jealous fear
Murdered her, & hid her in her bosom, embalming her for fear
She should arise again to life. Embalmed in Enion's bosom
Enitharmon remains a corse—such thing was never known
In Eden, that one died a death never to be revived.
225 Urthona stood in terror, but not long; his spectre fled
To Enion, & his body fell. Tharmas beheld him fall
Endlong, a raging serpent rolling round the holy tent.
The sons of war, astonished at the glittering monster, drove
Him far into the world of Tharmas, into a caverned rock.

230 'But Urizen, with darkness overspreading all the armies,
Sent round his heralds, secretly commanding to depart
Into the north. Sudden with thunder's sound, his multitudes
Retreat from the fierce conflict, all the sons of Urizen at once
Mustering together in thick clouds, leaving the rage of Luvah
235 To pour its fury on himself, & on the eternal Man.

'Sudden down fell they all together into an unknown space,

i *215. coulter*] Part of a plough: the vertical cutting blade just ahead of the
share.
i *230*. When Urthona has been overthrown, Urizen betrays Luvah by
withdrawing his forces. Luvah is left 'raging in the abyss'—this is not a
military campaign envisaged in detail—and his wrath, finding no enemy,
recoils on himself and on the Man, leaving Urizen's power undisputed.
The allegory is that passion and rationalism have allied to overthrow the
prophetic imagination in Man; and then passion, unbalanced, has run wild,
giving the rational spirit an excuse to take control of the entire Man who,
unable to handle this internal war, gives reason this undue authority
(ii *211–16*).
i *232. north*] Belongs to Urthona, but now usurped by Urizen (*186*).

Deep, horrible, without end. Separated from Beulah far beneath,
The Man's exteriors are become indefinite, opened to pain
In a fierce hungering void, & none can visit his regions.
[19]   Jerusalem his emanation is become a ruin;
241   Her little ones are slain on the top of every street
And she herself led captive & scattered into the indefinite.
Gird on thy sword, O thou most mighty in glory & majesty!
Destroy these oppressors of Jerusalem, & those who ruin Shiloh!'

245   So spoke the messengers of Beulah. Silently removing,
The Family Divine drew up the universal tent
Above high Snowdon, & closed the messengers in clouds around
Till the time of the end. Then they elected seven, called the Seven
Eyes of God, & the Seven Lamps of the Almighty.
250   The seven are one within the other, the seventh is named Jesus–
The Lamb of God blessed for ever, & he followed the Man,
Who wandered in mount Ephraim seeking a sepulchre,
His inward eyes closing from the Divine Vision, & all
His children wandering outside from his bosom, fleeing away.

[20]   The daughters of Beulah beheld the emanation; they pitied,
256   They wept, before the inner gates of Enitharmon's bosom,
And of her fine wrought brain, & of her bowels within her loins.
Three gates within, glorious & bright, open into Beulah
From Enitharmon's inward parts; but the bright female terror
260   Refused to open the bright gates. She closed and barred them fast,
Lest Los should enter into Beulah through her beautiful gates.

The emanation stood before the gates of Enitharmon

i *238.* For B. the true, eternal human form has a clear, definite, but not
rigid, outline. A fall from perfection will be accompanied by a loss of this
clear certainty of active, living feature.
i *240. his*] Albion's (the 'Man's'). When B. began *Four Zoas* the 'Man' had
no emanation; his only division was into Urthona, Urizen, etc., with their
counterparts. Later the 'Man' became Albion, who has an emanation,
Jerusalem. Cp. i *17n.*
i *248. seven*] Cp. *Milton* pl.14.*42n.* The seven are guardians of fallen 'man'
on behalf of the Divine Family; but they are in turn proved inadequate
though benevolent, except the last, Jesus. Cp. *Revelation* iv 5: 'there were
seven lamps of fire burning before the throne, which are the seven Spirits
of God'.
i *252. Ephraim*] The holy mountain of the seceded Northern Kingdom
(see *172n* on Shiloh).
i *255. the emanation*] Probably Jerusalem (cp. *240*), but possibly Enitharmon.
i *256. three gates*] Cp. *Milton* extra pl.5.*5–10n* (p. *569*). The gates of Eni-
tharmon's bosom, first closed against Los, burst open in viia *319*; cp. also
v *177*, viii *20–9.*

Weeping. The daughters of Beulah silent in the porches
Spread her a couch. Unknown to Enitharmon, here reposed
265 Jerusalem, in slumbers soft, lulled into silent rest.
Terrific raged the eternal wheels of intellect; terrific raged
The living creatures of the wheels in the wars of eternal life.
But perverse rolled the wheels of Urizen & Luvah, back reversed,
Downwards & outwards consuming in the wars of eternal death.

End of the First Night

Night the Second

For the textual problems, see Night i headnote (p. 291). The Second Night
takes up the story of Los and Enitharmon, and describes the flowering of
their mutual scorn into a quarrel, which lasts until after the birth of Orc
in the Fifth Night. First, in a passage of much textual confusion (13),
Enitharmon sings a song which tends to glorify the dominance of the
female; Los retaliates, and Enitharmon calls in Urizen (50) to establish her
ascendancy. After an exchange of threats, Los and Urizen settle an uneasy
peace (83), and they all sit down to a feast in the presence of Urizen's
armies. But the mood is unhappy; Los and Enitharmon regard each other
with mutual scorn, a song is sung (139ff) which describes the warlike chaos
which has come upon the world: and finally, a lament is heard from Enion,
driven by her children, Los and Enitharmon, to the verge of non-entity.
Thus all the Zoas, the elemental spirits within the 'man', are in conflict with
one another, threatening him with 'eternal death' (204), and he sinks
down (207–10), unable to keep his illness under control any longer.

Line 211 was once the beginning of another Night, and then perhaps
the beginning of the main story (the twice-erased word First may still be
read in the heading, as well as an erased Third). The 'Man' is ill, and wearily
hands over his power to one of the Zoas, Urizen–thus disturbing the whole
balance of his nature. (He sleeps in pain until the Ninth Night, when he
wakes and reassumes command over himself.) From this point B. develops
the myth of Urizen, which with added material takes him from the Second
to the Seventh Night (see general headnote, p. 288). The major difference
is in the place and nature of Urizen. In Urizen he is one among many
equals in the republic of Eternity, and he commits the treason of arrogating
sole power to himself. In Four Zoas he is one of the four great spirits who
are parts of the eternal Man. Eternity is seen, not simply as a republic,
but as 'one Man', made up of many living beings who are part of him, the
Four Zoas being the four major living principles which, in balance with
one another, make up the 'Man'.

Urizen's creation proceeds in Night ii; it is an attempt to secure his
power against his enemies and still more the encroaching abyss (225–31).

i 266. the wheels] Cp. Ezekiel i 4–25, where Ezekiel's vision of 'four living
creatures'–source of the Zoas–and of dazzling wheels is described. But to
B. wheels are often dead, mechanical things.

11*

Yet in the glory of his creation he is unhappy (*506–9*), enviously regarding
Los and Enitharmon, to whose continuing quarrel B. now turns (*512–29*):
and the Night ends with another lament from Enion (*602–33*), a comment
on the nature of life under Urizen, and one of the finest passages in B.'s
epics.

NIGHT THE SECOND

[9b]   But the two youthful wonders wandered in the world of Tharmas.
     'Thy name is Enitharmon', said the fierce prophetic boy;
     'While thy mild voice fills all these caverns with sweet harmony,
     O, how our parents sit & mourn in their silent secret bowers!'

[10]   But Enitharmon answered with a dropping tear & frowning,
   6 Dark as a dewy morning when the crimson light appears:
     'To make us happy let them weary their immortal powers,
     While we draw in their sweet delights, while we return them scorn
     On scorn to feed our discontent; for if we grateful prove
 10 They will withhold sweet love, whose food is thorns & bitter roots.
     We hear the warlike clarions, we view the turning spheres,
     Yet thou in indolence reposest, holding me in bonds.
     Hear! I will sing a song of death; it is a song of Vala.
     The fallen Man takes his repose: Urizen sleeps in the porch.
 15 Luvah and Vala woke & flew up from the human heart
     Into the brain; from thence upon the pillow Vala slumbered.
     And Luvah seized the horses of light, & rose into the chariot of day.

ii *1. the world of Tharmas*] Cp. i *201*, where Urthona's spectre is driven 'far
into the world of Tharmas' where the children are now wandering.
ii *2. prophetic boy*] Los.
ii *13–31. a song of Vala*] This is a usurpation story, but it has arrived at its
present form through the drastic revision of an entirely different earlier
text which apparently concerned Luvah and Vala, and described how
Vala's misery affected Luvah: it was probably another legend of female
dominance of the Man through jealousy and guile. The final version given
here tells how Luvah and Vala usurp Urizen's place in the brain of the
Eternal Man. While Luvah takes over Urizen's horses of light Vala puts
dreams into the Eternal Man's mind, dreams in which Enitharmon has a
place (*15*). The anxious words originally spoken by Luvah to Vala are
now spoken by the 'Man' to Enitharmon, in whose power he is. In the
guise of 'a song of Vala' Enitharmon is trying to make Los jealous. He
knocks her down (*32*):

    The main verbal alterations are shown in the notes: the textual develop-
ment, as far as it has been traced, may be found in *Erdman 1966* and the
Bentley edition.

    Other legends of the domination of man–both by Vala–are told in
iii *41*ff and viia *237*ff, and there are many occasional references.
ii *14. fallen*] *1st rdg del.* Eternal (so also in *35* and *39*).

Sweet laughter seized me in my sleep; silent & close I laughed,
For in the visions of Vala I walked with the mighty fallen one,
20 I heard his voice among the branches, & among sweet flowers:

"'Why is the light of Enitharmon darkened in dewy morn?
Why is the silence of Enitharmon a terror, & her smile a whirlwind?
Uttering this darkness in my halls, in the pillars of my holy ones,
Why dost thou weep as Vala & wet thy veil with dewy tears,
25 In slumbers of my night-repose, infusing a false morning,
Driving the female emanations all away from Los?
I have refused to look upon the universal vision;
And wilt thou slay with death him who devotes himself to thee—
Once born for the sport & amusement of man, now born to
   drink up all his powers?"

[11]   'I heard the sounding sea; I heard the voice weaker and weaker;
31 The voice came & went like a dream—I awoke in my sweet bliss.'

Then Los smote her upon the earth. 'Twas long ere she revived.
He answered, darkening more, with indignation hid in smiles:

'I die not, Enitharmon, though thou singest thy song of death,
35 Nor shalt thou me torment. For I behold the fallen Man
Seeking to comfort Vala; she will not be comforted.
She rises from his throne and seeks the shadows of her garden,
Weeping for Luvah lost, in the bloody beams of your false
   morning.
Sickening lies the fallen Man, his head sick, his heart faint.
40 Mighty achievement of your power! Beware the punishment.
I see invisible descend into the gardens of Vala
Luvah walking on the winds; I see the invisible knife,

ii *18–19.* These are added lines; *19* written before *18.*
ii *21. Enitharmon darkened in] 1st rdg del.* Vala darkened in her.
ii *22. Enitharmon a terror] 1st rdg del.* Vala lightning: *2nd rdg del.* Enitharmon
a cloud.
ii *24. as Vala] 1st rdg del.* O Vala.
ii *26–9.* These lines, which were added piecemeal and revised, are not part
of the early 'song' referred to in the note on *13.*
ii *34–47.* Here again considerable revision, presumably for the same pur-
pose as in *13–32,* has altered the sense to conform with B.'s latest story.
ii *36.* In Enitharmon's version the Man has been comforting her, not Vala
(*21*ff): Los says she is distorting the truth but in *40* lays all the blame for
the Man's sickness on Enitharmon. This is an error for (as we know) Los's
own fallen state, including his belligerence and this very quarrel, is another
part of Man's sickness.
ii *40.* For nine added but deleted lines, see appendix, p. 464.
ii *42–3.* i.e. 'I foresee the bloodshed that will come of this'.

I see the shower of blood; I see the swords & spears of futurity.
Though in the brain of man we live, & in his circling nerves,
45 Though this bright world of all our joy is in the human brain,
Where Urizen & all his hosts hang their immortal lamps,
Thou ne'er shalt leave this cold expanse where watery Tharmas
    mourns.'

So spoke Los. Scorn & indignation rose upon Enitharmon.
Then Enitharmon reddening fierce stretched her immortal hands:

50 'Descend, O Urizen, descend with horse & chariots!
Threaten not me, O visionary; thine the punishment!
The human nature shall no more remain, nor human acts
Form the rebellious spirits of heaven, but war & princedom and
    victory & blood.'

[12] Night darkened as she spoke; a shuddering ran from east to west.
55 A groan was heard on high. The warlike clarions ceased. The
    spirits
Of Luvah & Vala shuddered in their orb, an orb of blood.

Eternity groaned & was troubled at the image of eternal death.
The wandering Man bowed his faint head, and Urizen descended.
And the one must have murdered the other if he had not
    descended.
60 Indignant muttering low thunders Urizen descended,
Gloomy sounding: 'Now I am God from eternity to eternity.'

Sullen sat Los, plotting revenge. Silent he eyed the prince
Of light. Silent the prince of light viewed Los. At length a brooded
Smile broke from Urizen, for Enitharmon brightened more and
    more.
65 Sullen he lowered on Enitharmon, but he smiled on Los,

Saying: 'Thou art the lord of Luvah. Into thine hands I give
The prince of love, the murderer. His soul is in thine hands.
Pity not Vala, for she pitied not the Eternal Man,
Nor pity thou the cries of Luvah. Lo, these starry hosts,
70 They are thy servants, if thou wilt obey my awful law.'

Los answered furious: 'Art thou one of those who when most
    complaisant

ii 44–53. Los claims that the brain (usually given to Urizen, but in the song,
15–17, taken over by Luvah and Vala) belongs to himself and Enitharmon
by right: but threatens her with perpetual exile (cp. 1 and n). Los (or
Urthona) normally belongs in the heart, Luvah in the loins (despite 15,
which is unusual, but a reminder of B.'s inconsistency).
ii 59. the one . . . the other] Los and Enitharmon.
ii 71. complaisant] This is the sense; B. has complacent, which may have this
meaning.

Mean mischief most? If you are such, lo! I am also such.
One must be master: try thy arts, I also will try mine.
For I perceive thou hast abundance which I claim as mine.'

75 Urizen startled stood, but not long: soon he cried:
'Obey my voice, young demon! I am God from eternity to eternity!'

Thus Urizen spoke, collected in himself in awful pride:

'Art thou a visionary of Jesus, the soft delusion of Eternity?
Lo, I am God the terrible destroyer, & not the saviour!
80 Why should the Divine Vision compel the sons of Eden
To forego each his own delight to war against his spectre?
The spectre is the man. The rest is only delusion & fancy.'

So spoke the prince of light, & sat beside the seat of Los.
Upon the sandy shore rested his chariot of fire.

85 Ten thousand thousand were his hosts of spirits on the wind,
Ten thousand thousand glittering chariots shining in the sky,
They pour upon the golden shore beside the silent ocean,
Rejoicing in the victory; & the heavens were filled with blood.

The earth spread forth her table wide, the night a silver cup
90 Filled with the wine of anguish, waited at the golden feast;
But the bright sun was not as yet; he filling all the expanse
Slept as a bird in the blue shell that soon shall burst away.

Los saw the wound of his blow; he saw, he pitied, he wept.
Los now repented that he had smitten Enitharmon; he felt love
95 Arise in all his veins; he threw his arms around her loins
To heal the wound of his smiting.

They ate the fleshly bread, they drank the nervous wine,

---

ii 78. The description of Los as *a visionary of Jesus* is confusing. These
lines are a very late pencil addition: by the time B. had written Night viii,
this is what Los had become, because Los developed and changed radically
as B. worked at the poem. But in this context Los is still a spoilt child, as is
Enitharmon.

ii 80–2. The evil error into which Urizen has fallen.

ii 85–6. *Ten thousand thousand*] Urizen's host descends to take a bloodless
victory, which Los and Enitharmon must accept. The spirits, the sea, the
reception of honour, are all derived from *Revelation*, iv–v, but the direct
allusion is to *Paradise Lost* vi 767–70, where God appears: 'Attended with
ten thousand thousand Saints / He onward came; far off his coming
shone; / And twenty thousand (I their number heard) / Chariots of
God. . . .'

ii 97. *ate*] B. has *eat*.

[13]   They listened to the elemental harps & sphery song,
        They viewed the dancing hours, quick sporting through the sky
100   With winged radiance, scattering joys through the ever-changing
            light.

        But Luvah & Vala standing in the bloody sky
        On high remained alone, forsaken in fierce jealousy.
        They stood above the heavens forsaken, desolate, suspended in
            blood.
        Descend they could not, nor from each other avert their eyes.
105   Eternity appeared above them as One Man enfolded
        In Luvah's robes of blood & bearing all his afflictions.
        As the sun shines down on the misty earth, such was the vision.

        But purple night & crimson morning & golden day descending
        Through the clear changing atmosphere displayed green fields
            among
110   The varying clouds, like paradises stretched in the expanse,
        With towns & villages & temples, tents, sheep-folds & pastures,
        Where dwell the children of the elemental worlds in harmony;
        Not long in harmony they dwell, their life is drawn away
        And wintry woes succeed—successive driven into the void
115   Where Enion craves, successive drawn into the golden feast.

        And Los & Enitharmon sat in discontent & scorn.
        The nuptial song arose from all the thousand thousand spirits
        Over the joyful earth & sea, and ascended into the heavens.
        For elemental gods their thunderous organs blew, creating
120   Delicious viands, demons of waves their watery echoes woke.
        Bright souls of vegetative life, budding and blossoming
[14]   Stretch their immortal hands to smite the gold & silver wires,
        And with immortal voice soft warbling fill all earth & heaven,
        With doubling voices & loud horns wound round sounding

ii *98. sphery song*] The music of the spheres.
ii *113. Not long in harmony*] Los and Enitharmon will disturb it (see *116*,
and the song beginning on *128*).
ii *116. discontent and scorn*] Still angry with one another, perhaps also scorn-
ing what they see. The phrase indicates the true nature of the social
'pleasure' of the feast.
ii *121. vegetative life*] Rooted in the soil of the fallen world, not immortal.
ii *122. Stretch their immortal hands*] Recalling *Europe 13*, 'Stretch forth your
hands and strike the elemental strings', spoken by Los as he calls the spirits
to an earlier feast of Los and Enitharmon: both lines deriving from Milton's
At a Solemn Music, 12–13: 'And the cherubic host in thousand choirs /
Touch the immortal harps of golden wires'.
ii *124. loud horns wound round*] The valveless French horn, in common use
in duets in pleasure gardens.

125 Cavernous dwellers filled the enormous revelry responsing.
       And spirits of flaming fire on high governed the mighty song.

       And this the song sung at the feast of Los & Enitharmon:

       'Ephraim called out to Zion: Awake, O brother mountain,
       Let us refuse the plough & spade, the heavy roller & spiked
130 Harrow. Burn all these cornfields, throw down all these fences.
       Fattened on human blood & drunk with wine of life is better far

       'Than all these labours of the harvest & the vintage. See the river,
       Red with the blood of men, swells lustful round my rocky knees;
       My clouds are not the clouds of verdant fields & groves of fruit,
135 But clouds of human souls; my nostrils drink the lives of men.

       'The villages lament. They faint outstretched upon the plain.
       Wailing runs round the valleys, from the mill & from the barn;
       But most the polished palaces, dark, silent, bow with dread,
       Hiding their books & pictures underneath the dens of earth.

140 'The cities send to one another saying, "My sons are mad
       With wine of cruelty. Let us plait a scourge, O sister city!
       Children are nourished for the slaughter; once the child was fed
       With milk; but wherefore now are children fed with blood?

[15]   '"The horse is of more value than the man. The tiger fierce
145 Laughs at the human form. The lion mocks & thirsts for blood."
       They cry, "O spider, spread thy web! Enlarge thy bones &, filled
       With marrow, sinews & flesh, exalt thyself, attain a voice!

       'Call to thy dark-armed hosts, for all the sons of men muster
            together
       To desolate their cities. Man shall be no more. Awake, O hosts!"
150 The bowstring sang upon the hills. Luvah & Vala ride
       Triumphant in the bloody sky, & the human form is no more.

ii *128. Ephraim, Zion*] The holy mountains of Israel and Judah, the Northern
and Southern divided kingdoms of the O.T. The ascription of such bloody
sentiments to them illustrates the corruption of the world, or the singers'
view of it: and also B.'s awareness of the nature of the European war.
ii *144.* The tiger is destructive; the human form is the epitome of beautiful
completeness and coordination.
ii *148. muster together*] Perhaps a reference to the renewal of the war with
France in 1803, or to any period of its intensification.
ii *150ff.* The events of this passage are part of the song, not part of the
narrative of the poem. In it the demons describe a victory of Urizen over
Luvah: which presages that of *282*ff.

'The listening stars heard, & the first beam of the morning started
    back;
He cried out to his father, "Depart! depart!" But sudden seized
And clad in steel—& his horse proudly neighed, he smelt the
    battle
155 Afar off, rushing back. Reddening with rage the mighty father

'Seized his bright sheephook studded with gems & gold; he swung
    it round
His head, shrill sounding in the sky; down rushed the sun with noise
Of war. The mountains fled away, they sought a place beneath.
Vala remained in deserts of dark solitude, nor sun nor moon

160 'By night nor day to comfort her (she laboured in thick smoke).
Tharmas endured not, he fled howling. Then a barren waste
    sunk down,
Conglobing in the dark confusion. Meantime Los was born
And thou, O Enitharmon—hark, I hear the hammers of Los!

[16] 'They melt the bones of Vala & the bones of Luvah into wedges:
165 The innumerable sons & daughters of Luvah closed in furnaces
Melt into furrows. Winter blows his bellows; ice & snow
Tend the dire anvils. Mountains mourn, & rivers faint & fail.

'There is no city nor cornfield nor orchard—all is rock & sand!
There is no sun nor moon nor star, but rugged wintry rocks
170 Justling together in the void, suspended by inward fires.
Impatience now no longer can endure. Distracted Luvah,

'Bursting forth from the loins of Enitharmon, thou fierce terror,
Go howl in vain! Smite, smite his fetters! Smite, O wintry
    hammers!
Smite, spectre of Urthona, mock the fiend who drew us down
175 From heavens of joy into this deep. Now rage, but rage in vain!'

Thus sang the demons of the deep; the clarions of war blew loud.
The feast redounds, & crowned with roses & the circling vine,

ii *152.* Urizen is prince of light, and *the first beam* is his messenger, the *he*
of *153.*
ii *155. The mighty father*] Urizen, retaliating against Luvah.
ii *164. the bones of Vala . . . Luvah*] Cp. the melting of Luvah in the fires of
Vala in *282–326* below–note that here Vala is melted also. The iron,
smelted in the furnace, runs out along 'furrows' (*166*) to the mould.
ii *171–5.* The song now foretells what actually happens at the beginning of
Night v, where Orc (the fallen form of Luvah) is born to Enitharmon
(v *37*) but fettered by Los and the spectre of Urthona (v *104–12*).
ii *177. redounds*] A favourite word of B.'s, rather odd here; but *O.E.D.* gives
a meaning 'resound, reverberate', though marking it obsolete after 1632.

The enormous bride & bridegroom sat. Beside them Urizen
With faded radiance sighed, forgetful of the flowing wine,
180   And of Ahania his pure bride; but she was distant far.

But Los & Enitharmon sat in discontent & scorn,
Craving the more the more enjoying, drawing out sweet bliss
From all the turning wheels of heaven & the chariots of the slain,
At distance far in night repelled, in direful hunger craving,
185   Summers & winters round revolving in the frightful deep.

[17]   Enion blind & age-bent wept upon the desolate wind:

'Why does the raven cry aloud & no eye pities her?
Why fall the sparrow & the robin in the foodless winter?
Faint, shivering, they sit on leafless bush, or frozen stone,
190   Wearied with seeking food across the snowy waste–the little
Heart cold and the little tongue consumed, that once in
          thoughtless joy
Gave songs of gratitude to waving cornfields round their nest.

'Why howl the lion & the wolf? Why do they roam abroad?
Deluded by summer's heat, they sport in enormous love,
195   And cast their young out to the hungry wilds & sandy deserts.

[18]   'Why is the sheep given to the knife? The lamb plays in the sun:
He starts, he hears the foot of man, he says, "Take thou my wool
But spare my life;" but he knows not that winter cometh fast.

'The spider sits in his laboured web, eager watching for the fly;
200   Presently comes a famished bird & takes away the spider;
His web is left all desolate, that his little anxious heart
So careful wove & spread it out with sighs and weariness.'

This was the lamentation of Enion round the golden feast.
Eternity groaned and was troubled at the image of eternal death
205   Without the body of Man, an exudation from his sickening limbs.

ii *180. Ahania*] Urizen's emanation.
ii *181.* This line recalls *116.*
ii *186. Enion* was left (i *138*) after she had been driven to the void of non-
entity by the scorn of Los and Enitharmon. Compare this lament with
597ff.
ii *187–90.* Unlike the literary lion and wolf of *193*, this passage gives the
impression of being at least to some extent derived from observation.
ii *198. the winter cometh*] When he will suffer without his fleece (but sheep
are shorn in late spring so that the wool can grow again before winter)–or
the reference may be to slaughter for winter food (an out-of-date practice
by 1800).

Now Man was come to the palm tree & to the oak of weeping
Which stand upon the edge of Beulah; & he sunk down
From the supporting arms of the Eternal Saviour, who disposed
The pale limbs of his eternal individuality
210 Upon the Rock of Ages, watching over him with love & care.

       *   *   *

[23] Rising upon his couch of death Albion beheld his sons;
Turning his eyes outward to self, losing the Divine Vision,
Albion called Urizen & said: 'Behold these sickening spheres!
Whence is this voice of Enion that soundeth in my porches?
215 Take thou possession! Take this sceptre! Go forth in my might.
For I am weary, & must sleep in the dark sleep of death.
Thy brother Luvah hath smitten me; but pity thou his youth,
Though thou hast not pitied my age, O Urizen, prince of light.'

Urizen rose from the bright feast like a star through the evening sky,
220 Exulting at the voice that called him from the feast of envy.
First he beheld the body of Man, pale, cold; the horrors of death
Beneath his feet shot through him as he stood in the human brain,

ii *206–10*. B. adds to the picture of Enion watching at the Feast, a further aspect–that of the Divine Family. The effect of the wickedness of Los and Enitharmon, Urizen and all the Zoas, is expressed in terms of the myth of the weakened Albion.

     Palm tree and *oak of weeping*] M. J. Tolley has suggested a connection between two Deborahs, in *Genesis* xxxv 8 and *Judges* iv 5. In the first, a certain Deborah, nurse of Rebecca, Jacob's wife, dies and is buried beneath an oak, *Allon-bachuth* (A. V. margin translates, 'Oak of weeping') at Bethel. The second is near Bethel also, and refers to the palm tree where Deborah the prophetess gave judgment. The reference to two Deborahs appears incidental: the heart of the allusion is Jacob's experience at Bethel. There he laid his head on a stone pillar, and in his sleep saw a vision of God (*Genesis* xxviii 10–19). In B., dreams are an entry to Beulah. Albion also sleeps on stone, and is watched by the Divine love and care. Perhaps he also will see a vision of God, a vision which is not merely a dream, but an eternal reality. Cp. also *Milton* pl.15.*1–16* and *Jerusalem* pl.48.*1–4*.

ii Page 23. Once the beginning of a Night: still the beginning of Urizen's active dominion. See Night i headnote. The heading now stands as 'VALA / Night the [*erasure*]'.

ii *211. Albion*] (*1st rdg del.* The Man) B.'s later name for the archetypal Man; it implies also that the nation of Britain can stand for *The Man*.

ii *215. take this sceptre*] The symbol of handing over power. The illustration below shows the Man, aged, lying down to sleep.

ii *217. Luvah hath smitten me*] Cp. i *235*. Luvah's attack on Urizen had turned on himself and the Man.

ii *218. prince of light*] Urizen is equated with Lucifer and Satan.

ii *222. the human brain*] The brain of the 'Man', Urizen's home.

And all its golden porches grew pale with his sickening light.
No more exulting, for he saw eternal death beneath;
225   Pale, he beheld futurity; pale, he beheld the abyss,
Where Enion, blind & age-bent, wept in direful hunger craving,
All ravening like the hungry worm, & like the silent grave.

[24]   Mighty was the draught of voidness to draw existence in.

Terrific, Urizen strode above; in fear & pale dismay
230   He saw the indefinite space beneath, & his soul shrunk with
        horror.
His feet upon the verge of non-existence his voice went forth.

Luvah & Vala, trembling & shrinking, beheld the great
        workmaster,
And heard his word, 'Divide, ye bands, influence by influence.
Build we a bower for Heaven's darling in the grisly deep;
235   Build we the mundane shell around the rock of Albion.'
The bands of Heaven flew through the air, singing & shouting to
        Urizen:
Some fixed the anvil, some the loom erected, some the plough
And harrow formed, & framed the harness of silver & ivory,
The golden compasses, the quadrant & the rule & balance.

ii *229ff.* Cp. *Paradise Lost* vii 131ff, the creation of the world. But in B.
'Lucifer' is enthroned as creator, and he creates through fear of the abyss,
not to fill a gap left by rebels. B. draws on many details of Milton's account.

ii *230. the indefinite space*] Cp. *Paradise Lost* vii 211–12: '. . . the vast im-
measurable abyss, / Outrageous as a sea, dark, wasteful, wild'.

ii *232. the great workmaster*] Cp. Bacon (whose thought was anathema to
B.), *Advancement of Learning* II xiv 9: 'For if that great work-master had
been of an human disposition, he would have cast the stars into some
pleasant and beautiful works and orders, like the frets in the roofs of
houses; whereas one can scarce find a posture in square, or triangle, or
straight line, amongst such an infinite number. . . .' But though this
phraseology is remarkably relevant, B. could have found the phrase in
Paradise Lost iii 696.

ii *233. bands*] Bands (or gangs) of Urizen's servants.

ii *234. Heaven's darling*] In *Paradise Lost* ii 350–1 and 373, Beelzebub refers
to newly created man as 'favoured more of him who rules above' and
'his darling sons'.

ii *235. the mundane shell*] The enclosing firmament which confines and
restricts the material world: cp. *458*, and note at *Milton* pl.34.31.

ii *237–40.* At first sight a rather improbable mixture of tools and imple-
ments of various trades: but B., later in the Night, develops each trade—
blacksmithing, ironmoulding, farming and carpentry—in turn (*327–82*).

ii *239. the golden compasses*] From *Paradise Lost* vii 225, where they were
'. . . prepared / In God's eternal store, to circumscribe / This Universe,
and all created things'.

240   They erected the furnaces, they formed the anvils of gold, beaten
           in mills
         Where winter beats incessant, fixing them firm on their base.
         The bellows began to blow & the lions of Urizen stood round the
           anvil
[25]   And the leopards covered with skins of beasts tended the roaring
           fires;
         Sublime, distinct, their lineaments divine of human beauty.
245   The tigers of wrath called the horses of instruction from their
           mangers:
         They unloosed them & put on the harness of gold & silver & ivory.

         In human forms distinct they stood round Urizen, prince of light,
         Petrifying all the human imagination into rock & sand.
         Groans ran along Tyburn's brook, and along the river of Oxford
250   Among the Druid temples. Albion groaned on Tyburn's brook,
         Albion gave his loud death groan. The Atlantic mountains
           trembled,
         Aloft the moon fled with a cry, the sun with streams of blood
         From Albion's loins fled. All peoples and nations of the earth
         Fled with the noise of slaughter, & the stars of heaven fled.
255   Jerusalem came down in a dire ruin over all the earth;
         She fell cold from Lambeth's vales in groans & dewy death,
         The dew of anxious souls, the death-sweat of the dying
         In every pillared hall & arched roof of Albion's skies.
         The brother & the brother bathe in blood upon the Severn,
260   The maiden weeping by, the father & the mother with

ii *243. leopards*] B. might have heard of the West African 'leopard-man'
cults, which involved human sacrifice by celebrants dressed in leopard
skins; but no direct source has been found.

ii *245.* Cp. *Marriage,* p. 110 above.

ii *248.* A sketch below shows Urizen manipulating huge compasses.

ii *249. Tyburn*] The place where criminals were hanged, near the site of the
Marble Arch. Oxford, as a place of learning, is sometimes associated with
oppressive adherence to the past.

ii *250. Druid temples*] Cp. notes on *Europe 72* and *Jerusalem 27.*

ii *255. Jerusalem*] In B.'s later myth, Jerusalem, Albion's emanation, is
involved in his fall, and is enslaved (as a woman) or razed (as a city) until
he rises again from his sleep of death. See i *17, 19, 240–4;* viii *576–8,* and
especially the poem in *Jerusalem 27.*

ii *256. Lambeth's vales*] B.'s home 1791–1800. Also the home of the Arch-
bishop of Canterbury, head of English official and organized religion. But
cp. *Milton* pl.26.48.

ii *259. the Severn*] Two civil-war battles were fought on the Severn:
Shrewsbury (1403) and Tewkesbury (1471). But see *n* below.

ii *260. The maiden*] No one in *Vala;* it it a sort of stock ballad-scene.

The maiden's father & her mother fainting over the body,
And the young man, the murderer, fleeing over the mountains.
Reuben slept on Penmaenmawr & Levi slept on Snowdon.
Their eyes, their ears, nostrils & tongues roll outward; they behold
265   What is within now seen without; they are raw to the hungry wind,
They become nations far remote in a little & dark land.
The daughters of Albion girded around their garments of
          needlework,
Stripping Jerusalem's curtains from mild demons of the hills,
Across Europe & Asia to China & Japan, like lightnings
270   They go forth, & return to Albion on his rocky couch:
Gwendolen, Ragan, Sabrina, Gonorill, Mehetabel, Cordella,
Boadicea, Conwenna, Estrild, Gwinefred, Ignoge, Cambel—
Binding Jerusalem's children in the dungeons of Babylon.

ii *263–6. Reuben* belongs chiefly to *Jerusalem*, and the ideas of these lines
may be understood fully only in the context of that poem, especially
pls 15.*1–29*, 30.*43–54*, 32.*1–13*. The chief ideas here are: (*a*) that the two,
Reuben and Levi, are faithless children, and *asleep*; (*b*) their faculties are
turned inwards and limited, as human faculties are limited in this material
world. B. introduces the pair here within Urizen's creation as examples of
eternal natures corrupted. Reuben was disinherited as 'unstable as water'
(*Genesis* xlix 4) for his incest; Levi was the father of the tribe of priests.
See *Jerusalem* pl. 30.*43n*. For *outward* see *Jerusalem* pl. 12.*55n*.
  Snowdon and *Penmaenmawr*, the great mountains of northern Wales,
are associated by B. with the bards of old, inspired men who maintained
the great patriarchal tradition. Perhaps B. is indicating that even they have
only earthbound intuitions.
ii *266. They become nations . . .*] Intermittently and rather obscurely, B.
develops in *Jerusalem* pls 63.*1–64.5*, 64.*35–8*, 71.*1–5* the image of Albion
and Canaan as a single holy land, which in the time of Albion's despair is
split into two, the separated parts rolling far away from one another into
their present situations. This line alludes to that catastrophe: Reuben and
Levi are parted from Albion, and have become two of the twelve tribes
or nations in the remote land of Canaan. Line *264* is a reference to the idea
developed in *Jerusalem* pl.71.*6–9*. Lines *263–75*, an addition to the original
text, describe the evil which comes upon disintegrating Albion in his sleep.
ii *267–8. needlework . . . curtains*] The one is artificial, the other eternal. The
veil of the temple which tore at Christ's death (*Matt.* xxvii 51) was of
needlework.
271–2. the daughters of Albion] The names are chosen from the legendary
history of Ancient Britain (i.e. pre-Roman Britain) and so belong to the
Druid age. They are much used in *Jerusalem*; see pl.5.*43–4* for details.
ii *273*. The transportation of the Jews of Jerusalem to Babylon is described
in *2 Kings* xxv, and is the background of *Ezekiel*. *Revelation* uses the
opposition of Babylon and Jerusalem to symbolize evil and the city of

They play before the armies, before the hounds of Nimrod,
275 While the prince of light on Salisbury Plain among the Druid
         stones . . .

Rattling the adamantine chains & hooks, heave up the ore
In mountainous masses, plunged in furnaces, & they shut & sealed
The furnaces a time & times; all the while blew the north
His cloudy bellows, & the south & east & dismal west;
280 And all the while the plough of iron cut the dreadful furrows
In Ulro beneath Beulah, where the dead wail night & day.

Luvah was cast into the furnaces of affliction & sealed,
And Vala fed in cruel delight the furnaces with fire.
Stern Urizen beheld, urged by necessity to keep
285 The evil day afar, & if perchance with iron power
He might avert his own despair. In woe & fear he saw
[26] Vala encircle round the furnaces where Luvah was closed.
In joy she heard his howlings, & forgot he was her Luvah,
With whom she walked in bliss, in times of innocence & youth.

290 Hear ye the voice of Luvah from the furnaces of Urizen:

'If I indeed am Vala's king, & ye, O sons of men,
The workmanship of Luvah's hands in times of everlasting,
When I called forth the earth-worm from the cold & dark obscure
I nurtured her, I fed her with my rains & dews, she grew
295 A scaled serpent, yet I fed her though she hated me;
Day after day she fed upon the mountains in Luvah's sight.
I brought her through the wilderness, a dry & thirsty land,
And I commanded springs to rise for her in the black desert
Till she became a dragon, winged, bright & poisonous.
300 I opened all the floodgates of the heavens to quench her thirst,

God. Cp. also *Galatians* iv 25: 'Jerusalem . . . is in bondage, with her
children'. The image is biblical, not B.'s invention.
ii *274. Nimrod*] In *Genesis* x 9, 'the mighty hunter' and a ruler of wide
lands; to B. a fierce tyrant.
ii *275. Salisbury Plain*] Site of Stonehenge. Lines *249–75* are an added
passage; probably a line between *275* and *276* was missed out in copying.
ii *282–9.* Also in *Jerusalem* pl.7.*30–7*: cp. *Revelation* xx 3, where Satan is
sealed in the bottomless pit. Luvah was betrayed by Urizen at the beginning
of the story (i *210, 230*ff) after a brief and sinister collusion.
ii *283.* Vala has betrayed her counterpart; in viib Vala also takes Urizen's
side against Orc (who is a degraded form of Luvah).
ii *299.* The four drawings on this page show variations on this dragon, two
of them heavily emphasizing Vala's sexual poison. The opposite page
shows Vala, as a woman, smirking at Luvah, who is wasted to skin and
bone.

[27] And I commanded the great deep to hide her in his hand,
      Till she became a little weeping infant a span long,
      I carried her in my bosom as a man carries a lamb,
      I loved her, I gave her all my soul & my delight;
305   I hid her in soft gardens & in secret bowers of summer,
      Weaving mazes of delight along the sunny paradise,
      Inextricable labyrinths. She bore me sons & daughters,
      And they have taken her away & hid her from my sight.
      They have surrounded me with walls of iron & brass. O Lamb
310   Of God clothed in Luvah's garments, little knowest thou
      Of death eternal—that we all go to eternal death,
      To our primeval chaos, in fortuitous concourse of incoherent
      Discordant principles of love & hate. I suffer affliction
      Because I love, for I was love; but hatred awakes in me,
315   And Urizen, who was faith & certainty, is changed to doubt.
      The hand of Urizen is upon me, because I blotted out
      That human delusion to deliver all the sons of God
      From bondage of the human form. O first born son of light,
      O Urizen my enemy, I weep for thy stern ambition
320   But weep in vain. Oh, when will you return, Vala the wanderer?'

[28] These were the words of Luvah, patient in afflictions,
      Reasoning from the loins in the unreal forms of Ulro's night.

      And when Luvah age after age was quite melted with woe,
      The fires of Vala faded like a shadow, cold & pale,
325   An evanescent shadow; last she fell, a heap of ashes
      Beneath the furnaces, a woeful heap in living death.
      Then were the furnaces unsealed with spades, & pickaxes

ii *309–13.* An addition written over an erased passage. It expresses Luvah's disillusionment; but his view is erroneous, as the poem later shows (see *321–2* and *473–5*).

ii *310–3.* In *106* it is made clear that Jesus is 'clothed in Luvah's garments' in order to redeem him. Luvah misinterprets this here as Vala does in viii *145*. Cp. *Jerusalem* pl.29.8.

ii *316–7.* In fact, Luvah was striking at the Man's balance and personality. There can be no freedom for the Man's separate elements if the whole is disintegrated.

ii *321–2.* These lines reject Luvah's views; reasoning is not from the loins. His 'patience' is alien to his passionate nature and misguided.

ii *324.* Vala has destroyed Luvah and, unwittingly, herself also. But Luvah reappears as Orc in v *17*, and Vala's shadow also returns in viia *317*, with dire results.

ii *327. the furnaces unsealed*] B. refers to the simple kind of blast furnace (in common use before the introduction of coke) which he had doubtless seen in Surrey. The ore, broken and mixed with marl, was put in alternate

Roaring let out the fluid, the molten metal ran in channels,
Cut by the plough of ages held in Urizen's strong hand
330 In many a valley, for the bulls of Luvah dragged the plough.
With trembling horror, pale, aghast the children of man
Stood on the infinite earth & saw these visions in the air,
In waters, & in earth beneath; they cried to one another,
'What? are we terrors to one another? Come, O brethren, wherefore
335 Was this wide earth spread all abroad? Not for wild beasts to roam!'
But many stood silent & busied in their families,
And many said: 'We see no visions in the darksome air.
Measure the course of that sulphur orb, that lights the darksome day.
Set stations on this breeding earth, & let us buy & sell.'
340 Others arose & schools erected, forming instruments
To measure out the course of heaven. Stern Urizen beheld
In woe his brethren & his sons, in darkening woe lamenting
Upon the winds, in clouds involved, uttering his voice in thunders,
Commanding all the work with care & power & severity.
345 Then seized the lions of Urizen their work, & heated in the forge
Roar the bright masses, thundering beat the hammers, many a pyramid
Is formed & thrown down thundering into the deeps of non-entity.
Heated red hot they hissing rend their way down many a league
Till resting each his centre finds; suspended there they stand,
350 Casting their sparkles dire abroad into the dismal deep.
For measured out in ordered spaces the sons of Urizen
With compasses divide the deep; they the strong scales erect
[29] That Luvah rent from the faint heart of the fallen Man,
And weigh the massy cubes, then fix them in their awful stations.
355 And all the time, in caverns shut, the golden looms erected
First spun, then wove the atmospheres. There the spider & worm

layers with charcoal; the furnace was lit and closed, the heating being assisted by a blast of air provided by bellows and escaping through a high chimney. The metal, when molten, ran out into moulds when a plug at the base of the furnace was removed. The *spades and pickaxes* were probably used for digging out the moulds. The passage takes up the building of Urizen's world from *247*.

ii *332. the infinite earth*] *Not* the finite world Urizen is having built. Cp. the reaction of the Eternals against Urizen in *Urizen* 44ff.

ii *337*. These *many* were seduced to Urizen's vision, defying imagination and seeing only the material world.

ii *346. pyramid*] Altered from 'globe'. In the following pages B. systematically replaces spherical images with angular ones, such as 'cube'.

ii *353. Luvah rent*] This act is not mentioned elsewhere.

Plied the winged shuttle, piping shrill through all the listening
    threads.
Beneath the caverns roll the weights of lead & spindles of iron;
The enormous warp & woof rage direful in the affrighted deep.
360   While far into the vast unknown the strong-winged eagles bend
    Their venturous flight, in human forms distinct; through darkness
      deep
    They bear the woven draperies; on golden hooks they hang abroad
    The universal curtains, & spread out from sun to sun
    The vehicles of light; they separate the furious particles
365   Into mild currents as the water mingles with the wine.
    While thus the spirits of strongest wing enlighten the dark deep,
    The threads are spun & the cords twisted & drawn out. Then the
      weak
    Begin their work, & many a net is netted many a net
[30]   Spread & many a spirit caught; (innumerable the nets,
370   Innumerable the gins & traps), & many a soothing flute
    Is formed & many a corded lyre outspread over the immense.
    In cruel delight they trap the listeners, & in cruel delight
    Bind them, condensing the strong energies into little compass.
    Some became seed of every plant that shall be planted; some
375   The bulbous roots, thrown up together into barns & garners.
    Then rose the builders; first the architect divine his plan
    Unfolds—the wondrous scaffold reared all round the infinite.
    Quadrangular the building rose, the heavens squared by a line.
    Trigon & cubes divide the elements in finite bonds;
380   Multitudes without number work incessant; the hewn stone
    Is placed in beds of mortar mingled with the ashes of Vala.
    Severe the labour, female slaves the mortar trod, oppressed.

ii *358. weights ... spindles*] The weights on a loom to keep the warp
tightly stretched. In *Milton* pl.7.1, and presumably here, the spindle belongs
to the spinning machine.

ii *359. warp and woof*] The warp is the series of threads stretched along the
loom; the woof is the thread woven across it. The words were in common
poetic use without specific allusion to the details of the process.

ii *361. human forms*] Eternal, not yet fallen.

ii *368. net*] Like the curtain of *360–5*, this is an irresistible woven fabric that
ties down the spirit. The drawing immediately below shows a man making
a net.

ii *370. soothing flute*] The connection of oppression and seductiveness goes
back in B. at least to *In a Myrtle Shade* of the early 1790s (p. 153) and
Europe 17–28, 33–41, etc.

ii *381. ashes of Vala*] From *326.*

ii *382. female slaves*] This and *430–2* probably derive from the use of women
to mix mortar for building.

Twelve halls, after the names of his twelve sons, composed
The wondrous building, & three central domes, after the names
385 Of his three daughters, were encompassed by the twelve bright
        halls,
Every hall surrounded by bright paradises of delight
In which are towns & cities, nations, seas, mountains & rivers.
Each dome opened toward four halls, & the three domes
        encompassed
The golden hall of Urizen, whose western side glowed bright
390 With ever-streaming fires, beaming from his awful limbs.

His shadowy feminine semblance here reposed on a white couch,
Or hovered o'er his starry head, & when he smiled she brightened
Like a bright cloud in harvest; but when Urizen frowned she wept
In mists over his carved throne, & when he turned his back
395 Upon his golden hall & sought the labyrinthine porches
Of his wide heaven, trembling, cold, in paling fears she sat,
A shadow of despair. Therefore toward the west Urizen formed
A recess in the wall, for fires to glow upon the pale
Female's limbs in his absence; & her daughters oft upon
400 A golden altar burnt perfumes, with art celestial formed
Foursquare, sculptured & sweetly engraved to please their
        shadowy mother.
Ascending into her misty garments the blue smoke rolled to revive
Her cold limbs in the absence of her lord. Also her sons
With lives of victims, sacrificed upon an altar of brass
405 On the east side, revived her soul, with lives of beasts & birds
Slain on the altar up ascending into her cloudy bosom.
Of terrible workmanship the altar, labour of ten thousand slaves;
One thousand men of wondrous power spent their lives in its
        formation.
It stood on twelve steps named after the names of her twelve sons
410 And was erected at the chief entrance of Urizen's hall.
When Urizen returned from his immense labours & travels
Descending she reposed beside him, folding him around
In her bright skirts. Astonished & confounded he beheld

ii *383*ff. Urizen's *twelve sons* and *three daughters* are an idea not fully de-
veloped. Four sons are named in *Urizen 430–7*; and below, viia *488*, one
(Thiriel) is mentioned. The daughters reappear in vi *5–23* and viia *95*ff,
where they are named—Eleth, Uveth and Ona.
ii *391. His shadowy feminine semblance*] Not a true emanation; she is a
shadow of himself, and has no true separate existence (see note on *Ema-
nation*, i *17*). Yet the entire division of *413–16* makes matters worse, for
the shadow should be subordinate to its person of origin, and for it to
take on a pretence of humanity is a great evil.
ii *400. with art celestial formed*] i.e. the altar. The 'art' is cruelty.

Her shadowy form now separate, he shuddered & was silent,
415 Till her caresses & her tears revived him to life & joy.
Two wills they had, two intellects, & not as in times of old.
This Urizen perceived & silent brooded in darkening clouds;
To him his labour was but sorrow, & his kingdom was repentance.
He drave the male spirits all away from Ahania,
420 And she drave all the females from him away.

Los joyed & Enitharmon laughed, saying, 'Let us go down
And see this labour & sorrow.' They went down to see the woes
Of Vala, & the woes of Luvah, to draw in their delights.
And Vala like a shadow oft appeared to Urizen.
[31] The king of light beheld her mourning among the brick kilns, compelled
426 To labour night & day among the fires. Her lamenting voice
Is heard when silent night returns & the labourers take their rest:

'O Lord, wilt thou not look upon our sore afflictions
Among these flames incessant labouring? Our hard masters laugh
430 At all our sorrow. We are made to turn the wheel for water,
To carry the heavy basket on our scorched shoulders, to sift
The sand & ashes, & to mix the clay with tears & repentance.
I see not Luvah as of old; I only see his feet
Like pillars of fire travelling through darkness & non-entity.
435 The times are now returned upon us; we have given ourselves
To scorn, and now are scorned by the slaves of our enemies.
Our beauty is covered over with clay & ashes, & our backs
Furrowed with whips, & our flesh bruised with the heavy basket.
Forgive us, O thou piteous one whom we have offended, forgive
440 The weak remaining shadow of Vala that returns in sorrow to thee.'

Thus she lamented day & night, compelled to labour & sorrow.
Luvah in vain her lamentations heard; in vain his love
Brought him in various forms before her—still she knew him not,
[32] Still she despised him, calling on his name & knowing him not,
445 Still hating, still professing love, still labouring in the smoke.

ii 419–20. So with Los and Enitharmon in i 160–1.
ii 425–32. See note on 382.
ii 433–4 are written in the margin at this place, though B. did not mark
where they should go in.
ii 435. i.e. 'the wheel has come full circle'.
ii 441–3. Characteristically, B. puts Vala in various situations: faded to
ashes (326, 381); one of the female labourers (382, 425–38); and still ig-
noring the imprisoned Luvah, here as in 283. The consistent feature is that
both she and Luvah are governed by the will of Urizen, and cannot follow
their own natures.

And Los & Enitharmon joyed, they drank in tenfold joy
From all the sorrow of Luvah & the labour of Urizen;
And Enitharmon joyed, plotting to rend the secret cloud,
To plant divisions in the soul of Urizen & Ahania.

450 But infinitely beautiful the wondrous work arose
In sorrow & care, a golden world whose porchēs round the
  heavens
And pillared halls & rooms received the eternal wandering stars:
A wondrous golden building—many a window, many a door,
And many a division let in & out into the vast unknown,
455 *Cubed in window square* immoveable; within its walls & ceilings
The heavens were closed, and spirits mourned their bondage night
  and day.
And the Divine Vision appeared in Luvah's robes of blood.

Thus was the mundane shell builded by Urizen's strong power.

Sorrowing went the planters forth to plant, the sowers to sow:
460 They dug the channels for the rivers, & they poured abroad
The seas & lakes, they reared the mountains & the rocks & hills
On broad pavilions, on pillared roofs & porches & high towers
In beauteous order. Thence arose soft clouds & exhalations,
Wandering even to the sunny cubes of light & heat.
465 For many a window, ornamented with sweet ornaments,
Looked out into the world of Tharmas, where in ceaseless torrents
His billows roll, where monsters wander in the foamy paths.

On clouds the sons of Urizen beheld heaven walled round;
They weighed & ordered all, & Urizen comforted saw
470 The wondrous work flow forth, like visible out of the invisible.
For the divine Lamb, even Jesus, who is the Divine Vision,
Permitted all, lest Man should fall into eternal death.

ii *451. sorrow and care*] *1st rdg del.* songs and joy: so also in *478*.
ii *455. Cubed in window square*] *1st rdg del.* Circled in infinite orb. The
second reading is also erased; yet it is supported by the reference to 'cubes'
and 'window' in *469–70*. If B. hesitated to choose either reading, an editor
hesitates to reject either. See also *346n*.
ii *457. the Divine Vision*] Luvah has been sacrificed, but the Divine Vision
takes his place in the sacrifice. B. uses this term to avoid the monarchic
implications of the word *God*, but sometimes uses the name *Jesus* or *the
Saviour* (e.g. ii *208*). Thus B. regards the Divine Vision as a person.
robes of blood] A mark of Luvah's sufferings, from *101–7*, throughout the
poem.
ii *466. Tharmas*] Named for the first time in this Night, by his charac-
teristic domain – the sea.
ii *471–5*. Written over erasures; the addition justifies Urizen's world, on
account of 'necessity'.

For when Luvah sunk down, himself put on the robes of blood
Lest the state called Luvah should cease, & the Divine Vision
475 Walked in robes of blood till he who slept should awake.

Thus were the stars of heaven created like a golden chain,
To bind the body of man to heaven from falling into the abyss:
Each took his station, & his course began with sorrow & care,
In sevens & tens & fifties, hundreds, thousands, numbered all
480 According to their various powers, subordinate to Urizen
And to his sons in their degrees, & to his beauteous daughters,
Travelling in silent majesty along their ordered ways
In right-lined paths outmeasured, by proportions of number,
     weight,
And measure; mathematic motion wondrous along the deep
485 In fiery pyramid or cube or unornamented pillar
Of fire far shining, travelling along even to its destined end,
Then falling down a terrible space, recovering in winter dire
Its wasted strength, it back returns upon a nether course,
Till fired with ardour fresh recruited in its humble season
490 It rises up on high all summer till its wearied course
Turns into autumn. Such the period of many worlds.
Others, triangular, right-angled course maintain, others obtuse,
Acute, scalene, in simple paths; but others move
In intricate ways biquadrate—trapeziums, rhombs, rhomboids,
495 Parallelograms, triple & quadruple, polygonic—
In their amazing hard subdued course in the vast deep.

[34] And Los & Enitharmon were drawn down by their desires,
Descending sweet upon the wind, among soft harps & voices,
To plant divisions in the soul of Urizen & Ahania,
500 To conduct the voice of Enion to Ahania's midnight pillow.

Urizen saw, & envied; & his imagination was filled.

ii *474. the state called Luvah*] The idea of *states*, developed in B.'s late
period, differentiates individual personality, which is eternal, from its oc-
casional appearances, its *states*. B. deals with these states mythically, as if
they were persons, but wishes to make it clear that this is only a literary
device. Cp. *Milton* pl. *32.10n* and *Jerusalem* pl.*31.13n*.
i *478.* Cp. *451n.*
ii *485. unornamented pillar*] *1st rdg del.* ornamented pillar square.
ii *486. its*] A star's. In *478–96* B. varies between singular and plural in
referring to the stars.
ii *493. scalene*] A triangle with unequal sides.
ii *494. biquadrate*] The square of the square; i.e. to the fourth power. But
since B. then lists quadrangles, perhaps that is all he means. His mathemat-
ical terms do not seem to bear precise intentions.
ii *496. hard subdued*] *1st rdg del.* fructifying.

Repining, he contemplated the past in his bright sphere,
Terrified with his heart & spirit at the visions of futurity
That his dread fancy formed before him in the unformed void.

505 For Los & Enitharmon walked forth on the dewy earth,
Contracting or expanding their all-flexible senses—
At will to murmur in the flowers, small as the honey bee;
At will to stretch across the heavens & step from star to star;
Or standing on the earth erect, or on the stormy waves
510 Driving the storms before them, or delighting in sunny beams
While round their heads the elemental gods kept harmony.

And Los said: 'Lo! the lily pale & the rose reddening fierce
Reproach thee, & the beamy gardens sicken at thy beauty.
I grasp thy vest in my strong hand in vain, like water-springs
515 In the bright sands of Los, evading my embrace. Then I alone
Wander among the virgins of the summer: "Look!" they cry.
"The poor forsaken Los, mocked by the worm, the shelly snail,
The emmet & the beetle!" Hark, they laugh & mock at Los!'

Enitharmon answered: 'Secure now from the smitings of thy
   power,
520 Demon of fury, if the god enraptured me enfolds,
In clouds of sweet obscurity my beauteous form dissolving,
Howl thou over the body of death—'tis thine! But if among the
   virgins
Of summer I have seen thee sleep, & turn thy cheek delighted
Upon the rose or lily pale, or on a bank where sleep
525 The beamy daughters of the light, starting they rise, they flee
From thy fierce love. For though I am dissolved in the bright god,
My spirit still pursues thy false love over rocks & valleys.'

Los answered: 'Therefore fade I, thus dissolved in raptured trance:
Thou canst repose on clouds of secrecy, while o'er my limbs
530 Cold dews & hoary frost creeps, though I lie on banks of summer
Among the beauties of the world. Cold & repining, Los
Still dies for Enitharmon, nor a spirit springs from my dead corse.

ii *511. the elemental gods*] The 'elements'; i.e. the features of the weather
personified–a piece of commonplace poetic diction. They sang the song
in *119*ff; and sing again in v *42*ff and viib *143*ff.
ii *512ff.* The sense of this passage, *512–92* (all added material) divides into
two at *554.* Its theme is the flirtatious deceitfulness and jealousy of Eni-
tharmon, which bring out similar feelings in an unhappy Los.
ii *518. emmet*] Ant.
ii *520–3. the god*] Urizen, 'the bright god' (*526*), whom Los determines to
make jealous (*548*). Enitharmon says, in effect: 'I will let *the god* embrace
me if I like; but you must not behave as I do'. Los says: 'I shall do, but I
am still unhappy because you reject me'.

Then I am dead, till thou revivest me with thy sweet song—
Now taking on Ahania's form, & now the form of Enion.
535 I know thee not as once I knew thee, in those blessed fields
Where memory wishes to repose among the flocks of Tharmas.'

Enitharmon answered: 'Wherefore didst thou throw thine arms
      around
Ahania's image? I deceived thee & will still deceive.
Urizen saw thy sin, & hid his beams in darkening clouds;
540 I still keep watch, although I tremble & wither across the heavens
In strong vibrations of fierce jealousy; for thou art mine,
Created for my will, my slave—though strong, though I am weak.
Farewell! the god calls me away. I depart in my sweet bliss!'

She fled, vanishing on the wind, and left a dead cold corse
545 In Los's arms. Howlings began over the body of death.
Los spoke: 'Thy god in vain shall call thee if by my strong power
I can infuse my dear revenge into his glowing breast,
Then jealousy shall shadow all his mountains, & Ahania
Curse thee, thou plague of woeful Los, & seek revenge on thee!'

550 So saying, in deep sobs he languished till dead he also fell.
Night passed, & Enitharmon ere the dawn returned in bliss.
She sang o'er Los, reviving him to life (his groans were terrible),
But thus she sang: 'I seize the sphery harp, I strike the strings.

'At the first sound the golden sun arises from the deep
555 And shakes his awful hair.
The echo wakes the moon to unbind her silver locks.
The golden sun bears on my song,
And nine bright spheres of harmony rise round the fiery king.

'The joy of woman is the death of her most best beloved,
560 Who dies for love of her
In torments of fierce jealousy & pangs of adoration.
The lovers' night bears on my song,
And the nine spheres rejoice beneath my powerful control.

'They sing unceasing, to the notes of my immortal hand:
565 The solemn silent moon
Reverberates the living harmony upon my limbs,
The birds & beasts rejoice & play,
And every one seeks for his mate to prove his inmost joy.

ii 536. *the flocks of Tharmas*] The exact reference is not clear, though a
sense of pastoral peace is.
ii 542. This line sums up Enitharmon's creed.
ii 554. Compare the st. form with that of *Europe 161–91*. This is more
regular.

'Furious & terrible they sport, & rend the nether deeps;
570   The deep lifts up his rugged head
And lost in infinite humming wings vanishes with a cry;
The fading cry is ever dying,
The living voice is ever living in its inmost joy.

'Arise! you little glancing wings, & sing your infant joy!
575   Arise & drink your bliss!
For every thing that lives is holy, for the source of life
Descends to be a weeping babe;
For the earthworm renews the moisture of the sandy plain.

'Now my left hand I stretch to earth beneath
580   And strike the terrible string:
I wake sweet joy in dens of sorrow, & I plant a smile
In forests of affliction,
And wake the bubbling springs of life in regions of dark death.

'Oh, I am weary. Lay thine hand upon me or I faint;
585   I faint beneath these beams of thine,
For thou hast touched my five senses & they answered thee.
Now I am nothing, & I sink
And on the bed of silence sleep, till thou awakest me!'

Thus sang the lovely one in rapturous delusive trance.
590   Los heard; reviving he seized her in his arms, delusive hopes
Kindling. She led him into shadows, & thence fled outstretched
Upon the immense, like a bright rainbow, weeping, & smiling,
        and fading.

Thus lived Los, driving Enion far into the deathful infinite,
That he may also draw Ahania's spirit into her vortex.
595   Ah, happy blindness! Enion sees not the terrors of the uncertain;
Thus Enion wails from the dark deep (the golden heavens tremble):

[35]   'I am made to sow the thistle for wheat, the nettle for a nourishing
        dainty;
I have planted a false oath in the earth, it has brought forth a
        poison tree;
I have chosen the serpent for a counsellor, & the dog
600   For a schoolmaster to my children.
I have blotted out from light & living the dove & nightingale,
And I have caused the earthworm to beg from door to door.

ii 574. As in *Visions* 214–a strange equation of the innocent Oothoon and
Enitharmon.
ii 593. Enion] Before the addition of 512–92 to the MS, this was an im-
mediate continuation from 511. B. wishes to introduce Enion's new lament.
ii 599. Taken from *Visions* 119–120.

I have taught the thief a secret path into the house of the just,
I have taught pale artifice to spread his nets upon the morning.
605 My heavens are brass, my earth is iron, my moon a clod of clay,
My sun a pestilence burning at noon & a vapour of death in night.

'What is the price of experience? Do men buy it for a song,
Or wisdom for a dance in the street? No: it is bought with the
     price
Of all that a man hath, his house, his wife, his children.
610 Wisdom is sold in the desolate market where none come to buy,
And in the withered field where the farmer ploughs for bread in
     vain.

'It is an easy thing to triumph in the summer's sun
And in the vintage, & to sing on the waggon loaded with corn;
It is an easy thing to talk of patience to the afflicted,
615 To speak the laws of prudence to the houseless wanderer,
[36] To listen to the hungry ravens' cry in wintry season,
When the red blood is filled with wine, & with the marrow of
     lambs.

'It is an easy thing to laugh at wrathful elements,
To hear the dog howl at the wintry door, the ox in the slaughter-
     house moan;
620 To see a god on every wind, & a blessing on every blast—
To hear sounds of love in the thunderstorm that destroys our
     enemy's house,
To rejoice in the blight that covers his field, & the sickness that
     cuts off his children,
While our olive & vine sing & laugh round our door & our
     children bring fruits & flowers.

'Then the groan & the dolour are quite forgotten, & the slave
     grinding at the mill,
625 And the captive in chains, & the poor in the prison, & the soldier
     in the field
When the shattered bone hath laid him groaning among the
     happier dead.

ii 605. Cp. *Deuteronomy* xxviii 23, 'And thy heaven that is over thy head
shall be brass, and the earth that is under thee shall be iron'. The passage
describes the state of an accursed land.
ii 607. Cp. *Job*, xxviii 12-15, 'Where shall wisdom be found?... it can-
not be gotten for gold'.
ii 619. Taken from *Urizen* 447-8.
ii 621. enemy's] B. has *enemies*, unpuctuated; but the next line makes the
singular clear.

'It is an easy thing to rejoice in the tents of prosperity.
Thus could I sing, & thus rejoice; but it is not so with me!'

Ahania heard the lamentation, & a swift vibration
630   Spread through her golden frame. She rose up ere the dawn of day
When Urizen slept on his couch, drawn through unbounded space,
On to the margin of non-entity the bright female came.
There she beheld the spectrous form of Enion in the void,
And never from that moment could she rest upon her pillow.

End of the Second Night

Night the Third

Night the Third is concerned with Urizen and Ahania, taking up the last
lines of Night ii. Ahania tries to comfort Urizen (*1–10*), but he reveals the
source of his unhappiness—the foreknowledge that 'a boy' (*13*) (that is,
Orc) will come to overpower him. Ahania then (*39–99*) reveals her own
vision, which is another version of Enitharmon's vision in viia *234*ff; as
also in ii *14*ff–a passage which underwent much revision, apparently be-
ginning as a story of Vala similar to Ahania's. (The present version is
presumably the latest of the three.)

The consistent elements in each repetition of the story are that the
Eternal Man walks with Vala, that Urizen 'sleeps in the porch', and that
Luvah usurps a power that is not rightly his. In Night iii, Ahania tells
how, with Urizen asleep and unable to guard the Man and maintain the
balance with him, the Man begins to worship a shadow of himself. He is
seduced by Vala (Luvah's counterpart), mistakes Urizen's sleep for 'faded
splendour' and is thus entranced by the bright shadow (*42–60*); but this is
Luvah in disguise (*61–5*), and the Man realizes, too late, that he has wor-
shipped a part of himself that is unworthy, and that he has neglected the
rest (*73*). In reaction, he struggles against the part, Luvah, and throws him
out (*74–85*). The result is internal tumult and chaos as Luvah and Vala
go down to his heart 'where Paradise and its joys abounded', and turn it
into a place of 'fury and rage' (*90–1*). This may be seen as an allegory of
man rejecting a passion which has taken hold of him, and changing to an
extreme of self-control.

Urizen turns violently on Ahania, as Los had turned on Enitharmon in
ii *32*. He sees her vision as an attempt to enslave him to her will, and
throws her 'from his bosom obdurate' (*126*). The result is disastrous; his
whole carefully-built world falls into chaos. Tharmas emerges from this
chaos (*147–55*), but Enion, who is hated by Tharmas, withers away even
from what she was ('blind and age-bent', *172*) to a mere voice singing a
lament, as in the Nights i and ii.

ii *628*. Cp. *Job* ix 35, 'Then would I speak, and not fear him; but it is not
so with me'.
ii *634. she*] Ahania.

In the interchange between Urizen and Ahania, it should be realized
that the speeches are at least partly dramatic. That is, the two persons
speak in character, giving their own views, and not necessarily B.'s. It
seems that Ahania's warning to Urizen is meant genuinely to help him;
she feels that he should have been satisfied with his original position as
prince of light. Urizen's exclamation, 'Am I not God?', is both evil and
manifestly untrue; on the other hand, his suspicions of Ahania's intentions
are probably well founded, for the feminine deceitfulness which seeks to
gain power by seductive persuasion – associated here (116), as so often, with
moralistic chastity – is one of B.'s commonest dislikes. Neither Urizen nor
Ahania is entirely right or wrong; both are parts of fallen humanity, and
so partake of its errors, and also of its glimpses of fragmentary light.

[37]   NIGHT THE THIRD
Now sat the king of light on high upon his starry throne,
And bright Ahania bowed herself before his splendid feet:

'O Urizen, look on me; like a mournful stream
I embrace round thy knees & wet my bright hair with my tears:
5   Why sighs my lord? Are not the morning stars thy obedient sons?
Do they not bow their bright heads at thy voice? At thy command
Do they not fly into their stations, & return their light to thee?
The immortal atmospheres are thine; there thou art seen in glory
Surrounded by the ever-changing daughters of the light.
10 Why wilt thou look upon futurity, darkening present joy?'

She ceased. The prince his light obscured, & the splendours of his
        crown
[38] Enfolded in thick clouds, from whence his mighty voice burst forth:

'O bright *Ahania*, a boy is born of the dark ocean,
Whom Urizen doth serve, with light replenishing his darkness.
15 I am set here a king of trouble, commanded here to serve
And do my ministry to those who eat of my wide table.
All this is mine; yet I must serve, & that prophetic boy
Must grow up to command his prince. But hear my determined
        decree:
Vala shall become a worm in Enitharmon's womb,

iii *1*. See ii *416–18*.
iii *2*. Illustrated at the foot of the page.
iii *13*. *Ahania*] 'Shadow' is pencilled above, but both words are deleted.
The *boy* is Orc, another form of Luvah, Urizen's old enemy. In v *18–42*
he is born to Enitharmon and Los; in viib Orc wars against Urizen, but
this prophecy is not entirely fulfilled.
iii *19*. See ii *211–18*, where the Man gave his sceptre to Urizen.

20   Laying her seed upon the fibres, soon to issue forth,
      And Luvah in the loins of Los a dark & furious death.
      Alas for me! what will become of me at that dread time?'

      Ahania bowed her head & wept seven days before the king,
      And on the eighth day, when his clouds unfolded from his throne,
25   She raised her bright head, sweet perfumed, & thus with heavenly
         voice:

      'O prince, the eternal one hath set thee leader of his hosts;
[39] Leave all futurity to him, resume thy fields of light.
      Why didst thou listen to the voice of Luvah that dread morn
      To give the immortal steeds of light to his deceitful hands,
30   No longer now obedient to thy will? Thou art compelled
      To forge the curbs of iron & brass, to build the iron mangers,
      To feed them with intoxication from the winepresses of Luvah,
      Till the divine vision & fruition is quite obliterated.
      They call thy lions to the fields of blood, they rouse thy tigers
35   Out of the halls of justice, till these dens thy wisdom framed
      Golden & beautiful—but Oh, how unlike those sweet fields of bliss
      Where liberty was justice & eternal science was mercy!
      Then, O my dear lord, listen to Ahania, listen to the vision,
      The vision of Ahania in the slumbers of Urizen.
40   When Urizen slept in the porch and the Ancient Man was smitten,

      'The darkening Man walked on the steps of fire before his halls,

iii 27–9. In ii 17 Luvah steals the horses of light while Urizen is asleep; in
i 187–92 the idea is Urizen's, and Luvah denounces it as a trick. The present
version seems to be a third, in which Luvah has tricked Urizen. Cp. also
viia 234 and ix 92. Most of these stories are seen through the eyes of the
teller; but in any case B. had clearly no fixed idea in his mind.
    Line 27 replaces two deleted lines:

        Raise then thy radiant eyes to him raise thy obedient hands
        And comforts shall descend from heaven into thy darkning clouds.

iii 30. No longer now obedient] i.e. the horses.
iii 34. The eternal order, where lions and tigers have a valuable place, is
disturbed, and they become destructive beasts.
iii 40. According to Ahania, the downfall of the Man was largely due to
Urizen's sleep and neglect of duty. But, as in Enitharmon's song (ii 14ff),
Vala is the real source of trouble, 'deluding' Albion. As Los is hidden, the
insights of neither intellect nor imagination are available.
iii 41–98. These lines were copied on to Jerusalem pl.43.33–80, where they
are spoken by two messengers in another context. To prepare for this trans-
fer, B. made alterations in pencil on the pages of Four Zoas, changing
singular to plural where necessary, Man to Albion, and marking 68–72 for
omission, since they are Ahania's words to Urizen. These pencil alter-
ations, made for Jerusalem only, are here ignored. See also 98n.

And Vala walked with him in dreams of soft deluding slumber.
He looked up and saw thee, prince of light, thy splendour faded,
But saw not Los nor Enitharmon, for Luvah hid them in shadow,
[40] In a soft cloud outstretched across; and Luvah dwelt in the cloud.

46 'Then Man ascended mourning into the splendours of his palace;
Above him rose a shadow from his wearied intellect
Of living gold, pure, perfect, holy; in white linen pure he hovered,
A sweet entrancing self-delusion, a watery vision of Man,
50 Soft exulting in existence, all the Man absorbing.

'Man fell upon his face prostrate before the watery shadow,
Saying, "O Lord, whence is this change? Thou knowest I am
    nothing."
And Vala trembled and covered her face, and her locks were
    spread on the pavement.

'I heard, astonished at the vision, and my heart trembled within
    me;
55 I heard the voice of the slumberous Man, and thus he spoke,
Idolatrous to his own shadow, words of Eternity uttering:

'"Oh, I am nothing when I enter into judgment with thee.
If thou withdraw thy breath I die and vanish into Hades;
If thou dost lay thine hand upon me, behold I am silent;
60 If thou withhold thine hand I perish like a fallen leaf.
Oh, I am nothing, and to nothing must return again;
If thou withdraw thy breath, behold I am oblivion!"'

'He ceased: the shadowy voice was silent; but the cloud hovered
    over their heads
[41] In golden wreaths, the sorrow of Man, and the balmy drops fell
    down.
65 And lo! that son of Man, that shadowy spirit of the fallen one,
Luvah, descended from the cloud. In terror Man arose.

iii 47. *shadow*] Of the sleeping Urizen ('his sleeping intellect').

iii 48. *pure, perfect, holy*] In appearance, not truth.

iii 55. Man, having given up proper judgment, is not truly awake, and so 'slumberous'.

iii 57–8. Cp. *Psalm* cxliii 2, 7: 'And enter not into judgment with thy servant; for in thy sight shall no man living be justified . . . hide not thy face from me, lest I be like unto them that go down into the pit'.

iii 65. *that son of Man*] Luvah, in this myth, is a 'son' of the Man–not his master, as he seeks to be. But B. is aware of the biblical use of the phrase and opposes it to the *Lamb of God* (as in ii *310, 471*; viia *411*), who takes Luvah's place. B. argues (e.g. i *14*) that the gods of the heathen are actually man's own creations, which he has elevated to undeserved worship, instead of treating them as the vivid and valuable imaginative concepts they are.

Indignant rose the awful Man and turned his back on Vala—
'Why roll thy clouds in sickening mists? I can no longer hide
The dismal vision of mine eyes, O love and life and light!
70 Prophetic dreads urge me to speak; futurity is before me
Like a dark lamp. Eternal death haunts all my expectation,
Rent from eternal brotherhood we die, and are no more!
'I heard the voice of the fallen Man starting from his sleep:
'"Whence is this voice crying, *Enion!* that soundeth in my ears?
75 O cruel pity! O dark deceit! Can love seek for dominion?"'
'And Luvah strove to gain dominion over the fallen Man:
They strove together above the body where Vala was enclosed,
And the dark body of Man left prostrate upon the crystal pavement,
Covered with boils from head to foot, the terrible smitings of
      Luvah.
80 'Then frowned the fallen Man & put forth Luvah from his
        presence
(I heard him: frown not Urizen; but listen to my vision),
[42] 'Saying: "Go & die the death of Man for Vala, the sweet wanderer.
I will turn the volutions of your ears outward & bend your nostrils
Downward, & your fluxile eyes englobed roll round in fear;
85 Your withering lips & tongue shrink up into a narrow circle,
Till into narrow forms you creep. Go, take your fiery way
And learn what 'tis to absorb the Man, you spirits of pity & love!"
'O Urizen, why art thou pale at the visions of Ahania?
Listen to her who loves thee, lest we also are driven away.
90 'They heard the voice & fled, swift as the winter's setting sun,
And now the human blood foamed high; I saw that Luvah & Vala

iii 67. The Man realizes he has been betrayed.
iii 68–72. As Urizen smoulders, Ahania grows fearful.
iii 74–5. The Man, turning away from Vala, can hear Tharmas crying for Enion.
iii 77–8. Vala had assumed a *body* while walking with the Man; but it was not an essential part of her being; she was merely enclosed in it. Likewise, the Man leaves his body lying while he wrestles with Luvah spiritually.
iii 79. Cp. *Job* ii 7: '[Satan] smote Job with sore boils from the sole of his foot unto his crown.'
iii 83–7. These lines are derived from the description of Urizen's own fate in *Urizen 218–46*.
iii 84. *fluxile*] Implying that in Eternity the eyes were infinitely variable.
iii 91–2. The Eternal Man is vast, and Luvah and Vala are parts of his being. In this sense they are so minute, relative to him, that they travel down his veins as if down a river. Cp. viia *282–3*: 'the veins / Which now my rivers were become.'

Went down the human heart where paradise & its joys abounded,
In jealous fears, in fury & rage, & flames rolled round their fervid
    feet,
And the vast form of nature like a serpent played before them;
95 And as they went in folding fires & thunders of the deep,
Vala shrunk in like the dark sea that leaves its slimy banks,
And from her bosom Luvah fell far as the east & west,
And the vast form of nature like a serpent rolled between.'

She ended. From his wrathful throne burst forth the black
    hailstorm:

100 'Am I not God?' said Urizen, 'Who is equal to me?
Do I not stretch the heavens abroad, or fold them up like a
    garment?'

He spoke, mustering his heavy clouds around him black, opaque.
[43] Then thunders rolled around, & lightnings darted to & fro;
His visage changed to darkness, & his strong right hand came forth
105 To cast Ahania to the earth. He seized her by the hair
And threw her from the steps of ice that froze around his throne,

Saying: 'Art thou also become like Vala? Thus I cast thee out!
Shall the feminine indolent bliss, the indulgent self of weariness,
The passive idle sleep, the enormous night & darkness of death,
110 Set herself up to give her laws to the active masculine virtue?
Thou little diminutive portion that darest be a counterpart!
Thy passivity, thy laws of obedience & insincerity
Are my abhorrence. Wherefore hast thou taken that fair form?
Whence is this power given to thee? Once thou wast in my breast,
115 A sluggish current of dim waters, on whose verdant margin
A cavern shagged with horrid shades, dark, cool & deadly, where

iii *92–3*. Beside these lines in the margin of the MS is material for two lines
that might have been meant to go in, e.g. after 'foamed high', but were
never fitted in: 'Albion clos'd the Western Gate & / shut America out by
the Atlantic / for a Curse and hidden horror / and an altar of victims to
Sin / & Repentance.'
iii *94, 98*. Nature is material, transient and mortal; the serpent is one of
B.'s favourite images of evil.
iii *98*. Two lines written as one, in pencil, follow: 'Whether this is Jeru-
salem or Babylon we know not All is confusion, all is tumult, and we
alone are escaped.' These lines are a version of *Jerusalem* pl.43.*81–2*, and
were presumably intended to go there, as they do not fit this context.
See *41n.*
iii *116*. Cp. Milton, *Comus* 420, 428–30: ''Tis chastity, my brother,
chastity . . . / Yea, there where very desolation dwells, / By grots and
caverns shagged with horrid shades, / She may pass on with unblenched
majesty.' B. usually associated such exclusive chastity with hypocrisy.

I laid my head in the hot noon after the broken clods
Had wearied me. There I laid my plough, & there my horses fed.
And thou hast risen with thy moist locks into a watery image,
120   Reflecting all my indolence, my weakness & my death,
To weigh me down beneath the grave into non-entity
Where Luvah strives, scorned by Vala age after age wandering,
Shrinking & shrinking from her lord & calling him the tempter.
And art thou also become like Vala? Thus I cast thee out!'

125   So loud in thunders spoke the king, folded in dark despair,
And threw Ahania from his bosom obdurate. She fell like lightning.
Then fled the sons of Urizen from his thunderous throne petrific;
They fled to east & west & left the north & south of heaven.
A crash ran through the immense, the bounds of destiny were
        broken;
130   The bounds of destiny crashed direful, & the swelling sea
Burst from its bonds, in whirlpools fierce roaring with human voice,
Triumphing even to the stars at bright Ahania's fall.

Down from the dismal north the prince in thunders & thick clouds,
[44]   As when the thunderbolt down falleth on the appointed place,
135   Fell down, down, rushing, ruining, thundering, shuddering
Into the caverns of the grave & places of human seed,
Where the impressions of despair & hope enroot forever,
A world of darkness. Ahania fell far into non-entity.

She continued falling. Loud the crash continued, loud & hoarse.
140   From the crash roared a flame of blue sulphureous fire; from the
        flame
A dolorous groan that struck with dumbness — all confusion,
Swallowing up the horrible din in agony on agony.
Through the confusion like a crack across, from immense to
        immense,
Loud, strong, a universal groan of death, louder
145   Than all the wracking elements, deafened & rended worse
Than Urizen & all his hosts in cursed despair down rushing.

iii *117–21*. In this passage Urizen recalls another occasion when, he says,
Ahania tempted him. In his tiredness once, she, like a reflection in a pool,
showed him a depressing image of himself.
iii *127. the sons of Urizen*] In effect, Urizen's world — not only the world
he has made, but all that is associated with him.
iii *129. Destiny*] See i *66n* and *171* below.
iii *136*. So in viib *121*. It may continue the anatomical idea of vastness
of *91–2*. Cp. also the, dedicatory poem, 'The caverns of the grave I've
seen' (dated 1808, p. 614).

But from the dolorous groan one like a shadow of smoke appeared,
And human bones, rattling together in the smoke & stamping
The nether abyss, & gnashing in fierce despair, panting in sobs
150 Thick, short, incessant bursting, sobbing, deep despairing,
  stamping, struggling—
Struggling to utter the voice of Man, struggling to take the features
  of Man, struggling
To take the limbs of Man. At length emerging from the smoke
Of Urizen dashed in pieces from his precipitant fall,
Tharmas reared up his hands & stood on the affrighted ocean.
155 The dead reared up his voice, & stood on the resounding shore,

Crying: 'Fury in my limbs, destruction in my bones & marrow,
My skull riven into filaments, my eyes into sea jellies,
Floating upon the tide, wander bubbling & bubbling,
Uttering my lamentations & begetting little monsters,
160 Who sit mocking upon the little pebbles of the tide
In all my rivers, & on dried shells that the fish
[45] Have quite forsaken. O fool! fool! to lose my sweetest bliss!
Where art thou, Enion? Ah, too near, too cunning, too far off
And yet too near! Dashed down I send thee into distant darkness
165 Far as my strength can hurl thee. Wander there, & laugh & play
Among the frozen arrows. They will tear thy tender flesh.
Fall off, afar from Tharmas; come not too near my strong fury,
Scream & fall off & laugh at Tharmas, lovely summer beauty—
Till winter rends thee into shivers as thou hast rended me.'

170 So Tharmas bellowed o'er the ocean, thundering, sobbing, bursting.
The bounds of destiny were broken, & hatred now began
Instead of love to Enion. Enion, blind & age-bent,
Plunged into the cold billows living a life in midst of waters.
In terrors she withered away to Entuthon Benithon,
175 A world of deep darkness where all things in horrors are rooted.
These are the words of Enion heard from the cold waves of despair:

'O Tharmas! I had lost thee, & when I hoped I had found thee—

iii *147*. B. brings Tharmas back into the story, having shut him away in
i *68*, when he was as good as 'dead' (*155*).
iii *157–62*. These images are natural enough to suggest direct observation,
probably after B.'s removal to Felpham in Sept. 1800. But see iv *265n*.
iii *164*. On the reverse of this page (there is no room on the same side)
Tharmas is drawn driving Enion away.
iii *174*. *Entuthon Benithon*] As the description suggests, a gloomy place of
dark forests in Ulro: see viii *29n*. This is almost B.'s first use of a mythical
place-name since the very early poems *Thel* and *Tiriel*; in the later epics
such names grow increasingly important.

O Tharmas, do not thou destroy me quite, but let
A little shadow, but a little showery form of Enion
180 Be near thee, loved terror. Let me still remain, & then do thou
Thy righteous doom upon me; only let me hear thy voice!
Driven by thy rage I wander like a cloud into the deep,
Where never yet existence came, there losing all my life.
I back return, weaker & weaker; consume me not away
185 In thy great wrath. Though I have sinned, though I have rebelled,
Make me not like the things forgotten as they had not been;
Make not the thing that loveth thee a tear wiped away.'

Tharmas replied, riding on storms (his voice of thunder rolled):

'Image of grief, thy fading lineaments make my eyelids fail.
190 What have I done? Both rage & mercy are alike to me.
Looking upon thee, image of faint waters, I recoil
From my fierce rage into thy semblance. Enion, return!
Why does thy piteous face evanish like a rainy cloud
[46[Melting, a shower of falling tears, nothing but tears? Enion!
195 Substanceless, voiceless, weeping, vanished, nothing but tears!
    Enion,
Art thou for ever vanished from the watery eyes of Tharmas?
Rage, rage shall never from my bosom, winds & waters of woe
Consuming, all to the end consuming: love and hope are ended!'

For now no more remained of Enion in the dismal air,
200 Only a voice eternal wailing in the elements,

Where Enion blind & age-bent wandered, Ahania wanders now.
She wanders in eternal fear of falling into the indefinite,
For her bright eyes behold the abyss. Sometimes a little sleep
Weighs down her eyelids, then she falls, then starting wakes in
    fears,
205 Sleepless to wander round repelled on the margin of non-entity.

The End of the Third Night

Night the Fourth

In Night iii Urizen's creation, laboriously built in Night ii, was hurled into
ruins; in Night iv Tharmas takes a hand in order to try to limit the disaster.
Tharmas, revived in iii *145–54*, is now living in the abyss (where all the
Zoas have fallen, except Luvah), mourning the loss of his emanation
Enion. In a quarrelsome meeting with Los (iv *34*ff) Tharmas carries away
Enitharmon, and this shatters Los's personality. Although B. has hitherto
treated Los and Enitharmon as two separate persons, this division is a

iii *197*. i.e. 'rage shall never leave my bosom. . . .' There is no punctuation
in the MS.

division of Los himself, and it results in the appearance of Los's spectre (see *63n*). (This discrepancy between this and Night i is explained by the fact that Night i, as we now have it, was written later, when B. was intent on introducing new ideas—even though at the expense of narrative consistency. Note also that in *Urizen* Los divides when he is deluded by pity; and here Tharmas is the pitying spirit, who causes the division of Los and Enitharmon, both as the Spectre describes it (*93–100*) and by carrying her away (*56*).)

But Tharmas in turn claims to be God (*129–32*), an evil aspiration which seizes the four Zoas in turn. He returns Enitharmon to Los at the price of obedience: for they are to stay in his dominion, the sea (*71*), and Los is to work with his spectre according to Tharmas's directions. Tharmas, whose nature is compassionate, is overcome by the loss of Enion; to save her from complete dissolution he orders Los to 'rebuild these furnaces' (*149*)—to save something from the ruins of Urizen's world. At this point, B. recalls and quotes *Urizen*, where Los's labours turn the ruined Urizen into a definite form, the physical form of man, to save him from formless chaos.

NIGHT THE FOURTH

But Tharmas rode on the dark abyss, the voice of Tharmas rolled
Over the heaving deluge. He saw Los & Enitharmon emerge
In strength & brightness from the abyss; his bowels yearned over
    them.
They rose in strength above the heaving deluge, in mighty scorn,
5 Red as the sun in the hot morning of the bloody day.
Tharmas beheld them, his bowels yearned over them,

And he said: 'Wherefore do I feel such love & pity?
Ah, Enion! Ah, Enion! Ah, lovely, lovely Enion!
How is this? All my hope is gone for ever, fled
10 Like a famished eagle, eyeless, raging in the vast expanse.
Incessant tears are now my food, incessant rage & tears.
Deathless for ever now, I wander seeking oblivion
In torrents of despair in vain; for if I plunge beneath
Stifling I live; if dashed in pieces from a rocky height
15 I reunite in endless torment. Would I had never risen
From death's cold sleep beneath the bottom of the raging ocean!
And cannot those who once have loved ever forget their love?
Are love & rage the same passion? They are the same in me!
Are those who love, like those who died, risen again from death
20 Immortal, in immortal torment, never to be delivered?

iv *2–6*. Similarly, in ii *497–504*, Los and Enitharmon come to look at Urizen's world, and Urizen is envious of their brightness.
iv *12. Deathless*] See *15–16* and *83*; Tharmas fell in i *68* into the ocean, but has now reappeared.

Is it not possible that one risen again from death
Can die? When dark despair comes over, can I not
Flow down into the sea, & slumber in oblivion? Ah, Enion!
[48]   Deformed I see these lineaments of ungratified desire—
25   The all-powerful curse of an honest man be upon Urizen & Luvah!
But thou, my son, glorious in brightness, comforter of Tharmas,
Go forth: rebuild this universe beneath my indignant power,
A universe of death & decay. Let Enitharmon's hands
Weave soft delusive forms of man above my watery world,
30   Renew these ruined souls of men through earth, sea, air & fire,
To waste in endless corruption. Renew thou, I will destroy.
Perhaps Enion may resume some little semblance
To ease my pangs of heart & to restore some peace to Tharmas.'

Los answered in his furious pride, sparks issuing from his hair:
35   'Hitherto shalt thou come, no further. Here thy proud waves cease.
We have drunk up the Eternal Man by our unbounded power;
Beware lest we also drink up thee, rough demon of the waters!
Our god is Urizen the king, king of the heavenly hosts.
We have no other god but he, thou father of worms & clay,
40   And he is fallen into the deep, rough demon of the waters,
And Los remains god over all, weak father of worms & clay.
I know I was Urthona, keeper of the gates of heaven,
But now I am all-powerful Los, & Urthona is but my shadow.'

Doubting stood Tharmas in the solemn darkness; his dim eyes
45   Swam in red tears. He reared his waves above the head of Los
In wrath, but pitying back withdrew with many a sigh.
Now he resolved to destroy Los, & now his tears flowed down.

iv 25. Tharmas regards himself as the 'honest man', destroyed by the
quarrels of others.
iv 26. *my son*] Los. He and Enitharmon are born of Enion in i *121–2*.
iv 30–1. To give finite material form to 'these ruined souls' is to continue
their existence, though the world of the four elements is corrupt. It is not
clear if Tharmas's intention is good–the salvation of some humanity from
Urizen's ruins–or evil–revenge.
iv 31–2. Los is to be the builder, Tharmas the destroyer, in the never-
ending cycle of life and death. Enion (iii *200*) has faded away and may
vanish unless given a definite form.
iv 41. *weak father*] Scornfully addressed to Tharmas.
iv 43. In fact the opposite is true.
iv 44. *solemn*] The first of a series of alterations where B. realizing that he
is overworking the word 'dismal', replaces it with another word. The
others are: *griding (60)*, *dreary (121*, and v *5)*, *griding (v 93)*, *accursed (102)*,
deadly (178), *dreary (180)*: in vi, *dreary (79)*, *gloomy (166)*: in viii *566, flaming*.

In scorn stood Los; red sparks of blighting from his furious head
Flew over the waves of Tharmas. Pitying, Tharmas stayed his
   waves;

50 For Enitharmon shrieked amain, crying: 'O my sweet world,
Built by the architect divine whose love to Los & Enitharmon
Thou, rash abhorred demon, in thy fury hast o'erthrown!'

[49] 'What sovereign architect', said Tharmas, 'dare my will control?
For if I will I urge these waters, if I will they sleep
55 In peace beneath my awful frown: my will shall be my law!'

So saying in a wave he raped bright Enitharmon far
Apart from Los, but covered her with softest brooding care,
On a broad wave in the warm west, balming her bleeding wound.

Oh, how Los howled at the rending asunder! All the fibres rent,
60 Where Enitharmon joined to his left side, in griding pain.
He falling on the rocks bellowed his dolour, till the blood
Stanched, then in ululation wailed his woes upon the wind.

And Tharmas called to the dark spectre who upon the shores

iv *51–2. The architect divine*] Urizen.
demon] Tharmas.
iv *56.* On the back of this page, Enitharmon is drawn, carried on a wave.
iv *59.* Los, like the other three, Tharmas, Luvah and Urizen, is now
separated from his emanation.
iv *60. his left side*] Possibly his 'inferior' side.   *griding* was taken from
Milton; it means 'fiercely painful'.
iv *63. the dark spectre*] The spectre of Urthona (*dark* Urthona, *America*
Prel. 1), and so of Los, who is the fallen Urthona.
The SPECTRE appears in B. for the first time here as an active figure,
since the passage about the spectre of Tharmas in i *70–115* was written
later than this. This passage reads as if the spectre was invented by B. for
this particular occasion; then, as often happened, he saw more and more
possibilities in the idea as he used and developed it. A *spectre* is, of course,
first of all a *ghost*. In *Four Zoas* the spectre (here and later, of Urthona:
in i, the spectre of Tharmas) is a creature arising out of the disintegration
of a personality. Urthona's spectre henceforth exists as a being separate
from Los, though normally subordinate to him, and is as often as not a
good influence. This separateness is the chief evil; the parted spectre sums
up the need for union between the person and his spectre himself in viia
335–52. The spectre is part of the personality which should obey, and be
mastered: a useful servant but an evil master. Here, in iv, he has memories–
admittedly rather garbled–of a happy life in Eden which he, unlike most
of B.'s evil figures, does not reject as illusory. In viia his power is both evil
and good. He seduces Enitharmon's *shadow* (viia *215*ff), and from their
union the Shadowy Female, Vala, is let loose on the world, thus leading

With dislocated limbs had fallen. The spectre rose in pain,
65   A shadow blue, obscure, & dismal. Like a statue of lead
Bent by its fall from a high tower, the dolorous shadow rose.

'Go forth', said Tharmas, 'works of joy are thine. Obey & live.
So shall the spongy marrow issuing from thy splintered bones
Bonify, & thou shalt have rest when this thy labour is done.
70   Go forth, bear Enitharmon back to the eternal prophet.
Build her a bower in the midst of all my dashing waves;
Make first a resting place for Los & Enitharmon, then
Thou shalt have rest. If thou refusest, dashed abroad on all
My waves, thy limbs shall separate in stench & rotting, & thou
75   Become a prey to all my demons of despair & hope.'

The spectre of Urthona, seeing Enitharmon, writhed
His cloudy form in jealous fear & muttering thunders hoarse,
And casting round thick glooms, thus uttered his fierce pangs of
      heart:

'Tharmas, I know thee. How are we altered, our beauty decayed!
80   But still I know thee, though in this horrible ruin whelmed.
Thou, once the mildest son of Heaven, art now become a rage,
A terror to all living things. Think not that I am ignorant
That thou art risen from the dead, or that, my power forgot,
[50]   I slumber here in weak repose. I well remember the day,
85   The day of terror & abhorrence,

to ultimate disaster in viii. Yet (viia *332*) he is also the mediator of recon-
ciliation between Enitharmon *herself* (not her shadow) and Los; and after
this reconciliation he disappears, and the united pair become Eden's chief
instruments in the remedying of the Man's sickness.
   For the imagery of the spectre, see *Jerusalem* pl.6.*1n*.
iv *71*. Los and Enitharmon are to be reunited at the price of living in
Tharmas's dominion.
iv *76ff*. Characteristically, the spectre, who is a mere shadow of Urthona,
claims to be the true Urthona. Yet he remembers the days before the fall,
although his narrative may be garbled, especially in *105–10*, where the
flight of Urthona and Enitharmon to Tharmas does not accord with the
story in Night i. But this may be due only to B.'s writing the two accounts
at different times.
iv *84–9*. This is the first mention of Beulah; see headnote viia, and note on
Milton pl.30.*1*. The *sons of Beulah* are unusual but in the passage in viia
Beulah is the dwelling of the fallen Man, and his family of 'many sons/And
many daughters' (viia, *249–50*). In Bunyan's Beulah, the land on the border
of heaven, one would expect to find 'sons and daughters', but B.'s de-
veloping notion of Beulah later stressed the daughters, and the sons dis-
appear.
iv *85*. This line is left metrically incomplete.

When fleeing from the battle, thou, fleeting like the raven
Of dawn outstretching an expanse where ne'er expanse had been,
Drew'st all the sons of Beulah into thy dread vortex, following
Thy eddying spirit down the hills of Beulah. All my sons
90 Stood round me at the anvil, where new-heated the wedge
Of iron glowed furious, prepared for spades & mattocks.
Hearing the symphonies of war loud sounding, all my sons
Fled from my side; then pangs smote me, unknown before. I saw
My loins begin to break forth into veiny pipes, & writhe
95 Before me in the wind, englobing, trembling with strong vibrations.
The bloody mass began to animate. I bending over
Wept bitter tears incessant. Still beholding how the piteous form,
Dividing & dividing from my loins, a weak & piteous
Soft cloud of snow, a female pale & weak, I soft embraced
100 My counterpart & called it love. I named her Enitharmon,
But found myself & her together issuing down the tide
Which now our rivers were become, delving through caverns huge
Of gory blood, struggling to be delivered from our bonds.
She strove in vain; not so Urthona strove, for breaking forth
105 A shadow, blue, obscure, & dismal from the breathing nostrils
Of Enion I issued into the air, divided from Enitharmon.
I howled in sorrow. I beheld thee rotting upon the rocks;
I, pitying, hovered over thee; I protected thy ghastly corse
From vultures of the deep. Then wherefore shouldst thou rage
110 Against me, who thee guarded in the night of death from harm?'

Tharmas replied: 'Art thou Urthona, my friend, my old companion,
With whom I lived in happiness before that deadly night
When Urizen gave the horses of light into the hands of Luvah?
Thou knowest not what Tharmas knows. Oh, I could tell thee tales
115 That would enrage thee as it has enraged me, even
From death, in wrath & fury. But now come, bear back
Thy loved Enitharmon, for thou hast her here before thine eyes.
[51] But my sweet Enion is vanished, & I never more
Shall see her, unless thou, O shadow, wilt protect this son
120 Of Enion, & him assist to bind the fallen king,
Lest he should rise again from death in all his dreary power.

The day] Described in i *209–29*.
iv *114*. Tharmas recognizes the spectre as Urthona's, and sees that he can-
not now see or remember the truth. Tharmas's memory carries back to the
time before the Fall; but he too is fallen, and the reader cannot trust his
version entirely, as his own desire for power is shown in *129*.
iv *119*. *This son / Of Enion*] Los himself; *the fallen king* is Urizen. Here as
elsewhere (e.g. *Jerusalem* pls 8.*21*–10.*6*) B. has a task given to the spectre,
whose evil nature can be used to good effect, if controlled.

Bind him, take Enitharmon for thy sweet reward, while I
In vain am driven on false hope—hope, sister of despair.'

Groaning the terror rose & drave his solid rocks before
125 Upon the tide, till underneath the feet of Los a world
Dark, dreadful, rose; & Enitharmon lay at Los's feet.
The dolorous shadow joyed; weak hope appeared around his head.

Tharmas before Los stood, & thus the voice of Tharmas rolled:

'Now all comes into the power of Tharmas. Urizen is fallen
130 And Luvah hidden in the elemental forms of life & death.
Urthona is my son. O Los, thou art Urthona, & Tharmas
Is God. The Eternal Man is sealed, never to be delivered:
I roll my floods over his body, my billows & waves pass over him,
The sea encompasses him, & monsters of the deep are his
   companions.
135 Dreamer of furious oceans, cold sleeper of weeds & shells,
Thy eternal form shall never renew; my uncertain prevails against
   thee,
Yet, though I rage, God over all. A portion of my life
That in eternal fields in comfort wandered with my flocks
At noon, & laid her head upon my wearied bosom at night,
140 She is divided; she is vanished, even like Luvah & Vala.
O why did foul ambition seize thee, Urizen, prince of light?
And thee, O Luvah, prince of love, till Tharmas was divided?
And I—what can I now behold but an eternal death
Before my eyes, & an eternal weary work to strive
145 Against the monstrous forms that breed among my silent waves?
Is this to be a god? Far rather would I be a man—
To know sweet science, & to do with simple companions,
Sitting beneath a tent & viewing sheepfolds & soft pastures.
Take thou the hammer of Urthona, rebuild these furnaces.

iv *131*. Urthona is Tharmas's equal in eternity; it is only since the Fall
(Night i) that Tharmas is parent of Los.

iv *132*. In *Revelations* xx 1–3 Satan is sealed in the pit, but allowed to
escape after a thousand years.

iv *134–5*. The sea is Tharmas's dominion; he claims that the man is in his
power.

iv *136*. *My uncertain*] Contrasted with *eternal form*; the one shapeless,
indefinite, deathly, and the other (if restored) living, real and sure.

iv *137–40*. Refers to Enion.

iv *141–2*. Tharmas blames everyone but himself.

iv *147*. *science*] Skill or understanding rather than mere abstract learning.
Note the very last line of the poem, ix *852*–'sweet science reigns'.

iv *149*. Urizen's furnaces (ii *282*, *327*, etc.), in his fall destroyed (iii *140–6*).

150 Dost thou refuse? Mind I the sparks that issue from thy hair?
[52] I will compel thee to rebuild by these my furious waves.
  Death choose, or life. Thou strugglest in my waters, now choose life
  And all the elements shall serve thee to their soothing flutes.
  Their sweet inspiriting lyres thy labours shall administer,
155 And they to thee only. Remit not, faint not, thou my son.
  Now thou dost know what 'tis to strive against the god of waters.'

  So saying Tharmas on his furious chariots of the deep
  Departed far into the unknown & left a wondrous void
  Round Los. Afar his waters bore on all sides round, with noise
160 Of wheels & horses, hoofs & trumpets, horns & clarions.

  Terrified Los beheld the ruins of Urizen beneath,
  A horrible chaos to his eyes, a formless unmeasurable death,
  Whirling up broken rocks on high into the dismal air,
  And fluctuating all beneath in eddies of molten fluid.

165 Then Los with terrible hands seized on the ruined furnaces
  Of Urizen. Enormous work—he builded them anew,
  Labour of ages in the darkness & the war of Tharmas;
  And Los formed anvils of iron petrific; for his blows
  Petrify with incessant beating many a rock, many a planet.

170 But Urizen slept in a stonied stupor in the nether abyss,
  A dreamful horrible state. In tossings on his icy bed
  Freezing to solid all beneath, his grey oblivious form
  Stretched over the immense heaves in strong shudders, silent his
    voice,
  In brooding contemplation stretching out from north to south
175 In mighty power. Round him Los rolled furious
  His thunderous wheels, from furnace to furnace, tending diligent
  The contemplative terror, frightened in his scornful sphere,
  Frightened with cold infectious madness—in his hand the thundering
  Hammer of Urthona, forming under his heavy hand the hours,
[53] The days & years, in chains of iron round the limbs of Urizen,
181 Linked hour to hour & day to night, & night to day & year to year
  In periods of pulsative furor. Mills he formed & works
  Of many wheels resistless in the power of dark Urthona.

  But Enitharmon wrapped in clouds wailed loud; for as Los beat

iv *150. sparks*] See *48*.
iv *161*. B. continues to rework the material of earlier poems as far as viia *107*
(approx.). Note his alteration of the division of Los (*56–62* above) from
Urizen 286ff. As in *Urizen*, Los increasingly becomes the prophet-black-
smith, rather than the playboy of *Europe* and the early Nights of *Four Zoas*.
Lines *201–45*, *279–86* are almost the same as *Urizen 170–274*. In *Four Zoas*
the division of Enitharmon from Los precedes the binding of Urizen.

185 The anvils of Urthona, link by link the chains of sorrow
     Warping upon the winds & whirling round in the dark deep
     Lashed on the limbs of Enitharmon, & the sulphur fires,
     Belched from the furnaces, wreathed round her. Chained in
         ceaseless fire,
     The lovely female howled, & Urizen beneath deep groaned
190 Deadly, between the hammers, beating grateful to the ears
     Of Los. Absorbed in dire revenge, he drank with joy the cries
     Of Enitharmon & the groans of Urizen, fuel for his wrath
     And for his pity, secret feeding on thoughts of cruelty.

     The spectre wept at his dire labours, when from ladles huge
195 He poured the molten iron round the limbs of Enitharmon,
     But when he poured it round the bones of Urizen, he laughed
     Hollow upon the hollow wind, his shadowy form obeying
     The voice of Los. Compelled he laboured round the furnaces.

     And thus began the binding of Urizen, day & night in fear.
200 Circling round the dark demon with howlings, dismay & sharp
         blightings
     The prophet of Eternity beat on his iron links, & links of brass;
     And as he beat round the hurtling demon, terrified at the shapes
     Enslaved humanity put on, he became what he beheld,
     Raging against Tharmas his god, & uttering
205 Ambiguous words blasphemous, filled with envy, firm resolved
     On hate eternal. In his vast disdain he laboured, beating
     The links of fate, link after link, an endless chain of sorrows.

[54] The eternal mind bounded began to roll eddies of wrath ceaseless,
     Round & round, & the sulphureous foam surging thick
210 Settled, a lake bright & shining clear, white as the snow:

     Forgetfulness, dumbness, necessity, in chains of the mind locked up,
     In fetters of ice shrinking, disorganized, rent from Eternity.
     Los beat on his fetters & heated his furnaces
     And poured iron solder, and solder of brass.

215 Restless the immortal, enchained, heaving dolorous,
     Anguished unbearable, till a roof, shaggy wild, enclosed
     In an orb his fountain of thought.

     In a horrible dreamful slumber, like the linked chain,
     A vast spine writhed in torment upon the wind,
220 Shooting pained ribs like a bending cavern,
     And bones of solidness froze over all his nerves of joy.
     A first age passed, a state of dismal woe.

iv *186*. *Warping*] Throwing or twisting about—an unusual sense.
iv *191*. *revenge*] For her spitefulness.

From the caverns of his jointed spine down sunk with fright
A red round globe, hot burning, deep, deep down into the abyss,
225 Panting, conglobing, trembling, shooting out ten thousand branches
Around his solid bones: & a second age passed over.

In harrowing fear rolling, his nervous brain shot branches
On high into two little orbs, hiding in two little caves;
Hiding carefully from the wind his eyes beheld the deep.
230 And a third age passed, a state of dismal woe.

The pangs of hope began in heavy pain, striving, struggling.
Two ears in close volutions from beneath his orbs of vision
Shot spiring out & petrified as they grew: and a fourth
Age passed over & a state of dismal woe.

235 In ghastly torment sick hanging upon the wind,
Two nostrils bent down to the deeps.
[55a] And a fifth age passed & a state of dismal woe.

In ghastly torment sick, within his ribs bloated round
And a craving hungry cavern. Thence arose his channelled
240 Throat; then like a red flame a tongue of hunger
And thirst appeared: and a sixth age passed of dismal woe.

Enraged & stifled with torment he threw his right arm to the north,
His left arm to the south, shooting out in anguish deep,
And his feet stamped the nether abyss, in trembling, howling and
    dismay
245 And a seventh age passed over & a state of dismal woe.

The Council of God on high, watching over the body
Of Man, clothed in Luvah's robes of blood, saw & wept,
Descending over Beulah's mild moon-covered regions.
The daughters of Beulah saw the Divine Vision; they were
    comforted

iv 225. The illustration seems to show the globe forming; but its content
is not altogether clear.
iv 227. After this line B. wrote, then deleted, the line which follows it in
Urizen (220): 'Round the branches of his heart.' As B. was combining
short lines into longer ones, the probable reason for the deletion was a
problem in versification.
iv 246–78. These lines are added at the end of the text, but are marked to
go between 245 and 279. This addition is intended to remind the reader
that even though the Eternal Man seems to be dead, having handed his
power to Urizen in ii 211 and fallen into the sleep of death on his rock, he
is cared for by those in Beulah, and may be resurrected–as he is in the
Ninth Book. B. draws on the story of the resurrection of Lazarus in John 11.
He illustrates it at the foot of the text.

250 And as a double female form, loveliness & perfection of beauty,
    They bowed the head & worshipped, & with mild voice spoke
        these words:

[56] 'Lord, Saviour, if thou hadst been here our brother had not died;
    And now we know that whatsoever thou wilt ask of God
    He will give it thee; for we are weak women & dare not lift
255 Our eyes to the divine pavilions. Therefore in mercy thou
    Appearest clothed in Luvah's garments that we may behold thee
    And live. Behold! Eternal death is in Beulah! Behold,
    We perish & shall not be found unless thou grant a place
    In which we may be hidden under the shadow of wings!
260 For if we who are but for a time & who pass away in winter
    Behold these wonders of Eternity, we shall consume.'

    Such were the words of Beulah, of the feminine emanation.
    The empyrean groaned throughout. All Eden was darkened.
    The corse of Albion lay on the Rock, the sea of time & space
265 Beat round the Rock in mighty waves, & as a polypus

iv 250. *double female form*] i.e. in the form of Martha and Mary, the two sisters of Lazarus, whose words B. adapts in 252ff.

iv 252. Taken from Martha's saying on the death of Lazarus in *John* xi 21–2: 'Lord, if thou hadst been here, my brother had not died. But I know, that even now, whatsoever thou wilt ask of God, God will give it thee.'

our brother] The Eternal Man.

iv 257. See *84–9*.

iv 258. The phraseology is biblical, but this is not a direct allusion.

iv 259. *Psalm* xvii 8: 'Hide me under the shadow of thy wings.'

iv 261. The sense is imperfect because the following lines are erased and written over: but *consume* may have a passive meaning 'be consumed'.

iv 265 POLYPUS] There are thousands of species of these simple sea animals now classified among the *Cnidaria*. They were called *polypus* (the term is not now in scientific use) on account of the many stinging tentacles which fringe the often inverted mouth. There are different types; the sea anemones (depicted by B. in his colour-plate *Newton*, and in *Jerusalem* pl.28) and many corals; the jellyfish (*Book of Los 166*; see also *Four Zoas* iii *157–9*); and, most important in B., the *hydroids*. B.'s knowledge of all these creatures is more than that of the casual seaside observer, since he is aware that, in spite of their very different appearances, all are types of polypus. Yet he gives his polypus a heart once(*Jerusalem* pl.67.37) though there he may be thinking of the many-legged octopus or cuttle-fish.

    The hydroid polyp consists commonly of a body and a stalk. It uses the stalk to attach itself to a convenient base; the body (now technically known as a *zooid*) is a stomach with a mouth ringed by tentacles to trap the animal's prey, which is poisoned by stinging cells on the tentacles and body and drawn into the mouth. Many species are 'colonial'; that is, one such

That vegetates beneath the sea the limbs of Man vegetated
In monstrous forms of death, a human polypus of death.

The Saviour mild & gentle bent over the corse of death,
Saying: 'If ye will believe, your brother shall rise again.'
270 And first he found the limit of opacity, & named it *Satan*
In Albion's bosom (for in every human bosom these limits stand).

polyp may extend itself by putting out a *stolon*, which resembles a root (or
the runner of a strawberry), from which other complete individual polyps
arise. A polyp may also 'bud' out on the stalk, so that a 'colony' of polyps
branches out from the stolon and stalks–individuals, yet held together
(see *Milton* pl. 29.30, *Jerusalem* pl. 29.19–23). As an alternative to this form
of reproduction, the zooid which 'buds' off may be, not another polyp,
but a special form which produces free forms, *medusae*, which break free
and swim off. Medusae are sexual and reproduce by the fertilization of
eggs, which grow into new hydroids. Their significance in B. is that the
various jellyfish are the medusa stage of creatures of a different class of
Cnidaria (though not hydroids), and he can therefore include them among
the various types of *polypus*.

B. was affected by the apparently parasitic rooting of the *polypus*; its
tentacles and poison, and most of all by the indefinite and endless ramifica-
tions of the colonial forms. He had surely seen them, perhaps in an aqua-
rium, waving their tentacles in sinister silence. The image affected him
profoundly; for its associations with the branching systems of nerves and
veins, with the clutching images of web and tree, and with the kind of
cancer called *polypus*, see *Milton* pls 24.37, 34.24; *Jerusalem* pls 15.4, 66.48,
69.3 and notes.

iv 269. 'Your brother shall rise again' is also quoted from the Lazarus
story, *John* xi 23, though B. here as in 253–5 puts the plural in the place of
the biblical 'thou'.

iv 270–2. LIMITS] As in *Milton* pl.13.20 and *Jerusalem* pl.42.29ff. B. uses the
Cartesian scheme of the universe for his own ends. According to Descartes
there were three fundamental elements; the light-giving (e.g. the sun), the
translucent (the ether) and the opaque (e.g. the earth). B. takes light to be
the imaginative power. Hence the *opaque* is of Ulro, Satanic. The *limit of
translucence* is the border between the lesser element which can let light
pass, and the dark, dead element which repels light. It is thus the very
farthest point a human being can go to, and still live. That this limit is
fixed, so that a person cannot become 'opaque' and die, is the mercy of
God. But when he has gone so far, he is near spiritual death–and that is
Satan's state.

Similarly, if a person were to limit his faculties infinitely, he would
vanish and cease to be. There is, in the same mercy, a *limit of contraction*
fixed, and he cannot shrink his faculties below that limit. In our narrow
material world, we are at that limit–called Adam, for we are 'children of
Adam'.

And next he found the limit of contraction, & named it *Adam*,
While yet those beings were not born, nor knew of good or evil.

Then wondrously the starry wheels felt the Divine Hand. Limit
275 Was put to eternal death. Los felt the limit & saw
The finger of God touch the seventh furnace, in terror;
And Los beheld the hand of God over his furnaces
Beneath the deeps in dismal darkness beneath immensity.

[55b] In terrors Los shrunk from his task; his great hammer
280 Fell from his hand, his fires hid their strong limbs in smoke,
For with noises ruinous, hurtlings & clashings & groans
The immortal endured, though bound in a deadly sleep.
Pale terror seized the eyes of Los as he beat round
The hurtling demon, terrified at the shapes
285 Enslaved humanity put on, he became what he beheld.
He became what he was doing, he was himself transformed.

Spasms seized his muscular fibres writhing to & fro, his pallid lips
Unwilling moved as Urizen howled, his loins waved like the sea
At Enitharmon's shriek, his knees each other smote, & then he
     looked
290 With stony eyes on Urizen, & then swift writhed his neck
Involuntary to the couch where Enitharmon lay.
The bones of Urizen hurtle on the wind, the bones of Los
Twinge, & his iron sinews bend like lead & fold
Into unusual forms, dancing & howling, stamping the abyss.

[56b]   *End of the Fourth Night*

Night the Fifth

This Night falls into two parts. Lines *1–184* continue the story of Los and
Enitharmon, with the birth of Orc and his subsequent binding in the Chain
of Jealousy. From about *143* Los and Enitharmon become more like
husband and wife and less like the squabbling children they were in the
earlier Nights. Los is repentantly concerned for Enitharmon's unhappiness
and tries, ineffectively, to free Orc for her sake. There may be some auto-

iv *274. the starry wheels*] The stars in their circling courses.
iv *274–8*. This is the regenerate Los of viia *332*ff.
iv *286*. Here B. wrote 'Bring in here the Globe of Blood as in the B
of Urizen'. The globe of blood in *Urizen* became Enitharmon, who
already exists here. B. did not think of any new purpose for it, and so
could not 'bring it in' after all.
     At the bottom of this page is this erased pencil: 'Christs Crucifix shall
be made an excuse for Executing Criminals'–an ironic comment on the
resurrection theme of the page.

biographical source for this. B. certainly saw himself as a prophet, and
Catherine's name seems to appear in *Enitharmon*; lines *177–82* may refer to
a vision of Catherine's; but conjecture must be cautious in the absence of
any facts to which we can pin events in the poem. In any case, the poems
have a wider meaning than the events which may have given them birth.

In *41–2* the identification of Luvah and Orc is a new development, which
enables B. to work the stories of Orc, the rebel of the two *Prophecies*, into
Four Zoas, the Fuzon myth of *Urizen* and *Ahania* having proved unsatis-
factory. Orc is Luvah in his fallen state, as Los is the fallen Urthona. Orc
is born to Los and Enitharmon, and Vala, Luvah's emanation, is also born
to them in viia. For the associations of Orc/Luvah to Christ, see *41n.*

The last part of Night v (*183–241*) returns us to Urizen, who laments
his fall. Thus this Night, like ii and iii, ends in a lament.

[57]   NIGHT THE FIFTH

Infected, mad, he danced on his mountains high & dark as heaven.
Now fixed into one steadfast bulk his features stonify;
From his mouth curses, & from his eyes sparks of blighting.
Beside the anvil cold he danced with the hammer of Urthona—
5   Terrific, pale. Enitharmon, stretched on the dreary earth,
Felt her immortal limbs freeze, stiffening pale, inflexible.
His feet shrunk withering from the deep, shrinking & withering,
And Enitharmon shrunk up, all their fibres withering beneath—
As plants withered by winter, leaves & stems & roots decaying,
10   Melt into thin air; while the seed driven by the furious wind
Rests on the distant mountain's top. So Los & Enitharmon,
Shrunk into fixed space, stood trembling on a rocky cliff.
Yet mighty bulk & majesty & beauty remained; but unexpansive.
As far as highest zenith from the lowest nadir, so far shrunk
15   Los from the furnaces, a space immense, & left the cold
Prince of light bound in chains of intellect among the furnaces.
But all the furnaces were out & the bellows had ceased to blow.

He stood trembling & Enitharmon clung around his knees.
Their senses unexpansive in one steadfast bulk remain.

v *1. He*] Los.   *Infected, mad* and the ensuing lines suggest that B. is
thinking of rabies. Los and Enitharmon lose their immortal, infinite form
(described in ii *505*ff), and become 'unexpansive' (*13*) though still mighty.
v *4. The anvil cold*] He has given up working.
v *15. The furnaces* are Urizen's, used in the making of his dominion in
Night ii and repaired by Los in iv *165*ff.
v *18. He*] Los. With this physical restriction, the cycle of birth and death
begins (*36–7*).
v *18–22.* B. illustrated these lines on p. 58.

20 The night blew cold & Enitharmon shrieked on the dismal wind,
[58] Her pale hands cling around her husband, & over her weak head
     Shadows of eternal death sit in the leaden air.

     But the soft pipe, the flute, the viol, organ, harp & cymbal,
     And the sweet sound of silver voices calm the weary couch
25 Of Enitharmon, but her groans drown the immortal harps.
     Loud & more loud the living music floats upon the air;
     Faint & more faint the daylight wanes. The wheels of turning
        darkness
     Began in solemn revolutions. Earth convulsed with rending pangs
     Rocked to & fro, & cried sore at the groans of Enitharmon.
30 Still the faint harps & silver voices calm the weary couch;
     But from the caves of deepest night ascending in clouds of mist
     The winter spread his wide black wings across from pole to pole.
     Grim frost beneath & terrible snow, linked in a marriage chain,
     Began a dismal dance. The winds around on pointed rocks
35 Settled like bats innumerably, ready to fly abroad.
     The groans of Enitharmon shake the skies, the labouring earth—
     Till from her heart rending his way a terrible child sprang forth,
     In thunder smoke & sullen flames & howling & fury & blood.

     Soon as his burning eyes were opened on the abyss
40 The horrid trumpets of the deep bellowed with bitter blasts.
     The enormous demons woke & howled around the new-born king,
     Crying: 'Luvah, king of love, thou art the king of rage & death!'
     Urizen cast deep darkness round him; raging Luvah poured
     The spears of Urizen from chariots round the eternal tent.
45 Discord began, then yells & cries shook the wide firmament.

v <i>34</i>. The imagery of pointed rocks and bats is distinctly 'Gothic'.
v <i>41</i>. As in <i>Urizen</i>, Orc is born of Enitharmon, and is chained by the
jealous Los. Here, however, he turns out to be the fallen form of Luvah.
He is still the rebel of the two <i>Prophecies</i> (<i>America</i> and <i>Europe</i>), and is
destined to conquer Urizen (iii <i>13–14</i>): but by viiia–b B. has changed his
mind, and Orc becomes the corrupted servant of Urizen, his free spirit
gone but his violence remaining. Note the allusions to Christ: in <i>America</i>
37ff Orc is related to resurrecting humanity; in <i>Europe</i> <i>1–4</i> there are allu-
sions to the Nativity: here the phrase <i>new-born king</i> and the choir of demons
(instead of angels) who hymn his birth have a similar purpose. There is a
general similarity also between this choir of demons and their strophic song
(<i>46–65</i>) and Milton's <i>Nativity Ode</i>: earlier, in <i>Europe</i>, B. had used the same
material in a rather similar way. But Orc is always Christ with a differ-
ence—he comes with war and revolt, not peace. In B.'s earlier poems this
was the beginning of a new age: in the political disillusionment of the
later poems this was the violence of Antichrist. Cp. iii <i>65n</i>.
v <i>43</i>. The demons sing of the beginning of the fall (narrated in i <i>182ff</i>).

[59]   'Where is sweet Vala, gloomy prophet? Where the lovely form
       That drew the body of Man from Heaven into this dark abyss?
       Soft tears & sighs, where are you? Come forth, shout on bloody
           fields!
       Show thy soul, Vala, show thy bow & quiver of secret fires!

50   'Draw thy bow, Vala, from the depths of hell! Thy black bow draw,
       And twang the bow-string to our howlings! Let thine arrows black
       Sing in the sky as once they sang upon the hills of light,
       When dark Urthona wept in torment of the secret pain.

       'He wept & he divided, & he laid his gloomy head
55   Down on the Rock of Eternity, on darkness of the deep,
       Torn by black storms & ceaseless torrents of consuming fire.
       Within his breast his fiery sons chained down, & filled with cursings,

       'And breathing terrible blood & vengeance, gnashing his teeth with
           pain,
       Let loose the enormous spirit in the darkness of the deep,
60   And his dark wife, that once fair crystal form, divinely clear,
       Within his ribs producing serpents whose souls are flames of fire.

       'But now the times return upon thee! Enitharmon's womb
       Now holds thee, soon to issue forth. Sound, clarions of war!
       Call Vala from her close recess in all her dark deceit.
65   Then rage on rage shall fierce redound out of her crystal quiver!'

       So sung the demons round red Orc & round faint Enitharmon.
       Sweat & blood stood on the limbs of Los in globes, his fiery eyelids
       Faded; he roused, he seized the wonder in his hands & went
       Shuddering & weeping through the gloom & down into the deeps.

70   Enitharmon nursed her fiery child in the dark deeps,
       Sitting in darkness; over her Los mourned in anguish fierce,
       Covered with gloom. The fiery boy grew, fed by the milk
       Of Enitharmon. Los around her builded pillars of iron

v 46. Note the four-line sts from here to 65–the 'demons' song'. Cp.
Urizen's lament v 190–241. The demons ask for Vala; since Luvah has
appeared in the form of Orc, where is his counterpart?

v 49. secret fires] Of her sexual allurements.

v 53–61. These lines describe the disintegration of Urthona, the enormous
spirit (spectre in Jerusalem pl.36.32) and Enitharmon 'his dark wife' break-
ing out from his inner being. It is a version of the fall of Urthona varied
from i 214ff, iv 89ff.

v 56–61. These lines recur, with minor alterations, in Jerusalem pl.36 [40]
as 39–40, 38, 32, 41–2.

v 59. The enormous spirit] The spectre of Urthona, separated in iv 59–66.

v 73–6. builded pillars . . . Golgonooza] Los builds a tower to surround
Enitharmon against the dangers he foresees from Orc. His motive at this

[60]   And brass & silver & gold fourfold in dark prophetic fear;
  75   For now he feared eternal death & uttermost extinction.
       He builded Golgonooza on the lake of Udan Adan;
       Upon the limit of translucence then he builded Luban.
       Tharmas laid the foundations & Los finished it in howling woe.

       But when fourteen summers & winters had revolved over
  80   Their solemn habitation, Los beheld the ruddy boy
       Embracing his bright mother, & beheld malignant fires
       In his young eyes, discerning plain that Orc plotted his death.
       Grief rose upon his ruddy brows, a tightening girdle grew
       Around his bosom like a bloody cord. In secret sobs
  85   He burst it, but next morn another girdle succeeds
       Around his bosom. Every day he viewed the fiery youth
       With silent fear, & his immortal cheeks grew deadly pale—
       Till many a morn & many a night passed over in dire woe,
       Forming a girdle in the day & bursting it at night.
  90   (The girdle was formed by day; by night was burst in twain,
       Falling down on the rock, an iron chain link by link locked.)

       Enitharmon beheld the bloody chain of nights & days
       Depending from the bosom of Los, & how with griding pain
       He went each morning to his labours with the spectre dark,
  95   Called it the Chain of Jealousy. Now Los began to speak
       His woes aloud to Enitharmon, since he could not hide
       His uncouth plague. He seized the boy in his immortal hands,
       While Enitharmon followed him weeping in dismal woe
       Up to the iron mountain's top, & there the jealous chain
 100   Fell from his bosom on the mountain. The spectre dark
       Held the fierce boy; Los nailed him down, binding around his limbs

       point is chiefly jealousy; yet Orc does cause great distress to her as the
       poem goes on (e.g. viib *8off*). Later this tower developed into one of B.'s
       great conceptions—the infinite and beautiful city built by Los as a barrier
       against the onset of darkness and evil. Here is the germ of the idea, no
       more, but it is significant as an example of the manner in which B.'s
       images grew as he saw them more and more profoundly. Cp. viia *429*,
       viii *25n*, *Jerusalem* pls *12.21–14.34*.
       v *77*. For the *limit of translucence* see iv *270n*. Luban becomes the gate
       where Los's city of hope and light, Golgonooza, looks out into the darkness
       of Udan-Adan and Ulro. Cp. viia *429*; viii *29*; *Milton* pls *24.49, 27[26].24*,
       28.21; *Jerusalem* pl.*13.24*. This passage is one of B.'s earliest expressions of
       this image—or are lines *76–7* later than the rest?
       v *79ff*. The *fourteen years* are found in *America* 'Preludium' *2*; the jealousy of
       Los in the form of a girdle which becomes the Chain of Jealousy is in
       Urizen 379–95. The design on this page of the MS also illustrates it.
       v *94–95*. Perhaps a line has been missed out in copying.

The accursed chain. Oh, how bright Enitharmon howled & cried
Over her son! Obdurate, Los bound down her loved joy.
[61]   The hammer of Urthona smote the rivets in terror of brass
105   Tenfold. The demon's rage flamed tenfold, forth rending,
Roaring, redounding, loud, loud, & louder, & fired
The darkness, warring with the waves of Tharmas & snows of
        Urizen.
Crackling the flames went up with fury from the immortal demon;
Surrounded with flames the demon grew, loud howling in his fires.
110   Los folded Enitharmon in a cold white cloud in fear,
Then led her down into the deeps & into his labyrinth,
Giving the spectre sternest charge over the howling fiend.

Concentred into love of parent, storgous appetite, craving,
His limbs bound down mock at his chains; for over them a flame
115   Of circling fire unceasing plays, to feed them with life & bring
The virtues of the eternal worlds. Ten thousand thousand spirits
Of life lament around the demon; going forth & returning
At his enormous call they flee into the heavens of heavens
And back return with wine & food. Or dive into the deeps
120   To bring the thrilling joys of sense to quell his ceaseless rage.
His eyes, the lights of his large soul, contract or else expand:
Contracted they behold the secrets of the infinite mountains,
The veins of gold & silver & the hidden things of Vala,
Whatever grows from its pure bud or breathes a fragrant soul;
125   Expanded they behold the terrors of the sun & moon,
The elemental planets & the orbs of eccentric fire.
His nostrils breathe a fiery flame. His locks are like the forests
Of wild beasts: there the lion glares, the tiger & wolf howl there,
And there the eagle hides her young in cliffs & precipices.
130   His bosom is like starry heaven expanded; all the stars
Sing round. There waves the harvest & the vintage rejoices, the
        springs
Flow into rivers of delight; there the spontaneous flowers

v *108. demon*] Orc, flames being one of his characteristics.

v *112.* Cp. viia *328*, where the spectre hands over to Vala, with disastrous
results.

v *113.storgous*] From Gk.'storgé', parental affection for a child. But the word
can refer to family affection in general, and B. seems to go further, using
it to refer to Orc's desire for Enitharmon.

v *117. lament*] For 'rejoice' deleted.

v *121-6.* Immortal, infinite senses need no lenses to magnify small or
distant objects.

v *126. orbs of eccentric fire*] Comets, whose orbits are usually elongated
ellipses. See also vi *317-19n.*

Drink, laugh & sing, the grasshopper, the emmet & the fly;
The golden moth builds there a house & spreads her silken bed.
[62]   His loins enwove with silken fires are like a furnace fierce,
136   As the strong bull in summer-time, when bees sing round the heath,
Where the herds low after the shadow & after the water spring,
The numerous flocks cover the mountain & shine along the valley.
His knees are rocks of adamant & ruby & emerald;
140   Spirits of strength in palaces rejoice in golden armour,
Armed with spear & shield they drink & rejoice over the slain.
Such is the demon, such his terror in the nether deep.

But when returned to Golgonooza, Los & Enitharmon
Felt all the sorrow parents feel. They wept toward one another,
145   And Los repented that he had chained Orc upon the mountain;
And Enitharmon's tears prevailed, parental love returned—
Though terrible his dread of that infernal chain. They rose
At midnight, hasting to their much-beloved care.
Nine days they travelled through the gloom of Entuthon Benithon;
150   Los, taking Enitharmon by the hand, led her along
The dismal vales & up to the iron mountain's top, where Orc
Howled in the furious wind. He thought to give to Enitharmon
Her son in tenfold joy & to compensate for her tears,
Even if his own death resulted; so much pity him pained.

155   But when they came to the dark rock & to the spectrous cave,
Lo! the young limbs had strucken root into the rock, & strong
Fibres had from the Chain of Jealousy enwove themselves
In a swift vegetation round the rock & round the cave
And over the immortal limbs of the terrible fiery boy.
160   In vain they strove now to unchain, in vain with bitter tears
To melt the Chain of Jealousy. Not Enitharmon's death
Nor the consummation of Los could ever melt the chain,
Nor unroot the infernal fibres from their rocky bed.
Nor all Urthona's strength, nor all the power of Luvah's bulls—
165   Though they each morning drag the unwilling sun out of the deep—
Could uproot the infernal chain, for it had taken root
[63]   Into the iron rock, & grew a chain beneath the earth
Even to the centre, wrapping round the centre; &, the limbs

v *133*. There seems to be a hiatus here, unless *laugh & sing* belongs to the
insects, which would be a construction not easily parallelled in B.'s verse,
(though grasshoppers do 'laugh and sing'). B. has a point in the MS after
sing, nowhere else.
v *149*. *Entuthon Benithon*] Where Enion was lost—a fearsome world of
darkness (iii *174*).
v *162*. *consummation*] As usual in B., 'a burning-up'.
v *164*. *Luvah's bulls* drag the sun; he is 'lord of day' in *211*.

Of Orc entering with fibres, became one with him, a living chain
170 Sustained by the demon's life. Despair & terror & woe & rage
Enwrap the parents in cold clouds, as they bend howling over
The terrible boy, till fainting by his side the parents fell.

Not long they lay: Urthona's spectre found herbs of the pit;
Rubbing their temples he revived them. All their lamentations
175 I write not here; but all their afterlife was lamentation.

When satiated with grief they returned back to Golgonooza,
Enitharmon on the road of Dranthon felt the inmost gate
Of her bright heart burst open, & again close, with a deadly pain.
Within her heart Vala began to reanimate in bursting sobs,
180 And when the gate was open she beheld that dreary deep
Where bright Ahania wept. She also saw the infernal roots
Of the Chain of Jealousy, & felt the rendings of fierce howling Orc,
Rending the caverns like a mighty wind pent in the earth.
Though wide apart as furthest north is from the furthest south,
185 Urizen trembled where he lay, to hear the howling terror.
The rocks shook; the eternal bars, tugged to & fro, were rifted.
Outstretched upon the stones of ice, the ruins of his throne,
Urizen shuddering heard; his trembling limbs shook the strong
    caves.

The woes of Urizen, shut up in the deep dens of Urthona:

190 'Ah, how shall Urizen the king submit to this dark mansion?
Ah, how is this? Once on the heights I stretched my throne sublime;

v *170–2.* On the facing page, B. illustrates this with a drawing varied from
that at the head of the Preludium to *America.*
v *175.* This detail is not in *Urizen.* Perhaps it has a personal meaning.
v *177. Dranthon*] The only other reference in the whole of B. is the deleted
line after viia *452–*'the caverned rocks of Dranthon'.
v *179. Vala*] Born of Enitharmon's shadow in viia *313.*
v *180.* Enitharmon's imaginative powers are momentarily awoken. Cp.
B.'s letter to Thomas Butts, 23 Sept. 1800, just after arriving in Felpham–
'I met a plough on my first going out at my gate the first morning after
my arrival, and the ploughboy said to the ploughman, "Father, the gate is
open"–I have begun to work, and find that I can work with greater
pleasure than ever'. Cp. also the opening by Sin of the gate between Hell
and Chaos in *Paradise Lost* ii 871–84. The parallel is not exact: Sin's act is
evil, but the momentary opening of Enitharmon's heart is vision. Sin
cannot reclose the gates of Hell; Enitharmon's heart remains barred until
viia *323–4.*
v *182–3.* B. has a space here which the sense seems to contradict.
v *185. The howling terror*] Orc.
v *189. Urizen shut up . . .*] Cp. iv *170–84.*

The mountains of Urizen, once of silver where the sons of wisdom
    dwelt
And on whose tops the virgins sang, are rocks of desolation.

'My fountains, once the haunt of swans, now breed the scaly
    tortoise,
195 The houses of my harpers are become a haunt of crows,
The gardens of wisdom are become a field of horrid graves,
And on the bones I drop my tears, & water them in vain.

[64] 'Once, how I walked from my palace in gardens of delight,
The sons of wisdom stood around, the harpers followed with harps,
200 Nine virgins clothed in light composed the song to their immortal
    voices,
And at my banquets of new wine my head was crowned with joy.

'Then in my ivory pavilions I slumbered in the noon,
And walked in the silent night among sweet-smelling flowers
Till on my silver bed I slept, & sweet dreams round me hovered;
205 But now my land is darkened & my wise men are departed.

'My songs are turned to cries of lamentation
Heard on my mountains, & deep sighs under my palace roofs—
Because the steeds of Urizen, once swifter than the light,
Were kept back from my lord, & from his chariot of mercies.

210 'Oh, did I keep the horses of the day in silver pastures?
Oh, I refused the lord of day the horses of his prince!
O did I close my treasures with roofs of solid stone,
And darken all my palace walls with envyings & hate?

'O fool! to think that I could hide from his all-piercing eyes
215 The gold & silver & costly stones, his holy workmanship!
O fool! could I forget the light that filled my bright spheres
Was a reflection of his face, who called me from the deep?

'I well remember: for I heard the mild & holy voice
Saying: "O light, spring up & shine!" & I sprang up from the deep.
220 He gave to me a silver sceptre & crowned me with a golden crown,
And said: "Go forth & guide my son who wanders on the ocean."

v *200. Nine virgins*] Perhaps B. was thinking of the nine Muses, or of the
nine spheres (sun, moon, five planets, the star-sphere and the firmament).
v *211. the lord of day*] Luvah: in *164* it is his bulls who drag the sun, but
here the lines seem to refer to the Divine Vision; Luvah had never been
Urizen's lord, but an equal.
v *218–21. the mild and holy voice*] That of the Divine Vision; the phrase is
not otherwise used except satirically. This st. can be allegorically inter-
preted: that Thought has failed to act as a guide, preferring to rule, and
has ruined both Love and Imagination thereby; cp. *241*.

'I went not forth. I hid myself in black clouds of my wrath;
I called the stars around my feet in the night of councils dark.
The stars threw down their spears & fled naked away:
225 We fell. I seized thee, dark Urthona! In my left hand falling

'I seized thee, beauteous Luvah; thou art faded like a flower,
And like a lily is thy wife Vala, withered by winds.
When thou didst bear the golden cup at the immortal tables
Thy children smote their fiery wings, crowned with the gold of
    heaven;

[65] 'Thy pure feet stepped on the steps divine, too pure for other feet,
231 And thy fair locks shadowed thine eyes from the divine effulgence;
Then thou didst keep with strong Urthona the living gates of Heaven.
But now thou art bound down with him, even to the gates of Hell,

'Because thou gavest Urizen the wine of the Almighty
235 For steeds of light, that they might run in thy golden chariot of
    pride.
I gave to thee the steeds, I poured the stolen wine,
And drunken with the immortal draught fell from my throne
    sublime.

'I will arise, explore these dens, & find that deep pulsation
That shakes my caverns with strong shudders. Perhaps this is the
    night
240 Of prophecy, & Luvah hath burst his way from Enitharmon.
When thought is closed in caves, then love shall show its root in
    deepest Hell.'

End of the Fifth Night

v *223. America* 'b' *5* is similar.
v *224.* So in 'The Tiger', p. 214 above.
v *232. thou*] Luvah throughout.
v *234.* In other versions it is said that Urizen was asleep; this is the first
suggestion that Luvah had made him drunk.
v *238.* B. returns to the narrative as in *Urizen*, left behind at *103*.
v *239–40. the night/Of prophecy*] The night prophesied in iii *13*ff, that Orc
(Luvah) will come to conquer Urizen.
v *241.* A Blakean aphorism. Thought is closed in the restricting caves of
our material existence: but even at the worst love's power can be shown.
The 'love' that is to be shown in viii is the Divine Mercy, greater than
Luvah's love, and more than Urizen can envisage. Orc's chain is rooted
'even to the centre' of Hell (*168*); note *42*, and the paradox involved–
'Luvah, king of love, thou art the king of rage and death'.

Night the Sixth

This Night follows the journey of Urizen as he 'explores his dens', in a
sequence owing much to Satan's journey through Chaos in *Paradise Lost* ii.
He meets three women, his daughters, who refuse to know him, and he
curses them (*35*). This curse is later seen to cause still greater trouble in his
ruined world (*138–43*). He meets Tharmas, who pleads with him that they
should destroy one another (*64–6*), but Urizen ignores him and continues
his journey through the abyss of his ruined world (*72ff*). In horror at its
chaos, he determines to rebuild it as he built the palace in ii for fear of the
abyss; but he rebuilds, not the golden palace, but a hard, fixed, rigid,
mechanical world of laws (*224ff*), like that in *Urizen 50–84*. Yet chaos is
not overcome and he still wanders (*258ff*) until Tharmas, Orc and the
spectre of Urthona oppose him (*295ff*).

[66]　　　　　　　　*[Full page drawing]*

[67]　　　　　　　NIGHT THE SIXTH

So Urizen arose, & leaning on his spear explored his dens;
He threw his flight through the dark air to where a river flowed,
And taking off his silver helmet filled it & drank;
But when, unsatiated his thirst, he assayed to gather more,
5　Lo! three terrific women at the verge of the bright flood,
Who would not suffer him to approach, but drove him back with
　　storms.

Urizen knew them not, & thus addressed the spirits of darkness:

'Who art thou, eldest woman, sitting in thy clouds?
What is that name written on thy forehead? What art thou?
10　And wherefore dost thou pour this water forth in sighs & care?'

She answered not, but filled her urn & poured it forth abroad.

'Answerest thou not?' said Urizen, 'Then thou mayest answer me,
Thou terrible woman clad in blue, whose strong attractive power
Draws all into a fountain at the rock of thy attraction.
With frowning brow thou sittest, mistress of these mighty waters!'

She answered not, but stretched her arms & threw her limbs
　　abroad.

'Or wilt thou answer, youngest woman clad in shining green?
With labour & care thou dost divide the current into four.

vi. page 66. A group of nude sketches, dominated by a standing male figure,
seen from the back, and holding a globe on his head.
vi 5. B.'s three women may derive from Lear's three daughters, or the
three Fates of Greek legend, who look into past, present and future. But
though Urizen's three silent daughters are awesome, he does not develop
any similar characteristics in them.

Queen of these dreadful rivers, speak & let me hear thy voice!'
[68]   They reared up a wall of rocks, and Urizen raised his spear.
  21   They gave a scream, they knew their father; Urizen knew his
               daughters.
          They shrunk into their channels, dry the rocky strand beneath
               his feet,
          Hiding themselves in rocky forms from the eyes of Urizen.

          Then Urizen wept, & thus his lamentation poured forth:

  25   'O horrible, O dreadful state—those whom I loved best,
          On whom I poured the beauties of my light, adorning them
          With jewels & precious ornament, laboured with art divine
          Vests of the radiant colours of heaven, & crowns of golden fire!
          I gave sweet lilies to their breasts & roses to their hair,
  30   I taught them songs of sweet delight, I gave their tender voices
          Into the blue expanse, & I invented with laborious art
          Sweet instruments of sound. In pride encompassing my knees
          They poured their radiance above all. The daughters of Luvah
               envied
          At their exceeding brightness, & the sons of Eternity sent them
               gifts.
  35   Now will I pour my fury on them & I will reverse
          The precious benediction! For their colours of loveliness
          I will give blackness; for jewels, hoary frost; for ornament,
               deformity;
          For crowns, wreathed serpents; for sweet odours, stinking
               corruptibility;
          For voices of delight, hoarse croakings inarticulate through frost.
  40   For laboured fatherly care & sweet instruction, I will give
          Chains of dark ignorance & cords of twisted self-conceit,
          And whips of stern repentance, & food of stubborn obstinacy—
          That they may curse Tharmas their god, & Los his adopted son;
          That they may curse & worship the obscure demon of destruction;
  45   That they may worship terrors & obey the violent!
          Go forth, sons of my curse; go forth, daughters of my abhorrence!'

          Tharmas heard the deadly scream across his watery world,
          And Urizen's loud-sounding voice lamenting on the wind,
          And he came riding in his fury. Froze to solid were his waves:
[69]   Silent in ridges he beheld them stand round Urizen,
  51   A dreary waste of solid waters. For the king of light

          vi *20*. Originally the order of the clauses was reversed: 'Then Urizen ...
          but they. . . .'
          vi *44. the obscure demon*] Orc. Urizen says 'Let them worship the other
          Zoas—and suffer the effects!'
          vi *45*. Taken from *Visions 23*.

13+B.

Darkened his brows with his cold helmet, & his gloomy spear
Darkened before him. Silent on the ridgy waves he took
His gloomy way. Before him Tharmas fled, & flying fought,

55   Crying: 'What & who art thou, cold demon? Art thou Urizen?
Art thou like me risen again from death—or art thou deathless?
If thou art he, my desperate purpose hear, & give me death:
For death to me is better far than life, death my desire,
That I in vain in various paths have sought. But still I live.

60   The body of man is given to me; I seek in vain to destroy,
For it surges forth in fish & monsters of the deeps,
And in these monstrous forms I live in an eternal woe.
And thou, O Urizen, art fallen never to be delivered!
Withhold thy light from me for ever, & I will withhold

65   From thee thy food. So shall we cease to be & all our sorrows
End, & the Eternal Man no more renew beneath our power.
If thou refusest, in eternal flight thy beams in vain
Shall pursue Tharmas, & in vain shalt crave for food. I will
Pour down my flight through dark immensity, eternal falling.

70   Thou shalt pursue me but in vain, till starved upon the void
Thou hangst, a dried skin shrunk up, weak wailing in the wind.'

So Tharmas spoke; but Urizen replied not. On his way
He took, high bounding over hills & deserts, floods & horrible
    chasms.
Infinite was his labour, without end his travel. He strove

75   In vain, for hideous monsters of the deeps annoyed him sore—
Scaled & finned with iron & brass they devoured the path before
    him;
Incessant was the conflict. On he bent his weary steps,
Making a path toward the dark world of Urthona. He rose
With pain upon the dreary mountains, & with pain descended

80   And saw their grisly fears, & his eyes sickened at the sight.
The howlings, gnashings, groanings, shriekings, shudderings,
    sobbings, burstings
Mingle together to create a world for Los. In cruel delight

[70a] Los brooded on the darkness, nor saw Urizen with a globe of fire
Lighting his dismal journey through the pathless world of death,

85   Writing in bitter tears & groans in books of iron & brass
The enormous wonders of the abysses, once his brightest joy.

For Urizen beheld the terrors of the abyss wandering among
The ruined spirits, once his children & the children of Luvah,

---

vi *72ff.* This passage recalls–in general–Satan's journey through Chaos in
Paradise Lost ii 890–1033. Cp. also the wanderings of Tiriel.
74. travel.] See *Europe* 'Prel.' *6n.*

Scared at the sound of their own sigh that seems to shake the
    immense
90 They wander, moping, in their heart a sun, a dreary moon,
A universe of fiery constellations in their brain,
An earth of wintry woe beneath their feet, & round their loins
Waters or winds or clouds, or brooding lightnings & pestilential
    plagues.
Beyond the bounds of their own self their senses cannot penetrate,
95 As the tree knows not what is outside of its leaves & bark,
And yet it drinks the summer joy & fears the winter sorrow,
So in the regions of the grave none knows his dark compeer,
Though he partakes of his dire woes & mutual returns the pang,
The throb, the dolour, the convulsion in soul-sickening woes,

100 The horrid shapes & sights of torment in burning dungeons & in
Fetters of red-hot iron, some with crowns of serpents & some
With monsters girding round their bosoms, some lying on beds of
    sulphur,
On racks & wheels. He beheld women marching o'er burning
    wastes
Of sand, in bands of hundreds & of fifties & of thousands, strucken
    with
105 Lightnings which blazed after them upon their shoulders in their
    march,
In successive volleys; with loud thunders swift flew the king of light
Over the burning deserts. Then the deserts passed; involved in
    clouds
Of smoke, with myriads moping in the stifling vapours, swift
Flew the king, though flagged, his powers labouring, till over rocks

vi 92–9. In the margin opposite these lines is the rhymed couplet in
crayon, not marked for entry:

    Till thou dost injure / the distrest
    Thou shalt never have peace / within thy breast.

This seems to be a cryptic author's comment, not part of the text, to the
effect that 'You must tell the truth, even if it hurts the person who hears it'.
vi 97. *the regions of the grave*] Our material world which (see note above)
the prophet must shape for its own good.
vi 99. Followed by three deleted lines, the first replacing the second:

    Not so closd up the Prince of Light now darkend wandring among
    [For Urizen beheld the terrors of the Abyss wandring among]
    The Ruined Spirits once his Children & the Children of Luvah

vi 100. Much that Urizen sees is recognizable in certain human conditions,
e.g. the slavery in *103–4*.

110   And mountains faint, weary, he wandered, where multitudes were
             shut
        Up in the solid mountains & in rocks which heaved with their
             torments.
        Then came he among fiery cities & castles built of burning steel;
        Then he beheld the forms of tigers & of lions, dishumanized men.
        Many in serpents & in worms stretched out enormous length
115   Over the sullen mould, & slimy tracks obstruct his way,
        Drawn out from deep to deep, woven by ribbed
        And scaled monsters; or armed in iron shell, or shell of brass
        Or gold, a glittering torment shining & hissing in eternal pain—
        Some as columns of fire or of water, sometimes stretched out in
             height,
120   Sometimes in length, sometimes englobing, wandering in vain,
             seeking for ease.
        His voice to them was but an inarticulate thunder, for their ears
        Were heavy & dull, & their eyes & nostrils closed up.
        Oft he stood by a howling victim, questioning in words
        Soothing or furious; no one answered, everyone wrapped up
125   In his own sorrow howled regardless of his words, nor voice
        Of sweet response could he obtain, though oft assayed with tears.
        He knew they were his children, ruined in his ruined world.

[71a]   Oft would he stand & question a fierce scorpion glowing with gold;
        In vain—the terror heard not; then a lion he would seize
130   By the fierce mane, staying his howling course—in vain the voice
        Of Urizen, in vain the eloquent tongue. A rock, a cloud, a
             mountain
        Were now not vocal as in climes of happy Eternity,
        Where the lamb replies to the infant voice & the lion to the man
             of years,
        Giving them sweet instructions; where the cloud, the river & the
             field
135   Talk with the husbandman & shepherd. But these attacked him sore,
        Seizing upon his feet & rending the sinews, that in caves
        He hid, to recure his obstructed powers with rest & oblivion.
[70b]   Here he had time enough to repent of his rashly threatened curse—
        He saw them cursed beyond his curse; his soul melted with fear.
[71b]   He could not take their fetters off, for they grew from the soul,
  141   Nor could he quench the fires, for they flamed out from the heart,

        vi *110–11.* Miners, perhaps.
        vi *113–14.* The illustration shows a dragon with human hands and feet.
        vi *119. height*] B. has *heighth*.
        vi *130. his*] The lion's.
        vi *138.* The curse of *35–46.*

Nor could he calm the elements because himself was subject.
So he threw his flight in terror & pain & in repentant tears.

When he had passed these southern terrors, he approached the
  east,
145 Void, pathless, beaten with iron, sleet & eternal hail & rain.
No form was there, no living thing, & yet his way lay through
This dismal world. He stood a while, & looked back o'er his former
Terrific voyage—hills & vales of torment & despair—
Sighing & wiping a fresh tear; then turning round he threw
150 Himself into the dismal void. Falling he fell & fell,
Whirling in unresistible revolutions, down & down
In the horrid bottomless vacuity, falling, falling, falling
Into the eastern vacuity, the empty world of Luvah.

The Ever-pitying One who seeth all things saw his fall,
155 And in the dark vacuity created a bosom of clay.
When wearied, dead he fell; his limbs reposed in the bosom of slime.
As the seed falls from the sower's hand, so Urizen fell, & death
Shut up his powers in oblivion. Then as the seed shoots forth
In pain & sorrow, so the slimy bed his limbs renewed;
160 At first an infant weakness. Periods passed; he gathered strength,
But still in solitude he sat; then rising, threw his flight
Onward, though falling, through the waste of night, and ending
  in death,
And in another resurrection to sorrow & weary travel.
But still his books he bore in his strong hands, & his iron pen;
165 For when he died they lay beside his grave, & when he rose
He seized them with a gloomy smile. For wrapped in his death
  clothes
He hid them, when he slept in death; when he revived, the clothes
Were rotted by the winds, the books remained still unconsumed,
Still to be written & interleaved with brass & iron & gold
170 Time after time—for such a journey none but iron pens
Can write, and adamantine leaves receive; nor can the man who
  goes
[72] The journey, obstinate refuse to write time after time.

vi *145. iron . . . rain*] *1st rdg del.* eternal . . . snow.
vi *152.* Milton's 'vast vacuity' into which Satan falls 'ten thousand fathom
deep', *Paradise Lost* ii 934.
vi *154. The Ever-pitying One*] B. rarely names God.
vi *155.* Luvah, the passionate one, belongs to the heart. He is absent, but
an imitation of his home, the *bosom*, is created temporarily for Urizen's
sake.
vi *172. obstinate*] B. has no punctuation; the meaning seems to be that
refusal would be obstinate.

Endless had been his travel; but the Divine Hand him led,
For infinite the distance & obscured by combustions dire,
175　By rocky masses frowning in the abysses revolving erratic
Round lakes of fire in the dark deep, the ruins of Urizen's world.
Oft would he sit in a dark rift & regulate his books,
Or sleep such sleep as spirits eternal, wearied in his dark
Tearful & sorrowful state, then rise, look out & ponder
180　His dismal voyage, eyeing the next sphere though far remote,
Then darting into the abyss of night his venturous limbs,
Through lightnings, thunders, earthquakes & concussions, fires
　　　and floods,
Stemming his downward fall, labouring up against futurity,
Creating many a vortex, fixing many a science in the deep;
185　And thence throwing his venturous limbs into the vast unknown,
Swift, swift, from chaos to chaos, from void to void, a road
　　　immense.

For when he came to where a vortex ceased to operate,
Nor down nor up remained; then if he turned & looked back
From whence he came, 'twas upward all. And if he turned and
　　　viewed
190　The unpassed void, upward was still his mighty wandering,
The midst between, an equilibrium grey of air serene,
Where he might live in peace, & where his life might meet repose.

But Urizen said: 'Can I not leave this world of cumbrous wheels,
Circle o'er circle, nor on high attain a void
195　Where self-sustaining I may view all things beneath my feet;
Or sinking through these elemental wonders, swift to fall,
I thought perhaps to find an end, a world beneath of voidness,
Whence I might travel round the outside of this dark confusion?
When I bend downward, bending my head downward into the
　　　deep,
200　'Tis upward all, which way soever I my course begin.
But when a vortex formed on high, by labour & sorrow & care,

vi *184. vortex*] See *Milton* pl.15.21*n*, p. 508 below. In the Cartesian theory,
the universe consisted of a series of vortices, each centred on a star or
similar body.
science] B.'s objection is not to *science* (cp. iv *147* and ix *852*), but to *fixed*
science: the word means *learning* as a whole rather than physical science alone.
vi *193. cumbrous wheels*] These have not been mentioned: but to B. formless
chaos and mechanical rigidity were equal enemies of the imaginative life.
The heavy machinery of B.'s day had little functional beauty or precision,
to make it attractive.
vi *197.* Urizen longs for death–not life–but finds he can only escape from
one vortex into another. He cannot get away from this universe of eternal,
moving vortices.

And weariness begins on all my limbs, then sleep revives
My wearied spirits; waking then 'tis downward all, which way
Soever I my spirits turn. No end I find of all.
205 Oh, what a world is here—unlike those climes of bliss
Where my sons gathered round my knees. O thou poor ruined world,
Thou horrible ruin! once like me thou wast all glorious,
And now like me partaking desolate thy master's lot,
Art thou, O ruin, the once-glorious Heaven? Are these thy rocks
210 Where joy sang in the trees & pleasure sported on the rivers,
[73] And laughter sat beneath the oaks & innocence sported round
Upon the green plains, & sweet friendship met in palaces,
And books & instruments of song & pictures of delight?
Where are they? Whelmed beneath these ruins in horrible
destruction!
215 And if eternal falling I repose on the dark bosom
Of winds & waters, or thence fall into a void where air
Is not, down falling through immensity, ever & ever,
I lose my powers, weakened every revolution till a death
Shuts up my powers; then, a seed in the vast womb of darkness,
220 I dwell in dim oblivion. Brooding over me the enormous worlds
Reorganize me—shooting forth in bones & flesh & blood
I am regenerated, to fall or rise at will or to remain
A labourer of ages, a dire discontent, a living woe,
Wand'ring in vain. Here will I fix my foot, & here rebuild.
225 Here mountains of brass promise much riches in their dreadful
bosoms.'

So he began to dig, forming of gold, silver & iron
And brass, vast instruments to measure out the immense & fix
The whole into another world, better suited to obey
His will, where none should dare oppose his will, himself being king
230 Of all, & all futurity be bound in his vast chain.
And the sciences were fixed, & the vortexes began to operate
On all the sons of men, & every human soul terrified
At the turning wheels of heaven shrunk away inward, withering
away.

vi *209–11.* The sketch shows the present state–three dejected women under
a leafless tree.
vi *225.* This line is an insertion, preparing for the changes in the next line.
vi *226. So . . . iron*] *1st rdg:* 'So saying, he began to form of gold silver and
iron.' 'Dig' was inserted above 'form', and 'saying' deleted, presumably
to make room for both 'dig' and 'form'. 'To dig, forming' is more
characteristic of B. than 'to dig and form'.
vi *233.* The souls shrink with the shrinking of the diameter of the vortex
as it draws them in.

Gaining a new dominion over all his sons & daughters,
235 And over the sons & daughters of Luvah in the horrible abyss—
For Urizen lamented over them in a selfish lamentation,
Till a white woof covered his cold limbs from head to feet.
Hair white as snow covered him in flaky locks terrific,
Overspreading his limbs. In pride he wandered weeping,
240 Clothed in aged venerableness, obstinately resolved,
Travelling through darkness; & wherever he travelled, a dire web
Followed behind him, as the web of a spider dusky & cold,
Shivering across from vortex to vortex drawn out from his mantle
     of years,
A living mantle adjoined to his life & growing from his soul,

245 And the web of Urizen stretched direful, shivering in clouds,
And uttering such woes, such bursts, such thunderings—
The eyelids expansive as morning, & the ears
As a golden ascent winding round to the heavens of heavens.
(Within the dark horrors of the abysses, lion or tiger or scorpion).

[74] For every one opened within into eternity at will—
251 But they refused, because their outward forms were in the abyss,
And the wing-like tent of the universe, beautiful, surrounding all,
Or drawn up or let down at the will of the Immortal Man
Vibrated in such anguish. The eyelids quivered:
255 Weak & weaker their expansive orbs began shrinking,
Pangs smote through the brain & a universal shriek
Ran through the abysses, rending the web, torment on torment.

Thus Urizen in sorrows wandered many a dreary way,
Warring with monsters of the deeps in his most hideous pilgrimage,
260 Till his bright hair scattered in snows, his skin barked o'er with
     wrinkles.

vi 234. his] Urizen's. He also gains power over his chief enemy, Luvah.
vi 236. Urizen's lamenting creates a false religion. If he had not made this
corrupt world he would not need to lament; these are not tears of remorse,
but of false pity.
vi 237. woof] Fabric: a 'poetic' usage.
vi 241. In Urizen 461–8 called the Net of Religion.
vi 246–50. The sense is obscure, perhaps because of an omission. The eye-
lids and ears belonging to all living creatures, including such horrors as
lion, tiger or scorpion are 'expansive'–'opened to Eternity at will'. But
because they have fallen into the abyss of Urizen's universe, they refuse
the vision.
vi 250–1. within . . . outward] B. insists on the need for proportion in the
soul, a balance between the inward-looking and the outward-looking. If
these are separated, the inward man withers and the outward becomes a
mere shell.

Four caverns rooting downwards, their foundations thrusting forth,
The metal, rock & stone in ever-painful throes of vegetation—
The cave of Orc stood to the south, a furnace of dire flames
Quenchless unceasing. In the west the cave of Urizen;
265 For Urizen fell as the midday sun falls down into the west.
North stood Urthona's steadfast throne, a world of solid darkness
Shut up in stifling obstruction, rooted in dumb despair.
The east was void. But Tharmas rolled his billows in ceaseless
eddies,
Void, pathless, beat with snows eternal & iron hail & rain
270 All through the caverns of fire & air & earth, seeking
For Enion's limbs, nought finding but the black seaweed and
sickening slime,
Flying away from Urizen that he might not give him food,
Above, beneath, on all sides round in the vast deep of immensity,
That he might starve the sons & daughters of Urizen, on the winds
275 Making between horrible chasms into the vast unknown.
All these around the world of Los cast forth their monstrous births.
(But in eternal times the seat of Urizen is in the south,
Urthona in the north, Luvah in east, Tharmas in west.)

And now he came into the abhorred world of dark Urthona
280 By providence divine conducted—not bent from his own will
Lest death eternal should be the result; for the will cannot be
violated—
Into the doleful vales where no tree grew nor river flowed,
Nor man nor beast nor creeping thing, nor sun nor cloud nor star:
Still he with his globe of fire immense in his venturous hand
285 Bore on, through the affrighted vales, ascending & descending,
O'erwearied, or in cumbrous flight he ventured o'er dark rifts,
Or down dark precipices, or climbed with pain and labour huge,
Till he beheld the world of Los from the peaked rock of Urthona,
And heard the howling of red Orc distincter & distincter.
[75] Redoubling his immortal efforts through the narrow vales,
291 With difficulty down descending, guided by his ear
And by his globe of fire, he went down the vale of Urthona,
Between the enormous iron walls built by the spectre dark.

vi 261. *Four caverns*] In 277–8, Urizen, prince of light, belongs in the south.
the direction of the midday sun. Orc/Luvah, the bright youth, should be
in the east with the rising sun, and Tharmas in the west. But all is now dis-
ordered: the eternal homes of the Zoas have become four caverns.
vi 279. *He*] Urizen.
vi 284. This is illustrated at the foot of the page.
vi 288. *the peaked rock*] So Satan arrived 'on Niphates' top' to view the
Earth (*Paradise Lost* iii 742).

13*

Dark grew his globe, reddening with mists; and full before his
        path,
295   Striding across the narrow vale, the shadow of Urthona,
      A spectre vast, appeared, whose feet & legs with iron scaled
      Stamped the hard rocks, expectant of the unknown wanderer—
      Whom he had seen wandering his nether world when distant far—
      And watched his swift approach. Collected, dark, the spectre
        stood;
300   Beside him Tharmas stayed his flight & stood in stern defiance,
      Communing with the spectre who rejoiced along the vale.
      Round his loins a girdle glowed with many-coloured fires;
      In his hand a knotted club whose knots like mountains frowned,
      Desert among the stars, then withering with its ridges cold.
305   Black scales of iron arm the dread visage, iron spikes instead
      Of hair shoot from his orbed skull, his glowing eyes
      Burn like two furnaces; he called with voice of thunder.

      Four winged heralds mount the furious blasts & blow their trumps—
      Gold, silver, brass, & iron clangours clamouring rend the shores.
310   Like white clouds rising from the vales, his fifty-two armies
      From the four cliffs of Urthona rise glowing around the spectre.
      Four sons of Urizen the squadrons of Urthona led in arms
      Of gold & silver, brass & iron; he knew his mighty sons.

      Then Urizen arose upon the wind, back many a mile
315   Retiring into his dire web, scattering fleecy snows
      As he ascended, howling loud. The web vibrated strong,
      From heaven to heaven, from globe to globe. In vast eccentric paths

vi 295. shadow] Altered from 'shade'. The meeting with the spectre is
reminiscent of Satan's meeting with Death and Sin who barred his way
out of Hell (Paradise Lost ii 643ff). The spectre's iron scales on feet and legs
recall Sin who 'ended foul in many a scaly fold' (Paradise Lost ii 651); and
also, perhaps, Apollyon who was 'hideous to behold; he was clothed in
scales. . . .'
vi 302–3. girdle . . . club] Suggesting the constellation of Orion, and the
legendary Hercules.
vi 304. Desert] i.e. 'making a desert'.
vi 308–10. Adapted from 14–17 of the rejected plate c of America.
vi 309. shores] 1st rdg del. deeps. America c has shores.
vi 317–9. In 1705 the astronomer Halley published his calculations to show
that comets are part of the solar system, turning on very elliptical orbits.
Previously it had been thought that they were only temporary visitors,
drawn towards the sun for a while and then released. Descartes explained
them as falling from one vortex to another, being drawn in and then escap-
ing. B. saw this with moral overtones, as an endless and purposeless suc-
cession in the life of a fallen personality or world.

Compulsive rolled the comets at his dread command, the dreary way
Falling with wheel impetuous down among Urthona's vales
320 And round red Orc, returning back to Urizen gorged with blood.
Slow roll the massy globes at his command, & slow o'erwheel
The dismal squadrons of Urthona, weaving the dire web
In their progressions, & preparing Urizen's path before him.

End of the Sixth Night

Night the Seventh (a)

B. labelled two Nights as 'the Seventh'. There has been much critical
discussion of this anomaly, and many scholars believe that viib, which as
a whole was undoubtedly written earlier, was rejected by B. He did not
finally reject either, since he retained both sets of pages of the MS and
did not draw lines across the page–his method of cancelling large parts of
Night i. The present edition retains both viia and viib for this reason.
Further, there is a continuity in the narrative which justifies this retention.
It is impossible to prove, but not difficult to conjecture, why B. should
have labelled two Nights 'the Seventh'. The MS of i–iii shows that he
changed his mind several times about the numbering, and at some stage
he may have found that he had ten Nights, not nine. This was a problem
he never solved, but he had more important compositional problems, and
this one could wait. Night viib has undergone little revision, and remains in
a distinctly earlier state than viia, which has been extensively rewritten,
having been increased in length from about 320 lines to almost 500 by the
addition of important new material. The first part of viia, however,
appears to belong to the same date as vi and viib.

Night viia continues the narrative with Urizen's confrontation of Orc;
but B. now becomes more interested in Orc than in Urizen. Urizen's Tree
of Mystery shoots up to become increasingly important in the following
books. Orc is drawn under its power and changes into a serpent, losing
his human form entirely (152–6). But he is still chained to his rock, and the
myth alters its setting as Orc and Urizen disappear, while Enitharmon, Los
and the spectre of Urthona return (166ff).

B. achieves this change of setting by distinguishing two levels of exist-
ence–reality, and Urizen's ruined, spectral world, inhabited by shadows,
which Enitharmon cannot enter. Her shadow enters it, however, and is
tempted by the spectre of Urthona in a passage reminiscent of the tempta-
tion of Eve by Satan. In the upper world, Enitharmon knows nothing of
this; but when her shadow, having been seduced by Urthona's spectre,
gives birth to a monstrous shadow child (Vala's shadow, as foretold in
iii 20), her whole being in the upper world is shaken. This is one of the
climaxes of the poem: for now begins both the predominance of evil, as
we shall see in viib, and yet the beginning of redemption and liberation. In
the shadowy world, Urthona's spectre hands over control of the chained

Orc to the shadow (*332*) and goes up to the upper world. There he helps
the reconciliation of Los and Enitharmon (in the long addition mentioned
above). Night viia ends as they unite to work to redeem Urizen, Orc and
others, in a beautiful passage where B. draws upon his own experiences of
artistic creation.

[76]   *[Full-page drawing]*

[77]   NIGHT THE SEVENTH [a]

Then Urizen arose. The spectre fled, & Tharmas fled;
The darkening spectre of Urthona hid beneath a rock,
Tharmas threw his impetuous flight through the deeps of
     immensity,
Revolving round in whirlpools fierce all round the caverned
     worlds.

5   But Urizen silent descended to the caves of Orc, & saw
A caverned universe of flaming fire. The horses of Urizen,
Here bound to fiery mangers, furious dash their golden hoofs,
Striking fierce sparkles from their brazen fetters; fierce his lions
Howl in the burning dens, his tigers roam in the redounding smoke
10 In forests of affliction; the adamantine scales of justice
Consuming in the raging lamps of mercy poured in rivers
The holy oil rages through all the caverned rocks. Fierce flames
Dance on the rivers & the rocks, howling & drunk with fury.
The plough of ages & the golden harrow wade through fields
15 Of gory blood; the immortal seed is nourished for the slaughter.
The bulls of Luvah, breathing fire, bellow on burning pastures
Round howling Orc, whose awful limbs cast forth red smoke & fire,
That Urizen approached not near, but took his seat on a rock
And ranged his books around him, brooding envious over Orc.

20 Howling & rending his dark caves the awful demon lay.
Pulse after pulse beat on his fetters, pulse after pulse his spirit
Darted & darted higher & higher to the shrine of Enitharmon;

viia. page 76. A sketch of a male figure, nude, with arms raised.
viia *5ff*. In Orc's cave Urizen sees what Orc stands for: if this fiery creature
had his way, Urizen's own properties and all the universe would be aflame.
viia *7. bound to fiery mangers*] Instead of being out in the fields of light at
Urizen's work.
viia *8–16*. Cp. viib *107–9*, especially the phrase 'the tiger in redounding
smoke', and the bull, lion and tiger.
viia *22*. In v *80–1* Los 'beheld the ruddy boy embracing his bright mother',
and the chain that binds Orc grew from Los's jealousy.
viia *23–6*. An epic simile, leading to the lightning-struck 'blighted tree'
of *27*.

As when the thunder folds himself in thickest clouds,
The watery nations couch & hide in the profoundest deeps,
25   Then bursting from his troubled head with terrible visages &
        flaming hair
His swift-winged daughters sweep across the vast black ocean.

Los felt the envy in his limbs like to a blighted tree,
[78]   For Urizen, fixed in envy, sat brooding & covered with snow.
His book of iron on his knees, he traced the dreadful letters,
30   While his snows fell & his storms beat to cool the flames of Orc,
Age after age, till underneath his heel a deadly root
Struck through the rock—the root of Mystery accursed shooting up
Branches into the heaven of Los. They, pipe-formed, bending down
Take root again, wherever they touch again branching forth
35   In intricate labyrinths, o'erspreading many a grisly deep.

Amazed started Urizen, when he found himself compassed round
And high roofed over with trees. He arose, but the stems
Stood so thick, he with difficulty & great pain brought
His books out of the dismal shade, all but the book of iron.
40   Again he took his seat & ranged his books around
On a rock of iron, frowning over the foaming fires of Orc.

And Urizen hung over Orc & viewed his terrible wrath.
Sitting upon an iron crag at length his words broke forth:

'Image of dread, whence art thou? Whence is this most woeful
        place?
45   Whence these fierce fires but from thyself? No other living thing
In all this chasm I behold. No other living thing

viia *31*. Cp. 'The Human Abstract' in *Experience* (p. 216), *Ahania 103–15*,
and *Jerusalem* pl.28.*14*ff. B. has taken the idea of the tree that roots itself
as its branches touch the ground from the banyan tree; cp. *Paradise Lost*
ix 1101ff: 1104–7 read: 'Branching so broad and long, that in the ground /
The bended twigs take root, and daughters grow / About the mother tree,
a pillared shade / High overarched, and echoing walks between'. B.'s
tree branches above in the heavens, and its roots similarly branch out in
the abyss–an inverted, perverted image of the heavens. Cp. *Marriage*,
iv *139* p. 116. This may owe something to Yggdrasil, the ash of Norse
myth, on whose life the world was said to depend; its roots were spread
in the misty underworld of Niflheim. The overtones of evil are B.'s, but
he knew the Norse myth through P. H. Mallet's *Northern Antiquities*
(1770), which contains a translation of the Edda. Note also how B. associ-
ates the branching of the tree with the branching of the human nerves
and veins, 'pipe-formed' (*Book of Los* ch. iii) and with the other monstrous
image of the *polypus* (*Four Zoas* iv *265*).
viia *42*ff. Note how Urizen and Orc interpret differently what they see.

Dare thy most terrible wrath abide. Bound here to waste in pain
Thy vital substance in these fires, that issue new & new
Around thee; sometimes like a flood, & sometimes like a rock
50   Of living pangs, thy horrible bed glowing with ceaseless fires
Beneath thee & around. Above a shower of fire now beats,
Moulded to globes & arrowy wedges, rending thy bleeding limbs;
And now a whirling pillar of burning sands to overwhelm thee,
Steeping thy wounds in salts infernal & in bitter anguish;
55   And now a rock moves on the surface of this lake of fire
To bear thee down beneath the waves in stifling despair.
Pity for thee moved me to break my dark & long repose,
And to reveal myself before thee in a form of wisdom;
Yet thou dost laugh at all these tortures & this horrible place,
60   Yet throw thy limbs these fires abroad, that back return upon thee;
While thou reposest, throwing rage on rage, feeding thyself
With visions of sweet bliss far other than this burning clime.
Sure thou art bathed in rivers of delight, on verdant fields
Walking in joy, in bright expanses sleeping on bright clouds
65   With visions of delight, so lovely that they urge thy rage
Tenfold with fierce desire to rend thy chain, & howl in fury
And dim oblivion of all woe & desperate repose—
Or is thy joy founded on torment which others bear for thee?'

Orc answered: 'Curse thy hoary brows! What dost thou in this
          deep?
70   Thy pity I condemn; scatter thy snows elsewhere!
[79]   I rage in the deep, for lo! my feet & hands are nailed to the
          burning rock.
Yet my fierce fires are better than thy snows. Shuddering thou
          sittest:
Thou art not chained; why shouldst thou sit cold grovelling,
          demon of woe,
In tortures of dire coldness? Now a lake of waters deep
75   Sweeps over thee, freezing to solid; still thou sitst, closed up
In that transparent rock, as if in joy of thy bright prison,
Till overburdened with its own weight, drawn out through
          immensity,·
With a crash breaking across the horrible mass comes down.
Thundering & hail & frozen iron, hailed from the element,
80   Rends thy white hair; yet thou dost, fixed obdurate, brooding sit,
Writing thy books. Anon a cloud filled with a waste of snows
Covers thee, still obdurate, still resolved, & writing still;
Though rocks roll o'er thee, though floods pour, though winds,
          black as the sea
Cut thee in gashes, though the blood pours down around thy
          ankles,

85 Freezing thy feet to the hard rock, still thy pen obdurate
Traces the wonders of futurity, in horrible fear of the future.
I rage furious in the deep, for lo! my feet & hands are nailed
To the hard rock, or thou shouldst feel my enmity & hate
In all the diseases of man, falling upon thy grey accursed front.'

90 Urizen answered: 'Read my books: explore my constellations:
Enquire of my sons, & they shall teach thee how to war:
Enquire of my daughters, who accursed in the dark depths
Knead bread of sorrow by my stern command: for I am God
Of all this dreadful ruin. Rise, O daughters, at my stern command!'

95 Rending the rocks Eleth & Uveth rose, & Ona rose,
Terrific with their iron vessels, driving them across
In the dim air. They took the book of iron & placed above
On clouds of death, & sang their songs, kneading the bread of Orc.
Orc listened to the song compelled, hungering on the cold wind
That swagged heavy with the accursed dough. The hoar frost raged
100 Through Ona's sieve; the torrent rain poured from the iron pail
Of Eleth, & the icy hands of Uveth kneaded the bread.
The heavens bow with terror underneath their iron hands,
Singing at their dire work the words of Urizen's book of iron,
105 While the enormous scrolls rolled dreadful in the heavens above:
And still the burden of their song in tears was poured forth—
'The bread is kneaded: let us rest, O cruel father of children!'

But Urizen remitted not their labours upon his rock,
[80] And Urizen read in his book of brass in sounding tones:

110 'Listen, O daughters, to my voice! Listen to the words of wisdom!
So shall you govern over all. Let moral duty tune your tongue,
But be your hearts harder than the nether millstone,
To bring the shadow of Enitharmon beneath our wondrous tree:
That Los may evaporate like smoke & be no more;
115 Draw down Enitharmon to the spectre of Urthona,
And let him have dominion over Los the terrible shade.

'Compel the poor to live upon a crust of bread by soft mild arts.
Smile when they frown, frown when they smile; & when a man
    looks pale

viia *89.* So in *America 177ff*, Orc drives the plagues, which originated in
Albion's Angel, servant of Urizen, back again.
viia *95. Eleth, Uveth and Ona*] Urizen's three daughters of vi *5–23*.
viia *117ff.* B. is bitter about the methods of poor relief in his time by
which, as he saw it, the rich kept the poor in poverty while pretending to
help them. Cp. *Song of Los (Asia)*.
viia *122. temper*] Equanimity, 'good' temper, moderation in the face of
provocation.

With labour & abstinence, say he looks healthy & happy—
120   And when his children sicken, let them die. There are enough
Born, even too many, & our earth will be overrun
Without these arts. If you would make the poor live with temper,
With pomp give every crust of bread you give, with gracious cunning
Magnify small gifts, reduce the man to want a gift, & then give
    with pomp:
125   Say he smiles if you hear him sigh; if pale say he is ruddy:
Preach temperance, say he is overgorged & drowns his wit
In strong drink, though you know that bread & water are all
He can afford. Flatter his wife, pity his children, till we can
Reduce all to our will, as spaniels are taught with art.
130   Lo! how the heart & brain are formed in the breeding womb
Of Enitharmon, how it buds with life & forms the bones,
The little heart, the liver & the red blood in its labyrinths:
By gratified desire, by strong devouring appetite, she fills
Los with ambitious fury that his race shall all devour.'

135   Then Orc cried: 'Curse thy cold hypocrisy! Already round thy
    tree,
In scales that shine with gold & rubies thou beginnest to weaken
My divided spirit. Like a worm I rise in peace, unbound
From wrath. Now when I rage, my fetters bind me more:
O torment! O torment! A worm compelled! Am I a worm?
140   Is it in strong deceit that man is born? In strong deceit
Thou dost restrain my fury that the worm may fold the tree.
Avaunt, cold hypocrite! I am chained or thou couldst not use me
    thus.
The man shall rage, bound with this chain; the worm in silence
    creep.
Thou wilt not cease from rage. Grey demon, silence all thy storms:
145   Give me example of thy mildness, king of furious hail-storms!
Art thou the cold attractive power that holds me in this chain?
I well remember how I stole thy light, & it became fire
Consuming. Thou knowest me now, O Urizen, prince of light:
And I know thee! Is this the triumph, this the godlike state
150   That lies beyond the bounds of science in the grey obscure?'

Terrified Urizen heard Orc, now certain that he was Luvah,
And Orc began to organize a serpent body,

viia 130–4. Here Enitharmon is no more than the universal Mother, as in
the Preludium to Europe. The word 'Woman' might be used instead
of her name; similarly in 134, Los might read 'her men-folk'.
viia 147. Orc speaks as Luvah, who stole the light in ii 17; see 151.
viia 152. organize] This usually implies creative activity: yet the next lines
show that Orc's efforts have perverted results.

Despising Urizen's light & turning it into flaming fire,
Receiving as a poisoned cup receives the heavenly wine,
155 And turning affection into fury & thought into abstraction,
A self-consuming dark devourer, rising into the heavens.

Urizen envious brooding sat, & saw the secret terror
Flame high in pride, & laugh to scorn the source of his deceit,
Nor knew the source of his own, but thought himself the sole author
[81] Of all his wandering experiments in the horrible abyss.
161 He knew that weakness stretches out in breadth & length; he knew
That wisdom reaches high & deep, & therefore he made Orc,
In serpent form compelled, stretch out & up the mysterious tree.
He suffered him to climb that he might draw all human forms
165 Into submission to his will; nor knew the dread result.

Los sat in showers of Urizen, watching cold Enitharmon.
His broodings rush down to his feet producing eggs that hatching
Burst forth upon the winds above the Tree of Mystery.
Enitharmon lay on his knees. Urizen traced his verses;
170 In the dark deep the dark tree grew. Her shadow was drawn down,
Down to the roots; it wept over Orc—the shadow of Enitharmon:

Los saw **her** stretched, the image of death, upon his withered
    valleys:
Her shadow went forth & returned. Now she was pale as snow

viia *154. poisoned cup . . . heavenly wine*] An allusion to the Last Supper.
Perhaps 'it' is missing after 'Receiving'.
viia *155. affection*] 1st rdg del. wisdom.
viia *157. envious* of Orc's youth and life.
viia *159. of his own*] Urizen's own deceit. He did not even know that he
was sinful, or that his 'wandering experiments' were the inevitable deeds
of a creature trapped in evil.
viia *164.* Cp. *John* iii 14: 'And as Moses lifted up the serpent in the wilder-
ness, even so must the Son of man be lifted up' and xii 32: 'And I, if I be
lifted up from the earth, will draw all men unto me.' Moses, like Urizen,
is the Lawgiver; and he could never envisage Christ, as Urizen did not
envisage Orc.
viia *166.* The narrative of Los and Enitharmon is taken up from v *183*,
where their wretchedness over Orc's imprisonment and the Chain of
Jealousy is described. The 'husband-and-wife' relationship of v *143–75* is
absent, replaced by the old suspicion (which suggests that v contains later
revisions which the MS does not show). Nor is there any trace in these
lines of Enitharmon's deep grief of v *174–83*. But later in this Night these
return (*319*ff).
viia *171. shadow* here means, not the real Enitharmon, but a phantasm, a
projection of her personality which appeared like her.

When the mountains & hills are covered over & the paths of men
    shut up;
175 But when her spirit returned as ruddy as a morning when
The ripe fruit blushes into joy in heaven's eternal halls,
Sorrow shot through him from his feet; it shot up to his head,
Like a cold night that nips the roots & shatters off the leaves.
Silent he stood o'er Enitharmon, watching her pale face.
180 He spoke not, he was silent, till he felt the cold disease.
Then Los mourned on the dismal wind in his jealous lamentation:

'Why can I not enjoy thy beauty, lovely Enitharmon?
When I return from clouds of grief in the wandering elements,
Where thou in thrilling joy, in beaming summer loveliness
185 Delectable reposest, ruddy in my absence, flaming with beauty;
Cold, pale in sorrow at my approach, trembling at my terrific
Forehead & eyes, thy lips decay like roses in the spring—
How art thou shrunk! Thy grapes that burst in summer's vast
    excess,
Shut up in little purple covering, faintly bud & die.
190 Thy olive trees, that poured down oil upon a thousand hills,
Sickly look forth & scarcely stretch their branches to the plain;
Thy roses that expanded in the face of glowing morn,
[82] Hid in a little silken veil, scarce breathe & faintly shine;
Thy lilies that gave light what time the morning looked forth
195 Hid in the vales faintly lament, & no one hears their voice.
All things beside the woeful Los enjoy the delights of beauty.
Once, how I sang & called the beasts & birds to their delights.
Nor knew that I alone, exempted from the joys of love,
Must war with secret monsters of the animating worlds.
200 Oh that I had not seen the day! Then should I be at rest,
Nor felt the stingings of desire, nor longings after life.
For life is sweet to Los the wretched; to his winged woes
Is given a craving cry that they may sit at night on barren rocks,
And whet their beaks, & snuff the air & watch the opening dawn,
205 And shriek, till at the smells of blood they stretch their bony wings,
And cut the winds like arrows shot by troops of destiny.'

Thus Los lamented in the night, unheard by Enitharmon,
For the shadow of Enitharmon descended down the Tree of
    Mystery.
The spectre saw the shade, shivering over his gloomy rocks

viia *176.* Followed by two deleted lines:

    She secret joyed to see: she fed herself on his despair.
    She said I am avenged for all my sufferings of old.

viia *182–206.* A passage similar to ii *512–18.*
viia *187. in the*] *1st rdg del. in early.*

210   Beneath the Tree of Mystery, which in the dismal abyss
       Began to blossom, in fierce pain shooting its writhing buds
       In throes of birth, & now, the blossoms falling, shining fruit
       Appeared of many colours, & of various poisonous qualities
       Of plagues, hidden in shining globes that grew on the living tree.
215   The spectre of Urthona saw the shadow of Enitharmon
       Beneath the Tree of Mystery among the leaves & fruit.

       Reddening the demon strong prepared the poison of sweet love.
       He turned from side to side in tears, he wept & he embraced
       The fleeting image, & in whispers mild wooed the faint shade:

220   'Loveliest delight of men, Enitharmon—shady hiding
       In secret places, where no eye can trace thy watery way,
       Have I found thee? Have I found thee? Tremblest thou in fear?
       Because of Orc, because he rent his discordant way
       From thy sweet loins of bliss? Red flowed thy blood,
225   Pale grew thy face, lightnings played around thee, thunders
          hovered
       Over thee, & the terrible Orc rent his discordant way.
       But the next joy of thine shall be in sweet delusion,
       And its birth in fainting & sleep, & sweet delusions of Vala.'

       The shadow of Enitharmon answered: 'Art thou, terrible shade,
230   Set over this sweet boy of mine, to guard him lest he rend
[83]   His mother to the winds of heaven? Intoxicated with
       The fruit of this delightful tree, I cannot flee away
       From thy embrace: else be assured, so horrible a form
       Should never in my arms repose. Now listen: I will tell
235   Thee secrets of eternity which ne'er before unlocked
       My golden lips, nor took the bar from Enitharmon's breast—

viia 210. *abyss* See 31n.

viia 214. The tree, which attracts Enitharmon, grows dangerous fruit, and is used by the serpent Orc for his own malicious purposes. It clearly derives from 'the tree of the knowledge of good and evil' (*Genesis* ii 17). But it is the Tree of Mystery, one of B.'s most powerful creations, and its influence is intoxicating (311). The illustration to this page shows a woman turning a starry wheel—Enitharmon on the side of evil—in contrast to p. 104, where the woman is shown pushing the wheel away—on a page where Enitharmon is working for good.

viia 215. B. again uses *Paradise Lost* as a source, where, in ix 494, Satan as a serpent slides up to Eve 'among the leaves and fruit', flatters her and, after a disputation, wins her over. Here Orc is the serpent, but the tempter is the Spectre of Urthona.

viia 217. The adjective *strong* is used solely of Urthona among the Zoas.

viia 228. *sweet*] Written over 'woe'.

Among the flowers of Beulah walked the Eternal Man, & saw
Vala, the lily of the desert: melting in high noon
Upon her bosom in sweet bliss he fainted. Wonder seized
240   All Heaven: they saw him dark; they built a golden wall
Round Beulah. There he revelled in delight among the flowers.
Vala was pregnant & brought forth Urizen, prince of light,
First-born of generation. Then behold, a wonder to the eyes
Of the now fallen Man, a double form Vala appeared! A male
245   And female, shuddering pale: the fallen Man recoiled
From the enormity, & called them *Luvah & Vala*, turning down
The vales to find his way back into Heaven—but found none,
For his frail eyes were faded & his ears heavy & dull.

'Urizen grew up in the plains of Beulah. Many sons
250   And many daughters flourished round the holy tent of man,
Till he forgot Eternity, delighted in his sweet joy
Among his family, his flocks & herds & tents & pastures.

'But Luvah close conferred with Urizen in darksome night,
To bind the father & enslave the brethren. Nought he knew
255   Of sweet Eternity: the blood flowed round the holy tent, & riven
From its hinges, uttering its final groan all Beulah fell
In dark confusion. Meantime Los was born & Enitharmon,
But how I know not; then forgetfulness quite wrapped me up
A period, nor do I more remember, till I stood
260   Beside Los in the cavern dark, enslaved to vegetative forms,
According to the will of Luvah who assumed the place
Of the Eternal Man, & smote him. But thou, spectre dark,
Mayest find a way to punish Vala in the fiery south,
To bring her down subjected to the rage of my fierce boy.'

[84]   The spectre said: 'Thou lovely vision, this delightful tree

viia *237*. Yet another version of the story of the seduction of the Eternal
Man by Vala. Cp. ii *13n*, iii *41*. It does not agree with Enitharmon's Song
in Night ii; but here her shadow has a different purpose in telling the tale.
viia *241*. Cp. iv *84n*. This is not the Beulah of *Milton* pl.30.*1* and the late
additions to *The Four Zoas* (e.g. i *84–9*, iv *248*ff), but the less distinctive
place of iv *88–9*–a simpler and earlier use of Bunyan's Beulah, a 'holiday'
land just outside heaven.
viia *248*. Because he had fallen, he had lost the imaginative power necessary
to live in Heaven.
viia *253*. Another narrative of the seizing of power from the Man by
Urizen and Luvah; cp. i *182*ff. Like the rest of Enitharmon's speech, many
details do not fit the earlier narrative. This is probably her error, but may
be due to B.'s changing mind.
viia *263*. But the south belongs to Urizen: the implication is that something
must be wrong.

266 Is given us for a shelter from the tempests of void & solid,
    Till once again the morn of ages shall renew upon us,
    To reunite in those mild fields of happy Eternity,
    Where thou & I in undivided essence walked about
270 Embodied, thou my garden of delight & I the spirit in the garden.
    Mutual there we dwelt in one another's joy, revolving
    Days of eternity, with Tharmas mild & Luvah sweet melodious
    Upon our waters. This thou well rememberest. Listen I will tell
    What thou forgettest—they in us & we in them alternate lived,
275 Drinking the joys of Universal Manhood. One dread morn—
    Listen, O vision of delight—one dread morn of gory blood
    The Manhood was divided, for the gentle passions, making way
    Through the infinite labyrinths of the heart & through the nostrils
        issuing
    In odorous stupefaction, stood before the eyes of Man,
280 A female bright. I stood beside my anvil dark; a mass
    Of iron glowed bright, prepared for spades & ploughshares:
        sudden down
    I sunk, with cries of blood issuing downward in the veins
    Which now my rivers were become, rolling in tubelike forms
    Shut up within themselves, descending down I sunk along
285 The gory tide even to the place of seed, & there dividing
    I was divided in darkness & oblivion. Thou an infant woe,
    And I an infant terror in the womb of Enion.
    My masculine spirit scorning the frail body issued forth
    From Enion's brain, in this deformed form leaving thee there
290 Till times passed over thee; but still my spirit returning hovered
    And formed a male to be a counterpart to thee, O love
    Darkened & lost. In due time issuing forth from Enion's womb
    Thou & that demon Los wert born. Ah, jealousy & woe!
    Ah, poor divided dark Urthona, now a spectre wandering
295 The deeps of Los, the slave of that creation I created.
    I labour night & day for Los. But listen, thou my vision,
    I view futurity in thee; I will bring down soft Vala
    To the embraces of this terror, & I will destroy
    That body I created. Then shall we unite again in bliss.

300 'Thou knowest that the spectre is—in every man—insane, brutish,
    Deformed—that I am thus a ravening devouring lust, continually
    Craving & devouring. But my eyes are always upon thee, O lovely

viia 265. The tree is only 'lovely and delightful' in the spectre's eyes.
viia 297. This is the punishment asked for by Enitharmon (263).
viia 298. This terror] Orc. This happens in viib.
viia 299. Los, Urthona's fallen form, will vanish in the reunited Urthona.
viia 300. So in i 93–4, and Jerusalem pl.33.4.

Delusion, & I cannot crave for anything but thee; not so
The spectres of the dead, for I am as the spectre of the living.
305   For till these terrors planted round the gates of eternal life
Are driven away & annihilated, we never can repass the gates.'

[85]   Astonished, filled with tears, the spirit of Enitharmon beheld
And heard the spectre. Bitterly she wept, embracing fervent
Her once-loved lord, now but a shade, herself also a shade,
310   Conferring times on times among the branches of that tree.

Thus they conferred among the intoxicating fumes of Mystery,
Till Enitharmon's shadow, pregnant in the deeps beneath,
Brought forth a wonder horrible. While Enitharmon shrieked
And trembled through the worlds above, Los wept. His fierce soul
         was terrified
315   At the shrieks of Enitharmon, at her tossings, nor could his eyes
         perceive
The cause of her dire anguish, for she lay the image of death,
Moved by strong shudders till her shadow was delivered. Then she
         ran
Raving about the upper elements in maddening fury.

She burst the gates of Enitharmon's heart with direful crash,

viia *303. thee; not*] These words are on different lines, the following between
them being deleted:
                              . . . and till
          I have thee in my arms and am again united to Los
          To be one body and one spirit with him. . . .
viia *304*. The spectre of Urthona claims that his longing is for life, so that
he is unlike other spectres, who dream only destructively (whether they
know this or not).
viia *305-6*. So in *Genesis* iii 24 the gate of Paradise was guarded to prevent
the re-entry of mankind. Cp. *Paradise Lost* xii 643-4: '. . . the gate / With
dreadful faces thronged and fiery arms.' Note also B.'s use of the idea of re-
entry into Paradise in *The Gates of Paradise* (p. 841) and in *The Everlasting
Gospel* iii *23-6*: 'The Christian trumpets loud proclaim / Through all the
world in Jesus' name / Mutual forgiveness of each vice– / And oped the
Gates of Paradise.' This is a version of the theme of salvation, central in
B.'s writings and especially, in this form, in the long epics.
viia *312-14*. As Enitharmon's shadow in the abyss brings forth 'a wonder
horrible' the real Enitharmon above suffers in sympathy. Los (*315-16*)
cannot tell why until her shadow 'in the deeps beneath' has given birth.
viia *314-15*. B. makes a space between these lines which the sense does not
require.
viia *319. She*] Somewhat obscure. The general meaning is that because of
this trial Enitharmon's heart was shattered. 'She' is probably Enitharmon's

320 Nor could they ever be closed again; the golden hinges were broken,
And the gates broke in sunder & their ornaments defaced
Beneath the Tree of Mystery. For the immortal shadow shuddering
Brought forth this wonder horrible. A cloud she grew & grew,
Till many of the dead burst forth from the bottoms of their tombs,
325 In male forms without female counterparts or emanations,
Cruel and ravening with enmity & hatred & war,
In dreams of Ulro dark delusive, drawn by the lovely shadow.

The spectre, terrified, gave her charge over the howling Orc.
Then took the Tree of Mystery root in the world of Los,
330 Its topmost boughs shooting a fibre beneath Enitharmon's couch;
The double-rooted labyrinth soon waved around their heads.

But then the spectre entered Los's bosom—every sigh & groan
Of Enitharmon bore Urthona's spectre on its wings.
Obdurate Los felt pity; Enitharmon told the tale
335 Of Urthona. Los embraced the spectre, first as a brother,
Then as another self—astonished, humanizing & in tears,
In self-abasement giving up his domineering lust.

'Thou never canst embrace sweet Enitharmon, terrible demon,
    till

shadow, but may be the 'wonder horrible', Vala, child of the shadow. This
line marks the crisis in Enitharmon's regeneration. For the closing of the
gates, see i *260* and v *177–9*, with v *180n.*
viia *321. broke*] A past participle, equal to *broken* in the previous line. This
form was quite correct, and is commonly found until the early nineteenth
century.
viia *324.* At the Day of Judgment the dead will rise from their graves: B.
has inverted this idea before, e.g. *Europe 147–50* where instead the angels fall
'seeking their graves' when the last trumpet blows. Here there is the idea of
the dead descending into the shadowy land where the roots of the Tree of
Mystery spread. Cp. viib *295.*
viia *325.* Cp. viii *243.*
viia *327. dark*] *1st rdg* del. sweet.
viia *328. terrified*] *1st rdg* smiled &, (the ' &' not deleted). Cp. v *112*: now
Vala tends Orc instead of the spectre, until Orc breaks free (viib *133*) and,
to her delight, 'rends' her (viib *139, 208–10*).
viia *330. boughs . . . fibre*] *1st rdg. del.* branches . . . stem.
viia *332–3.* The spectre is drawn back by the realization that the true
Enitharmon is in sympathy with her shadow, and he hopes to find Los
also in sympathy with himself. These lines are written over *End of the
Seventh Night* erased.
viia *336–7* refer to the spectre.
viia *338.* The spectre speaks: the *demon* is Los.

Thou art united with thy spectre, consummating by pains and
 labours
340 That mortal body, & by self-annihilation back returning
To life eternal. Be assured I am thy real self,
Though thus divided from thee, & the slave of every passion
Of thy fierce soul. Unbar the gates of memory; look upon me,
Not as another, but as thy real self. I am thy spectre,
345 Though horrible & ghastly to thine eyes, though buried beneath
The ruins of the universe. Hear what inspired I speak, & be silent.
Thou didst subdue me in old times by thy immortal strength
When I was a ravening, hungering & thirsting, cruel lust & murder.
If we unite in one, another better world will be
350 Opened within your heart & loins & wondrous brain,
Threefold as it was in Eternity & this the fourth universe
Will be renewed by the three & consummated in mental fires.
But if thou dost refuse, another body will be prepared
[86] For me & thou annihilate, evaporate, & be no more.
355 For thou art but a form & organ of life, & of thyself
Art nothing, being created continually by mercy & love divine.'

Los furious answered: 'Spectre horrible, thy words astound my ear
With irresistible conviction. I feel I am not one of those
Who when convinced can still persist—though furious, controllable
360 By reason's power. Even I, already, feel a world within
Opening its gates, & in it all the real substances
Of which these in the outward world are shadows which pass away.
Come then into my bosom, & in thy shadow arms bring with thee
My lovely Enitharmon. I will quell my fury, & teach
365 Peace to the soul of dark revenge, & repentance to cruelty.'

So spoke Los, & embracing Enitharmon & the spectre.
Clouds would have folded round, in ecstasy & love uniting,
[87] But Enitharmon trembling fled, & hid beneath Urizen's tree.

viia *343–4*. Over *The End of the Seventh Night* erased. (The first 'End'
would have been after *331*, the second after *337*, for *338*ff are in a smaller,
sharper pen.)
viia *356*. In having no eternal life, but going through the endless cycle of
birth and death.
viia *361–2*. Between these lines is a fairly detailed drawing–made before
B. had to use the spaces for text, and filling most of the page–of a nude
female kneeling up, smiling, head on one side, her hands pressing her
breasts. Around the more finished drawing are vaguely sketched loops,
perhaps suggesting children. She is Vala, earth-mother and earth-ruler, who
dominates by the twin female powers of motherhood and seduction: the
poem is drawing towards her triumph. This design was once the tailpiece
for viia, or frontispiece for viib, before lines *338*ff were added.

But mingling together with his spectre, the spectre of Urthona
370 Wondering beheld the centre opened, by Divine Mercy inspired.
He in his turn gave tasks to Los, enormous, to destroy
That body he created—but in vain, for Los performed
Wonders of labour.
They builded Golgonooza; Los labouring builded pillars high,
375 And domes terrific in the nether heavens. For beneath
Was opened new heavens, & a new earth beneath & within:
Threefold, within the brain, within the heart, within the loins,
A threefold atmosphere sublime, continuous from Urthona's world,
But yet having a limit twofold, named *Satan* & *Adam*.

380 But Los stood on the limit of translucence, weeping & trembling,
Filled with doubts, in self-accusation beheld the fruit
Of Urizen's mysterious tree; for Enitharmon thus spake:

'When in the deeps beneath I gathered of this ruddy fruit,
It was by that I knew that I had sinned, & then I knew
385 That without a ransom I could not be saved from eternal death,
That life lives upon death, & by devouring appetite
All things subsist on one another. Thenceforth in despair
I spend my glowing time. But thou art strong & mighty
To bear this self-conviction: take then, eat thou also of
390 The fruit, & give me proof of life eternal, or I die.'

viia *369ff.* What follows, being part of a later text than most of the Night,
is not in the main stream of the narrative of Urizen, Orc and Los in the
ruins of Urizen's universe, but a sort of gloss on it, made probably when
B. was considering his work some time, perhaps a long time, later.
viia *370. the centre*] The centre of the earth, the traditional site of Hell.
viia *371–3.* These lines are an insertion written as one line with strokes
after *destroy* and *performed*–but the second stroke seems partly erased, and
perhaps *372–3* should be a single line.
viia *377. Threefold*] B.'s ideal was fourfold vision, but the threefold vision
had great power. Cp. letter to Butts, 22 Nov. 1802 (p. 475) *83–8*; and i *256.*
viia *378–80.* Cp. *Milton* pl.13.21; the lines mean that the 'threefold at-
mosphere sublime' reached from Urthona's universal world to the nether
heavens, but could not pass below a certain limit of opacity or contraction,
both marks of death. Cp. iv *270n.*
viia *381. beheld*] *1st rdg del.* gathered.
viia *385. ransom*] This line is not a verbal reminiscence, but refers to the
idea (expressed, in order to be upset, by Paul e.g. in *Romans* v 12: 'So
death passed upon all men, for that all have sinned'), that man can only
be saved from eternal death by a ransom–provided by Christ's death.
Enitharmon's despair leads her to think she is doomed, and she wants Los to
prove his possession of eternal life by also eating the supposedly poisonous
fruit (*390*).

Then Los plucked the fruit & ate & sat down in despair,
And must have given himself to death eternal, but
Urthona's spectre, in part mingling with him, comforted him,
Being a medium between him & Enitharmon. But this union
395   Was not to be effected without cares, & sorrows, & troubles
Of six thousand years of self-denial and of bitter contrition.

Urthona's spectre terrified beheld the spectres of the dead:
Each male formed without a counterpart, without a concentring
     vision.
The spectre of Urthona wept before Los, saying: 'I am the cause
400   That this dire state commences; I began the dreadful state
Of separation, & on my dark head the curse & punishment
Must fall, unless a way be found to ransom & redeem.

'But I have thee, my *counterpart vegetating* miraculous:
These spectres have no *counterparts*, therefore they raven
405   Without the food of life. Let us create them counterparts,
For without a created body the spectre is eternal death.'

Los trembling answered: 'Now I feel the weight of stern repentance.
Tremble not so, my Enitharmon; at the awful gates
Of thy poor broken heart I see thee like a shadow, withering
410   As on the outside of existence. But look! behold! take comfort!
Turn inwardly thine eyes, & there behold the Lamb of God
Clothed in Luvah's robes of blood descending to redeem.
O spectre of Urthona, take comfort! O Enitharmon,
Couldst thou but cease from terror & trembling & affright,
415   When I appear before thee in forgiveness of ancient injuries.
Why shouldst thou remember & be afraid? I surely have died in
     pain
Often enough to convince thy jealousy & fear & terror.
Come hither, be patient, let us converse together, because
I also tremble at myself & at all my former life.'

viia *391.* Cp., *Paradise Lost* ix 781: 'Forth reaching to the fruit, she plucked,
she ate.'
viia *396.* The six thousand years of the world, from its supposed creation
in 4004 B.C. to our own time. See *Marriage* iv *66n.*
viia *403-6.* In the margin but marked for insertion. B. evidently was
groping for some word preferable to 'Counterpart'; in the second line
he even left a gap to fill in after 'Counter'; in the first, after deleting the
whole word, he underlined 'Coun' as if to try again. Meanwhile (appar-
ently) he had written and deleted 'Vegetative' or 'Vegetating' above
'Counterpart'; though he rejected it, the only reading B. left us with which
to fill the gap, and make sense in context, is 'Vegetating Counterpart' or
'Counterpart, Vegetating miraculous'.
viia *412.* Cp. ii *309-10,* iii *65n*; also viii *53.* A key image.

420 Enitharmon answered: 'I behold the Lamb of God descending
     To meet these spectres of the dead. I therefore fear that he
     Will give us to eternal death, fit punishment for such
     Hideous offenders—uttermost extinction in eternal pain,
     An ever-dying life of stifling & obstruction, shut out
425 Of existence, to be a sign & terror to all who behold,
     Lest any should in futurity do as we have done in Heaven.
     Such is our state, nor will the Son of God redeem us but destroy.'
[88-89]
[90] So Enitharmon spoke, trembling & in torrents of tears.

     Los sat in Golgonooza in the gate of Luban, where
430 He had erected many porches, where branched the mysterious
          tree,
     Where the spectrous dead wail, & sighing thus he spoke to
          Enitharmon:

     'Lovely delight of men, Enitharmon, shady refuge from furious
          war,
     Thy bosom translucent is a soft repose for the weeping souls
     Of those piteous victims of battle. There they sleep in happy
          obscurity,
435 They feed upon our life; we are their victims. Stern desire
     I feel to fabricate embodied semblances in which the dead
     May live before us in our places & in our gardens of labour
     Which now, opened within the centre, we behold spread abroad,
     To form a world of sacrifice of brothers & sons & daughters,
440 To comfort Orc in his dire sufferings. Look! my fires enlume afresh
     Before my face ascending with delight, as in ancient times.'

viia. Page 88. The only writing on this page, the engraved side of one of
the two leaves (87 and 90), made by cutting in half B.'s print of *Edward and
Elenor* (1793), is the following prose aphorism: 'The Christian Religion
teaches that No Man is Indifferent to you but that every one is Either
your friend or your enemy. He must necessarily be either the one or the
other And that he will be equally profitable both ways if you treat him
as he deserves.'
viia. Page 89 contains the other half of the *Edward and Elenor* engraving.
viia *429. Luban*] See viii *25n.*
viia *436.* Cp. the later lines *452ff*, and *n.*
viia *437. labour*] The change from 'pleasure' (*1st rdg*) looks odd; but B.
felt pleasure in the labours of art. He probably made the change so that the
reader might not think he meant 'enervating pleasure'.
viia *438.* Looking up and around from the centre of a vortex. Cp. vi
184–92.
viia *439. sacrifice*] *1st rdg del.* life and love.
viia *440.* Ever since Orc was bound (v *101*) Los and Enitharmon have
tried to ease his sufferings; this is the only method that has any effect.

Enitharmon spread her beaming locks upon the wind, & said:
'O lovely, terrible Los! wonder of Eternity! O Los, my defence
          and guide!
Thy works are all my joy, & in thy fires my soul delights.
445   If mild they burn in just proportion, & in secret night
And silence build their day, in shadow of soft clouds & dews.
Then I can sigh forth on the winds of Golgonooza piteous forms
That vanish again into my bosom. But if thou, my Los,
Wilt in sweet moderated fury fabricate forms sublime,
450   Such as the piteous spectres may assimilate themselves into,
They shall be ransoms for our souls that we may live.'

So Enitharmon spoke, & Los, his hands divine inspired, began
To modulate his fires studious. The loud roaring flames
He vanquished with the strength of art, bending their iron points
455   And drawing them forth delighted upon the winds of Golgonooza,
From out the ranks of Urizen's war & from the fiery lake
Of Orc, bending down as the binder of the sheaves follows
The reaper, in both arms embracing the furious raging flames.
Los drew them forth out of the deeps, planting his right foot firm
460   Upon the iron crag of Urizen, thence springing up aloft
Into the heavens of Enitharmon in a mightly circle.

And first he drew a line upon the walls of shining heaven,
And Enitharmon tinctured it with beams of blushing love.
It remained permanent, a lovely form inspired, divinely human,
465   Dividing into just proportions. Los unwearied laboured
The immortal lines upon the heavens, till with sighs of love
Sweet Enitharmon, mild entranced, breathed forth upon the wind

viia 450. The spectres (397–8, 404–6) are no more than ghosts; Los will give
them bodies to live in. In them, B. represents the poor, earthly natures of
men.
viia 451. I.e. 'they can then be substitutes for us' (cp. 385n) 'that we may
live'. But the result is different (cp. 477–80).
viia 452. This is followed by a deleted line: 'To hew the caverned rocks of
Dranthon into forms of beauty'. The passage 452–94 is clearly an imagin-
ative interpretation of B.'s own sensation in the act of artistic creation, the
exaltation reaching its height at the end.
viia 453. I.e. 'studious to modulate his fires'.
viia 458. A remarkable image drawn from life: had B. experienced also
the 'fiery' prickling of an armful of wheat?
viia 463. Catherine, B.'s wife, often coloured his engravings for him, and
467–8 may indicate that she helped with the actual printing. The colouring
(which raised the price of an engraving) was often handed out by engravers,

The spectrous dead. Weeping the spectres viewed the immortal works
Of Los, assimilating to those forms, embodied & lovely,
470   In youth & beauty in the arms of Enitharmon mild reposing.

First Rintrah & then Palamabron, drawn from out the ranks of war,
In infant innocence reposed on Enitharmon's bosom.
Orc was comforted in the deeps, his soul revived in them;
As the eldest brother is the father's image, so Orc became
475   As Los, a father to his brethren, & he joyed in the dark lake,
Though bound with chains of jealousy, & in scales of iron & brass.

But Los loved them & refused to sacrifice their infant limbs,
And Enitharmon's smiles & tears prevailed over self-protection.
They rather chose to meet eternal death than to destroy
480   The offspring of their care & pity. Urthona's spectre was comforted,
But Tharmas most rejoiced in hope of Enion's return,
For he beheld new female forms born forth upon the air,
Who wove soft silken veils of covering, in sweet raptured trance,
Mortal & not as Enitharmon, without a covering veil.

485   First his immortal spirit drew Urizen's shadow away,
From out the ranks of war separating him in sunder,
Leaving his spectrous form which could not be drawn away.
Then he divided Thiriel, the eldest of Urizen's sons;
Urizen became Rintrah, Thiriel became Palamabron,
490   Thus dividing the powers of every warrior.
Startled was Los; he found his enemy Urizen now
In his hands—he wondered that he felt love & not hate.
His whole soul loved him; he beheld him an infant
Lovely, breathed from Enitharmon; he trembled within himself.

[End of the Seventh Night (a)]

Night the Seventh (b)

The text of viib has undergone much less alteration than that of viia. The regeneration of Los and Enitharmon in viia is ignored. The only apparently

e.g. to families of children; it was not normally considered 'art'. B. would probably have loathed the idea of subjecting children to the imprisonment of such sweated labour; but in any case every process was to him artistic, and Enitharmon is said to colour 'with beams of blushing love'.
viia *485. his*] Los's.
viia *488.* Cp. *Urizen 430–7* where Urizen's sons Thiriel, Utha, Grodna and Fuzon are born. Rintrah and Palamabron, however, are *Los's* sons: by this B. means that Los has drawn Urizen into his influence–cp. *491–2.*

late material is in *285–98*, though these are not an interpolation in the
present MS, unlike the related passage in iv *246–78*.

B. has made one major textual change; *1–120* originally followed
121–298, but he has inserted clear directions that the two halves of the
Night should be reversed. Night viia ends with signs of hope; in Night viib
all is confusion. We return to the shadow world where Urizen's influence
is at its most malign, and Vala's power is growing. In the first half of the
Night we see three Zoas in turn – Urizen with the fearsome products of his
evil, the secret temple and the cruel machines; the unregenerate Los
opposing him; and Tharmas threatening war. Enitharmon cries out in
fear, but the shadowy troops gather for war.

In the second half (as it now is) Orc appears. In transferring this passage
to the end, B. has delayed till last the revelation of the worst evil. So far the
Zoas have threatened war (e.g. at the end of vi); but it only begins when
Orc breaks free. The time is now ripe; and the now-liberated Orc is the
corrupted serpent form created by Urizen in viia. Vala has tended him,
hoping to seduce him by soft treatment, but he breaks his chain. The war
begins in earnest (viib *141*); Vala joins Urizen's side (*197*) and Orc attacks
her. But 'she joyed in the conflict' (*210*) and the real effect is to destroy
Orc entirely, except for his evil serpent-shadow. Vala delights in the
savagery, since cruel sensuality is her nature, and it is now only a matter of
time before (in Night viii) she can dominate all creation. Yet at this point
she feels, not happiness, but melancholy (*277*), for an evil person, even in
triumph, cannot feel joy. The last lines, however, remind us of the hope of
Beulah.

[91]
[95b]   NIGHT THE SEVENTH [b]

But in the deeps beneath the roots of Mystery in darkest night,
Where Urizen sat on his rock, the shadow brooded:
Urizen saw & triumphed, & he cried to his warriors:

'The time of prophecy is now revolved, & all
5   This universal ornament is mine & in my hands—
The ends of heaven, like a garment will I fold them round me,
Consuming what must be consumed. Then in power & majesty
I will walk forth through those wide fields of endless eternity,
A god & not a man, a conqueror in triumphant glory;
10   And all the sons of everlasting shall bow down at my feet!'

viib *1*. This line is the fifteenth on p. 95. See headnote.
viib *2*. *The shadow*] Vala watching over Orc (viia *328*).
viib *3*. *his warriors*] *1st rdg del.* the Shadowy female.
viib *6*. Cp. *Psalm* civ 2: 'Who coverest thyself with light as with a garment,
who stretchest out the heavens like a curtain.' Note Urizen's association
with light, and B.'s dislike of veils and coverings.
viib *10*. Followed by the deleted line: 'The shadowy voice answered O
Urizen Prince of Light.'

First trades & commerce, ships & armed vessels he builded
   laborious,
To swim the deep; & on the land children are sold to trades
Of dire necessity, still labouring day & night; till all
Their life extinct, they took the spectre form in dark despair:
15 And slaves in myriads in ship-loads burden the hoarse-sounding
   deep,
Rattling with clanking chains. The universal empire groans.

And he commanded his sons found a centre in the deep,
And Urizen laid the first stone, & all his myriads
Builded a temple in the image of the human heart;
[96] And in the inner part of the temple—wondrous workmanship—
20 They formed the secret place, reversing all the order of delight,
That whosoever entered into the temple might not behold
The hidden wonders, allegoric of the generations
Of secret lust, when hid in chambers dark the nightly harlot
25 Plays in disguise, in whispered hymn & mumbling prayer. The
   priests
He ordained, & priestesses clothed in disguises bestial,
Inspiring secrecy, & lamps they bore; intoxicating fumes
Roll round the temple. And they took the sun that glowed o'er Los,
And with immense machines down rolling the terrific orb

viib *19*. Cp. *Genesis* i 26–7: 'God created man in his own image.' Urizen's
temple is merely an imitation, an image, not the real, living thing. This
'temple' is in human form–a body dedicated to a Urizenic life–cp.
I *Corinthians* vi 19: 'Your body is the temple of the Holy Ghost which is in
you.'
viib *21*. *the secret place*] Alludes to *Ezekiel* vii 22, where it refers to the
inmost and holiest part of the temple, where only the High Priest might
enter once a year on the Day of Atonement. B. takes the phrase and
associates it with secret acts, specifically acts of lust. See, in *Ezekiel* viii, the
'abominations' of Babylonian religions: 'creeping things, and abominable
beasts, and all the idols . . .' (verse 10); dark temples thickly clouded with
incense (vv. 11–12); women weeping for Tammuz (v. 14); and men with
their backs to the Jewish temple altar worshipping the sun in the east
(v. 16). B. also uses the phrase *secret place* to indicate the kind of religious
ritual that is reserved for the priesthood alone. This ritual, he believed, was
designed only to deceive the people. The two associations here run to-
gether: in *25* B. may also have had temple prostitution in mind, but these
lines are a wider denunciation of ecclesiastical oppressiveness. The illustration
shows three worshippers at a phallic shrine. Cp. *Jerusalem* pl. 44.*33n*, *34n*.
viib *26*. *bestial*] B. spells it *beastial*, as usual: here he probably means 'imi-
tating beasts'.
viib *29*. *Machines* have objectionable associations to B.; cp. *171–83*.

30 Compelled. The sun reddening, like a fierce lion in his chains
Descended, to the sound of instruments that drowned the noise
Of the hoarse wheels, & the terrific howlings of wild beasts
That dragged the wheels of the sun's chariot, & they put the sun
Into the temple of Urizen to give light to the abyss,
35 To light the war by day, to hide his secret beams by night.
For he divided day & night in different ordered portions—
The day for war, the night for secret religion in his temple.

Los reared his mighty stature: on earth stood his feet; above
The moon his furious forehead, circled with black bursting thunders,
40 His naked limbs glittering upon the dark blue sky, his knees
Bathed in bloody clouds, his loins in fires of war where spears
And swords rage, where the eagles cry & the vultures laugh, saying:
'Now comes the night of carnage, now the flesh of kings & princes
Pampered in palaces for our food, the blood of captains nurtured
45 With lust & murder for our drink. The drunken raven shall
        wander
All night among the slain & mock the wounded that groan in the
        field.'

Tharmas laughed furious among the banners, clothed in blood,
Crying: 'As I will I rend the nations all asunder, rending
The people. Vain their combinations—I will scatter them!
50 But thou, O son, whom I have crowned and enthroned, thee
        strong
I will preserve though enemies arise around thee numberless.
I will command my winds & they shall scatter them, or call
[97] My waters like a flood around thee. Fear not, trust in me,
And I will give thee all the ends of heaven for thy possession.
55 In war shalt thou bear rule, in blood shalt thou triumph for me—
Because in times of everlasting I was rent in sunder,
And what I loved best was divided among my enemies.
My little daughters were made captives, & I saw them beaten
With whips along the sultry sands. I heard those whom I loved
60 Crying in secret tents at night, & in the morn compelled
To labour. And behold, my heart sunk down beneath

viib 37. Followed by the beginning of a line immediately deleted: 'Urizen named it Pande . . .' (i.e. Pandemonium, from *Paradise Lost* i 756).
viib 38. This is not Los, the sensitive artist of the end of viia, but the fierce and callous Los of the original version and of *Europe* 206–8 'in snaky thunders clad'.   *Stature* replaces 'forehead' *del.*
viib 50. Los is the son of Tharmas's spectre in i 179–92; and, e.g., in iv 26 and 131 Tharmas speaks to Los as 'son'. There also they are united against Urizen.
viib 56ff. Tharmas was 'divided' in i 17ff; what follows here is imaginative enlargement on that.

In sighs & sobbings, all dividing, till I was divided
In twain, & lo! my crystal form that lived in my bosom
Followed her daughters to the fields of blood. They left me naked,
65 Alone, & they refused to return from the fields of the mighty.
Therefore I will reward them as they have rewarded me.
I will divide them in my anger, & thou, O my king,
Shalt gather them from out their graves & put thy fetter on them,
And bind them to thee that my crystal form may come to me.'

70 So cried the demon of the waters, in the clouds of Los.
Outstretched upon the hills lay Enitharmon; clouds & tempests
Beat round her head all night; all day she riots in excess.
But night or day Los follows war, & the dismal moon rolls over her,
That when Los warred upon the south reflected the fierce fires
75 Of his immortal head into the north upon faint Enitharmon.
Red rage the furies of fierce Orc, black thunders roll round Los,
Flaming his head, like the bright sun seen through a mist, that
      magnifies
His disc into a terrible vision to the eyes of trembling mortals.

And Enitharmon trembling & in fear uttered these words:

80 'I put not any trust in thee, nor in thy glittering scales;
Thy eyelids are a terror to me, & the flaming of thy crest,
The rushing of thy scales confound me, thy hoarse rushing scales,
And if that Los had not built me a tower upon a rock
I must have died in the dark desert, among noxious worms.
85 How shall I flee, how shall I flee into the tower of Los?

viib 63. *my crystal form*] Enion.

viib 72. As with Los in *38*, this Enitharmon is the unredeemed figure of
Nights i–viia *206*.

viib 77–8. Note the use of direct observation, and cp. *Milton* pl.22.6 and
letter to Butts (22 Nov. 1802, p. 474) 55–8:

> Then Los appeared in all his power:
> In the sun he appeared, descending before
> My face in fierce flames; in my double sight
> 'Twas outward a Sun: inward Los in his might.

viib 79. She addresses Orc, the *shadow of jealousy* of *90* (though it has been
suggested that she addresses Tharmas, that the *glittering scales* are fish-scales
of the sea-god. In this case the *shadow of jealousy* would be Urthona's
spectre).

viib 83. *a tower*] In iv 73–4 Los surrounded her with pillars of fourfold
metals 'in dark prophetic fear' against Orc. (This became Golgonooza, but
here, probably because this is an early text, that development is not
noticed.)

14+B.

My feet are turned backward & my footsteps slide in clay,
And clouds are closed around my tower, my arms labour in vain!
Does not the god of waters in the wracking elements
Love those who hate, rewarding with hate the loving soul?
[98]   And must not I obey the god, thou shadow of jealousy?
91   I cry, the watchman heareth not; I pour my voice in roarings:
"Watchman, the night is thick & darkness cheats my rayey sight."
Lift up, lift up, O Los! awake my watchman, for he sleepeth.
Lift up, lift up! Shine forth, O light; watchman, thy light is out!
95   O Los, unless thou keep my tower, the watchman will be slain.'

So Enitharmon cried upon her terrible earthy bed,
While the broad oak wreathed his roots round her, forcing his dark way
Through caves of death into existence. The beech long-limbed
          advanced
Terrific into the pained heavens. The fruit trees, humanising,
100   Showed their immortal energies in warlike desperation,
Rending the heavens & earths & drinking blood in the hot battle,
To feed their fruit, to gratify their hidden sons & daughters,
That far within the close recesses of their secret palaces
Viewed the vast war & joyed, wishing to vegetate
105   Into the worlds of Enitharmon. Loud the roaring winds
Burdened with clouds howl round the couch. Sullen the woolly
          sheep
Walks through the battle; dark & fierce, the bull his rage
Propagates through the warring earth. The lion raging in flames,
The tiger in redounding smoke, the serpent of the woods
110   And of the waters, & the scorpion of the desert irritate
With harsh songs every living soul. The Prester Serpent runs
Along the ranks crying: 'Listen to the Priest of God, ye warriors!
This cowl upon my head he placed in times of everlasting,
And said:"Go forth & guide my battles. Like the joined spine
115   Of Man I made thee, when I blotted Man from life & light.
Take thou the seven diseases of Man, store them for times to come

viib 96–111. As the war comes nearer, both vegetable and animal creations
are affected by the growing tension.
viib 111–19. the Prester Serpent] (Illustrated on this page of the MS.) An
image of those clergy who use the prestige and authority of religion to
strengthen the most evil acts of state–in particular, to justify wars. In their
arrogance and treachery the cobra's hood becomes the priest's cowl, and
his venom the ecclesiastical power to curse. The name suggests Prester
John, the legendary Christian priest-king of the medieval orient–a figure
bound to be detested by B. The Prester Serpent is not Orc, who is still
bound–though in serpent form–to the Tree of Mystery and the rock.
But he is a realization of Orc; in B.'s terms, a 'son' of Orc.

In store-houses, in secret places that I will tell thee of,
To be my great & awful curses at the time appointed." '
The Prester Serpent ceased. The war-song sounded, loud & strong
120 Through all the heavens: Urizen's web vibrated, torment on
torment.
[91] Thus in the caverns of the grave & places of human seed,
The nameless shadowy vortex stood before the face of Orc.
The shadow reared her dismal head over the flaming youth,
With sighs & howling & deep sobs that he might lose his rage
125 And with it lose himself in meekness, she embraced his fire.
As when the earthquake rouses from his den his shoulders huge
Appear above the crumbling mountain. Silence waits around him
A moment; then astounding horror belches from the centre,
The fiery dogs arise, the shoulders huge appear.
130 So Orc rolled round his clouds upon the deeps of dark Urthona,
Knowing the arts of Urizen were pity & meek affection.
Silent as despairing love & strong as jealousy—
Jealous that she was Vala, now become Urizen's harlot
135 And the harlot of Los & the deluded harlot of the kings of earth,
His soul was gnawn in sunder—
The hairy shoulders rend the links, free are the wrists of fire.
Red rage redounds; he roused his lions from his forests black;

viib 120. Urizen's web] Cp. vi 236-46. After this line B. wrote 'Then I
heard the Earthquake &c' referring to a lost passage–or to some revision
of 126. Next follows the inked, and earlier, direction to bring in 'Thus in
the Caverns of the Grave &c as it stands now'.
viib. 121. This Night originally began here. Thus] 1st rdg Now.
places of human seed] B. again represents the action as taking place in the
universe of the body of the Man: cp. iii 136-7n.
viib 122. Cp. the Preludiums to America and Europe, where the female is
respectively 'the shadowy daughter of Urthona' and 'the nameless
Shadowy Female'. Here the vortex is Vala (134): B. is reusing the same
phrases as in America and Europe for a more developed set of ideas. In
America Urthona's daughter is Orc's loving guard; when he breaks free and
rapes her she is delighted. Here Vala seeks to reduce Orc to her power, in
her character as the seductive, dominating female; Orc refuses her wiles
and ignores her female desirability, later attacking her to try to destroy
her (139-42, 208-9).
Vortex] In Descartes's system, each star is the centre of a vortex, with a
portion of the universe centres on it (cp. Milton pl.15.21n). Vala is a vortex
because she is one of the universal powers: and perhaps because, like a
whirlpool, her empty heart is greedy.
viib 133-7. Cp. America Preludium 21-2. There also, in the Prophecy,
war follows.

They howl around the flaming youth, rending the nameless
　　shadow,
140　And running their immortal course, through solid darkness borne.

Loud sounds the war song round red Orc in his fury,
And round the nameless Shadowy Female in her howling terror,
When all the elemental gods joined in the wondrous song:

'Sound the war trumpet, souls clad in attractive steel!
145　Sound the shrill fife, serpents of war! I hear the northern drum.
Awake, I hear the flappings of the folding banners!

'The dragons of the north put on their armour,
Upon the eastern sea direct they take their course:
The glittering of their horses' trapping stains the vault of night.

150　'Stop we the rising of the glorious king! Spur, spur your clouds
[92]　Of death! O northern drum, awake! O hand of iron, sound
The northern drum! Now give the charge, bravely obscured

With darts of wintry hail. Again the black bow draw;
Again the elemental strings to your right breasts draw,
155　And let the thundering drum speed on the arrows black!'

The arrows flew from cloudy bow all day, till blood
From east to west flowed like the human veins, in rivers
Of life upon the plains of death & valleys of despair:

viib *141. his fury*] *1st rdg* his triumphant fury.
viib *144ff*. This passage is obscure; it is not clear who is involved and who
speaks. Being a song, it may have no narrative meaning, and its events
need not be the events of the poem at this point. It is not even clear whether
the song is meant to contain all of *144–206*. In any case, these lines are
made up of a number of discrete passages: *144–58* (in three-line sts),
159–66, 167–83, 184–206. Lines *144–9, 150–9* seem to be antiphonal, the
first made by those who see the northern armies moving, the second by
someone who commands them. *north* and *iron* are normally attributes of
Urthona, so that Los, as well as Urizen, Vala and Orc, seems to be in-
volved. But the passage is better taken as song than as narrative. The songs
of 'the elemental gods' elsewhere (ii *128ff*, v *42ff*) deal with primeval
history, not present events. See also *161–6n, 167n*.
viib *145–7. northern drum ... dragon of the north*] Besides referring to
Urthona, they may have some reference to the armies of Russia fighting
on the side of reaction in the Napoleonic war.
serpent] A wind-band instrument, now obsolete, but widely used in B.'s
time.
viib *150. the glorious king*] Possibly Urizen, to whom these terms most
often apply. But in the context the phrase might refer to Orc–who,
however, is neither a king nor glorious. See *144n*.
viib *159. victory*] But the battle is renewed in *184*.

'Now sound the clarions of victory, now strip the slain!
160 Clothe yourselves in golden arms, brothers of war!'
They sound the clarions strong, they chain the howling captives,
They give the oath of blood, they cast the lots into the helmet;
They vote the death of Luvah, & they nailed him to the tree;
They pierced him with a spear, & laid him in a sepulchre,
165 To die a death of six thousand years, bound round with desolation.
The sun was black, & the moon rolled a useless globe through
heaven.

—Then left the sons of Urizen the plough & harrow, the loom,
The hammer & the chisel, & the rule & compasses;
They forged the sword, the chariot of war, the battle axe,
170 The trumpet fitted to the battle; & the flute of summer
And all the arts of life they changed into the arts of death,
The hour glass contemned because its simple workmanship
Was as the workmanship of the ploughman; & the water-wheel
That raises water into cisterns broken & burned in fire,
175 Because its workmanship was like the workmanship of the shepherd;
And in their stead intricate wheels invented, wheel without wheel,
To perplex youth in their outgoings, & to bind to labours
Of day & night thy myriads of eternity—that they might file
And polish brass & iron, hour after hour, laborious workmanship,
180 Kept ignorant of the use, that they might spend the days of
wisdom

viib 161–6. This seems to be an intrusive passage; it certainly does not fit
the sequence as a whole (cp. 144n). Luvah is Orc, but Orc is not now
destroyed (cp. 208); Luvah was crushed by Urizen in Night i, and this is a
back-reference to those events.
There are two allusions: to the Druid practice mentioned by Caesar, of
sacrificing prisoners or criminals before a battle, to ensure victory; and,
in 162–4, to the crucifixion. Lines 145–66 associate the Druids, the Romans
at the death of Christ, and contemporary politics in a condemnation of all
such inhumanity.
viib 161–207. These lines recur in Jerusalem pl.65.6–56, with variations.
viib. 167–83. This is the voice of B., not of the 'elemental gods'. Yet their
song is resumed at 184 without comment. Although the MS of page 92
shows no sign of alteration, it seems likely that both this passage and the
preceding six lines (see 161n) were interpolations at an earlier stage of
composition.
viib 172. B. condemns the mechanization of manufacture, especially its
application to armaments.
viib 176. without] 'Outside'.
viib 178–81. The workman at a machine only sees one process, in contrast
with the craftsman who manufactures the whole product.

In sorrowful drudgery to obtain a scanty pittance of bread;
In ignorance to view a small portion & think that all,
And call it 'demonstration', blind to all the simple rules of life.

185 'Now, now the battle rages round thy tender limbs, O Vala!
Now smile among thy bitter tears! Now put on all thy beauty!
Is not the wound of the sword sweet, & the broken bone delightful?
Wilt thou now smile among the slain, when the wounded groan in
the field?

[93] 'Lift up thy blue eyes, Vala, & put on thy sapphire shoes,
O melancholy Magdalen; behold the morning breaks.
190 Gird on thy flaming zone, descend into the sepulchre.
Scatter the blood from thy golden brow, the tears from thy silver
locks;
Shake off the waters from thy wings & the dust from thy white
garments.
Remember all thy feigned terrors on the secret couch,
When the sun rose in glowing morn with arms of mighty hosts
195 Marching to battle, who was wont to rise with Urizen's harps,
Girt as a sower with his seed to scatter life abroad.

'Arise, O Vala! Bring the bow of Urizen, bring the swift arrows
of light!
How raged the golden horses of Urizen, bound to the chariot of
love,
Compelled to leave the plough to the ox, to snuff up the winds of
desolation,
200 To trample the cornfields in boastful neighing! This is no gentle
harp,
This is no warbling brook, nor shadow of a myrtle tree,
But blood, & wounds, & dismal cries & clarions of war,

viib *184*. Vala is the seductress who enjoys the torments of others; the song
asks, ironically, if war is also pleasing to her when she is in the midst of it.
viib *189*. An added line, also found in *Jerusalem* pl.65.38. Mary Magdalene
with other women went down to the grave of Jesus after his death (*Matthew*
xxvii 61, xxviii 1): Luvah's crucifixion here replaces Christ's, for Vala
should have taken the side of Luvah, her counterpart.
viib *193. feigned terrors*] The *couch* is Urizen's; Vala has betrayed Luvah and
turned to Urizen, ousting Ahania. The dawn is no longer heralded by
Urizen with light and music, for he is still with Vala who, by her pretence
of sexual fear, is leading him on and destroying his manhood by luring
him away from his proper tasks.
viib *194–6*. These images are not as confused as they may seem; they are a
compression of images of the sun, for Urizen was once prince of light.
The *glowing morn* is a red, threatening dawn.
viib *195. who*] The sun.

And hearts laid open to the light by the broad grisly sword,
And bowels hidden in hammered steel ripped forth upon the
    ground.
205 Call forth thy smiles of soft deceit; call forth thy cloudy tears.
We hear thy sighs in trumpets shrill when morn shall blood renew.'

So sung the demons of the deep. The clarions of war blew loud.
Orc rent her, & his human form, consumed in his own fires,
Mingled with her dolorous members strewn through the abyss.
210 She joyed in all the conflict, gratified, & drinking tears of woe.
No more remained of Orc but the serpent round the Tree of
    Mystery.
The form of Orc was gone; he reared his serpent bulk among
The stars of Urizen in power, rending the form of life
Into a formless indefinite & strewing her on the abyss,
215 Like clouds upon the winter sky broken with winds & thunders.
This was to her supreme delight. The warriors mourned,
    disappointed;
They go out to war with strong shouts & loud clarions—O pity!
They return with lamentations, mourning & weeping.

Invisible or visible, drawn out in length, or stretched in breadth,
220 The Shadowy Female varied in the war in her delight,
Howling in discontent black & heavy, uttering brute sounds,
Wading through fens among the slimy weeds, making lamentations
To deceive Tharmas in his rage, to soothe his furious soul,

viib *204. in hammered steel*] 1st rdg del. in darkness are.
viib *208.* Vala was Luvah's counterpart; now both are so corrupted that
they can only do violence to one another. Here military and sexual
ferocity are deliberately confused together. Luvah was also consumed by
his own rage (against Urizen) in i *235.*
viib *210.* Although Orc attacks her, Vala 'joys', for she sees that his spirit
is given over to the cruelty by which she reigns. In the left margin are
two lines, the first in pencil and the second in ink, which seem not part of
the text but an aphoristic comment upon it:

> Unorganized Innocence, an Impossibility.
> Innocence dwells with Wisdom but never with Ignorance.

viib *211–3.* Orc has had this serpent form since viia (see notes viia *152, 164*),
as a kind of superficial form or appearance. Now the real Orc has gone,
and only the appearance remains. B.'s use of the serpent image of Orc, as
against the seductive Vala, may invite a Freudian interpretation, but the
imagery is traditional.
viib *220. varied*] Varied her form, as in *219.* She now turns her attention
to Tharmas, having captured Urizen and Orc. She appeals to his sense of
pity, his major attribute.

To stay him in his flight, that Urizen might live, though in pain.
225   He said: 'Art thou bright Enion? Is the shadow of hope returned?'

And she said: 'Tharmas, I am Vala, bless thy innocent face!
Doth Enion avoid the sight of thy blue watery eyes?
Be not persuaded that the air knows this, or the falling dew.'

Tharmas replied: 'O Vala, once I lived in a garden of delight;
[94]   I wakened Enion in the morning & she turned away
231   Among the apple trees, & all the gardens of delight
Swam like a dream before my eyes. I went to seek the steps
Of Enion in the gardens, & the shadows compassed me
And closed me in a watery world of woe, where Enion stood
235   Trembling before me like a shadow, like a mist, like air.
And she is gone, and here alone I war with darkness & death.
I hear thy voice, but not thy form see. Thou & all delight
And life appear & vanish, mocking me with shadows of false hope.
Hast thou forgot that the air listens through all its districts, telling
240   The subtlest thoughts shut up from light in chambers of the moon?'

'Tharmas, the moon has chambers where the babes of love lie hid,
And whence they never can be brought in all eternity
Unless exposed by their vain parents. Lo, him whom I love
Is hidden from me, & I never in all eternity
245   Shall see him. Enitharmon & Ahania, combined with Enion,
Hid him in that outrageous form of Orc which torments me for sin,
For all my secret faults, which he brings forth upon the light
Of day. In jealousy & blood my children are led to Urizen's war
Before my eyes, & for every one of these I am condemned
250   To eternal torment in these flames. For though I have the power
To rise on high, yet love here binds me down; & never, never
Will I arise, till him I love is loosed from this dark chain.'
Tharmas replied: 'Vala, thy sins have lost us heaven & bliss;
Thou art our curse, and till I can bring love into the light
255   I never will depart from my great wrath.'

viib 224. Cp. vi 64–71, where Tharmas proposes to starve Urizen, so that
they might both end their useless lives.
viib 229–32. The *garden of delight*, the *apple trees*, the *morning* hint at the
Garden of Eden, somewhat in the phraseology of the *Song of Songs*.
viib 234. *watery world of woe*] The watery chaos associated with Tharmas in
this poem.
viib 245–6. This is false, but Vala wants Tharmas to believe it, and not
blame her for the first fall of the Man. Tharmas is not deceived (253).
viib 252. *this dark chain*] Orc was bound in the Chain of Jealousy; yet (137)
he has broken it. B. has not troubled to maintain complete consistency;
Orc is really still bound by the sins of all the Zoas.

So Tharmas wailed wrathful, then rode upon the stormy deep,
Cursing the voice that mocked him with false hope, in furious
    mood.
Then she returns, swift as a blight upon the infant bud,
Howling in all the notes of woe to stay his furious rage,
260 Stamping the hills, wading or swimming, flying furious, or falling,
Or like an earthquake rumbling in the bowels of the earth,
Or like a cloud beneath & like a fire flaming in high,
Walking in pleasure of the hills or murmuring in the dales,
Like to a rushing torrent beneath & a falling rock above,
265 A thundercloud in the south, & a lulling voice heard in the
    north.

And she went forth, & saw the forms of life & of delight
Walking on mountains, or flying in the open expanse of heaven.
She heard sweet voices in the winds, & in the voices of birds
That rose from waters; for the waters were as the voice of Luvah,
270 Not seen to her like waters or like this dark world of death.
Though all those fair perfections (which men know only by name)
In beautiful, substantial forms appeared, & served her
As food or drink or ornament, or in delightful works
To build her bowers (for the elements brought forth abundantly
275 The living soul in glorious forms, & every one came forth,
Walking before her shadowy face & bowing at her feet).
But in vain delights were poured forth on the howling melancholy:
For her delight the horse his proud neck bowed & his white mane,
And the strong lion deigned in his mouth to wear the golden bit,
280 While the far beaming peacock waited on the fragrant wind,
To bring her fruits of sweet delight from trees of richest wonders,
And the strong-pinioned eagle bore the fire of heaven in the
    night season.
Wooed & subdued into eternal death the demon lay
In rage against the dark despair, the howling melancholy;
[95a] For far & wide she stretched through all the worlds of Urizen's
    journey,
286 And was adjoined to Beulah, as the polypus to the rock.
Mourning, the daughters of Beulah saw, nor could they have
    sustained

viib 277. in vain ...] Vala, for all her power, cannot know true delight,
for her soul is evil. Only the Eternal Man, when he returns to his true,
balanced nature, can enjoy life in this way. The usurping Zoas, and Vala,
must be unhappy.
viib 283. the demon] Perhaps Tharmas, with whom Vala has been dealing;
but 'demon' usually means Orc.
viib 284. rage against] 1st rdg del. anguish for.
viib 286. polypus] See iv 265n.

14*

The horrid sight of death and torment, but the eternal promise
They wrote on all their tombs and pillars and on every urn;
290 These words—*If ye will believe, your brother shall rise again,*
In golden letters ornamented with sweet labours of love,
Waiting with patience for the fulfilment of the promise divine.

And all the songs of Beulah sounded comfortable notes,
Not suffering doubt to rise up from the clouds of the Shadowy
          Female.
295 Then myriads of the dead burst through the bottoms of their
          tombs,
Descending on the Shadowy Female's clouds in spectrous terror,
Beyond the limit of translucence on the lake of Udan-Adan:
These they named *Satans*, and in the aggregate they named them
          Satan.

[98b]   *End of the Seventh Night [b]*

Night the Eighth

B. has complicated this Night almost as much as the First by his alter-
ations; but his intentions in assembling the material of Night viii are
easier to understand. The theme is *the apparent victory of evil* in its most
dangerous and cruel female form. There are two parallel stories of disaster:
the first (*A*) is the continuation of the story of Urizen and Vala to its
catastrophe in the triumph of Vala, who overcomes Urizen and the
others (*468*). This ends in laments from Ahania and–more hope-
fully–Enion. This, the original story, was then elaborated. In (*B*.) the
material of the second story, already met in the earlier Nights, emerges in
the Council of God and the redeemed Los and Enitharmon, who watch over
the unfolding tragedy. (Thus Los appears in two forms: the fierce, unre-
generate Los of (*A*), and the labouring prophet of (*B*), who was regenerated
in viia.) The major new development–which becomes the central theme
–is that the Lamb of God has taken the place (*53–6*) of Urizen's chief
enemy and victim, Luvah; and neither Urizen not Vala can destroy his
Divine Humanity, though they must seem to. He must suffer the death they
condemn him to, so that in ix his life may spread through everything
they have corrupted. There is also (*C*) the introduction of Jerusalem, who

viib *289. urn*] Funeral urn (as stated in *Jerusalem* pl.53.28; cp. also pl.11.2n).
viib *290 John* xi 23, 25, 40: see also iv 252–69, where B. uses extensively
the story of the resurrection of Lazarus, from which this saying comes.
viib *295.* Cp. viia *324* and note.
viib *297–8.* For *limits* see iv *270n*; the idea is taken up in viii 3. The
spectrous dead are a multitude of various spirits: the saying 'Satan is abroad
in the world' means that a variety of persons, all in the same State, or
of the same nature, are active. The collective result of their actions is
satanic–is Satan.

is the biblical figure, a city and a people seen as a woman, beloved though weak and sometimes faithless. This receives less emphasis, but remains an important theme, for Jerusalem counterbalances Vala.

The earliest state of the present MS contained the narrative thus elaborated: and the specifically Christian material is still further elaborated by the later additions. The original story (A), in which Vala first flatters, then overcomes Urizen, and thereafter the other Zoas, remains undeveloped except by additions which bring it into line with the new. The additions are: (D) the enemies of Jesus, the Lamb of God, are Urizen and Vala; but these are enlarged into a council, the *Synagogue of Satan*, in the midst of whom appears a still greater evil, the harlot Rahab. The Synagogue is another image of Urizen, and Rahab is a form of Vala. Thus we now have the two parallel myths in full, and two climaxes—the triumph of Vala over the Zoas (A); and (B) the apparent triumph of Rahab (dominating the Synagogue) over Jesus at the crucifixion (*313–18*). These are in effect the same thing; a vision and its reinterpretation.

(E) Into this fits a further refinement of Rahab, her 'daughter' Tirzah, who is the sum of all the heathen; she is revealed in her song. (F) In a long and puzzling addition, Los faces Rahab and tells how many of his sons and daughters, of whom the unfallen Satan was one, were led astray and separated into a little round world (our world) which was guarded by a succession of emissaries, leading up to Jehovah—and then Jesus. At this point, in a crowning line of rhetoric (*395*) the meaning of the digression becomes clear; Los is telling Rahab that her triumph is vain, for by causing the death of Jesus she has permitted life to enter into her world of death—as the divine mercy had planned.

Thus the Night may be analysed roughly as follows (an asterisk indicates an added page), though close study will reveal this as only an approximate guide.

(B)	The Council of God and the work of Los	(*1– 56*)
(A)	Urizen restarts his war, but succumbs to Vala	(*52–173*)
(C)	Jerusalem appears	(*174–191*)
	(B, D) Los and Enitharmon versus Satan and Rahab	(*192–236*)★
(B)	The Lamb confronts the Synagogue of Satan	(*237–266*)
(D)	Rahab appears among the Synagogue	(*267–283*)
	(E) The song of Tirzah	(*283–310*)
(B, C)	The crucifixion	(*311–328*)
	(F) Los's children	(*329–401*)★★★
(A)	Urizen's fall and Vala's ultimate triumph	(*402–471*)
(A)	The laments of Ahania and Enion	(*472–571*)
(B, C, D)	The triumph of Rahab	(*572–582*)
(D)	Rahab's changing form	(*583–599*)★

The reader who finds the sequence difficult would do well to miss out at the first reading the passages indented in this table. The sequence of lettering (A) to (F) does not indicate a chronological sequence of composition except conjecturally and approximately.

[99]   NIGHT THE EIGHTH
      Then all in great Eternity met in the Council of God
      As one Man, even Jesus, upon Gilead & Hermon,
      Upon the limit of contraction to create the fallen Man.
      The fallen Man stretched like a corse upon the oozy rock
    5 Washed with the tides, pale, overgrown with weeds
      That moved with horrible dreams. Hovering high over his head
      Two winged immortal shapes, one standing at his feet
      Toward the east, one standing at his head toward the west,
      Their wings joined in the zenith overhead.
   10 Such is a vision of all Beulah hovering over the sleeper.

      The limit of contraction now was fixed & man began
      To wake upon the couch of death. He sneezed seven times.
      A tear of blood dropped from either eye; again he reposed
      In the Saviour's arms, in the arms of tender mercy & loving
          kindness.

   15 Then Los said: 'I behold the Divine Vision through the broken
          gates
      Of thy poor broken heart'—astonished, melted into compassion
          and love.
      And Enitharmon said, 'I see the Lamb of God upon Mount Zion.'
      Wondering with love & awe they felt the Divine Hand upon them.

      For nothing could restrain the dead in Beulah from descending
   20 Unto Ulro's night; tempted by the Shadowy Female's sweet

viii *1. met in*] *1st rdg del.* which is called.
viii *2. Gilead and Hermon*] Mountains on the borders of the Holy Land,
and 'upon the limit'–as far out on the frontier as an eternal human being
may safely go without dissolution: see iv *270n.*
viii *3.* i.e. to give the Man a body (which will keep a semblance of reality)
when he has reached the limit beyond which he could pass only to go into
non–entity–to cease to be. So it is with Albion in *Jerusalem.* The Night
opens with the Man in a state of inner warfare–the war of Urizen–but
with the prophetic voice of Los now audible within him.
viii *4–9.* For two distinct cancelled passages, see appendix, p. 464 below.
This passage describes one of B.'s own pictures, *Christ in the Sepulchre*
(1800–05), reproduced in Blunt, *The Art of W.B.* (1959) pl.37b.
viii *11. limit of contraction*] See iv *270n.*
viii *12.* In 2 *Kings* iv 35, the Shunammite child, when Elisha restored him
to life, sneezed seven times.
viii *15. Then Los said I behold*] *1st rdg del.* Then Los beheld; *2nd rdg.* Then
first Los beheld. This takes up from the end of viia; this is the new, recon-
ciled pair.
viii *19.* Referring to viib *295.*

Delusive cruelty they descend away from the daughters of Beulah
And enter Urizen's temple. Enitharmon pitying & her heart
Gates broken down, they descend through the gate of pity,
The broken heart-gate of Enitharmon. She sighs them forth upon
    the wind
25 Of Golgonooza: Los stood receiving them—
For Los could enter into Enitharmon's bosom & explore
Its intricate labyrinths, now the obdurate heart was broken—
[100a] From out the war of Urizen & Tharmas receiving them,
Into his hands. Then Enitharmon erected looms in Luban's gate
30 And called the looms *Cathedron*; in these looms she wove the
    spectres
Bodies of vegetation, singing lulling cadences to drive away
Despair from the poor wandering spectres, and Los loved them

viii 22. *Urizen's temple*] The 'secret temple' of viib 20ff.

viii 24. *Enitharmon*] Followed by a deletion: 'which joins to Urizen's
temple / Which is the Synagogue of Satan. . . .'

viii 25. GOLGONOOZA] Cp. v 73n, viia 429, *Milton* pl.27(26).25 and especially
Jerusalem pls 12.21–14.34, where the picture of Golgonooza is most
elaborated. So far in *Four Zoas*: (a) it is built in Ulro, region of chaos and
darkness, in the grim forest valleys of *Entuthon Benithon*, near the dark lake
of *Udan-Adan* (q.v. *Jerusalem* pl.13.38). (b) Its purpose is to act as a city of
guard, to keep watch on Ulro and to serve as a refuge for spirits fleeing
from death in Ulro. Los also tries to dissuade those who, in despair, want
to leave it. Golgonooza thus resembles Nehemiah's Jerusalem, a city being
built in a hostile land, where watch had to be kept continually. (c) In *Four
Zoas* viia (33, 374–82, 429–31) the Tree of Mystery grows up through
Golgonooza in the porch of Luban, and Los has to watch it; but this is not
referred to elsewhere, and the idea seems to be dropped. (d) The Porch or
Gate of *Luban*, facing East towards the lands of darkness (viii 214) is the
gate where Los keeps special watch. All spirits passing between Ulro and
Golgonooza, coming or going, pass through it. Enitharmon's looms,
called *Cathedron*, are built in Luban, and here she works at her redemptive
weaving, by which she creates the clothing of human form for lost–i.e.
formless–souls. Like Los, she must be at hand to help those who seek
refuge in Golgonooza, and those whose despair is drawing them out.

viii 28–9. Between these lines a marginal note 'Los stood &c' is resonably
interpreted in *Erdman 1965* to mean that nearly all p. 90 (viia 429–92) was
once intended to go here. Thus viia 492 'In his hands' would become
viii 29 'Into his hands'. Pp. 87/90 are one consecutive late passage, written
on distinctive sheets, and B. may well have been uncertain whether or not
to put half of it later–jumping viib, which consists almost entirely of early
material in which B. was losing interest. For the detailed comment, see
Erdman 1965 (p. 758) where the conclusion is reached that B.'s latest de-
cision was to leave the passage where it now is.

With a parental love, for the Divine Hand was upon him
And upon Enitharmon, & the Divine Countenance shone
35 In Golgonooza. Looking down the daughters of Beulah saw
With joy the bright light, & in it a human form;
And knew he was the Saviour, even Jesus, & they worshipped.

Astonished, comforted, delighted, in notes of rapturous ecstasy
All Beulah stood astonished. Looking down to eternal death
40 They saw the Saviour beyond the pit of death & destruction.
For whether they looked upward they saw the Divine Vision,
Or whether they looked downward still they saw the Divine Vision
Surrounding them on all sides beyond sin & death & Hell.

Enitharmon wove in tears, singing songs of lamentation
45 And pitying comfort, as she sighed forth on the wind the spectres;
Also the vegetated bodies which Enitharmon wove
Opened within their hearts & in their loins & in their brain
To Beulah, & the dead in Ulro descended from the war
Of Urizen & Tharmas & from the Shadowy Female's clouds.

50 And some were woven single & some twofold, & some threefold,
In head or heart or reins, according to the fittest order
Of most merciful pity & compassion to the spectrous dead.
[101a] When Urizen saw the Lamb of God clothed in Luvah's robes
Perplexed & terrified he stood (though well he knew that Orc
55 Was Luvah—but he now beheld a new Luvah, or one
Who assumed Luvah's form & stood before him opposite).
But he saw Orc, a serpent-form augmenting times on times
In the fierce battle, & he saw the Lamb of God & the world of Los
Surrounded by his dark machines. For Orc augmented swift
60 In fury, a serpent wondrous among the constellations of Urizen.
A crest of fire rose on his forehead, red as the carbuncle;
Beneath down to his eyelids scales of pearl, then gold & silver
Immingled with the ruby, overspread his visage down
His furious neck writhing contortive; in dire budding pains

viii 36. human] Equal to divine.
viii 44–52. Cp. viia 467. Enitharmon continues the saving task of giving
form to the spectres who would otherwise vanish. It is an inferior, *vegetated*
form, but better than non-entity. For the threefold order of 50–1, see i 94
and especially *Milton* pl.5.6–10.
viii 52. Lines 82–93 originally followed here.
viii 53ff. Urizen is perplexed by his failure to subdue all things to order.
B. deliberately stresses the confusion; and the ambiguity helps him to turn
away from Golgonooza and back to the battle scene.
The Lamb of God] Cp. viia 151 and 411–12. Luvah, as Orc, has deteriorated
into the serpent: but the Lamb has taken his place.
viii 60. Cp. viib 212–13. There is a lesser constellation named *Serpens*.

65 The scaly armour shot out. Stubborn down his back & bosom
    The emerald, onyx, sapphire, jasper, beryl, amethyst
    Strove in terrific emulation which should gain a place
    Upon the mighty fiend—the fruit of the mysterious tree
    Kneaded in Uveth's kneading-trough. Still Orc devoured the food
70 In raging hunger; still the pestilential food in gems & gold
    Exuded round his awful limbs, stretching to serpent length
    His human bulk, while the dark Shadowy Female brooding over
    Measured his food morning & evening in cups & baskets of iron.

    With tears of sorrow incessant she laboured the food of Orc—
75 Compelled by the iron-hearted sisters, daughters of Urizen—
    Gathering the fruit of that mysterious tree, circling its root
    She spread herself through all the branches in the power of Orc.

    Thus Urizen in self-deceit his warlike preparations fabricated.
    And when all things were finished, sudden waved among the stars,
80 His hurtling hand gave the dire signal. Thunderous clarions blow,
    And all the hollow deep rebellowed with the wondrous war.

viii 66. Five of the jewels are among the twelve used in the garnishing of
the Holy City in *Revelation* xxi 19–20, where only onyx does not appear
(but sardonyx, one of its varieties, does). In Ezekiel's condemnation of Tyre,
'the covering cherub', *Ezekiel* xxviii 13 reads: 'every precious stone was
thy covering, the sardius, topaz and the diamond, the beryl, the onyx and
the jasper, the sapphire, the emerald, and the carbuncle, and gold.' The
allusion is to the *Covering Cherub* (see *Milton* 37.8n).
viii 68. *Upon the mighty fiend*] 1st rdg del. On the immortal fiend.
viii 69. *Uveth*] Cp. viia *95–102*. The food she and her sisters prepare for
Orc keeps him in subjection to Urizen, in spite of his hostility.
viii 72–3. (Cp. *America* Preludium *1–4*.) This seems to contradict viib,
where Orc broke free from the Shadowy Female, Vala: there is a similar
contradictory mention of the chain in viib *252*. As myth, this is explicable
in that Orc's spirit is enslaved by Urizen, even after he has broken free.
As yet Vala is controlled by Urizen's daughters; later in viii she dominates
Urizen himself. This echoes her servitude to Urizen when tending Luvah
in ii *425–7*.
viii 74. *laboured*] The syntax is not clear, but the sense is. B. has no punctua-
tion at all in *74–7*.
viii 76. *circling its root*] So also in *165*. In Norse myth the world-ash Ygg-
drasil was encircled by a serpent which attacked its roots and at the last day
brought it down. Vala is as fateful.
viii 78–81. Urizen prepares a new offensive. So the Treaty of Amiens in
1802 was used to prepare for more war, which came in 1803. The following
lines may have been inspired by new devices of war, which were being
eagerly developed by numerous enthusiasts at the turn of the century.
viii 79–80. Originally: 'his hurtling hand / Among the stars.'

[100b] But Urizen his mighty rage let loose in the mid-deep.
    Sparkles of dire affliction issued round his frozen limbs,
    Horrible hooks & nets he formed, twisting the cords of iron
85 And brass, & molten metals cast in hollow globes, & bored
    Tubes in petrific steel, & rammed combustibles, & wheels
    And chains & pullies fabricated all round the heavens of Los—
    Communing with the serpent of Orc in dark dissimulation,
    And with the Synagogue of Satan in dark sanhedrim,
90 To undermine the world of Los & tear bright Enitharmon
[101a] To the four winds, hopeless of future. All futurity
    Seems teeming with endless destruction, never to be repelled:
    Desperate remorse swallows the present in a quenchless rage.

    Terrified & astonished, Urizen beheld the battle take a form
95 Which he intended not: a shadowy hermaphrodite black & opaque—
    The soldiers named it Satan—but he was yet unformed & vast.
    Hermaphroditic it at length became, hiding the male
    Within as in a tabernacle, abominable, deadly.

    The battle howls; the terrors, fired, rage in the work of death.
100 Enormous works Los contemplated, inspired by the Holy Spirit.
    Los builds the walls of Golgonooza against the stirring battle,
    That only through the gates of death they can enter to Enitharmon;
    Raging they take the human visage & the human form,

viii *83. Paradise Lost* vi *766*: 'Of smoke and bickering flame, and sparkles dire.'

viii *85–6. globes*] Perhaps shrapnel (cannon balls were solid), which was tested on the Thames in 1803; the *tubes* are cannon.

rammed combustibles] The explosives rammed down a muzzle-loading cannon.

viii *89.* This reads like an added line, though it is not so in the MS. The *Synagogue of Satan* is a council, opposed to the *Council of God*, and only active in this Night (cp. *261*ff). B. uses the idea to link Urizen, the villain of his original story, with his newer conception of Vala and Satan opposing the Divine Vision and the Council of God, with Christ in Luvah's sacrificial robes of blood (*262*) and their servants Los and Enitharmon (*90*). In *John* xi 47, after the raising of Lazarus (for which see iv *252*ff and viib *290*) 'then gathered the chief priests and the pharisees a council' to concert their antagonism to Jesus. See also *Revelation* ii 9: 'I know the blasphemy of them which say they are Jews, and are not, but are the synagogue of Satan.' For a different imaginative interpretation of the same idea, cp. ix *265–9*.

viii *94–8.* Written in the margin without a guide-line, but probably meant to come at the end of the transferred passage *82–93*, which ends here.

viii *95. hermaphroditic*] *1st rdg del.* male. See notes at *Milton* pls 14.*37*, 37.*6–8.*

Feeling the hand of Los in Golgonooza, & the force
105 Attractive of his hammers beating, & the silver looms
Of Enitharmon singing lulling cadences on the wind.
They humanize in the fierce battle, where in direful pain
Troop by troop the bestial droves rend one another; sounding loud
The instruments of sound, & troop by troop in human forms they urge
[102] The dire confusion till the battle faints. Those that remain
111 Return in pangs & horrible convulsions to their bestial state.
For the monsters of the elements, lions or tigers or wolves,
Sound loud the howling music, inspired by Los & Enitharmon
sounding loud. Terrific men
They seem to one another, laughing terrible among the banners;
115 And when, the revolution of their day of battles over,
Relapsing in dire torment, they return to forms of woe,
To moping visages returning, inanimate though furious,
No more erect though strong, drawn out in length they ravin
For senseless gratification, & their visages thrust forth
120 Flatten above & beneath, & stretch out into bestial length.
Weakened they stretch beyond their power in dire droves till war begins,
Or secret religion in their temples, before secret shrines.

And Urizen gave life & sense by his immortal power
To all his engines of deceit, that linked chains might run
125 Through ranks of war spontaneous, & that hooks & boring screws
Might act according to their forms by innate cruelty.
He formed also harsh instruments of sound
To grate the soul into destruction, or to inflame with fury
The spirits of life, to pervert all the faculties of sense
130 Into their own destruction—if perhaps he might avert
His own despair, even at the cost of every thing that breathes.

Thus in the temple of the sun his books of iron & brass
And silver & gold he consecrated, reading incessantly
To myriads of perturbed spirits through the universe.

viii *102. they*] The 'terrors' (*99*) who wish to destroy Enitharmon. But Los forces them instead to 'humanize' (*107*)–the first step towards redemption–so that she can try to work on them.

viii *106.* The *cadences* come from the tinkling of the weights hanging from the loom: cp. *Milton* pl.6.5–6.

viii *108. bestial*] B. spells it *beastial*, perhaps with deliberate semantic intention.

viii *124. linked chains*] Chain-shot, twin pieces of shot joined by a short chain.

viii *127–8.* Meaning trumpets, drums, pipes, etc. used in war.

135   They propagated the deadly words, the Shadowy Female absorbing
        The enormous sciences of Urizen, ages after ages exploring
        The fell destruction. And she said: 'O Urizen, prince of light,
        What words of dread pierce my faint ear! What falling shows
            around
        My feeble limbs enfold my destined misery!
140   I alone dare the lash abide to sit beneath the blast
        Unhurt, & dare the inclement forehead of the king of light;
        From dark abysses of the times remote fated to be
[103]   The sorrower of eternity, in love with tears. Submiss I rear
        My eyes to thy pavilions: hear my prayer, for Luvah's sake!
145   I see the murderer of my Luvah clothed in robes of blood—
        He who assumed my Luvah's throne in times of everlasting.
        Where hast thou hid him whom I love? In what remote abyss
        Resides that god of my delight? Oh, might my eyes behold
        My Luvah! Then could I deliver all the sons of god
150   From bondage of these terrors, & with influences sweet,
        As once in those eternal fields, in brotherhood & love
        United we should live in bliss, as those who sinned not.
        The Eternal Man is sealed by thee, never to be delivered.
        We are all servants to thy will, O king of light! Relent
155   Thy furious power, be our father & our loved king!
        But if my Luvah is no more, if thou hast smitten him
        And laid him in the sepulchre, or if thou wilt revenge
        His murder on another, silent I bow with dread.

        'But happiness can never come to thee, O king, nor me,
160   For he was source of every joy that this mysterious tree
        Unfolds in allegoric fruit. When shall the dead revive?
        Can that which has existed cease, or can love & life expire?'

        Urizen heard the voice & saw the shadow. Underneath
        His woven darkness, & in laws & deceitful religions,
165   Beginning at the Tree of Mystery, circling its root,
        She spread herself through all the branches in the power of Orc,
        A shapeless & indefinite cloud, in tears of sorrow incessant,
        Steeping the direful web of religion. Swagging heavy it fell
        From heaven to heaven through all its meshes, altering the
            vortexes,

viii *145–6*. Referring to Christ: Vala is lying, cp. ii *106* and viii *53*. Urizen
caused the death of Luvah. Her baneful influence has itself caused the
bondage she says she can abolish. But she imagines Urizen to be Lord of
all and in this light misinterprets the vision of Christ as Luvah.
viii *149–150*. Cp. ii *317–18*, where Luvah speaks.
viii *150*. *these terrors*] 1st rdg del. the human form.
viii *153*. Similar to iv *132*.
viii *156–7*. This happened at viib *164–5*.

170 Misplacing every centre. Hungry desire & lust began,
        Gathering the fruit of that mysterious tree, till Urizen,
        Sitting within his temple furious, felt the numbing stupor;
        Himself tangled in his own net in sorrow, lust, repentance.

        Enitharmon wove in tears, singing songs of lamentations
175 And pitying comfort, as she sighed forth on the wind the spectres
        And wove them bodies, calling them her beloved sons and
                daughters,
        Employing the daughters in her looms; & Los employed the sons
        In Golgonooza's furnaces, among the anvils of time & space,
        Thus forming a vast family, wondrous in beauty & love.
180 And they appeared a universal female form, created
        From those who were dead in Ulro, from the spectres of the dead.

[104a] And Enitharmon named the female Jerusalem the holy;
        Wondering she saw the Lamb of God within Jerusalem's veil—
        The Divine Vision, seen within the inmost deep recess
185 Of fair Jerusalem's bosom, in a gently beaming fire.

        Then sang the sons of Eden round the Lamb of God, & said:
        'Glory! Glory! Glory to the holy Lamb of God,
        Who now beginneth to put off the dark satanic body!
        Now we behold redemption. Now we know that life eternal
190 Depends alone upon the Universal Hand, & not in us
        Is aught but death, in individual weakness sorrow & pain.

[113a] 'We behold with wonder Enitharmon's looms & Los's forges,

        viii *172*. The beginning of the end. Vala's acts gradually envelop all the
        Zoas in this 'numbing stupor'.
        viii *174-5*. So in *44-5* above. From here to *402* B. turns from Urizen and
        treats the triumph of evil in another form–Satan and Rahab at the cruci-
        fixion of Christ.
        viii *181*. Cp. viia *214n*, on illustration to p. 82.
        viii *182*. *Jerusalem* here is the sum of all lost souls seeking redemption.
        Normally she is the emanation of Albion, the Eternal Man (i *240*). This
        passage may well be B.'s original poetic vision of Jerusalem, derived from
        the biblical image of the personified city, beloved by God in spite of her
        disobedience and–particularly in *Revelation*–his bride. B. brings in this
        image of redemption just as Urizen's world is coming to its destined
        catastrophe.
        viii *192-228*. These lines, written on a separate sheet with directions for
        their insertion here, use the idiom of *Milton* and *Jerusalem*. Rahab and
        Tirzah, etc., do not belong to the earlier form of *Four Zoas*, though B.
        assimilates them in Night viii by equating them with the triumphant Vala.
        See *174n* and *267n*.

And the spindles of Tirzah & Rahab, and the mills of Satan and
 Beelzeboul.
In Golgonooza Los's anvils stand & his furnaces rage;
195 Ten thousand demons labour at the forges, creating continually
The times & spaces of mortal life—the sun, the moon, the stars
In periods of pulsative furor; beating into wedges & bars,
Then drawing into wires the terrific passions & affections
Of spectrous dead. Thence to the looms of Cathedron conveyed
200 The daughters of Enitharmon weave the ovarium & the integument
In soft silk, drawn from their own bowels in lascivious delight,
With songs of sweetest cadence to the turning spindle & reel,
Lulling the weeping spectres of the dead, clothing their limbs
With gifts & gold of Eden. Astonished, stupefied with delight,
205 The terrors put on their sweet clothing on the banks of Arnon,
Whence they plunge into the river of space for a period till
The dread sleep of Ulro is past. But Satan, Og & Sihon
Build mills of resistless wheels to unwind the soft threads, and
 reveal
Naked of their clothing the poor spectres before the accusing
 heavens,
210 While Rahab & Tirzah far different mantles prepare, webs of
 torture,
Mantles of despair, girdles of bitter compunction, shoes of
 indolence,
Veils of ignorance, covering from head to feet with a cold web.

'We look down into Ulro: we behold the wonders of the grave.
Eastward of Golzonooza stands the lake of Udan-Adan in
215 Entuthon Benithon, a lake not of waters but of spaces,
Perturbed, black & deadly in its islands & its margins.
The mills of Satan and Beelzeboul stand round the roots of
 Urizen's tree,

viii *193. Satan* is a miller in the Bard's Song in *Milton* pl.8.*4–5* etc., where
he has his accepted place in Eden before his fall. Here he is working
against Los (see *207*ff), in his traditional form.
viii *194.* Followed by two deleted lines, which are used in another context
in *Milton* pl.24.*63–4*:

> The hard dentant hammers are lulld by the flute lula lula
> The bellowing furnaces blare by the long sounding Clarion.

viii *205. Arnon*] 1st rdg del. the Moon. The Arnon being a border of Israel
(see map, p. *575*), the souls are seen to be standing on the brink of earthly
life. Cp. also *Milton* pl.34.*30*, where B. uses the fact that the Arnon flows
into the *Dead* Sea.
viii *207. Og and Sihon*] Enemies of the Israelites, i.e. of God's chosen people.
Cp. *Milton* pl.22.*33*.

For this lake is formed from the tears & sighs & death sweat of
    the victims
Of Urizen's laws, to irrigate the roots of the Tree of Mystery.
220   They unweave the soft threads, then they weave them anew in the
    forms
Of dark death & despair, & none from eternity to eternity could
    escape,
But thou, O universal humanity, who is one Man blessed for ever,
Receivest the integuments woven. Rahab beholds the Lamb of
    God:
She smites with her knife of flint, she destroys her own work
225   Times upon times, thinking to destroy the Lamb blessed for ever.
He puts off the clothing of blood, he redeems the spectres from
    their bonds,
He awakes the sleepers in Ulro. The daughters of Beulah praise
    him:
They anoint his feet with ointment, they wipe them with the hair
    of their head.

[104b] 'We now behold the ends of Beulah, & we now behold
Where death eternal is put off eternally.
231   Assume the dark satanic body in the virgin's womb,
O Lamb Divine; it cannot thee annoy, O pitying one.
Thy pit is from the foundation of the world, & thy redemption
Begun already in eternity. Come then, O Lamb of God!
235   Come, Lord Jesus, come quickly!'

So sang they in Eternity looking down into Beulah.

The war roared round Jerusalem's gates; it took a hideous form.
Seen in the aggregate, a vast hermaphroditic form
Heaved like an earthquake, labouring with convulsive groans

---

viii *224. knife of flint*] The 'sharp knives' with which the Israelites were
circumcized(*Joshua* v 2, A. V. margin) to mark their acceptance of the Law.
viii *227.* Cp. the allusions to Mary, Martha and Lazarus (the sleeper
awoken by Christ) in iv *246*ff: B. here adopts the traditional identification
of this Mary and Mary Magdalene (*228*).
viii *228. John* xii 3: 'Mary . . . anointed the feet of Jesus, and wiped his
feet with her hair.'
viii *229. ends*] i.e. borders. In the MS this line originally followed *191*
without a space.
viii *234–5.* Cp. *Revelation* xxii 20: '"Surely I come quickly." Amen. Even
so, come, Lord Jesus.'
viii *237.* To be read literally; the war *is* Satan; see *247*.
viii *238. aggregate*] A nearer view (*247*) shows 'multitudes'; a distant,
aggregate view shows one man.

240 Intolerable. At length an awful wonder burst
 From the hermaphroditic bosom: *Satan* he was named,
 Son of perdition; terrible his form dishumanized, monstrous,
 A male without a female counterpart, a howling fiend
 Forlorn of Eden & repugnant to the forms of life,
245 Yet hiding the Shadowy Female Vala as in an ark & curtains,
 Abhorred, accursed, ever dying an eternal death,
 Being multitudes of tyrant men in union blasphemous
 Against the divine image, congregated assemblies of wicked men.

 Los said to Enitharmon: 'Pitying I saw,
250 Pitying the Lamb of God descended through Jerusalem's gates
 To put off Mystery time after time, & as a man
 Is born on earth so was he born of fair Jerusalem
 In mystery's woven mantle & in the robes of Luvah.'

 He stood in fair Jerusalem, to awake up into Eden
255 The fallen Man, but first to give his vegetated body
 To be cut off & separated that the spiritual body may be revealed.
[105] The Lamb of God stood before Satan opposite
 In Entuthon Benithon, in the shadows of torments & woe,
 Upon the heights of Amalek; taking refuge in his arms
260 The victims fled from punishment; for all his words were peace.

 Urizen called together the Synagogue of Satan in dire sanhedrim
 To judge the Lamb of God to death as a murderer & robber,
 As it is written: *He was numbered among the transgressors.*

 Cold, dark, opaque, the assembly met twelvefold in Amalek.
265 Twelve rocky unshaped forms, terrific forms of torture & woe,
 Such seemed the Synagogue to distant view. Amidst them beamed
 A false feminine counterpart lovely, of delusive beauty,

viii *241.* Cp. *Milton* pl.14 *37n.* Satan is a fearsome male, inhabited and animated by the female spirit of evil, Rahab.
viii *242. Son*] B. wrote 'Sons' and altered it to 'Son'.
viii *243.* Cp. viia *325.*
viii *255. Give . . . body*] *1st rdg del.* 'rend the Veil of Mystery', followed by the deleted line: 'And then call Urizen & Luvah & Tharmas & Urthona.'
viii *257–318.* An early draft of *257–66, 284–6a, 313–18* in one consecutive passage is found on a separate sheet known as p. 145. One inserted passage, *286b–312,* is written into the main text of p. 105; the other lines (*267–83*) were added in the margin and are therefore the latest.
viii *257 Satan* (p. 105) replaces *Urizen* (p. 145).
viii *259. Amalek*] Enemies of Israel, as were Canaan and Moab (*284*). *1st rdg* (altd. on p. 145) Entuthon.
viii *261.* Cp. *89* above and note.
viii *262. robber*] As worse than Barabbas.
viii *263.* From *Isaiah* liii 12, *Mark* xv 28, *Luke* xxii 37.

viii *267*. See *257n*.

A false feminine counterpart] Summarizes all the evils embodied in the 'sisters' Rahab and Tirzah, who are different but complementary representations of the worst forms of feminine evil–beautiful but repulsive, alluring but heartless, seeking man out only to destroy him. In *Milton* pls. 38.*15–27*, 40.*17–22* she is found in the heart of Satan. The earliest personification of *Mystery* as a woman–in date of composition–seems to be ix *654–66*, but here she is most developed.

RAHAB is not the friendly, if unvirtuous, woman of *Joshua* ii 1–22, vi 17–25, but the great harlot of *Revelation* xvii 3–5: 'I saw a woman sit upon a scarlet coloured beast, full of names of blasphemy, having seven heads and ten horns. And the woman was arrayed in purple and scarlet colour, and decked with gold and precious stones and pearls, having a golden cup in her hand full of abominations and filthiness of her fornication. And upon her forehead was a name written, MYSTERY, BABYLON THE GREAT, THE MOTHER OF HARLOTS AND ABOMINATIONS OF THE EARTH.' She is glittering, sensual, cruel, powerful and power-loving; but she is no more than an illusion, a 'state' of Vala. Vala is an eternal soul (*273–5*), and when in ix she returns to innocence and purity Rahab vanishes as the illusory monster she is. She is variously associated by B. with different evils and vices, such as Moral Virtue (*Milton* pl.40.*21*), or Deism (*Four Zoas* viii *618–20*), since B. sees the same mental evils at work in these different activities. Cp. also *Milton* pls 17.*11*, 33.*20*, 37.*43*, 38.*23*, *Jerusalem* pl. 75.*18–20*

TIRZAH is closely connected with Rahab, often as a kind of twin (e.g. *Jerusalem* pl. 5.*40–5*, where they each represent six of the twelve Daughters of Albion), but sometimes (*Milton* pl.19.*54*) as a daughter of Rahab. In the Bible she was, first, one of the daughters of Zelophehad (*Numbers* xxvii 1–2) who were allowed to inherit their father's goods, as he had no sons. Thus the law of male inheritance was changed for them–to B. a case of feminine insinuation. Secondly, Tirzah was the capital of the Northern Kingdom, and thus the rival of Jerusalem, both in religious politics and in beauty (*Song of Songs* vi 4: 'Thou art beautiful, O my love, as Tirzah, comely as Jerusalem'). B. takes the usual Southern viewpoint that Jerusalem is the Holy City, and Tirzah the false renegade, and so associates her with the heathen tribes of Amalek, Canaan and Moab (*283–4*). Her character is different from Rahab's. Rahab is a false queen; Tirzah is a cruel tormentor. She desires the Eternal Man with a passionate, selfish, insatiable devouring desire, torturing him and claiming that she must do so for his own good, thus justifying her sadism on 'moral' grounds, and ruthlessly crushing all his attempts to be free. In 'To Tirzah' (p. 591) she is 'mother of my mortal part': here (*309*) she binds man 'upon the stems of vegetation'. She is the power of Nature that restricts humanity to a material existence which may be beautiful, but is a cruel torment to the free human spirit. In both places her claims to authority over mankind are rejected.

B. was very aware of the evils which arise when the desirability of the female is converted to corrupt ends. Hence the glamorous Rahab and

Dividing & uniting at will in the cruelties of holiness—
Vala drawn down into a vegetated body now triumphant.
270   The Synagogue of Satan clothed her with scarlet robes & gems,
And on her forehead was her name written in blood: MYSTERY.
When viewed remote she is one, when viewed near she divides
To multitude (as it is in Eden so permitted, because
It was the best possible in the state called Satan, to save
275   From death eternal & to put off Satan eternally).

The Synagogue created her from fruit of Urizen's tree
By devilish arts abominable, unlawful, unutterable,
Perpetually vegetating in detestable births
Of female forms, beautiful through poisons hidden in secret,
280   Which give a tincture to false beauty. There was hidden within
The bosom of Satan the false Female, as in an ark & veil
Which Christ must rend & her reveal. Her daughters are called
Tirzah, she is named Rahab, their various divisions are called
The daughters of Amalek, Canaan, & Moab, binding on the
     stones
285   Their victims & with knives tormenting them, singing with tears
Over their victims. Hear ye the song of the females of Amalek:

'O thou poor human form, O thou poor child of woe,
Why dost thou wander away from Tirzah? Why me compel to
     bind thee?
If thou dost go away from me I shall consume upon the rocks.

Tirzah, combining in Vala, are often more to be feared and hated than the
aggressive male figures, whether Urizen, Satan or the Covering Cherub,
whom they dominate.

viii 274. *state*] See *Jerusalem* pl.31.13n.

viii 280–3. *there was hidden . . . called*] An afterthought to this late addition
(cp. *257n*).

viii 284. *Amalek*] Added on p. 105.

Stones] 1st rdg, p. 145, stones; 2nd rdg, p. 105, stems.

viii 286. *Hear ye . . .*] See *257–318n*.

viii 287–309. This passage is not on p. 145 (see *257n*). It appears to be
drawn from the song of Tirzah in *Jerusalem* pls 67.44–68.9, where five and
a half more lines are found. The short line *302* seems to be due to the
omission of references not relevant to *Four Zoas*.

viii 288. *Why dost thou wander . . .*] See note on Tirzah, *267*. Tirzah is the
renegade religion, and Amalek, etc., are heathen tribes; the separated
tribes are identified with the heathens, and are trying to force Man, in the
form of Israel (hence the place-names) into apostasy. But to B. apostasy
means refusal of the Divine Vision, and so Tirzah is shown (*288, 298–9*) as
wishing to bind the free, imaginative, 'wandering' living form 'on the
stems of vegetation' to this dead, law-bound material life.

290 These fibres of thine eyes that used to wander in distant heavens
Away from me I have bound down with a hot iron;
These nostrils that expanded with delight in morning skies
I have bent downward with lead molten in my roaring furnaces;
My soul is seven furnaces, incessant roars the bellows
295 Upon my terribly flaming heart; the molten metal runs
In channels through my fiery limbs: O love! O pity! O pain!
O the pangs, the bitter pangs of love forsaken!
Ephraim was a wilderness of joy where all my wild beasts ran;
The river Kanah wandered by my sweet Manasseh's side—
300 'Go, Noah, fetch the girdle of strong brass: heat it red hot,
Press it around the loins of this expanding cruelty—
Shriek not so, my only love!
Bind him down, sisters, bind him down on Ebal, mount of cursing.
Mahlah, come forth from Lebanon, & Hoglah from Mount Sinai,
305 Come, circumscribe this tongue of sweets, & with a screw of iron
Fasten this ear into the rock; Milcah, the task is thine.
Weep not so, sisters, weep not so; our life depends on this,
Or mercy & truth are fled away from Shechem & Mount Gilead—
Unless my beloved is bound upon the stems of vegetation.'

viii *298. Ephraim*] A tribe in central Palestine, south of Manasseh.
viii *299. The river Kanah* flows into the sea, and is the boundary between Ephraim and the western part of Manasseh. Kanah, Manasseh, Ephraim, Shechem and Gilead all lay in the Northern Kingdom. Its fault, in Tirzah's eyes, is 'wandering'.
Manasseh] One of the tribes of Israel that settled beyond Jordan. B. often uses the name in *Milton* (e.g. pls 20.3 and 24.2-6), implying that it was a faithless tribe.
viii *299.* Followed by deleted line: 'To see the boy spring into heaven sounding from my sight.'
viii *300. Noah*] Not the patriarch, but a woman, one of the daughters of Zelophehad, with Milchah, Mahlah, Hoglah and Tirzah. See *267n.*
viii *303. Ebal*] A mountain in central Palestine. Cp. *Deuteronomy* xxvii 4-8: '... in mount Ebal ... shalt thou build an altar unto the Lord thy God, an altar of stones: thou shalt not lift up any iron tool upon them ... and thou shalt offer burnt offerings thereon unto the Lord thy God ... and thou shalt write upon the stones all the words of this law very plainly', and xxvii 12-13: 'These shall stand upon mount Gerizim to bless the people ... and these shall stand upon mount Ebal to curse; Reuben, Gad and Asher, and Zebulun, Dan and Naphtali.' There follows a series of twelve prohibitions, each beginning 'Cursed be he that. ...'
viii *308. Shechem* (now Nablus)] is a city to the west of Jordan opposite Gilead, and between Mounts Gerizim and Ebal, near the border of Manasseh and Ephraim. The Law was accepted there (*Joshua* viii 30) and the secession of the Northern Kingdom ratified there (*1 Kings* xii).

310 Such are the songs of Tirzah, such the loves of Amalek.
      The Lamb of God descended through the twelve portions of
          Luvah,
      Bearing his sorrows and receiving all his cruel wounds.

[106a] Thus was the Lamb of God condemned to death.
      They nailed him upon the Tree of Mystery, weeping over him,
315 And then mocking & then worshipping, calling him 'Lord' & 'King':

      Sometimes as twelve daughters lovely, & sometimes as five
      They stood in beaming beauty, & sometimes as one, even Rahab
      Who is Mystery, Babylon the great, the mother of harlots.

      Jerusalem saw the body dead upon the cross; she fled away,
320 Saying: 'Is this eternal death? Where shall I hide from death?
      Pity me, Los, pity me, Urizen; & let us build
      A sepulchre & worship death in fear while yet we live—
      Death, god of all, from whom we rise, to whom we all return!
      And let all nations of the earth worship at the sepulchre
325 With gifts & spices, with lamps rich embossed, jewels & gold.'

      Los took the body from the cross, Jerusalem weeping over;
      They bore it to the sepulchre which Los had hewn in the rock
      Of eternity for himself. He hewed it, despairing of life eternal.

[113b] But when Rahab had cut off the mantle of Luvah from
      The Lamb of God it rolled apart, revealing to all in heaven
331 And all on earth the Temple & the Synagogue of Satan, and
          Mystery—

viii *310. loves*] Ironically meant.
viii *311. the twelve portions*] Suggests the twelve tribes, equating Israel and
Luvah, and both with mankind.
viii *313.* This refers back to *262*: *267–309* are an enlargement of *264*.
viii *315.* As in the crucifixion: *Matthew* xxvi 67–8, xxvii 36–44.
viii *316. Sometimes as twelve*] The number of the Daughters of Albion in
Jerusalem (and ii *267–73* above).   *sometimes as five*] The daughters of
Zelophehad (*300–06*).
viii *318.* For one line added above, and ten below this line, see appendix,
p. 465. In the MS, *402* follows: *319–28* are a marginal addition, and
329–401 are on two other leaves.
viii *319.* B. continues the parallel with the Crucifixion narrative, with Los
taking the part of Joseph of Arimathea and Jerusalem that of the women
(*Matthew* xxvii 55–61). Like Christ's disciples, they mourn because they
do not understand his sufferings. Cp. *572–5*.
viii *321–2.* Jerusalem's attitude is that of Christ's followers after the cruci-
fixion, failing to understand. In this sense Jerusalem, as in the Bible, stands
for 'God's people' collectively.
viii *329–44* (p. 113b). Another added passage (see *318n*).

Even Rahab in all her turpitude. Rahab divided herself.
She stood before Los in her pride among the furnaces,
Dividing & uniting in delusive feminine pomp, questioning him.

335 He answered her, with tenderness & love not uninspired;
Los sat upon his anvil stock, they sat beside the forge;
Los wiped the sweat from his red brow, & thus began
To the delusive female forms shining among his furnaces:

'I am that shadowy prophet who six thousand years ago
340 Fell from my station in the eternal bosom. I divided
To multitude, & my multitudes are children of care & labour.
O Rahab, I behold thee. I was once like thee a son
Of pride, and I also have pierced the Lamb of God in pride and
    wrath.
Hear me repeat my generations, that thou mayst also repent.
[115] And these are the sons of Los & Enitharmon: Rintrah, Palamabron,
346 Theotormon, Bromion, Antamon, Ananton, Ozoth, Ohana,
Sotha, Mydon, Ellayol, Natho, Gon, Harhath, Satan,
Har, Ochim, Ijim; Adam; Reuben, Simeon, Levi, Judah, Dan,
    Naphtali,
Gad, Asher, Issachar, Zebulun, Joseph, Benjamin; David,
    Solomon;
350 Paul, Constantine, Charlemagne, Luther, Milton.
These are our daughters: Ocalythron, Elynittria, Oothoon,
    Leutha,

viii *339–40.* So in *Milton* pl.22.*15–16.*

viii *342.* As the veil of the Temple, which hid the Holy of Holies from the
eyes of the people, tore at Christ's death (*Matthew* xxvii 51), so here a
mystery is laid open – the true nature of Rahab.

viii *345–95* (p. 115). This is another added passage, used as a continuation
of the addition *329–44,* but perhaps once intended for another purpose;
several third person pronouns have been changed to the first person; and
see *367n.*

viii *345–53.* Of the thirty-eight sons named, the first four are named in
Milton pl.24.*11–12* as Los's sons, as are Antamon, Ozoth and Sotha in
Milton pl.28.*13,21,29.* Har and Ijim belong to *Tiriel,* written but not en-
graved many years before. Besides Satan and Adam, the twelve biblical
names – from Reuben to Benjamin – are the sons of Israel, also called sons
of Los; some appear in *Milton* pl.24, and all in *Jerusalem* pl.16.*35–60.* Paul
to Luther are among the corrupt 'Churches' in *Milton* pl.37.*41.* The other
seven, Ananton, Ohana, and Mydon to Harhath, seem to have been in-
vented to fill out the list.

viii *351.* Of the eighteen daughters, six of the first eight (not Elythiria and
Enanto) occur in *Europe,* and seem here to be merely re-used names,
though the first four are also found in *Milton* pls 10.*14–19,* 13.*36–44;*

Elythiria, Enanto, Manathu-Vorcyon, Ethinthus; Moab, Midian;
Adah, Zillah, Caina, Naamah, Tamar, Rahab, Tirzah, Mary;
And myriads more of sons & daughters to whom our love increased,
355 To each according to the multiplication of their multitudes.
But Satan accused Palamabron before his brethren; also he
        maddened
The horses of Palamabron's harrow, wherefore Rintrah and
        Palamabron
Cut him off from Golgonooza. But Enitharmon in tears
Wept over him, created him a space closed with a tender moon,
360 And he rolled down beneath the fires of Orc, a globe immense,
Crusted with snow in a dim void. Here by the arts of Urizen
He tempted many of the sons & daughters of Los to flee
Away from me. First Reuben fled, then Simeon, then Levi, then
        Judah,
Then Dan, then Naphtali, then Gad, then Asher, then Issachar,
365 Then Zebulun, then Joseph, then Benjamin, twelve sons of Los—
And this is the manner in which Satan became the tempter.

'There is a state named Satan—learn distinct to know, O Rahab,
The difference between states, & individuals of those states.
The state named Satan never can be redeemed in all eternity;
370 But when Luvah in Orc became a serpent he descended into
That state called Satan. Enitharmon breathed forth on the winds
Of Golgonooza her well-beloved, knowing he was Orc's human
        remains.

Moab and Midian were unfriendly neighbours of Israel; the remainder are
names of biblical women; cp. also *Jerusalem* pl.62.8–12n. Only Mary is
important. B. may mean Magdalen, the prostitute, to parallel Rahab
'the Canaanitess'; but he may mean the mother of Jesus, who wanted to
hold him back–cp. 'To Tirzah' (p. 591).
viii *356–9*. B. uses the Bard's story, from *Milton* pls 7–9, to tell how his
children were corrupted. See also *366–84* below. In that story, Satan,
brother to Rintrah and Palamabron, starts a quarrel which results in his
own separation from heaven.
viii *361–6*. In *Milton* pls 23.61–24.4 Los says that some of his sons have left
him, but does not directly blame Satan there.
viii *367*. *Rahab*] *1st rdg del.* Mortals: a piece of tinkering to make the
passage fit the confrontation of Los and Rahab.
viii *367–9*. Cp. *Milton* extra pl.32.22, and note below.
viii *370*. B. is trying here to assimilate the Bard's mythology from *Milton*
to that of *Four Zoas*. In *Milton* Satan is fallen, hidden away in 'a space'
by Enitharmon so that his condition will not worsen (cp. also the fate of
Tharmas in i *78–92*). B. now says that the corruption of Orc into a serpent
(viib) is another case of the same fall, using the tradition which equates the
Genesis serpent with Satan. See note on *states, Milton* pl.32.*10n*, p. 573.

She tenderly loved him above all his brethren; he grew up
In mother's tenderness. The enormous worlds rolling in Urizen's
    power
375 Must have given Satan, by these mild arts, dominion over all;
Wherefore Palamabron, being accused by Satan to Los,
Called down a great solemn assembly. Rintrah in fury & fire
Defended Palamabron, & rage filled the universal tent.

'Because Palamabron was good-natured, Satan supposed he
    feared him,
380 And Satan not having the science of wrath but only of pity
Was soon condemned, & wrath was left to wrath, & pity to pity.
Rintrah & Palamabron cut sheer off from Golgonooza
Enitharmon's moony space, & in it Satan & his companions.
They rolled down, a dim world crusted with snow, deadly & dark.

385 'Jerusalem, pitying them, wove them mantles of life & death
Times after times. And those in Eden sent Lucifer for their guard.
Lucifer refused to die for Satan & in pride he forsook his charge.
Then they sent Molech; Molech was impatient. They sent
Molech impatient, they sent Elohim, who created Adam
390 To die for Satan. Adam refused but was compelled to die
By Satan's arts. Then the eternals sent Shaddai;
Shaddai was angry. Pachad descended; Pachad was terrified.
And then they sent Jehovah, who leprous stretched his hand to
    eternity.
Then Jesus came, & died willing beneath Tirzah & Rahab.
395 Thou art that Rahab: lo, the tomb! what can we purpose more?

[116] 'Lo! Enitharmon terrible & beautiful in eternal youth—
Bow down before her, you her children, & set Jerusalem free!'

Rahab, burning with pride & revenge, departed from Los.
Los dropped a tear at her departure, but he wiped it away in hope.
400 She went to Urizen in pride; the prince of light beheld
Revealed before the face of heaven his secret holiness.

[106b] Darkness & sorrow covered all flesh; Eternity was darkened.

    Urizen sitting in his web of deceitful religion

viii *376. Palamabron*] *1st rdg del.* Rintrah and Palamabron. The alteration
agrees with *Milton* pls 7–9.
viii *376–94*. These lines follow quite closely but much more briefly the
narrative of *Milton* pls 8.46–9.45 and 13.17–27. See notes there.
viii *385*. Satan in his restricted globe becomes our material world, watched
by the Seven, for whom see *Milton* pl.14.42n.
viii *402*. After the additions (cp. *318n*, *329n*) we return to Urizen, caught
as at *171–3* by Vala in his own net of false religion.

Felt the female death, a dull & numbing stupor such as ne'er
405 Before assaulted the bright human form. He felt his pores
Drink in the deadly dull delusion. Horrors of eternal death
Shot through him. Urizen sat stonied upon his rock;
Forgetful of his own laws, pitying he began to embrace
The Shadowy Female. Since life cannot be quenched, life exuded:
410 His eyes shot outwards, then his breathing nostrils drawn forth,
Scales covered over a cold forehead & a neck outstretched
Into the deep to seize the shadow; scales his neck & bosom
Covered, & scales his hands & feet, upon his belly falling
Outstretched through the immense, his mouth wide opening
          tongueless,
415 His teeth a triple row, he strove to seize the shadow in vain,
And his immense tail lashed the abyss, his human form a stone,
A form of senseless stone remained in terrors on the rock,
Abominable to the eyes of mortals who explore his books.
His wisdom still remained & all his memory, stored with woe:

420 And still his stony form remained in the abyss immense,
Like the pale visage in its sheet of lead that cannot follow.
Incessant stern disdain his scaly form gnaws inwardly,
With deep repentance for the loss of that fair form of man.
With envy he saw Los, with envy Tharmas, & the spectre
425 With envy, & in vain he swam around. His stony form
No longer now erect, the king of light outstretched in fury
Lashes his tail in the wild deep; his eyelids like the sun
Arising in his pride enlighten all the grisly deeps;
His scales transparent give forth light like windows of the
          morning;
430 His neck flames with wrath & majesty; he lashes the abyss,
Beating the deserts & the rocks; the deserts feel his power,
They shake their slumbers off, they wave in awful fear,
Calling the lion & the tiger, the horse & the wild stag,

viii *404*. He is the first to feel it: in *454-7* it spreads to Tharmas and Los.
viii *407. stonied*] Not 'astonished' but 'turned to stone'. See *420*.
viii *411*. Urizen's scales, fang-like teeth, and (*426*) his fall 'outstretched'
recall B.'s early use of the image of Nebuchadnezzar (e.g. in the design on
pl.24 of *Marriage*). Cp. also Leviathan in *Job* 41.
viii *416-7*. Perhaps B. was thinking of a fossil skeleton.
viii *424. the spectre*] *1st rdg del*. Urthona–a correction to remind us that the
real Urthona is not yet redeemed.
viii *425-6*. In the MS there is a narrow but uncertain space here. But the
syntax seems to require that 'his stony form . . . erect' should be read as
one phrase, for there seems to be no sense in 'he swam around his stony
form'. B. has no punctuation of any sort.

[107] The elephant, the wolf, the bear, the lamia, the satyr.
435   His eyelids give their light around, his folding tail aspires
      Among the stars, the earth & all the abysses feel his fury.
      When as the snow covers the mountain, oft petrific hardness
      Covers the deeps, at his vast fury moaning in his rock,
      Hardens the lion & the bear trembling in the solid mountain:
440   They view the light, & wonder, crying out in terrible existence
      (Up bound the wild stag & the horse) 'Behold the king of pride!'

      Oft doth his eye emerge from the abyss into the realms
      Of his eternal day, & memory strives to augment his ruthfulness;
      Then weeping he descends in wrath, drawing all things in his fury
445   Into obedience to his will, & now he finds in vain
      That not of his own power he bore the human form erect,
      Nor of his own will gave his laws in times of everlasting.
      For now fierce Orc in wrath & fury rises into the heavens,
      A king of wrath & fury, a dark enraged horror,
450   And Urizen repentant forgets his wisdom in the abyss,
      In forms of priesthood, in the dark delusions of repentance,
      Repining in his heart & spirit that Orc reigned over all,
      And that his wisdom served but to augment the indefinite lust.

      Then Tharmas & Urthona felt the stony stupor rise
455   Into their limbs. Urthona shot forth a vast fibrous form;
      Tharmas like a pillar of sand rolled round by the whirlwind,
      An animated pillar rolling round & round in incessant rage.

      Los felt the stony stupor, & his head rolled down beneath
      Into the abysses of his bosom; the vessels of his blood
460   Dart forth upon the wind in pipes writhing about in the abyss,
      And Enitharmon, pale & cold, in milky juices flowed
      Into a form of vegetation, living, having a voice
      Moving in rootlike fibres, trembling in fear upon the earth.

      And Tharmas gave his power to Los, Urthona gave his strength
465   Into the youthful prophet for the love of Enitharmon,

viii 434. *lamia*] 'A fabulous monster, supposed to have the body of a
woman and to prey upon human beings, and suck the blood of children'
(OED).
viii 446–8. The 'will' and 'power' were the Man's, not Orc's.
viii 458. This is the early form of Los, not the inspired Los of the late
additions (e.g. *15–33, 336*ff). As Urthona he also feels 'the stony stupor'
(*454–5*).
viii 464–7. This may be an adjustment, to permit all the Zoas in the first
story to be overwhelmed, and yet permit the redeemed Los and Enithar-
mon of the new story to operate. But it is not an addition to the MS.

And of the nameless Shadowy Female in the nether deep,
And for the dread of the dark terrors of Orc & Urizen.

Thus in a living death the nameless shadow all things bound.
All mortal things made permanent that they may be put off
470 Time after time by the Divine Lamb who died for all,
And all in him died, & he put off all mortality.

[108] Tharmas on high rode furious through the afflicted worlds,
Pursuing the vain shadow of hope, fleeing from identity
In abstract false expanses, that he may not hear the voice
475 Of Ahania wailing on the winds. In vain he flies, for still
The voice incessant calls on all the children of men:
For she spoke of all in heaven; & all upon the earth
Saw not as yet the Divine Vision. Her eyes are toward Urizen,
And thus Ahania cries aloud to the caverns of the grave:

480 'Will you keep a flock of wolves & lead them? Will you take the
         wintry blast
For a covering to your limbs, or the summer pestilence for a tent
         to abide in?
Will you erect a lasting habitation in the mouldering churchyard,
Or a pillar & palace of eternity in the jaws of the hungry grave?
Will you seek pleasure from the festering wound, or marry for a
         wife
485 The ancient leprosy, that the king & priest may still feast on your
         decay,
And the grave mock & laugh at the ploughed field, saying:
"I am the nourisher, thou the destroyer: in my bosom is milk
         and wine
And a fountain from my breasts: to me come all multitudes,
To my breath: they obey, they worship me: I am a goddess and
         queen."
490 But listen to Ahania, O ye sons of the murdered one:

viii 468. As in the later additions Rahab triumphs at the crucifixion (311–8),
so here the earlier narrative reaches its climax in the triumph of Vala.
viii 469–71. An addition to the MS, glossing the earlier, more complete,
statement of disaster. The 'permanence' is 'a living death' because it is
incapable of change, adaptation, or any living movement.
viii 472. Tharmas's 'stupor' in the previous lines does not prevent B. in-
serting another image of his wretchedness. Note that a new page begins
here.
viii 474. *abstract false expanses*] Three words indicating B.'s distaste for
formlessness and indefiniteness, and the falseness of Tharmas's pity now.
viii 480–3. Cp. *Visions 211, 152–3*.
viii 486. Cp. *Song of Los (Asia) 59–64*.
viii 490. *the murdered one*] i.e. the Man (*494*).

Listen to her whose memory beholds your ancient days;
Listen to her whose eyes behold the dark body of corruptible
  death,
Looking for Urizen in vain. In vain I seek for morning:
The Eternal Man sleeps in the earth, nor feels the vigorous sun,
495 Nor silent moon, nor all the hosts of heaven move in his body.
His fiery halls are dark, & round his limbs the serpent Orc
Fold without fold encompasses him, and his corrupting members
Vomit out the scaly monsters of the restless deep;
They come up in the rivers & annoy the nether parts
500 Of Man who lays upon the shores, leaning his faded head
Upon the oozy rock, enwrapped with the weeds of death.
His eyes sink hollow in his head, his flesh covered with slime
And shrunk up to the bones. Alas! that Man should come to this:
His strong bones beat with snows & hid within the caves of night
505 Marrowless, bloodless, falling into dust, driven by the winds.
Oh, how the horrors of eternal death take hold on Man!
His faint groans shake the caves & issue through the desolate
  rocks.
[109] And the strong eagle now with numbing cold, blighted of feathers,
Once like the pride of the sun, now flagging in cold night,
510 Hovers with blasted wings aloft, watching with eager eye
Till Man shall leave a corruptible body. He famished hears him
  groan,
And now he fixes his strong talons in the pointed rock,
And now he beats the heavy air with his enormous wings.
Beside him lies the lion dead, & in his belly worms
515 Feast on his death, till universal death devours all,
And the pale horse seeks for the pool to lie him down & die—
But finds the pools filled with serpents devouring one another.
He droops his head & trembling stands, & his bright eyes decay.
These are the visions of my eyes, the visions of Ahania'.

520 Thus cries Ahania. Enion replies from the caverns of the grave:

'Fear not, O poor forsaken one! O land of briars & thorns,
Where once the olive flourished, & the cedar spread his wings!
Once I wailed desolate like thee; my fallow fields in fear
Cried to the churchyards, & the earthworm came in dismal state.
525 I found him in my bosom, & I said, "The time of love
Appears upon the rocks & hills in silent shades", but soon
A voice came in the night, a midnight cry upon the mountains:

---

viii 500–4. There is a similar passage in *Jerusalem* pl.94.1–11.
viii 511. *corruptible body*] B. looks forward to the Man's spiritual resurrec-
tion in this phrase from *1 Corinthians* xv 40–54.
15+B.

Awake! the bridegroom cometh! I awoke to sleep no more.
But an eternal consummation is dark Enion,
530   The watery grave. O thou cornfield, O thou vegetater happy,
More happy is the dark consumer: hope drowns all my torment.
For I am now surrounded by a shadowy vortex, drawing
The spectre quite away from Enion, that I die a death
Of bitter hope, although I consume in these raging waters.
535   The furrowed field replies to the grave; I hear her reply to me:
"Behold! the time approaches fast that thou shalt be as a thing
Forgotten; when one speaks of thee he will not be believed.
When the Man gently fades away in his immortality,
When the mortal disappears in improved knowledge, cast away
540   The former things, so shall the mortal gently fade away,
And so become invisible to those who still remain."
Listen: I will tell thee what is done in the caverns of the grave.
[110]   The Lamb of God has rent the veil of Mystery, soon to return
In clouds & fires around the rock & the mysterious tree.
545   As the seed waits eagerly, watching for its flower & fruit,
Anxious, its little soul looks out into the clear expanse
To see if hungry winds are abroad with their invisible army;
So Man looks out in tree & herb & fish & bird & beast,
Collecting up the scattered portions of his immortal body
550   Into the elemental forms of every thing that grows.
He tries the sullen north wind riding on its angry furrows;
The sultry south when the sun rises, & the angry east
When the sun sets, when the clods harden & the cattle stand
Drooping, & the birds hide in their silent nests. He stores his
        thoughts
555   As in a storehouse, in his memory he regulates the forms
Of all beneath & all above, & in the gentle west
Reposes where the sun's heat dwells. He rises to the sun,
And to the planets of the night, & to the stars that gild
The zodiac, & the stars that sullen stand to north & south.
560   He touches the remotest pole & in the centre weeps,
That Man should labour & sorrow & learn & forget & return
To the dark valley whence he came, to begin his labours anew.
In pain he sighs; in pain he labours in his universe,

viii *528. Awake! the bridegroom cometh*] From *Matthew* xxv 6 (which reads
'Behold', not 'Awake'), the parable of the wise and foolish virgins.
viii *529–30*, i.e. 'Enion, who was dark, a watery grave, is now burnt up
and revived by hope'.
viii *543*. Cp. *329–34*.
viii *548*. Man's modern study of his natural surroundings, and his journeys
over the earth (551ff) are signs that his sense of wonder and his imagination
are awake.

Screaming in birds over the deep, & howling in the wolf
565 Over the slain, & moaning in the cattle, & in the winds,
And weeping over Orc & Urizen in clouds & flaming fires;
And in the cries of birth & in the groans of death his voice
Is heard throughout the universe: wherever a grass grows
Or a leaf buds the Eternal Man is seen, is heard, is felt,
570 And all his sorrows, till he reassumes his ancient bliss.'

Such are the words of Ahania & Enion. Los hears & weeps.
And Los & Enitharmon took the body of the Lamb
Down from the cross & placed it in a sepulchre, which Los had
    hewn
For himself in the Rock of Eternity, trembling & in despair.
575 Jerusalem wept over the sepulchre two thousand years.

[111] Rahab triumphs over all: she took Jerusalem
Captive, a willing captive, by delusive arts impelled
To worship Urizen's dragon form, to offer her own children
Upon the bloody altar. John saw these things revealed in heaven
580 On Patmos Isle, & heard the souls cry out to be delivered;
He saw the harlot of the kings of earth, & saw her cup
Of fornication, food of Orc & Satan, pressed from the fruit of
    Mystery.
But when she saw the form of Ahania weeping on the void
And heard Enion's voice sound from the caverns of the grave
585 No more spirit remained in her. She secretly left the Synagogue
    of Satan;
She communed with Orc in secret, she hid him with the flax

viii 566. *Flaming*] *1st rdg del.* dismal–cp. iv *44* for a series of similar changes
from *dismal.*
viii 571. Followed by eight deleted lines: see appendix, p. *465* below.
Lines *2–3* of these are written over an erased 'The End of the Eighth
Night'; *571* is interpolated; this 'End' was probably *570.*
viii *572–5.* Cp. *326–8.*
viii *579–82.* The references to *Revelation* are to vi 9–16: 'I saw under the
altar the souls of them that were slain for the word of God ... And they
cried with a loud voice, saying, How long, O Lord, holy and true, dost
thou not judge and avenge our blood on them that dwell on the earth? ...
and it was said unto them, that they should rest yet for a little season. ...'
And for the harlot, *Revelation* xvii *3–5,* see *267n.*
viii *585. She*] Rahab. Cp. the Queen of Sheba's reaction to the sight of
Solomon's grandeur (*1 Kings* x *5*): 'There was no more spirit in her.'
viii *586.* In *Joshua* ii 6, Rahab of Jericho, the harlot, to save the two Jewish
spies 'had brought them up to the roof of the house, and hid them with
the stalks of flax, which she had laid in order upon the roof'.

That Enitharmon had numbered away from the heavens,
She gathered it together to consume her harlot robes
In bitterest contrition, sometimes self-condemning repentant,
590 And sometimes kissing her robes & jewels & weeping over them;
Sometimes returning to the Synagogue of Satan in pride,
And sometimes weeping before Orc in humility & trembling.
The Synagogue of Satan therefore uniting against Mystery,
Satan divided against Satan, resolved in open sanhedrim
595 To burn Mystery with fire & form another from her ashes:
For God put it into their heart to fulfil all his will.

The ashes of Mystery began to animate. They called it Deism
And Natural Religion. As of old, so now anew began
599 Babylon, again in infancy, called Natural Religion.

[110b]   *End of The Eighth Night*

                   [Full-page drawing]

                   Night the Ninth

The Ninth Night relates the complete redemption of the Eternal Man. B.
bases the Night largely on *Revelation*, and its apocalyptic narrations of the
coming of the heavenly city. The first eighty-eight lines, in which Los
begins the Last Judgment, are later than the rest, *1–13* being latest of all.
Los does not directly bring in the new day; on the contrary, confusion in-
creases; but out of the chaotic movement some order can finally come.
The Eternal Man, sick and asleep on his rock (*93*), feels the 'war within
his members' (*97*) and, faint though he is, rouses himself to call for Urizen,
the Prince of Light, to whom he had handed his authority at the beginning
of Book ii when he first lay down to sleep.
    The first part of the salvation of Man is thus the regeneration of Urizen,
who had been trapped in a stony dragon form since viii *407*. Urizen is
afraid and reluctant, but the Man commands him and he dares not disobey.
He is now renewed as a young man 'glorious bright exulting in his joy'
(*189*), no longer an aged tyrant. The Man shows him the future, and the

viii *587. heavens*] See *Milton 37.35n.*
viii *593–9*. B. allegorizes the replacing of older false religion, with its
emphasis on mysterious revelation, by the new false religion of deism, the
intellectually popular 'rationalised' religion of the eighteenth century.
viii *597–9*. An addition, an explanatory afterthought.
viii page 112. A drawing of a distracted woman, restrained by a man (both
nude): probably Los and Enitharman from Night v, from which this page
may have been displaced (perhaps as frontispiece). Its presence in viii
seems accidental, due only to B.'s use of the other side for the additional
lines *576–590*.

restoration to him of Ahania, and he confesses his past errors (*223*). At this 'the bursting universe explodes' (*228*), the dead rise, and pay off old scores in a scene of riot and revenge (*233–275*) reminiscent of the Gordon riots of 1780 (which Blake had seen) and the worst days of the French revolutionary mob. Suddenly a divine light shines on the scene as the Man sees Christ descending from heaven (*270–2*)–at the moment when a prisoner revenges himself on an unjust judge (*273–5*). The terror fades away, and the Man rises to meet the vision (*284*). But he may not; he is not yet pure, and the second stage of the judgment, which now begins, must be passed through before the Man is fully redeemed.

This stage, which fills the rest of the Night, is the story of the harvest and vintage of souls. All human souls are seed to be sown, reaped, the corn thrashed and the grapes crushed, so that the Bread and Wine of Ages can be made. This is more an imaginative than an allegorical conception. The farming year begins as Urizen ploughs the ground and sows the seed. As he rests and the seed grows, the poem turns to the redemption of Luvah and Vala in summer-time. Orc, the inferior form of Luvah, is burnt away and consumed (*355*), and Luvah and Vala are temporarily dismissed from eternity. In an idyllic interlude we read of Vala's new childhood (*386ff*), and then of her care for the newly growing Tharmas and Enion (*481ff*).

When the summer is over and the harvest ripe, Urizen brings in the corn (*576ff*); then, after a harvest feast (*584ff*), he thrashes the corn. The chaff–the hosts of mystery, the effects of his own evil-doing in the earlier part of the poem–is blown away over the sea. It is now the turn of Luvah, who is renewed and so able to carry out his task, the vintage. In the terrible passage which follows the purgatorial sufferings of the souls are seen as evil is crushed out of them in the winepress. What remains is their true essence; and the wine and bread are made (*803–17*) as autumn gives way to winter. Man is himself renewed, and again free in the beautiful and infinite universe, as he had been before his long sleep on the cold rock.

The genuine elements of allegory in this Night are worth distinguishing. Urizen represents reason and the reasoning powers of man, first in *162–85*, where he regrets all his organizing activities–building, commerce, industry–since he has looked too carefully at the future and, in trying to control it, has destroyed the pleasures of man: and second, in his relations with Luvah. The Man makes him the master of Luvah; that is to say, the passions must be controlled by sense and reason. Urthona in a similar manner is the intuitive and creative power of imagination, and Tharmas, the spirit of care and tenderness. Yet the whole Night cannot be interpreted in these terms, and it is an impoverishment of the imagination both of B. and of the reader to attempt to do so. The conceptions of the harvest and the vintage of souls, of the bread and wine, of the growing year from spring to winter, are a kind of poetry not to be consciously interpreted by abstract equivalents. That would be to lay one's head upon the rock.

The significant figures in this Night are the Man, his Zoas and their emanations; the Night is fairly unmarked by alterations, and the later accumulations, in particular Satan and Rahab, so powerful in viii, are unimportant after the added opening passage.

[117]   NIGHT THE NINTH

being the Last Judgment

And Los & Enitharmon builded Jerusalem, weeping
Over the sepulchre & over the crucified body,
Which to their phantom eyes appeared still in the sepulchre.
But Jesus stood beside them in the spirit separating
5   Their spirit from their body. Terrified at non-existence—
For such they deemed the death of the body—Los his vegetable
     hands
Outstretched: his right hand branching out in fibrous strength
Seized the sun; his left hand like dark roots covered the moon,
And tore them down, cracking the heavens across from immense
     to immense.
10   Then fell the fires of eternity with loud & shrill
Sound of loud trumpet, thundering along from heaven to heaven,
A mighty sound articulate: '*Awake, ye dead, & come*
To judgment from the four winds! Awake & come away!'
Folding like scrolls of the enormous volume of heaven & earth,
15   With thunderous noise & dreadful shakings, rocking to & fro
The heavens are shaken & the earth removed from its place,
The foundations of the eternal hills discovered.
The thrones of kings are shaken; they have lost their robes and
     crowns.
The poor smite their oppressors, they awake up to the harvest;
20   The naked warriors rush together down to the sea-shore
Trembling before the multitudes of slaves now set at liberty;
They are become like wintry flocks, like forests stripped of leaves.
The oppressed pursue like the wind; there is no room for escape.

ix *1*. This refers back to viii *572–3*. Los builds Golgonooza; his building
Jerusalem is unusual, although B. treats her, biblically, as a city (e.g. i *240*,
viii *250–4*).
ix *7*. Cp. *Matthew* xxiv 29–31: 'The sun [shall] be darkened, and the moon
shall not give her light, and the stars shall fall from heaven . . . and then
shall all the tribes of the earth mourn . . . and [the Son of Man] shall send
his angels with a great sound of a trumpet.'
ix *14*. Cp. *Revelation* vi 14–15: 'The heaven departed as a scroll when it
is rolled together, and every mountain and island were moved out of their
places. And the kings of the earth, and the great men, and the rich men . . .
hid themselves in the dens and in the rocks of the mountains.'

The spectre of Enitharmon let loose on the troubled deep
25   Wailed shrill in the confusion, & the spectre of Urthona
[118] Received her in the darkening south. Their bodies lost, they stood
Trembling & weak—a faint embrace, a fierce desire, as when
Two shadows mingle on a wall. They wail & shadowy tears
Fell down & shadowy forms of joy mixed with despair & grief,
30   Their bodies buried in the ruins of the universe,
Mingled with the confusion. Who shall call them from the grave?

Rahab & Tirzah wail aloud in the wild flames; they give up
themselves to consummation.

The books of Urizen unroll with dreadful noise; the folding
serpent
Of Orc began to consume in fierce raving fire; his fierce flames
35   Issued on all sides gathering strength, in animating volumes,
Roaming abroad on all the winds, raging intense, reddening
Into resistless pillars of fire, rolling round & round, gathering
Strength from the earths consumed & heavens & all hidden
abysses,
Wherever the eagle has explored or lion or tiger trod,
40   Or where the comets of the night or stars of asterial day
Have shot their arrows or long-beamed spears in wrath & fury.

And all the while the trumpet sounds. From the clotted gore and
from the hollow den
Start forth the trembling millions into flames of mental fire,
Bathing their limbs in the bright visions of eternity.

45   Then like the doves from pillars of smoke, the trembling families
Of women & children throughout every nation under heaven
Cling round the men, in bands of twenties & of fifties, pale
As snow that falls around a leafless tree upon the green.

ix 24. *The spectre of Enitharmon*] Her shadow–forgotten since viia *322–7.*
The spectre of a female emanation or counterpart is unusual, but B. has
grown used to Enitharmon as a personality in herself–understandably, in
view of her partial origin in Catherine Blake.
ix 28. This is surely from direct observation, suggesting one source of B.'s
notion of the 'shadowy spectre'.
ix 32. An added line. Except in *66–9,* and especially *654–66,* Rahab–after
her great invasion of Night viii–plays very little part in ix.
ix 37. *resistless*] Irresistible.
ix 40. *asterial*] *1st rdg del.* eternal. This is *not* the eternal world.
ix 42. *sounds*] Followed by a deletion: 'Awake ye dead and come / To
judgement'.
ix 43–4. B.'s vision of the longed-for day when everyone on earth will be
able to see with a visionary eye.

Their oppressors are fallen, they have stricken them: they awake
to life.
50 Yet pale the just man stands erect & looking up to heaven.
Trembling & strucken by the universal stroke the trees unroot,
The rocks groan horrible & run about. The mountains and
Their rivers cry with a dismal cry; the cattle gather together,
Lowing they kneel before the heavens; the wild beasts of the
forests
55 Tremble, the lion shuddering asks the leopard: 'Feelest thou
The dread I feel, unknown before? My voice refuses to roar,
And in weak moans I speak to thee. This night
Before the morning's dawn the eagle called the vulture,
The raven called the hawk; I heard them from my forests black
60 Saying, "Let us go up far, for soon I smell upon the wind
A terror coming from the south." The eagle & hawk fled away
At dawn, & ere the sun arose the raven & vulture followed.
Let us flee also the north!' They fled. The sons of men
Saw them depart in dismal droves. The trumpet sounded loud,
65 And all the sons of Eternity descended into Beulah.

[119] In the fierce flames the limbs of Mystery lay consuming with
howling
And deep despair. Rattling go up the flames around the
Synagogue
Of Satan. Loud the serpent Orc raged through his twenty-seven
Folds. The Tree of Mystery went up in folding flames;
70 Blood issued out in mighty volumes, pouring in whirlpools fierce
From out the flood-gates of the sky. The gates are burst; down
pour
The torrents, black upon the earth; the blood pours down incessant.
Kings in their palaces lie drowned; shepherds, their flocks, their
tents
Roll down the mountains in black torrents—cities, villages,
75 High spires & castles, drowned in the black deluge. Shoal on shoal

ix 61. *terror . . . from the south*] Orc, bound there by Urizen.
ix 65. *The sons . . . descended* from Eternity, to be ready in Beulah, the
frontier between heaven and earth.
ix 66–80. Written over the erased title *Vala | Night the Ninth | Being | The
Last Judgement*. Thus the previous pages, as well as these lines, are an addi-
tion: since 81–8 are in the margin, the Night originally began at 89. Lines
66–88 seem, by their substance, to be later than 1–65 (pp. 117–18) and of
the same period as the added 32.
ix 68. *twenty-seven*] This is an 'imperfect' number, short of the perfect
fourfold seven–cp. *Jerusalem* pl.35.13: 'He is the twenty-eighth, and is four-
fold.' See also i 150n and *Milton* pl.37.35n.

Float the dead carcases of men & beasts driven to & fro on waves
Of foaming blood, beneath the black incessant sky, till all
Mystery's tyrants are cut off & not one left on earth.

And when all tyranny was cut off from the face of earth,
80   Around the dragon form of Urizen & round his stony form,
The flames rolling intense through the wide universe
Began to enter the holy city. Entering, the dismal clouds
In furrowed lightnings break their way, the wild flames whirring
   up
The bloody deluge, living flames winged with intellect
85   And reason; round the earth they march in order, flame by flame.
From the clotted gore & from the hollow den
Start forth the trembling millions into flames of mental fire
Bathing their limbs in the bright visions of Eternity.

Beyond this universal confusion, beyond the remotest pole
90   Where their vortexes begin to operate, there stands
A horrible rock far in the south. It was forsaken when
Urizen gave the horses of light into the hands of Luvah.
On this rock lay the faded head of the Eternal Man,
Enwrapped round with weeds of death, pale, cold, in sorrow
   and woe,
95   He lifts the blue lamps of his eyes & cries with heavenly voice,
Bowing his head over the consuming universe he cried:

'O weakness & O weariness! O war within my members!
My sons exiled from my breast pass to & fro before me,

ix *80.* Urizen fell into dragon form in viii *410*ff, though 'still his stony form
remained' (*420*): in viia *75–6* he is described by Orc as 'closed up / In that
transparent rock'.
ix *82. Began . . . holy city*] *1st rdg del.* Began to draw near to the Earth.
ix *83. whirring*] A doubtful reading.
ix *86–8.* Repeated from *42–4*, for no clear reason.
ix *89. Beyond*] *1st rdg del.* Without. The Night first began here (see *66n*):
this line refers back to the chaos of viii *468.*
ix *90. their vortexes . . . operate*] Their probably means 'the Zoas''; the
vortex is an organized system (cp. *Milton* pl.15.*21n*) in the universe, and
the sense of this obscure line is then 'beyond the furthest boundary of the
universe influenced by the Zoas'.
ix *91.* The south should have been Urizen's (vi *266*ff, especially *277–8*).
ix *92.* So in the key passage, i *187–9*, and the earlier iii *27–9*; in ii *17* Luvah
stole them.
ix *93.* Since ii *216* the man has 'slept the dark sleep of death': he now, by
an act of will, resumes the authority he had voluntarily laid down.
ix *98–103, 105–11.* These lines also occur in *Jerusalem* pl.19.*1–7,9–14* in the
third person and with other minor alterations

15*

My birds are silent on my hills, flocks die beneath my branches;
100 My tents are fallen, my trumpets & the sweet sounds of my harp
Is silent on my clouded hills, that belch forth storms & fires!
My milk of cows, & honey of bees, & fruit of golden harvest,
Are gathered in the scorching heat, & in the driving rain;
My robe is turned to confusion, & my bright gold to stones.
105 Where once I sat I weary walk, in misery & pain;
For from within my withered breast grown narrow with my woes
The corn is turned to thistles, & the apples into poison,
The birds of song to murderous crows, my joys to bitter groans,
[*120*] The voices of children in my tents to cries of helpless infants.
110 And all exiled from the face of light & shine of morning,
In this dark world, a narrow house, I wander up & down.
I hear Mystery howling in these flames of consummation.
When shall the Man of future times become as in days of old?
O weary life; why sit I here & give up all my powers
115 To indolence, to the night of death, when indolence & mourning
Sit hovering over my dark threshold?. Though I arise, look out
And scorn the war within my members, yet my heart is weak
And my head faint. Yet will I look again unto the morning.
Whence is this sound of rage, of men drinking each others' blood,
120 Drunk with the smoking gore & red, but not with nourishing
　　　wine?'

The Eternal Man sat on the rocks & cried with awful voice:

'O prince of light, where art thou? I behold thee not as once
In those eternal fields, in clouds of morning stepping forth
With harps & songs, where bright Ahania sang before thy face
125 And all thy sons & daughters gathered round my ample table.
See you not all this wracking furious confusion?
Come forth from slumbers of thy cold abstraction, come forth!
Arise to eternal births, shake off thy cold repose!
Schoolmaster of souls, great opposer of change, arise!
130 That the eternal worlds may see thy face in peace & joy,
That thou, dread form of certainty, mayest sit in town & village,
While little children play around thy feet in gentle awe,
Fearing thy frown, loving thy smile, O Urizen, Prince of Light!'

ix *101. Is*] In *Jerusalem* pl.19.4 this reads *Are*.
ix *112*. An addition, as *32*.
ix *119. Whence?*] The man realizes that the war is *within* him (but note that
the Man is a collective being, as well as an individual): and it is in his own
power to end it. Cp. viii *3n.*
ix *122*. Cp. ii *213*, where Urizen, prince of light, was entrusted by the
Man with the authority he has so misused.
ix *127. Come forth*] Christ's words to Lazarus in the tomb (*John* xi 43).

He called; the deep buried his voice, & answer none returned.

135 Then wrath burst round. The Eternal Man was wrath; again he
     cried:

'Arise, O stony form of death! O dragon of the deeps!
Lie down before my feet, O dragon! Let Urizen arise!
O how couldst thou deform those beautiful proportions
Of life & person? For as the person, so is his life proportioned.
140 Let Luvah rage in the dark deep even to consummation,
For if thou feedest not his rage it will subside in peace.
But if thou darest obstinate refuse my stern behest
Thy crown & sceptre I will seize, & regulate all my members
In stern severity & cast thee out into the indefinite
145 Where nothing lives, there to wander. And if thou returnest
     weary,
Weeping at the threshold of existence, I will steel my heart
Against thee to eternity & never receive thee more.
Thy self-destroying beast-formed science shall be thy eternal lot;
My anger against thee is greater than against this Luvah,
150 For war is energy enslaved, but thy religion
The first author of this war; & the distracting of honest minds
Into confused perturbation, & strife & honour & pride,
Is a deceit so detestable that I will cast thee out
If thou repentest not, & leave thee as a rotten branch to be burned
155 With Mystery the harlot, & with Satan for ever & ever.
Error can never be redeemed in all eternity,
But sin, even Rahab, is redeemed in blood & fury & jealousy—
That line of blood that stretched across the windows of the
     morning
Redeemed from error's power. Wake, thou dragon of the deeps!'
[121] Urizen wept in the dark deep, anxious his scaly form

ix *136. form . . . dragon*] Urizen, now seen in his fallen shape.
ix *140.* As in i *234–5*, where Urizen broke thieves' faith with Luvah.
ix *150. energy enslaved*] 1st rdg honest energy. This does not necessarily
imply a change of opinion; B. may have thought that 'honest' conveyed
the wrong idea.
ix *155–9.* Added, as *32* and *112.* The image is drawn from the exclusion of
Rahab's household from the fate of Jericho by the scarlet thread tied in her
window when the city was sacked at dawn(*Joshua* ii 18, 19, vi 15–25).
ix *163. futurity*] 1st rdg the past. Cp. iii *10* and *27* where Ahania asks the
scheming Urizen, 'Why wilt thou look upon futurity, darkening present
joy?' B. sees Urizen in all the planning and designing of man, who compli-
cates his life by structures and machines. Unlike Los's labours of love,
Urizen's are labours of fear and misery.

161   To reassume the human, & he wept in the dark deep,
    Saying: 'O that I had never drank the wine nor eat the bread
    Of dark mortality, nor cast my view into futurity, nor turned
    My back darkening the present, clouding with a cloud,
165   And building arches high & cities, turrets & towers & domes
    Whose smoke destroyed the pleasant garden, & whose running
        kennels
    Choked the bright rivers, burdening with my ships the angry deep,
    Through chaos seeking for delight, & in spaces remote
    Seeking the eternal which is always present to the wise,
170   Seeking for pleasure, which unsought falls round the infant's path,
    And on the fleeces of mild flocks who neither care nor labour.
    But I, the labourer of ages whose unwearied hands
    Are thus deformed with hardness, with the sword & with the spear,
    And with the chisel & the mallet, I, whose labours vast
175   Order the nations, separating family by family,
    Alone enjoy not. I am alone in misery supreme,
    Ungratified give all my joy unto this Luvah & Vala.
    Then go, O dark futurity! I will cast thee forth from these
    Heavens of my brain, nor will I look upon futurity more.
180   I cast futurity away & turn my back upon that void
    Which I have made, for lo! futurity is in this moment.
    Let Orc consume, let Tharmas rage, let dark Urthona give
    All strength to Los & Enitharmon, & let Los self-cursed
    Rend down this fabric, as a wall ruined & family extinct.
185   Rage, Orc; rage, Tharmas! Urizen no longer curbs your rage.'

    So Urizen spoke. He shook his snows from off his shoulders and
        arose
    As on a pyramid of mist, his white robes scattering
    The fleecy white—renewed he shook his aged mantles off
    Into the fires. Then, glorious bright, exulting in his joy,
190   He sounding rose into the heavens, in naked majesty,
    In radiant youth—when lo! like garlands in the eastern sky
    When vocal May comes dancing, from the east Ahania came
    Exulting in her flights; as when a bubble rises up
    On to the surface of a lake, Ahania rose in joy.
195   Excess of joy is worse than grief—her heart beat high, her blood

---

ix *166. kennels*] The open drains down the middle of the streets. In his life-
time B. must have seen the beginning of the worst choking of the
beauty of London.
ix *178, 179, 180, 181. futurity*] 1st rdg del. remembrance (cp. *163n*).
ix *186. snows*] An attribute of Urizen since his first appearance in *America*
208, but in *Four Zoas* specifically introduced in viia *28*.

Burst its bright vessels; she fell down dead, at the feet of Urizen
Outstretched, a smiling corse. They buried her in a silent cave;
Urizen dropped a tear, the Eternal Man darkened with sorrow.

The three daughters of Urizen guard Ahania's death couch,
200   Rising from the confusion in tears & howlings & despair,
Calling upon their father's name upon their rivers dark.

And the Eternal Man said: 'Hear my words, O prince of light:
[122] Behold Jerusalem, in whose bosom the Lamb of God
Is seen. Though slain before her gates, he self-renewed remains
205   Eternal & I through him awake from death's dark vale.
The times revolve; the time is coming when all these delights
Shall be renewed, & all these elements that now consume
Shall reflourish. Then bright Ahania shall awake from death,
A glorious vision to thine eyes, a self-renewing vision:
210   The spring, the summer to be thine, then sleep the wintry days
In silken garments spun by her own hands against her funeral.
The winter thou shalt plough & lay thy stores into thy barns,
Expecting to receive Ahania in the spring with joy:
Immortal thou, regenerate she; & all the lovely sex
215   From her shall learn obedience & prepare for a wintry grave,
That spring may see them rise in tenfold joy & sweet delight.
Thus shall the male & female live the life of eternity,
Because the Lamb of God creates himself a bride & wife,
That we his children evermore may live in Jerusalem,
220   Which now descendeth out of heaven, a city yet a woman,
Mother of myriads redeemed & born in her spiritual palaces,
By a new spiritual birth, regenerated from death.'
Urizen said: 'I have erred & my error remains with me.
What chain encompasses, in what lock is the river of light confined,
225   That issues forth in the morning by measure, & the evening by
carefulness?

ix *196–213*. Ahania here resembles Persephone, in that she is restored to
Urizen for the spring and summer of each year, and sleeps away from him
each winter; presumably B. was deliberately borrowing the myth, in a
form which is also found in i *56–9*. Urizen's eternal year is to be like an
earthly working day–work first, domestic pleasure afterwards. When
Urizen rests after his work, Ahania reappears (*341*). Here and after the
violence of *228–75* B. shows that the Man can only be redeemed in a new
creation, not by will alone.
ix *220*. Cp. *Revelation* xxi 2: 'And I John saw the holy city, new Jerusalem,
coming down from God out of heaven, prepared as a bride adorned for
her husband.'
ix *224*. *Lock*] The kind of lock used on inland waterways, which in B.'s
lifetime had undergone their greatest extension in England.

Where shall we take our stand to view the infinite & unbounded,
Or where are human feet? For lo! our eyes are in the heavens.'
He ceased: for, riven link from link, the bursting universe explodes.
All things reversed flew from their centres; rattling bones
230   To bones join, shaking, convulsed; the shivering clay breathes;
Each speck of dust to the earth's centre nestles round & round
In pangs of an eternal birth, in torment & awe & fear.
All spirits deceased, let loose from reptile prisons, come in shoals;
Wild furies from the tiger's brain & from the lion's eyes,
235   And from the ox & ass come moping terrors, from the eagle
And raven, numerous as the leaves of autumn. Every species
Flock to the trumpet, muttering over the sides of the grave and
        crying
In the fierce wind, round heaving rocks & mountains filled with
        groans,
On rifted rocks suspended in the air by inward fires.
240   Many a woeful company, & many on clouds & waters,
Fathers & friends, mothers & infants, kings & warriors,
Priests & chained captives, met together in a horrible fear.
And every one of the dead appears as he had lived before,
[123] And all the marks remain of the slave's scourge & tyrant's crown,
245   And of the priest's o'ergorged abdomen & of the merchant's thin
Sinewy deception, & of the warrior's outbraving & thoughtlessness,
In lineaments too extended & in bones too straight & long.

They show their wounds, they accuse, they seize the oppressor.
        Howlings began
On the golden palace, songs & joy on the desert. The cold babe
250   Stands in the furious air; he cries; the children of six thousand
        years
Who died in infancy rage furious, a mighty multitude rage furious,
Naked & pale standing on the expecting air to be delivered,

ix 229. The attractive compulsion of gravity ceases. Cp. *Ezekiel* xxxvii 7–
the vision of the valley of dry bones when, after Ezekiel spoke, 'there was
a noise, and behold a shaking, and the bones came together, bone to his
bone'.
ix 233. *Reptile prisons*] A conflation of two images: first, an image of dun-
geons loathsome with reptiles; second, B.'s common use of the serpent to
symbolize coiling, constricting mental imprisonment. Further, *234–6* con-
tain the notion that an animal's nature springs from a spirit hidden inside it.
ix 247. *straight*] B. has *strait*, but the context does not allow the meaning
'narrow'.
ix 248. *They*] The oppressed.
ix 249. *The cold babe*] A figure invented for the occasion, representing all
suffering children. Not Orc, who is always 'fiery'.

Rend limb from limb the warrior & the tyrant; reuniting in pain
The furious wind still rends around—they flee in sluggish effort.

255 They beg, they entreat; in vain now, they listened not to entreaty.
They view the flames, red rolling on through the wide universe
From the dark jaws of death beneath, & desolate shores remote—
These covering vaults of heaven & these trembling globes of earth.
One planet calls to another, & one star enquires of another:
260 'What flames are these coming from the south? What noise,
      what dreadful rout
As of a battle in the heavens? Hark! heard you not the trumpet
As of fierce battle?' While they spoke the flames come on
      intense, roaring;

They see him whom they have pierced, they wail because of him;
They magnify themselves no more against Jerusalem, nor
265 Against her little ones. The innocent accused before the judges
Shines with immortal glory. Trembling the judge springs from
      his throne,
Hiding his face in the dust beneath the prisoner's feet & saying,
'Brother of Jesus, what have I done? Entreat thy lord for me.
Perhaps I may be forgiven?' While he speaks the flames roll on.

270 And after the flames appears the cloud of the Son of Man
Descending from Jerusalem with power and great glory;
All nations look up to the cloud & behold him who was crucified.

The prisoner answers, 'You scourged my father to death before
      my face
While I stood bound with cords & heavy chains. Your hypocrisy
275 Shall now avail you nought.' So speaking he dashed him with his
      foot.

ix 254. they] The warrior and tyrant.
ix 263-4. Cp. Revelation i 7: 'Behold, he cometh with clouds; and every
eye shall see him, and they also which pierced him: and all kindreds of the
earth shall wail because of him.'
ix 265. The innocent] Anyone falsely accused, who is thereby a brother to
Jesus, himself falsely accused. B. may not have deliberately intended to
relate this scene to the Synagogue of Satan (viii 89ff), but there is a simi-
larity; the false judge has become the self-convicted criminal.
ix 270-1. Cp. Luke xxi 27: 'And then they shall see the Son of man coming
in a cloud with power and great glory.'
ix 273-5. These lines do not accord with B.'s doctrine of forgiveness: they
show, as does the entire passage, what happens to oppressors when their
victims get loose. The sufferers themselves are still to be purified by the
flail and the winepress (647ff).

The cloud is blood; dazzling upon the heavens, & in the cloud
Above, upon its volumes is beheld a throne & a pavement
Of precious stones, surrounded by twenty-four venerable patriarchs,
And these again surrounded by four wonders of the Almighty
280   Incomprehensible, pervading all, amidst & round about,
Fourfold each in the other reflected. They are named Lifes in
                Eternity—
Four starry universes, going forward from eternity to eternity.
And the fallen Man who was arisen upon the Rock of Ages
[124]   Beheld the vision of God, & he arose up from the rock,
285   And Urizen arose up with him walking through the flames
To meet the Lord coming to judgment. But the flames repelled
                them
Still to the rock; in vain they strove to enter the consummation
Together, for the redeemed Man could not enter the consummation.

Then seized the sons of Urizen the plough; they polished it
290   From rust of ages, all its ornaments of gold & silver & ivory
Reshone across the field immense, where all the nations
Darkened like mould in the divided fallows, where the weed
Triumphs in its own destruction. They took down the harness
From the blue walls of heaven, starry-jingling, ornamented
295   With beautiful art, the study of angels, the workmanship of demons
When heaven & hell in emulation strove in sports of glory.

ix 277. The throne, twenty-four elders, and the four beasts are found in
Revelation iv 4–6.
ix 279–82. Cp. *Revelation* iv 6: 'And before the throne there was a sea of
glass like unto crystal: and in the midst of the throne, and round about the
throne, were four beasts full of eyes before and behind.' The Greek word
for 'beasts' is ζῷα, zoa, which could also be translated, as in *281*, 'lifes'.
This, then, may be the beginning of B.'s idea of the fourfold grouping of
the Zoas; he does not identify the four beasts or 'lifes' here with Urizen,
Luvah, Urthona and Tharmas, and the word *Zoa* only appears in the title
of this poem in a very late revision.
ix 281. *Lifes*] B. has 'Life's'; but as elsewhere (e.g. in ii *120*, where the MS
has *Eccho's*), the -'s may only signify a plural.
ix 283. *Rock of Ages*] The phrase is not in the main biblical text, but is
found in the margin of the A.V. at *Isaiah* xxvi 4 as an alternative for
'everlasting strength' (in 'The Lord Jehovah is everlasting strength'). It
was in common use among nonconformist hymn writers (e.g. besides
Toplady, it occurs in John Newton and the Paraphrases), but B. uses it
in a pejorative sense.
ix 287. The thought of repentance is not enough; a change of activity is
needed, as the rest of the Night shows.
ix 288. *redeemed*] 1st rdg fallen.
ix 289. This is a reversal of what happened in ii *345*ff, and viib *167*ff.

The noise of rural work resounded through the heavens of heavens.
The horses neigh from the battle, the wild bulls from the sultry
   waste,
The tigers from the forests & the lions from the sandy deserts:
300   They sing, they seize the instruments of harmony, they throw away
The spear, the bow, the gun, the mortar; they level the fortifications,
They beat the iron engines of destruction into wedges,
They give them to Urthona's sons. Ringing the hammers sound
In dens of death, to forge the spade, the mattock & the axe,
305   The heavy roller to break the clods, to pass over the nations.

The sons of Urizen shout; their father rose; the eternal horses
Harnessed, they called to Urizen, the heavens moved at their call.
The limbs of Urizen shone with ardour. He laid his hand on the
   plough;
Through dismal darkness drave the plough of ages over cities
310   And all their villages, over mountains & all their valleys,
Over the graves & caverns of the dead, over the planets
And over the void spaces, over sun & moon & star & constellation.

Then Urizen commanded, & they brought the seed of men—
The trembling souls of all the dead stood before Urizen,
315   Weak wailing in the troubled air, east, west & north & south.
[125] He turned the horses loose & laid his plough in the northern
   corner
Of the wide universal field, then stepped forth into the immense.

Then he began to sow the seed. He girded round his loins
With a bright girdle, & his skirt filled with immortal souls.
320   Howling & wailing fly the souls from Urizen's strong hand.

For from the hand of Urizen the myriads fall like stars
Into their own appointed places; driven back by the winds
The naked warriors rush together down to the sea shores.
They are become like wintry flocks, like forests stripped of leaves,
325   The kings & princes of the earth cry with a feeble cry,

ix *306*. Urizen takes charge again of his steeds, which had been taken over
by Luvah, and puts them to proper use–an agricultural and productive
use. This is the beginning of a process of sowing and reaping souls, which
ends in the making of bread at the culmination of the poem.
ix *308. ardour*] Followed by deletion:

> He rose up from the Rock
> The Fallen Man wondring beheld.

ix *316*. Urizen has finished the ploughing; he sows broadcast, not with a
drill.
ix *325*. The sowing of souls is reminiscent of the parable of the sower
(*Luke* viii 5–15): according to B., it is kings and princes who fall on stony
ground.

Driven on the unproducing sands & on the hardened rocks;
And all the while the flames of Orc follow the vent'rous feet
Of Urizen, & all the while the trump of Tharmas sounds.
Weeping & wailing fly the souls from Urizen's strong hand;
330 The daughters of Urizen stand with cups & measures of foaming
          wine,
Immense upon the heavens with bread & delicate repasts.

Then follows the golden harrow in the midst of mental fires,
To ravishing melody of flutes & harps & softest voice;
The seed is harrowed in, while flames heat the black mould & cause
335 The human harvest to begin. Towards the south first sprang
The myriads, & in silent fear they look out from their graves.

Then Urizen sits down to rest, & all his wearied sons
Take their repose on beds. They drink, they sing, they view the
          flames
Of Orc in joy, they view the human harvest springing up.
340 A time they give to sweet repose till all the harvest is ripe.

And lo! like the harvest moon, Ahania cast off her death clothes.
She folded them up in care, in silence, & her brightening limbs
Bathed in the clear spring of the rocks, then from her darksome cave
Issued in majesty divine. Urizen rose up from his couch
345 On wings of tenfold joy, clapping his hands, his feet, his radiant
          wings
In the immense; as when the sun dances upon the mountains,
A shout of jubilee in lovely notes responds from daughter to
          daughter, ·
From son to son, as if the stars beaming innumerable
Through night should sing, soft warbling, filling earth & heaven;
350 And bright Ahania took her seat by Urizen in songs & joy.

The Eternal Man also sat down upon the couches of Beulah,
Sorrowful that he could not put off his new risen body
In mental flames; the flames refused, they drove him back to
          Beulah

ix *327. the flames of Orc*] Like the sun on earth, they cause the seed to grow.
ix *336.* A vivid image of seedlings.
ix *337–8.* Urizen is a farmer, and his family bring him refreshments in
the field.
ix *351. the couches of Beulah*] Cp. *Milton* pl.34.9ff, where they are used by
those as yet unresurrected. The Eternal Man is not yet fully redeemed; he
wishes to go straight into eternity, into the 'mental flames', leaving his
body behind. But the flames are driving him towards a complete redemp-
tion.

(His body was redeemed to be permanent through the mercy
divine).

[126] And now fierce Orc had quite consumed himself in mental flames,
356 Expending all his energy against the fuel of fire.
The regenerate Man stooped his head over the universe, & in
His holy hands received the flaming demon & demoness of smoke,
And gave them to Urizen's hands. The immortal frowned, saying:

360 'Luvah & Vala, henceforth you are servants. Obey & live.
You shall forget your former state; return & love in peace
Into your place, the place of seed, not in the brain or heart.
If gods combine against Man, setting their dominion above
The human form divine, thrown down from their high station
365 In the eternal heavens of human imagination, buried beneath
In dark oblivion with incessant pangs, ages on ages,
In enmity & war first weakened, then in stern repentance,
They must renew their brightness, & their disorganized functions
Again reorganize till they resume the image of the human,
370 Cooperating in the bliss of man, obeying his will,
Servants to the infinite & eternal of the human form.'

Luvah & Vala descended & entered the gates of dark Urthona,
And walked from the hands of Urizen in the shadows of Vala's
garden
Where the impressions of despair & hope for ever vegetate
375 In flowers, in fruits, in fishes, birds & beasts, & clouds & waters—
The land of doubts & shadows, sweet delusions, unformed hopes.
They saw no more the terrible confusion of the wracking universe,
They heard not, saw not, felt not all the terrible confusion;
For in their orbed senses within closed up they wandered at will.
380 And those upon the couches viewed them, in the dreams of Beulah,

ix *357. regenerate Man*] *1st rdg* Ancient Man.
ix *358. The demon and demoness*] Luvah and Vala. The degenerate form
of Luvah, Orc, is now consumed; they, and their passionate natures, are
to be servants, not the master of man.
ix *365. imagination*] *1st rdg del.* 'thought' – usually a less lively process, for B.,
than imagination.
ix *373.* At the time of the Fall, the Man had walked in Vala's Garden
(ii *37, 41*: but especially *19–20*): the beauties of that garden are deluding –
vegetated (374) – and limited (*379*), but they provide a place of rest and
renewal for Luvah and Vala, and later for Tharmas and Enion (*481ff*).
The narrative of this renewal continues to *555*, a digression filling in the
summer-time when Urizen's crop is growing. Then the harvest is de-
scribed.
ix *380. The couches*] Of those awaiting redemption in Beulah: see *351n.*

As they reposed from the terrible wide universal harvest.
Invisible Luvah in bright clouds hovered over Vala's head,
And thus their ancient golden age renewed. For Luvah spoke
With voice mild from his golden cloud upon the breath of morning:

385 'Come forth, O Vala, from the grass & from the silent dew;
Rise from the dews of death: for the Eternal Man is risen!'

She rises among flowers & looks toward the eastern clearness;
She walks, yea runs! Her feet are winged on the tops of the bending
    grass;
Her garments rejoice in the vocal wind & her hair glistens with dew.

390 She answered thus: 'Whose voice is this, in the voice of the
    nourishing air,
In the spirit of the morning awaking the soul from its grassy bed?

[127] Where dost thou dwell? For it is thee I seek, & but for thee
I must have slept eternally, nor have felt the dew of thy morning.
Look how the opening dawn advances with vocal harmony;

395 Look how the beams foreshow the rising of some glorious power!
The sun is thine; he goeth forth in his majestic brightness.
O thou creating voice that callest, & who shall answer thee?'

'Where dost thou flee, O fair one? Where dost thou seek thy
    happy place?'

'To yonder brightness, there I haste, for sure I came from thence;

400 Or I must have slept eternally nor have felt the dew of morning.'

'Eternally thou must have slept, nor have felt the morning dew,
But for yon nourishing sun; 'tis that by which thou art risen.
The birds adore the sun, the beasts rise up & play in his beams,
And every flower & every leaf rejoices in his light.

405 Then, O thou fair one, sit thee down, for thou art as the grass;
Thou risest in the dew of morning & at night art folded up.'

'Alas! am I but as a flower? Then will I sit me down,

ix *387*. The east belongs to Luvah.

ix *388*. Cp. *Aeneid* vii 808–9 (Camilla): *illa vel intactae segetis per summa volaret/gramina nec teneras cursu laessisset aristas* (She flies with almost untouched sandals over the top of the grain, Nor bends the slender stalks in her course).

ix *402*. In their limited temporary world (*372–9*) this is the best they can see. We know that their awakening is due to the Divine Mercy, and the rejuvenation of the Eternal Man.

ix *407*. Vala speaks. Cp. *Thel 6–14* (and *8, 12–13*, etc.):

Ah! Thel is like a watry bow, and like a parting cloud . . .
Ah! gentle may I lay me down, and gentle rest my head,
And gentle sleep the sleep of death. . . .

Then will I weep, then I'll complain & sigh for immortality,
And chide my maker—thee, O sun, that raisedst me to fall!'

410   So saying she sat down & wept beneath the apple trees:

'Oh, be thou blotted out, thou sun that raisedst me to trouble,
That gavest me a heart to crave & raisedst me, thy phantom,
To feel thy heat & see thy light & wander here alone—
Hopeless, if I am like the grass & so shall pass away.'

415   'Rise, sluggish soul, why sitst thou here? Why dost thou sit and
      weep?
Yon sun shall wax old & decay, but thou shalt ever flourish.
The fruit shall ripen & fall down, & the flowers consume away,
But thou shalt still survive. Arise, oh dry thy dewy tears!'

'Ha! Shall I still survive? Whence came that sweet & comforting
      voice,
420   And whence that voice of sorrow? O sun, thou art nothing now to
      me.
Go on thy course rejoicing, & let us both rejoice together;
I walk among his flocks & hear the bleating of his lambs—
Oh, that I could behold his face & follow his pure feet;
I walk by the footsteps of his flocks; come hither, tender flocks!
425   Can you converse with a pure soul that seeketh for her maker?
You answer not; then am I set your mistress in this garden:
I'll watch you & attend your footsteps. You are not like the birds
[128]   That sing & fly in the bright air, but you do lick my feet
And let me touch your woolly backs. Follow me as I sing,
430   For in my bosom a new song arises to my lord:

"Rise up, O sun, most glorious minister & light of day!
Flow on, ye gentle airs, & bear the voice of my rejoicing;
Wave freshly clear, waters flowing around the tender grass,
And thou, sweet smelling ground, put forth thy life in fruits and
      flowers."
435   Follow me, O my flocks, & hear me sing my rapturous song.
I will cause my voice to be heard on the clouds that glitter in the
      sun;
I will call & who shall answer me? I will sing, who shall reply?
For from my pleasant hills, behold the living, living springs

The lyrical style is similar, but the sentiment is not. Thel's complaint is
that her existence is purposeless, and her death will be unnoticed. Vala's
is more selfish, for her redemption is only beginning.
ix *415*. Luvah speaks.
ix *419*. Vala speaks. She has learnt to give the sun and all the material
world its true value. She can now enjoy it, not minding that she will, in
time, be parted from it, for it is only a limited vision.

Running among my green pastures, delighting among my trees.
440 I am not here alone, my flocks; you are my brethren,
And you, birds that sing & adorn the sky, you are my sisters:
I sing & you reply to my song; I rejoice & you are glad.
Follow me, O my flocks; we will now descend into the valley.
Oh, how delicious are the grapes flourishing in the sun!
445 How clear the spring of the rock, running among the golden sand!
How cool the breezes of the valley! And the arms of the branching
        trees
Cover us from the sun; come & let us sit in the shade.
My Luvah here hath placed me in a sweet & pleasant land,
And given me fruits & pleasant waters, & warm hills & cool
        valleys.
450 Here will I build myself a house, & here I'll call on his name;
Here I'll return when I am weary, & take my pleasant rest.'

So spoke the sinless soul, & laid her head on the downy fleece
Of a curled ram who stretched himself in sleep beside his mistress;
And soft sleep fell upon her eyelids, in the silent noon of day.

455 Then Luvah passed by & saw the sinless soul
And said, 'Let a pleasant house arise to be the dwelling-place
Of this immortal spirit growing in lower Paradise.'

He spoke, & pillars were builded, & walls as white as ivory;
The grass she slept upon was paved with pavement as of pearl;
460 Beneath her rose a downy bed & a ceiling covered all.

Vala awoke. 'When in the pleasant gates of sleep I entered,
I saw my Luvah like a spirit stand in the bright air;
Round him stood spirits like me who reared me a bright house—
And here I see thee, house, remain, in my most pleasant world.

[129] 'My Luvah smiled: I kneeled down, he laid his hands on my head;
466 And when he laid his hand upon me, from the gates of sleep I came
Into this bodily house, to tend my flocks in my pleasant garden.'

So saying, she arose & walked round her beautiful house;
And then from her white door she looked to see her bleating lambs;
470 But her flocks were gone up from beneath the trees into the hills.

ix 448. *A sweet and pleasant land*] Much of the phraseology of this ode is
quasi-biblical, but there are few actual borrowings. Note the psalmlike
parallelism of 445–51.
ix 453. A ram is more often noted for its fierceness: Vala's innocence has
tamed the lord of the flock. Cp. the illustration to *America* pl.7, where two
children lie asleep on 'a curled ram'.
ix 455–7. Vala has cast off her sin and become an innocent child; her new
being now must grow.

'I see the hand that leadeth me doth also lead my flocks'.
She went up to her flocks & turned oft to see her shining house.
She stopped to drink of the clear spring & eat the grapes & apples;
She bore the fruits in her lap, she gathered flowers for her bosom;
475 She called to her flocks, saying, 'Follow me, O my flocks'.

They followed her to the silent valley beneath the spreading trees,
And on the river's margin she ungirded her golden girdle.
She stood in the river & viewed herself within the watery glass,
And her bright hair was wet with the waters. She rose up from
          the river,
480 And as she rose, her eyes were opened to the world of waters.
She saw Tharmas sitting upon the rocks beside the wavy sea;
He stroked the water from his head & mourned faint through
          the summer vales.

And Vala stood on the rocks of Tharmas, & heard his mournful
          voice:

'O Enion, my weary head is in the bed of death.
485 For weeds of death have wrapped around my limbs in the hoary
          deeps.
I sit in the place of shells & mourn, & thou art closed in clouds.
When will the time of clouds be past, & the dismal night of
          Tharmas?
Arise, O Enion, arise, & smile upon my head
As thou dost smile upon the barren mountains and they rejoice.
490 When wilt thou smile on Tharmas, O thou bringer of golden day?
Arise, O Enion, arise, for lo! I have calmed my seas.'

So saying, his faint head he laid upon the oozy rock,
And darkness covered all the deep; the light of Enion faded
Like a faint flame quivering upon the surface of the darkness.

495 Then Vala lifted up her hands to heaven to call on Enion.
She called, but none could answer her, & the echo of her voice
          returned:

'Where is the voice of God that called me from the silent dew?
Where is the lord of Vala? Dost thou hide in clefts of the rock?
Why shouldst thou hide thyself from Vala, from the soul that
          wanders desolate?'

ix 480–1. Note the dreamlike changes, here and at 500–4. A sketch on
p. 124, of an aged man facing a young woman on a flower, might illustrate
this scene; although B. does not usually separate text and illustration so
widely.
ix 481. The story of the reunion of Tharmas and Enion, and their redemp-
tion, now begins. Vala has grown from childhood to a kind of motherhood.

500   She ceased, & light beamed round her like the glory of the
          morning,
[130]   And she arose out of the river & girded on her golden girdle.

And now her feet step on the grassy bosom of the ground
Among her flocks, & she turned her eyes toward her pleasant house,
And saw in the doorway beneath the trees two little children playing.
505   She drew near to her house & her flocks followed her footsteps;
The children clung around her knees, she embraced them and
          wept over them:

'Thou, little boy, art Tharmas, & thou, bright girl, Enion.
How are ye thus renewed & brought into the gardens of Vala?'

She embraced them in tears, till the sun descended the western hills,
510   And then she entered her bright house leading her mighty children,
And when night came the flocks laid round the house beneath
          the trees.
She laid the children on the beds which she saw prepared in the
          house,
Then last herself laid down & closed her eyelids in soft slumbers.

And in the morning when the sun arose in the crystal sky,
515   Vala awoke & called the children from their gentle slumbers:

'Awake, O Enion, awake! & let thine innocent eyes
Enlighten all the crystal house of Vala. Awake, awake,
Awake! Tharmas, awake, awake, thou child of dewy tears!
Open the orbs of thy blue eyes & smile upon my gardens.'

520   The children woke & smiled on Vala. She kneeled by the golden
          couch,
She pressed them to her bosom & her pearly tears dropped down:
'O my sweet children! Enion, let Tharmas kiss thy cheek.
Why dost thou turn thyself away from his sweet watery eyes?
Tharmas, henceforth in Vala's bosom thou shalt find sweet peace.
525   Oh, bless the lovely eyes of Tharmas & the eyes of Enion!'

They rose, they went out wandering, sometimes together,
          sometimes alone.
'Why weepest thou, Tharmas, child of tears, in the bright house
          of joy?
Doth Enion avoid the sight of thy blue heavenly eyes,
And dost thou wander with my lambs, & wet their innocent faces
530   With thy bright tears because the steps of Enion are in the gardens?
Arise, sweet boy, & let us follow the path of Enion.'

So saying, they went down into the garden among the fruits,

ix 527. Vala speaks.

And Enion sang among the flowers that grew among the trees:
And Vala said, 'Go, Tharmas, weep not. Go to Enion.'

[131] He said, 'O Vala, I am sick, & all this garden of pleasure
536   Swims like a dream before my eyes; but the sweet-smelling fruit
       Revives me to new deaths. I fade even like a water lily
       In the sun's heat, till in the night on the couch of Enion
       I drink new life, & feel the breath of sleeping Enion;
540   But in the morning she arises to avoid my eyes;
       Then my loins fade & in the house I sit me down & weep.'

       'Cheer up thy countenance, bright boy, & go to Enion.
       Tell her that Vala waits her in the shadows of her garden.'

       He went with timid steps, & Enion, like the ruddy morn
545   When infant spring appears in swelling buds & opening flowers
       Behind her veil withdraws, so Enion turned her modest head.

       But Tharmas spoke: 'Vala seeks thee, sweet Enion, in the shades,
       Follow the steps of Tharmas, O thou brightness of the gardens.'
       He took her hand; reluctant she followed in infant doubts.

550   Thus in eternal childhood straying among Vala's flocks,
       In infant sorrow & joy alternate, Enion & Tharmas played
       Round Vala in the gardens of Vala & by her river's margin.
       —They are the shadows of Tharmas & of Enion in Vala's world.

       And the sleepers who rested from their harvest work beheld these
           visions;
555   Thus were the sleepers entertained upon the couches of Beulah.

       When Luvah & Vala were closed up in their world of shadowy
           forms
       Darkness was all beneath the heavens; only a little light
       Such as glows out from sleeping spirits appeared in the deeps
           beneath,
       As when the wind sweeps over a cornfield, the noise of souls
560   Through all the immense borne down by clouds swagging in
           autumnal heat,
       Muttering along from heaven to heaven; hoarse roll the human
           forms
       Beneath thick clouds; dreadful lightnings burst & thunders roll,

ix 553. *The shadows*] Vala's world is temporary, a limited world where she
is to 'reorganize' (368–76). Only shadows can live there–it is not the world
of living reality. But as events in dreams have their effect on the living
personality, so Luvah, Vala, Tharmas and Enion are changed by what
happens to them in the dream world of Vala's garden.

ix 554. Cp. 337–40: we are recalled to Urizen's work from the story of
Luvah and Vala (cp. 373n).

Down pour the torrent floods of heaven on all the human harvest.
Then Urizen sitting at his repose on beds in the bright south
565 Cried: 'Times are ended!' He exulted; he arose in joy, he exulted,
He poured his light & all his sons & daughters poured their light
To exhale the spirits of Luvah & Vala through the atmosphere.
And Luvah & Vala saw the light, their spirits were exhaled
In all their ancient innocence; the floods depart, the clouds
570 Dissipate or sink into the seas of Tharmas. Luvah sat
Above on the bright heavens in peace; the spirits of men beneath
Cried out to be delivered, & the spirit of Luvah wept
Over the human harvest, & over Vala the sweet wanderer.
In pain the human harvest waved, in horrible groans of woe;
[132] The universal groan went up, the Eternal Man was darkened.
576 Then Urizen arose & took his sickle in his hand.
There is a brazen sickle & a scythe of iron hid
Deep in the south, guarded by a few solitary stars;
This sickle Urizen took, the scythe his sons embraced
580 And went forth & began to reap; & all his joyful sons
Reaped the wide universe, & bound in sheaves a wondrous
      harvest.
They took them into the wide barns with loud rejoicings, and
      triumph
Of flute & harp & drum & trumpet, horn & clarion.
The feast was spread in the bright south, & the regenerate Man
585 Sat at the feast rejoicing, & the wine of eternity
Was served round by the flames of Luvah all day & all the night.
And when morning began to dawn upon the distant hills
A whirlwind rose up in the centre, & in the whirlwind a shriek,
And in the shriek a rattling of bones, & in the rattling of bones

ix 577. The 'head' of the constellation Leo, the lion, is shaped like a sickle.
It is somewhat isolated and therefore distinctive. There are no constellations
named 'sickle' or 'scythe'. In *Revelation* xiv 14, where an angel comes to
harvest souls, 'having a sharp sickle', and in B. there are two harvests—
corn and grapes (576–83, 647–53, 690–723).
ix 582–4. The traditional celebrations after a successful harvest, including
the band: B. turns the feast into a magnificent banquet. Cp. the unhappy
feast in ii 89ff.
ix 588–91. Cp. the appearance of Tharmas in iii 139ff, where the sequence
is a crash, a flame, a dolorous groan: and also the appearance of God to
Elijah in 1 *Kings* xix 11–12 after 'a great and strong wind . . . and after
the wind an earthquake . . . and after the earthquake a fire . . . and after
the fire a still small voice'. But now Enion, not Tharmas appears; and it is
the real Enion, not a shadow; renewed with Vala in the limited world,
and now ready for the real world–Eternity.

590 A dolorous groan, & from the dolorous groan in tears
     Rose Enion like a gentle light. And Enion spoke, saying:

     'O dreams of death! the human form dissolving, companied
     By beasts & worms & creeping things, & darkness & despair!
     The clouds fall off from my wet brow, the dust from my cold
         limbs
595 Into the sea of Tharmas. Soon renewed, a golden moth
     I shall cast off my death-clothes & embrace Tharmas again.
     For lo! the winter melted away upon the distant hills,
     And all the black mould sings. She speaks to her infant race, her
         milk
     Descends down on the sand; the thirsty sand drinks & rejoices,
600 Wondering to behold the emmet, the grasshopper, the jointed worm;
     The roots shoot thick through the solid rocks, bursting their way;
     They cry out in joys of existence. The broad stems
     Rear on the mountain stem after stem, the scaly newt creeps
     From the stone & the armed fly springs from the rocky crevice.
605 The spider, the bat burst from the hardened slime crying
     To one another, "What are we, & whence is our joy & delight?
     Lo, the little moss begins to spring & the tender weed
     Creeps round our secret nest." Flocks brighten the mountains,
     Herds throng up the valley, wild beasts fill the forests.'

610 Joy thrilled through all the furious form of Tharmas, humanizing;
     Mild he embraced her whom he sought, he raised her through the
         heavens,
     Sounding his trumpet, to awake the dead; on high he soared
     Over the ruined worlds, the smoking tomb of the eternal prophet.

[133] The Eternal Man arose; he welcomed them to the feast.
615 The feast was spread in the bright south & the Eternal Man
     Sat at the feast rejoicing, & the wine of Eternity
     Was served round by the flames of Luvah all day & all the night.

     And many Eternal Men sat at the golden feast to see
     The female form now separate. They shuddered at the horrible
         thing—

ix *610–12.* Cp. the brutal sexuality of Tharmas's spectre in i *108–15.*
whom he sought] A reminder of Tharmas's long quest throughout the poem.
ix *613.* In iv *165* Los began to rebuild Urizen's golden world which had
been hurled into ruins in iii, but he was trapped by the chaos and 'became
what he beheld'. The *smoking tomb* is not otherwise mentioned.
ix *615–17.* Repeated from *585–87.*
ix *619.* This is strange here, as the word *now* suggests a new phenomenon,
though the emanations have long been separate, and are soon to be fully
reunited. The separation of the person into sexes is a common mark of the
fallen world (cp. *Jerusalem* pl.44.*33*) and it is so represented in *Urizen 315–25,*

620　Not born for the sport and amusement of man, but born to drink
　　　　up all his powers—
　　　They wept to see their shadows; they said to one another, 'This is
　　　　sin!
　　　This is the generative world!' They remembered the days of old;

　　　And one of the Eternals spoke; all was silent at the feast:

　　　'Man is a worm wearied with joy; he seeks the caves of sleep
625　Among the flowers of Beulah in his selfish cold repose,
　　　Forsaking brotherhood & universal love in selfish clay,
　　　Folding the pure wings of his mind, seeking the places dark,
　　　Abstracted from the roots of science. Then enclosed around
　　　In walls of gold we cast him like a seed into the earth,
630　Till times & spaces have passed over him. Duly every morn
　　　We visit him, covering with a veil the immortal seed;
　　　With windows from the inclement sky we cover him, & with walls
　　　And hearths protect the selfish terror, till divided all
　　　In families we see our shadows born; & thence we know⎫
635　That man subsists by brotherhood & universal love.　　　⎬ *Ephesians*
　　　We fall on one another's necks, more closely we embrace.⎭ *iii 10*

where Enitharmon is 'the *first* female form now separate'. In *Vala* there
have been separate females from the beginning of the fall. This may be a
contrivance to introduce the Eternal's words at *624*. There are other
anomalies: the unusual construction (*618–19*) 'many Eternal Men sat ...
to see'; B.'s normal style is more likely to be 'many Eternal Men sat ...
weeping (*or* trembling *or* darkened) to see. ...' And there is some contra-
diction in the presence of many Eternal Men; for Night ix as a whole is
dealing with the redemption of the one Universal Man, who is all men;
and this leaves no room, and normally no relevance, for other Eternals.
B. elsewhere has many Eternals, but not in Night ix–or elsewhere in *The
Four Zoas*, except as the Council of God. At the feast in ii, no one is
present but the elements of the Man, and servants. All these considerations
seem to suggest that B. has converted the Man's feast for Urizen and the
others into a feast among Eternals, momentarily, in order to fit in the
speech beginning 'Man is a worm' (*624–39*). The other Eternals then dis-
appear, and the rest of the Night is concerned only with the one Man and
his elements–the four Zoas, and their families.

ix *620*. Almost the same as ii *29*, where Los thus describes Enitharmon.

ix *622. generative*] *1st rdg del.* Vegetative.

ix *628. science*] *1st rdg del.* Nature.

ix *634*. The earthly desire for family life is a demonstration of man's
eternal need, in his nature, for 'Brotherhood and Universal Love'.
Ephesians iii 10 reads: '. . . to the intent that now unto the principalities
and powers in heavenly places might be known by [i.e. through] the church

Not for ourselves, but for the Eternal Family we live.
Man liveth not by self alone, but in his brother's face
Each shall behold the Eternal Father, & love & joy abound.'

640 So spoke the Eternal at the feast: they embraced the new-born Man,
Calling him Brother, image of the Eternal Father. They sat down
At the immortal tables, sounding loud their instruments of joy,
Calling the morning into Beulah; the Eternal Man rejoiced.

When morning dawned, the Eternals rose to labour at the vintage.
645 Beneath they saw their sons & daughters, wondering inconceivable
At the dark myriads in shadows in the worlds beneath.

The morning dawned. Urizen rose, & in his hand the flail
Sounds on the floor, heard terrible by all beneath the heavens;
Dismal loud redounding, the nether floor shakes with the sound,
[134] And all nations were threshed out & the stars threshed from their
husks.

651 Then Tharmas took the winnowing fan; the winnowing wind
furious
Above veered round, by the violent whirlwind driven west and
south,
Tossed the nations like chaff into the seas of Tharmas.

'O Mystery!' Fierce Tharmas cries: 'Behold, thy end is come:
655 Art thou she that made the nations drunk with the cup of religion?

the manifold wisdom of God.' The quotation is related to the phrase
'thence we know': B. tells how the Eternals *know*, through seeing the
necessity of brotherhood in the physical world, that so Man subsists. Cp.
Jerusalem pl.96.26–8.
ix *644*. Vintage is an incorrect word to use of corn harvesting, but B. takes
the association from *Revelation* xiv 15–20.
ix *645–6*. The punctuation is editorial, and proposes *wondering* as in appo-
sition to *they*–the Eternals wonder, not the sons and daughters. There is
no punctuation in the MS.
ix *647*. The harvest, left at *583*, continues with the threshing.
ix *650–1*. The threshing flail loosens the grain from the chaff; the wind or
a fan winnows the chaff away.
ix *654*. *Mystery*] The Rahab of viii *313–34*, *576–96*. But *Mystery* goes
behind her to the Tree of Mystery in viia *31*ff, which shoots up from the
errors of Urizen. The annihilation of Mystery, then, is the annihilation of
all that sprang from Urizen's evil-doing in the heart of the poem, as well
as of the delusive harlot Rahab. For these lines cp. *Revelation* xviii, where
the sudden and complete overthrow of 'that great city Babylon', elsewhere
equated with Mystery (*Revelation* xvii 5, quoted at viii *267n*), is lyrically
described at length in terms similar to these.

Go down, ye kings & councillors & giant warriors!
Go down into the depths, go down & hide yourselves beneath!
Go down, with horse & chariots & trumpets of hoarse war!

'Lo! how the pomp of Mystery goes down into the caves!
660   Her great men howl & throw the dust & rend their hoary hair;
Her delicate women & children shriek upon the bitter wind,
Spoiled of their beauty, their hair rent & their skin shrivelled up.
Lo, darkness covers the long pomp of banners on the wind,
And black horses & armed men & miserable bound captives.
665   Where shall the graves receive them all, & where shall be their
        place,
And who shall mourn for Mystery, who never loosed her captives?

'Let the slave grinding at the mill run out into the field;
Let him look up into the heavens & laugh in the bright air;
Let the enchained soul, shut up in darkness & in sighing,
670   Whose face has never seen a smile in thirty weary years,
Rise & look out—his chains are loose, his dungeon doors are open.
And let his wife & children return from the oppressor's scourge.

'They look behind at every step & believe it is a dream:
Are these the slaves that groaned along the streets of Mystery?
675   Where are your bonds & taskmasters? Are these the prisoners?
Where are your chains, where are your tears? Why do you look
        around?
If you are thirsty, there is the river: go bathe your parched limbs.
The good of all the land is before you; for Mystery is no more!'

Then all the slaves from every earth in the wide universe
680   Sing a new song, drowning confusion in its happy notes
(While the flail of Urizen sounded loud, & the winnowing wind of
        Tharmas)
So loud, so clear in the wide heavens; & the song that they sung
        was this,
Composed by an African black, from the little earth of Sotha:

'Aha! Aha! How came I here so soon in my sweet native land?
685   How came I here? Methinks I am as I was in my youth,
[135] When in my father's house I sat & heard his cheering voice;

ix *667–73*. So in *America 42–8*.
ix *674*. The slave trade was abolished in 1807 in British territories and
ships, but the agitation had preceded it for years. The allusion is also
biblical, for Mystery is Babylon (*654n*), the city which enslaved the Jews
in later Old Testament times, and which, in *Revelation*, is used as a 'cover'
name for Rome.

Methinks I see his flocks & herds & feel my limbs renewed;
And lo, my brethren in their tents & their little ones around them!'

The song arose to the golden feast, the Eternal Man rejoiced:
690 Then the Eternal Man said: 'Luvah, the vintage is ripe: arise!
The sons of Urizen shall gather the vintage with sharp hooks,
And all thy sons, O Luvah, bear away the families of earth.
I hear the flail of Urizen; his barns are full, no room
Remains, & in the vineyards stand the abounding sheaves beneath
695 The falling grapes, that odorous burst upon the winds. Arise!
My flocks & herds trample the corn, my cattle browse upon
The ripe clusters; the shepherds shout for Luvah, prince of love!
Let the bulls of Luvah tread the corn, & draw the loaded waggon
Into the barn, while children glean the ears around the door.
700 Then shall they lift their innocent hands & stroke his furious nose,
And he shall lick the little girl's white neck, & on her head
Scatter the perfume of his breath, while from his mountains high
The lion of terror shall come down, & bending his bright mane
And couching at their side, shall eat from the curled boy's white lap
705 His golden food, and in the evening sleep before the door.'

'Attempting to be more than Man we become less', said Luvah,
As he arose from the bright feast, drunk with the wine of ages.
His crown of thorns fell from his head, he hung his living lyre
Behind the seat of the Eternal Man & took his way,
710 Sounding the song of Los, descending to the vineyards bright.
His sons, arising from the feast with golden baskets, follow,
A fiery train—as when the sun sings in the ripe vineyards.
Then Luvah stood before the winepress; all his fiery sons
Brought up the loaded waggons with shoutings; ramping tigers play
715 In the jingling traces, furious lions sound the song of joy
To the golden wheels circling upon the pavement of heaven; & all
The villages of Luvah ring: the golden tiles of the villages
Reply to violins & tabors, to the pipe, flute, lyre & cymbal.

ix 690. The vintage, like the harvest of 577ff (q.v. note), derives from
Revelation xiv where, after the harvest, an angel 'thrust in his sickle into
the earth, and gathered the vine of the earth, and cast it into the great wine-
press of the wrath of God' (xiv 19). B.'s winepress follows in *721ff*.
ix 708. *His crown of thorns*] In viib *163–5* Luvah is said to be crucified as
Christ was, and throughout the poem they are associated in this way.
ix 710. *The song of Los*] B. may be recalling *Asia* (p. 245) which fore-
shadows the imminent overthrow by Orc of kings and priests, who serve
the evil Urizen. *Asia* ends with the revival of the dead for judgment in
terms suggesting a Bacchanalia (*62–4*): 'And milk and blood and glandous
wine / In rivers rush and shout and dance, / On mountain, dale and plain.'
ix 718. *pipe, flute, lyre and cymbal*] The first two may be real village instru-
ments, but the last two are certainly biblical.

       Then fell the legions of Mystery in maddening confusion
720   Down, down, through the immense, with outcry, fury & despair
       Into the winepresses of Luvah. Howling fell the clusters
       Of human families through the deep. The winepresses were filled,
       The blood of life flowed plentiful, odours of life arose
       All round the heavenly arches & the odours rose, singing this song:

[136] 'O terrible winepresses of Luvah! O caverns of the grave!
726   How lovely the delights of those risen again from death.
       O trembling joy! Excess of joy is like excess of grief.'

       So sang the human odours round the winepresses of Luvah.

       But in the winepresses is wailing, terror & despair.
730   Forsaken of their elements they vanish & are no more;
       No more but a desire of being, a distracted ravening desire,
       Desiring like the hungry worm & like the gaping grave.
       They plunge into the elements, the elements cast them forth
       Or else consume their shadowy semblance. Yet they, obstinate
735   Though pained to distraction, cry: 'Oh, let us exist, for
       This dreadful non-existence is worse than pains of eternal birth!
       Eternal death who can endure? Let us consume in fires,
       In waters stifling, or in air corroding, or in earth shut up.
       The pangs of eternal birth are better than the pangs of eternal
         death!'

740   How red the sons & daughers of Luvah! How they tread the
         grapes,

ix *719*. The harvest is in two parts–corn and grapes. *Mystery* is destroyed in both; by Urizen and by Luvah. The corn, which becomes bread, may signify Thought, and the grapes, which become wine, Feeling; cp. B.'s letter to Mrs Flaxman (14 Sept. 1800): 'The Bread of sweet thought and the wine of delight.' As always, one must beware of too narrow an interpretation, but the associations with Urizen and Luvah make this one plausible.

ix *724. odours*] Tharmas belongs to the tongue (i *96–8*), Urthona to the ear (i *12*), Urizen as prince of light to the eyes; thus the nose is left for Luvah.

ix *730. they*] There is no direct antecedent, but the sense is clear. *The human families (722)* are thrown into the press, and the truth they embody– that which is real in them–remains as the essence from which the wine is made; the falsehood, the parasitic *mystery*, deprived of the elements of the material world which gave it temporary form, vanishes and is annihilated.

ix *732. gaping*] *1st rdg del.* silent.

ix *740–68.* This passage is repeated in *Milton* pl.24(27).*3–41*, with certain alterations and additions. The additions there do not elucidate its context in *Four Zoas*.

Laughing & shouting, drunk with odours; many fall o'erwearied;
Drowned in the wine is many a youth & maiden. Those around
Lay them on skins of tigers or the spotted leopard or wild ass
Till they revive, or bury them in cool grots making lamentation.

745 But in the winepresses the human grapes sing not nor dance:
They howl & writhe in shoals of torment, in fierce flames
      consuming,
In chains of iron & in dungeons, circled with ceaseless fires
In pits & dens & shades of death, in shapes of torment & woe.
The plates, the screws and racks & saws & cords & fires & floods,
750 The cruel joy of Luvah's daughters, lacerating with knives
And whips their victims, & the deadly sports of Luvah's sons.

Timbrels & violins sport round the winepresses. The little seed,
The sportive root, the earthworm, the small beetle, the wise
      emmet
Dance round the winepresses of Luvah. The centipede is there,
755 The ground spider with many eyes, the mole clothed in velvet,
The earwig armed, the tender maggot, emblem of immortality,
The slow slug, the grasshopper that sings & laughs & drinks—
The winter comes, he folds his slender bones without a murmur—
There is the nettle that stings with soft down, & there
760 The indignant thistle whose bitterness is bred in his milk
And who lives in the contempt of his neighbour; there all the idle
      weeds
That creep about the obscure places show their various limbs
Naked in all their beauty, dancing round the winepresses.

They dance around the dying & they drink the howl & groan;
[137] They catch the shrieks in cups of gold, they hand them to one
      another.
766 These are the sports of love, & these the sweet delights of amorous
      play—

ix 745. The Dionysiac passions of Luvah express his nature; but the process
of purification is torment for those being purified.

ix 751. whips] The MS has 'whipt': Milton pl.24(27).36 has 'whips'.

ix 756. maggot] These were supposed to arise in dead flesh by spontaneous
birth.

ix 760. milk] i.e. his sap.

ix 764–7. The children of Luvah here have some of the nature of the un-
redeemed Vala, who enjoyed the cruel side of love play; and in 792–5 the
Eternal Man gives them in their turn a corrective punishment. The passage
is, however, partly allegorical and partly poetic imagination. The allegori-
cal part is that the children of Luvah are the representatives of various
sensual delights in man, which are by nature uncontrollable, which can be
cruel, and which have to be given rein in some way, but restrained at times.

16+B.

Tears of the grapes, the death sweat of the cluster, the last sigh
Of the mild youth who listens to the luring songs of Luvah.

The Eternal Man darkened with sorrow—& a wintry mantle
770 Covered the hills. He said, 'O Tharmas, rise; O Urthona!'

Then Tharmas & Urthona rose from the golden feast, satiated
With mirth & joy. Urthona, limping from his fall, on Tharmas
        leaned;
In his right hand his hammer. Tharmas held his shepherd's crook
Beset with gold: gold were the ornaments formed by sons of Urizen.

775 Then Enion & Ahania & Vala & the wife of dark Urthona
Rose from the feast, in joy ascending to their golden looms.
There the winged shuttle sang, the spindle & the distaff & the reel
Rang sweet the praise of industry. Through all the golden rooms
Heaven rang with winged exultation. All beneath howled loud;
780 With tenfold rout & desolation roared the chasms beneath,
Where the wide woof flowed down & where the nations are
        gathered together.

Tharmas went down to the winepresses & beheld the sons and
        daughters
Of Luvah quite exhausted with the labour & quite filled
With new wine, that they began to torment one another, and to
        tread
785 The weak. Luvah & Vala slept on the floor o'erwearied.

Urthona called his sons around him; Tharmas called his sons
Numerous: they took the wine, they separated the lees,
And Luvah was put for dung on the ground by the sons of Tharmas
        & Urthona.
They formed heavens of sweetest woods, of gold & silver & ivory,
790 Of glass & precious stones. They loaded all the waggons of heaven
And took away the wine of ages with solemn songs & joy.

Luvah & Vala woke, & all the sons & daughters of Luvah
Awoke. They wept to one another & they reascended
To the Eternal Man in woe. He cast them wailing into

ix 769. The year, which began with Urizen's sowing, has ended.
ix 772. *Urthona limping*] This is not referred to elsewhere; it equates
Urthona with Hephaestus, the lame smith of the Greek pantheon.
ix 777. *reel*] The bobbin of spun thread fitting into the weaving shuttle.
ix 779. *All beneath*] The legions of *Mystery* going down to annihilation.
ix 798. *Urthona*] Of the four Zoas, the least in need of redemption, the
last to arise in heaven, and with least ado. His spectre and Enitharmon's
were destroyed in ix 31. His is the final part in the making of the bread,
and the most creative.

795   The world of shadows through the air till winter is over & gone.
But the human wine stood wondering; in all their delightful
    expanses
The elements subside; the heavens rolled on with vocal harmony.

Then Los, who is Urthona, rose in all his regenerate power.
The sea that rolled & foamed with darkness & the shadows of
    death
800   Vomited out & gave up; all the floods lift up their hands,
Singing & shouting to the Man; they bow their hoary heads
And murmuring in their channels flow & circle round his feet.

[138] Then dark Urthona took the corn out of the stores of Urizen;
He ground it in his rumbling mills; terrible the distress
805   Of all the nations of earth, ground in the mills of Urthona.
In his hand Tharmas takes the storms, he turns the whirlwind
    loose
Upon the wheels, the stormy seas howl at his dread command,
And eddying fierce, rejoice in the fierce agitation of the wheels
Of dark Urthona. Thunders, earthquakes, fires, water, floods
810   Rejoice to one another; loud their voices shake the abyss,
Their dread forms tending the dire mills. The grey hoar-frost was
    there,
And his pale wife, the aged snow (they watch over the fires,
They build the ovens of Urthona). Nature in darkness groans,
And men are bound to sullen contemplations in the night.
815   Restless they turn on beds of sorrow, in their inmost brain
Feeling the crushing wheels—they rise, they write the bitter words
Of stern philosophy, & knead the bread of knowledge with tears
    and groans.

Such are the works of dark Urthona. Tharmas sifted the corn,
Urthona made the bread of ages, & he placed it
820   In golden & in silver baskets, in heavens of precious stone,
And then took his repose in winter, in the night of time.

The sun has left his blackness & has found a fresher morning,
And the mild moon rejoices in the clear & cloudless night,
And Man walks forth from midst of the fires, the evil is all
    consumed:

ix *800*. Cp. *Revelation* xx 13: 'And the sea gave up the dead which were in
it.'
ix *822–3*. Taken from *America 49–50*.
ix *824–5*. Man has destroyed all the evil in himself, and can look at infinity
without being harmed; earlier (*288*) he could not. Cp. also Vala's attempt
to walk at will in creation, in viib *266–85*; then her only reward was
melancholy.

825   His eyes behold the angelic spheres arising night & day;
      The stars consumed like a lamp blown out, & in their stead, behold!
      The expanding eyes of Man behold the depths of wondrous worlds.
      One earth, one sea beneath; nor erring globes wander, but stars
      Of fire rise up nightly from the ocean, & one sun
830   Each morning like a new-born man issues with songs of joy,
      Calling the ploughman to his labour & the shepherd to his rest.
      He walks upon the eternal mountains raising his heavenly voice,
      Conversing with the animal forms of wisdom night & day
      That, risen from the sea of fire, renewed walk o'er the earth.

835   For Tharmas brought his flocks upon the hills & in the vales;
      Around the Eternal Man's bright tent the little children play,
      Among the woolly flocks. The hammer of Urthona sounds
      In the deep caves beneath, his limbs renewed; his lions roar
      Around the furnaces, & in evening sport upon the plains.
840   They raise their faces from the earth, conversing with the Man:

      'How is it we have walked through fires & yet are not consumed?
      How is it that all things are changed, even as in ancient times?'

[139] The sun arises from his dewy bed, & the fresh airs
      Play in his smiling beams, giving the seeds of life to grow,
845   And the fresh earth beams forth ten thousand thousand springs of
          life.
      Urthona is arisen in his strength, no longer now
      Divided from Enitharmon, no longer the spectre Los.
      Where is the spectre of prophecy? Where the delusive phantom?
      Departed; and Urthona rises from the ruinous walls
850   In all his ancient strength to form the golden armour of science
      For intellectual war. The war of swords departed now,
      The dark religions are departed, & sweet science reigns.

End of the Dream

[Design]

      ix *827. expanding*] i.e. of infinite vision.
      ix *832. He*] The Man.
      ix *848. The spectre of prophecy*] Urthona's spectre, of iv–viia, which was
      sometimes in the right, but could not be trusted.
      ix *850. science*] Knowledge and understanding.
      ix *Design*. Below the text, most of the page is taken up with the figure
      of a young man springing up from a globe.

APPENDIX

The following are passages of some length that are still clearly visible in the MS, but have been cancelled from the text. Single lines and couplets similarly cancelled will be found in the footnotes; there are also signs in several places that B. has erased long passages, but as these have been overwritten it has proved impossible to recover them. The text of these passages has been modernized.

(a) Night i 1–3 as given above are the result of much alteration. At first there were seven lines:

1 This is the Dirge of Eno which shook the heavens with wrath;
2 And thus beginneth the Book of Vala which whosoever reads
3 If with his Intellect he comprehend the terrible sentence,
6 The heavens shall quake, the earth shall move, and shudder, and the mountains
7 With all their woods, the streams and valleys, wail in dismal fear.
4 To hear the sound of long resounding strong heroic verse
5 Marshalled in order for the day of intellectual battle.

The marginal numbers, added later, indicate a changed order. Various corrections were also made, which taken together would give the following text; the italicized words are an intermediate state. The altered numbering of lines is used here; but it is not altogether possible to tell at what time B. intended which changes. Finally B. numbered the lines yet again 1–3, ignoring the unwanted lines, and this gives the first three lines as printed in the main text.

> This is the Song of Enitharmon which shook the heavens with wrath,
> And thus beginneth the Book of Vala which whosoever reads
> If with his intellect he comprehend the terrible sentence,
> Hearing the march of long resounding strong heroic verse
> Marshalled in order for the day of intellectual battle,
> The heavens quake, the earth (*moves*) was moved and (*shudders*) shuddered, and the mountains
> With all their woods, the streams and valleys, wailed in dismal fear.

*

(b) After i 98, at the foot of p. 5 (see notes on p. 462):

> 'What have I done?' said Enion, 'Accursed wretch! What deed!
> Is this a deed of love? I know what I have done. I know
> Too late now to repent. Love is changed to deadly hate;
> A life is blotted out, and I alone remain possessed with fears!
> 5 I see the shadow of the dead within my soul wandering
> In darkness and solitude, forming seas of doubt and rocks of repentance.
> Already are my eyes reverted, all that I behold
> Within my soul has lost its splendour, and a brooding fear
> Shadows me o'er, and drives me outward to a world of woe!'
> 10 So wailed she, trembling before her own created phantasm,
> Who animating times on times by the force of her sweet song . . .

b 1. Accursed wretch] Since there is no punctuation, it may be that B. did not intend this to be part of the speech.

b 3. Love . . . hate] Probably first read: ' ?Alone ?possessed by deadly fears'.

b 4. A life] Perhaps a slip for *All life.*

b 5. shadow] Originally *remembrance*: *soul* was *eyes.*

b 6. seas . . . repentance] Originally read: 'seas of trouble and rocks of sorrow'.

b 11. This line (in pencil) replaces the following; but both are replaced by *99–103* of the main text:

> But standing on the rocks, her woven shadows, glowing bright . . .

*

(*c*) After line i *106*, thirty lines on p. 6, and seventeen on p. 7–a single sequence. Lines *48–59*, the rest of p. 7, are treated thus; *48–50* also cancelled; *51–6* not cancelled, but altered on a separate sheet (known as p. 143); *57–9* cancelled. Thus of the sixty-seven lines on pp. 6–7, only the first eight lines on p. 6 can stand in the text. The following text incorporates all B.'s alterations; these are many. The textual problems may be followed in the facsimile and in *Erdman 1965*, pp. 741–3. Italicized words and lines were deleted, but not replaced.

[6]   Searching for glory, wishing that the heavens had eyes to see,
       And courting that the earth would ope her eyelids, and behold
       Such wondrous beauty repining in the midst of all his glory,
       That nought but Enion could be found to praise, adore, and love.
5   Three days in self-admiring raptures on the rocks he flamed,
       And three dark nights repined the solitude: but the third morn
       Astonished, he found Enion hidden in the darksome cave.

       She spoke: 'What am I? wherefore was I put forth on these rocks,
       Among the clouds to tremble in the wind in solitude?
10 Where is the voice that lately woke the desert? Where the face
       That wept among the clouds, and where the voice that shall reply?
       No other living thing is here. The sea, the earth, the heaven,
       And Enion desolate! Where art thou, Tharmas?–O return!'

       Three days she wailed, and three dark nights, sitting among the rocks,
15 While the bright spectre hid himself among the backing clouds.
       Then sleep fell on her eyelids in a chasm of the valley.
       The sixteenth morn, the spectre stood before her manifest.

       The spectre thus spoke: 'Who art thou, diminutive husk and shell?
       Broke from my bonds I scorn my prison; I scorn, and yet I love.
               Art thou not my slave, and shalt thou dare
20 To smite me with thy tongue? Beware lest I sting also thee!
       If thou hast sinned and art polluted, know that I am pure
       And unpolluted, and will bring to rigid strict account
       All thy past deeds. Hear what I tell thee! Mark it well! Remember!
       This world is thine in which thou dwellest: that within thy soul,
25 That dark and dismal infinite where Thought roams up and down

Is mine; and there thou goest when with one sting of my tongue,
Envenomed thou rollst inwards to the place whence I emerged!'

She trembling answered, 'Wherefore was I born, and what am I? –
A sorrow and a fear, a living torment and naked victim!
30   I thought to weave a covering for my sins from wrath of Tharmas:
[7] *Examining the sins of Tharmas I soon found my own.*
O slay me not: thou art his wrath embodied in deceit.
I thought Tharmas a sinner and murdered his emanations,
His secret loves and graces – Ah me, wretched! What have I done?
35   For now I find that all those emanations were my children's souls,
And I have murdered them with cruelty above atonement.
Those that remain have fled from my cruelty into the deserts;
And thou the delusive tempter to these deeds sittest before me.
And art thou Tharmas? All thy soft delusive beauty cannot
40   Tempt me to murder my own soul, and wipe my tears and smile
In this thy world – not mine: though dark, I feel my world within.'

The spectre said: 'Thou sinful woman! Was it thy desire
That I should hide thee with my power, and delight thee with my
    beauty?
And now thou dark'nest in my presence! Never from my sight
45   Shalt thou depart to weep in secret. In my jealous wings
I evermore will hold thee, when thou goest out or comest in.
'Tis thou hast darkened all my world, O woman, lovely bane!'

Thus they contended all the day among the caves of Tharmas,
Twisting in fearful forms and howling, howling, harsh shrieking;
50   Howling, harsh shrieking; mingled, their bodies join in burning
    anguish,
Mingling his horrible brightness with her tender limbs; then high
    she soared
Shrieking above the ocean, a bright wonder *that* nature *shuddered at,*
Half woman and half spirit; all his lovely changing colours mix
With her fair crystal clearness; in her lips and cheeks his poisons rose
55   In blushes like the morning, and his scaly armour softening;
A monster lovely in the heavens or wandring on the earth,
With spirit voice incessant wailing; in incessant thirst,
Beauty all blushing with desire, mocking her fell despair,

Wandering desolate, a wonder abhorred by gods and men . . .

c 15. *backing*] An uncertain reading.
c 19. *Art thou* . . .] This is on the same line as 'The spectre thus spoke', but
the rest of *18–19* was inserted later.
c 24–6. *thine* . . . *mine*] Originally the other way round, *mine . . . thine.*
c 38. This line began *Among wild beasts to roam* (continuing *37*), but the
words were deleted.
c 51–6. These lines remain in the main text, with alterations.
c 52. *nature*] *1st rdg del.* 'Beulah'. B. retained the deleted words (in italics)
in his later text on p. 143.

(*d*) After i *127*, in the middle of p. 8:

> But those in great Eternity met in the Council of God
> As One Man, hovering over Gilead and Hermon:
> (He is the good Shepherd; he is the Lord and Master,
> To create Man morning by morning, to give gifts at noonday.)
> 5   Enion brooded o'er the rocks; the rough rocks, groaning, vegetate–
> Such power was given to the solitary wanderer–
> The barked oak, the long-limbed beech, the chestnut tree, the pine,
> The pear-tree mild, the frowning walnut, the sharp crab, and apple sweet,
> The rough bark opens; twittering peep forth little beaks and wings–
> 10   The nightingale, the goldfinch, robin, lark, linnet and thrush;
> The goat leaped from the craggy cliff, the sheep awoke from the mould;
> Upon its green stalk rose the corn, waving innumerable,
> Enfolding the bright infants from the desolating winds.

d 1–2. Cp. i *164* and viii *1–2*.
d 3–4. These lines are inserted (the brackets are editorial), and derive from an erased passage on p. 99 (under viii *4–9*–see (*f*) below) and ultimately form *Jerusalem* pl. *34.23*.
d 13. the bright infants] Los and Enitharmon (see main text).

*

(*e*) Written in the margin of p. 11 and marked to follow ii *40*, but then deleted:

> Refusing to behold the Divine Image which all behold
> And live thereby: he is sunk down into a deadly sleep;
> But we, immortal in our own strength, survive by stern debate,
> Till we have drawn the Lamb of God into a mortal form.
> 5   And that he must be born is certain; for One must be All,
> And comprehend within himself all things both small and great.
> We therefore, for whose sake all things aspire to be and live
> Will so receive the Divine Image that amongst the Reprobate
> He may be devoted to destruction from his mother's womb.

e 2. he] The fallen Man (see ii *39* in main text).
e 3. immortal in our own strength] A fallacy.
e 8. Reprobate . . . devoted to destruction] A concept developed in *Milton* (q.v. pls 11.*21–2* and 26.*32–8*).

*

(*f*) Lines viii *4–9* are written in the space where five lines had been erased. These can be partially read as follows; they appear to have been continuous with *1–3* of the main text which is therefore printed here (in italics):

> *Then all in great Eternity met in the Council of God*
> *As one Man, even Jesus, upon Gilead and Hermon,*
> *Upon the limit of contraction to create the fallen Man:*

He is . . .
5 He is the Good Shepherd; he is the Lord and Master;
He is the Shepherd of Albion; he is all in all:–
In Eden, in the Garden of God, and in heavenly Jerusalem
To create Man morning by morning, to give gifts at noonday.

f 4. One or two words in this line can be conjecturally read (see *Erdman 1965*, p. 757): the evidence is that, as is to be expected, the line gives attributes of Jesus.
f 5. As in *f 4*, He is Jesus.
f 6. Shepherd of Albion] The reading of this phrase is uncertain.

*

(*g*) After viii *9, overhead*, the words at the end of the line, plus the first five out of six in the margin (the sixth of these lines was not cancelled, and is *10* of the main text):

but other wings
They had which clothed their bodies like a garment of soft down,
Silvery-white, shining upon the dark blue sky in silence;
Their wings touched the heavens, their fair feet hovered above
The swelling tides; they bent over the dead corse like an arch,
5 Pointed at top in highest heavens of precious stones and pearl.

*

(*h*) p. 106 is copied from a draft on a separate sheet, known as p. 145. This sheet contains the following lines, which B. erased in the draft and did not transfer to p. 106. Of the following lines, *h 2* (in italics) was not erased, and so appears in the main text as viii *318*:

In which is Tirzah untranslucent, an opaque covering,
Who is Mystery, Babylon the great, the mother of harlots.
And Rahab stripped off Luvah's robes from off the Lamb of God.
Then first she saw his glory, and her harlot form appeared
5 In all its turpitude beneath the divine light; and of Luvah's robes
She made herself a mantle.
Also the vegetated bodies which Enitharmon wove in her looms
Opened within the heart and in the loins and in the brain
To Beulah; and the dead in Beulah descended through their gates.
10 And some were woven onefold, some twofold, and some threefold
In head or heart or reins according to the fittest order
Of most mournful pity and compassion to the spectrous dead.

h 6. This line shows no sign of completion. The theme of the next lines is different from that of *1–6*.

*

(*j*) After viii *571* (itself an interpolation), eight deleted lines:

But Rahab hewed a sepulchre in the Rock of Eternity,
And, placing in the sepulchre the body which she had taken

16*

From the divine Lamb, wept over the sepulchre, weaving
Her web of Religion around the sepulchre times after times, beside
    Jerusalem's gate:
5 But as she wove, behold! the bottom of the sepulchre
Rent, and a door was opened through the bottom of the sepulchre
Into Eternity. And as she wove, she heard a voice behind her
    calling her:
She turned, and saw the Divine Vision, and her

j 1. hewed] 1st rdg del. built.

j 2-3. Written over 'The End of the Eighth Night' erased.

j 4. Her web of religion] This web was originally attributed to Urizen (cp.
vi 241ff, and *Urizen 462-9*).

j 8. The passage ends thus, in mid-sentence; there is no sign of its com-
pletion.

*

(k) There are three fragments, one a torn piece of paper. These are known
as pp. 141–2, 143–4 (the torn piece) and 145 respectively (the reverse of p.
145 is blank). For pp. 143–4, see (c) above; but the text of p. 143 is used in
the main text, p. 298 above. Page 144 contains only a sketch, and above it
only the torn-off words:

That I should hide thee with my power, and . . .
And now thou darkenest in my presence, never from my sight

For p. 145, see (h) above. This leaves pp. 141–2: these contain a number of
bits of verse, separated from one another by lines across the page. None is
used in the final text, but most seem to be notes for the fall of Tharmas
and Enion into sexual division, in Night i.

[141] Beneath the veil of Vala rose Tharmas from dewy tears.
The eternal Man bowed his bright head, and Urizen, prince of light,
Astonished looked from his bright portals, calling thus to Luvah:
'O Luvah in the——————————————————————————
5   Astonished looked from his bright portals. Luvah, king of love,
Awakened Vala. Ariston ran forth with bright Onana,
And dark Urthona roused his shady bride from her deep den.
Awaking from his stony slumber
Pitying they viewed the new-born demon, for they could not love
10 After their sin——————————————————————
Male-formed the demon; mild athletic force his shoulders spread,
And his bright feet firm as a brazen altar: but the parts
To love devoted, female. All astonished stood the hosts
Of heaven, while Tharmas with winged speed flew to the sandy
    shore.
15 He rested on the desert wild and on the raging sea.
He stood and stretched his wings &c——————

<hr>

With printless feet scorning the concave of the joyful sky,
Female her form, bright as the summer: but the parts of love
Male, and her brow radiant as day, darted a lovely scorn.
20 Tharmas beheld from his high rocks &——————————

[142] The ocean calm, the clouds fold round, and fiery flames of love
    Enwrap the immortal limbs struggling in terrific joy
    Not long: thunders, lightnings, swift rending and blasting winds
    Sweep o'er the struggling copulation; in fell writhing pangs
25 They lie, in twisting agonies beneath the covering heavens.

The womb impressed, Enion fled and hid in verdant mountains;
Yet here his heavenly orbs &c

From Enion pours the seed of life and death in all her limbs;
    Frozen in the womb of Tharmas rush the rivers of Enion's pain:
30 Trembling he lay, swelled with the deluge, stifling in the anguish

k 1. Vala] *1st rdg del.* ?Enion.
k 3. This line deleted. The first word read *Astonish*–a clear slip (see *k 5*).
k 4. This unfinished line deleted, evidently in the process of composition.
k 6. Onana] The reading is uncertain.
k 8. This line interpolated, then deleted.
k 10. This phrase deleted.
k 14. shore] Altered to 'ocean', but the alteration then deleted.
k 16. The continuation is not found elsewhere.
k 20. The ' &' may, as in *k 16*, and *27* on p. 142, mean ' &c'. But here also the continuation is not extant.
k 21–5. An essay for the 'love-scene' of Tharmas's spectre and Enion, *i 102–15.*

All these '*k*' fragments imply an earlier form of the fall of Tharmas (see i headnote) rejected in favour of the present one. The final text derives this fall ultimately from the quarrel of Urizen and Luvah over the Man: *k 1–2* of p. 141 suggest that the Man's fall is due to Vala, and that Urizen and Luvah (*k 2–6*) are still unfallen. This fits the narrative of ii *13*ff and iii *40*ff. The mention of Ariston, and the state of Tharmas as a newly-created hermaphrodite, imply that the pattern of *Four Zoas* was not settled when these notes were made.

22 'When Klopstock England defied'

Date. August–September 1800 (when Blake left Lambeth), although the evidence is not final, and the verses may date from about 1797. Klopstock (German author of the epic *Messias*, and known as 'the German Milton') had for some time been decrying the potentialities and achievements of English verse, and in particular criticising a supposed coarseness, which he traced to Swift. Rodney G. Dennis has observed that Hayley may have shown Blake, before or after the removal to Felpham, the August 1800 issue of the London journal, *The German Museum*. This contained comparison by Klopstock of English and German verse translations of Homer, contrived to the disadvantage of English. B. replied appropriately, in these verses written on the original p. 1 (now p. 5) of the NB.

> When Klopstock England defied,
> Uprose terrible Blake in his pride.
> For old Nobodaddy aloft
> Farted and belched and coughed,
> 5 Then swore a great oath that made Heaven quake,
> And called aloud to English Blake.
> Blake was giving his body ease
> At Lambeth beneath the poplar trees;
> From his seat then started he
> 10 And turned himself round three times three.
> The moon at that sight blushed scarlet red,
> The stars threw down their cups and fled,
> And all the devils that were in hell
> Answered with a ninefold yell.
> 15 Klopstock felt the entripled turn,
> And all his bowels began to churn,
> And his bowels turned round three times three
> And locked in his soul with a ninefold key,
> That from his body it ne'er could be parted
> 20 Till to the last trumpet it was farted.
> Then again old Nobodaddy swore
> He ne'er had seen such a thing before—
> Since Noah was shut in the ark,
> Since Eve first chose her Hell-fire spark,
> 25 Since 'twas the fashion to go naked,
> Since the old anything was created;
> And so feeling he begged him to turn again
> And ease poor Klopstock's ninefold pain.
> From pity then he reddened round
> 30 And the spell removed and unwound.
>
> If Blake could do this when he rose up from shite,
> What might he not do if he sat down to write?

¶ 19. 3. *Nobodaddy* appears also in two other places in the NB: 'To Nobodaddy' (p. 155), and 'Let the Brothels of Paris be opened' (p. 168). Both are at the end of the book, where B. was writing with the pages upside-down, and can be dated Oct. 1792–Jan. 1793. B. repeats *3–4* here from 'Let the Brothels. . . .'
30. Followed by two del. lines

> It spun back on the stile
> Whereat Klopstock did smile.

23 Poems in letters (i) 1800

These poems are found in letters written at the beginning of B.'s stay at Felpham and show his feelings about the new life he saw beginning. Flaxman, a fellow-artist, was at this time, as can be seen, a great friend of B.'s, although later B.'s attitude changed, as the verses on p. 473 below show. Thomas Butts was a constant friend, and, not being an artist, was never involved in B.'s professional quarrels.

I

TO MY DEAREST FRIEND, JOHN FLAXMAN

I bless thee, O Father of Heaven and Earth, that ever I
  saw Flaxman's face.
Angels stand round my spirit in Heaven, the blessed
  of Heaven are my friends upon Earth.
When Flaxman was taken to Italy, Fuseli was given
  to me for a season,
And now Flaxman hath given me Hayley, his friend
  to be mine, such my lot upon Earth.
5 Now my lot in the Heavens is this; Milton loved me in
  childhood and showed me his face;
Ezra came with Isaiah the prophet, but Shakespeare
  in riper years gave me his hand;
Paracelsus and Behmen appeared to me; terrors
  appeared in the Heavens above
And in Hell beneath, and a mighty and awful change
  threatened the Earth.

¶ 23. This letter bears the postmark '12 o'clock 12 Sp. 1800'.
i 1–3. Flaxman ... Fuseli] B. met Flaxman about 1780; according to Gilchrist he met Fuseli a little later. But Flaxman did not go to Italy until 1787 (staying until 1794), and Gilchrist's ambiguity may be noted: 'To the list of ... friends was afterwards added Henry Fuseli. ... In 1780, Fuseli ... became a neighbour, lodging in Broad Street, where he remained until 1782' (Life of W.B., ch v). But on 26 Aug. 1799, B. wrote to George Cumberland, 'even Johnson and Fuseli have discarded my graver' –hence, perhaps, the phrase 'for a season'. Fuseli (originally Heinrich Füsslich) was a Continental intellectual, and his crucial influence on B. c. 1790 remains to be properly investigated. Flaxman was a Swedenborgian.
i 6. Ezra] The Book of Ezra describes the return of the exiles to Jerusalem, its rebuilding, and the dangers of their intermarriage with the local people. It is not a part of the Bible that has obviously influenced B., despite its subject-matter.
i 7. Paracelsus and Behmen] Renaissance mystical writers; for Behmen (the common eighteenth-century spelling of Boehme) see headnote to Urizen, p. 248 above.

The American War began. All its dark horrors passed
      before my face
10   Across the Atlantic to France. Then the French
      Revolution commenced in thick clouds,
   And my angels have told me that seeing such visions
      I could not subsist on the Earth
   But by my conjunction with Flaxman, who knows to
      forgive nervous fear.

II

TO MY DEAR FRIEND, MRS. ANNA FLAXMAN
   H[ercules] B[uildings] Lambeth, 14 Sepr 1800
   This song to the flower of Flaxman's joy,
   To the blossom of hope for a sweet decoy;
   Do all that you can, or all that you may,
   To entice him to Felpham and far away,
5   Away to sweet Felpham, for Heaven is there;
   The ladder of angels descends through the air;
   On the Turret its spiral does softly descend,
   Through the village then winds, at my cot it does end.
   You stand in the village and look up to Heaven;
10   The precious stones glitter on flights seventy-seven,
   And my brother is there, and my friend and thine
   Descend and ascend with the bread and the wine.
   The bread of sweet thought and the wine of delight
   Feeds the village of Felpham by day and by night,
15   And at his own door the blessed Hermit does stand,
   Dispensing unceasing to all the whole land.

III

   To my friend Butts I write
   My first vision of light:
   On the yellow sands sitting,
   The sun was emitting
5   His glorious beams
   From heaven's high streams.
   Over sea, over land,
   My eyes did expand
   Into regions of air,

ii. This poem is written at the foot of a letter from Catherine Blake to
Mrs Flaxman, and signed 'W. Blake'. The Blakes moved to Felpham on
the 18th.
ii 16. *the blessed Hermit*] Hayley. The 'Turret' (7) was his new house; its
walls ensured complete privacy.
iii. Letter dated 2 Oct. 1800.

10   Away from all care;
      Into regions of fire,
      Remote from desire;
      The light of the morning
      Heaven's mountains adorning,
15   In particles bright
      The jewels of light
      Distinct shone and clear—
      Amazed and in fear
      I each particle gazed,
20   Astonished, amazed:
      For each was a man
      Human-formed. Swift I ran,
      For they beckoned to me,
      Remote by the sea,
25   Saying, 'Each grain of sand,
      Every stone on the land,
      Each rock and each hill,
      Each fountain and rill,
      Each herb and each tree,
30   Mountain, hill, earth and sea,
      Cloud, meteor and star
      Are men seen afar '.
      I stood in the streams
      Of heaven's bright beams
35   And saw Felpham sweet
      Beneath my bright feet,
      In soft female charms;
      And in her fair arms
      My shadow I knew,
40   And my wife's shadow too,
      And my sister and friend.
      We like infants descend
      In our shadows on earth,
      Like a weak mortal birth;
45   My eyes more and more
      Like a sea without shore
      Continue expanding,
      The heavens commanding,
      Till the jewels of light,
50   Heavenly men beaming bright,
      Appeared as one man,
      Who complacent began
      My limbs to enfold
      In his beams of bright gold;
55   Like dross purged away

All my mire and my clay,
Soft-consumed in delight
In his bosom sun-bright
I remained. Soft he smiled,
60   And I heard his voice mild,
Saying, 'This is my fold,
O thou ram horned with gold—
Who awakest from sleep
On the sides of the deep,
65   On the mountains around,
The roarings resound
Of the lion and wolf,
The loud sea and deep gulf.
These are guards of my fold,
70   O thou ram horned with gold.'
And the voice faded mild;
I remained as a child;
All I ever had known
Before me bright shone.
75   I saw you and your wife
By the fountains of life.
Such the vision to me
Appeared on the sea.

IV

TO MRS. BUTTS

Wife of the friend of those I most revere,
Receive this tribute from a harp sincere.
Go on in virtuous seed, sowing on mould
Of human vegetation, and behold
5   Your harvest springing to eternal life,
Parent of youthful minds, and happy wife.

24 On the Virginity of the Virgin Mary and Joanna Southcott

Date: c. late 1802. Joanna Southcott was a Devonshire working girl who became convinced that she was the vehicle of a divine revelation. Her adherents grew in numbers, and in 1801 she gained some attention in

iii *62. Ram horned with gold*] B. himself; a reminiscence of, but not a direct reference to, the ram seen in a vision by Daniel (ch. viii); though that ram (which signified Egypt) was overcome by a goat.
iv. Lines written at the end of the letter which contains the previous poem.

London, where she arrived in May 1802. In October 1802 she proclaimed
that she was to give birth to the second Christ; and this is probably the
period of B.'s poem, which was written on p. 2 (now p. 6) of the Note-
book. In May 1813 she declared that she was pregnant with this child,
whom she named Shiloh in unfulfilled anticipation; she died on 27 Dec.
1814.

> Whate'er is done to her she cannot know,
> And if you ask her she will swear it so.
> Whether 'tis good or evil none's to blame;
> No one can take the pride, no one the blame.

25 Poems in letters (ii) 1802-3

The letters of 1800 (No. 23 above) show B.'s enthusiasm at the prospects
for his stay at Felpham. The letter, and the passage of verse given below,
show how those hopes had faded. The second piece is the end of a letter in
which B. has described his encounter with John Scholfield (see Chrono-
logical Table above, p. xviii).

i [TO THOMAS BUTTS, 22 NOVEMBER 1802]

> With happiness stretched across the hills
> In a cloud that dewy sweetness distils,
> With a blue sky spread over with wings
> And a mild sun that mounts and sings,
> 5 With trees and fields full of fairy elves
> And little devils who fight for themselves,
> Remembering the verses that Hayley sung
> When my heart knocked against the root of my tongue;
> With angels planted in hawthorn bowers
> 10 And God himself in the passing hours,
> With silver angels across my way
> And golden demons that none can stay;
> With my father hovering upon the wind
> And my brother Robert just behind
> 15 And my brother John, the evil one,
> In a black cloud making his moan—
> Though dead, they appear upon my path
> Notwithstanding my terrible wrath;

¶ 25.i 14-15. *Robert*] B.'s favourite brother, whom he tended continuously
for the fortnight before his death in 1787, and whom B. claimed to con-
verse with many times afterwards. Little is known of *John*, except the
report of Frederick Tatham, who knew B., that he 'lived a few reckless
days, enlisted as a soldier, and died', having at one time begged his bread
from William.

They beg, they entreat, they drop their tears,
20 Filled full of hopes, filled full of fears,
With a thousand angels upon the wind
Pouring disconsolate from behind
To drive them off—and before my way
A frowning thistle implores my stay.
25 What to others a trifle appears
Fills me full of smiles or tears;
For double the vision my eyes do see,
And a double vision is always with me:
With my inward eye 'tis an old man grey,
30 With my outward a thistle across my way.
'If thou goest back,' the thistle said,
'Thou art to endless woe betrayed:
For here does Theotormon lower,
And here is Enitharmon's bower,
35 And Los the terrible thus hath sworn,
Because thou backward dost return,
Poverty, envy, old age and fear
Shall bring thy wife upon a bier;
And Butts shall give what Fuseli gave,
40 A dark black rock and a gloomy cave.'

I struck the thistle with my foot
And broke him up from his delving root:
'Must the duties of life each other cross?
Must every joy be dung and dross?
45 Must my dear Butts feel cold neglect,
Because I give Hayley his due respect?
Must Flaxman look upon me as wild
And all my friends be with doubts beguiled?
Must my wife live in my sister's bane,
50 Or my sister survive on my love's pain?
The curses of Los, the terrible shade,
And his dismal terrors make me afraid.'

So I spoke and struck in my wrath
The old man weltering upon my path.
55 Then Los appeared in all his power;
In the sun he appeared, descending before
My face in fierce flames—in my double sight
'Twas outward a sun, inward Los in his might.

'My hands are laboured day and night,
60 And ease comes never in my sight;

i 49. An allusion to the constant disagreement between the two women
(both called Catherine).

My wife has no indulgence given,
Except what comes to her from Heaven.
We eat little, we drink less—
This earth breeds not our happiness.
65 Another sun feeds our life's streams;
We are not warmed with thy beams.
Thou measurest not the time to me
Nor yet the space that I do see;
My mind is not with thy light arrayed,
70 Thy terrors shall not make me afraid.'

When I had my defiance given,
The sun stood trembling in heaven;
The moon that glowed remote below
Became leprous and white as snow,
75 And every soul of men on the earth
Felt affliction and sorrow and sickness and dearth.
Los flamed in my path and the sun was hot
With the bows of my mind and the arrows of thought.
My bowstring fierce with ardour breathes,
80 My arrows glow in their golden sheaves;
My brothers and father march before;
The heavens drop with human gore.

Now I a fourfold vision see,
And a fourfold vision is given to me.
85 'Tis fourfold in my supreme delight
And threefold in soft Beulah's night
And twofold always. May God us keep
From single vision and Newton's sleep!

II

Oh, why was I born with a different face?
Why was I not born like the rest of my race?
When I look each one starts; when I speak I offend.
Then I'm silent and passive and lose every friend.

5 Then my verse I dishonour, my pictures despise,
My person degrade and my temper chastise;
And the pen is my terror, the pencil my shame,
And my talents I bury, and dead is my fame.

I am either too low or too highly prized;
10 When elate I am envied, when meek I'm despised.

ii. From a letter to Thomas Butts, 16 Aug. 1803. See p. 582, lines 21-2.

26 'He is a cock would'

Date: after Aug. 1803; the verse may allude to Pte Cock, who supported
Scholfield's perjury when B. was charged with sedition in Aug. 1803.
Probably not later than the Sussex Assizes, when B. was acquitted, in
Jan. 1804. It is written sideways in the margin of p. 29 of the Notebook.

> He is a cock would,
> And would be a cock if he could.

27 Notebook drafts, *c.* 1804

These poems are found together in the first pages of the Notebook,
wherever earlier drawings did not interfere, after the 'Klopstock' poem
of 1800 and the 'Joanna Southcott' poem of *c.* 1802. The only poem in
this group which contains a clue to its own date is the 'Grey Monk' draft,
which seems to belong to 1804. This poem, and 'The Golden Net',
appear in the Pickering MS (which is itself of uncertain date, but it con-
tains one poem, 'Mary', belonging to mid-1803; see pp. 475 and 582).
The pages of the Notebook were at some time disarranged; the poems are
here given in the original order of the pages.

I THE GOLDEN NET

> Beneath the white-thorn, lovely may,
> Three virgins at the break of day:
> 'Alas for woe! alas for woe!'
> They cry, and tears for ever flow.
> 5   The one was clothed in flames of fire,
> The other clothed in iron wire,
> The other clothed in tears and sighs.

¶ 26. *1–2. 1st rdg.*

> He is a Cock won't
> And would be a Crow if he could.

¶ 27.i. Notebook p. 6, now p. 14. Cp. Pickering MS version, p. 577
below; the only significant alteration is *1–2,* which were altered from the
Pickering MS form in the draft, to give the above opening. This change
may have been made at any time; either B. made the change later than the
date of the Pickering MS, or he altered the draft and then returned to his
original version. Note the similarity of *1* to *Milton* pl.31.55.

i *1.* This line is not in the Pickering MS version, where the above *2* is *1,*
and another line follows it. That was also the uncorrected draft on this
page.

i *5–13* were written in this order, but at one stage were numbered 3, 4,
5, 6, 1, 2, 7, 8, 9.

Dazzling bright before my eyes,
They bore a net of golden twine
10   To hang upon the branches fine.
[Pitying I wept to see the woe
That love and beauty undergo,
To be consumed with burning fires
And in ungratified desires,]
15   And in tears clothed night and day,
Melted all my soul away.
When they saw my tears, a smile
That did Heaven itself beguile
Bore the golden net aloft,
20   As by downy pinions soft
O'er the morning of my day.
Underneath the net I stray,
Now entreating Flaming Fire,
Now entreating Iron Wire,
25   Now entreating Tears and Sighs—
Oh, when will the morning rise?

II THE BIRDS

He. Where thou dwellest, in what grove,
Tell me, fair one, tell me, love,
Where thou thy charming nest dost build,
O thou pride of every field?

5   *She.* Yonder stands a lonely tree,
There I live and mourn for thee;
Morning drinks my silent tear,
And evening winds my sorrows bear.

He. O thou summer's harmony,
10   I have lived and mourned for thee;
Each day I mourn along the wood,
And night hath heard my sorrows loud.

She. Dost thou truly long for me,
And am I thus sweet to thee?
15   Sorrow now is at an end,
O my lover, and my friend!

i *11–14.* Cancelled: but the following alternative attempt was itself rejected (here printed as corrected):

Wings they had that soft enclose
Round their body when they chose
They would let them down at will
Or make translucent . . .

ii. Notebook p. 6, now p. 14. The *He* and *She* are B.'s.

> *He.* Come, on wings of joy we'll fly
>   To where my bower hangs on high;
>   Come, and make thy calm retreat
> 20   Among green leaves and blossoms sweet.

III 'I SAW A MONK . . .'

This poem is conjecturally dated 1804 as B.'s reflections on the renewed war and his private troubles (see below and p. 485). Most editors have reaction to the pacifist sermons of Richard Warner. Most editors have dated the poem, and the group in which it occurs, earlier–largely on the grounds that half of this poem is contained in the Pickering MS, which also contains 'Mary' which must have been written by Aug. 1803. However, a draft of 'Mary' is not in this group, or anywhere in the Notebook, and there is no particular reason to suppose that all the Pickering MS poems were composed at the same time. Since B. chose only two of this group (this poem and 'The Golden Net') for the Pickering MS and omitted the others, it is probable that he was selecting from a fairly large number of available drafts written over two or three years at least. Lines *25–8* also suggest composition after B. returned to London in 1803, when he was finding difficulty in getting a living as well as his anxieties over the charge of sedition (see p. 485).

In the following draft, B. numbered the first four stanzas 1–4, the two additional stanzas (see *45–8n*) 5–6; these were used in *Jerusalem* pl.52, as was the last stanza, though it is not numbered. The rest of the poem was used in the Pickering MS (see p. 584) in the order: stanzas 5, 4, 6–10, 14, 11. Stanzas 4 and 14 were used in both poems.

> I saw a monk of Charlemagne
> Arise before my sight;
> I talked with the grey monk where he stood
> In beams of infernal light.
>
> 5   Gibbon arose with a lash of steel,
>   And Voltaire with a racking wheel:

iii *1. Charlemagne*] Originally *Constantine.*

iii *5–8.* Two rejected variants to this stanza are written by it:

> (*a*)   Gibbon plied his lash of steel
>   Voltaire turned his racking wheel
>   Charlemagne & his barons bold
>   Stood by & mocked in iron and gold.
>
> (*b*)   The wheel of Voltaire whirl'd on high
>   Gibbon aloud his lash does ply,
>   Charlemagne & his clouds of war
>   Muster around the polar star.

The present *7* was composed after these variants had been rejected; *3* of (*a*) originally stood in its place.

The Schools, in clouds of learning rolled,
Arose with war in iron and gold.

'Thou lazy monk,' they sound afar,
10 'In vain condemning glorious war!
And in thy cell thou shalt ever dwell.
Rise, War, and bind him in his cell!'

The blood red ran from the grey monk's side,
His hands and feet were wounded wide,
15 His body bent, his arms and knees
Like to the roots of ancient trees.

'I see, I see,' the mother said,
'My children will die for lack of bread.
What more has the merciless tyrant said?'
20 The monk sat down on her stony bed.

His eye was dry, no tear could flow;
A hollow groan first spoke his woe.
He trembled and shuddered upon the bed;
At length with a feeble cry he said:

25 —When God commanded this hand to write
In the studious hours of deep midnight,
He told me that all I wrote should prove
The bane of all that on earth I love.

My brother starved between two walls,
30 His children's cry my soul appals;
I mocked at the rack and griding chain,
My bent body mocks at their torturing pain.

Thy father drew his sword in the north,
With his thousands strong he is marched forth;
35 Thy brother has armed himself in steel
To avenge the wrongs thy children feel.

But vain the sword and vain the bow,
They never can work war's overthrow.
The hermit's prayer and the widow's tear
40 Alone can free the world from fear.

The hand of vengeance sought the bed
To which the purple tyrant fled;
The iron hand crushed the tyrant's head,
And became a tyrant in his stead.

iii 9. *1st rdg del.* Seditious Monk said Charlemaine.
iii 44. *1st rdg del.* And usurped the tyrants throne & bed.

45 Until the tyrant himself relent,
   The tyrant who first the black bow bent,
   Slaughter shall heap the bloody plain.
   Resistance and war is the tyrant's gain.

   But the tear of love and forgiveness sweet,
50 And submission to death beneath his feet—
   The tear shall melt the sword of steel,
   And every wound it has made shall heal.

   A tear is an intellectual thing,
   And a sigh is the sword of an angel king,
55 And the bitter groan of the martyr's woe
   Is an arrow from the Almighty's bow.

IV MORNING

   To find the western path,
   Right through the gates of wrath
   I urge my way.
   Sweet mercy leads me on
5 With soft repentant moan;
   I see the break of day.

   The war of swords and spears
   Melted by dewy tears
   Exhales on high;
10 The sun is freed from fears,
   And with soft grateful tears
   Ascends the sky.

iii 45–8. This stanza is omitted in *Jerusalem*, which has at this point two other stanzas (beginning 'When Satan first . . .' and 'Titus! Constantine! Charlemagne!'): both of these are drafted on this MS page, and numbered 5 and 6. The latter is linked to the main draft by the catch, 'A tear is an &c'–i.e. to the second (not the *Jerusalem*) form of *53*.

iii 49–52. This stanza was not deleted, but was not used in either the *Jerusalem* or Pickering MS poems. It seems to be a variant of the next stanza; or the similarity of the two may have led to the abandonment of this one.

iii 53. *A tear is*] *1st rdg del.* 'For the tear'. In the Pickering MS and in *Jerusalem*, the reading is 'For a tear'; see note on 45–8.

iii 55. *of the martyr's*] *1st rdg del.* for anothers.

iv. Notebook p. 8, now p. 12.

iv 1. *western*, especially in B.'s later poetry, does not imply sunset, but freedom, virtue and the gate to Eternity. Cp. *Jerusalem* pl.5.68n.

V

Terror in the house does roar;
But pity stands before the door.

VI

Mock on, mock on, Voltaire, Rousseau!
Mock on, mock on—'Tis all in vain!
You throw the sand against the wind,
And the wind blows it back again.

5   And every sand becomes a gem
Reflected in the beams divine;
Blown back they blind the mocking eye,
But still in Israel's paths they shine.

The atoms of Democritus
10   And Newton's particles of light
Are sands upon the Red Sea shore,
Where Israel's tents do shine so bright.

VII

My spectre around me night and day
Like a wild beast guards my way;
My emanation far within
Weeps incessantly for my sin.

v. Notebook p. 8, now p. 12.
vi. Notebook p. 9, now p. 7.
vi *1. Voltaire*, etc.] All associated with rationalism, and attacked especially
in the preface to *Jerusalem* ch. 3, pl.52, the plate containing one form of
'The Grey Monk' (iii above) which is drafted on the opposite page of the
Notebook to this.
vii. Notebook pp. 13/12 (now pp. 3/2).
vii *1. spectre*] See *Four Zoas* iv *63n*, *Jerusalem* pl.6.1*n*: the spectre is that
part of the personality which is aggressive, ruthless and domineering; B.
envisages it as male, and often draws it as a kind of bat-winged evil angel.
vii *3. emanation*] Ideally a part of the personality which 'emanates' or is
sent out—the person's link with others. See *Four Zoas* i *17n*. The emanation
is feminine; kind by nature, but needing to be controlled by the person.
Otherwise, as here, she tends to develop her own brand of self-will,
domineering through insinuation. Thus this poem contains reflections on
the internal conflict of the personality, and also on relations between man
and woman.
vii *4.* After stanza 1, two deleted stanzas; the first numbered 2, the other 4,
then 5; after alterations these appeared thus:

5 A fathomless and boundless deep,
  There we wander, there we weep.
  On the hungry craving wind
  My spectre follows thee behind.

  He scents thy footsteps in the snow
10 Wheresoever thou dost go,
  Through the wintry hail and rain—
[*He.*] 'When wilt thou return again?

  'Dost thou not in pride and scorn
  Fill with tempests all my morn,
15 And with jealousies and fears
  Fill my pleasant nights with tears?

  'Seven of my sweet loves thy knife
  Has bereaved of their life;
  Their marble tombs I built with tears,
20 And with cold and shuddering fears.

  'Seven more loves weep night and day
  Round the tombs where my loves lay,
  And seven more loves attend each night
  Around my couch with torches bright;

    Thy weeping thou shall neer give oer
    I sin against thee more & more
    And never will from sin be free
    Till she forgives & comes to me.

    Thou hast parted from my side
    Once thou wast a virgin bride
    Never shalt thou a true love find
    My Spectre follows thee Behind.

Two other stanzas, also deleted, were written to replace these:

    A deep winter dark and cold
    Within my heart thou didst unfold
    A Fathomless & boundless deep
    There we wander, there we weep

    When my Love did first begin
    Thou didst call that Love a Sin
    Secret trembling night & day
    Driving all my Loves away.

The first of these was numbered 2, the second 3, then 4. The definitive second stanza was written last of all, at the very end of the draft, using material from the above, but at once numbered 2.

vii *12.* The spectre speaks, but the sequence of pleading and response is an editorial interpretation. B. left no quotation marks.

25   'And seven more loves in my bed
    Crown with wine my mournful head,
    Pitying and forgiving all
    Thy transgressions great and small.

    'When wilt thou return and view
30   My loves, and them to life renew?
    When wilt thou return and live?
    When wilt thou pity as I forgive?

[*She.*] 'Never, never I return:
    Still for victory I burn!
35   Living, thee alone I'll have,
    And when dead I'll be thy grave.'

    'Through the heaven and earth and hell
    Thou shalt never, never quell:
    I will fly and thou pursue,
40   Night and morn the flight renew.'

[*He.*] 'Till I turn from female love
    And root up the infernal grove,
    I shall never worthy be
    To step into Eternity—

45   'And to end thy cruel mocks
    Annihilate thee on the rocks,
    And another form create
    To be subservient to my fate.

    'Let us agree to give up love
50   And root up the infernal grove;
    Then shall we return and see
    The worlds of happy Eternity,

    'And throughout all Eternity
    I forgive you, you forgive me.
55   As our dear Redeemer said,
    This the wine, and this the bread.'

[*'Postscript'*]
[*He.*] 'O'er my sins thou sit and moan;
    Hast thou no sins of thy own?

vii *41. Till I*] *1st reading del.* Till thou.
vii *43. I shall*] *1st rdg del.* Thou shalt.
vii *53–6.* This stanza is in pencil; so are the next four, the first two of which
are numbered 1, 2, as if to begin a new poem.
vii. '*Postscript*'] The spectre speaks. ('Postscript' is an editorial description.)
vii *57. my sins thou*] *1st rdg thy* sins I.
vii *58. Hast . . . own*] *1st rdg.* Have I no sins of my own.

O'er my sins thou sit and weep
60   And lull thy own sins fast asleep!'

[*She*.] 'What transgressions I commit
Are for thy transgressions fit;
They thy harlots, thou their slave,
And my bed becomes their grave.'

65 [*He*.] 'Poor pale pitiable form
That I follow in a storm,
Iron tears and groans of lead
Bind around my aching head;

'And let us go to the highest downs
70   With many pleasing wiles.
The woman that does not love your frowns
Will never embrace your smiles.'

VIII

When a man has married a wife, he finds out whether
Her knees and elbows are only glued together

28 Milton

Four copies are known: the two earlier ones (A and B) have the text printed here. Copy C adds pls 3, 4, 10, 18, 32; D has these and also pl.5. These additional plates are largely digressive, and are given on pp. 566–74; one important reason for B.'s adding them seems to have been to bring the total of plates to fifty. In copies C and D the Preface (pl.1) is omitted, and pls 25–7 are arranged 26, 25, 27: hence the dual marginal numbering of these plates. As usual with B., the titlepage date is earlier than the completion of engraving; copies A and B are on paper watermarked 1808, and the latest plate in these copies (pl.6) is filled with London references, reminiscent of *Jerusalem*. But the poem seems to be based on two personal experiences of which we have no proof, but which we can conjecture from the text (15.47–50, 21.4–14; 35.42–5, 36.16–32, 42.24–30). The first was an inspiration in a shaft of light which struck B.'s foot as he was fastening his shoe in Lambeth (22.11)–i.e. before Sept. 1800. The second was a moment (35.42) of profound ecstasy as a lark sang and the scent of wild thyme filled the air, one day during his stay in Felpham, 1800–03. The poem lies between these two events; the first was the primary inspiration

vii *59. my sins thou*] *1st rdg.* thy sins I.
vii *60. thy*] *1st rdg del.* my.
viii. Notebook p. 14 (now p. 4).

which made B. feel himself the wearer of Los's prophetic mantle, which placed him in the line of Milton, and led him to write this poem in which he attempts to reshape Milton's work; the second experience, though it forms a climax to the poem, may not have been part of its original plan. Date of composition, then, *c.* 1800–04; of engraving, *c.* 1809. There is a facsimile in the Blake Trust series (1967).

Two other features are datable around 1803–04. B. lived at Felpham, a village on the Sussex coast near Bognor, from Sept. 1800 to Sept. 1803. He left because he felt that his patron, William Hayley, was interfering intolerably with his private work–probably the writing of *Milton*–and B. records an archetypal version of this quarrel in the Bard's Song, which he adds to the beginning of the poem (2.*24*–14.*3*). After returning to London, B. found business affairs very pressing, and the composition of this section probably belongs to late 1803 and early 1804. An earlier Felpham allusion is to B.'s cottage, which Hayley rented for him. At first it pleased B. greatly–'though small it is well proportioned, and if I should ever build a palace it would be only my cottage enlarged' (letter to Butts, 23 Oct. 1800): but with time its dampness caused his wife, Catherine, constant ill-health (pl. 36.*31–2*).

The second feature, the last major event of the Felpham stay, was B.'s argument with a soldier named Scholfield, whom he ejected from his garden. In return, Scholfield had B. charged with sedition. It was an illiberal age, and war had lately been renewed with France; the charge was dangerous. It must have caused B. great anxiety until, with Hayley's active aid, the jury at the Quarter Sessions in Jan. 1804 found B. not guilty. B. immortalized Scholfield as one of the leading evil 'sons of Albion' in *Jerusalem*, and named him once in *Milton* (19.*59*).

The starting-point of *Milton* is B.'s belief in the importance of the artist in national life. Milton had been the greatest, most inspired English poet, yet he had gone astray. The poet should show others the eternal world of imaginative truth, and act as a national seer and leader. But Milton had shown a false image of God as a law-giving tyrant beyond the clouds, not as a merciful brother among and in men. B.'s beliefs were fiercely contrary to Milton's; and the poem *Milton* is an imaginary narrative describing how Milton's soul in heaven was purified, and how the malign influence of the old Milton was to be countered when the spirit of the new Milton descended, in another generation, to B. himself.

The narrative has four parts: (A) the Bard's song; (B) Milton's journey to self-renewal; (C) the journey of Ololon, Milton's emanation, seeking him; (D) a description of the works of Los, which is really a digression, though it fills eight plates (22.*27–29*).

(A) The Bard's song retells the story of the fall of Satan in Blakean terms, drawing on B.'s own experience with Hayley. Satan's error is to assume activities not rightly his, and to display a self-righteous arrogance by which he shuts himself out of Heaven. Milton, hearing the song, realizes that Satan's errors are his own (14.*30*).

In (B) Milton leaves Heaven to return to earth to renew his spirit. This is the most complex part of the narrative: Milton is still an infinite spirit and can be seen in many forms and places at once:

(i) He descends into the abyss and returns to earth. Here his new prophetic spirit begins to reform the old religious errors which he had himself once sustained (Milton's struggle with Urizen, 19.4ff).

(ii) At the same time, Milton continues his journey into the present day, coming to B. himself and inspiring him (15.47).

(iii) At the same time, being an immortal soul lost in the abyss, Milton is sick and lies in a coma, while the daughters of Beulah tend him (15.9–14).

(iv) At the same time, being an immortal soul on a divine errand, he walks 'though darkened' in Heaven, attended by the seven Angels of the Presence (15.3ff): but soon they are all driven out of Heaven and go to 'join the watchers of the Ulro' (20.50).

(C) Those responsible for driving Milton out of Heaven are the heavenly tribe of Ololon, who in remorse follow him and meet him (37.1–15) in B.'s own cottage garden at Felpham. Here Ololon is manifested, not as a host of heaven, but as 'one female . . . a virgin of twelve years' (36.16–17) and as Milton's emanation. Thus Milton is reunited with his emanation, and the evil in both of them is rejected, though not yet annihilated. The poem ends with the promise of new inspirations from the now purified spirit of Milton.

(D) The works of Los are interpolated at the end of the First Book, where B., inspired by Milton, is taken into Golgonooza, Los's beautiful city, the outpost of Heaven in Ulro, and shown its wonders.

The cosmology of *Milton* is almost as fully developed as that of *Jerusalem*. Eternal, infinite, truly human beings live in Heaven, or Eden, where the Divine Vision enfolds them all. Around Eden is Beulah, a place of rest for weaker spirits from the fiery exhilaration of Eden (30.1–31.7). It is also a place which mortals may see and even enter in dreams and visions. The danger is that it may be taken to be Heaven itself, which it is not; that error is deadly. Beyond Beulah is the 'abyss'; furthest of all from Eden is Ulro, or chaos, the place of formlessness and non-entity. But Eden cares even for Ulro, and Los is set there, constantly building and rebuilding the beautiful city of Golgonooza, which guards against chaos and is a refuge for souls escaping from chaos. Within the abyss are other places, whose position is not so well defined. (In *Jerusalem* pl.12.45ff the fourfold pattern Eden-Beulah-Generation-Ulro emerges, but it is not laid out in *Milton*.) In the abyss, perhaps even in Ulro, but close to Beulah, are the 'couches of the dead', i.e. of the spiritually dead, such as Albion (England), who may seem to lower forms of life to be alive, but who are asleep to eternal life. Here also is the 'mundane shell', the enclosed universe which contains our world of generation–that is, of physically limited life and death. This is a region which has fallen from Eternity, yet is saved from the complete annihilation of Ulro: hence it is near both to 'Satan's seat' and to Golgonooza (17.*29*, 20.*37–9*). Both are within reach of mortal man; he may approach one and find the other. The 'abyss' is the place of much of the action, where B. does not choose to specify more precisely.

The entire action of 35.*42–42.28*, in so far as it takes place in the mortal world of generation, takes place in that single moment of lark song and the smell of wild thyme at Felpham in which, it has been suggested, B. was inspired with the vision which in part led to the writing of *Milton*. Spatially, B. insists on the infiniteness of the action, and personally he insists on the variable form of the immortal; so that Ololon, for example, a multitude descending through Beulah to seek for Milton's sleeping form, 'turns a corner' as it were in a fourth dimension, and is seen as a young girl coming into B.'s garden at Felpham. So also Milton himself can, as described above, be seen in several manifestations at once. This insistence on the infinite, on not being bound by physical limitations, is the chief difficulty of the poem which, when this is understood, becomes much clearer. For the meaning of the extended use of italics, see 2.*26n*; for the use of ampersands, p. xxiii.

MILTON
A Poem in 2 Books
To Justify the Ways of God to Men

Pl. 1

PREFACE

The stolen and perverted writings of Homer and Ovid, of Plato and Cicero, which all men ought to contemn, are set up by artifice against the sublime of the Bible. But when the new age is at leisure to pronounce, all will be set right, & these grand works of the more ancient,

5   and consciously & professedly inspired men, will hold their proper rank, & the daughters of memory shall become the daughters of

¶ 28. *Titlepage*] 'in 2 Books' first read 'in 12 Books', which copies C and D oddly retain.

1. *Preface*] This was deleted from the two later copies of *Milton*. See headnote.

1.*1*. Cp. B.'s *Descriptive Catalogue* to his exhibition in 1809: 'No man can believe that either Homer's Mythology, or Ovid's, were the production of Greece, or Latium; neither will anyone believe, that the Greek statues, as they are called, were the invention of Greek Artists . . . [they] are evidently copies, though fine ones, from greater works of the Asiatic Patriarchs. The Greek Muses are daughters of Mnemosyne, or Memory, and not of Inspiration or Imagination, therefore not authors of such sublime conceptions.' (See II: *Erdman 1965*, p. 521).

1.*2*. *contemn*] Despise.

by artifice] Artificially: they are not 'naturally' the chief writings of the world.

inspiration. Shakespeare & Milton were both curbed by the general malady & infection from the silly Greek & Latin slaves of the sword.

10   Rouse up, O young men of the new age! Set your foreheads against the ignorant hirelings! For we have hirelings in the camp, the court and the university, who would, if they could, for ever depress mental and prolong corporeal war. Painters, on you I call! Sculptors! Architects! Suffer not the fashionable fools to depress your powers

15   by the prices they pretend to give for contemptible works or the expensive advertising boasts that they make of such works; believe Christ & his apostles that there is a class of men whose whole delight is in destroying. We do not want either Greek or Roman models, if we are but just & true to our own imaginations, those worlds of eternity

20   in which we shall live for ever—in Jesus our Lord.

> And did those feet in ancient time
> Walk upon England's mountains green?
> And was the holy Lamb of God
> On England's pleasant pastures seen?

1.6. daughters of memory] In later Greek mythology, the nine Muses were the daughters of Mnemosyne, or memory. B. means that true religion and understanding is imaginative, not traditional. In *Four Zoas* i *14* (and iii *65n*) he says that the heathen gods were the imaginative creations of men, falsely elevated. See especially 14.*29*, p. 506 below.

1.8. slaves of the sword] Homer's and Virgil's epics were of war: B.'s pacificism erupts.

1.12–13. mental and . . . corporeal war] The first is the strife of minds and ideas and so creative; the second of arms and so destructive.

1.14. fashionable fools] Ignorant patrons who admire art because it is fashionable to do so. In a letter to Butts (6 July 1803) B. wrote: 'I regard fashion in poetry as little as I do in painting; so, if both poets and painters should alternately dislike (but I know the majority of them will not) I am not to regard it at all.'

1.17. a class of men] This is not a direct reference to any passage in the Bible. See B.'s *Descriptive Catalogue*, p. 27 (*Erdman 1965*, p. 529): 'As there is a class of men, whose whole delight is the destruction of men, so there is a class of artists, whose whole art and science is fabricated for the purpose of destroying art.'

1.18. models] Cp. *1n*.

1.19–20. imaginations . . . Lord] A careful and deliberate sequence of ideas, containing much of B.'s later thought.

1.21–28. did those feet] The first two stanzas are to be understood 'mentally': i.e. there was a golden age before the Fall, when Christ, the divine humanity, walked about England–'here' where B. and his reader were, not in a far-off land. So, in *Revelation* xxi, the Lamb is always present in Jerusalem.

25   And did the Countenance Divine
        Shine forth upon our clouded hills?
        And was Jerusalem builded here
        Among these dark Satanic mills?

        Bring me my bow of burning gold;
30   Bring me my arrows of desire;
        Bring me my spear—O clouds, unfold!
        Bring me my chariot of fire!

        I will not cease from mental fight,
        Nor shall my sword sleep in my hand,
35   Till we have built Jerusalem,
        In England's green and pleasant land.

Would to God that all the Lord's people were prophets!

Numbers xi 29.

Pl. 2   BOOK THE FIRST

Daughters of Beulah! Muses who inspire the poet's song!
Record the journey of immortal Milton through your realms
Of terror & mild moony lustre, in soft sexual delusions
Of varied beauty, to delight the wanderer & repose
5   His burning thirst & freezing hunger! Come into my hand

1.27–8. Was Jerusalem, the city of God, here, where Satan's mills
now are (see note below)? B. imagines that before the Fall England was a
Holy Land and London a Holy City, the Jerusalem of the Bible: but the
Fall has separated them, and reduced London to the state in which we
now see it. Cp. *Jerusalem* pl.27.

1.28. *dark Satanic mills*] Milton's Samson was 'eyeless . . . at the mill with
slaves' (*Samson Agonistes* 41); this is the source of B.'s use of *mill* as a place . . .
of slavery. The phrase refers not so much to the mills built for the new
industries, as to Satan's enslavement of the mind, the beginning of human
error. B. would, of course, have recognized the evils of the Industrial
Revolution as one more demonstration of the presence of Satan's mills in
Albion; and, for the image, cp. *Jerusalem* 15.14–20.

2.1. *Daughters of Beulah*] Beulah is the land of rest on the borders of Heaven;
the daughters of that land have the task of caring for human wanderers
in their earthly life (see pl.30.1n).

2.3. *sexual delusions*] Mere shadows and images of reality. In eternity, the
human form is one; in lesser, distorted states, it is divided–for example,
as separate and different sexes. B. is not attacking Beulah for its 'delusions',
as long as they are understood to belong to the land of rest and not the
land of waking life.

2.4–5. *The wanderer*] Man on earth.

17+B.

By your mild power descending down the nerves of my right arm
From out the portals of my brain, where by your ministry
The eternal great Humanity Divine planted his Paradise,
And in it caused the spectres of the dead to take sweet forms
10   In likeness of himself. Tell also of the false tongue, vegetated
Beneath your land of shadows, of its sacrifices and
Its offerings, even till Jesus, the image of the invisible God,
Became its prey—a curse, an offering & an atonement
For death eternal in the heavens of Albion & before the gates
15   Of Jerusalem, his emanation, in the heavens beneath Beulah.

Say first: what moved Milton—who walked about in Eternity
One hundred years, pondering the intricate mazes of providence;
Unhappy though in heaven, he obeyed, he murmured not, he was
    silent,
Viewing his sixfold emanation scattered through the deep
20   In torment—to go into the deep her to redeem & himself perish?
What cause at length moved Milton to this unexampled deed?—
A bard's prophetic song! For sitting at eternal tables,
Terrific among the sons of Albion in chorus solemn & loud,
A bard broke forth. All sat attentive to the awful man.

25   *Mark well my words; they are of your eternal salvation.*

Three classes are created by the hammer of Los & woven

2.*10*. FALSE TONGUE] This expressed the earthly misunderstanding of truth.
The source is *Psalm* cxx 2–4: 'Deliver my soul, O Lord, from lying lips,
and from a deceitful tongue. What shall be given unto thee? or what shall
be done unto thee, thou false tongue? Sharp arrows of the mighty, with
coals of juniper.' The False Tongue speaks through man with the voice
of Satan, when the Divine Voice should speak, and demands 'sacrifices
and offerings'. In the scheme of *Four Zoas* (see introduction, p. 290 above)
Tharmas is associated with the Tongue and also with the Western Gate
which opens from the universe of Man into Eternity. But the Western
Gate is closed in Night i, and the Gate of the Tongue is closed (i *98*), and
the tongue cannot speak of Eternity any more. The False Tongue is its
Satanic imitation, and what professes to be truth is spoken by the False
Tongue, as shown in *11–15* above. See also *Jerusalem* 14.2–9.
2.*16*. Milton died in 1674.
2.*17*. *intricate mazes*] Like the fallen angels of *Paradise Lost* ii 561, who
'reasoned high / And found no end, in wandering mazes lost'.
2.*18*. *he obeyed*] Out of a false notion of what was expected of him.
2.*19*. *sixfold emanation*] Milton's three wives and three daughters.
2.*21–2*. The narrative begins here; several plates (to 13.44) are taken up
with the Bard's song, which reveals to Milton his own error.
2.*26*. *Three classes*] Explained in 7.*1–3*, p. 492. The comments of pl.6. *32–35*

Pl. 6 *From Golgonooza, the spiritual fourfold London eternal,*
In immense labours & sorrows, ever building, ever falling,
Through Albion's four forests which overspread all the earth—
From London Stone to Blackheath east, to Hounslow west,
5 *To Finchley north, to Norwood south; and the weights*
Of Enitharmon's loom play lulling cadences on the winds of Albion,
From Caithness in the north to Lizard Point in the south.

Loud sounds the hammer of Los, & loud his bellows is heard
Before London to Hampstead's breadths & Highgate's heights, to
10 *Stratford & old Bow, & across to the gardens of Kensington*
On Tyburn's brook. Loud groans Thames beneath the iron forge
Of Rintrah & Palamabron, of Theotormon & Bromion, to forge the
instruments
Of harvest, the plough & harrow to pass over the nations.

The Surrey hills glow like the clinkers of the furnace. Lambeth's vale—
15 *Where Jerusalem's foundations began; where they were laid in ruins,*

are later. The next plate (6) is an interpolation; the sense continues in 7.1,
though the beginning and end of 6 are made to fit. The new reader will
find it simplest to overlook the italicized lines and read on from 2.26 to 7.1,
although all four copies contain pl.6. The two later copies also contain
three more plates (3–5), which will be found on pp. 566ff. below. These
amplify the theme of the labours of Los, including the creation of Satan,
but complicate the narrative of the Bard's song.

6.1. *the spiritual fourfold London eternal*] For Golgonooza, see *Four Zoas* viii
25n. Los's work is envisaged as a cosmic myth, 'spiritual' and 'eternal'.
But the sphere of his activities resembles London: (a) since though the theme
is eternal it cannot be envisaged by the mortal mind except in definite
earthly forms, (b) since it is worked out in London as fully as anywhere
else in the universe. *Fourfold* implies an absolute completeness. Los's work
is creative in making living 'human' forms for lost souls whose formless-
ness would otherwise be non-existence.
6.4. *London Stone*] Traditionally, the milestone used by the Romans as the
base from which they measured their roads. See also *Jerusalem* pl.8.27n.
6.5. *weights*] Tensioning weights, to hold the warp stretched on the loom.
Their 'lulling cadence' arises from their clinking together as they swing
with the shaking of the loom.
6.12. These are the four faithful sons of Los: cp. 24.10–12. Theotormon
and Bromion here are not the characters of *Visions of the Daughters of
Albion*.
6.14. *clinkers*] The raked-out and glowing slag from a blast-furnace (for
details see *Four Zoas* ii 327n). B. would have seen such furnaces on the
Surrey hills, though they were going out of business.
6.14–17. *Lambeth's vale*] The subject of *gleams* in 17.

Where they were laid in ruins from every nation, & oak groves rooted—
Dark gleams before the furnace-mouth, a heap of burning ashes.
(When shall Jerusalem return & overspread all the nations?
Return, return to Lambeth's vale, O building of human souls!)
20   *Thence stony Druid temples overspread the island white,*
And thence from Jerusalem's ruins—from her walls of salvation
And praise—through the whole earth were reared; from Ireland
To Mexico & Peru west, & east to China & Japan; till Babel,
The spectre of Albion, frowned over the nations in glory & war.
25   *(All things begin & end in Albion's ancient Druid rocky shore,*
But now the starry heavens are fled from the mighty limbs of Albion.)

[Design]

Loud sounds the hammer of Los, loud turn the wheels of Enitharmon:
Her looms vibrate with soft affections, weaving the web of life
Out from the ashes of the dead; Los lifts his iron ladles
30   *With molten ore—he heaves the iron cliffs in his rattling chains*
From Hyde Park to the alms-houses of Mile-end & old Bow.
Here the three classes of mortal men take their fixed destinations,
And hence they overspread the nations of the whole earth, & hence
The web of life is woven & the tender sinews of life created
35   *And the three classes of men, regulated by Los's hammers, & woven*
Pl. 7   By Enitharmon's looms & spun beneath the spindle of Tirzah:
The first, the Elect from before the foundation of the world;

6.16. oak groves] Where the Druids worshipped; see *20.*

6.19. building of human souls] Jerusalem is not a set of buildings, but (as for
the prophets of the Bible) a spiritual creation, the sum of the people who
make up the community.

6.20. It was supposed that Stonehenge and other stone circles were places
of Druid worship. B. follows the Druidists of his age in this error.

6.23. Babel is also Babylon, a vision of all that is evil in Albion.

6.25. All things . . . shore] So in *Jerusalem* pls 27 and *46.15.* The idea that
the ancient Britons possessed the wisdom of the patriarchs is the 'begin-
ning': the 'end' is that the new age will begin when Britain (Albion)
wakes up.

6.26. This line closely resembles *Jerusalem* pls.*27.16*; *70.32*; *75.27.*

6. Design: This covers half the page. Dominated by a huge Stonehenge-
like trilithon, with a rocking-stone in front of it, a tiny traveller on horse-
back rides through it towards the stone; through it a waning moon,
clouds and stars are seen.

7.1. Tirzah] See *17.11n.* Los and Enitharmon are normally the enemies
of Tirzah; they are 'prophetic' and imaginative, she the queen of 'vegeta-
tive' nature. But both, though in hostility, deal with the forms created in
this mortal world, and this is probably B.'s way of saying, 'Three classes
of souls are found in the fallen world'.

The second, the Redeemed; the third, the Reprobate & formed
To destruction from the mother's womb. Follow with me my
 plough!
5 Of the first class was Satan. With incomparable mildness
His primitive tyrannical attempts on Los—with most endearing
 love
He soft entreated Los to give to him Palamabron's station;
For Palamabron returned with labour wearied every evening.
Palamabron oft refused; and as often Satan offered
10 His service, till by repeated offers and repeated entreaties
Los gave to him the harrow of the Almighty—alas, blamable,
Palamabron feared to be angry lest Satan should accuse him of
Ingratitude, & Los believe the accusation through Satan's extreme
Mildness. Satan laboured all day; it was a thousand years!
15 In the evening returning terrified, overlaboured & astonished,
Embraced soft with a brother's tears Palamabron, who also wept.

Mark well my words; they are of your eternal salvation.

Next morning Palamabron rose. The horses of the harrow
Were maddened with tormenting fury, & the servants of the harrow,
20 The gnomes, accused Satan, with indignation, fury and fire.
Then Palamabron, reddening like the moon in an eclipse,
Spoke, saying, 'You know Satan's mildness and his self-imposition,
Seeming a brother, being a tyrant, even thinking himself a brother
While he is murdering the just. Prophetic I behold
25 His future course through darkness & despair to eternal death.
But we must not be tyrants also; he hath assumed my place
For one whole day, under pretence of pity and love to me.

7.2–3. See 11.17–22 and especially 26.27ff. The three classes derive from
traditional Calvinist theology, but B. inverts the moral judgment while
retaining the scheme.
7.4. *womb . . . follow*] These words are on different lines, with two deleted
half-lines between them in part conjecturally read in *Erdman 1965* in one
copy as: 'The Reprobate are first / ?who . . . by for the ?glorification. . . .'
7.5. The Bard now tells the true story of the fall of Satan (not that of
Paradise Lost). Satan and Palamabron are sons of Los (*Four Zoas* viii *345–7*,
also *356–63*, where this story is summarized).
mildness] Pretending to be good-natured, while acting tyrannically. The
passage is a reflection of the gentle destruction of B.'s plans by Hayley,
B.'s patron of 1800–03. According to B., Hayley should have stuck to the
duties assigned to him by his nature, without interfering with B.'s pro-
phetic task. Note 23.
7.21. *moon in an eclipse*] At a solar eclipse, the moon is black; but when the
earth eclipses the moon at full, the moon, instead of disappearing, glows
a deep coppery colour.

My horses hath he maddened and my fellow servants injured.
How should he—he!—know the duties of another? O foolish
    forbearance!
30 Would I had told Los all my heart! But patience, O my friends,
All may be well: silent remain, while I call Los and Satan.'

Loud as the wind of Beulah that unroots the rocks & hills
Palamabron called, and Los & Satan came before him,
And Palamabron showed the horses & the servants. Satan wept
35 And, mildly cursing Palamabron, him accused of crimes
Himself had wrought. Los trembled; Satan's blandishments almost
Persuaded the prophet of eternity that Palamabron
Was Satan's enemy, & that the gnomes, being Palamabron's friends,
Were leagued together against Satan through ancient enmity.
40 What could Los do? How could he judge, when Satan's self
    believed
That he had not oppressed the horses of the harrow, nor the servants?

So Los said, 'Henceforth, Palamabron, let each his own station
Keep; nor in pity false, nor in officious brotherhood, where
None needs, be active.' Meantime Palamabron's horses
45 Raged with thick flames redundant, & the harrow maddened with
    fury.
Trembling Palamabron stood, the strongest of demons trembled,
Curbing his living creatures; many of the strongest gnomes
They bit in their wild fury, who also maddened like wildest beasts.

Mark well my words; they are of your eternal salvation.

Pl. 8 Meanwhile wept Satan before Los, accusing Palamabron,
Himself exculpating with mildest speech; for himself believed
That he had not oppressed nor injured the refractory servants.
But Satan returning to his mills (for Palamabron had served
5 The mills of Satan as the easier task) found all confusion,
And back returned to Los, not filled with vengeance but with tears,
Himself convinced of Palamabron's turpitude. Los beheld
The servants of the mills drunken with wine & dancing wild
With shouts & Palamabron's songs, rending the forests green
10 With echoing confusion, though the sun was risen on high.

Then Los took off his left sandal, placing it on his head,

7.45. *thick flames redundant*] Cp. 'these redundant locks' (*Samson Agonistes*
568).

8.4–10. This may reflect B.'s individualistic treatment of Hayley's prosaic
tasks.

8.11. By this unfortunate image Los probably signifies that the order of all
things is disturbed; head and foot are confused. The *left* foot has sinister
connotations.

Signal of solemn mourning. When the servants of the mills
Beheld the signal they in silence stood, though drunk with wine.
Los wept. But Rintrah also came, and Enitharmon on
15 His arm leaned trembling, observing all these things,

And Los said, 'Ye genii of the mills, the sun is on high,
Your labours call you. Palamabron is also in sad dilemma.
His horses are mad, his harrow confounded, his companions
 enraged.
Mine is the fault. I should have remembered that pity divides the
 soul
20 And man unmans; follow with me my plough. This mournful day
Must be a blank in nature. Follow with me, and tomorrow again
Resume your labours, & this day shall be a mournful day.'

Wildly they followed Los & Rintrah, & the mills were silent.
They mourned all day, this mournful day of Satan & Palamabron;
25 And all the Elect & all the Redeemed mourned one toward another
Upon the mountains of Albion among the cliffs of the dead.
They ploughed in tears. Incessant poured Jehovah's rain, &
 Molech's
Thick fires, contending with the rain, thundered above, rolling
Terrible over their heads. Satan wept over Palamabron.
30 Theotormon & Bromion contended on the side of Satan,
Pitying his youth & beauty, trembling at eternal death.
Michael contended against Satan in the rolling thunder;
Thulloh, the friend of Satan, also reproved him (faint their reproof).

But Rintrah, who is of the Reprobate, of those formed to destruction,
35 In indignation for Satan's soft dissimulation of friendship
Flamed above all the ploughed furrows, angry, red & furious,
Till Michael sat down in the furrow, weary, dissolved in tears.
Satan, who drave the team beside him, stood angry & red;
He smote Thulloh & slew him, & he stood terrible over Michael
40 Urging him to arise. He wept! Enitharmon saw his tears,
But Los hid Thulloh from her sight, lest she should die of grief.
She wept; she trembled. She kissed Satan; she wept over Michael;
She formed a space for Satan & Michael & for the poor infected.
Trembling she wept over the space, & closed it with a tender moon.

8.*19. pity . . . soul*] So in *Urizen 288.*
8.*27. Molech*] A god worshipped in fire (cp. 37.*21*): but here the rain
and fire are simply an imaginative interpretation of a storm.
8.*32. Michael*] An archangel traditionally opposed to Satan, as in *Jude* 9
and *Paradise Lost* vi: otherwise see note below.
8.*33. Thulloh*] A 'friend', not listed among Los's sons anywhere. The
name is apparently B.'s invention, his character undefined.
8.*43. She formed a space*] She isolated them, as if in a vacuum, so that they

45   Los secret buried Thulloh, weeping disconsolate over the moony
        space.
     But Palamabron called down a great solemn Assembly,
     That he who will not defend truth may be compelled to
     Defend a lie, that he may be snared & caught & taken.

Pl. 9   And all Eden descended into Palamabron's tent
        Among Albion's Druids & Bards, in the caves beneath Albion's
        Death couch, in the caverns of death, in the corner of the Atlantic.
        And in the midst of the great Assembly Palamabron prayed:
        'O God, protect me from my friends, that they have not power over
5   me,
        Thou hast given me power to protect myself from my bitterest
          enemies.'

     Mark well my words; they are of your eternal salvation.

     Then rose the two witnesses, Rintrah & Palamabron.
     And Palamabron appealed to all Eden & received
10   Judgement, & lo! it fell on Rintrah & his rage,
     Which now flamed high & furious in Satan against Palamabron
     Till it became a proverb in Eden: 'Satan is among the Reprobate'.

     Los in his wrath cursed heaven & earth; he rent up nations,
     Standing on Albion's rocks among high-reared Druid temples
15   Which reach the stars of heaven & stretch from pole to pole.
     He displaced continents, the oceans fled before his face;
     He altered the poles of the world, east, west & north & south—
     But he closed up Enitharmon from the sight of all these things.

     For Satan, flaming with Rintrah's fury hidden beneath his own
        mildness,
20   Accused Palamabron before the assembly of ingratitude, of malice.
     He created seven deadly sins, drawing out his infernal scroll

would not infect the rest. B. envisages the creation as Satan sent into a
lower 'sphere' of life, where his now limited faculties may function. See
also extra pl. 10. 6–7 (p. 571) and Four Zoas i 90.

9.2. *Druids and Bards*] An allusion to the notion that heavenly wisdom and
insight have been transmitted from the beginning of the world through
the British bardic tradition.

9.3. *Albion's / Death couch*] A constant theme in *Milton* and *Jerusalem*,
and one added to *The Four Zoas*, is that Albion (personifying England) is
asleep as if dead, and that the universe is waiting for him to awake. *Jerusalem*
is the story of his death and revival. The action takes place 'in the corner
of the Atlantic' which is the heavenly equivalent of England. Cp.
15.36ff.

9.10. A mistaken judgment discussed in 11.15ff.

9.12. *Satan . . . Reprobate*] Because of his anger (*19*).

Of moral laws and cruel punishments upon the clouds of Jehovah,
To pervert the Divine Voice in its entrance to the earth
With thunder of war & trumpets' sound, with armies of disease,
25 Punishments & deaths mustered & numbered; saying, 'I am God alone,
There is no other! Let all obey my principles of moral individuality.
I have brought them from the uppermost innermost recesses
Of my eternal mind; transgressors I will rend off for ever,
As now I rend this accursed family from my covering!'

30 Thus Satan raged amidst the Assembly, & his bosom grew
Opaque against the Divine Vision. The paved terraces of
His bosom inwards shone with fires, but the stones, becoming opaque,
Hid him from sight in an extreme blackness and darkness.
And there a world of deeper Ulro was opened, in the midst
35 Of the Assembly; in Satan's bosom a vast unfathomable abyss.

Astonishment held the Assembly in an awful silence; & tears
Fell down as dews of night, & a loud solemn universal groan
Was uttered from the east & from the west & from the south
And from the north: & Satan stood opaque, immeasurable,
40 Covering the east with solid blackness round his hidden heart,
With thunders uttered from his hidden wheels, accusing loud
The Divine Mercy for protecting Palamabron in his tent.

Rintrah reared up walls of rocks & poured rivers & moats
Of fire round the walls; columns of fire guard around
45 Between Satan & Palamabron in the terrible darkness.

And Satan, not having the science of wrath but only of pity,
Rent them asunder & wrath was left to wrath, & pity to pity.
He sunk down, a dreadful death unlike the slumbers of Beulah.

The separation was terrible. The dead was reposed on his couch

9.21. B. commonly equates Satan with the law-giving God, opposing both to Jesus: this Miltonic Satan-Jehovah is a usurper. These lines, apparently out of context, recapitulate Urizen's actions in *Urizen 68–84*.
9.23. i.e. the earthly notion of God's voice. See 11.*10–14*.
9.26. *moral individuality*] i.e. 'each man for himself', regarding his own virtue, and not considering the needs of all humanity.
9.31. *opaque*] A sign of spiritual death. See *Four Zoas* iv *270n*; and 13.*20n* below.
9.34. *Ulro*] The abyss of chaos and death; see headnote.
9.43. As in Urizen *112–16*.
9.45–8. Satan did not understand the good purpose of Rintrah's barriers.
9.46. So in *Four Zoas* viii *380*.

17*

50 Beneath the couch of Albion, on the seven mountains of Rome,
    In the whole place of the Covering Cherub, Rome, Babylon & Tyre.
    His spectre raging furious descended into its space;

(I)   [*Full-plate illustration*]

Pl. 11 He set his face against Jerusalem, to destroy the eon of Albion.

    But Los hid Enitharmon from the sight of all these things
    Upon the Thames, whose lulling harmony reposed her soul,
    Where Beulah lovely terminates in rocky Albion,
5   Terminating in Hyde Park, on Tyburn's awful brook.

    And the mills of Satan were separated into a moony space
    Among the rocks of Albion's temples, and Satan's Druid sons
    Offer the human victims throughout all the earth, and Albion's
    Dread tomb, immortal on his rock, overshadowed the whole earth,
10 Where Satan, making to himself laws from his own identity,
    Compelled others to serve him in moral gratitude & submission,
    Being called God, setting himself above all that is called God.
    And all the spectres of the dead, calling themselves sons of God,
    In his synagogues worship Satan under the unutterable name.

15 And it was enquired why in a great solemn Assembly

9.50. Rome, which B. saw as the centre of oppression, both in empire and
religion.
9.51. the Covering Cherub] See note on *37.8. Ezekiel* xxviii 16 denounces
Tyre under the name of 'covering cherub'.

Plate 10, a later addition, will be found on p. 570 below. Between 9 and 10
is I. *full-plate illustration*, showing a male nude on a plinth, agonized amid
flames (illustrating Satan, *9.11,19*); a male and female watch.

11.1. eon] This word occurs only in *Jerusalem* pl.*19.16*: and in *36.41*, a line
also found in *Four Zoas* v *60*, where the word *wife* stands in the place of *Eon*.
Jerusalem is Albion's emanation.
11.4. Beulah lies between heaven and earth (see *30.1n*); its contact with
earth–doubtless through some personal experience of B.'s–is near Tyburn,
not far from B.'s home after 1803. Tyburn as the place of execution of
criminals, is called 'awful' (but cp. *Jerusalem* pls *34.55ff*, *43.1–4*).
11.6–8. With Satan set apart from the immortals 'his Druid sons' pervert
with their human sacrifices the divine wisdom they have received.
11.12. See note on *9.21*.
11.13. spectres of the dead] Literally, ghosts: meaning earthbound people
who think they are alive, and like good Christians go to church–to
worship a false image of God. And see *John* viii 41ff.
11.14. the unutterable name] In late Old Testament times God's name was
held to be too holy to speak–a sign of the distance which separated him
from men.
11.15–16. Satan has banished himself: the blame was (*9.10*) laid on Rin-
trah's wrath.

The innocent should be condemned for the guilty. Then an Eternal
   rose,

Saying, 'If the guilty should be condemned, he must be an eternal
   death,
And one must die for another throughout all eternity.
Satan is fallen from his station & never can be redeemed
20 But must be new created continually, moment by moment;
And therefore the class of Satan shall be called the Elect, & those
Of Rintrah the Reprobate, & those of Palamabron the Redeemed—
For he is redeemed from Satan's Law, the wrath falling on Rintrah.
And therefore Palamabron dared not to call a solemn Assembly
25 Till Satan had assumed Rintrah's wrath in the day of mourning,
In a feminine delusion of false pride, self-deceived.'

So spake the Eternal, and confirmed it with a thunderous oath.
But when Leutha, a daughter of Beulah, beheld Satan's
   condemnation
She down descended into the midst of the great solemn Assembly,
30 Offering herself a ransom for Satan, taking on her his sin.

Mark well my words; they are of your eternal salvation.

And Leutha stood glowing with varying colours, immortal,
   heart-piercing
And lovely, & her moth-like elegance shone over the Assembly.

At length, standing upon the golden floor of Palamabron,
35 She spake: 'I am the author of this sin; by my suggestion
My parent-power Satan has committed this transgression.

11.17–23. This argument has several threads: (*a*) the need for redemption
through sacrifice of others (*17–18, 23*): (*b*): the necessity that fallen
beings be kept in a continual state of change, so that they may not rigidify
(*19–20*): (*c*) the three classes defined (*21–2*). The *Elect* are predestined–not
to heaven, but to death. The *Reprobate* are punished–not in Hell, but in
their self-sacrificing expiation of the sins of others.

11.26. *feminine delusion*] Self-deceiving against one's better knowledge.

11.28. LEUTHA] She appears elsewhere (*Daughters of Albion 4, Europe 170,
Book of Los 2*), but is not given a definite character before this. She now
appears as Satan's emanation (*Four Zoas* i *17n*) and clearly derives from
Milton's *Sin* in *Paradise Lost* ii (see 11.*32–3*, 12.*2–39* below). But ten
years earlier, in *Europe 170–5*, she is already 'many-coloured' and 'silken',
a 'sweet smiling pestilence'. B. seems not to have determined her precise
role, and references to her must be read according to their immediate
context.

11.*32. varying colours* indicate a deceptive nature; Leutha is not altogether
to be trusted.

I loved Palamabron & I sought to approach his tent,
But beautiful Elynittria with her silver arrows repelled me;
Pl. 12 For her light is terrible to me. I fade before her immortal beauty.
—O, wherefore doth a dragon-form forth issue from my limbs
To seize her new-born son? Ah me! the wretched Leutha!
This to prevent, entering the doors of Satan's brain night after night,
5   Like sweet perfumes I stupefied the masculine perceptions
And kept only the feminine awake. Hence rose his soft
Delusory love to Palamabron, admiration joined with envy,
Cupidity unconquerable. My fault, when at noon of day
The horses of Palamabron called for rest and pleasant death,
10   I sprang out of the breast of Satan, over the harrow beaming
In all my beauty, that I might unloose the flaming steeds
As Elynittria used to do. But too well those living creatures
Knew that I was not Elynittria, & they brake the traces.
But me the servants of the harrow saw not, but as a bow
15   Of varying colours on the hills; terribly raged the horses.
Satan, astonished and with power above his own control,
Compelled the gnomes to curb the horses, & to throw banks of sand
Around the fiery flaming harrow in labyrinthine forms,
And brooks between to intersect the meadows in their course.
20   The harrow cast thick flames; Jehovah thundered above;

11.37. I loved Palamabron] As the next lines show, Leutha's dissatisfaction
with her lot is the cause of Satan's similar dissatisfaction; the result is
disastrous.

12.1. a dragon-form] Cp. Paradise Lost ii 650–3, 'The one seemed Woman
to the waist and fair, / But ended foul in many a scaly fold / Voluminous
and vast, a serpent armed / With mortal sting . . .' and ii 781–5, 'At last
this odious offspring whom thou seest [i.e. Death] . . . / Tore through my
entrails, that with fear and pain / Distorted, all my nether shape thus
grew / Transformed . . .' See also America 55; and Revelation xii 4: 'the
dragon stood before the woman which was to be delivered, for to devour
her child as soon as it was born.'

12.4. entering . . . brain] Cp. Paradise Lost iv 799–809, where Satan in the
form of a toad tempts the sleeping Eve, 'Assaying by his devilish art to
reach / The organs of her fancy, and with them forge / Illusions as he
list, phantasms and dreams'.

12.5–6. See note on 11.26.

12.9. pleasant death] 'Death' in Eden is only rest: there is no death in our
sense, except banishment, the kind Satan has forced upon himself.

12.18–19. labyrinthine . . . brooks to intersect] Note B.'s dislike of all that is
not straightforward. (But note Four Zoas viii 27, Jerusalem pl.98.18.)

12.20–39. These lines show how the effects of Leutha's crime enlarge and
increase. Each attempt to calm the horses and gnomes makes them wilder,
so that still fiercer measures are taken by the incompetent Satan and Leutha.

Chaos & Ancient Night fled from beneath the fiery harrow.
The harrow cast thick flames & orbed us round in concave fires,
A hell of our own making. See, its flames still gird me round!
Jehovah thundered above; Satan in pride of heart
25 Drove the fierce harrow among the constellations of Jehovah,
Drawing a third part in the fires as stubble north & south—
To devour Albion and Jerusalem, the emanation of Albion—
Driving the harrow in pity's paths. 'Twas then, with our dark fires
Which now gird round us (Oh eternal torment), I formed the serpent
30 Of precious stones & gold, turned poisons on the sultry wastes.
The gnomes in all that day spared not; they cursed Satan bitterly.
To do unkind things in kindness! With power armed, to say
The most irritating things in the midst of tears & love—
These are the stings of the serpent. Thus did we by them, till thus
35 They in return retaliated, & the living creatures maddened.
The gnomes laboured, I weeping hid in Satan's inmost brain;
But when the gnomes refused to labour more, with blandisihments
I came forth from the head of Satan; back the gnomes recoiled
And called me *Sin*, & for a sign portentous held me. Soon
40 Day sunk & Palamabron returned. Trembling I hid myself
In Satan's inmost palace of his nervous fine-wrought brain.
For Elynittria met Satan with all her singing women,
Terrific in their joy, & pouring wine of wildest power.
They gave Satan their wine; indignant at the burning wrath,
45 Wild with prophetic fury, his former life became like a dream.
Clothed in the serpent's folds, in selfish holiness demanding purity

12.21. Chaos and Ancient Night] Taken from *Paradise Lost* ii 970.
12.29. I formed the serpent] Rather a gratuitous introduction, but B. is
drawing as many parallels with the fall of Satan in *Paradise Lost* as he can,
and he uses the image extensively in the following lines.
12.32–3. Another reflection of the 'irritating things' Hayley used to do.
12.36. hid . . . brain] The emanation is, in Eden, a part of the whole person,
not a permanently separate counterpart.
12.37–9. Cp. *Paradise Lost* ii 759–61: 'back they recoiled afraid / At first,
and called me *Sin*, and for a sign / Portentous held me; but familiar
grown, / I pleased, and with attractive graces won / The most averse. . . '
12.42. Elynittria met Satan . . .] B. continues with an incident which ex-
plains Satan's separation from Leutha. The emanation's place is with her
mate; the events of the day have driven her desire for Palamabron out of
her mind; it returns in *13.38*.
12.44. the burning wrath] i.e. of the contest with the horses and the gnomes.
12.46. demanding purity] The moralistic law–see *9.26*. Satan has called
Leutha 'Sin' (*39*) and expelled her; whereas she should be an emanation,
to be enjoyed and controlled. Expulsion of an emanation is a rift in
personality.

Being most impure, self-condemned to eternal tears, he drove
Me from his inmost brain, & the doors closed with thunder's sound.
O Divine Vision, who didst create the female to repose

50   The sleepers of Beulah, pity the repentant Leutha. My

Pl. 13 Sick couch bears the dark shades of eternal death enfolding
The spectre of Satan; he furious refuses to repose in sleep.
I humbly bow in all my sin before the throne divine.
Not so the sick one; alas! what shall be done him to restore,

5   Who calls the individual law holy, and despises the Saviour,
Glorying to involve Albion's body in fires of eternal war?'

Now Leutha ceased; tears flowed; but the Divine Pity supported
her.

'All is my fault! We are the spectre of Luvah the murderer
Of Albion. O Vala! O Luvah! O Albion! O lovely Jerusalem!

10   The sin was begun in eternity & will not rest to eternity,
Till two eternities meet together. Ah! lost! lost! lost! for ever!'

So Leutha spoke. But when she saw that Enitharmon had
Created a new space to protect Satan from punishment,
She fled to Enitharmon's tent & hid herself. Loud raging

15   Thundered the Assembly dark & clouded, & they ratified
The kind decision of Enitharmon & gave a time to the space,
Even six thousand years, & sent Lucifer for its guard.
But Lucifer refused to die & in pride he forsook his charge,
And they elected Moloch, and when Moloch was impatient

20   The Divine Hand found the two limits; first of opacity, then of
contraction.

13.8. *Luvah*] One of the Four Zoas, 'brother' of Los; see *Four Zoas*, head-
note and iii *65n*. The sense of these lines is that Satan (with Leutha) is guilty
of the sin of overweening dominating passion that ruined Albion (*9.3n*).
13.17. *six thousand years*] Counting the creation from 4004 B.C. to an
imminent end of the world: the Fall will not endure beyond its limit. See
Marriage iv *66n*.
13.17–24. The Gods of the earth are given the task of looking after the
fallen world, but all are inadequate until Jesus comes. Each has his own
fault–pride, impatience, etc., and only Jesus will die. See the similar but
shorter narrative in *Four Zoas* viii *374–95*.
13.18. *Lucifer* is proud, and will not descend to the world of death. B.
distinguishes him from Satan.
13.20–1. Satan could not deteriorate below certain limits. B. repeats the
idea in *Jerusalem* pl.*42,29–31*, and adds (*42.35–7*): 'But there is no limit
of expansion! there is no limit of translucence! / In the bosom of man for
ever from eternity to eternity! / Therefore I break thy bonds of righteous-
ness; I crush thy messengers!'
13.20. OPACITY and CONTRACTION] In Cartesian cosmology, the three
forms of matter range from the luminous through the translucent to the

Opacity was named *Satan*, contraction was named *Adam*.
Triple Elohim came—Elohim wearied, fainted: they elected
    Shaddai.
Shaddai angry, Pahad descended: Pahad terrified, they sent
    Jehovah,
And Jehovah was leprous—loud he called, stretching his hand to
    Eternity.
25 For then the body of death was perfected in hypocritic holiness
Around the Lamb, a female tabernacle woven in Cathedron's
    looms.
He died as a Reprobate, he was punished as a transgressor.
Glory! Glory! Glory to the Holy Lamb of God!
I touch the heavens as an instrument to glorify the Lord.

30 The Elect shall meet the Redeemed: on Albion's rocks they shall
    meet,
Astonished at the transgressor, in him beholding the Saviour.

opaque. The sun is luminous, the ether is translucent, the earth is opaque.
(B. says that opacity is due to sin). *Expansion* is one of he three 'elements' in
the system, together with *motion* and *form*; and these are the essentials for
being. B. endows this theory with a moral and religious significance. See
Four Zoas iv 270n.

13.22. *Triple Elohim*] Elohim is literally a plural, 'gods', used of God in
certain sections of the Old Testament, in particular *Genesis* i, where he
creates the world: but not specifically 'triple'. B. regards him as the creator
of this fallen world, and Jehovah ('Lord God' of *Genesis* ii 4–iii 24, the
Eden story) as the god who required obedience. Hence the Elohim's
entry after *20–1*, when the limits on the fallen world had been laid down,
and Elohim was deputed to administer it.

Shaddai] In *Exodus* vi 3, 'I appeared unto Abraham . . . by the name of
God Almighty', the last two words an approximate translation of El (god)
Shaddai. B. converts Shaddai and Pahad (see note below) into names. Since
Abraham's God was Shaddai, he precedes Pahad.

13.23. *Pahad*] *Genesis* xxxi 42: in Jacob's dispute with Laban, 'Except the
God of my father, the God of Abraham, and the fear of Isaac, had been
with me. . . .' The word translated *fear* is *pahad*, 'dread', which B. uses by
a sort of inversion of meaning, for his 'terrified' God.

13.26–34. *Around the Lamb*] The Seventh (see 14.42), the only faithful
guardian.

13.26. *A female tabernacle . . . looms*] A false, enclosing wrap which could
not be escaped. For *tabernacle* see *Jerusalem* pl.44.34n.

Cathedron] See *Four Zoas* viii 25; Enitharmon erects her looms on the borders
of Ulro, to weave earthly forms for lost souls.

13.27. *He*] The Lamb.

And the Elect shall say to the Redeemed, 'We behold it is of divine
Mercy alone, of free gift & election that we live.
Our virtues & cruel goodnesses have deserved eternal death.'
35   Thus they weep upon the fatal brook of Albion's river.
But Elynittria met Leutha in the place where she was hidden,
And threw aside her arrows & laid down her sounding bow;
She soothed her with soft words & brought her to Palamabron's bed
In moments new created for delusion, interwoven round about.
40   In dreams she bore the shadowy spectre of sleep & named him
        Death.
In dreams she bore Rahab, the mother of Tirzah & her sisters,
In Lambeth's vales, in Cambridge & in Oxford, places of thought—
Intricate labyrinths of times and spaces unknown that Leutha lived
In Palamabron's tent, and Oothoon was her charming guard.'
45   —The Bard ceased. All considered, and a loud resounding murmur
Continued round the halls, & much they questioned the immortal
Loud-voiced Bard; & many condemned the high-toned song,
Saying, 'Pity & love are too venerable for the imputation
Of guilt.' Others said, 'If it is true, if the acts have been performed,
50   Let the Bard himself witness. Where hadst thou this terrible song?'
The Bard replied: 'I am inspired; I know it is truth, for I sing
Pl. 14 According to the inspiration of the poetic genius,
Who is the eternal all-protecting Divine Humanity,
To whom be glory & power & dominion evermore. Amen!'
                              [Design]

13.32. Elect . . . Redeemed] See pl.7.2n. The Elect have believed that their
salvation is by miraculous chance of an arbitrary divine decree (17.33–4):
now they see the truth. *Election* here means choice, i.e. the soul's accept-
ance of the gift.

13.35. fatal brook] Tyburn Brook, which ran near the place where criminals
were executed (see map p. 621).

13.40. she] Leutha.

In dreams] Leutha is the mother of all 'feminine' delusions seen by mortal
men; as the emanation of Satan she is linked with him in his fall. Note the
terms *delusion, interwoven, intricate, labyrinths, unknown.*

13.41. *Rahab, Tirzah* and their unholy sisters embody the most sinister of
female evils on earth; cp. *Four Zoas* viii *267n.*

13.44. Oothoon] Cp. *Visions 198–204*, where also Oothoon promises
to bring other girls to Theotormon as Elynittria brings Leutha to Pala-
mabron's bed.

13.48. pity and love] Both have been criticized by the Bard; the pity of
Los and Palamabron for Satan, and Leutha's love for Palamabron, have
both produced ill, because they were falsely conceived.

Design: Between the lines are recumbent figures; one supine, one half-
raised, one half-turned to rock.

Then there was great murmuring in the heavens of Albion
5 Concerning generation & the vegetative power, & concerning
The Lamb, the Saviour. Albion trembled to Italy, Greece & Egypt,
To Tartary & Hindustan & China, & to great America,
Shaking the roots & fast foundations of the earth in doubtfulness.
The loud-voiced Bard terrified took refuge in Milton's bosom.

10 Then Milton rose up from the heavens of Albion ardorous.
The whole assembly wept prophetic, seeing in Milton's face
And in his lineaments divine the shades of death & Ulro.
He took off the robe of the promise & ungirded himself from the oath
of God.

And Milton said, 'I go to eternal death! The nations still
15 Follow after the detestable gods of Priam, in pomp
Of warlike selfhood, contradicting and blaspheming.
When will the Resurrection come to deliver the sleeping body
From corruptibility? O when, Lord Jesus, wilt thou come?
Tarry no longer: for my soul lies at the gates of death.
20 I will arise & look forth for the morning of the grave.
I will go down to the sepulchre to see if morning breaks.
I will go down to self-annihilation & eternal death,
Lest the Last Judgement come & find me unannihilate,
And I be seized & given into the hands of my own selfhood.
25 The Lamb of God is seen through mists & shadows, hovering
Over the sepulchres in clouds of Jehovah & winds of Elohim,
A disc of blood, distant, & heavens & earths roll dark between.
What do I here before the Judgement? Without my emanation?

14.4. *The heavens of Albion*] The 'heavenly' Albion–which may be seen
as one man, or as a world, spread out into hills, valleys, rivers, etc., as well
as animals and men. Cp. *Jerusalem* pl.71.*15–19*, *Four Zoas* v *121–42*. The
infinite sight of heaven may 'expand' and see these details, or 'contract'
and see one man.
14.*13*. That is, he was willing to be lost eternally. This is the decisive act
of the poem, prepared in 2.*16–20*, and B. places a full-page illustration
of it on the next plate.
14.*14*. *I go!*] A statement of intention.
14.*17–24*. 'Death' here is final, spiritual death. 'The morning of the
grave' is spiritual resurrection, which the 'sleeping body' must undergo
if it is to live eternal life. B. plays upon the two sorts of death–of the
earthly body, which is supposed to sleep till Judgment Day; and mortal
life, which is itself only a kind of sleep or death. Milton has died from
mortal life, but his divided spirit is still not alive in eternal life. For this,
he must be 'annihilated' and remade–hence his wish to 'go down to the
sepulchre'. For *20* cp. *Four Zoas* ix *116–18*.

With the daughters of memory & not with the daughters of
        inspiration?
30   I in my selfhood am that Satan; I am that evil one,
      He is my spectre! In my obedience to loose him from my hells
      To claim the hells, my furnaces, I go to eternal death.'

      And Milton said, 'I go to eternal death!' Eternity shuddered,
      For he took the outside course, among the graves of the dead
35   A mournful shade. Eternity shuddered at the image of eternal death.

      Then on the verge of Beulah he beheld his own shadow—
      A mournful form, double, hermaphroditic, male & female
      In one wonderful body. And he entered into it
      In direful pain; for the dread shadow, twenty-seven-fold,
40   Reached to the depths of direst Hell, & thence to Albion's land,
      Which is this earth of vegetation on which now I write.

14.29. Cp. 1.6n.

14.30–1. Milton's sin had been that of the usurper Satan of the Bard's song
in that he supported tyranny and that his mind was attuned to it. 'That
Satan' is the corrupted, dominating part of Milton's own personality, his
spectre (see *Four Zoas* iv *63n*, *Jerusalem* pl.6.1n). Milton is now able to
identify himself with Satan instead of treating him with self-righteous
distaste, as he did in *Paradise Lost*.

14.32. 'To claim the hells (of destruction) as my furnaces (of purification
and creation).' Milton is to go down to Hell, as Christ did, in an act of
self-sacrifice, to redeem those who were there.

14.34. *the outside course*] Cp. 17.29: 'travellers from eternity pass outward
to Satan's seat'.

14.36. *his own shadow*] His spectral form, and fallen; but such a body must
be the vehicle of his spirit as he travels in the grosser lower regions where
the spiritual body of heaven cannot go.

14.37–8. HERMAPHRODITIC, *male and female . . . body*] Self-contradictory and
therefore nothing; male and female, yet neither one nor the other, nor (as
in Eternity) both in unity. It is essentially a creature of the fallen sexual
world, because in Eden human beings have no sex, but are both sexes
blended in one, mingled far more deeply and fully than is possible in two-
sexed mankind. The hermaphrodite, 'self-dividing' (19.33), is in effect
a summary of the sexual world where male and female depend on one
another, yet are at odds with one another. The ultimate form of evil, the
Covering Cherub (37.8n), is a hermaphrodite, a female 'dragon red
and hidden harlot' dominating, from within, a male giant. *Jerusalem*
pl.90.52–5 is also an interesting comment.

14.39. *twenty-sevenfold*] Cp. 17.24, 37.35n.

The seven Angels of the Presence wept over Milton's shadow.

(II)   [*Full-plate illustration*]

Pl. 15

As when a man dreams, he reflects not that his body sleeps,
Else he would wake; so seemed he entering his shadow. But
With him the spirits of the seven Angels of the Presence
Entering, they gave him still perceptions of his sleeping body,
5 Which now arose and walked with them in Eden, as an eighth

14.42. SEVEN ANGELS OF THE PRESENCE] Cp. *Four Zoas* i *248*, 'They elected
seven, called the Seven / Eyes of God and the Seven Lamps of the Al-
mighty'. The word 'elected' identifies the Seven as the guardians of
pl.13.*17* above (also *Four Zoas* viii *386*ff and *Jerusalem* pl.55.*31*), as does the
name Lucifer in the list of guardians and among the Seven Angels in extra
pl.32.*8–9* (p. 573 below). With Milton in 15.5 they make Eight. In
39.*3–13* the Seven defy Satan, Milton's spectre: with the redeemed
Milton 'the Starry Eight became one Man, Jesus the Saviour'. Thus the
Seven, in general, appear as guardians and advisers of humanity; in
Milton in particular they are his companions and protectors, who go into
the fallen world with him (15.*3*) in order to maintain his vision of
eternity (15.*5–7* and extra pl.32). See also *Isaiah* lxiii 9: 'In all their
affliction he was afflicted, and the angel of his presence saved them . . .':
and *Exodus* xxxiii 14.

  Revelation has many sevens, mostly agents of divine purpose: spirits
i 4, v 6) 'sent forth into all the earth'; candlesticks (i 12, 20, ii 1); stars
(i 16, ii 1)–the last two the churches, the emissaries of Christ in the world;
in *Revelation* viii 2 and xv 1ff the seven angels stand before God and scatter
calamities on the earth; these belong to the Lamb who (v 6) has 'seven
horns and seven eyes, which are the seven Spirits of God sent forth into
all the earth'. This passage is the basis of B.'s Seven Angels, though his
Divine Mercy does not dispense wrath as in *Revelation* (contrast Satan in
38.*54–5*), but accompanies the souls of individuals for their safety. In
1800, though the roads were safer than they had been, it would still be
prudent for travellers to journey in a group rather than alone.

II. Full-plate illustration to 14.*13*; Milton, throwing off his robe and girdle,
steps on to a dark globe, with the sun setting behind, its aura fading.

15.*1–16*. A description of three simultaneous states of being: the Seven
with Milton in Eden; their emanations tending him in Beulah; he travels
alone with both unknown to him. Yet all three states are real. Cp. 20.*15*ff
and headnote on p. 487.

15.*4. perceptions . . . body*] See 14.*42n*. The phrase is obscure but seems
to mean that they made him perceive heavenly things, though his 'spiritual
body' was asleep. Note also the similarity to Jacob's dream at Bethel
(*Genesis* xxviii).

Image, divine though darkened, and though walking as one walks
In sleep. And the Seven comforted and supported him.

Like as a polypus that vegetates beneath the deep
They saw his shadow vegetated underneath the couch
10   Of death. For when he entered into his shadow, himself,
His real and immortal self, was as appeared to those
Who dwell in immortality, as one sleeping on a couch
Of gold, & those in immortality gave forth their emanations
Like females of sweet beauty, to guard round him & to feed
15   His lips with food of Eden in his cold & dim repose.
But to himself he seemed a wanderer lost in dreary night.

Onwards his shadow kept its course among the spectres, called
Satan; but swift as lightning passing them, startled the shades
Of Hell beheld him in a trail of light as of a comet
20   That travels into chaos. So Milton went guarded within.

The nature of infinity is this: that everything has its
Own vortex, & when once a traveller through Eternity
Has passed that vortex, he perceives it roll backward behind
His path, into a globe itself enfolding like a sun

15.8. *polypus*] See *Four Zoas* iv *265* and a similar use of the image at *Jerusalem* pl.18.*40*.

15.9–*10*. *the couch of death*] Albion's (*9.3n*).

15.*17*. Here Milton begins a progress which recalls that of *Paradise Lost* ii 629ff: 'Satan with thoughts inflamed of highest design, / Puts on swift wings, and toward the Gate of Hell / Explores his solitary flight.'

15.*17–18*. *spectres, called / Satan*] Cp. *Four Zoas* viib *298*, where B. describes the spectres of the spiritually dead scattering through the abyss: 'in the aggregate they named them Satan.'

15.*21*. VORTEX] Descartes proposed in his cosmology that the universe was composed of a continuous range of vortices, each with a star at its centre. Thus a body (e.g. a comet) travelling through one vortex would, on passing beyond it, immediately enter the influence of another. (B. had probably met Descartes's theories indirectly through the writings of Henry More, 1614–87.) B. adds that a person so travelling would see the vortex in which he was, as we see this world partially and outspread. But in our state 'confined beneath the moony shade' (*33*) he would only see the vortex that had been left behind from the outside, its curved walls rolled up as if into a globe–a separate, distant object. Yet a heaven, an eternal world, lies there: and those unknown, apparently dead worlds are worlds of beauty like our own. Milton (*19*) travels like a comet, but so fast that he is drawn into the influence of no vortex.

15.*23–4*. He cannot see the infinite thing itself; he can, for example, see the sun.

25 Or like a moon, or like a universe of starry majesty,
    While he keeps onwards in his wondrous journey on the earth—
    Or like a human form, a friend with whom he lived benevolent.
    As the eye of man views both the east & west, encompassing
    Its vortex, & the north & south, with all their starry host,
30 Also the rising sun & setting moon, he views surrounding
    His cornfields and his valleys of five hundred acres square.
    Thus is the earth one infinite plane, and not as apparent
    To the weak traveller confined beneath the moony shade.
    Thus is the heaven a vortex passed already, & the earth
35 A vortex not yet passed by the traveller through eternity.

    First Milton saw Albion upon the Rock of Ages,
    Deadly pale, outstretched and snowy cold, storm-covered—
    A giant form of perfect beauty outstretched on the rock
    In solemn death; the sea of time & space thundered aloud
40 Against the rock, which was enwrapped with the weeds of death.
    Hovering over the cold bosom, in its vortex Milton bent down
    To the bosom of death (what was underneath soon seemed above).
    A cloudy heaven mingled with stormy seas in loudest ruin;
    But as a wintry globe descends precipitant through Beulah bursting
45 With thunders loud and terrible, so Milton's shadow fell,
    Precipitant loud-thundering into the sea of time & space.

[Design]

    Then first I saw him in the zenith as a falling star,
    Descending perpendicular, swift as the swallow or swift;
    And on my left foot, falling on the tarsus, entered there;
50 But from my left foot a black cloud redounding spread over Europe.

    Then Milton knew that the three heavens of Beulah were beheld
    By him on earth in his bright pilgrimage of sixty years

15.28–35. Man sees to right and left over 180°; he cannot see the extent
and comprehensiveness of infinity, but it is there, just as east and west are
there, part of one continuous entity. Both the outside and inside of the
'vortex' exist and are real.

15.41. Milton goes down to Albion; as he comes closer (42) he pierces the
clouds and enters the mortal world again (46).

Design: This shows a star falling on a man's foot, left; right, a woman
weeping (47–50). It seems to embody a vivid personal experience: in 21.
12–13 B. describes it, and this design is then enlarged into a full plate
and used twice (after pls 29 and 33).

15.51. three heavens] The beauty and delight of female head, heart and
loins; see 5.6, p. 569 below (a later passage). Milton had seen the whole
range of feminine beauty in his wives and daughters.

Pl. 16 (III)   *[Full-page illustration]*

Pl. 17   *[Design]*

In those three females, whom his wives, & those three whom his
    daughters
Had represented & contained, that they might be resumed
By giving up of selfhood; & they distant viewed his journey
In their eternal spheres, now human, though their bodies remain
    closed
5 In the dark Ulro till the Judgement. Also Milton knew they and
Himself was human, though now wandering through death's vale
In conflict with those female forms, which in blood & jealousy
Surrounded him, dividing & uniting without end or number.

He saw the cruelties of Ulro, & he wrote them down
10 In iron tablets; and his wives & daughters' names were these:
Rahab & Tirzah, & Milcah & Mahlah & Noah & Hoglah.
They sat ranged round him as the rocks of Horeb round the land

Plate 16. This full-page design shows the struggle of Milton and Urizen
(*19.4–14*). Above, in a separate division, the immortals in Eden rejoice,
playing various instruments. Below the design is the caption *To annihilate
the Self-hood of Deceit and False Forgiveness*. Reproduced in Keynes, *W.B.'s
Engravings*, pl.99.

17.1. The design at the top of the page shows the six females, three seated,
three in a dance. Although interrupted by designs, *15.52–17.1* are con-
tinuous.

17.1–3. The eternal nature of the six females (in sum, Milton's emanation),
partially represented on earth by the wives and daughters. By giving up
their earthly, self-centred individuality, they would resume their heavenly
form and place and combine with Milton.

17.5–7. *they and himself* in eternity made up *one* eternal human being
(hence *was*, not *were*). But on earth he was at odds with them; and they
represent all earthly female faults and errors.

17.9–17. Milton in his journey sees a vision of himself and the meaning of
the tainted work he did on earth.

17.11. *Rahab and Tirzah*] See *Four Zoas* viii *267*.
Milcah and Mahlah and Noah and Hoglah] *Numbers* xxvi 33 (also xxvii 1 and
xxxvi 11): 'Mahlah and Noah, Hoglah, Milcah and Tirzah'–Zelophehad
had no sons and these were his daughters, who were allowed to inherit
from him. Thus they embody the female insinuation into male inheritance
–a monstrous regiment of women. (Cp. also *Four Zoas* viii *300*ff.) Milton
himself had been similarly misled on earth.

17.12. *rocks of Horeb*] Or Sinai, the source of moral law. See *16–17*.

Of Canaan, & they wrote in thunder, smoke & fire
His dictate; and his body was the rock Sinai—that body
15   Which was on earth born to corruption. And the six females
Are Hor & Peor & Bashan & Abarim & Lebanon & Hermon,
Seven rocky masses terrible in the deserts of Midian.

But Milton's human shadow continued journeying above
The rocky masses of the mundane shell in the lands
20   Of Edom & Aram & Moab & Midian & Amalek.
(The mundane shell is a vast concave earth: an immense
Hardened shadow of all things upon our vegetated earth,
Enlarged into dimensions & deformed into indefinite space,
In twenty-seven heavens & all their hells, with chaos
25   And ancient night & purgatory. It is a cavernous earth
Of labyrinthine intricacy, twenty-seven folds of opaqueness,
And finishes where the lark mounts. Here Milton journeyed
In that region called Midian, among the rocks of Horeb.
For travellers from Eternity pass outward to Satan's seat,
30   But travellers to Eternity pass inward to Golgonooza.)
Los, the vehicular terror, beheld him, & divine Enitharmon
Called all her daughters, saying, 'Surely to unloose my bond

17.13–14. *His dictate*] Milton's daughters are said to have acted as his amanuenses in the blindness of his later life. B. conflates Milton's poetry and its moral source–the Law of Sinai.

17.16. *Hor . . . Hermon*] All are mountains and mountainous regions, from Hor to the south to Hermon north of Palestine's borders. B. sets them all in Midian, the hostile land S.S.E. of biblical Palestine, by a sort of moral ellipsis; all are hostile, threatening, and overhanging. Hermon is the highest point of Lebanon. See map, p. 575.

17.17. *Seven*] Milton (Sinai) is the seventh (see *14*).

17.19. *the mundane shell*] The enclosing universe beneath the firmament, shut off from eternity. See 34.31 and *Jerusalem* pl.13.33n.

17.20. *Edom . . . Amalek*] Tribes bordering on Palestine.

17.24. *twenty-seven heavens*] Also *26*: the space between earth and firmament is filled with this range of heavens varying, not in translucence, but in obscurity. See 37.35n.

17.27. *where the lark mounts*] An idea, developed in pl.35.61ff, that the singing lark rises to a point where it comes to the gate of eternity.

17.29–30. Because the traveller from Eden, coming to this world, leaves heaven for hell and vice versa. 'Outward' because he moves towards a world of superficial, objective appearances; 'inward' he goes to the heart of things. See *Jerusalem* 12.55n.

17.31. *vehicular*] Because he is the form taken, within time and space, of the eternal Urthona, whose personality he 'carries'. This idea, unimportant in *Milton*, is fully developed in *The Four Zoas*.

Is this man come. Satan shall be unloosed upon Albion.'
Los heard in terror Enitharmon's words. In fibrous strength
35 His limbs shot forth like roots of trees against the forward path
Of Milton's journey. Urizen beheld the immortal man,
Pl. 19 And he also darkened his brows, freezing dark rocks between
The footsteps & infixing deep the feet in marble beds,
That Milton laboured with his journey, & his feet bled sore
Upon the clay now changed to marble. Also Urizen rose
5   And met him on the shores of Arnon & by the streams of the brooks.

Silent they met, and silent strove among the streams of Arnon
Even to Mahanaim, when with cold hand Urizen stooped down
And took up water from the river Jordan, pouring on
To Milton's brain the icy fluid from his broad cold palm.
10 But Milton took of the red clay of Succoth, moulding it with care

17.33. *Satan shall be unloosed*] Both Los and Enitharmon misinterpret
Milton's new role, as he journeys in his 'shadow' form, for they do not
realize that he has renounced his earlier falsehoods. In *Revelation* xx Satan
is first locked up, then unloosed, by an angel, 'to deceive the nations', but
also to be annihilated. B. uses the image of unloosing, but has changed the
circumstances. This is the selfish Enitharmon of *Jerusalem* 87.12–24, seeing
her link with Los as 'bondage'. Los tries to obstruct the Satan that he thinks
he sees. But Milton is not Satan.
17.35. *like roots of trees*] A design at the foot of the page illustrates this,
with Urizen, 'his arms and knees / Like to the roots of ancient trees'
(*Jerusalem* pl.52 poem 734–5). In *Jerusalem* the image is not derogatory.
For Plate 18 see appendix, p. 571 below.

19.5. ARNON] A river in a steep valley, flowing into the Dead Sea: to B. it
was also a frontier–the border between Moab and the Israelites (speci-
fically Reuben, *Joshua* xiii 15). Milton (*Paradise Lost* i 399) refers to the
cruel worship of Moloch as far as Arnon.
19.7. *Mahanaim's* historical position is uncertain, but it was nowhere near
Arnon (see map). The line suggests a struggle over the border area of trans-
Jordanian Israel. The angels of God met Jacob at Mahanaim shortly before
his struggle at Jabbok (*Genesis* xxxii 1–2). Cp. also *Paradise Lost* xi 213–15:
'Not that more glorious when the angels met / Jacob in Mahanaim, where
he saw / The field pavilioned with his guardians bright. . . .' The illustra-
tion on pl.16 shows Milton struggling with Urizen beneath a group of
singing angels.
19.9. *icy fluid*] This is a sort of pseudo-baptism (to death, not life): the
struggle repeats Jacob's struggle with the angel at the ford of the Jabbok
and is one of the critical acts in *Milton*. Urizen tries to petrify, Milton to
redeem (29).
19.10. *Succoth*, where Hiram the brass-founder made ornaments and
utensils for Solomon's temple, 1 *Kings* vii 46: 'In the plain of Jordan . . .
in the clay ground between Succoth and Zarthan.' The *red clay* alludes to

Between his palms and filling up the furrows of many years,
Beginning at the feet of Urizen & on the bones
Creating new flesh on the demon cold and building him,
As with new clay, a human form in the valley of Beth Peor.
15 (Four universes round the mundane egg remain chaotic:
    One to the north, named Urthona; one to the south, named
        Urizen;
    One to the east, named Luvah; one to the west, named Tharmas.
    They are the four Zoas that stood around the throne divine.
    But when Luvah assumed the world of Urizen to the south,
20 And Albion was slain upon his mountains & in his tent,
    All fell towards the centre in dire ruin, sinking down.
    And in the south remains a burning fire, in the east a void,
    In the west, a world of raging waters, in the north a solid,
    Unfathomable, without end. But in the midst of these
25 Is built eternally the universe of Los and Enitharmon,
    Towards which Milton went—but Urizen opposed his path.)
    The man and demon strove many periods. Rahab beheld,
    Standing on Carmel; Rahab and Tirzah trembled to behold
    The enormous strife, one giving life, the other giving death
30 To his adversary. And they sent forth all their sons & daughters
    In all their beauty to entice Milton across the river.
    The twofold form hermaphroditic and double-sexed,

the creation of man from the red earth (*Genesis* ii 7); note the association
of the words *Adam*; *adamah* (ground); *adom* (red): and cp. *Marriage* i 13.
19.14. *the valley of Beth Peor*] Where the Israelites rested before entering
the promised land (*Deuteronomy* iii 27–9). Moses was buried there: 'but
no man knoweth of his sepulchre unto this day' (*Deuteronomy* xxxiv 6).
19.15–26. An interpolation of material derived from the myth of *The Four
Zoas* (q.v. headnote) and not relevant to Milton's struggle, though perhaps
intended to 'explain' who Urizen was. Line 26 is an attempt to make it fit.
Jerusalem pl.59.10–17 is almost identical, and *Milton* 34.32–9 very similar.
19.19. Luvah's usurpation of dominion over Albion is one of the chief
causes of the Fall in *Four Zoas* (i 182ff).
19.27. *Rahab* is the leading female principle of evil (*Four Zoas* viii 267n),
with her sister Tirzah. They come to Urizen's aid by trying to distract
Milton. B. has identified them with Milton's wives and daughters (17.11),
the female influences in his previous life.
19.31. *to entice Milton*] But Milton's task, like that of Moses, lay outside
the promised land. Carmel is on the coast, and so on the far side of Palestine
from the scene of these events.
19.32. *twofold form hermaphroditic*] The creature which symbolizes the
sexual creation, bound to but never satisfied by sex, held together yet 'self-
dividing'. The aggressive male form is dominated by an inner female
cruelty; the beautiful female by a male lust for power. Cp. 14.37n.

The female-male & the male-female, self-dividing, stood
Before him in their beauty, & in cruelties of holiness,
35   Shining in darkness, glorious upon the deeps of Entuthon,

Saying, 'Come thou to Ephraim! Behold the Kings of Canaan!
The beautiful Amalekites! Behold the fires of youth
Bound with the Chain of Jealousy by Los & Enitharmon!
The banks of Cam, cold learning's streams, London's dark-frowning
        towers
40   Lament upon the winds of Europe in Rephaim's vale,
Because Ahania, rent apart into a desolate night,
Laments, & Enion wanders like a weeping inarticulate voice,
And Vala labours for her bread & water among the furnaces.
Therefore bright Tirzah triumphs, putting on all beauty

19.35. Entuthon] The dark forest of evil (cp. *Four Zoas* viii *25n*).

19.36–20.6. They try to lure Milton away from his task, saying that Canaan—the land which, like Moses, he must not yet enter—needs a king. The passage is somewhat inconsequential and a logically continuous theme must not be looked for. The general idea is that the 'Twofold' speaker claims that Milton believes in a lost dream and is therefore wasting his time; for the world belongs to Rahab and Tirzah, cruel and oppressive, and Albion is in their power. Since Milton's quest is a step towards the awakening of Albion, they wish to dissuade him from continuing.

19.36–45. This is one of Blake's compressed passages, where he throws allusions from other poems and outside sources hastily together; the meanings of individual phrases are less than the drift of the whole. The passage deals with universal desolation, and *37–8*, *39–40*, *41–3* are different manifestations of it. Lines *44–62* describe the sadistic pleasure of Tirzah's cruelty in her creation (and malformation) of the fallen 'vegetable' world.

19.36. Ephraim] The holy mountain of the Northern Kingdom, which had broken away from the kingdom whose capital was Jerusalem.

19.37–8. Amalekites] The traditional enemies of Israel: *Exodus* xvii 16: 'The Lord will have war with Amalek from generation to generation.'

19.38. Chain of Jealousy] In *Urizen* 377ff and *Four Zoas* v *79–95*, *155–72*, after the birth of his child Orc, Los was impelled to bind him with this chain, which denies the child the freedom his fiery nature demands, and which Los himself is unable to break.

19.40. REPHAIM'S VALE] A valley S.W. of Jerusalem and N. of Bethlehem where the Philistines camped and were defeated by David more than once (*2 Samuel* v 18, xxiii 13). Thus it is a home of evil; but the name means 'valley of shades of the dead', and is therefore linked in B.'s imagery with 'spectre' and with Satan.

19.41–3. Ahania, Enion and *Vala*] In *Four Zoas* (ii *424ff*, iii *199–205*) Ahania and Enion are emanations driven into a solitary existence in the abyss; Vala is enslaved by Urizen.

45 And all perfection in her cruel sports among the victims.
Come, bring with thee Jerusalem with songs on the Grecian lyre!
In natural religion, in experiments on men,
Let her be offered up to holiness! Tirzah numbers her;
She numbers with her fingers every fibre ere it grow.
50 Where is the Lamb of God? Where is the promise of his coming?
Her shadowy sisters form the bones, even the bones of Horeb,
Around the marrow, and the orbed skull around the brain.
His images are born for war, for sacrifice to Tirzah!
To Natural Religion! To Tirzah, the daughter of Rahab the holy!
55 She ties the knot of nervous fibres into a white brain,
She ties the knot of bloody veins into a red-hot heart.
Within her bosom Albion lies embalmed, never to awake;
Hand is become a rock, Sinai & Horeb is Hyle & Coban;
Skofield is bound in iron armour before Reuben's gate.
60 She ties the knot of milky seed into two lovely heavens,
Pl. 20 Two yet but one, each in the other sweet reflected, these
Are our three heavens beneath the shades of Beulah, land of rest.
Come then to Ephraim & Manasseh, O beloved one!
Come to my ivory palaces, O beloved of thy mother,
5 And let us bind thee in the bands of war & be thou King
Of Canaan and reign in Hazor where the twelve tribes meet.'

So spoke they as in one voice. Silent Milton stood before
The darkened Urizen; as the sculptor silent stands before

19.46. *Bring Jerusalem*] Personified as a captive at the triumph of Babylon
(with which Rahab is associated). The *Grecian lyre*, the *Natural Religion*, and
the *experiments* are all expressions of the cold classical mind, which is mind
in error (cp. *Preface*).

19.48. *numbers*] An act of impersonal callousness.

19.51. *form the bones*] Man, the image of Christ, is forced into a misshapen
earthly mould (see *53*). In a similar passage in *Jerusalem* 80.69–78, Gwen-
dolen petrifies Hand 'against the Lamb of God'.

19.54. *natural religion*] Cp. *46n*.

19.57. *embalmed*] Seeming alive, but dead and in her power.

19.58. *Hand . . . Hyle and Coban*] Three of Albion's sons, who represent
aspects of him (see *Jerusalem* headnote, p. 624). For 'Skofield' see headnote.

20.2. *three heavens*] Cp. extra 5.6 (p.569). Tirzah's heavens of brain, heart
and loins are mere natural, animal beauties and not the genuine heavens
of Beulah, which admit the earthbound man momentarily to Eternity.

20.3. *Ephraim and Manasseh*] Born in Egypt (*Genesis* xlvi 20), the two sons
who inherited Joseph's place among the Israelite tribes. Later these tribes
were in the northern or renegade kingdom.

20.6. *Hazor*] The chief town among the Canaanite kingdoms in N.
Palestine before the Israelite invasion. In *Joshua* xi 1–10 the king of Hazor
led twelve hostile tribes against the Israelites and was decisively defeated.

His forming image (he walks round it patient labouring).
10   Thus Milton stood forming bright Urizen, while his mortal part
Sat frozen in the rock of Horeb, and his redeemed portion
Thus formed the clay of Urizen; but within that portion
His real human walked above in power and majesty
Though darkened; and the seven Angels of the Presence attended
him.

15   O how can I, with my gross tongue that cleaveth to the dust,
Tell of the fourfold Man, in starry numbers fitly ordered?
Or how can I with my cold hand of clay? But thou, O Lord,
Do with me as thou wilt; for I am nothing, and vanity.
If thou choose to elect a worm, it shall remove the mountains.
20   For that portion named the Elect, the spectrous body of Milton,
Redounding from my left foot into Los's mundane space,
Brooded over his body in Horeb against the Resurrection,
Preparing it for the great consummation. Red the cherub on Sinai
Glowed, but in terrors folded round his clouds of blood.

25   Now Albion's sleeping humanity began to turn upon his couch,
Feeling the electric flame of Milton's awful precipitate descent.
Seest thou the little winged fly, smaller than a grain of sand?
It has a heart like thee, a brain open to Heaven & Hell,
Withinside wondrous & expansive. Its gates are not closed;
30   I hope thine are not. Hence it clothes itself in rich array;
Hence thou art clothed with human beauty, O thou mortal man.
Seek not thy heavenly father then beyond the skies;
There Chaos dwells & Ancient Night, & Og & Anak old.
For every human heart has gates of brass & bars of adamant,
35   Which few dare unbar, because dread Og & Anak guard the gates
Terrific, & each mortal brain is walled & moated round
Within, & Og & Anak watch here; here is the seat

20.15–16. How can I . . . tell] B. has just attempted such a fourfold descrip-
tion (10–14). See Four Zoas i 1–15.
20.20–2. For that portion] Milton's self-righteous 'elect' mind, which con-
trolled him when he wrote on earth, was still trying to preserve its corrupt
existence; his prophetic soul remained in William Blake.
20.21. my left foot] Cp. 15.49.
20.23–4. When Moses received the Law, 'there were thunders and light-
nings, and a thick cloud upon the mount' (Sinai)–Exodus xix 16.
20.31. human] We would probably say divine.
20.37. OG and ANAK watch here to prevent man from using his imagination.
Og was a king of Bashan, defeated by the Israelites (Deuteronomy iii 1): the
'children of Anak' lived in Hebron, within the promised land: 'And there
we saw the giants, the sons of Anak . . . and we were in our own sight as
grasshoppers' (Numbers xiii 33): but, of course, the Israelites overcame

Of Satan in its webs. For in brain and heart & loins
Gates open behind Satan's seat to the city of Golgonooza,
40 Which is the spiritual fourfold London in the loins of Albion.

Thus Milton fell through Albion's heart, travelling outside of
   humanity
Beyond the stars in chaos, in caverns of the mundane shell.

But many of the Eternals rose up from eternal tables.
Drunk with the spirit, burning round the couch of death they stood,
45 Looking down into Beulah, wrathful, filled with rage.
They rend the heavens round the watchers in a fiery circle,
And round the shadowy eighth; the Eight close up the couch
Into a tabernacle and flee with cries down to the deeps,
Where Los opens his three wide gates, surrounded by raging fires.
50 They soon find their own place & join the watchers of the Ulro.

Los saw them and a cold pale horror covered o'er his limbs.
Pondering, he knew that Rintrah & Palamabron might depart,
Even as Reuben & as Gad, gave up himself to tears.
He sat down on his anvil-stock and leaned upon the trough,
55 Looking into the black water, mingling with it tears.

At last when desperation almost tore his heart in twain
He recollected an old prophecy in Eden recorded
And often sung to the loud harp at the immortal feasts—
That Milton of the land of Albion should up ascend
60 Forwards from Ulro from the Vale of Felpham and set free

them. Cp. 31.49 and 37.50. The giants are fierce guards, but B. nowhere
suggests that they are really dangerous; their appearance is their only
threat, and whoever slips past them may enter the gate of Golgonooza.
20.37–9. *the seat / of Satan . . . Golgonooza*] In *17.29–30* B. has shown the
closeness of these two opposed places; the traveller going sees one and
returning sees the other. Satan *seems* to prevent all passage by his power;
yet intellectual and sensual joy in earthly things are a passage, which he
cannot close, to Golgonooza. (*Four Zoas* viii *25n*; and *Milton 27.23–29.65*.)
20.43–5. The Eternals, like Los, do not understand Milton's act; they think
of it as rejection of heaven, not realizing that it is Milton's search for re-
demption through death.
20.47. *the shadowy eighth* is Milton (*15.3–7*), in the 'persona' that remains
in heaven. The Eight, expelled from Eden, go down to Golgonooza, where
Los keeps watch over Ulro (*50*).
20.52–3. *Reuben and Gad* were faithless sons of Los (*Four Zoas* viii *362–4*);
Los fears that Milton will tempt his remaining sons to flee as Satan tempted
the rest.
20.54. *the trough*] Where the blacksmith cools the red-hot iron on which he
is working.

Orc from his Chain of Jealousy. He started at the thought
Pl. 21 And down descended into Udan-Adan; it was night,
And Satan sat sleeping upon his couch in Udan-Adan:
His spectre slept, his shadow woke (when one sleeps the other wakes).

But Milton entering my foot, I saw in the nether
5 Regions of the imagination, also all men on earth
And all in heaven saw in the nether regions of the imagination,
In Ulro beneath Beulah, the vast breach of Milton's descent.
But I knew not that it was Milton, for man cannot know
What passes in his members till periods of space & time
10 Reveal the secrets of Eternity; for more extensive
Than any other earthly things are man's earthly lineaments.

And all this vegetable world appeared on my left foot,
As a bright sandal formed immortal of precious stones & gold:
I stooped down & bound it on to walk forward through Eternity.

15 There is in Eden a sweet river, of milk & liquid pearl,
Named Ololon, on whose mild banks dwelt those who Milton drove
Down into Ulro. And they wept in long resounding song
For seven days of Eternity, and the river's living banks,
The mountains, wailed, & every plant that grew in solemn sighs
    lamented.

20 When Luvah's bulls each morning drag the sulphur sun out of the
    deep,
Harnessed with starry harness, black & shining, kept by black slaves
That work all night at the starry harness, strong and vigorous
They drag the unwilling orb. At this time all the family
Of Eden heard the lamentation, and providence began.
25 But when the clarions of day sounded they drowned the
    lamentations;

20.61. Cp. 19.38. Los realizes that this longed-for event may be imminent.
21.1. Udan-Adan] The dark lake of Ulro, over which Los keeps watch.
Here it seems less a lake than a region of darkness–cp. Four Zoas viii 215,
'A lake not of waters but of spaces.'

21.4–11. B. and the whole world feel (perhaps unconsciously), rather than
see, the effects of Milton's act.
21.10–11. A man's identity ranges beyond his earthly limitations, and links
him with others in ways not understandable on earth.
21.15–16. A sweet river . . . Named Ololon] In 41.29–30 identified with
Milton's separated emanation, but at this point in the narrative this is not
realized or revealed. Ololon is a place, and also the dwellers in that place;
and they, as is possible in Eternity, later unite into one person (36.13–20).
21.16. those who Milton drove] Those who drove Milton . . .– the Eternals
of 20.43.

And when night came all was silent in Ololon, & all refused to lament
In the still night, fearing lest they should others molest.

Seven mornings Los heard them, as the poor bird within the shell
Hears its impatient parent bird, and Enitharmon heard them,
30 But saw them not, for the blue mundane shell enclosed them in.

And they lamented that they had in wrath & fury & fire
Driven Milton into the Ulro; for now they knew too late
That it was Milton the Awakener. They had not heard the bard
Whose song called Milton to the attempt; and Los heard these
    laments.
35 He heard them call in prayer all the Divine Family;
And he beheld the cloud of Milton stretching over Europe.

But all the Family Divine collected as four suns
In the four points of heaven, east, west & north & south,
Enlarging & enlarging till their discs approached each other;
40 And when they touched, closed together southward in one sun
Over Ololon. And as one man, who weeps over his brother
In a dark tomb, so all the Family Divine wept over Ololon,

Saying, 'Milton goes to eternal death!' So saying they groaned
    in spirit
And were troubled; & again the Divine Family groaned in spirit.

45 And Ololon said, 'Let us descend also, & let us give
Ourselves to death in Ulro among the transgressors.
Is virtue a punisher? O no! How is this wondrous thing,
This world beneath, unseen before, this refuge from the wars
Of great Eternity, unnatural refuge, unknown by us till now?
50 Or are these the pangs of repentance? Let us enter into them.

Then the Divine Family said: 'Six thousand years are now
Accomplished in this world of sorrow; Milton's angel knew
The universal dictate, and you also feel this dictate.
And now you know this world of sorrow and feel pity. Obey
55 The dictate! Watch over this world, and with your brooding wings
Renew it to eternal life. Lo! I am with you always;
But you cannot renew Milton. He goes to eternal death.'

So spake the Family Divine as one man, even Jesus,
Uniting in one with Ololon, & the appearance of one man,

21.30. them] Ololon.
21.45. Ololon, as one female figure, will unite (36.16) with Milton's lost
emanation: and this descent, similar to Milton's, leads to their meeting in
the lower world (48.1–3), their purification and reunion (42.3–15).
21.53. The universal dictate that after 6,000 years the entire creation will feel
the coming of the Last Days. See 13.17n.

60 Jesus the Saviour, appeared coming in the clouds of Ololon.
Pl. 22 Though driven away with the seven starry ones into the Ulro,
Yet the Divine Vision remains everywhere for ever. Amen.
And Ololon lamented for Milton with a great lamentation.

While Los heard indistinct in fear what time I bound my sandals
5 On to walk forward through Eternity, Los descended to me;
And Los behind me stood, a terrible flaming sun, just close
Behind my back, I turned round in terror, & behold!
Los stood in that fierce glowing fire, & he also stooped down
And bound my sandals on in Udan-Adan. Trembling I stood
10 Exceedingly, with fear & terror, standing in the vale
Of Lambeth, but he kissed me and wished me health
And I became one man with him, arising in my strength;
'Twas too late now to recede. Los had entered into my soul;
His terrors now possessed me whole. I arose in fury & strength.

15 'I am that shadowy prophet who six thousand years ago
Fell from my station in the eternal bosom. Six thousand years
Are finished; I return. Both time & space obey my will.
I in six thousand years walk up & down: for not one moment
Of time is lost, nor one event of space unpermanent,
20 But all remain; every fabric of six thousand years
Remains permanent, though on the earth where Satan
Fell and was cut off all things vanish & are seen no more,
They vanish not from me & mine; we guard them first & last.
The generations of men run on in the tide of time,
25 But leave their destined lineaments permanent, for ever & ever.'

So spoke Los as we went along to his supreme abode.

Rintrah and Palamabron met us at the gate of Golgonooza,
Clouded with discontent & brooding in their minds terrible things.

21.60. Cp. *Matthew* xxvi 64: 'Hereafter shall ye see the Son of man . . .
coming in the clouds of heaven.' The whole of Eternity is identified with
Ololon's descent, which is a 'Last Judgment'—'Whenever any individual
rejects error and embraces truth a Last Judgment passes on that indi-
vidual': *A Vision of the Last Judgment (Erdman, 1965*, p. 551).

22.5. *Los descended to me*] B. is interpreting a personal experience. With
Los's descent Milton's spirit has entered B. (*15.47–50, 21.4–14*), and Los
has left Golgonooza for Ulro to find Milton (*21.1*). Hence his appearance
to B., the Milton of his own age. This scene is illustrated in plate IV
between pls 22 and 23.

22.15. Los speaks in B. Lines *15–16* also occur in *Four Zoas* viii *339–40*
(p. 419) in another context.

22.27. *Golgonooza*] See *Four Zoas* viii *25n*.

They said: 'O father most beloved, O merciful parent,
30 Pitying and permitting evil, though strong & mighty to destroy,
Whence is this shadow terrible? Wherefore dost thou refuse
To throw him into the furnaces? Knowest thou not that he
Will unchain Orc & let loose Satan, Og, Sihon & Anak,
Upon the body of Albion? For this he is come. Behold it written
35 Upon his fibrous left foot black, most dismal to our eyes.
The Shadowy Female shudders through heaven in torment inexpressible,
And all the daughters of Los prophetic wail—yet in deceit
They weave a new religion from new jealousy of Theotormon!
Milton's religion is the cause; there is no end to destruction.
40 Seeing the churches at their period in terror & despair,
Rahab created Voltaire, Tirzah created Rousseau,
Asserting the self-righteousness against the universal Saviour,
Mocking the confessors & martyrs, claiming self-righteousness
With cruel virtue—making war upon the Lamb's Redeemed,
45 To perpetuate war & glory, to perpetuate the laws of sin.
They perverted Swedenborg's visions in Beulah & in Ulro,
To destroy Jerusalem as a harlot & her sons as reprobates,

22.31. *This shadow terrible*] Milton, who has descended to Ulro in a shadowy (mortal) form, and appears now in the form of B. himself. Los's sons misunderstood him, as Los once did (17.34–6).

22.33. SIHON] An Amorite king of the Heshbon region, across the Jordan E.N.E. of the Dead Sea. The Israelite victories over him and Og became proverbial–'and what ye did unto . . . Sihon and Og, whom ye utterly destroyed' (*Joshua* ii 10). B. regularly links Sihon, Og and Anak together as threatening giants. For Og and Anak see 20.37n.

22.35. *most . . . eyes*] Probably referring to 'foot': B. has no punctuation mark after 'eyes', but his punctuation is on the whole rhetorical rather than grammatical.

22.36. *The Shadowy Female*] Here a very shadowy figure; she is a kind of mother-spirit of mortal nature.

22.40. From this point B. gives way to an outburst of his own feelings. The spirits of evil, Rahab and Tirzah, have been very active in his age. The idea of 'Churches' (i.e. religious eras) is treated in 37.35.

22.41. *Voltaire* and *Rousseau*] B. vents his hatred against them for their abstract theorizing. He presumably disliked Voltaire's self-assured scepticism (from the pride of Rahab) and Rousseau's rationalistic perfectionism (from Tirzah, queen of Nature, which Rousseau claimed to follow).

22.46. *Swedenborg's visions*] Swedenborg described the revelations and angelic explanations that had come to him when he was carried in the spirit to these places. B. implies that he had only seen Beulah, not Eden, the true heaven; but in any case the good in him had been perverted by the churches (50–4), who preferred mystery to sight.

To raise up Mystery the Virgin Harlot, mother of war,
Babylon the great, the abomination of desolation.
50 O Swedenborg, strongest of men, the Samson shorn by the
    churches,
Showing the transgressors in Hell, the proud warriors in Heaven,
Heaven as a punisher & Hell as one under punishment,
With laws from Plato & his Greeks to renew the Trojan gods
In Albion & to deny the value of the Saviour's blood.
55 But then I raised up Whitefield, Palamabron raised up Wesley;
And these are the cries of the churches before the two witnesses'
Faith in God, the dear Saviour, who took on the likeness of men,
Becoming obedient to death, even the death of the cross:
"The witnesses lie dead in the street of the great city;
60 No faith is in all the earth; the book of God is trodden under foot.
He sent his two servants, Whitefield & Wesley. Were they prophets
Or were they idiots or madmen? Show us miracles!"

(IV)   *[Full-plate illustration]*

Pl. 23 —Can you have greater miracles than these? Men who devote
Their life's whole comfort to entire scorn & injury & death?
Awake! thou sleeper on the Rock of Eternity, Albion, awake!
The trumpet of Judgement hath twice sounded; all nations are
    awake,
5 But thou art still heavy and dull. Awake, Albion, awake!

22.48. *Mystery*] The personification of religious evil: cp. 33.20n, 38.23,
and on Rahab, *Four Zoas* viii 267n.
22.53. *With laws from Plato*] A reference to Plato's *Laws*, or rather to its
title.
22.55. *Whitefield and Wesley*] The two famous evangelists of eighteenth-
century England.
22.56-8 *witnesses'/Faith*] This interpretation is editorial (derived from
Erdman 1965 pp. 117 and 729); the plate has no raised comma. But Erdman
breaks the biblical quotation (see below) in two when he says that the
churches' cries begin at line *58*. Other editions have 'witnesses: Faith',
implying that the 'cries' begin at 'Faith . . .'. This is unsatisfactory, since
the churches here are evil, while Blake quotes the Bible as a believer. Erd-
man now agrees that the churches' cries do not begin at *58* but at *59*. The
reply may begin at *61* or pl.23.1. See *Philippians* II 7-8: 'But made himself
of no reputation, and took upon him the form of a servant, and was made
in the likeness of men: And being found in fashion as a man, he humbled
himself, and became obedient unto death, even the death of the cross.'
22.59. *the great city*] Babylon, whose spiritual power is seen in London,
where faith is dead.
IV. *Full-plate illustration.* Two nude male figures, illustrating 22.4-8.

Lo, Orc arises on the Atlantic. Lo, his blood and fire
Glow on America's shore. Albion turns upon his couch;
He listens to the sounds of war, astonished and confounded;
He weeps into the Atlantic deep, yet still in dismal dreams
10 Unawakened, and the Covering Cherub advances from the east.
How long shall we lay dead in the street of the great city?
How long beneath the Covering Cherub give our emanations?
Milton will utterly consume us & thee, our beloved father!
He hath entered into the Covering Cherub, becoming one with
15 Albion's dread sons; Hand, Hyle & Coban surround him as
A girdle, Gwendolen & Conwenna as a garment woven
Of war & religion. Let us descend & bring him chained
To Bowlahoola, O father most beloved, O mild parent!
Cruel in thy mildness, pitying and permitting evil
20 Though strong and mighty to destroy, O Los our beloved father!'

Like the black storm, coming out of chaos, beyond the stars.
It issues through the dark & intricate caves of the mundane shell,
Passing the planetary visions, & the well-adorned firmament;
The sun rolls into chaos & the stars into the deserts,
25 And then the storms become visible, audible & terrible,
Covering the light of day, &, rolling down upon the mountains,
Deluge all the country round. Such is a vision of Los.
When Rintrah & Palamabron spoke. And such his stormy face
Appeared, as does the face of heaven when covered with thick
    storms,
30 Pitying and loving, though in frowns of terrible perturbation.
But Los dispersed the clouds, even as the strong winds of Jehovah,
And Los thus spoke: 'O noble sons, be patient yet a little.
I have embraced the falling death, he is become one with me.
O sons, we live not by wrath; by mercy alone we live.
35 I recollect an old prophecy in Eden recorded in gold, and oft
Sung to the harp: that Milton of the land of Albion

23.6. As in *America*, where Orc is champion of the revolt of the American colonies against Britain. Line *9* means that England does not recognize the freedom this foretells.

23.10. *the Covering Cherub*] The ultimate manifestation of Satanic evil. See 37.*8n*.

23.11. *lay*] Grammatically acceptable in B.'s day.

23.13–14. These are misconceptions, as we know.

23.15–16. *Hand, Hyle and Coban . . . Gwendolen and Conwenna*] Sons and daughters of Albion, representing the perverted nature of the unredeemed English people. For a full discussion, see *Jerusalem* headnote, p. 624.

23.17–20. Los's sons wish to attempt to 'redeem' him by force (an impossibility); cp. *Jerusalem* pl.39.*1–10*.

23.21. An extended simile in Milton's epic manner.

Should up ascend forward from Felpham's vale, & break the Chain
Of Jealousy from all its roots. Be patient therefore, O my sons.
These lovely females form sweet night & silence & secret
40 Obscurities to hide from Satan's watch-fiends human loves
And graces, lest they write them in their books, & in the scroll
Of mortal life, to condemn the accused who, at Satan's bar,
Tremble in spectrous bodies continually, day & night,
While on the earth they live in sorrowful vegetations
45 Oh when shall we tread our winepresses in heaven & reap
Our wheat with shoutings of joy, & leave the earth in peace?
Remember how Calvin & Luther in fury premature
Sowed war & stern division between papists & protestants!
Let it not be so now. O go not forth in martyrdoms & wars!
50 We were placed here by the universal brotherhood & mercy,
With powers fitted to circumscribe this dark Satanic death,
And that the seven Eyes of God may have space for redemption.
But how this is as yet we know not, & we cannot know
Till Albion is arisen; then patient wait a little while.
55 Six thousand years are passed away; the end approaches fast.
This mighty one is come from Eden; he is of the Elect
Who died from earth & he is returned before the Judgement. This
    thing
Was never known; that one of the holy dead should willing return.
Then patient wait a little while, till the last vintage is over,
60 Till we have quenched the sun of Salah in the Lake of Udan-Adan.
O my dear sons! leave not your father, as your brethren left me.
Twelve sons successive fled away in that thousand years of sorrow,
Pl. 24 Of Palamabron's harrow, & of Rintrah's wrath & fury.

23.39. *These lovely females*] The daughters of Beulah (cp. 30.*1*–31.*7*). They
safeguard the sacred truths that Los's sons fear will be lost.
23.47. *Calvin and Luther*] In *Four Zoas* viii *350*, Luther is a son of Los.
Perhaps here B. intends both to be Los's sons. If so, in addition to drawing
the obvious moral of these lines, B. is also using them as examples of divine
purpose perverted–as Rintrah and Palamabron wish to pervert their
genuine desire to save Albion from Milton's spectre.
23.60. *the sun of Salah*] An obscure phrase. Salah was the father of Eber
(*Genesis* x 24) who was the founder of the Hebrew race. M. J. Tolley sug-
gests a pun on *son* and *sun*: in any case the sense seems to be that Salah,
father of all Hebrews, is thus father of a mistaken religion, which must be
'quenched' in non-entity before 'the last vintage' can be complete. In the
following lines, Los reminds his sons how the twelve Israelite tribes–also
his sons, having his divine tasks to perform–were faithless to him. For an
elaboration of the legend, see *Four Zoas* viii *345*–*65*.

24.*1*. Referring to the primordial events narrated in the Bard's song.

Reuben & Manazzoth & Gad & Simeon & Levi,
And Ephraim & Judah were generated because
They left me, wandering with Tirzah. Enitharmon wept
5   One thousand years, and all the earth was in a watery deluge.
We called him Menassheh because of the generations of Tirzah,
Because of Satan: & the seven Eyes of God continually
Guard round them. But I, the fourth Zoa, am also set
The watchman of Eternity; the three are not, & I am preserved.
10 Still my four mighty ones are left to me in Golgonooza:
Still Rintrah fierce, and Palamabron mild & piteous,
Theotormon filled with care, Bromion loving science.
You, O my sons, still guard round Los. O wander not & leave me.
Rintrah, thou well rememberest when Amalek & Canaan
15 Fled with their sister Moab into that abhorred void.
They became nations in our sight beneath the hands of Tirzah.
And Palamabron, thou rememberest when Joseph, an infant
Stolen from his nurse's cradle wrapped in needlework
Of emblematic texture, was sold to the Amalekite,
20 Who carried him down into Egypt, where Ephraim & Menassheh

24.2. *Manazzoth*] This seems to be a Hebrew word, but is unknown to
the Bible. B. had been studying Hebrew, and this looks like his own
formation of the feminine plural of *Manasseh*. Probably he means 'the
female Manassites', united in one figure and taking the place of a male,
to remind us of Tirzah and her sisters, from the tribe of Manasseh (17.*11n*).
The names listed are taken from the twelve tribes of Israel (23.*62*).

24.3. *generated*] Made to live in this mortal world.

24.4. *wandering with Tirzah*] Not the historical Tirzah (17.*11n*), but B.'s
derived figure, sister of the Whore of Babylon, and queen of nature (*Four
Zoas* viii 267*n*; and 19.*28* above).

24.6. *Menassheh*] Manasseh, in a more strictly Hebraic form (from the
Hebrew *nasheh*, 'cause to forget'): so named by Joseph (*Genesis* xli 51):
'For God, said he, hath made me forget all my toil, and all my father's
house.' His mother, and Ephraim's, was an Egyptian.

24.9–10. *the three . . . my four mighty ones*] 'The three' are the other three
Zoas (Urizen, Tharmas, Luvah) whose fall is narrated in *Four Zoas*. The
'four' are Los's remaining faithful sons, Rintrah, Palamabron, Theo-
tormon and Bromion.

24.14–15. *Amalek and Canaan . . . Moab*] Gentile nations, traditional
enemies of Israel: but originally children of Los.

24.18–19. *needlework*] B. uses the word with a sinister meaning in *Four
Zoas* ii 267. Its many colours are probably 'emblematic' of fickleness.

24.19. *Amalekite*] Joseph was in fact sold to the Ishmaelites—a tribe related
to the Israelites, but, like the Amalekites, generally hostile to them.

24.20. *Ephraim and Manasseh*] Joseph's sons, whose descendants took his
place among the twelve tribes. The reference is to the Exodus, but Moses,
who gathered the tribes together, was a Levite.

Gathered my sons together in the sands of Midian.
And if you also flee away & leave your father's side,
Following Milton into Ulro, although your power is great,
Surely you also shall become poor mortal vegetations
25 Beneath the moon of Ulro. Pity then your father's tears.
When Jesus raised Lazarus from the grave I stood & saw
Lazarus (who is the vehicular body of Albion the Redeemed)
Arise into the Covering Cherub who is the spectre of Albion,
By martyrdoms to suffer—to watch over the sleeping body,
30 Upon his rock beneath his tomb. I saw the Covering Cherub
Divide fourfold into four Churches when Lazarus arose:
Paul, Constantine, Charlemagne, Luther. Behold, they stand
    before us
Stretched over Europe & Asia! Come, O sons, come, come away!
Arise, O sons, give all your strength against eternal death,
35 Lest we are vegetated, for Cathedron's looms weave only death,

24.21. *sands of Midian*] In the Sinai desert, where the Israelites met the
Midianites (*Exodus* xviii 1).

24.26. Los contrasts the fall of his sons into Ulro with the resurrection of
Lazarus, which typifies all resurrection, including Milton's.

24.27. *The vehicular body*] 'An incarnation', 'a living example', but not
more. Cp. 17.31.

24.27ff. Lazarus is the image of the redeemed creation of the future. He
returned to this life–i.e. to mortality. This redeemed part of Albion must
enter the corrupted empty form (the spectre of Albion), not run away
from it, in order to redeem the whole. (Albion appears here in three forms:
the redeemed, Lazarus, *27*; the spectre, the Covering Cherub, *28*; and the
sleeping figure on the rock, *29*.) The spectre replies by augmenting his
activities through the institution-creating saints of the church. (For the
Covering Cherub, see 37.8n: B. also equates Lazarus and the fallen Man
(Albion) in *Four Zoas* iv 252ff.)

24.32. *Paul, Constantine, Charlemagne, Luther*] (In *Four Zoas* viii 350 these
are Los's sons, but B. seems not to have had that passage in mind here.)
Paul systematized Christian thought; in *Jerusalem* pl.56.32 B. associates
him with the establishment of female domination (which is seen in the
'tidying-up' of life). Constantine was chiefly a warrior, but is known as the
emperor of Rome who, though no Christian, decreed the toleration of
Christianity in the Roman Empire in A.D. 313, having won a battle in 312
after a superstitious adoption of the Christian cross as a battle sign. Charle-
magne revived the Empire in his own person in 800 and associated it with
the church. Luther was a reformer of the church, but his reforms brought
further wars. Their spirit of aggression and their perversion of Christianity
dominate Europe.

24.35-6. *Cathedron . . . Bowlahoola and Allamanda*] Parts of the city of
Golgonooza. Cathedron (*Four Zoas* viii 25) is the place where Enitharmon,

A web of death; & were it not for Bowlahoola & Allamanda
No human form, but only a fibrous vegetation,
A polypus of soft affections without thought or vision
Must tremble in the heavens & earths through all the Ulro space!
40 Throw all the vegetated mortals into Bowlahoola.
But as to this Elected form who is returned again,
He is the signal that the last vintage now approaches,
Nor vegetation may go on till all the earth is reaped!'

So Los spoke. Furious they descended to Bowlahoola & Allamanda,
45 Indignant, unconvinced by Los's arguments & thunders rolling.
They saw that wrath now swayed, & now pity absorbed him;
As it was, so it remained, & no hope of an end.

Bowlahoola is named Law by mortals; Tharmas founded it,
Because of Satan, before Luban in the city of Golgonooza.
50 (But Golgonooza is named Art & Manufacture by mortal men.)

In Bowlahoola Los's anvils stand & his furnaces rage;
Thundering the hammers beat, & the bellows blow loud,
Living, self-moving, mourning, lamenting & howling incessantly.
Bowlahoola through all its porches feels, though too fast founded
55 Its pillars & porticoes to tremble at the force

Los's emanation, weaves. When she works with him the work is good;
but on its own, Los now says, her work brings only ill, since it is then
uninspired. Only he can give it life. She creates 'soft affections', which
need the masculine virtues of strength and form if they are not to be cor-
rupted. Los and his sons, in Bowlahoola and Allamanda (see *51–67*, and
25.42–63 below), carry out their part of the work.
24.48. Here the narrative of Milton ends for a time, to be resumed in the
Second Book (pl.30). The remainder of the First Book is (to 26.64) a
description both of the terrors of Los's work in Golgonooza, and (26.65–
29.65) of its beauties. See headnote. Bowlahoola is Los's forge (Allamanda
is his farm; see 25.42ff). The equation with Law is confusing if taken as a
definition, or allegorical interpretation; it is more in the nature of an
equivalent. The vision comes first; then B. finds something similar, though
necessarily less than it, on earth. Law (B. refers primarily to the profession –
cp. 25.55ff) is fierce, firm and heavy-handed; hence the equivalence. But
Los's work is greater than Law alone. Tharmas, one of Los's brother Zoas,
drove Los to the founding of Golgonooza in *Four Zoas* iv 151ff.
24.49. *Because of Satan*] i.e. because of his sin and fall.   *Luban*] Cp. *Four
Zoas* v 77: the gate of Golgonooza 'upon the limit of translucence'.
24.50. *Art and Manufacture*] Creative occupations. This is all 'mortal men'
can see of the eternal city; cp. 25.55–63.
24.51ff. The essence of Bowlahoola is control; hence B.'s references to
Law (48), and the Stomach (67) which digests and sorts out very various
materials. The two ideas are otherwise separate.

Of mortal or immortal arm. And softly lilling flutes
Accordant with the horrid labours make sweet melody.

The bellows are the animal lungs, the hammers the animal heart,
The furnaces the stomach for digestion—terrible their fury!
60 Thousands & thousands labour, thousands play on instruments,
Stringed or fluted, to ameliorate the sorrows of slavery.
Loud sport the dancers in the dance of death, rejoicing in carnage:
The hard dentant hammers are lulled by the flutes' lula lula;
The bellowing furnaces' blare by the long sounding clarion.
65 The double drum drowns howls & groans, the shrill fife shrieks &
cries;
The crooked horn mellows the hoarse raving serpent, terrible but
harmonious.
(Bowlahoola is the stomach in every individual man.)

Los is by mortals named Time; Enitharmon is named Space.
But they depict him bald & aged who is in eternal youth,
70 All-powerful, and his locks flourish like the brows of morning.
He is the spirit of prophecy, the ever-apparent Elias.
Time is the mercy of Eternity; without time's swiftness,
Which is the swiftest of all things, all were eternal torment.
All the gods of the kingdoms of earth labour in Los's halls:
75 Every one is a fallen son of the spirit of prophecy;
He is the fourth Zoa, that stood around the throne divine.

Pl. 25 But the winepress of Los is eastward of Golgonooza, before the seat
(27) Of Satan. (Luvah laid the foundation, & Urizen finished it in
howling woe.)

24.58. Cp. *48n* on similar equivalences. They must be understood by the
feelings rather than by the mind: B. envisages the power of the animal
body.

24.65. The double drum] The kettledrums or timpani, being tunable to
definite notes, were usually played in pairs, one carried on each side of a
horse in a mounted band.

24.66. the serpent] A wooden instrument, conical in section, with holes like
a flute and a mouthpiece like a trombone. The tube was about seven feet
long, and was therefore twisted into a serpent shape. Well played, it had
a rich, 'harmonious' tone, but could easily deteriorate into rough, ill-
tuned coarseness.

24.76. the fourth Zoa] *Revelation* iv 6: 'And round about the throne, were
four beasts (*zoa*) full of eyes before and behind.' For B.'s development of
the Zoas, see *24.9n*, and, in full detail, *Four Zoas* headnote (p. 287).

Plate 25 (27). In copies C and D this plate precedes pl.28; hence the number
27 in brackets. It describes the winepress of Luvah, ready for *26.1–2*.
Lines *3–41* are an altered version of *Four Zoas* ix *740–68*, with some addi-
tions and changes of position. In *Four Zoas* this is always the winepress of

How red the sons & daughters of Luvah! Here they tread the grapes:
Laughing & shouting, drunk with odours many fall o'erwearied;
5   Drowned in the wine is many a youth & maiden. Those around
Lay them on skins of tigers & of the spotted leopard & the wild ass
Till they revive, or bury them in cool grots, making lamentation.

This winepress is called War on earth; it is the printing-press
Of Los, and here he lays his words in order above the mortal brain,
10   As cogs are formed in a wheel to turn the cogs of the adverse wheel.

Timbrels & violins sport round the winepresses; the little seed,
The sportive root, the earth-worm, the gold beetle, the wise emmet
Dance round the winepresses of Luvah; the centipede is there,
The ground-spider with many eyes, the mole clothed in velvet,
15   The ambitious spider in his sullen web, the lucky golden spinner,
The earwig armed, the tender maggot, emblem of immortality,
The flea, louse, bug, the tape-worm—all the armies of disease,
Visible or invisible to the slothful vegetating man.
The slow slug, the grasshopper that sings & laughs & drinks
20   (Winter comes, he folds his slender bones without a murmur).
The cruel scorpion is there, the gnat, wasp, hornet & the honey bee,
The toad & venomous newt, the serpent clothed in gems & gold;
They throw off their gorgeous raiment; they rejoice with loud
    jubilee
Around the winepresses of Luvah, naked & drunk with wine.

[Design]

Luvah; in *Milton* it is the winepress of Los (*1*) worked by the children of
Luvah; and in *8* B. glosses the press as 'call'd War on earth'. B. expands
five lines about insects to ten in *13–22*.

25.1. the winepress is from *Revelation* xiv 19–20: 'And the angel thrust in
his sickle into the earth, and gathered the vine of the earth, and cast it into
the great winepress of the wrath of God. And the winepress was trodden
without the city, and blood came out of the winepress, even unto the
horse bridles. . . .'

25.6. on skins of tigers . . .] Like Dionysus, god of wine and the vintage,
who was torn to pieces by frenzied women followers, the Mænads.

25.8. This is an afterthought, a gloss added by B. when transcribing the
passage from *Four Zoas*. See *30n.*

25.10. If the driving wheel goes clockwise, the driven wheel must go anti-
clockwise. Los's acts are similar in appearance, but contrary in effect, to
those of warriors on earth.

25.11. Timbrels] A biblical instrument, like a tambourine, whereas the
violin would be a normal dance-instrument in B.'s day.

25.22. venomous newt] The venom is a mistaken folk-belief.

25. Design. In the paragraph break, several of the creatures of the previous
lines are depicted.

18★

25   There is the nettle that stings with soft down, and there
     The indignant thistle, whose bitterness is bred in his milk,
     Who feeds on contempt of his neighbour; there all the idle weeds
     That creep around the obscure places show their various limbs,
     Naked in all their beauty dancing round the wine-presses.

30   But in the winepresses the human grapes sing not nor dance:
     They howl & writhe in shoals of torment, in fierce flames consuming,
     In chains of iron & in dungeons circled with ceaseless fires,
     In pits & dens & shades of death, in shapes of torment & woe—
     The plates & screws & racks & saws & cords & fires & cisterns,
35   The cruel joys of Luvah's daughters, lacerating with knives
     And whips their victims, & the deadly sport of Luvah's sons.

     They dance around the dying, & they drink the howl & groan;
     They catch the shrieks in cups of gold, they hand them to one
          another.
     These are the sports of love, & these the sweet delights of amorous
          play—
40   Tears of the grape, the death-sweat of the cluster, the last sigh
     Of the mild youth who listens to the luring songs of Luvah.

     But Allamanda (called on earth, Commerce) is the cultivated land
     Around the city of Golgonooza in the forests of Entuthon.
     Here the sons of Los labour against death eternal; through all
45   The twenty-seven heavens of Beulah, in Ulro, seat of Satan,
     Which is the false tongue beneath Beulah (it is the sense of touch)

25.30. The agony of the winepress in *Four Zoas* is, as in *Revelation,* part
of redemption, pressing out the good juice from the useless skin. Here it
is out of context, but *8–10* may imply the same purpose. The winepress
of Los redeems; the press of war on earth destroys without redemption
through cruelties which resemble Tirzah's (19.44ff).
25.42. Allamanda] Cp. *Bowlahoola,* 24.48n. The ref. to 'commerce' is a
little confusing; but cp. 24.58n. Allamanda is the farming area around
Golgonooza, which keeps the city supplied–as commerce keeps our own
cities alive.
25.43. Golgonooza . . . Entuthon] Cp. *Four Zoas* viii 25n. Entuthon is the
forest of darkness surrounding Golgonooza.
25.44–5. Beulah here (as in 26.39n), is somewhat ambivalent. Though it is
on the borders of heaven, and the home of heavenly spirits (30.1n), it is
open to corruption. Yet it is not usually said to belong with the 'twenty-
seven heavens' (cp. 17.23–6) of the 'deformed' mortal universe, being
above and beyond crude mortality. B. seems to be inconsistent here, and
again in 26.39. The sense is that of *43:* Los's sons labour in the land of
death itself against death. See also 27.20n.
25.46. the false tongue beneath Beulah] See note on 2.10: in *Four Zoas* i 96–8
Tharmas is associated with the tongue; and Tharmas is fallen. The idea,

The plough goes forth in tempests & lightnings & the harrow cruel
In blights of the east; the heavy roller follows in howlings of woe.

Urizen's sons here labour also, & here are seen the mills
50 Of Theotormon, on the verge of the Lake of Udan-Adan.
These are the starry voids of night, & the depths & caverns of earth.
These mills are oceans, clouds & waters ungovernable in their fury;
Here are the stars created & the seeds of all things planted,
And here the sun & moon receive their fixed destinations.

55 But in Eternity the four arts—poetry, painting, music,
And architecture (which is science)—are the four faces of man.
Not so in time & space; there three are shut out. And only
Science remains, through mercy by means of science, the three
Become apparent in time & space, in the three professions:
60 Poetry in religion: Music, law: Painting in physic & surgery,
That man may live upon earth till the time of his awakening;
And from these three, science derives every occupation of men.
And science is divided into Bowlahoola & Allamanda.

Pl. 26 Loud shout the sons of Luvah at the winepresses, as Los descended
(25) With Rintrah & Palamabron in his fires of resistless fury.

The winepress on the Rhine groans loud, but all its central beams
Act more terrific in the central cities of the nations,
5 Where human thought is crushed beneath the iron hand of power.
There Los puts all into the press, the oppressor & the oppressed
Together, ripe for the harvest & vintage, & ready for the loom.

They sang at the vintage: 'This is the last vintage, & seed
Shall no more be sown upon earth, till all the vintage is over,
10 And all gathered in, till the plough has passed over the nations,
And the harrow & heavy thundering roller upon the mountains.'

scattered in places through *Jerusalem* (e.g. pl.14.26), is that 'the gate of the
tongue is closed' (the gate which leads into eternity). What purports to be
that gate is therefore false, a gate to Ulro, 'beneath Beulah'.
25.56. *science*] B., as normal in the period, means 'learning'.
25.60. This line was erased from the plate before the two later copies were
printed.

Plate 26 (25). See pl.25n.
26.3. *on the Rhine*] The border between France and Germany. The cam-
paigns of 1800–10 were not centred on the Rhine, but it is an adequate
symbol of them.
26.5. Censorship, whether formal or not, was effective in Britain as else-
where in Europe, in that political views which were recognizably dissident
were treated as seditious or treasonable, and suppressed.
26.7. *harvest and vintage . . . loom*] The first two are Los's duty, the third
Enitharmon's, in their redemptive work.

And loud the souls howl round the porches of Golgonooza
Crying, 'O God, deliver us to the heavens or to the earths,
That we may preach righteousness & punish the sinner with death!'
15   But Los refused, till all the vintage of earth was gathered in.

And Los stood & cried to the labourers of the vintage in voice of
     awe:

'Fellow labourers! The great vintage & harvest is now upon earth.
The whole extent of the globe is explored; every scattered atom
Of human intellect now is flocking to the sound of the trumpet.
20   All the wisdom which was hidden in caves & dens, from ancient
Time, is now sought out from animal & vegetable & mineral.
The Awakener is come, outstretched over Europe. The vision of
     God is fulfilled:
The Ancient Man upon the rock of Albion awakes,
He listens to the sounds of war, astonished & ashamed;
25   He sees his children mock at faith & deny providence.
Therefore you must bind the sheaves not by nations or families:
You shall bind them in three classes; according to their classes
So shall you bind them, separating what has been mixed
Since men began to be wove into nations by Rahab & Tirzah,
30   Since Albion's death & Satan's cutting-off from our awful fields,
When under pretence to benevolence the Elect subdued all
From the foundation of the world. The Elect is one class: you
Shall bind them separate; they cannot believe in eternal life
Except by miracle & a new birth. The other two classes—
35   The Reprobate who never cease to believe, and the Redeemed,
Who live in doubts & fears perpetually tormented by the Elect,
These you shall bind in a twin-bundle for the consummation—
But the Elect must be saved from fires of eternal death,

26.12–15. Cp. *Revelation* vi 9–11: 'I saw under the altar the souls of them
that were slain for the word of God . . . And they cried with a loud voice,
saying, How long, O Lord, holy and true, dost thou not judge and avenge
our blood on them that dwell on the earth? . . . and it was said unto them,
that they should rest yet for a little season, until their fellow servants also
and their brethren, that should be killed as they were, should be fulfilled.'
Los refuses the cry for vengeance.
26.23. *Albion*] See 9.3n, 15.36ff.
26.27. *Three classes*] See 11.21–2 and note.
26.38. Traditionally, the Elect are safe from Hell. But B.'s fires are purga-
torial, and the Elect are saved from them only because they are too corrupt-
the flames would destroy, not purify them.
from] Not in the text, but the sense requires it. There are several slips on
this plate; the others involve letters only.

To be formed into the churches of Beulah that they destroy not the
      earth.
40   For in every nation & every family the three classes are born,
      And in every species of earth: metal, tree, fish, bird & beast.
      We form the mundane egg, that spectres, coming by fury or amity
      All is the same, & every one remains in his own energy.
      Go forth, reapers, with rejoicing; you sowed in tears,
45   But the time of your refreshing cometh; only a little moment
      Still abstain from pleasure & rest, in the labours of Eternity,
      And you shall reap the whole earth from pole to pole, from sea to
      sea,
      Beginning at Jerusalem's inner court, Lambeth ruined and given
      To the detestable gods of Priam, to Apollo, and at the Asylum
50   Given to Hercules, who labour in Tirzah's looms for bread,
      Who set pleasure against duty, who create Olympic crowns
      To make learning a burden, & the work of the Holy Spirit strife;
      To Thor & cruel Odin, who first reared the polar caves.
      Lambeth mourns, calling Jerusalem; she weeps & looks abroad
55   For the Lord's coming, that Jerusalem may overspread all nations.
      Crave not for the mortal & perishing delights, but leave them
      To the weak, & pity the weak as your infant care; break not
      Forth in your wrath lest you also are vegetated by Tirzah.
      Wait till the Judgement is past, till the creation is consumed,
60   And then rush forward with me into the glorious spiritual
      Vegetation, the supper of the Lamb & his Bride, and the
      Awakening of Albion, our friend and ancient companion.'

      So Los spoke. But lightnings of discontent broke on all sides round,
      And murmurs of thunder rolling, heavy, long & loud over the
         mountains,

26.39. *churches of Beulah*] As in 27.20n.
26.48–9. *Lambeth . . . gods of Priam, to Apollo*] Very near B.'s Lambeth
house in Hercules Buildings (1791–1800) was a crossroads, Asylum Cross,
dominated by three decaying pleasure gardens–two named 'Flora', the
third the 'Apollo Gardens'. Nearby was the Royal Asylum for Female
Orphans and a little way off a Charity School, where the children lived
by sweated labour. There may also be a reference to Lambeth Palace, the
residence of the Archbishop of Canterbury; one would expect such a
district to be a centre of worship, 'Jerusalem's inner court'. See map p. 621.
26.51. *Olympic crowns*] An uncertain allusion. The reference is to the
crowning of champions at Greek athletic festivals, but the immediate
application is not sure.
26.53. No allusions similar to those in *48–50* have been traced for this line.
26.58. Probably a warning to himself: do not be carried away by anger or
you will become embittered and hardened as the charity children be-
come (*50*).

65   While Los called his sons around him to the harvest & the vintage.

    Thou seest the constellations in the deep & wondrous night;
They rise in order & continue their immortal courses
Upon the mountains & in vales, with harp & heavenly song,
With flute & clarion, with cups & measures filled with foaming
     wine.
70   Glittering the streams reflect the vision of beatitude,
And the calm ocean joys beneath & smoothes his awful waves.
Pl. 27   These are the sons of Los, & these the labourers of the vintage.
(26)   Thou seest the gorgeous clothed flies that dance & sport in summer
Upon the sunny brooks & meadows; every one the dance
Knows in its intricate mazes of delight artful to wave,
5   Each one to sound his instruments of music in the dance,
To touch each other & recede, to cross & change & return.
These are the children of Los. Thou seest the trees on mountains:
The wind blows heavy, loud they thunder through the darksome
     sky,
Uttering prophecies & speaking instructive words to the sons
10   Of men. These are the sons of Los, these the visions of Eternity.
But we see only as it were the hem of their garments
When with our vegetable eyes we view these wondrous visions.

    There are two gates through which all souls descend. One southward

26.66. The rest of the First Book is taken up with an interpretation of
natural beauty seen with the imaginative (not merely observing) eye.

27.13. *two gates*] Derived from the *Odyssey* xiii 109–12 (Chapman's trans-
lation, Bk xiii, lines 145ff): 'There is a port, / That th'aged sea-God
Phorcys makes his fort, / Whose earth the Ithacensian people own . . . /
From forth the haven's high crest / Branch the well-brawn'd arms of an
olive-tree / Beneath which runs a cave from all sun free, / Cool, and de-
lightsome, sacred to th'access / Of Nymphs whose surnames are the
Naiades; / In which flew humming bees, in which lay thrown / Stone
cups, stone vessels, shuttles all of stone, / With which the Nymphs their
purple mantles wove, / In whose contexture art and wonder strove; / In
which pure springs perpetually ran; / To which two entries were; the
one for man, / On which the North breathed; th'other for the Gods, / On
which the South; and that bore no abodes / For earthy men, but only
deathless feet / Had there free way.' The Neo-Platonists, as B. knew, gave
this a spiritual meaning; the cave was mortal life, the northern gate the
entry of souls to the world, the southern their departure, as well as the gate
used by transient immortals. The Naiads resemble Enitharmon and her
daughters, weaving mortal clothing for immortal souls; but there is no
Ulro in this scene. Los (*16*) must be bending his back against the east.

From Dover Cliff to Lizard Point, the other toward the north—
15   Caithness & rocky Durness, Pentland & John Groat's House.

[*Design*]

The souls descending to the body wail on the right hand
Of Los, & those delivered from the body on the left hand.
For Los against the east his force continually bends
Along the valleys of Middlesex, from Hounslow to Blackheath,
20   Lest those three Heavens of Beulah should the creation destroy,
And lest they should descend before the north & south gates.
Groaning with pity, he among the wailing souls laments.

And these the labours of the sons of Los in Allamanda,
And in the city of Golgonooza, & in Luban, & around
25   The Lake of Udan-Adan, in the forests of Entuthon Benython
Where souls incessant wail, being piteous passions & desires
With neither lineament nor form, but like to watery clouds.
The passions & desires descend upon the hungry winds,
For such alone sleepers remain—mere passion & appetite;
30   The sons of Los clothe them & feed, & provide houses & fields.

And every generated body in its inward form
Is a garden of delight & a building of magnificence,
Built by the sons of Los in Bowlahoola & Allamanda,
And the herbs & flowers & furniture & beds & chambers
35   Continually woven in the looms of Enitharmon's daughters,

27.14–15. These are all rocky cliffs, at the north and south extremities of Britain (Albion). B. drew them in the spaces below *15* and *43*, the two designs perhaps signifying the two gates of *13–17*.
27.19. *Hounslow to Blackheath*] From west to east of London; both were 'heaths'.
27.20. *three Heavens*] These are the female beauties (*5.6*, p. *569* below). Beulah is a twilight land though close to Eden, and though its intentions are good, the results of its acts may be evil, unless governed by Los's artistic skill; fallen creation is not strong enough to support the force of such beauty when revealed. B. may again be thinking of the Naiads of the cave of mortality between the two gates (*13*).
27.23–30. All the names of *23–5* are place-names round Golgonooza, Los's outpost in Ulro (*Four Zoas* viii *25n*). There Los and Enitharmon (*35–6*) take in the lost, disorganized souls and give them definite form, the beginning of life and activity.
27.31 *every generated body*] These are fallen bodies, not the immortal forms of eternity; yet the seed of eternity is within them.
27.36. *Cathedron*] In Golgonooza, where Enitharmon weaves spiritual clothing for naked souls (see notes on *13*, *19* and *23* above). The limitations of *24.35* are not mentioned; for when in harmony with Los, Enitharmon's work is redemptive.

In bright Cathedron's golden dome with care & love & tears.
For the various classes of men are all marked out determinate
In Bowlahoola, & as the spectres choose their affinities,
So they are born on earth, & every class is determinate—
40 But not by natural, but by spiritual power alone, because
The natural power continually seeks & tends to destruction
Ending in death, which would of itself be eternal death.
And all are classed by spiritual & not by natural power.

[*Design*]

(And every natural effect has a spiritual cause, & not
45 A natural: for a natural cause only seems; it is a delusion
Of Ulro, & a ratio of the perishing vegetable memory.)
Pl. 28 Some sons of Los surrounded the passions with porches of iron &
silver,
Creating form & beauty around the dark regions of sorrow,
Giving to airy nothing a name & a habitation
Delightful—with bounds to the infinite putting off the indefinite
5 Into most holy forms of thought (such is the power of inspiration).
They labour incessant, with many tears & afflictions,
Creating the beautiful house for the piteous sufferer.

Others cabinets richly fabricate of gold & ivory,
For doubts & fears unformed & wretched & melancholy.
10 The little weeping spectre stands on the threshold of death
Eternal, & sometimes two spectres like lamps quivering,
And often malignant they combat (heart-breaking, sorrowful and
piteous)—
Antamon takes them into his beautiful flexible hands,
As the sower takes the seed, or as the artist his clay
15 Or fine wax, to mould artful a model for golden ornaments.
The soft hands of Antamon draw the indelible line,
Form immortal, with golden pen, such as the spectre admiring
Puts on the sweet form. Then smiles Antamon bright through his
windows.

27. *Design*. See *27.14n*.
27.44–6. B.'s passing comment.
28.1. *Some sons of Los*] The poets (see note below).
28.3. *Giving . . . habitation*] From *A Midsummer Night's Dream* v 14–17:
'And, as imagination bodies forth / The forms of things unknown, the
poet's pen / Turns them to shapes, and gives to airy nothing / A local
habitation and a name.' B. alters the emphasis: to him Theseus's 'airy
nothing' is the unseen imaginative reality.
28.7–20. The spectre, a shadowy unrealized being, is given form and so
life by Antamon, who (with Theotormon, Sotha, and Ozoth in *21, 29*)
is one of Los's sons and works for him.

The daughters of beauty look up from their loom & prepare
20 The integument soft for its clothing with joy & delight.

But Theotormon & Sotha stand in the gate of Luban, anxious
(Their numbers are seven million & seven thousand & seven
hundred);
They contend with the weak spectres; they fabricate soothing forms—
The spectre refuses, he seeks cruelty; they create the crested cock—
25 Terrified, the spectre screams & rushes in fear into their net
Of kindness & compassion, & is born a weeping terror.
Or they create the lion & tiger in compassionate thunderings—
Howling the spectres flee; they take refuge in human lineaments.

The sons of Ozoth within the optic nerve stand fiery glowing
30 (And the number of his sons is eight million & eight);
They give delights to the man unknown, artificial riches
They give to scorn, & their possessors to trouble & sorrow & care,
Shutting the sun, & moon, & stars, & trees, & clouds, & waters,
And hills, out from the optic nerve & hardening it into a bone
35 Opaque, & like the black pebble on the enraged beach,
While the poor indigent is like the diamond which, though clothed
In rugged covering in the mine, is open all within,
And in his hallowed centre holds the heavens of bright Eternity.
Ozoth here builds walls of rocks against the surging sea,
40 And timbers cramped with iron cramps bar in the joys of life
From fell destruction in the spectrous cunning or rage. He creates
The speckled newt, the spider & beetle, the rat & mouse,
The badger & fox; they worship before his feet in trembling fear.

But others of the sons of Los build moments & minutes & hours,
45 And days & months & years & ages & periods, wondrous buildings!
And every moment has a couch of gold for soft repose
(A moment equals a pulsation of the artery);

28.*19. daughters of beauty*] Enitharmon's daughters.
28.*21–8.* Theotormon and Sotha persuade by making the spectres experience real evil. *Luban* is the porch of Golgonooza facing Ulro.
28.*22, 30.* Multiples of seven are less perfect than multiples of eight: Theotormon and Sotha dispense fright, Ozoth prepares delight.
28.*24. the crested cock*] Cock-fighting was still a common pastime.
28.*29. The sons of Ozoth*] They give the narrow-minded man the vision apt to his narrowness.
28.*36–41. the diamond,* which may look like a common pebble until it is skilfully flaked. Its brilliance is hidden inside it. No man is entirely lost and visionless, though he may repress vision into what we now call the Unconscious. Ozoth protects this vision.
28.*41–3. He creates...*] None of these animals is commonly loved, but they also are creatures of the imagination.

And between every two moments stands a daughter of Beulah
To feed the sleepers on their couches with maternal care.
50   And every minute has an azure tent with silken veils,
And every hour has a bright golden gate carved with skill,
And every day & night has walls of brass & gates of adamant,
Shining like precious stones & ornamented with appropriate signs;
And every month a silver-paved terrace builded high,
55   And every year invulnerable barriers with high towers,
And every age is moated deep with bridges of silver & gold,
And every seven ages is encircled with a flaming fire.
Now seven ages is amounting to two hundred years:
Each has its guard, each moment, minute, hour, day, month & year.
60   All are the work of fairy hands of the four elements;
The guard are angels of providence on duty evermore.
Every time less than a pulsation of the artery
Is equal in its period & value to six thousand years;
Pl. 29   For in this period the poet's work is done, & all the great
Events of time start forth & are conceived in such a period,
Within a moment, a pulsation of the artery.

The sky is an immortal tent built by the sons of Los;
5   And every space that a man views around his dwelling-place,
Standing on his own roof, or in his garden on a mount
Of twenty-five cubits in height, such space is his universe;
And on its verge the sun rises & sets; the clouds bow
To meet the flat earth & the sea in such an ordered space.
10   The starry heavens reach no further, but here bend & set
On all sides, & the two poles turn on their valves of gold,
And if he move his dwelling-place, his heavens also move
Where'er he goes, & all his neighbourhood bewail his loss.
Such are the spaces called 'Earth', & such its dimension.
15   As to the false appearance which appears to the reasoner,

28.63. *equal . . . to six thousand years*] Equal to all time.

29.6-7. *a mount of twenty-five cubits*] Hayley's new house, the 'Marine
Turret' (still standing) – originally intended to be built as a tower but finally
a house surmounted by a turret.

29.11. *valves*] The original meaning (*OED*) is 'one of the halves or leaves
of a double or folding door'; Johnson's *Dictionary* simply says 'a folding
door'. To B. the two poles are not axles, but doors to infinity.

29.12. *his heavens also move*] As a nomad moves his tent (*4*) and as the
wandering Israelites moved theirs.

29.15. *that false appearance*] The scientific view and explanation of the sun.
Cp. *A Vision of the Last Judgment* (Erdman, 1965 p. 555): '"What," it
will be questioned, "when the sun rises, do you not see a round disc of
fire somewhat like a guinea?" O no, no! I see an innumerable company of
the Heavenly host crying: Holy, Holy, Holy is the Lord God Almighty!'

As of a globe rolling through voidness, it is a delusion of Ulro.
The microscope knows not of this, nor the telescope; they alter
The ratio of the spectator's organs, but leave objects untouched.
For every space larger than a red globule of man's blood
20 Is visionary & is created by the hammer of Los;
And every space smaller than a globule of man's blood opens
Into Eternity, of which this vegetable earth is but a shadow.
The red globule is the unwearied sun, by Los created
To measure time & space to mortal men; every morning
25 Bowlahoola & Allamanda are placed on each side
Of that pulsation & that globule, terrible their power.

But Rintrah & Palamabron govern over day & night
In Allamanda & Entuthon Benython where souls wail,
Where Orc incessant howls, burning in fires of eternal youth,
30 Within the vegetated mortal nerves; for every man born is joined
Within into one mighty polypus, & this polypus is Orc.

But in the optic vegetative nerves sleep was transformed
To death in old time by Satan, the father of Sin & Death
(And Satan is the spectre of Orc, & Orc is the generate Luvah).

35 But in the nerves of the nostrils, accident being formed
Into substance & principle, by the cruelties of demonstration
It became opaque & indefinite; but the Divine Saviour
Formed it into a solid by Los's mathematic power.
He named the opaque *Satan*: he named the solid *Adam*.

40 And in the nerves of the ear (for the nerves of the tongue are
closed)

29.31. *this polypus is Orc*] The image is of the 'colonial' organism of polyp
creatures (see *Four Zoas* iv *265*), in which although the polyps are struc-
turally interconnected they behave as individuals. B. contrasts this 'chained'
union with the free mingling of eternal souls (cp. 'mighty and mysterious
commingling, enemy with enemy', 38.3 below). Men are associated in an
unnatural way, so that they become, not an immortal community, free at
heart, but a formless band, striving hopelessly and destructively for freedom
from their rivals or enemies, as Orc does.
29.34. Luvah is the passionate Zoa of the Four: he appears as Orc the rebel
in this world ('generate'); Satan the rebel and enemy is his perverted form.
29.35–9. *Accident*–the particular form occasionally taken by an Eternal
reality–is seen by logical minds on earth as the 'substance and principle'
(the reality and the essence) as if the momentary appearance were the sum
of the eternal reality. This would be utterly evil and false (*opaque and in-
definite*) but for the divine act which limits such distortions.
29.39. *Satan and Adam*] See 13.20–1.
29.40. *tongue*] Cp. 2.10n.

On Albion's rock Los stands, creating the glorious sun each
    morning;
And when unwearied in the evening he creates the moon,
Death to delude, who all in terror at their splendour leaves
His prey, while Los appoints, & Rintrah & Palamabron guide
45 The souls clear from the rock of death, that Death himself may wake
In his appointed season when the ends of heaven meet.

Then Los conducts the spirits to be vegetated into
Great Golgonooza, free from the four iron pillars of Satan's throne
(Temperance, prudence, justice, fortitude, the four pillars of
    tyranny),
50 That Satan's watch-fiends touch them not before they vegetate.

But Enitharmon and her daughters take the pleasant charge,
To give them to their lovely heavens till the great Judgement Day.
Such is their lovely charge; but Rahab & Tirzah pervert
Their mild influences. Therefore the seven Eyes of God walk round
55 The three heavens of Ulro, where Tirzah & her sisters
Weave the black woof of death upon Entuthon Benython,
In the vale of Surrey where Horeb terminates in Rephaim.
The stamping feet of Zelophehad's daughters are covered with
    human gore
Upon the treadles of the loom; they sing to the winged shuttle.
60 The river rises above its banks to wash the woof;
He takes it in his arms, he passes it in strength through his current.
The veil of human miseries is woven over the ocean
From the Atlantic to the great south sea, the Erythrean.

Such is the world of Los, the labour of six thousand years.
65 Thus nature is a vision of the science of the Elohim.

End of the First Book.

29.48–9. *the four iron pillars . . . Temperance, prudence, justice, fortitude*] A
common Stoic set of virtues.
29.57. *the vale of Surrey*] No particular vale seems to be meant. B., when
living in Lambeth, was on the Surrey side of the Thames.
Horeb terminates in Rephaim] Horeb is in Sinai, and the Valley of Rephaim
(see 19.40n) to the south of Jerusalem (as Lambeth is south of London) – about
230 miles apart as the crow flies. Horeb is the place of Law-giving, and the
Valley of Rephaim, 'Valley of the shades of the dead', a place sometimes
occupied by the Philistines. The mountain of Law stretches its malign
influence close to Jerusalem and London
29.58. *Zelophehad's daughters*] Tirzah and her sisters (17.11 and 19.44ff
above).
29.64. *Such*] All the descriptions from 26.66 to 29.63.
29.65. *the science of Elohim*] The knowledge held by the creator.

(V)   *[Full-plate illustration]*

Pl. 30   BOOK THE SECOND
There is a place where contrarieties are equally true.
This place is called *Beulah;* it is a pleasant lovely shadow
Where no dispute can come, because of those who sleep.

V. *Full-plate illustration*: An enlargement of the interlinear figure on pl.15. A nude male, startled and throwing himself backwards to the left of the picture, as a star strikes his left foot; he is labelled WILLIAM (cp. full-pl. illustration VI, after pl. 33). Reproduced in Keynes' *W.B.'s Engravings* pl.100.

Plate 30. The heading of the second Book is a design of small human figures, which incorporates, in *reversed* writing, the sayings:

> How wide the Gulf and Unpassable! between Simplicity
> and Insipidity.
> Contraries are Positives
> A Negation is not a Contrary.

The reversed writing implies a secret hidden from common sight.
30.*1*. For *negations* and *contraries* see *Jerusalem* pl.10.7.

BEULAH] Another important passage on Beulah is *Four Zoas* i *78–90*, stressing the 'mild and pleasant rest', its night setting, its flowers and its feminine loveliness, 'given in mercy to those who sleep.' This passage in *Milton*, and also *Jerusalem* pl.48.*13–17*, refers to souls from Eden wishing to rest; the *Four Zoas* passage refers to 'those who sleep' in less happy worlds–for them, as in *Milton* 15.*12–16*, Beulah is a place where they are cared for. Beulah has passed into the folk-lore of evangelical Nonconformity, not directly from its obscure source in *Isaiah*, but from Bunyan. In keeping with this tradition, B.'s source for Beulah is in *Pilgrim's Progress*, where Christian and Hopeful towards the end of their journey, having 'got over the *Enchanted Ground*, and entering into the country of *Beulah*, whose air was very sweet and pleasant, . . . solaced themselves there for a season. Yea, here they heard continually the singing of birds, and saw every day the flowers appear on the earth, and heard the voice of the turtle in the land. In this country the sun shineth night and day: wherefore this was beyond the Valley of the *Shadow of Death*, and also out of the reach of Giant *Despair*. . . . Here they were within sight of the city they were going to, also here met them some of the inhabitants thereof, for in this land the Shining Ones commonly walked, because it was upon the borders of heaven.'–This only differs from B.'s Beulah in one important feature, that his is a 'moony' land of night, love, and sleep. Hence the 'Shining Ones' meet yet earthbound travellers chiefly as watchers and nurses–'the daughters of Beulah'. Nor has B. the linear view of Bunyan's pilgrimage; the traveller can enter Beulah in vision and dream at any time,

Into this place the sons & daughters of Ololon descended
5 With solemn mourning, into Beulah's moony shades & hills,
Weeping for Milton; mute wonder held the daughters of Beulah,
Enraptured with affection sweet and mild benevolence.

Beulah is evermore created around Eternity, appearing
To the inhabitants of Eden around them on all sides.
10 But Beulah to its inhabitants appears, within each district,
As the beloved infant in his mother's bosom, round encircled
With arms of love & pity & sweet compassion. But to
The sons of Eden the moony habitations of Beulah
Are from great Eternity a mild & pleasant rest.

15 And it is thus created: lo, the eternal great Humanity—
To whom be glory & domination evermore, Amen—
Walks among all his awful family, seen in every face
As the breath of the Almighty. Such are the words of man to man
In the great wars of Eternity, in fury of poetic inspiration,
20 To build the universe stupendous mental forms creating.

But the emanations trembled exceedingly, nor could they
Live, because the life of Man was too exceeding unbounded.
His joy became terrible to them, they trembled & wept,
Crying with one voice: 'Give us a habitation, & a place
25 In which we may be hidden under the shadow of wings.

and can look from it into paradise at any time. B.'s Shining Ones create
Beulah as a refuge for emanations, who are female; and Beulah is a femi-
nine world, designed for the creatures who, alone, could not bear the
strenuous activity of Eden (21–7). The male being may be seen there (but
he must not live there), for it is a place of recreation, and of sexual delight.
Yet the sexes are not irremediably distinguished, for they may return to
the united life in Eden at will. *Jerusalem* pls 30.*34–7*, 69.*14–29*, and the
following passage, 79.*73–7*, are important expressions of this:

O Vala! Humanity is far above
Sexual organization and the visions of the night of Beulah
Where Sexes wander in dreams of bliss among the emanations
. . . . till the time of sleep is past.

It is, therefore, only a place to rest in, and any being who tries to pretend
that it is the real life of Humanity–i.e. of Eternity–is committing a
serious error. It is a place of 'Threefold' life, not of the highest 'Fourfold'
life of Eden.
30.*4.* This refers back to 20.*45–60.*
30.*8. evermore*] Creation is a continuous process; it must be, to endure.
30.*10. Beulah to its inhabitants*] i.e. it surrounds them as a mother's embrace
surrounds a child.

For if we, who are but for a time, & who pass away in winter,
Behold these wonders of Eternity, we shall consume.
But you, O our fathers & brothers, remain in Eternity.
But grant us a temporal habitation. Do you speak
30 To us; we will obey your words, as you obey Jesus
The Eternal, who is blessed for ever & ever. Amen.'

So spake the lovely emanations, & there appeared a pleasant
Mild shadow above, beneath, & on all sides round.
Pl. 31 Into this pleasant shadow all the weak & weary,
Like women & children, were taken away as on wings
Of dovelike softness, & shadowy habitations prepared for them.
But every man returned & went, still going forward through
5 The bosom of the Father in Eternity on Eternity;
Neither did any lack or fall into error, without
A shadow to repose in, all the days of happy Eternity.

Into this pleasant shadow Beulah all Ololon descended.
And when the daughters of Beulah heard the lamentation
10 All Beulah wept, for they saw the Lord coming in the clouds.
(And the shadows of Beulah terminate in rocky Albion.)

And all nations wept in affliction, family by family.
Germany wept towards France & Italy; England wept & trembled
Towards America; India rose up from his golden bed,
15 As one awakened in the night. They saw the Lord coming
In the clouds of Ololon with power & great glory.

And all the living creatures of the four elements wailed
With bitter wailing; these in the aggregate are named *Satan*
And *Rahab*. They know not of regeneration, but only of generation.
20 The fairies, nymphs, gnomes & genii of the four elements,

30.*26. pass away*] Emanations 'pass away' and revive again, like Persephone.
So with Ahania in *Four Zoas* ix *194–216*.

31.*10. the Lord coming*] From *Matthew* xxvi 64: as Jesus prophesies of himself. This is the beginning of the Last Judgment–not of the world, but of Milton. The *clouds* are 'the clouds of Ololon' (*16*).

31.*13. wept towards*] Suggests a statuesque composition, similar to that of many of B.'s drawings.

31.*17. the living creatures*] See note on 24.*76*.

31.*20. fairies, nymphs, gnomes & genii*] Respectively of air, water, earth and fire. The same four kinds of spirits guard the gates of Golgonooza in *Jerusalem* pl.13.*26–9*, but here they are servants of Satan, not of Los. Thus B. sees them as spirits of the elements of the fallen world, with its qualities–evil (as here) in that it is fallen–or hopeful, in the slight vision of eternity which it affords.

Unforgiving & unalterable—these cannot be regenerated
But must be created, for they know only of generation.
These are the gods of the kingdoms of the earth—in contrarious
And cruel opposition, element against element, opposed in war

25   Not mental, as the wars of Eternity, but a corporeal strife,
In Los's halls continual labouring, in the furnaces of Golgonooza.
Orc howls on the Atlantic; Enitharmon trembles; all Beulah weeps.

Thou hearest the nightingale begin the song of spring;
The lark sitting upon his earthy bed, just as the morn

30   Appears, listens silent; then springing from the waving cornfield loud
He leads the choir of day—trill, trill, trill, trill,
Mounting upon the wings of light into the great expanse,
Re-echoing against the lovely blue & shining heavenly shell.
His little throat labours with inspiration; every feather

35   On throat & breast & wings vibrates with the effluence divine.
All nature listens silent to him, & the awful sun
Stands still upon the mountain looking at this little bird
With eyes of soft humility & wonder, love & awe.
Then loud from their green covert all the birds begin their song:

40   The thrush, the linnet & the goldfinch, robin & the wren
Awake the sun from his sweet reverie upon the mountain;
The nightingale again assays his song, & through the day
And through the night warbles luxuriant, every bird of song
Attending his loud harmony with admiration & love.

45   *This is a vision of the lamentation of Beulah over Ololon.*

Thou perceivest the flowers put forth their precious odours,
And none can tell how from so small a centre comes such sweets,
Forgetting that within that centre Eternity expands
Its ever-during doors that Og & Anak fiercely guard.

50   First, ere the morning breaks, joy opens in the flowery bosoms,
Joy even to tears, which the sun rising dries; first the wild thyme
And meadow-sweet, downy & soft waving among the reeds,
Light springing on the air, lead the sweet dance. They wake
The honeysuckle sleeping on the oak (the flaunting beauty

55   Revels along upon the wind); the white-thorn, lovely may,

31.22. *created*] i.e. put into generation in our world and given some kind
of form.
31.28. *begin the song of spring*] The dawn chorus of birds.
31.45, 63. The experiences we have of beauty are momentary visions of
the greater reality of Eternity.
31.49. *Its ever-during doors*] Cp. *Paradise Lost* vii 205–7: 'Heaven opened
wide / Her ever-during gates, harmonious sound / On golden hinges
moving. . . .'
Og & Anak] Cp. 20.37n. They attempt to deter the soul from imaginative
sallies.

'Opens her many lovely eyes. Listening the rose still sleeps—
None dare to wake her; soon she burst her crimson-curtained bed
And comes forth in the majesty of beauty. Every flower—
The pink, the jessamine, the wall-flower, the carnation,
60   The jonquil, the mild lily—opes her heavens. Every tree
And flower & herb soon fill the air with an innumerable dance,
Yet all in order sweet & lovely. Men are sick with love.
Such is a vision of the lamentation of Beulah over Ololon.

Pl. 33 And the Divine Voice was heard in the songs of Beulah, saying:
'When I first married you, I gave you all my whole soul;
I thought that you would love my loves, & joy in my delights,
Seeking for pleasures in my pleasures, O daughter of Babylon.
5   Then thou wast lovely, mild & gentle; now thou art terrible
In jealousy, & unlovely in my sight, because thou hast cruelly
Cut off my loves in fury, till I have no love left for thee.
Thy love depends on him thou lovest, & on his dear loves
Depend thy pleasures, which thou hast cut off by jealousy.
10   Therefore I show my jealousy, & set before you death.
Behold Milton descended to redeem the female shade
From death eternal; such your lot, to be continually redeemed
By death & misery of those you love, & by annihilation.
When the sixfold female perceives that Milton annihilates
15   Himself—that, seeing all his loves by her cut off, he leaves
Her also, entirely abstracting himself from female loves,
She shall relent in fear of death; she shall begin to give

31.*62.* Echoing *Song of Songs* ii *5*: 'I am sick of love'.

For pl.32 see p. *573.*

Plate 33. Another 'Song of Beulah', this time made relevant to the narra-
tive of Milton (*11–17*).

33.*2. you*] Babylon. This is a song of God to fallen humanity, resembling
in general the similar declarations by the prophets, 'controversies' of God
with the wayward Jews who would see Jerusalem enslaved by Babylon
(*22*). But here Babylon herself is a wayward child of God. This is a de-
velopment of the Rahab myth (*Four Zoas* viii *267n*, and *335, 399*) whereby
B. hopes that even Rahab, the harlot of Babylon, may turn out to be a real,
redeemable person.

33.*14. the sixfold female*] With whom, as appears in 41.*29–30*, Ololon will
identify themselves.

33.*17–18*. Cp. *Visions 199–204*, where Oothoon promises to catch for
Theotormon 'girls of mild silver or of furious gold' for his bed. Note also
the stories of Old Testament polygamy, such as *Genesis* xxx, when the
barren Rachel, jealous of the child-bearing of Leah, her senior wife, gives
her own handmaid Bilhah to her husband Jacob, to bear children on her
behalf. Later Leah likewise lent her maid Zilpah to Jacob. B. sees this as
real love, the opposite of 'Whoredoms' (*20*).

Her maidens to her husband, delighting in his delight.
And then, & then alone, begins the happy female joy,
20   As it is done in Beulah; & thou, O Virgin Babylon, Mother of
          Whoredoms,
Shalt bring Jerusalem in thine arms in the night watches and,
No longer turning her a wandering harlot in the streets,
Shalt give her into the arms of God, your Lord & Husband.'

Such are the songs of Beulah in the lamentations of Ololon.

[Design]

(VI)   *[Full-plate illustration]*

Pl. 34 And all the songs of Beulah sounded comfortable notes
To comfort Ololon's lamentation, for they said,
'Are you the fiery circle that late drove, in fury & fire,
The eight immortal starry ones down into Ulro dark,
5   Rending the heavens of Beulah with your thunders & lightnings?
And can you thus lament & can you pity & forgive?
Is terror changed to pity? O wonder of Eternity!'

And the four states of Humanity in its repose

33.20. O Virgin Babylon, Mother of Whoredoms] Cp. *5.27*ff: a conflation of
Isaiah xlvii 1: 'Come down, and sit in the dust, O virgin daughter of
Babylon', and the 'scarlet woman' of *Revelation* xvii 5: '. . . upon her
forehead was a name written, MYSTERY, BABYLON THE GREAT, THE MOTHER
OF HARLOTS AND ABOMINATIONS OF THE EARTH.' The evil mind, not promis-
cuity, makes the virgin into a harlot.

Design: Beneath the text a diagram, illustrating *34.31–48*, showing the
four worlds of the Zoas, as four circles meeting at a common centre (and
therefore overlapping, being 'fallen together'). In the centre of this 'dire
ruin', the Mundane Egg, filled with flames. 'Milton's Track' is marked
coming from the S.E. through 'Satan' (marked within the egg; the limit
of Opacity) to 'Adam' (the limit of Contraction). This track thus crosses
the 'Urizen' (S.) and 'Luvah' (E.) circles. The whole design is surrounded
by flames. (Reproduced in the editions of Keynes and Erdman.)

VI. Full-plate illustration: This is the mirror-image of plate *V* between pls 29
and 30, and is labelled *Robert*–B.'s brother (d. 1787), with whom B.
still conversed.

34.2. they] The daughters of Beulah.

34.3–4. the fiery circle] Cp. *20.43*ff when this event happened.

34.4. Eight] Milton and the Seven Angels (cp. *14.42n*).

34.8–18. the four states] The repose is the sleep of death, which we call
mortal life. The pattern is not used elsewhere, and seems to be invented
for this narrative alone, to prepare for Ololon's descent into the most un-
pleasant of the four choices. The association with parts of the body is an

Were showed them. First of Beulah, a most pleasant sleep
10 On couches soft, with mild music, tended by flowers of Beulah—
Sweet female forms, winged or floating in the air spontaneous.
The second state is Alla, & the third state Al-Ulro;
But the fourth state is dreadful; it is named Or-Ulro.
The first state is in the head, the second is in the heart,
15 The third in the loins & seminal vessels, & the fourth
In the stomach & intestines, terrible, deadly, unutterable.
And he whose gates are opened in those regions of his body
Can from those gates view all these wondrous imaginations.

But Ololon sought the Or-Ulro & its fiery gates,
20 And the couches of the martyrs & many daughters of Beulah
Accompanying them down to the Ulro with soft melodious tears—
A long journey & dark, through chaos in the track of Milton's
    course,
To where the contraries of Beulah war beneath negation's banner.

Then viewed from Milton's track they see the Ulro: a vast polypus
25 Of living fibres down into the sea of time & space growing,
A self-devouring monstrous human death, twenty-seven fold.
Within it sit five females & the nameless shadowy mother,
Spinning it from their bowels with songs of amorous delight
And melting cadences, that lure the sleepers of Beulah down
30 The River Storgé (which is Arnon) into the Dead Sea.

example of B.'s wish to see everything in human terms. It may be signifi-
cant that the Zoas (p. 290 above) are associated with the same four parts
of the body; in which case Ololon chooses the region of Tharmas, the
compassionate Zoa. But this is not the sense of *13, 16*.

34.21. *them*] Ololon, who is a collective personality (*21.15–17*).

34.23. Where contrasting but complementary things (called 'contraries' in
Beulah–see *Jerusalem* pl.10.*7n*) are supposed to be incompatibles, and made
mutually exclusive; one must destroy the other.

34.24. *polypus*] An indefinite, formless being whose ramifications spread
its tentacles everywhere. See *Four Zoas* iv *265* and *Jerusalem* pl.15.2. In
Jerusalem pl.66.*48* B. alludes to the similarity of the spreading colony of a
polypus to the network of veins and nerves in the body. Here the polypus
is enclosed in a shell by Los (*31*), as the nerves are contained and given form
in the body. B. uses the notion of Ulro as polypus again at *35.19–22, 36.13*
and *37.6*off below.

34.27. *five females*] The five sisters, including Tirzah: cp. *17.11* and *19.30*
above. They spin spiderlike, to make web-traps. The 'Shadowy Mother'
here seems to be Rahab, not Vala the 'Shadowy Female' of *Four Zoas*.

34.30. *Storgé* (*which is Arnon*)] A transliteration from Greek, meaning
'parental affection'. Cp. *Four Zoas* v *113*, where Orc degenerates into
'Love of parent, storgous appetite, craving'. Arnon (cp. *19.5*) is the river

Around this polypus Los continual builds the mundane shell.

(Four universes round the universe of Los remain chaotic:
Four intersecting globes, & the egg-formed world of Los
In midst, stretching from zenith to nadir, in midst of chaos.
35 One of these ruined universes is to the north, named Urthona;
One to the south—this was the glorious world of Urizen;
One to the east, of Luvah: one to the west, of Tharmas.
But when Luvah assumed the world of Urizen in the south,
All fell towards the centre sinking downward in dire ruin.)

40 Here in these chaoses the sons of Ololon took their abode,
In chasms of the mundane shell which opens on all sides round.
Southward, & by the east within the breach of Milton's descent
To watch the time, pitying & gentle, to awaken Urizen;
They stood in a dark land of death, of fiery corroding waters,
45 Where lie in evil death the four immortals, pale and cold,
And the Eternal Man, even Albion, upon the Rock of Ages.
Seeing Milton's shadow some daughters of Beulah trembling
Returned, but Ololon remained before the gates of the dead.

And Ololon looked down into the heavens of Ulro in fear.
50 They said: 'How are the wars of man, which in great Eternity
Appear around, in the external spheres of visionary life,
Here rendered deadly within the life & interior vision!
How are the beasts & fishes, & plants & minerals
Here fixed into a frozen bulk, subject to decay & death!

dividing the promised land from heathendom; and, as this line says, it
runs into the *Dead* Sea. The idea is that false, soothing affection is deadly
to the soul.
34.31. *the* MUNDANE SHELL] Cp. *Jerusalem* pl.13.*33n*. The shell (or egg, *33*) is
the enclosed and enclosing universe in which we live (see note on design
below 33.*24*). The egg image is originally Platonic, though it also occurs
in Swedenborg–the egg is oval, a misshapen form inferior to the perfect
sphere. Within its hard enclosing walls it traps the vision and aspirations
of man; yet Los works within it. There is a point of eternity in its heart
(*Jerusalem* pl.13.*35*)–perhaps B. is thinking of the life-germ in an egg? The
sixth design in *The Gates of Paradise* shows an infant cherub breaking
through an egg (as also 21.*28–30* above).
    In this passage B. explains the design at the foot of pl.33. The worlds of
the four Zoas (34.*8n*) stretch both within and beyond the mundane egg.
Milton's act in eternity, the vision of which struck B. (15.*47*), made a path
through the chaotic ruins of the Zoas into our enclosed world.
34.*32–9*. Cp. 19.*15–21* above and note: also *Jerusalem* pl.59.*10–17*.
34.*38*. This dispute between Luvah and Urizen (variously told) is the basis
of the *Four Zoas* narrative.
34.*45*. *the four immortals*] The four Zoas.

55 Those visions of human life & shadows of wisdom & knowledge
Pl. 35 Are here frozen to unexpansive deadly destroying terrors.
And war & hunting, the two fountains of the river of life,
Are become fountains of bitter death & of corroding hell,
Till brotherhood is changed into a curse & a flattery
5 By differences between ideas, that ideas themselves (which are
The Divine Members) may be slain in offerings for sin.
O dreadful loom of death! O piteous female forms compelled
To weave the woof of death! On Camberwell Tirzah's courts,
Mahlah's on Blackheath, Rahab & Noah dwell on Windsor's
heights,
10 Where once the cherubs of Jerusalem spread to Lambeth's vale.
Milcah's pillars shine from Harrow to Hampstead, where Hoglah
On Highgate's heights magnificent weaves, over trembling Thames,
To Shooter's Hill, and thence to Blackheath, the dark woof. Loud,
Loud roll the weights & spindles over the whole earth, let down
15 On all sides round to the four quarters of the world, eastward on
Europe to Euphrates & Hindu, to Nile & back in clouds
Of death across the Atlantic to America north & south!'

So spake Ololon in reminiscence astonished; but they
Could not behold Golgonooza without passing the polypus,
20 A wondrous journey not passable by immortal feet, & none
But the Divine Saviour can pass it without annihilation.
For Golgonooza cannot be seen, till having passed the polypus
It is viewed on all sides round by a fourfold vision;
Or till you become mortal & vegetable in sexuality.
25 Then you behold its mighty spires & domes of ivory & gold.

And Ololon examined all the couches of the dead,
Even of Los & Enitharmon, & all the sons of Albion,
And his four Zoas terrified & on the verge of death.
In midst of these was Milton's couch, & when they saw eight
30 Immortal starry ones, guarding the couch in flaming fires,
They thunderous uttered all a universal groan, falling down

35.5. *differences*] i.e. arguments, quarrels.
35.6. *members*] i.e. limbs.
35.8–13. *Camberwell ... Shooter's Hill*] In B.'s day, places surrounding
London, though now mostly well within the boundaries. See map on
p. 619. For *Tirzah* and her sisters, see 17.11n.
35.14. *weights and spindles* (of the looms)] See 6.5n.
35.24. *Or till you become mortal*] This does not contradict 20–3. 'Ordinary'
spirits are in danger of losing their immortality when faced by such
dangers; but the Saviour can pass them – and the fallen inhabitants of the
regions are already trapped by them. These see Golgonooza by imagina-
tion.
35.31. *They*] Ololon.

Prostrate before the starry eight, asking with tears forgiveness,
Confessing their crime with humiliation and sorrow.
Oh how the starry eight rejoiced to see Ololon descended—
35 And now that a wide road was open to Eternity,
By Ololon's descent through Beulah to Los & Enitharmon.

For mighty were the multitudes of Ololon, vast the extent
Of their great sway, reaching from Ulro to Eternity,
Surrounding the mundane shell outside in its caverns
40 And through Beulah, and all silent forbore to contend
With Ololon, for they saw the Lord in the clouds of Ololon.

There is a moment in each day that Satan cannot find,
Nor can his watch-fiends find it; but the industrious find
This moment & it multiply. And when it once is found
45 It renovates every moment of the day if rightly placed.
In this moment Ololon descended to Los & Enitharmon,
Unseen beyond the mundane shell southward in Milton's track.

Just in this moment when the morning odours rise abroad
(And first from the wild thyme), stands a fountain in a rock
50 Of crystal flowing into two streams; one flows through Golgonooza
And through Beulah to Eden, beneath Los's western wall;
The other flows through the aerial void & all the churches,
Meeting again in Golgonooza beyond Satan's seat.

The wild thyme is Los's messenger to Eden, a mighty demon—
55 Terrible, deadly & poisonous his presence in Ulro dark—
Therefore he appears only a small root creeping in grass,
Covering over the rock of odours his bright purple mantle
Beside the fount, above the lark's nest in Golgonooza.
Luvah slept here in death, & here is Luvah's empty tomb.
60 Ololon sat beside this fountain on the rock of odours.

Just at the place to where the lark mounts is a crystal gate.

35.42. *There is a moment*] One of the critical points in the poem. The rest of
the narrative, including the redemption of Milton, takes place in such an
infinite moment, bounded by the wild thyme and the song of the lark
(35.54, 61; 42.29–30). See headnote.
35.59. *Luvah's empty tomb*] In *Four Zoas* Luvah is the sufferer whose place
is taken by Christ, and imagery derived from the crucifixion narrative is
commonly applied to Luvah. Ololon sits by the tomb, as the women
watched over Jesus.
35.61–2. Cp. *42n*. The larks penetrate the 'cavernous earth / Of labyrin-
thine intricacy, twenty-seven folds of opaqueness' (17.25–6). Their flight
and their song defeats evil. The twenty-seven Churches, which thus sur-
round the mortal earth like a fog (37.35n), are a sequence of manifestations
of religious error, of which Luther (62), the would-be reformer, is the last.

It is the entrance of the first heaven, named *Luther*: for
The lark is Los's messenger through the twenty-seven churches,
That the seven Eyes of God, who walk even to Satan's seat
65 Through all the twenty-seven heavens, may not slumber nor sleep.
But the lark's nest is at the gate of Los, at the eastern
Gate of wide Golgonooza, & the lark is Los's messenger.
Pl. 36 When on the highest lift of his light pinions he arrives
At that bright gate, another lark meets him, & back to back
They touch their pinions, tip tip, and each descend
To their respective earths, & there all night consult with angels
5 Of providence, & with the Eyes of God all night in slumbers
Inspired; & at the dawn of day send out another lark
Into another heaven to carry news upon his wings.
Thus are the messengers dispatched till they reach the earth again
In the east gate of Golgonooza. And the twenty-eighth bright
10 Lark met the female Ololon descending into my garden.
(Thus it appears to mortal eyes & those of the Ulro heavens,
But not thus to immortals; the lark is a mighty angel.)
For Ololon stepped into the polypus within the mundane shell.
They could not step into vegetable worlds without becoming
15 The enemies of Humanity, except in a female form,
And as one female, Ololon and all its mighty hosts
Appeared—a virgin of twelve years. Nor time nor space was
To the perception of the virgin Ololon; but as the
Flash of lightning—but more quick—the virgin in my garden
20 Before my cottage stood (for the Satanic space is delusion).
For when Los joined with me he took me in his fiery whirlwind.
My vegetated portion was hurried from Lambeth's shades;

The lark penetrates the latest and nearest, and he and his companions
work back (35.*67*–36.*12*) to Eternity.
35.*64*. *seven Eyes*] Cp. 14.*42n*. The angelic guardians of Milton and of
humanity.
Satan's seat] At the end of the road from Eternity (17.*29*), yet in the curve of
infinity, close to Golgonooza (20.*37*–*9*).

36.*9*. *twenty-eighth*] The number twenty-seven is associated with such
groups of fallen and incomplete errors as the twenty-seven Churches and
twenty-seven Heavens; twenty-eight is a complete, fourfold number,
used, e.g. of the 'Friends of Albion' in *Jerusalem*. Thus, though the number
of Heavens is incomplete, the number of larks is complete.
36.*10*. *the female Ololon*] The 'multitudes' of 35.*37* have united into one
girl, who will soon be seen as the emanation of Milton. The explanation
of *13*–*15* below is unconvincing: B. wishes to stress the infinity of eternal
nature, and thus shows Ololon both as multitudes and as one. This passage
is the change of aspect. An emanation is always female (*Four Zoas* i *17n*).
The specific age, 'twelve years', here suggests an actual visit.

He set me down in Felpham's vale & prepared a beautiful
Cottage for me that in three years I might write all these visions
25   To display nature's cruel holiness, the deceits of natural religion.
Walking in my cottage garden sudden I beheld
The virgin Ololon & addressed her as a daughter of Beulah:

'Virgin of Providence, fear not to enter into my cottage.
What is thy message to thy friend? What am I now to do?
30   Is it again to plunge into deeper affliction? Behold me
Ready to obey, but pity thou my shadow of delight.
Enter my cottage, comfort her, for she is sick with fatigue.'

[*Design*]

Pl. 37   The virgin answered: 'Knowest thou of Milton who descended,
Driven from Eternity. Him I seek, terrified at my act
In great Eternity, which thou knowest. I come him to seek.'

So Ololon uttered in words distinct the anxious thought.
5   Mild was the voice, but more distinct than any earthly
That Milton's shadow heard; & condensing all his fibres
Into a strength impregnable of majesty & beauty infinite
I saw he was the Covering Cherub; & within him Satan

36.*31–2. my shadow of delight . . . is sick*] B.'s letters contain repeated
references to his wife Catherine's continual sickness while at Felpham: e.g.
to his brother James, 30 Jan. 1803: 'My wife has had Agues and Rheuma-
tisms almost ever since she has been here.' (*Erdman 1965*, p. 694.)
Design: A drawing labelled 'Blake's Cottage at Felpham', showing B. in
his garden, and the virgin Ololon descending (36.*10*): in Keynes, *W.B.'s
Engravings*, pl.101.

37.*2. my act* of driving Milton from Eternity (20.*43–8*, 21.*31*).
37.*6. Milton's shadow heard*] All the evils represented by Milton 'condense'
into one figure, as the multitudes of Ololon had also done. The confronta-
tion of Milton, his emanation and his shadow is being prepared.
37.*8.* THE COVERING CHERUB] B.'s great image of male evil. The description
covers 6–*43*. The biblical source is in the denunciation of Tyre in *Ezekiel*
xxvii–xxviii, first on the grounds of conceit and arrogance in beauty,
secondly for claiming godhead–'thine heart is lifted up, and thou hast
said, I am a God, I sit in the seat of God' (xxviii 2); and finally for betraying
God's trust–'Thou wast perfect in thy ways from the day that thou wast
created, till iniquity was found in thee' (xxviii 15). These are the chief
elements of B.'s Covering Cherub–great beauty, inner corruption, and
an arrogant assumption of divine power. B. adds three other important
features at different times: (*a*) the Cherub is he who drove Adam and Eve
from Paradise, and guards the gates (*Jerusalem* pl.14.*2*, 'the Cherub at the
Tree of Life'): (*b*) in *Jerusalem* pl.96.*17* he is in the cloud which over-
shadows Jesus and Albion–the cloud which covered Jesus and his three

And Rahab, in an outside which is fallacious, within
10 Beyond the outline of identity, in the selfhood deadly.
And he appeared the Wicker Man of Scandinavia, in whom
Jerusalem's children consume in flames among the stars,

Descending down into my garden, a human wonder of God
Reaching from heaven to earth, a cloud & human form.
15 I beheld Milton with astonishment, & in him beheld
The monstrous churches of Beulah, the gods of Ulro dark—
Twelve monstrous dishumanized terrors, synagogues of Satan,
A double twelve & thrice nine: such their divisions.

And these their names & their places within the mundane shell:

20 In Tyre & Sidon I saw Baal & Ashtaroth; in Moab, Chemosh;
In Ammon, Molech—loud his furnaces rage among the wheels
Of Og, & pealing loud the cries of the victims of fire.
And pale his priestesses enfold in veils of pestilence, bordered
With war, woven in looms of Tyre & Sidon by beautiful Ashtaroth.

disciples on the mountain-top at the Transfiguration (*Matthew* xvii *5*):
(*c*) the Cherub, for all his pride, is dominated by a lust within himself that
he cannot control, the female harlot Rahab (*8–9* and *38.15–27*). Satan and
the Cherub are not always distinguishable. B. has no interest in Tyre, but
is captivated by this image of the mighty, glorious figure who seeks to
usurp divinity, yet is inwardly corrupt and therefore doomed.

37.9. *within*] i.e. within Satan, deep in his selfish heart.

37.10. *the outline of identity*] Cp *Jerusalem* pls *18.2* and *71.6–9*. An outline
gives form and identifies the creature. The common outline 'spread
without' marks a thing off from the outer world. The 'outline spread
within' marks off the inner nature, and identifies its soul.

37.11. *the Wicker Man of Scandinavia*] Caesar's *Gallic Wars* vi 16 refers to
Druid (not Scandinavian) human sacrifice by burning. B. (*Jerusalem*
pl.47.3–7) sees this sadism as an escape of uncontrolled wildness, a savagery
which also finds an outlet in war.

37.15ff. B. sees in Milton's mistaken theology all the idols and false gods
denounced by Milton himself in *Paradise Lost* i *392–513*.

37.17. *synagogues of Satan*] The phrase derives from *Revelation* ii *9*, a
scornful reference to churches that fail in their task. B.'s idea, used chiefly
in *Four Zoas* viii *89*ff, and *Jerusalem* pl.89.5–8, is of a religious group de-
voted to Satan.

37.18. The numbers are explained in *34–5*.

37.19. *within the mundane shell*] 'This is the way these infinite powers are
revealed in the history of our mortal world.'

37.20. *Baal and Ashtaroth*] Respectively the chief male and female deities
of the Phœnecians and Canaanites.

Chemoch; Molech] These national deities of trans-Jordan were each wor-
shipped on occasion by the sacrifice in fire of living children.

19+B.

25   In Palestine Dagon, sea-monster worshipped o'er the sea;
      Thammuz in Lebanon, & Rimmon in Damascus curtained;
      Osiris, Isis, Orus, in Egypt—dark their tabernacles on Nile,
      Floating with solemn songs, & on the lakes of Egypt nightly
      With pomp, even till morning break, & Osiris appear in the sky.
30   But Belial of Sodom & Gomorrha, obscure demon of bribes
      And secret assasinations, not worshipped nor adored but
      With the finger on the lips & the back turned to the light;
      And Saturn, Jove & Rhea of the isles of the sea remote.
      These twelve gods are the twelve spectre sons of the Druid Albion.

35   And these the names of the twenty-seven heavens & their churches:

37.25. *Dagon*] Commonly supposed, as by Milton, to be 'upward man and
downward fish' (*Paradise Lost* i 462–3): a Philistine god, but found by
them on the mainland and altered to their sea-going life (i.e. not brought
'o'er the sea', but worshipped as a sea-god).
37.26. *Thammuz*] (biblical *Tammuz*). A dying–reviving god of vegetation
and fertility. Milton mentions the practice of religious prostitution
(*Paradise Lost* i 454) and places his worship in Lebanon.
Rimmon] The god of Naaman of Damascus (*2 Kings* v 18: *Paradise Lost* i
467–8).
curtained] As befits a hidden, secret god. See *40*. The detail is not in the Bible
or Milton, but (like *tabernacle* in *27*) indicates the nature of such false gods.
37.27. *Osiris, Isis, Orus*] Osiris was husband and brother of Isis, and father
of Orus (Milton's spelling; but usually Horus). Like Thammuz, he was a
god of fertility–in Egypt through the annual Nile flood. Despite *29*, he
was by no means a sun-god; this idea is not Milton's.
37.30. *Belial*] Not originally a god at all (the word means *wickedness*), and
not in the Bible associated with Sodom and Gomorrah. B. takes the clue
from *Paradise Lost* i 501–3:

          . . . then wander forth the sons
          Of Belial, flown with insolence and wine.
          Witness the streets of Sodom . . .

37.33. *Saturn, Jove and Rhea*] From *Paradise Lost* i 512–13; Milton also
mentions Crete.
37.34. *spectre sons*] Ashtaroth, Isis and Rhea were female: but there are
only eleven males besides. Osiris, Isis and Orus count as a trinity, and the
whole group is thus twelve. Britain (Albion) worships this kind of divinity,
a perversion of the truth once known in the ancient, supposedly pre-
patriarchal Druid tradition.
37.35. THE TWENTY-SEVEN HEAVENS AND THEIR CHURCHES] The mantling
clouds of religious error that surround our mortal universe (17.21ff). The
number is incomplete, one less than the ideal twenty-eight (cp. 36.9n).
The imaginative man must penetrate this obscurity before he can see the
vision of eternity. The ensuing lists of patriarchs, fathers and ecclesiastics

Adam, Seth, Enos, Cainan, Mahalaleel, Jared, Enoch,
Methuselah, Lamech; these are giants mighty, hermaphroditic.
Noah, Shem, Arphaxad, Cainan the second, Salah, Heber,
Peleg, Reu, Serug, Nahor, Terah; these are the female-males,
40 A male within a female hid as in an ark & curtains;
Abraham, Moses, Solomon, Paul, Constantine, Charlemagne,
Luther; these seven are the male-females, the dragon forms,
Religion hid in war, a dragon red & hidden harlot.

(All these are seen in Milton's shadow, who is the Covering Cherub

divides religious history into epochs, each one a 'church', which pretends
to present religious truth, but is in error. Lines *35–43*, with two extra lines,
recur in *Jerusalem* pl.*75.10–20*. Swedenborg is the source for a series of
'Churches' which aim at spiritual truth, but end in error, but his scheme is
much simpler than B.'s, comprising only four 'Churches'. B. may perhaps
also have adopted something of Boehme's scheme of seven Churches, but
this is more doubtful. See Raine, *B. and Tradition*, i 325ff.

37.36. Adam, Seth, Enos] B. uses the spelling of *Genesis* v (not *1 Chronicles* i):
but his list (to *Abraham*) is that of *Luke* iii in reverse – the genealogy of Christ.

37.37. Lamech] Last of the patriarchs before Noah and the Flood.

giants mighty, hermaphroditic] Mighty but self-defeating; see notes to *39, 42*.

37.38. Cainan] Named in *Luke*, not in *Genesis* or *Chronicles*.

37.39. Terah] Father of Abraham, directly descended from Noah.

female-males] B.'s own idea; the suggestion is of effeminacy, but see *42n*.
In the *Four Zoas* fragment (*k*, p. 466), Tharmas and Enion are similarly
described: 'Male form'd the demon mild: athletic force his shoulders
spread / . . . but the parts / To love devoted, female. . . .' 'Female her form;
bright as the summer, but the parts of love / Male. . . .'

37.40. in an ark and curtains] As God was hidden from the Jews (*Exodus*
xxv 10ff, xxvi 1–14, 31–7).

37.41–2. Abraham . . . Luther] B.'s choice of the most famous religious
names in the history of the world, at once in government and religion.
Paul is the exception, but even he made a point of the Christian necessity
for civil obedience. The list omits such reformers as Josiah (*2 Kings* xxii–
xxiii) and such thinkers as Augustine: and, most significantly, the key
figure – Christ himself – whose nature the rest misinterpreted.

37.42. The male-females] (See *8–9* and *40.17–22*.) An outward appearance
of power is inwardly dominated by womanish lusts. In *38.23* Satan is such
a person; in *Four Zoas* viii *266–7* Rahab similarly appears in the midst of
the male Sanhedrin. Of the three types in *35–43*, only this really interested
B. It seems he invented the other two for the nonce in order to complete a
pattern.

37.43. a dragon red and hidden harlot] The monster of *Revelation* xii 3 –
'behold a great red dragon . . . and [it] was cast out, that old serpent,
called the Devil, and Satan, which deceiveth the whole world' – and
the harlot of *Revelation* xvii 3–5 (quoted in *33.20n*).

45   The spectre of Albion, in which the spectre of Luvah inhabits,
In the Newtonian voids between the substances of creation.
For the chaotic voids outside of the stars are measured by
The stars, which are the boundaries of kingdoms, provinces
And empires of Chaos, invisible to the vegetable man.
50   The kingdom of Og is in Orion; Sihon is in Ophiuchus;
Og has twenty-seven districts; Sihon's districts twenty-one.
From star to star, mountains & valleys, terrible dimension
Stretched out, compose the mundane shell, a mighty incrustation
Of forty-eight deformed human wonders of the Almighty,
55   With caverns whose remotest bottoms meet again beyond
The mundane shell in Golgonooza; but the fires of Los rage
In the remotest bottoms of the caves, that none can pass
Into Eternity that way, but all descend to Los,
To Bowlahoola & Allamanda, & to Entuthon Benython.

37.45. i.e. 'This evil creature is the dominant evil power now controlling
Britain–a nation dominated by the spectre of Luvah (which means,
roughly, "by perverted passions").' This line is an additional comment.
37.46. *Newtonian voids*] Newton did not need to suppose the *ether*, tenuous
matter filling the universe, and binding all the heavenly bodies together.
Still less had he any room for 'music of the spheres' in his cosmology.
The only links are the distant forces of attraction; otherwise his stars and
planets move on their determined paths in everlasting silence, isolation and
night. B. envisages the constellations in *47–59* as being the entrances to
infinite chasms of chaos stretching away from us.
37.50. *Og . . . Sihon*] See 20.37n and 22.33n; and especially the note below.
The hostile kingdoms are not merely little forgotten princedoms. They
manifest a principle that is spread across the stars.
Orion . . . Ophiuchus] The first a spectacular constellation, the second much
less well-known; rather straggling and indeterminate. This concerns B.
less than its situation (see *54n*). Cp. *Paradise Lost* ii 709: 'the length of
Ophiuchus huge / In th'arctic sky, and from his horrid hair / Shakes
pestilence and war.' Ophiuchus is 'the serpent-bearer': Laocoön, in B.'s
engraving, is labelled 'Ophiuchus'.
37.54. *forty-eight*] The total number of constellations in the system tradi-
tional since Ptolemy thus reformed it in his *Amagest, c.* A.D. 150. (After
1600, other constellations were added.) Ptolemy has twenty-one 'northern',
twelve 'zodiacal' and fifteen 'southern': B. unites the latter pair under the
'southern' constellation Orion, making his favourite 'evil' number twenty-
seven, leaving the rest under the 'northern' Ophiuchus. Orion and Ophiuchus
lie in opposite regions on the star sphere. B. sees them as 'deformed' animal
or human figures, according to their astronomical names. See also 38.1.
37.59. Souls must enter Golgonooza through Los's hands, and cannot slip
through to invade Eternity without meeting his power.
Entuthon Benython] A region of Ulro, but Golgonooza is there; it is the
alien centre of Los's redeeming activities.

60 The heavens are the Cherub, the twelve gods are Satan,

(VII) [*Full-plate illustration*]

Pl. 38 And the forty-eight starry regions are cities of the Levites,
The heads of the great polypus, fourfold twelve enormity
In mighty & mysterious commingling, enemy with enemy,
Woven by Urizen into sexes from his mantle of years.)

5 And Milton, collecting all his fibres into impregnable strength,
Descended down a paved work of all kinds of precious stones
Out from the eastern sky—descending down into my cottage
Garden, clothed in black; severe & silent he descended.
The spectre of Satan stood upon the roaring sea & beheld
10 Milton within his sleeping humanity. Trembling & shuddering
He stood upon the waves, a twenty-sevenfold mighty demon,
Gorgeous & beautiful; loud roll his thunders against Milton.

37.*60. twelve gods*] The twelve signs of the Zodiac. In this and the next
line B. relates his scheme of Heavens, etc., to biblical figures of evil.

VII. *Full-plate illustration*: An eagle hovers over a nude pair (probably
Albion and Jerusalem, his emanation: see *Jerusalem* pl.94.*1–15*) who lie in a
slackened caress of unsatisfied desire, on rocks by the sea. Keynes, *W.B.'s
Engravings*, pl.102.

38.*1. cities of the Levites*] Forty-eight cities all over Israel were given to the
priestly tribe of Levi, instead of land. Cp. *Numbers* xxxv 7.

38.*2. fourfold*] Denotes perfection: here the perfection of enormity.
See 34.*24n.*

38.*4–5.* The space here is editorial, not found on the plate, and is meant to
indicate the renewal of narrative. Line 5 refers back to 37.*6–8.*

38.*5–14.* There is some intentional ambiguity in this figure of Milton.
Line 5 clearly echoes 37.*6*ff: but though *8* may be taken two ways—as indi-
cating the grimness, or the dignity, of puritanism—it contrasts with the
'thunderous' and 'gorgeous' spectre. But Milton, the eternal spirit, is
within the spectre, which surrounds or 'covers' him like a garment. He
entered it in order to return to Generation (14.*36*), but soon he will cast
it off.

38.*6. paved work*] From *Exodus* xxiv 10: 'And they saw the God of Israel:
and there was under his feet as it were a paved work of a sapphire stone....'
This is part of the narrative of the Law-giving, with which the Shadow of
Milton is thus associated.

38.*10. his sleeping humanity*] *his* means 'his own'; see note above; *sleeping
humanity* indicates an eternal soul shut off from heavenly life, as Milton
sleeps in 15.*10–12*, which this echoes. The spectre realizes that he, be-
longing as he does to Milton, belongs to life, not death; and although he
hates this, he dare not attack it (*14*, and 39.*19*), for to do so would be to
destroy himself. The essential fact is the confrontation of Milton and his
spectre, Satan; see headnote, p. 485.

Loud Satan thundered, loud & dark upon mild Felpham shore;
Not daring to touch one fibre he howled round upon the sea.

15   I also stood in Satan's bosom & beheld its desolations—
A ruined man, a ruined building of God not made with hands;
Its plains of burning sand, its mountains of marble terrible,
Its pits & declivities flowing with molten ore, & fountains
Of pitch & nitre, its ruined palaces & cities & mighty works,
20   Its furnaces of affliction, in which his angels & emanations
Labour with blackened visages among its stupendous ruins,
Arches & pyramids & porches, colonnades & domes,
In which dwells Mystery, Babylon; here is her secret place;
From hence she comes forth on the churches in delight;
25   Here is her cup filled with its poisons, in these horrid vales,
And here her scarlet veil woven in pestilence & war.
Here is Jerusalem bound in chains, in the dens of Babylon.

In the eastern porch of Satan's universe Milton stood & said:

'Satan, my spectre, I know my power thee to annihilate
30   And be a greater in thy place, & be thy tabernacle,
A covering for thee to do thy will—till one greater comes
And smites me as I smote thee, & becomes my covering.
Such are the laws of thy false heavens, but laws of Eternity
Are not such. Know thou, I come to self-annihilation.
35   Such are the laws of Eternity, that each shall mutually
Annihilate himself for other's good, as I for thee.
Thy purpose & the purpose of thy priests & of thy churches
Is to impress on men the fear of death; to teach
Trembling & fear, terror, constriction, abject selfishness.
40   Mine is to teach men to despise death, & to go on
In fearless majesty annihilating self, laughing to scorn
Thy laws & terrors, shaking down thy Synagogues as webs.
I come to discover before Heaven & Hell the self-righteousness
In all its hypocritic turpitude, opening to every eye
45   These wonders of Satan's holiness, showing to the earth
The idol-virtues of the natural heart, & Satan's seat

38.25. *her cup*] From *Revelation* xvii 4: 'having a golden cup in her hand
full of abominations': cp. *Four Zoas* viii *267n*.

38.26. *her scarlet veil*] The biblical Harlot is 'arrayed in purple and scarlet'–
B.'s detail of the veil reminds us that Rahab is Vala, the 'Shadowy Female'
who, in *Four Zoas*, sought to entrap all creation.

38.28. *Satan's universe*] The Covering Cherub, now envisaged as a world, as
in the previous lines.

38.42. *synagogues*] Cp. *37.17n*.

38.46. *the natural heart*] The heart of man in this world, out of touch with
eternity (A Pauline phrase: cp. 1 *Corinthians* xv 39–49, and 'To Tirzah',
p. 591).

Explore, in all its selfish natural virtue, & put off
In self-annihilation all that is not of God alone:
To put off self & all I have, ever & ever. Amen.'

50 Satan heard, coming in a cloud, with trumpets & flaming fire,
Saying: 'I am God, the judge of all, the living & the dead.
Fall therefore down & worship me; submit thy supreme
Dictate to my eternal will, & to my dictate bow.
I hold the balances of right & just, & mine the sword.
55 Seven angels bear my name & in those seven I appear;
But I alone am God, & I alone in heaven & earth
Of all that live dare utter this. Others tremble & bow
Pl. 39 Till all things become one great Satan, in holiness
Opposed to mercy; and the divine delusion, Jesus, be no more.'

Suddenly around Milton on my path the starry seven
Burned terrible! My path became a solid fire, as bright
5 As the clear sun, & Milton silent came down on my path
And there went forth from the starry limbs of the seven, forms
Human, with trumpets innumerable, sounding articulate
As the seven spake; & they stood in a mighty column of fire,
Surrounding Felpham's vale, reaching to the mundane shell,
saying:

10 'Awake, Albion, awake! Reclaim thy reasoning spectre! Subdue
Him to the Divine Mercy; cast him down into the lake
Of Los, that ever burneth with fire, ever & ever. Amen.
Let the four Zoas awake from slumbers of six thousand years!'

Then loud the furnaces of Los were heard & seen as seven heavens
15 Stretching from south to north over the mountains of Albion.

Satan heard; trembling round his body, he encircled it;
He trembled with exceeding great trembling & astonishment,
Howling in his spectre round his body, hungering to devour,
But fearing for the pain; for if he touches a vital,

38.55. *seven angels*] But the Angels of the Presence are not the emissaries
of fear of *Revelation* xvi, where they 'pour out the vials of the wrath of
God upon the earth'; but 'forms human' (39.6-7), and they support
Milton, not the spectre. Cp. 14.42*n*.
39.3. *the starry seven*] The Angels of the Presence: cp. 38.55*n*.
39.11. *the lake*] *Revelation* xx 10: 'And the devil that deceived them was
cast into the lake of fire and brimstone . . . and shall be tormented day and
night for ever and ever.' But this is Los's lake, and the fire is the redeeming
fire of divine inspiration and activity. Cp. *Jerusalem* pl.37 illustration.
39.18. *his spectre round his body*] The spectre is derived from a whole body
and personality, but is always in opposition to it.

20   His torment is unendurable. Therefore he cannot devour,
     But howls round it as a lion round his prey continually.
     Loud Satan thundered, loud & dark upon mild Felpham's shore,
     Coming in a cloud with trumpets & with fiery flame
     An awful form eastward, from midst of a bright paved-work
25   Of precious stones by cherubim surrounded—so permitted
     (Lest he should fall apart in his eternal death) to imitate
     The eternal great Humanity Divine, surrounded by
     His cherubim & seraphim in ever-happy Eternity.
     Beneath sat Chaos: Sin on his right hand, Death on his left;
30   And Ancient Night spread over all the heaven his mantle of laws.
     He trembled with exceeding great trembling & astonishment.

     Then Albion rose up in the night of Beulah on his couch
     Of dread repose, seen by the visionary eye; his face is toward
     The east, toward Jerusalem's gates; groaning he sat above
35   His rocks. London & Bath & Legions & Edinburgh
     Are the four pillars of his throne; his left foot near London
     Covers the shades of Tyburn; his instep from Windsor
     To Primrose Hill, stretching to Highgate & Holloway;
     London is between his knees, its basements fourfold.
40   His right foot stretches to the sea on Dover cliffs, his heel
     On Canterbury's ruins; his right hand covers lofty Wales,
     His left Scotland; his bosom girt with gold involves
     York, Edinburgh, Durham & Carlisle, & on the front
     Bath, Oxford, Cambridge, Norwich; his right elbow
45   Leans on the rocks of Erin's land, Ireland, ancient nation.
     His head bends over London; he sees his embodied spectre
     Trembling before him with exceeding great trembling & fear.
     He views Jerusalem & Babylon, his tears flow down;

39.24–5. from midst . . . by cherubim surrounded] Reminiscent of Solomon's
temple, *1 Kings* vi 29–30: 'And he carved the walls of the house round
about with carved figures of cherubims [etc.] . . . And the floor of the
house he overlaid with gold. . . .'
39.29–30. Chaos, Sin, Death, Ancient Night] Reminiscences of the associ-
ation of Satan, Sin and Death in *Paradise Lost* ii 643ff, much used by B. in
12.36ff. 'Chaos and Ancient Night' *ibid.* ii 970, occurs above: *12.21, 20.33*.
39.32ff. Albion] The map of Great Britain becomes a giant attempting to
rise from sleep.
39.35. Legions] Caerleon, the City of Legions, considered by Geoffrey of
Monmouth the noblest city in Wales.
39.37–8. For the London place-names, see map on p. 619.
39.43–4. York . . . Norwich] All cathedral cities, the first four northern, the
second southern.
39.48. Jerusalem and Babylon] i.e. their history. Cp. *33.21–3*, where Jerusalem
is oppressed by Babylon.

He moved his right foot to Cornwall, his left to the rocks of Bognor.
50 He strove to rise to walk into the deep, but strength failing
Forbade; & down with dreadful groans he sunk upon his couch
In moony Beulah. Los, his strong guard, walks round beneath the
moon.

Urizen faints in terror striving among the brooks of Arnon
With Milton's spirit. As the ploughman or artificer or shepherd
55 While in the labours of his calling sends his thought abroad
To labour in the ocean or in the starry heaven, so Milton
Laboured in chasms of the mundane shell,—though here before
My cottage 'midst the starry seven, where the virgin Ololon
Stood trembling in the porch. Loud Satan thundered on the
stormy sea,
60 Circling Albion's cliffs in which the fourfold world resides,
Though seen in fallacy outside—a fallacy of Satan's churches.

(VIII)   *[Full-plate illustration]*

Pl. 40 Before Ololon Milton stood & perceived the eternal form
Of that mild vision. Wondrous were their acts—by me unknown
Except remotely; and I heard Ololon say to Milton,

'I see thee strive upon the brooks of Arnon. There a dread
5 And awful man I see, o'ercovered with the mantle of years.
I behold Los & Urizen, I behold Orc & Tharmas,
The four Zoas of Albion, & thy spirit with them striving,
In self-annihilation giving thy life to thy enemies.
Are those who contemn religion & seek to annihilate it
10 Become in their feminine portions the causes & promoters

39.49. *Bognor*] Near Felpham. B. made this 'left foot' move.
39.53. Taken up from 19.6–14.
39.57–9. *though here before my cottage*] All this had taken place in the
single moment (35.42ff) of the girl's appearance (36.16ff). Milton is
facing his spectre in Eternity, while still struggling with Urizen, and ap-
pearing to Blake in his cottage. The importance of these simultaneous but
discrete acts is stated in 20.15ff.
39.61. *Though seen in fallacy outside*] I.e. though we see the externals of the
land alone; but it is really a world of humanity. Letter to Butts, 2 Oct.
1800 (p. 471):

–Each grain of sand,
Every stone on the land, . . .
Cloud, meteor and star
Are men seen afar.

VIII. Full-plate illustration: Milton raising the feeble Urizen (39.53).

40.5. *man*] Urizen. Cp. 19.11, 'the furrows of many years'. Ololon does
not know him, though recognizing him in another form in the next line.
19*

Of these religions? How is this thing, this Newtonian phantasm,
This Voltaire & Rousseau, this Hume & Gibbon & Bolingbroke,
This Natural Religion, this impossible absurdity?
Is Ololon the cause of this? Oh, where shall I hide my face?
15 These tears fall for the little ones, the children of Jerusalem,
Lest they be annihilated in thy annihilation.'

No sooner she had spoke but Rahab Babylon appeared
Eastward upon the paved-work across Europe & Asia,
Glorious as the midday sun, in Satan's bosom glowing—
20 A female hidden in a male, religion hidden in war,
Named 'Moral Virtue'; cruel twofold monster shining bright,
A dragon red & hidden harlot which John in Patmos saw.

And all beneath the nations innumerable of Ulro
Appeared—the seven kingdoms of Canaan & five Baalim
25 Of Philistia, into twelve divided, called after the names

40.11. Newtonian phantasm] Newton's dream-world, which we call 'real'.
40.12. Voltaire, Rousseau, Hume, Gibbon, Bolingbroke] All philosophers of
the eighteenth century. Voltaire, Hume and Gibbon were strongly
rationalistic, the first, however, less so than he seems. Rousseau was a very
different figure, a sentimentalist, but B. always sees him as a part of the
same movement, worshipping man as he is (in this world), and seeking his
perfection by rational means. Bolingbroke was primarily a politician, but
enjoyed some reputation as a philosopher, with for example, *Reflections
concerning Innate Moral Ideas* (1752). B. accuses them of supporting mys-
teries.
40.14. cause] B. saw, not a single chain of act-and-consequence, but a
relation between *all* wicked acts and *all* ill effects. This is not as irrational
as it seems. The person who is cruel to a child is involved in Cruelty, and
partly responsible for the continuation of all forms of cruelty in the future;
and in the one act justifies other people's cruel acts of the past. Cp. 'Auguries
of Innocence' (p. 585), e.g. 'A Robin Redbreast in a cage / Puts all
Heaven in a rage.' Ololon's own fault was that of 20.43–50.
40.20. Cp. 37.42–3.
40.23. beneath] B. conceives the sight more as one of his own formal
paintings of many figures, than as an imaginary scene in the narrative.
40.24. seven kingdoms] Those overrun by the Israelites: 'the Hittites, and
the Girgashites, and the Amorites, and the Canaanites, and the Perizzites,
and the Hivites, and the Jebusites, seven nations greater and mightier than
thou' (*Deuteronomy* vii 1).
40.24–5. five Baalim / Of Philistia] Cp. *Joshua* xiii 3, 'the five lords of the
Philistines' (i.e. of Gaza, Ashdod, Ashkelon, Gath and Ekron). These are
the enemies of Israel, the biblical 'nations' or heathen, who inhabited
Palestine itself. (But *Baalim* is not a word the Bible uses of Philistine gods:
the word *lords* above is *seren*: *Baalim* is a Canaanite title.)

Of Israel, as they are in Eden—mountain, river & plain,
City & sandy desert intermingled beyond mortal ken.

But turning toward Ololon in terrible majesty, Milton
Replied: 'Obey thou the words of the inspired man!
30   All that can be annihilated must be annihilated,
That the children of Jerusalem may be saved from slavery.
There is a negation, & there is a contrary:
The negation must be destroyed to redeem the contraries.
The negation is the spectre, the reasoning power in man.
35   This is a false body, an incrustation over my immortal
Spirit, a selfhood which must be put off & annihilated alway.
To cleanse the face of my spirit by self-examination,

[Design]

Pl. 41   *[Design]*

To bathe in the waters of life; to wash off the not-human
I come in self-annihilation & the grandeur of inspiration,
To cast off rational demonstration by faith in the Saviour;
To cast off the rotten rags of memory by inspiration;
5   To cast off Bacon, Locke & Newton from Albion's covering;
To take off his filthy garments, & clothe him with imagination;
To cast aside from poetry all that is not inspiration,
That it no longer shall dare to mock with the aspersion of madness
Cast on the inspired, by the tame high finisher of paltry blots
10   Indefinite, or paltry rhymes, or paltry harmonies;
Who creeps into state government like a caterpillar to destroy;
To cast off the idiot questioner who is always questioning
But never capable of answering, who sits with a sly grin
Silent plotting when to question, like a thief in a cave;
15   Who publishes doubt & calls it knowledge; whose science is despair,

40.*30.* What can be annihilated is unreal, a fantasy, and therefore must be destroyed.

40.*32. contrary]* That which is different and perhaps sometimes in opposition, but complementary. Cp. 30.*1* and especially *Jerusalem* pl.10.*7n.*

40. *Design*: Among trees, a snake coils and faces a man.

41. *Design*: Figures joining hands in a dance.

41.*5. Bacon, Locke and Newton]* A trio often found in B. as the source of the modern rational thought he hated.

41.*8. the aspersion of madness]* B.'s visionary life called forth this aspersion from a number of people of common–but limited–sense.

41.*9. the tame high finisher of paltry blots / Indefinite]* Perhaps Reynolds; but the condemnation goes on to cover all artists who rate technique above inspiration.

41.*15. doubt]* B.'s name for scientific knowledge, or any knowledge based on scepticism. It depends (*16–17*) on overturning the works of others.

Whose pretence to knowledge is envy, whose whole science is
To destroy the wisdom of ages to gratify ravenous envy,
That rages round him like a wolf day & night without rest.
He smiles with condescension; he talks of benevolence & virtue;
20   And those who act with benevolence & virtue, they murder time
     on time.
These are the destroyers of Jerusalem, these are the murderers
Of Jesus, who deny the faith & mock at eternal life;
Who pretend to poetry, that they may destroy imagination
By imitation of nature's images drawn from remembrance.
25   These are the sexual garments, the abomination of desolation
Hiding the human lineaments as with an ark & curtains
Which Jesus rent & now shall wholly purge away with fire,
Till generation is swallowed up in regeneration,'

Then trembled the virgin Ololon & replied in clouds of despair:

30   'Is this our feminine portion, the sixfold Miltonic female?
Terribly this portion trembles before thee, O awful man!
Although our human power can sustain the severe contentions
Of friendship, our sexual cannot, but flies into the Ulro.
Hence arose all our terrors in Eternity, & now remembrance
35   Returns upon us. Are we contraries, O Milton, thou & I?
O Immortal! how were we led to war the wars of death?
Is this the void outside of existence, which if entered into
Pl. 42 Becomes a womb, & is this the death-couch of Albion?
Thou goest to eternal death, & all must go with thee.'

So saying the virgin divided sixfold, & with a shriek
Dolorous that ran through all creation, a double sixfold wonder,
5   Away from Ololon she divided & fled into the depths
Of Milton's shadow, as a dove upon the stormy sea.

41.25. sexual garments] The clothing of mortal flesh which the soul wears
in this world.
41.26. ark and curtains] The Ark of the Covenant was kept in the Temple,
hidden behind curtains: 'there was nothing' in the ark save the two tablets
of stone which Moses put there at Horeb' (*1 Kings* viii 9). When Jesus
died, the curtain split (*Matthew* xxvii 51)–a symbol of the end of the old
dispensation.
41.32. human] The real human, known only in Eden. The *contentions of
friendship* are the frank, even fierce disputes which may arise among true
friends without destroying the friendship.
41.34. our terrors, which caused Ololon to drive Milton from Heaven
(20.43ff).
41.35. contraries] Cp. 40.32.

42.4. a double sixfold wonder] This is Ololon's evil part, which joins the
Shadow to be annihilated. Ololon finally surrenders to Milton.

Then as a moony ark Ololon descended to Felpham's vale
In clouds of blood, in streams of gore, with dreadful thunderings
Into the fires of intellect that rejoiced in Felpham's vale
10 Around the starry eight. With one accord the starry eight became
One man Jesus the Saviour, wonderful! Round his limbs
The clouds of Ololon folded as a garment dipped in blood,
Written within & without in woven letters, & the writing
Is the divine revelation in the literal expression—
15 A garment of war; I heard it named the woof of six thousand years.

And I beheld the twenty-four cities of Albion
Arise upon their thrones to judge the nations of the earth;
And the immortal Four in whom the twenty-four appear fourfold
Arose around Albion's body. Jesus wept & walked forth
20 From Felpham's vale, clothed in clouds of blood, to enter into
Albion's bosom, the bosom of death, & the Four surrounded him
In the column of fire in Felpham's vale. Then to their mouths the
    Four
Applied their four trumpets & them sounded to the four winds.

Terror struck in the vale. I stood at that immortal sound;
25 My bones trembled. I fell outstretched upon the path
A moment, & my soul returned into its mortal state,
To resurrection & judgement in the vegetable body.
And my sweet shadow of delight stood trembling by my side.

Immediately the lark mounted with a loud trill from Felpham's vale,
30 And the wild thyme from Wimbledon's green & empurpled hills;
And Los & Enitharmon rose over the hills of Surrey.
Their clouds roll over London with a south wind; soft Oothoon
Pants in the vales of Lambeth, weeping o'er her human harvest.
Los listens to the cry of the poor man, his cloud
35 Over London in volume terrific, low bended in anger.

42.15. *a garment of war*] Of spiritual war.
42.16. *twenty-four cities*] In 39.35–44 twelve are named. See *Jerusalem* (headnote), where the twenty-four cities are named, and summed up in 'the immortal Four', Verulam, London, York and Edinburgh (*Jerusalem* pl.46.23–4). They are Albion's friends and advisers, who stand by him in his trouble.
42.18. *Four ... twenty-four*] *Ezekiel* i and *Revelation* iv, where twenty-four elders surround the throne, seven lamps stand before it, and the four beasts are 'in the midst of the throne, and round about' it (*Revelation* iv 6). Also found in *Four Zoas* ix 278–84; and see note above.
42.29–30. *the lark ... thyme*] The whole vision from 35.48 has lasted a moment.
42.30. *Wimbledon*] Then south of London, though now part of it.
42.32. *soft*] For 'softly'.

Rintrah & Palamabron view the human harvest beneath;
Their winepresses & barns stand open; the ovens are prepared,
The waggons ready; terrific, lions & tigers sport & play.
All animals upon the earth are prepared in all their strength
Pl. 43 To go forth to the great harvest & vintage of the nations.

Finis

[Design]

42. *Design*: Oothoon flying over a cornfield (42.32).
Plate 43. The line of text is at the top. Otherwise, this is a full-plate design
of a female figure with arms raised, standing between two winged angels.

Extra Plates

Plates 3, 4, 5
As stated in the headnote, these are found only in the two later copies C
and D (pl.5 is not in C). It seems that the earliest text was simply pls 2 and
7: pl.6 was the first to be interposed (in all copies), with first and last lines
suitably composed to fit. Then pls 3 and 4 were added, and finally, in the
last copy only, pl.5. At each stage B. arranged suitable links, deleting 7.*1*
when he had used the same idea in 3.*1*.

Pl. 3 By Enitharmon's looms when Albion was slain upon his mountains
And in his tent, through envy of living form, even of the Divine Vision,
And of the sports of wisdom in the human imagination,
Which is the divine body of the Lord Jesus, blessed for ever.
5 *Mark well my words; they are of your eternal salvation.*

Urizen lay in darkness & solitude, in chains of the mind locked up.
Los seized his hammer & tongs; he laboured at his resolute anvil
Among indefinite druid rocks & snows of doubt & reasoning.

Refusing all definite form, the abstract horror roofed, stony hard;
10 *And a first age passed over, & a state of dismal woe!*

3.*1*. This line is intended to continue the sentence begun in 2.*26*: 'Three
classes are created by the hammer of Los, and woven. . . .'
3.*2*. *Through envy* . . .] Britain is spiritually dead, having clung to material-
istic ideas and refused to accept imaginative reality.
3.*6–27*. These lines are an abbreviated version of the appearance of the
fallen human form in *Urizen 196–254*.
3.*8*. *indefinite druid rocks*] Rocks are hard and unyielding, and the Druids
were (in B.'s eyes) the priests of a tyrannical and cruel religion. Indefinite-
ness was anathema to B. who, as an engraver, liked firm outline, and in
person was given to downright judgments. Line *9* further illustrates his
feelings.

Down sunk with fright a red round globe, hot burning; deep,
Deep down into the abyss, panting, conglobing, trembling.
And a second age passed over, & a state of dismal woe.

Rolling round into two little orbs, & closed in two little caves
15 The eyes beheld the abyss, lest bones of solidness freeze over all.
And a third age passed over & a state of dismal woe.

From beneath his orbs of vision, two ears in close volutions
Shot spiring out in the deep darkness & petrified as they grew.
And a fourth age passed over, & a state of dismal woe.

20 Hanging upon the wind, two nostrils bent down into the deep.
And a fifth age passed over, & a state of dismal woe.

In ghastly torment sick, a tongue of hunger & thirst flamed out.
And a sixth age passed over, & a state af dismal woe.

Enraged & stifled without & within, in terror & woe, he threw his
25 Right arm to the north, his left arm to the south, & his feet
Stamped the nether abyss, in trembling & howling & dismay.
And a seventh age passed over, & a state of dismal woe.

Terrified, Los stood in the abyss & his immortal limbs
Grew deadly pale. He became what he beheld: for a red
30 Round globe sunk down from his bosom into the deep; in pangs
He hovered over it, trembling & weeping. Suspended it shook
The nether abyss in tremblings: he wept over it, he cherished it
In deadly sickening pain, till separated into a female, pale
As the cloud that brings the snow. All the while from his back
35 A blue fluid exuded in sinews, hardening in the abyss,
Till it separated into a male form howling in jealousy.
Within labouring, beholding without—from particulars to generals
Subduing his spectre, they builded the looms of generation;
They builded great Golgonooza times on times, ages on ages.
40 First Orc was born; then the Shadowy Female; then all Los's
family.
At last Enitharmon brought forth Satan, refusing form in vain:
The miller of Eternity made subservient to the great harvest,
That he may go to his own place, prince of the starry wheels
Pl. 4 Beneath the plough of Rintrah & the harrow of the Almighty

3.28–36. A variation on the material of *Urizen 279–315*: but here, in addition to the female emanation, the spectre of Los grows out of his back.
3.38. the looms of generation weave active forms for this material world, which, though fallen, is better than chaos.
3.41. Satan tried to 'refuse form': see *9.35.*
3.42. miller of Eternity] Satan. He has his place in Eternity, but he must keep to it, for there he fulfils his special character.

4.1. This plate was also designed to read on from *2.26* (see *3.1n*), but at an earlier stage in composition, before pl.3 was inserted.

In the hands of Palamabron, where the starry mills of Satan
Are built beneath the earth & waters of the mundane shell.
Here the three classes of men take their sexual texture: woven.
5   The sexual is threefold; the human is fourfold.

'If you account it wisdom when you are angry to be silent, and
Not to show it, I do not account that wisdom, but folly.
Every man's wisdom is peculiar to his own individuality.
O Satan, my youngest born, art thou not prince of the starry hosts
10 And the wheels of heaven, to turn the mills day & night?
Art thou not Newton's pantocrator, weaving the woof of Locke?
To mortals thy mills seem everything, & the harrow of Shaddai
A scheme of human conduct invisible & incomprehensible.
Get to thy labours at the mills, & leave me to my wrath!'

                                   [*Design*]

15 Satan was going to reply, but Los rolled his loud thunders:

'Anger me not! Thou canst not drive the harrow in pity's paths.
Thy work is eternal death, with mills & ovens & cauldrons.
Trouble me no more: thou canst not have eternal life!'

So Los spoke, Satan trembling obeyed, weeping along the way.
20 *Mark well my words; they are of your eternal salvation.*

Between South Molton Street & Stratford Place, Calvary's foot,
Where the victims were preparing for sacrifice, their cherubim
Around their loins poured forth their arrows, & their bosoms beam

4.3. *mundane shell*] This fallen, material world: see 16.21–7 and especially
34.31.
4.6–8. Los speaks, words be related to the Blake–Hayley quarrel (see head-
note, p. 485). The lines are part of the quarrel between Satan and Palamabron:
Los reproves Satan for trying to leave his own task for someone else's.
4.11. *pantocrator*] The 'Universal Lord'; Newton's description of a
'Urizenic' God in his *Principia*.
4.12. *Shaddai*] 'Almighty' (see note on 13.23); one of the Seven Angels
of the Presence.
4. *Design*: Trilithons, huge stones with a tiny figure.
4.21. *South Molton Street*] B. lived here (at no. 17) after leaving Felpham
in Sept. 1803. It runs at a sharp angle into Oxford Street, opposite *Stratford
Place*, and Tyburn Brook (which follows the windings of Marylebone
Lane) passes close by, though now underground. (Map, p. 621). The ground
slopes up to the site of Tyburn gallows from the brook, and B. therefore
identifies this point with *Calvary's foot*.
4.22. *their cherubim*] Their spiritual guardians: perhaps in one sense B. him-
self, working nearby at his spiritual tasks.
4.23–5. *Around their loins . . .*] The victims, seen imaginatively, are not
dying but full of preparations for a new life.

With all colours of precious stones, & their inmost palaces
25 Resounded with preparation of animals wild & tame
(Mark well my words! Corporeal friends are spiritual enemies).
Mocking druidical, mathematical proportion of length, breadth,
height,
Displaying naked beauty, with flute & harp & song!

[*Design*]

Pl. 5 Palamabron with the fiery harrow in morning returning
From breathing fields: Satan fainted beneath the artillery:
Christ took on sin in the virgin's womb, & put it off on the cross.

All pitied the piteous, & was wrath with the wrathful; & Los
heard it.

5 And this is the manner of the daughters of Albion in their beauty:
Every one is threefold in head & heart & reins, & every one
Has three gates into the three heavens of Beulah which shine
Translucent, in their foreheads & their bosoms & their loins,
Surrounded with fires unapproachable: but whom they please
10 They take up into their heavens in intoxicating delight.
For the Elect cannot be redeemed, but created continually
By offering & atonement, in the cruelties of moral law.
Hence the three classes of men take their fixed destinations:
They are the two contraries, & the reasoning negative.

4.24. their inmost palaces] The vision changes; man is seen as a living city—
not a rigid, monumental one.
4. Design: A hill surmounted by three trilithons—symbols of the British
Druid priesthood, but recalling the three crosses on Calvary; other tri-
lithons in the distance. In the foreground, four female figures, gowned;
two spinning with distaff and spindle, two mourning.

Plate 5 is found only in copy D. It provides a rather confused collection of
additions to, and comments on, the Bard's story of Palamabron.
5.3. The three acts (of Palamabron, Satan and Christ) are simultaneous and
parallel. Satan introduced artillery into the war against heaven (*Paradise
Lost* vi 484ff).
5.5. DAUGHTERS OF ALBION] Here simply 'Englishwomen'; but B. sees them
imaginatively. Female beauty is a gate to the lesser dream-heaven of
Beulah. Cp. *Jerusalem* pl.14.*16–24n*; the concept is applied to Enitharmon
in *Four Zoas* i 255, ff.
5.11. Elect] B.'s lowest class, the self-righteous, who would take a negative
view of female 'intoxicating delight' (cp. 11.*17ff*). They are those against
whom Paul argues in *Galatians* and *Romans*, who cannot feel virtuous
without repeatedly fulfilling the earthly rites of blood or money sacrifice.
For may turn on *whom they please* (9): i.e. they do *not* please to take the
Elect.
5.14. For *contrary* and *negative* see *Jerusalem* pl.10.*7n*.

15 While the females prepare the victims, the males at furnaces
And anvils dance the dance of tears & pain: loud lightnings
Lash on their limbs as they turn the whirlwinds loose upon
The furnaces, lamenting around the anvils: & this their song.

'Ah weak & wide astray! Ah shut in narrow doleful form,
20 Creeping in reptile flesh upon the bosom of the ground!
The eye of man, a little narrow orb closed up & dark,
Scarcely beholding the great light conversing with the void:
The ear, a little shell in small volutions shutting out
All melodies, & comprehending only discord and harmony:
25 The tongue, a little moisture fills, a little food it cloys;
A little sound it utters, & its cries are faintly heard—
Then brings forth moral virtue the cruel Virgin Babylon.

Can such an eye judge of the stars? & looking through its tubes
Measure the sunny rays that point their spears on Udan-Adan
30 Can such an ear, filled with the vapours of the yawning pit,
Judge of the pure melodious harp struck by a hand divine?
Can such closed nostrils feel a joy? or tell of autumn fruits
When grapes & figs burst their covering to the joyful air?
Can such a tongue boast of the living waters? or take in
35 Ought but the vegetable ratio, & loathe the faint delight?
Can such gross lips perceive? alas! folded within themselves
They touch not ought, but pallid turn & tremble at every wind!'

Thus they sing, creating the three classes among druid rocks.
Charles calls on Milton for atonement: Cromwell is ready:
40 James calls for fires in Golgonooza, for heaps of smoking ruins
In the night of prosperity and wantonness which he himself created
Among the daughters of Albion, among the rocks of the druids;
When Satan fainted beneath the arrows of Elynittria
And mathematic proportion was subdued by living proportion.

Pl. 10Then Los & Enitharmon knew that Satan is Urizen,
Drawn down by Orc & the Shadowy Female into generation.

5.19–26. This passage occurs, rather differently, in *Jerusalem* pl.49.*32–41.*
5.27. Cp. *Everlasting Gospel* i *33–4,* p. 847 below. The 'Virgin' can produce only such a child of repression and harshness as this. Did B. imply birth-cries in *27*?
5.29. Udan-Adan] The dark lake of Ulro.
5.35. vegetable ratio] The understanding of truth as perceived by material (vegetable) nature. B. uses the word 'ratio' in a characteristic way; see *32.35n* and p. 877 below.
5.40–1. Cp. *Song of Los (Asia) 19–22.*
5.43. Cp. Leutha's speech, 11.35ff. esp. 12.*42–5.*

10.1–2. B. makes the connection between Satan and Urizen (see *7.9,* *8.19n* and *9.43n*) explicit. The myth has developed since *Urizen* (1794), including its rewriting in *Four Zoas*. None of the earlier forms make Orc

Oft Enitharmon entered weeping into the space, there appearing
An aged woman raving along the streets (the space is named
5   Canaan) then she returned to Los weary, frighted as from dreams.

(The nature of a female space is this: it shrinks the organs
Of life till they become finite, & itself seems infinite.
And Satan vibrated in the immensity of the space! Limited
To those without, but infinite to those within, it fell down and
10 Became Canaan—closing Los from Eternity in Albion's cliffs—
A mighty fiend against the Divine Humanity, mustering to war.)

'Satan, ah me, is gone to his own place,' said Los! 'Their God
I will not worship in their churches, nor king in their theatres. -
Elynittria! whence is this jealousy running along the mountains?
15 British women were not jealous when Greek & Roman were jealous.
Every thing in Eternity shines by its own internal light: but thou
Darkenest every internal light with the arrows of thy quiver,
Bound up in the horns of jealousy to a deadly fading moon:
And Ocalythron binds the sun into a jealous globe,
20 That every thing is fixed, opaque, without internal light!'

So Los lamented over Satan, who triumphant divided the nations.

[Design]

🐝

Pl. 18 And Tharmas, demon of the waters, & Orc, who is Luvah.

The Shadowy Female, seeing Milton, howled in her lamentation,
Over the deeps outstretching her twenty-seven heavens over Albion.

And thus the Shadowy Female howls, in articulate howlings:

a *cause* of Urizen's fall; on the contrary, he is elsewhere a *product* of the fallen universe which Urizen has made.

10.*5. Canaan*] A home of false religions, but also the promised land of Israel.

10.*6–7.* Thus Satan is so small that the space in which he is confined seems infinite–to himself alone, not to the immortals outside.

10.*11. fiend*] Satan, not Los.

10.*12–13.* Reflecting B.'s extreme religious views and his feelings which would lead him (for example) to abhor the practice of standing up to the National Anthem.

10.*14. Elynittria*] Palamabron's emanation, as appears in 11.*38*ff.

10.*19. Ocalythron*] Only a name, though perhaps Rintrah's emanation; cp. *Europe 49*, where the names are linked.

Design: A stone doorway, and an aged woman running (see *4*).

18.*3. Twenty-seven*] See 37.*35*n.

18.*4. The Shadowy Female*, not recognizing or not approving the true significance of Milton's act, means to lament it; but she reveals her own nature. The substance of her lamentations is cruelty and misery; she will cause cruelty and misery on earth, weaving them into a mourning

5   'I will lament over Milton in the lamentations of the afflicted!
     My garments shall be woven of sighs, & heart-broken lamentations:
     The misery of unhappy families shall be drawn out into its border,
     Wrought with the needle with dire sufferings, poverty, pain & woe
     Along the rocky island, & thence throughout the whole earth.
10   There shall be the sick father & his starving family! there
     The prisoner in the stone dungeon, & the slave at the mill!
     I will have writings written all over it in human words,
     That every infant that is born upon the earth shall read
     And get by rote as a hard task of a life of sixty years.
15   I will have kings enwoven upon it, & counsellors, & mighty men:
     The famine shall clasp it together with buckles & clasps,
     And the pestilence shall be its fringe, & the war its girdle;
     To divide into Rahab & Tirzah, that Milton may come to our tents!
     For I will put on the human form, & take the image of God,
20   Even pity & humanity: but my clothing shall be cruelty.
     And I will put on holiness as a breastplate & as a helmet,
     And all my ornaments shall be of the gold of broken hearts,
     And the precious stones of anxiety, & care & desperation & death,
     And repentance for sin & sorrow & punishment & fear,
25   To defend me from thy terrors, O Orc! my only beloved!'

     Orc answered: 'Take not the human form, O loveliest! Take not
     Terror upon thee! Behold, how I am & tremble lest thou also
     Consume in my consummation; but thou mayest take a form
     Female & lovely, that cannot consume in man's consummation.
30   Wherefore dost thou create & weave this Satan for a covering?
     When thou attemptest to put on the human form, my wrath
     Burns to the top of heaven against thee in jealousy & fear.
     Then I rend thee asunder, then I howl over thy clay & ashes:
     When wilt thou put on the female form as in times of old,
35   With a garment of pity & compassion like the garment of God?
     His garments are long-sufferings for the children of men:
     Jerusalem is his garment, & not thy Covering Cherub, O lovely
     Shadow of my delight, who wanderest seeking for the prey!'

     So spoke Orc, when Oothoon & Leutha hovered over his couch
40   Of fire, in interchange of beauty & perfection in the darkness;
     Opening interiorly into Jerusalem & Babylon, shining glorious
     In the Shadowy Female's bosom. Jealous her darkness grew:

garment, to make the earth mourn. Towards the end the purpose changes;
it is now to protect herself from Orc, whom she loves and fears. It may be
that the passage as a whole was already written, and 5 was added in order
to make it suit here.

18.*19*. 'I will pretend that such cruelties are God's will'—a common theme.

18.*26* Orc is heroic here, not corrupted as in *Four Zoas* viia.

18.*28* *Consume in my consummation*] See note on *consummation*, p. 877.

18.*32*. Her action has the opposite effect to that intended.

18.*38*. *shadow*] Not the reality.

Howlings filled all the desolate places in accusations of sin,
In female beauty shining in the unformed void: & Orc in vain
45 Stretched out his hands of fire, & wooed: they triumph in his pain.

Thus darkened the Shadowy Female tenfold, & Orc tenfold
Glowed on his rocky couch against the darkness: loud thunders
Told of the enormous conflict. Earthquakes beneath, around,
Rent the immortal females, limb from limb & joint from joint,
50 And moved the fast foundations of the earth to wake the dead.
Urizen emerged from his rocky form & from his snows,

❦

Pl. 32 And Milton oft sat upon the couch of death, & oft conversed
In vision & dream beatific with the seven Angels of the Presence:

'I have turned my back upon these Heavens builded on cruelty.
My spectre still wandering through them follows my emanation;
5 He hunts her footsteps through the snow & the wintry hail & rain.
The idiot reasoner laughs at the man of imagination,
And from laughter proceeds to murder by undervaluing calumny.'

Then Hillel, who is Lucifer, replied over the couch of death;
And thus the seven angels instructed him, & thus they converse:

10 'We are not individuals but states: combinations of individuals.
We were angels of the Divine Presence: & were druids in
Annandale,

18.51. Leads on to 19.1.

Plate 32.
This is not found in copies A and B. In copy C, the order is pls 31-32-33:
in copy D, pls 31-33-32. As both pls 32 and 33 are distinct and complete
'Visions of Beulah', this variation is not important.

32.4-5. spectre and emanation, broken fragments of personality, are at odds:
one hunts, the other flees. Cp. 'My spectre around me', p. 481.

32.8. Hillel] In Isaiah xiv 12, 'O Lucifer, son of the morning', the Hebrew
word for Lucifer is Helel. But Hillel was also a Rabbi living shortly before
the time of Christ, whose teaching in many respects resembled Christ's:
he may thus be thought of as the true Lucifer–'light-bearer'.

32.10-38. STATES] The crucial lines in this passage are 22-3. The angels (10)
are only one realization, or State, of the individual. B. wishes to find a way
of condemning Sin but not the sinner. The evildoer is 'in a state' of sin–of
Satan–but he himself is an immortal soul, or individual. When he is re-
deemed, his sinful nature is destroyed; but he himself returns to eternal life.
But while he is in a state of sin, his personality belongs to sin. Thus Satan
is the immortal Lucifer in a sinful state. When his sin is destroyed, he
ceases to be Satan, but he does not cease to exist. He puts off the State, and
is revealed in his true form as Lucifer. This idea of States was very import-
ant to B., who held the individual dear as an immortal and precious soul.
Cp. Four Zoas viii 367-9, Jerusalem pl.31.13n, and esp. pl. 49. 65-75.

Compelled to combine into form by Satan, the spectre of
   Albion,   כֹ

Who made himself a God & destroyed the human form   רבים
   divine.   as multitudes

But the Divine Humanity & Mercy gave us a human   Vox Populi
   form

15 Because we were combined in freedom & holy brotherhood;
    While these combined by Satan's tyranny, first in the blood of war
    And sacrifice, & next in chains of imprisonment, are shapeless rocks
    Retaining only Satan's mathematic holiness; length, breadth & height,
    Calling the human imagination–which is the Divine Vision &
      fruition

20 In which man liveth eternally–madness & blasphemy, against
    Its own qualities, which are servants of humanity, not gods or
      lords.
    Distinguish therefore states from individuals in those states.
    States change: but individual identities never change nor cease:
    You cannot go to eternal death in that which can never die.

25 Satan & Adam are states created into twenty-seven churches;
    And thou, O Milton, art a state about to be created,
    Called *Eternal Annihilation*; that none but the living shall
    Dare to enter: & they shall enter, triumphant over death
    And hell & the grave: states that are not, but ah! seem to be.

30 'Judge then of thy own self: thy eternal lineaments explore;
    What is eternal & what changeable? & what annihilable?
    The imagination is not a state: it is the human existence itself!
    Affection or love becomes a state, when divided from imagination.
    The memory is a state always, & the reason is a state

32.*11. Annandale*] Iron Age hill forts, the 'Deil's Dyke', and a rocking stone
in Annandale would be adequate as Druid relics for B. But John Adlard
has pointed out that B. may have been thinking of certain oak groves in
Annandale, taking them, according to common tradition, to be druidical.
See also *Jerusalem* 63.*1.*

32.*12–13.* The Hebrew word should read כרבים: the mistake is B.'s, who
apparently wanted to write *Kerabim*, the Hebrew for 'as multitudes', but in-
stead wrote a word suggesting *Cherubim*, though approximately; the letters
as they stand (R to L) are: kh, r, b, m. The trilingual gloss recalls the three
languages in which Christ's accusation was posted on his cross (Greek,
Latin, Hebrew: cp. *Luke* xxiii 38). See note on the Covering Cherub, 37.*8.*
32.*18.* Cp. 4.*27* (another interpolated plate): 'Mocking druidical math-
ematical proportion of length, breadth, height.'
32.*26. a state about to be created*] i.e. about to be given mortal form in the
material world.
32.*29. states that are not*] They are essentially unreal; only the true, inner
personality is real.

BIBLICAL PALESTINE
to illustrate Blake's works

Tribal names.......ASHER

0   10   20   30
Miles

Damascus ●

Sidon

ARAM

Mt Hermon

Lebanon

Beth-Rehob

Tyre

Hazor

OG'

BASHAN

ASHER

NAPHTALI

Land of Cabul

Mt Carmel

ZEBULUN

ISSACHAR

MANASSEH

GILEAD

MANASSEH

Tirzah

Mahanaim?

AMMON

R. Kanah

Mt Ebal

Shechem

Mt Gerizim

Adam

R. Jabbok

Succoth

EPHRAIM

R. Jordan

Shiloh

GAD

Zaretan

DAN

Boundary of northern and
southern kingdoms.

Jericho

Rabbath

SIHON

Ekron

BENJAMIN

Gilgal

Heshbon

Ashdod

Jerusalem

Stone of
Bohan

Mt Peora

Gath?

Vale of
Rephaim

Mt Nebo

Ashkelon

Bethlehem
Ephratha

Machpelah

PHILISTIA

JUDAH?

REUBEN

Gaza

Hebron
(Mamre)

Salt or Dead Sea

Abarim Mts.

R. Arnon

AMALEK

MOAB

EDOM

K.C.JORDAN

35   Created to be annihilated & a new ratio created.
Whatever can be created can be annihilated: forms cannot.
The oak is cut down by the axe, the lamb falls by the knife;
But their forms eternal exist, for ever. Amen! Hallelujah!'

Thus they converse with the dead, watching round the couch of
death.

40   For God himself enters death's door always with those that enter,
And lays down in the grave with them, in visions of Eternity:
Till they awake & see Jesus, & the linen clothes lying
That the females had woven for them, & the gates of their Father's
house.

29 The 'Pickering Manuscript'

This MS is so-called after a nineteenth-century owner. It can only be dated
conjecturally, but in a letter of 16 Aug. 1803 B. quotes a line from 'Mary',
with a continuation adapted to his own state (see p. 475). 'Long John
Brown' and 'William Bond' are poems with a similar village background,
perhaps suggesting a like date within the Felpham period. 'The Grey
Monk' is derived from the Notebook (see p. 478), and seems to derive
from a combination of circumstances in 1804; it carries 'The Golden
Net', in the same group in the Notebook, with it. These details suggest
that the Pickering MS is not earlier than 1804 as it stands. The development
of thought and imagery of 'The Mental Traveller' to some extent supports
this, though this poem may be as early as 1801–02. The other poems pro-
vide no clues. These considerations suggest a date for the MS, which is a
neat fair copy (with a few alterations, notably in 'The Mental Traveller'),
of about 1805: most editors, however, from Sampson (1905) to Erdman
(1965) have preferred, partly on subjective grounds, partly on the evidence
of 'Mary', a date *c.* 1803.

I THE SMILE

There is a smile of love,
And there is a smile of deceit;
And there is a smile of smiles
In which these two smiles meet.

5   And there is a frown of hate,
And there is a frown of disdain;
And there is a frown of frowns
Which you strive to forget in vain,

32.35. *ratio*] A rational scheme. See *OED*'s first meaning 'rationale',
('obs. rare'): with the example: 'In this consists the ratio and essential
ground of the Gospel Doctrine' (1752).

For it sticks in the heart's deep core,
10 And it sticks in the deep backbone;
And no smile that ever was smiled,
But only one smile alone

That betwixt the cradle and grave
It only once smiled can be;
15 But when it once is smiled
There's an end to all misery.

II THE GOLDEN NET

Three virgins at the break of day—
'Whither young man, whither away?
Alas for woe! alas for woe!'
They cry, and tears for ever flow.
5 The one was clothed in flames of fire,
The other clothed in iron wire,
The other clothed in tears and sighs,
Dazzling bright before my eyes.
They bore a net of golden twine
10 To hang upon the branches fine.
Pitying I wept to see the woe
That love and beauty undergo;
To be consumed in burning fires
And in ungratified desires,
15 And in tears clothed night and day,
Melted all my soul away.
When they saw my tears, a smile
That did heaven itself beguile
Bore the golden net aloft
20 As on downy pinions soft,
Over the morning of my day.

¶ 29.ii 1. *Three virgins*] Virginal not for their purity, but because they repel the man whose desire they have encouraged. The tears (4), as so often in B., are artificial.

ii 9. *a net*] The lover is trapped by his pity for the virgins, who have invited him to come to them, but will grant him only imprisonment where he can see them. The *net* is an image used by B. in *Urizen, Four Zoas* vi, and *Jerusalem*; he often calls it Urizen's 'net (or web) of religion', but other characteristics are seen here—it traps a man through his own weakness and is used by the female for her own ends.

ii 11. *Pitying*] A dangerous emotion for B., as it 'divides the soul, and man unmans' (*Milton* pl.8.19–20). The speaker pities the virgins for their ungratified desire, and so they capture him.

Underneath the net I stray,
Now entreating Burning Fire
Now entreating Iron Wire
25   Now entreating Tears and Sighs.
Oh, when will the morning rise?

III THE MENTAL TRAVELLER

I travelled through a land of men,
A land of men and women too,
And heard and saw such dreadful things
As cold earth wanderers never knew.

5   For there the babe is born in joy
That was begotten in dire woe,
Just as we reap in joy the fruit
Which we in bitter tears did sow;

And if the babe is born a boy
10   He's given to a woman old,
Who nails him down upon a rock,
Catches his shrieks in cups of gold.

She binds iron thorns around his head,
She pierces both his hands and feet,
15   She cuts his heart out at his side
To make it feel both cold & heat.

Her fingers number every nerve
Just as a miser counts his gold;
She lives upon his shrieks and cries—
20   And she grows young as he grows old,

Till he becomes a bleeding youth
And she becomes a virgin bright;
Then he rends up his manacles
And binds her down for his delight.

iii *10. a woman old*] She resembles Vala who, in her other semblances as
Rahab, or Tirzah, appears in the three long epics and behaves like the
woman here. In *Four Zoas* viii *287*ff, *Milton* pl.19.*48*ff, *Jerusalem* pl.67.*24–5*,
*41*ff, Tirzah torments man as the woman does here in *11–20*, in order to
control him. It is her intent to keep him bound to this world so that she
may dominate. The image of *20* is found only in this poem.
iii *12. cups of gold*] Deriving from the cup of the Scarlet Woman who, in
Revelation xvii 4, holds 'a golden cup . . . full of abominations'.
iii *13–15.* The references to the crucifixion are clear.
iii *23. he rends up . . .*] So Orc tears himself free and seizes the virgin in the
early *America* (Preludium), and also in *Four Zoas* viib *137*. But the outcome

25   He plants himself in all her nerves
     Just as a husbandman his mould,
     And she becomes his dwelling-place
     And garden, fruitful seventyfold.

     An aged shadow soon he fades,
30   Wandering round an earthly cot,
     Full filled all with gems and gold
     Which he by industry had got.

     And these are the gems of the human soul:
     The rubies and pearls of a lovesick eye,
35   The countless gold of the aching heart,
     The martyr's groan, and the lover's sigh.

     They are his meat, they are his drink:
     He feeds the beggar and the poor
     And the wayfaring traveller;
40   For ever open is his door.

     His grief is their eternal joy,
     They make the roofs and walls to ring—
     Till from the fire on the hearth
     A little female babe does spring!

45   And she is all of solid fire
     And gems and gold, that none his hand
     Dares stretch to touch her baby form,
     Or wrap her in his swaddling-band.

     But she comes to the man she loves,
50   If young or old, or rich or poor;
     They soon drive out the aged host,
     A beggar at another's door.

     He wanders weeping far away
     Until some other take him in;
55   Oft blind and age-bent, sore distressed,
     Until he can a maiden win.

     And to allay his freezing age
     The poor man takes her in his arms:
     The cottage fades before his sight,

is different here; her desirability drains the vitality from him and so per-
petuates female dominance.
iii 45–8. The woman, as mother, binds the man, as child, in swaddling-
bands; no man can do the same to a woman. Thus she dominates him as
mother or mistress; and (51) causes her new man-subject to drive out the
now useless old one.
iii 59–60 indicate a Felpham date, as do the references to cottage life and
hospitality throughout the poem.

60   The garden and its lovely charms;

       The guests are scattered through the land
       (For the eye altering, alters all);
       The senses roll themselves in fear,
       And the flat earth becomes a ball,

65   The stars, sun, moon, all shrink away—
       A desert vast without a bound,
       And nothing left to eat or drink
       And a dark desert all around.

       The honey of her infant lips,
70   The bread and wine of her sweet smile,
       The wild game of her roving eye
       Does him to infancy beguile.

       For as he eats and drinks he grows
       Younger and younger every day;
75   And on the desert wild they both
       Wander in terror and dismay.

       Like the wild stag she flees away;
       Her fear plants many a thicket wild,
       While he pursues her night & day,
80   By various arts of love beguiled,

       By various arts of love and hate,
       Till the wide desert planted o'er
       With labyrinths of wayward love,
       Where roams the lion, wolf and boar,

85   Till he becomes a wayward babe
       And she a weeping woman old.
       Then many a lover wanders here,
       The sun and stars are nearer rolled,

       The trees bring forth sweet ecstasy
90   To all who in the desert roam,
       Till many a city there is built,
       And many a pleasant shepherd's home.

       But when they find the frowning babe
       Terror strikes through the region wide;

iii *64. flat earth*] B. believed that the earth was flat, or round, according to the observer's vision. Thus, in *Milton* pl.15.23ff, the 'traveller through eternity' sees one universe, which he has left, rolled up behind him like a ball, while the one he is entering is spread out before him extended and flat.

iii *84. roams*] So the MS. *Erdman 1965*, p. 777 suggests that the 'lion, wolf and boar' are all manifestations of the single man, pursuing the 'stag' of 77.

95   They cry, 'The Babe! the Babe is born!'
    And flee away on every side.

    For who dare touch the frowning form
    His arm is withered to its root,
    Lions, boars, wolves, all howling flee
100   And every tree does shed its fruit;

    ' And none can touch that frowning form,
    Except it be a woman old;
    She nails him down upon the rock,
    And all is done as I have told.

IV THE LAND OF DREAMS

    'Awake, awake! my little boy,
    Thou wast thy mother's only joy.
    Why dost thou weep in thy gentle sleep?
    Awake! thy father does thee keep.'

5   'O what land is the land of dreams?
    What are its mountains and what are its streams?
    O father, I saw my mother there
    Among the lilies by waters fair.

    'Among the lambs clothed in white
10   She walked with her Thomas in sweet delight:
    I wept for joy, like a dove I mourn;
    O when shall I again return?'

    'Dear child, I also by pleasant streams
    Have wandered all night in the land of dreams,
15   But though calm and warm the waters wide,
    I could not get to the other side.'

    'Father, O father, what do we here
    In this land of unbelief and fear?
    The land of dreams is better far
20   Above the light of the morning star.'

iii *95. the Babe is born!*] Heralding the birth, as Christ's birth was heralded–
but here there is fear, not joy, for everyone recognizes the terrible power
of this being. This is not necessarily an evil power; it may only be the
vitality of its human force that makes it dangerous. This is in line with B.'s
idea of a heaven of fierce flames and infinite vigour: cp. *Milton* pl.30.*21–2*:
'Nor could they [the female emanations] live / Because the life of Man was
too exceeding unbounded.'
iii *101–2. none can touch . . . woman old*] Man is a terrible, fierce and vital
creature–tamed by the woman.

V MARY

Sweet Mary, the first time she ever was there
Came into the ballroom among the fair.
The young men and maidens around her throng,
And these are the words upon every tongue:

5   'An angel is here from the heavenly climes!
Or again does return the golden times?
Her eyes outshine every brilliant ray,
She opens her lips—'tis the month of May!'

Mary moves in soft beauty and conscious delight
10   To augment with sweet smiles all the joys of the night,
Nor once blushes to own to the rest of the fair
That sweet love and beauty are worthy our care.

In the morning the villagers rose with delight
And repeated with pleasure the joys of the night;
15   And Mary arose among friends to be free—
But no friend from henceforward thou, Mary, shalt
see!

Some said she was proud, some called her a whore,
And some when she passed by shut to the door.
A damp cold came o'er her, her blushes all fled,
20   Her lilies and roses are blighted and shed.

'O why was I born with a different face,
Why was I not born like this envious race?
Why did heaven adorn me with bountiful hand,
And then set me down in an envious land?

25   'To be weak as a lamb and smooth as a dove,
And not to raise envy is called Christian love;
But if you raise envy, your merit's to blame
For planting such spite in the weak and the tame.

'I will humble my beauty, I will not dress fine;
30   I will keep from the ball and my eyes shall not shine;
And if any girl's lover forsakes her for me
I'll refuse him my hand, and from envy be free.

She went out in morning attired plain and neat;
'Proud Mary's gone mad!' said the child in the street.
35   She went out in morning in plain neat attire,
And came home in evening bespattered with mire.

---

v 21. B. quoted this line, with a different continuation, in his letter to
Butts, 16 Aug. 1803 (p. 475).

She trembled and wept, sitting on the bed-side;
She forgot it was night and she trembled and cried;
She forgot it was night, she forgot it was morn,
40 Her soft memory imprinted with faces of scorn—

With faces of scorn and with eyes of disdain
Like foul fiends inhabiting Mary's mild brain.
She remembers no face like the human-divine—
All faces have envy, sweet Mary, but thine.

45 And thine is a face of sweet love in despair,
And thine is a face of mild sorrow and care,
And thine is a face of wild terror and fear
That shall never be quiet till laid on its bier.

VI THE CRYSTAL CABINET

The maiden caught me in the wild
Where I was dancing merrily,
She put me into her cabinet
And locked me up with a golden key.

5 This cabinet is formed of gold
And pearl and crystal shining bright,
And within, it opens into a world
And a little lovely moony night.

Another England there I saw,
10 Another London with its Tower,
Another Thames and other hills,
And another pleasant Surrey bower,

Another maiden like herself,
Translucent, lovely, shining clear,
15 Threefold each in the other closed—
Oh, what a pleasant trembling fear!

vi 3–4. This image of love goes as far back as *Poetical Sketches* (pp. 8–9). Was B. also inspired by a triple mirror?

vi 9. *Another . . .*] The lover sees the world anew with 'other eyes'.

vi 12. *Surrey bower*] Unidentified; not likely to be Lambeth, though that is in Surrey; Felpham is in Sussex.

vi 15. *Threefold*] The female land of Beulah is threefold–one short of four-fold perfection. (See also *8*, and *Jerusalem 69.16–24* and *Milton 30.1n.*) This poem reflects B.'s attitude to Beulah misused–a use of its female charms, and its pleasant limitations, as if they were all that humanity needs. The image of a pleasant enclosing space created for man to rest in–usually a feminine creation; the 'moony night' of *8*, and the 'translucent' loveliness of *14*: all are facets of Beulah developed in the three long epics.

Oh, what a smile, a threefold smile,
Filled me that like a flame I burned.
I bent to kiss the lovely maid
20   And found a threefold kiss returned.

I strove to seize the inmost form
With ardour fierce and hands of flame,
But burst the crystal cabinet
And like a weeping babe became,

25   A weeping babe upon the wild,
And weeping woman, pale, reclined;
And in the outward air again
I filled with woes the passing wind.

VII THE GREY MONK

'I die, I die!' the mother said,
'My children die for lack of bread –
What more has the merciless tyrant said?'
The monk sat down on the stony bed.

5   The blood red ran from the grey monk's side,
His hands and feet were wounded wide,
His body bent, his arms and knees
Like to the roots of ancient trees.

His eye was dry, no tear could flow;
10   A hollow groan first spoke his woe,
He trembled and shuddered upon the bed;
At length with a feeble cry he said:

'When God commanded this hand to write
In the studious hours of deep midnight,
15   He told me the writing I wrote should prove
The bane of all that on earth I loved.

'My brother starved between two walls;
His children's cry my soul appals.
I mocked at the rack and griding chain,
20   My bent body mocks their torturing pain.

'Thy father drew his sword in the north;
With his thousands strong he marched forth;

vi *21. seize the inmost form*] He tries to go beyond the kiss, and beyond the
threefold, and breaks the illusion.
vi *24–6.* Cp. 'The Mental Traveller' for the weeping babe and women.
vii. For draft, see p. 478 above: for its probable origins in early 1804, see
headnote, draft and *Jerusalem* pls. 36.*61n* and 37.*1*.

Thy brother has armed himself in steel
To avenge the wrongs thy children feel.

25 'But vain the sword, and vain the bow;
They never can work war's overthrow.
The hermit's prayer, and the widow's tear
Alone can free the world from fear.

'For a tear is an intellectual thing,
30 And a sigh is the sword of an angel king,
And the bitter groan of the martyr's woe
Is an arrow from the Almighty's bow.'

The hand of vengeance found the bed
To which the purple tyrant fled;
35 The iron hand crushed the tyrant's head,
And became a tyrant in his stead.

VIII AUGURIES OF INNOCENCE

To see a world in a grain of sand
And a heaven in a wild flower,
Hold infinity in the palm of your hand
And eternity in an hour.
5 A robin redbreast in a cage
Puts all Heaven in a rage,
A dove-house filled with doves and pigeons
Shudders Hell through all its regions.
A dog starved at his master's gate
10 Predicts the ruin of the state.
A horse misused upon the road
Calls to Heaven for human blood.
Each outcry of the hunted hare
A fibre from the brain does tear.
15 A skylark wounded in the wing,
A cherubim does cease to sing.

vii 29. *intellectual*] In B.'s vocabulary, this means 'existing in the realms of the mind and of imagination': not merely 'academic'.
vii 32. B. has no quotation marks; the MS does not show where the Monk's speech ends.
viii. These couplets are written down in a fair copy but in no evident order. Different alternative arrangements have been suggested by Sampson (1905) and Erdman (1965). Lines 55–62 seem to benefit by rearrangement thus: 59–62, 55–58, so that 'it should be so' (55) has an evident antecedent. But it is not impossible that 55 refers back to 53–4, the sense continuing to 59: then a new sequence begins at 60. The apparent reiteration and looseness of the entire series should not be permitted to obscure its excellence.

20+B.

The gamecock clipped and armed for fight
Does the rising sun affright.
Every wolf's and lion's howl
20   Raises from Hell a human soul.
The wild deer wandering here and there
Keeps the human soul from care.
The lamb misused breeds public strife,
And yet forgives the butcher's knife.
25   The bat that flits at close of eve
Has left the brain that won't believe.
The owl that calls upon the night
Speaks the unbeliever's fright.
He who shall hurt the little wren
30   Shall never be beloved by men.
He who the ox to wrath has moved
Shall never be by woman loved.
The wanton boy that kills the fly
Shall feel the spider's enmity.
35   He who torments the chafer's sprite
Weaves a bower in endless night.
The caterpillar on the leaf
Repeats to thee thy mother's grief.
Kill not the moth nor butterfly,
40   For the Last Judgement draweth nigh.
He who shall train the horse to war
Shall never pass the polar bar.
The beggar's dog and widow's cat—
Feed them and thou wilt grow fat.
45   The gnat that sings his summer's song
Poison gets from slander's tongue.
The poison of the snake and newt
Is the sweat of envy's foot;
The poison of the honey bee
50   Is the artist's jealousy.
The prince's robes and beggar's rags
Are toadstools on the miser's bags.
A truth that's told with bad intent
Beats all the lies you can invent.
55   It is right it should be so;
Man was made for joy and woe,
And when this we rightly know
Through the world we safely go.
Joy and woe are woven fine,
60   A clothing for the soul divine.
Under every grief and pine
Runs a joy with silken twine.

The babe is more than swaddling bands:
Throughout all these human lands
65 Tools were made and born were hands—
Every farmer understands.
Every tear from every eye
Becomes a babe in eternity;
This is caught by females bright
70 And returned to its own delight.
The bleat, the bark, bellow and roar
Are waves that beat on heaven's shore.
The babe that weeps the rod beneath
Writes *Revenge!* in realms of death.
75 The beggar's rags fluttering in air
Does to rags the heavens tear.
The soldier armed with sword and gun
Palsied strikes the summer's sun.
The poor man's farthing is worth more
80 Than all the gold on Afric's shore.
One mite wrung from the labourer's hands
Shall buy and sell the miser's lands;
Or if protected from on high
Does that whole nation sell and buy.
85 He who mocks the infant's faith
Shall be mocked in age and death.
He who shall teach the child to doubt
The rotting grave shall ne'er get out.
He who respects the infant's faith
90 Triumphs over hell and death.
The child's toys and the old man's reasons
Are the fruits of the two seasons.
The questioner who sits so sly
Shall never know how to reply.
95 He who replies to words of doubt
Doth put the light of knowledge out.
The strongest poison ever known
Came from Caesar's laurel crown.
Nought can deform the human race
100 Like to the armour's iron brace.
When gold and gems adorn the plough
To peaceful arts shall envy bow.
A riddle, or the cricket's cry,
Is to doubt a fit reply.
105 The emmet's inch and eagle's mile
Make lame philosophy to smile.
He who doubts from what he sees
Will ne'er believe, do what you please.

If the sun and moon should doubt
110   They'd immediately go out.
To be in a passion you good may do,
But no good if a passion is in you.
The whore and gambler by the state
Licenced build that nation's fate.
115   The harlot's cry from street to street
Shall weave old England's winding sheet;
The winner's shout, the loser's curse
Dance before dead England's hearse.
Every night and every morn
120   Some to misery are born;
Every morn and every night
Some are born to sweet delight.
Some are born to sweet delight,
Some are born to endless night.
125   We are led to believe a lie
When we see not through the eye,
Which was born in a night to perish in a night,
When the soul slept in beams of light.
God appears and God is light
130   To those poor souls who dwell in night,
But does a human form display
To those who dwell in realms of day.

IX LONG JOHN BROWN AND LITTLE MARY BELL

Little Mary Bell had a fairy in a nut,
Long John Brown had the devil in his gut;
Long John Brown loved little Mary Bell,
And the fairy drew the devil into the nut-shell.

5   Her fairy skipped out and her fairy skipped in,
He laughed at the Devil saying 'Love is a sin!'
The Devil he raged and the Devil he was wroth,
And the Devil entered into the young man's broth.

He was soon in the gut of the loving young swain,
10   For John ate and drank to drive away love's pain.
But all he could do he grew thinner & thinner,
Though he ate and drank as much as ten men for his
dinner.

Some said he had a wolf in his stomach day and night,
Some said he had the Devil, and they guessed right.

ix. As in 'The Fairy' (c. 1792, p. 161) and 'A fairy skipped' (?1805, p. 591),
the fairy is mischievous, and in particular an instigator of flirtations. So in
'William Bond' below.

15   The fairy skipped about in his glory, joy and pride,
And he laughed at the Devil till poor John Brown died.

Then the fairy skipped out of the old nutshell—
And woe and alack for pretty Mary Bell!
For the Devil crept in when the fairy skipped out—
20   And there goes Miss Bell with her fusty old nut.

X WILLIAM BOND

I wonder whether the girls are mad,
And I wonder whether they mean to kill,
And I wonder if William Bond will die,
For assuredly he is very ill.

5   He went to church in a May morning
Attended by fairies, one, two and three;
But the angels of providence drove them away,
And he returned home in misery.

He went not out to the field nor fold,
10   He went not out to the village nor town,
But he came home in a black, black cloud,
And took to his bed and there lay down.

And an angel of providence at his feet,
And an angel of providence at his head,
15   And in the midst a black, black cloud,
And in the midst the sick man on his bed.

And on his right hand was Mary Green,
And on his left hand was his sister Jane,
And their tears fell through the black, black cloud
20   To drive away the sick man's pain.

'O William, if thou dost another love,
Dost another love better than poor Mary,
Go and take that other to be thy wife
And Mary Green shall her servant be.'

x. The first stanza is almost indistinguishable from a Wordsworthian *Lyrical Ballads* opening. This *may* indicate direct influence from the first or second edition; or, with equal probability, merely that B. was responsive—especially perhaps at Felpham–to the same influences as Wordsworth.
x *6–7. fairies . . . angels of providence*] For *fairies* see ix above. The *angels* are more ambiguous: sometimes B.'s angels are protective (see note on the contemporary 'Angels of the Presence', *Milton* pl.14.42); but they may also be over-prudent guardians.

25 'Yes, Mary, I do another love;
　　Another I love far better than thee,
　　And another I will have for my wife—
　　Then what have I to do with thee?

　　'For thou art melancholy pale
30 And on thy head is the cold moon's shine;
　　But she is ruddy and bright as day,
　　And the sunbeams dazzle from her eyne.'

　　Mary trembled and Mary chilled
　　And Mary fell down on the right-hand floor,
35 That William Bond and his sister Jane
　　Scarce could recover Mary more.

　　When Mary woke and found her laid
　　On the right hand of her William dear,
　　On the right hand of his loved bed,
40 And saw her William Bond so near,

　　The fairies that fled from William Bond
　　Danced around her shining head;
　　They danced over the pillow white,
　　And the angels of providence left the bed.

45 'I thought love lived in the hot sunshine,
　　But oh, he lives in the moony light;
　　I thought to find love in the heat of day,
　　But sweet love is the comforter of night.'

　　Seek love in the pity of others' woe,
50 In the gentle relief of another's care, ·
　　In the darkness of night and the winter's snow,
　　In the naked and outcast, seek Love there.

30 To Tirzah

This poem is in *Songs of Experience*, but in the later copies only. The style of lettering dates the plate after mid-1803, and the poem probably belongs to 1804–05 or after 1809 (i.e. with the writing of *Milton* or the rewriting of *Four Zoas*). Tirzah first appears in *Milton* (see pl.17.11n), and again in *Jerusalem* and *Four Zoas* (especially viii *283*ff). She is the cruel queen of earthly life, who torments the soul of man and binds him as a sacrifice to mortal existence. Cp. also *Jerusalem* pls. *56.3–43*, *64.12–17*.

x *32*. *eyne*] A word B. would find in ballads.
x *45*, *49*. The quotation marks are editorial; B. has none.

TO TIRZAH

Whate'er is born of mortal birth
Must be consumed with the earth,
To rise from generation free;
Then what have I to do with thee?

5 The sexes, sprung from shame and pride,
Blowed in the morn—in evening died.
But mercy changed death into sleep;
The sexes rose to work and weep.

Thou mother of my mortal part,
10 With cruelty didst mould my heart,
And with false self-deceiving tears,
Didst bind my nostrils, eyes and ears,

Didst close my tongue in senseless clay
And me to mortal life betray.
15 The death of Jesus set me free.
Then what have I to do with thee?

31 'A fairy skipped'

Date. Uncertain. The poem is found on the reverse of a pencil drawing of
the infant Hercules. There is no external evidence of date, but *11–12* are
reminiscent of Beulah (see *Milton* pl.30.1n), and *13–14* of B.'s later de-
velopment of the idea of self-sacrifice. The matter of the poem–female

¶ 30.4. *What have I . . .?*] From *Matthew* xii 46–50, where Christ's mother
and brothers came to see him as he was teaching, and having asked 'Who
is my mother? and who are my brethren?' he answered by pointing to his
followers. The actual words are not found in this passage, but are addressed
to Jesus himself by two demon-possessed men (*Matthew* viii 29): 'What
have we to do with thee, Jesus, thou Son of God?'; and by the woman with
whom Elijah lodged (*1 Kings* xvii 18), who said when her son died, 'What
have I to do with thee, O thou man of God?'—whereupon Elijah revived
the child. B. has taken the idea from one place, and the phrase from his
memory of several.
7–8. The sleep, and the tearful labour, are those of this mortal world, the
home of restricted, sexual 'life'.
10. with cruelty] To B. parental upbringing and guidance is often seen as
cruel; cp. 'Infant Sorrow' and 'A Little Boy Lost' (*Songs of Experience*,
pp. 213 and 217). Tirzah's cruelty is most fully developed in *Four Zoas* viii
282–310.
Design: Below the text two female figures are raising a fallen man; an old
man offers him a drink. On the old man's gown is inscribed 'It is raised a
spiritual Body' (*1 Corinthians* xv 44, from Paul's discussion of the resurrec-
tion of the soul and the body).

adornment—may suggest a London rather than a Felpham origin. Keynes
dated the poem *c.* 1793, perhaps from the other 'fairy' poems in the Note-
book and *Europe*, but this would seem far too early. Cp. the previous poem.

> A fairy skipped upon my knee,
> Singing and dancing merrily.
> I said, 'Thou thing of patches, rings,
> Pins, necklaces and suchlike things,
> 5 Disguiser of the female form,
> Thou paltry, guilded poisonous worm!'
> Weeping he fell upon my thigh
> And thus in tears did soft reply:
> 'Knowest thou not, O fairies' lord,
> 10 How much by us contemned, abhorred,
> Whatever hides the female form
> That cannot bear the mental storm?
> Therefore in pity still we give
> Our lives to make the female live,
> 15 And what would turn into disease
> We turn to what will joy and please.'

32 'Grown old in love . . .'

On p. 54 of the Notebook. If it is to be taken literally, and B. was forty-
nine when he wrote it, this couplet dates from mid-1806 to mid-1807.

> Grown old in love from seven till seven times seven,
> I oft have wished for hell for ease from heaven.

33 To the Queen

This is the dedication of B.'s drawings to the edition of Blair's *The Grave*,
published by Cromek in 1808. It was intended to accompany B.'s vignette
of Queen Charlotte; Cromek returned the vignette with an insulting
letter, but printed the verses.

> The door of death is made of gold
> That mortal eyes cannot behold;

¶ 31.5. *Disguiser . . . form*] The fairy is the spirit which encourages women
to adorn themselves, in a sort of 'disguise'. The fairy's reply is that woman
must protect herself, at least in this world, if not in Eternity, from the over-
whelming vitality of 'mental' (i.e. spiritual) energy. This the fairy helps
her to do by the arts of feminine allurement (see *15–16*).

But, when the mortal eyes are closed,
And cold and pale the limbs reposed,
5   The soul awakes and wondering sees
In her mild hand the golden keys.
The grave is heaven's golden gate,
And rich and poor around it wait;
O Shepherdess of England's fold,
10   Behold this gate of pearl and gold!

To dedicate to England's Queen
The visions that my soul has seen,
And, by her kind permission, bring
What I have borne on solemn wing
15   From the vast regions of the grave,
Before her throne my wings I wave,
Bowing before my Sovereign's feet;
'The grave produced these blossoms sweet
In mild repose from earthly strife–
20   The blossoms of Eternal Life!'

34 Miscellaneous Notebook Verses, *c.* 1807–9

These verses and epigrams are scattered between pp. 21 and 89 of B.'s Notebook. On pp. 604–19 below are further verses which can be more certainly assigned to dates between 1809 and 1812; the verses below are much less certainly datable. They are unlikely to be before late 1806, but they may well overlap the later groups and may belong to any date up to about 1813. Since they chiefly concern B.'s business and artistic affairs around 1808–09, they are grouped together here, in the order they appear in the Notebook; the page is indicated in square brackets in the margin of the text.

The affairs referred to are: (*a*) Cromek's swindling of B. by asking him to design illustrations to Blair's *Grave*, and then giving the more profitable engraving of the designs to a fashionable engraver, Schiavonetti (who was unaware of the understanding); (*b*) Stothard's exhibition in May 1807 of a painting of the Canterbury Pilgrims, done at the suggestion of Cromek, who had stolen the idea from B. in 1806 (though Stothard seems to have been an innocent party, B. thought the worst); (*c*) attacks on B. in the *Examiner*, by Leigh and Robert Hunt, from August 1808, culminating in the insulting review of B.'s exhibition, in September 1809; and (*d*) B.'s exhibition which opened in May 1809; see also pp. 604ff below. In these verses, B. used the following abbreviations: Cr–– for Cromek, F–– for Flaxman, S–– for Stothard, and H–– for Hayley (except nos. ii and v: see notes).

20*

I

[21]   You don't believe, I won't attempt to make ye.
        You are asleep, I won't attempt to wake ye.
        Sleep on, sleep on, while in your pleasant dreams
        Of reason you may drink of life's clear streams.
  5   Reason and Newton, they are quite two things,
        For so the swallow and the sparrow sings.
        Reason says *Miracle*; Newton says *Doubt*—
        Aye, that's the way to make all Nature out:
        Doubt, doubt and don't believe without experiment!
 10   That is the very thing that Jesus meant
        When he said 'Only believe'; believe and try,
        Try, try and never mind the reason why!

II

[24]   The Sussex men are noted fools
           And weak is their brain pan;
           I wonder if H—— the painter
           Is not a Sussex man?

III

[24]   ... old acquaintance we'll renew:
        Prospero had one Caliban and I have two.

IV

[25]   Madman I have been called, fool they call thee:
        I wonder which they envy, thee or me?

V TO H——

[25]   You think Fuseli is not a great painter. I'm glad—
        This is one of the best compliments he ever had.

¶ 34.i *11. said*] After this word, B. first wrote 'Rich'; he must have had in mind the advice of Jesus to the rich man to give up all his possessions and follow him, with the later comment, 'With God all things are possible' (*Matthew* xix 21–6).

ii *1. Sussex men*] Sussex has long had a reputation, among Londoners, for 'backwardness'.

ii *3. H——*] The accepted reference is to Samuel Haines (1778–1848), an engraver and painter, as B. was. Work by both is in Boydell's *Shakespeare* (1802) and Hayley's *Life of Romney* (1809).

iii *1*. This line is written over an erasure, which can be partially read: 'Look(?) ... Flaxman & Stothard do'. Thus the identity of the 'two Calibans' is clear. B. may have intended to retain the first two words in his new line: '*Look? how old* ...'.

v. *To H——*] Robert Hunt, who decried Fuseli in 1806.

VI TO F––

[26]   I mock thee not, though I by thee am mocked:
Thou call'st me madman, but I call thee blockhead.

VII

[26]   He's a blockhead who wants a proof of what he can't
perceive––
And he's a fool who tries to make such a blockhead
believe.

VIII

[27]   S–– in childhood on the nursery floor
Was extreme old and most extremely poor.
He is grown old and rich and what he will;
He is extreme old and extreme poor still.

IX TO NANCY F––

[27]   How can I help thy husband's copying me?
Should that make differences 'twixt me and thee?

X

[27]   Of H––'s birth this was the happy lot:
His mother on his father him begot.

XI

[29]   Cr–– loves artists as he loves his meat.
He loves the art; but 'tis the art to cheat.

XII

[29]   A petty sneaking knave I knew––
'O Mr Cr––, how do ye do?'

XIII

[30]   He has observed the golden rule,
Till he's become the golden fool.

[30]   ### XIV TO S––D
You all your youth observed the golden rule
Till you're at last become the golden fool.

vi. *To F––*] Flaxman, B.'s staunch friend through many years. A very
open and honest man, he was not put off by B.'s hostility about this time.
viii 1. *S––*] Stothard, unlike B., was a successful and influential artist.
ix. *Nancy F––*] Ann Flaxman, the sculptor's wife. See p. 286 above.
xiv. 'Stothard's subservience to accepted standards, not his genius, has
brought him wealth.' Lines *3–5* allude to the fable of Æsop.

I sport with Fortune, merry, blithe and gay,
Like to the lion sporting with his prey.
5 Take you the hide and horns, which you may wear;
Mine is the flesh, the bones may be your share.

[31] XV MR STOTHARD TO MR CROMEK
'For Fortune's favours you your riches bring,
But Fortune says she gave you no such thing.
Why should you be ungrateful to your friends,
Sneaking and backbiting and odds and ends?'

MR CROMEK TO MR STOTHARD
'Fortune favours the brave, old proverbs say;
But not with money; that is not the way,
Turn back, turn back, you travel all in vain;
Turn through the iron gate down Sneaking Lane.'

XVI
[31] I am no Homer's hero you all know;
I profess not generosity to a foe.
My generosity is to my friends
That for their friendship I may make amends.
The generous to enemies promotes their ends,
And becomes the enemy and betrayer of his friends.

XVII
[32] The angel that presided o'er my birth
Said, 'Little creature formed of joy and mirth,
Go, love without the help of any king on earth.'

[34] XVIII ON F—— AND S——
I found them blind, I taught them how to see,
And now they know neither themselves nor me.
'Tis excellent to turn a thorn to a pin,
A fool to a bolt, a knave to a glass of gin.

XIX
[34] P—— loved me not as he loved his friends
For he loved them for gain to serve his ends.

xvii *3. king*] Altered in the MS from *Thing* (as all edns print except
Erdman 1965), though not very clearly.

xviii. Cp. iii. Lines *1–2* appear also on p. 33 of the *Descriptive Catalogue*,
1809, (*Erdman 1965*, p. 531).

xix *1.* P——] Probably Richard Phillips, whose portrait of B. was engraved
in Cromek's edition of Blair's *Grave* (see headnote).

He loved me and for no gain at all—
But to rejoice and triumph in my fall.

XX

[34] To forgive enemies H–– does pretend,
Who never in his life forgave a friend.

[35]

XXI TO F––

You call me mad, 'tis folly to do so,
To seek to turn a madman to a foe:
If you think as you speak, you are an ass,
If you do not, you are but what you was.

[35]

XXII ON H––Y'S FRIENDSHIP

When H––y finds out what you cannot do,
That is the very thing he'll set you to.
If you break not your neck 'tis not his fault,
But pecks of poison are not pecks of salt;
5 And when he could not act upon my wife—
Hired a villain to bereave my life.

XXIII

[36] Some men created for destruction come
Into the world and make the world their home;
Be they as vile and base as e'er they can,
They'll still be called the world's honest man.

[36]

XXIV ON S––

You say reserve and modesty he has,
Whose heart is iron, his head wood and his face brass.
The fox, the owl, the beetle, and the bat
By sweet reserve and modesty get fat.

xxii. The last line is manifestly unfair; Hayley was B.'s best friend in the
Scholfield affair (see *Milton*, headnote). The line comes from 'Fair Elenor'
68 (p. 8), but is not therefore less serious. But cp. *Milton* pl. 7.23–4,
'Seeming a brother, being a tyrant, even thinking himself a brother /
While he is murdering the just ...' and pl.32.6–7, 'The idiot reasoner
laughs at the man of imagination, / And from laughter proceeds to murder
by undervaluing calumny.' Pl.32 of *Milton* is a late addition, suggesting
a late date for this epigram.

xxiii 3–4. *1st rdg del.* 'Friend Caiaphas is one, do what he can, / He'll. ...'

xxiv 3–4. These lines were quoted, also with reference to Stothard, in the
Descriptive Catalogue, p. 33, altered by removal of the rhyme:

> The fox, the owl, the spider, and the mole
> By sweet reserve and modesty get fat.

XXV

[37] IMITATION OF POPE: A COMPLIMENT TO THE LADIES

Wondrous the gods, more wondrous are the men;
More wondrous, wondrous still the cock and hen.
More wondrous still the table, stool, and chair—
But ah! more wondrous still the Charming Fair!

[37]
XXVI TO H––

Thy friendship oft has made my heart to ache.
Do be my enemy, for friendship's sake.

XXVII

[37] Cosway, Frazer, and Baldwin of Egypt's lake,
Fear to associate with Blake.
This life is a warfare against evils,
They heal the sick, he casts out devils.
Hayley, Flaxman and Stothard are also in doubt,
Lest their virtue should be put to the rout.
One grins, t'other spits and in corners hides,
And all the virtuous have shown their backsides.

[37]
XXVIII AN EPITAPH

Come, knock your heads against this stone,
For sorrow that poor John Thompson's gone.

[37]
XXIX ANOTHER

I was buried near this dike—
That my friends may weep as much as they like.

[37]
XXX ANOTHER

Here lies John Trot, the friend of all mankind;
He has not left one enemy behind.
Friends were quite hard to find, old authors say,
But now they stand in everybody's way.

XXXI

[38] My title as a genius thus is proved:
Not praised by Hayley, nor by Flaxman loved.

xxvii 1. *Cosway*] Richard Cosway, a fashionable painter, who had taught at
Parr's art school (where B. was taught), and a Swedenborgian. George
Baldwin, (1743?–1826), a traveller, once consul-general in Egypt, inclined
to mysticism. *Frazer*] Uncertain; the painter Alexander Fraser has
been suggested, but he did not arrive in London till 1813.
xxxi 1. *a genius*] Altered from 'an artist'.

XXXII

[39]   If I e'er grow to man's estate
Oh, give to me a woman's fate.
May I govern all, both great and small,
Have the last word; and take the wall.

[41]   XXXIII ON H—— THE PICK-THANK
I write the rascal thanks till he and I
With thanks and compliments are quite drawn dry.

[41]   XXXIV CROMEK SPEAKS
'I always take my judgement from a fool
Because his judgement is so very cool,
Not prejudiced by feelings great or small.'
Amiable state! he cannot feel at all.

[41]   XXXV ENGLISH ENCOURAGEMENT OF ART
[*First reading*]

If you mean to please everybody, you will
Set to work both ignorance and skill.
For a great multitude are ignorant
And skill to them seems raving and rant,
5   Like putting oil and water into a lamp:
'Twill make a great splutter with smoke and damp.
For there is no use, as it seems to me,
Of lighting a lamp when you don't wish to see.

[*Final reading*]

ENGLISH ENCOURAGEMENT OF ART

Cromek's opinions put into rhyme

If you mean to please everybody, you will
Menny wouver both bunglishness and skill.
For a great conquest are bunglery

xxxv. Two versions are presented here, separating the two layers of
composition. The first was a 'straight' version of B.'s interpretation of
Cromek's ideas. Then he inserted the subtitle, 'and tampered with the
words in a punning burlesque of the speaker's pronunciation and thought'
(*Erdman 1965*, p. 787).
xxxv(1) 6. *damp*] Fumes.
xxxv(2) 2. *Menny wouver*] 'Manoeuvre', perhaps; but Morton Paley
suggests an allusion to Meynheer Philips Wouverman (1620–68), a Dutch
painter of skill, detail, and high finish.
xxxv(2) 3. *conquest*] Success. A second reading, between *multitude* and *con-
quest*, was *madjority*, which it is a pity to lose.

And jenous looks to ham like mad rantery,
5 Like displaying oil and water into a lamp—
'Twill hold forth a huge splutter with smoke and damp.
For it's all sheer loss, as it seems to me,
Of displaying up a light when we want not to see.

XXXVI

[41] When you look at a picture, you always can see
If a man of sense has painted he:
Then never flinch but keep up a jaw
About freedom and Jenny suck awa',
5 And when it smells of the lamp we can
Say all was owing to the skilful man.
For the smell of water is but small;
So e'en let ignorance do it all.

XXXVII

[42] You say their pictures well painted be,
And yet they are blockheads, you all agree.
Thank God, I never was sent to school
To be flogged into following the style of a fool.

XXXVIII

[42] The errors of a wise man make your rule
Rather than the perfections of a fool.

[43]   XXXIX THE WASHER-WOMAN'S SONG
I washed them out and washed them in—
And they told me it was a great sin.

XL

[43] Great things are done when men and mountains meet:
This is not done by jostling in the street.

XLI

[46]   I give you the end of a golden string—
Only wind it into a ball,

xxxv(2) *4. jenous*] Genius.   *ham*] Them.
xxxvi. Another Cromekian poem.
xxxvi *4. Jenny suck awa'*] 'Je ne sais quoi'.
xxxvi *5–8.* These lines are so written that they might belong to the previous poem, though they probably belong to this one.
xxxix. Probably alludes to B.'s own technique of water-colouring.
xli. A draft for the verse at the head of *Jerusalem* pl.77, the Preface to Chapter 3.

It will lead you in at heaven's gate
Built in Jerusalem's wall.

XLII

[47]   If you play a game of chance, know before you begin,
If you are benevolent you will never win.

[50]   ### XLIII WILLIAM COWPER, ESQUIRE
For this is being a friend just in the nick;
Not when he's well but waiting till he's sick.
He calls you to his help; be you not moved
Until by being sick his wants are proved.

5   You see him spend his soul in prophecy;
Do you believe it a confounded lie,
Till some bookseller, and the public fame
Proves there is truth in his extravagant claim.

For 'tis atrocious in a friend you love,
10   To tell you anything that he can't prove;
And 'tis most wicked in a Christian nation
For any man to pretend to inspiration!

XLIV

[50]   The only man that e'er I knew
Who did not make me almost spew
Was Fuseli; he was both Turk and Jew—
And so, dear Christian friends, how do you do?

XLV

[56]   Why was Cupid a boy?
And why a boy was he?
He should have been a girl
For ought that I can see.

xliii. This poem began as 'Epitaph for William Cowper, Esq.', and the
first four lines, now almost lost, began 'Here lies the Man'. The word
'Hayley' is legible, showing that the poem is addressed to him. B. accuses
Hayley of enthusiasm for Cowper, whose life he wrote, only when his
fame was sure–not at the time of his real need, when he might have been
saved from depression and insanity. The deletions broaden the accusation
to the entire 'Christian Nation'(*11*).

xliv. This was written over the deleted first stanza of xliii: did B. intend it
to replace it, with the word 'Friend' as the link?
xliv 3. *Turk and Jew*] Fuseli was neither. He was Swiss by birth.

For he shoots with his bow
5   And the girl shoots with her eye,
And they both are merry and glad
And laugh when we do cry.

And to make Cupid a boy
10   Was the Cupid-girl's mocking plan;
For a boy can't interpret the thing
Till he is become a man.

And then he's so pierced with care
And wounded with arrowy smarts,
15   That the whole business of his life
Is to pick out the heads of the darts.

'Twas the Greeks' love of war
Turned love into a boy,
And woman into a statue of stone—
20   And away fled every joy.

[63]
XLVI

Great men and fools do often me inspire;
But the greater fool the greater liar.

[64]
XLVII FROM CRATETOS

Me time has crook'd. No good workman
Is he. Infirm is all that he does.

XLVIII

[70] Some people admire the work of a fool,
For it's sure to keep your judgment cool;
It does not reproach you with want of wit—
It is not like a lawyer serving a writ!

[73]
XLIX TO GOD

If you have formed a circle to go into,
Go into it yourself and see how you would do.

xlv *19. a statue of stone*] Perhaps the statue of Pygmalion's creation, with which he fell in love, and which Aphrodite turned into a living woman for him.

xlvii. A translation of a Greek epigram, attributed to Crates of Thebes, a Cynic philosopher (*fl. c.* 325 B.C.). B.'s translation is not perfect; the meaning of the original is, 'For time has bent me; though a skilled craftsman, yet he makes all things weaker'. This is an interesting reflection on the limitation of B.'s Greek; he knew enough to translate, but not enough to translate faultlessly. He also misunderstood the ascription by Stobaeus, in whose anthology the epigram is found, reading the genitive κράτητος ('of Crates') as a nominative.

L

[73]   Since all the riches of this world
        May be gifts from the Devil and earthly kings,
        I should suspect that I worshipped the Devil
        If I thanked my God for worldly things.

LI

[78]   To Chloe's breast young Cupid slyly stole;
        But he crept in at Myra's pocket hole.

LII

[79]   'Now art has lost its mental charms
        France shall subdue the world in arms'.
        So spoke an angel at my birth,
        Then said: 'Descend thou upon earth;
5   Renew the arts on Britain's shore
        And France shall fall down and adore;
        With works of art their armies meet,
        And war shall sink beneath thy feet.
        But if thy nation arts refuse
10   And if they scorn the immortal Muse,
        France shall the arts of peace restore
        And save thee from the ungrateful shore.'

        Spirit who lov'st Britannia's Isle,
        Round which the fiends of commerce smile . . .

LIII

[79]   Nail his neck to the cross, nail it with a nail;
        Nail his neck to the cross. Ye all have power over his
            tail.

LIV

[89]   I rose up at the dawn of day—
        'Get thee away get thee away!,
        Pray'st thou for riches? Away, away!
        This is the throne of Mammon grey.'

lii *2. France shall subdue*] France's ascendancy continued until the Russian disaster of 1812, and was at its height from about 1809. Cp. also 20 ii *n*, p. 287).

lii *12. thee . . . the ungrateful*] *1st rdg del.* thy works . . . Britain's.

liii. This couplet implies the triple association of Christ, Orc, and the serpent, which runs through B.'s longer poems from *America* to *Four Zoas*: here B. speaks to hypocritical 'believers'.

5 Said I, 'This sure is very odd:
  I took it to be the Throne of God.
  For everything besides I have;
  It is only for riches that I can crave.

  'I have mental joy and mental health,
10 And mental friends and mental wealth;
  I've a wife I love and that loves me;
  I've all but riches bodily.

  'I am in God's presence night and day,
  And he never turns his face away;
15 The Accuser of Sins by my side does stand
  And he holds my money-bag in his hand;

  'For my worldly things God makes him pay,
  And he'd pay for more if to him I would pray;
  And so you may do the worst you can do,
20 Be assured, Mr. Devil, I won't pray to you.

  'Then if for riches I must not pray,
  God knows I little of prayers need say.
  So as a church is known by its steeple,
  If I pray it must be for other people.

25 'He says if I do not worship him for a God
  I shall eat coarser food and go worse shod;
  So as I don't value such things as these,
  You must do, Mr. Devil, just as God please.'

LV

[93] A woman scaly and a man all hairy
  Is such a match as he who dares
  Will find the woman's scales scrape off the man's
   hairs.

35 Miscellaneous Verses, 1809–12

These verses fall into the following groups: (A) those printed in the *Advertisement* and *Descriptive Catalogue* of B.'s exhibition, which opened in May 1809. (B) those found in B.'s marginalia to Reynolds's *Discourses*, where they may be given this late date (cp. p. 286 also). (In 1809–10 B. was anxious to go into print to defend himself against orthodoxy, and may be supposed to have re-read the *Discourses* to find ammunition for counter-attack.) (C) similar verses, of about the same date, but found in the Note-book; (D) Notebook verses directly attached to, or arising from, the *Public Address*. (This was eventually left incomplete, and is only known in this draft, belonging to *c.* mid-1810.); (E) verses which, either on biblio-graphical grounds or through allusions, can be shown to be later than the Address. The latest datable allusion (no. xl) is to the death of Cromek, 12 March 1812.

At the time of writing these verses, the Notebook was beginning to be full. When he wrote the *Last Judgement* commentary and the *Public Address* he had to fit passages in wherever he could, and was beginning to write over the fainter sketches. The verses and epigrams are also squeezed in where there is room; within the groups listed above, they are here printed in page order, but this cannot be taken to prove anything concerning relative dates. (A new facsimile edition and study of the Notebook, ed. D. V. Erdman, is in preparation.)

(A) Verses belonging to the *Advertisement* and the *Descriptive Catalogue*, May 1809.

I

In the last battle that Arthur fought, the most
     beautiful was one
That returned, and the most strong another; with them
     also returned
The most ugly, and no other beside returned from the
     bloody field.

The most beautiful the Roman warriors trembled
     before and worshipped;
5 The most strong, they melted before him and dissolved
     in his presence:
The most ugly they fled with outcries and contortion
     of their limbs.

¶ 35.i. These verses are found in the printed advertisement of B.'s ex-hibition; it is dated by hand 15 May 1809. The verses are the subject of one of the main pictures in the exhibition, the other being the *Canterbury Pilgrims*. This picture is described as 'Three Ancient Britons overthrowing the Army of armed Romans . . . –From the Welsh Triads'. (The form of *triad* is well exemplified in these lines of B.'s.) The triad, which B. loosely adapts to make two verses, is not otherwise known in English. S. F. Damon, in his *Blake Dictionary* (1965) p. 443, gives a translation by David Jenkins: 'Three men escaped from the battle of Camlan, . . . Morfran, because of his ugliness, everyone, deeming him to be a devil, avoided him. Sandde being so fair and beautiful, no-one raised a hand against him, thinking him to be an angel; and Glewlwyd, because of his size and strength, everyone fled before him.' (B. may have learnt of this triad from the Welsh national-ist Owen Pugh.) He has turned Camlan, Arthur's last battle against the Saxons, into a battle against the Romans (whose culture B. despised), and has added other details.

II

The fox, the owl, the spider and the mole
By sweet reserve and modesty get fat.

III

I found them blind; I taught them how to see,
And now they know me not nor yet themselves.

(B) Verses written as marginalia to Reynolds's *Discourses*, *c.* 1809–10.

Cp. the verses in group (C) below, and note. Other verses written in the *Discourses c.* 1798–1802 are given on p. 286 above.

IV

Some look, to see the sweet outlines
And beauteous forms that love does wear;
Some look, to find out patches, paint,
Bracelets and stays and powdered hair.

V

When nations grow old, the arts grow cold,
And commerce settles on every tree,
And the poor and the old can live upon gold,
For all are born poor, aged sixty-three.

VI ON THE VENETIAN PAINTER

He makes the lame to walk we all agree;
But then he strives to blind those who can see.

VII

A pair of stays to mend the shape
Of crooked humpy woman
Put on, O Venus! Now thou art
Quite a Venetian Roman.

VIII

Venetian, all thy colouring is no more
Than bolstered plasters on a crooked whore.

ii and iii are found in B.'s printed *Descriptive Catalogue* of his exhibition.
ii. Taken from ¶ 34.xxiv (p. 597 above), with the rhyme removed.
iii. Taken from ¶ 34.xviii (p. 596 above) and turned to unrhymed verse.
vi. *Venetian*] B. detested the sensuous style of such painters as Titian for its softness of line and rich colouring.

IX

O reader, behold the philosopher's grave;
He was born quite a fool—but he died quite a knave.

(C) Verses on art, artists, and artistic technique, *c.* 1809-10.

Cp. the verses above, on similar topics, found as marginalia to Reynolds's *Discourses,* whereas the following are found in the Notebook. B. expressed his opinions on colour and line forcefully in the published *Descriptive Catalogue* (May 1809) and the unpublished *Public Address* (1810), which is also in the Notebook. B.'s chief point is that the soul of art is in the outline drawing—with which the painter must start. The sensuousness, subtlety and sweep of colour of the styles of Titian, Rubens and Rembrandt produce only amorphous monstrosities. B.'s prejudices arise from his own profession of engraver, particularly as he adhered to the old hard-lined style which was going out of fashion–one of the causes of his unpopularity in contrast with the softer engraving of Bartollozzi and Schiavonetti (cp. xxxi, xxxiii, xl below).

X

[21]   No real style of colouring ever appears
        But advertising in the newspapers—
        Look, there you'll see Sir Joshua's colouring;
        Look at his pictures—all has taken wing!

XI

[26]   Can there be anything more mean,
        More malice in disguise,
        Than praise a man for doing what
        That man does most despise?
5   Reynolds lectures exactly so
        When he praises Michael Angelo.

XII

[28]   Sir Joshua praises Michael Angelo—
        'Tis Christian mildness when knaves praise a foe.
        But 'twould be madness, all the world would say
        Should Michael Angelo praise Sir Joshua.
        Christ used the Pharisees in a rougher way.

XIII

[29]   Sir Joshua praised Rubens with a smile
        By calling his the ornamental style,

xi. B. could not understand Reynolds's ability to see the virtues of opposing techniques. For Reynolds on Michaelangelo, see xvn.
xii 3–5. The rhyme implies the old pronunciation of final '-a' and '-ah'.

And yet his praise of Flaxman was the smartest
When he called him the 'ornamental artist'.
5   But sure, such ornaments we well may spare
As crooked limbs and lousy heads of hair.

XIV FLORENTINE INGRATITUDE

[32] Sir Joshua sent his own portrait to
The birthplace of Michael Angelo,
And in the hand of the simpering fool
He put a dirty paper scroll,
5   And on the paper to be polite
Did *Sketches by Michael Angelo* write.
The Florentines said "Tis a Dutch-English boor,
Michael Angelo's name writ on Rembrandt's door.'
The Florentines call it an English fetch,
10   For Michael Angelo did never sketch;
Every line of his has meaning
And needs neither suckling nor weaning.
'Tis the trading English-Venetian cant
To speak Michael Angelo & act Rembrandt.
15   It will set his Dutch friends all in a roar
To write *Mch. Ang.* on Rembrandt's door,
But you must not bring in your hand a lie,
If you mean that the Florentines should buy.
Giotto's circle or Apelles' line
20   Were not the work of sketchers drunk with wine,
Nor of the city clerks' merry-hearted fashion,
Nor of Sir Isaac Newton's calculation;
Nor of the city clerks' idle facilities,
Which sprang from Sir Isaac Newton's great abilities.

25   These verses were written by a very envious man,
Who whatever likeness he may have to Michael Angelo
Never can have any to Sir Jehoshuan.

---

xiv *Florentine Ingratitude*] Reynolds was elected to the Florentine Academy, and this required him to paint a self-portrait and send it to the Academy.

xiv *9. fetch*] Defined by Johnson as 'a stratagem by which anything is indirectly performed; by which one thing seems intended and another done'.

xiv *19. Giotto*] (1266–1337) Said to have been able to draw a perfect circle freehand.

Apelles] (fourth century B.C.) He challenged his friend Protogenes to the freehand drawing of straight lines.

XV A PITIFUL CASE

[33]   The villain at the gallows tree
When he is doomed to die,
To assuage his misery
In virtue's praise does cry.

5   So Reynolds, when he came to die
To assuage his bitter woe,
Thus aloud did howl and cry
'Michael Angelo! Michael Angelo!'

XVI TO THE ROYAL ACADEMY

[33] A strange erratum in all the editions
Of Sir Joshua Reynolds's Lectures
Should be corrected by the young gentlemen
And the Royal Academy's directors:

5 Instead of *Michael Angelo*
Read *Rembrandt*; for it is fit
To make mere common honesty
In all that he has writ.

XVII

[38]   I Rubens am a statesman and a saint—
Deceptions? O no—so I'll learn to paint.

XVIII TO ENGLISH CONNOISSEURS

[38] You must agree that Rubens was a fool
And yet you make him master of your school,
And give more money for his slobberings
Than you will give for Raphael's finest things.
5 I understand Christ was a carpenter
And not a brewer's servant, my good sir.

XIX

A Pretty Epigram for the Entertainment of
those who have Paid Great Sums in the
Venetian and Flemish Ooze

Nature and art in this together suit:
What is most grand is always most minute.
Rubens thinks tables, chairs and stools are grand,
But Raphael thinks a head, a foot, a hand.

xv. This verse and the next are inspired by the closing words of the
fifteenth and last of Reynolds's *Discourses to the Royal Academy* (Dec. 1790):
'I should desire that the last words which I should pronounce in this
Academy, and from this place, might be the name of MICHAEL ANGELO.'

XX

[38] These are the idiot's chiefest arts—
      To blend and not define the parts.
      The swallow sings in courts of kings—
      That fools have their high finishings.
5   And this the prince's golden rule—
      The laborious stumble of a fool.
      To make out the parts is the wise man's aim,
      But to lose them the fool makes his foolish game.

XXI

[39] Raphael, sublime, majestic, graceful, wise—
      His executive power must I despise?
      Rubens, low, vulgar, stupid, ignorant—
      His power of execution I must grant!
      Learn the laborious stumble of a fool
      And from an idiot's actions form my rule?
      Go send your children to the slobbering school!

XXII

[39] The cripple every step drudges & labours,
      And says, 'Come learn to walk of me, good
            neighbours'.
      Sir Joshua in astonishment cries out:
      'See what great labour pain him, & modest doubt!'
5   Newton and Bacon cry, being badly nursed,
      'He is all experiments from last to first'—
      He walks and stumbles as if he crep'
      And how high laboured is every step!

XXIII ON THE GREAT ENCOURAGEMENT
given by English Nobility and Gentry to Correggio, Rubens,
Rembrandt, Reynolds, Gainsborough, Catalani,
DuCrowe and Dilbury Doodle.

      As the ignorant savage will sell his own wife
      For a sword or a cutlass, a dagger or knife,
      So the taught savage Englishman spends his whole
            fortune
      On a smear or a squall to destroy picture or tune.

xxiii. Correggio (1489–1534) was a painter related to the sensuous Venetian
school. *Catalani* may be one of several Italian painters. *DuCrowe* is pre-
sumably B.'s spelling of *Ducros* (1748–1810), a Swiss landscape painter.
'*Dilbury Doodle*' is a flippant title for any bad pretender to art.

5   And I call upon Colonel Wardle
    To give these rascals a dose of caudle.

XXIV

[40] All pictures that's painted with sense and with thought
      Are painted by madmen, as sure as a groat:
      For the greater the fool, in the pencil more blest,
      And when they are drunk they always paint best.
      They never can Raphael it, Fuseli it, nor Blake it;
      If they can't see an outline, pray how can they make it?
      When men will draw outlines, begin you to jaw them;
      Madmen see outlines and therefore they draw them.

XXV

[43] When I see a Rubens, Rembrandt, Correggio,
      I think of the crippled Harry and slobbering Joe,
      And then I question thus, 'Are artists' rules
      To be drawn from the works of two manifest fools?'
      Then God defend us from the arts, I say,
      Send battle, murder, sudden death, oh pray!
      Rather than be such a blind human fool
      I'd be an ass, a hog, a worm, a chair, a stool.

XXVI

[46] Delicate hands and heads will never appear
      While Titian's (etc., as in the Book of Moonlight, p. 5).

XXVII TO VENETIAN ARTISTS

[61] That God is colouring Newton does show,
      And the Devil is a black outline all of us know.
      Perhaps this little fable may make us merry:
      A dog went over the water without a wherry.
5   A bone which he had stolen he had in his mouth,
      He cared not whether the wind was north or south,
      As he swam he saw the reflection of the bone—
      'This is quite perfection, one generalizing tone.

xxiii 5. *Colonel Wardle* gained great popularity in February and March 1809
by attacking, in the Commons, the corruptions of the Duke of York in the
army.

xxiii 6. *caudle*] A medicinal potion.

xxiv 1–2. *thought / groat*] Such a rhyme is not unknown in B., cp. the
rhyme *hot / thought* in his letter to Butts, 22 Nov. 1802.

xxvi. *The Book of Moonlight* is lost.

xxvii. *To Venetian Artists*] Artists of the school of Titian and Correggio.

Outline? There's no outline, there's no such thing—
10   All is chiaroscuro, poco pen; it's all colouring!'
Snap! Snap! he has lost shadow and substance too;
He had them both before: now how do ye do?
'A great deal better than I was before:
Those who taste colouring love it more and more.'

(D) Verses from the period of drafting the *Public Address,* mid-1810.

XXVIII

[21]   And in melodious accents I
Will sit me down and cry, *I! I!*

XXIX

[40]   Give pensions to the learned pig,
Or the hare playing on a tabor.
Anglus can never see perfection
But in the journeyman's labour.

XXX

[40]   The Cunning-sures and the Aim-at-yours.

XXXI   BLAKE'S APOLOGY FOR HIS CATALOGUE
[62–3,
65] Having given great offence by writing in prose,
I'll write in verse as soft as Bartolloze.

xxvii *10. chiaroscuro*] The technique of light and darkness.
poco pen] With little evidence of drawing, and an emphasis on shape and mass of colour.

xxviii. This follows the declaration: 'I demand therefore of the amateurs of art the encouragement which is my due. If they continue to refuse, theirs is the loss, not mine, and theirs is the contempt of posterity. I have enough in the approbation of fellow-labourers; this is my glory and exceeding great reward. I go on and nothing can hinder my course.' The verse seems to depict B. as a public speaker; *I* in *2* standing for *Aye.*

xxix *1–2.* These were common side-shows at fairs.
xxix *3. Anglus can never see*] Lines *3–4* appear in the draft of the *Public Address,* a prose addition, with this phrase reading: 'Can Anglus never discern. . . .' *Anglus* means 'the typical Englishman'.

xxx. A parody of 'the connoisseurs and amateurs', a phrase which occurs in the *Public Address,* on p. 63 of the Notebook.

xxxi. *Blake's Apology . . .*] This exists in a first, much revised draft on pp.

Some blush at what others see no crime in,
But nobody sees any harm in rhyming.
5 Dryden in rhyme cries 'Milton only planned';
Every fool shook his bells throughout the land.
Tom Cooke cut Hogarth down with his clean graving;
Thousands of connoisseurs with joy ran raving.
Thus Hayley on his toilette seeing the soap
10 Cries, 'Homer is very much improved by Pope!'
Some say I've given great provision to my foes,
And that now I lead my false friends by the nose.
Flaxman and Stothard smelling a sweet savour
Cry, 'Blakified drawing spoils painter and engraver!'
15 While I, looking up to my umbrella,
Resolved to be a very contrary fellow,
Cry, looking quite from 'skumference to centre,
'No one can finish so high as the original inventor.'
Thus poor Schiavonetti died of the Cromek,
20 A thing that's tied around the *Examiner's* neck.
This is my sweet apology to my friends,
That I may put them in mind of their latter ends.

62-3; the text here is that of the fair copy on p. 65. The draft on p. 62 arises from a passage in the *Public Address*, which it immediately follows on the page (Keynes in fact considered it a part of the text of the Address): 'Nor can an original invention exist without execution, organized and minutely delineated and articulated, either by God or Man. I do not mean smoothed up and niggled and poco-pen'd, ⟨and all the beauties picked out and blurred and blotted⟩ but drawn with a firm ⟨and decided⟩ hand at once like Fuseli and Michael Angelo and Shakespeare and Milton.' Phrases enclosed thus ⟨ ⟩ are additions, very likely later than the verses.

xxxi 2. *Bartolloze*] *1st rdg del.* feather pillows. Bartollozi (1727-1815) was a successful Italian engraver, who settled in England and was popular for his style of 'softening' the lines. B. proudly continued to use the old and unfashionable style of hard-lined engraving.

xxxi 7. *Tom Cooke* 'engraved after Hogarth' and 'wished to give to Hogarth what he could take from Raphael; that is, outline and mass and colour, but he could not...' (*Public Address* p. 60).

xxxi 19-20. *Schiavonetti ... Cromek ... Examiner*] See headnote to no. xxxiv, p. 593. There was no relationship between *The Examiner* and Cromek's firm. The deleted lines following in the draft give B.'s notions of *The Examiner's* attack:

> Who cries, All art is a fraud and genius a trick
> And Blake is an unfortunate lunatic.

The title was then crowded in above this addition, 'Blake's Apology' being directed against *The Examiner*.

XXXII

[66] Call that the public voice which is their error?
      Like as a monkey peeping in a mirror—
      Admires all his colours brown and warm,
      And never once perceives his ugly form.

(E) Verses later than the *Public Address,* late 1810–*c.* 1812.

XXXIII

[23] Was I angry with Hayley who used me so ill,
      Or can I be angry with Felpham's old mill?
      Or angry with Flaxman or Cromek or Stothard,
      Or poor Schiavonetti whom they to death bothered?
  5   Or angry with Macklin or Boydell or Bowyer,
      Because they did not say, 'O what a beau ye are!'
      At a friend's errors anger show,
      Mirth at the errors of a foe!

XXXIV

[87] The caverns of the grave I've seen
      And these I showed to England's Queen:
      But now the caves of hell I view
      Who shall I dare to show them to?
  5   What mighty soul in beauty's form
      Shall dauntless view the infernal storm?

xxxii. This follows the statement in the *Public Address*: 'England will never rival Italy while we servilely copy what the wise Italians Raphael and Michael Angelo scorned—nay abhorred—as Vasari tells us.' After the verse B. adds only the sentence: 'What kind of intellects must he have who sees only the colours of things and not the forms of things?'

xxxiii *3–4.* See headnote, p. 593. Schiavonetti died on 7 June 1810.

xxxiii *5. 1st rdg del.* Boydell or Bowyer or Basire. All three, as well as Macklin, had employed B. to make engravings; Basire (whom he tried to bring into a line now deleted, between *2* and *3*) was the master to whom B. was apprenticed.

xxxiii *6.* Written over the erased line: 'Mirths all your sufferings convey sir' (which indicates the pronunciation of *Basire,* with which this would have rhymed).

xxxiv *1–2.* Referring to B.'s designs for Blair's *Grave,* dedicated to the Queen (see p. 592).

xxxiv *3–4.* B. refers to the painting *A Vision of the Last Judgement,* for which he was at this time preparing a commentary in the Notebook, i.e. in late 1810. The commentary refers to a large painting, but one very similar to that on the same theme which went to the Egremonts' home, Petworth House, for which this poem is a dedication.

Egremont's Countess can control
The flames of hell that round me roll.
If she refuse I still go on
10   Till the heavens and earth are gone,
Still admired by noble minds,
Followed by envy on the winds.
Re-engraved time after time,
Ever in their youthful prime,
15   My designs unchanged remain;
Time may rage but rage in vain.
For above Time's troubled fountains
On the great Atlantic mountains,
In my golden house on high,
20   There they shine eternally.

XXXV

[38] Swelled limbs, with no outline that you can descry,
That stink in the nose of a stander-by,
But all the pulp washed, painted, finished with labour
Of an hundred journeymen's—how d'ye do, neighbour?

XXXVI

[60] I asked my dear friend Orator Prigg
'What's the first part of oratory?' He said, 'A great
      wig.'
'And what is the second?' Then dancing a jig
And bowing profoundly, he said 'A great wig.'
5   'And what is the third?' Then he snored like a pig
And puffing his cheeks, he replied, 'A great wig.'

So if a great painter with questions you push—
'What's the first part of painting?' He'll say 'A paint
      brush.'

xxxiv 7. *Egremont's Countess*] Officially, there was no countess; the Earl of
Egremont never married, and his mother had died in 1794. But he had had
several illegitimate children by Elizabeth Iliff, daughter of a master at
Westminster School, whom he later married privately; after the marriage
there was one legitimate child, a daughter. Elizabeth died in 1822, the Earl
in 1837, and the title passed to a nephew. Having no son to cause him
to have the marriage recognized, his wife was never established as Countess,
and the peerages ignore her. Nevertheless, B. clearly knew of her, and must
have assumed that she was countess. Three drafts exist of a letter to Ozias
Humphrey, describing the picture, and all refer to the 'Countess'. Of these,
one was found at Petworth; significantly, this copy has *Countess* corrected
to *Earl*–but not in B.'s hand (see G. L. Keynes' edn. of the *Letters*, nos. 86–8).
18. Atlantic] i.e., of Atlantis.

'And what is the second?' With modest blush
10 He'll smile like a cherub and say, 'A paint brush.'
'And what is the third?' He'll bow like a rush,
With a tear in his eye he'll reply, 'A paint brush.'
Perhaps this is all a painter can want—
But look yonder! That house is the house of Rembrandt.

XXXVII

[61] 'O dear Mother Outline, of knowledge most sage,
What's the first part of painting?' She said, 'Patronage'.
'And what is the second to please and engage?'
She frowned like a fury and said, 'Patronage'.
'And what is the third?' She put off old age,
And smiled like a siren, and said, 'Patronage'.

XXXVIII

[23] Anger and wrath my bosom rends—
I thought them the errors of friends:
But all my limbs with warmth glow—
I find them the errors of the foe.

XXXIX

[65] If men will act like a maid smiling over a churn
They ought not, when it comes to another's turn,
To grow sour at what a friend may utter,
Knowing and feeling that we all have need of butter.
False friends! Fie! Fie! Our friendship you shan't
        sever:
In spite, we will be greater friends than ever.

XL

[22] And his legs carried it like a long fork
Reached all the way from Chichester to York,
From York all across Scotland to the sea:
This was a man of men as seems to me.
5   Not only in his mouth his own soul lay,
But my soul also would he bear away.

---

xxxix 1-4. A milkmaid expects favours and flattery; men also expect the
same (note the pun on *butter*). Why then are they angry (another pun on
sour) when someone else is flattered, resenting the praise one of their
friends gives another?
xl 1-2. *his legs*] Cromek's; his parents lived in York. B., when at Felpham,
was near Chichester.
xl 6. *my*] Stewhard's (Stothard's).

Like as a pedlar bears his weary pack
So Stewhard's soul he buckled to his back.
But once, alas! committing a mistake
10 He bore the wretched soul of William Blake,
That he might turn it into eggs of gold ;
But neither back nor mouth those eggs could hold.
His under-jaw dropped as those eggs he laid,
And Stewhard's eggs are addled and decayed.
15 The *Examiner* whose very name is Hunt
Called Death a madman—trembling for the affront,
Like trembling hare sits on his weakly paper
·On which he used to dance and sport and caper.
Yorkshire Jack Hemp and gentle blushing Daw
20 Clapped Death into the corner of their jaw,
And Felpham Billy rode out every morn
Horseback with Death over the fields of corn,
Who with iron hand cuffed in the afternoon
The ears of Billy's lawyer and dragoon;
25 And Cur my lawyer, and Dady, Jack Hemp's parson,
Both went to law with Death to keep our ears on.
For how to starve Death we had laid a plot
Against his price; but Death was in the pot—
He made them pay his price, alack a day!
30 He knew both Law and Gospel better than they.
O that I ne'er had seen that William Blake,
Or could from death Assassinetti wake!
We thought (alas! that such a thought should be!)
That Blake would etch for him and draw for me;

xl 15. *Examiner . . . Hunt*] See headnote to ¶ 34, p. 593.

xl 17. *weakly*] (sic).

xl 19. *Yorkshire Jack Hemp . . . Daw*] A punning name for Flaxman; *Daw*
is probably Ann Flaxman, his wife, on the association of *Jack/Daw*. See
¶ 34.ix above, p. 595.

xl 20. *Death*] B. himself–because so many people associated with him had
died, as the notes show.

xl 21. *Felpham Billy*] William Hayley. It is unlikely that he actually rode
through the corn.

xl 24. *Billy's lawyer and dragoon*] The lawyer retained by Hayley to defend
B. in 1803–04 was Samuel Rose, who died very soon after the trial.
Scholfield, the dragoon (see p. 485) was, of course, nothing to do with
Hayley.

xl 25. *Cur, Dady*] Not identified, though Sampson proposed Dr B. H.
Malkin, who was a schoolmaster, not a parson.

xl 32. *Assassinetti*] Schiavonetti, engaged by Cromek to engrave B.'s
designs to Blair's *Grave*: he died on 7 June 1810.

·21 + B.

35   For 'twas a kind of bargain Screwmuch made,
That Blake's designs should be by us displayed,
Because he makes designs so very cheap.
Then Screwmuch at Blake's soul took a long leap—
'Twas not a mouse: 'twas Death in a disguise!
40   And, I, alas, live to weep out mine eyes,
And Death sits laughing on their monuments
On which he's written *Received the Contents*.
But I have writ, so sorrowful my thought is,
His epitaph; for my tears are aqua fortis:

45   *Come, artists, knock your heads against this stone,*
For sorrow that our friend Bob Screwmuch's gone.
And now the men upon me smile and laugh
I'll also write my own dear epitaph,
And I'll be buried near a dike
50   *That my friends may weep as much as they like.*
Here lies Stewhard the friend of all, etc. . . . .

XLI

[33] If it is true what the prophets write,
That the heathen gods are all stocks and stones,
Shall we for the sake of being polite
Feed them with the juice of our marrow bones?

5   And if Bezaleel and Aholiab drew
What the finger of God pointed to their view,
Shall we suffer the Roman and Grecian rods
To compel us to worship them as gods?
They stole them from the Temple of the Lord
10   And worshipped them that they might make inspired
     art abhorred.

The wood and stone were called the Holy Things,
And their sublime intent given to their kings:
All the atonements of Jehovah spurned,
And criminals to sacrifices turned.

xl 35. *Screwmuch*] Cromek (died 14 March 1812).
xl 42. *Received the Contents*] The tombstones act as invoices, which equates 'receipts' with epitaphs.
xl 45–50. Cp. the 1808 epigrams ¶ 34.xxviii and xxix, p. 598.
xl 51. *Stewhard*] Stothard, whose 'epitaph' is no. xxx, p. 598.

xli 5. *Bezaleel and Aholiab*] The two master craftsmen who (*Exodus* xxxi 2, 6) directed the manufacture of the Tabernacle, its furniture and ornaments, according to the instructions which Moses received on Sinai.
xli 8. *them*] The classics.

XLII

[52]   I will tell you what Joseph of Arimathea
        Said to my fairy. Was it not very queer?—
        Pliny and Trajan, what! are you here?
        Come listen to Joseph of Arimathea:
5   Listen patient and when Joseph has done,
        'Twill make a fool laugh and a fairy fun.

XLIII

[39]   The Hebrew nation did not write it:
        Avarice and Chastity did shite it.

xlii *1. Joseph of Arimathea* is sometimes supposed to have visited Britain and brought the knowledge of Christ. This is in keeping with B.'s feelings about the importance of Britain in the religious history of the world. It is therefore only right and proper that classical figures from the despised Roman world (cp. verse above)–Pliny the scholar, and Trajan the emperor–should listen to Joseph and B.

xliii. Keynes dates this 1793; but it is more in keeping with B.'s attitude in his later years, as the forgiving Saviour came to be more and more at the centre of his belief, while the old covenant, the laws and aggressive militarism of the Old Testament became more and more unsavoury to him.

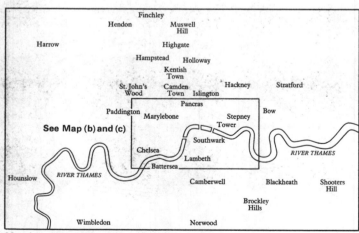

Map (a)   Blake's London ca. 1810

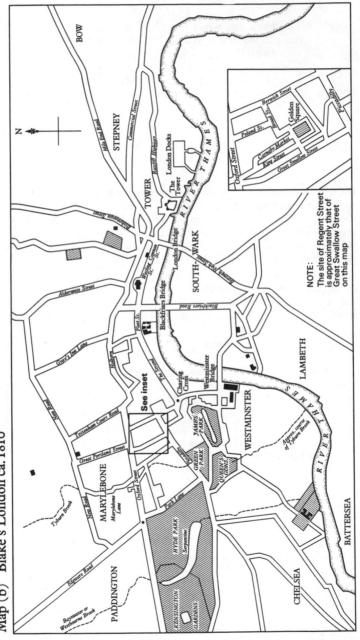

Map (b) Blake's London ca. 1810

BOW

STEPNEY

Mile End Road

Commercial Street

Ratcliff Highway

TOWER

London Docks

The Tower

RIVER THAMES

SOUTH-WARK

London Bridge

Blackfriars Bridge

Blackfriars Road

Borough High Street

LAMBETH

Bishopsgate Street

Wigmore Street

Old St. St.

Aldersgate Street

Fleet St.

Gray's Inn Lane

Holborn

The Strand

Charing Cross

Westminster Bridge

See inset

WESTMINSTER

Tottenham Court Road

Great Portland Street

MARYLEBONE

Marylebone Lane

New Road

Oxford Street

Pall Lane

JAMES'S PARK

GREEN PARK

QUEEN'S PARK

Approx. course of Tyburn Brook

RIVER THAMES

BATTERSEA

Tyburn brook

Edgware Road

PADDINGTON

Bayswater or Westbourne Brook

HYDE PARK

Serpentine

KENSINGTON GARDENS

CHELSEA

N

NOTE:
The site of Regent Street
is approximately that of
Great Swallow Street
on this map

Berwick Street

Poland St.

Broad St.

Golden Square

Piccadilly

Carnaby Market

King Street

Great Swallow Street

Oxford Street

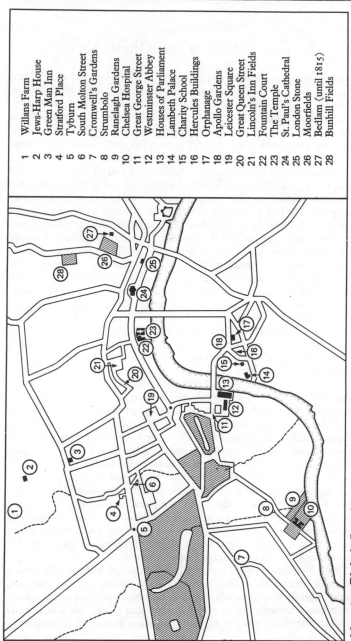

1 Willans Farm
2 Jews-Harp House
3 Green Man Inn
4 Stratford Place
5 Tyburn
6 South Molton Street
7 Cromwell's Gardens
8 Strumbolo
9 Ranelagh Gardens
10 Chelsea Hospital
11 Great George Street
12 Westminster Abbey
13 Houses of Parliament
14 Lambeth Palace
15 Charity School
16 Hercules Buildings
17 Orphanage
18 Apollo Gardens
19 Leicester Square
20 Great Queen Street
21 Lincoln's Inn Fields
22 Fountain Court
23 The Temple
24 St. Paul's Cathedral
25 London Stone
26 Moorfields
27 Bedlam (until 1815)
28 Bunhill Fields

Map (c) Blake's London ca. 1810

36 Jerusalem,
the Emanation of the Giant Albion

Jerusalem was being written *c.* 1804–07, but was conceived at Felpham, *c.* 1801–02 (see 3.*1*) and not certainly complete before 1820. The titlepage, which B. probably engraved early in a burst of enthusiasm, is dated 1804 (as is the titlepage of *Milton*), and B. probably began to *write* about that time, though the *engraving* must have begun after mid-1805, since all the remaining plates are in the late script B. adopted at that time. *Milton* must have had priority, being printed *c.* 1808–10; but in mid-1807 George Cumberland wrote, 'Blake has eng^d. 60 Plates of a new Prophecy!' which seems to be *Jerusalem*, since *Milton* was only forty-five plates long, and the remark implies that the 'new Prophecy' was to comprise more than sixty plates. The first known copy of *Jerusalem* is shown by the watermarks to have been *printed* no earlier than 1818–20. Although the work of engraving in 1807 suggests that B. regarded the poem as finished, there are signs shortly afterwards that he was revising it. The *Descriptive Catalogue* of 1809, when B. believed himself to stand on the verge of recognition, indicates that he still thought of the poem as almost ready for publication– 'Mr B. has in his hands poems of the highest antiquity . . . if every thing goes on as it has begun, the world of vegetation and generation may expect to be opened again to Heaven. . . .' But the 'Public Address', which he drafted in his Notebook in 1809–10 when his hopes of fame were fading, shows that revision had begun, though B. still seemed to think the poem would soon be published–'the manner in which I have routed out the nest of villains will be seen in a Poem concerning my Three years' Herculean labours at Felpham, which I will soon publish'. These villains are the Hunt brothers, whose *Examiner* attacked B. savagely in 1808 and 1809, and who appear in *Jerusalem* as the three-headed giant Hand, leader of the sons of Albion. To include Hand as an important figure B. must have revised the poem after 1808, though in 1807, as we have seen, he regarded it as finished. Another sign of revision is the abandonment of the original plan of twenty-eight chapters which were announced on the titlepage in its first state; pl.14 seems to have ended the first of these chapters at one time. Probably when B.'s ambitions failed, he turned to *Jerusalem* knowing that he need not hasten his revision, since the poem would bring him no advantage; and he had a private revenge to take on the Hunts. Perhaps the revised poem lay for some years while he had neither resources nor incentive to print it until, about 1818, a group of young disciples began to gather round him and encourage him to proceed.

This is a complex poem, but it is based on simple notions. The first is that of a personified Albion, subsuming all Britons, present, past and future, together with their island and its history. B. elevates this personification into a metaphysical theory (see pl.27 and notes), but it is at heart no more than this: Albion is an entity, a person in himself, looking upon and interacting with his own elements–primarily the people who cal themselves 'Britons'–whom B., adopting a more biblical usage, calls 'sons' or 'daughters' of Albion. In the abstract the idea is confusing, but it is no more so than the concept of a masque.

The second notion is the biblical image of the New Jerusalem, dear to nonconformists, affected as they were by the evangelical excitement of the period. In the Preface to chapter 3, B. proudly places himself in this tradition, which found great hope in the promise of 'Jerusalem the golden'. B. belonged to the generation of 'Guide me, O thou great Jehovah', and wrote in that spirit. As in the Bible, Jerusalem appears in many forms: as a city, beset by enemies (especially Babylon); as a woman, led astray and captive by Babylon, or redeemed, and a bride in Eternity.

His most remarkable achievement was to unite the two notions. Albion is elevated to more than political or economic greatness; B. sets him in universal and eternal greatness in the realms of ideal truth. Jerusalem becomes a vision to be realized at home, in England, among B.'s compatriots and in his own day. Albion–a name for England in very common literary use–is asleep, dreaming distorted ambitions of war and conquest, trapped by mistaken laws of 'righteousness', and therefore incapable of waking to the vision and freedom of his true destiny, which is embodied in Jerusalem; he scorns her love, forgiveness and joy as folly, or sin. B. cries to Albion repeatedly, 'Awake!', but only one figure is faithful–Los, who struggles against the perverted visions of Albion's children (i.e. of ordinary Englishmen and women). Los is the personification of the true artist, and of the imaginative spirit; therefore B. identifies himself with Los; but Los is greater than any one man. Whenever a man sees visions of eternity and gives them to the world in the vital forms of art, the spirit of Los is awake. He cannot bring about the millennium when Albion will awake; but he can keep the nature and possibility of that day continually alive before him in a multitude of forms.

In the title of his poem B. refers to his vision of '*Jerusalem, the emanation of the Giant Albion*'. This is not merely an obscure way of saying that Albion, or England, should look forward to the coming of the New Jerusalem described in *Revelation*. B. envisages a more complete union of profounder concepts. Albion has become more than a personification; he is an eternal reality, a living human personality in heaven. In B.'s vision, the person in Eternity attains a wholeness unknown on earth. All the opposing principles and characteristics found in earthly life–opposed although they are all recognized to be necessary in the community, whether distinguished by character, outlook, sex, or even by different forms of life and nature–are blended together. On earth no man can experience characteristics other than his own; he cannot know what it is to be a stone, or a horse, or even a woman. In Eternity, the individual contains all these forms, and their experiences, within himself (see pl.99); and therefore every person in this mortal life is a part of the eternal Albion. Even the wandering prostitute is Jerusalem, crushed by the cruelty of Albion's children (e.g. 62.4, 74.16–17; *Milton* 33.22; 'Auguries of Innocence' 115–6).

The *emanation* (see *Four Zoas* i 17n) is a part of a person–temporarily separated from him, but essentially belonging to him. B. usually embodies this in the separation of a female form from the total personality (which by a necessary contrast is shown as male, though male emanations are occasionally mentioned). Jerusalem, then, the Holy City and Bride of *Revelation*, is no more than a vision of a part of the eternal Albion, 'which John in Patmos saw' (*Milton* pl.40.22). The story of Israel in the Bible, and the legends and history of Britain, are inextricably mixed–the *earthly* manifestations of Albion's diseased dreams in *eternity*. The corrupted visions of God seen by the warlike Israelites and the aggressiveness of eighteenth-century England are symptoms of the same disease, afflicting not merely two nations on earth, but one–Albion–whose nature is universal. Albion is divided; his emanation has been dismissed from his presence (ch. 1), and so in history there are two separate nations which ought to be one. Hence the deliberate interweaving of biblical and British names and stories. The children of Israel are really also the children of Albion; Reuben, the eldest son of Israel, stands for the twelve tribes as Hunt stands for misguided Englishmen. Hence also the curious story of the 'rolling apart' of Canaan and Albion (63.41–3), and the passages assigning the children of Israel to parts of Britain (16.28ff, 71.1–72.31).

These assumptions, then, underlie the poem. Its narrative begins as, in Eternity, Albion rejects Jerusalem as a sinful partner; his depression deepens into sickness, and his corrupted sons take control of him in spite of his friends. The evil spreads; but Los, the faithful guardian, watches until the moment comes when divine inspiration wakens Albion, whose evil self is at last annihilated; and he is once more united with Jerusalem. Throughout the poem, B. insists on his ethic of perpetual forgiveness and self-sacrifice, and on the belief that man can only rise to infinite life when he abandons the constricted vision of objectivity and order, in nature and society, for the imaginative and compassionate vision which sees divine humanity in everything.

The Sons and Daughters of Albion

The pattern of the relationships is set out in pl.71, and this is generally adhered to, though the country attachments are not very important. The two sets of twelve are:

Hyle	Cambel–Boadicea
Hand	Gwendolen
Coban	Ignoge
Gwantok	Cordella
Peachey	Mehetabel
Brereton	Ragan
Slayd	Gonorill

Huttn	Gwinefred
Skofield	Gwineverra
Kox	Estrild
Kotope	Sabrina
Bowen	Conwenna

The sons are constant; in the list in *Four Zoas* ii *61–2* there is no Gwine-verra, and Cambel and Boadicea are separated. All the daughters are queens and princesses of British legendary history, except for Gwinefred, Cambel and Mehetabel. *Gwinefred* was an Anglo-Saxon saint; *Mehetabel* is a shadowy Edomite (i.e. alien) queen named in *Genesis* xxxvi 39; *Cambel* is a mystery. *Camber*, in Milton's *History of Britain*, is a man, and no closer name has been found. Boadicea is the only other queen not from pre-Roman legend. The daughters thus represent Britain through the ages.

The sons, on the other hand, are disguised *contemporaries* of B. Scholfield was his antagonist in the quarrel which led to B.'s indictment for 'assault and seditious words'; *Kox* is Cock, who supported Scholfield, and *Huttn* is Hutton, an officer who was involved. *Peachey, Brereton* and *Quantock* were the names of Justices at B.'s trial; *Bowen* was a lawyer who practised in the region and may have been involved. *Hylé* is Hayley, the disguise helped by Cockney pronunciation (B. was probably also aware that the word is Greek for *matter*). *Hand*, the three-headed enemy of Los, is the brothers Hunt, who signed editorials in their *Examiner* (which attacked B. in 1808–09) with the symbol of a hand. *Coban* may be Cromek, who employed B. in 1806–08, and swindled him. (Another suggestion for Coban is 'Bacon', who however was not a contemporary of B.'s, and whom he often attacks in his own name). *Kotope* looks like a form of Courthope, but has not been identified; nor has *Slayd* who, however, is often paired with Hutton and may perhaps have been another officer. The list as a whole contains 'the sons of England who keep the nation blind and asleep'.

Vala and Luvah

Vala is a major figure in *Jerusalem*, Luvah is not; but they must be considered together. In *Four Zoas* Vala was Luyah's emanation; in *Jerusalem* she is presented as Albion's, as the shadow of Jerusalem. *Vala* was the original title of *Four Zoas*, when she was the central evil figure of the poem, as she is in *Jerusalem*, where she appears in a number of guises. As herself, Vala appears in ch. 1 as Jerusalem's scornful partner who through jealousy causes Albion to reject Jerusalem, so that both Jerusalem and he fall into her power—under her net or veil. As *Babylon*, she appears as the historical city which took Jerusalem captive and drove her inhabitants into exile, and so Jerusalem is often shown imprisoned by Babylon. In *Revelation*, Babylon is called *Rahab*, and B. develops his great Queen of Mystery from this source. *Tirzah* is another revelation of Vala's evil; and the twelve daughters of Albion are together identified with her. In B.'s terminology, Babylon, Rahab and Tirzah are 'states' of Vala. They are temporary personae,

21*

which in Eternity will be annihilated; Vala is the real person, who in Albion's resurrection is purified and re-united with Jerusalem in Albion.

B. gives himself some trouble by reintroducing Luvah, who is now Vala's father, since she cannot be his emanation. She took her life from him, but belongs to Albion. This is an unsatisfactory expedient, but B. wished to use material (in particular pl.43) from the earlier myth of *Four Zoas*. These passages are best considered individually, as by-products of the main story, since B. never fully assimilated him to the myth. Sometimes he is identified with Albion's spectre, sometimes his enemy: but his appearance always signifies distress within Albion's soul.

The Prefaces

Having addressed the reading public at large at the outset, B. addresses the religious in three different groups, the last being the Christians, who should recognize the truth which has been revealed to them, though they clearly find it difficult to do so. The material of the chapters is not exclusively related to the object of the respective prefaces, though there is a good deal about Reuben in ch. 2, and about Voltaire and Rousseau in ch. 3. The prefaces give B. an opportunity to speak in his own voice.

Designs and Editions

Each chapter of twenty-three or twenty-four pages is closed by a full-page design; with frontispiece and titlepage this brings the total to exactly 100 plates. There are facsimile editions (now out of print) in the Blake Trust series, both in colour and in black-and-white; references to easily available reproductions of individual pages are given in the footnotes. The reader is referred to the abridged *Jerusalem*, ed. W. R. Hughes (London 1964). The most important aid to the reading of *Jerusalem* is a thorough knowledge of the historical books of the Old Testament, the Gospels, and *Revelation*. For Druidism see A. L. Owen's *The Famous Druids* (Oxford 1962), and for the occult sources D. Hirst's *Hidden Riches* (London 1963).

Chapter One

The first chapter describes the origins of the sickness of Albion, and has two main themes: the state of Albion himself, and the labours and problems of Los, who struggles endlessly to contain the evils resulting from Albion's state.

ANALYSIS

Epic introduction 4.1–5.

ALBION

(A) 4.6–5.15. Albion is presented in a state of wretchedness.

interjection 5.16–45. B. speaks of his own writing, and the visions that surround him.

(B) 5.46–65. Albion's twin emanations, Vala and Jerusalem, are shown, the first drawing the second away from their true home in Beulah, into the land of chaos, Ulro.

LOS

(C) *5.66–11.7.* Los, seeing and hearing this, sets to work, but is bedevilled by his spectre, his evil self, whom he must subdue.

(D) *11.8–12.20.* Los creates Erin, who will guard Albion.

(E) *12.21–14.34.* Los builds Golgonooza, the beautiful city which guards against chaos; it is fully described.

interjection 15.1–16.27. B. again describes the confused visions of the state of Albion and Europe as they appear to him.

(F) *16.28–17.63.* Los ties Albion to biblical history; and continues to seek out and expose the evil done by Albion's children.

ALBION

(G) *18.1–19.35.* Albion is incited by his sons to reject Jerusalem.

(H) *19.36–25.16.* Albion disputes with Jerusalem and Vala. He believes his love for Jerusalem is an unforgivable sin, and he rejects her in spite of her entreaties, and her declaration that no sin is unforgivable and that love is not sin. Vala casts her veil over Albion, and thus gains power over both the others.

Pl. 1   *[Frontispiece]*

¶ 36. A man, wearing hat and overcoat, carrying a globe-like lantern, enters a dark doorway with a pointed arch. No text. Round and above the arch, as revealed by a proof copy (facs. reproduced in the *Blake Trust* edn of *Jerusalem*, Rinder copy, and in G. L. Keynes: *Blake Studies* and *William Blake: Poet, Printer, Prophet*), these lines, deleted by engraving in all extant copies of the poem: (Above the arch)

> There is a Void, outside of Existence, which if entered into
> Englobes itself and becomes a Womb; such was Albion's Couch,
> A pleasant Shadow of Repose called Albion's lovely Land.
>
> His Sublime and Pathos become two rocks fixed in the Earth:
> 5 His Reason, his Spectrous Power, covers them above:
> Jerusalem his Emanation is a Stone laying beneath.
> O *Albion behold! Pitying* behold the Vision of Albion!

(On right side of arch)

> Half Friendship is the bitterest Enmity, said Los
> As he entered the Door of Death for Albion's sake inspired.
> 10 The long-sufferings of God are not for ever; there is a Judgement.

(On left side of arch, in reversed writing)

> Everything has its Vermin, O Spectre of the Sleeping Dead!

1–3 resemble *Milton* pl.41.*36–42.2*

7. Albion behold Pitying] A somewhat conjectural reading (the ! is editorial).

Pl. 2

JERUSALEM
The Emanation of The Giant Albion

Pl. 3   SHEEP   TO THE PUBLIC   GOATS

After my three years' slumber on the banks of the ocean, I again dis-
play my giant forms to the public: my former giants & fairies having
received the highest reward possible, the *love* and *friendship* of
those with whom to be connected is to be *blessed:* I cannot doubt
5   that this more consolidated & extended work will be as kindly
received.

The enthusiasm of the following poem, the author hopes *no reader
will think presumptuousness or arrogance when he is reminded that the Ancients
entrusted their love to their writing, to the full as enthusiastically as I have
10   who acknowledge mine for my Saviour and Lord, for they were wholly ab-
sorbed in their gods.* I also hope the reader will be with me, wholly one
in Jesus our Lord, who is the God *of Fire* and Lord *of Love* to whom
the Ancients looked and saw his day afar off, with trembling and
amazement.

15   The spirit of Jesus is continual forgiveness of sin: he who waits to
be righteous before he enters into the Saviour's kingdom, the divine
body, will never enter there. I am perhaps the most sinful of men; I
pretend not to holiness. Yet I pretend to love, to see, to converse with
daily, as man with man, & the more to have an interest in the Friend
20   of Sinners. Therefore *dear* reader, *forgive* what you do not approve,
and *love* me for this energetic exertion of my talent.

Pl. 2. *Titlepage.* The title written in large, ornamented 'copperplate' script,
surrounded by flying figures with butterfly wings. One, right, hovers with
hands over face as if in despair; across the foot of the page, beneath another
winged female figure resting, lies Jerusalem, asleep or in a swoon–a nude
female figure, whose limbs and wings are 'vegetating' into the form of a leaf.
At the very foot, the words: '1804/Printed by W. Blake Sth Molton St', in-
cised (i.e. added to the plate). The words 'In XXVIII Chapters' were del.
[Reproduced in G. L. Keynes, *William Blake: Poet, Printer, Prophet.*]

Pl. 3. *Sheep / Goats*] Doubtless implying that *Jerusalem* will divide the
people in a Last Judgment.

3.*1. my three years' slumber*] Refers to B.'s residence in Felpham, 1800–03.
The 'former giants and fairies' are presumably the Lambeth books.

3.*3.* The words printed in italics were erased from the plate, but have been
recovered by D. V. Erdman. B. thus left the text with large gaps, in the
sense as well as in the appearance.

3.*12.* The deletions *of Fire* and *of Love*, unlike the others, leave the text
making sense, and may not have been made with the same apparent rash-
ness as the others.

Reader, *lover* of books, *lover* of heaven,
And of that God from whom *all books are given*,
Who in mysterious Sinai's awful cave
25   To man the wondrous art of writing gave.
Again he speaks in thunder and in fire—
Thunder of thought, & flames of fierce desire.
Even from the depths of Hell his voice I hear,
Within the unfathomed caverns of my ear.
30   Therefore I print, nor vain my types shall be;
Heaven, Earth & Hell henceforth shall live in harmony.

32   *Of the measure in which the following poem is written*

We who dwell on earth can do nothing of ourselves; everything is
conducted by spirits, no less than digestion or sleep. *To note the last*
35 *words of Jesus*, Εδοθη μοι πασα εξουσια εν ουρανω και επι γης.
When this verse was first dictated to me I considered a monot-
onous cadence like that used by Milton & Shakespeare & all writers
of English blank verse, derived from the modern bondage of rhym-
ing, to be a necessary and indispensable part of verse. But I soon
40 found that in the mouth of a true orator such monotony was not only
awkward, but as much a bondage as rhyme itself. I therefore have
produced a variety in every line, both of cadences & number of syl-
lables. Every word and every letter is studied and put into its fit
place: the terrific numbers are reserved for the terrific parts, the
45 mild & gentle for the mild & gentle parts, and the prosaic for in-
ferior parts: all are necessary to each other. Poetry fettered, fetters
the human race. Nations are destroyed, or flourish, in proportion as
their poetry, painting and music are destroyed or flourish. The
primeval state of man was wisdom, art and science.

3.24. *Sinai's awful cave* and the giving of writing there is B.'s reading of
Exodus xxiv 4, 7, 12–15, where Moses went up Sinai, was hidden in a
cloud, and was given the Law: in verse 4 Moses writes; in verse 12 he is
'given the Law'.
3.32. *Of the measure*] Cp. Milton's justification of the use of blank verse in
his note *The Verse* at the head of *Paradise Lost*.
3.35. The deleted Greek means: 'All power is given unto me in heaven
and in earth' (*Matthew* xxviii 18). They are the first words of Christ's last
speech (in *Matthew*) before ascending to heaven. B. wrote the Greek as
shown, and without accents or breathings.
3.36. *monotonous*] Regular. The following explanation distinguishes be-
tween the *inspiration* B. received, and the care and skill which, as he recog-
nized, was necessary in setting it down.
3.38. *modern bondage of rhyming*] Milton's phrase (see 3.32n).

CHAPTER 1

Pl. 4   Of the sleep of Ulro, and of the passage through
Eternal death, and of the awaking to eternal life!

This theme calls me in sleep, night after night, & every morn
Awakes me at sunrise; then I see the Saviour over me,
5   Spreading his beams of love & dictating the words of this mild
song:

'Awake, awake, O sleeper of the land of shadows, wake, expand!
I am in you and you in me, mutual in love divine;
Fibres of love from man to man through Albion's pleasant land.
In all the dark Atlantic vale, down from the hills of Surrey,
10   A black water accumulates. Return, Albion, return!
Thy brethren call thee; and thy fathers and thy sons,
Thy nurses and thy mothers, thy sisters and thy daughters
Weep at thy soul's disease, and the Divine Vision is darkened.
Thy emanation that was wont to play before thy face,
15   Beaming forth with her daughters into the divine bosom—
Where hast thou hidden thy emanation, lovely Jerusalem,
From the vision and fruition of the Holy One?
I am not a God afar off, I am a brother and friend;
Within your bosoms I reside, and you reside in me.
20   Lo! we are one, forgiving all evil, not seeking recompense.
Ye are my members, O ye sleepers of Beulah, land of shades!'

Pl.4. At the top of this plate, between moon and a star, Μονος ο Ιεσους (sic)
'alone Jesus' is written in the heavens. The words are found in *John* viii 9,
but a likelier source is the transfiguration narrative in *Luke* ix 36 where
Jesus is seen alone after the vision and the cloud have passed. (There the
words are ὁ 'Ιησοῦς μόνος.) The transfiguration becomes important at the
final climax of the poem in pl.96.
4.1. *Ulro*] The region of non-entity (see introduction to *Milton*, p. 486).
The sleeper is Albion, representing both England and mankind as a whole.
4.6. *Awake!*] The song is addressed to Albion, not B.
Expand] Cp. 34.17–18.
4.8. *Fibres* . . .] i.e. 'fibres of love run. . . .' At the end of the line is the word
'Where!!' (*del.*).
4.16. *thy emanation, lovely Jerusalem*] See headnote.
4.17. *fruition*] Perhaps suggesting jealousy in Albion, and that he is hiding
Jerusalem where she may not have visions and then give birth by them?
4.21. *Beulah*] The region, just outside the highest heaven but in contact
with it, where spirits weary, or injured, or sick, may rest. In our material
world we can, in dreams and visions, enter Beulah (cp. 48.20 and especially
Milton pl.30.1n).

But the perturbed Man away turns down the valleys dark;
'Phantom of the overheated brain, shadow of immortality,
Seeking to keep my soul a victim to thy love, which binds
25 Man the enemy of man into deceitful friendships.
Jerusalem is not; her daughters are indefinite.
By demonstration man alone can live, and not by faith.
My mountains are my own, and I will keep them to myself:
The Malvern and the Cheviot, the Wolds, Plinlimmon & Snowdon
30 Are mine! Here will I build my laws of moral virtue.
Humanity shall be no more, but war & princedom & victory.'

So spoke Albion in jealous fears, hiding his emanation
Upon the Thames and Medway, rivers of Beulah, dissembling
His jealousy before the throne divine, darkening, cold.

Pl. 5 The banks of the Thames are clouded, the ancient porches of
    Albion are
Darkened; they are drawn through unbounded space, scattered
    upon
The void in incoherent despair. Cambridge & Oxford & London
Are driven among the starry wheels, rent away and dissipated,
5 In chasms & abysses of sorrow, enlarged without dimension,
    terrible.
Albion's mountains run with blood, the cries of war & of tumult

4.22. After this line, a deleted line: 'Saying: "We are not One; we are
Many, thou most simulative"....'

4.23. From *Macbeth* II i 38–9: 'a false creation / Proceeding from the heat-
oppressed brain'. In fact, Albion is rejecting truth by confusing it with
error, which he accepts (26–7).

4.30. *Here will I build . . .*] Perhaps thinking of the 'druid temples' spread
across England and Wales, signs of priestly oppression.

4.33. These are *rivers of Beulah* in being representative of places in the
spiritual imagination. Albion is hiding Jerusalem within his own domain
and not letting her out (*16–17*).

5.1–6. Albion is thrown into a tumult by his selfish withdrawal. Albion is,
in normal usage, the land of England and, in B.'s usage, a person in
eternity. B. associates the two usages and describes how the parts of Albion
(places in England as we know them) are dispersed in eternity. Albion can
be a land and a human figure, and can take other forms as well—hence the
porches (*1*).

5.3 *starry wheels*] The stars here (as often, though not without exception)
connote the Newtonian universe, which B. saw as a formless abyss. The
wheels are complex, calculated, mindless and irresistible devices of the
devil. Cp. 15.18–20.

5.6. War is one result of Albion's apostasy; but the line should be
understood imaginatively.

Resound into the unbounded night, every human perfection
Of mountain & river & city, are small & withered & darkened.
Cam is a little stream, Ely is almost swallowed up,
10 Lincoln & Norwich stand trembling on the brink of Udan-Adan,
Wales and Scotland shrink themselves to the west and to the north,
Mourning for fear of the warriors in the vale of Entuthon Benython.
Jerusalem is scattered abroad like a cloud of smoke through
       non-entity:
Moab & Ammon & Amalek & Canaan & Egypt & Aram
15 Receive her little ones for sacrifices and the delights of cruelty.

Trembling I sit day and night; my friends are astonished at me.
Yet they forgive my wanderings, I rest not from my great task—
To open the eternal worlds, to open the immortal eyes
Of man inwards into the worlds of thought—into Eternity
20 Ever expanding in the bosom of God, the human imagination.
O Saviour, pour upon me thy spirit of meekness & love;
Annihilate the selfhood in me, be thou all my life.
Guide thou my hand which trembles exceedingly upon the Rock
       of Ages,
While I write of the building of Golgonooza, & of the terrors of
       Entuthon;
25 Of Hand & Hyle & Coban, of Gwantok, Peachey, Brereton,
       Slayd & Huttn;
Of the terrible sons & daughters of Albion and their generations.

5.9. Ely . . . Cam] See *35.12n.*
5.10. Udan-Adan] The dark lake of Ulro, a sinister lake in a black forest, a
place of indefinite form, B.'s Acheron and Styx. Cp. *13.38ff.*
5.12. Entuthon-Benython] The forest in which Udan-Adan is found.
5.14. B. names tribes surrounding, and mostly hostile to, Israel. He accuses
them, among their pagan rites, of human sacrifice–a practice condemned
several times in the Old Testament (e.g. Ahaz in *2 Kings* xvi 3 'made his
son to pass through the fire, according to the abominations of the heathen'.
See also *Ezekiel* xvi 21, xx 26.).
5.24. Golgonooza] The city built by Los in the midst of Ulro as a bastion
of light against the power of darkness. See *12.25ff.*
5.25. Hand & Hyle] 'Sons of Albion' (see headnote), that is, lesser exten-
sions of Albion's fallen personality, who, in the course of *Jerusalem*, enact
in particular ways the evil that has come into his mind. All twelve are
named at *19.18.*
5.27–33. The four sons try to destroy Los's work, which, as will be seen,
is to maintain the remnants of eternity in Ulro by the building of Gol-
gonooza and his work at the anvil. (Cp. note on *Milton* pl.27.13: in Neo-
Platonic imagery a southern entry is for eternal spirits and a northern for
mortals, so that the sons of Albion may thus be described as assaulting the
spiritual gate and being driven out through the mortal gate: but it is not

Skofield, Kox, Kotope and Bowen revolve most mightily upon
The furnace of Los, before the eastern gate bending their fury.
They war to destroy the furnaces, to desolate Golgonooza,
30 And to devour the sleeping humanity of Albion in rage & hunger.
They revolve into the furnaces southward & are driven forth
    northward,
Divided into male and female forms time after time.
From these twelve all the families of England spread abroad.
The male is a furnace of beryl; the female is a golden loom.
35 I behold them, and their rushing fires overwhelm my soul
In London's darkness, and my tears fall day and night .
Upon the emanations of Albion's sons, the daughters of Albion,
Names anciently remembered but now contemned as fictions,
Although in every bosom they control our vegetative powers.
40 These are united into Tirzah and her sisters, on Mount Gilead:
Cambel & Gwendolen & Conwenna & Cordella & Ignoge.

certain that this was in B.'s mind.) The division into male and female is a
sign of fallen, imperfect nature.
5.28. *The furnace of Los*] An important image. Three kinds of furnace are
imagined: (*a*) Los, as blacksmith, has a hot, bellows-driven fire in which to
heat the iron that he holds in his tongs and shapes with his hammer; (*b*) as
iron-moulder, he uses a blast-furnace to smelt iron from ore (using the
processed summarized at *Four Zoas* ii *327*, though here the process is puri-
fying and not formative as in (*a*); (*c*) B. recalls the 'burning fiery furnace'
of *Daniel* iii, where men walked in the midst of the fire (cp. 31.5*n*). B. may
combine these images, as in 11.*8–12*, where Los looks into the furnace as
Nebuchadnezzar might have looked at Daniel; yet Erin, whom he then
sees, is a creation of his furnace as in different ways iron is manufactured
in the two kinds of furnace mentioned above. B.'s images often depart from
a simple depiction of either process in the search for imaginative expression.
5.34. *The male . . . the female*] So in 90.*27*, where the context clearly indi-
cates that these are furnaces and looms inimical to those of Los and Eni-
tharmon. The men and women of England that B. envisages are immortal
forms, intended to do Los's work, but only parodying it for evil.   *beryl*]
Chosen for its beauty, and hardness (cp. 'beryl and emerald immortal', in a
similar passage, 53.*9*).
5.37. *upon*] For or on behalf of.
5.38. The names of the daughters of Albion are drawn from the legendary
history of Ancient Britain (see headnote, p. 624). B. saw these legends, as
he saw the Druids, as imaginative realities. As against the rationalist, the
imaginative eye can see through and past such myths to the eternal verities
which they reveal. *contemned*] Despised.
5.39. *Our vegetative powers*] The powers by which we live this mortal,
earthly life, as distinct from the imaginative, eternal life.
5.40–5. Tirzah and Rahab are the two female powers of evil whom B.

And these united into Rahab in the Covering Cherub on Euphrates:
Gwineverra & Gwinefred, & Gonorill & Sabrina beautiful,
Estrild, Mehetabel & Ragan, lovely daughters of Albion;
45   They are the beautiful emanations of the twelve sons of Albion.

The starry wheels revolved heavily over the furnaces,
Drawing Jerusalem in anguish of maternal love
Eastward, a pillar of a cloud with Vala upon the mountains,
Howling in pain, redounding from the arms of Beulah's
    daughters,
50   Out from the furnaces of Los above the head of Los,
A pillar of smoke writhing afar into non-entity, redounding
Till the cloud reaches afar, outstretched among the starry wheels
Which revolve heavily in the mighty void above the furnaces.

O what avail the loves & tears of Beulah's lovely daughters?
55   They hold the immortal form in gentle hands & tender tears;
But all within is opened into the deeps of Entuthon Benython,
A dark and unknown night, indefinite, unmeasurable, without end—
Abstract philosophy warring in enmity against imagination
(Which is the Divine Body of the Lord Jesus, blessed for ever).
60   And there Jerusalem wanders with Vala upon the mountains,
Attracted by the revolutions of those wheels, the cloud of smoke
Immense. And Jerusalem & Vala weeping in the cloud
Wander away into the chaotic void, lamenting with her shadow
Among the daughters of Albion, among the starry wheels,
65   Lamenting for her children, for the sons & daughters of Albion.

Los heard her lamentations in the deeps afar. His tears fall
Incessant before the furnaces, and his emanation divided in pain,

derived from the Bible. Both are cruel, Tirzah like an oppressive mother,
Rahab like a domineering mistress. B. says, in effect, that the daughters
of Albion–the womanhood of Britain–are marked by the evil principles
figured in his Rahab and Tirzah. See *Four Zoas* viii *267n*.
5.46–53. The meaning of *46* is that of *27–8*. In the following lines B. is
using an image derived from watching the smoke blow up from the
chimney of a blast furnace; imaginatively this becomes Vala, as the roaring
of the furnace in *7.35–6* becomes Luvah's voice. The lines reiterate the
theme that evil influences from Albion are seeking to destroy the good that
remains in Albion at his heart–in his emanation Jerusalem.
5.54. *Beulah's lovely daughters*] They have the task, nurselike, of caring for
the souls of the lost, or those in danger of being lost, who sleep a deathly
sleep. But their powers are limited, and they can only tend the sleeper; they
cannot heal. See *Milton* pl.30.*1n*. They see Albion's outward appearance
as an immortal form; but all 'within' is a world of corruption.
5.66. The first part of the action proper begins: Los disputes with his
spectre who wishes to dominate him.

> Eastward toward the starry wheels. But westward, a black horror,
> Pl. 6 His spectre driven by the starry wheels of Albion's sons, black and

5.68. In *Jerusalem* the west is the direction of freedom and imagination; but Albion's Western Gate is closed (40.*3,17*) except in a few people (40.*33*). The east is the direction in which lay the reactionary kingdoms of Europe, and the war (45.*56*); further away lay Babylon (82.*36*). The 'current of creation' (77.*9*) runs with the sun from east to west. The north is the direction of ice and darkness, and the bloody religions of the old days (83.*19*), to which the south is the opposite, the direction of sun and light. Thus western and southern places, whether in London or Europe or the world, are associated with beauty and imagination; northern and eastern places with evil and death. In 12.*45ff* Eden is west, Beulah is south, Generation is north and Ulro is east: B.'s scheme of the cardinal points normally follows this pattern. The arrangement of *Four Zoas* (Urthona/Los north, Luvah east, Urizen south, Tharmas west; cp. vi *276–7* and *261n*) is found also from time to time in *Jerusalem*, and does not quite fit, though there also the west remains ideal and Luvah is in the east. But of the other two, 'strong Urthona' in the north is less corrupt than 'bright Urizen' in the south.

See also the note on the *false tongue* (*Milton* pl.2.*10*). Much depends on the west–the 'parent' sense or power (98.*17*; *Four Zoas* i 16), which is closed in this fallen world. In Eternity, the fourfold completeness of the cardinal points makes them, with the four rivers of paradise and the four Zoas, a mark of perfection and wholeness (98.*24–7*).

6.1. The SPECTRE (see design at foot of plate) first appeared in *Four Zoas* iv *62ff*, torn from Los when Tharmas separated him and Enitharmon. At first B. uses this *spectre* only as a ghost of the Los who had been a 'dolorous shadow'. But the image caught his imagination, and he used it and developed it throughout *Four Zoas, Milton* and *Jerusalem*, as well as 'My spectre around me' (p. 481). It is important that the idea did develop, and that it does not hold one meaning at all times. It is an image with many connotations, rather than an exact symbol.

There are a number of elements in the image. (*a*) The ordinary meaning– 'ghost', phantom of a person once alive. Spectres were common in the 'Gothic' horror-romances of the time. It is essentially *not real*; the shape of a person, a divided part of him, his copy, bodiless but unspiritual. B. often referred to it as a 'shadow', which hovers round a man, never able to leave him, but never touching him (e.g. 'My spectre around me'). It is an empty imitation of a man, not his real self–and so tragedy follows when a person depends on the shadow instead of the reality. Since the physical world is unreal, the man who lives only in it is living in dependence on an unreal mortal body–he is in spectrous form. (*b*) There is a further development of this, where the hovering spectre wishes to bite but dare not (11.*6–7*; *Milton* pl.39.*16–21*). This is derived from the *spectre, or vampire-bat* mentioned by Stedman in his *Travels*, published 1796, in which edition B.

Opaque, divided from his back; he labours and he mourns.

For as his emanation divided, his spectre also divided
In terror of those starry wheels. And the spectre stood over Los
5   Howling in pain, a blackening shadow, blackening, dark & opaque,
Cursing the terrible Los, bitterly cursing him for his friendship
To Albion, suggesting murderous thoughts against Albion.

Los raged and stamped the earth in his might & terrible wrath.

illustrated this bat: and he often gives bat-wings to his own spectres. The vampire bat sucks blood, and B.'s spectre is also vicious; but the shadow of a man cannot destroy the man without destroying itself. (*c*) Yet another element, though less important in the image, may be the Epicurean notion that creatures exhaled a sort of image of themselves 'composed of a very subtle matter' (Reid, *Essays on the Intellectual Powers of Man*, 1785–where the word 'spectre' is used for this 'image', the earliest *OED* reference to the use of the word in this way). By this 'spectre' men were said to perceive each other; B. may have had this in his mind, thinking that only in Eden do persons truly meet, not through spectral forms, but with nothing intervening.

In narrative use, there are two aspects of the spectre, one good, the other evil. In *Four Zoas* the good is often uppermost, in *Milton* chiefly the evil. The spectre in power is evil, a 'Hyde' figure, a corruption of a person's real and complete 'Jekyll' self. It seeks to dominate by force, and is a creature of darkness–hence the bat-wings with which it is shown, e.g. in the illustration to *Jerusalem* 6. It is male, aggressive and domineering, as against both the gentle female emanation and the subtle corruption of Rahab; and as against the true Human personality which contains and balances both male and female in itself. Sometimes B. uses the image of the hermaphrodite (e.g. *Milton* pl.14.*37*), which is a spectral form most strikingly seen in *Milton* pl.38.*15–27*, where the magnificent desolation of the male Satan is ruled by the hidden interior power of the female Rahab. This perpetuates the sexual division, yet is effectively neither male nor female.

When controlled for good, however, as in Los's building (*Four Zoas* iv *194*ff; *Jerusalem* 8.*30–60*), the spectre may be a valued and necessary aid, although often reluctant. In *Four Zoas* viia *333*ff the spectre of Los, with its dim memories of a higher state in another life, is instrumental in reconciling Los and Enitharmon. But there are no spectres in Eden; the spectre is unreal, a shadow, and must be annihilated in the end.

6.*2*. *He*] Los.

6.*6*. The spectre wishes to strengthen Albion's desire for death (4.*31*). B. in passages such as this identifies himself with Los, who works for the good of Albion, in spite of the spectral forces of those (such as Hayley) who try to prevent him, and in spite of the evil tendencies he sees within himself, which make him afraid to act because of the corruptions of Albion.

He stood and stamped the earth. Then he threw down his hammer
    in rage and
10 In fury; then he sat down and wept, terrified. Then arose
And chanted his song, labouring with the tongs and hammer.
But still the spectre divided, and still his pain increased.

In pain the spectre divided, in pain of hunger and thirst,
To devour Los's human perfection, but when he saw that Los

[Design]

Pl. 7 Was living, panting like a frighted wolf and howling
He stood over the immortal in the solitude and darkness,
Upon the darkening Thames, across the whole island westward,
A horrible shadow of death among the furnaces, beneath
5 The pillar of folding smoke. And he sought by other means
To lure Los: by tears, by arguments of science & by terrors,
Terrors in every nerve, by spasms & extended pains,
While Los answered unterrified to the opaque blackening fiend.

And thus the spectre spoke: 'Wilt thou still go on to destruction,
10 Till thy life is all taken away by this deceitful friendship?
He drinks thee up like water; like wine he pours thee
Into his tuns. Thy daughters are trodden in his vintage,
He makes thy sons the trampling of his bulls, they are ploughed
And harrowed for his profit. Lo! thy stolen emanation
15 Is his garden of pleasure. All the spectres of his sons mock thee.
Look how they scorn thy once admired palaces, now in ruins
Because of Albion, because of deceit and friendship! For lo!
Hand has peopled Babel & Nineveh; Hyle, Asshur & Aram;
Coban's son is Nimrod; his son Cush is adjoined to Aram

6. *Design*: Los in front of his furnace, leaning on his hammer, and looking
up to argue with his spectre, a bat-winged spirit who hovers over him.
(Reproduced in *Blake's Engravings*, ed. Keynes, pl.103.)

7.3. The shadow of night as it spreads across England from east to west.

7.5. *A pillar of folding smoke*] Cp. *5.48*.

7.9. The spectre speaks with the voice of worldly wisdom, saying that Los
is working for Albion, who only scorns his labour and misappropriates it.

7.14. *thy stolen emanation*] Apparently a reference to someone else's enjoy-
ment of advantages derived from a work of B.'s—perhaps Hayley, or
Cromek, both specified as sons of Albion. Emanations are stolen in *Four
Zoas*, e.g., ii *512–52*, iv *56*.

7.18–26. The great cities of the ancient world have been taken over and
corrupted by the wicked sons of Albion, and the patriarchs themselves have
also become vehicles of their evil will. These lines are based chiefly on
Genesis x, where Noah's descendants are listed. But B. is not consistent
with *Genesis*, in which Cush is Nimrod's *father* and is not linked with

20   By the daughter of Babel in a woven mantle of pestilence & war.
      They put forth their spectrous cloudy sails, which drive their
          immense
      Constellations over the deadly deeps of indefinite Udan-Adan.
      Kox is the father of Shem & Ham & Japheth; he is the Noah
      Of the flood of Udan-Adan. Huttn is the father of the seven
25   From Enoch to Adam; Skofield is Adam who was new
      Created in Edom. I saw it indignant, & thou art not moved!
      This has divided thee in sunder, and wilt thou still forgive?
      O, thou seest not what I see—what is done in the furnaces.
      Listen, I will tell thee what is done in moments to thee unknown:
30   Luvah was cast into the furnaces of affliction & sealed,
      And Vala fed in cruel delight the furnaces with fire.
      Stern Urizen beheld, urged by necessity to keep
      The evil day afar, & if perchance with iron power
      He might avert his own despair. In woe & fear he saw
35   Vala encircle round the furnaces where Luvah was closed.
      With joy she heard his howlings, & forgot he was her Luvah,
      With whom she lived in bliss in times of innocence & youth.
      Vala comes from the furnace in a cloud, but wretched Luvah
      Is howling in the furnaces, in flames among Albion's spectres,

Aram. The descent is: *Adam* to *Enoch* (seven, inclusive; cp. *24*) and Enoch
was *Noah's* great-grandfather. Of Noah's three sons *Ham*, *Shem* and
Japheth (*23*), Ham's son *Cush* was father of *Nimrod*, who reigned in *Babel*
and *Nineveh* (*18*). Shem's children included *Asshur* and *Aram* (assigned to
Hyle, *18*). Thus the spectrous sons of Albion are associated with each stage
in the patriarchal lineage, down to the founding of the tribes known to the
Bible in the warlike history echoed in *20–2*.
7.*19*. *Cush's* son *Nimrod* founded Babel, which is near *Aram*, both being on
the Euphrates. But the Cushites of the historical books were Ethiopians.
7.*25*. Edom was a traditional enemy of Israel; the 'Adam new created in
Edom' is an image of man falsely made, deceiving later generations.
7.*28*. *Thou seest not*] A blast-furnace is enclosed while in operation. But at
11.*8* Los opens the furnace.
7.*30–7*. These lines repeat *Four Zoas* ii *282–9*. There they refer to Urizen's
revenge on Luvah while the building of Urizen's palace was in progress.
Here the passage is a sudden digression into another of B.'s worlds; in the
terms of *Jerusalem*, this is a vision to be seen inside Los's furnace. It shows
how, in yet another way, evil is hanging over Los.
7.*39–40*. Cp. *5.46n* above. The sense is obscure. Who is 'forming' and
'preparing'?–Luvah, it seems; yet he is also the unwilling sacrifice. He is
'among Albion's spectres' as if they were in the same plight as his; yet in
41 he seems to be 'forming' them. What is clear is that through the agency
of Luvah, the passionate one, whose passion is here turned to evil use, the
'spectre sons of Albion' are turning against Los.

40 To prepare the spectre of Albion to reign over thee, O Los,
    Forming the spectres of Albion according to his rage—
    To prepare the spectre sons of Adam, who is Skofield, the ninth
    Of Albion's sons, & the father of all his brethren in the shadowy
    Generation. Cambel & Gwendolen wove webs of war & of
45 Religion to involve all Albion's sons, and when they had
    Involved eight, their webs rolled outwards into darkness,
    And Skofield the ninth remained on the outside of the eight,
    And Kox, Kotope, & Bowen, one in him, a fourfold wonder,
    Involved the eight. Such are the generations of the giant Albion,
50 To separate a law of sin to punish thee in thy members.'

    Los answered: 'Although I know not this, I know far worse than
       this.
    I know that Albion hath divided me and that thou, O my spectre,
    Hast just cause to be irritated. But look steadfastly upon me,
    Comfort thyself in my strength; the time will arrive
55 When all Albion's injuries shall cease, & when we shall
    Embrace him tenfold bright, rising from his tomb in immortality.
    They have divided themselves by wrath; they must be united by
    Pity. Let us therefore take example & warning, O my spectre.
    Oh, that I could abstain from wrath! O that the Lamb
60 Of God would look upon me & pity me in my fury,
    In anguish of regeneration, in terrors of self-annihilation.
    Pity must join together those whom wrath has torn in sunder,
    And the religion of generation, which was meant for the destruction
    Of Jerusalem, become her covering till the time of the end.

7.43. *The father of all his brethren*] Of all his own brothers (not Albion's);
an echo of Milton's phrase, 'fairest of all her daughters, Eve' (*Paradise Lost*
iv 324). Skofield, the trooper who accused B. of sedition, is the great
enemy, and from him may be derived all the evil to be found partially in
the rest.

7.43–4. *the shadowy | Generation*] This mortal life.

7.47. *outside*] The outside is the shell, the superficial appearance (cp. *12.55n*).
Skofield sums up the rest, and the evils of the rest are seen in the form of
Skofield.

7.48. *One in him*] An anti-Trinity.

7.50. *To separate a law of sin*] Separation is usually evil in B.–man's mani-
fold interrelated activities are now to be divided apart, analysed, and made
subject to moral law.

7.56. *tenfold*] One more than Skofield's nine, a perfect number. See note
on *Four Zoas* i 150.

7.63–4. The religions known in this world ('generation') are formed in a
temporal mould; they are not divine, but earthly. Yet, since nothing better
is available, it is they who must preserve the divine truth 'till the time
of the End'.

65 Oh holy generation, *image* of regeneration!
  O point of mutual forgiveness between enemies,
  Birthplace of the Lamb of God incomprehensible!
  The dead despise & scorn thee, & cast thee out as accursed,
  Seeing the Lamb of God in thy gardens & thy palaces,
70 Where they desire to place the Abomination of Desolation.
  Hand sits before his furnace; scorn of others & furious pride
  Freeze round him to bars of steel & to iron rocks beneath
  His feet. Indignant self-righteousness like whirlwinds of the north
Pl. 8 Rose up against me thundering from the brook of Albion's river,
  From Ranelagh & Strumbolo, from Cromwell's Gardens & Chelsea,
  The place of wounded soldiers; but when he saw my mace
  Whirled round from heaven to earth trembling he sat; his cold
5 Poisons rose up, & his sweet deceits covered them all over
  With a tender cloud. As thou art now, such was he, O spectre.
  I know thy deceit & thy revenges, & unless thou desist
  I will certainly create an eternal hell for thee. Listen!
  Be attentive! Be obedient! Lo! the furnaces are ready to receive
  thee.

7.65. This line shows a change in B.'s attitude to 'generation', which in earlier writings was almost all evil (e.g. the myth of *The Book of Urizen*, and Urizen's creation in *Four Zoas*). But the 'Holy Generation' here probably refers specifically to Jerusalem, seen in this passage as the earthly manifestation of heaven.

Image] Deleted, but retouched into legibility in two of the five copies.

7.68. *The dead*] The spiritually dead.

7.70. *Daniel* xii 11, and especially *Matthew* xxiv 15: 'When ye therefore shall see the abomination of desolation, spoken of by Daniel the prophet, stand in the holy place. . . .' The holy place is in the heart of the Temple in Jerusalem (hence B.'s allusion). (In *Matthew*, also *Mark* xiii 14 and *Luke* xxi 20, the exact allusion varies, but relates to the unrest which culminated in the destruction of the Temple in A.D. 70. All three N.T. passages remind the reader of *Daniel*, and the time when the statue of Zeus was set up in the Temple, the added phrase in *Matthew* and *Mark* 'whoso readeth, let him understand' giving latitude to the reader's interpretation.)

7.71. *Hand*] B. says what he thinks of Robert Hunt and the *Examiner*, who in 1808 had scornfully criticized him (see pp. xix and 593).

8.1. *The brook*] Tyburn, which flowed near the place of public execution.

8.2. *Ranelagh & Strumbolo, Cromwell's Gardens*] Popular places of entertainment; Chelsea Hospital, the home for invalided soldiers, was next to Ranelagh. All these places are in the west; they are seen here as places of licentious, not innocent, amusement, and they blemish the virtue of the west. See map, p. 621.

8.6. B. sees in himself the beginnings of the same faults that corrupted Hand or Hunt.

10   I will break thee into shivers & melt thee in the furnaces of death;
I will cast thee into forms of abhorrence & torment if thou
Desist not from thine own will, & obey not my stern command.
I am closed up from my children; my emanation is dividing
And thou my spectre art divided against me. But mark:
15   I will compel thee to assist me in my terrible labours. To beat
These hypocritic selfhoods on the anvils of bitter death
I am inspired. I act not for myself; for Albion's sake
I now am what I am, a horror and an astonishment,
Shuddering the heavens to look upon me. Behold what cruelties
20   Are practised in Babel & Shinar, & have approached to Zion's hill!'

While Los spoke, the terrible spectre fell shuddering before him,
Watching his time with glowing eyes to leap upon his prey.
Los opened the furnaces in fear. The spectre saw to Babel & Shinar,
Across all Europe & Asia; he saw the tortures of the victims.
25   He saw now from the outside what he before saw & felt from
      within.
He saw that Los was the sole, uncontrolled lord of the furnaces.
Groaning he kneeled before Los's iron-shod feet on London Stone,
Hungering & thirsting for Los's life, yet pretending obedience,
While Los pursued his speech in threatenings loud & fierce:

30   'Thou art my pride & self-righteousness; I have found thee out.
Thou art revealed before me in all thy magnitude & power;
The uncircumcised pretences to chastity must be cut in sunder.
Thy holy wrath & deep deceit cannot avail against me,
Nor shalt thou ever assume the triple form of Albion's spectre,

8.*15*. Los, the imaginative man, makes even his evil tendencies work for
him; if he does not, they will destroy him. Cp. *30*ff.
8.*20. Babel and Shinar*] The region from which the Babylonians, and
Assyrians, who caused so much destruction, came; *23–4* point out that
their spirit now governs the modern world.
8.*22*. A characteristic of the spectre; one's evil self, although subdued,
remains dangerous and must always be watched. B. may have seen a
trained lion or similar beast.
8.*26*. The furnaces, though terrible, are constructive, a part of the black-
smith's essential equipment.
8.*27. London Stone*] An ancient relic, supposed to have been set as the datum-
point for milestones along the Roman roads. It had stood for centuries on
the south side of Cannon Street, but was moved in 1742, and in 1798 was
built into the wall of the church of St Swithun (destroyed in 1941) on the
north side. (It is still on the same site, now built into the wall of the Bank
of China.) It was popularly supposed to be a stone where Druid victims
were slaughtered, and this is its chief connotation for B.
8.*34. The triple form*] Cp. 7.*48n*. Los will not permit his spectre to go the
way of Albion's.

35 For I am one of the living. Dare not to mock my inspired fury,
   If thou wast cast forth from my life, if I was dead upon the
        mountains,
   Thou mightest be pitied & loved, but now I am living. Unless
   Thou abstain ravening I will create an eternal hell for thee.
   Take thou this hammer, & in patience heave the thundering
        bellows;
40 Take thou these tongs, strike thou alternate with me; labour
        obedient.
   Hand & Hyle & Coban, Skofield, Kox & Kotope labour
        mightily;
   In the wars of Babel & Shinar, all their emanations were
   Condensed. Hand has absorbed all his brethren in his might;
   All the infant loves & graces were lost, for the mighty Hand

[Design]

Pl. 9 Condensed his emanations into hard opaque substances,
   And his infant thoughts & desires into cold, dark, cliffs of death.
   His hammer of gold he seized, & his anvil of adamant;
   He seized the bars of condensed thoughts to forge them
5 Into the sword of war, into the bow & arrow,
   Into the thundering cannon & into the murdering gun.
   I saw the limbs formed for exercise contemned, & the beauty of
   Eternity looked upon as deformity, & loveliness as a dry tree.
   I saw disease forming a body of death around the Lamb
10 Of God, to destroy Jerusalem, & to devour the body of Albion,
   By war & stratagem to win the labour of the husbandman;

[Design]

   Awkwardness armed in steel, folly in a helmet of gold,
   Weakness with horns & talons, ignorance with a ravening beak.
   Every emanative joy forbidden as a crime,
15 And the emanations buried alive in the earth with pomp of religion;
   Inspiration denied, genius forbidden by laws of punishment.
   I saw terrified; I took the sighs & tears, & bitter groans;
   I lifted them into my furnaces to form the spiritual sword

8.41ff. Los describes the enemy he has to work against.

8.42. emanations] Turned from living and beautiful counterparts to rigid
forms. See Four Zoas i 17n.

8. Design: A woman drags a crescent moon, harnessed to her breast and
thighs, through the clouds.

9. Design: Right a shepherd piping to his sheep, while left wild animals
lie in wait; a kneeling, praying figure is interposed between them and the
sheep.

That lays open the hidden heart; I drew forth the pang
20 Of sorrow red-hot; I worked it on my resolute anvil.
I heated it in the flames of Hand, & Hyle, & Coban
Nine times. Gwendolen & Cambel & Gwineverra

[Design]

Are melted into the gold, the silver, the liquid ruby,
The crysolite, the topaz, the jacinth, & every precious stone.
25 Loud roar my furnaces and loud my hammer is heard.
I labour day and night, I behold the soft affections
Condense beneath my hammer into forms of cruelty,
But still I labour in hope, though still my tears flow down,
That he who will not defend truth may be compelled to defend
30 A lie—that he may be snared & caught & snared & taken,
That enthusiasm & life may not cease. Arise, spectre, arise!'

Thus they contended among the furnaces with groans & tears.
Groaning, the spectre heaved the bellows, obeying Los's frowns,
Till the spaces of Erin were perfected in the furnaces
35 Of affliction, & Los drew them forth, compelling the harsh spectres

[Design]

Pl. 10 Into the furnaces & into the valleys of the anvils of death,
And into the mountains of the anvils & of the heavy hammers,
Till he should bring the sons & daughters of Jerusalem to be
The sons & daughters of Los, that he might protect them from
5 Albion's dread spectres. Storming, loud, thunderous & mighty,
The bellows & the hammers move, compelled by Los's hand.

And this the manner of the sons of Albion in their strength:
They take the two contraries which are called *qualities*, with which
Every substance is clothed; they name them *good & evil*.

9.21. The sons and daughters of Albion are shown in two situations; as
opposing Los (5.27) and as subject to his power in the furnaces. Thus, for
example, an artist may be obstructed and frustrated by philistinism, but
hopes in his turn to use even the philistine for the purposes of art.
9. *Design*: A bowed figure left; centre, a strip showing a woman fondling
and feeding a serpent.
9.23-4. gold . . . jacinth] Biblical jewellery, featured particularly in Aaron's
vestments (*Exodus* xxviii) and the building of New Jerusalem (*Revelation*
xxi 19-21).
9.34. The spaces of Erin] See 11.8n.
9. *Design*: A group of women lament over the dead body of a man
(Albion?).

Plate 10. This is an added plate, later than pls 9 and 11, and made to fit
between them: pl.9 has the catchword *To* (cp. 11.*1*).

10   From them they make an abstract, which is a negation
Not only of the substance from which it is derived,
A murderer of its own body, but also a murderer
Of every divine member. It is the reasoning power,
An abstract objecting power that negatives everything
15   This is the spectre of man—the holy reasoning power;
And in its holiness is closed the Abomination of Desolation.

Therefore Los stands in London building Golgonooza,
Compelling his spectre to labours mighty; trembling in fear
The spectre weeps, but Los unmoved by tears or threats remains.

20   'I must create a system, or be enslaved by another man's;
I will not reason & compare; my business is to create.'

So Los, in fury & strength, in indignation & burning wrath.
Shuddering the spectre howls; his howlings terrify the night:
He stamps around the anvil, beating blows of stern despair;
25   He curses heaven & earth, day & night & sun & moon;
He curses forest, spring & river, desert & sandy waste,
Cities & nations, families & peoples, tongues & laws,
Driven to desperation by Los's terrors & threatening fears.

Los cries: 'Obey my voice & never deviate from my will,
30   And I will be merciful to thee. Be thou invisible to all
To whom I make thee invisible, but chief to my own children.
O spectre of Urthona, reason not against their dear approach,
Nor them obstruct with thy temptations of doubt & despair.
O shame, O strong & mighty shame, I break thy brazen fetters!

10.7–16. B. distinguishes between CONTRARIES and NEGATIONS. Negations, such as *good and evil, beautiful and ugly,* affirm one quality and simultaneously deny the other. Contraries, such as *elegant* and *grotesque,* are contrasting but complementary qualities. B. says that the analysis which insists that opposites must be exclusive destroys not only what it denies, but also what it affirms. Cp. 17.33ff, B.'s fullest exposition of the concept.
10.17. *Golgonooza*] The city built by Los in the heart of Ulro, an outpost which by his continual labour he maintains and guards so that evil may not be absolutely triumphant.
in London] Not meaning that London is Golgonooza – far from it – but that even in London, the scene of B.'s common life, Golgonooza is being built.
10.20–1. These lines have been much quoted. Note that the important word is *create*, not *system*. B.'s idea of creation is that of continual creation and continual renewal. See 58.*15–18*.
10.*32. spectre of Urthona*] Cp. *Four Zoas* iv 76ff, the beginning of the servant-spectre of Los. In *Four Zoas* Los is the temporal name and form of the eternal Urthona; the spectre of Urthona is thus the spectre of Los.

35 If thou refuse, thy present torments will seem southern breezes
To what thou shalt endure if thou obey not my great will.'

The spectre answered: 'Art thou not ashamed of those thy sins
That thou callest thy children? Lo! the Law of God commands
That they be offered upon his altar. (O cruelty & torment,
40 For thine are also mine!) I have kept silent hitherto,
Concerning my chief delight; but thou has broken silence;
Now I will speak my mind. Where is my lovely Enitharmon,
O thou my enemy, where is my great sin? She is also thine!
I said: "Now is my grief at worst, incapable of being
45 Surpassed", but every moment it accumulates more & more,
It continues accumulating to eternity. The joys of God advance,
For he is righteous; he is not a being of pity & compassion,
He cannot feel distress; he feeds on sacrifice & offering,
Delighting in cries & tears & clothed in holiness & solitude.
50 But my griefs advance also, for ever & ever without end.
O that I could cease to be! Despair—I am despair,
Created to be the great example of horror & agony; also my
Prayer is vain. I called for compassion: compassion mocked,
Mercy & pity threw the gravestone over me & with lead
55 And iron bound it over me for ever. Life lives on my
Consuming, & the Almighty hath made me his contrary,
To be all evil, all reversed & for ever dead, knowing
And seeing life, yet living not. How can I then behold
And not tremble? How can I be beheld & not abhorred?'

60 So spoke the spectre shuddering, & dark tears ran down his
        shadowy face,
Which Los wiped off, but comfort none could give, or beam of hope.
Yet ceased he not from labouring at the roarings of his forge,
With iron & brass building Golgonooza in great contendings
Till his sons & daughters came forth from the furnaces
65 At the sublime labours; for Los compelled the invisible spectre

10.37–8. To the dull earthly mind, the products of an imaginative mind
are dangerous and sinful.
10.42–3. The spectre is Los's shadow; he is an *image* of Los (not the real
Los). Thus Enitharmon, as counterpart or emanation of Los, stands in the
same relation as Los does to the spectre, who thinks himself real, and Los
is false. But the spectre reveals himself by the description of his love as Sin.
10.47. A false, spectrous view of God. The spectre's misery in the following
lines derives from this false notion.
10.61. *comfort none could give*] Los will not comfort the spectre in spectrous
terms: and the spectre does not understand Los's terms.

Pl. 11   [*Design*]

To labours mighty, with vast strength, with his mighty chains,
In pulsations of time, & extensions of space, like urns of Beulah.
With great labour upon his anvils, & in his ladles the ore
He lifted, pouring it into the clay ground prepared with art;
5 Striving with systems to deliver individuals from those systems,
That, whenever any spectre began to devour the dead,
He might feel the pain as if a man gnawed his own tender nerves.

Then Erin came forth from the furnaces, & all the daughters of
    Beulah
Came from the furnaces, by Los's mighty power for Jerusalem's
10 Sake, walking up and down among the spaces of Erin,
And the sons and daughters of Los came forth in perfection lovely.
And the spaces of Erin reached from the starry height to the
    starry depth.

Los wept with exceeding joy & all wept with joy together.
They feared they never more should see their father, who
15 Was built in from eternity in the cliffs of Albion.
But when the joy of meeting was exhausted in loving embrace,
Again they lament: 'O what shall we do for lovely Jerusalem,
To protect the emanations of Albion's mighty ones from cruelty?

11. *Design*: A creature with woman's body and legs, and swan's wings, neck and head, rests its head on the surface of the lake it floats in (perhaps drinking). See design at the foot. The swan swimming on the sea and spitting out a milky liquid is a symbol used by alchemists of arsenic, not as a poison, but as a substance 'mediating' between alchemical stages, and thus valuable in the process.

11.2. *urns of Beulah*] Funeral urns (stated in 53.28). In Beulah the ashes of the spiritually 'dead' are carefully tended; thus their existence is prolonged in some form, however reliquary, and this 'extension' of the pause between life and annihilation gives time for the renewal of the spirit.

11.3. Los is blacksmith and also ironfounder, preparing sand moulds on the ground, into which he pours the molten metal.

11.5. *with*] i.e. 'against, or 'among'.

11.7. *He*] The spectre. This line describes a characteristic of the spectre.

11.8. *Erin*] One of the leaders of the daughters of Beulah, now created by Los for Albion's sake. As B. visualises the island of England as the giant Albion, stretched out in sleep, so he sees the neighbouring island Ireland as a beautiful woman, Erin, who sits by him, watches over him, and shields him from the full force of the destructive Atlantic waves. She appears in *Jerusalem* only. The daughters of Beulah operate in limited 'spaces' (*12*) where their beatific influence is best felt.

11.12. *spaces*] See 2n and 12n.

11.14. *their father*] Albion.

Sabrina & Ignoge begin to sharpen their beamy spears
20 Of light & love; their little children stand with arrows of gold.
Ragan is wholly cruel; Skofield is bound in iron armour;
He is like a mandrake in the earth before Reuben's gate;
He shoots beneath Jerusalem's walls to undermine her foundations.
Vala is but thy shadow, O thou loveliest among women,
25 A shadow animated by thy tears, O mournful Jerusalem!

[Design]

Pl. 12 'Why wilt thou give to her a body whose life is but a shade,
Her joy and love a shade (a shade of sweet repose)?
But animated and vegetated she is a devouring worm.
What shall we do for thee, O lovely mild Jerusalem?'

5 And Los said: 'I behold the finger of God in terrors.
Albion is dead; his emanation is divided from him,
But I am living, yet I feel my emanation also dividing.
Such thing was never known. O pity me, thou all-piteous-one;
What shall I do, or how exist, divided from Enitharmon?
10 Yet why despair? I saw the finger of God go forth
Upon my furnaces, from within the wheels of Albion's sons,
Fixing their systems permanent, by mathematic power
Giving a body to falsehood that it may be cast off for ever,
With demonstrative science piercing Apollyon with his own bow.

11.*19–21.* These lines are a *lament* for of the souls of Sabrina, etc.

11.*22. mandrakes . . . before Reuben's gate*] In *Genesis* xxx 14 Reuben brings mandrakes (which supposedly induce in others desire for the person who eats them) to his mother, Leah, to regain for her Jacob's love. The allusion may be to the family discord which this action brought, when Leah quarrelled with Jacob's other wife Rachel.

11.*23–5.* Jerusalem is imagined first as a city, then as a woman. Vala, who in *Four Zoas* was the evil female spirit eventually redeemed and brought back to a state of Jerusalem-like innocence, is made in *Jerusalem* into the 'other side' of Jerusalem herself, a 'shadow' form.

11. *Design*: An evil-seeming female figure, bejewelled, swims through the water (beneath the swan-woman at the top of the page).

12.*1–4.* Vala is not 'real': she lives in the unimaginative, dead, dream-world. Would it not be kinder to leave her so, both for her own sake and that of all creation? Los, in 5ff (especially *13*), says not.

12.*3. animated and vegetated*] In mortal form, not in true 'life' (*1*).

12.*7. dividing*] Not 'dividing in two', but 'dividing from me'–as in the previous line.

12.*12.* The hand of God acts even in the most godless places; error is made unchangeable and rigid, so that its lifelessness will reveal it to be error.

12.*14. Apollyon*] 'The angel of the bottomless pit' in *Revelation* ix 11, who was in command of the creatures that tormented the godless for a limited time. Apollyon is more famous as the demon in *Pilgrim's Progress* who

15 God is within & without; he is even in the depths of hell.'

Such were the lamentations of the labourers in the furnaces.
And they appeared within & without, encircling on both sides
The starry wheels of Albion's sons, with spaces for Jerusalem,
And for Vala the shadow of Jerusalem, the ever-mourning shade,
20 On both sides, within & without beaming gloriously.

Terrified at the sublime wonder, Los stood before his furnaces.
And they stood around, terrified with admiration at Erin's spaces,
For the spaces reached from the starry height to the starry depth;
And they builded Golgonooza, terrible eternal labour.

25 What are those golden builders doing? Where was the burying-
    place
Of soft Ethinthus? Near Tyburn's fatal tree? Is that
Mild Zion's hill's most ancient promontory, near mournful
Ever-weeping Paddington? Is that Calvary & Golgotha
Becoming a building of pity & compassion? Lo!
30 The stones are pity and the bricks well-wrought affections,
Enamelled with love & kindness, & the tiles engraven gold,
Labour of merciful hands. The beams & rafters are forgiveness;
The mortar & cement of the work, tears of honesty; the nails
And the screws & iron braces are well-wrought blandishments,
35 And well-contrived words, firm fixing, never forgotten,
Always comforting the remembrance; the floors, humility,
The ceilings, devotion; the hearths, thanksgiving.
Prepare the furniture, O Lambeth, in thy pitying looms!
The curtains, woven tears & sighs, wrought into lovely forms

attacks Christian in the Valley of Humiliation. The name is Greek ('De-
stroyer').

12.*17. they*] The labourers: who, Los sees, are active in the midst of the
works of evil, ensuring that Jerusalem and even Vala are given spaces—
'room to breathe'—so that they are not crushed in the wheels.

12.*25*. Cp. *Milton* pl.27.*23*ff for another long sequence on the work of Los
in Golgonooza. B. breaks in here with his own thoughts.

12.*26. Ethinthus*] A name only: cp. *Europe 158* and *Four Zoas* viii *352*.
Tyburn] The place of public execution (see map). In the next lines, B.
associates the Holy Land, and Calvary in particular, with London and
Tyburn. Los's labourers (now builders of Golgonooza, not at the furnace)
are creating beauty even there by their pity and compassion.

12.*28. Paddington*] A little N.W. of B.'s South Molton St home; a no-
torious shanty-town in his childhood, but new building in 1811—the
creation of real houses—revealed relics of old Tyburn executions.

12.*38. Lambeth*] Where B. had lived from 1791 to 1800 and written much
of his early work. Cp. also *Milton* pl.26.*48n*, where B. refers to the sweated
labour in orphanage workshops in Lambeth.

40 For comfort. There the secret furniture of Jerusalem's chamber
Is wrought; Lambeth the bride, the Lamb's wife loveth thee.
Thou art one with her & knowest not of self in thy supreme joy.
Go on, builders, in hope,' though Jerusalem wanders far away
Without the gate of Los among the dark Satanic wheels.

45 Fourfold the sons of Los in their divisions. And fourfold
The great city of Golgonooza: fourfold toward the north
And toward the south fourfold, & fourfold toward the east & west,
Each within other toward the four points—that toward
Eden, and that toward the world of generation,
50 And that toward Beulah, and that toward Ulro.
(Ulro is the space of the terrible starry wheels of Albion's sons.)
But that toward Eden is walled up till time of renovation;
Yet it is perfect in its building, ornaments & perfection.

And the four points are thus beheld in great Eternity—
55 West, the circumference; south, the zenith; north,
The nadir; east, the centre, unapproachable for ever.
These are the four faces towards the four worlds of humanity
In every man; Ezekiel saw them by Chebar's flood.
And the eyes are the south, and the nostrils are the east,
60 And the tongue is the west, & the ear is the north.

12.45. The description of Golgonooza begins. As with the description of
the temple in *Ezekiel* xl–xliii, B. stresses the formal proportions of the
building. In particular, he uses the notion of *fourfold* completeness. Cp.
13.*6n*.
12.52. The west gate is closed; cp. 5.*68n*.
12.55–6. CIRCUMFERENCE ... CENTRE] B. is rather inconsistent, in that
'outside', 'without', often refer to corrupt superficiality, and 'inside',
'within' to the deeper realities of the individual heart. But 'the centre' is
a traditional name for Hell, and the *circumference* here is the bounding line,
the *outline* which shows a visible living form. Cp. 18.2, and *Milton* pl.37.9,
which seem to represent a moral reversal of this image: the *outside* is
'fallacious', and truth lies in the heart. The two notions are reconciled at
71.*6–8*: 'What is above is within, for everything in Eternity is trans-
lucent: / The circumference is within: without is formed the selfish
centre, / And the circumference still expands, going forward to Eternity.'
12.*58*. Cp. *Ezekiel* i 1: '... as I was among the captives by the river of
Chebar, that the heavens opened, and I saw visions of God'; and verses
5–6 '... came the likeness of four living creatures. And this was their
appearance; they had the likeness of a man. And every one had four faces,
and every one had four wings.' Ezekiel does not refer to eyes, nostrils,
tongue and ears: his four faces are those of a man, a lion, an ox and an
eagle.

And the north gate of Golgonooza toward generation
Has four sculptured bulls terrible, before the gate of iron,
And iron the bulls. And that which looks toward Ulro,
Clay-baked & enamelled, eternal glowing as four furnaces,
65   Turning upon the wheels of Albion's sons with enormous power.
And that toward Beulah four—gold, silver, brass, & iron.
Pl. 13   And that toward Eden four, formed of gold, silver, brass, & iron.
The south, a golden gate, has four lions, terrible, living;
That toward generation four, of iron carved wondrous;
That toward Ulro four, clay-baked, laborious workmanship;
5   That toward Eden four, immortal gold, silver, brass & iron.
The western gate fourfold is closed, having four cherubim
Its guards, living, the work of elemental hands (laborious task!)
Like men hermaphroditic, each winged with eight wings.
That towards generation, iron; that toward Beulah, stone;
10   That toward Ulro, clay; that toward Eden, metals.
But all closed up till the Last Day, when the graves shall yield ·
their dead.
The eastern gate fourfold, terrible & deadly its ornaments,
Taking their forms from the wheels of Albion's sons, as cogs
Are formed in a wheel to fit the cogs of the adverse wheel.
15   That toward Eden eternal ice, frozen in seven folds
Of forms of death. And that toward Beulah stone
(The seven diseases of the earth are carved, terrible).
And that toward Ulro forms of war, seven enormities.
And that toward generation, seven generative forms.
20   And every part of the city is fourfold, & every inhabitant fourfold.
And every pot & vessel & garment & utensil of the houses,
And every house, fourfold; but the third gate in every one
Is closed as with a threefold curtain of ivory & fine linen & ermine.

12.61. i.e. 'has four bulls facing Generation, northwards'; Ulro is the evil
east, Eden, the closed gate, is west, and Beulah is the golden south.

12.66. B.'s four favourite metals: cp. *America* 75 and pl.*c.15* and *Daniel* ii
32–3, the image of gold, silver, brass, iron and clay.

13.6. *fourfold*] Cp. the closing lines of the letter to Butts (22 Nov. 1802),
p. 475 above. Fourfold is the form of perfection. In the following lines,
sixty-four thousand is the cube of four multiplied by a thousand. Similarly,
in *Revelation* vii 4 the number 'one hundred and forty-four thousand' is
made up of the perfect number twelve, squared and multiplied by a
thousand. The squaring or cubing of the number completes its mystic
perfection; the thousand indicates the hosts of spirits. G. H. Harper shows
in a comprehensive essay in *W.B.: Essays presented to S. Foster Damon*
(1969) the importance of B.'s constant usage of 4, 8, 16, 32, 64 as numbers of
wholeness, and of 3, 7, 12, 27 as numbers of incomplete, broken, sexual
mortality.

And Luban stands in middle of the city; a moat of fire
25 Surrounds Luban, Los's palace & the golden looms of Cathedron.
And sixty-four thousand genii guard the eastern gate;
And sixty-four thousand gnomes guard the nothern gate;
And sixty-four thousand nymphs guard the western gate;
And sixty-four thousand fairies guard the southern gate.
30 Around Golgonooza lies the land of death eternal, a land
Of pain & misery & despair & ever-brooding melancholy,
In all the twenty-seven heavens, numbered from Adam to Luther,
From the blue mundane shell, reaching to the vegetative earth.
The vegetative universe opens like a flower from the earth's
centre,
35 In which is Eternity. It expands in stars to the mundane shell
And there it meets Eternity again, both within and without, .

13.24. Luban, Cathedron] See *Four Zoas* v *77n* for Luban, the gate opening
from Golgonooza towards Ulro; in viia *429* it is a place of 'many porches'
surrounding and watching the Tree of Mystery. Here it is in the centre of
the city, but this does not, in Blake's terms, contradict either of these
earlier pictures, though the present scheme of fourfold gates is a later de-
velopment than Luban. Cathedron is the name of the looms which
Enitharmon erected 'in Luban's gate' to give the spectres of lost souls
'bodies of vegetation' when they escaped from Ulro, in order to save them
from annihilation. See *Four Zoas* viii *25n*.
13.26–9. Cp. *Milton* pl.31.20: 'the fairies, nymphs, gnomes and genii of
the four elements'. They are servants of the four Zoas, and are attached
thus: fairies (air)–Urizen; nymphs (water)–Tharmas; gnomes (earth)–
Urthona (Los); genii (fire)–Luvah. The compass points here are appro-
priate to their Zoas, a good example of B.'s liking for patterns.
13.32. the twenty-seven heavens] Cp. *Milton* pl.37.35. These are the labyrin-
thine clouds of error which surround the mortal world, manifest particu-
larly in the religious errors which have beset it.
13.33 The MUNDANE SHELL] In *Urizen* the physical universe was separated
from Eternity when Urizen encased himself in rocks to hide from the
eternal flames. This casing became our universe, which is bounded by the
earth and by the arching firmament above our heads. The image is con-
tinued here, though B. no longer describes it as Urizen's formation. There
are two simultaneous images; the encasing shell (or egg; cp. *Milton*
pl.34.*31n*), and the flower. The first emphasizes the face of the earth from
eternity; the second describes the face of the earth within the shell. It is a
vortex, opening to eternity at two points–the wide, open mouth, and the
infinitesimally small centre. In *Milton* pl.17.*29–30* the open mouth spreads
towards the heavens and is the entry to earth past 'Satan's seat' (whence, in
Paradise Lost iv, Satan views the earth–and the twenty-seven heavens (*32*)
are in layers above the earth); the second entry is the re-entry to eternity
by Golgonooza.

And the abstract voids between the stars are the Satanic wheels.
There is the cave, the rock, the tree, the lake of Udan-Adan,
The forest, & the marsh, & the pits of bitumen deadly,
40   The rocks of solid fire, the ice valleys, the plains
Of burning sand, the rivers, cataract & lakes of fire,
The islands of the fiery lakes, the trees of malice, revenge,
And black anxiety, & the cities of the salamandrine men.
(But whatever is visible to the generated man
45   Is a creation of mercy & love from the Satanic void.)
The land of darkness, flamed but no light & no repose;
The land of snows, of trembling, & of iron hail incessant;
The land of earthquakes & the land of woven labyrinths;
The land of snares & traps & wheels & pit-falls & dire mills,
50   The voids, the solids; & the land of clouds & regions of waters
With their inhabitants in the twenty-seven heavens beneath
        Beulah—
Self-righteousnesses conglomerating against the Divine Vision,
A concave earth, wondrous, chasmal, abyssal, incoherent,
Forming the mundane shell above, beneath, on all sides
        surrounding
55   Golgonooza. Los walks round the walls night & day.

He views the city of Golgonooza & its smaller cities,
The looms & mills & prisons & work-houses of Og & Anak,
The Amalekite, the Canaanite, the Moabite, the Egyptian,
And all that has existed in the space of six thousand years—
60   Permanent, & not lost, not lost nor vanished, & every little act,
Word, work, & wish, that has existed, all remaining still
In those Churches ever consuming & ever building, by the spectres
Of all the inhabitants of earth wailing to be created—
Shadowy to those who dwell not in them, mere possibilities,
65   But to those who enter into them they seem the only substances.
For everything exists, & not one sigh nor smile nor tear,

13.*38. There*] In the vegetative universe. For the cave where Orc is bound,
the rock where Urizen sits brooding, and the Tree of Mystery which
sprang up under his foot, see *Four Zoas* viia *5-32*.

13.*43. salamandrine men*] An unexplained phrase; the association of sala-
manders is with fire.

13.*53. a concave earth*] A universe like the inside of an egg.

13.*57-8. The looms . . . of Og and Anak . . . Egyptian*] These are not Gol-
gonooza's looms, but are built by surrounding enemies. The nations
named were all enemies of the Israelites (and therefore of Jerusalem), as
were Og and Anak (cp. 48.*63*).

13.*62. Churches*] The stages of error (cp. *32n* above) created by the deluded
spectres who inhabit the fallen, mortal world. They go on building and re-
building as their creations crumble. So does Los; but his continual creation
of Golgonooza is a creation of an image of eternal beauty.

Pl. 14 One hair nor particle of dust, not one can pass away.

He views the Cherub at the Tree of Life, also the serpent
Orc the first-born, coiled in the south, the dragon Urizen,
Tharmas the vegetated tongue, even the devouring tongue—
5 A threefold region, a false brain, a false heart,
And false bowels, altogether composing the false tongue
Beneath Beulah, as a watery flame revolving every way,
And as dark roots and stems, a forest of affliction, growing
In seas of sorrow. Los also views the four females:
10 Ahania, & Enion, & Vala, & Enitharmon lovely.
And from them all the lovely beaming daughters of Albion.
Ahania & Enion & Vala are three evanescent shades;
Enitharmon is a vegetated mortal wife of Los,
His emanation, yet his wife till the sleep of death is past.

15 Such are the buildings of Los & such are the woofs of
Enitharmon.

And Los beheld his sons, & he beheld his daughters—
Every one a translucent wonder, a universe within,
Increasing inwards, into length & breadth, & height,
Starry & glorious, & they every one in their bright loins
20 Have a beautiful golden gate which opens into the vegetative
world;
And every one a gate of rubies & all sorts of precious stones
In their translucent hearts, which opens into the vegetative world;
And every one a gate of iron dreadful & wonderful,
In their translucent heads, which opens into the vegetative world.
25 And every one has the three regions; childhood, manhood, & age.
But the gate of the tongue, the western gate, in them is closed,
Having a wall builded against it, & thereby the gates

14.2. *the Cherub*] The angel (called by B. the Covering Cherub); see
Milton pl.37.8n) who drove, and keeps, Adam and Eve out of Paradise
(*Genesis* iii 24).
14.2-6. The references here are to the narrative of *Four Zoas* as in 13.38
above: they exemplify the ruinous state of the universe. In *Four Zoas* the
universe is seen as the 'universal Man'; hence the anatomical allusions.
Cp. *Milton* pl.2.10n.
14.10. These are the emanations of the Zoas–of Urizen, Tharmas, Luvah
and Los respectively. They are (*11*) the 'mothers' of all the different kinds
of women in England–of the 'daughters of Albion'.
14.16-24. *his daughters . . . a universe within . . .*] A description of the three
'gates' of female beauty which are approaches to Beulah–i.e. to the verge
of Paradise–even to the earthbound man. Similar passages occur in *Four
Zoas* i 255-61 and *Milton* pl.5.5-10 (p. 569).
14.25 REGIONS] In all there are four regions; see 18.1, 25.14, 42.79, 65.4 and

Eastward & southward & northward are encircled with flaming
fires.
And the north is breadth, the south is height & depth;
30   The east is inwards, & the west is outwards every way.
And Los beheld the mild emanation Jerusalem, eastward bending
Her revolutions toward the starry wheels in maternal anguish,
Like a pale cloud arising from the arms of Beulah's daughters:
In Entuthon Benython's deep vales beneath Golgonooza.

[*Design*]

Pl. 15   And Hand & Hyle rooted into Jerusalem by a fibre
Of strong revenge, & Skofield vegetated by Reuben's gate
In every nation of the earth till the twelve sons of Albion
Enrooted into every nation: a mighty polypus growing
5   From Albion over the whole earth: such is my awful vision.

—I see the fourfold Man, the humanity in deadly sleep
And its fallen emanation, the spectre & its cruel shadow.
I see the past, present & future, existing all at once
Before me; O Divine Spirit, sustain me on thy wings,
10   That I may awake Albion from his long & cold repose!
For Bacon & Newton, sheathed in dismal steel, their terrors hang
Like iron scourges over Albion; reasonings like vast serpents
Enfold around my limbs, bruising my minute articulations.

I turn my eyes to the schools & universities of Europe

98.*32*. Three is the number of mortal incompleteness, and requires the
fourth for absolute wholeness. 25.*14* and 98.*31–4* suggest that the fourth is
the age beyond mortality–death; or eternity.
14.*30*. inwards . . . outwards] Cp. 12.*55n*: the east is typically evil, the west
good.
14.*31*. Jerusalem is drawn by the malevolent influences of the east; although
her movement has a virtuous origin it is dangerous, as 15.*1–2* show.
14. Design: Albion sleeps; a rainbow is over the starry heavens above him,
and an angelic female figure hovers over him. Above this design the words
End of the 1st Chap: are deleted.
15.*2*. Skofield vegetated by Reuben's Gate] Reuben was the eldest son of
Israel, and is thus identified with the leader of Albion's sons. Skofield
besets him 'in every nation'–i.e. the same evil influence may be
seen, *mutatis mutandis*, in every nation, affecting its weak point (for
Reuben was a weak character). B. develops a myth of Reuben in 30.*43ff*.
The word *vegetate* refers to the ramifying growth of the polypus (see *Four
Zoas* iv *267n*), which might spread over everything and into every corner.
See also 18.*40* and 69.*1–3*.

15 And there behold the loom of Locke whose woof rages dire,
Washed by the water-wheels of Newton. Black the cloth
In heavy wreaths folds over every nation; cruel works
Of many wheels I view, wheel without wheel, with cogs tyrannic
Moving by compulsion each other: not as those in Eden, which
20 Wheel within wheel in freedom revolve, in harmony & peace.

I see in deadly fear in London: Los raging round his anvil
Of death, forming an axe of gold: the four sons of Los
Stand round him cutting the fibres from Albion's hills,
That Albion's sons may roll apart over the nations
25 While Reuben enroots his brethren in the narrow Canaanite
From the limit Noah to the limit Abram, in whose loins
Reuben in his twelvefold majesty & beauty shall take refuge,
As Abraham flees from Chaldea shaking his gory locks.
But first Albion must sleep, divided from the nations.

30 I see Albion sitting upon his rock in the first winter,
And thence I see the chaos of Satan & the world of Adam
When the Divine Hand went forth on Albion in the midwinter
And at the place of death, when Albion sat in eternal death
Among the furnaces of Los in the valley of the son of Hinnom.—

15.15–16. *Locke, Newton*] Two great seventeenth-century English rational-
ists. Locke rationalized thought and freedom; Newton rationalized the
stars.

15.18. *without*] Outside. These lines illustrate very neatly B.'s notion of
wheels, which he often uses as an image of callousness.

15.22. *the four sons of Los*] Rintrah, Palamabron, Theotormon and Bromion:
he had many, but only these remained faithful (cp. *Four Zoas* viii *344–66*
and *Milton* pl.24.*10*).

15.24–5. See *Four Zoas* ii *266n*, and pls 63–4, 71 below. B. imagines Albion
and Canaan as one Holy Land in Eternity. But Albion's despair and fear
have corrupted him; the two lands split and 'roll apart', and the twelve
tribes ('Reuben's brethren') settle and 'enroot' in Canaan, a narrow 'little
and dark land' (*Four Zoas* ii *266*). For the distinction of Abram and
Abraham, see *Genesis* xvii 5.

15.25–9. This myth is fully developed in ch. 3. Cp. also 27.*1n*. Albion was
once the Holy Land, but the two have 'rolled apart', and in the patriarchal
history from Noah to Abraham we have the story of this wandering apart,
and the establishment of a separate Jewish nation, in the narrow land of
Canaan. Cp. also *Limits*, at *Four Zoas* iv *270*.

15.34. *the son of Hinnom*] In 2 *Chronicles* xxxiii 6, King Manasseh, the
idolator, 'caused his children to pass through the fire in the valley of the
son of Hinnom', i.e. sacrificed them–among other evil practices. In
xxviii 3 Ahaz is also said to have burnt his children there. But the 'furnaces
of Los' are not those furnaces: the idea is that Los's struggle to create
continues everywhere, even there.

[Design]

Pl. 16 Hampstead, Highgate, Finchley, Hendon, Muswell Hill rage loud
Before Bromion's iron tongs & glowing poker reddening fierce.
Hertfordshire glows with fierce vegetation; in the forests
The oak frowns terrible, the beech & ash & elm enroot
5 Among the spiritual fires; loud the cornfields thunder along
The soldier's fife; the harlot's shriek; the virgin's dismal groan;
The parent's fear; the brother's jealousy: the sister's curse
Beneath the storms of Theotormon; & the thundering bellows
Heaves in the hand of Palamabron, who in London's darkness
10 Before the anvil watches the bellowing flames. Thundering
The hammer loud rages in Rintrah's strong grasp, swinging loud
Round from heaven to earth, down falling with heavy blow
Dead on the anvil, where the red-hot wedge groans in pain.
He quenches it in the black trough of his forge: London's river
15 Feeds the dread forge, trembling & shuddering along the valleys.

Humber & Trent roll dreadful before the seventh furnace,
And Tweed & Tyne anxious give up their souls for Albion's sake.
Lincolnshire, Derbyshire, Nottinghamshire, Leicestershire,
From Oxfordshire to Norfolk on the lake of Udan-Adan
20 Labour within the furnaces, walking among the fires
With ladles huge & iron pokers over the island white.

15. Design: A running man, arms outstretched, met by a smaller figure
who rises or floats up to meet him.

16.1. Continuing the blacksmith's labours of Los and his sons, now in
London and England. (The place names are all suburbs of North London.)
In the turmoil, Los's sons struggle at their work, obstructed (as in *3–4*) by
the vegetative world, or aided (as in *17*).

16.19. B. insists on the closeness of the 'known' world to that of the
imagination.

16.21. Albion] 'The white (island).'

16.28–58. Before the Fall, Albion was the Holy Land; cp. *27.1–3nn*,
38.68–70n. B. therefore identifies counties of Wales, England and Scotland
with the lands of the twelve tribes of Israel, though the associations are
quite arbitrary; there is, for example, no geographical equivalence since,
e.g., the southernmost tribe (Simeon) is given Cardigan (on the Welsh
west coast), three northerly English counties and three middle Scottish
counties. The purpose seems to be formal and rhetorical: to recollect the
Old Testament passages where boundaries are carefully delineated (e.g.
Joshua xii–xxi), and to attempt the solemnity which absolute formality
can bring, as in *Paradise Lost* i 407–11: 'From Aroer to Nebo and the wild /
Of southmost Abarim; in Hesebon / And Horonaim, Seon's realm, be-

Scotland pours out his sons to labour at the furnaces;
Wales gives his daughters to the looms; England, nursing mothers
Gives to the children of Albion & to the children of Jerusalem.
25 From the blue mundane shell even to the earth of vegetation
Throughout the whole creation which groans to be delivered:
Albion groans in the deep slumbers of death upon his rock.

Here Los fixed down the fifty-two counties of England & Wales,
The thirty-six of Scotland, & the thirty-four of Ireland
30 With mighty power, when they fled out at Jerusalem's gates
Away from the conflict of Luvah & Urizen, fixing the gates
In the twelve counties of Wales; & thence gates looking every way
To the four points conduct to England & Scotland & Ireland,
And thence to all the kingdoms & nations & families of the earth.
35 The gate of Reuben in Carmarthenshire: the gate of Simeon in
Cardiganshire: & the gate of Levi in Montgomeryshire;
The gate of Judah, Merionethshire: the gate of Dan, Flintshire:
The gate of Naphtali, Radnorshire: the gate of Gad, Pembroke-
shire:
The gate of Asher, Carnarvonshire: the gate of Issachar,
Brecknockshire:
40 The gate of Zebulun, in Anglesey & Sodor: so is Wales divided.
The gate of Joseph, Denbighshire: the gate of Benjamin
Glamorganshire,
For the protection of the twelve emanations of Albion's sons.

And the forty counties of England are thus divided: in the gates
Of Reuben; Norfolk, Suffolk, Essex. Simeon; Lincoln, York,
Lancashire.
45 Levi; Middlesex, Kent, Surrey. Judah; Somerset, Gloucester,
Wiltshire.
Dan; Cornwall, Devon, Dorset. Naphtali; Warwick, Leicester,
Worcester.
Gad; Oxford, Bucks, Hertford. Asher; Sussex, Hampshire,
Berkshire.

yond / The flow'ry vale of Sibma, clad with vines. / And Elealè to
th'Asphaltic Pool.' But Milton does not equal B.'s strictness, which owes
more to Old Testament 'legal prose'.
16.30–1. Cp. *Four Zoas* viii 25ff where Los and Enitharmon care for the
lost souls who escape from the war of Urizen and Orc, who is Luvah.
16.31–4. B. imagines gates opening from the eternal world into Wales,
land of the bards; thence the influence spreads throughout Britain and so
to the whole world. Note also the numerology of *four* and *twelve*.
16.48. *Huntingdon, Cambridge*] The plate has *Huntgn Camb*; the abbrevi-
ations are doubtless due to cramped space. So with certain other names.

Issachar; Northampton, Rutland, Nottingham. Zebulun;
    Bedford, Huntingdon, Cambridge.
Joseph; Stafford, Shropshire, Hereford. Benjamin; Derby,
    Cheshire, Monmouth;
50 And Cumberland, Northumberland, Westmorland & Durham
    are
    Divided in the gates of Reuben, Judah, Dan & Joseph.

And the thirty-six counties of Scotland; divided in the gates
Of Reuben; Kincardine, Haddington, Forfar. Simeon; Ayr,
    Argyll, Banff.
Levi; Edinburgh, Roxburgh, Ross. Judah; Aberdeen, Berwick,
    Dumfries.
55 Dan; Bute, Caithness, Clackmannan. Naphtali; Nairn, Inverness,
    Linlithgow.
Gad; Peebles, Perth, Renfrew. Asher; Sutherland, Stirling,
    Wigtown.
Issachar; Selkirk, Dunbarton, Glasgow. Zebulun; Orkney,
    Shetland, Skye.
Joseph; Elgin, Lanark, Kinross. Benjamin; Cromarty, Moray,
    Kirkcudbright.
Governing all by the sweet delights of secret amorous glances
60 In Enitharmon's halls builded by Los & his mighty children.

All things acted on earth are seen in the bright sculptures of
Los's halls; & every age renews its powers from these works,
With every pathetic story possible to happen, from hate or
Wayward love, & every sorrow & distress is carved here.
65 Every affinity of parents, marriages & friendships are here
In all their various combinations wrought with wondrous art:
All that can happen to man in his pilgrimage of seventy years.
Such is the 'divine written law' of Horeb & Sinai:
And such the holy gospel of Mount Olivet & Calvary.

Pl. 17 His spectre divides & Los in fury compels it to divide:
To labour in the fire, in the water, in the earth, in the air,
To follow the daughters of Albion as the hound follows the scent
Of the wild inhabitant of the forest, to drive them from his own:
5 To make a way for the children of Los to come from the furnaces.

16.52. B., wanting a multiple of twelve, seems to have adapted an alpha-
betical list of the 33 Scottish counties. Cromarty was distinct from Ross
until 1889; but he has left out 'the Kingdom of Fife', and has divided Orkney
and Shetland, added Glasgow and Skye, and duplicated Moray (as Moray
and Elgin).
16.59. This is an unexpected line, implying as it does 'female secret delu-
sion' rather than Los's saving strength; but cp. 69.14–22.
16.62. Los's halls] B. returns to Golgonooza; there the 'fixing' is done.

But Los himself against Albion's sons his fury bends—for he
Dare not approach the daughters openly lest he be consumed
In the fires of their beauty & perfection, & be vegetated beneath
Their looms, in a generation of death, & resurrection to forget-
fulness.
10 They woo Los continually to subdue his strength; he continually
Shows them his spectre, sending him abroad over the four points
of heaven,
In the fierce desires of beauty & in the tortures of repulse! He is
The spectre of the living pursuing the emanations of the dead.
Shuddering they flee: they hide in the druid temples in cold
chastity,
15 Subdued by the spectre of the living & terrified by undisguised
desire.
For Los said: Though my spectre is divided, as I am a living man
I must compel him to obey me wholly, that Enitharmon may not
Be lost, & lest he should devour Enitharmon. Ah me,
Piteous image of my soft desires & loves, O Enitharmon!
20 I will compel my spectre to obey; I will restore to thee thy
children.
No one bruises or starves himself to make himself fit for labour.

'Tormented with sweet desire for these beauties of Albion,
They would never love my power if they did not seek to destroy
Enitharmon. Vala would never have sought & loved Albion
25 If she had not sought to destroy Jerusalem; such is that false
And generating love—a pretence of love to destroy love,
Cruel hypocrisy, unlike the lovely delusions of Beulah,
And cruel forms, unlike the merciful forms of Beulah's night.

17.6ff. Los's masculinity is not proof against feminine wiles; he has to turn
the brutish side of his nature against them.
17.13. The living] Los.
the dead] Albion.
17.14. druid temples in cold chastity] The Druid temples (cp. Europe 72n)
were seen as cruel sites of an evil religion. After 6–12 'chastity' may seem
a strange attribute for the daughters of Albion: but here it is associated
with cold heartlessness, the evil of a patriarchal, oppressive religion.
Besides, their true, lascivious nature is repressed by that religion under the
disguise of prudery.
17.16. divided] i.e. 'divided away from me'. Cp. 12.6–7.
17.21. i.e. he will not deprive Enitharmon of her joy (in her children)
since there is no purpose in doing so, and only loss to her. If the sense is
reflexive, it implies also that Enitharmon's weakness is his also, since she is
a part of him. This deprivation of her children is not developed elsewhere.
17.24. Vala's desire to supplant Jerusalum in Albion's love is the theme
of pls.20–3.

'They know not why they love nor wherefore they sicken & die,
30 Calling that Holy Love which is envy, revenge & cruelty;
Which separated the stars from the mountains, the mountains
     from man,
And left man, a little grovelling root, outside of himself.
Negations are not contraries; contraries mutually exist;
But negations exist not. Exceptions & objections & unbeliefs
35 Exist not; nor shall they ever be organised for ever & ever.
If thou separate from me, thou art a negation, a mere
Reasoning & derogation from me, an objecting & cruel spite
And malice & envy; but my emanation, alas! will become
My contrary. O thou negation, I will continually compel
40 Thee to be invisible to any but whom I please, & when
And where & how I please, & never, never shalt thou be
     organized
But as a distorted & reversed reflection in the darkness
And in the non-entity. Nor shall that which is above
Ever descend into thee, but thou shalt be a non-entity for ever.
45 And if any enter into thee, thou shalt be an unquenchable fire,
And he shall be a never-dying worm, mutually tormented by
Those that thou tormentest, a hell & despair for ever & ever.'

So Los in secret with himself communed, & Enitharmon heard
In her darkness & was comforted, yet still she divided away
50 In gnawing pain from Los's bosom in the deadly night—
First as a red globe of blood trembling beneath his bosom.
Suspended over her he hung, he enfolded her in his garments
Of wool; he hid her from the spectre, in shame & confusion of
Face. In terrors & pains of hell & eternal death, the
55 Trembling globe shot forth self-living; & Los howled over it,
Feeding it with his groans & tears day & night without ceasing.
And the spectrous darkness from his back divided in temptations,
And in grinding agonies, in threats, stiflings, & direful strugglings.

'Go thou to Skofield: ask him if he is Bath or if he is Canterbury.

17.33. Negations . . . contraries] Cp. 10.7n.
17.36. thou] Los speaks to his spectre (as shown in 42): in spite of 48, for
his spectre is part of himself.
17.41. organized] B. distinguishes between the killing restraint of regulated
system, and the 'organization' of an organism, a living creature whose
organization is part of its nature, not imposed from outside.
17.45. fire . . . worm] Mark ix 42–3: 'into hell . . . where their worm dieth
not, and the fire is not quenched.'
17.51. Cp. 6.2. In Urizen 286–323 Enitharmon appears from a globe of
blood drawn from Los by his pity for Urizen. The growth of the spectre
from his back is not in Urizen, but appears in Milton pl.3.34–6 (p. 567).
17.59. Another unexpected change; Bath and Canterbury feature later in the

60 Tell him to be no more dubious: demand explicit words.
Tell him: I will dash him into shivers, where & at what time
I please. Tell Hand & Skofield they are my ministers of evil
To those I hate; for I can hate also as well as they!'

Pl. 18 From every one of the four regions of human majesty
There is an outside spread without & an outside spread within,
Beyond the outline of identity both ways, which meet in one—
An orbed void of doubt, despair, hunger, & thirst & sorrow.
5 Here the twelve sons of Albion, joined in dark assembly,
Jealous of Jerusalem's children, ashamed of her little ones
(For Vala produced the bodies. Jerusalem gave the souls)
Became as three immense wheels, turning upon one another
Into non-entity, and their thunders hoarse appal the dead
10 To murder their own souls, to build a kingdom among the dead:

[*Design*]

'Cast! Cast ye Jerusalem forth, the shadow of delusions,
The harlot daughter, mother of pity and dishonourable
forgiveness,
Our father Albion's sin and shame! But father now no more,
Nor sons, nor hateful peace & love, nor soft complacencies
15 With transgressors meeting in brotherhood around the table,
Or in the porch or garden. No more the sinful delights
Of age & youth, and boy & girl, and animal & herb,
And river & mountain, and city & village, and house & family,
Beneath the oak & palm, beneath the vine & fig-tree
20 In self-denial—but war and deadly contention between
Father & son, and light & love! All bold asperities
Of haters met in deadly strife, rending the house & garden,

poem (pls 41–6), but this seems to be a rhetorical question. *Skofield* is
an evil demon and a dissembler, neither east nor west–'dubious' and
not 'explicit'.

18.*1*. A new section, though connected to the previous lines in that both
concern the sons of Albion.
18.*2*. Cp. 71.*6–9*: the inner world leads to Eternity, the outside is the
superficial edge of things only.
18. *Design*: Symmetrically, two winged figures, a man L with lilies in his
hair a woman R with roses in hers, float apart from one another. From
their outstretched arms two smaller figures (a male from the woman's arm,
and vice versa) fly together, to embrace and kiss. All against a night sky,
with two crescent moons turned into boats with a simple square sail. (Cp.
Los's lament, 56.*18–19*: 'the moon, a ship / In the British ocean!')
18.*11*. The sons of Albion speak: their attitudes are all wrong. They
suspect (as in *12*: cp. *7*) anything that is not earthly; and delight in war.

The unforgiving porches, the tables of enmity, and beds
And chambers of trembling & suspicion, hatreds of age & youth,
25 And boy & girl, & animal & herb, & river & mountain,
And city & village, and house & family. That the perfect
May live in glory, redeemed by sacrifice of the Lamb
And of his children before sinful Jerusalem, to build
Babylon, the city of Vala, the Goddess Virgin-Mother.
30 She is our mother! Nature! Jerusalem is our harlot sister
Returned with children of pollution, to defile our house
With sin & shame. Cast! Cast her into the potter's field!
Her little ones she must slay upon our altars, & her aged
Parents must be carried into captivity, to redeem her soul,
35 To be for a shame & a curse, & to be our slaves for ever!'

So cry Hand & Hyle, the eldest of the fathers of Albion's
Little ones—to destroy the divine Saviour, the friend of sinners,
Building castles in desolated places, & strong fortifications.
Soon Hand mightily devoured & absorbed Albion's twelve sons;
40 Out from his bosom a mighty polypus, vegetating in darkness,
And Hyle & Coban were his two chosen ones, for emissaries
In war. Forth from his bosom they went and returned
Like wheels from a great wheel reflected in the deep.
Hoarse turned the starry wheels, rending a way in Albion's loins
45 Beyond the night of Beulah. In a dark & unknown night,
Outstretched his giant beauty on the ground in pain & tears:

Pl. 19   *[Design]*

His children exiled from his breast pass to & fro before him;
His birds are silent on his hills, flocks die beneath his branches,

18.*26. the perfect*] i.e. the 'perfect' according to moral Law; the sacrifice is
demanded and taken, not a self-sacrifice.
18.*32. The potter's field*] *Matthew* xxvii 7: the field bought 'to bury strangers
in' with the bribe-money thrown back by Judas when he went to hang
himself; i.e. a place to bury the rejected.
18.*33. she must slay*] i.e. offer her children in human sacrifice–not merely
suffer in having them taken from her–as renegade kings of Judah sacrificed
their children. Cp. note on 15.34. Besides, these are children of inspiration
and love, and must not be allowed to live.
18.*40. polypus*] See 15.2n and *Four Zoas* iv 265n.
18.*44–5. The night of Beulah* is for renewal. Albion's life is destroyed, and
his night is a time of spiritual misery and death.

19 Design: At the foot of the page, in the setting sun, Albion lies on his
rock, with mourning figures round him and others ascending round and
above the text, with the weariness of slaves.
19.*1–7, 9–14.* These lines, with minor alterations, occur in *Four Zoas* ix
98–103, 105–11.

His tents are fallen, his trumpets & the sweet sound of his harp
Are silent on his clouded hills, that belch forth storms & fire.
5 His milk of cows, & honey of bees, & fruit of golden harvest,
Is gathered in the scorching heat, & in the driving rain.
Where once he sat he weary walks in misery & pain,
His giant beauty & perfection fallen into dust;
Till from within his withered breast, grown narrow with his woes,
10 The corn is turned to thistles & the apples into poison,
The birds of song to murderous crows, his joys to bitter groans,
The voices of children in his tents to cries of helpless infants.
And, self-exiled from the face of light & shine of morning,
In the dark world (a narrow house!) he wanders up & down,
15 Seeking for rest & finding none; & hidden far within
His eon weeping in the cold & desolated earth.

All his affections now appear withoutside: all his sons—
Hand, Hyle & Coban, Gwantok, Peachey, Brereton, Slayd &
  Huttn,
Skofield, Kox, Kotope & Bowen, his twelve sons (Satanic mill,
20 Who are the spectres of the Twenty-four, each double-formed),
Revolve upon his mountains, groaning in pain beneath
The dark incessant sky, seeking for rest & finding none;
Raging against their human natures, ravening to gormandize
The human majesty and beauty of the Twenty-four—
25 Condensing them into solid rocks with cruelty & abhorrence.
Suspicion & revenge, & the seven diseases of the soul,
Settled around Albion & around Luvah in his secret cloud.

19.16. *eon*] Emanation: a form also used in *36.41* below, and *Milton*
pl.*11.1*. Eon is used of Jerusalem only, and is probably borrowed from the
Gnostic word *aeon*, an emanation of the Supreme Being.
19.17. *withoutside*] Separated and alienated from him. Cp. *12.55n*.
19.19. *Satanic mill*] A place of mental slavery (cp. *Milton* pl.*1.28n*).
19.20. *the Twenty-four*] The twenty-four 'friends of Albion', the cathedral
cities of Britain, who in pls 36ff try to save Albion: they are named in
36.48–61 and *41.1–19*. At *41.23–4* there are four more, in whom the
twenty-four are summed up–a total of twenty-eight. B. therefore some-
times refers to *twenty-four* and sometimes to *twenty-eight*. The sons of
Albion are the false side of him, the 'friends' the good. Both are sides of
the same coin.
19.26. *seven diseases*] B. will not speak of sins, but of a more organic failing.
19.27. *Luvah in his secret cloud*] Cp. *43.33ff*, especially *37–42* and *55–7*. This
passage is best seen in its original context, in *Four Zoas* iii *41ff*. There Vala
(Luvah's counterpart or emanation) seduced the Eternal Man, or Albion.
A result of this was that he began to worship the image of Luvah seen in a
cloud; for in falling under Vala's influence he had in part also fallen under
Luvah's. Yet Luvah was his enemy and tried to subdue him. B. later adds

Willing the Friends endured, for Albion's sake, & for
Jerusalem his emanation shut within his bosom,
30   Which hardened against them more & more, as he builded
        onwards
On the gulf of death in self-righteousness, that rolled
Before his awful feet, in pride of virtue for victory.
And Los was roofed in from eternity in Albion's cliffs
Which stand upon the ends of Beulah, and withoutside all
35   Appeared a rocky form against the Divine Humanity.

Albion's circumference was closed; his centre began darkening
Into the night of Beulah, & the moon of Beulah rose
Clouded with storms. Los his strong guard walked round beneath
        the moon,
And Albion fled inward among the currents of his rivers.

40   He found Jerusalem upon the river of his city, soft reposed
In the arms of Vala, assimilating in one with Vala
The lily of Havilah; & they sang soft through Lambeth's vales,

Jerusalem as the emanation of Albion to this myth: so that in turning to
Vala exclusively Albion dethrones Jerusalem.
19.28. *Friends*] The twenty-four cities.
19.33–4. Albion is connected with Beulah, but outside it, 'a rocky form'
separated from the worlds of eternity.
19.36. *circumference*] Cp. 12.55n.
19.37. Because Albion was cut off from the eternal world, his 'heart' began
to weaken. The *centre* would retain its life longer than the *circumference*, but
in time even the centre loses contact with eternity, and the only contact it
retains is through 'the night of Beulah', through dreams. *Centre* and *cir-
cumference* belong not to a circle, but to a vortex, in which the centre can
reach the outside without crossing the circumference–by going 'down the
whirlpool'.
19.39. *His rivers*] The rivers of Paradise (*Genesis* ii 10). Albion, turning
inward, to his home, is here equated with Adam. In returning to Paradise,
he finds Jerusalem and Vala on one of its four rivers. See *42n.*
19.40. The next sequence of narrative begins: Albion's feeling of despair
over his love for Vala and Jerusalem. Jerusalem and Vala seem to be in their
unfallen state, united and complementary to one another. The *sweet
moony night* (*43*) is the restful night of Beulah, inhabited by the feminine
emanations when the full vigour of Eden is too much for them–cp.
Milton pls 30–1. *The river of* (*Albion's*) *city* is the Thames.
19.42. *The lily of Havilah*] Cp. *Four Zoas* viia *238*: 'Vala the lily of the
desert'. Havilah is mentioned half a dozen times in the Bible, as a tribe or
a place, but this particular phrase does not appear. B. probably knew that
the Hebrew means 'sand', and seems to have realized that Havilah was
desert land; this phrase thus implies beauty in the midst of desolation. In

In a sweet moony night & silence that they had created,
With a blue sky spread over with wings, & a mild moon,
45 Dividing & uniting into many female forms—Jerusalem
Trembling; then in one commingling in eternal tears,
Sighing to melt his giant beauty on the moony river.

[Design]

Pl. 20 *[Design]*

But when they saw Albion fallen upon mild Lambeth's vale
Astonished, terrified, they hovered over his giant limbs.
Then thus Jerusalem spoke, while Vala wove the veil of tears,
Weeping in pleadings of love in the web of despair:

5 'Wherefore has thou shut me into the winter of human life,
And closed up the sweet regions of youth & virgin innocence
Where we live, forgetting error, not pondering on evil,
Among my lambs & brooks of water, among my warbling birds,
Where we delight in innocence before the face of the Lamb,
10 Going in & out before him in his love & sweet affection?'

Vala replied weeping & trembling, hiding in her veil:

'When winter rends the hungry family & the snow falls
Upon the ways of men, hiding the paths of man & beast,

[Design]

Then mourns the wanderer; then he repents his wanderings & eyes
15 The distant forest; then the slave groans in the dungeon of stone,
The captive in the mill of the stranger, sold for scanty hire.
They view their former life; they number moments over & over,
Stringing them on their remembrance as on a thread of sorrow.
Thou art my sister and my daughter; thy shame is mine also.
20 Ask me not of my griefs; thou knowest all my griefs.'

Jerusalem answered with soft tears over the valleys:

Genesis ii 11 Havilah 'where there is gold' is watered by one of the four
rivers of Paradise.
Design. See note at head of this plate.

20. *Design*: Two figures float towards one another, symmetrically.
20.1. *Lambeth*] B.'s home from 1791–1800, a suburb of London on the
south of the Thames; but this allusion may not be fundamental here. Albion
has fallen so that he lies along the Thames, in this fallen material world.
20.11. Whereas Jerusalem tries to remind Albion of happy days, Vala
dwells on their present unhappiness, and 'hides in her veil'. As yet, how-
ever, Vala is not fallen and evil, though the last line of her speech (20)
shows impatience and refusal of sympathy.

'O Vala, what is sin, that thou shudderest & weepest
At sight of thy once-loved Jerusalem? What is sin but a little
Error & fault that is soon forgiven? But mercy is not a sin,
25   Nor pity nor love nor kind forgiveness. Oh, if I have sinned
Forgive & pity me! Oh, unfold thy veil in mercy & love!

[Design]

Slay not my little ones, beloved virgin daughter of Babylon,
Slay not my infant loves & graces, beautiful daughter of Moab!
I cannot put off the human form; I strive but strive in vain.
30   When Albion rent thy beautiful net of gold & silver twine—
Thou hadst woven it with art, thou hadst caught me in the bands
Of love; thou refusedst to let me go. Albion beheld thy beauty,
Beautiful through our love's comeliness, beautiful through pity,
The veil shone with thy brightness in the eyes of Albion,
35   Because it enclosed pity & love, because we loved one another.
Albion loved thee; he rent thy veil, he embraced thee, he loved
thee.
Astonished at his beauty & perfection, thou forgavest his furious
love.
I redounded from Albion's bosom in my virgin loveliness.
The Lamb of God received me in his arms; he smiled upon us;
40   He made me his bride & wife, he gave thee to Albion.
Then was a time of love. Oh, why is it passed away?'

Then Albion broke silence & with groans replied:

Pl. 21   'O Vala, O Jerusalem, do you delight in my groans?
You, O lovely forms, you have prepared my death-cup.
The disease of shame covers me from head to feet. I have no hope;

20. *Designs*: Below *13* and *26*, different scenes of figures dragging ploughs
like flaming stars, or sowing starry seed in the furrows. The sky, with
three moons, stars and a comet, is seen above the upper design, between
11 and *12*: flames rising from the lower design are seen above *21*.

20.27. In *Milton* pl.33.*20* this idea appears in the phrase 'Virgin Babylon,
mother of whoredoms' to indicate the evil, self-righteous cruel nature of
Vala's virginity. But here, Babylon is still not quite lost, the virgin is still
pure. The phrase *daughter of Moab* in the next line has the same sense; Moab
was one of the often hostile tribes on the borders of Judah, east of the
Dead Sea.

20.29. *the human form*] The perfect form of divine humanity.

20.30. Vala had woven a net (or veil) which cut Jerusalem and herself off
from Albion: but Albion, for love of Vala, broke through it.

21.3ff. Albion has fallen into the major error of judging by standards of
Righteousness and Sin. All the elements of his being have been 'driven
forth'—i.e. have become separate entities, and he blames Vala—not for

Every boil upon my body is a separate & deadly sin.
5 Doubt first assailed me, then shame took possession of me.
Shame divides families: shame hath divided Albion in sunder.
First fled my sons, & then my daughters, then my wild animations,
My cattle next, last even the dog of my gate. The forests fled,
The corn-fields, & the breathing gardens outside separated,
10 The sea, the stars, the sun, the moon—driven forth by my disease!
All is eternal death, unless you can weave a chaste
Body over an unchaste mind. Vala, oh that thou wert pure!
That the deep wound of sin might be closed up with the needle
And with the loom, to cover Gwendolen & Ragan with costly robes
15 Of natural virtue (for their spiritual forms without a veil
Wither in Luvah's sepulchre). I thrust him from my presence,
And all my children followed his loud howlings into the deep.
Jerusalem, dissembler Jerusalem, I look into thy bosom,
I discover thy secret places. Cordella, I behold
20 Thee, whom I thought pure as the heavens in innocence & fear,
Thy tabernacle taken down, thy secret cherubim disclosed.
Art thou broken? Ah me, Sabrina, running by my side—
In childhood what wert thou? Unutterable anguish! Conwenna,
Thy cradled infancy is most piteous. O hide, O hide!
25 Their secret gardens were made paths to the traveller;
I knew not of their secret loves with those I hated most,
Nor that their every thought was sin & secret appetite.
Hyle sees in fear, he howls in fury over them. Hand sees

causing him to judge wrongly, but for her 'sin' (*12*)–for these are now
the only terms he can understand.
21.*13–14. needle* and *loom*] Albion wants to escape from sin by mechanical
means, by covering himself with a mere appearance of chastity, and by
hiding from sin–not by repudiating it.
21.*14. Gwendolen & Ragan*] Cp. 5.*40n*, and headnote. They are 'daughters
of Albion'.
21.*15. natural virtue*] The virtue of the natural world–not real virtue.
21.*16. Luvah's sepulchre*] Luvah, the passionate Zoa (see p. 290) is associated
with Christ in *Four Zoas* viii 250, and is crucified and laid in a sepulchre
(viib 163–4). The events of the present passage do not fit those of *Four
Zoas*; but the idea is clear. Albion has pushed Luvah out of the way, and
complains of the results. But he is unwilling to restore Luvah to his proper
place and thus regain his own spirituality.
21.*19. Cordella*] Another of the twelve daughters of Albion: so also
Sabrina (*22*) and Conwenna (*23*).
21.*25. Their*] His daughters'.
21.*26–7*. Albion is, of course, deluded: in his unfallen state he had not
hated, and his children's joys were not sin.
21.*28–49*. The drift of this is that the beautiful and truly virtuous daughters

In jealous fear: in stern accusation with cruel stripes
30   He drives them through the streets of Babylon before my face.
Because they taught Luvah to rise into my clouded heavens,
Battersea & Chelsea mourn for Cambel & Gwendolen.
Hackney & Holloway sicken for Estrild & Ignoge.
Because the Peak, Malvern & Cheviot reason in cruelty,
35   Penmaenmawr & Dhinas-bran demonstrate in unbelief.
Manchester & Liverpool are in tortures of doubt & despair,
Maldon & Colchester demonstrate. I hear my children's voices,
I see their piteous faces gleam out upon the cruel winds
From Lincoln & Norwich, from Edinburgh & Monmouth;
40   I see them distant from my bosom scourged along the roads,
Then lost in clouds. I hear their tender voices—clouds divide;
I see them die beneath the whips of the captains. They are taken
In solemn pomp into Chaldea across the breadths of Europe.
Six months they lie embalmed in silent death, worshipped,
45   Carried in arks of oak before the armies in the spring,
Bursting their arks they rise again to life, they play before
The armies. I hear their loud cymbals & their deadly cries.
Are the dead cruel? Are those who are enfolded in moral law
Revengeful? O that death & annihilation were the same!'

50   Then Vala answered, spreading her scarlet veil over Albion:

of Albion have been wrenched away from their true places in Albion's life
by his now fallen sons, such as Hyle and Hand. As the Jews were taken
captive to Babylon, so are they; and they reappear in Albion's sight cor-
rupted. Their songs are now cruel–as they remain throughout the poem
until Albion's redemption. The place-names, as related to the daughters,
have no specific significance; these references mean that every part of
England and Wales has suffered its own particular loss.
21.32–3. *Cambel, Gwendolen, Estrild, Ignoge*] Daughters of Albion: see
headnote.
21.35. *Penmaenmawr*] A mountain surrounded by ancient fortifications.
Dhinas-bran is the site of a medieval castle. Thus both are places of war in
Wales, the home of the Druids.   *demonstrate*] 'Prove by experimental
demonstration.'
21.37. *Maldon & Colchester*] B. has *Malden*, but all his allusions indicate
Maldon on the east coast. See 27.60n, 90.62n.
21.42. *Chaldea*] Of which Babylon was the capital.
21.44–7. A reference to the fertility religions which worshipped the dying
god who was resurrected in spring: and to the similar legend of Per-
sephone or Proserpine (a woman): and to the use of religion to hallow
war. Oak is associated with the Druids. The allusion seems to be a confla-
tion of these rather than a direct reference to one rite.
21.48. *Are the dead cruel?*] The spiritually dead are (note next line).
21.50. *scarlet*] Vala is becoming the 'Scarlet Woman'.

[*Design*]

Pl. 22   [*Design*]

'Albion, thy fear has made me tremble; thy terrors have surrounded
    me.
Thy sons have nailed me on the gates, piercing my hands & feet,
Till Skofield's Nimrod, the mighty huntsman Jehovah, came
With Cush his son, & took me down. He in a golden ark
5 Bears me before his armies, though my shadow hovers here.
The flesh of multitudes fed & nourished me in my childhood;
My morn & evening food were prepared in battles of men.
Great is the cry of the hounds of Nimrod along the valley
Of vision; they scent the odour of war in the valley of vision!
10 All love is lost—terror succeeds & hatred instead of love,
And stern demands of right & duty instead of liberty.
Once thou wast to me the loveliest son of heaven; but now
Where shall I hide from thy dread countenance & searching eyes?
I have looked into the secret soul of him I loved,
15 And in the dark recesses found sin & can never return.'

Albion again uttered his voice beneath the silent moon:

'I brought love into light of day, to pride in chaste beauty;
I brought love into light, & fancied innocence is no more.'

Then spoke Jerusalem: 'O Albion, my father Albion,
20 Why wilt thou number every little fibre of my soul,
Spreading them out before the sun like stalks of flax to dry?
The infant joy is beautiful, but its anatomy
Horrible, ghast & deadly; nought shalt thou find in it
But dark despair & everlasting brooding melancholy.'

25 Then Albion turned his face toward Jerusalem & spoke:

'Hide thou, Jerusalem, in impalpable voidness, not to be

21. *Design*: Illustrates *40–3*.

22. *Design*: A female figure, perhaps Leda, and a swan.

22.2. The connection of Vala with the crucifixion is unusual, though she is
Luvah's emanation (see note on 21.*16*). But since she is in error, her words
are in any case to be treated as probably false. She claims to be released only
by the warlike Nimrod, who uses her to goad his armies to more wars.

22.3. Although the names are biblical, the reference is not. B. uses the
biblical story of the ark, a sacred mystery, which was carried before the
Israelites when they set out from Sinai (cp. *Numbers* x 33): but the details
(e.g. the gold) are his own.

22.15. But she should have forgiven any fault she might have found.

22.20–4. So in *Four Zoas* i 28–32, where *number* reads *examine*, and *dark*
reads *death*.

Touched by the hand nor seen with the eye! O Jerusalem,
Would thou wert not & that thy place might never be found!
But come, O Vala, with knife & cup, drain my blood
30 To the last drop, then hide me in thy scarlet tabernacle.
For I see Luvah whom I slew, I behold him in my spectre
As I behold Jerusalem in thee, O Vala, dark & cold.'

Jerusalem then stretched her hand toward the moon & spoke:

'Why should punishment weave the veil with iron wheels of war,
35 When forgiveness might it weave with wings of cherubim?'

Loud groaned Albion from mountain to mountain & replied:

Pl. 23 'Jerusalem, Jerusalem, deluding shadow of Albion,

[Design]

Daughter of my fantasy, unlawful pleasure, Albion's curse!
I came here with intention to annihilate thee; but
My soul is melted away, enwoven within the veil.
5 Hast thou again knitted the veil of Vala, which I for thee
Pitying rent in ancient times? I see it whole and more
Perfect, and shining with beauty!'
                                    —'But thou, O wretched father!'
Jerusalem replied, like a voice heard from a sepulchre:
'Father, once piteous! Is pity a sin? Embalmed in Vala's bosom
10 In an eternal death for Albion's sake, our best beloved.
Thou art my father & my brother; why hast thou hidden me
Remote from the Divine Vision, my Lord & Saviour?'

Trembling stood Albion at her words in jealous dark despair:

[Design]

He felt that love & pity are the same—a soft repose,
15 Inward complacency of soul, a self-annihilation.
'I have erred, I am ashamed, & will never return more;

22.*29–30*. This self-torment is characteristic of the fallen soul.
22.*34–5*. These lines are illustrated at the foot of the page, where cherubim
hover over iron gear-wheels.
23. *Design*: A female angelic figure with large eagle's wings, and feathers
growing down from her limbs, reclines and sleeps.
23.*1–7*. Albion's speech is confused by his error; he does not understand
the nature either of Jerusalem or of the veil.
23.*16ff*. Albion misinterprets love and pity. The second is intended for the
unfortunate, but is a dangerous emotion, for it inhibits remedial action
('pity . . . man unmans', *Milton* pl.8.*19–20*). The first leads a person to
understanding another's needs, and to acting thereon, even though the

I have taught my children sacrifices of cruelty. What shall I
    answer?
I will hide it from Eternals! I will give myself for my children!
Which way soever I turn, I behold humanity and pity.'

20 He recoiled, he rushed outwards, he bore the veil whole away;
His fires redound from his dragon altars in errors returning.
He drew the veil of moral virtue, woven for cruel laws,
And cast it into the Atlantic deep, to catch the souls of the dead.
He stood between the palm tree & the oak of weeping
25 Which stand upon the edge of Beulah, & there Albion sunk
Down in sick pallid langour. These were his last words,
    relapsing,
Hoarse from his rocks, from caverns of Derbyshire & Wales
And Scotland, uttered from the circumference into Eternity:

[*Design*]

'Blasphemous sons of feminine delusion, God in the dreary void
30 Dwells from eternity, wide separated from the human soul.
But thou, deluding image—by whom imbued, the veil I rent—
Lo! here is Vala's veil whole, for a law, a terror & a curse.
And therefore God takes vengeance on me; from my clay-cold
    bosom

action may be unpleasant in its immediate effects. Los, according to the
Bard's Song in *Milton*, once forgot this, with disastrous results. Albion
believes he will be condemned for his error, and cannot accept the forgive-
ness of the Eternals. His only wish is to hide his error, not to admit it and
end it; he is afraid and too ashamed to return to truth.

23.20. *outwards*] Towards the superficial, outward appearance of things,
accepting Vala's veil whole and unchallenged. Thus in *28* he speaks 'from
the circumference into eternity' against the inner life. Cp. *12.55*.

23.21. *dragon altars*] The altars of the 'Dragon Temples' of the Druids (a
mistaken notion of William Stukeley's, commonly accepted in B.'s time:
cp. *Europe 72n*).

23.23. *the Atlantic deep*] Connotes evil to B. for it overwhelmed the beauti-
ful land of Atlantis. The *veil* becomes a fishing-net.

23.24. So in *Four Zoas* ii *204*, where also Albion is on the point of lapsing
into a deathly sleep. For the *palm* and *oak* see *Four Zoas* i *206n*.

23.27. *caverns*] Perhaps B. refers to the pot-holes, the underground caverns
of Derbyshire.

23. *Design* (in one with that at foot of the plate): Struggling figures; above
trapped in caves and roots of trees, below in rocks beneath the earth's
surface.

23.31 *the veil I rent*] An allusion to *20.30–41*: Albion now regards his love
as 'delusion'. Yet the veil is delusion, and if he ceased to believe in it, it
would dissolve.

My children wander, trembling victims of his moral justice.
35   His snows fall on me & cover me, while in the veil I fold
My dying limbs. Therefore, O manhood, if thou art aught
But a mere fantasy, hear dying Albion's curse:
May God who dwells in this dark Ulro & voidness, vengeance take,
And draw thee down into this abyss of sorrow & torture,
40   Like me thy victim. O that death & annihilation were the same!

[Design]

Pl. 24   *[Design]*

'What have I said? What have I done? O all-powerful human
     words,
You recoil back upon me in the blood of the Lamb slain in his
     children.
Two bleeding contraries, equally true, are his witnesses against me.
We reared mighty stones; we danced naked around them,
5   Thinking to bring love into light of day, to Jerusalem's shame
Displaying our giant limbs to all the winds of heaven. Sudden
Shame seized us, we could not look on one another for abhorrence:
     the blue
Of our immortal veins & all their hosts fled from our limbs,
And wandered distant in a dismal night clouded & dark;
10   The sun fled from the Briton's forehead, the moon from his mighty
     loins;
Scandinavia fled with all his mountains filled with groans.

[Design]

'Oh, what is life & what is man? Oh, what is death? Wherefore
Are you, my children, natives in the grave to where I go?
Or are you born to feed the hungry ravenings of destruction,
15   To be the sport of accident, to waste in wrath & love a weary
Life, in brooding cares & anxious labours that prove but chaff?

23. *Design*: See note on design above.

24. *Design*: A crescent moon floats on the waves, cradling a figure.

24.2. *recoil*] Albion has wished that the Divine Humanity be drawn 'down
into this abyss' (23.39): then has a glimpse of the truth–that though Christ
has been crucified, this has glorified him, not destroyed him. But Albion
cannot accept the implications.

24.4. There may be a double reference here to the erection of the Druid
temples such as Stonehenge, and to the orgiastic dances there, attributed to
sisterhoods of witches. Neither ritual succeeded in destroying Jerusalem;
they only succeeded in bringing shame to Albion.

24. *Design*: Mourning figures carried by the waves of the design above,
which continues down the margin.

Thy pillars of ivory & gold, thy curtains of silk & fine
Linen, thy pavements of precious stones, thy walls of pearl
20 And gold, thy gates of thanksgiving, thy windows of praise,
Thy clouds of blessing, thy cherubims of tender mercy,
Stretching their wings sublime over the little ones of Albion.
O human imagination! O divine body I have crucified,
I have turned my back upon thee into the wastes of moral law.
25 There Babylon is builded in the waste, founded in human
desolation.
O Babylon, thy watchman stands over thee in the night;
Thy severe judge all the day long proves thee, O Babylon,
With provings of destruction, with giving thee thy heart's desire.
But Albion is cast forth to the potter, his children to the builders
30 To build Babylon, because they have forsaken Jerusalem.
The walls of Babylon are souls of men, her gates the groans
Of nations, her towers are the miseries of once happy families.
Her streets are paved with destruction, her houses built with death,
Her palaces with hell & the grave, her synagogues with torments
35 Of ever-hardening despair, squared & polished with cruel skill.
Yet thou wast lovely as the summer cloud upon my hills
When Jerusalem was thy heart's desire in times of youth & love.
Thy sons came to Jerusalem with gifts, she sent them away
With blessings on their hands & on their feet, blessings of gold,
40 And pearl & diamond; thy daughters sang in her courts;
They came up to Jerusalem; they walked before Albion.
In the Exchanges of London every nation walked,
And London walked in every nation, mutual in love & harmony.
Albion covered the whole earth, England encompassed the nations,
45 Jerusalem covered the Atlantic mountains & the Erythrean,
From bright Japan & China to Hesperia, France & England.
Mount Zion lifted his head in every nation under heaven,
And the Mount of Olives was beheld over the whole earth.
The footsteps of the Lamb of God were there: but now no more,

24.29. Albion is shapeless clay, to be moulded against his will.

24.36. As Jerusalem is both city and woman, so Babylon the city is Vala the woman; cp. 19.40–1. In the following lines the friendship of the two is seen in terms of the cities.

24.42. *Exchanges*] Cp. 27.103. B. sees the commercial exchanges as places designed for fraternal and international commerce, not mere money-making.

24.45. i.e. before the ocean had overwhelmed Atlantis. *The Erythrean* is the Red Sea; to B. the eastern ocean, equivalent to the Atlantic in the west. Lines 46–7 therefore mean that Jerusalem enfolded the whole earth.

24.46. *Hesperia*] Italy.

50   No more shall I behold him; he is closed in Luvah's sepulchre.
       Yet why these smitings of Luvah, the gentlest mildest Zoa?
       If God was merciful this could not be. O Lamb of God,
       Thou art a delusion, & Jerusalem is my sin. O my children,
       I have educated you in the crucifying cruelties of demonstration,
55   Till you have assumed the providence of God & slain your father.
       Dost thou appear before me who liest dead in Luvah's sepulchre?
       Dost thou forgive me, thou who wast dead & art alive?
       Look not so merciful upon me, O thou slain Lamb of God!
       I die, I die in thy arms, though hope is banished from me!'
60   Thundering the veil rushes from his hand, vegetating knot by
       Knot, day by day, night by night; loud roll the indignant Atlantic
       Waves & the Erythrean, turning up the bottoms of the deeps.
Pl. 25 And there was heard a great lamenting in Beulah. All the regions
       Of Beulah were moved as the tender bowels are moved; & they
       said:

       'Why did you take vengeance, O ye sons of the mighty Albion,
       Planting these oaken groves, erecting these dragon temples?
5   Injury the Lord heals, but vengeance cannot be healed.
       As the sons of Albion have done to Luvah, so they have in him
       Done to the divine Lord & Saviour, who suffers with those that
           suffer.
       For not one sparrow can suffer, & the whole universe not suffer also,
       In all its regions, & its Father & Saviour not pity & weep.
10   But vengeance is the destroyer of grace & repentance in the bosom
       Of the injurer—in which the Divine Lamb is cruelly slain.
       Descend, O Lamb of God, & take away the imputation of sin
       By the creation of states & the deliverance of individuals, evermore,
           Amen!'
       Thus wept they in Beulah over the four regions of Albion.
15   But many doubted & despaired, & imputed sin & righteousness
       To individuals & not to states; and these slept in Ulro.

[*Design*]

24.*50–2*. Albion's fall has perverted Luvah: cp. 19.*27n*. But Albion will not
see his own fault, and instead denies the mercy of God.
24.*56*. i.e. 'thou . . . who liest'.

25.*1*. It is the duty of Beulah to watch over sufferers in other worlds.
25.*4*. The Druids were said to worship in oak groves, and to have built
great stone temples and made human sacrifices there.
25.*13*. states] Cp. *Milton* pl.*32.22* and note: also *Jerusalem* 31.*13n*.
25. *Design* (covering most of the plate): Albion, tormented by three of his
daughters. His body is covered with sun, moon, and the stars of Orion and
of the Pleiades; one of the females is twisting the umbilical cord (facs. in
Keynes, *W.B.'s Engravings*, pl.105).

Pl. 26   *[Design, bearing the words]*

Such visions have appeared to me
as I my ordered race have run.
Jerusalem is named Liberty
Among the sons of Albion.

Chapter 2

The theme of this chapter is the further weakening of Albion. At the end of ch. 1 he said 'Hope is banished from me' (24.*60*), and this cry is repeated at 47.*18*; after this he is laid on his couch as if dead. Thus there is little advancement of narrative: the chapter, however, is not designed as a narrative. It is designed to show the nature of Albion's weakness, its effects, and the ineffectiveness of different kinds of outside help. He can only be saved by his own response to the Divine Mercy, for which the time is not yet ripe.

The chapter consists of a number of sequences: disputations among differing groups of figures; declarations; episodic incidents; and some narrative. Certain passages may be detached as of special importance. (1) The narrative of *Reuben*, 30.*43–58*, 32.*1–24*. Albion is identified with Israel, 'the sons of Albion' with the Israelites, and (30.*36*) their leader Hand with Reuben. After Albion's fall, his eldest son, Reuben, is driven out of the 'holy land' of Eternity, and becomes the first of mortal men. (2) Lines 33.*1–45.39* consist of a number of distinct passages but, as a whole, are an account of Los's attempts to save Albione. Hexhorts him and brings the 'friends of Albion' to help him, but they fail when they try to use force; and Bath, one of the 'friends', teaches that they must wait for the preparations of the Divine Vision. Los searches London but fails to find the cause of Albion's error. (3) Lines 45.*40–48.12* contain the chief piece of narrative in the chapter. Vala asserts her control over Albion; his sons determinedly compose him to sleep; but the Divine Mercy prepares a couch for him on which he may sleep with hope of reawakening. (4) Lines 48.*13–50.30*; Los creates Erin to watch over Albion; she and the daughters of Beulah end the chapter with their mourning. Within all these sequences there are many subdivisions, and the poem moves, in so far as it moves at all, only slowly. The incidents contained in these sequences are often self-contained, and do not, with the exception of parts of (2) and all (3) above, advance the main action.

There are two different arrangements of the plates of this chapter. That given here was used in the earliest two copies; B. then altered it for two copies, and returned to the original order for the fifth and last copy. Both arrangements seem to have given him some satisfaction. Plates 29–46 are

26. *Full-page design*: *Hand*, encircled by flames, with a serpent coiling round his outstretched arms: *Jerusalem* watches in fear; the figures are labelled.

therefore given double numbers, thus: pl.29(33): the number in brackets indicates the place of the plate in the alternative arrangement. Because of the nature of the material, the different orders do not affect the thread of thought very seriously. In the footnote references the first number only is given.

Pl. 27   To the Jews

Jerusalem the emanation of the giant Albion! Can it be? Is it a truth that the learned have explored? Was Britain the primitive seat of

27.1. Jerusalem . . . Albion!] This idea is central to *Jerusalem*. Cp. *38.68n*. For *emanation*, see *Four Zoas* i *17n*; here Jerusalem is (*a*) the essential counterpart of Albion's being, as wife is to husband, as the New Jerusalem is to Christ in *Revelation*: (*b*) his creation–as, in Neo-Platonic thought, an emanation is an ethereal spirit, externalized from the person, but existing only as a reflection of that person. Jerusalem, the Holy City of the Bible, is thus an emanation, not of a distant land in a mysterious past, but of Britain, the nation to whom B. was addressing himself. This Preface is dedicated 'To the Jews': B. wishes to identify his nation and its history with theirs. Hence he also feels the need to describe the separation of the two lands, which he envisages were once literally one (e.g. *38.69–70*, *63.41–2*).

The *Giant Albion* is B.'s development of the idea of Adam Kadmon, the Universal Man referred to in *13–14*; the idea may have come to B. through Swedenborg, but originated in the Jewish mystical traditions of the Kabbala. The Universal Man is the basis of the *Four Zoas*, but in *Jerusalem* B. specifies that the Man is to be seen in Albion, Britain, on his island-rock, rather than as an ancestor of the Jews (see note below).

27.2–3. Was Britain . . . religion?] These ideas are by no means original to B., who is drawing on a long tradition of reputable, if not always orthodox, thought. Briefly, this held that the patriarchs of *Genesis* possessed divine wisdom drawn directly from those who, like Abraham, spoke to God; that this wisdom spread over the whole world. Later the sins of men lost them this divine contact, until it was restored by the coming of Christ. B. combines this with the theory that the druids, Britain's ancient religious men, were themselves the original patriarchs– thus uniting Jewish and British legend, and setting the scene of patriarchal activity in Albion. Hence the repeated identification of Albion and biblical Palestine in *Jerusalem*, and in the famous prefatory poem to *Milton*. *The learned* (*2*) refers to a series of earnest if bewildered antiquaries, from William Stukeley (1687–1765) who associated the druids with the patriarchs, to Jacob Bryant (1715–1804) who, in his *New System* (1774) associated all ancient religions with one another. B. adds that, as the patriarchal religion was corrupted so also the druids, with all Albion, were corrupted, building their stone temples (as B. and his age thought), for human sacrifice. But the strain of wisdom was never entirely lost.

Cp. *Descriptive Catalogue* v: 'Mr B. has in his hands poems of the highest

the patriarchal religion? If it is true, my title-page is also true—that
Jerusalem was & is the emanation of the giant Albion. It *is* true and
5 cannot be controverted. Ye are united, O ye inhabitants of earth, in
one religion, the religion of Jesus—the most ancient, the eternal, &
the everlasting gospel. The wicked will turn it to wickedness, the
righteous to righteousness. Amen! Huzza! Selah!
  '*All things begin & end in Albion's ancient druid rocky shore.*'
10 Your ancestors derived their origin from Abraham, Heber, Shem,
and Noah, who were druids, as the druid temples (which are the
patriarchal pillars & oak groves) over the whole earth witness to this
day.
  You have a tradition, that man anciently contained in his mighty
15 limbs all things in heaven & earth: this you received from the druids.
  '*But now the starry heavens are fled from the mighty limbs of Albion.*'
  Albion was the parent of the druids; & in his chaotic state of sleep
Satan & Adam & the whole world was created by the Elohim.

antiquity. Adam was a Druid, and Noah; also Abraham was called to suc-
ceed the druidical age, which began to turn allegoric and mental significa-
tion into corporeal command, whereby human sacrifice would have de-
populated the earth. All these things are written in Eden. . . . The antiqui-
ties of every nation under heaven, is no less sacred than that of the Jews.
They are the same thing as Jacob Bryant, and all antiquaries have proved.
How other antiquities came to be neglected and disbelieved, while those of
the Jews are collected and arranged, is an enquiry, worthy of both the
Antiquarian and the Divine. All had originally one language, and one
religion, this was the religion of Jesus, the everlasting Gospel. Antiquity
preaches the Gospel of Jesus. . . .' (*Erdman 1965*, pp. 533–34). See also
Marriage iv *39–41*.
27.8. *Amen! Huzza! Selah!*] B. unites Jewish and British ejaculations.
(*Selah* is not an ejaculation, but was commonly supposed to be.)
27.9. So in *Milton* pl.6.*25* (the plate is a late addition) and *Jerusalem*
46.*15*. It appears to be a kind of slogan with B.
27.16. So in *Milton* pl.6.*25* and see *Jerusalem* 30.*20–1*, *70.32*, *75.27*. The
universal man, who contained all nature in his own being, is disintegrated;
the universe is turned into a host of separated entities.
27.18. *Satan and Adam*] The two 'limits' (cp. *Four Zoas* iv *270n*) of the
Fall; man was divinely prevented from deteriorating beyond them.
Created by the Elohim] Creation is the fixed state of being in this mortal
world; better than chaos, but fallen from eternity. In *Genesis* i, the bame of
God who creates is *Elohim*. In 2.*4* another narrative begins (but B., like all
his age, would read only one continuous story): this includes the specifically
earthly creation of man ('out of the dust'); the separation of woman from
him; the prohibition, and the fall. In this part, God is called *Jah*, or *Jehovah*.
B. often distinguishes the creating Elohim from the law-giving Jehovah,
taking his cue from Neo-Platonism, directly or indirectly.

20   The fields from Islington to Marybone,
        To Primrose Hill and Saint John's Wood,
          Were builded over with pillars of gold,
        And there Jerusalem's pillars stood.

        Her little ones ran on the fields,
        The Lamb of God among them seen
25   And fair Jerusalem his bride,
        Among the little meadows green.

        Pancras & Kentish Town repose
        Among her golden pillars high,
          Among her golden arches which
30   Shine upon the starry sky.

        The Jews-Harp House & the Green Man,
        The ponds where boys to bathe delight,
          The fields of cows by Willan's farm,
        Shine in Jerusalem's pleasant sight.

35   She walks upon our meadows green,
        The Lamb of God walks by her side,
          And every English child is seen
        Children of Jesus & his Bride,

        Forgiving trespasses and sins,
40   Lest Babylon with cruel Og,
          With moral & self-righteous law
        Should crucify in Satan's synagogue!

        What are those golden builders doing
        Near mournful ever-weeping Paddington,
45   Standing above that mighty ruin
        Where Satan the first victory won,

        Where Albion slept beneath the fatal tree
        And the druid's golden knife
          Rioted in human gore,
50   In offerings of human life?

27. poem. This, as far as *82*, is almost a summary of ch. 1. For the London place-names, see map on p. 621.
27.*32*. *boys*] Includes B. himself; these were places he would have known as a child.
27.*40–2*. i.e. lest the enemies of true religion should set up their false laws of cruelty. In *Four Zoas* viii *89*, *261*ff, the synagogue of Satan is set against Los and the council of God, and seen as the religious forces that crucified Christ.
27.*43*. These are the builders of Golgonooza, working in the midst of ruin: cp. 12.25.

They groaned aloud on London Stone,
They groaned aloud on Tyburn's brook;
Albion gave his deadly groan,
And all the Atlantic mountains shook.

55   Albion's spectre from his loins
Tore forth in all the pomp of war,
Satan his name; in flames of fire
He stretched his druid pillars far.

Jerusalem fell from Lambeth's Vale,
60   Down through Poplar & Old Bow,
Through Maldon & across the sea,
In war & howling, death & woe.

The Rhine was red with human blood,
The Danube rolled a purple tide;
65   On the Euphrates Satan stood
And over Asia stretched his pride.

He withered up sweet Zion's hill,
From every nation of the earth;
He withered up Jerusalem's gates
70   And in a dark land gave her birth.

He withered up the human form
By laws of sacrifice for sin
Till it became a mortal worm
(But oh, translucent all within!).

75   The Divine Vision still was seen,
Still was the human form divine
Weeping in weak & mortal clay;
O Jesus, still the form was thine!

And thine the human face & thine
80   The human hands & feet & breath,

27.51–2. *London Stone* . . . *Tyburn*] Places of execution or sacrifice in ancient
and modern times.
27.55. B., in a typical compression, relates war, brutal sexuality, and false
religion. Cp. 47.3.
27.60–1. Jerusalem falls eastwards, to the lands of war and superstition,
where she is now embedded. Maldon (cp. 21.37) is on the East Coast, and
supposed (by Camden and others) to be the site of the Roman Camulo-
dunum.
27. 63–4. As in Napoleon's campaigns of 1805–6.
27. 65–6. Cp. 8.19–24.
27. 68. What is true of Albion is true of all nations.

Entering through the gates of birth
And passing through the gates of death.

And, O thou Lamb of God, whom I
Slew in my dark self-righteous pride,
85   Art thou returned to Albion's land,
And is Jerusalem thy Bride?

Come to my arms & never more
Depart, but dwell for ever here.
Create my spirit to thy love,
90   Subdue my spectre to thy fear.

Spectre of Albion, warlike fiend,
In clouds of blood & ruin rolled,
I here reclaim thee as my own,
My selfhood, Satan, armed in gold.

95   Is this thy soft family love,
Thy cruel patriarchal pride
Planting thy family alone,
Destroying all the world beside?

A man's worst enemies are those
100   Of his own house & family;
And he who makes his law a curse,
By his own law shall surely die.

In my exchanges every land
Shall walk, & mine in every land
105   Mutual shall build Jerusalem:
Both heart in heart & hand in hand.

If humility is Christianity, you, O Jews, are the true Christians.
if your tradition that man contained in his limbs all animals is true,
and they were separated from him by cruel sacrifices, and when
110 compulsory cruel sacrifices had brought humanity into a feminine
tabernacle, in the loins of Abraham & David, the Lamb of God,
the Saviour, became apparent on earth as the prophets had fore-
told! The return of Israel is a return to mental sacrifice & war. Take
up the cross, O Israel, & follow Jesus!

27.99. Cp. *Matthew* x 36: 'And a man's foes shall be they of his own house-
hold.' B. does not refer to actual strife, but to the hindering of a man by
family influences. B. uses the same words in 41.25–6.
27.103. Cp. 24.42.
27.110. *feminine tabernacle*] The tabernacle was the place of worship set up
under Moses (*Exodus* xxv–xxvii). Feminine domination is usually seen by
B. as cruel; the religion of Rahab and Tirzah, as chs 2–3 repeatedly show, is
characterized by a kind of vicious, perverted sexuality.

Pl. 28   CHAPTER 2
                                 [*Design*]
Every ornament of perfection, and every labour of love,
In all the Garden of Eden, & in all the golden mountains
Was become an envied horror, & a remembrance of jealousy;
And every act a crime, and Albion the punisher & judge.

5   And Albion spoke from his secret seat and said:

'All these ornaments are crimes, they are made by the labours
Of loves, of unnatural consanguinities and friendships
Horrid to think of when enquired deeply into, and all
These hills & valleys are accursed witnesses of sin.
10 I therefore condense them into solid rocks, steadfast,
A foundation & certainty & demonstrative truth,
That man be separate from man; & here I plant my seat.'

Cold snows drifted around him; ice covered his loins around.
He sat by Tyburn's brook, and underneath his heel, shot up
15 A deadly tree—he named it *Moral Virtue*, and the *Law
Of God* who dwells in chaos hidden from the human sight.

The tree spread over him its cold shadows (Albion groaned),
They bent down, they felt the earth and again enrooting
Shot into many a tree; an endless labyrinth of woe.

20 From willing sacrifice of self, to sacrifice of (miscalled) enemies
For atonement Albion began to erect twelve altars,
Of rough unhewn rocks, before the potter's furnace.

28. *Design*: The upper half of the page shows a couple embracing on a
floating lily–perhaps referring to *1–2*. As in *Song of Songs* ii 6, 'His left
hand is under my head, and his right hand doth embrace me'; her arms
embrace him likewise.
28.*13*. Albion has behaved as Urizen does in the myth of *Urizen* and
Four Zoas: the effects are the same–cp. *Four Zoas* viia *28–35*.
28.*15 A deadly tree*] B. uses the same image in the 'Tree of Mystery' in
Four Zoas, q.v. viia *31n*.
28.*20–7*. Albion's family disintegrates: it was a single entity, but now he
is hostile to his sons, who in turn attack Jerusalem.
28.*22. rough unhewn rocks*] As in *Joshua* viii 30–2, after Joshua had annihil-
ated the people of Ai, and hanged their king on a tree, he raised an altar to
God in the presence of all the twelve tribes. This altar, in obedience to the
command in *Deuteronomy* xxvii 5, was 'an altar of whole stones, over
which no man hath lift up any iron. . . . And he wrote there upon the
stones a copy of the law of Moses.'
potter's furnace] Cp. *53.27–9*. In death and life, souls are unshaped and shaped
like clay in a pottery.

23 + B.

He named them *Justice*, & *Truth*. And Albion's sons
Must have become the first victims, being the first transgressors;
25 But they fled to the mountains to seek ransom, building a strong
    Fortification against the divine humanity & mercy,
    In shame & jealousy to annihilate Jerusalem.

Pl. 29 Turning his back to the Divine Vision, his spectrous
(33) Chaos before his face appeared, an unformed memory.

Then spoke the spectrous chaos to Albion, darkening cold,
From the back & loins where dwell the spectrous dead:

5 'I am your rational power, O Albion, & that human form
  You call divine is but a worm seventy inches long,
  That creeps forth in a night & is dried in the morning sun:
  In fortuitous concourse of memories accumulated & lost,
  It ploughs the earth in its own conceit, it overwhelms the hills
10 Beneath its winding labyrinths, till a stone of the brook
   Stops it in midst of its pride among its hills & rivers.
   Battersea & Chelsea mourn, London & Canterbury tremble;
   Their place shall not be found as the wind passes over.
   The ancient cities of the earth remove as a traveller;
15 And shall Albion's cities remain when I pass over them
   With my deluge of forgotten remembrances over the tablet?'

[Design]

So spoke the spectre to Albion. (He is the great selfhood,
Satan, worshipped as God by the mighty ones of the earth,
Having a white dot called a centre from which branches out
20 A circle in continual gyrations. This became a heart,
   From which sprang numerous branches varying their motions,
   Producing many heads—three or seven or ten, & hands & feet

28.24. Must] i.e. would inevitably.

28.25. ransom] A reference to the theology that a stern, unyielding God demanded a ransom for sin, which was provided by Christ as a scapegoat.

29.1-2 his spectrous / Chaos] His spectre; nihilistic, chaos-making creature.

29.4. back and loins] Los's spectre grew from his back (17.57)—not from the heart. The Spectre's message is the logical conclusion of a materialistic belief.

29.8. fortuitous concourse] A famous phrase from Cicero, referring to the random atoms of Democritus' theory. See *OED* 'Concourse' 3.

29.10. a stone of the brook] So David took 'five smooth stones out of the brook' (1 *Samuel* xvii 40) and killed Goliath in his pride.

Design: A man ploughs with two man-headed lions—cp. *9* and *32*.

29.19. a white dot] B. parodies the 'contemplator's' notion of a heart and of life. Note the resemblance of this image to the *polypus* image (see 66.48n and *Four Zoas* iv 267n).

Innumerable at will of the unfortunate contemplator,
Who becomes his food. Such is the way of the devouring power.)

25 And this is the cause of the appearance in the frowning chaos.
Albion's emanation, which he had hidden in jealousy,
Appeared now in the frowning chaos, prolific upon the chaos,
Reflecting back to Albion in sexual reasoning hermaphroditic.

Albion spoke: 'Who art thou that appearest in gloomy pomp,
30 Involving the Divine Vision in colours of autumn ripeness?
I never saw thee till this time, nor beheld life abstracted,
Nor darkness immingled with light on my furrowed field.
Whence camest thou? Who art thou, O loveliest? The
      Divine Vision
Is as nothing before thee; faded is all life & joy.'

35 Vala replied in clouds of tears, Albion's garment embracing:

'I was a city & a temple built by Albion's children.
I was a garden planted with beauty; I allured on hill & valley
The river of life to flow against my walls & among my trees.
Vala was Albion's bride & wife in great Eternity,
40 The loveliest of the daughters of Eternity, when in day-break
I emanated from Luvah over the towers of Jerusalem
And in her courts, among her little children offering up
The sacrifice of fanatic love. Why loved I Jerusalem?
Why was I one with her embracing in the vision of Jesus?

29.23–4. The 'contemplator' who worships (18) this metaphysical creation
of his own is nevertheless devoured by it.
29.26. *Albion's emanation*] Vala (35): she is 'the cause' (25).
29.28. *Sexual reasoning* is *hermaphroditic* because it is sterile. The sexual
world is the world after the Fall, when humans can no longer live together
in true unity and love, but can only struggle for a sexual imitation of it.
29.36ff. In these lines Vala is Babylon, the city opposing Jerusalem.
Babylon was a great city and religious centre, famous for its artificial
gardens; the great river Euphrates ran by it. In *Revelation* Babylon is the
great and evil city which is supplanted by the holy Jerusalem, on the true
River of Life; and Jerusalem, not Babylon, is the Bride. Hence Vala lies:
her memory of Eternity (39–46) is embittered and distorted.
29.41. *I emanated from Luvah*] Vala was Luvah's 'child' and became Albion's
wife (ignoring Jerusalem's position, described in ch. 1, as 'co-wife'). This
amends the myth of *Four Zoas* (where she is Luvah's emanation and wife,
but set out to seduce Albion, thus causing his ruin), making it more
suitable for *Jerusalem*. B. maintains this fairly consistently, in spite of
passages borrowed from *Four Zoas*, e.g. 7.35–7, 'her Luvah, / With whom
she lived in bliss', and 43.33ff; and in spite of Vala's position as Jerusalem's
shadow–an integral but lesser part of her.

45   Wherefore did I loving create love, which never yet
     Immingled God & man—when thou & I hid the Divine Vision
     In cloud of secret gloom which behold involve me round about,
     Know me now, Albion: look upon me. I alone am beauty;
     The imaginative human form is but a breathing of Vala.
50   I breathe him forth into the heaven from my secret cave,
     Born of the woman to obey the woman, O Albion the mighty.
     For the divine appearance is brotherhood, but I am Love

Pl. 30   Elevate into the region of brotherhood with my red fires.'
(34)   'Art thou Vala?' replied Albion, 'image of my repose?
       O how I tremble, how my members pour down milky fear!
       A dewy garment covers me all over, all manhood is gone;
5   At thy word & at thy look death enrobes me about
       From head to feet, a garment of death & eternal fear.
       Is not that sun thy husband & that moon thy glimmering veil?
       Are not the stars of heaven thy children? Art thou not Babylon?
       Art thou Nature, mother of all? Is Jerusalem thy daughter?
10   Why have thou elevate inward, O dweller of outward chambers,
       From grot & cave beneath the moon, dim region of death
       Where I laid my plough in the hot noon, where my hot team fed,
       Where implements of war are forged, the plough to go over the
           nations,
       In pain girding me round like a rib of iron in heaven? O Vala!
15   In Eternity they neither marry nor are given in marriage:
       Albion the high cliff of the Atlantic is become a barren land.'

       Los stood at his anvil; he heard the contentions of Vala—
       He heaved his thundering bellows upon the valleys of Middlesex.
       He opened his furnaces before Vala; then Albion frowned in anger
20   On his rock ere yet the starry heavens were fled away

30.2–16. Albion is overwhelmed, and takes Vala at her own valuation
(7–9), losing his masculine strength under her influence.
30.9. Both statements are false: Nature is not an eternal spirit, being a
limited creation; and Jerusalem is daughter neither of Nature nor Vala.
Albion has accepted the physical universe as the total reality, and elevated
Vala, who veiled his sight in this way, to be queen of the universe.
30.10. 'Why has your outgoing turned to ingoing: why have you reversed
the true order?'
30.15. A glimmer of truth: taken from *Matthew* xxii 30, which reads: 'In
the resurrection they. . . .'
30.19. Los opens his furnaces to show Albion the visions revealed within
it (cp. 8.23). Albion resents what he sees.
30.20. Cp. 27.16n, 70.32, and 75.27, the last line of ch. 3.
starry heavens] Refers to Albion's containing–in his eternal state–all things
within him. When the fallen world was formed, he disintegrated (24.6–10)

From his awful members. And thus Los cried aloud
To the sons of Albion, & to Hand, the eldest son of Albion:

'I hear the screech of childbirth loud pealing, & the groans
Of death, in Albion's clouds dreadful uttered over all the earth.
25 What may man be? Who can tell? But what may woman be
To have power over man from cradle to corruptible grave?
There is a throne in every man; it is the throne of God.
This, woman has claimed as her own & man is no more.
Albion is the tabernacle of Vala & her temple,
30 And not the Tabernacle & Temple of the Most High!
O Albion, why wilt thou create a female will,
To hide the most evident God in a hidden covert, even
In the shadows of a woman & a secluded Holy Place,
That we may pry after him as after a stolen treasure
35 Hidden among the dead, & mured up from the paths of life?
Hand, art thou not Reuben enrooting thyself into Bashan,
Till thou remainest a vaporous shadow in a void? O Merlin,
Unknown among the dead where never before existence came,
Is this the female will, O ye lovely daughters of Albion? To
40 Converse concerning weight & distance in the wilds of Newton &
Locke?'

So Los spoke, standing on Mam Tor, looking over Europe &
Asia;
The graves thunder beneath his feet from Ireland to Japan.

and the heavens etc., fell away from him to assume independent existences.
As yet, this catastrophe is not quite complete.
30.23ff. By childbirth the woman becomes the mother of the man–cp. *A
Mental Traveller*, p. 578; he comes under female domination in this fallen
world, first from mother, then from wife or mistress.
30.36. This prepares for 43ff, q.v. note. Hand is the spirit of such enemies
of imagination as the carping critics of the *Examiner*, the Hunt brothers,
who scorned visionaries like B. But such critics represent forces far greater
than themselves.
30.37. MERLIN] A British magician of King Arthur's court, and so associated
with the druids: but Merlin fell under the seductive, Vala-like powers of
Nimue, or Vivien. He is the type of the wise man who allowed his super-
natural, imaginative powers to be swamped by female wiles. In 32.23 he
is again linked with Reuben, in 88.18 with King Arthur, his legendary
ward who was also a victim of woman. For his Prophecy, see p. 160.
30.40. Not a self-evident relationship: but B. is connecting two pet
hatreds: that of materialism and that of female domination.
30.41. *Mam Tor*] A hill in the Peak District of Derbyshire. The graves
may be the 'pot-holes', the natural underground caverns in the limestone.
Their thunder is ominous, and worldwide. At this point a new theme
begins–Los's treatment of Reuben.

Reuben slept in Bashan like one dead in the valley,
Cut off from Albion's mountains & from all the earth's summits,
45   Between Succoth & Zaretan beside the Stone of Bohan,
While the daughters of Albion divided Luvah into three bodies.
Los bended his nostrils down to the earth, then sent him over
Jordan to the land of the Hittite. Everyone that saw him
Fled; they fled at his horrible form, they hid in caves
50   And dens, they looked on one another & became what they
beheld.

30.43. REUBEN is a strange figure, an offshoot of the myth of Albion's fall.
As the eldest son of Israel, he is also the senior son of Albion according to
the theory propounded in pl.27, and represents the typical weaknesses of
fallen man. In the Bible, he is involved in too many dubious love-adven-
tures: in *Genesis* xxx *14* he finds mandrakes for a love-potion for his
mother Leah to capture his father's attentions: in xxxv 22 he 'went and lay
with Bilhah his father's concubine'—mother of his half-brothers Dan and
Naphtali. Later he was disinherited (*Genesis* xlix *3–4*) for being 'unstable
as water.' (B.'s phrase, in 81.*10*, is 'wandering Reuben.') The Reubenites,
with Gad and half Manasseh, settled east of Jordan, outside the promised
land proper. Thus B. takes him as the type of backslider, the easily cor-
rupted man who falls under female influence. In *Jerusalem* this means falling
under the veil of Vala, and B. goes on to show how this veil enwraps him.
Left to himself, he would go into a deathly sleep, but Los drives him to
activity, and limits his perceptions (30.*47*ff) to the scope they can retain
whilst in Vala's limited world. Thus he becomes the first earthly man–as
he was Israel's first-born.
30.43–5. *Bashan . . . Succoth and Zaretan . . . Stone of Bohan*] See map,
p. 575. Reuben sleeps in the land of Og, a place hostile to true religion.
The valley implies the Jordan rift valley which cuts Reuben off, as stated
in *44*. *Succoth* and *Zaretan* are in the valley respectively e?st and west of
Jordan, but the *Stone of Bohan* is not between them. Succoth and Zaretan
are both associated allusively with the creation of Adam: see 32.*5n* and
Milton pl.19.*6–14* (where the clay of Succoth is used by Milton to remould
Urizen to life: this allusion is not made here, however). The *Stone of
Bohan the Reubenite* is mentioned twice as a boundary stone (*Joshua* xv 6,
xviii 17): B. only seems interested in the association of Reuben with
a stone–always, to B., an evil influence, implying rigidity, death and often
sacrifice. In 74.*34* B. says that Reuben sleeps on London Stone.
30.46. An allusion to an event not mentioned elsewhere.
30.47. This is the first of three similar acts: Los forms a physical organ–
nostril, eyes, tongue–in Reuben and sends him out of the holy land. On
each occasion he infects all he meets. (The third occasion is on 32, being
interrupted by 31.)
30.48. *land of the Hittite*] The first of the Gentile nations Reuben is sent
into; the others are not named ('over Jordan', *54* and 32.*13*).

Reuben returned to Bashan; in despair he slept on the stone.
(Then Gwendolen divided into Rahab & Tirzah in twelve
    portions.)
Los rolled his eyes into two narrow circles, then sent him
Over Jordan. All terrified fled: they became what they beheld.

55 (If perceptive organs vary, objects of perception seem to vary.
If the perceptive organs close, their objects seem to close also.
'Consider this, O mortal man, O worm of sixty winters,' said
    Los:
'Consider sexual organization & hide thee in the dust!')

Pl. 31   [Design]
(35)

Then the Divine Hand found the two limits, Satan and Adam,
In Albion's bosom: for in every human bosom those limits stand.
And the Divine Voice came from the furnaces, as multitudes
    without
Number, the voices of the innumerable multitudes of Eternity.
5 And the appearance of a man was seen in the furnaces,
    Saving those who have sinned from the punishment of the law

30.52. This contradicts 5.40ff, where Rahab and Tirzah are divided into
the twelve Daughters of Albion, including Gwendolen: it is difficult to
see B.'s exact meaning in this line, except that it parallels the equally
obscure 46.
30.55–8. The story of Reuben is interrupted (resuming at 32.1) by a
comment on the previous line. Reuben's perceptions are being restricted
by Los so that he can only see the material world. B. points out that
Reuben's state only means that what he–and the others who 'became
what they beheld'–can see is limited; it does not mean that eternity beyond
those limits does not exist. See Gates of Paradise 47n. For sexual organisation
see 29.28n.
31. Design: This plate is really one design with the text superimposed. The
design shows Jehovah creating Eve. Jehovah hovers above the text against
a background of flames; below, Adam lies asleep, while Eve, looking up at
Jehovah, has risen out of Adam's body as far as her waist. But Jehovah is
also Jesus, for the nail-marks are clear on his hands and feet. The design
and text are integral (note 9–16), but the plate is an interpolation between
30.57 and 32.1.
31.1. the two limits] See 27.18 above, and Four Zoas iv 270n.
31.3–5. As Nebuchadnezzar saw a fourth man 'like the Son of God'
walking in the furnace with the three Jews (Daniel iii 25). But note the
'multitudinous' nature of B.'s Divine Voice. The reference to furnaces
may have caused the plate to be inserted here, following 30.19.

(In pity of the punisher whose state is eternal death),
And keeping them from sin by the mild counsels of his love.

'Albion goes to eternal death: in me all eternity
10   Must pass through condemnation, and awake beyond the grave.
No individual can keep these laws, for they are death
To every energy of man, and forbid the springs of life;
Albion hath entered the state Satan. Be permanent, O state.
And be thou for ever accursed, that Albion may arise again!
15   And be thou created into a state. I go forth to create
States, to deliver individuals evermore. Amen.'

So spoke the voice from the furnaces, descending into non-entity.

[Design]

Pl. 32   *[Design]*
(36)
Reuben returned to his place; in vain he sought beautiful Tirzah,
For his eyelids were narrowed, & his nostrils scented the ground;
And sixty winters Los raged in the divisions of Reuben,
Building the moon of Ulro, plank by plank & rib by rib.

31.11. these laws] Jehovah (who is shown in the plate) was the law-giver.
For years this had earned B.'s fiercest condemnation; now he says that
Jehovah, who wanted to redeem Albion, restricted Albion's life so that he
would have to turn to God for redemption, instead of wandering, forever
lost, in Chaos.
31.13. the state Satan] For STATES see the text of 49.65–75, and *Milton*
pl.32.22n. 'Satan' is Albion's name–and personality–at the moment: he
is 'in the state of' being Satanic. But he is an individual, and so cannot
remain in the same state for ever. Satan, rather like a familiar spirit, may
dwell in many men at many times and always be the same; but he is an
illusion and will die, while the individual personality, once redeemed, will
live. Therefore do not say that a person 'is evil': but that he 'is in an evil
state.' 'The oak dies as well as the lettuce, but its eternal image and in-
dividuality never dies . . .' (*Vision of the Last Judgement, Erdman 1965*, p. 545).
31.17. Beneath this line, the deleted line (the italicized words are uncertain
but proposed by D. V. Erdman): 'To govern the evil by good; and *States
abolish Systems.*'

32. Design: An illustration of *4*.
32.1. Tirzah is a being in eternity, though evil: Reuben would not find
her here, though she is mother of Nature.
32.3–4. Los laboured sixty years at the task of giving Reuben his material,
saving form. The moon may not seem to be directly connected with
Reuben, but the process is the same–that of creating a shapely material
universe (Generation) in order to save living creatures from the chaos of
Ulro.

 5 Reuben slept in the cave of Adam, and Los folded his tongue
   Between lips of mire & clay, then sent him forth over Jordan.
   In the love of Tirzah he said, 'Doubt is my food day & night'.
   All that beheld him fled howling and gnawed their tongues
   For pain; they became what they beheld. In reasonings Reuben
       returned
10 To Heshbon; disconsolate he walked through Moab, & he stood
   Before the furnaces of Los in a horrible dreamful slumber,
   On Mount Gilead looking toward Gilgal, and Los bended
   His ear in a spiral circle outward, then sent him over Jordan.
   The seven nations fled before him; they became what they beheld.
15 Hand, Hyle & Coban fled; they became what they beheld.
   Gwantok & Peachey hid in Damascus beneath Mount Lebanon,
   Brereton & Slayd in Egypt. Huttn & Skofield & Kox
   Fled over Chaldea in terror, in pains in every nerve.
   Kotope & Bowen became what they beheld, fleeing over the
       earth;
20 And the twelve female emanations fled with them agonising.

   Jerusalem trembled, seeing her children driven by Los's hammer
   In the visions of the dreams of Beulah on the edge of non-entity.
   Hand stood between Reuben & Merlin, as the reasoning spectre

32.5. *cave of Adam*] Chiefly 'the cave of mortality where Adam lived': but
also with a verbal allusion to the city of Adam near Zaretan (*Joshua* iii 16).
32.7. *In the love of Tirzah*] For *Tirzah* see *Four Zoas* viii *267n.* Reuben is
now a lost wanderer; he infects all mankind, and this passage, to *42*, de-
scribes the devastation this causes among mankind. Reuben is sent abroad,
but repeatedly returns.
32.9. *reasonings*] Which require doubt.
32.10. *Heshbon*] On the northern boundary of Reubenite land, and as-
signed to Reuben, but later taken over by the tribe of Gad. It was orig-
inally the city of Sihon. Moab was the tribe living south of Reuben; B.
seems to imply that Moab (and Bashan, 30.43–51) were 'home' to Reuben.
32.12. Reuben is looking into the Promised land; Gilgal was the Israelites'
first camp after crossing Jordan. Note that Reuben is already 'across'
Jordan this time, but Los sends him further abroad.
32.14. *seven nations*] Seven tribes occupied the promised land before the
Israelite invasion. Cp. *Milton* pl.40.24n. They are scattered, losing their
community and cohesion, and carry Reuben's disease with them over the
earth, as do the sons of Albion (*15–20*) who are identified with the tribes
of Israel.
32.22. i.e. Jerusalem is in Beulah on the verge of Non-entity, and sees the
visions.
32.23. See notes on Merlin and Hand at 30.36–7; Hand is the leader of the
sons of Albion, and thus another manifestation of Reuben, first-born of
the Israelites under the vision of the identity of Albion and Israel in pl.27.

23*

Stands between the vegetative man & his immortal imagination.
25 And the Four Zoas clouded rage, east & west & north & south;
They change their situations in the universal man.
Albion groans; he sees the elements divide before his face,
And England, who is Britannia, divided into Jerusalem & Vala.
And Urizen assumes the east, Luvah assumes the south
30 In his dark spectre ravening from his open sepulchre,

And the Four Zoas who are the four eternal senses of man
Became four elements, separating from the limbs of Albion
(These are their names in the vegetative generation):
And accident & chance were found hidden in length, breadth
& height.
35 And they divided into four ravening deathlike forms,
Fairies & genii & nymphs & gnomes of the elements.
These are states permanently fixed by the Divine Power.
The Atlantic continent sunk round Albion's cliffy shore,
And the sea poured in amain upon the giants of Albion,
40 As Los bended the senses of Reuben. Reuben is Merlin
Exploring the three states of Ulro: creation, redemption,
& judgement.

Merlin was the prophet of Albion (see p. 160, xxxii *n*) in the legends of
Arthur. Hand stands where?–perhaps in opposition to Jerusalem. Both
Merlin and Reuben fell through desire for a woman: B. implies that the
philistine enemies of imagination in this world are of the same kind.
32.25. These lines are another indication of cosmic disruption. In their
rightful place (cp. *Four Zoas* vi *277–8*), Urizen belongs to the south, and
Luvah to the east.
32.32. separating] Albion once contained all elements in himself (cp. *27.16n*).
32.33. These] 'These above', referring back to the Zoas, and not to the
content of the deleted line between *33* and *34*, which has been conjec-
turally restored by D. V. Erdman: 'West weighing, east & north dividing
Generation, south . . . ing.'
32.35. These lines refer to the supremacy of rationality. A probable inter-
pretation is: 'all the forms of nature were supposed to be the result of
accident and chance', though under the Divine Vision forms are created
and shapes given meaning by the imaginative creator (*55* below). The
following two lines are an imaginative picture of the sciences, creatures of
the material elements, ravening over the earth. Lines *38–40* revert to an
old theme of B.'s–the deluge which destroyed the beautiful land of
Atlantis. Returning to Reuben (cp. *24*), B. says that he has fallen into the
theological error of believing that redemption is a process according to a
law, beginning with creation and ending with judgement–whereas, in B.'s
belief, all these are continually repeated, and involved in one another–
creation is a form of redemption, redemption is a form of judgement.

And many of the Eternal Ones laughed after their manner:

'Have you known the judgement that is arisen among the
Zoas of Albion, Where a man dare hardly to embrace
45   His own wife, for the terrors of chastity that they call
By the name of morality? Their daughters govern all
In hidden deceit; they are vegetable, only fit for burning.
Art & science cannot exist but by naked beauty displayed.'

Then those in great Eternity who contemplate on death
50   Said thus: 'What seems to be, is—to those to whom
It seems to be—& is productive of the most dreadful
Consequences to those to whom it seems to be, even of
Torments, despair, eternal death. But the Divine Mercy
Steps beyond and redeems man in the body of Jesus. Amen!
55   And length, breadth, height again obey the Divine Vision.
    Hallelujah!'

Pl. 33   [*Design*]
(37) And one stood forth from the Divine Family, & said:

'I feel my spectre rising upon me. Albion, arouse thyself!
Why dost thou thunder with frozen spectrous wrath against us?
The spectre is, in giant man, insane and most deformed.
5   Thou wilt certainly provoke my spectre against thine in fury!
He has a sepulchre hewn out of a rock ready for thee,
And a death of eight thousand years, forged by thyself, upon
The point of his spear, if thou persistest to forbid with laws
Our emanations, and to attack our secret supreme delights.'

10 So Los spoke: but when he saw blue death in Albion's feet,

---

32.*42–8* and *49–55*. Both passages are general remarks, inserted here; they would be relevant to any sequence describing the chaos in mankind, except that the last line, *55*, refers back to *34*.

33. *Design*: Above, a scene supported on a winged globe: Albion, under an oak tree, faints into the arms of a radiant figure.

33.*1* This line was added by incising after the plate was completed. The phrase 'Divine Family' is distinguished from the rest by being written in copperplate, not B.'s usual italic. Albion becomes once more the subject of the verse. The opening line was perhaps added to relate it to 'the eternal ones' of 32.*42*; but the scene returns to that of pl.29; Los arguing with the somnolent Albion, trying to stop him falling asleep.

33.*4*. So in *Four Zoas* i *93* and viia *300–01*.

33.*10*. *blue*] The plate had *pale*, but B. altered it: in one of the five copies he altered it back again.

Again he joined the Divine Body, following, merciful;
While Albion fled more indignant, revengeful, covering

[*Design*]

Pl. 34   His face and bosom with petrific hardness, & his hands
(38)   And feet, lest any should enter his bosom & embrace
His hidden heart. His emanation wept & trembled within him,
Uttering not his jealousy, but hiding it as with
5   Iron & steel, dark & opaque, with clouds & tempests brooding.
His strong limbs shuddered upon his mountains high & dark.

Turning from universal love, petrific he went,
His cold against the warmth of Eden raged, with loud
Thunders of deadly war (the fever of the human soul),
10 ·   Fires & clouds of rolling smoke. But mild the Saviour followed
him,
Displaying the eternal vision, the divine similitude,
In loves & tears of brothers, sisters, sons, fathers, & friends
Which if man ceases to behold, he ceases to exist,

Saying: 'Albion, our wars are wars of life, & wounds of love,
15   With intellectual spears, & long winged arrows of thought.
Mutual in one another's love & wrath all-renewing
We live as one man; for contracting our infinite senses
We behold multitude; or expanding, we behold as one,
As one man all the universal family; & that one man
20   We call Jesus the Christ—& he in us, & we in him,
Live in perfect harmony in Eden, the land of life,
Giving, receiving, & forgiving each other's trespasses.
He is the good shepherd, he is the lord & master;
He is the shepherd of Albion, he is all in all,
25   In Eden, in the garden of God, & in heavenly Jerusalem.

33.12. fled] The image contradicts that of Albion asleep, but co-operates with it. In the following pages, B. uses the two images–of Albion lying sick on his couch, and of Albion running away from the Divine Vision. Both are images of Albion's error, and B. uses one or the other as the situation requires. In the previous pages, Reuben's sleep, and his fleeing, are also aspects of his ancestor Albion's disease.

33. Design: Jerusalem lies on her couch with a spectre, a vampire bat, hovering over her; sun and crescent moon in the background.

34.14. A very important passage, being a summary of B.'s idea of the ideal infinite state of EDEN. The argument here is that the energetic communal activity which Albion fears and labels 'sin' is creative, not destructive. It cannot harm him. This submergence of individuality does not destroy personality, but enhances it. Cp. *55.36–46, 71.15–19, 88.3–15,* also *Four Zoas* ii *505*ff, v *121–42*; and *Paradise Lost* viii *622–29.*

If we have offended, forgive us, take not vengeance against us.'

Thus speaking, the Divine Family follow Albion:
I see them in the vision of God upon my pleasant valleys.

I behold London, a human awful wonder of God.
30 He says: 'Return, Albion, return, I give myself for thee:
My streets are my ideas of imagination.
Awake, Albion, awake, & let us awake up together.
My houses are thoughts, my inhabitants, affections—
The children of my thoughts walking within my blood-vessels,
35 Shut from my nervous form which sleeps upon the verge of
    Beulah
In dreams of darkness, while my vegetating blood, in veiny pipes,
Rolls dreadful through the furnaces of Los, & the mills of Satan.
For Albion's sake, & for Jerusalem thy emanation
I give myself, & these my brethren give themselves for Albion.'

40 So spoke London, immortal guardian. I heard in Lambeth's
    shades:
In Felpham I heard & saw the visions of Albion;

34.*28–9*, *40–3*. 'I' in these lines is B. himself.
34.*31*. Everything seen in this world is a shadow of reality; the real London
is in Eternity, the London where B. lived a reflection of the real one. Yet
the eternal London is involved in Albion's fall.
34.*33–4*. B. sees London imaginatively as a living creature, her streets
blood-vessels, the people on the streets—not, in modern terminology, as
bacteria—but as *thoughts*. London is seen as a living being, capable of self-
sacrifice.
34.*40–2*. B. first saw London imaginatively while he was living in Lambeth
(before autumn 1800) and the vision continued at Felpham (1800–03). Now
(after 1803) he is writing about it in his house in South Molton Street.
34.*45*. *Verulam*] The Roman town close by the site of St Alban's. Here B.
begins to introduce the twenty-eight FRIENDS OF ALBION, the cities of
England, in their 'human forms'. Albion's *Sons* are corrupt, seeking to
draw him into evil: his *Friends* try to draw him away, or else are willing
to sacrifice themselves for him. B. sees that all Albion is in spiritual danger;
but there are some faithful Britons left who try to recall Britain to a true
sense of values. These he embodies, not as individuals (as the *Sons* are) but
as cities–organized and undying forms of humanity. Verulam and Canter-
bury are not always included in the list of twenty-eight; see note on 36.*45*.
Here the four chief cities are Verulam (seat of the earliest Christianity in
Roman Britain), Canterbury (where Christianity was reintroduced to the
Kentish tribes), York (seat of the second archbishopric), and Edinburgh
(in Scotland, not England, and not in B.'s time the seat of an Episcopalian
bishop; but capital of Scotland, and centre of the Scottish church).

I write in South Molton Street, what I both see and hear
In regions of humanity, in London's opening streets.

I see thee, awful parent land in light, behold I see!
45 Verulam, Canterbury, venerable parent of men,
Generous immortal guardian, golden clad. For cities
Are men, fathers of multitudes, & rivers & mountains
Are also men; every thing is human, mighty, sublime.
In every bosom a universe expands as wings
50 Let down at will around, & called the universal tent.
York, crowned with loving kindness: Edinburgh, clothed
With fortitude, as with a garment of immortal texture
Woven in looms of Eden, in spiritual deaths of mighty men
Who give themselves, in Golgotha, victims to justice; where
55 There is in Albion a gate of precious stones & gold
(Seen only by emanations, by vegetations viewless)
Bending across the road of Oxford Street; it from Hyde Park
To Tyburn's deathful shades admits the wandering souls
Of multitudes who die from earth. This gate cannot be found

Pl. 35   *[Design]*
(39)
By Satan's watch-fiends; though they search numbering every
        grain
Of sand on earth every night, they never find this gate.
It is the Gate of Los. Withoutside is the mill, intricate, dreadful
And filled with cruel tortures; but no mortal man can find the
        mill
5 Of Satan, in his mortal pilgrimage of seventy years,
For human beauty knows it not, nor can mercy find it. But
In the fourth region of humanity, Urthona named,

34.54–5. *where / There is*] This reads awkwardly, as if B. were fitting in a
passage previously composed.
34.55. See 29.1–4. B. has stood on Oxford Street looking over Hyde Park,
past Tyburn, the place of execution (i.e. the English Golgotha) and has
seen, probably in a rainbow, the Gate he here describes.
35. *Design*: Above, a rank of archers mounted on flying horses (only the
nearest, a grim, bearded figure, is seen) turn to shoot their arrows behind
and down. Underneath, a setting sun. As on pls 31 and 33, the text is in a
panel on the design. (Reproduced in Keynes, *W.B.'s Engravings*, pl.110.)
35.6–11. Los's work has hitherto been unimpeded by the forces of Ulro
directly: now the threatening clouds gather round the gates of Golgonooza.
Evil (B. refers to Rahab, and to the moral law which now holds Albion
fast) gains momentum: Albion, fearful, runs away (11) from Los–but
pauses on the threshold of Golgonooza. In the ensuing pages B. tells the
story of how Los and the Friends of Albion try to prevent him from going
out and falling into the chaos and death of Ulro outside.

Mortality begins to roll the billows of eternal death
Before the Gate of Los. (Urthona here is named Los,
10   And here begins the system of moral virtue, named Rahab.)

Albion fled through the Gate of Los, & he stood in the gate.

(Los was the friend of Albion who most loved him. In
     Cambridgeshire
His eternal station, he is the twenty-eighth, & is fourfold.)
Seeing Albion had turned his back against the Divine Vision,
15   Los said to Albion: 'Whither fleest thou?' Albion replied:

'I die. I go to eternal death; the shades of death
Hover within me & beneath, & spreading themselves outside
Like rocky clouds, build me a gloomy monument of woe.
Will none accompany me in my death, or be a ransom for me
20   In that dark valley? I have girded round my cloak, & on my feet
Bound these black shoes of death, & on my hands death's iron
     gloves.
God hath forsaken me, & my friends are become a burden,
A weariness to me, & the human footstep is a terror to me.'

Los answered, troubled, & his soul was rent in twain:
25   'Must the wise die for an atonement? Does mercy endure
     atonement?
No! It is moral severity, & destroys mercy in its victim.'
So speaking, not yet infected with the error & illusion,

[Design]

Pl. 36   Los shuddered at beholding Albion, for his disease
(40)   Arose upon him pale & ghastly, & he called around

35.*12. Cambridgeshire*] B. associates Ely ('scribe of Los', 41.6), in this
county, Cambridge University and–almost certainly, though not ex-
plicitly–Milton, who went to Cambridge. Milton, the great artificer of
the poetic imagination, is Los's ageless representative in Albion.
35.*13. twenty-eighth*] There were twenty-eight Friends of Albion. See 36.*3n.*
35.*16.* Albion replies with the determinism of depression. He believes that
he is a sinner, that his sin can only be atoned by a ransom, that God is his
enemy, and that the ransom will not be paid. According to B., sin is de-
stroyed by forgiveness, not payment (cp. 61.*17*ff).
35.*20–1.* Cp. the command to the Israelites on the institution of the
Passover (*Exodus* xii 11): 'And thus ye shall eat it: with your loins girded,
your shoes on your feet, and your staff in your hand'–ready for instant
escape after the angel of God had struck the first-born of Egypt. This is a
reminiscence; echoing, not the choice and salvation of God, but the sense of
his arbitrary power, the doom of those who have incurred his wrath, and
the recognition of an endless journey before Albion.

The Friends of Albion. Trembling at the sight of eternal death
The four appeared with their emanations in fiery
5 Chariots. Black their fires roll, beholding Albion's house of
         eternity.
Damp couch the flames beneath, and silent, sick, stand shuddering
Before the porch of sixteen pillars. Weeping every one
Descended & fell down upon their knees round Albion's knees,
Swearing the oath of God, with awful voice of thunders round
10 Upon the hills & valleys; & the cloudy oath rolled far & wide.

'Albion is sick,' said every valley, every mournful hill
And every river; 'Our brother Albion is sick to death.
He hath leagued himself with robbers, he hath studied the arts
Of unbelief, envy hovers over him. His friends are his abhorrence,
15 Those who give their lives for him are despised;
Those who devour his soul are taken into his bosom.
To destroy his emanation is their intention.
Arise, awake, O friends of the giant Albion;
They have persuaded him of horrible falsehoods,
20 They have sown errors over all his fruitful fields.'

The Twenty-four heard. They came trembling on watery
         chariots,
Borne by the living creatures of the third procession

36.3–4. THE FRIENDS OF ALBION] B. chooses the cathedral cities of England,
of which there were twenty-seven in his day, the number having been
unchanged since the reign of Henry VIII. They were as listed in 36.47–61,
41.1–19, with Canterbury, York and London. B. takes the first twenty-four
as the main group of 'Friends', but wanting four more–for twenty-eight,
the number of completeness–he uses Verulam or Edinburgh to complete
the Four: cp. 34.45n. (He is not consistent, however: at 34.45 the four
are Verulam, Canterbury, York and Edinburgh, excluding London, a
city B. has just specially treated. At 41.24 London replaces Canterbury:
at 57.1 Bath joins London, York and Edinburgh. Edinburgh, in Presby-
terian Scotland, had no cathedral, but is the centre of the Church of
Scotland.) The twenty-four are summed up in the four–perhaps because,
as leading cities, they speak for and represent the Church in England, but
largely because of B.'s liking for the 'fourfold' pattern. B. was no friend
of bishops and archbishops, or of any sort of ecclesiastical authority, and
the vision of the Friends of Albion should be taken as B.'s view of the
actual goodness bestowed by Christianity on Britain over the centuries,
as summarized in the 'human forms' of the cities and of the most famous
four.
36.7. the porch of sixteen pillars] Anticipating 48.1–12.
36.21. trembling . . . watery] Ominous words, implying uncertainty and
weakness–realized in 37.23.

Of human majesty; the living creatures wept aloud as they
Went along Albion's roads, till they arrived at Albion's house.
25 Oh, how the torments of eternal death waited on man—
And the loud-rending bars of the creation ready to burst,
That the wide world might fly from its hinges, & the immortal
        mansion
Of man for ever be possessed by monsters of the deeps,
And man himself become a fiend, wrapped in an endless curse,
30 Consuming & consumed forever in flames of moral justice.
For had the body of Albion fallen down, & from its dreadful ruins
Let loose the enormous spectre on the darkness of the deep,
At enmity with the merciful & filled with devouring fire,
A netherworld must have received the foul enormous spirit,
35 Under pretence of moral virtue, filled with revenge & law,
There to eternity chained down, & issuing in red flames
And curses, with his mighty arms brandished against the heavens
Breathing cruelty, blood & vengeance, gnashing his teeth with
        pain,
Torn with black storms & ceaseless torrents of his own consuming
        fire,
40 Within his breast his mighty sons chained down & filled with
        cursings,
And his dark eon, that once fair crystal form divinely clear,
Within his ribs producing serpents whose souls are flames of fire,
But, glory to the Merciful One, for he is of tender mercies!
And the Divine Family wept over him as one man.
45 And these the Twenty-four in whom the Divine Family
Appeared; & they were one in him, a human vision—
Human-Divine, Jesus the Saviour, blessed for ever & ever!
Selsey, true friend, who afterwards submitted to be devoured

36.26. *the creation*] Normally, in the later poems, a necessary evil, but still
an evil. These lines, however, do not seem to carry this connotation; the
creation is 'the immortal mansion of Man', and it seems as if B. is simply
thinking of the possible dissolution of all the beauty man sees around him –
setting doctrine aside for the moment.
36.41. *eon*] Emanation, a word used of Albion's emanation only, thrice
(see 19.16 and *Milton* pl.11.1).
36.45. The list of the twenty-four Friends begins. It continues on pl.41,
and the four intervening plates were probably placed here later. Both
pls 37 and 40 begin with *Bath*, and so we may suppose the following se-
quence of development: (*a*) pls 36 and 41 alone; (*b*) pls 36/40/41; (*c*) com-
plete as printed.
36.48. *Selsey*] Owing to coastal erosion, the site of the village and church
at Selsey had to be transferred further inland to Chichester (which is near
Felpham) in 1075.

By the waves of despair, whose emanation rose above
50 The flood, & was named Chichester, lovely, mild & gentle—Lo!
Her lambs bleat to the sea-fowls' cry, lamenting still for Albion.

Submitting to be called the son of Los, the terrible vision,
Winchester stood devoting himself for Albion; his tents
Outspread with abundant riches, & his emanations
55 Submitting to be called Enitharmon's daughters, & be born
In vegetable mould, created by the hammer & loom
In Bowlahoola & Allamanda, where the dead wail night & day.

(I call them by their English names—English, the rough basement.
Los built the stubborn structure of the language, acting against
60 Albion's melancholy, who must else have been a dumb despair.)

Gloucester & Exeter & Salisbury & Bristol, & benevolent Bath;
Pl. 37 Bath who is Legions: he is the seventh, the physician and
(41) The poisoner, the best & worst in heaven & hell,
Whose spectre first assimilated with Luvah in Albion's
mountains.

36.57. *Bowlahoola & Allamanda*] Cp. *Milton* pls 24.51–66 and 25.42–8. The
first is the place in Golgonooza where Los set up his forge; the second the
fields round Golgonooza where his sons labour to feed the city. In *Milton*
neither is a place for looms: that is usually *Cathedron*.
36.61. *benevolent Bath*] Probably B.'s admiration for Bath derives from the
preaching of the Bath clergyman Richard Warner, whose pacifist sermons
and writings in 1804–08 might seem to B. the voice of 'benevolent Bath',
potent against the warlike sons of Albion. Note Bath's speech on pl.40.

37.1. *Bath who is Legions*] The word *Legions* has two connotations: (*a*) the
name of the evil spirit who, in the story of 'the Gadarene swine', possessed
a man (*Mark* v 9)–his name was 'Legion' (singular); (*b*) more directly
relevant, the city of Caerleon, also called (e.g. by Milton in his *History of
Britain*) 'Caerlegion'. Caerleon is far from Bath, and in *Milton* pl.39.35 B.
distinguishes the two; his purpose in here identifying the two is not clear.
Bath is a city of healing springs, and hence 'the physician'; but Merlin's
famous Prophecy (in Geoffrey of Monmouth's *History*) foretells that 'the
baths will grow cold at Bath and its healing waters bring forth death.' B.
here stresses the worst, as pls 40–41 stress the best. In 75.2 'Bath stood . . .
with Merlin and Bladud and Arthur': thus B. associates Bath with ancient
British legend. Bladud is supposed to have founded Bath; he was a necro-
mancer, sometimes said to be powerful among the early druids. 'The
poisoner' probably refers to this relation of Bath with corrupt druid
religion.
37.3. An obscure line. Luvah is the passionate, sometimes lustful element in
Albion; this unites him with Bath ('the poisoner') to attack Jerusalem-in-
Albion. In 54.11 Albion sees 'his sons assimilate with Luvah': Bath is not

A triple octave he took, to reduce Jerusalem to twelve,
5　To cast Jerusalem forth upon the wilds to Poplar & Bow,
　To Maldon & Canterbury in the delights of cruelty.
　The shuttles of death sing in the sky to Islington & Pancras
　Round Marybone to Tyburn's river, weaving black melancholy
　　　as a net,
　And despair as meshes closely wove over the west of London,
10　Where mild Jerusalem sought to repose in death & be no more.
　She fled to Lambeth's mild vale & hid herself beneath
　The Surrey hills where Rephaim terminates. Her sons are
　　　seized
　For victims of sacrifice, but Jerusalem cannot be found—hid
　By the daughters of Beulah, gently snatched away & hid in
　　　Beulah.

15　There is a grain of sand in Lambeth that Satan cannot find
　Nor can his watch-fiends find it; 'tis translucent & has many
　　　angles.
　But he who finds it will find Oothoon's palace, for within,
　Opening into Beulah, every angle is a lovely heaven.
　But should the watch-fiends find it, they would call it sin,
20　And lay its heavens & their inhabitants in blood of punishment.

one of the twelve 'sons of Albion', but as a part of him is in some sense a child. Bath's place in druidism (see note above) makes him the first to corrupt.

37.4. *reduce . . . to twelve*] Cp. 74.23ff where B. tries to explain how sixteen 'sons of Jerusalem' become twelve 'sons of Albion'. The *triple octave* (3 × 8 = 24) may be part of the same arithmetic, using also the idea of 19.20 that the twelve sons are 'spectres of the twenty-four': but no certain explanation has yet been made. See 16.52n and 74.23n.

37.5–6. *Poplar and Bow . . . Maldon and Canterbury*] Places to the east of London and of England respectively. See map, and 5.68n for the significance of 'east'.

37.7–8. *Islington, Pancras, Mary(le)bone, Tyburn*] Moving from east to west across the northern outskirts of London.

37.12. *Rephaim*] A camp of the Philistines; cp. *Milton* pl.19.40n.

37.15. *a grain of sand*] B. lived in Lambeth from 1791 to 1800, as obscure as a grain of sand near the Archbishop of Canterbury's palace; but he found the opening to Oothoon's greater palace.

37.17. *Oothoon*] The heroine of *Visions*, a poem written fifteen years or more earlier. There she maintains the freedom of true love. In *Milton* pl.13.44 she is the fallen Leutha's 'charming guard'; here she cares for Jerusalem and Vala. Thus in the long epics she becomes a daughter of Beulah, caring especially for female spirits in their sickness, but always retaining her association in B.'s mind with the beauty of sexual love.

Here Jerusalem & Vala were hid in soft slumberous repose,
Hid from the terrible east, shut up in the south & west.

The Twenty-eight trembled in death's dark caves; in cold despair
They kneeled around the couch of death in deep humiliation
25　And tortures of self-condemnation, while their spectres raged
　　within.
The Four Zoas in terrible combustion clouded rage,
Drinking the shuddering fears & loves of Albion's families,
Destroying by selfish affections the things that they most admire,
Drinking & eating, & pitying & weeping, as at a tragic scene
30　The soul drinks murder & revenge, & applauds its own holiness.

They saw Albion endeavouring to destroy their emanations.

[Design]

Pl. 38　They saw their wheels rising up poisonous against Albion:
(43)　Urizen, cold & scientific; Luvah, pitying & weeping;
　　Tharmas, indolent & sullen; Urthona, doubting & despairing;
　　Victims to one another & dreadfully plotting against each other
5　To prevent Albion walking about in the four complexions.

37.22. See 5–8nn above.
37.24. *in deep humiliation*] The twenty-eight cities are aware of their own
faults which in part have brought Albion to this state. They have come to
Albion's side voluntarily, though in 42.48 Albion believes that Hand and
Hyle have captured them. In a sense, they have, as this despair is congruent
with the moralistic religion of Albion. Los (38.12) goes to the opposite
extreme in rousing them.
37.26. All the elements of the universe, of Albion and of man are disturbed.
37.31. *they*] The twenty-four Friends: cp. 33.8 and 42.13.
37. *Design*: A bowed figure sits with his head on a book on his knees;
beside him a scroll with, in reversed writing, the words:

> Each man is in his Spectre's power
> Until the arrival of that hour
> When his Humanity awake
> And cast his Spectre into the lake.

Reversed writing usually implies a truth which is hidden from the blind.

38.1. *Their wheels*] The machinations of the perverted spirits of the Zoas,
described in 2–3. In their unfallen states, their characteristics are intelli-
gence, love, compassion, prophecy respectively.
38.5. *the four complexions*] A phrase not used elsewhere; referring to the
fourfold range of human characteristics represented by the unfallen Zoas;
but they, being fallen, obstruct him.

They saw America closed out by the oaks of the western shore,
And Tharmas dashed on the rocks of the altars of victims in
    Mexico.
'If we are wrathful, Albion will destroy Jerusalem with rooty
    groves;
If we are merciful, ourselves must suffer destruction on his oaks.
10 Why should we enter into our spectres to behold our own
    corruptions?
O God of Albion, descend, deliver Jerusalem from the oaken
    groves!'

Then Los grew furious, raging: 'Why stand we here trembling
    around,
Calling on God for help and not ourselves in whom God dwells,
Stretching a hand to save the falling man? Are we not four,
15 Beholding Albion upon the precipice ready to fall into
    non-entity,
Seeing these heavens & hells conglobing in the void? Heavens
    over hells
Brooding in holy hypocritic lust, drinking the cries of pain
From howling victims of law, building heavens twenty-seven-fold;
Swelled & bloated general forms, repugnant to the Divine
20 Humanity, who is the only general & universal form,
To which all lineaments tend & seek with love & sympathy.
All broad & general principles belong to benevolence,
Who protects minute particulars, every one in their own identity.
But here the affectionate touch of the tongue is closed in by
    deadly teeth,
25 And the soft smile of friendship & the open dawn of benevolence
Become a net & a trap, & every energy rendered cruel,
Till the existence of friendship & benevolence is denied.
The wine of the Spirit & the vineyards of the Holy One
Here turn into poisonous stupor & deadly intoxication,
30 That they may be condemned by law & the Lamb of God be
    slain.

38.6. *America*] The western land of the free.

oaks] The sacred tree of the oppressive druid religion; hence the *groves* of *8*.
Remember also 'Heart of oak are our ships'.

38.7. *altars of victims*] The human sacrifices of Central American pre-
Spanish religions (which, as 'pre-Christian', would be largely associated
with druidism to B.).

38.14. *four*] Los, as Urthona, is one of the Zoas.

38.15. *upon the precipice*] The image changes from that of 37.24, but not
the idea.

38.16–18. *heavens twenty-seven-fold*] An image fully developed in *Milton*,
of the clouds of error surrounding the world; cp. *Milton* pl.37.35.

And the two sources of life in eternity, hunting & war,
Are becoming the sources of dark & bitter death & of corroding
    hell.
The open heart is shut up in integuments of frozen silence
That the spear that lights it forth may shatter the ribs & bosom.
35 A pretence of art to destroy art! A pretence of liberty
To destroy liberty, a pretence of religion to destroy religion!
Oshea and Caleb fight; they contend in the valleys of Peor
In the terrible family contentions of those who love each other.
The armies of Balaam weep; no women come to the field;
40 Dead corses lay before them, & not as in wars of old.
(For the soldier who fights for truth, calls his enemy his brother:
They fight & contend for life, & not for eternal death.)
But here the soldier strikes, & a dead corse falls at his feet;
Nor daughter nor sister nor mother come forth to embosom the
    slain,
45 But death, eternal death, remains in the valleys of Peor.
The English are scattered over the face of the nations. Are these
Jerusalem's children? Hark! hear the giants of Albion cry at
    night:

38.31. *hunting and war*] Cp. 34.14, 'our wars are wars of life'.
38.37–40. *Oshea and Caleb* . . .] B. conflates a series of incidents in *Numbers*
xxii–xxv, xxxi. Oshea (Joshua) and Caleb were among the representatives
of the twelve tribes sent to spy out the Promised Land in *Numbers* xiii–xiv,
and the only two to insist that Israel would conquer. Thereafter they were
increasingly favoured, and in *Numbers* xxvii 18–23 Joshua was appointed
Moses' successor.
Balaam] The Moabite prophet who refused to curse the Israelites and
blessed them instead (*Numbers* xxii–xxiv). In *Numbers* xxv a plague
falls on the Israelites at *Peor* for consorting with Gentile women and
worshipping their gods: in ch. xxxi, after the Midianites were defeated,
Moses commanded that they should all be killed, except for the virgins,
on the grounds (xxxi 16) that the plague at Peor, due to the apostasy of the
people–allegedly caused by Balaam–should not be repeated.
    B. says therefore: 'Oshea and Caleb lead armies to war, bringing death
to people who want to live as families' (the Israelites had been taking wives
among the Gentiles who, the priests insisted, were enemies). Balaam was
a prophet, not a soldier: B.'s reference to his 'armies' may be taken as a
reference to his frustrated *spiritual* force and vision. Instead of union be-
tween Gentile and Jew, the field is strewn with the 'dead corses' of the
ritually slain; 'no women come to the field' to mourn them or help them
because even the women are driven away (as in *Numbers* xxv) or them-
selves killed or enslaved (as in *Numbers* xxxi).
38.45. *valleys of Peor*] See previous note.
38.46. *scattering*] Denotes disintegration.

"We smell the blood of the English; we delight in their blood on
        our altars!
    The living & the dead shall be ground in our rumbling mills
50   For bread of the sons of Albion, of the giants Hand & Skofield!"
    Skofield & Kox are let loose upon my Saxons. They accumulate
    A world in which man is by his nature the enemy of man,
    In pride of selfhood unwieldy stretching out into non-entity,
    Generalizing art & science till art & science is lost.
55   Bristol & Bath, listen to my words, & ye seventeen, give ear!
    It is easy to acknowledge a man to be great & good while we
    Derogate from him in the trifles & small articles of that goodness,
    Those alone are his friends who admire his minutest powers.
    Instead of Albion's lovely mountains & the curtains of Jerusalem
60   I see a cave, a rock, a tree deadly & poisonous, unimaginative;
    Instead of the mutual forgivenesses, the minute particulars, I see
    Pits of bitumen ever burning, artificial riches of the Canaanite
    Like lakes of liquid lead; instead of heavenly chapels built
    By our dear Lord I see worlds crusted with snows & ice.
65   I see a wicker idol woven round Jerusalem's children. I see
    The Canaanite, the Amalekite, the Moabite, the Egyptian,
    By demonstrations the cruel sons of quality & negation,
    Driven on the void in incoherent despair into non-entity.
    I see America closed apart, & Jerusalem driven in terror

38.48. This cry is derived from the folk-tale giants' rhyme–and shows a
simple source for a part of B.'s unpleasant notion of giants.

38.54. It is a basic principle with B. that to generalize is destructive; truth
lies in particularity.

38.55. *seventeen*] The group of the 'Friends of Albion' named in 41.*1–19*,
not counting Bath.

38.60. In *Four Zoas*, Orc (the fallen Luvah) is imprisoned in a cave (viia *5*);
Urizen sits on a rock (viia *18*); and the tree of Mystery shoots up from
beneath his foot (viia *31f*). Cp. also *Jerusalem* pl.13.*38*.

38.62. *pits of bitumen*] Bitumen was known as "Jew's pitch" in B.'s day,
when the supply was chiefly from the Middle East. B. would know of the
extensive deposits in the Dead Sea. Cp. *Isaiah* xxxiv 9–10, referring to the
judgement of Edom: 'the land thereof shall become burning pitch. It shall
not be quenched night or day . . .'

38.65. *a wicker idol*] A reference to the druid sacrifice by burning. Cp.
47.*5–6*.

38.66. All these were enemies of the Israelites.

38.68–70. Cp. 27.*1–2n*. B. imagines a time before the Fall when Britain
and Judaea, London and Jerusalem, were one; when Atlantis stood above
the waves. But in the cataclysm of the Fall, the Atlantic overwhelmed
Atlantis and divided America from Albion while Albion and Judaea broke
apart from one another. (See also 39.*14–17* in text.)

70 Away from Albion's mountains, far away from London's spires.
    I will not endure this thing! I alone withstand to death
    This outrage. Ah me, how sick & pale you all stand round me.
    Ah me, pitiable ones, do you also go to death's vale?
    All you my friends & brothers, all you my beloved companions,
75 Have you also caught the infection of sin & stern repentance?
    I see disease arise upon you. Yet speak to me & give
    Me some comfort. Why do you all stand silent? I alone
    Remain in permanent strength. Or is all this goodness & pity
        only
    That you may take the greater vengeance in your sepulchre?'

80 So Los spoke. Pale they stood around the house of death,
    In the midst of temptations & despair, among the rooted oaks,
    Among reared rocks of Albion's sons. At length they rose

Pl. 39   [Design]
(44)
    With one accord in love sublime, & as on cherub's wings
    They Albion surround with kindest violence, to bear him back
    Against his will through Los's gate to Eden. Fourfold, loud,
    Their wings waving over the bottomless immense, to bear
5   Their awful charge back to his native home. But Albion dark,
    Repugnant, rolled his wheels backward into non-entity.
    Loud roll the starry wheels of Albion into the world of death,
    And all the gate of Los, clouded with clouds redounding from
    Albion's dread wheels, stretching out spaces immense between,
10 That every little particle of light & air became opaque,
    Black & immense, a rock of difficulty & a cliff
    Of black despair—that the immortal wings laboured against
    Cliff after cliff, & over valleys of despair & death,
    The narrow sea between Albion & the Atlantic continent.
15 Its waves of pearl became a boundless ocean, bottomless,
    Of grey obscurity, filled with clouds & rocks & whirling waters,
    And Albion's sons ascending & descending in the horrid void.

38.72. You] The Friends of Albion.
38.80. The Friends of Albion—the cities of Britain—are involved in Albion's
(Britain's) destiny, and so must be affected to some extent by his fall. Yet
it is not inevitable, because Britain has fallen, that every Briton should be
lost, and Los begs the Friends of Albion to be faithful.

39. Design: A winged ark floats on the waves, watched by angels.
39.3. i.e. Albion is trying to escape from Golgonooza into Ulro; his
Friends try to carry him back the other way through the gate into Eden.
The gate of Los is also the gate seen in B.'s vision in 34.55ff. But Albion
cannot be saved without an act of will on his own behalf.

But as the will must not be bended but in the day of divine
Power, silent, calm & motionless, in the mid-air sublime,
20 The Family Divine hover around the darkened Albion.

(Such is the nature of the Ulro that whatever enters
Becomes sexual, & is created, & vegetated, & born.)
From Hyde Park spread their vegetating roots beneath Albion
In dreadful pain, the spectrous uncircumcized vegetation
25 Forming a sexual machine, an aged virgin form,
In Erin's land toward the north, joint after joint; & burning
In love & jealousy immingled & calling it religion.
And feeling the damps of death they with one accord delegated
    Los,
Conjuring him by the Highest that he should watch over them,
30 Till Jesus shall appear. And they gave their power to Los
Naming him 'the spirit of prophecy', calling him Elijah.

Strucken with Albion's disease they become what they behold;
They assimilate with Albion in pity & compassion;
Their emanations return not, their spectres rage in the deep.
35 The slumbers of death came over them around the couch of
    death,
Before the gate of Los & in the depths of non-entity
Among the funaces of Los, among the oaks of Albion.
(Man is adjoined to man by his emanative portion,

39.21. In the following lines, note the words connoting evil–*sexual*,
vegetated, spectrous, uncircumcised, machine, aged virgin, jealousy–all in oppo-
sition to freedom and life. This is Albion's fate.
39.26. Erin] See 11.8*n*: the place from which the Friends can watch Albion.
39.28. *they*] The Friends of Albion. Cp. the fate of those who saw the fate
of Reuben in 30.50ff. B. has to reconcile the fate of the twenty-four cities,
bound to Albion's destiny and so condemned with him; but also his
friends, and therefore trying like angels to raise him.
39.31. Elijah, who defied the priests of Baal and was faithful when all
Israel was unfaithful, embodies the spirit of prophecy which B. sums up
and personifies in Los.
39.34. In Eden the emanation may separate for a time from the Human
Form, but always for a purpose, returning in due course; only when the
personality is disintegrating does the emanation fail to return. See note
below.
39.38–42. This is a detached passage of comment, especially on *34* above.
It uses the Epicurean notion that from everything *emanates* an image of
itself, which is perceived by the recipient. B. goes further, and says that
there is a meeting of substances as well as perception. B. says that the true
vision of beauty (Jerusalem) is to be contrasted with the false vision of
reason (Vala): one is imaginative and real, the other rational and dead.

Who is Jerusalem in every individual man, and her
40   Shadow is Vala, builded by the reasoning power in man.
O search & see, turn your eyes inward. Open, O thou world
Of love & harmony in man, expand thy ever-lovely gates!)

They wept into the deeps a little space; at length was heard
The voice of Bath, faint as the voice of the dead in the house of
    death—

Pl. 40   [Design]
(45)
Bath, healing city, whose wisdom in midst of poetic
Fervour mild spoke through the western porch, in soft gentle
    tears;

'O Albion, mildest son of Eden, closed is thy western gate.
Brothers of Eternity, this man whose great example
5   We all admired & loved, whose all-benevolent countenance, seen
In Eden, in lovely Jerusalem, drew even from envy
The tear, & the confession of honesty, open & undisguised,
From mistrust & suspicion—the man is himself become
A piteous example of oblivion, to teach the sons
10   Of Eden that however great & glorious, however loving
And merciful the individuality, however high
Our palaces & cities, & however fruitful are our fields,
In selfhood, we are nothing, but fade away in morning's breath.
Our mildness is nothing; the greatest mildness we can use
15   Is incapable and nothing. None but the Lamb of God can heal
This dread disease, none but Jesus. O Lord, descend and save!
Albion's western gate is closed; his death is coming apace.
Jesus alone can save him; for alas, we none can know
How soon his lot may be our own. When Africa in sleep

40. *Design*: At the top, enclosing *1–2*: a crouching figure is enmeshed in
the twisted branches of a tree; a flying female figure escapes over the waves
to the right. Under the water, beneath *2*, a large fish swallows smaller ones.
40.2. *western porch*] Because Bath is in the west; and because the western
porch is in the direction of Eden, and Bath is here one of the most en-
lightened Friends of Albion. There is a probable origin of B.'s admiration
for Bath in the fearless preaching and writing of Richard Warner in
1804–08, whose denunciation of war is echoed in the quietism of these
lines (for full detail, see D. V. Erdman, *Blake, Prophet Against Empire*, 1954,
pp. 440–4). Bath rejects the use of force, already shown futile after Los's
attempt (38.*81*ff), and waits for the inspiration of Jesus. But only the
blessed ('whose western gates are open', *34*) can hear him, though he ap-
pears as a 'Divine Vision' (*38*).
40.19. The story of Africa, here personified, seems to have been invented
for this passage, and is not found elsewhere; *in sleep* implies 'in spiritual

20 Rose in the night of Beulah, & bound down the sun & moon,
His friends cut his strong chains, & overwhelmed his dark
Machines in fury & destruction, & the man reviving repented.
He wept before his wrathful brethren, thankful & considerate
For their well-timed wrath. But Albion's sleep is not
25 Like Africa's, and his machines are woven with his life.
Nothing but mercy can save him, nothing but mercy interposing,
Lest he should slay Jerusalem in his fearful jealousy.
O God, descend, gather our brethren, deliver Jerusalem.
But that we may omit no office of the friendly spirit,
30 Oxford, take thou these leaves of the Tree of Life. With
    eloquence
That thy immortal tongue inspires, present them to Albion.
Perhaps he may receive them, offered from thy loved hands.'

So spoke, unheard by Albion, the merciful son of heaven
To those whose western gates were open, as they stood weeping
35 Around Albion. But Albion heard him not; obdurate, hard,
He frowned on all his friends, counting them enemies in his
    sorrow.

And the seventeen—conjoining with Bath, the seventh
In whom the other ten shone manifest, a Divine Vision—
Assimilated & embraced eternal death for Albion's sake.

death', that Africa did not know what he was doing–as if sleep-walking.
40.30. Oxford] B.'s admiration for Oxford as a centre of poetic vision was
traced unconvincingly (by Damon) to Shelley, who was sent down in 1811
for circulating the pamphlet *The Necessity of Atheism*. But Shelley did not
emerge as a poet until *Alastor*, 1816, though his prose pamphlets *may* have
been the 'eloquence' referred to. A more probable source is the now-
forgotten Fellow of Oriel, Edward Marsh, 'my much admired and respectd
Edward the Bard of Oxford whose verses still sound upon my ear like the
distant approach of things mighty and magnificent . . .' (letter to Hayley,
27 Jan. 1804). No poetry by Marsh is known, but the letter, and Gilchrist's
remarks, shows that he read poetry, including B.'s own, with an 'elo-
quence' very pleasing to B.
the leaves of the Tree of Life 'were for the healing of the nations' (*Revelation*
xxii 2): cp. also 41.9 below. The leaves suggest a garland–a classical allu-
sion fitting for Oxford.
40.37–8. seventeen . . . the seventh . . . the other ten] In 37.1 Bath is 'the
seventh' of the friends there listed. By pl.36 B. had listed eleven cities
before breaking off (including 'the Four', 34.45,51). In pl.41 he lists eight-
een; Bath is the twice-mentioned name (36.61, 41.1), seventh on pl.36,
and the pivot of the list. 'The other ten' are therefore those listed in pls 34
and 36; at this point Bath is greater even than 'the Four in whom the
twenty-four appeared' (41.23).

40 And these the names of the eighteen combining with those ten:
Pl. 41 Bath, mild physician of Eternity, mysterious power,
(46) Whose springs are unsearchable & knowledge infinite.
Hereford, ancient guardian of Wales, whose hands
Builded the mountain palaces of Eden, stupendous works.
5 Lincoln, Durham & Carlisle, counsellors of Los,
And Ely, scribe of Los, whose pen no other hand
Dare touch. Oxford, immortal bard, with eloquence
Divine, he wept over Albion, speaking the words of God
In mild persuasion, bringing leaves of the Tree of Life:

10 'Thou art in error, Albion, the land of Ulro.
One error not removed will destroy a human soul.
Repose in Beulah's night till the error is removed.
Reason not on both sides. Repose upon our bosoms,
Till the plough of Jehovah, and the harrow of Shaddai
15 Have passed over the dead to awake the dead to Judgement.'
But Albion turned away, refusing comfort.

Oxford trembled while he spoke, then fainted in the arms
Of Norwich, Peterborough, Rochester, Chester awful,
Worcester,
Lichfield, Saint David's, Llandaff, Asaph, Bangor, Sodor,
20 Bowing their heads devoted. And the furnaces of Los
Began to rage. Thundering loud the storms began to roar
Upon the furnaces, & loud the furnaces rebellow beneath.

And these the Four in whom the Twenty-four appeared fourfold:
Verulam, London, York, Edinburgh, mourning one towards
another:

40.*40.* This line is a late addition, incised into the plate, so as to connect it with pl.41.

41.*1. physician*] Because of the medicinal wells at Bath.

41.*3. Hereford*] A cathedral city with a great castle covering the approach to South Wales.

41.*6. Ely*] In Cambridgeshire, and so associated with the university (cp. 35.*12n*): also a town with an ancient and famous tradition in her own right, though no great 'scribe' can be specified in Ely itself.

41.*14. Shaddai*] 'The Almighty' (*Exodus* vi 3); God as he appeared to Abraham, Isaac and Jacob. God must plough and turn over the land before it can be fertile again. In *Four Zoas* ix *313–36* souls are planted so that they can grow and be reaped.

41.*19. Asaph . . . Sodor*] The bishoprics of *St Asaph's* and *Sodor and Man* (i.e. the Isle of Man and the southern Hebrides, the Norse *Sudreyjar*).

41.*23. the Four*] First mentioned in 36.*3*, q.v. note.

25 'Alas, the time will come, when a man's worst enemies
Shall be those of his own house & family, in a religion
Of generation, to destroy by sin & atonement happy Jerusalem,
The bride & wife of the Lamb. O God, thou art not an avenger.'

[Design]

Pl. 42 Thus Albion sat, studious of others in his pale disease,
Brooding on evil: but when Los opened the furnaces before him
He saw that the accursed things were his own affections,
And his own beloved's. Then he turned sick, his soul died within
him.
5 Also Los sick & terrified beheld the furnaces of death
And must have died, but the Divine Saviour descended
Among the infant loves & affections, & the Divine Vision wept
Like evening dew on every herb upon the breathing ground.

Albion spoke in his dismal dreams: 'O thou deceitful friend,
10 Worshipping mercy & beholding thy friend in such affliction!
Los, thou now discoverest thy turpitude to the heavens.
I demand righteousness & justice, O thou ingratitude!
Give me my emanations back, food for my dying soul.
My daughters are harlots, my sons are accursed before me.
15 Enitharmon is my daughter, accursed with a father's curse.
Oh, I have utterly been wasted! I have given my daughters to
devils.'

So spoke Albion in gloomy majesty, & deepest night
Of Ulro rolled round his skirts from Dover to Cornwall.

41.25. So in 27.99–100.
41. *Design*: Covers almost half the page; an aged man sits with a veiled
woman in a chariot drawn by lions, with serpents for wheels and demons
on the lions' backs urging them on. The shaft is also a serpent, and another
curls round beyond the chariot. (Reproduced in Blunt, *The Art of W.B.*,
pl.50b; Keynes, *W.B.'s Engravings* pl.107; and Sloss and Wallis edn
(O.U.P.) i, p. 530.)
42.2. Cp. 30.14.
42.3. *the accursed things*] (a) In a moment of insight (the 'furnaces') Albion
sees that he has oppressed by law the most desirable things in life; and (b)
conversely he also sees that what he really wants to do is what is forbidden.
41.13. Albion wants his emanations as sacrifices, not as forgiven children.
See 37.31.
42.21. *these little ones*] The children of Albion's imagination. Cp. *Matthew*
xviii 6, 14: 'whoso shall offend one of these little ones which believe in me,
it were better for him that a millstone were hanged about his neck. . . .
Even so it is not the will of your Father which is in heaven, that one of these
little ones should perish.'

Los answered: 'Righteousness & justice I give thee in return
20 For thy righteousness, but I add mercy also, & bind
Thee from destroying these little ones. Am I to be only
Merciful to thee & cruel to all that thou hatest?
Thou wast the image of God surrounded by the four Zoas.
Three thou hast slain; I am the fourth—thou canst not destroy me.
25 Thou art in error; trouble me not with thy righteousness.
I have innocence to defend & ignorance to instruct.
I have no time for seeming & little arts of compliment,
In morality & virtue, in self-glorying & pride.
There is a limit of opaqueness, & a limit of contraction
30 In every individual man, & the limit of opaqueness
Is named Satan, & the limit of contraction is named Adam.
But when man sleeps in Beulah, the Saviour in mercy takes
Contraction's limit, & of the limit he forms woman—that
Himself may in process of time be born, man to redeem.
35 But there is no limit of expansion; there is no limit of
        translucence
In the bosom of man for ever from eternity to eternity!
Therefore I break thy bonds of righteousness; I crush thy
        messengers
That they may not crush me & mine. Do thou be righteous,
And I will return it; otherwise I defy thy worst revenge.
40 Consider me as thine enemy, on me turn all thy fury;
But destroy not these little ones, nor mock the Lord's anointed.
Destroy not by moral virtue the little ones whom he hath chosen—
The little ones whom he hath chosen in preference to thee.
He hath cast thee off for ever; the little ones he hath anointed.
45 Thy selfhood is for ever accursed from the Divine Presence.'

So Los spoke; then turned his face & wept for Albion.

Albion replied: 'Go, Hand & Hyle, seize the abhorred friend,
As you have seized the twenty-four rebellious ingratitudes

42.29. Cp. 31.1 and note on *Four Zoas* iv 270. B. now adds the idea that
by his incarnation Christ took the *worst* (most contracted) form possible
to humanity, in order to prevent man passing that limit. The suggestion
that woman was formed next, solely for the purpose of his eventual in-
carnation, is only found here in B. Elsewhere the separation of the sexes
is one of the evils of the Creation and Fall.
42.44. *thee*] As the next line says, this refers to Albion's Selfhood, not to
Albion's true Humanity. The Humanity may always be forgiven, but the
Selfhood must be annihilated.
42.47. *friend*] Presumably 'Friend of Albion': or perhaps B.'s own error for
fiend.
42.48. In 36.21 the Friends come to Albion's side; but they are weak, and

To atone for you, for spiritual death. Man lives by deaths of men.
50 Bring him to justice before Heaven here upon London Stone,
Between Blackheath & Hounslow, between Norwood & Finchley.
All that they have is mine: from my free generous gift,
They now hold all they have. Ingratitude to me,
To me their benefactor, calls aloud for vengeance deep!'

55 Los stood before his furnaces awaiting the fury of the dead;
And the Divine Hand was upon him, strengthening him mightily.

The spectres of the dead cry out from the deeps beneath
Upon the hills of Albion; Oxford groans in his iron furnace,
Winchester in his den & cavern; they lament against
60 Albion, they curse their human kindness & affection;
They rage like wild beasts in the forests of affliction;
In the dreams of Ulro they repent of their human kindness.

'Come up, build Babylon! Rahab is ours & all her multitudes
With her in pomp & glory of victory. Depart,
65 Ye twenty-four, into the deeps; let us depart to glory!'

Their human majestic forms sit up upon their couches
Of death; they curb their spectres as with iron curbs.
They enquire after Jerusalem in the regions of the dead,
With the voices of dead men, low, scarcely articulate,
70 And with tears cold on their cheeks they weary repose.

'O when shall the morning of the grave appear, & when
Shall our salvation come? We sleep upon our watch,
We cannot awake, and our spectres rage in the forests.
O God of Albion, where art thou? Pity the watchers.'

75 Thus mourn they. Loud the furnaces of Los thunder upon
The clouds of Europe & Asia, among the serpent temples.

in 37.23 are overcome by despair, which is equivalent to being Hand and
Hyle.
42.51. i.e. east, west, south and north–the whole of London: Albion's
words express, one after another, his errors–fear, selfishness, cruelty.
42.56. Again in 46.9, Los, finding his furnaces dead, calls for divine aid.
42.57. A distinction is made between the *spectres of the dead*, i.e. of spiritually
lost Britons, here identified with the twenty-four, who in these lines cry
for vengeance (following the lead of Albion himself) as many inhabitants
of those cities in our earthly experience are prone to do: and the true
humanity of the Friends, who keep the faith.
42.75. The cities of Albion are involved in his fate, and cannot leave him.
Los meanwhile acts freely over the whole world, as the following lines
show.

And Los drew his seven furnaces around Albion's altars,
And as Albion built his frozen altars, Los built the mundane shell,
In the four regions of humanity, east & west & north & south,
80 Till Norwood & Finchley & Blackheath & Hounslow covered the
     whole earth.
This is the net & veil of Vala among the souls of the dead.

Pl. 43 Then the Divine Vision like a silent sun appeared above
(29)   Albion's dark rocks, setting behind the gardens of Kensington
        On Tyburn's river, in clouds of blood, where was mild Zion hill's
        Most ancient promontory; & in the sun a human form appeared.
5   And thus the Voice Divine went forth upon the rocks of Albion:

        'I elected Albion for my glory; I gave to him the nations
        Of the whole earth. He was the Angel of my Presence, & all
        The sons of God were Albion's sons & Jerusalem was my joy.
        The reactor hath hid himself through envy. I behold him:
10   But you cannot behold him till he be revealed in his system.
        Albion's reactor must have a place prepared; Albion must sleep
        The sleep of death, till the man of sin & repentance be revealed.
        Hidden in Albion's forests he lurks. He admits of no reply
        From Albion but hath founded his reaction into a law
15   Of action, for obedience to destroy the contraries of man.
        He hath compelled Albion to become a punisher & hath
          possessed

42.77–8. Los opposes his heat to Albion's frost. At 13.53 the mundane shell is a creation of Ulro *against* Los in Golgonooza: here B. sees the shell from the other side–as a limitation of chaos.

43.1. Standing near Tyburn, B. would be able to see the winter sunset over Kensington Gardens, which lie south of west from the end of Oxford Street.

43.7. *the Angel of my Presence*] An angel close to God, to be entrusted with the most solemn messages, and carrying the equivalence of God's presence: in *Exodus* xxxiii 14 he is promised as a companion to Moses, and in *Isaiah* lxiii 9 he saved the Israelites in their affliction.

43.9. *the reactor*] The word is used here only, and seems to refer to the Spectre of Albion. B. is following a particular train of thought, and uses a new term–which, however, he does not put to common use. Lines *14–15* suggest that B. is thinking of the error which supposes *reaction* to be true and independent *action*, so that Albion supposes this reaction to be the only truth. B. also uses a special name, *eon*, for Albion's emanation (19.*16*, 36.*41*): this may be its parallel.

43.12. *The man of sin and repentance*] The man who believes that sin is real, and must be atoned for by Repentance–a fallacy to B., who believed instead in active Forgiveness.

43.15. *for obedience*] i.e. demanding obedience to law, which will destroy...

Himself of Albion's forests & wilds, and Jerusalem is taken,
The city of the woods in the forest of Ephratah is taken.
London is a stone of her ruins; Oxford is the dust of her walls;
20 Sussex & Kent are her scattered garments; Ireland her holy
            place;
And the murdered bodies of her little ones are Scotland & Wales.
The cities of the nations are the smoke of her consummation,
The nations are her dust: ground by the chariot wheels
Of her lordly conquerors, her palaces levelled with the dust.
25 I come that I may find a way for my banished ones to return.
Fear not, O little flock, I come. Albion shall rise again.'

So saying, the mild sun enclosed the human family.

Forthwith from Albion's darkening rocks came two immortal
            forms,
Saying: 'We alone are escaped, O merciful Lord & Saviour.
30 We flee from the interiors of Albion's hills & mountains,
From his valleys eastward, from Amalek, Canaan & Moab,
Beneath his vast ranges of hills surrounding Jerusalem.

'Albion walked on the steps of fire before his halls

43.18. *Ephratah*] Bethlehem; the name means 'fruitful land'. The *city* here
is clearly Jerusalem, however. Present-day Britain is all that remains of the
beautiful city and civilization of old with which B. identifies her.
43.22. *consummation*] B. spells it so but, as always, means 'burning'.
43.27. An image of the setting sun closing down the folds of darkness on to
the gardens and streets—see *1n* and 'Albion's *darkening* rocks' in *28*.
43.28 *rocks*] B. has *locks*; the emendation was suggested by Joanne Witge.
Cp. line 2.
43.33–82. These lines are taken from the vision of Ahania in *Four Zoas* iii
46–98, with slight alterations. In both poems, the speaker is describing the
origin of man's troubles. In *Jerusalem*, however, the references to Vala and
Luvah are not self-evident. Full notes are given in the original context,
p. 332 above; the general sense is that Albion is deluded into a fascination
for one part of himself—Vala—at the expense of the rest, and of proportion.
Vala is the feminine counterpart of Luvah, who is now worshipped by
Albion as God (*41*). When Luvah steps down from the cloud in which he
has disguised himself, Albion is shocked, and finally turns his back on Vala
(*57*). Then, the fascination broken, he hears the call of other forgotten
elements of his being (*58–60*), Tharmas and Enion. Luvah and Albion
struggle (*61*) with the result that Albion's body is marked, as Job's was, but
he repulses Luvah's attempt to dominate him, and drives Luvah and Vala
away (*66–71*). This is not victory, as he remains a disordered being, for
they are essential parts of him. The passage may allegorize a man's falling
under the domination of his passions, which he then repudiates and tries
to forgo. The result is (*73–5*) that the human heart is in a turmoil.

And Vala walked with him in dreams of soft deluding slumber.
35 He looked up & saw the prince of light with splendour faded.
Then Albion ascended mourning into the porches of his palace.
Above him rose a shadow from his wearied intellect
Of living gold, pure, perfect, holy; in white linen pure he
    hovered,
A sweet entrancing self-delusion, a watery vision of Albion,
40 Soft exulting in existence, all the man absorbing.

'Albion fell upon his face prostrate before the watery shadow,
Saying: "O Lord, whence is this change? Thou knowest I am
    nothing!"
And Vala trembled & covered her face, & her locks were spread
    on the pavement.

'We heard, astonished at the vision, & our hearts trembled
    within us;
45 We heard the voice of slumberous Albion, & thus he spake,
Idolatrous to his own shadow, words of Eternity uttering:

'"Oh, I am nothing when I enter into judgement with thee.
If thou withdraw thy breath I die & vanish into Hades;
If thou dost lay thine hand upon me, behold I am silent;
50 If thou withhold thine hand, I perish like a fallen leaf.
O I am nothing, and to nothing must return again.
If thou withdraw thy breath, behold I am oblivion!"

'He ceased. The shadowy voice was silent, but the cloud hovered
    over their heads
In golden wreaths, the sorrow of man, & the balmy drops fell
    down.
55 And lo! that son of man, that shadowy spirit of mild Albion,
Luvah, descended from the cloud; in terror Albion rose.
Indignant rose the awful man, & turned his back on Vala.

'We heard the voice of Albion starting from his sleep:

'"Whence is this voice crying, *Enion!* that soundeth in my ears?
60 O cruel pity! O dark deceit! Can love seek for dominion?"

'And Luvah strove to gain dominion over Albion.
They strove together above the body where Vala was enclosed;
And the dark body of Albion left prostrate upon the crystal
    pavement,

43.35. *prince of light*] Urizen, one of the four Zoas, who should watch
Albion and advise him against such follies as that which follows.
43.59–60. In *Four Zoas*, one result of the disorder within Man was that
Enion, counterpart of Tharmas, one of the four Zoas, had been driven out
to 'the margin of non-entity', and Tharmas was continuously seeking her.

Covered with boils from head to foot, the terrible smitings of
Luvah.

65   'Then frowned the fallen man & put forth Luvah from his
presence,
Saying: "Go & die the death of man for Vala the sweet wanderer.
I will turn the volutions of your ears outward, & bend your nostrils
Downward, & your fluxile eyes englobed roll round in fear;
Your withering lips & tongue shrink up into a narrow circle,
70   Till into narrow forms you creep. Go take your fiery way,
And learn what 'tis to absorb the man, you spirits of pity & love!"

'They heard the voice & fled swift as the winter's setting sun.
And now the human blood foamed high, the spirits Luvah & Vala
Went down the human heart where paradise & its joys abounded,
75   In jealous fears & fury & rage, & flames roll round their fervid feet:
And the vast form of nature like a serpent played before them.
And as they fled in folding fires & thunders of the deep,
Vala shrunk in like the dark sea that leaves its slimy banks,
And from her bosom Luvah fell far as the east & west.
80   And the vast form of nature like a serpent rolled between—
Whether of Jerusalem's or Vala's ruins congenerated we know not.
All is confusion, all is tumult; & we alone are escaped.'

So spoke the fugitives: they joined the Divine Family, trembling.

Pl. 44   [*Design*]
(30)
And the two that escaped were the emanation of Los & his
Spectre, for wherever the emanation goes, the spectre
Attends her as her guard, & Los's emanation is named
Enitharmon, & his spectre is named Urthona. They knew
5   Not where to flee; they had been on a visit to Albion's children,

43.*67–70.* The fate also of Reuben (30.*47–56,* 32.*2–6*).
43.*81.* Probably Vala's, but the escaping pair are confused. Moreover, B.
must add these lines to the end of the *Four Zoas* passage to bring it into line
with the myth of *Jerusalem.*
43.*83. trembling*] Altered from 'Albion ?slept'.
44. *Design:* The two flying forms come to Los, who holds his arms out to
welcome them.
44.*4. his spectre is named Urthona*] This is a new idea; normally, in 10.*32*
and in *Four Zoas,* Urthona is the eternal, unfallen Los. Perhaps B. now
thinks he has no further use for that myth, but might use the name for the
Spectre. But he keeps to the old use in *14.*
44.*5.* This passage may derive from the abortive attempt by Hayley to be
B.'s patron. Hayley's efforts to help B.'s career in his own way are com-
mented on in *9–10;* it is more important to see the use B. makes of it in the

And they strove to weave a shadow of the emanation
To hide themselves, weeping & lamenting for the vegetation
Of Albion's children, fleeing through Albion's vales in streams of
gore.

Being not irritated by insult, bearing insulting benevolences,
10   They perceived that corporeal friends are spiritual enemies.
They saw the sexual religion in its embryon uncircumcision,
And the Divine Hand was upon them, bearing them through
darkness
Back safe to their humanity as doves to their windows.
Therefore the sons of Eden praise Urthona's spectre in songs,
15   Because he kept the Divine Vision in time of trouble.
They wept & trembled, & Los put forth his hand & took them in
Into his bosom, from which Albion shrunk in dismal pain,
Rending the fibres of brotherhood, & in feminine allegories
Enclosing Los: but the Divine Vision appeared with Los,
20   Following Albion into his central void among his oaks.

And Los prayed & said: 'O Divine Saviour, arise
Upon the mountains of Albion as in ancient time. Behold,
The cities of Albion seek thy face. London groans in pain
From hill to hill, & the Thames laments along the valleys.
25   The little villages of Middlesex & Surrey hunger & thirst;
The twenty-eight cities of Albion stretch their hands to thee,
Because of the oppressors of Albion in every city & village.

narrative. The two messengers had been to visit Hand, Skofield and the
rest, and had had to escape.
44.6. A difficult line. If the reference is still to B.'s private affairs, it may
mean that they used Catherine's ill-health as an excuse and a smoke-screen
in which to escape from Felpham. The immediate meaning is obscure: a
shadow of an Emanation is normally the female equivalent of the Spectre.
44.9–11. Hayley meant well, and tried to show B. the facts of economic
life; B. regarded this as 'insulting benevolence'. In 11 he declares that
Hayley's attitude contains in embryo all the faults of the materialism he
hates–sexual connoting the fallen state where one person is set against
another; uncircumcision because it is a false religion.
44.13. windows] The windows of their dovecots.
44.18. feminine allegories] An allegory to B. is normally a false representa-
tion; 'feminine' in such a context implies the kind of error propagated
by Vala. That Los should be so enclosed means that his imaginative creat-
ions, and the purpose in life of their creator, are hedged about with false
notions of the purpose of poetry and art, which weaken its prophetic
impact.
44.20. his central void among his oaks] Two ideas connoting spiritual death;
the oaks are the oaks of druid religion, and of British warships.

They mock at the labourer's limbs, they mock at his starved
    children,
They buy his daughters that they may have power to sell his sons;
30   They compel the poor to live upon a crust of bread by soft mild arts;
They reduce the man to want, then give with pomp & ceremony.
The praise of Jehovah is chanted from lips of hunger & thirst.

'Humanity knows not of sex: wherefore are sexes in Beulah?
In Beulah the female lets down her beautiful tabernacle
35   Which the male enters magnificent between her cherubim,
And becomes one with her, mingling, condensing in self-love
The rocky law of condemnation & double generation, & death.
Albion hath entered the loins, the place of the Last Judgement;

44.33. *Humanity ... sex*] Humanity is the form of life in Eternity; sex is
unknown there, as it began only when Eve was created (*Genesis* ii 22);
Christ's saying in *Matthew* xxii 30 (quoted by B. at 30.*15* above) may be
taken to support this. *Beulah* (q.v. *Milton* pl.30.*1n*) is the blessed land on
the borders of Eternity, essentially a place for rest, where emanations go in
the form of women and children (*Milton* pl.31.*1–3*). Eternals go there only
for relaxation; then they should return to Eden, where (69.*43*):

    'Embraces are comminglings from the head even to the feet,
    And not a pompous High Priest entering by a Secret Place.'

Why then should there be sex in Beulah? Male and female unite, retain-
ing their own separate forms and identities–not in the total 'commingling'
of Eden, where there is no male or female. However, this separation-in-
union has one great effect. It forces evil ('self-love ... death', *36–7*) into a
fixed, 'condensed' form which (*40*) the Lord can rend, as the veil of the
temple rent at Christ's death. Cp. 69.*14–31*; elsewhere, sexual delight is
one of the joys of Beulah (37.*15–19*: *Milton* pl. *5.5–10, 33.17–20*).
44.*34–40*. The imagery is that of the TABERNACLE in *Exodus* xxv, where
the sanctuary was curtained off (cp. *39–40*), leading to the Holy of Holies,
which was again curtained off. There was kept the Ark, on which was the
mercy-seat, symbolizing the Presence of God; but the Presence was hidden
by two cherubim, in one piece with the mercy-seat. The Holy of Holies
was unapproachable (B.'s 'secret place'), being entered only once a year,
by the High Priest alone, after the most careful purification, on the Day of
Atonement (cp. 'Last Judgement', *38*). B. is impressed by the powerful
sense of restriction and compulsion in the ritual, and blends it with the
sense of restriction and compulsive necessity in sex. Cp. *Four Zoas* viib *21n*.
44.*38–9*. *Last Judgement*] In his commentary on his painting *A Vision of the
Last Judgement*, B. says: 'Whenever any individual rejects error and em-
braces truth, a Last Judgement passes upon that individual.' Any area of
human experience which can lead to heightened sensitivity and inspiration,
including sex, can produce such a 'last judgement', a revelation of truth.
Here Albion's union with the deluding, selfish and moralistic Vala, blessed

And Luvah hath drawn the curtains around Albion in Vala's
  bosom;
40 The dead awake to generation. Arise, O Lord, & rend the veil.'
  So Los in lamentations followed Albion. Albion covered
Pl. 45 His western heaven with rocky clouds of death & despair.
(31) Fearing that Albion should turn his back against the Divine
  Vision,
  Los took his globe of fire to search the interiors of Albion's
  Bosom, in all the terrors of friendship, entering the caves
5 Of despair & death, to search the tempters out, walking among
  Albion's rocks & precipices, caves of solitude & dark despair;
  And saw every minute particular of Albion degraded & murdered,
  But saw not by whom; they were hidden within in the minute
  particulars
  Of which they had possessed themselves—& there they take up
10 The articulations of man's soul, & laughing throw it down
  Into the frame, then knock it out upon the plank, & souls are baked
  In bricks to build the pyramids of Heber & Terah. But Los

by Luvah (the spirit of passion) who draws the curtains round them to
enclose them in the mystery of the secret place, sets in motion greater forces
than either of them can understand. Children will be born (*40*) and brought
out of chaos into the world of mortal life where the hand of God, ripping
the curtain, Vala's veil, can reach them and free them.

45.3. Los's search gives us B.'s imaginative review of the state of London
in his day.

45.7. *minute particular*] B. laid much stress on this phrase. The minute par-
ticular is a living detail, as against the vague, formless generalities B.
detested. Hence his admiration of painters who draw, and particularize, as
against his detestation of those who lay on a spread of colour (*Descriptive
Catalogue* xv (*Ruth*), Keynes 1957, p. 585: *Erdman 1965*, p. 540: 'Such art
of losing the outlines is the art of Venice and Flanders; it loses all character,
and leaves what some people call, expression . . . expression cannot exist
without character as its stamina; and neither character nor expression can
exist without firm and determinate outline.') As in art, so in morality and
all things. In the context of *17*, 'minute particular' seems to mean simply
'children'–the children of the streets.

45.9ff. B. has seen brickmakers at work: they would take a brick-mould,
pack it with clay, knock the shaped clay on to a board, and put the row of
bricks to bake in a kiln. So in 24.31, 'the walls of Babylon are souls of men'.
The *articulations* may be the straw which binds the bricks together, as [the
articulations of the body, though hidden, give it its living form.

45.12. *Heber & Terah*] Ancestors of the Hebrews; but B. associates them
(against the genealogies of *Genesis* x), with the tribes of the region of the
Euphrates, the land where towers such as the tower of Babel (*Genesis* xi 1–9)
were built for worship in false religions: built, B. says, from the tormented

Searched in vain; closed from the minutia he walked difficult.
He came down from Highgate through Hackney & Holloway
    towards London
15 Till he came to Old Stratford, & thence to Stepney & the Isle
Of Leutha's Dogs, thence through the narrows of the river's side,
And saw every minute particular, the jewels of Albion, running
    down
The kennels of the streets & lanes as if they were abhorred.
Every universal form was become barren mountains of moral
20 Virtue, and every minute particular hardened into grains of sand,
And all the tendernesses of the soul cast forth as filth & mire
Among the winding places of deep contemplation intricate
To where the Tower of London frowned dreadful over
    Jerusalem—
A building of Luvah, builded in Jerusalem's eastern gate to be
25 His secluded court. Thence to Bethlehem, where was builded
Dens of despair in the house of bread; enquiring in vain
Of stones & rocks he took his way, for human form was none:
And thus he spoke, looking on Albion's city with many tears:

'What shall I do? What could I do? If I could find these
    criminals
30 I could not dare to take vengeance; for all things are so constructed
And builded by the Divine Hand that the sinner shall always
    escape,
And he who takes vengeance alone is the criminal of providence.
If I should dare to lay my finger on a grain of sand

souls of men. However, Abraham lived at Ur; and *Terah* was his father,
and *Heber* (or *Eber*) his distant ancestor.
45.14–16. See map. The walk would then be through satellite villages; as B.
puts it, it is not a straight route, unless Hackney and Holloway are re-
versed, when it would be a walk of about fifteen miles.
45.18. kennels] Open drains.
45.19–21. Virtue, and all other perfections, instead of being parts of the
nature of the soul, and issuing in particular acts according to circumstance,
have been hardened into a Moral Law, which regards neither circumstance
nor individuality–and it has become immoral to the truly virtuous or
compassionate, or tender.
45.24. Luvah] Represented in these pages (43.56ff) as Albion's enemy; and
the Tower is at the eastern end of London.
45.25. Bethlehem] i.e. 'house of bread'. The lunatic asylum, where patients
were imprisoned rather than tended, was called Bedlam (= Bethlehem) and
was moved from Moorfields to Lambeth Road, very near B.'s old home, in
1815. (This building is now the Imperial War Museum.) Though Los
might have crossed London Bridge to Southwark, B. probably refers to
Moorfields, the site of scandals about maltreatment in 1807 and 1814.

In way of vengeance, I punish the already punished. Oh, whom,
35 Should I pity if I pity not the sinner who is gone astray?
O Albion, if thou takest vengeance, if thou revengest thy wrongs,
Thou art for ever lost! What can I do to hinder the sons
Of Albion from taking vengeance, or how shall I them persuade?'

So spoke Los, travelling through darkness & horrid solitude.
40 And he beheld Jerusalem in Westminster & Marybone,
Among the ruins of the Temple; & Vala who is her shadow,
Jerusalem's shadow, bent northward over the island white.
At length he sat on London Stone, & heard Jerusalem's voice:

'Albion, I cannot be thy wife. Thine own minute particulars
45 Belong to God alone, & all thy little ones are holy.
They are of faith & not of demonstration. Wherefore is Vala
Clothed in black mourning upon my river's currents? Vala, awake!
I hear thy shuttles sing in the sky, & round my limbs
I feel the iron threads of love & jealousy & despair.'

50 Vala replied: 'Albion is mine. Luvah gave me to Albion
And now receives reproach & hate. Was it not said of old,
"Set your son before a man & he shall take you & your sons
For slaves: but set your daughter before a man & she
Shall make him & his sons & daughters your slaves for ever?"
55 And is this faith? Behold the strife of Albion & Luvah
Is great in the east, their spears of blood rage in the eastern heaven.
Urizen is the champion of Albion, they will slay my Luvah;
And thou, O harlot daughter, daughter of despair, art all
This cause of these shakings of my towers on Euphrates.
60 Here is the house of Albion, & here is thy secluded place,
And here we have found thy sins, & hence we turn thee forth
For all to avoid thee, to be astonished at thee for thy sins—
Because thou art the impurity & the harlot, & thy children
Children of whoredoms, born for sacrifice, for the meat & drink

45.40–1. These places are in the west of London: the Temple (named after
the Knights Templars) is the western boundary of the city of London. For
London Stone see 8.27n.
45.41. *shadow*] The evil self of the female emanation, as the spectre is the
evil self of the whole personality. (Note that this definition is true of
Jerusalem; also in *Four Zoas* viia. Elsewhere 'shadow' is only another word
for 'spectre'.)
45.5off. This passage is partly allegory. Vala claims that Luvah (the pas-
sionate side of man) is oppressed (or repressed) by Albion, who is under the
domination of Urizen, prince of reason. Vala, who is the type of female
domination (an enervating domination by means of secret desire, re-
stricted vision, etc.) hates Jerusalem for the freedom of her actions, which
she calls sin and harlotry.

65 Offering, to sustain the glorious combat & the battle & war,
   That man may be purified by the death of thy delusions.'

   So saying she her dark threads cast over the trembling river,
   And over the valleys—from the hills of Hertfordshire to the hills
   Of Surrey, across Middlesex & across Albion's house
70 Of eternity; pale stood Albion at his eastern gate,

[Design]

Pl. 46 Leaning against the pillars, & his disease rose from his skirts;
(32)   Upon the precipice he stood, ready to fall into non-entity.

   Los was all astonishment & terror. He trembled, sitting on the Stone
   Of London. But the interiors of Albion's fibres & nerves were
      hidden
5 From Los; astonished he beheld only the petrified surfaces,
   And saw his furnaces in ruins, for Los is the demon of the furnaces;
   He saw also the four points of Albion reversed inwards.
   He seized his hammer & tongs, his iron poker & his bellows,
   Upon the valleys of Middlesex, shouting loud for aid divine.

10 In stern defiance came from Albion's bosom Hand, Hyle, Coban,
   Gwantok, Peachey, Brereton, Slayd, Huttn, Skofield, Kox, Kotope,
   Bowen, Albion's sons. They bore him a golden couch into the porch
   And on the couch reposed his limbs, trembling from the bloody
      field,
   Rearing their druid patriarchal rocky temples around his limbs.
15 (All things begin & end in Albion's ancient druid rocky shore.)

[Design]

45. *Design*: Two female figures; Vala holding the end of a thread with
which she has wound a net round Jerusalem's body.

46.2. *precipice*] i.e. upon the verge of Ulro, ready to fall into ultimate
chaos. This recalls 35.*11–16* and 39.*1–4*.

46.*6–12*. Los sees that he has neglected his work; Albion is in complete
disorder, and Los cannot see into his heart. The page is a notable example
of B.'s use of disparate images together–the furnace, the compass points,
the couch, and the druid temples.

46.*15*. So in 27.9, and *Milton* pl.6.25.

46. *Design*: Most of the plate is taken up by this. Vala, left, draping herself
in a black veil (45.47) faces Jerusalem and three children, all nude, centre
and right. One child springs and points upwards, the others cling to
Jerusalem. In the background: right, London churches; left, a cross on a
hill. (Reproduced in Keynes, *W.B.'s Engravings* pl.106.)

24*

Pl. 47 From Camberwell to Highgate, where the mighty Thames
      shudders along,
    Where Los's furnaces stand, where Jerusalem & Vala howl,
    Luvah tore forth from Albion's loins, in fibrous veins, in rivers
    Of blood over Europe—a vegetating root in grinding pain,
5   Animating the dragon temples, soon to become that holy fiend
    The wicker man of Scandinavia, in which cruelly consumed
    The captives reared to heaven howl in flames among the stars.
    Loud the cries of war on the Rhine & Danube with Albion's sons,
    Away from Beulah's hills & vales break forth the souls of the
      dead,
10   With cymbal, trumpet, clarion & the scythed chariots of Britain.

[Design]

And the veil of Vala is composed of the spectres of the dead.

47.1. Above this line, the deleted line: 'When Albion uttered his last
words, Hope is banished from me' (from *24.60*). The last line of this plate
is similar, but this does not make the erasure entirely necessary. B. may once
have had some other arrangements of plates in mind.
Camberwell, Highgate] From north to south of London; see map.
47.3–9. Cp. *27.55ff*:

    Albion's Spectre from his loins
    Tore forth in all the pomp of war:
    Satan his name; in flames of fire
    He stretched his druid pillars far . . .

    The Rhine was red with human blood,
    The Danube rolled a purple tide . . .

Substituting Luvah for Satan, the similarity is clear. B. thus relates sup-
pressed sexual passion to war–cp. *44.38–9*, where it is also related to priestly
religion.
47.5–6. The false spirit of priestly religion gets abroad, first producing the
druid temples which (following Stukeley's popular interpretation of
Avebury: see *Europe 72n*) B. saw as having serpent form; then the cruelty
of human sacrifice in man-shaped wicker idols (see *38.65* and *Milton*
pl.*37.11n*). This was a Druid custom, on certain occasions, not Scandinavian.
47.8. Neither Austerlitz nor Jena, Napoleon's two great victories of 1805
and 1806, is on the Danube or the Rhine; but they carried him through
Austria and Germany, lands associated with those rivers.
47.10. the scythed chariot] A historical detail that 'every schoolboy knows'.
47. Design (most of the plate): Three writhing figures, one male and two
female (cp. *6–8*). (Reproduced in Keynes, *W.B.'s Engravings*, pl.108.)
47.11. the dead] Usually B. means 'the spiritually dead', and so here refers
to the veil or binding force of Vala felt through the influence of evil men.
It may simply mean in addition 'the victims of war', so that the line means

Hark, the mingling cries of Luvah with the sons of Albion!
Hark & record the terrible wonder; that the punisher
Mingles with his victim's spectre, enslaved & tormented
15 To him whom he has murdered, bound in vengeance & enmity!
Shudder not, but write, & the hand of God will assist you.
Therefore I write Albion's last words: *Hope is banished from me.*

Pl. 48 These were his last words, & the merciful Saviour in his arms
Received him, in the arms of tender mercy, & reposed
The pale limbs of his eternal individuality
Upon the Rock of Ages. Then, surrounded with a cloud,
5 In silence the Divine Lord builded with immortal labour
Of gold & jewels a sublime ornament, a couch of repose,
With sixteen pillars, canopied with emblems & written verse.
Spiritual verse, ordered & measured, from whence time shall
reveal.
The five Books of the Decalogue, the books of Joshua & Judges,
10 Samuel, a double book, & Kings, a double book, the Psalms &
Prophets,
The fourfold Gospel, and the Revelations everlasting.
Eternity groaned & was troubled at the image of eternal death!

Beneath the bottoms of the graves, which is earth's central joint,
There is a place where contrarieties are equally true
15 (To protect from the giant blows in the sports of intellect,
Thunder in the midst of kindness, & love that kills its beloved:
Because death is for a period, & they renew tenfold).
From this sweet place maternal love awoke Jerusalem.
With pangs she forsook Beulah's pleasant lovely shadowy
universe
20 Where no dispute can come, created for those who sleep.

Weeping was in all Beulah, & all the daughters of Beulah

that Vala's power is made up of the evil natures (spectres) of the dead, who, instead of living for good, die and are turned to her account.
47.17. *I*] B. writes; Albion's words were deleted from the head of this page, but occur at 24.60.

48.6. *a couch*] The Bible, including only the books approved by Swedenborg.
48.13. Beulah is located at the 'joint' of the Earth and Eden, and of Ulro and Eden: Eden may be reached from either place by way of Beulah.
48.14. So in *Milton* pl.30.1.
a place] Beulah, free from strife—where contrary states exist at peace together.
48.18. Jerusalem, as an emanation, would have a 'second home' in Beulah; but at such a time of stress she cannot rest there.

Wept for their sister the daughter of Albion, Jerusalem,
When out of Beulah the emanation of the sleeper descended
With solemn mourning out of Beulah's moony shades & hills
25 Within the human heart, whose gates closed with solemn sound.

And this the manner of the terrible separation:
The emanations of the grievously afflicted friends of Albion
Concentre in one female form, an aged pensive woman.
Astonished, lovely, embracing the sublime shade, the daughters
of Beulah
30 Beheld her with wonder. With awful hands she took
A moment of time, drawing it out with many tears & afflictions
And many sorrows oblique across the Atlantic vale,
Which is the Vale of Rephaim dreadful from east to west,
Where the human harvest waves abundant in the beams of Eden,
35 Into a rainbow of jewels & gold, a mild reflection from
Albion's dread tomb, eight thousand & five hundred years
In its extension (every two hundred years has a door to Eden).
She also took an atom of space, with dire pain opening it, a centre
Into Beulah; trembling the daughters of Beulah dried
40 Her tears. She ardent embraced her sorrows, occupied in labours
Of sublime mercy in Rephaim's vale. Perusing Albion's tomb
She sat; she walked among the ornaments solemn mourning.
The daughters attended her shudderings, wiping the death-sweat.
Los also saw her in his seventh furnace, he also terrified
45 Saw the finger of God go forth upon his seventh furnace,
Away from the starry wheels to prepare Jerusalem a place—
When with a dreadful groan the emanation mild of Albion

48.29. i.e. the Daughters of Beulah embrace her (Erin, 51, 53). The phrase
sublime shade implies that, though the 'pensive woman' is not an eternal
form, but appears only through the blending together of the separated
emanations, she is sublime because her purpose is good.

48.30–41. Cp. *Four Zoas* i 139–43, and also *Milton* pl.28.46ff.

48.32–3. *the Atlantic Vale . . . Rephaim*] The Atlantic is the gulf that sep-
arates Albion from the west, and from America, B.'s land of freedom.
Rephaim (see *Milton* pl.19.40) is a valley just south of Jerusalem where the
Philistines camped. The 'pensive woman' Erin is creating a thing of
beauty—a rainbow—in opposition to the ugliness which is overcoming
Albion and the Friends of Albion. Under her the whole of earthly time and
space are developed, in whatever goodness and beauty they possess, out of
a moment of infinity. This is an act of divine mercy, like the first rainbow
(*Genesis* ix 13) which symbolized God's faithfulness to Noah.

48.42. *ornaments*] See 6.

48.47. Jerusalem herself is affected, and begins to turn away from the
Divine Mercy. The Daughters of Beulah 'receive' her—a word used when
they give attention to lost souls.

Burst from his bosom in the tomb like a pale snowy cloud,
Female & lovely, struggling to put off the human form,
50 Writhing in pain. The daughters of Beulah in kind arms received
Jerusalem, weeping over her among the spaces of Erin,
In the ends of Beulah, where the dead wail night & day.

And thus Erin spoke to the daughters of Beulah, in soft tears:

'Albion the vortex of the dead, Albion the generous,
55 Albion the mildest son of heaven, the place of holy sacrifice,
Where friends die for each other!—will become the place
Of murder, & unforgiving, never-awaking sacrifice of enemies.
The children must be sacrificed (a horror never known
Till now in Beulah), unless a refuge can be found
60 To hide them from the wrath of Albion's law that freezes sore
Upon his sons & daughters, self-exiled from his bosom.
Draw ye Jerusalem away from Albion's mountains:
To give a place for redemption, let Sihon & Og
Remove eastward to Bashan & Gilead, & leave
Pl. 49 The secret coverts of Albion & the hidden places of America.
Jerusalem, Jerusalem, why wilt thou turn away?
Come ye, O daughters of Beulah, lament for Og & Sihon
Upon the lakes of Ireland from Rathlin to Baltimore;
5 Stand ye upon the Dargle from Wicklow to Drogheda;
Come & mourn over Albion, the white cliff of the Atlantic,
The mountain of giants. All the giants of Albion are become

48.54. *vortex of the dead*] For *vortex* see *Milton* pl.14.21. The 'traveller through eternity' passes through the centre of a vortex into a new world; Erin says that the dying pass through Albion, who is such a vortex: that is his Eternal nature, lost now he is fallen.

48.58. *The children*] Albion's–the creations of his infinite life will be lost if he is lost. Cp. 15.34n.

48.63. *Sihon and Og*] Amorite kings living east of Jordan, who were defeated in turn by the Israelites on their way to cross the Jordan. They were not then driven across into Bashan and Gilead, but already lived in the east: B. speaks of primordial events.   *Anak* (see 49.56) is often associated with Og: they were a tribe of giants (*Numbers* xiii 33) who did live west of Jordan, in the hill country of Hebron, south of Jerusalem, and were wiped out by Joshua in one of his campaigns. Goliath, however, may have been of the tribe of survivors in the region of Gath. The trend of these lines is: let the evil ones leave the land where holiness should reign.

49.4. *Rathlin, Baltimore, Dargle, Wicklow, Drogheda*] Rathlin is an island off the extreme north-east of Ireland, Baltimore a town on the far south-west coast; the Dargle is a river near Dublin. Wicklow and Drogheda are on the east coast of Ireland, some distance north and south respectively of Dublin. Thus B. makes a circuit of Ireland.

Weak, withered, darkened, & Jerusalem is cast forth from Albion.
They deny that they ever knew Jerusalem, or ever dwelt in
　　Shiloh.
10 The gigantic roots & twigs of the vegetating sons of Albion,
Filled with the little ones, are consumed in the fires of their altars,
The vegetating cities are burned & consumed from the earth;
And the bodies in which all animals & vegetations, the earth &
　　heaven
Were contained in the all-glorious imagination are withered &
　　darkened;
15 The golden gate of Havilah, & all the garden of God,
Was caught up with the sun in one day of fury & war.
The lungs, the heart, the liver shrunk away far distant from man
And left a little slimy substance floating upon the tides.
In one night the Atlantic continent was caught up with the moon,
20 And became an opaque globe far distant, clad with moony beams.
The visions of eternity, by reason of narrowed perceptions,
Are become weak visions of time & space, fixed into furrows of
　　death,
Till deep dissimulation is the only defence an honest man has left.
O polypus of death! O spectre over Europe & Asia!
25 Withering the human form by laws of sacrifice for sin.
By laws of chastity & abhorrence I am withered up,
Striving to create a heaven in which all shall be pure & holy
In their own selfhoods, in natural selfish chastity, to banish pity
And dear mutual forgiveness, & to become one great Satan,
30 Enslaved to the most powerful selfhood, to murder the Divine
　　Humanity,
In whose sight all are as the dust, & who chargeth his angels with
　　folly.

49.9. Jerusalem and Shiloh were the two holy cities of Israel.

49.10–11. Another reference to the 'wicker man' (47.5–6n).

49.15. Havilah] Cp. 19.42n; Havilah is in Paradise. B. begins another
story, invented for this passage and not a part of a wider myth, of catas-
trophe at the time of the Fall.

49.23. Cp. the annotation to Watson's Apology for the Bible (Keynes p. 383,
Erdman 1965 p. 601): 'To defend the Bible in this year 1798 would cost a
man his life.' Clearly a personal thought from B.'s own experience. His
political and social conscience was alive, yet to be a confessed radical was
to be in serious danger. Even in private life he had to pretend to be more
grateful to Hayley than he really felt, and disguise his real feelings in the
figure of Hyle.

49.26. I] Erin is the speaker. But in the following line she refers to fallen
beings who seek to establish a moral law.

49.31. This refers to Satan, not the Divine Humanity.

Ah, weak & wide astray! Ah, shut in narrow doleful form!
Creeping in reptile flesh upon the bosom of the ground!
The eye of man, a little narrow orb, closed up & dark,
35 Scarcely beholding the great light, conversing with the void;
The ear, a little shell, in small volutions shutting out
True harmonies, & comprehending great as very small;
The nostrils, bent down to the earth & closed with senseless flesh,
That odours cannot them expand, nor joy on them exult;
40 The tongue, a little moisture fills, a little food it cloys,
A little sound it utters, & its cries are faintly heard.
Therefore they are removed; therefore they have taken root
In Egypt & Philistia, in Moab & Edom & Aram,
In the Erythrean Sea their uncircumcision in heart & loins
45 Be lost for ever & ever. Then they shall arise from self
By self-annihilation, into Jerusalem's courts & into Shiloh,
Shiloh the masculine emanation among the flowers of Beulah.
Lo! Shiloh dwells over France, as Jerusalem dwells over Albion:
Build & prepare a wall & curtain for America's shore.
50 Rush on, rush on, rush on, ye vegetating sons of Albion!
The sun shall go before you in day, the moon shall go

49.32–41. These lines, in a somewhat different form, recur in the latest
Milton plate, *5.19–26*, p. 570 above.
49.42. *They*] The fallen–sons, giants of Albion–including Sihon and Og,
who are variously referred to in this passage. In spite of their diversity they
are all names for children of the eternal man Albion.
49.43. Albion's children have left the holy land and gone to the homes of
its enemies. Apart from the episode of the Israelites in Egypt, the Old
Testament is full of complaints that they were prone to 'follow' the gods
of these tribes.
49.44. *Erythrean*] The Red Sea, where the armies of Pharaoh, pursuing
Moses, were swallowed up and lost: in general, the south sea, beyond the
land-mass to the east as the Atlantic is to the west.
49.47. A masculine emanation is unusual: perhaps B. means to say that
Jerusalem and Shiloh, though enemies, should really be complementary
to one another. At the time of writing, France and Britain, traditional
enemies for a century, were locked in an apparently endless war. So also
Judæa and Israel divided: but B. insists that such enmity among families
is devilish.
49.49–58. This is an evil act, intended to confine America: but God will
continue his redeeming work unperturbed. B.'s call to 'come on!' is
partly ironical, and partly to bring the rebels back to God's mercy in the
end. Thus the tomb of Albion, the giants Og, Sihon and Anak, are all
found to be useful to God, though apparently hostile to his wishes.
49.51. *The sun shall go before you*] A conflation of the pillars of fire and
smoke that led Moses across the desert, with a verbal reminiscence of

Before you in night. Come on, come on, come on! The Lord
Jehovah is before, behind, above, beneath, around.
He has builded the arches of Albion's tomb, binding the stars
55   In merciful order, bending the laws of cruelty to peace.
He hath placed Og & Anak, the giants of Albion, for their guards,
Building the body of Moses in the valley of Peor, the body
Of divine analogy, & Og & Sihon in the tears of Balaam,
The son of Beor, have given their power to Joshua & Caleb.
60   Remove from Albion, far remove these terrible surfaces:
They are beginning to form heavens & hells in immense
Circles, the hells for food to the heavens, food of torment,
Food of despair: they drink the condemned soul & rejoice
In cruel holiness in their heavens of chastity & uncircumcision.
65   Yet they are blameless, & iniquity must be imputed only
To the state they are entered into that they may be delivered.
Satan is the state of Death, & not a human existence,
But Luvah is named Satan, because he has entered that state—
A world where man is by nature the enemy of man—
70   Because the evil is created into a state, that men
May be delivered time after time evermore. Amen.
Learn therefore, O sisters, to distinguish the eternal human
That walks about among the stones of fire, in bliss & woe
Alternate, from those states or worlds in which the spirit travels.
75   This is the only means to forgiveness of enemies.
Therefore remove from Albion these terrible surfaces,
And let wild seas & rocks close up Jerusalem away from
Pl. 50   The Atlantic mountains where giants dwelt in intellect—
Now given to stony druids, & allegoric generation,
To the twelve gods of Asia, the spectres of those who sleep,
Swayed by a providence opposed to the Divine Lord Jesus:

Psalm cxxi 6: 'The sun shall not smite thee by day, neither the moon by
night.'
49.58–9. Balaam was *son of Beor*: for him, and *Joshua and Caleb* see 38.37n:
Joshua's name was originally *Oshea*.
49.60. In spite of what has preceded, Erin renews her plea that the enemies
of the divine mercy should be kept away so that their evil does not con-
taminate further.
49.65–71. For *states*, and the distinction between personal blame and the
fault of the 'state', see 31.13n. The idea is very important.
49.68. *Luvah* is mentioned because, in 44.39 and 47.3 he is said to have
conquered Albion.

50.2. *allegoric generation*] 'Allegory' signifies 'a lie' to B.
50.3. *The twelve gods of Asia*] Listed in *Milton* pl.37.20ff.
50.4. i.e. a god is worshipped who is called Providence; but this god 'pro-
vides' for one creature only at the expense of another.

5 A murderous providence, a creation that groans, living on death,
Where fish & bird & beast & man & tree & metal & stone
Live by devouring, going into eternal death continually.
Albion is now possessed by the war of blood, the sacrifice
Of envy Albion is become, & his emanation cast out.
10 Come, Lord Jesus, Lamb of God, descend! for if, O Lord,
If thou hadst been here, our brother Albion had not died.
Arise, sisters! Go ye & meet the Lord, while I remain—
Behold the foggy mornings of the dead on Albion's cliffs!

'Ye know that if the emanation remains in them,
15 She will become an eternal death, an avenger of sin,
A self-righteousness—the proud virgin-harlot, mother of war,
And we also, & all Beulah, consume beneath Albion's curse.'

So Erin spoke to the daughters of Beulah. Shuddering,
With their wings they sat in the furnace, in a night
20 Of stars; for all the sons of Albion appeared distant stars,
Ascending & descending into Albion's sea of death.
And Erin's lovely bow enclosed the wheels of Albion's sons.

Expanding on wing, the daughters of Beulah replied in sweet
    response:

'Come, O thou Lamb of God, & take away the remembrance of
    sin.
25 To sin & to hide the sin in sweet deceit is lovely!!
To sin in the open face of day is cruel & pitiless. But
To record the sin for a reproach, to let the sun go down

50.5. In *Romans* viii 22 'the whole creation groaneth', but Paul's image is of childbirth.

50.10. *Come, Lord Jesus!*] From *Revelation* xxii 20; the descent of the Lamb is the subject of *Revelation* xxi–xxii.

50.11. So, at the end of *Four Zoas* iv, and as in the story of Lazarus in *John* xi from which the cry is derived, the sisters call on Jesus when no hope seems possible. Line *12* recalls that when Jesus arrived after Lazarus' death, Mary stayed at home while Martha and the mourners went out.

50.14–17. The idea that the emanation must leave the dead body or be corrupted is new here, but not difficult. It probably derives from the thought of the soul leaving the body at death. Line *16* describes Rahab, the 'state' into which Jerusalem might fall.

50.22. *Erin's lovely bow*] Cp. 48.*35*: shown in the design on pl.14, without the wheels, which appear in a design on pl.22 closely resembling *23*.

50.25. the *!!* is B.'s.

50.27. *to let the sun . . . of the sin*] Cp. *Ephesians* iv 26: 'Be ye angry, and sin not: let not the sun go down upon your wrath' (that is, do not be afraid of anger, but do not keep it burning). The source of the idea, and the

In a remembrance of the sin, is a woe & a horror,
A brooder of an evil day, & a sun rising in blood.
30 Come then, O Lamb of God, & take away the remembrance of
sin!'

End of Chapter the Second

[Design]

Pl. 51   *[Full-page design]*

Chapter 3

Chapter 3 is the most difficult for the reader to keep his bearings in, since the
narrative sequence largely breaks down. There are several narrative pas-
sages, but they do not follow a recognizable 'plot', and they are inter-
spersed with reflective and expository passages which break such thread of
narrative as there is. B.'s purpose is not primarily to tell a story, but to
display the state of evil into which Albion has fallen; to show the nature
of that evil, and to show also the nature of the hope that remains over it
all. The Preface is addressed 'To the Deists', and in this chapter there are
many references to deism and rationalism–to B. the greatest evil of his
time. (There is also much material that might be thought to belong to
ch. 2, dedicated 'To the Jews'–such as the account of Jerusalem's sons in
pl.74, the origin of the tribes of Israel: it is not an exclusively 'anti-deist'
chapter.) The chapter consists, then, of a collection of passages which are
distinct from one another but united by their general theme, and which
have a certain narrative framework.

This framework may be described thus: (*a*) Albion falls into his Spectre's
power (*54.6–32*, *57.12–16*). Thereafter Albion, and his particular repre-
sentatives (his 'sons' and 'daughters') are 'spectrous' beings, entirely given
over to evil. The true Albion is asleep as if dead. (*b*) In the unfallen state,
Albion and the land of Israel (Canaan) were one (see pl.27); now they

phrase, is *Deuteronomy* xxiv 14–15: 'Thou shalt not oppress an hired ser-
vant . . . At his day thou shalt give him his hire, neither shall the sun go
down upon it.'
50. *Design*: Against a background of moon, comet and planet, the three-
headed figure of Hand (70.4) writhes on and above a rock rising from the
sea. Other figures twist about the sky above them.
51. *Design*: L, a gowned and crowned female with a fleur-de-lys sceptre,
on a stone throne, head bent. Centre, a seated male figure, head down
between his knees. R, a chained nude male, surrounded by flames, walks
away. All are despondent: Gilchrist (ch. xxi) suggested that 'Vala' and
Hayley were depicted in dejection at the discomfiture of Scholfield (the
chained figure) at B.'s trial, when the prosecution wanted to have B. led
off in chains. (Facsimile in Keynes, *W.B.'s Engravings* pl.109.)

divide (63.*41–4*). Jerusalem is separated from Albion and, as in the Bible, carried captive to Babylon–that is, in B.'s version, imprisoned by Rahab, who is the evil form of Vala. (In ch. 1, Vala turned on her sister Jerusalem and caused Albion to drive her away.) Rahab-Vala now gains control over Albion (64.*25*). (*c*) The fate of the children of Albion and Jerusalem, now enslaved by Vala. In eternity they were the same; in the division of Albion and Canaan they too are divided, into children of Albion and of Jerusalem. The latter are born on earth as the twelve tribes of Israel (74.*31–57*). Previously, the sons and daughters of Albion have made Luvah, Vala's parent, a victim of war and sacrifice in heaven (65.*5ff*): Vala takes them in this evil act (65.*65–79*) and pens them in their error in this mortal world, where they build Stonehenge, which incorporates all their errors and fixes them in their worship of these errors for all time (66.*8–14*). Much of the rest of the chapter is taken up with illustrations of the fallen state of the children of Albion, and Los's visionary work.

The chapter may also be considered not as narrative but as separate sequences. These may be grouped thus: (*a*) specifically narrative passages, as mentioned above; (*b*) episodes, such as the conversation of Jerusalem with the Divine Voice (60.*5–62.30*); (*c*) passages setting out relationships, either in Eternity or in the fallen world, such as the assignment of the heavenly Albion to the sons of Albion before the fall (71.*1–55*); (*d*) passages describing various figures and revealing their nature, such as Hand (70.*1–16*). B. wishes to present many aspects of the fallen Albion, not a single panorama, and the reader must expect to find therefore a series of discrete passages.

Pl. 52

Rahab is an }   To the Deists.   { *The spiritual States of*
Eternal State }   { *the soul are all eternal.*
                                          { *Distinguish between the*
                                          { *Man, & his present State.*

He never can be a friend to the human race who is the preacher of natural morality or Natural Religion. He is a flatterer who

52. Heading. *states*] See 31.*13n*.   *Deists*] Deism was the universal religion popular among rationalists and free-thinkers in the eighteenth century. Its chief features were its including all the creeds as variants of a single more general one, its rationalizing of the supernatural, and its acceptance of a Creator, on the hypothesis that the universe, organized as it is, was planned and set in motion by some being. This being, however, need not necessarily concern man further. B. objects to the rationalism, to the exclusion of the wonderful from creation, and to the basic assumption that knowledge of this material world, and that derived through it, is all the knowledge there can be–thus denying the eternal world of B.'s imagination.

52.2. *natural*] Since the rationalist would not accept morality as divinely ordained, he claimed that it was inborn in man, a natural element in him.

means to betray, to perpetuate tyrant pride & the laws of that
Babylon which he foresees shall shortly be destroyed, with the
5 spiritual and not the natural sword. He is in the state named Rahab:
which state must be put off before he can be the friend of man.

You, O deists, profess yourselves the enemies of Christianity—
and you are so. You are also the enemies of the human race & of
universal nature. Man is born a spectre or Satan & is altogether
10 an evil, & requires a new selfhood continually, & must continually
be changed into his direct contrary. But your Greek philosophy
(which is a remnant of Druidism) teaches that man is righteous
in his vegetated spectre—an opinion of fatal & accursed con-
sequence to man, as the ancients saw plainly by revelation to the
15 entire abrogation of experimental theory; and many believed what
they saw, and prophesied of Jesus.

Man must & will have some religion. If he has not the religion
of Jesus, he will have the religion of Satan, & will erect the
Synagogue of Satan, calling the prince of this world 'God'; and
20 destroying all who do not worship Satan under the name of God.
Will any one say: 'Where are those who worship Satan under
the name of God?' Where are they? Listen! Every religion that
preaches vengeance for sin is the religion of the enemy & avenger,
and not of the forgiver of sin; and their God is Satan, named by
25 the Divine Name. Your religion, O deists, 'Deism', is the worship
of the god of this world by the means of what you call Natural

To be moral, therefore, was only to fulfil his own higher nature. But
nature, says B. (in the Platonic tradition) is only a distorted reflection of
eternal, supernatural reality.

52.4. *he foresees*] In spite of himself, the deist feels these things instinctively.
What follows is nothing like genuine deist thought.

52.5. *Rahab*] See *Four Zoas* viii 267n: here B. means that the deist has
fallen into the sin of deluding men into accepting this material life and
form, and its fulfilments and pleasures, as ultimate. Cp. 90.63–6.

52.8–9. *enemies of universal nature*] The very principle of which they would
claim to be friends; their vision of the universe is too narrow.

52.9. *born a spectre or Satan*] All this world is a shadow, and man born into
it is only a false shadow of his true nature in eternity. In the next lines B.
reiterates his belief that continual change, continuous struggling towards
new ideals which change as the moments change, is essential in this evil
world if one is not to be petrified into a dead, rigid nature, 'good' only to
a false and legalistic morality. What is good now will not be good in the
future; man must change—sometimes even to something quite different—
his 'direct contrary'.

52.11. *Greek philosophy*] Like all ancient wisdom, it has its supposed source
in Druidism: see 27.2n.

52.13. *vegetated spectre*] His limited existence in this vegetated world.

Religion and Natural Philosophy, and of natural morality or self-righteousness, the selfish virtues of the natural heart. This was the religion of the Pharisees who murdered Jesus. Deism is the same &
30 ends in the same.

Voltaire, Rousseau, Gibbon, Hume charge the spiritually religious with hypocrisy. But how a monk, or a Methodist either, can be a hypocrite, I cannot conceive. We are men of like passions with others & pretend not to be holier than others. Therefore, when a
35 religious man falls into sin, he ought not to be called a hypocrite; this title is more properly to be given to a player who falls into sin, whose profession is virtue & morality & the making men self-righteous. Foote in calling Whitefield 'hypocrite' was himself one; for Whitefield pretended not to be holier than others: but confessed
40 his sins before all the world. Voltaire, Rousseau, you cannot escape my charge that you are Pharisees & hypocrites, for you are constantly talking of the virtues of the human heart, and particularly of your own, that you may accuse others & especially the religious, whose errors you, by this display of pretended virtue, chiefly design
45 to expose. Rousseau thought men good by nature; he found them evil & found no friend. Friendship cannot exist without forgiveness of sins continually. The book written by Rousseau called his *Confessions* is an apology & cloak for his sin & not a confession.

But you also charge the poor monks & religious with being the
50 causes of war, while you acquit & flatter the Alexanders & Caesars, the Louises & Fredericks, who alone are its causes & its

52.31. Voltaire, Rousseau, Gibbon, Hume] All rationalists, though of very differing complexions.

52.33. We] B. associates himself with monks and Methodists.

52.36. player] 'Hypocrite' derives from the Greek word for actor. B. disliked drama: cp. 37.29, 'as at a tragic scene / The soul drinks murder and revenge and applauds its own holiness.' The two references together suggest that B. saw drama's purpose as being to inculcate virtue by example, while its effect was to leave the audience 'righteous in their own conceit'.

52.38. Foote] (1720–77) wrote *The Minor* (1760), a successful farce which satirized the Methodists and George Whitefield (1714–70), the Calvinist Methodist, in particular. Foote unjustifiably satirized Whitefield's supposed self-interested hypocrisy.

52.45. Rousseau thought men good] A contrast of Rousseau's theory of the innate goodness of man with the maltreatment he alleged he received from society. (Rousseau's answer would be that this was a society deformed by custom.)

52.48. Confessions] B.'s opinion, though extreme, is not unsupported, either by other critics or by the book itself.

52.51. Louises and Fredericks] Louis XIV, in particular, but meaning the whole French monarchy; and Frederick II, 'the Great', the aggressive Prussian King (r. 1740–86).

actors. But the religion of Jesus, forgiveness of sin, can never be the
cause of a war nor of a single martyrdom.

Those who martyr others or who cause war are deists, but never
55   can be forgivers of sin. The glory of Christianity is to conquer by
forgiveness. All the destruction therefore in Christian Europe has
arisen from *Deism*, which is *Natural Religion*.

> I saw a monk of Charlemagne
> Arise before my sight;
60 > I talked with the grey monk as we stood
> In beams of infernal light.
>
> Gibbon arose with a lash of steel
> And Voltaire with a racking wheel;
> The Schools, in clouds of learning rolled,
65 > Arose with war in iron and gold.
>
> 'Thou lazy monk,' they sound afar,
> 'In vain condemning glorious war!
> And in your cell you shall ever dwell—
> Rise, war, and bind him in his cell.'
>
70 > The blood red ran from the grey monk's side;
> His hands and feet were wounded wide,
> His body bent, his arms and knees
> Like to the roots of ancient trees.
>
> When Satan first the black bow bent
75 > And the moral law from the Gospel rent,
> He forged the law into a sword
> And spilled the blood of mercy's Lord.
>
> Titus, Constantine, Charlemagne!

52. Poem. There is a draft in the Notebook (see p. 478); and a fair copy of
a different poem, 'The Grey Monk', drawn from the same draft, is in the
Pickering MS, of about 1802–3 (p. 584).

52.58. of Charlemagne] I.e. of his time. See *78n.*

52.61. infernal] The imagery of B.'s early period, when (as in *Marriage
of Heaven and Hell*) he maintained the paradox that Hell's living flames are
preferable to Heaven's traditional immobility.

52.62–3. Gibbon, Voltaire] Both given to irony and satiric 'lashing' of
irrationalism.

52.66. lazy] The MS first reading was: 'Seditious Monk', said Charlemagne.
B. first identified himself in his own dangerous radicalism with the monk,
and Charlemagne with George III; but by the alteration withdrew the
point.

52.78. Titus, Constantine, Charlemagne] The first two were Roman emperors.
Titus reigned A.D. 79–81, but has become famous by his destruction of

O Voltaire, Rousseau, Gibbon! Vain
80　　Your Grecian mocks and Roman sword
　　　Against this image of his Lord.

　　For a tear is an intellectual thing;
　　And a sigh is the sword of an angel king,
　　　And the bitter groan of a martyr's woe
85　Is an arrow from the Almighty's bow!

Pl. 53　　　　　　CHAPTER 3
But Los, who is the vehicular form of strong Urthona,
Wept vehemently over Albion where Thames currents spring
From the rivers of Beulah—pleasant river, soft, mild, parent stream.
And the roots of Albion's tree entered the soul of Los
5　As he sat before his furnaces clothed in sackcloth of hair,
In gnawing pain, dividing him from his emanation—
Enclosing all the children of Los time after time.

Their giant forms condensing into nations & peoples & tongues;
Translucent the furnaces, of beryl & emerald immortal,
10　And sevenfold each within other; incomprehensible
To the vegetated mortal eye's perverted & single vision.

Jerusalem in A.D. 70. *Constantine (274–337)*, was also a successful general.
He favoured Christianity, but B. prefers to see him as tyrant and politician
rather than as religious enthusiast. *Charlemagne* likewise claimed to uphold
Christianity, and became the first emperor of the reorganized Holy
Roman Empire of the west. B. sees him as warlord rather than as Christian.
52.82. In this stanza the stress is on the *power* of weakness that cares for
others; B. does not merely praise the tear, the sigh, etc.
53. Design: The heading shows a triple-crowned female figure (Vala)
enthroned on a sun-flower (or sea-anemone, a form of polypus: it rises
from the sea), surrounded by mystic signs of moon and stars, but dejected.
(Reproduced in Blunt, *Art of W.B.* pl.50d.) For melancholy Vala, see
65.37–8.
53.1. Los is found mourning the fall of Albion.
vehicular form] Means that Los is the eternal Urthona as he acts in the fallen
world of the poem. This was an important element in *Four Zoas*, but is
scarcely relevant to *Jerusalem*.
53.4. Albion's tree] Described in 28.14–19: it is the spreading, rooting
product of Albion's error. Los cannot avoid its effects.
53.8. This line was squeezed into a break, after *7* and *9* were written, but
in time to be etched with the rest of the plate.
Their giant forms] 'Their forms in vast eternity'. In the ensuing lines, B.
tells of the hidden existence of these eternal forms by which Los keeps
Vision alive in mortality.
53.9. Translucent] Capable of carrying the light of vision and truth.

The bellows are the animal lungs; the hammers, the animal heart;
The furnaces, the stomach for digestion. Terrible their fury
Like seven burning heavens ranged from south to north.

15 Here, on the banks of the Thames, Los builded Golgonooza,
Outside of the gates of the human heart, beneath Beulah
In the midst of the rocks of the altars of Albion. In fears
He builded it, in rage & in fury. It is the spiritual fourfold
London—continually building & continually decaying desolate.
20 In eternal labours, loud the furnaces & loud the anvils
Of death thunder incessant around the flaming couches of
The twenty-four Friends of Albion and round the awful Four
For the protection of the twelve emanations of Albion's sons
(The mystic union of the emanation in the Lord)—because
25 Man divided from his emanation is a dark spectre,
His emanation is an ever-weeping melancholy shadow.
But she is made receptive of generation through mercy
In the potter's furnace, among the funeral urns of Beulah,
From Surrey hills, through Italy and Greece, to Hinnom's vale.

Pl. 54 (In great Eternity, every particular form gives forth or emanates
Its own peculiar light, & the form is the Divine Vision;

53.12. 'Single vision' sees animal organs as merely physical devices for
maintaining life; true vision sees them as imaginative powers. These lines
are drawn from *Milton* pl.24.58–9.

53.15. B. reminds the reader of Golgonooza: it is built just outside the
closed gates of the human heart; it is made in the midst of the dangerous
chaos; its labours are continually renewed, as building and decay was
always evident in B.'s London, as in all great cities. From it, Los watches
Albion and the Friends imprisoned around him.

53.21. thunder . . . around] Their activity surrounds and protects.

53.23–4. Albion's sons are corrupt and evil; but only in their fallen state.
One day they may be reunited with their emanations and redeemed.

53.24. This line is added in the same way as *8*, but the brackets are editorial.

53.26–7. In *Four Zoas* Enion, separated from Tharmas, becomes a shadow
weeping in the void. But the Divine Mercy prevents this, B. says here, by
shaping the emanation into an earthly female form, so that she still has
life and purpose. Cp. also *42.32–4*.

53.28. potter's furnace . . . funeral urns] This world is like a pottery, because
souls can be reshaped into eternal forms: it is a funeral urn, because here
we sleep, dead to eternity but waiting for the resurrection (cp. *11.2n*).

54.1–5 form an interjection, perhaps a reflection on the use of the word
emanation in the previous lines, but not directly consequent on those lines.
Whereas there B. stresses the personality of the emanation, here he em-
phasizes that it is a part of the Form in which it originates.

And the light is his garment. This is Jerusalem in every man,
A tent & tabernacle of mutual forgiveness, male & female clothings.
5 And Jersualem is called LIBERTY among the children of Albion.)

—But Albion fell down, a rocky fragment from Eternity hurled
By his own spectre, who is the reasoning power in every man,
Into his own chaos, which is the memory between man & man.

The silent broodings of deadly revenge, springing from the
10 All-powerful parental affection, fills Albion from head to foot.
Seeing his sons assimilate with Luvah, bound in the bonds
Of spiritual hate, from which springs sexual love as iron chains,
He tosses like a cloud outstretched among Jerusalem's ruins
Which overspread all the earth; he groans among his ruined
    porches.

[*Design*]

15 But the spectre like a hoar-frost & a mildew rose over Albion
Saying: 'I am God, O sons of men! I am your rational power!
Am I not Bacon & Newton & Locke who teach humility to man,
Who teach doubt & experiment? And my two wings, Voltaire,
    Rousseau?

54.3. Jerusalem] Recalling the image of the Bride of Christ; the emanation
is the perfect counterpart for Everyman.
54.4. tent and tabernacle] The holy places which accompanied the Israelites
wherever they went, and the source of their strength.
clothings] An emanative garment, as in *3*, fitting different personalties and
needs.
54.5. Liberty] The cherished possession of Englishmen, or so they thought:
but B. believed that liberty was a lost emanation of Albion's, sought for
but not attained. This line, slightly varied, is inscribed on pl.26.
54.6. See *47.17*. This line takes up from there, where Albion had abandoned
hope and turned away from Los. There B. shows the Divine Mercy at
work: here he shows Albion's fate as seen by those who cannot see the
divine labour. The two visions are simultaneous views, from different
angles.
54.8. memory] Unimaginative (as in *Milton*, Preface): the national traditions
of Albion are dead memory, not continual imaginative creations.
54.11. Luvah] In this chapter, B. develops the theme of Albion's association
with Luvah–the figure (taken from *Four Zoas*) of Luvah–Orc, a cruel
demon of passion and lust, whose baleful influence spreads war.
54. Design: The rocky world, surrounded by flying figures, and marked
thus, showing the unreconciled opposites which divide this world:

                Reason
     Pity   THIS WORLD   *Wrath*
                Desire

Where is that friend of sinners, that rebel against my laws
20 Who teaches belief to the nations, & an unknown eternal life?
Come hither into the desert & turn these stones to bread!
Vain foolish man! Wilt thou believe without experiment?
And build a world of fantasy upon my great abyss,
A world of shapes, in craving lust & devouring appetite?'

25 So spoke the hard cold constrictive spectre: he is named Arthur,
Constricting into druid rocks round Canaan, Agag & Aram &
Pharaoh.

Then Albion drew England into his bosom in groans & tears;

54.21. From *Matthew* iv 2–4.

54.25. ARTHUR] The semi-mythical king of the Britons, who established a
court famed for justice in the dark ages after the fall of the Roman Empire.
Cp. *Descriptive Catalogue* v: 'The Ancient Britons', where B. identifies
Arthur with the Albion of *Jerusalem*: 'Arthur was a name for the constella-
tion Arcturus, or Boötes, the Keeper of the North Pole. And all the fables
of Arthur and his round table; of the warlike naked Britons; of Merlin; of
Arthur's conquest of the whole world; of his death, or sleep, and promise
to return again; of the Druid monuments, or temples; of the pavement of
Watling-street; of London Stone; of the caverns in Cornwall, Wales,
Derbyshire, and Scotland; of the Giants of Ireland and Britain; of the
elemental beings, called by us the by general name of Fairies . . . Mr B. has
in his hands poems of the highest antiquity. Adam was a Druid, and Noah;
also Abraham was called to succeed the Druidical age, which began to turn
allegoric and mental signification into corporeal command, whereby human
sacrifice would have depopulated the earth . . . The giant Albion, was
Patriarch of the Atlantic; he is the Atlas of the Greeks, one of those the
Greeks called Titans. The stories of Arthur are the acts of Albion, applied
to a Prince of the fifth century, who conquered Europe, and held the Em-
pire of the world in the dark age, which the Romans never again re-
covered.' The Spectre of Albion is thus seen in this warlike prince, whose
deeds, through the common link of the Druids, are seen in biblical wars
also. Since Arthur was a British king, he could be associated with the
Druids: and his magician-adviser, Merlin (cp. 30.37*n*) is a figure closely
resembling the popular notion of an idealized Druid.

54.26. Canaan . . . Pharaoh] All enemies of the Israelites at various times.
In *Milton* pl.17.*12–20*, a similar group of 'rocky masses' are outward
representations of the 'cruelties of Ulro'; they also include Aram and
Amalek (of which Agag was a king).

54.27. England is another form of Albion's emanation; see 32.*28*; 94.7,*20*;
95.*4, 22*; 96.*2*. The two complement one another like male and female:
B. often associates the female with *space* and *spaces*–the home-maker, the
less mobile and active partner. The tableau in the following lines presents
pictorially the alliance of spectre and emanation of Albion in hostility to

But she stretched out her starry night in spaces against him, like
A long serpent, in the abyss of the spectre; which augmented
30 The night with dragon wings covered with stars; & in the wings
Jerusalem & Vala appeared; & above, between the wings magnificent
The Divine Vision dimly appeared in clouds of blood, weeping.

[Design]

Pl. 55 When those who disregard all mortal things saw a Mighty One
Among the flowers of Beulah still retain his awful strength
They wondered, checking their wild flames. And many gathering
Together into an Assembly, they said, 'Let us go down
5 And see these changes!' Others said, 'If you do so, prepare
For being driven from our fields; what have we to do with the dead?
To be their inferiors or superiors we equally abhor;
Superior, none we know; inferior none. All equal share
Divine benevolence & joy, for the Eternal Man
10 Walketh among us, calling us his brothers & his friends,

him: the relationships of 'England' with the combination of Albion's double emanation, Jerusalem-and-Vala (for this duality see 19.40ff); and the constant presence of the Divine Vision. These lines are like a verbal sketch for a Blake design. (Vala is not, in *Jerusalem*, normally Luvah's emanation, as she is in *Four Zoas*. Cp. 64.19, where B. makes her Luvah's daughter, thus maintaining a close relationship but permitting her to be Albion's emanation, sister to Jerusalem.)

54. *Design*: Beneath clouds of insects, the three-headed Hand, and another figure (or four separate heads), with thrown-back, tormented faces.

55.1. This page contains the history of the Council of the Eternals, in which the choice of seven emissaries is made (30ff), and which B. uses in *Four Zoas* viii 377–94 and *Milton* pl.13.14–25, in each case with variations. The main idea in 'the seven Eyes' is that the image of God–Elohim, Jehovah, etc.–presented in the Old Testament is inaccurate, not the true God, who is Christ. This image is a collation of several viceroys, sent to control the evil situation in which man finds himself–and all the emissaries proved insufficient, until Christ himself, the Divine Vision, came. To this, in *Jerusalem*, B. adds, with a tenuous link, the passage about Generalities and Particulars, 56–66.

55.2. *his awful strength*] This is a sign that something is amiss, as Beulah is the place of rest, which would be disturbed by the appearance of such a majestic being. The *Mighty One* may be Albion, who has acted wrongly– although elsewhere he is said to be asleep and cared for by the daughters of Beulah: or Los, acting in such a way because of his mission. It is not explained, nor does it matter greatly. Albion, however, is a Mighty One in the sense that he is one of the Eternals; Los, the temporal form of Urthona, does not fit so well.

Forbidding us that veil which Satan puts between Eve & Adam,
By which the princes of the dead enslave their votaries,
Teaching them to form the serpent of precious stones & gold,
To seize the sons of Jerusalem & plant them in one man's loins,
15   To make one family of contraries—that Joseph may be sold
Into Egypt; for negation, a veil the Saviour born & dying rends.'

But others said: 'Let us to him who only is, & who -
Walketh among us, give decision. Bring forth all your fires!'

So saying, an eternal deed was done: in fiery flames
20   The universal concave raged—such thunderous sounds as never
Were sounded from a mortal cloud, not on Mount Sinai old,
Nor in Havilah where the cherub rolled his redounding flame.

Loud, loud, the mountains lifted up their voices, loud the forests!
Rivers thundered against their banks, loud winds furious fought,
25   Cities & nations contended in fires & clouds & tempests.
The seas raised up their voices & lifted their hands on high;
The stars in their courses fought, the sun, moon, heaven, earth—
Contending for Albion & for Jerusalem his emanation,
And for Shiloh, the emanation of France, & for lovely Vala.

30   Then far the greatest number were about to make a separation.
And they elected seven, called the *Seven Eyes of God;*
Lucifer, Molech, Elohim, Shaddai, Pahad, Jehovah, Jesus.

55.11. that veil] In the first place, the veil of modesty; hence the separation
between persons, exploited by those who wish to rule.
55.13. The serpent] An allusion to Orc, in *Four Zoas* viib, where he is the
slave of war. Cp. also *96.11–13*, and *Milton 12.29*ff.
55.14. one man's loins] A reference to the belief that the Promise of God was
to the seed of Abraham alone, which led to the notion of the Israelites as
'chosen' and the other nations separated as inferior.
55.15. one family] Only one, instead of the true range of variety which
contrary implies.
Joseph] Sold into slavery; later all the Israelites were in bondage—a nega-
tion of human nature, as are all the deeds of 'the dead' in *11–16*.
55.20. concave] Cp. *Paradise Lost* i 542: 'A shout that tore hell's concave.'
Or a slip for *conclave?*
55.22. Havilah] i.e. at the gate of Paradise, when the angel drove Adam
and Eve out. See *19.42n.*
55.23. B. has seen disputations of eternal spirits in earthly storms.
55.27. the stars . . . fought] Taken from Deborah's gloating triumph-song
at the death of Sisera, *Judges* v 20.
55.30. separation] i.e. so to separate the evil in the lower worlds that it
could not reach or contaminate their own. For the *Seven Eyes* see notes at
Milton pls *14.42, 13.17–24.*

They named the eighth; he came not, he hid in Albion's forests.
But first they said (& their words stood in chariots in array,
35 Curbing their tigers with golden bits & bridles of silver & ivory):

'Let the human organs be kept in their perfect integrity,
At will contracting into worms, or expanding into gods,
And then, behold, what are these Ulro visions of chastity?
Then as the moss upon the tree, or dust upon the plough,
40 Or as the sweat upon the labouring shoulder, or as the chaff
Of the wheat-floor, or as the dregs of the sweet wine-press—
Such are these Ulro visions, for though we sit down within
The ploughed furrow, listening to the weeping clods till we
Contract or expand space at will, or if we raise ourselves
45 Upon the chariots of the morning, contracting or expanding time,
Every one knows we are one family: one Man blessed for ever!'

Silence remained, & every one resumed his human majesty.
And many conversed on these things as they laboured at the furrow,
Saying: 'It is better to prevent misery than to release from misery.
50 It is better to prevent error than to forgive the criminal.
Labour well the minute particulars, attend to the little ones,
And those who are in misery cannot remain so long,
If we do but our duty. Labour well the teeming earth.'

They ploughed in tears; the trumpets sounded before the golden
    plough,
55 And the voices of the living creatures were heard in the clouds of
    heaven,
Crying: 'Compel the reasoner to demonstrate with unhewn
    demonstrations;
Let the indefinite be explored, and let every man be judged
By his own works. Let all indefinites be thrown into demonstrations,
To be pounded to dust & melted in the furnaces of affliction.
60 He who would do good to another must do it in minute
        particulars;
'General Good' is the plea of the scoundrel, hypocrite & flatterer.
For art & science cannot exist but in minutely organised
    particulars,

55.33. *eighth*] The eighth, in *Milton* pl.20.47, is Milton himself, who, as
that poem shows, was subdued by Albion's errors and not fully faithful to
his task.
55.55. *living creatures*] The four Zoas; but this reference is close to B.'s
source, the four creatures who in Ezekiel's vision heralded the approach of
God, and in *Revelation* iv surrounded his throne.
55.56. *unhewn*] Crude. These lines mean: let the error of Albion's deist
rationalists be made to show its falsity in practice, and thus condemn
itself.

And not in generalizing demonstrations of the rational power.
The infinite alone resides in definite & determinate identity;
65 Establishment of truth depends on destruction of falsehood
    continually—
On circumcision, not on virginity, O reasoners of Albion!'

So cried they at the plough. Albion's rock frowned above,
And the great voice of Eternity rolled above, terrible in clouds,
Saying: 'Who will go forth for us, & who shall we send before our
    face?'

Pl. 56 Then Los heaved his thundering bellows on the valley of
    Middlesex,
And thus he chaunted his song; the daughters of Albion reply:

'What may man be?—Who can tell? But what may woman be
To have power over man from cradle to corruptible grave?
5 He who is an infant, and whose cradle is a manger
Knoweth the infant sorrow, whence it came, and where it goeth,
And who weave it a cradle of the grass that withereth away.
This world is all a cradle for the erred wandering phantom,
Rocked by year, month, day & hour, and every two moments
10 Between dwells a daughter of Beulah to feed the human vegetable.
Entune, daughters of Albion, your hymning chorus mildly!
Cord of affection thrilling ecstatic on the iron reel,
To the golden loom of love, to the moth-laboured woof,
A garment and cradle weaving for the infantine terror,
15 For fear, at entering the gate into our world of cruel
Lamentation, it flee back & hide in non-entity's dark wild,

55.62. *science*] All knowledge–the present restricted meaning developed
later in the nineteenth century.
55.66. *circumcision*] A deliberate entry into the chosen society; virginity is
an attempt to justify oneself by withdrawal.
55.69. The Seven have already been elected; but this demand seems to
lead to Los, on the next plate, as the elected one who will obey the divine
will in the fallen world. This was the voice of God whom Isaiah heard–
'Whom shall I send, and who will go for us?'–*Isaiah* vi 8.
56.1. So at 30.18.
56.3–25. Cp. 30.25–6. Los's words do not derive directly from the matter
of the previous plate; but they are indirectly connected in that they are a
comment on one part of the nature of the fallen Albion. The Eternals had
referred to the sexuality of the fallen world (55.11–16); Los speaks of the
control this gives to woman, the mother of all–for good or ill.
56.7. Thus B. associates the two significant aspects of the mother: rocking
the cradle (when the child is entirely dependent on and subject to her), and
weaving the stuff which will clothe the man in a vision of the reality of
the material world. Los is concerned that they create a true vision.

Where dwells the spectre of Albion, destroyer of definite form.
The sun shall be a scythed chariot of Britain; the moon, a ship
In the British ocean created by Los's hammer—measured out
20 Into days & nights & years & months, to travel with my feet
Over these desolate rocks of Albion! O daughters of despair,
Rock the cradle, and in mild melodies tell me where found
What you have enwoven with so much tears & care, so much
Tender artifice: to laugh, to weep, to learn, to know,
25 Remember, recollect, what dark befel in wintry days.'

'O, it was lost for ever! and we found it not; it came
And wept at our wintry door. Look, look, behold, Gwendolen
Is become a clod of clay! Merlin is a worm of the valley!'

Then Los uttered with hammer & anvil: 'Chant, revoice!
30 I mind not your laugh, and your frown I not fear; and
You must my dictate obey. From your gold-beamed looms, trill
Gentle to Albion's watchman, on Albion's mountains; re-echo
And rock the cradle while, ah me, of that Eternal Man,
And of the cradled infancy in his bowels of compassion,
35 Who fell beneath his instruments of husbandry & became
Subservient to the clods of the furrow; the cattle and even
The emmet and earthworms are his superiors & his lords.'

Then the response came warbling from trilling looms in Albion:

'We women tremble at the light; therefore, hiding fearful
40 The Divine Vision with curtain & veil & fleshy tabernacle.'

Los uttered, swift as the rattling thunder upon the mountains:

56.18. Everything is seen by these fearful souls as if it belonged to them and
their way of life alone.
56.22. *Where found*] 'What is the source of the material you weave?'–but
they cannot see that the source is in a wider world than theirs, the infinite
world.
56.26. The daughters of Albion reply: they can only see the mortality of
the people round them. They are figures from ancient British history;
hence the allusion to Merlin.
56.32. Los, 'Albion's watchman', sees that the daughters of Albion have
no vision of their own, and so he can direct their vision.
56.33. *while*] Meanwhile. 'Re-echo my song of that Eternal Man; rocking
the cradle meanwhile.'
56.37. *earthworms*] The plate has 'earthworm', but B. added an *s* by pen in
the last copy.
56.39. But women cannot bear the full light of truth, and prefer a life
controlled by their own understanding, which is limited by their earthly
female nature.

'Look back into the Church Paul! Look! Three women around
The cross! O Albion, why didst thou a female will create?'

Pl. 57   [*Design*]

And the voices of Bath & Canterbury & York & Edinburgh cry
Over the plough of nations in the strong hand of Albion, thundering
    along
Among the fires of the druid & the deep black rethundering waters
Of the Atlantic, which poured in, impetuous—loud, loud, louder
    and louder!

5   And the great voice of the Atlantic howled over the druid altars,
    Weeping over his children in Stonehenge, in Maldon & Colchester,

56.42. In B.'s own crucifixion picture (*Jerusalem* pl.76, reproduced in
Blunt, *The Art of W.B.* pl.48a; Keynes', *W.B.'s Engravings* pl.115 and
Blake: Poet, Printer, Prophet) there are no women, but one man, who is
Albion. B. suggests that the women who weep at the cross fail to see the
positive act it is; they smother the vigour of reaction in mourning.

the Church Paul] One of the twenty-seven 'Churches' or religious estab-
lishments whose pervading errors have, in series, befogged the history of
the world: cp. *Milton* pl.37.35n. Paul is well-known for believing in keeping
women in their place: but B. disliked Paul's theology for its apparent stress
on the cruel God who demanded ransom (B. would assume that *Hebrews*
was written by Paul). Paul, as B. sees him, is caught up in an interpretation
of religion which is earthbound, and without Vision; and 'earthbound' is
as much as to say that it is under the dominion of the 'mother-figure'.
Alternatively, as the Church Paul comes between Solomon and Constan-
tine, B. may simply mean 'the New Testament age.'

57. Design: The text is set across the middle of a large globe, most of which
is thus obliterated. At the top of it two cities, York and London, are
sketched in; at the bottom, Jerusalem. Above the globe, two nude female
figures float (in a kneeling position, perhaps because of the space), their
arms and bodies bent as if in a kind of dance: beneath, another female
swims or floats in the surrounding abyss. From their hair and fingers
threads twist and extend over the background, which is also scattered with
stars. (Reproduced in Keynes, *W.B.'s Engravings* pl.111.)

57.1. This text might run straight on from pl.54, or equally well from
pl.55: but certainly not from the end of pl.56. The scene here is a new one—
Albion as a ploughman driving away from the Divine Vision. The plough-
ing on pl.55 is in the hands of the Eternals: when Albion handles the plough
the draught-creatures 'madden' and overrun him (*13–14*). The phrase
plough of nations (2) suggests an allegory of Albion's desire for international
political power.

57.5. the great voice of the Atlantic] A devouring, destructive power.

57.6. Weeping] Refers to the cities, who mourn over the oppression of
Albion's children. They speak *8–11.*

Round the rocky Peak of Derbyshire, London Stone & Rosamond's
bower:
'What is a wife, & what is a harlot? What is a church, & what
Is a theatre? Are they two & not one? Can they exist separate?
10 Are not religion & politics the same thing? Brotherhood is religion,
O demonstrations of reason, dividing families in cruelty & pride!'
But Albion fled from the Divine Vision, with the plough of nations
enflaming.
The living creatures maddened, and Albion fell into the furrow,
and
The plough went over him, & the living was ploughed in among
the dead.
15 But his spectre rose over the starry plough. Albion fled beneath the
plough
Till he came to the Rock of Ages, & he took his seat upon the rock.

Wonder seized all in Eternity to behold the Divine Vision open
The centre into an expanse! And the centre rolled out into an expanse.

[Design]

Pl. 58 In beauty the daughters of Albion divide & unite at will.
Naked and drunk with blood, Gwendolen, dancing to the timbrel
Of war, reeling up the street of London—she divides in twain

57.7. Rosamond's bower] Rosamond was a famous mistress of King Henry II.
Her 'bower' may mean the ruins of the Godstow nunnery near Oxford,
where she was said to have retired. B. names a series of stony places;
London Stone is not otherwise comparable with the Peak in Derbyshire.
57.8–9. Institutionalism sets up artificial divisions; and when it claims 'this
is good' it implies that 'the rest is evil'. But true vision takes good wherever
it finds it. Note that B. disliked theatres; cp. *52.36n.*
57.12. The following lines mark a turning-point: Albion's folly over-
whelms him, and only his spectre remains active.
57.16. the Rock of Ages] Where he was laid (48.4).
57.17–18. the centre] The centre of the englobed world, which opens out
like a vortex into an outspread world such as we see around us. Cp.
Milton pl.15.21ff and *n*, where B. explains this. Here the Divine Vision
acts to 'open out' Albion's world even when it is most corrupt.

Plate 58. The scene changes again; we return to the daughters of Albion—
not the bewildered matrons of pl.56, but the cruel sportive females who
are their more usual representation. From now on, most of this chapter is
concerned with the activity of the evil elements in fallen Albion.
58.3. Street] 'Possibly a mistake for Streets' (*Erdman 1965*): or a reference
to Watling Street, the Roman road which runs through London from
south-east to north-west and is its oldest thoroughfare. B. says in the
Descriptive Catalogue (quoted in note on *Arthur 54.25*) that his poetry treats

Among the inhabitants of Albion; the people fall around.
5   The daughters of Albion divide & unite in jealousy & cruelty;
The inhabitants of Albion at the harvest & the vintage
Feel their brain cut round beneath the temples, shrieking,
Bonifying into a skull, the marrow exuding in dismal pain.
They flee over the rocks bonifying; horses, oxen feel the knife.
10   And while the sons of Albion by severe war & judgement bonify,
The hermaphroditic condensations are divided by the knife,
The obdurate forms are cut asunder by jealousy & pity.

[Design]

Rational philosophy and mathematic demonstration
Is divided in the intoxications of pleasure & affection;
15   Two contraries war against each other in fury & blood,
And Los fixes them on his anvil, incessant his blows.
He fixes them with strong blows, placing the stones & timbers,
To create a world of generation from the world of deaths,
Dividing the masculine & feminine (for the commingling
20   Of Albion's & Luvah's spectres was hermaphroditic).

Urizen wrathful strode above, directing the awful building,

of 'Druid monuments . . . the pavement of Watling-street: of London Stone' (etc.), but in fact Watling Street is not elsewhere mentioned.
58.7. Perhaps a reference to the neolithic (to B., 'Druid') practice of trepanning.
58.8. B. returns to his *Creation* theme–the conversion of eternal Human forms into mortal 'human' forms. This is, in the *Four Zoas* ii, one of the deeds of Urizen; it is also an act of mercy in Los, who ensures that the mortal form is 'fixed' in such a way that it retains some reminiscence of eternity. Both Los and Urizen appear in the following lines.
58.11. *hermaphroditic condensations*] The eternal human forms have been depraved to a fixity–a condensation–which in eternity they did not have. They are hermaphroditic because they are infertile–neither male nor female, but a useless and monstrous mixture of both.
58. *Design*: A bat-winged figure flying away from the reader. The figure is obscure, but a comparison with the water-colour of the red dragon of *Revelation* xii (reproduced in Blunt, *The Art of W.B.* pl.58a) shows that the present design is a compression of the same figure.
58.13–16. An obscure passage: B. sins against his own warnings on Abstractions. He attributes 'intoxications . . .' to philosophy and demonstration. The meaning may be (a) that scientists (a post-Blakean word) are infatuated with their labours; (b) that the thinker and the experimentalist drift away from one another and (15) oppose one another where they should, as Contraries, complement one another.
58.21. *Urizen* suddenly appears; these lines are reminiscent of, but not the same as, *Four Zoas* ii *229ff.* There he begins to build a great palace for him-

As a mighty temple, delivering form out of confusion.
Jordan sprang beneath its threshold, bubbling from beneath
Its pillars; Euphrates ran under its arches; white sails
25 And silver oars reflect on its pillars, & sound on its echoing
Pavements where walk the sons of Jerusalem who remain
ungenerate.
But the revolving sun and moon pass through its porticoes;
Day & night, in sublime majesty & silence they revolve
And shine glorious within. Hand & Coban arched over the sun
30 In the hot noon, as he travelled through his journey; Hyle &
Skofield
Arched over the moon at midnight, & Los fixed them there
With his thunderous hammer; terrified the spectres rage & flee.
Canaan is his portico; Jordan is a fountain in his porch,
A fountain of milk & wine to relieve the traveller.
35 Egypt is the eight steps within; Ethiopia supports his pillars;
Lybia & the lands unknown are the ascent without;
Within is Asia & Greece, ornamented with exquisite art;
Persia & Media are his halls; his inmost hall is great Tartary,
China & India & Serbia are his temples for entertainment;
40 Poland & Russia & Sweden, his soft retired chambers;
France & Spain & Italy & Denmark & Holland & Germany
Are the temples among his pillars. Britain is Los's forge;
America, North & South, are his baths of living waters.

[*Design*]

Such is the ancient world of Urizen in the Satanic void,

self as Lord of the Universe, fearing the apparent insecurity of the freedom
in Eternity. Here he seems to be working with Los–which is very unusual.
The scene, with a definitely evil connotation, recurs in pl.66: here it is
justified in 22.

58.23. *Jordan . . . Euphrates*] These and the other place-names in *33–43* are
used in a 'Miltonic' way–for their rhetorical effect–rather than for any
particular allusive significance, except that they radiate from, but do not
include Palestine. There is a similarity in this rhetorical effect to that of the
description of Golgonooza in pls 12–14; but this is the world of Genera-
tion–our world, not Golgonooza: hence the place-names.

58. *Design*: A skeleton, prone, amid flames. 'Such is the ancient world . . .'
(44).

58.44. *in the Satanic void*] Note the reference to CONTINUAL CREATION in 50.
The 'Satanic void' is the abyss of non-entity, a vacuum in which all life
disappears. The world of Generation made by Urizen is a depraved world
of single unimaginative vision (cp. poem to Butts, 22 Nov. 1802, p. 473,
27–30, 83–8); at least it has that little vision. Yet it has no life of its own,
and if it is allowed to settle it will petrify, die, and vanish into the void.

45 Created from the valley of Middlesex by London's river
From Stonehenge and from London Stone, from Cornwall to
    Caithness.
The four Zoas rush around on all sides in dire ruin;
Furious in pride of selfhood, the terrible spectres of Albion
Rear their dark rocks among the stars of God—stupendous
50 Works! A world of generation continually creating out of
The hermaphroditic Satanic world of rocky destiny,
Pl. 59 And formed into four precious stones, for entrance from Beulah.

For the veil of Vala, which Albion cast into the Atlantic deep
To catch the souls of the dead, began to vegetate & petrify
Around the earth of Albion, among the roots of his tree.
5 This Los formed into the gates & mighty wall, between the oak
Of weeping & the palm of suffering beneath Albion's tomb.
Thus in process of time it became the beautiful mundane shell,
The habitation of the spectres of the dead, & the place
Of redemption & of awaking again into Eternity.

10 For four universes round the mundane egg remain chaotic.

Therefore Generation must be continually stirred up, continually changed
and altered–hence the cycle of birth and death–in order that the Divine
Mercy may continue to flow through it and keep it alive, ultimately to be
awakened into the full life of the fourfold vision of Eternity (see 59.7–9).
Thus although mortal life is transient and subject to the ravages of Time,
this is part of the mercy of Eternity.

58.45. B. alters the traditional picture of a Mesopotamian Creation, so as
to remind us that the act of Creation was not a far-off event; it had taken
place at home in London–and spiritually it is important to be reminded
that the struggle against the onset of the Satanic world is present and con-
temporary. The next lines stress the struggle to create, using primarily the
materials left in this Satanic void.

58.46. Cornwell, Caithness] Both are rocky coasts, at the extremes of Britain.

59.2. The veil, as a fishing net, goes back to 23.23, which B. quotes in 2–3.
This is a slight change of subject–from the creation of Urizen in the
Satanic void to the work of Los against Albion and Vala's veil: but it is
the same theme. Only continual labour can prevent the creeping paralysis
and destruction of life.

59.5. This] The veil, which trapped and enclosed the material world–first
made by Vala for her own purposes of dominion, but used by Los in the
opposite direction–to keep evil influences out of Generation as far as
possible.

59.7. mundane shell] As described in 58.23–43: cp. 13.33n and (for Egg),
Milton pl.34.31.

59.10–21. These, except for 14, also occur in Milton pl.19.15–25. The re-
introduction of the Four Zoas (see Four Zoas, headnote, p. 288) is confusing

One to the north, Urthona; one to the south, Urizen;
One to the east, Luvah; one to the west, Tharmas.
They are the four Zoas that stood around the Throne Divine
(Verulam, London, York & Edinburgh, their English names.).
15 But when Luvah assumed the world of Urizen southward,
And Albion was slain upon his mountain & in his tent,
All fell towards the centre, sinking downwards in dire ruin.
In the south remains a burning fire, in the east, a void,
In the west, a world of raging waters, in the north, solid darkness
20 Unfathomable, without end, but in the midst of these
Is built eternally the sublime universe of Los & Enitharmon;

[Design]

And in the north gate, in the west of the north, toward Beulah
Cathedron's looms are builded, and Los's furnaces in the south;
A wondrous golden building immense with ornaments sublime
25 Is bright Cathedron's golden hall, its courts, towers & pinnacles.

And one daughter of Los sat at the fiery reel, & another
Sat at the shining loom with her sisters attending round—
Terrible their distress, & their sorrow cannot be uttered!
And another daughter of Los sat at the spinning-wheel—
30 Endless their labour, with bitter food, void of sleep,
Though hungry they labour. They rouse themselves anxious,
Hour after hour labouring at the whirling wheel—
Many wheels, & as many lovely daughters sit weeping.
Yet the intoxicating delight that they take in their work
35 Obliterates every other evil; none pities their tears,

in *Jerusalem* and *Milton*, which are not really concerned with their story.
The present lines seem to be an attempt to relate the myth of the collapse
of order among the Zoas, described in *Four Zoas*, to the myth of Albion
(*15–16*) and of the Friends of Albion. B. also tried to relate the two poems
by making Albion the central figure of *Four Zoas*, writing in this name in
the place of the unnamed 'Universal Man'. See especially *Four Zoas* vi
261–78.
59.20–1. i.e. Golgonooza.
59. *Design*: Los's daughters at their spinning.
59.23. *Cathedron*] The place for Enitharmon's weaving, in Golgonooza—
the subject of 26ff. Los's daughters are of course Enitharmon's. The cir-
cumstances may well derive from the fate of the inmates of the Royal
Asylum for Female Orphans, very near B.'s old home (till 1800) in Lam-
beth.
59.28. B. contrasts the distress felt by women in the conditions of their life
with the exhilaration they feel at their work.
59.35. *None pities their tears*] The image of Los's daughters weaving is
probably drawn from what B. had seen in the sweated labour of girls'

Yet they regard not pity & they expect no one to pity.
For they labour for life & love, regardless of anyone
But the poor spectres that they work for, always, incessantly.

They are mocked by every one that passes by: they regard not,
40   They labour; & when their wheels are broken by scorn & malice
They mend them sorrowing with many tears & afflictions.

Other daughters weave on the cushion & pillow, network fine
That Rahab & Tirzah may exist & live & breathe & love.
Ah, that it could be as the daughters of Beulah wish!

45   Other daughters of Los, labouring at looms less fine,
Create the silk-worm & the spider & the caterpillar
To assist in their most grievous work of pity & compassion.
And others create the woolly lamb & the downy fowl
To assist in the work: the lamb bleats; the sea-fowl cries.
50   Men understand not the distress & the labour & sorrow
That in the interior worlds is carried on in fear & trembling,
Weaving the shuddering fears & loves of Albion's families.
Thunderous rage the spindles of iron, & the iron distaff
Maddens in the fury of their hands, weaving in bitter tears
55   The veil of goats-hair & purple & scarlet & fine twined linen.

Pl. 60 The clouds of Albion's druid temples rage in the eastern heaven,
While Los sat terrified beholding Albion's spectre (who is Luvah)
Spreading in bloody veins in torments over Europe & Asia—
Not yet formed, but a wretched torment unformed & abyssal
5   In flaming fire. Within the furnaces the Divine Vision appeared

charity schools in Lambeth (see *Milton* pl.26.*48n*). Normally weaving was man's work.

59.42. *network*] Here perhaps meaning an ornamental pattern, embroidered or woven in. The *cushion and pillow* may have no special point; or may suggest that these weavers are weaving dreams of eternity into the pillows on which Rahab and Tirzah will sleep. Perhaps even these two may be granted a true existence!–but in *44* B. fears not.

59.55. An allusion to the free gifts to the first tabernacle, *Exodus* xxxv 25–6: 'And all the women that were wise-hearted did spin with their hands, and brought that which they had spun, both of blue, and of purple, and of scarlet, and of fine linen. And all the women whose heart stirred them up in wisdom spun goats' hair.' The Bible and B. both stress the willingness and inspiration of the gifts.

60.2. At *58.20* B. recorded the 'commingling of Albion's and Luvah's spectres'. Its effect is seen here, while the Divine Vision is still seen to be active.

60.4. *Not yet formed*] Europe and Asia; creation has not gone so far yet. Cp. *Four Zoas* viii *94–8*.

On Albion's hills; often, walking from the furnaces in clouds
And flames among the druid temples & the starry wheels,
Gathered Jerusalem's children in his arms & bore them like
A shepherd in the night of Albion which overspread all the earth.

10 'I gave thee liberty and life, O lovely Jerusalem,
And thou hast bound me down upon the stems of vegetation.
I gave thee sheep-walks upon the Spanish mountains, Jerusalem;
I gave thee Priam's city and the isles of Grecia lovely.
I gave thee Hand & Skofield & the counties of Albion:
15 They spread forth like a lovely root into the Garden of God;
They were as Adam before me, united into one Man,
They stood in innocence & their skiey tent reached over Asia
To Nimrod's tower, to Ham & Canaan walking with Mizraim
Upon the Egyptian Nile, with solemn songs to Grecia
20 And sweet Hesperia, even to great Chaldea & Tesshina,
Following thee as a shepherd by the four rivers of Eden.
Why wilt thou rend thyself apart, Jerusalem?
And build this Babylon, & sacrifice in secret groves
Among the gods of Asia, among the foundations of pitch & nitre?

25 'Therefore thy mountains are become barren, Jerusalem;
Thy valleys, plains of burning sand; thy rivers, waters of death.
Thy villages die of the famine, and thy cities
Beg bread from house to house, lovely Jerusalem.
Why wilt thou deface thy beauty & the beauty of thy little ones
30 To please thy idols, in the pretended chastities of uncircumcision?
Thy sons are lovelier than Egypt or Assyria; wherefore
Dost thou blacken their beauty by a secluded place of rest,
And a peculiar tabernacle, to cut the integuments of beauty
Into the veils of tears and sorrows, O lovely Jerusalem?
35 They have persuaded thee to this; therefore their end shall come

60.10. A divine plea to Jerusalem, resembling those in the prophets:
Jerusalem is inevitably involved in Albion's fall.
60.11. *stems of vegetation*] In B.'s picture of the Crucifixion on pl.76,
Christ is crucified on an oak tree; the phrase implies 'earthly existence'.
60.16. *Adam*] Alluding to the meaning of the name–(*The*) *Man*.
60.18. *Nimrod's tower*] Babel, within Nimrod's kingdom as described in
Genesis x 9–10.
Mizraim] Egypt: in *Genesis* x 6 Mizraim and Canaan are sons of Ham.
60.20. *Tesshina*] An unexplained reference. Perhaps B. confused himself
with Hebrew script, and meant *Shinar* (the Babylonian region): in *Genesis*
x 10, xi 2 and elsewhere the word *erets* (land) precedes *Shinar*, and it is just
possible that he attached *ts* to Shinar, making it syllabic. But in that case,
he also missed off the pronounced and spelt *r*. No other explanation is
forthcoming. Shinar is at least in the same region as Chaldea.

And I will lead thee through the wilderness in shadow of my cloud,
And in my love I will lead thee, lovely shadow of sleeping Albion.'
This is the song of the Lamb, sung by slaves in evening time.

But Jerusalem faintly saw him, closed in the dungeons of Babylon.
40　Her form was held by Beulah's daughters, but all within unseen
She sat at the mills, her hair unbound, her feet naked,
Cut with the flints—her tears run down, her reason grows like
The wheel of Hand, incessant turning day & night without rest.
Insane she raves upon the winds, hoarse, inarticulate.
45　All night Vala hears, she triumphs in pride of holiness
To see Jerusalem deface her lineaments with bitter blows
Of despair, while the Satanic Holiness triumphed in Vala,
In a religion of chastity & uncircumcised selfishness,
Both of the head & heart & loins, closed up in moral pride.

50　But the Divine Lamb stood beside Jerusalem; oft she saw
The lineaments divine & oft the voice heard, & oft she said:

'O Lord & Saviour, have the gods of the heathen pierced thee?
Or hast thou been pierced in the house of thy friends?
Art thou alive, & livest thou for evermore? Or art thou
55　Not but a delusive shadow, a thought that liveth not?
Babel mocks saying, "There is no God nor Son of God",
That thou, O human imagination, O divine body, art all
A delusion. But I know thee, O Lord, when thou arisest upon
My weary eyes, even in this dungeon & this iron mill.
60　The stars of Albion cruel rise; thou bindest to sweet influences:
For thou also sufferest with me although I behold thee not;

60.36. *shadow of my cloud*] As Jehovah led the Israelites with his pillars of
smoke and fire.
60.40. A reminder that no person is ever beyond care, although imprisoned
in evil, as Jerusalem is. Her 'form' is her eternal form, her real 'spiritual
body'.
60.42. *reason*] Her mind is trapped in a cycle of despair and misery.
60.54. Jerusalem's questionings indicate her state: she is imprisoned in the
dead world of Babylon, away from vision; although not active in evil like
Vala or the sons and daughters of Albion she is not active in vision and
imagination, and therefore she is a fallen being. Yet she has not entirely
lost the vision, and wants to appeal to it (or him) if she can perceive it
clearly. Her fate is bound with Albion's; she cannot rise of her own will,
but must wait for him to awake and leave his rock.
60.60. i.e. the stars–the universe–of Albion is cruel; yours is a universe
of 'sweet influences'. (For B.'s vision of the *Stars of Albion* see *Milton*
pl.37.47ff.) The verbal reminiscence is *Job* xxxviii 31: 'Canst thou bind the
sweet influences of the Pleiades?'

And although I sin & blaspheme thy holy name, thou pitiest me—
Because thou knowest I am deluded by the turning mills
And by these visions of pity & love, because of Albion's death.'

65 Thus spake Jerusalem, & thus the Divine Voice replied:
'Mild shade of man, pitiest thou these visions of terror & woe?
Give forth thy pity & love, fear not! Lo, I am with thee always.
Only believe in me that I have power to raise from death
Thy brother who sleepeth in Albion. Fear not, trembling shade,
Pl. 61 Behold in the visions of Elohim Jehovah, behold Joseph & Mary
And be comforted, O Jerusalem, in the visions of Jehovah Elohim!'

She looked & saw Joseph the carpenter in Nazareth, & Mary
His espoused wife. And Mary said: 'If thou put me away from thee,
5 Dost thou not murder me?' Joseph spoke in anger & fury: 'Should I
Marry a harlot & an adulteress?' Mary answered; 'Art thou more
pure
Than thy Maker who forgiveth sins & calls again her that is lost?
Though she hates, he calls her again in love. I love my dear Joseph,
But he driveth me away from his presence. Yet I hear the voice of
God
10 In the voice of my husband—though he is angry for a moment, he
will not

60.66. *these visions*] Her persecutors.
60.67. *I am with thee always*] The words of Jesus after the resurrection, turned into the singular: *Matthew* xxviii 20, 'I am with you alway, even unto the end of the world.'
60.69. *thy brother*] This seems to be Albion himself, though Jerusalem is his emanation, not sister. The allusion, and the word *brother*, come from the story of Lazarus (*John* xi), which B. uses in *Four Zoas* iv 252ff, where Albion is 'brother' to the daughters of Beulah. Pl.61 is interpolated, and the sentence as it originally stood continued the resurrection theme (62.1).
Plate 61. The theme of this plate is eternal forgiveness, expressed in a story not used elsewhere in *Jerusalem*, and not related to the myth of Albion and Jerusalem. B. rewrites the story hinted at in *Matthew* i 19, which says that that Joseph found Mary pregnant and decided, of course, to break off the engagement, quietly so as to avoid scandal. In the Bible an angel appears and explains. B.'s view is different: the angel (16) does not justify Mary by showing divine intervention, but admits her 'sin' and appeals to the divine necessity of forgiveness. See also *Everlasting Gospel* iii, p. 848.
61.5–7. The implication is clear; that B. (as in *Everlasting Gospel* iii 3–6) doubted the authenticity of the *virgin* birth of Jesus, and thought in any case that the early anti-Christian legend *should* have been true (i.e. that Mary's pregnancy was adulterous, and the virgin birth idea was thought up to make it 'respectable')–because only thus could the Divine Mercy and Vision be seen: see *11–13*.

25*

Utterly cast me away. If I were pure, never could I taste the sweets
Of the forgiveness of sins! If I were holy I never could behold the
tears
Of love – of him who loves me in the midst of his anger in furnace
of fire!'
'Ah, my Mary': said Joseph, weeping over & embracing her
closely in
15   His arms: 'Doth he forgive Jerusalem, & not exact purity from her
who is
Polluted? I heard his voice in my sleep, & his angel in my dream,
Saying, "Doth Jehovah forgive a debt only on condition that it
shall
Be paid? Doth he forgive pollution only on conditions of purity?
That debt is not forgiven! That pollution is not forgiven!
20   Such is the forgiveness of the gods, the moral virtues of the
Heathen, whose tender mercies are cruelty. But Jehovah's salvation
Is without money & without price, in the continual forgiveness of
sins,
In the perpetual mutual sacrifice in great Eternity. For behold!
There is none that liveth & sinneth not. And this is the covenant
25   Of Jehovah: *If you forgive one another, so shall Jehovah forgive you,*
That he himself may dwell among you. Fear not then to take
To thee Mary thy wife, for she is with child by the Holy Ghost."'

Then Mary burst forth into a song! She flowed like a river of
Many streams in the arms of Joseph & gave forth her tears of joy
30   Like many waters—and emanating into gardens & palaces upon
Euphrates, & to forests & floods & animals wild & tame from
Gihon to Hiddekel, & to cornfields & villages & inhabitants
Upon Pison & Arnon & Jordan. And I heard the voice among
The reapers saying: 'Am I Jerusalem the lost adulteress? Or am I

61.*17*. The words of the biblical angel are (*Matthew* i 20): 'Joseph, thou
son of David, fear not to take unto thee Mary thy wife: for that which is
conceived in her is of the Holy Ghost . . .' (*26*). B. says that Mary's adultery
would not alter the divinity of the child's origin, or its essential fatherhood
in God.
61.*22*. *Without money and without price*] From *Isaiah* lv 1.
61.*30*. *gardens and palaces upon / Euphrates*] An allusion to the 'hanging
gardens' of Babylon. Mary is here a timeless being, a type of many women,
and of Jerusalem herself.
61.*31–3*. *Euphrates, Gihon, Hiddekel and Pison* are the four rivers of the
garden of Eden (*Genesis* ii 9–14): Arnon and Jordan flow into the Dead
Sea. B. has caught the voice of the prophets who saw salvation in images
of rivers bringing life to desert lands.
61.*34*. *the voice among the reapers*] Like Ruth's, the lonely stranger. The two

35 Babylon come up to Jerusalem?' And another voice answered,
        saying,

    'Does the voice of my Lord call me again? Am I pure through his
        mercy
    And pity? Am I become lovely as a virgin in his sight, who am
    Indeed a harlot drunken with the sacrifice of idols? Does he
    Call her pure as he did in the days of her infancy when she
40 Was cast out to the loathing of her person? The Chaldean took
    Me from my cradle. The Amalekite stole me away upon his camels
    Before I had ever beheld with love the face of Jehovah, or known
    That there was a God of mercy. O mercy, O Divine Humanity!
    O forgiveness & pity & compassion! If I were pure I should never
45 Have known thee; if I were unpolluted I should never have
    Glorified thy holiness, or rejoiced in thy great salvation!'

    Mary leaned her side against Jerusalem. Jerusalem received
    The infant into her hands in the visions of Jehovah. Times passed on:
    Jerusalem fainted over the cross & sepulchre. She heard the voice:
50 'Wilt thou make Rome thy patriarch druid, & the Kings of
        Europe his
    Horsemen? Man in the resurrection changes his sexual garments at
        will.
    Every harlot was once a virgin, every criminal an infant love.

Pl. 62   *[Design]*

voices who speak in these lines are those of 'lost adulteresses' who see in
the narrative of Mary and Joseph the source of a new freedom.
61.39–40. *her infancy . . . person*] From *Ezekiel* xvi 3–5: 'Thus saith the
Lord God unto Jerusalem;. . . And as for thy nativity, in the day thou
wast born thy navel was not cut, neither wast thou washed in water to
supple thee; thou wast not salted at all, nor swaddled at all. None eye
pitied thee, to do any of these unto thee, to have compassion upon thee;
but thou wast cast out in the open field, to the loathing of thy person, in
the day that thou wast born. And when I passed by thee, and saw thee
polluted in thine own blood, I said unto thee when thou wast in thy
blood, *Live.*'
61.40–1. *Chaldean . . . Amalekite*] The Chaldeans were from Babylon; both
nations were enemies of the Jews, but no specific allusion is made here.
61.47–9. *Jerusalem* here is both woman – the redeemed woman – and the
city which sees many events pass.
61.50. This is the choice made by the men who crucified Christ.

62. *Design*: At top and bottom of the text appear the head and feet of a
horrific figure, in agony. His head is encircled by a snake and his hands
grip the rock as if he were trying to pull himself up. Between his feet a
figure, tiny in proportion, stares up with his arms raised.

Repose on me till the morning of the grave. I am thy life.'

Jerusalem replied: 'I am an outcast: Albion is dead.
I am left to the trampling foot & the spurning heel;
A harlot I am called; I am sold from street to street.
5   I am defaced with blows & with the dirt of the prison.
And wilt thou become my husband, O my Lord & Saviour?
Shall Vala bring thee forth? Shall the chaste be ashamed also?
I see the maternal line, I behold the seed of the woman—
Cainah, & Ada & Zillah & Naamah wife of Noah,
10 Shuah's daughter & Tamar, & Rahab the Canaanitess,
Ruth the Moabite, & Bathsheba of the daughters of Heth,
Naamah the Ammonite, Zibeah the Philistine, & Mary.
These are the daughters of Vala, mother of the body of death.
But I thy Magdalen behold thy spiritual risen body.
15 Shall Albion arise? I know he shall arise at the Last Day.

62.2. This is not the Jerusalem of the previous plate, but the lost Jerusalem
of pl.60, who has not yet come to the vision of pl.61.

62.8–12. *maternal line*] This is a series of women in the line of motherhood
that leads to Jesus. *Cainah*, who is not in the Bible, means 'wife of Cain';
Lamech, supposedly her son, had two wives, *Ada* and *Zillah*, whose
daughter *Naamah* was. The line died out with Lamech's children because
he too was a murderer (*Genesis* iv 19–24). *Naamah* was traditionally the
troublesome *wife of Noah*, unnamed in the Bible; she is said to have been one
of the 'daughters of men' who slept with angels (*Genesis* vi 1–4). *Shua's
daughter* was a Canaanitess, wife of Judah with three sons but no grand-
children. Her son Er married a *Tamar* (not Absolom's beautiful sister);
when he died childless Tamar disguised herself and had children by Judah,
thus continuing the lineage, which became the royal lineage and ultimately
the lineage of David and of Jesus. *Rahab* is not the great Harlot of B.'s
poem, but the shadowy wife of the shadowy man Salmon (or Salma), often
identified as the friendly harlot of Jericho (*Joshua* ii). Her child was Boaz,
who married Ruth the Moabitess. *Bathsheba* was wife of Uriah the Hittite.
She was taken by David and became mother of Solomon, one of whose
wives, the second *Naamah*, twice noted in 1 *King's* xiv as an Ammonite,
was mother of the apostate king Rehoboam. *Zibeah* of Beer-sheba (not
identified as a Philistiness, but coming from beyond the southern borders)
was mother of the renegade king Jehoash. Thus the women have some or
all of these features: they are mothers; many are foreigners and even derived
from enemies of the Jews; their children are often wicked (but by no
means all); nevertheless, they belong to the chosen people, and most bore
sons in the line (recorded in *Matthew* i) from Abraham to Jesus. The list
numbers twelve, and may be taken as parallel to the twelve daughters of
Albion.

62.15. *Shall Albion arise?*] Another return to the Lazarus theme (see
60.69n); *John* xi 23–7: 'Jesus saith unto her, Thy brother shall rise again.

I know that in my flesh I shall see God; but emanations
Are weak, they know not whence they are, nor whither tend.'
Jesus replied: 'I am the resurrection & the life.
I die & pass the limits of possibility, as it appears
20 To individual perception. Luvah must be created
And Vala; for I cannot leave them in the gnawing grave,
But will prepare a way for my banished ones to return.
Come now with me into the villages, walk through all the cities.
Though thou art taken to prison & judgement, starved in the streets,
25 I will command the cloud to give thee food, & the hard rock
To flow with milk & wine; though thou seest me not a season,
Even a long season & a hard journey & a howling wilderness,
Though Vala's cloud hide thee, & Luvah's fires follow thee,
Only believe and trust in me. Lo, I am always with thee.'
30 So spoke the Lamb of God, while Luvah's cloud reddening above
Burst forth in streams of blood upon the heavens, & dark night
Involved Jerusalem. And the wheels of Albion's sons turned hoarse
Over the mountains, & the fires blazed on druid altars,
And the sun set in Tyburn's brook, where victims howl & cry.
35 But Los beheld the Divine Vision among the flames of the furnaces:
Therefore he lived & breathed in hope, but his tears fell incessant
Because his children were closed from him apart, & Enitharmon
Dividing in fierce pain. Also the vision of God was closed in clouds
Of Albion's spectres that Los in despair oft sat, & often pondered
40 On death eternal in fierce shudders upon the mountains of Albion

Martha saith unto him, I know that he shall rise again in the resurrection at
the last day. Jesus said unto her, I am the resurrection, and the life; he that
believeth in me, though he were dead, yet shall he live: And whosoever
liveth and believeth in me shall never die. Believest thou this? She saith
unto him, Yea, Lord: I believe that thou art the Christ, the Son of God,
which should come into the world.'
62.16. From *Job* xix 25.
62.20. *created*] i.e. given material form, in order that they shall not lose form
entirely. See *58.44n*.
62.25–8. Reminiscences of the Israelites in the wilderness, who ate quails
and manna from the heavens (*Exodus* xvi); for whom Moses brought
water from a rock (*Exodus* xvii); who were guided (misguided, as B. saw
it) by columns of fire and smoke (*Exodus* xiii 21–2).
62.29. *Lo . . . thee*] From *Matthew* xxviii 20, adapted: also quoted in 60.67.
62.30. *Luvah's cloud*] This image derives from *Four Zoas*, where Luvah is
involved in a cloud of blood, the disastrous effects of his desire to dominate
Albion (there usually called the Eternal Man). Here the cloud is the cloud
of his error–his lust for power. The image is introduced here to show the
promise of the Lamb coming through the terror of Luvah's war and op-
pression, where victims are sacrificed to false gods and false justice.

Walking & in the vales in howling fierce. Then to his anvils
Turning, anew began his labours, though in terrible pains.

[*Design*]

Pl. 63 Jehovah stood among the druids in the valley of Annandale,
When the four Zoas of Albion, the four living creatures, the
cherubim
Of Albion, tremble before the spectre in the starry harness of the
plough
Of nations. And their names are Urizen & Luvah & Tharmas and
Urthona.

5 Luvah slew Tharmas, the angel of the tongue, & Albion brought
him

Plate 63. From this point the chapter becomes a series of tableaux. The
reader must not expect narrative continuity. There is, nevertheless, con-
sistency of theme. The forces of good–Jehovah, Los, etc.–are ranged
against the forces–Albion's Spectre, his daughters, Vala, etc.–who are in
a state of evil. The incidents are momentary, not continuous, and there
are many unexplained changes of scene and persons. But the themes are
always those already met in the poem.

63.1. *Jehovah*] Not the tyrant of earlier books, but the merciful god of
pl.61. There are no druid remains in *Annandale*, but a number of old fortifi-
cations remain in the region, which is a valley opening southwards in
Dumfriesshire, in south-western Scotland. Jehovah's opposition to the
court of druids resembles–probably deliberately–the scene in *Four Zoas*
viii 256–65 where the Lamb of God faces the Synagogue of Satan. Cp. also
Milton pl.32.11.

63.2. *the cherubim*] They cover the mercy seat of God; like the Zoas, they
tremble at the sight of the spectre which assumes the trappings of godhead.
At 54.16 Albion's spectre says 'I am God!'; at 57.16 he sits on his Rock as if
it were a throne. For the *Zoas* see *Four Zoas* headnote: for the *Living
Creatures* see 55.55.n

63.3. *the Plough*] A constellation: hence its 'starry harness'. In 57.12–15
Albion tried to drive this plough but it overran him.

63.5. In this plate B. refashions some older material to new purposes,
blending different legends together–the four Zoas, the Israelite tribes, and
ancient British legend. B. now tells how Albion quarrels with the Zoa
Luvah, and how, in revenge, Vala causes an eruption of wickedness and
cruelty in Albion's own land, opposing as she does so the divine interven-
tion of Jehovah. The conflict of this myth with other myths is detailed in
the following notes. At 60.2 Albion's spectre is Luvah; here they are again
distinguished.

In *Four Zoas* Luvah does not kill Tharmas: in the First Night Tharmas
withers away by his own jealousy; then 'the gate of the Tongue is closed'.
It has been suggested that lines 5–8 are an allegory of the British attack on

To justice in his own city of Paris, denying the resurrection.
Then Vala, the wife of Albion, who is the daughter of Luvah,
Took vengeance twelve-fold among the chaotic rocks of the druids,
Where the human victims howl to the moon, & Thor & Friga
10 Dance the dance of death, contending with Jehovah among the
    cherubim.
The chariot wheels filled with eyes rage along the howling valley
In the dividing of Reuben & Benjamin bleeding from Chester's
    river.

The giants & the witches & the ghosts of Albion dance with
Thor & Friga, & the fairies lead the moon along the valley of
    cherubim,

the French Revolution, and the suppression of free speech (the tongue)
by Luvah-like war-fever. Cp. 66.15.

63.6. his own] i.e. Luvah's. In 55.29 'SHILOH the Emanation of France' is
associated with Vala as Albion with Jerusalem, suggesting that B. wishes
to identify France and Paris as the modern seat of Luvah and Vala, (spiri-
tually deriving from Shiloh of old, the holy city of the Northern Kingdom
of Israel)–against Britain and London–that is, Albion and Jerusalem the
emanation and city.

63.7. Vala] In Four Zoas, and often in Jerusalem, she is the emanation or
wife of Luvah; it is Albion's sin that he seeks to make her, who is only one
element of his being, his wife and mistress. But earlier in Jerusalem, B. has
made Jerusalem and Vala twin emanations of Albion in eternity (19.40ff);
so that B. has made Vala into Luvah's daughter for convenience, cp. 29.36n.
Vala now makes Albion's insensitivity rebound on himself; the cruelty he
shows to Luvah is seen in his own land–probably deriving from the
thought that Britain's reactionary policy against freedom in France has
brought oppression to Britain too.

63.9. Thor and Friga] The Scandinavian god of thunder, and the mother-
goddess wife of Odin. Although they are best known in Norse, not English,
mythology, B. put them in Jerusalem as part of Germanic tradition, once
recognized and worshipped in England.

63.10–11. cherubim . . . chariot wheels] In Ezekiel x there is a vision of four
cherubim, with four wheels, 'And their whole body and their backs, and
their hands, and their wings, and the wheels were full of eyes round about,
even the wheels which they four had' (Ezekiel x 12). They carry the throne
of Jehovah against the followers of false religions.

63.12. the dividing . . . from Chester's river] Probably referring to the
separation of the Holy Land from Albion (cp. 41 and 27.2n). Benjamin is
given Cheshire in 16.49.

63.14. fairies] In B.'s writings usually mischievous, sometimes (as here)
spiteful They debase the beauty of the moon: B. may be confusing Friga
with Freya, the moon-goddess, in whom, therefore, the moon was con-
nected with a false religion.

15 Bleeding in torrents from mountain to mountain, a lovely victim.
And Jehovah stood in the gates of the victim, & he appeared
A weeping infant in the gates of birth in the midst of heaven.

The cities & villages of Albion became rock & sand unhumanized—
The druid sons of Albion & the heavens a void around
        unfathomable,
20 No human form, but sexual, & a little weeping infant pale, reflected
Multitudinous in the looking-glass of Enitharmon, on all sides
Around in the clouds of the female on Albion's cliffs of the dead.

Such the appearance in Cheviot in the divisions of Reuben,

[Design]

When the cherubim hid their heads under their wings in deep
        slumbers,
25 When the druids demanded chastity from woman & all was lost.

'How can the female be chaste, O thou stupid druid?' cried Los,
'Without the forgiveness of sins in the merciful clouds of Jehovah,
And without the baptism of repentance to wash away calumnies
        and
The accusations of sin, that each may be pure in their neighbour's
        sight?
30 O when shall Jehovah give us victims from his flock & herds,
Instead of human victims by the daughters of Albion & Canaan?'

Then laughed Gwendolen, & her laughter shook the nations &
        families of

63.*16.* Here and in *20* the self-sacrifice of Jehovah is contrasted with the
cruelties of the world which almost–but not quite–obliterates him.

63.*21. Multitudinous*] The self-sacrifice of God can be seen in all sorts of
places by the person who catches its reflection 'in the looking-glass of
Enitharmon', whose work is to help lost souls.

63.*22. the female*] Not Enitharmon, but the female type of Vala and
Friga, the dominating female.

63.*23. Cheviot*] The hills on the border of Scotland and England (cp.
Annandale in *1*, although Annandale is not in the Cheviots, but further
west on the Dumfries coast).

63. *Design*: A nude woman lying in the coils of a serpentlike worm (it
has segments and no recognizable head); a radiant crescent moon behind.
'Such the appearance' (*23*) may refer to this design; the rounded Cheviot
hills being seen to the visionary eye as the curves of the woman's form,
made rigid in generation, as Reuben was (30.*43*ff).

63.*26. Los*] A reminder that Los is watching all these things in his furnaces
as they happen on earth.

The dead beneath Beulah, from Tyburn to Golgotha, and from
Ireland to Japan. Furious her lions & tigers & wolves sport before
35 Los on the Thames & Medway; London & Canterbury groan in
pain.
Los knew not yet what was done: he thought it was all in vision,
In visions of the dreams of Beulah among the daughters of Albion.
Therefore the murder was put apart in the looking-glass of
Enitharmon.

He saw in Vala's hand the druid knife of revenge & the poison cup
40 Of jealousy, & thought it a poetic vision of the atmospheres—
Till Canaan rolled apart from Albion across the Rhine, along the
Danube;
And all the land of Canaan suspended over the valley of Cheviot,
From Bashan to Tyre & from Troy to Gaza of the Amalekite.
And Reuben fled with his head downwards among the caverns

Pl. 64   [Design]

Of the mundane shell, which froze on all sides round Canaan on
The vast expanse, where the daughters of Albion weave the web

63.32. Gwendolen] One of the daughters of Albion who lives by sacrifice
and power (*58.2, 80.83*). Sacrifices include not only human religious sacri-
fices such as the druids were supposed to commit, but any sacrifice of
human joy, dignity or freedom to supposed religious or moral laws.
63.33. the dead beneath Beulah] Mankind on earth, dead to eternal life.
63.36. i.e. Los thought it was 'just poetry'—he did not realize the truth of
what he saw.
63.38. the murder] That of *5*.
63.41–3. This is in part the removal of Canaan from Albion eastwards into
its present position, Palestine: see *12* above. But *43* describes not a move-
ment but an area–from east to west and from extreme north (Troy is in
western Asia Minor) to south–the area, roughly speaking, of the tribes
among whom the Israelites found themselves, the worshippers of false
gods. Since the mundane shell 'freezes round Canaan' in *64.1*, the idea may
be that Canaan, the alien land, is separated from the heavenly Albion, and
becomes our world, a foreign land to us, separated from our true home in
heaven.
63.44. Reuben] One of the characteristics of B.'s Reuben is that he flees;
perhaps because his father Israel took from him his birthright as eldest son,
saying that he was as 'unstable as water'.

64. Design: A dejected but radiant female figure (Jerusalem?) leans away
from two smaller flying figures.
64.2–5. The daughters weave the female spell which hides eternity from
man. Sometimes this appears as the physical limitation of the world; some-
times it lies in the heart of man, in his own indefinite, unimaginative
thoughts.

Of ages & generations, folding & unfolding it like a veil of
    cherubim.
And sometimes it touches the earth's summits, & sometimes spreads
5   Abroad into the indefinite spectre, who is the rational power.
Then all the daughters of Albion became one before Los, even
    Vala!
And she put forth her hand upon the looms in dreadful howlings
Till she vegetated into a hungry stomach & a devouring tongue.
Her hand is a court of justice; her feet, two armies in battle;
10 Storms & pestilence in her locks; & in her loins earthquake
And fire, & the ruin of cities & nations & families & tongues.

She cries: 'The human is but a worm, & thou, O male, thou art
Thyself female. A male, a breeder of seed, a son & husband. And lo!
The Human-Divine is woman's shadow, a vapour in the summer's
    heat!
15 Go, assume papal dignity, thou spectre, thou male harlot! Arthur,
Divide into the kings of Europe in times remote—O woman-born
And woman-nourished & woman-educated & woman-scorned!'

'Wherefore art thou living,' said Los, '& man cannot live in thy
    presence?
Art thou Vala, the wife of Albion, O thou lovely daughter of Luvah?
20 All quarrels arise from reasoning: the secret murder, and
The violent man-slaughter—these are the spectre's double cave;
The sexual death, living on accusation of sin & judgement,
To freeze love & innocence into the gold & silver of the merchant.
Without forgiveness of sin, love is itself eternal death!'

25 Then the spectre drew Vala into his bosom, magnificent, terrific,

64.8. vegetated] Vala is not here the beautiful though fallen woman and
wife, but a cruel devourer. This is a view of woman at her worst—de-
vouring and bullying.
64.13. Thyself female] As far as Vala is concerned, the chief purpose of the
male is the same as that of the female—to breed: and, further, as a mere
accessory to the dominant female. She has no sense of the genuine re-
lationship of male and female, as seen in Los and Enitharmon, carrying out
different tasks to a common end.
64.15. papal dignity] Supposed power—the real power is in the hands of
the woman behind the throne.
Arthur] See 54.25. He was a king doomed by a woman.
64.20. reasoning] Quarrels arise when people think of one another as
separate objects, the material for rational processes, not with love, as re-
lated to their own nature; when bitterness becomes impossible.
64.25. In the midst of this series of discrete incidents, this act is one of the
critical points in the poem. Albion first turned away from vision; he
allowed his spectre to overpower him, he set himself up as God. Now he

Glittering with precious stones & gold, with garments of blood & fire.

He wept in deadly wrath of the spectre, in self-contradicting agony,
Crimson with wrath & green with jealousy, dazzling with love
And jealousy immingled; & the purple of the violet darkened deep
30 Over the plough of nations thundering in the hand of Albion's spectre.

A dark hermaphrodite they stood, frowning upon London's river;
And the distaff & spindle in the hands of Vala with the flax of
Human miseries turned fierce with the lives of men along the valley,
As Reuben fled before the daughters of Albion, taxing the nations.

35 Derby Peak yawned a horrid chasm at the cries of Gwendolen, & at
The stamping feet of Ragan upon the flaming treadles of her loom
That drop with crimson gore, with the loves of Albion & Canaan,
Opening along the valley of Rephaim, weaving over the caves of
   Machpelah

                          [Design]
Pl. 65   [Design]

To decide two worlds with a great decision: a world of Mercy, and
A world of Justice—the world of Mercy for salvation,
To cast Luvah into the wrath, and Albion into the pity,
In the two contraries of humanity, & in the four regions.

5 For in the depths of Albion's bosom in the eastern heaven,

takes a further step towards ultimate destruction; he draws Vala 'into his
bosom'—he takes her, and all she now stands for, as his. In Eternity, Albion
could take Jerusalem or Vala to himself in love and delight; in their present
corrupted state the result is 'magnificent, terrific'; but monstrous and
sterile: she is bound to dominate him.

64.34. taxing the nations] As Augustus did at the time of the birth of Christ:
Reuben is associated with imperial oppression. Cp. *98.53*.

64.35. Derby Peak] A height in the southern Pennines, which now sud-
denly becomes a chasm: the allusion is probably to the underground caves
of the region.

64.38. Rephaim] See *37.12* and *Milton* pl.19.*40*–a hostile place, but near
Jerusalem. At *Machpelah* was a great cave in which Abraham, his wife, his
son Isaac and grandson Jacob with their wives, were buried. It also is in
the hills south of Jerusalem.

64. Design: An aged and dejected figure, reclining.

65. Design: A chain descends the right margin.

65.1. To decide] Although the syntax is indistinct, it seems that Gwendolen
and Ragan wish to make this decision–a rigid division between those
favoured with salvation and those of whom justice will be demanded.

65.4. regions] See *14.25n*.

65.5–56. This passage is transferred from *Four Zoas* viib *161–206*, with
additions to relate it to Albion, both as a person and as a land. The original

They sound the clarions strong, they chain the howling captives.
They cast the lots into the helmet; they give the oath of blood in
    Lambeth,
They vote the death of Luvah, & they nailed him to Albion's tree
    in Bath;
They stained him with poisonous blue, they enwove him in cruel
    roots
10 To die a death of six thousand years bound round with vegetation.
The sun was black & the moon rolled a useless globe through
    Britain.

Then left the sons of Urizen the plough & harrow, the loom,
The hammer & the chisel, & the rule & compasses; from London
    fleeing
They forged the sword on Cheviot, the chariot of war & the
    battle-axe,
15 The trumpet fitted to mortal battle, & the flute of summer in
    Annandale.
And all the arts of life they changed into the arts of death in Albion.
The hour-glass contemned because its simple workmanship
Was like the workmanship of the ploughman, & the water-wheel
That raises water into cisterns, broken & burned with fire
20 Because its workmanship was like the workmanship of the shepherd.
And in their stead, intricate wheels invented, wheel without wheel;
To perplex youth in their outgoings, & to bind to labours in Albion

tells of the war in heaven between Luvah, Los and Tharmas on the one
hand, and Urizen and Vala on the other. This war is not a part of *Jerusalem*;
even in *Four Zoas* it is a very confused affair, with the sides not clearly
drawn. Out of context, as here in *Jerusalem*, it describes the turmoil in
Albion's bosom. The notes on the passage on p. 397 may be useful; those
below are intended to show what B. had in mind in fitting the passage to
Jerusalem.
65.6. *They*] Vala, or the Hermaphrodite, and the children of Albion.
65.8. *Luvah*] At the end of this sequence (66.15) Luvah is again identified
with France, crucified (65.7) by Albion–historically France's old enemy–
when Albion's corrupted nature vents itself in war on his neighbour. Vala,
Luvah's emanation and Albion's wife, 'drawn in by Albion's spectre'
(64.25), is invoked; her reaction produces further inner corruption (65.75ff),
as the evil of Albion rebounds on himself. But Luvah is also the passionate
Zoa, and the identification with France alone is insufficient. In torturing
him, Albion's children are hurting (in themselves also) all the virtues essen-
tial to man which B. could see in the French desire for liberty, and in all
man's desires for freedom and joy–dangerous though these desires are.
65.12. *the sons of Urizen*] Also out of place here; but they can be taken to
be other children of Albion–the artificers of England giving up their
peaceful occupations when drawn into the war.

Of day & night the myriads of eternity, that they may grind
And polish brass & iron hour after hour, laborious task!
25 Kept ignorant of its use, that they might spend the days of wisdom
In sorrowful drudgery, to obtain a scanty pittance of bread:
In ignorance to view a small portion & think that all,
And call it 'demonstration', blind to all the simple rules of life.

'Now, now the battle rages round thy tender limbs, O Vala!
30 Now smile among thy bitter tears: now put on all thy beauty.
Is not the wound of the sword sweet, & the broken bone delightful?
Wilt thou now smile among the scythes when the wounded groan in
the field?
We were carried away in thousands from London, & in tens
Of thousands from Westminster & Marybone in ships closed up;
35 Chained hand & foot, compelled to fight under the iron whips
Of our captains; fearing our officers more than the enemy.
Lift up thy blue eyes, Vala, & put on thy sapphire shoes;
O melancholy Magdalen, behold the morning over Maldon break;
Gird on thy flaming zone, descend into the sepulchre of Canterbury.
40 Scatter the blood from thy golden brow, the tears from thy silver
locks;
Shake off the waters from thy wings, & the dust from thy white
garments!
Remember all thy feigned terrors on the secret couch of Lambeth's
Vale,
When the sun rose in glowing morn, with arms of mighty hosts
Marching to battle (who was wont to rise with Urizen's harps
45 Girt as a sower with his seed to scatter life abroad over Albion):
Arise, O Vala! bring the bow of Urizen, bring the swift arrows of
light!
How raged the golden horses of Urizen, compelled to the chariot
of love!
Compelled to leave the plough to the ox, to snuff up the winds of
desolation,
To trample the cornfields in boastful neighings! this is no gentle
harp,

65.32. *scythes*] (in *Four Zoas* reads *slain*). Not scythes for reaping, but blades
fixed to chariot-wheels. B. does not limit his opposition to war to the
Napoleonic wars: all wars are of the same evil nature.
65.33–6. This refers to the forced enlistment of sailors into the Navy by the
press-gang, and the bad conditions generally on board ship, which led to
the mutiny at Spithead and the Nore in 1797. These lines are an interpola-
tion into the earlier text. The phrase in 36 is traditional.
65.37. This apparent change of direction is a new appeal to Vala to devote
herself to the battle. The allusion to 'Magdalen' who will 'descend into
the sepulchre' recalls the relation of Luvah to Christ in 8.

50 This is no warbling brook, nor shadow of a myrtle tree,
    But blood and wounds and dismal cries, and shadows of the oak;
    And hearts laid open to the light, by the broad grisly sword,
    And bowels hid in hammered steel ripped quivering on the ground.
    Call forth thy smiles of soft deceit; call forth thy cloudy tears!
55 We hear thy sighs in trumpets shrill when morn shall blood renew.'

So sang the spectre sons of Albion round Luvah's stone of trial,
Mocking and deriding at the writhings of their victim on Salisbury,
Drinking his emanation in intoxicating bliss, rejoicing in giant
    dance;
For a spectre has no emanation but what he imbibes from deceiving
60 A victim! Then he becomes her priest & she is his tabernacle
And his oak grove, till the victim rend the woven veil,
In the end of his sleep when Jesus calls him from his grave.

Howling the victims on the druid altars yield their souls
To the stern warriors; lovely sport the daughters round their
    victims,
65 Drinking their lives in sweet intoxication. Hence arose from Bath
Soft deluding odours, in spiral volutions intricately winding
Over Albion's mountains, a feminine indefinite cruel delusion.
Astonished, terrified, & in pain & torment, sudden they behold
Their own parent, the emanation of their murdered enemy
70 Become their emanation, and their temple and tabernacle!
They knew not this Vala was their beloved mother Vala, Albion's
    wife.

Terrified at the sight of the victim, at his distorted sinews,
The tremblings of Vala vibrate through the limbs of Albion's sons;
While they rejoice over Luvah in mockery & bitter scorn
75 Sudden they become like what they behold, in howlings & deadly
    pain!
Spasms smite their features, sinews & limbs; pale they look on one
    another:
They turn, contorted; their iron necks bend unwilling towards
Luvah; their lips tremble; their muscular fibres are cramped and
    smitten.
They become like what they behold! Yet immense in strength and
    power,
Pl. 66 In awful pomp & gold, in all the precious unhewn stones of Eden

65.50. *warbling brook . . . myrtle tree*] Clichés of poetic diction.
65.68–71. They suddenly realize that the smoke drifting up from the
sacrifice in 65–7, emanating from their victim Albion, is taking the female
form they themselves worship; for (though they do not know it) the
emanation of Albion is Vala. So also in 5.48–50, 7.38–9, Vala rises as a
cloud of smoke from the furnaces where Luvah has been cast; and she is
Jerusalem's shadow.

They build a stupendous building on the Plain of Salisbury; with
    chains
Of rocks round London Stone, of reasonings, of unhewn
    demonstrations
In labyrinthine arches (mighty Urizen the architect) through which
5 The heavens might revolve & eternity be bound in their chain;
Labour unparallelled! a wondrous rocky world of cruel destiny,
Rocks piled on rocks reaching the stars, stretching from pole to pole.
The building is Natural Religion, & its altars Natural Morality,
A building of eternal death, whose proportions are eternal despair.
10 Here Vala stood turning the iron spindle of destruction
From heaven to earth, howling, invisible! but not invisible
Her two covering cherubs (afterwards named Voltaire and
    Rousseau)
Two frowning rocks, on each side of the cove & stone of torture:
Frozen sons of the feminine tabernacle of Bacon, Newton & Locke.
15 For Luvah is France, the victim of the spectres of Albion.

Los beheld in terror: he poured his loud storms on the furnaces.
The daughters of Albion, clothed in garments of needlework,
Strip them off from their shoulders and bosoms; they lay aside
Their garments, they sit naked upon the stone of trial.
20 The knife of flint passes over the howling victim; his blood

66.2–9. *a stupendous building*] Stonehenge; its arches are not 'unhewn', but
they are not very carefully 'finished'. Line 5 refers to the alignment of
Stonehenge with the midsummer sun.

66.8. *The building is Natural Religion*] This does not mean 'this building
symbolizes Natural Religion alone', but rather that such an evil creation
is derived from an attitude of mind, which might create many such
temples, in religion, politics, or private life. Natural Religion is not an
elegant creation of sophisticated minds, but a creation such as this, a
refuge of despair.

66.12. B. in these lines imagines the megaliths of Stonehenge in terms of
the Hebrew Tabernacle, where the Mercy Seat of God is flanked and
covered by two cherubim. Vala now sits in the place of Albion's God; her
cherubim are soulless philosophers, who stand, not as golden cherubim,
but as the frozen rocks of Stonehenge. It was supposed that London Stone
(see 8.27n) had been a sacrificial stone, and random conjecture might derive
it from Stonehenge.

66.13. *cove*] Stonehenge has at its centre a stone known as the 'altar stone',
surrounded by a horseshoe of standing stones, B.'s 'cove'.

66.17. *needlework*] Artificial, woven garments: cp. *Four Zoas* ii 267n.

66.17–21. Illustrated by a marginal figure.

66.19. Stukeley's *Paleographica Britannica* iii (1752) includes such a figure in
the frontispiece.

66.20. *The knife of flint*] The ritual knife used for circumcision was made of

Gushes & stains the fair side of the fair daughters of Albion.
They put aside his curls, they divide his seven locks upon,
His forehead; they bind his forehead with thorns of iron.
They put into his hand a reed, they mock, saying: 'Behold
25　The King of Canaan whose are seven hundred chariots of iron!'
They take off his vesture whole with their knives of flint;
But they cut asunder his inner garments, searching with
Their cruel fingers for his heart, & there they enter in pomp,
In many tears; & there they erect a temple & an altar.
30　They pour cold water on his brain in front, to cause
Lids to grow over his eyes in veils of tears, and caverns
To freeze over his nostrils, while they feed his tongue from cups
And dishes of painted clay. Glowing with beauty & cruelty
They obscure the sun & the moon; no eye can look upon them.

35　Ah! alas! at the sight of the victim, & at sight of those who are
　　　　smitten,
All who see become what they behold; their eyes are covered
With veils of tears, and their nostrils & tongues shrunk up,
Their ears bent outwards; as their victim, so are they in the pangs
Of unconquerable fear, amidst delights of revenge earth-shaking!
40　And as their eye & ear shrunk, the heavens shrunk away.
The Divine Vision became first a burning flame, then a column
. Of fire, then an awful fiery wheel surrounding earth & heaven;
And then a globe of blood wandering distant in an unknown night.
Afar into the unknown night the mountains fled away—

flint; flint implements, commonly found on prehistoric sites in Britain, are
associated with 'Ancient Britons' and thus with Druids. The *victim* is
still Luvah: but any victim partakes of the same significance. See *Four Zoas*
viii 224.
66.*23–4*. The crucifixion imagery fits the repeated association of Luvah and
Christ; and (since Albion is said to be Luvah in this manifestation) of Albion
and Christ. The daughters of Albion are like pagan priests, sacrificing their
victim to a cruel god, and it has been pointed out that Clavigevo's *History
of Mexico* (trans. 1787) describes such cruelties as these, and those in 68.*32–5*.
66.*25*. A verbal allusion to *Judges* iv 3, where the Israelites suffer under the
King of Canaan, 'for he had nine hundred chariots of iron'.
66.*38. ear*] B. has 'ear'; but note the plurals in *36–7*.
66.*41*. The references are to various visions of God in the sun: by Moses in
the flame in the bush (*Exodus* iii 2–6), by the Israelites in the desert (*Exodus*
xiii 21), by Ezekiel (*Ezekiel* i).
globe of blood] A modern, circumscribed view of the sun, a single star in an
empty universe. (But cp. *Revelation* vi 12, 14: 'The sun became black . . .
and the moon became as blood, . . ., and every mountain and island were
moved out of their places.')

45 Six months of mortality; a summer: & six months of mortality; a
winter.
The human form began to be altered by the daughters of Albion,
And the perceptions to be dissipated into the indefinite, becoming
A mighty polypus named Albion's Tree. They tie the veins
And nerves into two knots, & the seed into a double knot.
50 They look forth; the sun is shrunk, the heavens are shrunk
Away into the far remote; and the trees & mountains withered
Into indefinite cloudy shadows in darkness & separation.
By invisible hatreds adjoined, they seem remote and separate
From each other; and yet are a mighty polypus in the deep.
55 As the mistletoe grows on the oak, so Albion's tree on eternity. Lo,
He who will not commingle in love, must be adjoined by hate!

They look forth from Stonehenge! from the cove round London
Stone
They look on one another; the mountain calls out to the mountain.
Plinlimmon shrunk away; Snowdon trembled; the mountains
60 Of Wales & Scotland beheld the descending war, the routed flying.
Red run the streams of Albion; Thames is drunk with blood,
As Gwendolen cast the shuttle of war, as Cambel returned the
beam.
The Humber & the Severn are drunk with the blood of the slain;
London feels his brain cut round; Edinburgh's heart is
circumscribed!
65 York & Lincoln hide among the flocks, because of the griding knife.

66.48. *A mighty polypus named Albion's Tree*] An important blending of two
images; the poisonous, spreading polypus (see *Four Zoas* iv *265n*) and the
spreading, clutching Tree of Mystery (see *Ahania 109ff*, *Four Zoas* viia
31ff). B. was aware, in a frightening way, of the resemblance between
these images and the branching ramifications of the nervous system and of
the blood vessels. The clutch seems inescapable, the ramifications endless;
yet the wandering, searching grasp is without form or mind. The matter
is treated fully by Paul Miner in 'The Polyp as a Symbol in... W.B.'
(*Texas Studies in Lang. and Lit.*, ii (1960), pp. 198ff).
    The polypus sticks to its stone like mistletoe to a tree (55); besides this
parasitic implication there is poison in the tentacles.
66.49. *knots*] Cp. a similar passage in *Milton* pl.19.55ff: this kind of thought
ties infinite realities into little physical strings.
66.55. *mistletoe*] A parasitic plant that feeds on and may destroy its host.
Both mistletoe and oak were sacred to the druids.
66.57. *the cove around London Stone*] Cp. *12* and *13* above, and notes.
66.59. *Plinlimmon, Snowdon*] Mountains of Wales.
66.62. *shuttle ... beam*] They are working a loom together.
66.64. *his brain cut round*] Cp. *58.7n*.

Worcester, & Hereford, Oxford & Cambridge reel & stagger,
Overwearied with howling: Wales & Scotland alone sustain the
   fight!
The inhabitants are sick to death; they labour to divide into days
And nights the uncertain periods, and into weeks & months. In
   vain
70 They send the dove & raven; & in vain the serpent over the
   mountains,
And in vain the eagle & lion over the fourfold wilderness.
They return not; but generate in rocky places desolate.
They return not; but build a habitation separate from man.
The sun forgets his course like a drunken man; he hesitates,
75 Upon the Chisledon hills, thinking to sleep on the Severn
In vain: he is hurried afar into an unknown night.
He bleeds in torrents of blood as he rolls through heaven above;
He chokes up the paths of the sky. The moon is leprous as snow,
Trembling & descending down, seeking to rest upon high Mona,
80 Scattering her leprous snows in flakes of disease over Albion.
The stars flee remote; the heaven is iron, the earth is sulphur,
And all the mountains & hills shrink up like a withering gourd,
As the senses of men shrink together under the knife of flint,
In the hands of Albion's daughters, among the druid temples,
Pl. 67 By those who drink their blood & the blood of their covenant.

66.66. The Friends of Albion suffer with him, and are weakened with
him.
Wales and Scotland] Perhaps the Celts, descendants in the unweakened line;
or B. may be thinking of the dislike of these two countries for episcopal
religion.
66.70. Noah sent out dove and raven, but of course not the other animals;
B. adds them because they all hide from man.
66.74. The sun in eternity had no fixed course, and rested where he chose;
now he is bound to a changeless circle.
66.75. Chisledon] On the Downs south of Swindon, between Avebury (site
of the 'dragon temple') and the White Horse: the lesser-known hill-fort
of Barbury is not far from Chisledon, but B. may not have known this.
66.79. Mona] A Druid centre at the time of the Roman invasions; an
island, almost certainly Anglesey, but often supposed to be Man, as here.
B.'s source is *Lycidas* 54, 'the shaggy top of Mona high'.

67.1. the blood of their covenant] An ironical contrast with the covenant of
Christ; the phrase derives (*a*) from Moses, 'Behold the blood of the
covenant' at the ritual dedication of the Israelites to Jehovah at Moreb
(*Exodus* xxiv 8): and (*b*) *Hebrews* xiii 20, 'the God of peace, that brought
again from the dead our Lord Jesus, that great shepherd of the sheep,
through the blood of the everlasting covenant'.

And the twelve daughters of Albion united in Rahab & Tirzah,
A double female; and they drew out from the rocky stones
Fibres of life to weave. For every female is a golden loom;
5 The rocks are opaque hardnesses covering all vegetated things.
And as they wove & cut from the looms in various divisions
Stretching over Europe & Asia from Ireland to Japan,
They divided into many lovely daughters, to be counterparts
To those they wove; for when they wove a male, they divided
10 Into a female to the woven male. In opaque hardness
They cut the fibres from the rocks, groaning in pain they weave—
Calling the rocks 'atomic origins of existence', denying eternity
By the atheistical Epicurean philosophy of Albion's tree.
Such are the feminine & masculine when separated from Man.
15 They call the rocks 'parents of men' & adore the frowning chaos,
Dancing around in howling pain clothed in the bloody veil,
Hiding Albion's sons within the veil, closing Jerusalem's
Sons without—to feed with their souls the spectres of Albion,
Ashamed to give love openly to the piteous & merciful man,
20 Counting him an imbecile mockery. But the warrior
They adore & his revenge cherish with the blood of the innocent.
They drink up Dan & Gad to feed with milk Skofield & Kotope,
They strip off Joseph's coat & dip it in the blood of battle.

Tirzah sits weeping to hear the shrieks of the dying. Her knife

67.2. A change of vision, but not a change of theme–the cruelties per-
petrated on mankind by the perverted 'female will'. For *Rahab* and *Tirzah*
see *Four Zoas* viii *267n*. The sons and daughters can divide or separate–like
all immortals–at will: see 64.6 (similar to this) and 69.1, where the sons
unite.
67.12. An example of B.'s self-interpretation which makes his work diffi-
cult to follow. The image of the weaving women has a much wider
meaning than *12–13* suggest. B. chooses one particular interpretation, be-
cause the mental similarity occurs to him, between the women who create
for themselves lovers of a kind they do not really want ('groaning in
pain'), and thinkers who create needlessly an unhappy philosophy.
67.15. *the rocks*] Stonehenge, which they have just built.
67.17–18. *Albion's sons . . . Jerusalem's sons*] This is developed later (pls
71–4); Albion's sons (Hand, Hyle, Skofield, etc.) are 'spectrous'; Jeru-
salem's (the twelve tribes of Israel) are lost figures of history, vainly fol-
lowing a mistaken idea of God, but still trying. At 63.41 Albion was
divided from Canaan, and this 'spectrous' division of his children followed.
67.22. *Dan and Gad*] Two of the tribes of Israel, not ordinarily connected
together. This line means, 'they sacrifice the true children to feed the
shadows of children'.
67.23. Joseph's coat was dipped in blood (*Genesis* xxxvii 31), but the *blood
of battle* is B.'s gloss.

25 Of flint is in her hand; she passes it over the howling victim.
The daughters weave their work in loud cries over the Rock
Of Horeb, still eyeing Albion's cliffs, eagerly seizing & twisting
The threads of Vala & Jerusalem, running from mountain to
    mountain
Over the whole earth. Loud the warriors rage in Beth Peor
30 Beneath the iron whips of their captains & consecrated banners.
Loud the sun & moon rage in the conflict; loud the stars
Shout in the night of battle, & their spears grow to their hands
With blood, weaving the deaths of the mighty into a tabernacle
For Rahab & Tirzah, till the great polypus of generation covered
    the earth.

35 In Verulam the polypus's head, winding around his bulk
Through Rochester, & Chichester, & Exeter & Salisbury
To Bristol, & his heart beat strong on Salisbury Plain,
Shooting out fibres round the earth, through Gaul & Italy
And Greece, & along the Sea of Rephaim into Judæa
40 To Sodom & Gomorrha; thence to India, China & Japan.

The twelve daughters in Rahab & Tirzah have circumscribed the
    brain
Beneath, & pierced it through the midst with a golden pin.
Blood hath stained her fair side beneath her bosom.

'O thou poor human form!' said she: 'O thou poor child of woe!

67.27. Horeb] Sinai, where the Law was given to Israel.
67.29. Beth Peor] Where the Israelites camped before entering the Promised
Land, and where Moses was buried. The invasion of Canaan was supposed
to be a divine command: hence the *consecrated banners* (*30*). (This phrase
may also refer to the practice of consecrating regimental flags in the
British and other armies.)
67.35. the polypus's head] The creature is spreading over the whole of
Britain, as the dragon temple was supposed to do (*Europe 72–3*). The five
English towns are all cathedral cities, and as such Friends of Albion.
Salisbury Plain, the polypus's heart, is the site of Stonehenge, the centre of
Vala's power and worship.
67.39. Sea of Rephaim] The valley of Rephaim is not a sea. B. may be
thinking of the original sense of the word, 'giants', referring to legendary
giants of a past age recalled by Hebrew legends. Thus *Sea of Rephaim* may
mean 'sea of the giants', some of whom lived on the southern coast of
Palestine.
67.44. In this passage the cruelty of Tirzah is again described, this time
emphasizing her belief that she is really doing good to the tortured Albion.
She does not wish to hurt him, but she must in order to 'reform' him–that
is, form him to her own desires, her puppet. There are associations with all

45 Why wilt thou wander away from Tirzah; why me compel to bind
  thee?
  If thou dost go away from me I shall consume upon these rocks.
  These fibres of thine eyes that used to beam in distant heavens
  Away from me, I have bound down with a hot iron;
  These nostrils, that expanded with delight in morning skies,
50 I have bent downward with lead melted in my roaring furnaces
  Of affliction, of love, of sweet despair, of torment unendurable.
  My soul is seven furnaces; incessant roars the bellows
  Upon my terribly flaming heart, the molten metal runs
  In channels through my fiery limbs. O love! O pity! O fear!
55 O pain! O the pangs, the bitter pangs of love forsaken!
  Ephraim was a wilderness of joy where all my wild beasts ran;
  The River Kanah wandered by my sweet Manasseh's side
  To see the boy spring into heavens sounding from my sight.
  Go, Noah, fetch the girdle of strong brass, heat it red-hot:
60 Press it around the loins of this ever-expanding cruelty.
  Shriek not so, my only love! I refuse thy joys, I drink
  Thy shrieks, because Hand & Hyle are cruel & obdurate to me.

[Design]

Pl. 68 Skofield, why art thou cruel? Lo, Joseph is thine—to make
  You one, to weave you both in the same mantle of skin.
  Bind him down, sisters, bind him down on Ebal, mount of cursing.
  Mahlah, come forth from Lebanon, & Hoglah from Mount Sinai:
5 Come, circumscribe this tongue of sweets; & with a screw of iron
  Fasten this ear into the rock! Milcah, the task is thine.
  Weep not so, sisters! weep not so! our life depends on this:
  Or mercy & truth are fled from away Shechem & Mount Gilead,

female dominion: and with the circumscription of the immortal soul in a
mortal universe. The passage that follows (*44–50, 52–61a, 68.3–9*) is also
found in and is the source of *Four Zoas* viii *287–309*.

67.56–7. Ephraim, Kanah, Manasseh] Place-names in Israel, Kanah being
part of the border between the other two. All are personified.

67.59. Noah] A sister of the biblical Tirzah (*Numbers* xxvi 33), as were
Mahlah, Hoglah and Milcah in 68.4–6 below.

67. Design: A victim racked out by chains on his feet and wrists.

68.2. Of course, this is not the way to make two beings one; souls may
unite in the bliss of eternity (cp. 34.*16* and 66.*56*).

68.3. Ebal] Scene of a comprehensive ritual curse: cp. *Four Zoas* viii *303n*
and *Deuteronomy* xxvii 4–13.

68.4. Lebanon . . . Sinai] North and south of Palestine respectively.

68.8. Shechem . . . Gilead] Cp. *Four Zoas* viii *308n*. These were places–a
town and a mountain–at about the same latitude, on opposite sides of
Jordan, and in Manasseh's land.

Unless my beloved is bound upon the stems of vegetation.'

10 And thus the warriors cry, in the hot day of victory, in songs:

'Look, the beautiful daughter of Albion sits naked upon the stone,
Her panting victim beside her; her heart is drunk with blood
Though her brain is not drunk with wine. She goes forth from Albion
In pride of beauty, in cruelty of holiness, in the brightness
15 Of her tabernacle, & her ark & secret place. The beautiful daughter
Of Albion delights the eyes of the kings; their hearts & the
Hearts of their warriors glow hot before Thor & Friga. O Molech!
O Chemosh! O Bacchus! O Venus! O double god of generation!
The heavens are cut like a mantle around from the cliffs of Albion
20 Across Europe; across Africa; in howling & deadly war
A sheet & veil & curtain of blood is let down from heaven,
Across the hills of Ephraim & down Mount Olivet to
The valley of the Jebusite. Molech rejoices in heaven;
He sees the twelve daughters naked upon the twelve stones,
25 Themselves condensing to rocks & into the ribs of a man.
Lo! they shoot forth in tender nerves across Europe & Asia:
Lo! they rest upon the tribes, where their panting victims lie.
Molech rushes into the kings in love to the beautiful daughters,
But they frown & delight in cruelty, refusing all other joy—
30 Bring your offerings, you first-begotten, pampered with milk &
        blood;
Your first-born of seven years old, be they males or females,
To the beautiful daughters of Albion! they sport before the kings
Clothed in the skin of the victim! blood, human blood is the life
And delightful food of the warrior! the well-fed warrior's flesh
35 Of him who is slain in war fills the valleys of Ephraim with
Breeding women, walking in pride & bringing forth under green
        trees
With pleasure, without pain; for their food is blood of the captive!
Molech rejoices through the land from Havilah to Shur: he rejoices

68.*17–18*. *Molech . . . Chemosh*] Gods worshipped by the sacrifice of
children. By the association with Bacchus and Venus, and by *30ff*, B.
associates their cruelty with sexual repression.
68.*18*. *double god of generation*] In 1 *Kings* xi 7 Molech and Chemosh are
closely associated, and some scholars identified the two as one.
68.*23*. *The valley of the Jebusite*] Jerusalem, or rather a valley approaching it.
68.*38*. *Molech rejoices*] Because he can win love (cp. *28*) by slaughter.
68.*38 from Havilah to Shur*] The phrase occurs in *Genesis* xxv 18, of the
Ishmaelites, the outcast tribes, who 'dwelt from Havilah unto Shur, that
is before Egypt, as thou goest toward Assyria'. Shur was somewhere south
of Palestine: the phrase means 'from far north-east to far south-west'.

In moral law & its severe penalties: loud Shaddai & Jehovah
40 Thunder above, when they see the twelve panting victims
On the twelve stones of power, & the beautiful daughters of Albion
(If you dare rend their veil with your spear you are healed of
    love!)
From the hills of Camberwell & Wimbledon, from the valleys
Of Walton & Esher, from Stonehenge & from Maldon's cove
45 Jerusalem's pillars fall in the rendings of fierce war
Over France & Germany, upon the Rhine & Danube.
Reuben & Benjamin flee; they hide in the Valley of Rephaim—
Why trembles the warrior's limbs when he beholds thy beauty
Spotted with victim's blood, by the fires of thy secret tabernacle
50 And thy ark & holy place? At thy frowns, at thy dire revenge
Smitten as Uzzah of old, his armour is softened; his spear
And sword faint in his hand, from Albion across Great Tartary—
O beautiful daughter of Albion, cruelty is thy delight;
O virgin of terrible eyes, who dwellest by valleys of springs
55 Beneath the mountains of Lebanon, in the city of Rehob in Hamath;
Taught to touch the harp, to dance in the circle of warriors
Before the kings of Canaan; to cut the flesh from the victim,
To roast the flesh in fire; to examine the infant's limbs
In cruelties of holiness; to refuse the joys of love; to bring
60 The spies from Egypt, to raise jealousy in the bosoms of the twelve

68.39. Shaddai and Jehovah] Two of the Seven Eyes of God (*55.30–3*). They
'thunder' against the activities of the twelve daughters, but are unable to
prevent them.

68.41. twelve stones of power] The twelve sacrificial stones of *28.21*.

68.42. For the mingling of sexual and religious symbolism, see *44.33n*,
34–40n. This passage adds the element of war.

68.43–4. Camberwell, Wimbledon, Walton, Esher] See map on p. *575*. They
are respectively east, south, west and north-east of London. *Stonehenge*
and *Maldon* are west and east. Maldon has no cove; but it is on the sea,
though the land is very flat. The disasters of *43–7* arise from man's de-
pendence on woman and his brutal carrying-out of her brutal demands.

68.49. thy] The daughter of Albion's.

68.51. Uzzah] Struck dead because, when the oxen drawing the ark of
God stumbled, he touched the ark to steady it (*2 Samuel* vi 3–7).

68.55. Rehob in Hamath] A town or district in Syria, otherwise Beth-
Rehob. B. errs in thinking it was in Hamath, which was a hundred miles
to the north. He takes his notion from *Numbers* xiii 21, where the spies
Joshua and Caleb are said to have surveyed the whole land as far as 'Rehob,
as men come to [on the way to] Hamath'.

68.58. To examine the infant's limbs] To make sure that the child is flawless
for the sacrifice.

Kings of Canaan, then to let the spies depart to Meribah Kadesh,
To the place of the Amalekite—I am drunk with unsatiated love;
I must rush again to war; for the virgin has frowned & refused.
Sometimes I curse, & sometimes bless thy fascinating beauty.
65 Once man was occupied in intellectual pleasures & energies,
But now my soul is harrowed with grief & fear & love & desire;
And now I hate & now I love, & intellect is no more;
There is no time for anything but the torments of love & desire.
The feminine & masculine shadows soft, mild & every-varying
70 In beauty, are shadows now no more, but rocks in Horeb.'

Pl. 69 Then all the males combined into one male, & every one
Became a ravening eating cancer growing in the female,
A polypus of roots of reasoning, doubts, despair & death,
Going forth & returning from Albion's rocks to Canaan,
5 Devouring Jerusalem from every nation of the earth.

Envying stood the enormous form, at variance with itself
In all its members, in eternal torment of love & jealousy,
Driven forth by Los time after time from Albion's cliffy shore,
Drawing the free loves of Jerusalem into infernal bondage,
10 That they might be born in contentions of chastity, & in
Deadly hate between Leah & Rachel, daughters of deceit & fraud,

68.61. *Meribah Kadesh*] The place in the wilderness where the Israelites
were encamped when they sent out the spies Caleb, et al. (*Numbers* xiii), who
looked over the land right up to Rehob: for their lack of faith the Israelites
were then condemned to a further forty years' wandering.
68.67. *now . . . love*] A famous quotation from Catullus, *Carmen* 85, 'Odi et
amo', available to B. in many translations, imitations and allusions.
68.70. *rocks in Horeb*] The place of the Law.

69.1. *combined*] Or 'conjoined'; B. tried both. The previous plates have
dealt with the evil nature of the daughters of Albion, both as a group of
twelve and as united: pls 69–70 deal with the sons of Albion, united into
one; first as a polypus, then as the three-headed giant Hand.
69.3. *polypus*] See 15.2n and *Four Zoas* iv 265n. The name *polypus* was given
to a form of cancer, chiefly found in the nose, which ramifies in a way that
somewhat resembles the growth of the marine hydroid species.
69.6. *at variance*] This contrasts with the unity of the human form, in
eternity, which may also be composed of many elements, but they are all
at one with one another.
69.10. Destroying the unlimited love of eternity by imposing the con-
straints of chastity upon it, as told in the following lines.
69.11. *Leah and Rachel*] The two wives of Jacob; daughters of Laban, who
tricked Jacob into serving seven years for the less attractive Leah, so that
he had to serve another seven for the desirable Rachel. Thereafter a rivalry
grew up between the sisters for the attentions of Jacob (*Genesis* xxix–xxx),

Bearing the images of various species of contention,
And jealousy & abhorrence & revenge & deadly murder;
Till they refuse liberty to the male, & not like Beulah
15 Where every female delights to give her maiden to her husband.
(The female searches sea & land for gratifications to the
Male genius, who in return clothes her in gems & gold
And feeds her with the food of Eden. Hence all her beauty beams;
She creates at her will a little moony night & silence
20 With spaces of sweet gardens & a tent of elegant beauty,
Closed in by a sandy desert & a night of stars shining,
And a little tender moon & hovering angels on the wing.
And the male gives a time & revolution to her space
Till the time of love is passed in ever-varying delights—
25 For all things exist in the human imagination)
And thence in Beulah they are stolen by secret amorous theft,
Till they have had punishment enough to make them commit
      crimes.
Hence rose the Tabernacle in the wilderness & all its offerings,
From male & female loves in Beulah & their jealousies;
30 But no one can consummate female bliss in Los's world without
Becoming a generated mortal, a vegetating death.

And now the spectres of the dead awake in Beulah. All
The jealousies become murderous, uniting together in Rahab,
A religion of chastity, forming a commerce to sell loves,
35 With moral law, an equal balance, not going down with decision.
Therefore the male, severe & cruel, filled with stern revenge,
Mutual hate returns, & mutual deceit & mutual fear.

Hence the infernal veil grows in the disobedient female—
Which Jesus rends & the whole druid law removes away
40 From the inner sanctuary—a false holiness hid within the centre
For the sanctuary of Eden is in the camp, in the outline,

so that, rather than see him beget children on the other, each of them gave
her servant-girl to him during a period of barrenness. This B. contrasts
with his picture of Beulah (*14ff*). The rest of the plate is something of a
digression, returning to Hand at *70.1*.
69.25-6. The brackets are editorial; but it seems that *14*b-*25* are a paren-
thesis, and that 'they' of *26-7* refers back to *9-10*. The male is 'punished'
and, repressed, creates a religion of repression. See 68.*42n*.
69.32. *Beulah*] A twilight land, a place where those who cannot bear the
full force of Eden may rest—and so open to infection from Ulro. Although
Beulah is also the land of the compassionate spirits who watch over fallen
spirits on behalf of the Divine Vision, this danger is always present, for if
the sleeping spirits awake unhealed they may run wild.
69.41. *is in the camp, in the outline*] i.e. is not a separated and 'Secret Place'
26+B.

In the circumference, & every minute particular is holy.
Embraces are comminglings from the head even to the feet,
And not a pompous High Priest entering by a Secret Place.

45　(Jerusalem pined in her inmost soul over wandering Reuben,
As she slept in Beulah's night hid by the daughters of Beulah.)

[*Design*]

Pl. 70 And this the form of mighty Hand sitting on Albion's cliffs
Before the face of Albion, a mighty threatening form:

His bosom wide & shoulders huge, overspreading, wondrous,
Bear three strong sinewy necks & three awful & terrible heads,
5　Three brains in contradictory council brooding incessantly.
Neither daring to put in act its councils, fearing each other,
Therefore rejecting ideas as nothing, & holding all wisdom
To consist in the agreements & disagreements of ideas,
Plotting to devour Albion's body of humanity & love.

10　Such form the aggregate of the twelve sons of Albion took, & such
Their appearance when combined: but often by birth-pangs and
　　loud groans
They divide to twelve; the key-bones & the chest dividing in pain

which the ordinary person may not enter, but an outside place, open to
everyone; not one little room, but everywhere is holy–'every minute
particular'. The tabernacle in the wilderness was surrounded by the camps
of the tribes, but remained a Holy Place distinct from the camp.
69.44. See 44.33n, 34n.
69.45. *the wandering Reuben*] A suggestion that B. thought of Reuben as
the Wandering Jew, doomed always to travel, never to rest. (The Wander-
ing Jew, however, is never connected with the disinherited Reuben; his
name is sometimes given as Joseph.)
69. *Design*: Two daughters of Albion dance round him.
70.1. *Hand*] One of the sons of Albion, but also (*10*) the form which they
take when united as one being. He is three-headed because B. took the
idea of Hand, the enemy of vision, from the three brothers Hunt (Robert,
John and Leigh) who produced the journal *The Examiner*. (There were
other brothers, but only these three were involved.) Hand is illustrated on
pl.50: see also headnote, p. 624.
70.4. See 69.6n.
70.10–16. These lines associate almost all the evils B. saw in Albion: the
philistinism of *The Examiner*; the evils represented by the twelve sons of
Albion; the rationalism of Bacon, Newton and Locke; the religious op-
pression and deceit of priesthoods. The oak groves of *16* are seen, in
another manner, as the huge stone trilithon of the design beneath: both
'overspread all the earth'.

Disclose a hideous orifice. Thence issuing, the giant-brood
Arise as the smoke of the furnace, shaking the rocks from sea to sea.
15 And there they combine into three forms, named Bacon & Newton
      & Locke,
In the oak groves of Albion which overspread all the earth.

[*Design*]

Imputing sin & righteousness to individuals, Rahab
Sat, deep within him hid—his feminine power unrevealed,
Brooding abstract philosophy, to destroy imagination, the Divine
20 Humanity; a threefold wonder—feminine, most beautiful; threefold
Each within other. On her white marble & even neck, her heart
Inorbed and bonified, with locks of shadowing modesty, shining
Over her beautiful female features, soft flourishing in beauty,
Beams mild, all love and all perfection, that when the lips
25 Receive a kiss from gods or men, a threefold kiss returns
From the pressed loveliness; so her whole immortal form threefold
Threefold embrace returns, consuming lives of gods & men;
In fires of beauty melting them, as gold & silver in the furnace.
Her brain enlabyrinths the whole heaven of her bosom & loins
30 To put in act what her heart wills—Oh, who can withstand her
      power?
Her name is Vala in Eternity; in time, her name is Rahab.

The starry heavens all were fled from the mighty limbs of Albion.

70. *Design* (covering half the page): A huge trilithon, five or six times as
high as the three figures who pass on the road beneath it. It overshadows
the countryside seen behind it, and a new moon is seen through its arch:
a visual image of the massive-shouldered giant Hand: cp. 63. *design. n.*
Reproduced in Blunt, *Art of W.B.* pl.48b; Keynes, *W.B.'s Engravings*,
frontispiece; (in colour) Keynes, *W.B., Poet, Printer, Prophet.*)
70.17. *Rahab*] The evil feminine harlot-principle controls the evil masculine
principle, although she is unseen. In this fallen world, Rahab rules all.
Cp. 64.25; the same theme appears in *Four Zoas* viii 576, where Rahab-
Vala conquers, and *Milton* pl.38.23–7; where she rules Satan from within.
70.27. *consuming*] The significant word.
70.31. *Vala*] Her name in B.'s myth of Eden and Ulro: in this world, the
reader knows her as the Harlot of *Revelation*; B. forgets that the naming of
that harlot as Rahab was his doing.
70.32. This line states the utter downfall of Albion (repeated as the last line
of the chapter, 75.27): he has lost his universality and become a single, self-
centred being: all the elements that should form parts of his being are now
externalized. The catchword *And* is altered from 'His': perhaps the text
of pl.19 was once intended to follow.

Pl. 71 And above Albion's land was seen the heavenly Canaan
        As the substance is to the shadow; and above Albion's twelve sons
        Were seen Jerusalem's sons, and all the twelve tribes spreading
        Over Albion. As the soul is to the body, so Jerusalem's sons
    5   Are to the sons of Albion: and Jerusalem is Albion's emanation.

        (What is above is within, for everything in Eternity is translucent:
        The circumference is within: without, is formed the selfish centre,
        And the circumference still expands, going forward to Eternity.
        And the centre has eternal states. These states we now explore.)

    10 And these the names of Albion's twelve sons, & of his twelve
            daughters
        With their districts. Hand dwelt in Selsey & had Sussex & Surrey
        And Kent & Middlesex, all their rivers & their hills of flocks &
            herds;
        Their villages, towns, cities, sea-ports, temples, sublime cathedrals;
        All were his friends, & their sons & daughters intermarry in Beulah.
    15 For all are men in Eternity; rivers, mountains, cities, villages,
        All are human; & when you enter into their bosoms you walk
        In heavens & earths, as in your own bosom you bear your heaven
        And earth; & all you behold, though it appears without it is within,
        In your imagination of which this world of mortality is but a
            shadow.

    20 Hyle dwelt in Winchester, comprehending Hampshire, Dorset,
            Devon, Cornwall;
        Their villages, cities, sea-ports, their cornfields & gardens, spacious

71.1–55. This passage refers back to 63.41–5, where the mortal and im-
mortal forms of Albion have separated, and describes the lost ideal.
71.6. B. associates the 'heavenly' (traditionally and in 1–3 'above') with
that 'within' the heart, and also – though paradoxically – with the outward-
looking 'circumference'. The selfish introspective heart encases itself in a
hard shell, and has no outward-facing circumference. Cp. 12.55n and 18.2:
B. is not altogether sure about the meanings of these terms.
71.9. The following passage describes in detail the association envisaged in 1,
and the original state of Albion in the perfection of eternity. The schematic
appearance of the whole should not cause the important and often beautiful
passages, interspersed in the list of countries, to be overlooked. B. has made
two slips. Wiltshire and Staffordshire are both named twice (26, 42; 34,
44), Lancashire not at all.
71.11. Hand . . . Selsey] Hand is the worst, the ringleader, yet Selsey
(36.48) is the type of self-sacrifice.
71.15–19. This passage, taken with 34.14–22, shows B.'s vision of the
Eternity and Infinity in which material limitations are forgotten.
71.20. Hyle . . . Winchester] 'Hyle' derives from 'Hayley', the self-satisfied
intellectual; Winchester, Alfred's centre of learning, has a famous school.

Palaces, rivers & mountains. And between Hand & Hyle arose
Gwendolen, & Cambel who is Boadicea; they go abroad & return
Like lovely beams of light from the mingled affections of the
brothers.
25 The inhabitants of the whole earth rejoice in their beautiful light.

Coban dwelt in Bath: Somerset, Wiltshire, Gloucestershire
Obeyed his awful voice; Ignoge is his lovely emanation;
She adjoined with Gwantok's children. Soon lovely Cordella arose.
Gwantok forgave & joyed over South Wales & all its mountains.

30 Peachey had North Wales, Shropshire, Cheshire & the Isle of Man.
His emanation is Mehetabel, terrible & lovely upon the
mountains.

Brereton had Yorkshire, Durham, Westmorland, & his emanation
Is Ragan; she adjoined to Slayd, & produced Gonorill far-beaming.

Slayd had Lincoln, Stafford, Derby, Nottingham, & his lovely
35 Emanation Gonorill rejoices over hills & rocks & woods & rivers.

Huttn had Warwick, Northampton, Bedford, Buckingham,
Leicester & Berkshire; & his emanation is Gwinefred beautiful.

Skofield had Ely, Rutland, Cambridge, Huntingdon, Norfolk,
Suffolk, Hertford & Essex: & his emanation is Gwineverra
40 Beautiful. She beams towards the east, all kinds of precious stones
And pearl, with instruments of music in holy Jerusalem.

Kox had Oxford, Warwick, Wilts: his emanation is Estrild;
Joined with Cordella she shines southward over the Atlantic.

Kotope had Hereford, Stafford, Worcester, & his emanation
45 Is Sabrina; joined with Mehetabel she shines west over America.

Bowen had all Scotland, the Isles, Northumberland & Cumberland;
His emanation is Conwenna, she shines a triple form
Over the north with pearly beams gorgeous & terrible;
Jerusalem & Vala rejoice in Bowen & Conwenna.

[Design]

50 But the four sons of Jerusalem that never were generated

71.23. At 80.58 Cambel is said to be Hand's counterpart, and at 80.67
Gwendolen is Hyle's.
71. Design: A narrow strip, showing a dejected, reclining female figure on
the right, and a swan on the left with its neck stretched along the ground,
its beak touching her foot, and its wings lifted.
71.50. In Milton pls 23.62–24.13 Los has sixteen sons; twelve leave him for
mortality and become the tribes of Israel 'in generation'. The four who

Are Rintrah and Palamabron and Theotormon and Bromion. They
Dwell over the four provinces of Ireland in heavenly light,
The four universities of Scotland, & in Oxford & Cambridge and
Winchester.

But now Albion is darkened & Jerusalem lies in ruins,
55   Above the mountains of Albion, above the head of Los.

And Los shouted with ceaseless shoutings & his tears poured down
His immortal cheeks, rearing his hands to heaven for aid divine.
But he spoke not to Albion, fearing lest Albion should turn his back
Against the Divine Vision, & fall over the precipice of eternal
       death.
60   But he receded before Albion & before Vala weaving the veil
With the iron shuttle of war among the rooted oaks of Albion,
Weeping & shouting to the Lord day & night, & his children
Wept round him as a flock, silent seven days of Eternity.

Pl. 72   And the thirty-two counties of the four provinces of Ireland
Are thus divided: the four counties are in the four camps—
Munster south in Reuben's gate, Connaught west in Joseph's gate,
Ulster north in Dan's gate, Leinster east in Judah's gate.

5   For Albion in Eternity has sixteen gates among his pillars,
But the four towards the west were walled up, & the twelve

are left are those here called 'sons of Jerusalem'—which is unusual, as they
are more often given to Los (cp. 15.22). The twelve sons of Albion are
'spectrous' forms of the twelve tribes, however, and this would lead B. to
shift the whole group from Los to Albion and Jerusalem. See 72.12.

71.53. The four Scottish universities were St Andrew's, Glasgow, Aber-
deen and Edinburgh.

71.56–63. Los ... spoke not] Perhaps deriving from B.'s choice not to attack
the political and social evils of Albion too openly. Los's work from here on
is to create forms from chaos and enliven them continually by imagination.
See 72.29ff, 73.29ff.

72.1. This reverts to the theme which was left at 71.52; the association of
places in Britain with spiritual figures. Here B. takes up in detail the divi-
sions of Ireland. These passages are evidently inspired by the geneological
lists of the Old Testament.

72.2. the four camps] The four camps into which the Israelites were divided
on their march through the wilderness. The four camps surrounded the
tabernacle in the order and direction that B. gives, except that the western
camp was Ephraim's; he was the junior but favoured son of Joseph. Cp.
Numbers ii 3, 10, 18, 25. The four camps contained three tribes each, and B.
retains the groupings in 18–27 below, except that Levi in the Israelite camp
had charge of the tabernacle itself, and the third tribe in that camp was Gad.

That front the four other points were turned four-square
By Los, for Jerusalem's sake, & called the Gates of Jerusalem,
Because twelve sons of Jerusalem fled successive through the gates.
10   But the four sons of Jerusalem who fled not but remained
Are Rintrah & Palamabron & Theotormon & Bromion,
The four that remain with Los to guard the western wall.
And these four remain to guard the four walls of Jerusalem
Whose foundations remain in the thirty-two counties of Ireland,
15   And in twelve counties of Wales, & in the forty counties
Of England & in the thirty-six counties of Scotland.
And the names of the thirty-two counties of Ireland are these:
Under Judah & Issachar & Zebulun are Louth, Longford,
East Meath, West Meath, Dublin, Kildare, King's County,
20   Queen's County, Wicklow, Catherlow, Wexford, Kilkenny.
And those under Reuben & Simeon & Levi are these:
Waterford, Tipperary, Cork, Limerick, Kerry, Clare.
And those under Ephraim, Manasseh & Benjamin are these:
Galway, Roscommon, Mayo, Sligo, Leitrim.
25   And those under Dan, Asher & Napthali are these:
Donegal, Antrim, Tyrone, Fermanagh, Armagh, Londonderry,
Down, Monaghan, Cavan. These are the land of Erin.
All these centre in London & in Golgonooza, from whence
They are created continually, east & west & north & south,
30   And from them are created all the nations of the earth,
Europe & Asia & Africa & America, in fury fourfold!
                        [*Design*]
And thirty-two the nations to dwell in Jerusalem's gates.

72.7. *four other points*] Surely there should be only *three*: north, east and
south?
72.10–12. This explains away the inconsistency noted at 71.50.
72.17. See notes on 71.1 and 71.9. B. groups the counties exactly according
to the four provinces (1–4).
72.28. *London*, B.'s home and place of work, is constantly connected with
Golgonooza, Los's place of work: the association of Erin with London
perhaps alludes to the political subordination of Ireland to London but
more probably to the spiritual connections—Ireland, land in the west,
relating to Golgonooza.
72.29. *created continually*] Cp. 58.44n. B., as the design below shows, at-
tached great stress to the essentially preservative nature of mortal transience.
72. *Design*: Two angels weep before a rocky globe showing the continents,
over which is inscribed: 'Continually Building, Continually Decaying
because of Love and Jealousy.'
72.32. *thirty-two*] This number is taken, not from the Bible, but apparently
from a fourfold eight, if the thirty-two nations given in *38–43* be divided

O come, ye nations! Come, ye people! Come up to Jerusalem!
Return, Jerusalem, & dwell together as of old! Return,
35   Return! O Albion, let Jerusalem overspread all nations
As in the times of old! O Albion, awake! Reuben wanders,
The nations wait for Jerusalem, they look up for the Bride.

France, Spain, Italy, Germany, Poland, Russia, Sweden, Turkey,
Arabia, Palestine, Persia, Hindustan, China, Tartary, Siberia,
40   Egypt, Lybia, Ethiopia, Guinea, Caffraria, Negroland, Morocco,
Congo, Zaara, Canada, Greenland, Carolina, Mexico,
Peru, Patagonia, Amazonia, Brazil, thirty-two nations:
And under these thirty-two classes of islands in the ocean,
All the nations, peoples & tongues throughout all the earth.

45   And the four gates of Los surround the universe within and
Without, & whatever is visible in the vegetable earth, the same
Is visible in the mundane shell (reversed in mountain & vale).
And a son of Eden was set over each daughter of Beulah to guard
In Albion's tomb the wondrous creation. And the fourfold gate
50   Towards Beulah is to the south: Fénelon, Guyon, Teresa,

into eight each from Europe, Asia, Africa and America. This means in-
cluding Turkey in Europe–and she was at this time a major European
power. A more doubtful necessity is the inclusion of Egypt in Asia, with
which, however, her history is largely linked. See 16.52n.

72.40. *Caffraria*] The land of the Kaffirs; i.e. African land south of Ethiopia.

72.41. *Zaara*] Sahara.

72.50–1. François *Fénelon* (1651–1751) was a teacher, spiritual adviser and
religious philosopher. He left many writings, and was regarded in the
eighteenth century as a great thinker. William Godwin, in *Political Justice*,
chose him as the type of the 'great mind' in his curious moral dilemma
when he asked which of two people, Fénelon or a servant-girl, should be
saved from a burning house if there was only time to rescue one–arguing
that logic and good sense would choose to rescue the obviously invaluable
Fénelon. He was a follower of Jeanne Marie *Guyon* (1648–1717); she taught
an extreme form of quietism, giving up the necessity for good works and
active good behaviour, and claiming that spiritual perfection was to be
found in ceaseless contemplation. She was accused of heresy and im-
prisoned in the Bastille, but later released. *St Teresa* (1515–82) was very
active as a reformer of her order, the Carmelites, which she returned to
most of the severity of its early rule; but most famous for her mystical
writings on the soul's search for God. George *Whitefield* (1714–70) was a
founder of Methodism but, unlike Wesley, Calvinist rather than Anglican
in theology; he was a great preacher. James *Hervey* (1714–58) an Anglican
rector, but prominent in early Methodism though he disagreed with
Wesley: famous in his day for *Meditations among the Tombs* (1746) and
other poems of religious reflection.

Whitefield & Hervey guard that gate, with all the gentle souls
Who guide the great winepress of love; four precious stones that
gate.

[Design]

Pl. 73 Such are Cathedron's golden halls in the city of Golgonooza.

And Los's furnaces howl loud—living, self-moving, lamenting
With fury & despair—& they stretch from south to north
Through all the four points. Lo! the labourers at the furnaces,
5 Rintrah & Palamabron, Theotormon & Bromion, loud labouring
With the innumerable multitudes of Golgonooza round the anvils
Of death. But how they came forth from the furnaces, & how long,
Vast & severe the anguish ere they knew their father, were
Long to tell—& of the iron rollers, golden axle-trees & yokes
10 Of brass, iron chains & braces, & the gold, silver & brass
Mingled or separate (for swords, arrows, cannons, mortars,
The terrible ball, the wedge, the loud-sounding hammer of
      destruction,
The sounding flail to thresh, the winnow to winnow kingdoms;
The water-wheel & mill of many innumerable wheels resistless)
15 Over the fourfold monarchy from earth to the mundane shell.

Perusing Albion's tomb in the starry characters of Og & Anak—
To create the lion & wolf, the bear, the tiger & ounce;

72. *Design*: A serpent, heading left; beneath it, in reversed writing:
'Women the comforters of men become the Tormentors & Punishers.'

73.*1*. This line does not seem to follow the text of the previous plates:
Cathedron is described on pl.59, and it may be that in an earlier arrange-
ment B. placed the two plates together. But the present order is fixed: all
existing copies of the poem adhere to it.

73.*2*. *Los's furnaces*] If a description of Cathedron had preceded, this would
continue the theme of the work of Los and Enitharmon. As it stands, it
refers back to 71.56ff.

73.*7*. *they*] The *multitudes* of *6*, who are cast like molten iron from Los's
furnaces: but being human forms, they are not inanimate.

73.*14*. *resistless*] Irresistible.

73.*15*. *fourfold*] This has the sense of *complete*, 'from earth to the top of the
sky', but B. does not elaborate.

73.*16*. *Perusing*] The four sons (Rintrah, etc.) were closely studying the
mortal world–not to 'number' it, like Satan's watch-fiends in 35.*1*, but
to see what could be done for its redemption.

the starry characters of Og and Anak] The constellations, the starry writing
of the enemy, which the four brothers study for the same purpose as in the
previous note; and they create living forms out of dead rocks. In *Milton*
pl.37.*50* the constellations are divided between Og and Sihon.

26*

To create the woolly lamb & downy fowl & scaly serpent,
The summer & winter; day & night; the sun & moon & stars;
20   The tree; the plant; the flower; the rock; the stone; the metal
Of vegetative nature by their hard restricting condensations.

[*Design*]

Where Luvah's world of opaqueness grew to a period, it
Became a *limit*, a rocky hardness without form & void,
Accumulating without end. Here Los, who is of the Elohim,
25   Opens the furnaces of affliction in the emanation,
Fixing the sexual into an ever-prolific Generation,
Naming the limit of opaqueness *Satan*, & the limit of contraction
Adam, who is Peleg & Joktan, & Esau & Jacob, & Saul & David.

(Voltaire insinuates that these limits are the cruel work of God,
30   Mocking the remover of limits & the resurrection of the dead,
Setting up kings in wrath, in holiness of Natural Religion,
Which Los with his mighty hammer demolishes time on time
In miracles & wonders in the fourfold desert of Albion,
Permanently creating, to be in time revealed & demolished:

73. *Design*: Los hammering at a wall around the sun (see *32* and *41*).
73.*22. Luvah*] Active for evil in Albion: this is the image of Luvah united
with Albion's spectre (*54.11*, *60.2*)–not the crucified Luvah of pls 65–7.
73.*23. limit*] This passage is somewhat obscure. The sense is: Luvah's
world reached the limit of Opacity (cp. *Four Zoas* iv *270n*)–that is, 'a
rocky hardness'. It accumulates without end, because it has no creative
purpose about it.
73.*24. Elohim*] The creator God of *Genesis* i, and one of B.'s *Seven Eyes of
God*–see *55.31* and *Milton* pl.14.*42n*.
73.*25. in the emanation*] The syntax is uncertain: there is no punctuation.
The editorial punctuation is based on a reading that 'the emanation, shaped
by Los at his furnaces, becomes the female, in a scheme of "ever-prolific
generation"–continually creating, continually renewing'.
73.*28. Peleg and Joktan*] Brothers, sons of Eber, father of all the Hebrews.
B. names three pairs of brothers, in parallel to Satan and Adam, who in B.'s
notion of 'limits' inevitably go together.
73.*29. Voltaire*] Not a direct allusion to Voltaire, but an allusion to his
sceptical attitude, and his agnosticism. B. says that Voltaire does not under-
stand that the forms taken by created things are the mercy, not the punish-
ment, of God.
73.*31.* Voltaire was no lover of despots, but he was no egalitarian either:
and B. does him no injustice in associating him with the rationalists of
eighteenth-century religion.   *Holiness* is ironic.

35 Satan, Cain, Tubal, Nimrod, Pharaoh, Priam, Bladud, Belin,
   Arthur, Alfred, the Norman Conqueror, Richard, John,
   And all the kings & nobles of the earth & all their glories.
   These are created by Rahab & Tirzah in Ulro, but around
   These, to preserve them from eternal death, Los creates
40 Adam, Noah, Abraham, Moses, Samuel, David, Ezekiel,
   Dissipating the rocky forms of death by his thunderous hammer.
   As the pilgrim passes while the country permanent remains,
   So men pass on; but states remain permanent for ever.)

   The spectres of the dead howl round the porches of Los
45 In the terrible family feuds of Albion's cities & villages,
   To devour the body of Albion, hungering & thirsting & ravening.
   The sons of Los clothe them & feed, & provide houses & gardens;
   And every human vegetated form in its inward recesses
   Is a house of pleasantness & a garden of delight, built by the
50 Sons & daughters of Los in Bowlahoola & in Cathedron.

   From London to York & Edinburgh the furnaces rage terrible.
   Primrose Hill is the mouth of the furnace & the iron door.

73.35. *Satan, etc.*] Eternal beings are revealed anew in each generation. In
27 Satan is a 'father' of mankind; here B. draws out the line of kings. It
moves from the antediluvian metal-worker *Tubal*, through the famous
hunter, the Hamite *Nimrod*, by way of *Pharaoh* (treated, as biblically, as a
proper name) and the classical *Priam* of Troy (for what is good in the
classics, according to B., came from the patriarchs: cp. Preface to *Milton*)
to ancient British history as traditionally told, and recorded by Milton in
his *History of Britain*. *Bladud, Belin* and *Arthur* are all from this source; and
so B. leads on to historical kings, coming up to date in the line which he
wisely deleted, since it presented King George as the latest in the descent
of Satan.
73.36. Beneath this, a line deleted from the plate: 'Edward Henry Elizabeth
James Charles William George.'
73.40. Beneath this, deleted from the plate: 'Pythagoras Socrates Euripides
Virgil Dante Milton.' On second thoughts, B. decided that the line of
virtue must be entirely biblical. Notice the ambiguity of his use of Adam,
who is Satan at *28*.
73.47. Any such work of mercy is the work of Los; the artist who feeds the
minds of otherwise savage men, and the person who in humanity dissolves
feuds and assists the victims.
73.53. *Primrose Hill*] In B.'s day, outside London to the north-west, with an
extensive view: cp. 27 *19–22* B. said to Crabb Robinson, 'I have
conversed with the spiritual sun–I saw him on Primrose Hill' (10 Dec.
1825).

Pl. 74 (The four Zoas clouded rage; Urizen stood by Albion,
With Rintrah and Palamabron and Theotormon and Bromion.
These four are Verulam & London & York & Edinburgh,
And the four Zoas are Urizen & Luvah & Tharmas & Urthona,
5   In opposition deadly, and their wheels in poisonous
And deadly stupor turned against each other loud & fierce;
Entering into the reasoning power, forsaking imagination,
They became spectres; & their human bodies were reposed
In Beulah by the daughters of Beulah, with tears & lamentations.

10   The spectre is the reasoning power in man, & when separated
From imagination, and closing itself as in steel, in a ratio
Of the things of memory, it thence frames laws & moralities
To destroy Imagination, the Divine Body, by martyrdoms & wars.)

Teach me, O Holy Spirit, the testimony of Jesus! Let me
15   Comprehend wondrous things out of the divine law!
I behold Babylon in the opening streets of London. I behold
Jerusalem in ruins wandering about from house to house.
This I behold; the shudderings of death attend my steps,
I walk up and down in six thousand years; their events are present
before me,
20   To tell how Los in grief & anger, whirling round his hammer on
high
Drave the sons & daughters of Albion from their ancient mountains.

74.1. *The four Zoas*] (Cp. 63.2ff.) Always doubtful elements in *Jerusalem*,
representing an earlier myth which is not fully assimilated to the present
one. Each reference to them needs to be accepted at its face-value. Here, as
often, their internecine strife is emphasized.

74.2. Sons of Jerusalem, or Los: cp. 71.50n, and 72.12 in the text.

74.3. This does not mean that every allusion to the Friends, and every
allusion to the four faithful sons, must be read with this indentification
literally in mind. B. is pointing out that the same essential spirit ani-
mates both groups of four. At 59.11–14 the Friends are the Zoas; if B.
intends that here, then the four faithful sons must be the warring Zoas
too: yet the purpose of introducing them was to have four figures who
were *not* corrupted. This passage seems to distinguish the Friends and the
Zoas.

74.16–17. *I behold Babylon in . . . London*] London and Jerusalem are identi-
cal in Eternity (cp. 27.1,2nn): but Jerusalem has been driven away; and now
London is inhabited by the evil spirit of Babylon, the city of Rahab, the
symbol of corruption and the negation of Jerusalem in *Revelation*.

74.19. *I walk . . . years*] i.e. 'I am aware of the whole of human his-
tory'.

They became the twelve gods of Asia opposing the Divine Vision.
The sons of Albion are twelve; the sons of Jerusalem sixteen.
I tell how Albion's sons by harmonies of concords & discords
25 Opposed to melody, and by lights & shades opposed to outline,
And by abstraction opposed to the visions of imagination,
By cruel laws, divided sixteen into twelve divisions:
How Hyle roofed Los in Albion's cliffs, by the affections rent
Asunder & opposed to thought, to draw Jerusalem's sons
30 Into the vortex of his wheels. Therefore Hyle is called Gog,
Age after age drawing them away towards Babylon—
Babylon, the rational morality deluding to death the little ones
In strong temptations of stolen beauty. I tell how Reuben slept
On London Stone, & the daughters of Albion ran around admiring
35 His awful beauty; with Moral Virtue the fair deceiver, offspring
Of good & evil, they divided him in love upon the Thames & sent
Him over Europe in streams of gore out of Cathedron's looms;
How Los drave them from Albion & they became daughters of
    Canaan—
Hence Albion was called the Canaanite, & all his giant sons.
40 Hence is my theme. O Lord my Saviour, open thou the gates

74.22. *the twelve gods of Asia*] Listed in *Milton* pl.37.20ff.

74.23ff. *the sons of Albion*] This passage (ending at 75.1) begins as a necessary adjustment and continues as a vision of the history of Israel. There are two sets of twelve 'sons': Hand, Hyle, Skofield, etc.; and the twelve tribes of Israel. The division of Albion and Canaan (63.42; 71.1) leaves the corrupt spiritual sons of Albion in Albion; and their counterparts in Israel are the historical twelve tribes. But (cp. 71.50n) B. has now given to Jerusalem the sixteen 'sons of Los' of *Milton* pl.23.61ff, who comprise the twelve sons of Israel plus Rintrah, Palamabron, Bromion and Theotormon. See 16.52n; the 'perfect' sixteen has been reduced to an 'imperfect' twelve.

74.28. *Hyle roofed Los in*] Hyle derives from *Hayley*, the well-meaning but intolerable patron who attempted to circumscribe B.'s work by misplaced 'affections'.

74.30. *Gog*] In *Ezekiel* xxxviii–xxxix, a king foretold as the type of heathendom who would invade Israel in the last days, only to be defeated with great slaughter. An allusion is also made in *Revelation* xx 8.

74.31. *Babylon*] Gog is not biblically associated with Babylon; the relation is B.'s: the temptations of Hayley, dangerous as Gog, appear 'age after age' trying to corrupt Jerusalem. The opposition of Jerusalem and Babylon, so important to B., is equally fundamental to biblical tradition, most especially in *Revelation*.

74.34. *London Stone*] In 30.45 the stone is the Stone of Bohan in Judah; B. links, as always, Britain and Canaan.

And I will lead forth thy words, telling how the daughters
Cut the fibres of Reuben, how he rolled apart & took root
In Bashan; terror-struck Albion's sons look toward Bashan!
They have divided Simeon; he also rolled apart in blood
45   Over the nations till he took root beneath the shining looms
Of Albion's daughters, in Philistia by the side of Amalek.
They have divided Levi; he hath shot out into forty-eight roots
Over the land of Canaan. They have divided Judah;
He hath took root in Hebron, in the land of Hand & Hyle.
50   Dan, Naphtali, Gad, Asher, Issachar, Zebulun roll apart
From all the nations of the earth to dissipate into non-entity.

I see a feminine form arise from the four terrible Zoas,
Beautiful but terrible, struggling to take a form of beauty,
Rooted in Shechem. This is Dinah, the youthful form of Erin.
55   The wound I see in South Molton Street & Stratford Place,
Whence Joseph & Benjamin rolled apart away from the nations.
In vain they rolled apart; they are fixed into the land of Cabul.

74.41. See 23n. In the following lines, B. describes how the twelve sons of
Israel (i.e. of Jerusalem) are 'divided' and 'roll apart'—i.e. are separated
from one another and from their true nature. The twelve are listed in the
order of their birth (*Genesis* xxix 32–xxx 24, xxxv 16–18), with Dinah
also in the order of birth: i.e. B. identifies their birth into this world with
their separation from eternity.

74.42–3. *Reuben . . . took root in Bashan*] The Reubenites, in the invasion of
the Promised Land, settled in Transjordan, but not in Bashan.

74.44. *Simeon* was granted land in the far south, as B. says, near the lands
ruled by the Philistines and the Amalekites.

74.47. *forty-eight*] The cities of the Levites, which they received instead of
land.

74.48. *Judah*] This 'rooting' of Judah in the region of Hebron (to the south
of Jerusalem) is also historical, as with Simeon.

74.52. *Dinah*] The only recorded daughter of Israel, and of course she did
not name a tribe. B. therefore associates her with Erin. She was beloved
by the young lord of Shechem, who (*Genesis* xxxiv 2) 'lay with her, and
defiled her'—this is commonly, but not necessarily, taken to mean rape;
and afterwards he was anxious to marry her. A bargain was made with
Israel and his sons, but treacherously broken by Dinah's full brothers (by
the same mother) Simeon and Levi, whose men killed all the men of
Shechem. Thus Dinah was trying to 'take root' in Shechem by marriage,
but was brutally prevented. So Erin (Ireland) was ill-treated by her
'brother' Albion over centuries of misrule.

74.57. *the land of Cabul*] A region near Carmel, granted by Solomon to
Hiram, king of Tyre in return for wood and gold provided for the great

[Design]

Pl. 75 And Rahab, Babylon the Great, hath destroyed Jerusalem.

Bath stood upon the Severn with Merlin & Bladud & Arthur,
The cup of Rahab in his hand, her poisons twenty-sevenfold.

And all her twenty-seven Heavens, now hid & now revealed,
5 Appear in strong delusive light of time & space, drawn out
In shadowy pomp, by the Eternal Prophet created evermore.
For Los in six thousand years walks up & down continually,
That not one moment of time be lost, & every revolution
Of space he makes permanent in Bowlahoola & Cathedron.

[Design]

10 And these the names of the twenty-seven Heavens & their Churches:
Adam, Seth, Enos, Cainan, Mahalaleel, Jared, Enoch,

temple. Hiram was dissatisfied (*1 Kings* ix 13) 'and said, What cities are
these which thou hast given me, my brother?–And he called them the
land of Cabul unto this day.' The name means 'as good as nothing'; but
it is in the land of Zebulun, not of Benjamin or of the two sons of Joseph,
Manasseh and Ephraim.

74. *Design*: Illustrates Dinah (*52–4*).

75.1. Historically, Babylon destroyed Jerusalem: but B. chooses his image
from *Revelation*, and Jerusalem is seen to be destroyed by the spiritual de-
generation of her sons in the previous lines. This line, with the last on the
plate, marks the nadir in the story of Jerusalem.

75.2. *Merlin and Bladud and Arthur*] Figures in Ancient British legend and
semi-history. Bladud founded Bath and, like Merlin, was a necromancer,
according to Milton's *History of Britain*; thus *Bath* in this line is 'the
poisoner' (37.1–2).

75.4. *twenty-seven Heavens*] See *Milton* pl.37.35n. In *Milton* these are repre-
sented as the clouds of unending religious error which have enwrapped the
world since its creation. They oppose Los's revitalizing work.

75. *Design*: A frieze-like series of angels in overlapping circles: an early
sketch of the famous *Job* illustrations no. 14, of the morning stars singing
together. This plate is reproduced in Keynes, *W.B.'s Engravings* pl.112.

75.10–20. Lines *10–17* and *20* are taken from *Milton* pl.37.35–43; *18a* is
from *Milton* pl.40.20; *19*, similar to *Four Zoas* viii *318*, *Milton* pls 22.48–9,
33.20, derives from *Revelation* xvii 5 (quoted in full at *Four Zoas* viii
267n).

75.10. *twenty-seven Heavens*] See *4n* above. The list is made up of biblical
and ecclesiastical names largely to complete the required number: for full
details see *Milton* pl.37.35n. They are a cycle (*24*) of unending religious

Methuselah, Lamech; these are the giants mighty, hermaphroditic.
Noah, Shem, Arphaxad, Cainan the second, Salah, Heber,
Peleg, Reu, Serug, Nahor, Terah: these are the female-males,
15   A male within a female hid as in an ark & curtains.
Abraham, Moses, Solomon, Paul, Constantine, Charlemagne,
Luther; these seven are the male-females: the dragon forms,
The female hid within a male. Thus Rahab is revealed—
Mystery, Babylon the Great, the Abomination of Desolation,
20   Religion hid in war, a dragon red & hidden harlot.
But Jesus, breaking through the central zones of death & hell
Opens Eternity in time & space, triumphant in mercy.

Thus are the heavens formed by Los within the mundane shell.
And where Luther ends Adam begins again in eternal circle
25   To awake the prisoners of death—to bring Albion again
With Luvah into light eternal, in his eternal day.

But now the starry heavens are fled from the mighty limbs of
    Albion.
[Design]

Pl. 76   *[Full-page design]*

Chapter 4

This chapter leads up to the final awakening of Albion and the redemption
of Jerusalem. But there is much more material before this, and so the
chapter falls into two distinct parts, dividing at the beginning of pl.94
when Albion begins to stir, awoken by 'the Breath Divine'. The remaining
plates contain fairly simple narrative, but pls 78–93 are much more com-
plex.

errors, varying in kind but not in nature. They are the products of the fall
into sexual creation–divided into male and female, and badly pieced
together again. In each one the ultimate evil, Rahab, reveals her power on
earth. The additions in this passage to its equivalent in *Milton* emphasize
the greater power of Jesus.

75.23. *formed by Los*] Although they are Rahab's (4) Los shapes them,
gives them recognizable form, and keeps them moving so that they will
not petrify, or turn into irredeemable chaos.

75. *Design*: Two female figures, daughters of Albion (or Rahab and
Tirzah; they are crowned) coiled with and embracing serpents.

Plate 76. *Full-page design*: The crucifixion, with Christ hanging on a
spreading oak tree, a radiant crown of thorns on his head, and Albion
beneath him, arms outspread like Christ's, looking up at him. (Reproduced
in Blunt, *Art of W.B.* pl.48a; Keynes, *W.B.'s Engraving* pl.113; *W.B., Poet,
Printer, Prophet*, frontispiece.) The figures are named in some copies.

Plates 78 to 86.*49*, and again pl.*90*, describe further the nefarious activities of the daughters of Albion, who now have taken the stage from his sons; they are watched by Los, whose labours never cease, and who sometimes manages to win a tactical victory. At the beginning of this section is a long lament by the imprisoned Jerusalem (78.*31*–80.*5*), and other speeches, by various figures, punctuate it. From 85.*14*–86.*32*. Los sings about the beauty of the eternal Jerusalem. But at 86.*50* a new section starts, with a rather strange reversion to the theme of Los's own troubles, referred to at the beginning of the poem when he was struggling with his spectre (pls 6–11). Now the spectre, long-subdued and almost forgotten, returns, rebellious as before, to accentuate the difficulties of a dispute between Los and Enitharmon. Hitherto, in *Jerusalem*, Los and Enitharmon have always worked together harmoniously at their different but parallel tasks. Now Enitharmon begins to be jealous, and (86.*50*–88.*48*) we get a partial recapitulation of the quarrel between the pair which fills up so much of *Four Zoas*. Los angrily refuses to give in to her jealousy and desire for domination, driving both his spectre and emanation Enitharmon hard. The dispute comes to an end as (pl.92) Los suddenly sees signs of hope in his furnaces. Enitharmon is distressed at the failure of her desires, but can do nothing. In *Four Zoas* viia *411*ff, a full reconciliation between the pair was made, to be followed by their working together in love: but in *Jerusalem* the theme fades out. It is tempting to conjecture that B., having filled all his vacant space, had no room for more; note that the loving cooperation, which in *Four Zoas* follows reconciliation after the long quarrel, is normal in *Jerusalem*; they only quarrel at this unexpected place at the end.

In the middle of this section, pl.89 opposes the vision of Jerusalem, with a description of the Covering Cherub, the figure in whom all male aggressive evil is summed up (and who, in pl.96, advances on Jesus and is annihilated). His appearance is sudden, but significant, in that now all the power of evil is assembled in order to overwhelm Los and those with him, and to devour Albion and Jerusalem. After this description, B. continues the theme of the daughters of Albion and Los's opposition in pl.90, leading, in pl.91, by way of the spectre back to the quarrel with Enitharmon, in pl.92. The chapter may be thus summarized:

A	78–86.*49*	The powers of evil triumphant; Los remains in opposition recalling Jerusalem in Eternity.
B	86.*50*–88	Los, Enitharmon and the spectre.
C	89	The Covering Cherub.
D	90	As *A*.
E	91	Los and his spectre (partly as *B*, but no mention of Enitharmon)
F	92–3	As *B*.
G	94–9	The awakening of Albion.

Pl. 77   To the Christians
Devils are   I give you the end of a golden string,
false religions.   Only wind it into a ball:
'*Saul, Saul,*   It will lead you in at Heaven's gate,
Why persecutest thou me?'   Built in Jerusalem's wall.

[*Design*]

5   We are told to abstain from fleshly desires that we may lose no time
from the work of the Lord. Every moment lost is a moment that can-
not be redeemed: every pleasure that intermingles with the duty of
our station is a folly unredeemable & is planted like the seed of a wild
flower among our wheat. All the tortures of repentance are tortures
10   of self-reproach on account of our leaving the Divine Harvest to the
enemy, the struggles of entanglement with incoherent roots. I know
of no other Christianity and of no other Gospel than the liberty both
of body & mind to exercise the divine arts of Imagination—Imagina-
tion, the real & eternal world of which this vegetable universe is but a
15   faint shadow, & in which we shall live in our eternal or imaginative
bodies, when these vegetable mortal bodies are no more. The apostles
know of no other gospel. What were all their spiritual gifts? What is
the Divine Spirit? Is the Holy Ghost any other than an intellectual
fountain? What is the harvest of the gospel & its labours? What is that
20   talent which it is a curse to hide? What are the treasures of heaven
which we are to lay up for ourselves—are they any other than mental
studies & performances? What are all the gifts of the gospel, are
they not all mental gifts? Is God a spirit who must be worshipped in
spirit & in truth, and are not the gifts of the Spirit everything to man?
25   O ye religious, discountenance everyone among you who shall pre-
tend to despise art & science! I call upon you in the name of Jesus!
What is the life of man but art & science? Is it meat & drink? Is not
the body more than raiment? What is mortality but the things relat-
ing to the body, which dies? What is immortality but the things
30   relating to the spirit, which lives eternally? What is the joy of heaven
but improvement in the things of the spirit? What are the pains of
hell but ignorance, bodily lust, idleness & devastation of the things of
the spirit? Answer this to yourselves, & expel from among you those
who pretend to despise the labours of art & science, which alone are
35   the labours of the gospel: is not this plain & manifest to the thought?

77.4. '*Saul . . . me*'] From *Acts* ix 4; the words of the vision of Jesus to
Saul, the religious man who persecuted Christians and who became Paul. The
language of the following passage is too full of New Testament references
to itemize each one; the sense is clear, the argumentative style not dis-
similar to Paul's.
77. *Design*: The stanza is central at the top, and underneath, R, is a picture
of a child following the thread and winding it up. The remarks '*Devils
are . . .*' are tucked away at the left-hand side.

Can you think at all & not pronounce heartily, that to labour in
knowledge is to build up Jerusalem: and to despise knowledge, is to
despise Jerusalem & her builders? And remember; he who despises
and mocks a mental gift in another, calling it pride & selfishness and
40 sin, mocks Jesus, the giver of every mental gift, which always appear
to the ignorance-loving hypocrite, as sins. But that which is a sin in
the sight of cruel man is not so in the sight of our kind God.

Let every Christian, as much as in him lies, engage himself
openly & publicly before all the world in some mental pursuit for
45 the building up of Jerusalem.

I stood among my valleys of the south
And saw a flame of fire, even as a wheel
Of fire surrounding all the heavens; it went
From west to east against the current of
50 Creation and devoured all things in its loud
Fury and thundering course round heaven and earth.
By it the sun was rolled into an orb;
By it the moon faded into a globe
Travelling through the night: for from its dire
55 And restless fury, man himself shrunk up
Into a little root a fathom long.
And I asked a watcher and a holy one
Its name? He answered, 'It is the wheel of religion.'
I wept and said, 'Is this the law of Jesus,
60 This terrible devouring sword turning every way?'
He answered, 'Jesus died because he strove
Against the current of this wheel: its name
Is Caiaphas, the dark preacher of death,
Of sin, of sorrow, and of punishment,
65 Opposing nature! It is Natural Religion:
But Jesus is the bright preacher of life,
Creating nature from this fiery law,
By self-denial and forgiveness of sin.
Go therefore, cast out devils in Christ's name;
70 Heal thou the sick of spiritual disease,
Pity the evil, for thou art not sent
To smite with terror and with punishments
Those that are sick, like to the Pharisees
Crucifying and encompassing sea and land

77.46–51. The vision is based on Ezekiel's vision in his opening verses.
But Ezekiel saw a cloud of fire coming from the *north*, and does not say
that it went from west to east. B. picks out the *wheel* from Ezekiel's
visions, and for the present ignores the 'living creatures'.
77.57. *a watcher* . . . *one*] The phrase is from *Daniel* iv 13: John also in-
quired of angels in *Revelation*; and Swedenborg conversed with them.

75   For proselytes to tyranny and wrath.
        But to the publicans and harlots go!
        Teach them true happiness, but let no curse
        Go forth out of thy mouth to blight their peace:
        For Hell is opened to Heaven: thine eyes beheld
80   The dungeons burst and the prisoners set free.'

    England! awake, awake, awake!
      Jerusalem thy sister calls!
   Why wilt thou sleep the sleep of death,
      And close her from thy ancient walls?

85   Thy hills and valleys felt her feet,
                            Gently upon their bosoms move:
                        Thy gates beheld sweet Zion's ways;
                            Then was a time of joy and love!

              And now the time returns again:
90   Our souls exult, and London's towers
              Receive the Lamb of God to dwell
                  In England's green and pleasant bowers.

CHAPTER 4
Pl. 78   [*Design*]
    The spectres of Albion's twelve sons revolve mightily
Over the tomb, & over the body, ravening to devour
The sleeping humanity. Los with his mace of iron
Walks round: loud his threats, loud his blows fall
5 On the rocky spectres, as the potter breaks the potsherds,
Dashing in pieces self-righteousnesses, driving them from Albion's
Cliffs, dividing them into male & female forms in his furnaces
And on his anvils, lest they destroy the feminine affections
They are broken. Loud howl the spectres in his iron furnace;
10 While Los laments at his dire labours, viewing Jerusalem,
Sitting before his furnaces clothed in sackcloth of hair;
Albion's twelve sons surround the forty-two gates of Erin,
In terrible armour, raging against the Lamb & against Jerusalem,
Surrounding them with armies to destroy the Lamb of God.

78. *Design*: The top half of the page is taken up with the chapter-heading
design: a dejected male figure with an eagle's beak and cock's comb facing
a setting sun.
78.2. *The tomb ... the body*] Albion's. The image is that of 46.*10*–48.*12*.
78.*12*. *Erin*] The leader of the daughters of Beulah caring for Albion (11.*8*).
forty-two] Why? In pl.72 there are thirty-two, not forty-two divisions
of Ireland, as there are thirty-two counties.

15 They took their mother Vala, and they crowned her with gold;
They named her Rahab, & gave her power over the earth,
The concave earth round Golgonooza in Entuthon Benython,
Even to the stars exalting her throne, to build beyond the throne
Of God and the Lamb, to destroy the Lamb & usurp the throne
of God,
20 Drawing their Ulro voidness round the fourfold humanity.
Naked Jerusalem lay before the gates upon Mount Zion,
The hill of giants, all her foundations levelled with the dust.
Her twelve gates thrown down, her children carried into captivity,
Herself in chains: this from within was seen in a dismal night
25 Outside, unknown before in Beulah; & the twelve gates were filled
With blood, from Japan eastward to the Giants' Causeway, west
Into Erin's continent. And Jerusalem wept upon Euphrates' banks
Disorganised; an evanescent shade—scarce seen or heard among
Her children's druid temples, dropping with blood—wandered
weeping,
30 And thus her voice went forth in the darkness of Philistia:
'My brother & my father are no more. God hath forsaken me;
The arrows of the Almighty pour upon me & my children;
I have sinned and am an outcast from the Divine Presence.
Pl. 79 My tents are fallen, my pillars are in ruins, my children dashed
Upon Egypt's iron floors, & the marble pavements of Assyria.
I melt my soul in reasonings among the towers of Heshbon;
Mount Zion is become a cruel rock; & no more dew
5 Nor rain, no more the spring of the rock appears, but cold,
Hard & obdurate are the furrows of the mountain of wine & oil.
The mountain of blessing is itself a curse & an astonishment;
The hills of Judæa are fallen with me into the deepest hell,
Away from the nations of the earth, & from the cities of the nations.
10 I walk to Ephraim; I seek for Shiloh; I walk like a lost sheep

78.*15*. *Vala*] 70.*17–31*, 75 (and indeed the second half of ch. 2 as a whole)
tell of the rise in the power of Vala-Rahab.
78.*26*. *the Giants' Causeway*] The spectacular range of 'steps' of basalt
rocks in Antrim at the far north of Ireland. See 89.*50–1*.
78.*28*. *Disorganised*] Disintegrated, or paralysed–incapable of human action.
78.*31–2*. *arrows of the Almighty*] From *Job* vi 4, the tenor of these lines is
like the lamenting of Job: but Job would not admit what Jerusalem in her
despair insists, that 'I have sinned'.
79.*3*. *Heshbon*] A Reubenite city originally in the land of Sihon (cp.
48.*63*) famous for its strength.
79.*7*. *mountain of blessing*] Perhaps Gerizim (*Four Zoas* viii *303n*), the place
from which ritual blessings were read to the Israelites as they crossed the
Jordan; but in this context more probably Jerusalem.
79.*10–13*. *Ephraim, Shiloh, Goshen, Gilead, Og*] The scrutiny covers

Among the precipices of despair. In Goshen I seek for light
In vain, and in Gilead for a physician and a comforter.
Goshen hath followed Philistia, Gilead hath joined with Og.
They are become narrow places in a little and dark land,
15 How distant far from Albion! His hills & his valleys no more
Receive the feet of Jerusalem, they have cast me quite away;
And Albion is himself shrunk to a narrow rock in the midst of the
    sea.
The plains of Sussex & Surrey, their hills of flocks & herds,
No more seek to Jerusalem nor to the sound of my holy-ones.
20 The fifty-two counties of England are hardened against me
As if I was not their mother; they despise me & cast me out.
London covered the whole earth, England encompassed the nations;
And all the nations of the earth were seen in the cities of Albion.
My pillars reached from sea to sea; London beheld me come
25 From my east & from my west. He blessed me and gave
His children to my breasts, his sons & daughters to my knees.
His aged parents sought me out in every city & village;
They discerned my countenance with joy, they showed me to their
    sons,
Saying: "Lo, Jerusalem is here! She sitteth in our secret chambers:
30 Levi and Judah & Issachar, Ephraim, Manasseh, Gad and Dan
Are seen in our hills & valleys; they keep our flocks & herds;
They watch them in the night, and the Lamb of God appears
    among us!"
The river Severn stayed his course at my command;
Thames poured his waters into my basins and baths;
35 Medway mingled with Kishon; Thames received the heavenly
    Jordan;
Albion gave me to the whole earth to walk up & down; to pour
Joy upon every mountain, to teach songs to the shepherd and
    ploughman.
I taught the ships of the sea to sing the songs of Zion.

Palestine centrally, north and south. *Shiloh*, the second city of the Israelites
and eventually capital of the northern kingdom is in *Ephraim*, in the
middle of the land. *Goshen* here is probably the Goshen conquered by
Joshua (*Joshua* x 41), which was not far from the south-eastern area where
the Philistines were. *Gilead* is beyond Jordan to the north-east of Palestine,
and its northern part was part of the territory of *Og*, king of Bashan: he
was defeated, and the Amorite border pushed northwards, so that northern
Gilead was given to Manasseh.
79.30ff. The 'holy land' should not be a tradition of a distant past; the land
of everyday life should be as holy as Palestine is said to be (i.e. as the
Palestine of prophetic vision, not of the warring tribes of history).
79.35. *The Medway*] Runs into the Thames estuary.
Kishon] The river running to the sea at the foot of Carmel.

Italy saw me, in sublime astonishment; France was wholly mine,
40 As my garden & as my secret bath; Spain was my heavenly couch,
I slept in his golden hills—the Lamb of God met me there.
There we walked as in our secret chamber among our little ones;
They looked upon our loves with joy; they beheld our secret joys,
With holy raptures of adoration rapt sublime in the visions of God.
45 Germany, Poland & the north wooed my footsteps; they found
My gates in all their mountains & my curtains in all their vales;
The furniture of their houses was the furniture of my chamber.
Turkey & Grecia saw my instruments of music; they arose,
They seized the harp, the flute, the mellow horn of Jerusalem's joy;
50 They sounded thanksgivings in my courts. Egypt & Lybia heard;
The swarthy sons of Ethiopia stood round the Lamb of God
Enquiring for Jerusalem—he led them up my steps to my altar.
And thou, America, I once beheld thee, but now behold no more
Thy golden mountains, where my cherubim & seraphim rejoiced
55 Together among my little ones. But now my altars run with blood,
My fires are corrupt; my incense is a cloudy pestilence
Of seven diseases. Once a continual cloud of salvation rose
From all my myriads; once the fourfold world rejoiced among
The pillars of Jerusalem, between my winged cherubim,
60 But now I am closed out from them in the narrow passages
Of the valleys of destruction, into a dark land of pitch & bitumen,
From Albion's tomb afar and from the fourfold wonders of God
Shrunk to a narrow doleful form in the dark land of Cabul.
There is Reuben & Gad & Joseph & Judah & Levi, closed up
65 In narrow vales; I walk & count the bones of my beloveds
Along the valley of destruction, among these druid temples
Which overspread all the earth in patriarchal pomp & cruel pride.
Tell me, O Vala, thy purposes, tell me wherefore thy shuttles
Drop with the gore of the slain, why Euphrates is red with blood?
70 Wherefore in dreadful majesty & beauty outside appears
Thy masculine from thy feminine, hardening against the heavens
To devour the human? Why dost thou weep upon the wind among
These cruel druid temples? O Vala! Humanity is far above
Sexual organisation, & the visions of the night of Beulah,
75 Where sexes wander in dreams of bliss among the emanations,

79.44. *rapt*] The text reads 'rapd', a normal abbreviation for 'raped': it could also perhaps be 'wrapped': but *rapt* gives the best sense.
79.45. *Germany, Poland and the north*] Within B.'s lifetime the centre of much strife. Poland was partitioned between 1772 and 1795.
79.48. *Turkey and Grecia*] Greece was a rebellious subject of Turkey.
79.54. *Thy golden mountains*] The legendary mountains of Atlantis, now flooded by the Atlantic.
79.73. This is an important qualification of the beauties of Beulah–that it is a place of rest only, not the place of eternal life.

Where the masculine & feminine are nursed into youth & maiden
By the tears & smiles of Beulah's daughters, till the time of sleep
    is past.
Wherefore then do you realize these nets of beauty & delusion
In open day to draw the souls of the dead into the light,
80 Till Albion is shut out from every nation under heaven,
Pl. 80 Encompassed by the frozen net and by the rooted tree?
I walk weeping in pangs of a mother's torment for her children.
I walk in affliction: I am a worm, and no living soul,
A worm going to eternal torment, raised up in a night
5 To an eternal night of pain, lost, lost, lost, for ever!'

Beside her Vala howled upon the winds in pride of beauty,
Lamenting among the timbrels of the warriors, among the captives
In cruel holiness; and her lamenting songs were from Arnon
And Jordan to Euphrates. Jerusalem followed, trembling,
10 Her children in captivity, listening to Vala's lamentation
In the thick cloud & darkness. And the voice went forth from
The cloud: 'O rent in sunder from Jerusalem, the harlot daughter,
In an eternal condemnation in fierce burning flames
Of torment unendurable! And if once a delusion be found
15 Woman must perish, & the heavens of heavens remain no more.
'My father gave to me command to murder Albion

80. *Design*: In the right margin figures struggling with coiling worms.
80.*1. net . . . tree*] The net or veil of Vala (21.*50*) and the Tree of Mystery
(28.*15*ff).
80.*3. I am a worm . . . soul*] Psalm xxii 6: 'But I am a worm, and no man; a
reproach of men, and despised of the people.' (This is the psalm which
begins 'My God, my God, why hast thou forsaken me?') B. changes the
word 'man' to 'living soul' partly because Jerusalem is female, partly
because the phrase is not tied to the 'generative earth'.
80.*6. howled*] Although Vala is triumphant, she cannot enjoy her supposed
triumph, since it is contrary to her true nature in Eternity. Her speech
betrays this contradiction.
80.*8–9. from Arnon . . . Euphrates*] From Israel to Babylon, as the captive is
carried away to the conqueror's home. Babylon is identified with Rahab,
who is Vala (cp. 75.*18–19*).
80.*12.* Vala's views are all distorted. Jerusalem is not a harlot (cp. 18.*11*ff,
and the disputation beginning at 20.*3*). There is no eternal condemnation;
and woman can only exist as part of humanity together with man–not as
a selfish entity.
80.*14. if once a delusion be found*] i.e. 'found out'–if one of woman's wiles
be discovered she is lost.
80.*16. My father*] Luvah. What follows is a lie, told to excuse her crime
by blaming others. At *23* she suddenly realizes how things have changed
for the worse since her act.

In unreviving death; my love, my Luvah, ordered me in night
To murder Albion, the king of men. He fought in battles fierce,
He conquered Luvah my beloved, he took me and my father,
20 He slew them. I revived them to life in my warm bosom.
He saw them issue from my bosom; dark in jealousy
He burned before me. Luvah framed the knife, & Luvah gave
The knife into his daughter's hand. Such thing was never known
Before in Albion's land—that one should die a death never to be
revived!
25 For in our battles we the slain men view with pity and love;
We soon revive them in the secret of our tabernacles.
But I, Vala, Luvah's daughter, keep his body embalmed in moral
laws
With spices of sweet odours of lovely jealous stupefaction
Within my bosom, lest he arise to life & slay my Luvah.
30 Pity me then, O Lamb of God! O Jesus, pity me!
Come into Luvah's tents, and seek not to revive the dead!'

So sang she: and the spindle turned furious as she sang.
The children of Jerusalem, the souls of those who sleep,
Were caught into the flax of her distaff, & in her cloud,
35 To weave Jerusalem a body according to her will,
A dragon form on Zion hill's most ancient promontory.

The spindle turned in blood & fire. Loud sound the trumpets
Of war; the cymbals play loud before the captains,
With Cambel & Gwendolen in dance and solemn song,
40 The cloud of Rahab vibrating with the daughters of Albion.
Los saw terrified, melted with pity & divided in wrath
He sent them over the narrow seas in pity and love,
Among the dour forests of Albion which overspread all the earth.
They go forth & return, swift as a flash of lightning,
45 Among the tribes of warriors, among the stones of power.
Against Jerusalem they rage through all the nations of Europe:
Through Italy & Grecia, to Lebanon & Persia & India.

80.23–6. Cp. 43.39–45, where a similar idea is expressed; there 'no women
come to the field' in contrast with the present passage (25–6, with their
strong sexual symbolism). Instead of reviving Albion, Vala prefers to
keep him 'embalmed'–that is, dead.
80.37. spindle] Tirzah's–she is a manifestation of Vala.
80.38. cymbals] An instrument mentioned in the Bible (e.g. Psalm cl 5,
2 Chronicles v 13) in contexts which, as here, imply a melodic instrument,
not merely percussion.
80.45. Stones of Power] See 68.41, where the daughters of Albion torment
their victims at Stonehenge on 'the twelve stones of power'.
80.47. From west to east–the direction of error 'against the current of
Creation' (77. poem 4).

The serpent temples through the earth, from the wide plain of
   Salisbury,
Resound with cries of victims, shouts & songs & dying groans
50 And flames of dusky fire, to Amalek, Canaan and Moab.
And Rahab like a dismal and indefinite hovering cloud
Refused to take a definite form. She hovered over all the earth,
Calling the definite 'Sin', defacing every definite form,
Invisible, or visible, stretched out in length or spread in breadth
55 Over the temples, drinking groans of victims, weeping in pity,
And joying in the pity, howling over Jerusalem's walls.

Hand slept on Skiddaw's top, drawn by the love of beautiful
Cambel, his bright, beaming counterpart, divided from him—
And her delusive light beamed fierce above the mountain,
60 Soft, invisible, drinking his sighs in sweet intoxication,
Drawing out fibre by fibre, returning to Albion's tree
At night and in the morning to Skiddaw. She sent him over
Mountainous Wales into the loom of Cathedron, fibre by fibre.
He ran in tender nerves across Europe to Jerusalem's shade
65 To weave Jerusalem a body repugnant to the Lamb.

Hyle on East Moor in rocky Derbyshire raved to the moon
For Gwendolen; she took up in bitter tears his anguished heart
That, apparent to all in Eternity, glows like the sun in the breast.
She hid it in his ribs & back; she hid his tongue with teeth
70 In terrible convulsions, pitying & gratified, drunk with pity,
Glowing with loveliness before him, becoming apparent
According to his changes. She rolled his kidneys round
Into two irregular forms, and looking on Albion's dread tree
She wove two vessels of seed, beautiful as Skiddaw's snow,

80.48. In pl.66 Stonehenge was the origin of corrupt religion. Strictly
speaking, the 'serpent temple' (as interpreted by Stukeley), was at Avebury,
which is in Salisbury Plain.
80.57. *Hand slept on Skiddaw*] A famous mountain in the Lake District;
Hand and Hyle are sons of Albion whose bones are these mountains. In
pl.71 Bowen is given Cumberland; Hand has south-east England. He is
now running after his counterpart, and so has been drawn away from home
to this desolate, rocky place, while she enjoys teasing him. So with Hyle
in the next passage. Like the episode of Reuben (30.51ff) these sections
describe a 'creation' into mortal form.
80.63. *Cathedron*] A place where Enitharmon works for redemption, by
weaving mortal forms for lost, formless souls. Cambel causes Hand to be
enwoven with fibres of mortal flesh. The association of the corrupt Cambel
with Cathedron is unusual.
80.66. Cp. this passage with *Milton* pls 19.44–20.6, where the same terms
and images are used.

75 Giving them bends of self-interest & selfish natural virtue.
    She hid them in his loins; raving he ran among the rocks,
    Compelled into a shape of 'moral virtue' against the Lamb,
    The invisible lovely one giving him a form according to
    His law, a form against the Lamb of God, opposed to mercy
80 And playing in the thunderous loom in sweet intoxication,
    Filling cups of silver & crystal with shrieks & cries, with groans
    And dolorous sobs—the wine of lovers in the winepress of Luvah.

    'O sister Cambel,' said Gwendolen, as their long beaming light
    Mingled above the mountain, 'What shall we do to keep
85 These awful forms in our soft bands? Distracted with trembling
Pl. 81 I have mocked those who refused cruelty & I have admired
    The cruel warrior, I have refused to give love to Merlin the piteous.
    He brings to me the images of his love & I reject in chastity
    And turn them out into the streets for harlots, to be food
5   To the stern warrior. I am become perfect in beauty over my
        warrior.
    For men are caught by love, woman is caught by pride,
    That love may only be obtained in the passages of death.
    Let us look, let us examine. Is the cruel become an infant
    Or is he still a cruel warrior? Look sisters, look! Oh piteous!
10 I have destroyed wandering Reuben who strove to bind my will;
    I have stripped off Joseph's beautiful integument for my beloved,
    The cruel one of Albion, to clothe him in gems of my zone.
    I have named him Jehovah of Hosts; humanity is become
    A weeping infant in ruined lovely Jerusalem's folding cloud.

                    [Design]

80.78. *the invisible lovely one*] Gwendolen, whom he seeks. He cannot come near her, but she can come at him. She is the 'playing' one of *80*.
80.82. *the winepress of Luvah*] Cp. *Four Zoas* ix *713ff*. The winepress is a place of joy for the workers, of suffering for the 'human grapes'. Here it is a place of Luvah-like excitement and desire, in which Gwendolen revels at Hyle's cost. B. returns to the idea at 82.*64*.

81.2. *Merlin*] A figure in Arthurian and therefore British legend goes with the British legendary queen Gwendolen: Merlin was enamoured of, and trapped by Nimue (or Vivien)—not Gwendolen—in early legend.
81.10. *wandering Reuben*] A key to part of B.'s notion of Reuben (see 30.*43n*). Reuben slept with his father Jacob's concubine, for which he was disinherited as too weak a character. B. agrees; Reuben leans too much on the casual beauty of women to be a 'strong' character.
81.11. Joseph's coat of many colours (*Genesis* xxxvii 3) is biblical, of course, but Gwendolen's allusion is not.
81.13. *him*] 'My beloved', Hyle—her counterpart.
81. *Design* (filling more than half the page): The twelve daughters of

15 In heaven love begets love, but fear is the parent of earthly love!
      And he who will not bend to love must be subdued by fear:
Pl. 82 I have heard Jerusalem's groans; from Vala's cries & lamentations
      I gather our eternal fate—outcasts from life and love!
      Unless we find a way to bind these awful forms to our
      Embrace, we shall perish annihilate, discovered our delusions.
 5 Look! I have wrought without delusion. Look! I have wept,
      And given soft milk mingled together with the spirits of flocks,
      Of lambs and doves, mingled together in cups and dishes
      Of painted clay. The mighty Hyle is become a weeping infant;
      Soon shall the spectres of the dead follow my weaving threads.'

10 The twelve daughters of Albion attentive listen in secret shades,
      On Cambridge and Oxford beaming, soft uniting with Rahab's
         cloud,
      While Gwendolen spoke to Cambel, turning soft the spinning reel,

Albion. All are nude: Gwendolen, her hair drawn up in a modish bun,
with her back towards us, points out the following lines, in reversed
writing, to the others:

       In Heaven the only Art of Living
       Is Forgetting and Forgiving   Especially to the Female
       But if you on Earth Forgive
       You shall not find where to Live

Her left hand is clasped behind her back, her left leg crossed in front of her
right (cp. 82.*17–19*). The other daughters face forwards: one is drawn at
full length, 'modestly' covering her nakedness with her hands; the others
are in the background. The scene illustrates 82.*10–20*. Reversed writing
usually indicates a hidden truth–here an unpalatable fact of B.'s ex-
perience. The phrase 'Especially to the Female' is a comment on the first
two lines, but is so placed that its sequence is not self-evident. It may mean
'these verses are for female reading'; or may continue the sense after
Forgiving.
81.*15–16*. These lines appear beneath the design in such a way that they
may not be part of the text. But the sentiment is Gwendolen's, not B.'s,
and fits her argument: that woman must try to subdue man, and reduce
even the cruel warrior to the state of an infant dependent on woman–for
each sex, she says in her error, necessarily fears the other: safety lies only
in power.
82. *Design*: A worm winds down the righthand margin (*47*). This plate
shows many signs of haste in preparation: see *43*, *47–8*, *67–8.*.
82.*3–4*. Vala's error of 80.*12*ff.
82.*5*. But weeping is suspect in B., and often hypocritical.
82.*11–12*. i.e. engaged in spinning and weaving, female household tasks.
The female influence spreads subtly–even among the druid temples, in
spite of druid majesty and power.

Or throwing the winged shuttle, or drawing the cords with softest
    songs.
The golden cords of the looms animate beneath their touches soft
15   Along the island white, among the druid temples, while Gwendolen
Spoke to the daughters of Albion standing on Skiddaw's top.

So saying, she took a falsehood & hid it in her left hand,
To entice her sisters away to Babylon on Euphrates.
And thus she closed her left hand and uttered her falsehood.
20   Forgetting that falsehood is prophetic, she hid her hand behind her,
Upon her back behind her loins, & thus uttered her deceit:

'I heard Enitharmon say to Los: "Let the daughters of Albion
Be scattered abroad and let the name of Albion be forgoten.
Divide them into three! Name them Amalek, Canaan & Moab.
25   Let Albion remain a desolation without an inhabitant,
And let the looms of Enitharmon & the furnaces of Los
Create Jerusalem, & Babylon & Egypt & Moab & Amalek,
And Helle & Hesperia, & Hindustan & China & Japan.
But hide America, for a curse, an altar of victims & a holy place".
30   See, sisters! Canaan is pleasant, Egypt is as the Garden of Eden,
Babylon is our chief desire, Moab our bath in summer.
Let us lead the stems of this tree; let us plant it before Jerusalem
To judge the friend of sinners to death without the veil,
To cut her off from America, to close up her secret ark,

82.17. *left hand*] Traditionally 'sinister': note the prominence of left hand
and foot in the design on pl.81.
82.22. This is a subtle distortion of Los's purpose. He does associate Albion
with the land of Canaan–not to destroy him, but to fulfil Albion's poten-
tialities as a Holy Land. He does 'create' Jerusalem, etc.–though not
because he likes to see the limited forms of creation, but only because he
must create these forms or see Albion disintegrate and die.
82.28. *Helle and Hesperia*] Greece (*Hellas*) and Italy, 'the Western Land' of
the Greeks.
82.29. Los will favour America–in B.'s eyes the land of freedom: but it is
the children of Albion who make altars and holy places. This is another
distortion of truth.
82.30-1. Gwendolen finds nations hostile to Israel and Jerusalem pleasant.
82.32. *this tree*] Albion's tree of 80.1,73–the Tree of Mystery (the allusion
is, as in *Four Zoas* viia 32, to the banyan tree, whose branches touch the
ground and take root).
82.33. *without the veil*] Outside the rituals of religion. Cp. *Hebrews* xiii 12:
'Jesus also . . . suffered without the gate.'
82.34-5. Note the strong sexual symbolism here in the image of the secret
Holy Place, as in 44.33ff, 69.43. B. is not the first author to associate bel-
ligerence with sexual frustration.

35 And the fury of man exhaust in war; woman permanent remain!
    See how the fires of our loins point eastward to Babylon.
    Look! Hyle is become an infant love. Look, behold, see him lie
    Upon my bosom! Look! Here is the lovely wayward form
    That gave me sweet delight by his torments beneath my veil.
40 By the fruit of Albion's tree I have fed him with sweet milk,
    By contentions of the mighty for sacrifice of captives.
    Humanity, the great delusion, is changed to war & sacrifice;
    I have nailed his hands on Bath Rabbim & his feet on Heshbon's
        wall.
    Oh, that I could live in his sight! Oh! that I could bind him to my
        arm!'

45 So saying, she drew aside her veil from Mam-Tor to Dovedale,
    Discovering her own perfect beauty to the daughters of Albion—
    And Hyle a winding worm beneath, & not a weeping infant.
    Trembling & pitying she screamed & fled upon the wind:
    Hyle was a winding worm and herself perfect in beauty;
50 The deserts tremble at his wrath; they shrink themselves in fear!

    Cambel trembled with jealousy. She trembled, she envied!

82.35. *Woman permanent*] Implies that virginity is completeness, which B.
holds as a falsehood.
82.37. *An infant love*] Hyle has been made subject to woman, as a baby is.
So in 8.
82.43. *Bath-Rabbim: . . . Heshbon*] (B. has 'Beth' in error). For Heshbon
see 79.3n and *Song of Songs* vii 3–4: 'Thy two breasts are like two young
roes that are twins. Thy neck is as a tower of ivory: thine eyes like the
fish-pools in Heshbon, by the gate of Bath-Rabbim: thy nose is as the
tower of Lebanon which looketh toward Damascus.' The contrast in
mood between original and B.'s echo is pointed.
feet] The copies all read 'hands', but it seems clear that B. meant to refer to
hands . . . & . . . feet.
82.45. Gwendolen had forgotten 'that falsehood is prophetic' (*20*). Her
words were lies, telling of what she wanted, not what was the truth. The
result is that she finds that half, the unpleasant half, of her picture has come
true. Her perfect beauty is useless.
82.45. *Mam-Tor to Dovedale*] In the Derbyshire hills (cp. 80.66).
82.47. This was at first two lines, as follows, but two half-lines have been
erased from the plate:

    And Hyle a winding worm beneath her loom upon the scales.
    Hyle was become a winding worm: and not a weeping infant.

winding worm] A ballad expression–the worm that devours the dead: and
so a symbol of the mortality of man.
82.51. *Cambel*] Envious of Gwendolen's power, in spite of its terrible
results. Her envy, running through the nerve-threads of creation, makes

The envy ran through Cathedron's looms into the heart
Of mild Jerusalem to destroy the Lamb of God. Jerusalem
Languished upon Mount Olivet, east of mild Zion's hill.

55 Los saw the envious blight above his seventh furnace
On London's Tower on the Thames. He drew Cambel in wrath
Into his thundering bellows, heaving it for a loud blast—
And with the blast of his furnace upon fishy Billingsgate,
Beneath Albion's fatal tree, before the gate of Los,
60 Showed her the fibres of her beloved to ameliorate
The envy. Loud she laboured in the furnace of fire
To form the mighty form of Hand according to her will—
In the furnaces of Los & in the winepress treading day & night.

Naked among the human clusters, bringing wine of anguish
65 To feed the afflicted in the furnaces, she minded not
The raging flames, though she returned instead of beauty
Deformity. She gave her beauty to another, bearing abroad
Her struggling torment in her iron arms, & like a chain
Binding his wrists & ankles with the iron arms of love.

70 Gwendolen saw the infant in her sister's arms. She howled
Over the forests with bitter tears, and over the winding worm
Repentant, and she also in the eddying wind of Los's bellows
Began her dolorous task of love, in the winepress of Luvah
To form the worm into a form of love by tears & pain.
75 The sisters saw: trembling ran through their looms, softening mild

Jerusalem weaker still (for Cambel is a daughter of Albion, a part of
Jerusalem's life; and so she can affect the state of Jerusalem).
82.58. Billingsgate] The fish-market, south of the Thames in the dock area.
It is not clear whether B. had any special purpose in choosing this place.
82.63. the winepress] Cp. 80.82. The picture of the winepress in *Four Zoas*
ix 729ff (derived from *Revelation* xiv 19–20) is of the treading-out of
human souls so that the good is drawn from them and the waste is left
behind. The grapes 'sing not nor dance' though the treaders of wine do.
Los's efforts are not entirely in vain; in spite of Cambel's evil intentions,
she is led to sacrifice herself and her beauty for Hand's benefit; and as
Gwendolen does the same for Hyle, in 78 Los is 'comforted'.
82.66. Two half-lines erased from the plate (cp. 47): before erasure the
lines read:
        ... tho she returned consumd day after day
  A redning skeleton in howling woe: instead of beauty ...

The sense is somewhat obscure: its drift is that Cambel is creating an
infant 'in the raging flames', as Gwendolen did: this is the desired form of
her counterpart Hand, deformed (as Hyle was, 47), not beautiful.

Towards London; then they saw the furnaces opened & in tears
Began to give their souls away in the furnaces of affliction.

Los saw & was comforted at his furnaces, uttering thus his voice:
'I know I am Urthona, keeper of the gates of Heaven,
80   And that I can at will expatiate in the gardens of bliss;
But pangs of love draw me down to my loins which are
Become a fountain of veiny pipes. O Albion, my brother!
Pl. 83   Corruptibility appears upon thy limbs, and never more
Can I arise and leave thy side, but labour here incessant
Till thy awaking! Yet, alas, I shall forget Eternity!   ,
Against the patriarchal pomp and cruelty labouring incessant,
5   I shall become an infant horror.—Enion! Tharmas! Friends,
Absorb me not in such dire grief.—O Albion, my brother,
Jerusalem hungers in the desert: affection to her children!
The scorned and contemnd youthful girl, where shall she fly?
Sussex shuts up her villages. Hants, Devon & Wilts,
10   Surrounded with masses of stone in ordered forms, determine then
A form for Vala and a form for Luvah, here on the Thames,
Where the victim nightly howls beneath the druid's knife,
A form of vegetation. Nail them down on the stems of Mystery!
Oh, when shall the Saxon return with the English, his redeemed
brother?

82.77. *Began to give* . . .] A significant point, not to be missed for its brief
treatment. Even Gwendolen and Cambel can repent: but by 84.*26* their
fear has the upper hand again.
82.*79ff.* Los's speech is very complex and difficult to interpret. The notes
below attempt to break it into portions (*a*) to (*h*), for easier understanding.
(*a*) The theme of the speech is the nature and difficulty of Los's task.
82.*80. expatiate*] 'Wander at will'–the original meaning of the word.
83.*5. Enion! Tharmas!*] (*b*) In *Four Zoas* they are a couple parted at the
beginning of the story, Enion fading to a lost voice in the void, Tharmas
the pitiful seeking her constantly without success.
83.*6–15.* (*c*) Los turns to Albion's plight, covered as he is with 'druid
temples' such as Stonehenge and Avebury (which in fact surrounds its
village), and takes severe measures–forcing Luvah and Vala to display
their cruel forms.
83.*7. affection*] The grammar here is unusual; a copying omission may well
be the cause, or he may have misread the MS word 'affliction'. In any case,
the sense of *6–9* is very compressed. Whatever Jerusalem's affection for her
children, Albion has little: the girl with an illegitimate 'love-child' finds
the homes of Albion shut against her (cp. 'Mary', p. 582). Jerusalem's
love is essentially free; see 18.*30–32*, 79.*41–44*.
83.*10. determine then*] An imperative, declaring his own intention.
83.*14. Saxon . . . English*] The German Saxon, parted from the Anglo-
Saxon by history and the North Sea.

15 Oh, when shall the Lamb of God descend among the reprobate?
    —I woo to Amalek to protest my fugitives; Amalek trembled.
    I call to Canaan & Moab in my night watches; they mourn:
    They listen not to my cry, they rejoice among their warriors.
    Woden and Thor and Friga wholly consume my Saxons,
20 On their enormous altars built in the terrible north,
    From Ireland's rocks to Scandinavia, Persia & Tartary,
    From the Atlantic sea to the universal Erythrean.
    —Found ye London, enormous city! Weeps thy river?
    Upon his parent bosom lay thy little ones, O land
25 Forsaken. Surrey and Sussex are Enitharmon's chamber,
    Where I will build her a couch of repose, & my pillars
    Shall surround her in beautiful labyrinths. Oothoon,
    Where hides my child? In Oxford hidest thou with Antamon?
    In graceful hidings of error, in merciful deceit
30 Lest Hand the terrible destroy his Affection, thou hidest her,
    In chaste appearances for sweet deceits of love & modesty
    Immingled, interwoven, glistening to the sickening sight.
    —Let Cambel and her sisters sit within the mundane shell,
    Forming the fluctuating globe according to their will.

83.15. reprobate] For B.'s three classes–the reprobate, the redeemed and
the elect–see Milton 7.2–3n.

83.16–22. (d) The alien nations show their nature, throughout the Old
World.

83.19. Woden] The Anglo-Saxon name for the Germanic high god: father
of wisdom and lord of the dead.

Thor] 'Thunder', a Herculean weather-god, usually friendly and humorous.
Friga] A goddess of love and motherhood, but often confused with the god
Frey and the goddess Freya, and her attributes are likewise often misread.
Of the three named by B. only Woden, as lord of the dead, demanded
human sacrifice–by hanging or in battle: not, as B. and his age assumed,
by slaughter on an altar.

83.23–32. (e) Los turns to Albion again, seeing various sights–London, the
southern counties, and Oxford, where Oothoon is hidden.

83.23. Found] An imperative, an order to his workers. In 25–7 also he
speaks as the overseer.

83.27–8. Oothoon . . . Antamon] The only reference to Antamon in Jerusa-
lem; in Four Zoas viii 346 he is a son of Los, and (351) Oothoon a daughter.
The two are not linked elsewhere. In Milton pl.28.13 he does Los's work.

83.30. Affection] B. altered a to A: perhaps stressing the idea of Affection
as a title similar to Emanation.

83.33–48. (f) He speaks of the daughters of Albion: within the creation
whose form was fixed by Los–the mundane shell–they are making a
world to suit themselves, which they control.

83.34. fluctuating globe] i.e. an indefinite form, a vague shape which can be
made to 'mean' what they like.

27 + B.

35 According as they weave the little embryon nerves & veins,
    The eye, the little nostrils, & the delicate tongue & ears
    Of labyrinthine intricacy, so shall they fold the world,
    That whatever is seen upon the mundane shell, the same
    Be seen upon the fluctuating earth woven by the sisters.
40 And sometimes the earth shall roll in the abyss, & sometimes
    Stand in the centre, & sometimes stretch flat in the expanse,
    According to the will of the lovely daughters of Albion.
    Sometimes it shall assimilate with mighty Golgonooza,
    Touching its summits; & sometimes divided roll apart
45 As a beautiful veil. So these females shall fold & unfold
    According to their will the outside surface of the earth,
    An outside shadowy surface superadded to the real surface;
    Which is unchangeable for ever & ever. Amen: so be it!
    —Separate Albion's sons gently from their emanations,
50 Weaving bowers of delight on the current of infant Thames
    Where the old parent still retains his youth—as I, alas!
    Retain my youth eight thousand and five hundred years,
    The labourer of ages in the valleys of despair.
    The land is marked for desolation, & unless we plant
55 The seeds of cities & of villages in the human bosom
    Albion must be a rock of blood; mark ye the points
    Where cities shall remain & where villages; for the rest,
    It must lie in confusion till Albion's time of awaking.
    Place the tribes of Llewellyn in America for a hiding place,
60 Till sweet Jerusalem emanates again into eternity.
    The night falls thick; I go upon my watch: be attentive.
    The sons of Albion go forth; I follow from my furnaces,
    That they return no more; that a place be prepared on Euphrates.
    Listen to your watchman's voice: sleep not before the furnaces.
65 Eternal death stands at the door: O God, pity our labours!'

83.40. The allusion here is to three cosmologies: the Copernican, with the
earth one of many planets in space; the Ptolemaic, with the earth at the
centre; and the legendary, such as that of *Genesis* i, with a flat earth floating
on a dish of waters.

83.43–5. The world may be a source of vision or a cause of obscurity.

83.49–51. (*g*) Another task–presumably to prevent the daughters of Albion
having their way with the sons (as Gwendolen hoped in her speech). The
cruel sons of Albion of the earlier part of the poem are here seen as infants,
following the action of 80.57–82.54.

83.51–65. (*h*) Los concludes his song with a general view of his work.

83.59. *tribes of Llewellyn*] The Welsh, who were driven from the whole of
Britain into the western mountains. They have no historical connection
with America before modern times: the connection of Wales and America
is the connection of the land of freedom with the land of patriarchs.

So Los spoke to the daughters of Beulah, while his emanation
Like a faint rainbow waved before him in the awful gloom
Of London, city on the Thames, from Surrey hills to Highgate.
Swift turn the silver spindles, & the golden weights play soft
70 And lulling harmonies beneath the looms from Caithness in the
       north
To Lizard Point & Dover in the south. His emanation
Joyed in the many weaving threads in bright Cathedron's dome,
Weaving the web of life for Jerusalem; the web of life
Down flowing into Entuthon's vales glistens with soft affections,
75 While Los arose upon his watch, and down from Golgonooza
Putting on his golden sandals to walk from mountain to mountain,
He takes his way, girding himself with gold, & in his hand
Holding his iron mace; the spectre remains attentive.
Alternate they watch in night, alternate labour in day,
80 Before the furnaces labouring, while Los all night watches
The stars rising & setting, & the meteors & terrors of night.
With him went down the dogs of Leutha, at his feet
They lap the water of the trembling Thames, then follow swift.
And thus he heard the voice of Albion's daughters on Euphrates:

85 'Our father Albion's land! Oh, it was a lovely land! And the
       daughters of Beulah
Walked up and down in its green mountains. But Hand is fled
Away, & mighty Hyle, & after them Jerusalem is gone. Awake,
Pl. 84 Highgate's heights & Hampstead's, to Poplar, Hackney & Bow,

83.*68–71*. There are many resemblances between this passage and *Milton*
pl.6.*1–13*. The *Surrey hills* were the site of the old ironworks; thence to
Highgate is south to north. *Caithness, Lizard* and *Dover* represent the entire
kingdom, from north to south-west and south-east extremities.
83.*69. the spindles*] The bobbins, and the *weights* of a loom. This is work of
the same kind, but opposite effect, to Vala's, in 80.*32–6*.
83.*74. Entuthon*] The dark region surrounding Golgonooza.
83.*78. The spectre*] Los's spectre, forgotten since ch. 1, when Los made
his spectre subservient to his will.
83.*82. the dogs of Leutha*] From the Isle of Dogs, in the loop of the
Thames. Cp. 45.*15*.
84.*1*. The sequence here from the previous plate is not very clear, and the
sentence 'Awake Highgate's heights . . .' seems to lack something. This
is no doubt partly due to B.'s tendency to compose plate by plate. The foot
of pl.83 is very crowded; one missing line would be sufficient, but there is
no room for it on pl.83 and–if this hypothetical line did exist in B.'s
mine–he did not squeeze it in at the top of pl.84 either. The idea is clearly:
'Awake, Albion–bring back the days when from Highgate's heights . . .'
(*Erdman 1965* remarks (p. 733) that pl.83 is 'different in technique and
lettering as well as content and that it obviously did not originally follow.

To Islington & Paddington & the brook of Albion's river.
We builded Jerusalem as a city & a temple; from Lambeth
We began our foundations, lovely Lambeth! O lovely hills
5 Of Camberwell, we shall behold you no more in glory & pride,
For Jerusalem lies in ruins & the furnaces of Los are builded there.
You are now shrunk up to a narrow rock in the midst of the sea;
But here we build Babylon on Euphrates, compelled to build
And to inhabit, our little ones to clothe in armour of the gold
10 Of Jerusalem's cherubims, & to forge them swords of her altars.
I see London blind & age-bent begging through the streets
Of Babylon, led by a child: his tears run down his beard.
The voice of wandering Reuben echoes from street to street
In all the cities of the nations; Paris, Madrid, Amsterdam.
15 The corner of Broad Street weeps, Poland Street languishes;
To Great Queen Street & Lincoln's Inn, all is distress & woe.

'The night falls thick, Hand comes from Albion in his strength:
He combines into a mighty one, the double Molech & Chemosh,
Marching through Egypt in his fury. The east is pale at his course;
20 The nations of India, the wild Tartar that never knew man
Starts from his lofty places & casts down his tents & flees away.
But we woo him all the night in songs. O Los, come forth, O Los,
Divide us from these terrors & give us power them to subdue!
25 Arise upon thy watches, let us see thy globe of fire
On Albion's rocks, & let thy voice be heard upon Euphrates!'

Thus sang the daughters in lamentation, uniting into one

Part of the daughters' song of building appears to be lost'). Yet the theme of
83.*85* is that of 84.*4*, etc.
84.*2. the brook of Albion's river*] Tyburn brook. See map (p. 621).
84.*5.* The daughters of Albion lament the land from which they were
exiled (in this resembling the daughters of Jerusalem who lamented in
Psalm cxxxvii and *Lamentations*); but, like the Jews of the Old Testament,
they do not admit that the original fault was their own. They cannot see
the purpose of Los's fierce furnaces.
84.*11.* This line is illustrated in the design at the foot of the page.
84.*15–16.* See map. The place-names are all in central London, then and
now. Beneath *16* three lines have been irrecoverably deleted.
84.*18. double Molech and Chemosh*] Cp. 68.*17n.*
84.*22.* The daughters of Albion want to use Los for their own ends, to
subdue the sons to their influence. The repentance of 82.*77* has been short-
lived.
84.*24. globe of fire*] With which he searched Albion (pl.45) to find those
responsible for Albion's fall; not the globe of blood of 86.*52*. This globe is
apt to show up the errors of Albion's children, not to help them in their
perverted aims.

With Rahab as she turned the iron spindle of destruction.
Terrified at the sons of Albion, they took the falsehood which
Gwendolen hid in her left hand. It grew & grew till it

[Design]

Pl. 85 Became a space & an allegory around the winding worm.
They named it Canaan, & built for it a tender moon.
Los smiled with joy, thinking on Enitharmon, & he brought
Reuben from his twelvefold wanderings & led him into it,
5 Planting the seeds of the twelve tribes & Moses & David,
And gave a time & revolution to the space, six thousand years.
He called it Divine Analogy; for in Beulah the feminine
Emanations create space, the masculine create time, & plant
The seeds of beauty in the space; listening to their lamentation
10 Los walks upon his ancient mountains in the deadly darkness,
Among his furnaces directing his laborious myriads watchful,
Looking to the east; & his voice is heard over the whole earth,
As he watches the furnaces by night & directs the labourers.

84.27. *spindle*] In 80.32 the spindle is Vala's, but she and Rahab are different
visions of the same personality.
84.28. *Terrified at the sons of Albion*] Because the daughters feared they were
going to lose their power over the aggressive sons.
84. *Design*: Illustrating 11; the boy seems to be leading the old man past a
classical church to a Gothic one. Cp. design to 'London' in *Experience*.

85.1–9. *the winding worm*] Hyle.
space] The daughters of Albion are working with a lie; nevertheless Los
finds he can do something with it, and he develops the long history of the
Jews out of it. That history is a history of falsehood–in religion and act,
for both the jealous God of the Old Testament and the cruel wars he
demanded were false–yet it was possible for the true redemption by
forgiveness to come out of it. Therefore Los uses it. In 7–9, B. sees *space*
as the home of female activity, *time* as the male's. In *Milton* pl.8.39–44
Enitharmon 'creates a space' to save Satan and Michael and 'closed it with
a tender moon' (cp. 2 here). In *Milton* pl.10.6–7 B. writes this gloss:
  The nature of a female space is this: it shrinks the organs
  Of life till they become finite, and itself seems infinite.
Thus the 'female space' is another version of the creation which does good
by limiting the damage caused by evil; though mortality, created as an
end in itself, would be evil. Note that 1 could well be the end of a sentence
in which the daughters of Beulah 'create' the space. This they do, e.g. in
Four Zoas i 90. In *Milton* (see above) Enitharmon acts likewise. It may well
be that B. has connected pls 84 and 85 by a kind of butt-joint, and that
originally Gwendolen was not the creator of this 'space'. In 82.20 a similar
line introduces her 'deceit'. Nevertheless, B. published the passage in the
form it now takes. *Allegory*] In B. usually means 'fallacy'.

And thus Los replies upon his watch; the valleys listen silent,
15　The stars stand still to hear. Jerusalem & Vala cease to mourn.
His voice is heard from Albion; the Alps & Apennines
Listen; Hermon & Lebanon bow their crowned heads,
Babel & Shinar look toward the western gate; they sit down
Silent at his voice, they view the red globe of fire in Los's hand
20　As he walks from furnace to furnace, directing the labourers.
And this is the song of Los, the song that he sings on his watch:

[Design]

'O lovely mild Jerusalem! O Shiloh of Mount Ephraim!
I see thy gates of precious stones, thy walls of gold & silver;
Thou art the soft reflected image of the sleeping man
25　Who, stretched on Albion's rocks, reposes amidst his twenty-eight
Cities, where Beulah lovely terminates in the hills & valleys of
　　Albion—
Cities not yet embodied in time and space. Plant ye
The seeds, O sisters, in the bosom of time, & space's womb,
To spring up for Jerusalem. Lovely shadow of sleeping Albion,
30　Why wilt thou rend thyself apart & build an earthly kingdom,
To reign in pride & to oppress, & to mix the cup of delusion?
O thou that dwellest with Babylon, come forth, O lovely one!

[Design]

Pl. 86 'I see thy form, O lovely mild Jerusalem, winged with six wings

85. *Design*: An ornament of leaves, to mark off the idyllic passage which
follows.

85.22. *Jerusalem . . . Shiloh*] Here identified as one Holy City, not the
hostile capitals of later Jewish history. A 'reflected image' is another way
of saying 'emanation'.

85.26–8. *Beulah lovely . . . time and space*] These things are seen in dreams
and visions, not in the material of time and space.

sisters] The daughters of Beulah (7–9).

85.32. Jerusalem was carried captive to Babylon (Rahab's city). But Los
regards her as having been in captivity to evil long before, in her dreams
and wars of conquest.

85. *Design* (covering about a third of the plate): A rather rough design
showing a female spinning plant-fibres out of a man. In the background,
the sun, moon, a star and a comet. This design illustrates 87.6–9.

86.1. *they form . . . Jerusalem . . . six wings*] In this passage, Albion and his
emanation Jerusalem are not always distinguished, since in Eternity they
are parts of one another. The six wings come from *Isaiah* vi 2, where the
seraphim cover their faces with one pair, their feet with another, and fly
with the third. Jerusalem's wings here cover head, bosom and loins. Note
that she is *threefold* (2)–only when united with Albion can she be perfect
and fourfold. Hers is the highest beauty of Beulah (cp. **14.**16ff).

In the opacous bosom of the sleeper, lovely threefold
In head & heart & reins, three universes of love & beauty.
Thy forehead bright: *Holiness to the Lord*, with gates of pearl
5 Reflects Eternity beneath thy azure wings of feathery down,
Ribbed delicate & clothed with feathered gold & azure & purple
From thy white shoulders shadowing, purity in holiness!
Thence feathered with soft crimson of the ruby, bright as fire,
Spreading into the azure wings, which like a canopy
10 Bends over thy immortal head in which Eternity dwells.
Albion, beloved land, I see thy mountains & thy hills
And valleys & thy pleasant cities: *Holiness to the Lord.*
I see the spectres of thy dead, O emanation of Albion.

'Thy bosom white, translucent, covered with immortal gems,
15 A sublime ornament not obscuring the outlines of beauty,
Terrible to behold for thy extreme beauty & perfection.
Twelvefold here all the tribes of Israel I behold
Upon the holy land: I see the river of life & tree of life;
I see the New Jerusalem descending out of Heaven
20 Between thy wings of gold & silver, feathered immortal,
Clear as the rainbow, as the cloud of the sun's tabernacle.

86.3. *three universes*] Described in turn, *4–13, 14–21, 22–32.* The whole
sequence draws heavily on the imagery of Aaron's vestments (*Exodus*
xxviii) and of the New Jerusalem (*Revelation* xxi).
86.4. *Holiness . . . Lord*] Cp. *Exodus* xxviii 36: 'And thou shalt make a
plate of pure gold, and grave upon it . . . HOLINESS TO THE LORD . . . And
it shall be upon Aaron's forehead, that Aaron may bear the iniquity of the
holy things.' *gates of pearl*] In *Revelation* xxi 21, 'the twelve gates' (of
the new Jerusalem) 'were twelve pearls; every several gate was one pearl'.
86.6. *gold, and azure and purple*] Aaron's vestments were to be of 'gold,
and blue, and purple, and scarlet, and fine linen' (*Exodus* xxviii 5, etc.).
The *purple, scarlet* and *fine linen* were echoed in 59.55; and here in the *white
shoulders* of Jerusalem.
86.14. *thy bosom . . . covered with immortal gems*] Aaron's breastplate was
set with twelve gems of different kinds, one for each of the twelve tribes
(*Exodus* xxviii 17–21).
86.17. *twelvefold*] Each tribe, in *Revelation* vii 4–8, is numbered twelvefold,
multiplied by a thousand.
86.18. *river of life and tree of life*] From *Revelation* xxii 1–2: 'And he
shewed me a pure river of water of life, clear as crystal proceeding out of
the throne of God and of the Lamb . . . on either side of the river was there
the tree of life . . . and the leaves of the tree were for the healing of the
nations.'
86.19. From *Revelation* xxi 2: 'And I John saw the holy city, new Jerusa-
lem, coming down from God out of Heaven, prepared as a bride adorned
for her husband.'

'Thy reins covered with wings translucent, sometimes covering
And sometimes spread abroad, reveal the flames of holiness
Which like a robe covers, & like a veil of seraphim
25 In flaming fire unceasing burns from eternity to eternity.
Twelvefold I there behold Israel in her tents.
A pillar of a cloud by day, a pillar of fire by night
Guides them. There I behold Moab & Ammon & Amalek;
There bells of silver round thy knees, living, articulate
30 Comforting sounds of love & harmony; & on thy feet
Sandals of gold & pearl, & Egypt & Assyria before me,
The isles of Javan, Philistia, Tyre and Lebanon.'

Thus Los sings upon his watch, walking from furnace to furnace.
He seizes his hammer every hour; flames surround him as
35 He beats. Seas roll beneath his feet, tempests muster
Around his head, the thick hailstones stand ready to obey
His voice in the black cloud. His sons labour in thunders
At his furnaces; his daughters at their looms sing woes.
His emanation separates, in milky fibres agonising
40 Among the golden looms of Cathedron, sending fibres of love
From Golgonooza with sweet visions for Jerusalem, wanderer.

(Nor can any consummate bliss without being generated
On earth of those whose emanations weave the loves
Of Beulah for Jerusalem & Shiloh, in immortal Golgonooza,
45 Concentring in the majestic form of Erin, in eternal tears

86.24. *a veil of seraphim*] Seraphim are only mentioned in the Bible at
Isaiah vi 2–6 (cp. *1n*), where they may be taken as a living veil before God,
though Isaiah says 'I saw the Lord'. The same word in Hebrew, however,
is used in three places in the Bible, but translated 'fiery flying serpent'
(*Numbers* xxi 6–8, *Isaiah* xiv 29, xxx 6). With the 'live coal' which the
seraph held in his hand to purify Isaiah in his vision, this accounts for the
flaming fire of 25.
86.28. *Moab, Ammon, Amalek*] Hostile nations on earth, reconciled in
Eternity.
86.29. *bells*] Such as surrounded the hem of Aaron's robe (*Exodus* xxviii 33).
86.31. *sandals*] B.'s addition, and not mentioned in the account of Aaron's
vestments.
86.32. *Javan*] Occasionally mentioned in the Old Testament, meaning
Greece: the word is cognate with 'Ionian'.
86.42–6. A difficult passage: 'No person can consummate bliss without be-
coming one of Los's agents in this mortal world, so great is Los's deter-
mination to turn all possible things to his reforming purpose.' They are
'generated' through 'those whose emanations weave, in Golgonooza,
earthly forms for them.' The emanations also 'concentre' (45) and 'view'
(46–7). For *Erin* see 48.27.

Viewing the winding worm on the deserts of Great Tartary,
Viewing Los in his shudderings, pouring balm on his sorrows.
So dread is Los's fury, that none dare him to approach
Without becoming his children in the furnaces of affliction.)

50 And Enitharmon like a faint rainbow waved before him,
Filling with fibres from his loins, which reddened with desire
Into a globe of blood beneath his bosom, trembling in darkness
Of Albion's clouds. He fed it with his tears & bitter groans,
Hiding his spectre in invisibility from the timorous shade
55 Till it became a separated cloud of beauty, grace & love,
Among the darkness of his furnaces dividing asunder, till
She separated stood before him, a lovely female, weeping,
Even Enitharmon separated outside. And his loins closed
And healed after the separation; his pains he soon forgot,
60 Lured by her beauty outside of himself in shadowy grief.
Two wills they had, two intellects: & not as in times of old.

Silent they wandered hand in hand, like two infants wandering
From Enion in the deserts, terrified at each other's beauty,
Envying each other yet desiring, in all-devouring love,

Pl. 87   *[Design]*

Repelling weeping Enion, blind & age-bent into the fourfold
Deserts. Los first broke silence & began to utter his love:

'O lovely Enitharmon, I behold thy graceful forms
Moving beside me, till intoxicated with the woven labyrinth
5 Of beauty & perfection my wild fibres shoot in veins
Of blood through all my nervous limbs. Soon overgrown in roots
I shall be closed from thy sight. Seize therefore in thy hand
The small fibres as they shoot around me, draw out in pity
And let them run on the winds of thy bosom. I will fix them
10 With pulsations; we will divide them into sons & daughters
To live in thy bosom's translucence as in an eternal morning.'

86.50. For comment on 86.50–88.58, see headnote, p. 793.
86.50–2. Cp. 82.81–2.
86.55. it] The 'shade', Enitharmon. This is the division of male and female.
86.61. So in *Four Zoas* ii 416.
86.63. *Enion*] In the myth of *Four Zoas*, the mother of Los and Enitharmon; in the present myth, where Enitharmon is parted directly from Los's substance (as in *Urizen*), she seems to have no real place. In *Four Zoas*, as here, they repel her and she drifts away forlorn.

87. *Design* (half the page): The scene of 1–2, with two figures watching on the left.
87.6–9. This is illustrated in the design at the foot of pl.85.

27*

Enitharmon answered: 'No! I will seize thy fibres & weave
Them—not as thou wilt but as I will, for I will create
A round womb beneath my bosom, lest I also be overwoven
15 With love. Be thou assured I never will be thy slave.
Let man's delight be love, but woman's delight be pride.
In Eden our loves were the same; here they are opposite.
I have loves of my own; I will weave them in Albion's spectre.
Cast thou in Jerusalem's shadows thy loves—silk of liquid
20 Rubies, jacinths, crysolites, issuing from thy furnaces. While
Jerusalem divides thy care, while thou carest for Jerusalem,
Know that I never will be thine. Also thou hidest Vala;
From her these fibres shoot to shut me in a grave.
You are Albion's victim; he has set his daughter in your path.'

Pl. 88 Los answered, sighing like the bellows of his furnaces:

'I care not; the swing of my hammer shall measure the starry
round.
When in Eternity man converses with man they enter
Into each other's bosom (which are universes of delight)
5   In mutual interchange—& first their emanations meet,
Surrounded by their children. If they embrace & commingle,
The human fourfold forms mingle also in thunders of intellect.
But if the emanations mingle not; with storms & agitations
Of earthquakes & consuming fires they roll apart in fear.
10 For man cannot unite with man but by their emanations,
Which stand, both male & female, at the gates of each humanity.
How then can I ever again be united as man with man
While thou, my emanation, refusest my fibres of dominion?
When souls mingle & join through all the fibres of brotherhood,
15 Can there be any secret joy on earth greater than this?'

Enitharmon answered: 'This is woman's world, nor need she any

87.14. The woman takes the creation of children, and so control of them,
for herself.
87.16. Cp. 81.6.
87.18. in Albion's spectre] She chooses the male spectre to work on, and
grants him the female emanation, Jerusalem—with the warning that be-
cause of this she will be jealous. This is the evil of sexuality; instead of an
ideal 'human' relationship between the complete Los-Enitharmon per-
sonality and the complete Albion-Jerusalem (as there would be in Eden),
there is only a set of contradicting desires and jealousies between one part
and the others: cp. Los's view of the ideal in 88.3–15.
87.24. Enitharmon is jealous because Los works to release Jerusalem; she
supposes that his intentions are dishonest.
88.2. Los measures time, with which he is often associated.

Spectre to defend her from man. I will create secret places,
And the masculine names of the places *Merlin* & *Arthur*.
A triple female tabernacle for moral law I weave,
20 That he who loves Jesus may loathe, terrified, female love,
Till God himself become a male subservient to the female.'

She spoke in scorn & jealousy, alternate torments, and
So speaking she sat down on Sussex shore, singing lulling
Cadences, & playing in sweet intoxication among the glistening
25 Fibres of Los, sending them over the ocean eastward into
The realms of dark death. (O perverse to thyself, contrarious
To thy own purposes!) For when she began to weave,
Shooting out in sweet pleasure, her bosom in milky love
Flowed into the aching fibres of Los; yet contending against him
30 In pride, sending his fibres over to her objects of jealousy
In the little lovely allegoric night of Albion's daughters
Which stretched abroad, expanding east & west & north & south
Through all the world of Erin & of Los & all their children.

A sullen smile broke from the spectre in mockery & scorn,
35 Knowing himself the author of their divisions & shrinkings.
    Gratified
At their contentions, he wiped his tears, he washed his visage:

'The man who respects woman shall be despised by woman,
And deadly cunning & mean abjectness only shall enjoy them.
For I will make their places of joy & love, excrementitious,
40 Continually building, continually destroying in family feuds.
While you are under the dominion of a jealous female,
Unpermanent for ever because of love & jealousy,
You shall want all the minute particulars of life.'

Thus joyed the spectre in the dusky fires of Los's forge, eyeing
45 Enitharmon, who at her shining looms sings lulling cadences,
While Los stood at his anvil in wrath, the victim of their love

88.18. Merlin & Arthur] Both great men among the Britons whose down-
fall could be traced to women. See, for Merlin 30.*37n*; for Arthur, 54.*25n*.
88.19. a triple female tabernacle] A set of enclosed places, in contrast with
the three open heavens of 86.*1–32*.
88.23. the Sussex shore] Where B. lived for three years. He regarded his
stay there as a time of subtle temptation to leave his prophetic duty and
devote himself to easier tasks, but no specific allusion is evident.
88.26. O perverse . . . !] The author's own comment, an interjection ad-
dressed to Enitharmon.

And hate—dividing the space of love with brazen compasses
In Golgonooza & in Udan-Adan, & in Entuthon of Urizen.

The blow of his hammer is Justice; the swing of his hammer,
Mercy;
50   The force of Los's hammer is Eternal Forgiveness. But
His rage or his mildness were vain; she scattered his love on the
wind
Eastward into her own centre, creating the female womb
In mild Jerusalem around the Lamb of God. Loud howl
The furnaces of Los, loud roll the wheels of Enitharmon.
55   The four Zoas in all their faded majesty burst out in fury
And fire. Jerusalem took the cup which foamed in Vala's hand
Like the red sun upon the mountains in the bloody day
Upon the hermaphroditic winepresses of love & wrath.

Pl. 89   Though divided by the cross & nails & thorns & spear
In cruelties of Rahab & Tirzah, permanent endure
A terrible indefinite hermaphroditic form,
A winepress of love & wrath, double, hermaphroditic,
5   Twelvefold in allegoric pomp, in selfish holiness,
The Pharisaion, the Grammateis, the Presbyterion,

88.48. Golgonooza] Set in the midst of the lake of Udan-Adan in the forest
of Entuthon Benithon, in Ulro: see Four Zoas v 76.
88.52. Eastward . . . centre] Both places of corruption; cp. 5.68, 12.55
Womb] Cp. 87.14.
88.56. Jerusalem succumbs still further to the power of Babylon, or Rahab-
Vala.
88.58. hermaphroditic winepresses] For the duality of the winepress, see
89.4; hermaphroditic indicates a sterile association of sexual forms, without
blending of personality such as that spoken of by Los in 3–15.
89.1–3. Endure] Plural because of the plurality of the 'hermaphroditic
form' ('twelvefold', 5). This is 'divided' within and against itself by the
activities of Rahab and Tirzah, who torture the male in order to retain
control over him (see 67.41–68.70). Yet the 'form' remains 'permanent'
on earth, i.e. it recurs again and again.
89.4. winepress] B. is not sure about his winepress; it can be an instrument
of righteousness and of purification (see Four Zoas ix 692ff and Jerusalem
pl.82.63), but also of cruelty and judgment for sin. It may therefore be
'double' for either of two reasons—the mixture of good and evil it repre-
sents or, more probably, because it is a cruelty under pretence of doing
good.
89.6–7. Pharisaion, etc.] i.e. 'the Pharisees, the scribes, the elders ('of the
people'), the High Priest, the priest and the Sadducees'. All were involved
in the condemnation of Jesus. B. has used Greek words; Pharisaion seems
to be neuter, a collective, but may be plural. If so, it is a genitive, which B.

The Archiereus, the Iereus, the Saddusaion, double
Each withoutside of the other, covering eastern heaven.

10 Thus was the Covering Cherub revealed, majestic image
Of selfhood, body put off, the Antichrist accursed,
Covered with precious stones, a human dragon terrible
And bright, stretched over Europe & Asia gorgeous:
In three nights he devoured the rejected corse of death.

15 His head dark, deadly, in its brain encloses a reflection
Of Eden all perverted: Egypt on the Gihon many-tongued
And many-mouthed; Ethiopia, Lybia, the Sea of Rephaim.
Minute particulars in slavery I behold among the brick-kilns
Disorganized; & there is Pharaoh in his iron court,
And the dragon of the River & the furnaces of iron.

mistook for a nominative. *Iereus* omits the *H* (cp. Eng. *hierarchy*) which
would transliterate the rough breathing sign over *i*. *Presbyterion* is un-
usual, but found in *Luke* xxii 66, 'the *elders of the people* and the chief
priests and scribes.'

89.8. Each withoutside] All surface and no heart; each taking precedence: cp.
12.55n, 71.6–8.

89.9. the Covering Cherub] The revelation of the Covering Cherub is a
climax in *Milton* (pl.37.6ff, where a note on the name will be found): there
also the climax comes shortly before the Cherub's overthrow–his revela-
tion is a sure step towards his rejection by all who see him. Note also how
the description of the Covering Cherub is similar in composition to, but
in contrast with, the description of the unfallen Jerusalem, in pl.86.

89.13. in three nights] The three nights between crucifixion and resurrection.
The meaning seems to be that the Cherub lives by the mortal form of man,
rejected by Christ in the resurrection. In *The Everlasting Gospel* vi 91–6
man's spectre is likened to a serpent, as the Cherub–also a spectral being–is
here a dragon.

> In three nights he devoured his prey,
> And still he devours the body of clay;
> For dust and clay is the serpent's meat,
> Which never was made for man to eat.

In *Genesis* iii 14 the serpent is condemned to eat dust: B. turns this to use
here; the serpent lives on death, man on life.

89.15–16. Gihon . . . Rephaim] *Gihon* was one of the four rivers of Paradise;
described in *Genesis* ii 10–14; here the Nile, with its estuary. B. introduces
the four rivers in turn (*24, 35, 38*). The Sea of Rephaim does not appear in
the Bible–see *37.12* and *Milton* pl.19.40n.

89.18. Disorganized] In chaos, unable to function according to their true
nature.

89.19. dragon of the River] Of the Nile. From *Ezekiel* xxix 3: 'Thus saith
the Lord God: Behold, I am against thee, Pharaoh king of Egypt, the

20 Outwoven from Thames & Tweed & Severn, awful streams,
    Twelve ridges of stone frown over all the earth in tyrant pride,
    Frown over each river—stupendous works of Albion's druid sons.
    And Albion's forests of oaks covered the earth from pole to pole.

    His bosom wide reflects Moab & Ammon, on the River
25 Pison, since called Arnon; there is Heshbon beautiful,
    The rocks of Rabbath on the Arnon, & the fish-pools of Heshbon
    Whose currents flow into the Dead Sea by Sodom & Gomorrah.
    Above his head high-arching wings, black, filled with eyes,
    Spring upon iron sinews from the scapulae & os humeri.
30 There Israel in bondage to his generalizing gods
    Molech & Chemosh; & in his left breast is Philistia,
    In druid temples over the whole earth with victims' sacrifice,
    From Gaza to Damascus, Tyre & Sidon, & the gods
    Of Javan, through the isles of Grecia & all Europe's kings.
35 Where Hiddekel pursues his course among the rocks

great dragon that lieth in the midst of his rivers, which hath said, My
river is mine own, and I have made it for myself.'
89.20. *Outwoven*] Spreading out from, originating in.
89.21. *Twelve ridges of stone*] B.'s notion of Stonehenge; cp. 68.24,41n.
89.24. *His*] The Cherub's.
89.24–7. The Cherub represents and contains the elements of the tribes
from beyond Jordan, i.e. outside the Promised Land, who were often
hostile to the chosen people.
Pison, since called Arnon] The *Pison* was another river of Paradise; B.
identified Gihon and the Nile in *15*, and here Pison with Arnon, the river
on the border of Israel and Moab–see map, and *Milton* pl.19.5n. Cp. also
61.33, the same names in a very different association.
89.26. *rocks of Rabbath*] Rabbath (Rabbah) was the scene of much fighting
against the Ammonites (2 *Samuel* xi, 1 *Chronicles* xx) but no rocks are par-
ticularly mentioned; they are B.'s imaginative detail.   *Heshbon*] Cp.
82.43n: it is not on the Arnon.   *Sodom and Gomorrah*] On the shores of
the Dead Sea, but probably not at the mouth of the Arnon; this again is
B.'s interpretation.
89.28. *filled with eyes*] As were the wheels in Ezekiel's vision (*Ezekiel* i),
and the four beasts before the throne of God in *Revelation* iv 6.
89.29. *scapulae and os humeri*] Shoulder-blades and upper arm-bone.
89.30–1. *his generalizing gods, Molech and Chemosh*] These were gods of
child sacrifice; to live and think by generalized and abstract notions, in-
stead of by human compassion, leads only to cruelty and destruction.
89.33–4. *Gaza . . . Europe's Kings*] This is a progression up the Palestinian
coast, westwards through Greece to the rest of Europe.
89.35. *Hiddekel*] The Tigris, and another of the four rivers of Paradise
(*Genesis* ii 14). Nineveh was on its banks, and Daniel saw a vision (*Daniel*
x 4) beside it. B. sees it as a river of error–hence the rocks.

Two wings spring from his ribs, of brass, starry, black as night,
But translucent their blackness as the dazzling of gems.
His loins enclose Babylon on Euphrates beautiful,
And Rome in sweet Hesperia. There Israel scattered abroad
40 In martyrdoms & slavery I behold: ah vision of sorrow!
Enclosed by eyeless wings, glowing with fire as the iron
Heated in the smith's forge, but cold the wind of their dread fury.

But in the midst of a devouring stomach, Jerusalem
Hidden within the Covering Cherub as in a tabernacle
45 Of threefold workmanship, in allegoric delusion & woe.
There the seven Kings of Canaan & five Baalim of Philistia,
Sihon & Og, the Anakim & Emim, Nephilim & Gibborim,
From Babylon to Rome: & the wings spread from Japan
Where the Red Sea terminates the world of generation & death,
50 To Ireland's farthest rocks where giants builded their Causeway
Into the Sea of Rephaim; but the sea o'erwhelmed them all.

A double female now appeared within the tabernacle;
Religion hid in war, a Dragon red & hidden Harlot
Each within other; but without a warlike mighty one
55 Of dreadful power, sitting upon Horeb, pondering dire
And mighty preparations, mustering multitudes innumerable
Of warlike sons among the sands of Midian & Aram.
For multitudes of those who sleep in Alla descend,
Lured by his warlike symphonies of tabret, pipe & harp,

89.38. Euphrates] The fourth river of Paradise.
89.43–5. This is the usual image of the Cherub–the Cherub who covers the
Mercy Seat to keep man from seeing God.
threefold workmanship] Denotes that something is lacking, for true divinity
(which is the apotheosis of humanity) is fourfold.
89.46. Cp. Milton pl.40.24n: they are the numbers of Canaanite tribes and
Philistine towns opposing Israel.
89.47. Anakim . . . Gibborim] All giants who had lived in or around Canaan
before the Israelites came.
89.52. See 75.15ff and Milton pls.37.35ff, 40.20ff. These lines are an inter-
pretation of Israelite history in the Old Testament. Horeb is Sinai, where
the Law was given; the multitudes innumerable are the seed of Abraham.
They are governed by a false vision of God–as a warlike mighty one who
gives laws; and the God who is hidden in the tabernacle of their highest
ritual is not the Divine Vision, but a god, or rather goddess, of female
cruelty, whose religion is war and whose war is excused as religion. Cp.
also Ezekiel xxviii 14, 'Those art the anointed cherub that covereth; and I
have set thee so: thou wast upon the holy mountain of God' (though this
would mean Jerusalem, it might remind B. of Horeb).
89.58. Alla] A part of Ulro–cp. Milton pl.34.12.

60   Burst the bottoms of the graves & funeral arks of Beulah;
      Wandering in that unknown night beyond the silent grave,
      They become one with the Antichrist & are absorbed in him.

Pl. 90 —The feminine separates from the masculine & both from man,
      Ceasing to be his emanations, life to themselves assuming!
      And while they circumscribe his brain, & while they circumscribe
      His heart, & while they circumscribe his loins, a veil & net
5   Of veins of red blood grows around them like a scarlet robe,
      Covering them from the sight of man like the woven veil of sleep,
      Such as the flowers of Beulah weave to be their funeral mantles
      But dark, opaque, tender to touch, & painful! & agonizing
      To the embrace of love, & to the mingling of soft fibres
10   Of tender affection: that no more the masculine mingles
      With the feminine, but the sublime is shut out from the pathos
      In howling torment, to build stone walls of separation, compelling
      The pathos to weave curtains of hiding secrecy from the torment.

      Bowen & Conwenna stood on Skiddaw, cutting the fibres
15   Of Benjamin from Chester's river. Loud the river; loud the Mersey
      And the Ribble thunder into the Irish sea, as the twelve sons
      Of Albion drank & imbibed the life & eternal form of Luvah.
      Cheshire & Lancashire & Westmorland groan in anguish:
      As they cut the fibres from the rivers he sears them with hot
20   Iron of his forge, & fixes them into bones of chalk & rock.
      Conwenna sat above; with solemn cadences she drew
      Fibres of life out from the bones into her golden loom.
      Hand had his furnace on Highgate's heights, & it reached
      To Brockley Hills across the Thames: he with double Boadicea

90.1. Another scene begins, with a general comment from B., describing
the nature and effects of the fall from Eternity. The material of this plate in
general resembles that of 80.57–85.13, the story of Gwendolen and Cambel.
90.14ff. Conwenna is Bowen's emanation. In 16.49 Benjamin is given
Derby, Cheshire and Monmouth. The nature of this action is not clear,
but Los's words in 28–38 may explain it–that Bowen and Conwenna are
separating Benjamin from the home assigned to him by Los so that they
may enjoy it for themselves. Chester's river is the Dee. B. often sees veins
as rivers of life-blood; here the rivers are veins of the counties' life.
90.18. Cheshire, etc.] The rivers named in 15–16 flow into the Irish Sea
from these respective counties.
90.19. they] Bowen and Conwenna; he is Bowen.
90.21-3. Conwenna has her looms; Bowen his furnaces, working for ill in
opposition to the looms of Enitharmon and the furnaces of Los.
90.24. Brockley Hills] To the south-east of London.
double Boadicea] She appears occasionally in the lists of the daughters of
Albion; in 71.23 B. explains this discrepancy by identifying her with

25 In cruel pride cut Reuben apart from the hills of Surrey,
     Commingling with Luvah & with the sepulchre of Luvah:
     For the male is a furnace of beryl: the female is a golden loom.

     —Los cries: 'No individual ought to appropriate to himself,
     Or to his emanation, any of the universal characteristics
30 Of David or of Eve, of the woman, or of the Lord,
     Of Reuben or of Benjamin, of Joseph or Judah or Levi.
     Those who dare appropriate to themselves universal attributes
     Are the blasphemous selfhoods & must be broken asunder.
     A vegetated Christ & a virgin Eve are the hermaphroditic
35 Blasphemy; by his Maternal Birth he is that Evil One.
     And his maternal humanity must be put off eternally,
     Lest the sexual generation swallow up regeneration.
     Come, Lord Jesus! take on thee the Satanic body of holiness!'

Cambel. 'Double' here may refer to this duality; or to the nature of the historical Boadicea, elevated as a heroine in legend, but yet warlike and cruel.
90.24–6. An obscure statement, partly clarified in the next passage (38). In 26 it is Hand who 'commingles'; Luvah here is clearly an Antichrist; his sepulchre resembles Christ's, but his 'commingling' with Hand is equally clearly to no good end. In *Four Zoas* Luvah causes his own downfall, and is almost destroyed: this is imaged by the 'robes of blood' which enwrap him. Jesus comes, takes the robes of blood on himself, and in *Four Zoas* viii is buried in the sepulchre (cp. 38 below); this is Rahab's triumph, but it is shortlived. Thus B. adapts the Gospel narrative to his own myth, retaining the essential themes unharmed. Here he intends to draw together all the forms of evil into 'One Great Satan' (43).
90.27. So in 5.34 (cp. also 53.9): the context of this line clarifies the sense, that these are the furnaces and looms of the corrupt children of Albion, beautiful but evil.
90.32–4. *a vegetated Christ and a virgin Eve*] The sense of these lines is: 'Those who dare say, "I am God" (as Albion did, 54.16), or "Lordship (or Womanhood) is seen ideally in me and nowhere else and in no other way", are making a claim they have no right to. To claim similar attributes for Christ is to *vegetate* him–to bring him down to the level of mortality, to narrow his nature; and this is blasphemous.' Eve is not of course said to remain a virgin; B. means that Mary, mother of Jesus, is falsely elevated as an image of universal motherhood–as a virgin, not as a mature woman. Taken together, these false notions of Christ and his mother result in a false religion with sterile values–a religion prolonging the divisions of 'sexual generation' (37) and Vala's domination (in 'Maternal Birth' not involving a male).
90.38. *Come, Lord Jesus*] John's prayer at the end of *Revelation* (also at 50.10). *take . . . the Satanic body*] In order to test, and disprove, its power to assimilate Christ's Divine Humanity and destroy it. This theme is further treated in *Four Zoas* viii.

So Los cried in the valleys of Middlesex in the spirit of prophecy,
40 While in selfhood Hand & Hyle & Bowen & Skofield appropriate
The divine names: seeking to vegetate the Divine Vision
In a corporeal & ever-dying vegetation & corruption.
Mingling with Luvah in one, they become One Great Satan.

Loud scream the daughters of Albion beneath the tongs & hammer;
45 Dolorous are their lamentations in the burning forge!
They drink Reuben & Benjamin as the iron drinks the fire;
They are red hot with cruelty; raving along the banks of Thames
And on Tyburn's brook among the howling victims, in loveliness;
While Hand & Hyle condense the little ones & erect them into
50 A mighty temple even to the stars: but they vegetate
Beneath Los's hammer, that life may not be blotted out.

—For Los said: 'When the individual appropriates universality
He divides into male & female; & when the male & female
Appropriate individuality, they become an Eternal Death,
55 Hermaphroditic worshippers of a God of cruelty & law!
Your slaves & captives you compel to worship a God of Mercy!
These are the demonstrations of Los, & the blows of my mighty
    hammer!'

So Los spoke. And the giants of Albion, terrified & ashamed
With Los's thunderous words, began to build trembling rocking-
    stones
60 (For his words roll in thunders & lightnings among the temples)
Terrified, rocking to & fro upon the earth, & sometimes
Resting in a circle in Maldon or in Strathness or Jura:

90.49. *condense*] The little ones (the 'minute particulars') are forced to lose their individuality in being 'condensed' into a single mass. Their virtues essentially belong to each of them as individuals, but now they are heaped together and one abstract notion of Virtue, or Right, arises. Los saves them by keeping one speck of life—although it is of the most degraded kind—alive in them. Cp. *9.1*.
90.50. *a mighty temple*] An allusion to the tower of Babel.
90.59. *rocking-stones*] Huge stones (smaller ones have been knocked over) which are found in various parts of the world, including Britain, balancing on a pivot of stone. Their origin is natural and accidental, but there was some speculation that they were put there by 'druids' such as those who built great monuments such as Stonehenge. B. draws both a trilithon and a rocking-stone in his design on *Milton* pl.6 (reproduced in the Sloss and Wallis edn. opposite p. 358).
90.62. *a circle in Maldon or in Strathness or Jura*] This suggests stone circles; Strathness refers to the deep valley in which the famous loch lies (though its usual name is Glen Mhor, 'The Great Glen'). There are stone circles

Plotting to devour Albion, & Los the friend of Albion;
Denying in private, mocking God & eternal life; & in public
65 Collusion, calling themselves Deists, worshipping the maternal
Humanity; calling it Nature, and Natural Religion.

But still the thunder of Los peals loud, & thus the thunder's cry:

'These beautiful witchcrafts of Albion are gratified by cruelty!
Pl. 91 It is easier to forgive an enemy than to forgive a friend—
The man who permits you to injure him deserves your vengeance;
He also will receive it. Go, spectre! obey my most secret desire,
Which thou knowest without my speaking; go to these fiends of
      righteousness,
5 Tell them to obey their humanities, & not pretend holiness
When they are murderers; as far as my hammer & anvil permit
Go, tell them that the worship of God is honouring his gifts
In other men; & loving the greatest men best, each according
To his genius, which is the Holy Ghost in man. There is no other
10 God, than that God who is the intellectual fountain of humanity;
He who envies or calumniates (which is murder & cruelty)
Murders the Holy One. Go, tell them this & overthrow their cup,
Their bread, their altar table, their incense & their oath,
Their marriage & their baptism, their burial & consecration.
15 I have tried to make friends by corporeal gifts but have only
Made enemies—I never made friends but by spiritual gifts,
By severe contentions of friendship & the burning fire of thought.
He who would see the Divinity must see him in his children.
One first, in friendship & love; then a divine family, & in the midst
20 Jesus will appear; so he who wishes to see a vision, a perfect whole,
Must see it in its minute particulars; organised—& not as thou,
O fiend of righteousness, pretendest; thine is a disorganised
And snowy cloud; brooder of tempest & destructive war.
You smile with pomp & rigour: you talk of benevolence & virtue!

in the north of Scotland at Muir of Ord and Cononbridge (not far from
Dingwall, and roughly in the Loch Ness area). For *Jura* B. has *Dura*,
reflecting the Gaelic spelling (and pronunciation) *Diura*. This island off
the west coast of Scotland is famous for the rocky caves on its coast, which
probably led B. to include it here, since it has no stone circles. Maldon has
prehistoric remains, but no stone circles.

91.1. Preceded by a deleted line, partly deciphered as 'Forgiveness of
Enemies ?can . . . only . . . God. . . .'
91.9. *genius*] Almost a pun, considering the original meaning of 'genius' as
'indwelling spirit'.
91.17. *severe contentions of friendship*] Disputes which are severe and hard,
but carried on in a spirit of friendship.

25   I act with benevolence & virtue & get murdered time after time!
You accumulate particulars, & murder by analysing, that you
May take the aggregate; & you call the aggregate Moral Law:
And you call that swelled & bloated form, a minute particular.
But general forms have their vitality in particulars: & every
30   Particular is a man; a divine member of the Divine Jesus!'

So Los cried at his anvil, in the horrible darkness weeping!

The spectre builded stupendous works, taking the starry heavens
Like to a curtain & folding them according to his will,
Repeating the Smaragdine Table of Hermes to draw Los down
35   Into the indefinite, refusing to believe without demonstration.
Los reads the stars of Albion: the spectre reads the voids
Between the stars, among the arches of Albion's tomb sublime,
Rolling the sea in rocky paths, forming Leviathan
And Behemoth, the war by sea enormous, & the war
40   By land astounding, erecting pillars in the deepest hell
To reach the heavenly arches. Los beheld undaunted; furious
His heaved hammer—he swung it round & at one blow,
In unpitying ruin driving down the pyramids of pride,
Smiting the spectre on his anvil, & the integuments of his eye

91.32. The spectre tries hard to disobey Los, although Los is driving him
to work.

91.34. *the Smaragdine Table of Hermes*] i.e. of Hermes Trismegistus. Plato
refers to an Egyptian god, or divine man, Theuth (Thoth): he was later
identified with Hermes, but also often thought of as a man so honoured
for his learning that he was called *Trismegistus* ('thrice-great'). In Gnosti-
cism he was again deified, but this is not relevant to the present reference.
B.'s notion is well summarized in the following quotation (D. Hirst,
Hidden Riches, 1964, pp. 123–4): 'The basic document for all alchemy is the
famous "Emerald Table of Hermes" or "Smaragdine Tablet", ascribed
to the semi-mythical philosopher Hermes Trismegistus, sometimes identi-
fied with the Egyptian scribe-god, Thoth. Its thirteen cryptic propositions
were accepted [in the early Renaissance] as the key to the secret of the
Philosopher's Stone and the mystery of the universe itself.' B.'s knowledge
of the Tablet, and of Hermes, appears to have been sketchy in the extreme,
for the propositions had little or nothing in common with the science of
demonstrative experiment with which B. identifies them.

91.38–9. *Leviathan and Behemoth*] B. drew these creatures (from *Job* xl 15,
xli 1) in his illustrations to *Job*, no. 14 (reproduced in Keynes, *W.B.'s
Engravings* pl.58). Leviathan was a sea-monster, Behemoth a land-monster
something like a hippopotamus. In his 1809 Exhibition B. showed paintings
of Nelson guiding the sea-war monster Leviathan, and of Pitt leading
Behemoth.

91.44–5. *integuments*] Los 'operates' on the spectre to release the con-
stricted powers of eye and ear.

45 And ear unbinding in dire pain, with many blows
Of strict severity self-subduing, & with many tears labouring.

Then he sent forth the spectre; all his pyramids were grains
Of sand, & his pillars dust on the fly's wing, & his starry
Heavens a moth of gold & silver mocking his anxious grasp.
50 Thus Los altered his spectre, & every ratio of his reason
He altered time after time, with dire pain & many tears
Till he had completely divided him into a separate space.

Terrified Los sat to behold trembling & weeping & howling:
'I care not whether a man is good or evil; all that I care
55 Is whether he is a wise man or a fool. Go! Put off holiness
And put on intellect, or my thundrous hammer shall drive thee
To wrath which thou condemnest, till thou obey my voice.'

So Los terrified cries, trembling & weeping & howling:
    'Beholding,
                    [Design]

Pl. 92 What do I see? The Briton, Saxon, Roman, Norman
            amalgamating
In my furnaces into one nation, the English; & taking refuge
In the loins of Albion. The Canaanite united with the fugitive
Hebrew, whom she divided into twelve, & sold into Egypt—
5 Then scattered the Egyptian & Hebrew to the four winds!
This sinful nation created in our furnaces & looms is Albion!'

So Los spoke. Enitharmon answered in great terror in Lambeth's
            vale:

91.46. *self-subduing*] For the spectre is himself. He subdues, not his true
nature, but his savage and corrupt nature.
91.47–9. *his*] The spectre's. The rigid facts which the spectre wants to
control turn out to be delicate things of beauty, untouchable and uncon-
trollable.
91.50. *every ratio of his reason*] Every system of hypotheses which his reason
erects, and by which it understands. Cp. *Milton* 32.35n, and p. 877.
91. *Design*: A woman supine, with head thrown back, and flower-like
mystical symbols on either side of her.

92.1. This is one of the first signs of hope; Albion, hitherto shattered and
disintegrated, is seen to display in the course of history the power of
brotherhood in uniting nations in himself.
92.4. *she*] Not clear from the context; perhaps Jacob and Rachel, or Judah
and Bathshua (*Genesis* xxviii, xxxviii); or the two nations as wholes (as in *1*).
92.7. *Enitharmon*] She began this sequence, in pl.87, by refusing to work
with Los. Now she realizes that what has begun to show in Albion is a
power too great for her female will to dominate.

'The poet's song draws to its period, & Enitharmon is no more.
For if he be that Albion I can never weave him in my looms;
10   But when he touches the first fibrous thread, like filmy dew

[Design]

My looms will be no more & I, annihilate, vanish for ever.
Then thou wilt create another female according to thy will.'

Los answered swift as the shuttle of gold: 'Sexes must vanish &
cease
To be, when Albion arises from his dread repose, O lovely
Enitharmon:
15   When all their crimes, their punishments, their accusations of sin;
All their jealousies, revenges, murders, hidings of cruelty in deceit
Appear only in the outward spheres of visionary space and time,
In the shadows of possibility by mutual forgiveness for evermore,
And in the vision & in the prophecy, that we may foresee & avoid
20   The terrors of Creation & Redemption & Judgement, beholding
them
Displayed in the emanative visions of Canaan in Jerusalem & in
Shiloh,
And in the shadows of remembrance, & in the chaos of the spectre—
Amalek, Edom, Egypt, Moab, Ammon, Asshur, Philistia, around
Jerusalem,
Where the druids reared their rocky circles to make permanent
remembrance
25   Of sin, & the Tree of Good & Evil sprang from the rocky circle &
snake

92. *Design* (half the page): Jerusalem, gowned, sitting and lamenting, with
dead (or sleeping) figures on the ground round her, and trilithons in the
background.
92.17. i.e. these evils will not exist, except as concepts, thought of only to
be avoided: or (22ff) in memories of these evil times. For *outward* see
71.6–8, 12.55n: here the idea is that these things will exist only as a far-
fetched imaginary notion.
92.23. The hostile nations in Israel's biblical history. *Asshur* is Assyria.
92.24–7. 'The druid priesthood insisted on the fearfulness of sin, to the ex-
clusion of more positive and truer doctrines (such as forgiveness); from this
arose a religion of moral law, stressing the rigid distinction of Good and
Evil; and so a hateful and restricted world view grew.'
92.25–6. *rocky circle and snake*] The alleged 'serpent temple' of Avebury.
Cp. *Europe 72n*.
Valley of Rephaim] Cp. *Milton pl.19.40*; here identified with the Thames;
hence the reference to Camberwell, in south-east London, south of the
river.

Of the druid, along the Valley of Rephaim from Camberwell to
    Golgotha,
And framed the mundane shell, cavernous in length, breadth &
    height.'

Pl. 93   [Design]

Enitharmon heard. She raised her head like the mild moon:

'O Rintrah! O Palamabron! What are your dire & awful purposes?
Enitharmon's name is nothing before you; you forget all my love.
The mother's love of obedience is forgotten, & you seek a love
5   Of the pride of dominion that will divorce Ocalythron &
    Elynittria
Upon East Moor in Derbyshire & along the valleys of Cheviot.
Could you love me, Rintrah, if you pride not in my love,
As Reuben found mandrakes in the field & gave them to his
    mother?
Pride meets with pride upon the mountains in the stormy day,

93. *Design*: Three kneeling accusing figures in line, their right hands point-
ing; they are labelled *Anytus, Melitus* and *Lycon* (the three accusers of
Socrates) respectively; and the names lead into the sentence engraved on
the thigh of the nearest, 'thought Socrates a Very Pernicious Man'.
Added sideways are the words 'So Caiaphas thought Jesus'. Reproduced
in Nonesuch Blake, 1927, 1946, 1957; *Erdman 1965*; Blunt, *Art of W.B.*
pl.51a.

93.2. *Rintrah and Palamabron*] In 72.*11*, 73.*5*, 74.*2* these are two of Jerusa-
lem's four faithful sons, after twelve had deserted her. But the whole
passage (*2–16*) echoes more closely *Milton* pl.24, where the same four sons
are sons of Los (cp. 74.*23n* above; and also 73.*49*, where these seem to be
Los's sons).

93.5. *Ocalythron and Elynittria*] Emanations of Rintrah and Palamabron
respectively: Elynittria appears in *Milton* pl.11.*37–8*, but Ocalythron is
little more than a name (*Europe 49, Milton* pl.10.*19*).

93.6. *East Moor . . . Cheviot*] High places (already associated with evil, e.g.
in 21.*34* and 80.*66*) which are on Albion's 'backbone' and may be said to
overshadow the island.

93.7–8. *Reuben . . . mandrakes*] At a time when, because of the barrenness
of his wives, Jacob was begetting children on their servant-girls whom they
provided for him, Reuben brought mandrake roots to his mother Leah,
for a love-potion. Leah refused to let Rachel share the mandrakes, and took
Jacob to her bed that night (*Genesis* xxx 14–16). Reuben's act favoured his
mother, and showed that he took a pride in her allurement of his father–
and so confirmed the power of the female (which is Enitharmon's real
interest). The phrase *pride meets pride* may recall the clash of Rachel and
Leah over the mandrakes, marked by haughtiness on both sides; but the
image is of two storm-clouds rolling up a hill. B. has no punctuation, and
some edns end the sentence at *my love*, linking *8–9*.

10   In that terrible day of Rintrah's plough & of Satan's driving the
         team.
         Ah! then I heard my little ones weeping along the valley!
         Ah! then I saw my beloved ones fleeing from my tent.
         Merlin was like thee, Rintrah, among the giants of Albion,
         Judah was like Palamabron. O Simeon! O Levi! ye fled away.
15   How can I hear my little ones weeping along the valley,
         Or how upon the distant hills see my beloved's tents?'

         Then Los again took up his speech as Enitharmon ceased:

         'Fear not, my sons, this waking death; he is become one with me.
         Behold him here! We shall not die, we shall be united in Jesus.
20   Will you suffer this Satan, this body of doubt that seems but is not,
         To occupy the very threshold of eternal life? If Bacon, Newton,
            Locke
         Deny a conscience in man, & the communion of saints & angels,
         Contemning the Divine Vision & fruition, worshipping the *deus*
         Of the heathen, the god of this world, & the goddess Nature,
25   Mystery, Babylon the Great, the druid dragon & hidden harlot,
         Is it not that signal of the morning which was told us in the
            beginning?'

         Thus they converse upon Mam-Tor: the graves thunder under
            their feet.
                                    [*Design*]

93.*10. the day of Rintrah's plough*] In *Milton* pls 7–8, Satan drove Palama-
bron's team at the harrow–not Rintrah's plough. Yet the echo is so clear
that it almost seems that B. had forgotten the details of his own story.
93.*13–15.* Enitharmon likens Rintrah and Palamabron, who are before her,
to sons she has lost–'my little ones'. See *2n*; in *Jerusalem*, the Israelite tribes
are sometimes children of Los, sometimes of Jerusalem. When B. wants a
figure of a querulous mother he uses Enitharmon. It would be out of place,
he feels, to put these words in Jerusalem's mouth, and so Enitharmon
speaks–in spite of any inconsistency.
93.*13. Merlin*] Identified with Reuben and Hand in 34.*36–7, 36.41.*
93.*14. Palamabron* remains faithful: *Judah* fled into generation.
93.*18. this waking death*] Satan, the spectral form of Albion, the Covering
Cherub–all one figure, the visible body of corrupted humanity. But Los
claims that he has drawn the sting of its terror, not by trying to destroy
it, but by sympathetic assimilation–a more terrible and effective method.
Thus Los is, at this point, identified with the Jesus of 90.*38.*
93.*26.* The signs of the Second Coming (*Matthew* xxiv 3ff) are disasters
and fears. So in *Four Zoas* viii *336–32, 394–9* (cp. *395n*).
93.*27. Mam-Tor*] The Derbyshire peak; in 30.*41* also its 'graves' (the lime-
stone caverns, or perhaps the lead-mines of the region) thunder.
93. *Design*: A nude female figure, reclining in a bath (or punt?).

Pl. 94   [*Design*]

Albion cold lays on his rock; storms & snows beat round him,
Beneath the furnaces & the starry wheels & the immortal tomb.
Howling winds cover him; roaring seas dash furious against him;
In the deep darkness broad lightnings glare, long thunders roll.

5   The weeds of death enwrap his hands & feet, blown incessant
And washed incessant by the for-ever restless sea-waves foaming
    abroad
Upon the white rock. England, a female shadow, as deadly damps
Of the mines of Cornwall & Derbyshire, lays upon his bosom heavy,
Moved by the wind in volumes of thick cloud, returning, folding
    round
10   His loins & bosom, unremovable by swelling storms & loud rending
Of enraged thunders. Around them the starry wheels of their giant
    sons
Revolve, & over them the furnaces of Los, & the immortal tomb
    around,
Erin sitting in the tomb to watch them unceasing night and day.
And the body of Albion was closed apart from all nations.

15   Over them the famished eagle screams on bony wings, and around
Them howls the wolf of famine; deep heaves the ocean black,
    thundering
Around the wormy garments of Albion—then pausing in deathlike
    silence:

Time was finished! The Breath Divine breathed over Albion
Beneath the furnaces & starry wheels and in the immortal tomb;
20   And England, who is Britannia, awoke from death on Albion's
    bosom.

94. *Design*: A group of nude figures lying down, heads thrown back.
94.*1*. This is illustrated at the foot of the page, though many details differ.
94.*5-14*. An imaginative vision of the island, Albion, as a man, asleep in
the midst of waves, the seaweed round the shores as 'weeds of death', and
the fog and clouds which are often considered characteristic of the island
as the 'female shadow' oppressing his spirit. Ireland, or Erin (*13*), is close
by, watching the sleeper, who is an island separated from the other nations
(of Europe).
94.*8. mines*] Tin in Cornwall; lead in Derbyshire.
94.*18*. The sudden climax is the act of divinity, foreseen by Los in the pre-
ceding plates.
94.*20. England, who is Britannia*] The feminine aspect of Albion, a compound
of his emanations. In 32.*28*, she is 'divided into Jerusalem and Vala': now
conversely the two emanations of Albion meet and are united in her.
(Note also 96.*2*.) This is the redemption of Albion by his emanation: in
turn, he awakes Jerusalem in 97.*1-5*.

She awoke pale & cold; she fainted seven times on the body of
    Albion:

'Oh, piteous sleep! Oh, piteous dream! O God, O God, awake: I
    have slain!
In dreams of chastity & moral law I have murdered Albion! Ah!
In Stonehenge & on London Stone & in the oak groves of Maldon
25 I have slain him in my sleep with the knife of the druid! O
    England!
O all ye nations of the earth, behold ye the jealous wife!
The eagle & the wolf & monkey & owl & the king & priest were
    there.'
                        [Design]

Pl. 95   [Design]

Her voice pierced Albion's clay-cold ear; he moved upon the rock.
The Breath Divine went forth upon the morning hills; Albion moved
Upon the rock; he opened his eyelids in pain, in pain he moved
His stony members, he saw England. Ah! shall the dead live again?

5   The Breath Divine went forth over the morning hills. Albion rose
    In anger, the wrath of God breaking, bright flaming on all sides
        around
    His awful limbs. Into the heavens he walked, clothed in flames,
    Loud thundering, with broad flashes of flaming lightning and pillars
    Of fire, speaking the words of Eternity in human forms, in direful
10 Revolutions of action & passion, through the four elements on all
        sides
    Surrounding his awful members. Thou seest the sun in heavy clouds
    Struggling to rise above the mountains. In his burning hand
    He takes his bow, then chooses out his arrows of flaming gold;
    Murmuring the bowstring breathes with ardour, clouds roll
        round the
15 Horns of the wide bow, loud sounding winds sport on the
        mountain brows

94. *Design*: Albion on his rock, England lying over him: in the background,
behind rocks and a trilithon, the sun rises.
94.23. *dreams*] For these are not reality, or truth.
94.27. This line probably a late addition during a rewriting of the page.
The text of pl.94 was first etched in the top half of pl.95, and was prob-
ably identical to the re-etched version except for this line.
95. *Design* (half the page): Albion rising on one knee, his right arm up-
lifted.

Compelling Urizen to his furrow & Tharmas to his sheepfold.
And Luvah to his loom. Urthona he beheld mighty labouring at
His anvil, in the great spectre Los unwearied labouring & weeping.
Therefore the sons of Eden praise Urthona's spectre in songs—
20 Because he kept the Divine Vision in time of trouble.

As the sun & moon lead forward the visions of heaven & earth,
England, who is Britannia, entered Albion's bosom rejoicing,
Rejoicing in his indignation, adoring his wrathful rebuke.
(She who adores not your frowns will only loathe your smiles.)

Pl. 96   [*Design*]

[As the sun & moon lead forward the visions of heaven & earth,
England, who is Britannia, entered Albion's bosom rejoicing.]

Then Jesus appeared standing by Albion, as the good shepherd
By the lost sheep that he hath found; & Albion knew that it
5 Was the Lord, the Universal Humanity, & Albion saw his form,
A man: & they conversed as man with man, in ages of eternity.
And the divine appearance was the likeness & similitude of Los.

Albion said: 'O Lord, what can I do? My selfhood cruel
Marches against thee deceitful from Sinai & from Edom
10 Into the wilderness of Judah to meet thee in his pride.
I behold the visions of my deadly sleep of six thousand years
Dazzling around thy skirts like a serpent of precious stones & gold.
I know it is my Self, O my divine creator & redeemer!'

95.16. Albion makes the three wandering Zoas return to their proper order
and function.

96. Design: On the right of *1–25* (which are therefore broken in two), an
aged figure embracing a female figure in a cloud of radiance.

96.1–2. Repeated from *95.21–2.* When B. rewrote pl.95 he seems to have
included them there; had he remade this pl. he would presumably have left
them out here.

96.3. good shepherd] The phrase is from *John* x 11; the allusion to the
parable of the lost sheep from *Matthew* xviii 12–14.

96.4–7. i.e. 'the Lord, the Universal Humanity' may take many forms; at
this moment he took the human form of Los, who was not solely 'the
Lord', but whose activities had been entirely devoted to the divine vision.

96.8–10. Like the proud armies of the Israelites marching from Sinai
through the desert, arrogant in their possession of a God-given law.

96.13. my Self] 'My Selfhood'–the Covering Cherub, who has been
waiting for his prey since pl.89, and who has yet to be dealt with. Albion
has put off his error on his awakening; but the accumulation of that error,
in the person of the Cherub, remains. Albion fears that it will overcome
the Redeemer, but is told that the Redeemer must die but may not be
overcome.

Jesus replied: 'Fear not, Albion: unless I die thou canst not live.
15 But if I die I shall arise again & thou with me;
This is friendship & brotherhood; without it man is not.'

So Jesus spoke, the Covering Cherub coming on in darkness
Overshadowed them & Jesus said: 'Thus do men in Eternity,
One for another to put off by forgiveness every sin.'

20 Albion replied: 'Cannot man exist without mysterious
Offering of self for another? Is this friendship & brotherhood?
I see thee in the likeness & similitude of Los my friend.'

Jesus said: 'Wouldest thou love one who never died
For thee, or ever die for one who had not died for thee?
25 And if God dieth not for man & giveth not himself
Eternally for man, man could not exist. For man is love,
As God is love. Every kindness to another is a little death
In the Divine Image, nor can man exist but by brotherhood.'

So saying the cloud overshadowing divided them asunder.
30 Albion stood in terror—not for himself but for his friend
Divine, & self was lost in the contemplation of faith
And wonder at the Divine Mercy & at Los's sublime honour.

'Do I sleep amidst danger to friends? O my cities & counties,
Do you sleep? Rouse up, rouse up! Eternal death is abroad!'

35 So Albion spoke & threw himself into the furnaces of affliction.
All was a vision, all a dream! The furnaces became
Fountains of living waters flowing from the Humanity Divine.
And all the cities of Albion rose from their slumbers, & all
The sons & daughters of Albion on soft clouds waking from sleep;
40 Soon all around remote the heavens burnt with flaming fires,
And Urizen & Luvah & Tharmas & Urthona arose into

96.17. *in darkness*] This scene recalls the Transfiguration (*Luke* ix 34) where
Peter, James and John, watching the vision of Christ with Moses and
Elijah are overshadowed by a cloud, which makes them afraid: afterwards
Jesus is found alone–for which see note on the heading of pl.4.
96.32. *Los's sublime honour*] For Jesus has chosen the form of Los in which
to meet the Cherub.
96.36. A collection of several biblical ideas: the furnaces are like the fur-
nace of *Daniel* which did not harm the three loyal Jews; and resemble
the traditional Hell, the lake of fire and brimstone into which the devil
was cast–but Hell itself turns into the fountain of living water offered by
Jesus, resembling the 'fountain of the water of life' in the New Jerusalem.
(*Daniel* iii, *Revelation* xx 10, *John* iv 10–15, *Revelation* xxi 6.) Thus, all the
evil and error was a dream, and vanished; and so did the affliction which
accompanied it.

Albion's bosom. Then Albion stood before Jesus in the clouds
Of heaven, fourfold among the visions of God in Eternity.

Pl. 97 'Awake! Awake, Jerusalem! O lovely Emanation of Albion,
Awake and overspread all nations as in ancient time—
For lo! the night of death is past and the eternal day
Appears upon our hills! Awake, Jerusalem, and come away!'

5 So spake the vision of Albion, & in him so spake in my hearing
The Universal Father. Then Albion stretched his hand into
        infinitude
And took his bow. Fourfold the vision: for bright beaming Urizen
Laid his hand on the south & took a breathing bow of carved gold;
Luvah his hand stretched to the east & bore a silver bow bright
        shining;
10 Tharmas westward a bow of brass pure flaming, richly wrought;
Urthona northward in thick storms a bow of iron terrible
        thundering.

And the bow is a male & female, & the quiver of the arrows of love
Are the children of this bow—a bow of mercy & loving-kindness,
        laying
Open the hidden heart in wars of mutual benevolence, wars of love;
15 And the hand of Man grasps firm between the male & female
        loves.
And he clothed himself in bow & arrows in awful state fourfold
In the midst of his twenty-eight cities, each with his bow breathing.

                    [Design]

Pl. 98   [Design]

Then each an arrow flaming from his quiver fitted carefully;
They drew fourfold the unreprovable string, bending through the
        wide heavens
The horned bow fourfold. Loud sounding flew the flaming arrow
        fourfold.

96.43. fourfold] i.e. complete and perfect.

97.7. Fourfold the vision] Albion's act is reflected in all the four parts of his
being (and, in 17, in the twenty-eight parts), for all four are now united
in him. The image is rather like the simultaneous movements of a person
reflected in a group of mirrors. (See 'The Crystal Cabinet,' p. 583.)
97.12. the bow is a male & female] Whole, not partial.
97. Design: A male figure, facing away, on a hill-top, his right hand lifted
over his head to shade his eyes against the radiance, his left hand resting
on a globe. (Reproduced in Keynes, W.B.'s Engravings pl.114.)
98. Design: A serpent coils leftwards across the top of the page.

Murmuring the bow-string breathes with ardour. Clouds roll
    round the horns
5 Of the wide bow; loud sounding winds sport on the mountain's
    brows.
The druid spectre was annihilate—loud thundering, rejoicing,
    terrific vanishing
Fourfold annihilation! And at the clangour of the arrows of intellect
The innumerable chariots of the Almighty appeared in Heaven:
And Bacon & Newton & Locke, & Milton & Shakespeare &
    Chaucer,
10 A man of blood-red wrath surrounding Heaven on all sides around,
Glorious, incomprehensible by mortal man: & each chariot was
    sexual threefold.

And every man stood fourfold; each four faces had. One to the
    west,
One toward the east, one to the south, one to the north. The horses
    fourfold,
And the dim chaos brightened beneath, above, around. Eyed as
    the peacock
15 According to the human nerves of sensation, the four Rivers of
    the Water of Life.

South stood the nerves of the Eye. East in rivers of bliss the nerves
    of the
Expansive Nostrils. West flowed the parent sense, the tongue.
    North stood
The labyrinthine Ear. Circumscribing & circumcising the
    excrementitious
Husk & covering into vacuum evaporating, revealing the
    lineaments of Man,
20 Driving outward the body of death in an eternal death and
    resurrection,

98.6. *druid spectre*] See note on 96.*13*.

98.7. *intellect*] As always in B., meaning 'imaginatively used mental
powers', not mere reason.

98.11. *each chariot was sexual threefold*] As is Beulah.   *Threefold* was
amended from 'twofold'. The great men of *9* are now redeemed, but not
complete in themselves; they represent partial activity–certain kinds of
thought and writing–and find their place in Heaven, where they are
assimilated into larger, fourfold beings.

98.*12–15*. The four faces belong to the four living creatures (*zoa*) of
Ezekiel i and *Revelation* iv: the horses to the famous four horsemen of
Revelation vi; there also the four living creatures of *Revelation* iv 6 are 'full
of eyes before and behind'. The four rivers are the rivers of Paradise
(*Genesis* ii 1–14) identified with the River of Life of *Revelation* xxii.

Awaking it to life among the flowers of Beulah, rejoicing in unity
In the four senses, in the outline, the circumference & form, for ever
In forgiveness of sins which is self-annihilation. It is the Covenant
    of Jehovah.
The four living creatures, chariots of Humanity Divine
    incomprehensible,
25 In beautiful paradises expand. These are the four rivers of paradise
And the four faces of humanity, fronting the four cardinal points
Of heaven, going forward, forward—irrestible from eternity to
    eternity.
And they conversed together in visionary forms dramatic, which
    bright
Redounded from their tongues in thunderous majesty, in visions,
30 In new expanses, creating exemplars of memory & of intellect—
Creating space, creating time according to the wonders divine
Of human imagination, throughout all the three regions immense
Of childhood, manhood & old age; & the all-tremendous
    unfathomable Non-ens
Of death was seen in regenerations—terrific or complacent, varying
35 According to the subject of discourse. And every word & every
    character
Was human, according to the expansion or contraction, the
    translucence or
Opaqueness of nervous fibres. Such was the variation of time and
    space,
Which vary according as the organs of perception vary, & they
    walked
To & fro in eternity as one man, reflecting each in each & clearly
    seen
40 And seeing according to fitness & order. And I heard Jehovah
    speak
Terrific from his Holy Place & saw the words of the mutual
    Covenant Divine
On chariots of gold & jewels, with living creatures starry and
With every colour. Lion, tiger, horse, elephant, eagle, dove, fly,
    worm,
And the all-wondrous serpent clothed in gems & rich array,
    humanize
45 In the forgiveness of sins according to the Covenant of Jehovah.
    They cry:

98.30. *exemplars*] Keeping memory and intellect in their proper subordinate
place. Time, place, age and death are 'created' for momentary interest,
as a story is, and then put away. Cp. 92.*17–18.*

98.34. *complacent*] Or 'complaisant'–i.e. pleasing, not terrifying.

98.44. *humanize*] i.e. 'take human form'.

'Where is the covenant of Priam, the moral virtues of the heathen?
Where is the Tree of Good & Evil that rooted beneath the cruel
    heel
Of Albion's spectre, the patriarch druid? Where are all his human
    sacrifices
For sin in war, & in the druid temples of the Accuser of Sin,
    beneath
50 The oak groves of Albion that covered the whole earth beneath
    his spectre?
Where are the kingdoms of the world & all their glory that grew
    on desolation,
The fruit of Albion's poverty-tree, when the triple-headed
    Gog-Magog giant
Of Albion taxed the nations into desolation, & then gave the
    spectrous oath?'.

Such is the cry from all the earth, from the Living Creatures of
    the earth
55 And from the great city of Golgonooza in the shadowy generation,

[*Design*]

And from the thirty-two nations of the earth among the living
    creatures:

98.46. *the covenant of Priam*] There was of course no such covenant; B.
makes a contrast with the 'covenant of Jehovah'. The classical attitude to
life sets out a false relationship. Nor have moral law and sacrifices of
humanity (whether physical or mental) any place in true human religion.
98.47. *Tree of Good and Evil*] The tree of *Genesis* iii, 'of the knowledge of
good and evil', identified with the Tree of Mystery, 28.*14ff*.
98.52. *the triple-headed . . . giant*] In *Ezekiel* xxxviii–xxxix, 'Gog, the land
of Magog' is denounced as an enemy of Israel, to be overthrown by the
Lord. In *Revelation* xx 8–9 this is drawn upon in the 'Gog and Magog'
who are overthrown at the last: but these represent all the hostile nations
of the world, and are not represented as a triple-headed giant. Hand, leader
of the once-corrupted sons of Albion, was triple-headed (70.4). Gog and
Magog are also famous statues outside the London Guildhall–home of
those whose mind and vision are single (like Hand's).
98.53. *taxed the nations*] As Caesar did at the time of Christ's birth (and
cp. 64.*34*); and as the British government had taxed the Americans.
98.55. I.e. the cry is even now, in the shadows of Generation, heard from
Golgonooza.
98. *Design*: A strip showing a row of lowly creatures–a snail, a frog, a
worm, a spider, a snake, and smaller butterflies and other insects.
98.56. *the thirty-two nations*] Listed in 72.*32–44*.

Pl. 99 All human forms identified, even tree, metal, earth & stone. All
   Human forms identified, living, going forth & returning wearied
   Into the planetary lives of years, months, days & hours—reposing
   And then awaking into his bosom in the life of Immortality.

5 And I heard the name of their emanations: they are named
   JERUSALEM.

The End of the Song
of Jerusalem

[Design]

Pl. 100 [Full-page illustration]

37 For the Sexes: The Gates of Paradise

This little book was an emblem book, headed 'For Children' (somewhat
ironically) when it was first published in 1793. Emblem books were still
far from extinct, and editions of Quarles, for example, were still being
published. In 1793 the text consisted simply of rather cryptic headings to
the designs, and these are not reproduced here. The 'Children' of the
first title were real children–B. was advertising an 'improving' book;
the irony lay in his conviction that 'improving' books for children were
really meant to hide from them the 'true nature of Experience. His booklet
revealed, parabolically, that the Gates of Paradise, as this world saw them,
were entered by the way of law. But fifteen or twenty years later (or even
more) B. saw deeper meanings in his designs. In a second version, dating
from some time after 1806, B. changed the heading to 'For the Sexes'–i.e.

99.1. All human forms] Note that inanimate things are stressed as having
a part in true humanity; nothing exists that is not human: cp. 98.43-44.
99.2-3. i.e. 'wearying themselves in the life of Eternity, then resting in
planetary lives' (of time and space, as measured by the movements of
planets). When rested, they awaken again in Eternity.
99.5. Jerusalem is universalized and, by implication, so is Albion, whose
emanation she is.
I heard . . .] The language of apocalyptic vision, as in Daniel and Revelation,
and B. thus places Jerusalem in this tradition.
99. Design: Under the text, and filling almost the whole page, a bearded
sage-like man accepts the embrace of a female figure who throws herself,
arms outstretched, into his arms. Behind them is the sun, and flames all
around. (Reproduced in Blunt, Art of W.B. pl.49c.)

Plate 100. Full-page illustration. In front of a 'dragon temple' stretched
along the ground, a male figure (Los) with sledge-hammer and tongs, with
two other labouring figures beside him, their backs turned.

28—B.

for those in the fallen state of mortality–and eventually the text was en-
larged to consist of a motto, a prologue, the sixteen design-headings (some-
times added to), a series of couplets entitled 'The Keys of the Gates', and
an epilogue or envoi 'To the Accuser', which alludes to B.'s late doctrine
of *states*, expounded e.g. in the final *Milton* pl.32–implying a date *c.* 1815.
The headings of the designs are printed in the notes with descriptions.
    The substance of these later versions is of the same matter as *Jerusalem*.
'The Keys' refers to the Hermaphrodite, the Veil (of Vala), the Mundane
Shell, the Spectre, and the Door of Death (which forms the frontispiece of
Jerusalem); and these, together with the ideas of the sexual life as being
characteristic of the fallen, material world (*21–4*), of this life as sleep
(*13*), and the Christianity of *20* and *40*, all belong to B.'s last period. The
'epilogue' has the same vocabulary as that used by B. in his reworking of
the Lord's Prayer in the last months of his life.
    The designs are reproduced in various editions and in Keynes, *W.B.'s
Engravings* pls 7–28. There is an interesting discussion in J. Beer, *Blake's
Humanism*, pp. 231–243, where the designs are also reproduced. There is
also a set of facsimiles in the Blake Trust edition (1969).

[PROLOGUE]

Mutual forgiveness of each vice:
Such are the Gates of Paradise.
Against the Accuser's chief desire
Who walked among the stones of fire
5   Jehovah's finger wrote the law;
Then wept, then rose in zeal and awe
And the dead corpse from Sinai's heat
Buried beneath his Mercy Seat.
O Christians, Christians, tell me why
10   You rear it on your altars high?

THE KEYS

The caterpillar on the leaf
Reminds thee of thy mother's grief.

¶ 37.5. As stated in *Exodus* xxxi 8.
7. *the dead corpse*] The Law, which God had repented of. In Christ he has
buried it; but Christians insist on reviving a Law.
The Keys. The frontispiece shows a caterpillar, and a chrysalis as a swaddled
baby. Beneath the design: (1793) 'What is Man!', and (late addition), the
couplet:

The sun's light when he unfolds it
Depends on the organ that beholds it.

13. The inset numbers refer to the designs which are 'keyed'. The

OF THE GATES

1. My eternal man set in repose;
The female from his darkness rose,
15   And she found me beneath a tree
A mandrake, and in her veil hid me.
Serpent reasonings us entice
Of good and evil: virtue and vice,
2. Doubt self-jealous, watery folly
20   3. Struggling through earth's melancholy,
4. Naked in air in shame and fear,
5. Blind in fire with shield and spear;
Two-horned reasoning, cloven fiction
In doubt, which is self-contradiction.
25   A dark hermaphrodite we stood,
Rational truth, root of evil and good.
Round me flew the flaming sword,
Round her snowy whirlwinds roared
Freezing her veil, the mundane shell.
30   6. I rent the veil where the dead dwell.

When weary man enters his cave
He meets his Saviour in the grave;
Some find a female garment there
And some a male, woven with care
35   Lest the sexual garments sweet
Should grow a devouring winding sheet.
7. One dies! Alas, the living and dead;

first shows a woman pulling up children (like mandrakes) under a tree,
headed (1793) 'I found him beneath a tree' (perhaps an ironical reference
to the 'discreet' legend told to inquisitive children concerning childbirth).
19–22. Designs 2–5 are entitled respectively (1793) *Water, Earth, Air, Fire*;
in the last version B. added the quatrain (one line per design):

> Thou waterest him with tears
> He struggles into life
> On cloudy doubts and reasoning cares
> That end in endless strife.

Each design shows a dejected figure in the relevant environment, except
Fire, which shows B.'s figure of the 'Dark Hermaphrodite'.
23–30. Design 6: An infant cherub breaking out of an eggshell, under-
written (1793): 'At length for hatching ripe he breaks the shell' (From
Dryden's Fable, *Palamon and Arcite*, 1069, as John Beer pointed out).
37. Design 7: A boy knocking down fairies with his hat; one lies on the
ground, the other is trying to escape. Subscription (1793) 'Alas!': later
enlarged to 'What are these? Alas! the female martyr! Is she also the
Divine Image?'

One is slain and one is fled.
8. In vain-glory hatched and nursed
40   By double spectres self-accurst.
My son, my son, thou treatest me
But as I have instructed thee!
9. On the shadows of the moon
Climbing through night's highest noon,
10. In Time's ocean falling drowned,
45   In aged ignorance profound,
11. Holy and cold, I clipped the wings
Of all sublunary things,
12. And in depths of my dungeons
50   Closed the father and the sons.
13. But when once I did descry
The Immortal Man that cannot die,
14. Through evening shades I haste away
To close the labours of my day.
15. The door of death I open found,
55   And the worm weaving in the ground.
16. Thou'rt my mother from the womb
Wife, sister, daughter to the tomb,
Weaving to dreams the sexual strife.
60   And weeping over the web of life.

39. *Design 8*: A youth aims a spear at a dejected old man who sits leaning on his sword: (1793) 'My son! my son!'
43. *Design 9*: A man climbs a ladder reaching to the moon: (1793) 'I want! I want!'
45. *Design 10*: Head and upstretched arm of a figure drowning in the sea: (1793) 'Help! Help!'
47. *Design 11*: An old man under a tree clips an infant cherub's wings. Subscribed (1793) 'Aged Ignorance': later addition, 'Perceptive organs closed their objects close.'
49. *Design 12*: Ugolino and his sons walled into prison. (1793): 'Does thy God, O Priest, take such vengeance as this?'
51. *Design 13*: The spirit of an old man rises from his body, while his wife and children watch amazed. (1793): 'Fear and Hope are–Vision.'
53. *Design 14*: Illustrates the title (1793): 'The traveller hasteth in the evening.'
55. *Design 15*: Illustrates the title (1793) 'Death's Door': an old man, leaning on a stick, enters a dark, massive stone doorway.
57. *Design 16*: A seated figure, in robe and hood, holding a wand, with a worm winding round. Underwritten (1793): 'I have said to the worm: Thou art my mother and my sister' (from *Job* xvii 14).

> *To the Accuser who is*
> *the God of this World*
> Truly, my Satan, thou art but a dunce
> And dost not know the garment from the man:
> Every harlot was a virgin once,
> Nor canst thou ever change Kate into Nan.
>
> 65 Though thou art worshipped by the names divine
> Of Jesus and Jehovah, thou art still
> The Son of Morn in weary night's decline,
> The lost traveller's dream under the hill.

[*Design*]

38 The Everlasting Gospel

'Nine widely-scattered entries in B.'s Notebook, three sections in a separate scrap of paper, and one cue line indicating a lost section' (*Erdman 1965*): one of these, a prose passage, is on a sheet of 1818 notepaper, and it is supposed that all the fragments date from this time. The rest are in verse, reproduced either in the main text or the footnotes in the following pages. Although the pieces are separate, the similarity in style and theme, and a recognizable development in handling, from theory to dramatic exposition, all make probable the conjecture that they were designed for a single poem or set of poems, never completed. The only doubtful section is iv, 'The Vision of Christ', which may possibly be an independent poem which was there before B. began *The Everlasting Gospel* at all.

Epilogue. The Accuser is Satan—as in *Job*.
61. Truly ... dunce. After Young, *Night Thoughts* viii 1417. Young argues that since man's mortal abilities are limited, reliance on them alone is folly, and worse (1410–13): 'World-wisdom much has done, and more may do, / In arts and sciences, in wars, and peace: / But art and science, like thy wealth, will leave thee, / And make thee twice a beggar at thy death.' And therefore, he concludes this 'Night', 'Satan, thy master, I dare call a dunce.' B. takes up the point, probably assuming Young's line to be well-known: the material world of nature, earthly life and appearances (*63–4*), is only a 'garment' for the real personality, the eternal soul. See note on *States*, p. 573.
68. An allusion to such common folk-tales as that of True Thomas, or Rip Van Winkle, in which a mortal is carried into a fairy hill where he loses many years of life in a short dream of magic. The 'Son of Morn' is 'Lucifer, son of the morning' (Isaiah, xiv, 12).
Design: A dark bat-winged figure (a spectre) hovers over the figure of a sleeping traveller.

The fragments are here assembled in two parts, with an epigrammatic coda (viii): first the earlier and more tentative verses in the most probable order of composition, headed *Early Drafts* (i–iv); then the three main sections (v–vii) which may well represent B.'s latest–though certainly not definitive–idea of the poem. (Two other brief fragments will be found on p. 854, in a note to vi.) The three major sections were probably written in the order *Chastity, Gentility, Humility*: but B. headed the last with the title *The Everlasting Gospel*, as if the poem were meant to start there. The couplet 'I am sure . . .' was perhaps B.'s ironic expression of his reasons for not finishing the poem, though public rejection of his works had not usually prevented him from continuing them: its appearance as a coda is attractive, but editorial.

The title derives from *Revelation* xiv 6, 'And I saw another angel fly in the midst of heaven, having the everlasting gospel to preach unto them that dwell on the earth. . . .' Although it was only tentatively attached, to the *Humility* section of the poem, it is apt, since the poem expresses strongly and clearly B.'s message concerning the true worship of God as he sees it. He takes the Christian traditions of 'gentle Jesus, meek and mild', and overturns them, showing that the deeds and words of Jesus display quite another kind of Saviour. Humility, chastity and gentleness emerge as virtues indeed–but almost unrecognizable to Wilberforce's Society for the Suppression of Vice. Although never completed, *The Everlasting Gospel* remains one of the most powerful expression of B.'s ideas, and a vigorous sequence of poetry.

Early Drafts

i

What can this Gospel of Jesus be?
What life and immortality?
What was it that he brought to light
That Plato and Cicero did not write?
5   The heathen deities wrote them all,
These moral virtues, great and small.
What is the accusation of sin
But moral virtues' deadly gin?

¶ 38.i. The following lines preceded this passage in the MS: 'There is not one moral virtue that Jesus inculcated but Plato & Cicero did inculcate before him: what then did Christ inculcate?–Forgiveness of Sins. This alone is the Gospel, and this is the life & immortality brought to light by Jesus, even the covenant of Jehovah, which is this: if you forgive one another your trespasses, so shall Jehovah forgive you, that he himself may dwell among you; but if you avenge, you murder the Divine Image, & he cannot dwell among you because you murder him: he arises again & you deny that he is arisen & are blind to spirit.'
i *8. gin*] Trap.

The moral virtues in their pride
10 Did o'er the world triumphant ride
In wars and sacrifice for sin,
And souls to Hell ran trooping in.
The Accuser, Holy God of all
This pharisaic worldly ball,
15 Amidst them in his glory beams
Upon the rivers and the streams.
Then Jesus rose and said to me,
'Thy sins are all forgiven thee.'
Loud Pilate howled, loud Cai'phas yelled
20 When they the Gospel light beheld.
It was when Jesus said to me,
'Thy sins are all forgiven thee'
The Christian trumpets loud proclaim
Through all the world in Jesus' name
25 Mutual forgiveness of each vice
And oped the Gates of Paradise.
The Moral Virtues in great fear
Formed the cross and nails and spear,
And the Accuser standing by
30 Cried out, 'Crucify! Crucify!
Our moral virtues ne'er can be,
Nor warlike pomp and majesty,
For moral virtues all begin
In the accusations of sin,
35 And all the heroic virtues end
In destroying the sinners' friend.
Am I not Lucifer the Great,
And you, my daughters in great state,
The fruit of my mysterious tree
40 Of good and evil and misery
And death and Hell, which now begin
On everyone who forgives Sin?'

II

If moral virtue was Christianity
Christ's pretensions were all vanity,

---

i *14. pharisaic worldly ball*] Three words expressing restriction and con-
striction.
i *17. me*] Originally 'men': the theorizing is beginning to give way to
dramatic expression.
i *21.* The line 'Jerusalem he said to me' is found deleted beneath this line.
ii *1.* Marked in the MS 'This to come first'–i.e. before i.

And Caiaphas and Pilate men
Praiseworthy, and the lion's den,
5   And not the sheepfold, allegories
Of God and Heaven and their glories.
The moral Christian is the cause
Of the unbeliever and his laws.
The Roman virtues' warlike fame
10   Take Jesus' and Jehovah's name:
For what is Antichrist but those
Who against sinners Heaven close
With iron bars in virtuous state,
And Rhadamanthus at the gate?

III

Was Jesus born of a virgin pure
With narrow soul and looks demure?
If he intended to take on sin
The mother should an harlot been,
5   Just such a one as Magdalen
With seven devils in her pen.
(Or were Jew virgins still more curst,
And more sucking devils nursed?)
Or what was it which he took on
10   That he might bring salvation?
A body subject to be tempted,
From neither pain nor grief exempted;
Or such a body as might not feel
The passions that with sinners deal?
15   Yes, but they say he never fell.—
Ask Caiaphas, for he can tell:

ii 14. *Rhadamanthus*] A mythical figure, son of Zeus and Europa: known as a ruler and judge renowned for justice. B. seems to take him as a type of judge after the fashion of Moses. After his death he was appointed one of the three judges of the destinies of spirits arriving in the underworld, and ruler of Elysium.

iii 4. B. may have known of the anti-Christian story current in the first century A.D., which said that the Virgin Birth was merely an 'explanation' of the unpalatable fact that Jesus was Mary's son by some passing Roman soldier—that Mary was indeed a harlot. B. declares that the notion, abhorrent to the orthodox, is essential and glorious.

iii 6. *seven devils*] Cp. vi 4*n*.

iii 16. The following lines are B.'s expression of Caiaphas' attitude, rather than words put, dramatically, into the mouth of Caiaphas.

'He mocked the Sabbath, and he mocked
The Sabbath's God, and he unlocked
The evil spirits from their shrines,
20   And turned fishermen to divines;
O'erturned the tent of secret sins,
And its golden cords and pins.
'Tis the bloody shrine of war
Pinned around from star to star,
25   Halls of justice, hating vice,
Where the devil combs his lice.
He turned the devils into swine
That he might tempt the Jews to dine;
Since which a pig has got a look
30   That for a Jew may be mistook.
"Obey your parents." What says he?
"Woman, what have I to do with thee?
No earthly parents I confess:
I am doing my Father's business."
35   He scorned earth's parents, scorned earth's God,
And mocked the one and the other's rod;
His seventy disciples sent
Against religion and government.
They by the sword of justice fell,
40   And him their cruel murderer tell.
He left his father's trade to roam,
A wandering vagrant without home,
And thus he others' labour stole,
That he might live above control.
45   The publicans and harlots he
Selected for his company,
And from the adulteress turned away
God's righteous law, that lost its prey . . .'

iii *17. mocked the Sabbath*] By doing forbidden things, unashamedly, on a number of well-known occasions. Cp. *Matthew* xii 8: 'The Son of man is Lord even of the sabbath day.'

iii *19. the evil spirits*] Those in possession of persons, later healed by Jesus. The spirits lived in the soul as if in a shrine.

iii *27–8. devils . . . dine*] The Gadarene swine, *Luke* viii 27–37, *Mark* v 1–19. The swine-devils are still devils, tempting and luring the Jews to transgression.

iii *32. Woman . . . thee*] See note on *To Tirzah*, p. 591 above. B. associates this saying with the teaching of the boy Jesus in the temple (*Luke* ii 42ff and below v 5–10, 'Was Jesus humble?').

iii *37–8. seventy disciples*] *Luke* x 1, 17, where Jesus despatches them throughout Palestine: but it is B.'s inference that they went 'against religion and government'.

29 + B.

IV

The vision of Christ that thou dost see
Is my vision's greatest enemy:
Thine has a great hook nose like thine,
Mine has a snub nose like to mine;
5 Thine is 'the Friend of All Mankind',
Mine speaks in parables to the blind;
Thine loves the same world that mine hates,
Thy Heaven-doors are my Hell-gates.
Socrates taught what Melitus
10 Loathed as a nation's bitterest curse,
And Caiaphas was, in his own mind,
A benefactor to mankind.
Both read the Bible day and night,
But thou read'st black where I read white.

THE EVERLASTING GOSPEL

V

Was Jesus humble, or did he
Give any proofs of humility,
Boast of high things with humble tone
And give with charity a stone?
5 When but a child he ran away
And left his parents in dismay.

iv 3–4. Elsewhere in the Notebook (p. 64) B. wrote, 'I always thought
Jesus Christ was a Snubby or I should not have worshipd him if I had
thought he had been one of those long spindle nosed rascals.'

iv 5. *Friend of All Mankind*] A weak character who could not oppose anyone
–cp. v 'Was Jesus humble?' See also p. 598, no. xxx, and p. 618, no. xl.

iv 6. *parables to the blind*] Obscure stories told to those most likely to find
them difficult.

iv 9. *Melitus*] One of Socrates's accusers, who demanded that he be put to
death for corrupting the young.

v. This, as explained in the headnote, appears in the Notebook *after* the
sections which in this edition follow it. But B. headed it with the title, and
seems to have intended the poem to begin here. This is a second draft; the
chief differences between it and the first draft (which appears elsewhere in
the Notebook) are shown in the notes below. Lines not in the first draft
are: *3–4, 21–4, 26–7, 31–58, 69–70, 85–106*. Lines *12–17* were first written
in the order *12-15-16-13-14-17*, but even in the first draft B. marked the
couplets in the margin with numbers indicating that they should be
switched.

v 4. *give . . . a stone*] *Matthew* vii 9 (*Luke* xi 11) 'What man . . . if his son
ask bread, will he give him a stone?'

v 6. *left his parents*] *Luke* ii 42–50.

When they had wandered three days long,
These were the words upon his tongue:
'No earthly parents I confess:
10   I am doing my Father's business'.
When the rich learned Pharisee
Came to consult him secretly,
Upon his heart with iron pen
He wrote: 'Ye must be born again.'
15   He was too proud to take a bribe;
He spoke with authority, not like a scribe.
He says with most consummate art,
'Follow me: I am meek and lowly of heart'—
As that is the only way to escape
20   The miser's net and the glutton's trap.
What can be done with such desperate fools
Who follow after the heathen schools?
I was standing by when Jesus died;
What I called 'humility' they called 'pride',
25   He who loves his enemies betrays his friends;
This surely is not what Jesus intends,
But the sneaking pride of heroic schools
And the scribes' and Pharisees' virtuous rules.
For he acts with honest triumphant pride;
30   And this is the cause that Jesus died.
He did not die with Christian ease;
Asking pardon of his enemies—
If he had Caiaphas would forgive;
Sneaking submission can always live—
35   He had only to say that God was the devil
And the devil was God, like a Christian civil,
Mild Christian regrets to the devil confess

v 8. *These were the words*] Not a direct quotation. In *Luke* ii 49 Jesus says,
'... Wist ye not that I must be about my Father's business?', and in
Matthew xii 46–50 he rejects the ties of earthly families (cp. also 'To
Tirzah', p. 590 above).

v 11. *the rich learned Pharisee*] Nicodemus, who came to Jesus by night to
consult him (*John* iii 1–21).

v 14. *Ye must be born again*] John iii 7.

v 15. *A bribe*] There is no specific reference in the Gospels to an attempt to
bribe Jesus; perhaps B. is thinking of Satan's tempting in the wilderness,
when he offered power to Jesus.

v 16. *authority* . . .] *Mark* i 22, *Matthew* vii 29.

v 18. *Follow me* . . . *heart*] *Matthew* xi 28–9.

v 27. i.e. 'Jesus, when he thinks of pride, thinks of–and condemns–the
arrogance found in those who consciously adhere to a moral code, whether
classical-heroic or Hebraic.'

For affronting him thrice in the wilderness:
He had soon been bloody Caesar's elf,
40 And at last he would have been Caesar himself—
Like Dr Priestley and Bacon and Newton.
Poor spiritual knowledge is not worth a button,
For thus the Gospel Sir Isaac confutes:
'God can only be known by his attributes,
45 And as for the indwelling of the Holy Ghost
Or of Christ and his Father—it's all a boast,
And pride and vanity of the imagination,
That disdains to follow this world's fashion.'
To teach doubt and experiment
50 Certainly was not what Christ meant.
What was he doing all that time
From twelve years old to manly prime?
Was he then idle, or the less
About his Father's business—
55 Or was his wisdom held in scorn
Before his wrath began to burn
In miracles throughout the land
That quite unnerved Caiaphas' hand?
If he had been Antichrist, creeping Jesus,
60 He'd have done any thing to please us;
Gone sneaking into synagogues,
And not used the elders and priests like dogs,
But humble as a lamb or ass
Obeyed himself to Caiaphas.
65 God wants not man to humble himself—
This is the trick of the ancient elf.
This is the race that Jesus ran:
Humble to God, haughty to man,
Cursing the rulers before the people
70 Even to the Temple's highest steeple;
And when he humbled himself to God,
Then descended the cruel rod:
'If thou humblest thyself thou humblest me;
Thou also dwell'st in Eternity.
75 Thou art a man; God is no more:

v 41. *Bacon and*] Reads 'Sir Isaac' in the first draft. Dr Priestley was the well-known Unitarian minister and scientist, discoverer of oxygen.
v 67–8 were in reverse order in the first draft.
v 73. Reads 'Why dost thou humble thyself to me' in the first draft.
v 75. This line contains a Swedenborgian doctrine, developed by B. Swedenborg was the opposite of Unitarian; to him God was the perfect,

Thy own humanity learn to adore,
For that is my spirit of life.
Awake! arise to spiritual strife,
And thy revenge abroad display
80   In terrors at the Last Judgement day.
God's mercy and long-suffering
Is but the sinner to judgement to bring.
Thou on the cross for them shalt pray—
And take revenge at the Last Day!'
85   Jesus replied, and thunders hurled,
'I never will pray for the world:
Once I did so when I prayed in the garden;
I wished to take with me a bodily pardon.'
Can that which was of woman born
90   In the absence of the morn,
When the soul fell into sleep
And archangels round it weep,
Shooting out against the light
Fibres of a deadly night,
95   Reasoning upon its own dark fiction
In doubt, which is self-contradiction . . .?
Humility is only doubt,
And does the sun and moon blot out,
Rooting over with thorns and stems
100   The buried soul and all its gems
(This life's dim windows of the soul)—
Distorts the heavens from pole to pole,

the divine Humanity. B. brings to this an imaginative conception of the infinite glory of true, eternal Man according to which this line does not diminish the grandeur of God in the least.

v 84. Followed by an altered but deleted couplet, which read:

> This corporeal life's a fiction
> And is made up of contradiction.

v 87. John xvii 9: 'I pray for them: I pray not for the world, but for them which thou hast given me; for they are thine.' Thus Jesus, in Gethsemane, did not pray for the world in so many words. B. probably means that Jesus, when he prayed (Matthew xxvi 39ff, Mark xiv 35-6, Luke xxii 42) 'if it be possible, let this cup pass from me', was praying to be given an excuse to let this world stay as it was–a moment of weakness.

v 89. Can that . . .] This sentence has no verb, and peters out at 96.

v 90. the morn] The true morning of eternal light.

v 91. sleep] Eternity is the only true waking; B.'s own myth of Albion, in Four Zoas and Jerusalem particularly, turns on Albion's sleeping the sleep of death–i.e. of mortal existence.

> And leads you to believe a lie
> When you see with, not through, the eye,
> 105   That was born in a night, to perish in a night,
> When the soul slept in the beams of light.

VI

> Was Jesus chaste, or did he
> Give any lessons of chastity?
> The morning blushed fiery red:
> Mary was found in adulterous bed.
> 5   Earth groaned beneath, and heaven above
> Trembled at discovery of love.
> Jesus was sitting in Moses' chair;

v *103–6*. Cp. 'Auguries of Innocence' *125–8*.

vi. On the same page as the first lines of this section, sideways in the margin, are the following lines:

> Did Jesus teach doubt or did he
> Give any lessons of Philosophy
> Charge Visionaries with deceiving
> Or call Men wise for not believing?

On the same page is a note 'This was spoke by my Spectre to Voltaire Bacon &c.'–which may refer to the marginal lines, as both deal with philosophers. On the page where this section ends and the 'Humility' section begins, there are the lines:

> Seeing this False Christ, in Fury & Passion
> I made my voice heard all over the Nation
> What are those &c.

There is no obvious section which the ' &c.' alludes to. *This False Christ* is probably the Shadow of *81–96* (for 'Shadow' see note on Spectre, p. 635 above).

vi 4. *Mary*] Mary Magdalene; the woman taken in adultery of *John* viii 3 is here identified with Mary, sister of Lazarus and Martha, who in *John* xii 3 anointed the feet of Jesus and wiped them with her hair (in *Matthew* xxvi 7 and *Mark* xiv 3 the woman is not named), and Mary Magdalene, who in *Mark* xvi 1–9 is the woman 'out of whom he had cast seven devils'. B.'s collation of Maries is not unfounded in gospel tradition. But note also *Jerusalem* pl.61, where Mary, the mother of Jesus, is treated as an adulteress, as in iii above.

vi 7. *in Moses' chair*] Figuratively speaking. The scribes appealed to Jesus, as a rabbi, to interpret the Law of Moses for them. (Cp. *John* viii 5: 'Now Moses in the law commanded us, that such should be stoned: but what sayest thou?') Thus they make him a Mosaic law-giver, and he accepts the authority but refuses to follow the tradition.

They brought the trembling woman there:
'Moses commands she be stoned to death'.
10 What was the sound of Jesus breath?
He laid his hand on Moses' law;
The ancient heavens in silent awe,
Writ with curses from pole to pole
All away began to roll.
15 The earth trembling and naked lay
In secret bed of mortal clay,
On Sinai felt the hand divine
Putting back the bloody shrine;
And she heard the breath of God
20 As she heard by Eden's flood:
'Good and evil are no more:
Sinai's trumpets, cease to roar!
Cease, finger of God, to write!
The heavens are not clean in thy sight;
25 Thou art good and thou alone,
Nor may the sinner cast one stone.
To be good only is to be
A devil, or else a Pharisee!
Thou Angel of the Presence Divine,
30 That didst create this body of mine,
Wherefore hast thou writ these laws
And created Hell's dark jaws?
My presence I will take from thee:
A cold leper thou shalt be

vi *18. Putting back*] i.e. putting back the curtain which, in the Jewish Tabernacle, veiled the Mercy Seat of God from the sight of the people (*Exodus* xxvi 1–14). *On Sinai* because that was the source of all these mysteries of law and ritual.

vi *20. by Eden's flood*] This act of Jesus was as mighty as the creation of man; earth trembled at both, B. says.

vi *23. finger of God*] *Exodus* xxxi 18, where the Law is given to Moses in the form of 'tables of stone, written with the finger of God'.

vi *28. devil*] B. originally wrote 'God'; but God is not concerned with 'being good', only with loving: so B. altered the word to *devil*–only a devil pretending to be God obeys the inhumane moral law.

vi *29. Angel of the Presence Divine*] The Law is not God's: it was invented by a jealous angel who wished to keep God apart from Man, and so locked Man up in a corrupted body, thinking that this corruption inevitably meant separation from God. But God, in Jesus, is in the body too. Later in the poem the Angel becomes 'the shadowy man' (*81*), not a real humanity, but a deathly shadow of God, and it is he, not God or man, who is cast out. He is the 'Covering Cherub' of *Milton* pls.37–38 and *Jerusalem* pl.89.

35   Though thou wast so pure and bright
     That Heaven was impure in thy sight,
     Though thy oath turned Heaven pale,
     Though thy covenant built Hell's jail,
     Though thou didst all to Chaos roll
40   With the serpent for its soul,
     Still the breath divine does move;
     And the breath divine is love!
     Mary, fear not: let me see
     The seven devils that torment thee.
45   Hide not from my sight thy sin,
     That forgiveness thou mayest win.
     Has no man condemned thee?'
     'No man, Lord!' 'Then what is he
     Who shall accuse thee? Come ye forth,
50   Fallen fiends of heavenly birth,
     That have forgot your ancient love,
     And driven away my trembling dove.
     You shall bow before her feet,
     You shall lick the dust for meat
55   And though you cannot love, but hate,
     Shall be beggars at Love's gate.
     What was thy love?—Let me see it:

vi 38. *Hell's jail*] i.e. the threat of the Law, that divine punishment will follow sin, created Hell, the place for that punishment (cp. *Romans* v 13: 'sin is not imputed when there is no law').

vi 44. *seven devils*] See *4n* above.

vi 47. So in *John* viii 10–11.

vi 51. From B.'s own song 'To the Muses' (*Poetical Sketches*, p. 13 above):

> How have you left the ancient love
> That bards of old enjoyed in you?

The fiends once knew what the Divine Love was, but have put it aside. The *Dove* is Mary: but the fiends have also driven away Peace.

vi 54. *lick the dust*] From here on B. uses the account of the punishment of the serpent (*Genesis* iii 14–15): '... upon thy belly shalt thou go, and dust shalt thou eat all the days of thy life: And I will put enmity between thee and the woman, and between thy seed and her seed; it shall bruise thy head, and thou shalt bruise his heel.' The actual phrase occurs in *Micah* vii 17: 'They shall lick the dust like a serpent.'

vi 56. *beggars*] As Lazarus in the parable begged at the rich man's gate, and as the rich man in turn begged of Lazarus after death (*Luke* xvi 19–26).

vi 57. *thy love*] Jesus speaks to Mary, changing from *you* (the fiends) to *thou* (Mary). Note B.'s attitude to Mary's adultery. It arose from various trivial causes (*60–2*), but ultimately it arose from the attitude to love as something shameful (*65–8*)–though in fact it is divine (*64*). Preoccupation

Was it love, or dark deceit?'
'Love too long from me has fled;
60   'Twas dark deceit to earn my bread;
'Twas covet, or 'twas custom, or
Some trifle not worth caring for—
That they may call a shame and sin
Love's temple that God dwelleth in,
65   And hide in secret hidden shrine
The naked human form divine,
And render that a lawless thing
On which the soul expands its wing.
But this, O Lord, this was my sin,
70   When first I let these devils in
In dark pretence to chastity,
Blaspheming love, blaspheming thee.
Thence rose secret adulteries,
And thence did covet also rise.
75   My sin thou hast forgiven me:
Canst thou forgive my blasphemy?
Canst thou return to this dark hell,
And in my burning bosom dwell,
And canst thou die, that I may live,
80   And canst thou pity and forgive?'
Then rolled the shadowy man away
From the limbs of Jesus to make them his prey,
An ever-devouring appetite,
Glittering with festering venoms bright,
85   Crying: 'Crucify this cause of distress,
Who don't keep the secrets of holiness!
All mental powers by diseases we bind,
But he heals the deaf and the dumb and the blind:

with legal chastity leads to a pretence that desire is not strong (70); and this pretence both destroys real love and, through repression, leads to adultery—which is evil in B.'s eyes, not because it is illegal, but because it is secret and selfish (73–4) and therefore blasphemous (76). B. does not now say, as he said in *Visions*, that promiscuity is a sign of virtue.

vi 64. *temple*] 1 *Corinthians* vi 19: 'Your body is the Temple of the Holy Ghost which is in you.' B. characteristically takes this to mean what it says.

vi 81. *the shadowy man*] See note on Spectre, p. 635; also p. 854 above. Here the spectre is the evil shadow of good Humanity, usurping the good man's place. Jesus is Lord because of his Mercy, Love and Vision. The Spectre claims lordship, but does so in order to tyrannize and destroy, not to re-create: he wants to swallow up the divine humanity of Christ, and reign, an evil lord of law, in his place.

vi 85. *Crying 'Crucify'*] The first reading was, 'Crying I've found him.'
   29*

Whom God has afflicted for secret ends
90   He comforts and heals, and calls them friends!'
But when Jesus was crucified,
Then was perfected his glittering pride,
In three nights he devoured his prey,
And still he devours the body of clay;
95   For dust and clay is the serpent's meat,
Which never was made for man to eat.

VII

Was Jesus gentle, or did he
Give any marks of gentility?
When twelve years old he ran away,
And left his parents in dismay.
5   When after three days' sorrow found—
Loud as Sinai's trumpet sound:
'No earthly parents I confess:
My heavenly Father's business!
Ye understand not what I say,
10   And angry, force me to obey.
Obedience is a duty then,
And favour gains with God and men.'
John from the wilderness loud cried;
Satan gloried in his pride:
15   'Come', said Satan, 'come away:
I'll soon see if you'll obey.
John for disobedience bled,
But you can turn the stones to bread?
God's high king and God's high priest

vi 92. *his*] The spectre's.

vi 93–6. The spectre, and all who share the spectre's nature and attitudes, live off dust, and their whole life is made of it. They still concentrate on earthly things and deeds, ignoring the divine reality which is man's true inheritance. Cp. *Jerusalem* pl.89.13.

vii 3. Cp. v 5 above, and *Luke* ii 42–50.

vii 6. *Sinai's trumpet*] Which heralded the giving of the Law.

vii 15. *Come, said Satan*] B. begins to allude to the story of the temptation of Christ, *Matthew* iv, *Luke* iv.

vii 17. *John*] Executed for crossing Herod (*Matthew* xiv 3–12).

vii 18. *stones to bread*] The first temptation, *Matthew* iv 3.

vii 19–24. *king . . . priest shall plant . . .*] The third temptation, to use divine power to gain earthly power (*Matthew* iv 8–9). Satan shows 'all the kingdoms of the world, and the glory of them; And saith unto him, All these things will I give thee, if thou wilt fall down and worship me.' B.'s version is adapted by interpreting 'serve me' as 'obey the powers-that-be'.

20 Shall plant their glories in your breast,
    If Caiaphas you will obey;
    If Herod you, with bloody prey,
    Feed with the sacrifice, and be
    Obedient: fall down, worship me!'
25 Thunders and lightnings broke around,
    And Jesus' voice in thunder's sound!—
    'Thus I seize the spiritual prey:
    Ye smiters with disease, make way!
    I come your king and god to seize—
30 Is God a smiter with disease?'
    The god of this world raged in vain:
    He bound old Satan in his chain,
    And bursting forth his furious ire
    Became a chariot of fire.
35 Throughout the land he took his course,
    And traced diseases to their source,
    He cursed the scribe and Pharisee,
    Trampling down hypocrisy.
    Where'er his chariot took its way
40 There Gates of Death let in the day,
    Broke down from every chain and bar;
    And Satan in his spiritual war
    Dragged at his chariot wheels. Loud howled
    The god of this world; louder rolled
45 The chariot wheels, and louder still
    His voice was heard from Zion's hill.
    And in his hand the scourge shone bright—
    He scourged the merchant Canaanite
    From out the Temple of his mind;

vii *29–30* refer to the exercise by Jesus of healing powers. The inference that Caiaphas is on the side of the 'smiters with disease' is not direct; B. has left Caiaphas for the moment. Nevertheless, to condemn Jesus—as Caiaphas and the priests did—is to condemn a healer, as the Gospels also point out. Of course there are more diseases than the physical ones.

vii *32. bound old Satan*] *Revelation* xx 2: 'And he laid hold on the dragon, that old serpent, which is the Devil, and Satan, and bound him a thousand years.' B. sees this, not as a vision of the 'last days', but as a fact realized in the life of Jesus.

vii *48. scourged the merchant Canaanite*] A reference to the clearing of the Temple courtyard of merchants and money-changers (*Matthew* xxi 12, *John* ii 13–17). (Only *John* mentions the scourge.) But the merchants considered themselves true Jews; it is B. who points out that their behaviour is that of heathens, as blasphemous as the Canaanites of history had been.

50   And in his body tight does bind
        Satan and all his hellish crew;
        And thus with wrath he did subdue
        The serpent bulk of Nature's dross,
        Till he had nailed it to the cross.
55   He took on sin in the virgin's womb
        And put it off on the cross and tomb,
        To be worshipped by the Church of Rome . . .

VIII

I am sure this Jesus will not do,
Either for Englishman or Jew.

39 The Ghost of Abel
A Revelation in the Visions of Jehovah
Seen by William Blake

In 1821 Byron's *Cain, a Mystery*–a romantic drama of Lucifer's tempting of Cain, and the killing of Abel, resembling in style an inferior *Faust Part II*–appeared, and B. replied with this little variation on it. B. picks up certain of Byron's themes: first, the chief argument of Lucifer and Cain, in which Jehovah is denounced for his treatment of Adam and Eve, first tempting and then punishing: 'Cursed be / He who first invented life that leads to death!' (*Cain* II ii 18–19). But B. uses this only to deny it: life does not lead to death; mortal 'life' is unreal, and only Eternity knows true life. From elsewhere in *Cain* B. takes up Adam's puzzled misery and Eve's fierce rejection of sin and sinner. Finally he takes up the biblical line Byron had reshaped–*Genesis* iv 10, which in *Cain* iii is spoken by 'the Angel of the Lord': 'The voice of thy slain brother's blood cries out, / Even from the ground, unto the Lord.' B. writes that the punishment of Cain is therefore due not to Jehovah, who only wishes forgiveness and reconciliation, but to the vindictiveness of Abel's shade.

The *Ghost of Abel* is B.'s only known attempt at the dramatic form except the *King Edward III* fragment in *Poetical Sketches*, over forty years earlier. There is a facsimile in the Sloss and Wallis edn of B. (1927) vol i.

vii *50*. Satan belongs in the material, transient, unreal body; not in the eternal life of the imaginative mind. Thus (*54*) the body is crucified and destroyed, not the life.

vii *55*. *took on sin*] (*a*) By taking material, and therefore corrupt form; (*b*) as iii shows, by his birth through the sin of Mary.

vii *56*. The first reading was 'And on the Cross he Seald its doom'.

vii *57*. This comment seems to be ironic–'only to be worshipped . . .', for B. was no lover of Roman Catholicism or any episcopalian denomination. The text ends suddenly and was surely not thought to be complete.

Pl. 1   To Lord Byron in the wilderness:
                              What doest thou
         here, Elijah? Can a poet doubt the visions of Jehovah?
         Nature has no outline; but Imagination has. Nature
         has no time; but Imagination has! Nature has no
         supernatural and dissolves: Imagination is Eternity.

                    *Scene: a rocky country. Eve fainted over the dead body
                    of Abel which lays near a grave. Adam kneels by her; Jehovah
                                                            stands above.*
Jeh.–   Adam!
Adam–   I will not hear thee more, thou spiritual voice!
         Is this Death?
Jeh.–   Adam!
Adam–   It is in vain: I will not hear thee
         Henceforth! Is this thy promise that the woman's seed
         Should bruise the serpent's head? Is this the serpent?
         Ah!
     5   Seven times, O Eve, thou hast fainted over the dead.
         Ah! Ah!
                              Eve revives

Eve–   Is this the promise of Jehovah? Oh it is all a vain
         delusion,

¶ 39.1. *What doest thou here, Elijah?*] *1 Kings* xix 9,13. When Elijah de-
stroyed the heathen prophets on Carmel, Jezebel threatened to kill him,
and he escaped in despair 'to Horeb, the mount of God' (and also, as
would not escape B., the mountain of the Law). There he heard the voice
of God, before and after the wind, earthquake and fire, 'What doest thou
here, Elijah?' So also Byron is resting on the old law, and not putting
himself vigorously into the new revelation of forgiveness.
1. *Nature has no outline*] In *Cain* II i, Lucifer shows Cain the distant worlds
of the universe, all beautiful, and all to die. B. controverts this: Nature is
not the truth, but only the veil over the truth, the shadow of the undying,
eternal reality.
Stage direction. *lays*] Common usage at this period, where we would
expect *lies.*
1.1. *I will not hear*] Adam's rejection of the spiritual is like Albion's in
Jerusalem. Yet he does not deny its existence (*17*)–only its strength.
1.3–4. *the woman's seed . . . serpent's head*] From *Genesis* iii 15: cp. also
Everlasting Gospel vi *53–4*: 'You shall bow before her feet, / You shall
lick the dust for meat.'
this] Abel's body, for he, not the Serpent, has been killed.
1.6. *delusion*] Eve's disaster destroys her faith, and she cannot see beyond
earthly life and death.

| | This death and this life and this Jehovah! |
| *Jeh.–* | Woman, lift thine eyes! |

A voice is heard coming on

Voice– O Earth, cover not thou my blood, cover not thou my
blood!

Enter the Ghost of Abel

Eve– Thou visionary phantasm, thou art not the real
. Abel!
Abel– Among the Elohim a human victim I wander; I am
their house,
11   Prince of the Air; and our dimensions compass zenith
and nadir.
Vain is thy covenant, O Jehovah! I am the accuser
and avenger
Of blood. O earth, cover not thou the blood of Abel!
Jeh.– What vengeance dost thou require?
Abel– Life for life! Life
for life!
Jeh.– He who shall take Cain's life must also die, O Abel.
16   And who is he? Adam; wilt thou, or Eve thou, do
this?
Adam– It is all a vain delusion of the all-creative imagination.
Eve, come away and let us not believe these vain
delusions:
Abel is dead and Cain slew him. We shall also die a
death
20   And then—what then? Be as poor Abel, a thought,
or as
This! Oh what shall I call thee, form divine, Father of
Mercies

Stage direction. *Ghost*] i.e. the spectre, Abel's evil, shadowy self–as Eve
immediately realizes. (For *Spectre* see *Jerusalem* pl.6.1n.)
1.10. Elohim] The God of *Genesis* i, the Creator, who restricts mankind in
this earthly form, away from the reality of Eternity. The Hebrew word is
plural, meaning literally *gods*, and this is the sense in which B. also uses it
here (cp. *2.22*). Jehovah (*12*) is the forgiving God, whom Abel's Spectre
or ghost denies.
1.17. delusion] To Adam the imagination is only the inventor of delusions,
not the creator of reality. But Adam is still capable of vision (*22*).

That appearest to my spiritual vision? Eve, seest thou
    also?
Eve– I see him plainly with my mind's eye. I see also Abel
    living,
Though terribly afflicted as we also are; yet Jehovah
    sees him
Pl. 2 Alive and not dead. Were it not better to believe vision
With all our might and strength, though we are fallen
    and lost?
Adam– Eve, thou hast spoken truly: let us kneel before his
    feet.

They kneel before Jehovah

Abel– Are these the sacrifices of eternity, O Jehovah—a
    broken spirit
  5 And a contrite heart? Oh, I cannot forgive! The
    Accuser hath
Entered into me as into his house, and I loathe thy
    tabernacles!
As thou hast said, so is it come to pass: my desire is
    unto Cain,
And he doth rule over me. Therefore my soul in fumes
    of blood
Cries for vengeance: sacrifice on sacrifice, blood on
    blood!
Jeh.– Lo, I have given you a lamb for an atonement
    instead
  11 Of the transgressor, or no flesh or spirit could ever
    live.
Abel– Compelled I cry, O earth, cover not the blood of
    Abel!

*Abel sinks down into the grave from which arises Satan
armed in glittering scales with a crown and a spear*

Satan– I will have human blood and not the blood of bulls or
    goats,
And no atonement, O Jehovah! The Elohim live on
    sacrifice
  15 Of men: hence I am God of men: thou human,
    O Jehovah.
By the rock and oak of the druid, creeping mistletoe
    and thorn,
Cain's city built with human blood, not blood of bulls
    and goats,

Thou shalt thyself be sacrificed to me thy God, on
Calvary!

Jeh.– Such is my will: *Thunders*
that thou thyself go to eternal death
20 In self-annihilation, even till Satan self-subdued
put off Satan
Into the bottomless abyss, whose torment arises for
ever and ever.

*On each side a Chorus of Angels entering sing the
following:*

The Elohim of the heathen swore vengeance for sin!
Then thou stoodst
Forth, O Elohim Jehovah, in the midst of the darkness
of the oath, all clothed
In thy covenant of the forgiveness of sins: 'Death,
O Holy! Is this brotherhood?'
25 The Elohim saw their oath eternal fire; they rolled
apart trembling over the
Mercy Seat, each in his station fixed in the firmament
by peace, brotherhood and love.

The curtain falls

The Voice of Abel's Blood [*Design*]

1822 W Blake's original stereotype was 1788

2.*19–21.* B.'s interpretation of the imprisonment of the Beast, Satan, in
the bottomless pit for a thousand years (*Revelation* xx 1–3).
2. *Design*: Figures in the margin: at the foot of the text, Cain leans despair-
ingly over Abel's body, while a fierce Satanic figure, labelled 'The Voice
of Abel's blood' rises from Abel.
1822 ... 1788] B.'s earliest attempt at illuminated printing seems to have
been a series of little tracts entitled *There is No Natural Religion* and *All
Religions are One*, which could very well belong to 1788.

Index of Titles and First Lines

Titles of books and single works are given in italic type; titles of individual poems in roman type; first lines in inverted commas.

Index to Notes

The following important figures, subjects or terms are specially annotated (V = *Visions of the Daughters of Albion*, Eu = *Europe*, FZ = *The Four Zoas*, M = *Milton*, J = *Jerusalem*, hn = headnote):

Note on Names and Key-words

Of all B.'s invented names, only three have a doubtful pronunciation, as follows:

Los: Pronounced as 'loss', though the *o* might be long.
Urizen: stress on the first syllable, *i* short.
Vala: derived from, and pronounced as, *veil*.

The following words occur so often that it is impracticable and unnecessary to annotate each occurrence repetitively: yet they are likely to be stumbling-blocks to the reader.

consummation: B. uses this regularly in a special sense to mean 'burning-up', as the phoenix burns, in a regenerative fire. Thus *consuming* is a form of *consummation*; but B. does not use the word in a more general sense.

enormous: usually, though not invariably, with its earlier sense of *monstrous*.

generative: pertaining to the mortal world where existence depends on sexual generation, and is not an immortal possession. In Eternity, beings do not die; if corrupted they *sleep*: but in mortality they can only be kept alive by repeated births.

globe: normally implies a contained and constricted enclosure.

ocean, sea: imply an uncontrolled, destructive, overwhelming power, without form or creativity.

vegetative: rooted in the mortal world (see *generative*) and unable to spring up into eternal life.

ratio: not 'proportion' (see *Milton* pl.32.*35n*), but a rational system derived from evidence provided by the perceptions of the senses, and so merely a reduction of this already limited evidence to a still more limited abstraction.

Note that many now obsolete past-participial forms such as *heart-broke* ('A Dream', *Songs of Innocence*, p. 64) were acceptable as 'good grammar' in the eighteenth century.